W9-DDK-099

THE DORLING KINDERSLEY
VISUAL
Encyclopedia

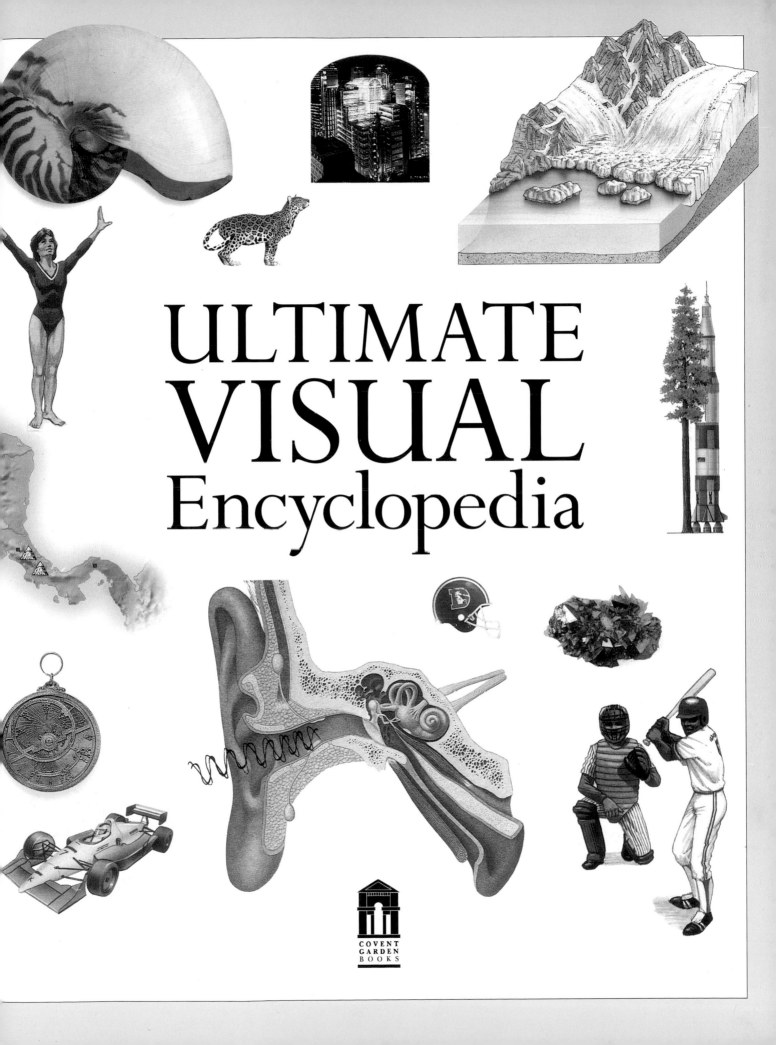

ULTIMATE
VISUAL
Encyclopedia

COVENT
GARDEN
BOOKS

**COVENT
GARDEN
BOOKS**

Senior Editor Anna Kruger **Senior Art Editor** Gillian Shaw

Section Editors
Sue Copsey, Marie Greenwood, Fran K. Jones, James Pickford

Editors
Huw Clough, Carey Denton, Deborah Murrell

US Editor
Jill Hamilton

Art Editors
Shirley Gwillym, Rebecca Johns, Floyd Sayers, Dominic Zwemmer

Designers
Wayne Holder, Marcus James, Joanna Pocock, Wilfrid Wood

DTP Designers
Mathew Birch, Carol Titchener, Noel Barnes

Picture Manager
Lorna Ainger

Research and Editorial Assistance
Alex Tinley, Leo Vita-Finzi, Tim Hetherington, Giles Portman, Deslie Lawrence

Production
Catherine Semark, Samantha Larmour

Deputy Editorial Director Sophie Mitchell **Deputy Art Director** Miranda Kennedy

Models in Human Body section are original SOMSO models

First American Edition, 1995
2 4 6 8 10 9 7 5 3 1

Published in the United States by
Dorling Kindersley Publishing, Inc.,
95 Madison Avenue
New York, New York 10016

Copyright © 1995
Dorling Kindersley Limited, London

This edition published 2001 for Covent Garden Books
All rights reserved under International and Pan-American Copyright Conventions.
No part of this publication may be reproduced, stored in a retrieval system, or
transmitted in any form or by any means, electronic, mechanical, photocopying,
recording, or otherwise, without the prior written permission of the copyright owner.
Published in Great Britain by Dorling Kindersley Limited.

Library of Congress Cataloging-in-Publication Data
The Dorling Kindersley visual encyclopedia
p.   cm.
Includes index.
ISBN 0-681-29015-3
1. Children's encyclopedias and dictionaries.
AG5.D72   1994
031- - dc20   94-45785
CIP

Reproduced by Colourscan, Singapore
Printed and bound in Hong Kong

CONSULTANTS

UNIVERSE
Professor Heather Couper
Television and radio broadcaster. Past president of the British Astronomical Association. International author.
Nigel Henbest
International writer and science broadcaster. Past consultant, Royal Greenwich Observatory and the Science and Engineering Research Coucil.
Doug Millard
Associate curator, Space Technology, Science Museum, London.

EARTH
Maurice Crewe
Fellow, Royal Meteorological Society.
Cally Hall
Museum geologist, Mineralogy Department, Natural History Museum, London.
Donna Rispoli
Ecology and energy consultant.
Bob Symes
Associate keeper, Department of Mineralogy, Natural History Museum, London.
Barbara Taylor
Internationally acclaimed science and natural history writer.
Warren Yasso
Professor of Natural Sciences, Teachers College, Columbia University. Textbook author.

LIVING WORLD
Keith Banister
Government consultant on fisheries, broadcaster, writer.
David Burnie
Zoologist, biologist, and internationally acclaimed writer of science and nature books.
Barry Clarke
Curator, Amphibians, Natural History Museum, London.
Joseph DiCostanzo
Researcher, Great Gull Island Project, American Museum of Natural History. Past president, Linnaean Society of New York.
Theresa Greenaway
Botanist and natural history author.
Miranda Macquitty
Zoologist and best-selling natural history author.

Matthew Robertson
Professional entomologist. Former Head Keeper, Invertebrate House, London Zoo.
Ray Rogers
Horticulturist and gardening editor.

HUMAN BODY
Dr. Sarah Brewer
General practitioner and medical author.
Dr. Thaddeus M. Yablonsky
Physician and medical consultant.

BELIEFS, CUSTOMS, AND SOCIETY
W. Owen Cole
Lecturer and writer in religious studies.
John Gray
Fellow in Politics, Jesus College, University of Oxford.
John Keyworth
Curator, Museum of the Bank of England.
James Nicholson
Financial journalist, *Guardian* newspaper.
Helen Watson
Lecturer in Anthropology; Fellow St. John's College, University of Cambridge.

ARTS AND THE MEDIA
Christopher Cook
Documentary film maker and arts presenter for BBC Radio. Film advisor, National Gallery, London.
Alistair Niven
Literature Director, Arts Council of England
Brigid Pepin
Lecturer Art History and Architecture, University of North London.
Penelope Vita-Finzi
Former lecturer, English Literature and Theatre, Thames Valley University, England.
Rodney Wilson
Film, Video, and Broadcasting Director, Arts Council of England.
Ann Wingate
Independent film producer, including *Howards End*

SPORTS
Norman Barrett
Sports writer and consultant.
David Heidenstam
Sports writer and editor.

SCIENCE
Peter Bailes
Collections information manager Science Museum, London.
Marina Benjamin
Science writer and journalist.
Jack Challoner
Formerly with the Education Unit, Science Museum, London. Science author.
Eryl Davies
Science and technology writer and consultant.
Kimi Hosoume
Mathematics and science educator, Lawrence Hall, University of California at Berkeley.
Carole Stott
Former curator of Astronomy, Greenwich Royal Observatory, London. Science author.

TRANSPORTATION, COMMUNICATIONS, AND INDUSTRY
Christine Heap
Curator, National Railway Museum, York, England.
Eric Kentley
Curator, National Maritime Museum, London.
Bob McWilliam
Senior curator, Civil Engineering, Science Museum, London.
Andrew Nahum
Senior curator, Aeronautics, Science Museum, London.
Lynda Springate, Anice Collette, Marie Tieche
Curators, National Motor Museum, Beaulieu, England.

INTERNATIONAL WORLD
Dorling Kindersley Cartography in conjunction with leading cartographic consultants, embassies, and consulates.

HISTORY
Brian Dooley
Political journalist. Former Senate aide to Edward Kennedy.
Margaret Mulvihill
Historian and writer.
Philip Wilkinson
Historian and writer.
Charles S.Wills
US History consultant.

HOW TO USE THIS BOOK

EACH PAGE OR DOUBLE-PAGE spread in *The Visual Encyclopedia* is a self-contained unit, carefully designed to present the maximum number of facts about its subject in the most accessible manner. Information on each page follows a clear, logical order, beginning with the main feature and most important factual topics, then moving on to records, strange comparisons, and fascinating, collectible facts.

Main feature
Focuses on the subject and provides the most important facts.

Running head – thematic
Tells readers which thematic section they are in.

Introduction
A brief text introduction defines the subject and provides a number of key facts.

Topic headings
Easy-to-find topic headings draw the reader to subfeatures within the main subject. Each page contains an average of 10 subject-related topics.

Detailed artwork
Stunning, full-color cutaway artwork stimulates learning and provides maximum information.

Key facts
Bulleted key facts and figures give the reader the most essential facts at a glance.

Boxed types
To provide maximum information, an example of every major type of plant, animal, or object is illustrated.

Clear labels and annotation
Identify types and special features and clarify complex information.

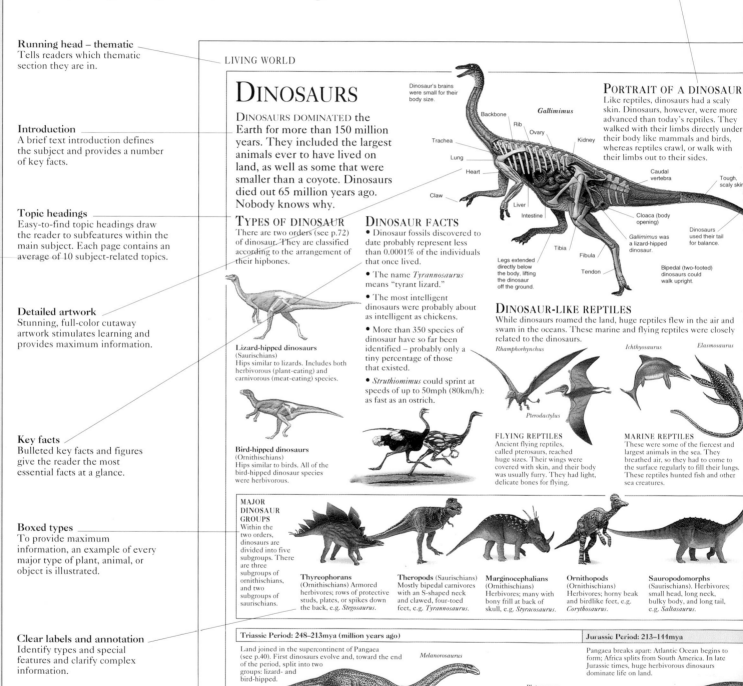

LIVING WORLD

DINOSAURS

DINOSAURS DOMINATED the Earth for more than 150 million years. They included the largest animals ever to have lived on land, as well as some that were smaller than a coyote. Dinosaurs died out 65 million years ago. Nobody knows why.

Dinosaur's brains were small for their body size.

Gallimimus

Backbone — Rib — Ovary — Kidney
Trachea —
Lung —
Heart —
Claw —
Liver —
Intestine —
Caudal vertebra
Tough, scaly skin
Cloaca (body opening)
Gallimimus was a lizard-hipped dinosaur.
Dinosaurs used their tail for balance.
Tibia — Fibula —
Tendon —
Legs extended directly below the body, lifting the dinosaur off the ground.
Bipedal (two-footed) dinosaurs could walk upright.

PORTRAIT OF A DINOSAUR
Like reptiles, dinosaurs had a scaly skin. Dinosaurs, however, were more advanced than today's reptiles. They walked with their limbs directly under their body like mammals and birds, whereas reptiles crawl, or walk with their limbs out to their sides.

TYPES OF DINOSAUR
There are two orders (see p.72) of dinosaur. They are classified according to the arrangement of their hipbones.

Lizard-hipped dinosaurs
(Saurischians)
Hips similar to lizards. Includes both herbivorous (plant-eating) and carnivorous (meat-eating) species.

Bird-hipped dinosaurs
(Ornithischians)
Hips similar to birds. All of the bird-hipped dinosaur species were herbivorous.

DINOSAUR FACTS
• Dinosaur fossils discovered to date probably represent less than 0.0001% of the individuals that once lived.

• The name *Tyrannosaurus* means "tyrant lizard."

• The most intelligent dinosaurs were probably about as intelligent as chickens.

• More than 350 species of dinosaur have so far been identified – probably only a tiny percentage of those that existed.

• *Struthiomimus* could sprint at speeds of up to 50mph (80km/h): as fast as an ostrich.

DINOSAUR-LIKE REPTILES
While dinosaurs roamed the land, huge reptiles flew in the air and swam in the oceans. These marine and flying reptiles were closely related to the dinosaurs.

Rhamphorhynchus
Ichthyosaurus
Elasmosaurus
Pterodactylus

FLYING REPTILES
Ancient flying reptiles, called pterosaurs, reached huge sizes. Their wings were covered with skin, and their body was usually furry. They had light, delicate bones for flying.

MARINE REPTILES
These were some of the fiercest and largest animals in the sea. They breathed air, so they had to come to the surface regularly to fill their lungs. These reptiles hunted fish and other sea creatures.

MAJOR DINOSAUR GROUPS
Within the two orders, dinosaurs are divided into five subgroups. There are three subgroups of ornithischians, and two subgroups of saurischians.

Thyreophorans
(Ornithischians) Armored herbivores; rows of protective studs, plates, or spikes down the back, e.g. *Stegosaurus*.

Theropods (Saurischians)
Mostly bipedal carnivores with an S-shaped neck and clawed, four-toed feet, e.g. *Tyrannosaurus*.

Marginocephalians
(Ornithischians)
Herbivores; many with bony frill at back of skull, e.g. *Styracosaurus*.

Ornithopods
(Ornithischians)
Herbivores; horny beak and birdlike feet, e.g. *Corythosaurus*.

Sauropodomorphs
(Saurischians). Herbivores; small head, long neck, bulky body, and long tail, e.g. *Saltasaurus*.

Triassic Period: 248–213mya (million years ago)	Jurassic Period: 213–144mya
Land joined in the supercontinent of Pangaea (see p.40). First dinosaurs evolve and, toward the end of the period, split into two groups: lizard- and bird-hipped.	Pangaea breaks apart: Atlantic Ocean begins to form; Africa splits from South America. In late Jurassic times, huge herbivorous dinosaurs dominate life on land.

Melanorosaurus
Coelophysis
Plateosaurus
Mussaurus
Herrerasaurus
Staurikosaurus
Technosaurus
Camptosaurus
Dryosaurus

70

MEASUREMENTS AND ABBREVIATIONS

Some words and measurements are abbreviated, or shortened, in *The Illustrated Factopedia*. The following list explains what the abbreviations stand for:

°C = degrees Celsius
°F = degrees Fahrenheit
mm = millimetre
cm = centimetre
m = metre
km = kilometre
sq km = square kilometre
km/h = kilometres per hour
in = inch

ft = foot
yd = yard
sq mile = square mile
mph = miles per hour
g = gram
kg = kilogram
oz = ounce
lb = pound
c. before a date = about

B.C. = before Christ
A.D. = Anno Domini, after the birth of Christ
b. = born
r. = reigned
d. = died
CIS = Commonwealth of Independent States (formerly Russia)

DINOSAURS

Running head – by subject
Helps guide readers to the subject they want to find out about.

DINOSAUR DISCOVERY

Pre-19th century: around the world, dinosaur fossils are believed to be curious things, including dragon bones in China, and giant human bones in parts of Europe.

1800 Dinosaur footprints found in Massachusetts, USA. Their discoverer claims they were made by the raven from Noah's Ark.

1820 *Iguanodon* teeth discovered in Tilgate Forest, Sussex, England, by doctor and fossil hunter Gideon Mantell (1790–1852) and his wife. He suspects they are the remains of ancient reptiles, but his theory is dismissed as heretical (anti-religious).

1834 First glimpse of what dinosaurs looked like provided by find of a partial skeleton near Maidstone, England, known as the Maidstone *Iguanodon*.

1841 The term dinosaur, from the Greek words for "terrible" and "lizard", is coined by English anatomist Richard Owen (1804–92).

Timelines
Present and illustrate key historical dates, people, events, and developments for every subject.

| 1800 | 1800 | 1820 | 1820 | 1830 | 1834 | 1840 | 1841 |

1851 First reconstruction of dinosaurs: *Iguanodon* and *Hylaeosaurus* models are made for the Great Exhibition at Crystal Palace, London, England. Results in huge public enthusiasm for dinosaurs. Before the *Iguanodon* is completed, the sculptor holds a dinner party inside it.

Dinner party in a model dinosaur

1877 One of the greatest dinosaur collections found at Como Bluff, Wyoming, USA, by O.C. Marsh (1831–99) of Yale College.

1947 Largest number of dinosaurs ever found together: more than 100 *Coelophysis* skeletons.

1987 Evidence to support theory of warm-blooded dinosaurs found by palaeontologists Tom Rich and Patricia Vickers-Rich of the Museum of Victoria, Australia. They discover dinosaur fossils in a part of South Australia that would have been inside the Antarctic Circle when these dinosaurs lived. The mean annual temperature in this region would then have been near freezing.

Leaellynasaura lived in polar regions.

Topic headings
Each main topic has its own look-up heading. There are 12 separate topics on this spread.

| 1850 | 1851 | 1870 | 1877 | 1940 | 1947 | 1980 | 1987 |

DINOSAUR RECORDS

SMALLEST DINOSAUR was probably *Wannanosaurus*, a bipedal carnivore that measured 60cm (2ft) long. It was about the size of a chicken.

MOST PRIMITIVE KNOWN DINOSAUR is *Eoraptor*, a 228 million-year-old bipedal carnivore that was about the size of a large dog.

SMALLEST DINOSAUR BRAIN is believed to have been that of the *Stegosaurus*. It was less than 5cm (2in) long.

LARGEST DINOSAUR EGGS were probably those of *Hypselosaurus*. They measured about 30cm (12in) long and contained an estimated 3.3 litres (6 pints) of fluid: roughly the same as the fluid in 60 hens' eggs.

EARTH SHAKER

The name *Seismosaurus* means "earth-shaking lizard". This enormous plant-eating dinosaur was 40m (131ft) in length: longer than an Airbus A320.

EXTINCTION THEORIES

About 65 million years ago the dinosaurs, together with many other animal species, became extinct. Other animal groups, including turtles, frogs, birds, and mammals, survived. There are many theories for this mass-extinction: below are two of the most widely accepted.

Exciting visual comparisons
Bring facts to life and make them memorable by placing them into interesting and unusual contexts.

Records
Provide the reader with all the record-breaking features smallest, largest, fastest, slowest, earliest, and latest of every subject.

LARGEST CARNIVORES

Dinosaur	Estimated length	
	m	ft
Acrocanthosaurus	12	39
Tyrannosaurus	12	39
Aliwalia	11	36
Allosaurus	11	36

GRADUAL EXTINCTION
Gradual changes in climate and vegetation caused by continental drift (see p.40) led to the dinosaurs' slow extinction over about 50,000 years. Warm, tropical conditions were replaced by cooler, more seasonal climates, and mammals slowly replaced dinosaurs as the dominant animal group.

Data tables
Give the reader essential data in an immediately accessible form.

WIDER GLIDER

The largest flying animal ever to have existed was *Quetzalcoatlus*, a flying reptile. Its wingspan measured about 12m (39ft) across: wider than the wingspan of a hang glider.

LARGEST HERBIVORES

Dinosaur	Estimated length	
	m	ft
Seismosaurus	40	131
Barosaurus	27	89
Diplodocus	27	89
Brachiosaurus	25	82

CATASTROPHES
The period when dinosaurs were dying out coincided with many volcanic eruptions in India. At the same time, a huge meteorite hit the Earth. Dust thrown into the atmosphere blocked out sunlight, and dinosaurs could not survive the resulting climate changes.

Detailed captions
Expand on the subject and reinforce the image.

| Cretaceous Period: 144–65mya | 65mya |

Continents split further apart, eventually drifting into their present-day positions. Dinosaurs continue to flourish; those on different continents evolve separately, leading to great diversity.

Dinosaurs become extinct, together with many other animal species.

Diplodocus
Stegosaurus
Saltasaurus
Tyrannosaurus
Iguanodon
Allosaurus
Scelidosaurus
Deinonychus
Hypsilophodon
Torosaurus

Amazing facts
Words and pictures combine to present little-known or amazing and unusual facts.

Page size
The Dinosaurs spread is shown slightly smaller than actual size.

71

7

CONTENTS

Earth's tectonic plates

Jupiter

Vostok
36.4m (119.5ft)

Saturn V
110.6m (363ft)

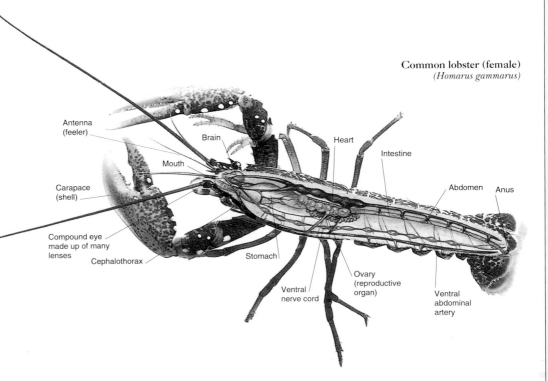

Common lobster (female)
(Homarus gammarus)

Antenna (feeler)

Brain

Heart

Intestine

Mouth

Carapace (shell)

Abdomen

Anus

Compound eye made up of many lenses

Cephalothorax

Stomach

Ventral nerve cord

Ovary (reproductive organ)

Ventral abdominal artery

113 HUMAN BODY

Muscle system

Flexors of forearm

Brachioradialis

Frontalis

Brachialis

Sternocleidomastoid

Trapezius

Pectoralis major

Rectus abdominis

Deltoid

Linea alba

Biceps brachii

External oblique

Tensor fasciae latae

Serratus anterior

Iliopsoas

Pectineus

Adductor longus

Vastus lateralis

Rectus femoris

Gracilis

Sartorius

Vastus medialis

Gastrocnemius

Tibialis anterior

Extensor muscles of foot

Flexor muscles of foot

Body systems

Skeletal system   *Circulatory system*   *Muscular system*   *Skin system*

Welsh guard   *Nun*   *Bolivian dancer*   *Arab woman*

Phenakistoscope

Two-person dinghy

Vaulting over

Pole vault

Isotopes

Fluorine–19 nucleus

Fluorine–18 nucleus

Nuclear-powered submarine

North and Central America

Japanese golfer

Traditional Arab head-dress

Bulgarians with rose petals

Decorative Islamic face-veil

West African children

South America

Africa

Asia

African elephants *Giraffe* *Mountain gorilla*

Kazakh yurts

369 HISTORY

425 INDEX

453 CREDITS

UNIVERSE AND SPACE

Starting with the formation and scale of the known Universe, and including the latest theories about how it might end, this section provides facts and figures about every aspect of outer space. Vital statistics are given for planets, stars, the Moon, comets, meteors, and asteroids, as well as key dates in space exploration and great discoveries in astronomy.

Universe • Stars • Night Skies • Sun and Solar System
Planets • Moon • Comets, Meteors, and Asteroids • Astronomy
Space Exploration • Rockets

UNIVERSE

THE KNOWN UNIVERSE contains an estimated 100 billion galaxies. They are grouped in massive superclusters and separated by vast empty spaces.

EVOLUTION OF THE UNIVERSE

The Universe is thought to have exploded into existence 13 billion years ago at the Big Bang. 300,000 years later ripples of matter began to form, followed 9.2 billion years later by the first known life forms.

13 billion years ago
At the time of the Big Bang, all matter and energy is concentrated into a single, tiny point.

3 minutes later
Atomic nuclei, the centres of atoms, begin to form out of the soup of sub-atomic particles.

300,000 years after Big Bang
The first ripples of matter emerge. They form the seeds of galaxies.

12 billion years ago
One billion years after Big Bang, the first galaxies evolve. Light from their stars begins its journey across space.

11 billion years ago
The stars of the Milky Way form from the break-up of a vast cloud of helium and hydrogen.

5 billion years ago
The Solar System is born out of a whirling cloud of gas studded with ice and rock.

3.8 billion years ago
Life evolves on Earth, the only planet known in the Universe to support living things.

FUTURE OF THE UNIVERSE

The empty spaces of the Universe may be full of dark matter, whose nature is not yet known. If there is enough dark matter, its gravity could reverse the Universe's expansion. If not, the Universe could expand forever.

Eternal Expansion
The most recent studies indicate that the Universe will expand forever. As stars and galaxies die, the Universe becomes a great empty void.

Turning point
Dark matter begins to drag in all the galaxies.

AFTER BIG BANG
The Universe could follow different courses.

Big Bang
A huge explosion creates all existing matter.

Big Crunch
All matter is contracted into a single point of infinite density.

Evolution
Stars and galaxies form.

Expansion or Contraction?
The Universe may grow forever, or reach a maximum size.

Present day
The Universe expands.

The next Universe?
After Big Crunch the Universe may end or it may be reborn in an entirely new form.

COBE
In 1992, data from COBE, Cosmic Background Explorer satellite, found evidence for the first ripples of matter in the Universe. These ripples were the beginnings of galaxies.

FAMOUS COSMOLOGISTS

Cosmologists study the origin and structure of the Universe.

Sir Isaac Newton (1642–1727) laid the foundations of modern astronomy with his theory of Universal Gravity. He stated that it was gravity that held the planets in their orbits.

Max Planck (1858–1947) published his quantum theory concerning the nature of energy in 1900. It explained that light could take the form of waves or particles.

Albert Einstein (1879–1955) His theories of relativity explained that light was the fastest thing in the Universe, and that matter and energy were the same thing.

Edwin Hubble (1889–1953) provided the first strong evidence that the Universe was expanding. In 1924 he discovered galaxies beyond the Milky Way.

Arno Penzias (born 1933) **Robert Wilson** (born 1936) discovered a constant level of background radiation in the Universe, left over from the Big Bang.

Stephen Hawking (born 1942) made major discoveries about the nature of black holes and contributed greatly to our understanding of gravity.

UNIVERSE SCALE

The Universe spans more than 26 billion light-years. A light-year, the distance light travels in one year, is equal to 9,461 billion km (5,875 billion miles).

Ground level

Flying at low altitude 1km (0.6 miles)

Orbiting at high altitude 1,000km (620 miles)

Earth from space 100,000km (62,000 miles)

Earth and Moon 1 million km (620,000 miles)

GALAXY TYPES

Galaxies are huge families of stars held together by their own gravity. They take different forms. The Milky Way is a spiral galaxy. Other types include elliptical, barred spiral, and irregular galaxies.

SPIRAL
Spiral galaxies are shaped like discs. They have two or more curved arms of densely packed stars that rotate around a central bulge.

BARRED SPIRAL
Barred spiral galaxies have a rigid central bar with spiral arms beginning at the bar's ends. The central bar, made up of millions of stars, rotates.

ELLIPTICAL
All the stars in elliptical galaxies formed at the same time. Elliptical galaxies range from the smallest to the largest galaxies of all.

CANNIBAL
Cannibal galaxies are a type of elliptical galaxy. They are so massive and exert such a powerful gravitational pull that they swallow up smaller galaxies.

IRREGULAR
Irregular galaxies have no definite shape and are small in size. New stars continue to form inside them and they are rich in gas and dust.

MAJOR NEARBY GALAXIES

Galaxy	Type	Mass (billion solar masses)	Distance (light-years)
Andromeda (M 31)	Spiral	300	2,500,000
Milky Way galaxy	Spiral	150	0
Galaxy in Triangulum (M 33)	Spiral	10	2,500,000
Large Magellanic Cloud	Irregular	10	160,000
NGC 205	Elliptical	10	2,500,000
NGC 221	Elliptical	3	2,500,000
Small Magellanic Cloud	Irregular	2	190,000
NGC 185	Elliptical	1	2,000,000
NGC 147	Elliptical	1	1,920,000

COSMIC DUST AND THE ZONE OF AVOIDANCE

A cosmic dust grain is about one millionth of a millimetre in diameter, smaller than a particle of smoke. Clouds of these grains dim our view of the Universe by scattering the light from stars. Until the invention of radio astronomy, parts of our galaxy were hidden.

The Zone of Avoidance
Before the 1950s, astronomers were puzzled that a dark, empty zone appeared to stretch around the sky, avoided by stars and distant galaxies.

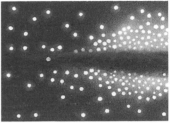

Exposing the Zone
New instruments were able to peer through the veil of dust. They revealed new stars and gas clouds at the galactic centre, and many distant galaxies.

MILKY WAY DATA

Age	About 11 billion years
Number of stars	200 billion
Diameter	100,000 light-years
Maximum thickness	20,000 light-years
Thickness at Sun	700 light-years
Distance of Sun from galactic centre	25,000 light-years
Time taken for Sun to orbit galactic centre	240 million years

GALACTIC CENTRE

This radio picture shows the centre of the Milky Way galaxy. It is a hot region of stars, possibly containing a black hole.

QUASAR FACTS

- Quasars are the violent centres of distant galaxies, brighter than the average galaxy.

- They are powered by huge black holes in their centres tearing matter apart.

- Remotest object in known Universe is quasar PC 1247 + 3406, 13.2 billion light-years away.

- In 1989, quasar PKS 0558-504 threw out as much energy in 3 minutes as the Sun throws out in 340,000 years.

- First discovered and nearest quasar is 3C–273, 2 billion light-years away. It is as bright as 200 galaxies combined.

X-ray photograph of quasar 3C-273

AMAZING JOURNEYS

A journey by jumbo jet to the nearest star, Proxima Centauri, would take 5 million years.

The flight time of a jumbo jet bound for the Sun would be 20 years.

A car driven at a steady speed of 88km/h (55mph) would reach space in two hours.

The Solar System
10 billion km
(6.2 billion miles)

Interstellar space
1,000 billion km
(620 billion miles)

Nearest stars
100 light-years

Milky Way Galaxy
100,000 light-years

Local Group of galaxies
6 million light-years

Extent of the known Universe
26 billion light-years

STARS

A STAR IS AN immense globe of fiery hydrogen gas powered by nuclear reactions at its core. Only gravity holds it together and stops it from exploding. In the first stage of its life, a star generates energy by fusing pairs of hydrogen atoms to form helium.

STAR TYPES

Most stars are part of a system composed of two or more stars. Mintaka (in Orion) consists of three stars, while Castor (in Gemini) has six. Stars form in close-knit groups from a nebula. About 60% stay in groups, held together by each other's gravity. Our Sun is unusual in being a single star.

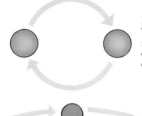

BINARY STARS
These stars of similar mass and size orbit a common centre of gravity, or central balance point.

ECLIPSING BINARY
One star in a pair regularly moves in front of the other. First we see a reduction, then a recovery in the star's light.

VARIABLE STAR
These stars vary in brightness. In some cases, explosions on the star's surface make it appear brighter than usual.

STAR RECORDS

FAINTEST KNOWN STAR
is brown star RG 0058.8-2807, with a visual brightness less than one millionth of the Sun's.

BRIGHTEST KNOWN SUPERNOVA
was SN 1006, which flared in April 1006. It was easily visible during the day.

FASTEST KNOWN PULSAR
is PSR 1937+214, which spins 642 times a second.

FEATHERWEIGHT

On Earth, the average bird's feather weighs very little. On the surface of a neutron star, however, the intense gravity would cause a medium-sized feather to weigh as much as two Apollo lunar landing modules weigh on Earth.

BIRTH AND LIFE OF A MASSIVE STAR

Every star begins life as an enormous cloud of dust and gas. This cloud collapses in on itself and the star begins to shine. Death comes in two ways. A star the mass of the Sun ends its life by swelling to a red giant and puffing off its outer layers of gas, which glow for a few thousand years as a planetary nebula. A massive star ends in a supernova.

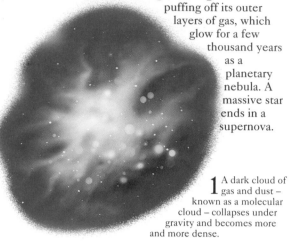

1 A dark cloud of gas and dust – known as a molecular cloud – collapses under gravity and becomes more and more dense.

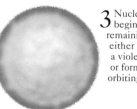

2 Parts of the cloud contract into clumps called protostars. These heat up, shrink, and become denser. Each protostar begins to spin and flattens into a disc.

3 Nuclear reactions begin. The remaining dust is either blown away by a violent stellar wind or forms planets orbiting the star.

4 On the main sequence, the star settles down into the major period of its lifespan. It shines steadily and radiates energy. Bigger and brighter stars burn hydrogen more quickly. They have shorter lifetimes.

STAR FACTS

• Red giant diameter: up to 100 times that of Sun. Red supergiant diameter: up to 1,000 times that of Sun.

• Energy released by a supernova in one minute is equivalent to total radiated by Sun in nine billion years.

• Average galaxy has 100 billion stars – it would take 1,000 years to count them all at a rate of 3 per second.

MAIN SEQUENCE STARS

The main sequence is the central period of a star's lifetime. A star's brightness, colour, surface temperature, size, and lifespan depend on its mass. Our Sun is a yellow star, a typical star of average size and temperature.

Brown dwarf 1,000°C (1,800°F)

Red dwarf 2,800°C (5,100°F)

Yellow star 5,500°C (9,900°F)

White star 10,000°C (18,000°F)

Blue/White star 16,000°C (28,800°F)

Blue star 24,000°C

NEAREST STARS

Star	Star type	Distance (light years)
Sun	Yellow main sequence	0.0
Proxima Centauri	Red dwarf	4.2
Alpha Centauri A	Yellow main sequence	4.3
Alpha Centauri B	Orange main sequence	4.3
Barnard's star	Red dwarf	5.9
Wolf 359	Red dwarf	7.6
Lalande 21185	Red dwarf	8.1
Sirius A	White main sequence	8.6
Sirius B	White dwarf	8.6
UV Ceti A	Red dwarf	8.9

SUPERNOVA REMAINS

One famous supernova was seen by Chinese astronomers in 1054. Its remains, a cloud of gas and dust particles called a nebula, can now be seen as the Crab nebula. This nebula is now expanding at a speed of 1500km/sec (930 miles/sec): 130 times the top speed of the Saturn V Moon rocket.

Crab nebula

COLLAPSED STARS

A star's life on the main sequence ends either in a supernova explosion or a planetary nebula. Depending on its size, the remaining corpse collapses into one of three forms: white dwarf, neutron star, or black hole.

WHITE DWARF

When the planetary nebula of a typical star disperses into space, all that remains is a superdense core known as a white dwarf. Star corpses of less than 1.4 times the Sun's mass (i.e. typical star corpses) become white dwarfs.

Solid core

Gas

Radius = 6,000km (3,700 miles)

NEUTRON STAR

Neutron stars form when supernova corpses between 1.4 and 3 times the mass of our Sun collapse into the most solid state of matter possible. These neutron stars are so dense that a pinhead of their matter would weigh a million tonnes.

Solid crust

1cm (0.39in) thick atmosphere

Noutron fluid

Possible solid core

Radius = 16km (10 miles)

PULSAR

Rotating neutron stars are called pulsars. Their spin creates an intense magnetic field around them, a million million times Earth's field. Like a lighthouse, a pulsar sends out beams of radiation from hot spots on or above its surface.

Axis of rotation

Beam of radiation from pulsar can be detected as it sweeps past Earth.

Hot spot

BLACK HOLE

A black hole is a region of powerful gravity surrounding a point of infinite density called a singularity. Nothing, not even light, can escape after falling past the event horizon (the "edge" of the black hole). Supernova corpses of more than three times the Sun's mass collapse into black holes.

Through the black hole

A black hole's gravity is so strong that an astronaut falling into it would be stretched apart. Tearing matter apart in this way creates enormous heat.

7 The core's contraction leads to a massive explosion called a supernova. The star shines as bright as a billion Suns as it blows apart. The core collapses in just one second.

6 Now a red supergiant, the swollen star swallows up its surrounding planets. Its core fuses carbon into iron, stops generating energy, and suddenly collapses under its own weight.

5 The star begins to swell when its central supply of hydrogen is exhausted. The core fuses helium into carbon. Its outer layers swell and glow red.

A black hole's gravity distorts space into a well.

Event horizon: point of no return

BRIGHTEST STARS TO THE NAKED EYE

Star	Star type	Distance (light-years)
Sun	Yellow main sequence	0.0
Sirius A	White main sequence	8.6
Canopus	White supergiant	200
Alpha Centauri	Yellow main sequence	4.3
Arcturus	Red giant	36
Vega	White main sequence	26
Capella	Yellow giant	42
Rigel	Blue/white supergiant	910
Procyon	Yellow main sequence	11
Achernar	Blue/white main sequence	85

NIGHT SKIES

ANCIENT PEOPLES INVENTED names for different groups of stars, called constellations, to help them find their way about the skies. The stars that belong to them form patterns that have been observed and recognized over thousands of years.

CELESTIAL SPHERES

The celestial sphere is the huge, revolving, hollow ball studded with stars that encloses Earth. In fact, it is Earth that rotates and the stars are scattered about in space; but the idea of a celestial sphere allows astronomers to plot the positions of stars and follow their movements.

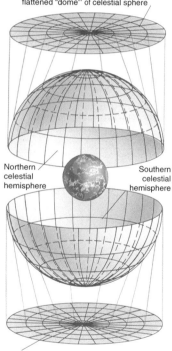

Map of northern skies – flattened "dome" of celestial sphere

Northern celestial hemisphere

Southern celestial hemisphere

Map of southern skies – flattened "bowl" of celestial sphere

OLDEST STAR MAP

The oldest example of a map of the heavens was discovered in 1987 on the ceiling of a tomb in Jiaotong University, Xian, China. It was painted in 25 B.C.

SKIES OF THE NORTHERN HEMISPHERE

The picture below shows the constellations an observer would see while standing at the North Pole and looking up into the night sky.

Pole position
In the Northern Hemisphere stars appear to revolve steadily about the star at the centre: Polaris, the Pole Star. This star lies directly along Earth's axis of rotation.

Betelgeuse: 400 times bigger than the Sun

Pisces
Cetus
Pegasus
Aries
Delphinus
Andromeda
Triangulum
Taurus
Sagitta
Cygnus
MILKY WAY
Perseus
Aquila
Cassiopeia
Orion
Cepheus
Auriga
Lyra
Polaris (North Star)
Draco
Ursa Minor
Gemini
Ophiuchus
Monoceros
Hercules
Canis Minor
Corona Borealis
Ursa Major
Cancer
Serpens Caput
Ursa Major
Leo Minor
Hydra
Boötes
Canes Venatici
Leo
Virgo

Vega: it will be the Pole Star in 14,000 A.D.. A "wobble" in the Earth's rotation makes the celestial poles slowly change position.

Castor: in fact a family of six stars

MONTHLY STARS

Stars that lie on the other side of the Sun from Earth cannot be seen at night – night-time observers face the other way. Earth, however, revolves around the Sun once a year. So, the best time to see those stars is during the months when they lie on the opposite side of Earth from the Sun. This is why different constellations are visible at different times of the year.

Celestial sphere

Stars visible from Earth in March

Earth in July

Sun

Earth in March

Earth in January

STARS OF THE ZODIAC

The Sun appears in front of each constellation of the zodiac on the dates shown. These astronomical dates differ from astrological ones by about one month.

Aries
the ram
21 April–
21 May

Taurus
the bull
22 May–
21 June

Gemini
the twins
22 June–
22 July

Cancer
the crab
23 July–
23 August

Leo
the lion
24 August–
22 September

Virgo
the virgin
23 September–
23 October

SKIES OF THE SOUTHERN HEMISPHERE

In the South, no bright star lies along Earth's axis of rotation, so there is no Pole Star. Southern stars, however, are more spectacular.

Milky Way
The Solar System lies in the plane of the Milky Way Galaxy. So, when we look up in the sky, we see a band of bright stars, and none of the Galaxy's spiral details.

Orion Nebula: a region of star formation.

Cetus

Aquarius

Sculptor

Piscis Austrinus

Fornax

Capricornus

Phoenix

Grus

Eridanus

Microscopium

Tucana

Indus

Aquila

Horologium

Caelum

Pavo

Sagittarius

Lepus

Hydrus

Dorado

Reticulum

Mensa

Corona Australis

Columba

Pictor

Volans

Apus

Chameleon

Ara

Canis Major

Carina

Triangulum Australe

Scorpius

Ophiuchus

Mono-ceros

Musca

Norma

Vela

Crux

Lupus

Puppis

MILKY WAY

Pyxis

Centaurus

Antila

Libra

Sirius: the brightest star in the sky

Hydra

Canopus: used by space probes as a navigation aid.

Corvus

Sextans

Crater

Spica: 70,000 times brighter than the Sun

Virgo

Alpha Centauri: a member of the closest star system to the Sun.

TRUE STAR DISTANCES

The stars in a constellation appear to lie in the same region. In reality, they may lie at great distances from each another, but have a similar brightness when seen from Earth.

Orion Nebula

Mintaka

Earth

Rigel

Betelgeuse

Constellation of Orion seen from Earth

light-years 0   1,000   2,000   3,000

Libra
the scales
24 October–
22 November

Scorpius
the scorpion
23 November–
21 December

Sagittarius
the archer
22 December–
20 January

Capricornus
the sea-goat
21 January–
18 February

Aquarius
the water-carrier
19 February–
20 March

Pisces
the fishes
21 March–
20 April

NIGHT SKY FACTS

• 2,000 years ago Sirius, the dog star, may have appeared red, and Romans used to sacrifice red dogs to it.

• Some "stars" seem to move very quickly across the night sky – these are in fact artificial satellites, reflecting the Sun's light at dawn or dusk.

• The Andromeda Galaxy is the furthest object visible to the naked eye – it lies 2.5 million light-years away.

• The ancient Chinese had constellations for every aspect of life – a celestial prison, a celestial stable, and a row of shops.

AURORAS

The Aurora Borealis (Northern Lights) and the Aurora Australis (Southern Lights) are colourful glowing lights that can be observed near the Poles. They are caused when the solar wind meets the Earth's atmosphere (see p.25).

CONSTELLATION CHANGES

The constellations seem fixed and eternal. Over hundreds of thousands of years, however, stars will change their positions, altering the overall shape.

1 "The Plough" as ancient people saw it 100,000 years ago

2 "The Plough" as it can be seen today

3 "The Plough" as it will be seen in 100,000 years

LARGEST CONSTELLATIONS

Constellation	Meaning	Area (% of visible sky)
Hydra	The Watersnake	6.32
Virgo	The Virgin	6.28
Ursa Major	The Great Bear	6.20
Cetus	The Whale	5.97
Hercules	Hercules the Hero	5.94

SUN AND SOLAR SYSTEM

THE SUN IS THE STAR at the heart of the Solar System. Its huge gravitational pull anchors the nine planets, the asteroids, and comets in their orbits. The nuclear-reactor core at the Sun's centre radiates light and heat throughout the entire Solar System.

Corona
The corona is a huge, thin halo of hot gas. It has a temperature of 1 million°C (1.8 million°F).

Corona seen at eclipse

ANATOMY OF THE SUN

Inside the core, nuclear fusion turns hydrogen into helium, creating energy that rises out into the photosphere, and from there into space.

Chromosphere
The chromosphere is a reddish outer layer of hydrogen that rises 1,000 km (620 miles) above the photosphere. It has a temperature of 4,000–8,000°C (7,200–14,400°F).

Convective zone
In the convective zone, rising and falling currents carry heat outwards towards the photosphere. It has a temperature of 1.5 million°C (2.7 million°F).

Photosphere
This is the surface layer of the Sun. Its white-hot hydrogen has a temperature of 5,500°C (9,900°F).

Radiative zone
The core's energy radiates outwards through this hydrogen layer. It has a temperature of 1.5 million–14 million°C (2.7 million–25.2 million°F).

Core
The hydrogen core works as a massive nuclear reactor. It fuses hydrogen to create helium at a temperature of 14 million°C (25.2 million°F).

SUN DATA

Age	5 billion years
Diameter	1,392,000km (865,000 miles)
Mass (Earth = 1)	332,946
Density (water = 1)	1.41
Distance from Earth	149.6 million km (92.9 million miles)
Distance from nearest star	40,000 billion km (24,900 billion miles)
Core Temperature	14 million°C (25.2 million°F)
Surface Temperature	5,500°C (9,900°F)
Luminosity	390 billion billion megawatts
Life Expectancy	5 billion years
Speed	240 million years to orbit the galaxy

SUN FACTS

- One square metre (10.8 sq ft) of Sun's surface shines as brightly as 600,000 100-watt lightbulbs.

- Biggest observed solar prominence reached height of 700,000km (435,000 miles) in one hour in 1946.

- In one second, Sun gives out 35 million times average annual electricity supply for the entire United States.

- Solar flares can interrupt radio communications on Earth, cause magnetic storms, and confuse birds flying long distances.

- Rotation of Sun's surface varies from 25 days at equator to 35 days at poles. Radiative zone rotates regularly every 27 days.

- If Sun's cooler outer layers were peeled off, dangerous radiation from its core would destroy life on Earth.

SURFACE FEATURES OF THE SUN

SPICULES
Spicules are straight jets of gas that occur in the chromosphere. They rise as high as 10,000km (6,200 miles) at speeds of 25km/sec (16 miles/sec). After 5-10 minutes they dissolve into the surrounding corona. Spicules are thought to be caused by magnetic fields. There are 100,000 on the Sun's surface at any time.

GRANULES
The Sun's surface is made up of millions of upsurging granules. A granule is about 1,000km (620 miles) across: an area the size of France.

Granule

France

SUNSPOTS
These areas of darker, cooler gas appear in pairs at a temperature of 4,000°C (7,200°F). They occur when the heat flow from the core is blocked by the Sun's magnetic field. Sunspot activity runs in 11.5-year cycles. It will peak next in 2001.

SOLAR FLARES
These enormous and unpredictable explosions occur in the Sun's atmosphere. Solar flares can throw billions of tonnes of the Sun's material out into space. These explosions release an amount of energy equivalent to a million million times that of the first nuclear bomb.

SOLAR PROMINENCES
Solar prominences are arched plumes of flaming hydrogen gas that hang in the lower corona, supported by the force of the Sun's magnetic field. Some prominences erupt into space as great arches at speeds of 400m/sec (900 mph).

EVOLUTION OF THE SUN AND SOLAR SYSTEM

The Solar System began life 5 billion years ago as a massive cloud of gas with rocky and icy particles. When the cloud collapsed under its own gravity, the Sun formed, and the grains clumped together to form the planets.

1 The Solar System begins as a spinning cloud of gas that contains particles of rock and ice, densest at the centre.

2 Gravity causes the cloud to collapse inwards. The Sun forms and begins to shine, melting ice in its inner region.

3 Rock grains nearest the Sun form planetesimals (minute planets). Further away, colder planetesimals are icy and rocky.

4 Rocky planetesimals crash into each other. Icy, rocky planetesimals grow in size as they draw in gas and dust.

Solar System to scale: outer planets move in large orbits around the Sun.

Pluto

The angle of Pluto's orbit around the Sun is steeper than that of the other planets.

Asteroid Belts

Saturn

Neptune

Uranus

Jupiter

The inner planets are dense, rocky bodies, close to the Sun.

Mars

Sun

Venus

Mercury

Earth

5 Rocky inner planets form first by gathering up other planetesimals. Further out, where there is less matter, outer planets form more slowly.

AMAZING SCALES

If the Sun's diameter were the height of an average adult, then Jupiter would be the size of the head. Earth would be slightly bigger than the iris of the eyeball.

HELIOSPHERE

The Sun's magnetic field or heliosphere extends beyond the edge of the Solar System. It is generated by the gale of hot, charged particles known as the solar wind that streams in spirals off the corona. The Sun also generates a sheet of electrical current, smaller than the heliosphere.

Cosmic radiation

Interstellar gases

Sheet of current flows through the heliosphere

Pluto

Sun

LARGEST BODIES IN THE SOLAR SYSTEM

Body	Maximum diameter	
	km	miles
Sun	1,392,000	865,000
Jupiter	142,984	88,846
Saturn	120,536	74,898
Uranus	51,118	31,763
Neptune	49,528	30,775
Earth	12,756	7,926
Venus	12,103	7,520
Mars	6,786	4,217
Ganymede (moon of Jupiter)	5,262	3,270
Titan (moon of Saturn)	5,150	3,200

DEATH OF THE SUN AND SOLAR SYSTEM

1 Five billion years from now, the Sun will swell to 100 times its present size, as its fuel begins to run low. Its outer layers will engulf Mercury, Venus, and possibly Earth.

2 After a further one million years, the Sun will have used up all its available hydrogen. Its gaseous outer layers will dissolve into space as a planetary nebula, a thin cloud of gas and dust particles.

3 The remaining core will finally become a white dwarf, a superdense star about the size of Earth. It will slowly cool off and fade to a black dwarf. The outer planets of the present Solar System will still orbit this dwarf, but at a much greater distance.

PLANETS

A PLANET IS A BODY that orbits the Sun, or any other star. Our Sun has nine known planets and they can be divided into two groups: the dense, rocky inner planets, and the gassy or icy outer planets.

THE INNER PLANETS

Mercury, Venus, Earth, and Mars are known as the inner planets or terrestrials. They are made up of rocks and metals, they are smaller than the outer gas giants, and their atmospheres contain very little of the gases hydrogen and helium. Earth, as far as we know, is the only planet where there is life.

Sun

RELATIVE SIZES

Pluto is the smallest planet and also the most distant. Jupiter is bigger than all the other planets put together.

Mercury   Venus   Earth   Mars

Jupiter

RELATIVE DISTANCES

The orbits of the four inner planets lie close to the Sun. Mercury, the nearest planet to the Sun, is 100 times closer than Pluto.

Mercury Venus Earth Mars   Jupiter   Saturn
Sun

MERCURY
It has the fastest orbiting speed around the Sun. Its huge impact crater, Caloris Basin, is 1,300km (800 miles) across.

Crust

Mantle

Core

VENUS
This is the deadliest planet. The atmosphere would crush a tin can; the heat would melt it; the acid clouds would dissolve it.

Crust

Mantle

Core

EARTH
Earth is the only planet known to have any quantity of water and oxygen, and to support life. Its surface is constantly moving due to plate tectonics (see p.40).

Crust

Mantle

Outer core

Inner core

MARS
Mars is the red planet: its plains are covered in rust. Meteors that left Mars billions of years ago have been found to contain minute structures that could be the fossil remains of simple life forms.

Crust

Mantle

Core

INNER PLANETS

	Mercury	Venus	Earth	Mars
Distance from Sun million km (million miles)	57.9 (36.0)	108.2 (67.2)	149.6 (93.0)	227.9 (141.6)
Diameter km (miles)	4,878 (3,031)	12,103 (7,520)	12,756 (7,926)	6,786 (4,217)
Time taken to circle Sun	87.97 days	224.70 days	365.26 days	686.98 days
Orbital speed around Sun km/sec (miles/sec)	47.89 (29.76)	35.03 (21.77)	29.79 (18.51)	24.13 (14.99)
Time taken to turn on axis	58 days, 16 hours	243 days, 14 mins	23 hours, 56 mins	24 hours, 37 mins
Mass (Earth = 1)	0.055	0.81	1	0.11
Density (water = 1)	5.43	5.25	5.52	3.95
Temperature Celsius (Fahrenheit)	(on surface) -180 to +430°C (-292 to +806°F)	(on surface) 465°C (869°F)	(on surface) -70 to +55°C (-94 to +131°F)	(on surface) -120 to +25°C (-184 to +77°F)
Number of moons	-	-	1	2

MARS' GIANT MOUNTAIN

Olympus Mons is the biggest volcano (extinct) in the Solar System.

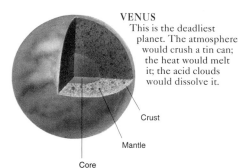

Olympus Mons 26km (16 miles) high

Everest 8.8km (5.5 miles) high

ATMOSPHERES

Scientists have identified various gases in the atmospheres of the planets. The giant planets all contain large quantities of helium and hydrogen.

GASES FOUND IN THE ATMOSPHERE

Sodium   Hydrogen   Carbon dioxide

Helium   Nitrogen   Oxygen   Methane

Mercury   Venus   Earth   Mars   Jupiter   Saturn   Uranus   Neptune   Pluto

THE OUTER PLANETS

Beyond the orbit of Mars lie the outer planets: Jupiter, Saturn, Uranus, Neptune, and Pluto. These planets, with the exception of Pluto, are not solid, but gigantic balls of swirling gases and liquids held together by gravity. Pluto is extremely small and made of rock and thick ice.

Pluto

Neptune

Saturn

Uranus

Uranus   Neptune   Pluto

JUPITER
Jupiter is the biggest and fastest spinning planet in the Solar System. It could contain 1,300 Earths.

Atmosphere

Liquid hydrogen

Metallic hydrogen

Core

SATURN
The diameter of its rings is almost the distance between Earth and the Moon. It has the lowest density. Set on a huge lake it would float.

Atmosphere

Liquid hydrogen

Metallic hydrogen

Core

URANUS
This planet has the most tilted axis and spins on its side. It has the longest-lasting seasons: each pole receives 42 years of sunlight then 42 years of darkness.

Atmosphere

Water, ammonia, methane

Core

NEPTUNE
Neptune's winds are the fastest in the Solar System at 2,000km/h (1,240mph). Its Great Dark Spot is as large as Earth.

Atmosphere

Water, ammonia, methane

Core

PLUTO
Pluto is the smallest, darkest, and coldest planet. It may just be the largest member of an outer asteroid belt called the Kuiper Belt.

Ice and frozen methane

Ice

Core

OUTER PLANETS

Jupiter	Saturn	Uranus	Neptune	Pluto
778.3 (483.6)	1,427 (886)	2,871 (1,784)	4,497 (2,794)	5,914 (3,675)
142,984 (88,846)	120,536 (74,898)	51,118 (31,763)	49,528 (30,775)	2,284 (1,419)
11.86 years	29.46 years	84.01 years	164.79 years	248.54 years
13.06 (8.12)	9.64 (5.99)	6.81 (4.23)	5.43 (3.37)	4.74 (2.95)
9 hours, 55 mins	10 hours, 40 mins	17 hours, 14 mins	16 hours, 7 mins	6 days, 9 hrs
318	95.18	14.5	17.14	0.0022
1.33	0.69	1.29	1.64	2.03
(at cloud tops) -150°C -238°F	(at cloud tops) -180°C -292°F	(at cloud tops) -210°C -346°C	(at cloud tops) -210°C -346°F	-220°C -364°F
16	18	15	8	1

PLANETARY MOON FACTS

• Saturn has the most moons of any planet in Solar System: 18. Jupiter comes second with 16.

• Europa, Jupiter's moon, has a surface of ice 97km (60 miles) thick.

• Titan, Saturn's moon, is thought to have cliffs of solid methane and rivers of liquid methane.

• Phobos, Mars' moon, is being dragged closer to Mars. In 30 million years, it will be destroyed by crashing on to the surface.

• Miranda, Uranus' moon, has canyons ten times deeper than Earth's Grand Canyon. It has an ice cliff 5.2km (3.23 miles) high.

• Callisto, Jupiter's moon, has a more cratered surface than any other body in Solar System.

Callisto, a moon of Jupiter

MERCURY LEAP
The record women's high jump on Earth is 2.09m (6ft 10.25in). On Mercury, where gravity is weaker, the same athlete would be able to jump more than twice as high. She could leap over an elephant in one bound.

MOON

THE MOON IS EARTH'S constant companion in space. Held by our planet's gravity, it revolves around Earth in its orbit of the Sun, like a satellite. The Moon, like Earth, is 4.6 billion years old. Unlike Earth, the Moon is dead, waterless, and airless.

THEORY OF MOON'S ORIGIN

Astronomers have put forward several theories to explain the mystery of the Moon's origin. The most popular theory holds that a body the size of Mars collided with Earth in its early days. The impact threw vast amounts of matter into space, and these fragments of rock came together to form the Moon.

PHASES OF THE MOON

As the Moon orbits Earth, it receives light from the Sun, and a changing portion of its illuminated face is visible from Earth. These portions are the Moon's phases.

Sun's rays

Earth

Moon's face invisible: new Moon

Moon's face fully visible: Full Moon

New Moon   Crescent   First quarter   Gibbous   Full Moon   Gibbous   Last quarter   Crescent

MOON DATA

Age	4.6 billion years
Diameter	3,476km (2,160 miles)
Mass (Earth=1)	0.012
Surface gravity (Earth=1)	0.16
Average distance from Earth	384,400km (238,000 miles)
Time taken to orbit Earth	27.3 days
Time taken to rotate on axis	27.3 days
Surface temperature	-155°C to 105°C (-247°F to 221°F)

NEAR SIDE OF THE MOON

The near side of the Moon always faces Earth and is always at least partially visible in our night sky, except at a new Moon.

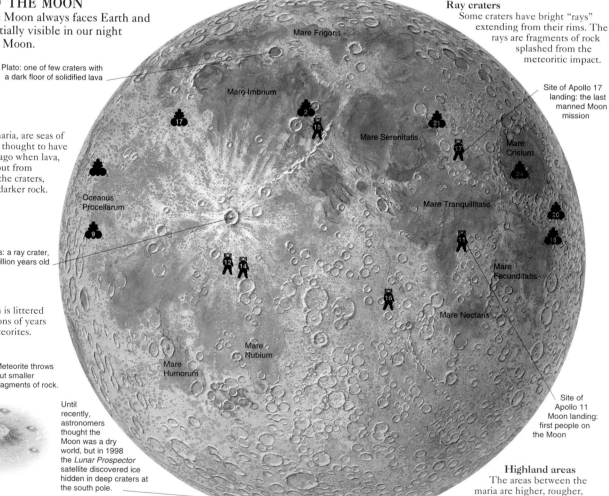

Plato: one of few craters with a dark floor of solidified lava

Mare Frigoris

Mare Imbrium

Maria

The dark areas, called maria, are seas of solidified lava. They are thought to have formed billions of years ago when lava, or molten rock, seeped out from beneath the crust to fill the craters, and then solidified into darker rock.

Oceanus Procellarum

Copernicus: a ray crater, about 800 million years old

Craters

The surface of the Moon is littered with craters formed billions of years ago by the impact of meteorites.

Meteorite throws out smaller fragments of rock.

Ejected rocks make craters surrounding main crater.

Mare Serenitatis

Mare Crisium

Mare Tranquillitatis

Mare Fecunditatis

Mare Nectaris

Mare Nubium

Mare Humorum

Until recently, astronomers thought the Moon was a dry world, but in 1998 the *Lunar Prospector* satellite discovered ice hidden in deep craters at the south pole.

Ray craters

Some craters have bright "rays" extending from their rims. The rays are fragments of rock splashed from the meteoritic impact.

Site of Apollo 17 landing: the last manned Moon mission

Site of Apollo 11 Moon landing: first people on the Moon

Highland areas

The areas between the maria are higher, rougher, and brighter than the maria.

MOON LANDINGS

– Apollo landings (USA)   – Luna landings (USSR)

MOON AND EARTH: GRAVITY AND TIDES

The Moon is so close to Earth that it exerts a strong pull on Earth's waters. This gravitational pull produces a bulge on the side of Earth facing the Moon, and a corresponding bulge on the opposite side. So, the oceans have two daily high tides.

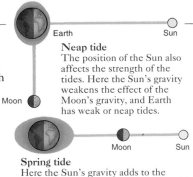

Neap tide
The position of the Sun also affects the strength of the tides. Here the Sun's gravity weakens the effect of the Moon's gravity, and Earth has weak or neap tides.

Spring tide
Here the Sun's gravity adds to the Moon's, and Earth has strong spring tides.

LUNAR AND SOLAR ECLIPSES

LUNAR ECLIPSE
When the Moon moves into the Earth's shadow, no sunlight is reflected off the Moon and it disappears from Earth's view. Normally the Moon passes above or below the shadow because its orbit is tilted at 5° from Earth's path.

SOLAR ECLIPSE
By chance, the Sun and Moon appear the same size in the sky. When, at a full Moon, the Moon lines up directly between Sun and Earth, its inner shadow creates a total eclipse. People in its outer shadow see a partial eclipse.

TOTAL LUNAR ECLIPSES

Date	Visible from
21 Jan 2000	Europe, Americas, Asia
16 July 2000	Pacific, Australasia, southwest Asia
9 Jan 2001	Australia, Asia, Africa, Europe
16 May 2003	Africa, Europe, Americas
8-9 Nov 2003	Asia, Africa, Europe, Americas

TOTAL SOLAR ECLIPSES

Date	Visible from
26 Feb 1998	North America, Hawaii, West Africa
11 Aug 1999	Europe, North Africa, Arabia, Greenland
21 June 2001	South Atlantic, southern Africa
4 Dec 2002	Southern Africa, southern Indian Ocean
23-24 Nov 2003	Southern Australasia, South America

NEAR AND FAR SIDE

The Moon spins on its axis in exactly the same time that it takes to complete an orbit of Earth. The same side always faces us and the far side remains invisible. The Moon wobbles on its axis, and at some places on its orbit it surges forward or slows down. As a result, we can actually see 59% of its surface from Earth.

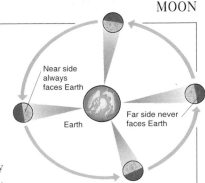

LASTING IMPRESSION

With no air, water, or volcanic activity to erode them, the footprints and tracks left by the Moon's astronauts will remain as they are for 100 million years.

FAR SIDE OF THE MOON

The far side always faces away from Earth, and is more cratered and rugged than the near side.

Clearer view
For astronomers, who need a clear view of space, the far side would be an excellent place to build an observatory. It is totally shielded from the reflective glare and stray electrical signals of Earth, and it has no atmosphere to dim the stars' images.

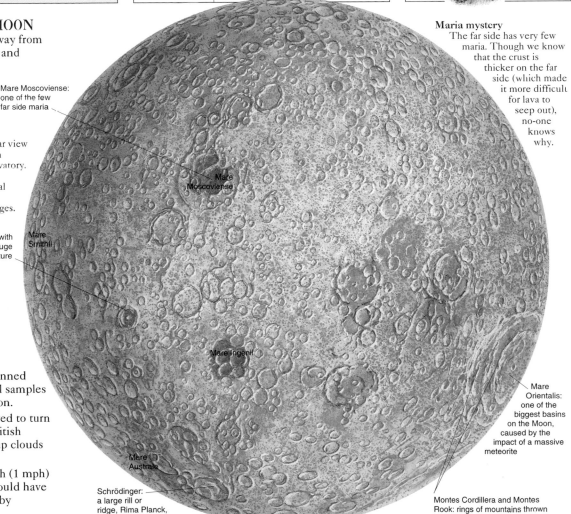

Mare Moscoviense: one of the few far side maria

Tsiolovsky: a crater with terraced walls and a huge central mountain structure

Mare Moscoviense

Mare Smithii

Mare Ingenii

Mare Australe

Schrödinger: a large rill or ridge, Rima Planck, extends from this crater

Maria mystery
The far side has very few maria. Though we know that the crust is thicker on the far side (which made it more difficult for lava to seep out), no-one knows why.

Mare Orientalis: one of the biggest basins on the Moon, caused by the impact of a massive meteorite

Montes Cordillera and Montes Rook: rings of mountains thrown up around Mare Orientalis

MOON FACTS

• Moon's first astronauts, Americans Neil Armstrong and Buzz Aldrin, landed in 1969 in Apollo XI.

• In 1970 Russian probe Luna 16 was the first unmanned spacecraft to bring back soil samples from the surface of the Moon.

• In 1950 the Moon appeared to turn blue after a forest fire in British Columbia, Canada, threw up clouds of smoke particles.

• A mistake of only 1.6km/h (1 mph) in Apollo XI's top speed would have led to it missing the Moon by 1,600km (1,000 miles).

COMETS, METEORS, AND ASTEROIDS

CHUNKS OF ROCK and metal, lumps of ice, and clouds of dust float far and wide in the Solar System. Scientists classify these wandering objects as comets, meteors, and asteroids. Rocky asteroids sometimes crash into planets or their moons, causing massive craters.

Dust tail

Gas tail

COMETS
Comets are chunks of ice and rock left over from the birth of the Solar System. Astronomers believe that these icy rocks are located in a zone called the Oort cloud, named after the Dutch astronomer Jan Oort (1900–92), that lies beyond the furthest planet in the Solar System.

DEFINITIONS
Comet An icy object orbiting the Sun. It produces steam when it nears the Sun and develops a tail of dust and gas.

Meteor A particle of rock that burns up in Earth's upper atmosphere, leaving a streak of light.

Asteroid A small rocky object in the Solar System. Asteroids range in size from 930km (578 miles) across down to dust particles.

Meteorite A piece of rock that has survived passage through Earth's atmosphere: thought to be a fragment of an asteroid, not of a comet.

MOST FREQUENTLY SEEN COMETS

Name	Period (years)
Encke	3.3
Grigg-Skjellerup	4.9
Honda-Mrkos-Pajdusakova	5.2
Tempel 2	5.3
Neujmin 2	5.4
Tuttle-Giacobini-Kresak	5.5
Tempel-Swift	5.7
Tempel 1	6.0
Pons-Winnecke	6.3
De Vico Swift	6.3

Jets of dust

Nucleus

Nucleus

Halley's comet photographed by the Schmidt telescope in 1986

HALLEY'S COMET
Every 76 years Halley's comet returns to the centre of the Solar System. In 1705, English astronomer Edmund Halley (1656–1742) correctly predicted its return in the year 1758. On the last return in 1986, the space probe Giotto penetrated to within 600km (370 miles) of the comet's nucleus.

COMET NUCLEUS
The nucleus is a chunk of rock and ice that lies at the comet's core. As the comet nears the Sun, the heat melts the ice. Gas jets spring from the Sun-facing side. Fragments of rock break off to form the dust tail.

Ice

Gas and dust jets

Rock

COMET TAIL
Each comet has a dust tail and a gas tail. These are blown back by the solar wind, which forces the dust and gas away from the Sun.

Gas tail forced back by electrically charged particles of the solar wind

Dust tail follows curve of comet's path

Sun

Comet recedes from Sun, but tail always points away from Sun

SO LONG
The comet with the longest known tail was the Great Comet of 1843, which trailed for 330 million km (205 million miles). The tail could have wrapped around Earth 7,000 times. It will not return to the centre of the Solar System until 2356.

COMET RECORDS
LONGEST KNOWN PERIOD of a comet is 24 million years. This comet, Delavan's comet, was last seen in 1914.

MOST FREQUENT COMET is Encke's comet, which returns every 3.3 years.

BRIGHTEST COMET this century was the Daylight Comet of 1910. It was as bright as the planet Venus.

METEORS
Meteors, or shooting stars, are streaks of light that appear briefly in the night sky. They occur when particles of rock or dust, left by comets, burn up in Earth's atmosphere at speeds of up to 70km/sec (43 miles/sec).

METEOR SHOWER
Comets leave trails of dust and debris along their orbits around the Sun. When Earth crosses one of these trails, the dust burns up in the atmosphere and we see a meteor shower in the sky.

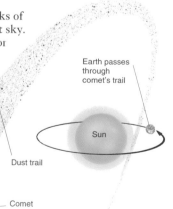

Earth passes through comet's trail

Sun

Dust trail

Comet

SHOOTING STAR
This long-exposure photograph shows a meteor from the Ursid meteor shower that occurs each year in December.

METEOR SHOWERS

Main showers (annual)	Date	Maximum number per hour
Quadrantids	3-4 Jan	50
Lyrids	22 April	10
Delta Aquarids	31 July	25
Perseids	12 Aug	50
Orionids	21 Oct	20
Taurids	8 Nov	10
Leonids	17 Nov	10
Geminids	14 Dec	50
Ursids	22 Dec	15

ASTEROIDS

Asteroids are pieces of rock smaller than planets that orbit the Sun. More than 4,000 have been found. They range in size from tiny fragments of rock to bodies hundreds of kilometres across.

Ceres
Ceres, discovered in 1801, is the biggest known asteroid with a diameter of 930km (578 miles). If Ceres were placed on Earth it would cover France.

Vesta
Vesta is smaller than Ceres, but its highly reflective surface makes it the brightest asteroid.

Psyche
Psyche is irregularly shaped, made of iron, and about 260km (160 miles) long – the size of Jamaica.

ASTEROID BELTS

Most asteroids lie in the Asteroid Belts between the orbits of Mars and Jupiter. The Trojan asteroids, though, follow Jupiter's orbit in two groups. Others orbit the Sun alone.

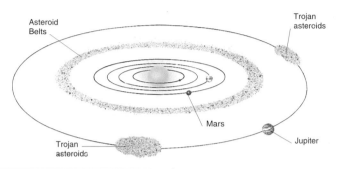

Asteroid Belts

Trojan asteroids

Mars

Jupiter

Trojan asteroids

ASTEROID FACTS

• An estimated 2,000 collisions have occurred between asteroids and Earth in the last 600 million years.

• If an asteroid of average size collided with Earth, it could destroy an entire country.

• In January 1991, an asteroid measuring about 10m (33ft) across passed between the Moon and Earth.

• In the future, asteroids could be mined for metals as resources on Earth grow scarce.

Captain James T. Kirk and Mr. Spock

• Asteroid 2309 is called Mr. Spock, after the character in the television series *Star Trek*.

• Ceres, the largest asteroid, contains a quarter of all the rock in the Asteroid Belts.

LARGEST ASTEROIDS

Name	First seen	Diameter	
		km	miles
Ceres	1801	930	578
Pallas	1802	607	377
Vesta	1807	519	322
Hygeia	1849	450	280
Euphrosyne	1854	370	230
Interamnia	1910	349	217
Davida	1903	322	200
Cybele	1861	308	191
Europa	1858	288	179
Patienta	1899	275	171

ARIZONA CRATER

On Earth, the best example of an asteroid impact crater is the Arizona Crater, USA, which is 1.2km (0.7 miles) in diameter, 180m (590ft) deep, and 50,000 years old.

Walking on the Moon
In order to prepare for their work on the surface of the Moon, the Apollo astronauts trained on the slopes of the Arizona Crater. Dressed in their spacesuits, they tested the Moon buggy and other equipment.

TUNGUSKA EVENT

In June 1908 a huge explosion occurred in the forested Tunguska region of Siberia, devastating an area of 3,900sq km (1,500sq miles). The shock wave was heard 1,000km (600 miles) away. The explosion is now thought to have been caused by an asteroid.

METEORITES

A meteorite is a piece of rock from space that escapes destruction in Earth's atmosphere, and is able to reach the ground. There are three kinds of meteorites stony, iron, and stony-iron.

Stony
Stony meteorites are the most common type. They consist mainly of the minerals olivine and pyroxene.

Iron
Iron meteorites come from small asteroids that broke up in space. They are rarer than stony meteorites.

Stony-iron
Stony iron meteorites contain both rock and metal. The picture shows bright metal enclosing the mineral olivine.

METEORITE RECORDS

OLDEST METEORITES
called carbonaceous chondrites, are 4.55 billion years old.

LARGEST METEORITE
lies at Grootfontein, Namibia. It is called Hoba, is 2.75m (9ft) long, made of iron, and weighs 59 tonnes: as much as eight elephants.

ONLY PERSON INJURED
was Mrs. A. Hodges of Alabama, USA. A 4kg (9lb) meteorite crashed through her roof in November 1954 and injured her arm.

ONLY FATAL METEORITE
killed a dog in Nakhla, Egypt in 1911.

FROM THE HAND OF GOD

The Black Stone of Mecca, housed in a shrine in Saudi Arabia, is the sacred stone of Islam. It is believed to be a meteorite that fell to Earth hundreds of years ago.

DUST COLLECTOR

Rock particles picked up from space add 10,000 tonnes to Earth's weight each year. This would be enough dust to give everyone on Earth two grams (0.07oz) per year.

ASTRONOMY

ASTRONOMY IS THE STUDY of the nature and movement of the heavenly objects in the Universe: planets, moons, comets, asteroids, stars, and galaxies.

Aristotle's Universe

335–323 B.C. Aristotle (384–322 B.C.), Greek physicist and philosopher, puts Earth at the centre of the Universe. This central belief dominates until the 15th century.

A.D. 137–145 Ptolemy (c.120–180), Greek astronomer, records the positions of 1,080 stars and divides them into 48 constellations in his book, *Almagest*. His system uses Aristotle's beliefs as its basis, and stands for 1,400 years.

Ptolemy

Timeline: 400 B.C. | 335 | 200 B.C. | A.D. | 137 | 200 A.D.

1543 Nicolas Copernicus (1473–1543), Polish monk, establishes the position of the Sun at the centre of the Universe in his book, *De Revolutionibus Orbium Caelestium*.

Nicolas Copernicus

1596 Tycho Brahe (1546–1601), Danish nobleman, publishes his great star catalogue, compiled from 1575 to 1595. His study fixes accurate positions for about 770 stars.

Tycho Brahe

1608 First telescope is thought to have been invented for military use by Dutch scientist Hans Lippershey (1570–1619).

1609 Elliptical motion of planets is established by German astronomer Johannes Kepler (1571–1630), overturning the theory of circular motion around the Sun.

Timeline: 1500 | 1543 | 1596 | 1600 | 1608 1609

17th-century telescope

Galileo

1610 Galileo (1564–1642), Italian scientist and the first systematic user of the telescope, discovers the moons of Jupiter and identifies sunspots and craters on the Moon. He shows that Venus has phases like the Moon, adding support to the idea that the Sun is the centre of the Universe.

1667 Isaac Newton (1642–1727), English scientist, lays down the laws of gravitation governing celestial bodies, marking the beginning of modern astronomy. In 1668 he invents and builds the first reflecting telescope.

Isaac Newton

1705 Edmund Halley (1658–1742), English astronomer, correctly predicts the return of Halley's comet in 1758.

Edmund Halley

Timeline: 1610 | 1667 | 1700 | 1705

1781 Uranus is discovered by German-born musician William Herschel (1738–1822). Six years later, he finds four of its moons. He discovers binary stars, catalogues thousands of clusters and nebulae, and reasons the existence of other galaxies.

William Herschel

1846 Neptune is discovered by German astronomers Johann Galle (1812–1910) and Heinrich D'Arrest (1822–1875).

1849 First star photographs are taken at Harvard Observatory, USA.

Fusion of hydrogen nuclei

Deuterium — positron
Hydrogen — gamma ray
proton
neutrino
Helium-3 | Helium-4

1907 Albert Einstein (1879–1955), German-born physicist, discovers mass can turn into energy. This leads to the theory of how the Sun shines – by fusing hydrogen atoms to make helium (see p.223).

Timeline: 1781 | 1800 | 1846 1849 | 1900 | 1907

1919 Expanding Universe is suggested by American astronomer Vesto Slipher (1875–1969), who proves that most galaxies are red-shifted.

1924–30 Big Bang theory (see p.18) is independently formulated by Belgian scientist Abbé Lemaître (1894–1966) and Russian scientist A. Friedmann (1888–1925).

Edwin Hubble

1929 Edwin Hubble (1889–1953), American astronomer, finds strong evidence for an expanding Universe.

1930 Pluto is discovered by American astronomer Clyde Tombaugh (born 1906).

1932 Radio signals from outside Earth are discovered by American engineer Karl Jansky (1905–50). His improvised aerial accidentally picks up radio waves from the Milky Way.

Karl Jansky

Timeline: 1919 | 1920 | 1924 | 1929 | 1930 | 1932 | 1950

1965 3K cosmic background radiation (believed to be the remains of Big Bang's radiation) is discovered by Americans Arno Penzias (born 1933) and Robert Wilson (born 1936).

Cosmic radiation radio antenna at New Jersey, USA.

1967 First pulsar (CP 1919) is identified by Belfast-born astronomer Jocelyn Bell (born 1943).

Jocelyn Bell

1986 Giotto space probe sends back the first pictures of a comet's nucleus (Halley's comet).

Giotto space probe (Europe)

1990 Hubble Space Telescope is launched, the first large optical telescope to be placed above Earth's atmosphere, where it has the clearest view of the Universe.

2001 Very Large Telescope – the largest telescope in the world – due to be completed.

Timeline: 1960 | 1965 1967 | 1970 | 1980 | 1986 | 1990 | 2001

DEVELOPMENT OF THE OPTICAL TELESCOPE

Early telescopes produced images that were blurred, suffered colour distortions, and showed only a small region of the sky. Better designs have produced more powerful telescopes.

REFRACTING TELESCOPE

The main glass lens focuses the starlight, while the eyepiece, a smaller lens, magnifies the image. It is called a refracting telescope because its main lens bends, or refracts, the light that enters. It can, however, introduce false colours and shows only a small region of the sky.

Refractor sees single bright galaxy.

SCHMIDT CAMERA

Estonian optical worker Bernhard Schmidt (1879–1935) made a telescope with a specially shaped lens at its front. This directs light onto a spherical mirror. The image can then be photographed on a curved plate, providing a much wider view of the sky than is usually possible.

Schmidt camera shows many galaxies at once.

REFLECTING TELESCOPE

A reflecting telescope uses a curved mirror to focus light at the bottom of the tube. A second small mirror directs the light to the side of the tube or behind the main mirror. The largest and most powerful telescopes are reflectors, and they reveal the most distant objects in the Universe.

Reflector shows faint distant galaxies.

ASTRONOMY RECORDS

LOWEST OBSERVATORY

This observatory lies in the Homestake Mine, 1.5km (0.9 miles) below ground level in South Dakota, USA. It detects minute particles from space, called neutrinos, that can pass straight through the Earth. An underground tank containing a special fluid shows when a neutrino passes through.

LARGEST SINGLE RADIO DISH

(305m/1,000ft diameter) is the Arecibo radio telescope. It is built into a natural valley in the hills of Puerto Rico.

OLDEST STANDING OBSERVATORY

is the Chomsung-Dae observatory, Kyongju, South Korea. It was built in A.D. 632.

Sensitive detectors surround the tank.

Lowest observatory

INSTRUMENTS OF OBSERVATION

Telescopes that observe visible light waves can study only some of the wavelengths that come from space. Telescopes that detect other wavelengths from the electromagnetic spectrum (see p.231), such as radio waves, give astronomers a fuller picture of the Universe.

ASTRONOMICAL MEASUREMENT

LIGHT-YEAR

A light-year is the distance travelled by light in one year. It is used as a measurement for vast distances and is equal to 9,461 billion km (5,879 billion miles). The light that we see today from the galaxy IC 4296 left its source 117 million years ago, when dinosaurs roamed Earth.

PARALLAX

A star appears to shift its position against the background of more distant stars if seen from opposite sides of Earth's orbit. An astronomer can thus calculate the distance of a star from Earth from the size of this parallax shift, together with the diameter of Earth's orbit.

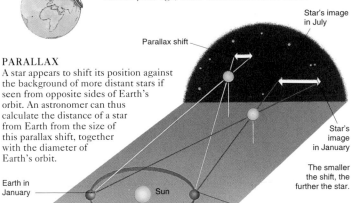

Star's image in July

Parallax shift

Star's image in January

The smaller the shift, the further the star.

Earth in January

Sun

Earth in July

RED SHIFT

Starlight can reveal the speed at which a star moves. If the star is moving away from Earth, its light waves are stretched out, shifting its colour towards the red end of the spectrum. Astronomers measure red shifts by looking for dark lines, caused by gas in the star's atmosphere absorbing light of particular colours.

Stationary star
If the star is not moving away from or towards Earth, an observer sees the dark "absorption lines at their true wavelengths.

Retreating star
If the star is moving away from Earth, its light waves are stretched and the absorption lines are red shifted.

MAJOR WORLD OBSERVATORIES

Observatories	Height	
	metres	feet
Keck Observatory, Mauna Kea, Hawaii, USA	4,205	13,796
Hale Observatory, Palomar, California, USA	1,706	5,597
Whipple Observatory, Mt. Hopkins, USA	2,600	8,530
Kitt Peak Observatory, Arizona, USA	2,064	6,672
V.L.A., Socorro, New Mexico, USA	2,124	6,968
Anglo-Australian Telescope, Siding Spring, Australia	1,165	3,822

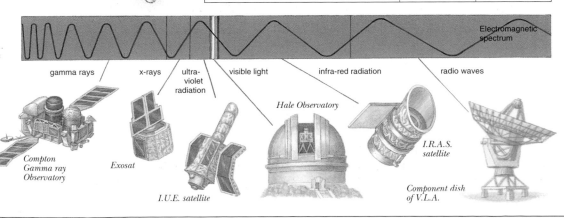

Electromagnetic spectrum

gamma rays   x-rays   ultra-violet radiation   visible light   infra-red radiation   radio waves

Compton Gamma ray Observatory

Exosat

I.U.E. satellite

Hale Observatory

I.R.A.S. satellite

Component dish of V.L.A.

SPACE EXPLORATION

IN OCTOBER 1957, THE USSR put *Sputnik 1* into orbit around the Earth; the great achievements of the Space Age had begun.

c.1200 Chinese use gunpowder rockets in battle, with handheld launching baskets.

1926 Liquid fuel rocket launched by US pioneer Robert Goddard.

1934 Liquid oxygen and alcohol rocket launched by German pioneer rocket scientist Wernher Von Braun (1912–77).

1944 German V2 rocket, designed and built by Von Braun, used against Britain in World War II.

V2 rocket

1965 US Mars probe *Mariner 4* finds no water or life on Mars. First spacewalk by Soviet cosmonaut Leonov in *Voskhod 2*. US manned craft *Gemini 6* meets *Gemini 7* in space.

Leonov's spacewalk

1966 USSR's *Luna 9* probe lands on Moon. First panoramic photos of Moon surface by US *Lunar Orbiter 1*. US manned craft *Gemini 8* docks with *Agena* rocket stage.

Luna 9

1968 Space observatory launched to study UV rays. Three US astronauts orbit Moon in *Apollo 8*.

1969 First people on Moon. US *Apollo 11* astronauts take rock samples.

Edwin M. Aldrin steps on to Moon's surface.

c.1200 | *1920* | *1926* | *1930* | *1934*

1965 | 1966 | 1968 | 1969

1974 Images of surface of Mercury sent by US *Mariner 10*.

1975 Images of surface of Venus sent by USSR's *Venera 9*. US and USSR craft, *Apollo 18* and *Soyuz 19*, meet in space.

Venera 9

Mariner 10

1976 US *Viking 1* **lands on Mars.** Surface tests confirm no life on Mars. Daily weather reports sent until Spring 1983.

1977 US *Voyagers 1* **and** *2* **launched** to outer planets and beyond.

Surface of Mars

Voyager probe

1974 | 1975 | 1976 | 1977

1982 Surface of Venus photographed in colour by USSR's *Venera 13*.

Surface of Venus

1984 Manned Manoeuvring Unit used by US astronaut Bruce McCandless to float untethered alongside shuttle *Challenger*. First retrieval and repair of a satellite, *Solar Maximum* satellite, in space. Satellite resumed observations immediately.

Bruce McCandless

Uranus

1986 *Voyager 2* finds ten moons and a ring system around Uranus. Shuttle *Challenger* explodes, killing crew of seven. Halley's comet returns, observed by four probes.

1982 | 1984 | 1986

SPACE FACTS

• Rivalry between the two great powers after World War II, the US and USSR, resulted in the "Space Race". Each side tried to show its superiority in space and rocket technology.

• One third of the world's population watched the *Apollo 11* Moon landing on television.

• More than 300 people in total have travelled into space.

• Everything becomes weightless when spacecraft leave Earth, so untethered objects float in mid-air. Liquid and food is stored in and eaten from sealed bags.

• Some spacesuits may have as many as 15 layers of different materials to protect and insulate.

• Inside a manned spacecraft, air is constantly being removed and purified. In a space station, this process has to continue for months or years at a time.

• The building in which *Saturn V* rockets were assembled was so large that small clouds sometimes formed in its roof.

• Cosmonauts aboard *Salyut 4* were not allowed to return to Earth when their air purifying system broke down, even when mould grew up the walls.

Salyut 4

Undersuit contains pipes for cool, flowing water to protect against Sun's heat.

Suit layers of nylon, dacron and kevlar

ASTRONAUT SUIT

Spacesuits have to be tough to protect the astronaut from small meteorites. Most have internal cooling systems to absorb the Sun's heat, and a dark, mirrored visor to shield the astronaut from the Sun's glare. Spacesuits are very heavy on Earth, but are weightless when in space.

SPACE RECORDS

LONGEST TIME SPENT IN SPACE was achieved by the Russian cosmonaut Valeri Polyakov, who spent 417 days, 17 hours on the space station *Mir* between January 1994 and March 1995.

FIRST MARRIED COUPLE IN SPACE were Americans Mark Lee and Judy Davis, on shuttle *Endeavour* in September 1992.

1957 First artificial satellite launched, USSR's *Sputnik 1*. First living creature in space, the dog Laika, in *Sputnik 2*.

1959 Far side of Moon photographed by USSR's *Luna 3*.

Laika in Sputnik 2

1961 First man in space, Soviet cosmonaut Yuri Gagarin (1934–68) in *Vostok 1*.

1962 US Mariner 2 approaches another planet, Venus.

Yuri Gagarin

1963 First woman in space, Soviet cosmonaut Valentina Tereshkova in *Vostok 6*.

1964 Detailed images of Moon taken by US probe *Ranger 7*.

Valentina Tereshkova

1940 | 1942 | 1950 | 1957 | 1959 | 1960 | 1961 | 1962 | 1963 | 1964

1970 USSR's Venera 7 is first probe to land on another planet (Venus). Moon samples brought back by automatic probe, USSR's *Luna 16*.

1971 USSR's Mars 3 lands on Mars. US *Mariner 9* begins orbiting Mars and sends images of its volcanoes. First orbiting space station launched, USSR's *Salyut 1*.

Venus

1972 Last manned mission to Moon (*Apollo 17*).

1973 First images of Jupiter taken by US *Pioneer 10*. First US manned space station, *Skylab*.

Mars

Jupiter

1970 | 1971 | 1972 | 1973

1979 US Pioneer 11 visits Saturn, six years after launch, finding new ring and moons. *Voyagers 1* and *2* pass Jupiter, finding active volcanoes on one moon, Io, and discovering three new moons, bringing total to 16.

Sulphur volcano on Io

1980–81 Voyager probes pass Saturn, take first detailed images of ring systems, and find new moons, bringing total to 18.

Saturn

1981 First reusable craft launched, US space shuttle *Columbia*.

Launch of Columbia

1979 | 1980 | 1981

1988 US shuttle launches resume with *Columbia*. Soviet space shuttle, *Buran*, tested.

Voyager 2

1989 Voyager 2 finds six new moons round Neptune, as well as Triton's nitrogen volcanoes. US COBE (Cosmic Background Explorer) satellite launched to study Big Bang's radiation.

1990 Hubble space telescope launched (with faulty mirror). US *Magellan* probe radar-maps Venus. *LDEF* (Long Duration Exposure Facility) satellite retrieved by space shuttle.

Hubble telescope

1994 Hubble space telescope mirror fault corrected by space shuttle astronauts.

1998 International Space Station construction is begun by space shuttle astronauts.

COBE satellite

1988 | 1989 | 1990 | 1994 | 1998

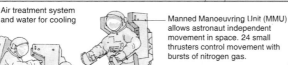

Air treatment system and water for cooling

Manned Manoeuvring Unit (MMU) allows astronaut independent movement in space. 24 small thrusters control movement with bursts of nitrogen gas.

Seams and seals must be airtight to withstand the vacuum of space.

SPACE STATION

A space station enables astronauts to live and work in space for long periods. Scientific experiments in low gravity that are impossible on Earth can be carried out over months or years. Space stations are too large to put into space all at once so are assembled in pieces on separate journeys.

Kvant 2 stores equipment that astronauts use when working outside *Mir*.

Small rockets on the side of *Mir* adjust its position to keep its orbit constant.

Solar panels keep *Mir* supplied with energy.

Docking port

Main module for living and working, 13m (42.65ft) long

Kristall, a module used for experiments in materials for electronic circuits

Floor and ceiling are painted different colours to help orientation.

Handrail aids astronauts when working outside.

Mir space station

WEIGHTLESSNESS

Astronauts in Mir *space station floating in weightless conditions.*

Long periods of weightlessness affect the human body in many ways: muscles weaken and waste away, so astronauts have to exercise regularly; blood and other fluids have no sense of "down", so circulation must be regularly checked; bacteria multiply at four times the normal rate; loss of balance can cause "space sickness".

ROCKETS

IN ORDER TO ESCAPE Earth's gravity, a rocket must reach 40,000km/h (24,900mph). Rockets burn fuel and liquid oxygen, ignited under pressure.

WHAT A BLAST!

The F1 engine of the *Saturn V* rocket (which carried the astronauts to the Moon) is the most powerful engine ever built. Each of its five nozzles is 3.81m (12.5ft) in diameter and 5.79m (19ft) high, as tall as a giraffe. At launch, each engine burns three tonnes of fuel every second.

External fuel tank (liquid oxygen and liquid hydrogen)

Solid fuel rocket booster

O-ring (joint between booster sections)

Vostok – 36.41m (119.5ft)

Payload container (*Vostok* manned capsule)

Orbital stage

Central rocket

Payload bay 18.3m (60ft) long

Orbiter

Boosters

Space shuttle – 58.4m (191.6ft)

Payload (satellite) inside casing

Third stage fuel tank (liquid oxygen and liquid hydrogen)

Protective cover

Second stage fuel tank (liquid fuel and nitrogen tetroxide)

Protective cover

First stage fuel tank (liquid fuel and nitrogen tetroxide)

Liquid fuel booster

Solid fuel booster

Ariane 44LP – 56.76m (186.2ft)

Launch escape tower

Apollo Command Module

Apollo Service Module

Apollo Lunar Module (inside protective cover)

Third stage fuel tank (liquid oxygen and liquid hydrogen)

Single stage-3 rocket

Protective cover

Second stage fuel tanks (liquid nitrogen and liquid oxygen)

Five stage-2 engines

Protective cover for engines above

First stage fuel tank (kerosene and liquid oxygen). Burns for 2.5 minutes before being jettisoned.

Stabilizing fin

Giraffe

Saturn V – 110.64m (363ft)

SPACE MISSION FACTS

● Rockets are designed in separate stages, so that when all the fuel from a stage has been used up, that stage drops away, and the next takes over.

● The first 11 US unmanned missions to the Moon were unsuccessful: *Rangers 4* and *6* hit the Moon but failed to transmit any data. The rest missed the Moon, *Ranger 3* overshooting by 59,500km (37,000 miles).

● On 28 January 1986, the US space shuttle *Challenger* exploded 73 seconds after launch. The crew of seven was killed in the world's worst space disaster.

● A hyphen instead of a minus sign keyed into a computer caused *Mariner 1*'s launch vehicle to crash into the Atlantic in 1962.

● Each shuttle launch releases 75 tonnes of hydrogen chloride into the atmosphere, as well as tonnes of pollutant waste from the solid fuel burned during lift-off.

● The Moon's astronauts left behind them the remains of six lunar landers, three moon buggies, and more than 50 tonnes of litter.

JUNK ALERT

One great danger facing astronauts and satellites is fragments of old rockets and satellites. This crater in a space shuttle window was made by a paint fleck travelling at high speed.

Solid fuel booster rockets, designed to be used 10 times, parachute back to Earth, and are later recovered from sea.

Shuttle reaches 130km (81 miles) at Mach 15. External tank released; burns up in Earth's atmosphere.

Solid fuel rocket boosters jettisoned 2 mins 5 secs after lift-off, at an altitude of 45km (28 miles). Shuttle now travelling at 4.5 times the speed of sound (Mach 4.5).

Shuttle engines put orbiter into circular orbit.

Liquid hydrogen from external fuel tank flows into orbiter engines at 3,100 litres/sec (820gal/sec).

Solid fuel (polybutadiene) burns for 2 mins. Each solid fuel rocket produces the thrust of 11 Boeing 747s at take-off.

Rupture in O-rings (joints) of left solid fuel booster caused 1986 *Challenger* shuttle explosion.

External fuel tank

Orbiter

Solid fuel rocket boosters

Main engines on orbiter take fuel from external tank. Two solid fuel boosters fire for take-off.

SATELLITE REPAIR JOB

In 1984, the shuttle *Challenger* retrieved and repaired the US *Solar Max* solar observatory while in space. One of the satellite's control systems had failed and it was falling towards Earth. The shuttle's robotic arm brought it into the cargo bay, where repairs were made. The satellite was then put back in orbit.

Orbiter remains in orbit for between 5 and 30 days. Mission can be carried out – new satellites put into orbit, old ones mended, experiments performed.

Cargo bay doors close. Engines rotate orbiter into re-entry position.

Orbiter manoeuvres into precise angle for re-entry. Begins 30-minute descent into atmosphere at Mach 22.4.

Parts of nose and wings reach 1,460°C (2,660°F) during re-entry. They are covered with 32,000 carbon or silica insulating tiles, each glued on by hand.

Orbiter makes four "S-shaped" circuits to break its speed of Mach 2.5, before making a gliding landing.

SPACE CENTRES

Launch site	Launches	Type of launch
Pletsetsk cosmodrome, USSR	1,056	Secret military satellites
Baikonur cosmodrome, USSR	693	Manned craft, probes, and satellites
Cape Canaveral (USAF), USA	1,045	Manned craft, probes, and satellites
Kennedy Space Center, USA	66	Apollo missions and space shuttle

FUTURE SHUTTLES

The present generation of US shuttles would be improved if they did not have to shed their huge fuel tanks at various stages after take-off. NASA are currently working on a "reusable launch vehicle" (RLV) that could travel into space and back with a single rocket stage.

Orbiter lands at a speed of 345km/h (214mph). It is towed, or flown on the back of a Boeing 747 jet, to next launch site.

EARTH

From Earth's formation to the strongest earthquakes and the biggest volcanic eruptions, this section provides every essential fact and figure about our wonderful planet.

Earth • Continents • Volcanoes • Earthquakes • Rocks and Minerals
Ocean Floor • Oceans and Islands • Mountains • Valleys and Caves • Glaciation
Rivers and Lakes • Weather • Climates • Deserts • Forests • Earth's Biosphere
Earth in Danger • Saving the Earth

EARTH

THE EARTH IS ONE OF THE NINE planets in the Solar System. It is the fifth largest in size, and is the only planet with plentiful oxygen and water: the necessary ingredients for life.

THEORY OF FORMATION

1 About 4.6 billion years ago, a dense cloud of gas and dust contracted to form the Sun. Other matter in the cloud formed solid lumps of ice and rock, and these joined together to form the planets.

2 Radioactivity in the rocks caused the new-born Earth to melt. Iron and nickel sank to form the Earth's core, while oceans of molten rock floated on the surface.

3 About 4 billion years ago, the Earth's crust began to form. At first there may have been many small platelets floating on the molten rock beneath.

4 Over millions of years the crust thickened and volcanoes erupted. Gases pouring out of volcanoes began to form the atmosphere, and water vapour condensed to fill the oceans.

ANATOMY OF THE EARTH

The Earth is made up of several layers of rock around a core of iron and nickel. The deeper the layer, the higher the temperature.

Atmosphere
Depth: approx. 640km
(400 miles)

Crust
Depth: 6–70km
(4–43 miles)
Composition: rocks
similar to those on
the surface

Mantle
Depth: approx. 2,900km
(1,800 miles)
Composition: mostly solid
rock; probably partly melted
80–150km (50–93 miles) down

Outer core
Depth: approx. 2,000km (1,240 miles)
Composition: mostly liquid iron,
nickel, and oxygen

Inner core
Diameter: 2,740km (1,700 miles)
Composition: solid iron and nickel
The temperature of the Earth's inner core is thought to
be about 4,500°C (8,100°F).

DEEPEST DRILLING INTO EARTH'S CRUST

The deepest mine in the world reaches 4.2km (2.6 miles) down into the Earth. A geological exploration has drilled more than 12km (7.5 miles) below the Earth's surface. Yet neither of these is anywhere near as deep as the bottom of the Earth's crust.

Depth (km)

Mount Everest:
8.85km (5.5 miles)

Depth
(miles)

Sea level

Sea level

A deep coal mine

Deepest mine:4.2km (2.6 miles)

Deepest
ocean drilling:
1.7km
(1.05 miles)

Deepest hole (still being drilled):
12.1km (7.4 miles)

Deepest hole projected to reach 15km (9.3 miles)

The Earth's crust is much thicker
beneath land than beneath the ocean.

CRUST

MANTLE

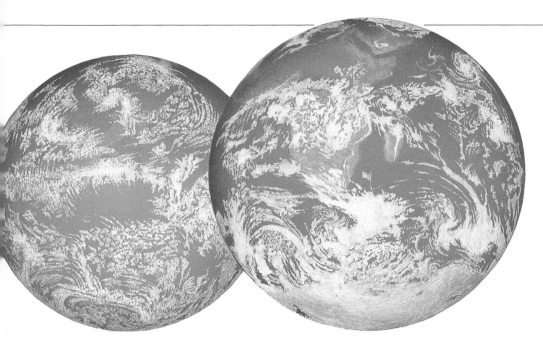

5 About 3.5 billion years ago most of the Earth's crust had formed, but the shapes of the continents looked very different from today. The oldest rocks on Earth date from just before this time.

6 Today the Earth is still changing. The crust has broken into huge plates (see pp.40–41) that are constantly being created and destroyed at their edges. The continents are always on the move, powered by forces deep inside the Earth.

EARTH DATA

Age	4.6 billion years
Mass	5,854 billion billion tonnes
Volume	1,083,218,915,000cu km (259,877,796,843cu miles)
Diameter at Equator	12,756km (7,926 miles)
Diameter at Poles	12,713km (7,899 miles)
Circumference at Equator	40,075km (24,901 miles)
Circumference at Poles	39,942km (24,819 miles)
Distance from the Sun	150 million km (93 million miles)
Time for one spin	23 hours, 56 minutes, 4 seconds
Time to orbit Sun	365 days, 6 hours, 9 minutes, 9.5 seconds

EARTH'S MAGNETIC FIELD

Molten iron flowing in the Earth's outer core generates electric currents. These currents create the Earth's magnetic field. This field – the magnetosphere – stretches more than 60,000km (37,000 miles) into space. Sometimes Earth's magnetic field flips: north becomes south and vice versa. No-one knows why this happens. The last pole reversal occurred about 30,000 years ago.

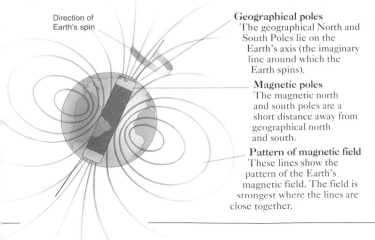

Direction of Earth's spin

Geographical poles
The geographical North and South Poles lie on the Earth's axis (the imaginary line around which the Earth spins).

Magnetic poles
The magnetic north and south poles are a short distance away from geographical north and south.

Pattern of magnetic field
These lines show the pattern of the Earth's magnetic field. The field is strongest where the lines are close together.

EARTH FACTS
• Proportion of land and sea:
Area of land: 29.2%
Area of sea: 70.8%

• If a car could travel non-stop around the Equator at 100km/h (62mph), it would take 16 days, 16 hrs, 45 mins. A car driving around Earth from North Pole to South Pole and back would finish 80 mins earlier, because Earth is not a perfect sphere.

• An excavator digging a hole at 1m (39ins) per min through the Earth would take 24 years to reach the other side.

JUST A PIN-PRICK
If the Earth were the size of an egg, the deepest hole ever drilled by humans would not even pierce its shell.

EARTH'S ATMOSPHERE
The atmosphere is the film of gases that surrounds the Earth. It is divided into four main layers – the troposphere, stratosphere, mesosphere, and thermosphere – and its composition is 78% nitrogen, 21% oxygen, and 1% water vapour and other gases. The atmosphere is held in place by gravity. It stops the Earth from becoming too hot or too cold, and shields the planet from the Sun's harmful ultraviolet rays.

Height

Satellite

1,00Ckm (620 miles)

THERMOSPHERE

80km (50 miles)

MESOSPHERE

50km (31 miles)

STRATOSPHERE

Weather balloon

Ozone layer

Aircraft

10km (6 miles)

TROPOSPHERE

EARTH

CONTINENTS

THE CONTINENTS ARE THE seven huge land masses that make up most of the Earth's land surface. They are always on the move, shifted around by forces deep inside the Earth. The concept of moving continents is known as continental drift.

EARTH'S TECTONIC PLATES

The Earth's crust is fragmented into vast pieces of rock, called tectonic plates. These slabs fit together like a huge jigsaw. Where the plates rise above sea level, they form continents and islands.

The Earth's crust is only 70km (43 miles) thick at its greatest depths.

CONTINENTAL DRIFT

1 Some 250 million years ago the continents were joined together in the giant super-continent of Pangaea (from the Greek word meaning "all lands"). About 200 million years ago Pangaea slowly began to break up.

2 By 135 million years ago Pangaea had split into two main land masses, Gondwanaland and Laurasia. North America and Europe split apart, and about 120 million years ago India began to drift north towards Asia.

3 Over the next 120 million years the continents drifted into their present-day positions. The Americas moved away from Europe and Africa; India joined on to Asia; Australia and Antarctica split apart.

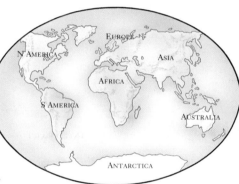

4 This is how the Earth might look 150 million years from now. Africa has split in two, and the larger section has drifted north to join Europe. Antarctica has joined Australia, and California has been crumpled against Alaska.

THE PLATES AND THEIR BOUNDARIES

The Earth's crust is made up of about 15 major plates. Plates that form the ocean floor are oceanic plates, and plates that form land are continental plates. Most plates are partly oceanic and partly continental. Scientists can locate the boundaries by monitoring earthquakes and volcanoes.

KEY

◀▶ Pulling apart

▶◀ Colliding

······· Subduction zone

– – – Uncertain boundary

—— Mid-ocean ridge

– – Transform fault

+++++ Rift valley

SECTION THROUGH THE EARTH'S CRUST

This illustration shows a cross-section of the Earth's crust at the Equator.

CONTINENT SIZES

Continent	Area	
	sq km	sq miles
Asia	44,485,900	17,176,090
Africa	30,269,680	11,687,180
North America	24,235,280	9,357,290
South America	17,820,770	6,880,630
Antarctica	13,209,000	5,100,020
Europe	10,530,750	4,065,940
Australasia	8,924,100	3,445,610

CONTINENT AND PLATE FACTS

- Europe and Africa would fit into Asia with room to spare.
- Europe and the Americas drift about 4cm (1.6in) further apart every year.
- The African Rift Valley grows about 1mm wider every year.
- Fossils of tropical plants are found as far north as Alaska, because North American land mass was once situated in tropics.
- Continental plates are up to 70km (43 miles) thick, but oceanic plates are only about 5km (3 miles) thick.

PROPORTION OF LAND PER CONTINENT

Asia 30%

Australasia 6%

Europe 7%

Antarctica 9%

South America 12%

North America 16%

Africa 20%

PLATE TECTONICS

Plate tectonics is the theory of how and why the Earth's plates move. At their boundaries, the plates may be colliding, pulling apart, or sliding past each other. These different types of motion build mountains, cause earthquakes and volcanoes, and create deep-sea trenches.

Chains of volcanoes often form at subduction zones.

Subduction zone

Rock melts when it is forced down into the mantle at a subduction zone.

Mid-ocean ridge

Convergence

Transform fault

TRANSFORM FAULT
Transform faults are boundaries where two plates are sliding past each other. Earthquakes often occur at this type of boundary, as the plates slip and judder past each other (see p.44). The San Andreas Fault in California, USA, is a transform fault.

CONVERGENCE
When two continental plates collide, the Earth's crust often buckles and folds as they push against each other, forcing up great mountain ranges. The Himalayas and the Andes were formed by colliding plates.

SUBDUCTION ZONE
When two plates collide, one plate sometimes rides over the other, forcing it down into the mantle. This type of boundary, called a subduction zone, often occurs at the edges of oceans where the thicker continental plate rides over the thinner oceanic plate. Deep ocean trenches form at these boundaries.

PULLING APART
Where two plates are pulling apart, molten rock from the mantle rises to fill the gap, creating new crust. When this type of boundary occurs beneath the sea, ridges of mountains called mid-ocean ridges form. On land, these boundaries create steep-sided rift valleys.

THEORIES OF MOVEMENT

Scientists have not yet identified exactly what makes the Earth's tectonic plates shift around, but there are several theories to explain their movements. The three main theories involve convection, gravity, and the different weights of hot and cold rock.

CONVECTION
Heat generated deep inside the Earth creates convection currents in the mantle. These currents slowly push the overlying plates around.

WEIGHT OF ROCK
Hot rock rising at mid-ocean ridges cools down as it moves further away from the ridge. As it cools it becomes heavier and sinks, pulling the rest of the plate down with it.

GRAVITY
The plates are about 2–3km (1–2 miles) higher at mid-ocean ridges than at ocean rims, so they could simply be sliding slowly downhill under the force of gravity.

AS FAST AS A FINGERNAIL GROWS

The tectonic plates move at different rates along their margins, and some plates move faster than others. The average rate of movement is approximately 2.5cm (1 inch) every year: about as fast as a finger-nail grows.

No land rises above the Pacific Ocean for thousands of miles.

Andes

Amazon Basin

PACIFIC OCEAN

SOUTH AMERICA

ATLANTIC OCEAN

Peru-Chile Trench

Mid-Atlantic Ridge

Pacific Plate

Nazca Plate

American Plate

African Plate

VOLCANOES

VOLCANOES OCCUR where magma (molten rock) from deep inside the Earth forces its way to the surface. The magma may erupt as red-hot lava, or may explode into clouds of ash and volcanic bombs. Volcanic activity also produces strange landscapes of gushing geysers, steaming lakes, and bubbling mud pools.

VOLCANIC AREAS
There are around 1,300 active volcanoes in the world, but only 20 or 30 erupt each year. Some of the major volcanoes are marked on this map. Most volcanoes are located on or close to the boundaries of the plates that make up the Earth's crust.

Many of the Earth's volcanoes lie beneath the oceans.

MAJOR ERUPTIONS

The eruption of Mount St. Helens, Washington, USA

MOUNT ST. HELENS
erupted in May 1980. The explosion was heard more than 350km (217 miles) away. Hot ash and gas rushed down the mountainside; 62 people died.

GREATEST VOLCANIC EXPLOSION
occurred when Krakatoa, Indonesia, blew up in 1883, hurling rocks 55km (34 miles) high. The explosion was heard in Australia, and generated a 40m (131ft) high seismic sea wave (see p.45); 36,000 people died.

GREATEST VOLCANIC ERUPTION
was Tambora on Sumbawa, Indonesia in 1815, which threw up more than 100cu km (24cu miles) of ash. The island was lowered by 1,250m (4,100ft); 92,000 people died.

MAJOR ACTIVE VOLCANOES
The number of volcanoes active in historic times is shown in parentheses after each region.

Name	Height		Latest eruption
	metres	feet	
Africa and Indian Ocean (14)			
Nyamuragira, Zaire	3,053	10,016	1989
Mt. Cameroon, Cameroon	4,070	13,353	1982
Antarctica (9)			
Erebus, Ross Island	3,794	12,448	1989
Asia (210)			
Kliuchevskoi, Siberia	4,850	15,912	1990
Kerinci, Indonesia	3,805	12,484	1970
SW Pacific (54)			
Ruapehu, New Zealand	2,796	9,173	1996
Europe and Middle East (20)			
Etna, Sicily, Italy	3,350	10,991	1992
Stromboli, Italy	926	3,038	1990
North America and Hawaii (56)			
Mount St. Helens, USA	2,549	8,362	1980
Mauna Loa, Hawaii	4,170	13,681	1984
Iceland and Atlantic (54)			
Pico de Teide, Canary Islands	3,713	12,181	1909
Central and South America (100)			
Sangay, Ecuador	5,230	17,159	1989
Popocatepetl, Mexico	5,465	17,930	1943
Llullaillaco, Chile	6,723	22,057	1877

ERUPTION SIZES
The amount of ash thrown out is a good indicator of the size of an eruption.

Mount Vesuvius Italy A.D. 79

Tambora Indonesia 1815

Krakatoa Indonesia 1883

Katmai Alaska 1912

Mount St. Helens Washington, USA 1980

El Chichón Mexico 1982

VOLCANO TYPES AND SHAPES
A volcano's shape depends mainly on the type of lava that comes out of it. Thick, sticky lava forms tall, steep-sided cones; thin, runny lava forms gently sloping lava shields and plateaux.

Clouds of ash and dust

Split in the Earth's crust

Lava

Lava

Side vent

Lava flow

Volcanic bomb

COMPOSITE VOLCANO
Composite cones are made of alternating layers of lava and volcanic ash.

Crater

Vent

Layers of ash

Main pipe

Layers of ash and lava

Side pipe

Magma chamber

CINDER VOLCANO
A cinder volcano is made up of layers of volcanic ash, and has a steep, conical shape. Each time the volcano erupts, another layer of ash is added.

FISSURE VOLCANO
Not all volcanoes form over a single hole. Sometimes a crack opens up in the Earth's crust, and runny lava flows out along its length, forming a plateau.

SHIELD VOLCANO
When the lava that erupts from a volcano is runny, it forms a gentle slope rather than a cone. These shield volcanoes often have many side vents.

TYPES OF LAVA

The type of lava flow that erupts from a volcano depends on several factors, such as the amount of gas it contains, and whether it is erupting on to land or into the sea. The two main types of lava flow, aa and pahoehoe, take their names from Hawaiian words.

PAHOEHOE LAVA
Pahoehoe lava is runny and fast-moving. When it cools, it resembles coils of rope.

PILLOW LAVA
Lava erupting into the sea cools quickly in the water, forming pillow lava – round lumps of rock.

AA LAVA
Aa lava is thicker and stickier than pahoehoe lava. It cools to form sharp, chunky rock.

TALLEST GEYSER

In 1903, the Waimangu Geyser in New Zealand erupted to a height of about 457m (1,500ft). This is higher than the Sears Tower in Chicago, USA, which is one of the world's tallest buildings. The Waimangu Geyser has not erupted since 1904.

Sears Tower *Waimangu Geyser*

VOLCANIC PRODUCTS

The solid products of volcanic eruptions and explosions are called pyroclasts. These include cinders, volcanic ash, and large chunks of solidified lava. Cinders and ash may blanket a huge area after an eruption.

VOLCANIC BOMB
Blobs of molten lava erupting high into the air may fall as volcanic bombs.

LAPILLI
These cinder fragments are called lapilli, from the Latin for "little stones".

PUMICE
Pumice forms from lava containing bubbles of gas. It is often so light that it can float on water.

VOLCANIC DUST
Dust thrown high into the atmosphere during an eruption may fall hundreds of kilometres away.

VOLCANIC RECORDS

LARGEST ACTIVE VOLCANO
is Mauna Loa, Hawaii, which has a diameter of 100km (62 miles).

HIGHEST ACTIVE VOLCANO
is Llullaillaco, Chile, which is 6,723m (22,057ft) high.

TALLEST ACTIVE GEYSER
is Steamboat Geyser, Wyoming, USA. It erupts to a height of 60–115m (195–380ft).

VOLCANO PHASES

Most volcanoes have three phases: an active volcano has erupted in recent historic times or is still erupting; a dormant volcano has been quiet for a long time but may erupt again; an extinct volcano has stopped erupting and is not expected to erupt again.

Castle Rock, Edinburgh, Scotland: the remains of an extinct volcano.

LARGEST VOLCANIC EXPLOSIONS

Scientists measure the size of a volcanic explosion according to the Volcanic Explosivity Index (VEI). This grades explosions on a scale of 0 (a non-explosive eruption) to 7 or 8 for the largest eruptions. There have so far been no known eruptions with a VEI of 8.

Volcano and location	Date	VEI
Crater Lake, Oregon, USA	c4895 B.C.	7
Kikai, Ryukyu Island, Japan	c4350 B.C.	7
Santorini (Thira), Greece	c1390 B.C.	6
Taupo, New Zealand	c130	7
Ilopango, El Salvador	c260	6
Oraefajokull, Iceland	1362	6
Long Island, New Guinea	c1660	6
Tambora, Indonesia	1815	7
Krakatoa, Indonesia	1883	6
Santa Maria, Guatemala	1902	6
Katmai (Novarupta), Alaska	1912	6

VOLCANOES ON OTHER PLANETS AND MOONS

Olympus Mons on Mars, which is the highest mountain in the Solar System, is an extinct volcano. The Moon also has extinct volcanoes, and there may be active volcanoes on Venus. Io, one of Jupiter's 16 moons, has active volcanoes that throw out plumes of gases up to 160km (100 miles) high.

Io's volcanoes throw out huge plumes of sulphurous gases.

VOLCANIC LANDSCAPE

Volcanic activity beneath the surface heats up water above and below the ground. This can create spectacular volcanic landscapes, called hydrothermal areas, where hot water, mud, and gases gush, bubble, and steam from vents in the ground.

HOT SPRING
A steaming hot spring forms when underground water is heated by warm rocks. As it gets hotter, the water rises to the surface.

BUBBLING MUD POOL
A pool of hot, bubbling mud may form where hot water mixes with mineral particles. Acidic volcanic gases corrode these particles from the surrounding rocks.

FUMAROLE
A fumarole is a vent that releases jets of steam and hot, volcanic gases. These gases often give off a smell of rotten eggs, because they contain sulphur.

GEYSER
A geyser is a tall jet of water that erupts when water trapped in underground chambers is heated to boiling point by hot rocks.

SINTER TERRACE
Minerals deposited by a hot spring as it emerges on to the surface may build up into a beautiful, strangely coloured sinter terrace.

EARTHQUAKES

EARTHQUAKES ARE caused by
movements of the massive plates
that make up the Earth's crust.
Each year scientists detect about
500,000 earthquakes and tremors
(small earthquakes). Most are so
small that they can hardly be felt,
but about 1,000 cause damage.
Severe earthquakes can reduce whole
cities to rubble.

EARTHQUAKE BELTS
Most earthquakes occur
on or near to the edges
of the Earth's
tectonic plates (see
pp.40–41). The
ten earthquakes
with the highest
known death tolls
are marked on
this map.

Earthquake belts usually
follow the edges of the
Earth's tectonic plates.

FOCUS AND EPICENTRE
The exact point at which an
earthquake occurs is the
focus. The point on
the Earth's surface
directly above the
focus is the
epicentre.

The earthquake is
strongest at the
epicentre.

The focus is
usually deep
inside the Earth.

Shock waves can
travel right through
the Earth to the other side.

CLOSE-UP OF AN EARTHQUAKE
Many earthquakes occur at
transform faults (see pp.40–41)
where the jagged edges of
two moving plates may
occasionally lock
together. Stress
builds up within
the plates, until
they suddenly
slip, making the
ground shake
violently.

The plates slip and lurch past each
other, causing an earthquake.

This fault line
marks the boundary
of two plates.

MEASURING EARTHQUAKES
The study of earthquakes is called
seismology. Scientists measure and
record earthquakes using seismometers.
The size of an earthquake is measured
either according to its magnitude (the
size of the shock waves and energy it
produces), or according to its effects.
Magnitude is usually measured by the
Richter scale; effects are graded on the
Modified Mercalli Intensity scale.

THE RICHTER SCALE
The Richter scale was devised by
American Charles F. Richter in the 1930s.

Charles F. Richter
(1900–1985)

Magnitude	Probable effects
1	Detectable only by instruments
2–3	Can just about be felt by people
4–5	Detectable within 32km (20 miles) of the epicentre. Possible slight damage within a small area
6	Fairly destructive
7	A major earthquake
8	A very destructive earthquake

THE MODIFIED MERCALLI INTENSITY SCALE
The Mercalli scale runs from I to XII. It grades earthquakes according to their effects,
such as damage to buildings. The original scale was devised by Italian Giuseppe Mercalli
(1850–1914) in 1902. It was later updated to create the Modified Mercalli Intensity scale.

I Not felt by people, but recorded by instruments. Animals may be uneasy. Doors may swing slowly.

II May be felt by a few people indoors, particularly those on upper floors.

III Felt indoors by several as a rapid vibration. Hanging objects may swing slightly.

IV Felt indoors by many, outdoors by a few. Standing cars rock. Dishes and windows rattle.

V Felt outdoors by most. Buildings tremble. Small objects are knocked over. Doors swing.

VI Felt by all: people afraid. Trees shake. Small bells ring. Dishes break. Pictures and books fall.

VII General alarm. Hard for people to stand. Chimneys crack. Plaster falls. Windows break.

VIII Difficult to drive. Considerable damage to buildings. Chimneys fall. Tree branches break.

IX General panic. Large cracks appear in the ground. Some buildings collapse.

X Water slops out of rivers. Underground pipes torn apart. Most buildings destroyed.

XI Few buildings remain standing. Bridges collapse. Railway lines buckle. Large landslides.

XII Almost all constructions destroyed. Waves seen on ground. Rivers change course.

EARTHQUAKE SIDE-EFFECTS

Earthquakes on land may flatten cities and towns, cause landslides and avalanches, and start fires. Earthquakes beneath the sea may cause giant waves called seismic sea waves or tsunamis. These can travel many kilometres across the ocean, building into a huge wall of water as they approach the coast.

FIRE
If an earthquake breaks gas mains, the slightest spark can cause huge fires.

LANDSLIDE
An earthquake may cause a huge chunk of mountainside to break away, burying all in its path.

SEISMIC SEA WAVE
A seismic sea wave can cause terrible devastation when it hits the coast.

WORST EARTHQUAKE DAMAGE ON RECORD

The most destructive earthquake happened in Kwanto, Japan in 1923. In nearby Tokyo, where many of the houses were built of wood and paper, the shaking ground overturned stoves, setting the houses on fire. A fire-storm then engulfed the city. Almost 144,000 people were killed, and 575,000 homes were destroyed.

Tokyo was devastated by the 1923 earthquake.

SAN ANDREAS FAULT

At the San Andreas Fault in California, USA, two plates are sliding past each other at a rate of about 5cm (2in) every year. Earthquakes and tremors happen frequently, and are sometimes severe. San Francisco sits on the San Andreas Fault.

San Andreas Fault, California, USA

WORST EARTHQUAKE DEATH TOLLS

Location	Date	Estimated deaths
Shansi, China	1556	830,000
Calcutta, India	1737	300,000
Tangshan, China	1976	255,000
Aleppo, Syria	1138	230,000
Damghan, Iran	856	200,000
Gansu, China	1920	200,000
Nr. Xining, China	1927	200,000
Ardabil, Iran	893	150,000
Kwanto, Japan	1923	144,000
Messina, Italy	1908	70–100,000

STRONGEST KNOWN EARTHQUAKES

Location	Date	Magnitude Richter scale
Colombia	1906	8.9
Morioka, Japan	1933	8.9
Lisbon, Portugal	1755	8.75
Assam, India	1897	8.7

SEISMIC SEA WAVE (TSUNAMI) RECORDS

HIGHEST SEISMIC SEA WAVE
was estimated at 85m (278ft) high: almost as high as New York's Statue of Liberty. It appeared on 24 April 1971 off Ishigaki Island, Japan.

FASTEST SEISMIC SEA WAVES
have been recorded travelling at approximately 900km/h (559mph): more than 300km/h (186mph) faster than the world water speed record of 556km/h (345mph), achieved by a hydroplane.

EARTHQUAKE-PROOF BUILDINGS

In earthquake-prone areas, specially designed buildings can lessen the effects of a serious earthquake. For example, a pyramidal or cone-shaped building is less likely to topple over than a building with vertical walls.

San Francisco's TransAmerica building

The central column of this Japanese pagoda helps to absorb earthquake shocks.

EARTHQUAKE FACTS

- Most earthquakes last less than a minute.
- Longest recorded earthquake lasted four minutes. Occurred on 27 March 1964 in Alaska, USA. It was one of the strongest known earthquakes, but killed only 115 people due to low population density.
- First instrument for recording earthquakes was the seismoscope, invented in China in A.D. 132.

- Earthquake shock waves travel through rock at approx. 25,000km/h (16,000mph): more than 20 times the speed of sound. They slow down in sand and mud.
- Some scientists believe animals can sense an earthquake's approach. Strange behaviour includes: dogs howling; chickens fleeing roosts; rats and mice leaving holes; fish thrashing about in ponds.

MOONQUAKES

Most moonquakes are caused by meteorites smashing into the Moon's surface. Moonquakes are monitored by seismometers left by American astronauts.

Seismometers on the Moon

ROCKS AND MINERALS

AT ANY POINT ON THE EARTH'S SURFACE, if you dig down far enough, you will come to rock. Rocks are the building blocks of the Earth's crust. There are many different types of rock, and they are all composed of one or more minerals.

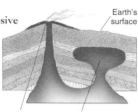

Limestone is a sedimentary rock (see below). About 75% of land is covered with sedimentary rocks.

ROCKS

The study of rocks is called geology. All types of rock fall into one of three categories: igneous, sedimentary, or metamorphic.

IGNEOUS ROCK

Igneous rock starts off deep within the Earth as magma (molten rock). The magma rises towards the surface where it may erupt from a volcano, or cool and solidify within the Earth's crust.

Basalt is an igneous rock.

Extrusive and intrusive igneous rock

Igneous rock that erupts from a volcano on to the Earth's surface is extrusive. Igneous rock that solidifies before it reaches the surface is intrusive.

Earth's surface

Extrusive igneous rock   Intrusive igneous rock

The Giant's Causeway in Northern Ireland is formed from basalt, an extrusive igneous rock.

Granite mountains in Yosemite, USA. These intrusive igneous rocks have been exposed by the erosion of overlying rocks.

SEDIMENTARY ROCK

Rocks are weathered into fragments that are carried away by water, wind, and ice. These sediments are laid down in lakes, rivers, sand dunes, and on the sea floor. Over millions of years they are compressed, forming layers of sedimentary rocks.

Sandstone is a sedimentary rock.

Ayers Rock (Uluru) in central Australia is composed of sandstone.

METAMORPHIC ROCK

Metamorphic rock is igneous or sedimentary rock that has been changed by heat and/or pressure. Heat may come from rising magma, and pressure may occur when rock is squeezed during mountain building.

Gneiss is a metamorphic rock.

This landscape in northwest Scotland is formed from gneiss.

GEOLOGICAL TIME CHART

Rocks are dated according to a geological timescale that divides the Earth's history into eras, periods, and epochs.

Era	Period	Million years ago
Cenozoic	Quaternary	
	Holocene (epoch)	0.01
	Pleistocene (epoch)	2
	Tertiary	
	Pliocene (epoch)	5
	Miocene (epoch)	25
	Oligocene (epoch)	38
	Eocene (epoch)	55
	Palaeocene (epoch)	65
Mesozoic	Cretaceous	144
	Jurassic	213
	Triassic	248
Paleozoic	Permian	286
	Carboniferous	360
	Devonian	408
	Silurian	438
	Ordovician	505
	Cambrian	590
	Precambrian (about 7 times longer than all the other periods combined)	4,600 (origin of Earth)

THE ROCK CYCLE

All rocks are constantly passing through a recycling process.

Igneous rocks are weathered away and washed into the ocean.

Mineral particles sink to the sea floor where they are compacted into sedimentary rock.

Heat from molten rock changes surrounding sedimentary and igneous rock into metamorphic rock.

Rock may melt and rise to the surface where it cools to form igneous rock.

MINERALS

A mineral is a natural, non-living substance. Examples include gold, silver, gypsum, quartz, and sulphur.

ROCK-FORMING MINERALS

Different combinations of minerals form different types of rock.

Granite is composed of the minerals quartz, feldspar, and mica.

Quartz

Feldspar

Mica

ORE MINERALS

Ore minerals contain metals, and about 80 types of pure metal are extracted from them.

Titanium
A light, strong metal used in aircraft manufacture.

Rutile – titanium ore

Jet airliner

Aluminium
Used in construction, and the manufacture of consumer goods, such as saucepans.

Bauxite – aluminium ore

Aluminium can

Lead
The softest common metal, used in batteries and engineering.

Galena – lead ore

Battery

Iron
Used in construction, and in the manufacture of steel.

Hematite – iron ore

Stainless steel fork

Copper
A good conductor, widely used in the electricity industry.

Chalcopyrite – copper ore

Copper pipe

Mercury
Used in scientific instruments, and in the manufacture of drugs and pesticides.

Cinnabar – mercury ore

Mercury thermometer

CRYSTALS

Crystals grow from molten minerals, or minerals that are dissolved in liquids, such as water. Of the Earth's rocks and minerals, 85% are formed from crystals.

Rock crystal – one form of quartz

Quartz
Hardness: 7
System: hexagonal/trigonal
One of the commonest minerals. Most popular material for crystal balls.

Azurite forms in regions of copper deposits.

Azurite
Hardness: 3.5
System: monoclinic
Bright blue mineral once used as a pigment (colouring).

Sulphur forms bright yellow crystals.

Sulphur
Hardness: 1.5–2.5
System: orthorhombic
Forms around volcano craters. Referred to in the Bible as "brimstone".

Pyrite has a metallic lustre.

Pyrite
Hardness: 6.5
System: cubic
Sometimes mistaken for gold, hence its popular name "fool's gold".

MINERAL HARDNESS

The hardness of a mineral is graded on a scale of 1 to 10, devised by German mineralogist Friedrich Mohs (1773–1839).

MOHS' SCALE

1: Talc

2: Gypsum

3: Calcite

4: Fluorite

5: Apatite

6: Orthoclase

7: Quartz

8: Topaz

9: Corundum

10: Diamond

CRYSTAL SYSTEMS

The geometrical shape in which a mineral crystallizes is called its crystal system. There are six main systems.

Cubic
Examples: diamond, galena, garnet

Tetragonal
Examples: zircon, rutile, vesuvianite

Hexagonal/ trigonal
Examples: corundum, beryl

Orthorhombic
Examples: sulphur, olivine, topaz

Monoclinic
Examples: malachite, gypsum

Triclinic
Examples: rhodonite, kyanite, turquoise

GEMSTONES

Gemstones are minerals valued for their beauty, rarity, and durability. There are about 100 types of gemstone. The most valuable include diamonds, emeralds, rubies, and sapphires.

Diamond

Diamond
Hardness: 10
System: cubic
Sources include: Russia, S. Africa, Australia, Brazil

Ruby

Emerald

Ruby
Hardness: 9
System: trigonal
Sources include: India, Thailand, Burma, Sri Lanka

Emerald
Hardness: 7–8
System: hexagonal
Sources include: Russia, USA, Zambia, Colombia

ORGANIC GEMSTONES

Organic gemstones are those that have a plant or animal origin. They include pearls, shell, jet, and amber.

Amber is the fossilized resin of trees.

BIRTHSTONES

Some gemstones are associated with different months of the year. The custom of wearing birthstones became popular in the 18th century.

January Garnet

February Amethyst

March Aquamarine

April Diamond

May Emerald

June Pearl

July Ruby

August Peridot

September Sapphire

October Opal

November Topaz

December Turquoise

GIANT GEMS

The largest diamond was the Cullinan, found in South Africa in 1905. It weighed the same as a pineapple.

The Cullinan diamond weighed 3,106 carats (0.6kg/1.37lb).

A pineapple

The largest pearl is the Pearl of Lao-tze, found in the Philippines in 1934 in the shell of a giant clam. It weighs about the same as a four-month-old baby.

The Pearl of Lao-tze, weighs 6.37kg (14lb 1oz).

A four-month-old baby

MINERAL STRUCTURE

A mineral's hardness depends on the arrangement of its atoms. Diamond and graphite are different forms of the same element – carbon – but their hardness varies because of their different internal structures.

Diamond
Diamonds are the hardest of all minerals. Each atom is strongly bonded to four others, forming a compact, rigid structure.

Diamond ring

Arrangement of diamond atoms

Graphite
In graphite, the atoms are arranged in layers that easily slip over each other. This gives graphite its weak structure.

Graphite is used in pencil lead.

Arrangement of graphite atoms

CARATS AND BEANS

The weight of a gemstone is measured in carats: one carat = 0.2g (0.007oz). The term carat comes from the Greek word for carob seed. These seeds were once used as weights.

Carob seed

1-carat ruby

The purity of gold is also measured in carats: the purest gold is 24 carat. This gold bar is 23.5 carats.

ROCK AND MINERAL FACTS

• More than half the gold mined returns to Earth: it is buried in bank vaults.

• The word crystal comes from the Greek *kyros*, meaning icy cold. It was once thought that rock crystal was ice that had frozen so hard it would never thaw.

• About one in every thousand oysters and one in every three thousand mussels contains a pearl.

OCEAN FLOOR

THE OCEAN FLOOR IS the largest landscape on Earth. Beneath the oceans are mountains as high as the Himalayas, rugged mountain ranges longer than any on land, vast plains, deep canyons, and trenches plunging thousands of metres into the Earth's crust. Most of this fascinating landscape is still unexplored.

SMOKERS

Smokers are tall, chimney-like vents on the ocean floor that belch out clouds of super-heated water. They occur at volcanically active spots on mid-ocean ridges.

Heated water erupts in tall jets.

Temperature of heated water may be up to 350°C (662°F).

"Chimneys" up to 50m (164ft) high build up from minerals deposited by the hot water.

Smokers were discovered in 1977 by the American submersible "Alvin".

Heated water rises back to the surface of the ocean floor.

Clams

Tube worms

Life around smokers
Smokers support strange life forms that derive energy not from the Sun, like other life forms on Earth, but from volcanic activity.

Water seeps deep down into the sea floor where it is heated by volcanic activity.

MAJOR RIDGES AND TRENCHES

The major features of the ocean floor form at the boundaries of the plates that make up the Earth's crust (see pp.40–41). Mid-ocean ridges form where two plates are pulling apart, and trenches form at subduction zones, where one plate is plunging beneath another.

Vast undersea mountain ranges form where two tectonic plates are pulling apart.

EUROPE
AFRICA
ASIA
N AMERICA
S AMERICA
AUSTRALIA
Indian Ocean
Atlantic Ocean
Pacific Ocean
Kuril Trench
Izu-Ogasawara Trench
Philippine Trench
Mariana Trench
Deepest point in the Ocean
Yap Trench
New Britain Trench
North New Hebrides Trench
Tonga Trench
Kermadec Trench
Highest Seamount
Deepest Submarine Canyon
Mid-Indian Ridge
Southwest Indian Ridge
Southeast Indian Ridge
Reykjanes Ridge
Mid-Atlantic Ridge
Puerto Rico Trench
East Pacific Rise

DEEPEST TRENCHES
The depth of deep-sea trenches is measured from sea level.

Trench	Ocean	Depth metres	Depth feet
Mariana Trench	West Pacific	10,920	35,827
Tonga Trench	South Pacific	10,800	35,433
Philippine Trench	West Pacific	10,057	32,995
Kermadec Trench	South Pacific	10,047	32,963
Izu-Ogasawara Trench	West Pacific	9,780	32,087
Kuril Trench	West Pacific	9,550	31,332
North New Hebrides Trench	South Pacific	9,175	30,102
New Britain Trench	South Pacific	8,940	29,331
Puerto Rico Trench	West Atlantic	8,605	28,232
Yap Trench	West Pacific	8,527	27,976

FEATURES OF THE OCEAN FLOOR
The ocean floor is where the Earth's crust is created and destroyed. Volcanic activity associated with mid-ocean ridges and subduction zones (see pp.40–41) creates many ocean floor features.

SUBMARINE CANYON
A river flowing off the land into the sea may carve a deep canyon in the ocean floor.

ABYSSAL PLAIN
About 3,500–5,500m (11,480–18,040ft) below sea level is a vast plain covered with deep sediment, called the abyssal plain.

SEAMOUNT
A seamount is an underwater volcano that rises 1,000m (3,280ft) or more above the surrounding plain.

Oil rig
Submarine canyon
Abyssal plain
Seamount
Mid-ocean ridges are about 1,000km (620 miles) wide.
As two tectonic plates pull apart, magma rises to fill the gap, forming new ocean floor.
Continental shelf
Continental slope
Continental rise

CONTINENTAL SHELF
The continental shelf is the gently sloping rim of a continent.

CONTINENTAL SLOPE
The continental slope descends steeply from the continental shelf to the abyssal plain.

CONTINENTAL RISE
Below the steep continental slope, sediment may collect to form a gentler slope: the continental rise.

MID-OCEAN RIDGE
A long, undersea mountain range runs along the mid-ocean ridge, where two tectonic plates are pulling apart.

OCEAN FLOOR SEDIMENT

Close to the coast, sediment consists mainly of mud, sand, and silt washed off the land by rivers. The deep ocean floor is blanketed with ooze (the remains of dead marine plants and animals). The amount of sediment and ooze can help scientists to calculate the age of the ocean floor.

Newly formed rock
At the mid-ocean ridge, the new volcanic rock of the ocean floor is almost free of sediment.

5 million years later
The rock has moved 500km (311 miles) from the ridge. Sediment has started to gather in hollows.

10 million years later
The rock has moved 1,000km (621 miles) from the ridge. It is covered with a thick blanket of sediment.

MAPPING THE OCEAN FLOOR

Early explorations of the ocean floor were made from ships using a lead weight and line to estimate depth. Scientists today use echo-sounding techniques, and special submarines – submersibles – that can descend to the very depths of the ocean.

The ship sends down a signal from its transmitter.

The time taken for the signal to bounce back to the ship indicates the depth of the ocean.

OCEAN FLOOR FACTS

• A particle of ooze sinks 0.3–3m (1–10ft) per day. At this rate, it would take 25 years for the remains of a dead shrimp to sink from the ocean surface to the floor of a deep-sea trench.

• The tube worm *Alvinella pompejana* can live on smoker walls where the temperature is 105°C (221°F) – higher than any land animal can tolerate.

• The Mariana trench could hold 28 Empire State Buildings standing on top of each other.

• Oldest parts of the ocean floor are about 200 million years old. Oldest rocks on land are about 3.5 billion years old.

• At a growth rate of about 2mm (0.08in) every million years, it takes 10 million years for a manganese nodule to reach the size of a grape.

FOUND ON THE OCEAN FLOOR

Many useful products are found on or under the ocean floor. They include diamonds, oil, gas, coal, sand, and metals from manganese nodules (potato-like lumps of minerals).

DIAMONDS
These are found in shallow waters off the coasts of Africa and Indonesia.

SAND, GRAVEL, AND LIMESTONE
These are found in coastal waters.

COAL
Coal is mined beneath the sea as well as on land.

OIL AND GAS
About 20% of oil comes from the ocean floor. Natural gas is found with oil deposits.

FORMATION OF OIL AND GAS

Under certain conditions, oil and gas form from the remains of dead plants and animals that accumulate on the floor of shallow seas.

Remains of dead marine organisms

Sea floor

Mud and sand form layer of sandstone.

Organic remains

Further sedimentary layers
Sandstone
Gas
Oil
Water

1 Dead plant and animal remains sink down to the floor of the continental shelf. Bacteria break the remains down into organic material.

2 Sediments of sand and mud washed off the land by rivers form layers of sandstone, covering the organic remains.

3 Increased pressure from further layers of sandstone and other sedimentary rock turns the organic remains into oil and gas.

HIGHEST SEAMOUNT AND DEEPEST SUBMARINE CANYON

The highest seamount is near the Tonga Trench between Samoa and New Zealand. The deepest submarine canyon is 40km (25 miles) south of Esperance, Australia.

On land
Mt. Everest
8,848m (29,028ft)

Beneath the sea
Highest seamount
8,705m (28,560ft)

Grand Canyon
1,676m (5,499ft)

Deepest submarine canyon 1,800m (5,906ft)

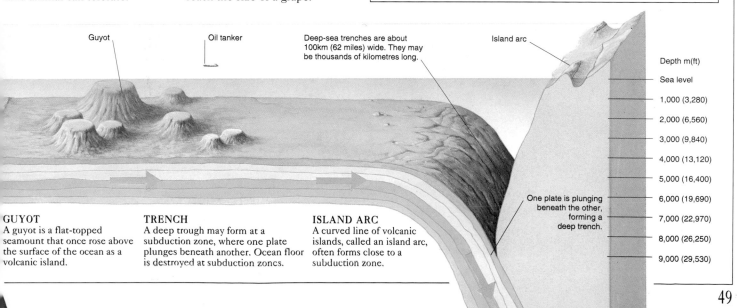

Guyot

Oil tanker

Deep-sea trenches are about 100km (62 miles) wide. They may be thousands of kilometres long.

Island arc

One plate is plunging beneath the other, forming a deep trench.

Depth m(ft)
Sea level
1,000 (3,280)
2,000 (6,560)
3,000 (9,840)
4,000 (13,120)
5,000 (16,400)
6,000 (19,690)
7,000 (22,970)
8,000 (26,250)
9,000 (29,530)

GUYOT
A guyot is a flat-topped seamount that once rose above the surface of the ocean as a volcanic island.

TRENCH
A deep trough may form at a subduction zone, where one plate plunges beneath another. Ocean floor is destroyed at subduction zones.

ISLAND ARC
A curved line of volcanic islands, called an island arc, often forms close to a subduction zone.

OCEANS AND ISLANDS

MORE THAN TWO-THIRDS of the Earth's surface lies beneath the oceans. Where the land rises above sea level it forms continents and islands. An island is a piece of land, smaller than a continent, that is surrounded by water.

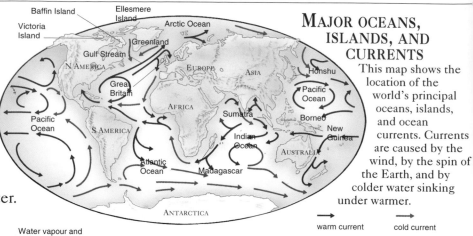

MAJOR OCEANS, ISLANDS, AND CURRENTS

This map shows the location of the world's principal oceans, islands, and ocean currents. Currents are caused by the wind, by the spin of the Earth, and by colder water sinking under warmer.

→ warm current　　→ cold current

FORMATION OF THE OCEANS

The oceans began to form many millions of years ago when the Earth was still cooling and solidifying following its early molten (liquid) state. Water vapour was thrown into the atmosphere by volcanoes.

Water vapour and carbon dioxide

1 As the young Earth cooled, volcanoes erupted, throwing out a mixture of gases that formed the early atmosphere.

2 When the atmosphere was saturated with water vapour, the vapour condensed, falling as rain. Rainwater began to collect in vast hollows.

3 The Earth cooled and volcanic eruptions became fewer. For the last 100 million years the volume of water in the sea has stayed about the same.

WAVE SEQUENCE

Most waves are caused by wind blowing across the surface of the sea. The height and power of waves depends on the speed of the wind and how far it has blown.

The water in a wave appears to be moving forwards, but in fact it moves in a circle.

The base of the wave is held back by the shore. The crest of the wave moves faster, toppling over when it reaches land.

Water reaches the base of the circle in the trough of a wave.

Water reaches the top of the circle at the crest of the wave.

OCEAN DATA

Total surface area	362 million sq km (139.8 million sq miles)
Total volume	1.35 billion cu km (324 million cu miles)
Mean (average) depth	3.5km (2.2 miles)
Weight of water	1.32×10^{18} tonnes
% of Earth's water	94%
Temperature range	-1.9°C to 36°C (28°F to 97°F)
Freezing temp. of sea water	-1.9°C (28°F)
Deepest known point	10,920m (35,827ft)

FORCE OF THE WAVES

When waves break on the shore, they exert a tremendous force. The weight of the sea hitting land can create pressures of more than 25 tonnes per square metre. This is 30 times as great as the

OCEAN FACTS

• More than 60% of the Earth's surface is covered by water deeper than 1.6km (1 mile).

• Average depth of Pacific Ocean: 3.94km (2.4 miles); average depth of Atlantic Ocean: 3.57km (2.2 miles).

• There is more gold dissolved in seawater than there is on land. The concentration is 0.000004 parts per million.

• The Gulf Stream ocean current contains about 100 times as much water as the combined volume of all the rivers in the world.

The Pacific Ocean covers more than a third of the Earth.

WHIRLPOOLS

Whirlpools are caused by a clash of tidal flows in places where the sea floor is uneven. Currents rush towards each other, and, if they hit a rocky shelf on the sea floor, water surges upwards, turning the surface into a seething mass.

OCEAN AND SEA AREAS

Pacific Ocean
165,384,000sq km (63,855,000sq miles)
45.7% of sea area

Atlantic Ocean
82,217,000sq km
(31,744,000sq miles)
22.7% of sea area

Indian Ocean
73,481,000sq km (28,371,000sq miles)
20.3% of sea area

Arctic Ocean
13,230,000sq km
(5,108,000sq miles)
3.65% of sea area

Other seas
27,688,000sq km
(10,690,000sq miles)
7.65 % of sea area

OCEAN ZONES

Depth
m(ft)
0

2,000
(6,560)

6,000
(19,690)

Bathyal zone
surface – 2,000m (6,560ft)

Light disappears about
100m (330ft) down

Temperature declines
rapidly about
300m (980ft) down

Abyssal zone
2,000–6,000m
(6,560–19,690ft)

Hadal zone
below 6,000m
(19,690ft)

The temperature of
the deep ocean is
close to freezing.

Over half of
deep-sea fish species
produce their own light.

MINERALS IN THE SEA

Minerals dissolved from rocks
by rivers are washed into the
oceans. The most abundant are
sodium and chlorine, which
together form salt. The average
salinity of the oceans is 33 to 38
parts salt per 1,000 parts water.

Potassium:
1.13%

Sulphate:
7.94%

Sodium:
30.79%

Calcium: 1.19%

Magnesium:
3.66%

Salt (sodium
chloride)
molecule

Chlorine: 55.29%

HEAPS OF SALT

The total amount of salt in
the world's oceans and seas
would cover Europe to a
depth of
5km
(3 miles).

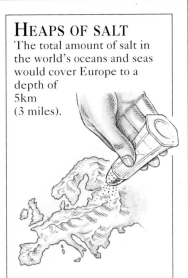

ISLANDS

Islands are found in seas,
rivers, and lakes. They range
in size from small mud and
sand islands measuring only
a few square metres, to
the largest, Greenland, which
measures more than
2 million square kilometres.

WORLD'S LARGEST ISLANDS

New Guinea
Western Pacific
Area: 792,493sq km
(305,981sq miles)

Borneo
Indian Ocean
Area: 725,416sq km
(280,083sq miles)

Greenland
Arctic Ocean
Area: 2,175,219sq km
(839,852sq miles)

Madagascar
Indian Ocean
Area: 587,009sq km
(226,644sq miles)

Baffin Island
Arctic Ocean
Area:
507,423sq km
(195,916sq miles)

Sumatra
Indian Ocean
Area: 427,325sq km
(164,990sq miles)

Great Britain
North Atlantic
Area: 218,065sq km
(84,195sq miles)

Honshu
NW Pacific
Area: 227,401sq km
(87,799sq miles)

Victoria Island
Arctic Ocean
Area:
217,278sq km
(83,891sq miles)

Ellesmere Island
Arctic Ocean
Area:
196,225sq km
(75,762sq miles)

TYPES OF ISLAND

There are four main types
of island.

CORAL ISLAND

A coral island forms when corals (tiny
marine organisms) grow up towards the
surface of the ocean from an underwater
platform in shallow water, such as the
peak of a seamount (see p.48). The
coral skeletons build up over many
years until they reach the surface.

*The Maldives in the Indian Ocean
are coral islands.*

VOLCANIC ISLAND

Volcanoes that erupt beneath the
ocean may eventually grow to reach
the surface, where they emerge as
islands. Volcanic islands often form
close to plate boundaries
(see pp.40–41).

*The volcanic island of Surtsey appeared
south of Iceland in the Atlantic
Ocean in 1963.*

ISLAND FORMED BY A
CHANGE IN SEA LEVEL

A rise in sea level, for example at the
end of an ice age, may cut off an area
of land from a continent, forming an
island. Great Britain was formed in this
way. Some pieces of land become
islands at high tide.

*Mont St. Michel in France becomes an island
each time the tide comes in.*

ISLAND ARC

An island arc is a chain of volcanic
islands that usually forms close to a
subduction zone (see pp.40–41).
Some island arcs contain many
thousands of islands. The Japanese
islands were formed in this way.

*Part of Indonesia, photographed from
the Space Shuttle in 1983. Indonesia is the
world's longest island arc.*

CORAL ATOLLS

An atoll is a ring-shaped coral island with
a lagoon in its centre. Atolls form
when a coral reef builds up
around a volcanic island, and
the island subsequently
sinks below sea level. As
the island sinks, the
coral continues
to grow.

A coral reef builds up,
fringing the volcanic island.

As the island starts
to sink, coral continues
to grow upwards.

The island has disappeared,
leaving a coral atoll.

Lagoon

OCEAN AND ISLAND RECORDS

GREATEST OCEAN CURRENT
is the Antarctic Circumpolar
Current (also known as the West
Wind Drift Current), which
flows at a rate of 130,000,000cu m
(4.3 billion cu ft) per second.

HIGHEST RECORDED WAVE
(excluding seismic sea waves)
was 34m (112ft) from trough to
crest, recorded in 1933 en route
from the Philippines to the USA.

REMOTEST ISLAND
is Bouvet Island, about 1,700km
(1,056 miles) from the nearest
land (Queen Maud Land on the
coast of eastern Antarctica).

LARGEST CORAL ATOLL
is Kwajalein in the Marshall
Islands, central Pacific Ocean.
Its reef is 283km (176 miles)
long, and encloses a lagoon of
2,850sq km (1,100sq miles).

MOUNTAINS

AS THE EARTH'S tectonic plates jostle and grind against each other, the crust may buckle and fold, throwing up lofty mountain ranges. Volcanoes also erupt at plate boundaries, sometimes building into high mountains.

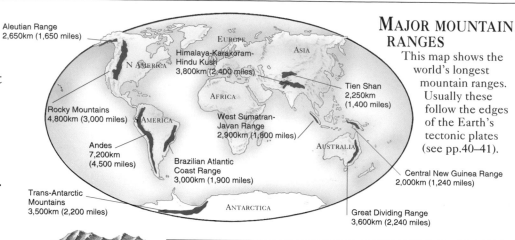

Aleutian Range
2,650km (1,650 miles)

Himalaya-Karakoram-Hindu Kush
3,800km (2,400 miles)

Tien Shan
2,250km
(1,400 miles)

Rocky Mountains
4,800km (3,000 miles)

West Sumatran-Javan Range
2,900km (1,800 miles)

Andes
7,200km
(4,500 miles)

Brazilian Atlantic Coast Range
3,000km (1,900 miles)

Central New Guinea Range
2,000km (1,240 miles)

Trans-Antarctic Mountains
3,500km (2,200 miles)

Great Dividing Range
3,600km (2,240 miles)

MAJOR MOUNTAIN RANGES

This map shows the world's longest mountain ranges. Usually these follow the edges of the Earth's tectonic plates (see pp.40–41).

TYPES OF MOUNTAIN

There are four main types of mountain.

FOLD MOUNTAINS

When two of the Earth's tectonic plates collide, the crust at the plate edges may crumple and fold under the strain, pushing up ranges of fold mountains.

Fold mountains form when the Earth's crust bends and buckles.

VOLCANOES

A volcano forms when magma (molten rock) from deep inside the Earth erupts on to the surface, building into a tall cone. Some of the highest mountains in the world are volcanoes.

Layers of lava build up into a mountain.

FAULT-BLOCK MOUNTAINS

Plate movements may squeeze layers of rock until they crack and snap. These cracks are faults. Mountains form when a slab or block of rock is squeezed upwards.

Fault-block mountains form where one slab or rock is thrust above another.

DOME MOUNTAINS

A large upwelling of molten rock (an igneous intrusion) beneath the Earth's surface may force up the overlying layers of rock into a huge hump. Mountains formed in this way are dome mountains.

Rising molten rock forces up overlying layers of rock into mountains.

WORLD'S HIGHEST MOUNTAINS

The ten highest mountains in the world are all in the Himalayas.

Name	Location	Height	
		metres	feet
Everest	Nepal/China	8,848	29,028
K2	Kashmir/China	8,611	28,251
Kanchenjunga	Nepal/Sikkim	8,598	28,208
Lhotse	Nepal/Tibet	8,511	27,923
Makalu	Nepal/Tibet	8,480	27,821
Cho Oyu	Nepal	8,201	26,906
Dhaulagiri	Nepal	8,172	26,811
Manaslu	Nepal	8,156	26,759
Nanga Parbat	Kashmir	8,126	26,660
Annapurna	Nepal	8,078	26,503

CLOSE-UP OF A MOUNTAIN

High mountains have several zones of vegetation, due to the drop in temperature at higher altitudes.

Nothing can survive

Specially adapted alpine species

Pine forest

Broadleaf forest

Wide range of vegetation

LIFE OF A MOUNTAIN

Young

YOUNG

Mountains that formed during the last few million years, or that are still growing, e.g. the Himalayas.

Mature

MATURE

Mountains several hundred million years old that have been eroded to a fraction of their former size, e.g. the Urals.

Ancient

ANCIENT

Mountains that have been eroded away until there are just a few hills on a low-lying peneplain.

The Eiffel Tower in Paris, France, is 300m (984ft) high.

Mt. Everest
Nepal/China
Asia
8,848m
(29,028ft)

Mt. Everest was first climbed on 29 May 1953 by New Zealander Edmund Hillary (born 1919) and Sherpa Tensing Norgay (1914–86) of Nepal.

Aconcagua
Argentina
South America
6,960m
(22,834ft)

Mt. McKinley
Alaska, USA
North America
6,194m
(20,320ft)

El'brus
Russia
Europe
5,642m
(18,510ft)

Vinson Massif
Antarctica
5,140m
(16,863ft)

Kilimanjaro
Tanzania
Africa
5,895m
(19,340ft)

Mt. Wilhelm
Papua New Guinea
Australasia
4,884m
(16,024ft)

HIGHEST MOUNTAIN PER CONTINENT

This illustration shows the comparative size of the highest mountain on each continent.

VALLEYS AND CAVES

THE FORCES OF EROSION are constantly attacking the land, changing its appearance. Rain flows into rivers that gash the landscape with valleys. In limestone areas, rainwater may seep into the rock, eating it away to form caves.

The river valley begins high in the mountains as a narrow gully.

In the river's upper course, the valley is a characteristic V-shape.

Cross-section of a river valley's upper course

FEATURES OF A VALLEY

A river valley usually begins in the mountains as a steep-sided gully cut by a fast-flowing stream. As it flows down towards lower ground, the river slows down and the valley widens. As it nears the sea the river flows across a wide, level flood plain. Some rivers fan out into a delta at their estuary (see pp.56–57).

As the river reaches the gentler slopes of its middle course, its rate of flow slows down.

The river meanders back and forth, widening the valley.

The valley floor is covered in a thick carpet of sand and mud.

Estuary (see p.56)

Delta (see p.56)

Cross-section of a river valley's lower course

TYPES OF VALLEY

Milford Sound, New Zealand

FJORD
In glaciated areas of the world, deep valleys are scoured out by glaciers. When a glacier melts, for example at the end of an ice age, the sea level may rise, flooding the valley to form a fjord.

CAVES

Caves are large, naturally occurring hollows in the ground, in cliffs, or in ice.

LIMESTONE CAVE
Most caves occur in limestone areas, because this type of rock is soluble (dissolves) in rainwater.

SEA CAVE
Waves crashing against cliffs erode the rocks, forming sea caves.

ICE CAVE
A stream of meltwater running beneath a glacier may carve out an ice cave.

LAVA CAVE
When the crust of a lava flow hardens, the molten lava beneath may flow out, leaving a lava cave.

CROSS-SECTION OF A LIMESTONE CAVE

Limestone dissolves in rainwater.

Rainwater eats away at the rock, forming a cave.

A stream plunges underground at a sink hole.

Waterfall

Stalactites grow down from the roof.

Water enlarges cracks and joints.

Stalagmites build up on the cave floor.

A stalactite and stalagmite have joined, forming a column.

RIFT VALLEY
Rift valleys form when a long, narrow block of land sinks between two faults, at places where two tectonic plates are pulling apart (see pp.40–41).

Grand Canyon, Arizona, USA

GORGE AND CANYON
A gorge is a deep ravine with walls that are almost vertical. A canyon is a gorge, usually with water flowing through it, found in the desert. The source of its river is often outside the valley.

LIMESTONE CAVE FEATURES

Water dripping in limestone caves leaves behind tiny amounts of calcite. These mineral deposits build up to form distinctive limestone cave features. It can take from four to four thousand years for a stalactite or stalagmite to grow one inch (2.5cm).

Curtain stalactite

Stalactite

Column

Stalagmite

Fir cone stalagmite

Plate stack stalagmite

VALLEY AND CAVE RECORDS

LONGEST FJORD is Nordvest Fjord, Greenland, which extends 313km (194 miles) inland.

LARGEST GORGE is the Grand Canyon in Arizona, USA, at 349km (217 miles) long and up to 1,676m (5,499ft) deep.

LARGEST CAVE CHAMBER is the Sarawak Chamber in Sarawak, Malaysia, which has an area of 162,700sq m (1,751,300sq ft). The cave chamber is 700m (2,300ft) long, and has an average width of 300m (980ft). The lowest part of the roof is 70m (230ft) high.

LONGEST CAVE SYSTEM is the Mammoth Cave system, Kentucky, USA, which is 560km (348 miles) long.

LONGEST STALACTITE is 6.2m (20ft 4in) long. It is in the Poll an Ionana, a cave in Co. Clare, Ireland.

TALLEST STALAGMITE is 32m (105ft) tall, in the Krásnohorska cave in the Czech Republic.

Size of tallest stalagmite compared to an adult

Valley of Kings, Egyptian desert

WADI
A wadi is a narrow, steep-sided desert valley that is usually dry. A wadi's characteristic shape is carved out by the flash floods that occur after torrential desert rainfall.

GLACIATION

MORE THAN A TENTH of the Earth's
surface is permanently covered
with ice. Ice sheets and sea ice
blanket the polar areas, and
ice caps and glaciers tumble
down the slopes of high mountain
ranges. Glaciers are found even on
mountains at the Equator.

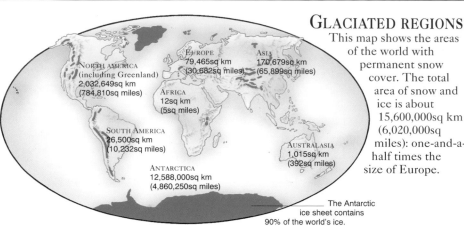

GLACIATED REGIONS

This map shows the areas
of the world with
permanent snow
cover. The total
area of snow and
ice is about
15,600,000sq km
(6,020,000sq
miles): one-and-a-
half times the
size of Europe.

EUROPE
79,465 km
(30,682sq miles)

ASIA
170,679 km
(65,899sq miles)

NORTH AMERICA
(including Greenland)
2,032,649sq km
(784,810sq miles)

AFRICA
12sq km
(5sq miles)

SOUTH AMERICA
26,500sq km
(10,232sq miles)

AUSTRALASIA
1,015sq km
(392sq miles)

ANTARCTICA
12,588,000sq km
(4,860,250sq miles)

The Antarctic
ice sheet contains
90% of the world's ice.

FORMATION OF
AN ICE CAP

1 Heavy winter snowfall
covers the land. Fresh
layers compress the
older snow beneath,
turning it into an
icy mass called firn.

2 The temperature rises in
summer, but on high ground
it is not warm enough to
melt the ice. Over
successive winters,
the blanket of firn
becomes thicker.

3 Eventually the firn forms
an ice cap. Gravity causes
it to flow down from
higher ground.
Tongues of ice fill
the valleys,
forming glaciers.

FEATURES OF
A GLACIER

Glaciers usually
begin high in the
mountains. Most
flow at a rate of up
to 2m (7ft) per day,
although glaciers
on steeper slopes
may flow much
more quickly. It
may take thousands
of years for ice to
reach the end of a
slow-moving glacier.

Headwall

Firn field

The crack
between the
headwall and the
firn field is the
Bergschrund.

Crevasses are
deep cracks in
the surface of
the glacier.

Lateral moraine is
carried along at the
side of the glacier.

The end of
the glacier is
the snout.

A stream of
meltwater flows out
from the snout.

A pyramidal peak forms when
a mountain is attacked by
glaciers from several sides.

The glacier starts in an
ice-worn hollow, called
a cirque or corrie.

A sharp ridge called an
arête forms between
two glaciers.

The glacier
scours out rocks,
forming debris
called moraine.

Medial moraine is
carried in the centre,
where two glaciers
have joined.

Terminal
moraine is
dumped at the snout.

FRESHWATER
RESERVOIR

More than 75% of the world's
fresh water is frozen in ice
sheets, ice caps, and glaciers.

Ice

Water

PROPORTION OF ICE

About 12% of sea and 10%
of land is permanently
covered with ice.

Sea   *Land*

ICE-SCULPTED LANDSCAPES

When glaciers retreat, for example at the end of an
ice age, they leave behind U-shaped valleys, fjords
(see p.53), and deep lakes. Piles of moraine form
drumlins (small hills) and moraine ridges.

Before glaciation: a V-shaped
river valley

Hanging valleys
open high on
the sides of the
main valley.

After glaciation: a U-shaped
river valley

LONGEST GLACIERS

The glaciers listed below are the longest in each of the major
glaciated regions of the world.

Glacier	Region	Length	
		km	miles
Lambert-Fisher Ice Passage	Antarctica	515	320
Petermanns Glacier	Greenland	200	124
Hubbard Glacier	Alaska-Yukon, N. America	128	80
Siachen Glacier	Karakoram, Asia	75	47
Skeidararjokull	Iceland	48	30
Tasman Glacier	New Zealand	29	18
Aletsch Gletscher	European Alps	24	15
Gyabrag Glacier	Himalayas	21	13

SNOWLINE

The snowline is the level that divides year-round snow from snow that melts during warmer weather. The closer an area is to the Equator, the higher the snowline.

Mt. Kenya, which is close to the Equator, has glaciers on its summit.

Mt. Vinson, Antarctica, is covered in snow and ice from foot to summit.

On the Equator
the snowline lies about 4,900m (16,000ft) high.

In the European Alps
the snowline lies about 2,700m (9,000ft) high.

In polar regions
the snowline lies at sea level.

ICE AGES

Ice ages occur when the Earth's climate becomes much cooler, and the amount of ice increases. Scientists believe there have been at least five ice ages over the last million years.

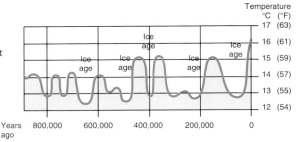

MOST RECENT ICE AGE

The last ice age began about 72,000 years ago, and ended about 10,000 years ago. This map shows the areas of the world that were covered with ice. The sea level was about 150m (490ft) lower than today, because so much water was locked up in ice.

Huge ice sheets covered much of North America, Europe, and Asia.

The land where New York now stands was covered with ice.

Southern Argentina was covered by an ice sheet.

Up to 30% of the Earth's surface was glaciated.

New Zealand was covered by an ice cap.

AVALANCHES

An avalanche is a mass of snow and ice that suddenly crashes down a mountainside. It may be up to 1km (0.6 miles) across, and can move at up to 320km/h (200mph). If a town or village lies in the path of an avalanche, houses may be flattened and people killed.

Heavy snowfall adds extra weight to the snow cover on this mountain slope.

The extra weight of snow, combined with a sudden rise in temperature, triggers an avalanche.

AVALANCHE FACTS

● An avalanche can generate winds of up to 300km/h (185mph).

● About 18,000 Austrian and Italian soldiers are thought to have been killed in a single day in 1916 by more than 100 avalanches in the Dolomites, northern Italy. Many of these avalanches were started by gunfire.

● The biggest avalanches usually occur on slopes with an angle of 30–40°.

SEA ICE

The sea freezes over when its temperature falls below -1.9°C (28°F). Sea ice is never more than about 5m (16ft) thick.

Sea ice off the western Antarctic coast

TALLEST ICEBERG

The tallest iceberg ever reported was 167m (550ft) high – taller than St. Paul's Cathedral, London. It was sighted off Greenland in 1958.

ICEBERGS

Icebergs are large chunks of ice that break off the end of ice sheets, ice caps, and glaciers, and float out to sea. The process of icebergs breaking off a body of ice is called calving.

The rising and falling tide, together with buffeting from the waves, breaks the iceberg off the end of the glacier.

Once an iceberg has broken away, its movements are controlled by ocean currents and the wind.

ICY RECORDS

FASTEST-MOVING GLACIER is the Quarayaq, Greenland, which can flow 20–24m (65–80ft) per day.
THICKEST ICE ever recorded is 5km (3 miles) deep, in Wilkes Land, Antarctica. This would reach over half way up Mt. Everest.

LARGEST ICEBERG The largest iceberg ever recorded was more than 335km (208 miles) long and 97km (60 miles) wide – an area three times the size of Cyprus.
GREATEST NUMBER OF DEATHS FROM AN AVALANCHE was 5,000 at Huaras, Peru, on 13 December 1941.

Only a small proportion of an iceberg – about 12% – is visible above the surface of the ocean. The remainder is hidden beneath the water.

ICEBERG FACTS

● About 10,000 icebergs a year break away from the glaciers of western Greenland.

● Scientists estimate that the average age of the ice in icebergs is 5,000 years.

RIVERS AND LAKES

MOST OF THE EARTH'S fresh water is frozen in ice, or is held in rocks below the surface as groundwater. Less than one per cent is contained in rivers and lakes, yet these features have a significant effect on the landscape.

MAJOR RIVERS AND LAKES

This map shows the world's major rivers and lakes. The largest lake (the Caspian Sea) covers an area almost as large as Japan, while the longest river (the Nile) could stretch from New York to Berlin.

Great Bear Lake
Mackenzie R.
Lake Superior
N AMERICA
Mississippi-Missouri R.
Lake Huron
Lake Michigan
EUROPE
Ob-irtysh R.
Lake Ladoga
Volga R.
Lena R.
ASIA
Lake Baikal
Amur R.
Yellow R.
Aral Sea
Caspian Sea
Nile R.
AFRICA
Yangtze R.
Mekong R.
Amazon R.
Congo R.
Lake Titicaca
S AMERICA
Lake Nyasa (Lake Malawi)
Lake Victoria
Lake Tanganyika
Ganges Delta
AUSTRALIA
Lake Eyre
Murray R.
ANTARCTICA

Antarctica has no rivers or lakes: all of its fresh water is frozen.

TYPES OF RIVER

PERENNIAL RIVER
Perennial rivers flow all year round. They are usually found in temperate and tropical areas (see pp.60–61), where rain falls throughout the year.

The Nile: a perennial river

SEASONAL RIVER
Seasonal rivers only flow during wet seasons. Many Mediterranean countries have seasonal rivers that flow in the wet winter season, but are dry in summer.

Seasonal river in Crete during summer.

EPHEMERAL RIVER
Ephemeral rivers are usually dry. Many desert rivers are ephemeral, for example the Todd River in central Australia hardly ever has water in it.

The Todd River in central Australia.

RIVER RECORDS

LONGEST EUROPEAN RIVER
is the Volga, Russia, which is 3,531km (2,194 miles) long.

LONGEST AUSTRALASIAN RIVER
is the Murray, Australia, which is 2,589km (1,609 miles) long.

LARGEST DELTA
is the Ganges and Brahmaputra delta, which covers about 75,000sq km (30,000sq miles). Sri Lanka would fit into it with room to spare.

HIGHEST WATERFALL
The Angel Falls in Venezuela have a total drop of 979m (3,212ft): almost three times as high as the Empire State Building.

FEATURES OF A RIVER
A river is a body of water that flows downhill in a channel, usually towards the ocean. Rivers have three sections: the upper course, middle course, and lower course.

Upper course
The young, fast-flowing river rushes down a steep gradient, cutting a V-shaped gully.

The river plunges over a shelf of hard rock, forming a waterfall.

The waterfall wears away the rock and moves slowly upstream, cutting a deep gorge.

Where the river flows down a steep slope of hard rock, it forms swirling rapids.

In its upper course, the river flows over obstacles.

The river cuts further into the bank, widening the meander (loop).

A meander cut off after flooding forms an oxbow lake.

Middle course
The mature river's gradient is more gentle, and its rate of flow slower. It flows around obstacles, forming meanders.

Lower course
In its old age, with almost no gradient, the river flows sluggishly and begins to dump its sediment. It frequently floods and changes course.

The river estuary is where fresh river water meets salty sea water.

The wide, flat floodplain is submerged when the river floods.

The river may block its own route with sediment, forcing it to split into separate streams. These fan out, forming a delta.

Many rivers begin in mountain ranges.

Rainfall runs off mountain slopes into the river system.

Tributary streams feed the main river.

RIVER WATER SOURCES
All rivers receive their water, either directly or indirectly, from precipitation (see pp.60–61).

OVERLAND FLOW
Rainfall runs down slopes into small streams. These tributaries eventually flow into the main river.

SPRING
Rain soaks into the ground and is absorbed into the aquifer – a layer of rock that can hold water. Where the water table (the upper surface of the groundwater) meets the ground surface, a spring may occur.

MELTWATER
Many rivers rise (begin) in glaciated regions of the world, where they are fed by melting snow and ice.

LONGEST RIVERS

River	Location	Length km	miles
Nile	Africa	6,695	4,160
Amazon	South America	6,439	4,001
Yangtze	Asia	6,379	3,964
Ob-Irtysh	Asia	5,410	3,362
Yellow	Asia	4,672	2,903
Amur	Asia	4,464	2,774
Lena	Asia	4,400	2,734
Congo	Africa	4,374	2,718
Mackenzie	North America	4,270	2,653
Mekong	Asia	4,184	2,600

TYPES OF LAKE

A lake is an inland body of water that collects in a hollow. The type of lake is determined by how it originally formed. Most lakes are fed by rivers (plus a small amount of rainfall), and most lose water into an outlet river. Some lakes, however, have no outlet and only lose water by evaporation. These lakes, such as Australia's Lake Eyre, are often salty.

EROSION

Lakes fill hollows scoured out by glaciers during ice ages, e.g. the lakeland plateau of Kuopio, Finland. When desert winds erode a deflation hollow (see p.62) to below the water table, groundwater may fill the depression, forming a lake.

Lakes in ice-worn hollows

Lake in a deflation hollow

EARTH MOVEMENT

When the Earth's crust is uplifted (see p.52), a body of water may be cut off from the sea, forming a lake. Similarly, when a rift valley forms (see p.53), water collects in the trough forming long, narrow lakes, e.g. Lake Nyasa, Africa.

Lake formed by crustal uplift

Rift valley lake

DEPOSITION

An oxbow lake forms when a meander is cut off from a river by the deposition of sediment. Deposition lakes also form when a landslide dams a river, and when sand bars and dunes cut off coastal waters from the sea.

Oxbow lake

Lake formed by a landslide

VOLCANIC ACTIVITY

Rainwater often collects in volcano craters, forming lakes such as Crater Lake in Oregon, USA. Some lakes, such as the Sea of Galilee in Israel, form when a river is dammed by a lava flow (see p.42).

Crater lake

Lake formed by a lava dam

EROSION AND DEPOSITION

Glaciers carve out U-shaped valleys and corries (see p.54) that may be dammed by moraine deposited when the ice retreats. Long, narrow ribbon lakes fill the valleys, and small, circular tarns fill the corries.

Ribbon lake

Tarn

DEEPEST LAKE

Lake Baikal in Siberia has a maximum depth of 1,620m (5,315ft). Its deepest point could swallow five Eiffel Towers standing on top of each other.

LARGEST LAKES

Lake	Location	Area	
		sq km	sq miles
Caspian Sea	Asia	370,980	143,236
Lake Superior	North America	82,098	31,698
Lake Victoria	Africa	69,480	26,826
Lake Huron	North America	59,566	22,999
Lake Michigan	North America	57,754	22,299
Aral Sea	Asia	37,056	14,307
Lake Tanganyika	Africa	32,891	12,699
Lake Baikal	Siberia	31,498	12,161
Great Bear Lake	Canada	31,327	12,095
Lake Nyasa (Malawi)	Africa	28,877	11,149

LAKE RECORDS

LARGEST EUROPEAN LAKE
is Lake Ladoga, Russia, which has an area of 17,702sq km (6,835sq miles).

LARGEST AUSTRALASIAN LAKE
is Lake Eyre, Australia, which has an area of 9,323sq km (3,600sq miles). This salt lake is usually dry.

LARGEST SOUTH AMERICAN LAKE
is Lake Titicaca in Peru and Bolivia, which has an area of 8,288sq km (3,200sq miles).

USES OF RIVERS AND LAKES

SOURCE OF FRESH WATER
Lakes and rivers supply water for factories and industry. They also provide fresh water for towns and cities.

TRANSPORTATION
Lakes and rivers have been used for centuries to transport goods.

ELECTRICITY
Hydro-electric power is generated by dammed rivers, and by waterfalls driving turbines.

FISHING
Some of the world's larger lakes and rivers support important fishing industries.

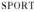

SPORT
Sports such as sailing and wind-surfing are carried out on lakes. Canoeing and rafting are popular on rivers.

IRRIGATION
Rivers are an important source of water for irrigating crops in many arid (dry) regions.

VANISHING LAKES

Most lakes are geologically short-lived, drying up within a million years. Most are filled in by sediment dumped by rivers; others disappear when rainfall dwindles (becomes less). The remnants of lakes form swamps, marshes, and bogs.

RIVER AND LAKE FACTS

• About 180,000cu m (6.4 million cu ft) of water flows out of the Amazon into the ocean every second: it would take just over a second to fill London's St. Paul's Cathedral.

• Each year rivers dump about 20 billion tonnes of sediment in the sea, shaving the equivalent of 3.13cm (1.2in) off the land every thousand years.

• Lake Geneva will be filled in by the River Rhône within approximately 40,000 years.

1 The river dumps its load of mud and gravel when it reaches the lake.

2 The sediment builds up, forming a sediment fan at one end of the lake.

3 Further sediment extends the fan out into the lake which shrinks, forming a shallow swamp.

4 The lake is completely filled in with sediment. Plants eventually cover the old lake site.

WEATHER

EVERYTHING called weather – from sun and rain to snow and hurricanes – occurs in the bottom layer of the Earth's atmosphere. This churning layer of gas is being heated and cooled constantly by wind, water, and the Sun.

WATER CYCLE

Water moves in a never-ending cycle. The Sun's heat evaporates water from seas, lakes, and rivers. As it rises into the atmosphere, the vapour cools and condenses into clouds. Eventually the droplets fall back to Earth as rain.

Plants release water vapour into the atmosphere.

Precipitation falls on high ground.

Wind

Water vapour cools to form clouds.

Water evaporates from the sea.

Water evaporates from lakes.

River carries water downstream.

Water seeps below ground and flows to the sea.

River flows into the sea.

TYPES OF CLOUD

Clouds are classified according to their shape, and their height above the ground.

Cirrostratus
5,000–13,000m (16,000–40,000ft)
Semi-transparent layer; causes halo around the Sun.

Cirrocumulus
5,000–13,000m (16,000–40,000ft)
Made of icy particles; resemble fish scales. Often called "mackerel sky".

Altostratus
2,000–7,000m (6,500–23,000ft)
Thin, watery layer; forms coloured ring (corona) around Sun and Moon.

Cirrus
5,000–13,000m (16,000–40,000ft)
Highest clouds; wispy.

Altocumulus
2,000–7,000m (6,500–23,000ft)
Lumpy globules of white and grey cloud.

Cumulonimbus
Massive, flat-topped storm clouds that may stretch up to 15,000m (49,000ft) above the ground. Can bring heavy showers, thunderstorms, hail, or tornadoes.

Stratocumulus
0–2,000m (0–6,500ft)
Low sheet of grey or white, lumpy clouds.

Cumulus
0–2,000m (0–6,500ft)
Puffy clouds; grey at the bottom, brilliant white at the top.

Nimbostratus
0–2,000m (0–6,500ft)
Thick multi-layered clouds covering the sky; bring continuous rain or snow.

Stratus
0–2,000m (0–6,500ft)
Lowest clouds; hide hills in fog.

FORMATION OF CLOUDS

Clouds form when water vapour in warm air rises, cools, and condenses. The highest clouds usually consist of tiny ice crystals; lower clouds are made up mostly of water droplets.

1 Warm air containing invisible water vapour rises from the ground.

2 As water vapour cools it condenses into droplets, forming a cloud.

3 Cloud goes on forming as long as warm, moist air continues to rise.

WEATHER FACTS

• The first thermometer was made in about 1600 by Italian scientist Galileo Galilei (1564–1642).

• There is enough water in the troposphere (see p.39) to flood the world to a depth of 1m (3.3ft).

• On any one day there may be 44,000 storms over the Earth.

• In 1888, 246 people died because of a hailstorm in Moredabad, India.

• Over a 30-year period in the USA, there was an average of 730 tornadoes a year, causing more than 100 deaths annually.

• During a tornado, one house can be destroyed, but another 20m (66ft) away can remain intact.

THE WORLD'S WINDS

Wind is air moving from one place to another. Winds always blow from areas of high pressure to areas of low pressure.

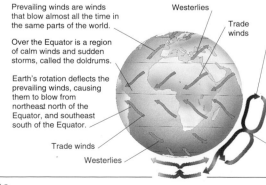

Prevailing winds are winds that blow almost all the time in the same parts of the world.

Over the Equator is a region of calm winds and sudden storms, called the doldrums.

Earth's rotation deflects the prevailing winds, causing them to blow from northeast north of the Equator, and southeast south of the Equator.

Westerlies

Trade winds

Trade winds

Westerlies

At the Equator the Sun is almost directly overhead. Its concentrated heat causes air to expand, rise, and billow out at high altitudes.

As it cools, the air sinks back to the surface just beyond the tropics, creating regions of high pressure. Winds blow from there back into the low-pressure zone around the Equator.

AIR PRESSURE

Cold air sinks, creating areas of high pressure called anticyclones, or highs. Warm air rises, creating areas of low pressure called depressions, lows, or cyclones.

Air sinks to the ground and spreads, absorbing moisture.

Anticyclone
An anticylone has descending air, light winds, and brings clear skies.

Air rises, forming clouds.

In the Southern Hemisphere, air in highs and lows circulates in the opposite direction to air flows in the Northern Hemisphere.

Depression
A depression often has rising air, strong winds, and may bring clouds, rain, or snow.

AIR MASSES AND FRONTS

Air masses are huge bodies of air that form over continents and oceans. They can be warm, cold, moist, or dry, depending on where they form. The boundary between two air masses is a front. As a front sweeps across the land, it usually brings a change in the weather.

Cold front Cold air moves in under warm air, bringing heavy rain followed by showers.

Cold air mass

Warm air mass

Warm front Long spells of rain occur as warm air rises above cold air, before the front arrives on the ground.

Warm, moist air mass

Cold, moist air mass

Occluded front An occluded front forms when a cold front overtakes a warm front, lifting warm air above it.

Cold air mass

Cold air mass

Warm air mass

Rain falls along the occluded front.

WEATHER WORDS

Blizzard A severe snowstorm with strong winds.

Dew Tiny drops of water that condense on cold objects near to the ground.

Fog Ground-level cloud: visibility less than 1km (0.6 miles).

Frost Ice crystals or frozen particles of moisture that form on cold surfaces.

Hail Pellets of ice that fall during storms.

Mist Thin fog: visibility 1–2km (0.6–1.25 miles).

Precipitation Rain, drizzle, hail, or snow.

Rainbow A seven-coloured arc that forms in the sky when sunlight shines through raindrops.

Squall A sudden increase in wind, accompanied by rain.

Waterspout A tornado that forms over an ocean or lake, sucking up water.

LIGHTNING

Lightning is the visible flash that occurs when electric energy is released from a cloud. It is often accompanied by thunder – a loud bang caused by rapidly expanding air.

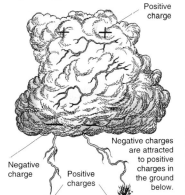

Positive charge

Negative charges are attracted to positive charges in the ground below.

Negative charge

Positive charges

BEAUFORT SCALE

In 1805, British Admiral Francis Beaufort (1774–1857) devised a scale of 12 wind forces for use in sailing. For many years this scale has been used on land as well as at sea, although winds of force 10, 11, and 12 rarely occur over land.

0 Calm. Chimney smoke rises straight up.

1 Light air. Smoke drifts gently. Wind speed 3km/h (2mph).

2 Light breeze. Leaves rustle. Wind speed 9km/h (6mph).

3 Gentle breeze. Flags flutter. Wind speed 15km/h (9mph).

4 Moderate wind. Small branches move. Wind speed 25km/h (16mph).

5 Fresh wind. Small trees sway. Wind speed 35km/h (22mph).

6 Strong wind. Difficult to control umbrellas. Wind speed 45km/h (28mph).

7 Near-gale. Large trees sway. Wind speed 56km/h (35mph).

8 Gale. Twigs break off trees. Wind speed 68km/h (43mph).

9 Severe gale. Slates and chimney pots blow off. Wind speed 81km/h (51mph).

10 Storm. Houses damaged; trees blow down. Wind speed 94km/h (59mph).

11 Severe storm. Serious damage to buildings. Wind speed 110km/h (69mph).

12 Hurricane. Widespread damage. Wind speed 117km/h (73mph).

TORNADO

A tornado is a violently whirling column of wind averaging 100m (300ft) across. It forms a funnel of cloud that can suck up objects lying in its path. Tornadoes last from a few minutes to two hours.

Tornadoes move at an average speed of 55km/h (35mph).

Rising air sucks up dirt, and objects as large as vehicles.

Base of tornado measures less than 1km (0.6 miles) across.

UNLUCKY STRIKES

US ex-park ranger Roy Sullivan was struck by lightning seven times in 35 years.

SHOCKING FACTS

• Twenty-one people died when a single bolt of lightning hit a hut near Umtali, Zimbabwe, on 23 December 1975.

• London, England, experiences an average of 4,200 lightning strikes per year.

• Every minute, there are about 6,000 flashes of lightning around the world.

• The longest lightning flashes measure up to 32km (20 miles). They occur in flat areas with very high clouds.

HURRICANE

A hurricane is a violent storm with winds spiralling inwards towards a centre of low pressure, called the eye. Some hurricanes remain over the ocean and last only a few days; others last from three to five weeks and devastate islands and coastal regions with violent winds, torrential rain, and huge waves.

Hurricanes range in size from 300km (200 miles) to 3,000km (2,000 miles) across.

Air spreads out from the top of the storm, forming a huge circle of cloud.

Many hurricanes move westwards at 19–28km/h (12–18mph).

The eye may be 50km (31 miles) across, with light winds and little cloud and rain.

A young storm may cross 2,000km (1,200 miles) of ocean on its way to becoming a hurricane.

Air spirals anticlockwise in the Northern Hemisphere, and clockwise in the Southern Hemisphere.

Deep cumulus clouds.

Winds of more than 117km/h (73mph) whirl around the eye, gusting to 360km/h (220mph).

WEATHER RECORDS

WETTEST DAY ON RECORD occurred when 1,870mm (73.63in) fell at Cilaos, Reunion Island, in March 1952.

WIND SPEED RECORD is 512km/h (318mph), recorded above a tornado in Oklahoma, USA, in 1999.

HIGHEST RECORDED TEMPERATURE is 58°C (136°F), at Azizia, Libya, in 1922. (Temperature readings are always taken in the shade.)

LOWEST RECORDED TEMPERATURE is -89°C (-128°F), at Vostok, Antarctica, in 1983.

CLIMATES

A REGION'S CLIMATE is its characteristic weather over a long period of time. The type of climate is determined by how near a region is to the Equator, and its distance from the sea.

DRY GRASSLAND
Vast expanses of dry grassland occur in the middle of some continents, where temperatures are extreme and there is not enough rainfall for forests to grow. These areas have very hot summers and very cold winters.

DESERT
Deserts are the hottest and driest climates in the world, receiving less than 250mm (10in) of rain per year. They are often found in areas of continents that are far from the sea, or in rain-shadow areas (see p.62). Only a few specially adapted plants can survive in the harsh desert climate.

TROPICAL GRASSLANDS
Tropical grasslands, such as the African savannah, occur between the equatorial forests and the hot, dry deserts. The climate is always hot, but the year is divided into a dry and a wet season. Vegetation consists of grasses that grow up to 2m (6ft) tall during the wet season, and low trees and bushes.

CLIMATIC ZONES
The world's climates run in broad zones each side of the Equator. There are many ways to classify climate: most use a combination of temperature and rainfall. A region's climate, together with the physical landscape, determines its characteristic vegetation.

KEY
- Polar and tundra
- Mountain regions
- Taiga
- Temperate forest
- Mediterranean
- Dry grassland
- Desert
- Tropical grassland
- Tropical rainforest

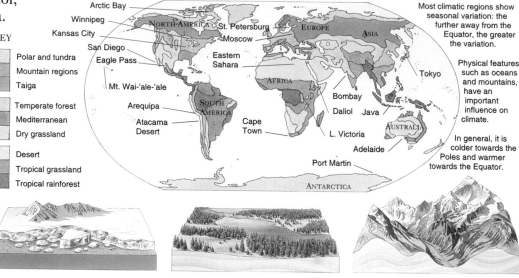

Arctic Bay
Winnipeg
Kansas City
San Diego
Eagle Pass
Mt. Wai-'ale-'ale
Arequipa
Atacama Desert
NORTH AMERICA
St. Petersburg
Moscow
EUROPE
ASIA
Eastern Sahara
AFRICA
SOUTH AMERICA
Cape Town
Bombay
Daliol
Java
L. Victoria
Tokyo
AUSTRALIA
Adelaide
Port Martin
ANTARCTICA

CLIMATE MAP
This map shows the major climatic zones of the world. Also marked are places featured on the page opposite: those holding climate records; cities featured in the city climate graphs; and the locations of some of the places listed in the temperature variations table.

Most climatic regions show seasonal variation: the further away from the Equator, the greater the variation.

Physical features, such as oceans and mountains, have an important influence on climate.

In general, it is colder towards the Poles and warmer towards the Equator.

POLAR AND TUNDRA REGIONS
In Polar regions all fresh water is frozen solid, so land plants cannot grow. The sea's surface is frozen, but underneath is a rich diversity of life. The land bordering the ice caps is the tundra. The temperature in this treeless land rises above freezing only for a few months each year.

TAIGA
Taiga is a Russian word meaning "cold forest". The taiga is a huge area of coniferous forest that lies south of the tundra, stretching across northern Canada, Scandinavia, and the Russian Federation. Four to six months of the year are dark, with the temperature falling well below 0°C (32°F).

MOUNTAIN REGIONS
On mountain ranges, temperature decreases with altitude. Although mountain climates vary according to how close a region is to the Equator, most have distinct vegetation zones that change with altitude. At the highest points, temperatures are often too low for vegetation to survive.

MEDITERRANEAN
The type of climate around the Mediterranean Sea is found in several other parts of the world, including California, USA. Summers are hot and dry, and winters are cool and wet. Plants in these regions, such as olive trees, have adapted to the dry summer conditions.

TEMPERATE FOREST
Temperate climates are rarely very hot or very cold: the average temperature is usually 10°C (50°F) or more for four months of the year, and below 5°C (41°F) for at least one month. In temperate regions, many types of plant, e.g. deciduous trees (see p.78), are dormant during winter.

TROPICAL RAINFOREST
In equatorial regions the climate is hot and wet all year round. The temperature remains at about 27–28°C (80–82°F), and it rains almost every day. This climate results in the most abundant plant and animal growth in the world: equatorial forests contain 50% of all plant and animal species.

PINK PEAKS
Winds sometimes pick up dust and sand that may eventually fall as coloured rain or snow. Pink snow has fallen on the European Alps, caused by seasonal winds from the Sahara desert picking up red sand.

CLIMATE PROPORTIONS
This table shows the percentage of the Earth that has each basic climate type.

Climate	Continent %	Ocean %	Total Earth %
Polar	17	19.5	18.8
Taiga	21.3	1.7	7.3
Moist temperate	15.5	31.9	27.2
Moist tropical	19.9	42.7	36.1
Dry	26.3	4.2	10.6

MICROCLIMATES
Microclimates are small areas that have their own climate. They include cities, where the air temperature may be 6°C (11°F) higher than the surrounding area. On this special satellite photograph of Paris, the hottest areas are blue, and the coolest areas are green.

CLIMATE FACTS
- In parts of the Atacama Desert, Chile, it has not rained for 400 years.

- In India, during the summer monsoon (see opposite page), up to 75% of annual rainfall may fall in just three months.

- In the tropics, the difference between the highest annual noon temperature and the lowest, may be only 2°C (3.6°F).

SEASONS

Seasons occur because different regions of the Earth are tilted towards the Sun at various times during the year.

In the tropics there are often just two seasons a year: wet, and dry.

SUN'S RAYS

Equatorial regions always receive the Sun's full heat.

Summer in the Southern Hemisphere

Regions between the Poles and the tropics have four seasons. They change slowly from spring to summer to autumn to winter.

In mid-winter, when the Southern Hemisphere is at its furthest from the Sun, the South Pole is in darkness all day.

The Poles have only two seasons: six months of winter and six months of summer.

The hemisphere tilted away from the Sun receives less sunlight. Days are short, bringing winter.

Seasons in the Northern Hemisphere are opposite to those in the Southern Hemisphere.

The hemisphere tilted towards the Sun receives more sunlight and heat, bringing summer.

SUN'S RAYS

Winter in the Southern Hemisphere

TEMPERATURE VARIATIONS

This table illustrates how a region's temperatures depend on its closeness to the Equator. These North American locations are situated at similar longitudes; some are on the map opposite.

Location/ Maximum Temp.	Minimum Temp.
Arctic Bay 11°C (52°F)	-28°C (-50°F)
Churchill 18°C (64°F)	-24°C (-11°F)
Winnipeg 26°C (79°F)	-14°C (7°F)
Minneapolis 28°C (82°F)	-6°C (22°F)
Kansas City 33°C (92°F)	3°C (37°F)
Dallas 35°C (95°F)	13°C (56°F)
Eagle Pass 38°C (100°F)	19°C (66°F)

CLIMATE RECORDS

Most of the climate records listed below are based on annual averages.

MOST THUNDER is experienced in parts of Java, and around Africa's Lake Victoria: thunderstorms occur 200–250 days per year.

DRIEST PLACE is the Atacama Desert, Chile, with an average of only 0.51mm (0.02in) of rain per year.

SUNNIEST PLACE is the Eastern Sahara, which has sunshine for more than 90% of daylight hours.

HOTTEST PLACE is Daliol, Ethiopia, where the average temperature over a six-year period was 34.4°C (94°F).

COLDEST PLACE is Polus Nedostupnost, Antarctica, which has an annual average temperature of -57.8°C (-72°F).

WINDIEST PLACE is Port Martin, Antarctica, which had a mean wind speed of 105km/h (65mph) over a one-month period.

MOST RAINY DAYS are experienced by Mount Wai-'ale-'ale (altitude 1,569m/ 5,148ft) on the Hawaiian island of Kauai, which has up to 350 days of rain per year.

MONSOONS

Monsoons are seasonal winds that affect large areas of the tropics and sub-tropics. In southern Asia, monsoons blow from southwest in summer, and northeast in winter.

Areas of the world that experience monsoons are marked in pink.

Himalayas
Rain cloud
Warm sea
Moist, southwest monsoon brings rain.
Indian Ocean

Dry northeast monsoon
Cool sea

Southwest monsoon
In early summer, the hot dry lands of Asia draw in warm, moisture-laden air from the Indian Ocean.

Northeast monsoon
In winter, cold dry air spreads out from central Asia, bringing chilly weather.

CLIMATE CHANGE

Factors that influence the world's climate include the atmosphere, volcanic eruptions, the oceans, the polar ice caps, and the biosphere (see p.64). The 1997/98 El Niño, a warm water current off the coast of South America, caused random and unpredictable changes in the world's weather.

Large volcanic eruptions throw dust and sulphur dioxide gas high into the atmosphere, where it forms a fine haze, blocking some of the Sun's heat.

Human activities such as deforestation, large-scale changes in land use, and the release of various chemicals into the air, can affect the world's climate.

CLIMATE FACTS

- At the Equator, the temperature is about 25–30°C (77–86°F) every day.

- The average temperature close to the South Pole is -50°C (-122°F). This is much colder than a deep freeze, which is about -18°C (0°F).

- Tundra regions are sometimes described as cold deserts, because their climate is so dry.

SOGGIEST SPOT

Hawaii's Mt. Wai-'ale-'ale receives an average of about 11,700mm (460.6in) of rain a year, making it the rainiest place in the world. If it did not drain away, this volume of rain would almost submerge a two-storey house.

CITY CLIMATES

These graphs show the average temperature and rainfall for various cities around the world. Locations are marked on the map on p.60.

Rainfall (mm)

Cape Town, S. Africa
J F M A M J J A S O N D

Adelaide, Australia
J F M A M J J A S O N D

Moscow, Russia
J F M A M J J A S O N D

Tokyo, Japan
J F M A M J J A S O N D

San Diego, USA
J F M A M J J A S O N D

Bombay, India
Temp. (°C)
J F M A M J J A S O N D

Arequipa, Peru
Temp. (°C)
J F M A M J J A S O N D

DESERTS

DESERTS ARE areas of land that receive less than 250mm (10in) of rain per year. They are barren regions of rugged hills, cliff-like canyons, and pebble or dune-covered plains. Low rainfall and high temperatures make life in the desert hard: only a few plant and animal species can survive.

Existing deserts

Areas at risk of desertification

MAJOR DESERTS

About 12% of land is covered with desert, and another third is thought to be at risk of desertification (see p.66).

Average rainfall in Death Valley, USA, is 38mm (1.5in) per year.

NORTH AMERICA   EUROPE   ASIA
Great Basin   Kara Kum
Chihuahuan   Gobi
AFRICA
Sonoran   Sahara
SOUTH AMERICA   Arabian
Atacama   Great Sandy
                                 AUSTRALIA
Namib   Great Victoria
Patagonian

Hot deserts, such as the Namib, have hot days and cold nights.

ANTARCTICA

Cold deserts, such as the Gobi, have hot summers and very cold winters.

Desert covers nearly 80% of Australia.

DESERT FEATURES

Weathering caused by fierce winds, huge temperature variations between day and night, and occasional fast-flowing water, forms distinctive desert features.

Mesas are steep-sided, table-like hills that form where layers of resistant rock protect softer rock beneath.

Deep canyons are usually fed by rain that falls outside the desert area.

Desert water courses, called wadis, are steep-sided with a flat floor. They are usually dry.

Buttes are isolated, flat-topped hills. They are similar to mesas, but smaller.

Mushroom-shaped pedestal rocks form where stones, blown by the wind, cut into the rock close to the ground.

Zeugen are parallel, flat-topped ridges with caps of hard, resistant rock perched on softer rock below.

Alluvial fans form where water flowing down wadis meets the desert plain and dumps its sediment.

Dry salt lake (playa)

Most oases form at deflation hollows where the water table (see p.56) is near the surface.

A shallow depression, called a deflation hollow, has been scooped out by the wind.

Hamada (rock pavement)

Barkhans

Seif dunes

Hard sandstone

Transverse dunes

SAND DUNES

Dunes develop in flat areas. They range from a few metres to 200m (660ft) high, and can be 900m (3,000ft) wide. There are several types of sand dune, including the four shown below.

BARKHANS
These crescent-shaped dunes with two horns may grow up to 30m (100ft) high. Barkhans are always moving.

Wind direction

Crescent-shaped dune

SEIFS
Seifs are long ridges of sand that occur where there is little sand and a powerful wind. They grow up to 215m (700ft) high.

Wind direction

Parallel dunes

TRANSVERSE DUNES
These long ridges of sand are separated by deep troughs. Transverse dunes form at right angles to the wind direction.

Wind direction

Dune at right angle to wind

STAR DUNES
These dunes form where several ridges of sand meet, and the wind comes from different directions.

Point where ridges meet

Wind direction

TYPES OF DESERT

CONTINENTAL DESERTS
Continental deserts, such as the Sahara (right), form because they are too far from the sea for winds to bring them much rain. Winds travel over thousands of kilometres of land before they reach these deserts, losing moisture as they do so.

RAIN-SHADOW DESERTS
Rain-shadow deserts, such as the Atacama desert in Chile (right), form next to mountain ranges. As winds rise up over the mountains, the moisture they carry falls as rain, so the winds are dry as they flow down the other side.

DEAD HOT
If a person spent a day in the Sahara with no shade, food, water, or clothes, their temperature would be about 46°C (115°F) by sunset, and they would have lost 2–3.5 litres (4–6 pints) of water. By nightfall they would be dead.

MIRAGES
Mirages are often seen in hot deserts. They occur when a layer of warm air next to the ground is trapped by cooler air above. Light bends towards the horizontal line of vision, and eventually travels upwards: the mirage is an upside-down "virtual" image.

Light rays travel straight through cool air.

Cool air

Observer

Warm air

Virtual image seen by observer

Light rays travelling through cool and warm air are bent.

LARGEST DESERTS

Desert	Area	
	sq km	sq miles
Sahara	8,600,000	3,320,000
Arabian	2,330,000	900,000
Gobi	1,200,000	463,000
Patagonian	673,000	260,000
Great Victoria	647,000	250,000
Great Basin	492,000	190,000
Chihuahuan	450,000	174,000
Great Sandy	407,000	157,000
Kara Kum	350,000	135,000
Sonoran	310,000	120,000

FORESTS

A THIRD OF THE Earth's land surface is covered by forest: areas of land with dense tree cover. Forests range from the vast, cold taiga of the Northern Hemisphere, to the steamy tropical rainforest of the Amazon Basin, which contains half of all known plant and animal species.

Emergent layer
The crowns of giant, scattered, emergent trees spread out above the canopy to form this layer.

Canopy layer
The canopy layer forms the dense forest roof about 30–40m (100–130ft) above the ground.

Most rainforest animals live in the canopy, where there is plenty of light, warmth, rainfall, and food.

Rainforest trees have long, slim trunks.

Understorey
The understorey layer of the rainforest consists of plants that thrive in shady places, such as palm trees, and young trees growing towards the canopy.

On the forest floor, dead organisms and leaf litter are quickly broken down in the warm, humid climate.

In the understorey, lianas and other climbing plants twine around the trees.

Forest floor
The shady rainforest floor is almost bare apart from a thin blanket of leaves. Many of the plants are fungi or parasites, which do not need light to make food.

CROSS-SECTION OF A FOREST

Forests consist of several layers of vegetation. This illustration shows the layers of a rainforest. Rainforests grow in parts of the world that receive more than 200cm (80in) of rainfall per year. They consist of broadleaved evergreen trees (see p.78), and cover about 6% of the Earth's land surface.

RAINFOREST DIVERSITY

About 750 species of tree grow in a single 10-hectare patch of rainforest in Malaysia. There are only 700 species of tree in the whole of North America.

FOREST FACTS

• An area of rainforest the size of a soccer pitch disappears every second, and more than 50 species of rainforest plants and animals become extinct every day.

• A single tree in Amazonia may be home to 43 species of ant – about the same number found in the whole of the British Isles.

• Forest destruction contributes to the loss of about 50 billion tonnes of topsoil every year.

• During the monsoon (see p.61), deforested areas of Nepal may experience up to 20,000 landslides in a single day.

• One in five of all birds lives in the Amazon rainforest.

RAINFOREST REGENERATION

When large gaps occur in a forest, through natural causes or human activity, it takes at least 100 years to return to its natural state. If the soil is degraded (spoiled), the forest may be replaced by scrubby vegetation only.

DESTRUCTION OF EARTH'S FORESTS

Ten thousand years ago, about half of the world's land surface was covered with trees. Today about 33% of those forests have been destroyed, and about 65% of what remains has been greatly changed. Half of the world's tropical rainforests have been felled this century.

Northwest America has lost much of its forest: 60% of the Canadian part and 90% of the US part has been felled.

90% of Central America's rainforest has gone.

The Amazon rainforest originally covered an area nearly two thirds the size of the USA. An area of the size of Europe has been felled.

Trees originally covered about 95% of western and central Europe. By the late Middle Ages, only 20% of the forest was left.

Since 1950, at least 40% of the Himalayan forest has been cut down.

The Ethiopian highlands have lost 90% of their trees this century

Present-day forest cover

EUROPE
NORTH AMERICA
ASIA
AFRICA
SOUTH AMERICA
AUSTRALIA

RAINFOREST PRODUCTS

Perfumes
Rainforest plants are used in the manufacture of perfumes and incense.

Rubber
Rubber was originally used by South American Indians to make toys. Rubber tapping is now an important forest industry around the world.

*Scarlet macaw
(Ara macao)*

Rattan
Rattan, a woody, climbing rainforest plant, is used to make furniture.

Drugs
One in four types of drug contains chemicals developed from rainforest species.

Insects
A weevil from the Cameroon forests is used to pollinate oil palms in Malaysia: a huge task that was once done by hand.

FOREST RECORDS

LARGEST FOREST
is the taiga (see p.60), which stretches in a wide band across the north of Europe, Asia, and North America.

LARGEST RAINFOREST
is the Amazon rainforest, which covers an area of 7 million sq km (2.7 million sq miles).

Natural, uncut forest

Forest is cut down and burned.

Land can be used for farming for about two years.

Two years after farming stopped, specialist "pioneer" species are established.

After 15 years, small primary (original) forest species appear.

After 60 years, primaries are the dominant species.

More than 100 years later, the forest has returned to its natural state.

EARTH'S BIOSPHERE

THE BIOSPHERE is the area of the Earth's surface and its immediate atmosphere that supports life. It stretches from the depths of the oceans to about 15km (9 miles) up into the atmosphere.

BIOSPHERE UNITS

Ecologists (scientists who study the relationship between living things and their environment) break down the biosphere into progressively smaller units, to make it simpler to study.

Earth
The only planet in the Universe known to support life.

Niche
The position of a plant or animal within an ecosystem (see below), including how it relates to other species.

Habitat
The natural home of a plant or animal. A habitat often contains a number of niches.

Ecosystem
The combination of a plant and animal community and its non-living environment.

Biosphere
Close to the ground, this living part of Earth, includes the atmosphere. It contains many different ecosystems.

OZONE LAYER

The ozone layer encircles the Earth at a height of 15–50km (9–30 miles). Ozone is the only gas in the atmosphere that can screen out ultraviolet rays from the Sun. Without this protective layer, all life on Earth would die.

Most of the ozone layer is contained in the stratosphere.

Sun's harmful ultraviolet rays

Ozone layer screens ultraviolet rays, preventing most of them from reaching Earth.

Stratosphere

Troposphere

Earth

EARTH'S CYCLES

Everything in nature is constantly being recycled. Living things take in water, carbon, nitrogen, and oxygen, and use them to live and grow. When they die, they decompose (break down), and the substances they are made of are recycled back into the biosphere and used again for new life. (See p.58 for the water cycle.)

CARBON CYCLE

All living things are based on the element carbon, which originates from carbon dioxide in the Earth's atmosphere. Green plants and some bacteria take in carbon dioxide and use it to make food. When animals eat plants they take in some of this carbon. Carbon dioxide returns to the atmosphere when animals breathe out, produce waste, and finally die and decompose.

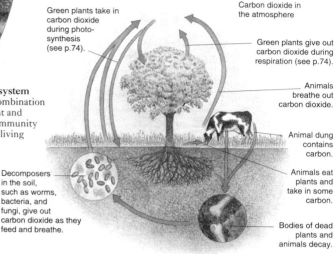

Green plants take in carbon dioxide during photo-synthesis (see p.74).

Carbon dioxide in the atmosphere

Green plants give out carbon dioxide during respiration (see p.74).

Animals breathe out carbon dioxide.

Animal dung contains carbon.

Animals eat plants and take in some carbon.

Bodies of dead plants and animals decay.

Decomposers in the soil, such as worms, bacteria, and fungi, give out carbon dioxide as they feed and breathe.

OXYGEN CYCLE

Living things take in oxygen from the air and use it to obtain energy from the food they eat. Plants and animals take in oxygen during respiration, and green plants release oxygen back into the atmosphere during photosynthesis.

Oxygen in the atmosphere

At night, plants take in oxygen and give out carbon dioxide.

In the daytime, plants take in carbon dioxide and give out oxygen during photosynthesis.

Animals breathe in oxygen and breathe out carbon dioxide.

Night

Day

NITROGEN CYCLE

All living things need nitrogen, but most cannot use nitrogen in the atmosphere directly: it has to be fixed (combined with other elements) by bacteria, algae, and some lichens, to form nitrates. Plants can take in nitrates, and animals obtain nitrogen by eating plants.

Nitrogen in the atmosphere

Decaying animal waste and dead organisms release nitrogen compounds into the soil.

Bacteria in roots and soil convert nitrogen compounds to nitrates.

Animals eat plants containing nitrates.

Other types of bacteria take in nitrates and release nitrogen back into the atmosphere.

BODIES OF WATER

Water circulates through the biosphere in a continuous cycle, in oceans, rivers, clouds, and as rain and snow. Living things also form part of this water cycle: the composition of almost all plants and animals, including humans, is nearly 75% water.

GAIA THEORY

The Gaia theory was developed in 1979 by British scientist James Lovelock (born 1919) (below), and American biologist Lynn Margulis (born 1938). The basis of the theory is that the Earth acts as a single living, self-sustaining organism that can regulate and organize itself. The hypothesis was named after Gaia, the Greek goddess of the Earth.

BIOSPHERE FACTS

• Ozone is spread so finely that, collected together, it would form a ring round the Earth no thicker than the sole of a shoe.

• Without life, the composition of the Earth's atmosphere would probably be very similar to that of the planet Mars.

• Humans are the first and only species to produce things that cannot be reabsorbed into the Earth's natural systems (non-biodegradable products). Most plastics are non-biodegradable.

• If life disappeared from Earth, nitrogen would move from the atmosphere to the oceans.

EARTH IN DANGER

THE ACTIVITIES OF the rapidly expanding human population create environmental problems that can upset the balance of the biosphere. Pollution and the destruction of the rainforests, for example, seriously threaten the future of life on Earth.

GLOBAL WARMING

Greenhouse effect
Carbon dioxide and certain other gases in the atmosphere act like glass in a greenhouse. They let the Sun's rays through, but trap some of the heat which would otherwise be reflected back into space. This greenhouse effect has always existed.

Sun's heat

Balanced conditions

Atmosphere

Trapped heat is reflected back to Earth.

Excess heat escapes into space.

Sun's heat

Out of balance

Extra heat reflected

Less heat escapes

Raising the temperature
Burning fossil fuels (see p.272) increases the amount of carbon dioxide in the atmosphere, which traps extra heat. If we continue to release heat-trapping gases, the Earth's temperature will rise, creating many problems.

OZONE HOLES

Holes in the ozone layer occur all over the world, with particularly large ones over the poles. The main cause is the release of chemicals that destroy the ozone layer, such as chlorofluorocarbons (CFCs), into the atmosphere. The thinning of the ozone layer means that more of the Sun's ultraviolet rays can reach Earth, leading to an increase in skin cancers, and damage to crops.

Chemicals released by factories pollute the air, rivers, lakes, and oceans.

More than a million tonnes of oil a year are deliberately discharged from tankers.

URBAN AIR POLLUTION

In many large cities, air pollution caused by vehicles and industry has become a serious problem. It causes human health problems such as eye irritation, coughs, and asthma, and damages plants and buildings.

12% of marine pollution is caused by shipping.

MARINE POLLUTION

The sea has always been a dumping ground for human wastes, but in the last century the amount of pollutants being discharged into the oceans has increased dramatically. This pollution causes problems such as toxic algae, health risks to bathers, and danger to aquatic life.

ACID RAIN

Acid rain is caused mainly by sulphur and nitrogen given off by power stations, industry, and vehicle engines. When these pollutants combine with water vapour, sunlight, and oxygen in the atmosphere, they create weak sulphuric and nitric acids. This mixture falls as rain, increasing the acidity of lakes and rivers. These unfavourable conditions often cause a decline in the numbers of animals and plants.

UPSETTING THE BALANCE

The use of chemicals, such as those in pesticides and fertilizers, can interfere with Earth's natural cycles. For example, the large amount of nitrogen used in farming can lead to pollution of the water supply.

DEFORESTATION

Forests are being felled for timber, and to create land for agriculture. This reduces biodiversity (range and number of species), leads to soil erosion, upsets cycles, and contributes to global warming.

Toxic algae
One of the most serious effects of marine pollution is toxic (poisonous) algae. Chemicals from sewage discharges, fertilizers, and industrial wastes nourish algae, causing a huge increase in their numbers and, consequently, the amount of poison entering the food chain (see p.108).

Toxic algae

Litter is unsightly and unhygienic, and can harm animals that eat it.

POLLUTION FACTS

- Most scientists believe that global warming will cause the average world temperature to rise by 1°C (1.8°F) by the year 2030, and by 4°C (7.2°F) by the end of the 21st century.
- In January 1989, Mexico City's smog (urban pollution) was so bad that schoolchildren were given the whole month off.
- About 50 outbreaks of toxic algae occur in Japanese waters every year.
- 2,200 Swedish lakes are nearly lifeless because of acid rain, and 80% of Norway's lakes are biologically dead or threatened.

POLLUTED CITIES

The table below shows the average number of days a year that the suspended particulate matter (soot and smoke) of some of the world's most polluted cities is above the World Health Organization's recommended standard.

City	Number of days above standard
New Delhi, India	294
Beijing, China	272
Tehran, Iran	174
Bangkok, Thailand	97
Madrid, Spain	60

WASTING EARTH'S RESOURCES

The world's industrialized nations use a far greater proportion of the Earth's resources than the developing nations, even though their combined population is small. The richest 20% of the world's population consumes 70% of the world's energy, 75% of its metals, 85% of its wood, and 60% of its food. Many resources are unnecessarily wasted: much of what people consume ends up on rubbish tips.

A FOREST A WEEK

It takes an entire forest – more than half a million trees – to supply Americans with their Sunday newspapers every week.

POPULATION GROWTH

Population growth creates huge pressure on the Earth's resources. This graph shows population growth over the last 1,000 years.

World

CIS

Asia

Europe

Africa

Oceania

North America

South America

About 250,000 babies are born every day.

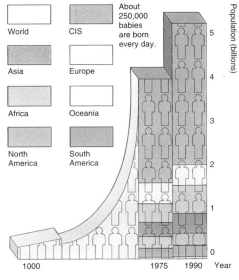

Population (billions)

1000   1975   1990   Year

SAVING THE EARTH

PEOPLE ARE beginning to accept responsibility for Earth's future. The main environmental problems have been recognized, and ways of reducing their impact are being explored. Positive steps towards the long-term survival of our planet are shown here, but there is still much work to be done.

LIMITING POPULATION GROWTH

Slowing down population growth is one of the most important factors in saving the Earth's diminishing resources. Ways include family planning, and improving standards of living. (In many countries, a large family is seen as a secure source of income.) Family planning measures introduced in Kerala, India, led to a 66% decline in the birth rate between 1983 and 1993.

PROMOTING ECOTOURISM

Tourism that benefits the environment is known as ecotourism. For example, money earned from tourism can be spent on the creation and management of national parks. A report by the US Forest Service showed that the potential earnings from forest recreational activities such as camping and canoeing are twice what could be made by selling the timber.

WAYS TO HELP THE ENVIRONMENT

- Use recycled paper and card.
- Recycle bottles, glass, cans, and waste paper.
- Avoid buying tropical hardwoods, such as mahogany.

REDUCING URBAN POLLUTION

Sharing cars, using public transport, cycling, and walking, all reduce vehicle use in urban areas. Catalytic converters can help to reduce pollution from cars. Working from home using technology such as computers ("telecommuting"), instead of travelling to an office, also reduces the number of vehicles on the roads.

Public transport   Cycling and walking   Public transport
Car sharing

HALTING DESERTIFICATION

Farming methods such as terracing (right) can reduce desertification and the loss of topsoil. In China, a "great green wall" of trees (the San Bei Forest Belt) has been planted to hold back the advancing desert. Somalia has begun a major anti-desertification programme that includes a ban on cutting trees for fuel.

Trees planted to hold back the desert

CONSERVING HABITATS AND SPECIES

Projects have been set up worldwide to conserve habitats and the species they contain. These include the establishment of national parks and other conservation areas – more than 5% of the world's total land area is now protected. The Convention on International Trade in Endangered Species (CITES) is an international treaty that has been signed by 122 countries. It aims to prevent trade in endangered plant and animal species, and in products such as animal skins and ivory.

The tiger is endangered.

REDUCING POLLUTION

Many countries are reducing sulphur dioxide emissions to prevent acid rain and global warming. The EC has ruled that large fossil-fuel power plants must cut emissions of sulphur dioxide by 60% by 2003. Ways of improving toxic waste treatment and disposal are also being explored. International treaties have been developed to regulate the dumping of waste at sea, and to control the discharge of other pollutants into the oceans.

- Walk, cycle, or use public transport instead of going by car whenever possible.
- Switch off lights and other appliances when not in use.
- When getting rid of an old refrigerator, make sure that its CFCs are safely removed.

USING RENEWABLE ENERGY

Fossil fuels (see p.272) will eventually run out. In the meantime, their use creates pollution and contributes to global warming. Cleaner, renewable methods of generating energy are being developed, including wind, wave, solar, and tidal power. Some countries, including Norway and Brazil, already obtain more than half their energy from renewable sources.

Hydro-electric power (right) is a clean, renewable energy source.

Wind turbines

Solar collectors trap sunlight to generate power.

REDUCING FIREWOOD USE

Tree cover is being lost where large amounts of wood are chopped for fire. Alternative, more efficient cooking methods are being introduced in some countries affected by this deforestation. In Kenya, where wood energy accounts for more than 75% of energy consumption, 180,000 jikos (charcoal-burning stoves) have been distributed (right).

SAVING THE RAINFORESTS

Many initiatives have been introduced to try to save the remaining areas of rainforest. Debt-swap deals, in which a country protects an area of forest in return for a reduction in their foreign debt, have been negotiated. Practices that do not damage the forest, such as rubber tapping, are being encouraged, together with trade in forest products such as spices, rattan, nuts, and medicinal plants. These products may be worth as much as timber.

Brazil nuts

Rubber tapping

- Start a compost heap for vegetable peelings and garden waste, such as leaves and grass cuttings.
- When ordinary lightbulbs are spent, replace them with energy-efficient, compact fluorescent lightbulbs.

PROTECTED AREAS OF THE WORLD

This table shows the percentage of land area worldwide (except Antarctica) that is protected in national parks or other conservation areas. It also shows the country with the most protected land.

Area	% land protected	Country with most protected land (%)
North & Central America	10.4	Panama 17.2
Europe	7.5	Austria 19
South America	5.7	Ecuador 37.7
Oceania	5.7	New Zealand 10.5
Africa	3.9	Botswana 17.2
Asia	2.1	Bhutan 19.7

LIVING WORLD

In this fascinating survey of the natural world, all living things are classified, and every major plant and animal group is illustrated. Stunning cut-away artworks show anatomical details, and there is a wealth of factual information about attack and defence, movement, and reproduction. Tables list record breakers from the heaviest to the most deadly.

Evolution • Fossils • Dinosaurs • Classifying Living Things
Plants • Flowers • Leaves • Trees • Food Plants • Fungi and Lichens
Micro-organisms • Animals • Invertebrates • Molluscs • Insects
Arachnids • Crustaceans • Amphibians • Reptiles • Fish
Birds • Domestic Birds • Mammals • Domestic Mammals
Animal Senses and Behaviour • Migration and Homes
Food Chains and Webs • Endangered Species
Animal Records and Comparisons

EVOLUTION

LIFE ON EARTH probably originated from chemicals dissolved in the oceans. From these simple beginnings, life has gradually developed into many different forms. All living things change as one generation succeeds another. This process is called evolution.

EVOLUTION TERMS

Variation Almost all living things vary in size, shape, colour, and strength: no two animals or plants are the same.

Adaptations These are certain features, such as colour, that may give one animal or plant a better chance of survival than another.

Inheritance Characteristics are passed on, or inherited, when living things reproduce. Most living things have a unique combination of characteristics.

Natural selection Through natural selection, inherited characteristics that help a living thing survive are passed on; those that do not gradually die out.

Competition/survival of the fittest More individuals are born than can survive. Strong, well-adapted individuals are more likely to survive than weak, poorly adapted individuals.

EVOLUTION OF THE ELEPHANT

Fossils reveal that several elephant-like species have existed and become extinct over the last 40 million years. It is likely that they were related, and that today's elephants evolved from them.

Trilophodon lived from 26 to 3 million years ago.

Platybelodon lived from 12 to 7 million years ago.

Woolly mammoth lived about 2 million years ago.

African elephant

Moenitherium lived about 38 million years ago.

ADAPTATION EXAMPLE

The 28 species of honeycreeper in the Hawaiian islands probably all evolved from one species. Each has a beak adapted for a particular way of feeding. Some are now extinct.

The iiwi's beak and tongue are adapted for sipping nectar.

The Kona grosbeak (now extinct) had a strong bill for crushing seeds.

The Kauai akialoa uses its long beak to probe for insects.

EVOLUTION FACTS

• Ninety-five per cent of all animals and plants that have ever existed on Earth have become extinct.

• Between 35 and 20 million years ago, giant rhinoceroses, such as *Paraceatherium*, roamed the Americas. This animal measured up to 8m (26ft) long and was as tall as a giraffe.

• Moas – the giant, flightless birds of New Zealand (now extinct) – show what could have happened in a world without mammals: birds would have become dominant. (New Zealand has no native mammals except for a few bats.)

• The earliest horse, *Hyracotherium*, was about the size of a modern fox terrier.

CHARLES DARWIN (1809–82)

The theory of evolution was developed by English naturalist Charles Darwin, and published in 1859 in his book *The Origin of Species*. Darwin developed his theory after studying the animals of the Galapagos Islands, which were unique, but similar to those on the South American mainland.

• Australia's largest ever marsupial (see p.102) was *Diprotodon optatum*, which was as big as a rhinoceros and weighed up to 1,500kg (3,307lb).

SLOTH GROWTH

During the Tertiary Period, South America was cut off from other landmasses, and there were few predators. Several types of mammal became gigantic, for example *Megatherium*, the giant ground sloth, grew to more than 6m (20ft) long.

PRECAMBRIAN	PALEOZOIC						MESOZO
	Cambrian	Ordovician	Silurian	Devonian	Carboniferous	Permian	Triassic

4,600–590mya (million years ago) Earth forms and gradually cools; atmosphere has no oxygen. First bacteria appear. Blue-green algae evolve and produce oxygen-rich atmosphere. Protists (single-celled organisms) develop. Non-flowering marine plants evolve and become abundant. First animals, including worms and jellyfish, appear.

590–505mya Invertebrates (see p.84) become widespread in the oceans. Trilobites are common. First molluscs (see pp.86–87) evolve.

505–438mya First crustaceans evolve. First, fish-like vertebrates (see p.84) appear: they have no fins or jaws.

438–408mya First fish with jaws evolve. Coral reefs flourish in the oceans. Huge sea scorpions hunt. On land, the first small plants appear.

408–360mya "Age of Fish." Fish dominate life in the seas. First insects evolve. First amphibians appear on land.

360–286mya "The Coal Age." Warm, damp climate; huge forests lay down remains that will turn into coal. First reptiles evolve from amphibians. Insects abundant.

286–248mya Earth cooler. Amphibians decline; reptiles diversify. Ferns and conifers widespread. Many species vanish in greatest mass extinction known.

248–213 Climate to warm conifers ferns for forests. First din evolve. man

FOSSILS

FOSSILS PROVIDE a history book of life on Earth. They are the remains of dead animals and plants that have been preserved naturally for thousands or millions of years. The study of fossils is called palaeontology.

FORMS OF FOSSILIZATION
Fossils are preserved in several different ways. Most are found in rocks, but fossils also occur in ice, tar, peat, and amber.

MINERALIZATION
This is the most common form of preservation. It occurs when the organic matter of a fossil is replaced by durable (long-lasting) minerals. Petrified wood is formed by mineralization.

Petrified wood

FREEZING
Low temperatures can preserve animal and plant remains. Well-preserved mammoths have been found in Siberian permafrost (permanently frozen ground). Flesh and skin, as well as bones, are preserved by freezing.

Fossilized mammoth

AMBER
Tree resin (sap) can trap and surround small animals such as insects and spiders. The resin, with the animal still intact inside, is fossilized, turning into amber.

Spider in amber

PEAT AND TAR
Animals and plants can be preserved in peat and tar. Human bodies more than 2,000 years old have been found in peat bogs, and animal remains up to 20,000 years old have been found in tar.

Human preserved in peat

TYPES OF FOSSIL
Any organism can be mineralized, provided it is buried by mud or sand before it rots away. Most fossils form on the sea bed, so the most common are those of sea creatures. Fossils of land animals and plants are much rarer.

Ammonites
Ammonites were marine (sea-dwelling) molluscs that became extinct about 65 million years ago. Their shells were often fossilized.

Archaeopteryx
Prehistoric flying animal believed to be the evolutionary link between reptiles and birds. Seven fossilized *Archaeopteryx* have been found.

Trilobites
Marine arthropods (see p.85) distantly related to the wood louse. They died out about 286 million years ago.

Soft-bodied animals
Most fossils are the remains of bones or shells. Fossils of soft-bodied animals, such as this dragonfly, are rare.

Coprolites
These are fossilized animal droppings. Dinosaur coprolites can measure more than 60cm (2ft) long.

Plant fossils
This fossilized poplar leaf is about 25 million years old. Modern poplar leaves are almost identical: these trees have hardly changed.

FOSSIL FACTS
• Fossils are found only in sedimentary rocks (see p.46). Marine limestones, shales, and some sandstones, contain the most fossils.

• Some ammonites measured up to 2m (6.6ft) in diameter.

FORMATION OF FOSSILS
This sequence shows how the remains of sea creatures may be fossilized and brought to the land surface.

MAMMOTH MISTAKE
For centuries, fossils were associated with myths and legends. Fossilized mammoth tusks discovered in about 1600 were believed at the time to be the horns of unicorns.

FOSSIL RECORDS
EARLIEST FOSSILS are prokaryotes (cells without nuclei) found in Western Australia, which are an estimated 3.5 billion years old.

LARGEST FOSSIL is a *Brachiosaurus* skeleton (see p.71), which is 22m (72ft) long.

1 Dead animals, such as fish, sink to the sea bed. Their remains are slowly buried by layers of sediment.

2 The lower layers of sediment turn to rock, and the animal remains are mineralized, becoming fossils.

3 Over many years the rock is folded, and the upper layers are eroded away.

4 The rock is eroded further, and the fossils are eventually exposed on the surface.

CENOZOIC								
Cretaceous	Tertiary						Quaternary	
	Palaeocene	Eocene	Oligocene	Miocene	Pliocene	Pleistocene	Holocene

...4mya	144–65mya	65–55mya	55–38mya	38–25mya	25–5mya	5–2mya	2m–10,000 years ago	10,000 years ago – today
...e much than ...Dinosaurs ...te life on ...rst bird, ...pteryx, from	First flowering plants evolve. Dinosaurs flourish. Period ends with mass extinction: sweeps away many species including all dinosaurs and ammonites.	Climate warm and damp. Flowering plants continue to evolve and, together with insect pollinators, become widespread.	Mammals continue to diversify, becoming larger and more numerous. Primates (apes, monkeys, and lemurs) evolve into many forms.	First human-like primates appear. Many early mammals become extinct. Giant flightless hunting birds flourish.	Climate cools; forests begin to decrease worldwide. Hoofed mammals, such as deer, flourish. Towards the end of the epoch, the first hominids evolve.	Climate cold and dry. Mammals reach peak of their diversity. Many land creatures similar to today's. Bony fish dominate life in the sea.	Time of ice ages. Many mammal species, including mammoths and sabre-toothed tigers, become extinct. *Homo sapiens* evolves.	Humans develop agriculture and technology; population expands.

DINOSAURS

DINOSAURS DOMINATED the Earth for more than 150 million years. They included the largest animals ever to have lived on land, as well as some that were smaller than a pet dog. Dinosaurs died out 65 million years ago. Nobody knows why.

TYPES OF DINOSAUR

There are two orders (see p.72) of dinosaur. They are classified according to the arrangement of their hip-bones.

Lizard-hipped dinosaurs
(Saurischians)
Hips similar to lizards. Includes both herbivorous (plant-eating) and carnivorous (meat-eating) species.

Bird-hipped dinosaurs
(Ornithischians)
Hips similar to birds. All of the bird-hipped dinosaur species were herbivorous.

DINOSAUR FACTS

• Dinosaur fossils discovered to date probably represent less than 0.0001% of the individuals that once lived.

• The name *Tyrannosaurus* means "tyrant lizard".

• The most intelligent dinosaurs were probably about as intelligent as chickens.

• More than 350 species of dinosaur have so far been identified: probably only a tiny percentage of those that existed.

• *Struthiomimus* could sprint at speeds of up to 80km/h (50mph): as fast as an ostrich.

PORTRAIT OF A DINOSAUR

Like reptiles, dinosaurs had a scaly skin. Dinosaurs, however, were more advanced than today's reptiles. They walked with their limbs directly under their body like mammals and birds, whereas reptiles crawl, or walk with their limbs out to their sides.

Dinosaurs' brains were small for their body size.

Gallimimus

Backbone
Rib
Ovary
Kidney
Trachea
Lung
Heart
Claw
Liver
Intestine
Tibia
Fibula
Tendon

Caudal vertebra

Tough, scaly skin

Cloaca (body opening)

Dinosaurs used their tail for balance.

Gallimimus was a lizard-hipped dinosaur.

Legs extended directly below the body, lifting the dinosaur off the ground.

Bipedal (two-footed) dinosaurs could walk upright.

DINOSAUR-LIKE REPTILES

While dinosaurs roamed the land, huge reptiles flew in the air and swam in the oceans. These marine and flying reptiles were closely related to the dinosaurs.

Rhamphorhynchus

Pterodactylus

Ichthyosaurus

Elasmosaurus

FLYING REPTILES

Ancient flying reptiles, called pterosaurs, reached huge sizes. Their wings were made of skin, and their body was usually furry. They had light, delicate bones for flying.

MARINE REPTILES

These were some of the fiercest and largest animals in the sea. They breathed air, so had to come to the surface regularly to fill their lungs. These reptiles hunted fish and other sea creatures.

MAJOR DINOSAUR GROUPS

Within the two orders, dinosaurs are divided into five sub-groups. There are three sub-groups of ornithischians, and two sub-groups of saurischians.

Thyreophorans
(Ornithischians) Armoured herbivores; rows of protective studs, plates, or spikes down the back, e.g. *Stegosaurus*.

Theropods (Saurischians)
Mostly bipedal carnivores with an S-shaped neck and clawed, four-toed feet, e.g. *Tyrannosaurus*.

Marginocephalians
(Ornithischians)
Herbivores; many with bony frill at back of skull, e.g. *Styracosaurus*.

Ornithopods
(Ornithischians)
Herbivores; horny beak and bird-like feet, e.g. *Corythosaurus*.

Sauropodomorphs
(Saurischians). Herbivores; small head, long neck, bulky body, and long tail, e.g. *Saltasaurus*.

Triassic Period: 248–213mya (million years ago)	Jurassic Period: 213–144mya

Land joined in the super-continent of Pangaea (see p.40). First dinosaurs evolve and, towards the end of the period, split into two groups: lizard- and bird-hipped.

Pangaea breaks apart: Atlantic Ocean begins to form; Africa splits from South America. In late Jurassic times, huge herbivorous dinosaurs dominate life on land.

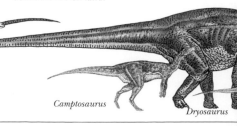

Melanorosaurus

Coelophysis

Plateosaurus

Mosasaurus

Herrerasaurus

Staurikosaurus

Technosaurus

Camptosaurus

Dryosaurus

DINOSAUR DISCOVERY

Pre-19th century: around the world, dinosaur fossils are believed to be various things, including dragon bones in China, and giant human bones in parts of Europe.

1800 Dinosaur footprints found in Massachusetts, USA. Their discoverer claims they were made by the raven from Noah's Ark.

1820 *Iguanodon* teeth discovered in Tilgate Forest, Sussex, England, by doctor and fossil hunter Gideon Mantell (1790–1852) and his wife. He suspects they are the remains of ancient reptiles, but his theory is dismissed as heretical (anti-religious).

1834 First glimpse of what dinosaurs looked like provided by find of a partial skeleton near Maidstone, England, known as the Maidstone *Iguanodon*.

1841 The term dinosaur, from the Greek words for "terrible" and "lizard", is coined by English anatomist Richard Owen (1804–92).

| 1800 | 1800 | 1820 | 1820 | 1830 | 1834 | 1840 | 1841 |

1851 First reconstruction of dinosaurs: *Iguanodon* and *Hylaeosaurus* models are made for the Great Exhibition at Crystal Palace, London, England. Results in huge public enthusiasm for dinosaurs. Before the *Iguanodon* is completed, the sculptor holds a dinner party inside it.

Dinner party in a model dinosaur

1877 One of the greatest dinosaur collections found at Como Bluff, Wyoming, USA, by O.C. Marsh (1831–99) of Yale College.

1947 Largest number of dinosaurs ever found together: more than 100 *Coelophysis* skeletons.

1987 Evidence to support theory of warm-blooded dinosaurs found by palaeontologists Tom Rich and Patricia Vickers-Rich of the Museum of Victoria, Australia. They discover dinosaur fossils in a part of South Australia that would have been inside the Antarctic Circle when these dinosaurs lived. The mean annual temperature in this region would then have been near freezing.

Leaellynasaura lived in polar regions.

| 1850 | 1851 | 1870 | 1877 | 1940 | 1947 | 1980 | 1987 |

DINOSAUR RECORDS

SMALLEST DINOSAUR
was probably *Wannanosaurus*, a bipedal carnivore that measured 60cm (2ft) long. It was about the size of a chicken.

MOST PRIMITIVE KNOWN DINOSAUR
is *Eoraptor*, a 228 million-year-old bipedal carnivore that was about the size of a large dog.

SMALLEST DINOSAUR BRAIN
is believed to have been that of the *Stegosaurus*. It was less than 5cm (2in) long.

LARGEST DINOSAUR EGGS
were probably those of *Hypselosaurus*. They measured about 30cm (12in) long and contained an estimated 3.3 litres (6 pints) of fluid: roughly the same as the fluid in 60 hens' eggs.

WIDER GLIDER

The largest flying animal ever to have existed was *Quetzalcoatlus*, a flying reptile. Its wingspan measured about 12m (39ft) across: wider than the wingspan of a hang glider.

EARTH SHAKER

The name *Seismosaurus* means "earth-shaking lizard". This enormous plant-eating dinosaur was 40m (131ft) in length: longer than an Airbus A320.

LARGEST CARNIVORES

Dinosaur	Estimated length	
	m	ft
Acrocanthosaurus	12	39
Tyrannosaurus	12	39
Aliwalia	11	36
Allosaurus	11	36

LARGEST HERBIVORES

Dinosaur	Estimated length	
	m	ft
Seismosaurus	40	131
Barosaurus	27	89
Diplodocus	27	89
Brachiosaurus	25	82

EXTINCTION THEORIES

About 65 million years ago the dinosaurs, together with many other animal species, became extinct. Other animal groups, including turtles, frogs, birds, and mammals, survived. There are many theories for this mass-extinction: below are two of the most widely accepted.

GRADUAL EXTINCTION
Gradual changes in climate and vegetation caused by continental drift (see p.40) led to the dinosaurs' slow extinction over about 50,000 years. Warm, tropical conditions were replaced by cooler, more seasonal climates, and mammals slowly replaced dinosaurs as the dominant animal group.

CATASTROPHES
The period when dinosaurs were dying out coincided with many volcanic eruptions in India. At the same time, a huge meteorite hit the Earth. Dust thrown into the atmosphere blocked out sunlight, and dinosaurs could not survive the resulting climate changes.

| Cretaceous Period: 144–65mya | 65mya |

Continents split further apart, eventually drifting into their present-day positions. Dinosaurs continue to flourish; those on different continents evolve separately, leading to great diversity.

Dinosaurs become extinct, together with many other animal species.

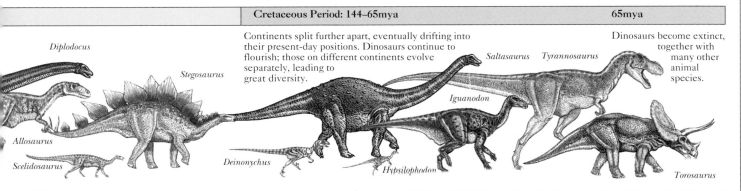

Diplodocus · *Stegosaurus* · *Saltasaurus* · *Tyrannosaurus* · *Iguanodon* · *Allosaurus* · *Scelidosaurus* · *Deinonychus* · *Hypsilophodon* · *Torosaurus*

CLASSIFYING LIVING THINGS

LIVING THINGS ARE classified in groups according to the features they have in common. The largest groups are the five kingdoms: animals, plants, fungi, protists, and monerans. Each kingdom is then subdivided into smaller and smaller groups.

KEY

These colours show the classification groupings used in the chart. All numbers of species are approximate. A division is the plant equivalent of a phylum.

	Kingdom		Class
	Phylum		Order
	Sub-phylum		Division

SCIENTIFIC NAMES

Many living things have different common names around the world. To avoid confusion, every species also has a two-part scientific name which is the same worldwide. The first part of the name gives the genus; the second part the species. This system was devised by Swedish botanist Carolus Linnaeus (1707–78). Larger groups, such as orders, also have a scientific name. Throughout the *Living World* section, scientific names are given wherever possible for species and genera.

CLASSIFYING A TIGER

This illustration shows how a biologist would classify a tiger.

Kingdom Animal (Animalia)
Many-celled organisms with no cell walls; cannot make their own food.

Phylum Chordate (Chordata)
Animals that have a single nerve cord at some time in their life.

Class Mammal (Mammalia)
Animals that suckle their young on milk and have fur or hair.

Order Carnivores (Carnivora)
Land mammals specialized for hunting.

Family Cats (Felidae)
Carnivores with sharp front claws that can be retracted (drawn in).

Genus Big cats (*Panthera*)
The five species of big cats: lion, tiger, leopard, snow leopard, and jaguar.

Species Tiger
(*Panthera tigris*)

Sponges
(Porifera) 9,000 species

Sea anemones, hydras, corals, jellyfish
(Cnidaria) 9,500 species

Comb jellies
(Ctenophora) 90 species

Flatworms, flukes, tapeworms
(Platyhelminthes) 15,000 species

Roundworms
(Nematoda) 20,000 species

Horsehair worms
(Nematomorpha) 250 species

Spiny-headed worms
(Acanthocephala) 1,150 species

Rotifers
(Rotifera) 2,000 species

Waterbears
(Tardigrada) 600 species

Worms and leeches
(Annelida) 18,600 species

Molluscs (Mollusca)

Sea squirts
(Ascidiacea) 2,500 species

Jawless fish
(Agnatha) 75 species

Sharks and rays
(Chondrichthyes) 800 species

Sharks, dogfish
Skates, rays

Bony fish
(Osteichthyes) 20,000 species

More than 20 orders including:
Eels
Herrings, anchovies
Salmon, trout
Carp
Catfish
Perch, marlins, swordfish, tunas
Flying fish

MONERANS (Monera)

Blue-green algae
(Cyanonta) 1,700 species

Bacteria
(Schizonta) 4,000 species

PROTISTS (Protista)

Golden algae
(Chrysophyta) 650 species

Amoebas, flagellates, opalinids
(Sarcomastigophora) 27,000 species

Sporozoans
(Sporozoa) 5,000 species

Ciliates
(Ciliophora) 8,000 species

FUNGI (Fungi)

Rusts and mildews
(Oomycetes) 600 species

Moulds
(Zygomycetes) 765 species

Sac fungi
(Ascomycetes) 29,000 species

Club fungi
(Basidiomycetes) 16,000 species

Fungi imperfecti
(Deuteromycetes) 17,000 species

Slime moulds
(Acrasiomycota) 6 species

PLANTS (Plantae)

Green algae
(Chlorophyta) 14,000 species

Red algae
(Rhodophyta) 5,000 species

Brown algae
(Phaeophyta) 1,500 species

Mosses and liverworts
(Bryophyta) 14,000 species

Ferns
(Pteridophyta) 12,000 species

Clubmosses
(Lycopodophyta) 1,000 species

Horsetails
(Sphenophyta) 40 species

ANIMALS (Animalia)

Velvetworms
(Onychophora)
100 species

Lampshells
(Brachiopoda)
300 species

Moss animals
(Bryozoa) 4,000 species

c.13 other small phyla
c.2,000 species

Chitons
(Polyplacophora) 500 species

Solenogasters
(Aplacophora) 5,540 species

Deep-sea limpets
(Monoplacophora) 10 species

Tusk shells
(Scaphopoda) 350 species

Gastropods
(Gastropoda) 35,000 species

Bivalves
(Bivalvia) 8,000 species

Cephalopods
(Cephalopoda) 600 species

Arthropods
(Arthropoda)

Horseshoe crabs
(Merostomata)
4 species

Millipedes
(Diplopoda)
10,000 species

Sea spiders
(Pycnogonida)
1,000 species

Centipedes
(Chilopoda)
2,500 species

Arachnids
(Arachnida)
73,000 species

Scorpions
Tick spiders
Micro-whip scorpions
Tail-less whip scorpions
Whip scorpions
Camel spiders
Pseudoscorpions
Harvestmen
Mites and ticks
Spiders

Echinoderms
(Echinodermata)
6,000 species in 5 orders including:

Starfish
(Asteroidea)
1,500 species

Brittle stars
(Ophiuroidea)
2,000 species

Sea urchins
(Echinoidea)
950 species

Sea cucumbers
(Holothuroidea)
900 species

Crustaceans
(Crustacea 55,400 species

Sand shrimps
(Cephalocarida)
9 species

Mystacocarideans
(Mystacocarida)
10 species

Branchiopods
(Branchiopoda)
1,000 species

Spiny sand shrimps
(Branchiura)
125 species

Mussel shrimps
(Ostracoda) 10,000 species

Barnacles
(Cirripedia) 1,220 species

Copepods
(Copepoda) 13,000 species

Crabs, lobsters, and shrimps
(Malacostraca) 30,000 species

Insects
(Insecta) 1,000,000 species

Springtails	Webspinners	Grylloblattids	Sucking lice	Ants, bees, wasps	Stylopids
Telson-tails	Dragonflies	Earwigs	Thrips	Dobson and alderflies	Caddisflies
Diplurans	Grasshoppers, crickets	Cockroaches	Booklice	Snakeflies	Butterflies and moths
Silverfish	Stick and leaf insects	Praying mantids	Zorapterans	Lacewings and antlions	Flies
Mayflies		Termites	Bugs	Scorpionflies	Fleas
Stoneflies		Biting lice	Beetles		

Chordates
(Chordata)

Amphibians
(Amphibia)
4,200 species

Frogs and toads
Newts and salamanders
Caecilians

Reptiles
(Reptilia)
6,000 species

Lizards and snakes
Turtles, tortoises, and terrapins
Crocodilians
Tuatara

Birds
(Aves) 9,000 species

Ostrich
Rheas
Cassowaries, emu
Kiwis
Albatrosses, petrels, shearwaters, fulmars
Pelicans, gannets, cormorants, frigatebirds, darters
Penguins
Grebes
Divers or loons
Tinamous
Herons, storks, ibises, flamingos
Ducks, geese, swans
Eagles, hawks, vultures, falcons, kites, buzzards
Pheasant, partridges, grouse, turkeys

Cranes, rails, coots, bustards
Wading birds, gulls, terns, auks
Sandgrouse
Pigeons, doves
Parrots
Cuckoos, roadrunners, turacos
Owls
Nightjars, frogmouths
Swifts, hummingbirds
Trogons
Mousebirds
Kingfishers, bee-eaters, rollers, hoopoes
Woodpeckers, toucans, barbets, honeyguides, puffbirds, jacamars
Passerines

Mammals
(Mammalia) 4,600 species

Monotremes
(egg-laying mammals)
Marsupials (pouched mammals)
Insectivores
Elephant shrews
Flying lemurs
Bats
Tree shrews
Primates
Edentates (anteaters, sloths, armadillos)
Pangolins
Aardvark
Hares, rabbits, pikas
Rodents

Whales and dolphins
Carnivores
Seals, sea lions, walrus
Elephants
Hyraxes
Sea cows
Odd-toed hoofed mammals
Even-toed hoofed mammals

Monocotyledons
80,000 species

Gymnosperms
(Gymnospermae)

Conifers
(Coniferopsida) 500 species

Cycads
(Cycadopsida) 100 species

Joint pines
(Gnetopsida) 70 species

Flowering plants
(Angiospermae)

Dicotyledons
170,000 species

PLANTS

PLANTS, UNLIKE ANIMALS, can manufacture their own food. This makes them the starting point of most food chains, and almost all other living organisms depend on them for food.

PLANT STRUCTURE

A scarlet runner bean (*Phaseolus coccineus*) is a typical flowering plant.

Flowers carry the reproductive parts of the plant.

Stem supports the foliage (leaves) and the flowers.

Leaves get their green colour from chlorophyll.

Fruits protect the plant's seeds. This runner bean's fruit is called a pod.

Beans are seeds. Each one contains all the nourishment it needs to grow into a new plant.

ROOTS
Roots anchor the plant into the ground, and draw up water and minerals from the surrounding soil.

Fine hairs near the growing tip take up water.

Vascular system (see p.77)

Root cap

Roots draw up water.

UNDERGROUND PARTS
Some plants have both roots and special storage organs, such as tubers or bulbs.

Tap root
A tap root has a large, central root and finer side-growing roots.

Carrot

Tuber
A tuber is a swollen stem or root in which the plant stores food.

Potato

TYPES OF PLANT

NON-FLOWERING

Algae
Algae are a large group of plants with no true roots, stems, or leaves.

Seaweeds
Seaweeds are marine algae, and may be red, brown, or green.

Mosses and liverworts
Mosses and liverworts have stems and leaves, but no true roots.

Ferns
Ferns have roots, stems, and fronds, and can grow as tall as trees.

FLOWERING

Grasses
Grasses have jointed stems, narrow leaves, and seedlike fruits.

Shrubs
Shrubs are short, woody plants, with a stem that divides at ground level.

Herbs
Herbs are flowering plants that die back after producing seeds.

Trees
Most trees, such as palms (see p.78), are flowering plants.

LIFE CYCLE

SEXUAL REPRODUCTION
Many plants reproduce by ova being fertilized by pollen, whether from the same flower or plant or a different one. This is sexual reproduction.

Life cycle of a poppy

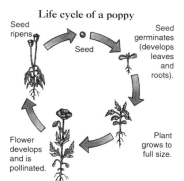

Seed ripens

Seed germinates (develops leaves and roots).

Seed

Plant grows to full size.

Flower develops and is pollinated.

ASEXUAL REPRODUCTION
Many plants can reproduce without pollination or fertilization taking place. This is called asexual reproduction.

New plants grow from tip of runner.

Plant sends out horizontal stems, called runners.

Strawberry plant (Fragaria)

PHOTOSYNTHESIS

In photosynthesis, chlorophyll in the leaves uses energy from the sun to combine carbon dioxide with water. This produces food in the form of carbohydrates (sugars and starches) and oxygen.

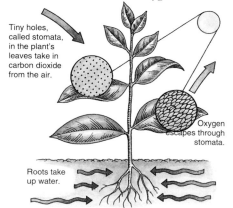

Tiny holes, called stomata, in the plant's leaves take in carbon dioxide from the air.

Oxygen escapes through stomata.

Roots take up water.

CHLOROPHYLL

Chlorophyll, a pigment, gives most leaves their green colour. It absorbs light from the sun, soaking up red and blue light, but reflecting green.

Red and blue light waves absorbed

Green light waves reflected

RESPIRATION

Plants, like humans, breathe constantly, taking up oxygen (O_2) and releasing carbon dioxide (CO_2). This process is called respiration. At twilight, plants produce equal amounts of oxygen and carbon dioxide. This is called the compensation point. Carbon dioxide is released during both day and night.

1 Daytime
Plant releases more oxygen than it uses in respiration.

2 Twilight
Compensation point. Plant produces both gases.

3 Night-time
The plant releases more carbon dioxide than it uses.

PIGMENTATION

Plants are not always green. Chlorophyll is present in most plants, but some also contain other pigments that affect their colour. These pigments may help the plant to photosynthesize in difficult conditions.

Brown seaweed (Phaeopyta)

Red seaweed (Rhodophyta)

PLANT HABITATS

Plants will grow wherever there is enough moisture, light, warmth, and nourishment in the soil. Some plants have developed particular ways of coping with extreme conditions.

Tropical
Most bromeliads (*Bromeliaceae* family) live in tropical rainforests, on tall trees where sunlight can reach their leaves.

Brackish and salt water
Mangroves (*Rhizophora*) have special pores in their roots to take in oxygen from the air.

Desert
Saguaro cactus (*Carnegia gigantea*) lacks leaves, reducing water loss. Its spines protect it from animals.

Aquatic
Water lilies (*Nymphaea*) have a waxy outer layer, so the leaves float; stomata are on the upper surface only.

Sand and shingle
Sand couch grass (*Elymus farctus*) has very long roots that can reach water below ground.

Alpine
Alpine anemone (*Pulsatilla alpina*) has white hairs on its leaves to reflect the heat of the alpine summer sun.

HORMONES

Plants, like humans, have hormones. These control whether a plant makes a leaf or a flower. They also ensure that its stem grows up towards the sun, and that its roots grow down towards underground water.

If a plant is turned on its side, its stem and roots soon change direction.

PLANT FACTS

• Air plants have no roots. They grow on tree branches in tropical and sub-tropical Americas, absorbing all the moisture they need from the air.

• Resurrection plants shrivel up in dry weather. As soon as it rains, they become green and begin to photosynthesize again.

• Ant plants have ants living in spaces, called domatia, in their stems. The ants protect the plants from attacks by other insects.

WEEDS

Daisy (Bellis perennis) Weeds are simply plants that grow in places where they are a nuisance to people, such as gardens or crop fields. Some are as colourful and sweet-smelling as garden flowers.

PLANT GROWTH RATES

Giant bamboo (*Dendrocalamus giganteus*) grows 90cm (3ft) in a day

Giant kelp (*Macrocystis pyrifera*) grows 30cm (12in) in a day.

Bermuda grass (*Cynodon dactylon*) grows 15cm (6in) in a day.

Albizzia falcataria grows 2cm (1in) in a day.

Eucalyptus regnans grows 1cm (0.5in) in a day.

PARASITES AND EPIPHYTES

Some plants cannot photosynthesize. Instead, they live and feed on other plants, taking their food from the stems or roots. These plants are called parasites. Epiphytes also live on other plants, but they take neither food nor water from them.

This epiphytic bromeliad (*Aechmea miniata*) grows on the bark of trees.

The plant traps water in the spaces formed by its overlapping leaf bases.

CARNIVOROUS PLANTS

Carnivorous (meat-eating) plants feed on small animals, such as insects, as well as producing their own food by photosynthesis. Insects provide minerals and other nutrients that help these plants to survive.

1 The Venus flytrap (*Dionaea muscipula*) attracts insects with its unusual leaf tips.

2 The insect touches sensory hairs, which trigger the two halves of the leaf to snap shut.

3 Comb-like teeth trap the insect, and the plant slowly digests it.

GIANT FRONDS

The Pacific giant kelp (*Macrocystis pyrifera*) has the longest fronds of any plant. Each frond can grow up to 120m (394ft), taller than the Statue of Liberty.

COMMON USES OF PLANTS

LEAVES

Panama hats, from the leaves of the jipijapa tree (*Carludovica palmata*).

Skin cream, including juice from the leaves of *Aloe vera*.

Ice cream, thickened with agar-agar from seaweeds (*Gelidium*).

SAP

FIBRE

Rubber, from the latex of the rubber tree (*Hevea brasiliensis*).

Rope, from the fibres of the hemp plant (*Cannabis sativa*).

Linen, from the fibres of the flax plant (*Linum usitatissimum*).

ENDANGERED PLANTS

Scientific name	Common name	Location
Phragmipedium exstaminodium	Chiapas slipper orchid	Mexico
Sarracenia oreophila	Green pitcher plant	USA
Marojejya darianii	Big-leaf palm	Madagascar
Euphorbia handiensis	(succulent)	Canary Islands
Kerriodoxa elegans	(palm)	Thailand
Swainsona recta	(pea)	Australia
Dicliptera dodsonii	(vine)	Ecuador
Punica protopunica	Socotran pomegranate	Socotra

FLOWERS

FLOWERS HELP ENSURE that a plant is pollinated, and protect its seeds until they are shed. Flowers are often scented, and may be brightly coloured. They consist of sepals, petals, stamens, and carpels.

INFLORESCENCES

Some plants produce a single flower on each flower stalk (pedicel). Many, though, have flowers arranged in groups on a main stalk (peduncle). This is called an inflorescence.

Single flower
Glory lily
(*Gloriosa superba*)

Pedicel
(flower stalk)

Raceme inflorescence
Orchid family
(*Cymbidium*)

Peduncle
(inflorescence stalk)

Spike inflorescence
Lobster claws
(*Heliconia peruviana*)

Peduncle
(no pedicels)

Spadix inflorescence
Painter's palette
(*Anthurium andreanum*)

Compound umbel inflorescence
Common elder
(*Sambucus nigra*)

Dichasial cyme inflorescence
Common lime
(*Tilia x europaea*)

Flower bud

Peduncle

FLOWER STRUCTURE

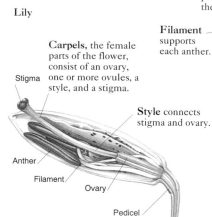

Stamens are the male parts of the flower. Each one consists of a filament and an anther.

Stigma is sticky to trap pollen.

Pollen is produced by the anthers.

Filament supports each anther.

Petals attract insects and guide them towards anthers and stigma.

Sepals protect flower while it is in bud.

Ovary contains one or more ovules with an ovum (egg cell) inside each.

Lily

Carpels, the female parts of the flower, consist of an ovary, one or more ovules, a style, and a stigma.

Stigma

Style connects stigma and ovary.

Anther

Filament

Ovary

Pedicel

POLLEN GRAIN
A pollen grain contains male gametes (reproductive cells). Once pollination has taken place, these male gametes can fertilize an ovum (female gamete).

FLOWER FACTS
• Most plants have both male and female reproductive organs in each flower. Some, such as willows (*Salix*), have either male or female flowers.

• The largest flower, giant rafflesia (*Rafflesia arnoldii*), grows up to 105cm (3.5ft) across and weighs up to 7kg (15.4lb).

Giant rafflesia   Hand

FLOWER EXAMPLES

Cockscomb
(*Celosia argentea cristata*)

Banksia
(*Banksia menziesii*)

Yellow calla lily
(*Zantedeschia*)

Cape cowslip
(*Lachenalia aloides*)

Urn plant
(*Aechmea*)

Guelder rose
(*Viburnum opulus*)

Hyacinth
(*Hyacinthus orientalis*)

Chrysanthemum
(*Chrysanthemum morifolium*)

Ice plant
(*Sedum*)

POLLINATION

Pollination is the transfer of pollen from anthers to a stigma. Many plants use insects to help spread their pollen. An insect feeding on a flower's nectar picks up pollen and carries it to the next flower.

Pollen sticks to stigma of next flower.

Bee picks up pollen from anthers.

FERTILIZATION

Once a flower has been pollinated, fertilization may take place. This process produces the seed, from which a new plant will grow.

One male gamete fuses with ovum to form embryo.

One male gamete fuses with polar nuclei to form endosperm.

1 Each pollen grain sends out a tube, which grows towards the ovary.

2 Two male gametes (reproductive cells) from the pollen grain enter the ovule.

3 The embryo plant and the endosperm (food store) develop inside the seed.

LEAVES

MOST LEAVES HAVE a stalk, called a petiole, and a blade, or lamina. Chlorophyll, a pigment that the leaves use in photosynthesis (see p.74), makes them green.

VASCULAR SYSTEM
The vascular system, made up of phloem and xylem, carries nutrients around the leaf.

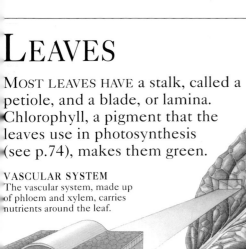

Phloem carries sugars around the plant.

Stoma (pore through which gases flow in and out)

Xylem carries water and minerals around the plant.

Midrib

LEAF STRUCTURE

Lamina

Vein

Phlox

Petiole

HEAVY SWEATER

Trees lose water through their leaves. An average birch tree with 200,000 leaves can lose up to 400 litres (106 gallons) on a hot day – enough to fill about 1,200 soft drink cans.

LEAF TEXTURES

Smooth, waxy leaves allow water to flow off, so they do not become waterlogged.

Rhododendron

Hard, spiky leaves help prevent the flower and leaf buds from being eaten by animals.

Holly

Hairy leaves trap a layer of air, so they do not burn in sunshine, or freeze in cold weather.

Tanacetum

Needle-shaped leaves offer little resistance to wind, preventing it from damaging the plant.

Cypress

LEAF EXAMPLES

Hornbeam maple
(Acer carpinifolium)

Conifer *(Taiwania cryptomerioides)*

Castor aralia
(Kalopanax pictus)

Asparagus
(Asparagus)

Burr oak
(Quercus macrocarpa)

Swiss cheese plant
(Monstera deliciosa)

Lily family
(Lilium)

Lungwort
(Pulmonaria officinalis)

Robinia
(Robinia x holdtii)

Sassafras
(Sassafras albidum)

Blue echeveria
(Echeveria)

Black wattle acacia
(Acacia mearnsii)

LEAF RECORDS

LARGEST LEAVES
belong to the raffia palm *(Raphia farinifera)* and the Amazonian bamboo palm *(Raphia taedigera)*, growing up to 20m (64ft) long.

SMALLEST LEAVES (Flowering plants) are those of a floating duckweed *(Wolffia angusta)*. Leaves grow to about 0.6mm (0.2in) long, and 0.3mm (0.1in) wide.

POISONOUS LEAVES
The leaves of many plants contain poisons. Rhubarb leaves contain high concentrations of oxalic acid, which is particularly dangerous for people suffering from rheumatism or arthritis. Jimson weed and aconite leaves can also cause sickness in humans.

Rhubarb *(Rheum rhaponticum)* leaves contain oxalic acid.

Jimson weed *(Datura stramonium)* leaves contain atropine.

Aconite *(Aconitum napellus)* leaves contain aconitine and ephedrine.

LEAF MOULD
When dead plants and leaves decay and are broken down, they form topsoil, which contains nutrients essential for plant growth.

Leaf litter   Centipede   Ant   Earthworm

Plants, such as this bluebell, thrive in the fertile topsoil.

1 Fallen leaves and dead plants lie on the surface. They slowly decompose, forming a layer called humus.

2 Tiny animals, such as earthworms, eat and excrete the humus, grinding it up finely and mixing it with the soil.

3 Valuable nutrients are released in the process, forming a rich layer of topsoil in which new plants grow.

LEAF RAFT
The leaves of the giant water lily *(Victoria amazonica)* can grow up to 2.4m (8ft) across. They can support the weight of a young child.

TREES

TREES ARE PLANTS at least six metres (20 feet) tall, with a single trunk (main stem). They are all perennial (live for many years), and most are broadleaved plants, which bear flowers.

LIFE CYCLE

Once a tree is mature, it can produce flowers, fruits, and seeds each year.

Seed grows into sapling (young tree).

Seed falls on fertile ground.

Fruit protects seed.

Fertilized flowers produce fruits.

Flower buds appear on mature tree in spring.

Buds appear in early spring. They will soon grow into flowers, called catkins.

English oak (*Quercus robur*) in spring and autumn

Leaves

Bark

Trunk

Roots

ROOTS

A tree's roots take up water from the soil. The vascular system (see p.77) transports the water around the tree.

TREE STRUCTURE

Broadleaved trees, like most flowering plants, have a main stem, or trunk, leaves, flowers, fruits, and seeds.

Fruit of the oak tree is a nut, called an acorn. Nuts are hard, dry fruits with only one seed.

INSIDE THE TRUNK

A tree trunk grows new layers of cells outside the old layers. Trees grow quickly in warm conditions and slowly in cold conditions, forming visible rings in the trunk. Heartwood consists of dead cells, containing chemicals such as tannins or resins, which can produce rich, deep colours.

Heartwood

Sapwood

One year's growth ring

Waterproof layer of cork

Bark

TYPES OF TREE

BROADLEAVED TREES

There are many thousands of species of broadleaved trees. Most are deciduous (shed their leaves seasonally).

Most broadleaved trees, as their name suggests, have broad, flat leaves.

All the trees in this group are angiosperms (flowering plants).

NEEDLE-LEAVED TREES

The group called needle-leaved trees includes pines, firs, and yews. There are over 500 species of needle-leaved trees, most of which are evergreen.

Many conifers have needle-shaped leaves, but some are strap-shaped, or even oval.

Most needle-leaved trees bear seeds in woody cones.

PALM TREES

The palm family contains about 2,800 species. Palms have only one growing point, called the apical bud. If this is damaged, the tree dies.

Palm trees have this name because the leaves are often shaped like a hand.

Palm trees, like broadleaved trees, are flowering plants.

HARDWOODS AND SOFTWOODS

Broadleaved trees are sometimes referred to as hardwoods, and conifers as softwoods. However, some conifers, such as Douglas fir and yew, produce harder wood than many broadleaved trees. Balsa, the softest of all, is a hardwood.

Pine is a softwood. Its timber is soft and open-grained.

Walnut is a hardwood with a distinctive colour.

TREES AROUND THE WORLD

Trees grow wherever there is at least 20cm (7.9in) of rain each year, and a temperature of at least 10°C (50°F) in summer. These conditions are not met in the white areas on the map. No trees grow in the Arctic tundra, in Antarctica, or on very high mountain tops.

EQUATOR

MAP KEY

Boreal forest (conifers)

Tropical rainforest (broadleaved)

Mangroves

Temperate forest (mixed)

Limited forest cover

Tropical dry forest (deciduous)

Limit of palm trees

BARK

A tree's bark consists of dead cells, which protect the living cells of the sapwood. As the tree grows, the outer layer of bark splits and is replaced by a new layer. Sometimes many layers are visible at the same time.

Younger, pinkish layer shows beneath peeling outer layer.

Lenticels (cell areas) allow the tree to breathe.

The paper birch (*Betula papyrifera*) has a very pale bark.

This cherry tree (*Prunus serrula*) has a dark, glossy bark.

River birch (*Betula nigra*) has bark that peels in flaky layers.

TREE RECORDS

TALLEST LIVING TREE is a coast redwood (*Sequoia sempervirens*) in Redwood National Park, USA. It is 111.25m (365ft) tall, about the same as an Apollo space rocket.

OLDEST KNOWN TREE, a bristlecone pine (*Pinus longaeva*) in Nevada, USA, was over 5,100 years old.

MOST DROUGHT-RESISTANT TREE, the baobab (*Adansonia digitata*) of Africa, can store up to 136,000 litres (35,900 gallons) of water in its swollen trunk.

Height m(ft)
111.25 (365)
90 (300)
60 (200)
30 (100)
0

LEAF FALL

In harsh conditions, leaves do not photosynthesize properly, and water lost from them cannot be replaced if the ground is dry or frozen. So a tree withdraws the useful substances from its leaves, and then sheds them.

Deciduous forest in autumn, New England, USA

TREE FACTS

- The Bishop pine (*Pinus muricata*) can reproduce only after a forest fire. It needs the heat of the fire to crack open its cones.

- One cubic metre (1.3 cubic yards) of dried ebony weighs 1,030kg (2,271lb). The same volume of balsa weighs only 160kg (234lb).

- Mangroves are the only trees that can grow in salty water. They have special roots that help them take in oxygen.

TRUNK ROAD

Californian redwoods (*Sequoia sempervirens*) grow up to 7.6m (25ft) across. It is sometimes easier to cut through the trunk than to remove the tree.

GROWTH RATES

Trees grow at different rates. Below and right are the heights of some trees after 15 years.

Adult human, 1.8m (6ft)

Juniper (*Juniperus*), 3m (10ft)

Oak (*Quercus*), 7.5m (25ft)

Birch (*Betula*), 9m (30ft)

Douglas fir (*Pseudotsuga*), 12.2m (40ft)

AUTUMN COLOURS

1 Chlorophyll is the first leaf pigment to break down when autumn arrives.

2 Other colour pigments, such as yellow carotenoids, now show through.

3 Carotenoids darken as they age, turning from yellow through orange to red.

4 Anthocyanins, from sugars in the leaves, give them a scarlet colour.

5 The tree deposits tannins in the leaves. These produce a dark brown colour.

6 A layer of cells, called the absission layer, forms at the base of the leaf stalk. Finally the leaf falls.

A maple leaf, as it dies, changes colour dramatically.

COMMON USES OF TREES

WOOD

Oak (*Quercus*) for furniture.

Sycamore (*Acer pseudoplatanus*) for violins.

Poplar (*Populus*) for buildings (some countries).

Ebony (*Diospyros*) for carving work.

PULP PRODUCTS

Paper is made from the pulp of many kinds of trees. Pulp is used for paper products such as kitchen paper, tissues, and books.

FIBRE PRODUCTS

Rayon fabric is made from cellulose using wood fibres from many species of trees.

SEED PRODUCTS

Kapok stuffing is made from the hairs that cover the seeds of the kapok or silk-cotton tree (*Ceiba pentandra*).

BARK

Cinnamon, from the bark of the cinnamon (*Cinnamomum zeylanicum*).

Cork, from the bark of the cork oak (*Quercus suber*).

SAP

Maple syrup from the sap of the sugar maple (*Acer saccharum*).

Chewing gum from the sap of the sapodilla tree (*Manilkara zapota*).

Turpentine from the sap of the longleaf pine (*Pinus palustris*).

Amber fossilized resin from conifer trees that are now extinct.

ENDANGERED TIMBER TREES

Scientific name	Common name	Location
Abies guatemalensis	(Fir)	North and Central America
Aniba duckei	Bois de rose	South America
Dalbergia nigra	Bahia rosewood	South America
Hopea erosa	(Dipterocarp family)	Southeast India
Rousselia erratica	(Nettle family)	Central America
Vatica soepadmoi	(Dipterocarp family)	Sumatra

FOOD PLANTS

MANY TYPES OF PLANT ARE important food sources for humans. They include fruits, vegetables, herbs, spices, and cereals.

FRUIT EXAMPLES

Fruits form an important part of the human diet. There is a huge variety of wild and cultivated fruits, some of which are shown below.

TEMPERATE

Apple
(*Malus domestica*)

Strawberry
(*Fragaria*)

Cherry
(*Prunus avium*)

TROPICAL

Papaya
(*Carica papaya*)

Durian
(*Durio zibethinus*)

Star fruit
(*Averrhoa carambola*)

NUTS

Walnut
(*Juglans regia*)

Brazil nut
(*Bertholletia excelsa*)

Hazelnut
(*Corylus avellana*)

GRAPE SCOTT!

One year's worldwide grape harvest would bury Manhattan Island, New York, to a depth of 124m (407ft).

TOP FIVE FRUIT

Fruit	Annual worldwide consumption (tonnes)
Bananas (*Musa*)	40,597,200
Apples (*Malus domestica*)	34,422,144
Oranges (*Citrus sinensis*)	30,853,920
Water-melons (*Citrullus lanatus*)	19,330,912
Plantains (*Musa*)	18,130,384

FRUIT RECORDS

LARGEST SEED
is the "double coconut" of the coco de mer palm (*Lodoicea maldivica*), which can weigh up to 25kg (55lb).

LARGEST TREE FRUIT
comes from the jackfruit tree (*Artocarpus heterophyllus*): it can weigh up to 50kg (110lb).

FOOD PLANT ANCESTORS

The size, shape, and flavour, of many food plants have been altered by selective breeding.

Wild tomatoes (Lycopersicon esculentum) *are about the size of grapes, and sweeter than cultivated tomatoes.*

*This primitive form of a corn plant (*Zea mays*) with its cob is much smaller than a modern corn cob.*

FRUIT

The fruit is the part of a flower that develops to contain the seed or seeds. Fruits can be succulent or dry. Succulent fruits, such as lemons, are fleshy and brightly coloured.

Pedicel (flower stalk)
Carpel (female parts of the flower)
Seed
Endocarp (inner layer of pericarp)
Exocarp (outer layer of pericarp)
Mesocarp (middle layer of pericarp)
Remains of style (see p.76)
Pericarp (fruit wall)
Vesicle (juice sac)
Lemon (*Citrus limon*)

NUTS

Nuts are a type of dry fruit. They have a hard wall around their seed.

Peduncle (inflorescence stalk)
Remains of stigma (see p.76)
Remains of male inflorescence (see p.76)
Remains of style (see p.76)
Spiky cupule (husk around fruit)
Woody pericarp (fruit wall)
Sweet chestnut (*Castanea sativa*)

SEEDS

Each fruit contains one or more seeds that will germinate and grow into new plants if conditions are suitable. Some types of fruit, such as cherries and peaches, contain just one seed. Other fruits, such as strawberries and apples, contain several seeds.

Hilum (point of attachment to ovary)
Testa (seed coat)
Lemon seed

DEVELOPMENT OF A FRUIT

A plant's fruit begins to form after fertilization has taken place (see p.76).

Development of a blackberry (*Rubus fruticosus*)

Ovaries begin to swell; stamens wither.

Carpels expand and become more fleshy.

Carpels continue to expand and begin to change colour.

Carpels mature into drupelets: small fleshy fruit with a single seed in each.

Drupelets ripen fully. Fruit is ready to eat.

FRUIT ORIGINS

This map shows the origins of several fruits now found worldwide.

KEY
- Cherries (Egypt)
- Peaches (China)
- Lemons (India)
- Water-melons (Africa)
- Strawberries (America)
- Passionfruit (Brazil)

VEGETABLE EXAMPLES

Vegetables can be leaves, tubers, flowers, stalks, or shoots.

LEAVES

Cabbage
(*Brassica oleracea*)

Spinach
(*Spinacia oleracea*)

Lettuce
(*Lactuca sativa*)

STALKS

Asparagus
(*Asparagus officinalis*)

Celery
(*Apium graveolens*)

Bean sprout
(*Vigna radiata*)

FLOWERS

Globe artichoke
(*Cynara scolymus*)

Cauliflower
(*Brassica oleracea*)

Broccoli
(*Brassica oleracea*)

ROOTS

Carrot
(*Daucus carota*)

Beetroot
(*Beta vulgaris*)

Turnip
(*Brassica rapa*)

VEGETABLES

The term vegetable describes an edible plant, or part of a plant. Some fruits, such as tomatoes and aubergines, are also commonly called vegetables.

VEGETABLE RECORDS

All of the following records are held by Mr. Bernard Lavery (born 1938) of Llanharry, Wales, UK. Mr. Lavery also holds three other world records for growing large vegetables.

LARGEST CABBAGE weighed 56.24kg (124lb).

LARGEST MARROW (*Cucurbita pepo*) weighed 49.05kg (108.1lb).

LONGEST PARSNIP (*Pastinaca sativa*) was 4.36m (14.3ft) long.

LONGEST CARROT was 5.14m (16.9ft) long.

LARGEST CELERY weighed 20.89kg (46lb).

LARGEST BRUSSELS SPROUT weighed 8.25kg (18.2lb).

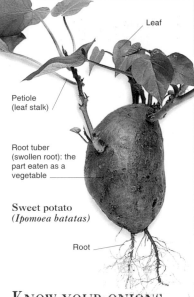

Leaf

Petiole (leaf stalk)

Root tuber (swollen root): the part eaten as a vegetable

Sweet potato
(*Ipomoea batatas*)

Root

KNOW YOUR ONIONS

Onions, chives, garlic, and leeks all belong to the lily family. Different parts of each plant are eaten as vegetables: the bulbs of onion and garlic, the stems of leeks, and the leaves of chives.

Onion
(*Allium cepa*)

Chives
(*Allium schoenoprasum*)

Garlic
(*Allium sativum*)

Leeks
(*Allium porrum*)

FRUIT AND VEGETABLE FACTS

• For 2,000 years the Chinese have considered lychees (*Litchi chinensis*) to be the finest fruits. Relays of horsemen took them to court, and in some districts, tax collectors demanded them as payment.

• Even the hottest chili pepper (*Capsicum frutescens*) derives all its heat from no more than 0.1% of the fruit.

• There are 6,000 varieties of potato in Peru.

TOP FIVE VEGETABLES

Vegetable	Annual worldwide consumption (tonnes)
Tomatoes (*Lycopersicon esculentum*)	57,525,248
Cabbages (*Brassica oleracea*)	34,418,560
Onions (*Allium cepa*)	25,943,344
Cucumbers/gherkins (*Cucumis sativus*)	15,851,327
Carrots (*Daucus carota*)	11,713,606

FRUIT EATEN AS VEGETABLES

Some foods usually regarded as vegetables are in fact fruits. Familiar examples are shown below.

Tomato
(*Lycopersicon esculentum*)

Peppers
(*Capsicum annum*)

Aubergine
(*Solanum melongena*)

Pumpkin
(*Cucurbita pepo*)

SPICE EXAMPLES

Spices are strongly flavoured plants used in cooking.

Cinnamon
(*Cinnamomum zeylandicum*)

Chili peppers
(*Capsicum frutescens*)

Cloves
(*Syzygium aromaticum*)

HERB EXAMPLES

Herbs are used to flavour food, and in medicine.

Basil
(*Ocimum basilicum*)

Coriander
(*Coriandrum sativum*)

Spearmint
(*Mentha spicata*)

FRUIT AND VEGETABLE PRODUCTS

Many products in daily use come from fruits and vegetables.

Vegetable dyes
Dyes are made from plants such as indigo (*Indigofera*) and henna (*Lawsonia inermis*).

Loofahs
People use dried loofahs (*Luffa cylindrica*), a tropical fruit, to wash in the bath.

Cooking oil
Cooking oils are extracted from several fruits and seeds, including olives (*Olea europaea*).

Chocolate
Chocolate comes from the beans of the cacao tree (*Theobroma*).

Face powder
Finely ground walnut (*Juglans regia*) shells are used to make cosmetic face powder.

Coffee
Coffee is produced from the ground beans of the *Coffea* tree.

COLOSSAL CUCUMBER

The largest cucumber ever grown weighed 9.1kg (20lb). This would have provided enough slices to make 1,137 cucumber sandwiches.

FUNGI AND LICHENS

FUNGI WERE ONCE CLASSIFIED as plants, but since about 1969 botanists have treated them as a separate kingdom. Most fungi are immobile, like plants, but cannot make their own food. Instead, they feed on living or dead plants or animals, dung, and other organic materials.

FUNGUS EXAMPLES

There are about 65,000 known species of fungus and 20,000 lichens. Many more may be discovered.

Orange peel fungus
(*Aleuria aurantia*)

Maze-gill
(*Daedalea quercina*)

Astraeus hygrometricus

Fly agaric
(*Amanita muscaria*)

Green wood-cup
(*Chlorosplenium aeruginascens*)

Clavulinopsis helvola

Scarlet hood
(*Hygrocybe coccinea*)

Chanterelle
(*Cantharellus cibarius*)

Common stinkhorn
(*Phallus impudicus*)

TYPES OF LICHEN

Lichens have a number of distinctive growth forms – some flat, others branching or bushy.

Fruticose
(*Cladonia portentosa*)

Foliose
(*Hypogymnia physodes*)

Squamulose
(*Cladonia floerkeana*)

TRUFFLE TREAT

Truffles (fungi that produce sporophores underground) are delicious. The White Truffle (*Tuber magnatum*) from Italy costs about £1,000 per kg.

FUNGUS AND LICHEN FACTS

• Fungus cells contain a light, strong substance called chitin. Chitin is also found in the cuticle, or outer layer, of some animals, such as insects.

• Lichen extracts produce orchil, the dye used for litmus paper, as well as the dyes once used to colour the wool in Scottish tartans.

Gills produce and store spores

Cap

Cap curls upwards to release the spores.

Stem

Cortinarius armillatus

Hyphae form the mycelium (main body) and anchor the sporophore (fruiting body).

LIFE CYCLE

Fungi reproduce through spores, which are the equivalent of a plant's seeds. The fungal mycelium spreads underground until it meets another mycelium of the same species. They bond together and, given the right conditions, produce a fruiting body that generally grows above ground.

Mature sporophore produces spores

Cap curls upwards to release spores

Spore germinates, and mycelium develops

Sporophore grows above ground level

Mycelium spreads; forms sporophore

SYMBIOTIC RELATIONSHIPS

Many fungi live in close association, or symbiotic relationships, with plants and animals. The three main kinds of symbiotic relationships are parasitic, mutualistic, and saprophytic.

PARASITIC
Some parasitic fungi cause galls and can even kill the plant they live on.

MUTUALISTIC
Many orchids need the presence of a fungus for their seeds to germinate.

SAPROPHYTIC
Some fungi live on dead wood, animals, and other organic matter in the soil.

FUNGUS RECORDS

LONGEST-LIVING MUSHROOM, *Ganoderma applanatum*, can live for as long as fifty years.

MOST IMPORTANT FUNGI belong to *Penicillium* genus. They are used in blue cheeses, and the antibiotic penicillin.

BIGGEST FRUITING BODY is giant puffball (*Lycoperdon gigantea*), which can measure up to 2m (6.6ft) in circumference.

FUNGUS STRUCTURE

Mushrooms and toadstools are the fruiting bodies of fungi. They grow up out of the soil to spread their spores (reproductive bodies).

LICHEN STRUCTURE

Lichens consist of fungi living in association with algae (simple plants) or cyanobacteria, the only organisms apart from plants that can photosynthesize.

Soredium may develop into a new lichen

Algal layer

Fungal mycelium

Hypogymnia physodes

Fairy ring

• Fairy rings form when hyphae grow outwards from a central point. Mushrooms sprout at the outer edge, forming a ring.

• Lichens are very sensitive to air pollution, and several kinds are used to indicate pollution levels.

POISONOUS FUNGI

Name	Poison	Symptoms
Fly agaric (*Amanita muscaria*)	muscarine	Stomach pain, hallucinations, delirium, convulsions; rarely fatal
Death cap (*Amanita phalloides*)	amanitine, phalloidine	Nausea, liver and kidney failure, abdominal pain; can be fatal
False morel (*Gyromitra esculenta*)	gyromitrin	Stomach pain, nausea, jaundice; can be fatal
Never eat wild mushrooms unless they have been identified by an expert as edible.		

MICRO-ORGANISMS

A MICRO-ORGANISM IS a life-form that is usually too small for the human eye to see. The most familiar are protists, bacteria, and viruses. Some micro-organisms are harmful, but many are vital: without them, life as we know it could not continue.

Cytoplasm

Nucleus

Food vacuole

Cell wall

Pseudopodia: extensions that flow out from the body.

Portrait of an amoeba
Amoebas are irregularly shaped protists that crawl about on the bottom of ponds.

PROTISTS

Protists are neither animals nor plants. They belong to a separate kingdom (see p.72). Protists have just one cell, which carries out all the functions necessary for them to live and reproduce. They live in watery environments, from damp soil and puddles, to lakes and oceans.

FEEDING

Many protists trap their food, which includes algae and other protists, by engulfing it with part of their jelly-like body.

TYPES OF PROTIST

There are more than 40,000 species of protist. Two phyla are shown below.

Ciliates
(Ciliophora)

Flagellates, amoebas, opalinids
(Sarcomastigophora)

REPRODUCTION

Most protists reproduce by splitting themselves in two. Each of the two halves then becomes a single cell. This process is called binary fission. Many types of bacteria also reproduce in this way.

A fully grown protist

The nucleus and cytoplasm split into two equal halves.

Two identical protists result

The amoeba's pseudopodia surround its prey.

Food is trapped, forming a food vacuole.

BACTERIA

Bacteria, together with blue-green algae, belong to the Moneran kingdom. Monerans are the simplest, and probably the most ancient, forms of life on Earth. Bacteria are found everywhere, from the depths of the oceans to the upper atmosphere.

Some bacteria have flagella.

Some types of bacteria look hairy.

A rigid wall protects the bacterium.

The cell wall may be surrounded by a slimy capsule.

Material stored in granules

Bacteria do not have a nucleus: their genetic material floats freely.

A fine membrane surrounds the cell contents.

Cell manufacturing machinery floats freely.

BACTERIA SHAPES

Bacteria are often classified according to their shape, which is spherical, rod-shaped, or curved.

Coccus   *Bacillus*   *Spirillum*

VIRUSES

A virus is a tiny package of chemicals surrounded by a protein coat. There are many virus shapes, including rod-shaped, round, and many-sided. They are all so small (the largest are about 0.0003mm) that they can be seen only with an electron microscope.

Influenza virus particles seen through an electron microscope. Viruses cause many diseases, from the common cold to yellow fever.

Head

DNA

Collar

Bacteriophage:
a virus that invades bacteria

Tail

Tail fibres

HOW A BACTERIOPHAGE VIRUS MULTIPLIES

A virus shows no signs of life until it invades the cell of a living organism. The bacteriophage is a complex virus that reproduces by invading bacteria cells. It is replicated at a rate of 300 every half an hour.

1 The virus injects DNA into the bacterium.

2 The bacterium makes copies of the virus's DNA.

3 The DNA develops into complete viruses.

4 The cell bursts open, releasing copies of the virus.

ARMPIT CITY

There are about 600 million bacteria in and on a human body. The skin of an armpit may be home to up to 800 bacteria per square millimetre (516,000 per square inch).

USEFUL BACTERIA

Bacteria are nature's most important recycling agents. They break down dead plants and animals, and return the materials to the ecosystem. Most bacteria are harmless to humans. Some are vital: without them we could not digest our food.

Bacteria are important in the production of many foods.

Vinegar

Cheese   *Yoghurt*

MICRO-ORGANISM FACTS

• It would take a ciliate (protist) about five minutes to swim the length of this page.
• One gram of soil may contain over 150,000 protists.

• The largest species of protist ever to have lived grew to over 20cm (7.9in) in diameter: the width of this page. It has now become extinct.

ANIMALS

MORE THAN A MILLION animal species have been discovered. They have adapted to just about every habitat: some even spend their entire life inside the body of another animal.

ANIMAL CHARACTERISTICS

Animals, unlike plants, cannot manufacture their own food, so they have to eat other organisms. They have many cells, can reproduce, and can sense and respond to their surroundings. Most animals move around at some stage in their lives.

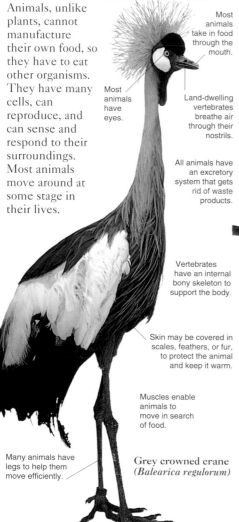

Most animals take in food through the mouth.

Most animals have eyes.

Land-dwelling vertebrates breathe air through their nostrils.

All animals have an excretory system that gets rid of waste products.

Vertebrates have an internal bony skeleton to support the body.

Skin may be covered in scales, feathers, or fur, to protect the animal and keep it warm.

Muscles enable animals to move in search of food.

Many animals have legs to help them move efficiently.

Grey crowned crane
(Balearica regulorum)

TYPES OF ANIMAL

INVERTEBRATES
About 97% of animal species are invertebrates (have no backbone). Some of the most important phyla (see p.72) are shown here.

Sea anemones, corals, jellyfish, hydras (Cnidaria)
Ring of tentacles armed with stinging cells surrounds the mouth.

Molluscs (Mollusca)
Most have a hard shell to protect their soft body. Includes snails and slugs, squid and octopuses, clams, mussels, and scallops.

Arthropods (Arthropoda)
Jointed limbs and a tough external skeleton. Includes insects, arachnids, and crustaceans.

Worms
At least ten phyla, including segmented worms (Annelida) and roundworms (Nematoda).

Starfish, sea urchins, and sea cucumbers (Echinodermata)
Marine; body usually made up of five identical parts.

VERTEBRATES
Only about 3% of animal species are vertebrates (animals with a backbone). There are more than 40,000 species, in seven classes (see p.72). Three of these classes are fish.

Fish (Agnatha, Chondrichthyes, Osteichthyes). Three classes: jawless fish, sharks and rays, and bony fish.

Amphibians (Amphibia)
Can live both on land and in water. Includes frogs, toads, newts, and salamanders.

Reptiles (Reptilia)
Scaly skin; most species lay eggs. Includes snakes, lizards, crocodiles, and turtles.

Birds (Aves)
Covered with feathers. Have wings, a beak, and no teeth. Most species can fly.

Mammals (Mammalia)
Feed young on milk produced in female's body. Most have fur or hair.

ANIMAL REPRODUCTION

The main function of an animal's life is to continue its species. Some animals reproduce without mating (asexual reproduction), but most mate with a partner to produce offspring (sexual reproduction).

Asexual reproduction
Some organisms, e.g. hydras, reproduce by budding: part of the parent becomes detached and forms a new individual.

Sexual reproduction
Most animals reproduce sexually: a cell from a male (a sperm) joins with a cell from a female (an egg). This egg grows into a new individual.

ANIMAL LIFESPANS

Lifespans range from a few days for some insects, to more than 200 years for a giant clam *(Tridacna)*. Most mammals have about the same number of heartbeats in their lifetime.

Elephants and shrews have a similar number of heartbeats during their lives, but the shrew's heart beats much faster during its short life.

LARVA'S LARDER

The female tarantula wasp *(Pepsis)* paralyzes a tarantula with her sting. She then bites off its legs to make it easier to carry, puts it in a burrow, and lays an egg on it. When the larva hatches, it feeds off the still-living spider.

ANIMAL FACTS

• Only about 0.3% of animal species are mammals, and only about 0.7% are birds. Most creatures on Earth are insects or worms.

• A large locust swarm can eat 80,000 tonnes of food in a day: equivalent to the amount of food eaten by 35,000 American families in a year.

FEEDING

Some animals have specialized diets, while others eat almost anything. Animals have evolved different teeth to suit their diet.

Mongoose skull

Carnivore
Meat-eater: sharp canine teeth

Gazelle skull

Herbivore
Plant-eater: flat molars

Moonrat skull

Insectivore
Insect-eater: sharp, pointed teeth

Monkey skull

Omnivore
Meat- and plant-eater: sharp and flat teeth

ANIMAL GROUPS

A cast of hawks
A covert of coots
A bazaar of guillemots
A pride of lions
A clowder of cats
A leap of leopards
A sloth of bears
A skulk of foxes
A labour of moles
A crash of rhinoceroses
A shrewdness of apes
A pod of dolphins

INVERTEBRATES

THE VAST MAJORITY of creatures are invertebrates – animals without a backbone. They include insects, spiders, crabs, worms, jellyfish, and corals. Many invertebrates are tiny, but others, such as the giant squid and the Japanese spider crab, can grow to be larger than humans.

TYPES OF INVERTEBRATE

There are more than a million known species of invertebrate, in about 30 phyla (see p.72). Some of the largest and most important phyla are shown below; the number of species in each is approximate.

Sponges
(Porifera)
9,000 species

Sea anemones, corals, jellyfish, hydras
(Cnidaria)
9,500 species

Flatworms, flukes, and tapeworms
(Platyhelminthes)
15,000 species

Roundworms
(Nematoda)
20,000 species

Molluscs
(Mollusca)
51,000 species

Worms and leeches
(Annelida)
18,600 species

Arthropods
(Arthropoda)
1,092,000 species

Starfish, sea urchins, and sea cucumbers
(Echinodermata)
6,000 species

PORTRAIT OF AN INVERTEBRATE

Invertebrates range from simple microscopic animals to complex, intelligent molluscs, such as octopuses. Invertebrates do not have an internal skeleton: their body shape is maintained either by a tough, external coat, called an exoskeleton, or by fluid pressing against the skin.

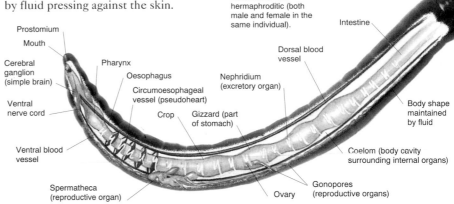

Earthworm

Body is formed of many identical segments

Clitellum (saddle)

Dorsal surface

Prostomium

Pygidium

Earthworms are hermaphroditic (both male and female in the same individual).

Intestine

Prostomium
Mouth
Cerebral ganglion (simple brain)
Pharynx
Oesophagus
Circumoesophageal vessel (pseudoheart)
Nephridium (excretory organ)
Dorsal blood vessel
Ventral nerve cord
Crop
Gizzard (part of stomach)
Body shape maintained by fluid
Ventral blood vessel
Coelom (body cavity surrounding internal organs)
Spermatheca (reproductive organ)
Ovary
Gonopores (reproductive organs)

LIFE CYCLE

There is a huge diversity of invertebrate life cycles. Most species lay eggs, then many pass through several larval stages that may look very different to the adult stage. Other species hatch as miniature adults. Some invertebrates, such as houseflies, live for just a few weeks, but others may live for many years: the giant clam (*Tridacna*) can live to be more than 200 years old.

Life cycle of a jellyfish

Adult

Female jellyfish releases fertilized larvae which settle on the sea-bed.

Larvae grow into small polyps called scyphistoma.

At the right temperature, polyps divide into eight-armed buds called ephyrae.

Ephyrae break free and become free-swimming adults.

TAPE MEASURE

The pork tapeworm (*Taenia solium*) can grow to over 7m (23ft) long inside the human body: as long as four adult humans. It has as many as 1,500 segments, each containing 80,000 tapeworm embryos. Tapeworms can cause death if they enter the bloodstream.

WORM FACTS

• Roundworms are probably the most numerous animals on Earth. 20,000 species have been discovered, but scientists believe there are at least 500,000 species.

• Up to 500 million hookworms may be found in a single human.

ECHINODERMS

Echinoderms include starfish, sea urchins, and sea cucumbers. An echinoderm's body is divided into five parts radiating out from a central point, and it moves using tiny, water-filled tube feet. All echinoderms live in the sea.

Starfish are among the strongest animals for their size: they can prize apart the shells of bivalve molluscs, such as scallops.

ARTHROPODS

This huge phylum contains the largest variety of creatures in the animal kingdom, including insects, crustaceans, spiders, centipedes, millipedes, and horseshoe crabs. All arthropods have a tough exoskeleton, jointed limbs, and a nerve cord running the length of the body.

The tiger centipede (Scolopendra hardwickii) is the largest species of centipede. It grows to just under 30cm (12in) long.

ZOOPLANKTON

Plankton is made up of small invertebrates (zooplankton) and plants (phytoplankton) that drift along in water currents. Zooplankton includes jellyfish, and the larvae of sea creatures such as starfish and crabs.

Zooplankton

INVERTEBRATE RECORDS

LARGEST JELLYFISH is the giant North Atlantic jellyfish (*Cyanea capillata*), which grows to more than 2m (6.6ft) in diameter, and may have tentacles nearly 37m (121.4ft) long.

LONGEST EARTHWORM is the *Mirochaetus* earthworm from South Africa, which grows up to 6m (19.7ft) long.

MOLLUSCS

MOLLUSCS FORM the second largest group of animals on Earth. They range from tiny snails to the giant squid, which grows as long as a sperm whale. Molluscs are found all over the world. They live in oceans and seas, in fresh water, and on land.

PORTRAIT OF A MOLLUSC

A typical mollusc has a soft body divided into the head, the foot, and a hump containing the main organs. This hump is covered by a fold of skin called the mantle. The body is usually protected by a hard shell.

Labels: Eye, Shell, Tentacle, Collar, Foot, Heart, Kidney, Lung, Mantle, Crop (digestive tract), Brain, Mucus gland, Mouth, Radula (toothed tongue), Reproductive organs, Salivary gland, Anus, Excretory gland, Sperm duct, Ovotestis (reproductive organ), Hermaphrodite duct, Stomach, Oviduct

Snails have both male and female reproductive organs.

Giant African land snail (*Achatina*)

TYPES OF MOLLUSC

There are more than 50,000 species of mollusc. They are divided into seven classes (see p.72).

Chitons
(Polyplacophora)
coat-of-mail shells
500 species

Solenogasters
(Aplacophora)
worm-like
marine molluscs
5,540 species

Monoplacophorans
(Monoplacophora)
deep-sea limpets
10 species

Tusk shells
(Scaphopoda)
350 species

Gastropods
(Gastropoda)
e.g. slug, snail, whelk
35,000 species

Bivalves
(Bivalvia)
two-shelled molluscs
e.g. oyster, clam
8,000 species

Cephalopods
(Cephalopoda)
squid, octopuses,
nautiluses, cuttlefish
600 species

LIFE CYCLE

Most molluscs lay eggs. Many marine (sea-dwelling) species hatch into tiny larvae. Other molluscs, such as some snails, hatch into miniature adults.

Life cycle of an oyster

Egg

Egg hatches into free-swimming larva, called a trochophore.

Larva grows larger, shell develops. This stage called a veliger larva.

Young adult sinks to sea bed and settles in suitable place.

MOLLUSC FACTS

• The giant clam (*Tridacna*) is the longest-lived animal in the world: it can live to be more than 200 years old.

• Larger species of octopus can measure up to 9m (30ft) across with their tentacles spread out.

• The mucus secreted by snails is so effective that they can crawl along the edge of a razor without cutting themselves.

• Limpets have such strong teeth on their radula that they leave scratch marks on rocks when they browse.

FEEDING

Bivalve molluscs are filter feeders, sifting tiny organisms from the water. Most other molluscs have a toothed tongue, called a radula, which they use to scratch food into their mouth.

Close-up of a snail's radula showing rows of rasping teeth

The giant clam's gills sift food from the water. The gills are also used for breathing.

MOLLUSC MOVEMENT

Some molluscs, such as mussels, anchor themselves to one place. Most molluscs, however, move around in search of food and to escape from predators.

BIVALVES

Some bivalves, e.g. scallops, suck in water then expel it rapidly by clapping their two shells together. This propels them through the water in a series of jerks.

GASTROPODS

Gastropods create a wave of muscle contractions that runs from the rear of the foot to the front. This wave slowly drags them along.

CEPHALOPODS

Cephalopods, such as squid, take in water then force it out again, pushing themselves rapidly backwards. They also have fins which they use to pull themselves forwards.

Slugs and snails secrete a slimy mucus that helps them to slide along.

This *Euglandina* snail is the fastest mollusc on land.

Squid can swim at speeds of up to 40km/h (25mph).

TOP OF THE CLASS

Octopuses are intelligent animals, and have the ability to learn. An octopus at London Zoo in England learned how to twist the lid off a jar to reach the crab inside.

Cross-section of a squid's mantle

Expanded mantle cavity takes in water

Contracted mantle cavity shoots out jet of water, propelling squid along

DEFENCE AND ATTACK

Molluscs have evolved several unique ways of protecting themselves from enemies. Many carnivorous (meat-eating) molluscs are also efficient predators.

STINGING

Some sea slugs eat jellyfish, and can swallow the stinging cells without being stung. The cells are then carried to the slug's back, where they protect it from enemies.

POISONOUS HARPOONS

Cone shells have long, barbed teeth on their radula. They thrust one of these into their prey like a harpoon, deliver a venomous sting, then pull the impaled victim back into their mouth.

SQUIRTING INK

Octopuses, squid, and cuttlefish squirt a cloud of ink at their enemy. This allows them to escape behind a dark screen. *Heteroteuthis*, a type of deep-sea squid, squirts a cloud of luminous bacteria to dazzle its enemies.

Squid squirting ink from its syphon

SAFETY IN SHELLS

Many molluscs, including gastropods and bivalves, retreat into their shell if danger threatens.

MOLLUSC FACTS

• The ink squirted by cuttlefish was the original sepia colouring used by artists.

• Several species of cone shell can kill a human with their sting.

• The Mediterranean fan mussel *(Pinna nobilis)* anchors itself to the sea bed with strong, golden-brown threads. These threads were once used to make "cloth of gold".

CHANGING COLOUR

Squid, octopuses, and cuttlefish can change colour in less than a second to blend in with their surroundings. They also change colour to indicate their mood. Male cuttlefish turn black with anger; octopuses turn white with fear, and blue with rage.

Cuttlefish with mottled brown and white colouring

The same cuttlefish has turned red. It is probably signalling to another cuttlefish.

MOLLUSC SHELLS

Mollusc shells are made of layers of calcium carbonate secreted from the mantle. They form in a huge variety of shapes, sizes, patterns, and colours.

Pacific thorny oyster

West African margin shells

Cockle shells

Royal cloak scallop

Marlinspike auger

Nautilus: the only cephalopod with a true external shell

Rose-branch murex

Limpet

Cuban land snail

Elephant tusk shell

Lammellose ormer

HOW PEARLS FORM

Some molluscs form pearls in their shells. Oyster pearls are highly valued.

1 A tiny piece of grit or a parasite lodges in the oyster's shell, causing irritation.

2 The oyster secretes mother-of-pearl (nacre) around the cause of irritation.

3 The pearl breaks free of the shell, removing the source of irritation.

Oyster shell

Pearl

PRIZE EYES

The giant Atlantic squid has the largest eyes of any animal in the world, each with a diameter of more than 40cm (15.7in).

MOLLUSC RECORDS

LARGEST MOLLUSC and the largest invertebrate (see p.84), is the giant Atlantic squid *(Archteuthis)*, which can grow up to 20m (66ft) long.

LARGEST BIVALVE MOLLUSC is the giant clam, which can weigh over 300kg (661lb): the equivalent of three large humans.

SMALLEST MOLLUSC is the gastropod *Ammonicera*, which is only 1mm (0.04in) long.

LONGEST SHELL was over 5m (16.4ft) long. It belonged to a prehistoric cephalopod.

LARGEST LAND SNAIL is the giant African land snail, which can grow up to 39cm (15.4in) from snout to tail.

It has taken just over one minute for this *Euglandina* snail to crawl along the bottom of these two pages.

INSECTS

THERE ARE MORE species of insect than of any other group of animals on Earth. For every human, there are an estimated 200 million insects. Insects live just about everywhere, including polar lands, deserts, rainforests, and even in pools of petrol.

PORTRAIT OF AN INSECT

Insects have three distinct body regions: the head, the thorax, and the abdomen. They have six jointed legs, and a tough outer skeleton called an exoskeleton. Most insects have wings at some stage during their life.

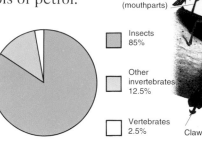

Antenna (feeler)

Thorax (middle section of the body)

Exoskeleton

Wing

Compound eye

Abdomen (rear part of the body)

Insects have no veins: blood flows freely around the body.

Foregut

Midgut

Heart

Ovary (reproductive organ)

Brain

Mandibles (mouthparts)

Anus

Ovipositor (egg-laying tool)

Hindgut

Ventral nerve cord

Air enters through holes (spiracles) in the insect's sides and goes directly to muscles and organs.

Katydid (female)

PROPORTION OF INSECTS

Insects make up about 85% of all the animal species on Earth.

Insects 85%

Other invertebrates 12.5%

Vertebrates 2.5%

Claw

TYPES OF INSECT

There are over a million known species of insect, with perhaps 30 million still to be discovered. They are grouped into 32 orders (see p.72), including those illustrated below.

Mayflies
(Ephemeroptera)
2,000 species

Dragonflies
(Odonata)
5,000 species

Grasshoppers, crickets
(Orthoptera)
20,000 species

Stick and leaf insects
(Phasmida)
2,500 species

Earwigs
(Dermaptera)
1,500 species

Cockroaches
(Blattodea)
3,700 species

Praying mantids
(Mantodea)
1,800 species

Termites
(Isoptera)
2,300 species

Biting lice
(Mallophaga)
2,700 species

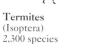

Bugs
(Hemiptera)
82,000 species

Beetles
(Coleoptera)
300,000 species

Ants, bees, and wasps
(Hymenoptera)
110,000 species

Butterflies and moths
(Lepidoptera)
136,800 species

Flies
(Diptera)
98,500 species

Fleas
(Siphonaptera)
1,800 species

LIFE CYCLES

The series of changes an insect goes through during its life is called its metamorphosis.

Complete metamorphosis: butterfly

Winged adult emerges from pupa

Egg

Young hatches as larva (grub)

Larva changes into pupa

Larva moults to grow larger

Incomplete metamorphosis: grasshopper

Winged adult emerges from final moult

Egg

Young hatches as wingless nymph

Nymph resembles adult

Nymph moults to grow larger

MOULTING

A young insect's tough exoskeleton cannot stretch, so the insect has to moult (shed its skin) several times in order to grow. The sequence below shows the final moult of a damselfly, as it changes from nymph to adult.

Two hours after leaving the water, the nymph has become an adult damselfly. Its old skin is left behind on the stalk.

Damselfly nymphs live under water, but climb out when they are ready to become adults.

The skin has split along the back of the thorax, and the adult head has emerged.

The young adult grips the plant stem and pulls itself up and away from its old skin.

It will take a few more days for the damselfly to develop its brilliant adult colours.

INSECT FACTS

• If all the animals on Earth were weighed, ants would make up 10% of the total.

• Queen termites can lay one egg per second for more than 14 years. This gives a total of more than 440,000,000 babies from one queen.

• A bee must visit over 4,000 flowers to make one tablespoon of honey.

["\n\n"]

INSECT WINGS

Wings enable an insect to escape from predators, and to fly to new areas in search of food.

Moth wing

Dragonfly wing

Beetle forewing (elytron)

INSECT VISION

An insect's compound eyes are made up of hundreds of individual lenses.

Dragonflies have the largest eyes of any insect.

INSECT RECORDS

LOUDEST INSECTS
are cicadas, which can be heard up to 400m (1,312ft) away.

FASTEST-FLYING INSECTS
are dragonflies, which have been recorded flying at speeds of over 50km/h (31mph).

FASTEST-RUNNING INSECT
is the American cockroach (*Periplaneta americana*), which can run at speeds of almost 5km/h (3mph).

GIANT DRAGONFLY
The biggest insect ever to have lived was a prehistoric dragonfly. It had a wingspan of 75cm (29.5in): about the same as a kestrel's.

DEFENCE AND ATTACK

Insects have developed many ways of defending themselves against enemies. These include camouflage, stinging, and squirting noxious chemicals. In several cases these methods are also useful for attacking prey.

CAMOUFLAGE
Many insects are so well-camouflaged that they are almost impossible for predators to spot. The green markings of this Javanese leaf insect (*Phyllium bioculatum*), complete with holes and brown edges, make it look just like a dying leaf.

The insect curls its body, completing its leafy disguise.

Imitation leaf midrib

Imitation leaf vein

When the Javanese leaf insect sits on a twig or branch, it blends in completely with its leafy surroundings.

Real leaf

INSECT HOMES

Bees, wasps, termites, and ants are the only insects that build permanent homes. These range from a simple hole in the ground to complex termite mounds up to 12m (39ft) high.

Common wasps (Vespula vulgaris) *build their nests from chewed-up wood fibres.*

This umbrella-shaped mound is home to the African termites Cubitermes.

Inside wasps' and bees' nests are combs of cells. A single larva develops in each cell.

HELPFUL INSECTS
BEES
Bees pollinate many types of crops, and produce honey (the first sweetener used by humans) and beeswax.

SILK MOTHS
Silk is produced from the cocoon (pupa) of the silk moth *Bombyx mori*. Each cocoon produces a thread of silk that may be over 1km (0.6 miles) long.

DUNG BEETLES
Dung beetles were introduced to Australia to eat the large amounts of dung produced by cattle.

HARMFUL INSECTS
FLEAS AND FLIES
Diseases carried by fleas and flies have caused more than half of all human deaths since the Stone Age.

BODY LICE
More than 3,800 body lice can live on one person. In unhygienic situations they can transmit disease.

KILLER BEES
An aggressive type of African honey bee (*Apis mellifera adansonii*) attacks humans without provocation. More than 300 people have been killed.

The orchid mantis (*Hymenopus coronatus*) is camouflaged as an orchid flower.

CHEMICALS
Ants squirt stinging formic acid from their abdomen at enemies.

STINGING
Wasps and bees defend themselves by delivering a painful sting.

MIMICRY
The hover fly's colours resemble the warning stripes of wasps. This may put off predators.

INSECT SIZES
Insects range from tiny wasps smaller than a full stop, to beetles as big as a human hand. (The insects below are not shown actual size.)

SMALLEST INSECTS
are fairyfly wasps, which measure only 0.2mm long.

HEAVIEST INSECTS
are the goliath beetles (*Goliathus*), which weigh up to 110g (3.9oz): about the same as an apple.

LONGEST INSECT
is the giant stick insect (*Pharnacia serratipes*), which measures up to 45cm (17.7in) from leg tip to leg tip.

Giant stick insect's leg, actual size

LARGEST WING-SPAN
is that of the owlet moth (*Thysania agripina*), which measures up to 30cm (12in) across.

ARACHNIDS

SOME OF THE world's least loved animals are arachnids. They include spiders, scorpions, ticks, and mites. Most arachnids live on land. They are found all over the world in almost every habitat: there is even a species of spider that lives high on Mount Everest.

TYPES OF ARACHNID

There are more than 73,000 species of arachnid, divided into ten orders (see p.72). Six orders are illustrated below.

Scorpions
(Scorpiones)
2,000 species

Whip scorpions
(Uropygi)
60 species

Camel spiders
(Solifugae)
900 species

Harvestmen
(Opiliones)
4,500 species

Mites and ticks
(Acari)
30,000 species

Spiders
(Araneae)
40,000 species

SPIDER ATTACK

All spiders are carnivorous (meat-eating), feeding mainly on insects and other spiders. They are skilful hunters, and have developed ingenious ways of capturing prey. After trapping a meal, they paralyze it with venom, then wrap it in silk.

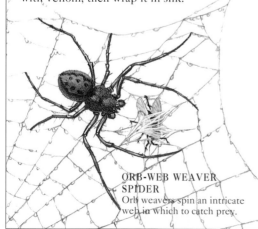

ORB-WEB WEAVER SPIDER
Orb weavers spin an intricate web in which to catch prey.

PORTRAIT OF AN ARACHNID

Arachnids have eight legs, and their body is divided into the cephalothorax (front and middle), and the abdomen (rear). They have a pair of leg-like or pincer-like pedipalps for feeling and feeding.

Pedipalp
Abdomen
Tail
Simple eye
Exoskeleton (outer skeleton)
Cephalothorax
Poison gland
Sting

Simple eye
Heart
Brain
Chela (claw of the pedipalp)
Oesophagus
Intestine
There are no veins: blood flows freely inside the body
Lung
Spiracle (air hole)
Ventral nerve cord
Claw
Muscles

Imperial scorpion
(Pandinus imperator)

LIFE CYCLE

Arachnids lay eggs that hatch into nymphs resembling adults. They moult (shed their skin) several times before they are mature. Some mites live just a few weeks; larger species of spider may live up to 30 years.

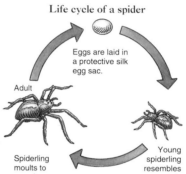

Life cycle of a spider

Eggs are laid in a protective silk egg sac.

Adult

Young spiderling resembles adult.

Spiderling moults to grow larger.

BALLOONING SPIDERS
Spiderlings can "balloon" from one area to another, travelling up to 2,000km (1,243 miles) at heights of more than 3,000m (9,843ft). They release a thread of silk from their abdomen, which is picked up by the wind.

ARACHNID RECORDS

MOST VENOMOUS SCORPION is the Israeli gold scorpion (*Leiurus quinquestriatus*).

LARGEST SPIDER WEB is spun by the tropical orb spider (*Nephila*). It measures up to 3m (10ft) across.

LARGEST ARACHNID is Leblondis' goliath bird-eating spider (*Theraphosa leblondi*): with a leg span of 28cm (11in), it can cover a dinner plate.

ARACHNID FACTS

• More people die from bee stings than from the bites and stings of all the venomous arachnids put together.

• There are more than 2 million spiders lurking in an average acre of countryside.

NET-CASTING SPIDER
The net-casting spider spins a sticky net that it holds between its front legs, ready to throw over a passing meal.

TRAPDOOR SPIDER
The trapdoor spider lives in a burrow sealed with a hinged door spun from silk. When an insect passes, it flips open the trapdoor and leaps on its prey.

JUMPING SPIDER
The jumping spider has short, strong legs, and can jump 40 times its body length. It anchors itself to the ground with a silk thread, then pounces on its prey.

BOLAS SPIDER
The bolas spider produces a scent that attracts moths, then twirls a thread of silk with a sticky blob on the end. Moths flying towards the scent are trapped on the end of the silk.

The jumping spider has excellent eyesight for keeping a lookout for prey.

CRUSTACEANS

CRUSTACEANS RANGE from tiny water fleas invisible to the human eye, to giant spider crabs with legs longer than a person. Most crustaceans are aquatic (live in water). They are found all over the world, from rivers and shorelines to the floors of the deepest oceans.

Antenna (feeler)

Antennule (feeler)

Carapace (shell)

Compound eye made up of many lenses

Cephalothorax

Common lobster (female) (*Homarus gammarus*)

Brain

Mouth

Stomach

Ventral nerve cord

Ovary (reproductive organ)

Ventral abdominal artery

Heart

Intestine

Dorsal abdominal artery

Abdomen

Anus

PORTRAIT OF A CRUSTACEAN

Most crustaceans have a body divided into three parts: the head, thorax (middle), and abdomen (rear). In some species the head and thorax are joined to form the cephalothorax. Crustaceans have two pairs of antennae, and compound eyes. The body is covered by a tough coat, called the exoskeleton.

TYPES OF CRUSTACEAN

There are more than 55,000 species of crustacean. They are grouped into eight classes (see p.72), including the four illustrated below.

Branchiopods (Branchiopoda) e.g. fairy shrimps, water fleas 1,000 species

Copepods (Copepoda) tiny marine and freshwater organisms 13,000 species

Barnacles (Cirripedia) 1,220 species

Malacostracans (Malacostraca) e.g. crabs, lobsters 30,000 species

LIFE CYCLE

Most crustaceans lay their eggs in water. After hatching, many species pass through several larval stages. Crustaceans moult (shed their skin) to grow bigger.

Life cycle of a shrimp

Adult

Egg

Egg hatches into first larval stage, called nauplius; has single eye; uses antennae for swimming.

Second larval stage, called zoea; has more appendages and two eyes.

Third stage, called mysis; uses limbs on thorax for swimming.

Final, post-larval stage, uses abdominal limbs for swimming.

CRUSTACEAN RECORDS

SMALLEST CRUSTACEANS are the water fleas *Alonella*, which grow only 0.25mm long.

HEAVIEST CRUSTACEAN is the North Atlantic lobster (*Homarus americanus*) which weighs up to 20kg (44lb).

LARGEST CRUSTACEAN is the Japanese spider crab (*Macrocheira kaempferi*): its leg span can reach nearly 4m (13ft).

Japanese spider crab

CRAB DEFENCE

Most crabs have a hardened exoskeleton, called a carapace, to protect them from predators. Many crabs also use camouflage, burrowing, and running away as effective defensive tactics.

PINCER POWER
The robber crab (*Birgus latro*) defends itself with formidable pincers. These are so strong that this crab could cut its way out of a cake tin.

RUNNING SIDEWAYS
Scuttling sideways is the fastest method of escape for many crabs. It is easier for them to enter their burrow sideways because of their body shape.

BURROWING
Many crabs, such as this ghost crab (*Ocypode*), burrow to escape predators. Their eyes may stick up above the ground, keeping a lookout for danger.

CAMOUFLAGE
Some crabs, such as this decorator crab (*Camposcia retusa*), cover their shell with plants and sea creatures to disguise themselves on the sea bed.

CRUSTACEAN FACTS

• Copepods are probably the most numerous animals on Earth, forming much of the plankton that floats in the ocean.

• The North Atlantic lobster (*Homarus americanus*) and the robber crab (*Birgus latro*) can live for over 50 years.

• Woodlice are the only crustaceans that have successfully adapted to life on land.

• A swarm of krill (malacostracans) can cover 440sq km (170sq miles) and weigh over 2 million tonnes.

• The pancarid, a type of shrimp, is only found in a single Tunisian pool the size of a bath.

SUPERSHRIMP

The mantis shrimp can deliver a blow with the same force as a small calibre rifle. It can easily punch its way out of a fish tank.

AMPHIBIANS

MOST AMPHIBIANS CAN live both on land and in water. They need a moist environment because their skin is not waterproof and they rapidly lose body water in dry conditions. Amphibians have, nevertheless, adapted to a wide range of habitats, even deserts. They are found on every continent except Antarctica.

TYPES OF AMPHIBIAN

There are more than 4,200 species of amphibian, divided into three orders (see p.72).

Frogs and toads
(Anura)
3,700 species

Caecilians
(Apoda)
170 species

Newts and salamanders
(Urodela)
350 species

AMPHIBIAN FEET

Amphibians' feet are adapted for their particular way of life. Many species have webbed feet for swimming, while others' feet enable them to burrow or climb.

The palmate newt (Triturus helveticus) has webbed feet for swimming.

The tiger salamander (Ambystoma tigrinum) has flattened feet for burrowing.

The White's treefrog (Litoria caerulea) has sticky discs on its toes for gripping leaves.

The African clawed toad (Xenopus) has webbed feet for swimming, and claws for gripping slippery surfaces.

PORTRAIT OF AN AMPHIBIAN

Amphibians are vertebrates (see p.84). Their skin has no hair or scales, and is important for keeping the correct balance of water in the body. Most adult amphibians have lungs, but can also breathe through their skin.

Brain
Vocal sac
Large bulging eyes
Eardrum
Shoulder blade (outline)
Spinal cord
Backbone
Heart
Lungs
Liver
Stomach
Kidney
Intestine

Adults can breathe through their skin.

European common toad
(*Bufo bufo*)

Frogs and toads have no tail.

LIFE CYCLE

Most amphibians lay their eggs in water. The young pass through a series of changes, called metamorphosis, before becoming adults. Lifespans range from a brief breeding season to more than 50 years for the Japanese giant salamander (*Andrias japonicus*).

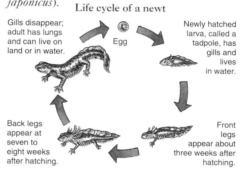

Life cycle of a newt

Gills disappear; adult has lungs and can live on land or in water.

Egg

Newly hatched larva, called a tadpole, has gills and lives in water.

Back legs appear at seven to eight weeks after hatching.

Front legs appear about three weeks after hatching.

AMPHIBIAN FACTS

• Young frogs are called froglets, and young toads are toadlets.

• Amphibian comes from the Greek words *amphi* and *bios*, meaning "double life", because amphibians can live both on land and in water.

• The smallest frog in the world, *Psyllophryne didactyla*, is smaller than a fingernail at just 10.4mm (0.41in) long.

• Poison-dart frogs are so-named because the indigenous (native) people of South America tip their arrows with their poison.

CARING FOR EGGS AND YOUNG

Many amphibians lay their eggs and then leave the young to fend for themselves. Others protect them in a variety of ways.

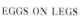

VOCAL SAC BROODER

The male Darwin's frog (*Rhinoderma*) swallows his tadpoles into his vocal sac for protection. When they become froglets, he spits them out one at a time.

CARRYING TO WATER

The poison-dart frog (*Dendrobates*) carries its newly hatched tadpoles on its back to a nearby pool or stream.

EGGS ON LEGS

The male midwife toad (*Alytes obstetricans*) wraps his string of eggs around his back legs and carries them until they are ready to hatch.

UNDER THE SKIN

The Surinam toad's (*Pipa pipa*) eggs are placed on the female's back. Her skin swells around them until they are almost covered. The young develop into toadlets under her skin, then hatch out of her back.

Eggs embedded in female toad's skin

LARGEST FROGS AND TOADS

Length is measured from the snout to the end of the body.

Common name	Scientific name	Size (approx) mm	in
Goliath frog	*Conraua goliath*	358	14
American bullfrog	*Pyxicephalus adspersus*	230	9
Cane toad	*Bufo marinus*	230	9
Rococo toad	*Bufo paracnemis*	230	9

BIG TADPOLE, LITTLE FROG

The South American paradoxical frog (*Pseudis paradoxa*) is larger when it is a tadpole than when it turns into an adult frog.

AMPHIBIAN COLOURS AND SHAPES

Amphibians have evolved a wide range of shapes and colours to suit their habitat and lifestyle. Many poisonous species are brightly coloured to warn predators to keep away, while others have colours and shapes that help them to blend in with their surroundings.

This brightly coloured golden mantella (Mantella aurantiaca) *is a poisonous frog from Madagascar.*

This South African shovel-nosed frog (Hemisus guttatus) *uses its shovel-shaped snout for burrowing.*

Mottled colouring helps disguise this South American horned toad (Ceratophrys).

The shape and colours of this Asian leaf frog (Megophrys nasuta) *resemble a dead leaf.*

The tiger salamander's (Ambystoma tigrinum) *spots are a signal to predators that it may make an unpleasant meal.*

Poison-dart frogs are the most poisonous of all amphibians. Their startling colours make them easier for enemies to spot and avoid.

The colours and shape of this Malaysian narrow-mouthed toad (Kaloula pulchra) *may fool predators into thinking it is a wet stone.*

The flattened shape of this burrowing frog (Rhinophrynus dorsalis) *helps it to slip easily through the soil.*

DEFENCE AND ATTACK

Amphibians are carnivorous (meat-eating), and many species rely on camouflage to stay hidden from prey as well as from predators. Other defensive tactics include oozing poison, looking fierce, and startling enemies.

SURPRISE

The fire-bellied toad (*Bombina bombina*) relies on its camouflage to stay hidden from enemies. But if it is attacked, the toad displays the bright warning colours on its belly, hoping that the startled predator will leave it alone.

SCARING TACTICS

If this Budgett's frog (*Lepidobatrachus asper*) is attacked, it puts on a fearsome display. It opens its mouth, screams, and makes loud grunting noises. If this performance fails to scare away the enemy, the frog may bite it.

STICKY TONGUE

Frogs have a long, sticky tongue for flicking out at prey, such as insects.

The tongue is attached to the front of the mouth.

European common frog (Rana temporaria) *attacking prey.*

LEAPING AND SWIMMING

If a frog is attacked, for example by a bird, it quickly leaps out of danger using its powerful back legs. If the frog is close to a pond or stream, it will dive into the water and swim out of the predator's reach.

LEAP FROG

The African sharp-nosed frog (*Ptychadena oxyrhynchus*) holds the frog long jump record. One individual leapt 5.35m (17.5ft) at the Calaveras County Frog Jubilee, California, in 1975.

CAMOUFLAGE

This European yellow-bellied toad (*Bombina variegata*) is almost completely hidden when it sits on a piece of bark.

Patches of green complete the toad's disguise.

Sharp rib

PRICKLY RIBS

The ribs of the Spanish sharp-ribbed salamander (*Pleurodeles waltl*) have needle-like tips. If a predator tries to eat it, the ribs pass through its skin giving the predator a sharp surprise.

Toad tries to make itself look bigger.

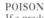

LOOKING FIERCE

This European common toad is confronting an enemy. It has puffed up its body, and is standing on its toes to make itself appear larger.

AMPHIBIAN RECORDS

LARGEST SALAMANDER
is the Japanese giant salamander, which grows up to 1.5m (5ft) long.

SMALLEST SALAMANDERS
are the Mexican lungless salamanders (*Thorius*), which grow only 14mm (0.55in) long.

MOST POISONOUS AMPHIBIAN
is the golden-yellow poison-dart frog (*Phyllobates terribilis*). The poison from the skin of a single frog could kill up to 20,000 mice.

MOST EGGS
are laid by the female cane toad (*Bufo marinus*): she can produce up to 35,000 eggs in one year.

POISON
If a predator tries to eat them, many amphibians ooze a nasty tasting poison from their skin. This should make the attacker spit them out.

If attacked, the red eft, the young form of the eastern newt (Notophthalmus viridescens), *secretes poison from special glands in its skin.*

An oriental fire-bellied toad (Bombina orientalis) *swimming away from danger.*

REPTILES

REPTILES RANGE from tiny lizards to snakes up to 10m (33ft) long. They live in oceans, lakes, rivers, and on land. All reptiles have a scaly skin. They depend on their surroundings for warmth, so they are more numerous in hot countries.

PORTRAIT OF A REPTILE

Most reptiles (excluding snakes) have four legs and a tail. Their scaly skin retains water inside the body, enabling them to live in dry, barren regions.

Nostril
Mouth
Brain
Oesophagus
Trachea (windpipe)
Heart
Lung
Liver
Stomach
Claw
Spinal cord
Small intestine
Bladder
Five toes
Kidney
Vertebral column (backbone)
Eye
Tail
Scaly skin

Eyed lizard (female)
(Lacerta lepida)

TYPES OF REPTILE

There are nearly 6,000 species of reptile, grouped into four orders (see p.72).

Lizards and snakes
(Squamata)
5,700 species

Crocodilians
(Crocodilia)
23 species

Tuatara
(Rhynochocephalia)
2 species

Turtles, tortoises, and terrapins
(Chelonia)
200 species

LIFE CYCLE

Most reptiles lay leathery-shelled eggs, although some give birth to fully developed young. Reptiles continue to grow after reaching maturity, so older individuals may reach a huge size.

Life cycle of a gecko

Egg

Gecko reaches maturity after about 18 months.

Egg hatches into young that resembles adult.

REPTILE SHELLS

Turtles, tortoises, and terrapins have a bony shell covered with horny plates or leathery skin. The shell is for protection, and often acts as a camouflage.

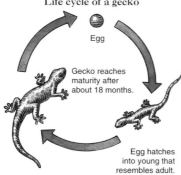

Tortoise
Tortoises usually have a strong, high-domed shell to protect the body from predators' jaws.

SLOUGHING

Snakes and lizards slough (shed) their skin from time to time, either in large flakes or in one piece. This allows them to grow, and replaces worn-out skin.

Turtle and terrapin
A turtle's shell is lighter and flatter than a tortoise's shell. The streamlined shape enables the turtle to glide through the water.

Soft-shelled turtle
These turtles have a light, flat, shell for buoyancy (floating), and for hiding in the sand and mud of the riverbed.

REPTILE SKINS

The outer layer of a reptile's skin is thickened, forming waterproof scales. These scales are composed of keratin: the same substance that hoofs, hair, and fingernails are made of.

Crocodilians
Crocodilians have a tough, armour-like skin made of rough, horny scales (scutes).
Caiman skin

Snakes
Most snakes have a smooth skin. The scales overlap so that the snake can bend easily.
Snake skin

Lizards
Lizard skins range from smooth and slippery, to rough and spiky.
Gecko skin

LONGEST SNAKE

The longest and heaviest snake in the world is the anaconda *(Eunectes murinus)*. The longest anaconda on record measured 10.26m (33.7ft): longer than a bus.

REPTILE COLOURS

CAMOUFLAGE

Many reptiles have skin colours and patterns that enable them to blend in with their surroundings, from bright green forest lizards, to dull brown desert snakes.

WARNING COLOURS

Many venomous snakes, such as the Eastern coral snake *(Micrurus fulvius)*, have bright colours to warn predators to keep away. Some harmless species have also developed these colours, to fool enemies into thinking they are dangerous.

The colours of this diadem snake *(Spalerosophis diadema cliffordi)* make it difficult to spot in its desert habitat.

The emerald tree skink *(Dasia smaragdina)* blends in with its leafy surroundings.

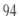

REPTILES ON THE ATTACK

Most reptiles are carnivorous (meat-eating). From deadly venom to sticky tongues and snapping jaws, they have evolved some of the most efficient methods of attack in the animal kingdom.

VENOM
Poisonous snakes, such as this green mamba (*Dendroaspis angusticeps*), kill prey by biting it, and injecting venom through their fangs.

CONSTRICTION
Pythons and boas, such as this anaconda, coil their body around their prey, slowly squeezing the animal until it suffocates.

STICKY TONGUE
Chameleons have a long tongue with a sticky tip that they shoot out at prey. The chameleon's tongue is as long as its body and tail combined.

REPTILE RECORDS

LARGEST CROCODILIAN is the saltwater crocodile (*Crocodylus porosus*), which can grow up to 6m (20ft) long.

LARGEST LIZARD is the Komodo dragon (*Varanus komodoensis*), which grows up to 3m (10ft) long.

SMALLEST REPTILE is the British Virgin Island gecko (*Sphaerodactylus parthenopion*), with a body just 18mm (0.7in) in length.

SNAPPING BEAKS
Tortoises and turtles do not have teeth: instead, they have a sharp, horny beak. Carnivorous turtles, such as snapping turtles, have strong jaws for grabbing and chopping up a passing meal.

This alligator snapping turtle (*Macroclemys*) has a pink, worm-like tongue for luring fish into its mouth.

Alligators can grow up to 50 new sets of teeth in a lifetime.

TERRIBLE TEETH
Crocodiles and their relatives have formidable sharp, pointed teeth for grabbing prey and tearing off chunks of flesh.

DEFENSIVE TACTICS

Many reptiles have developed effective ways of putting off their enemies. A predator attacking a reptile may receive an unpleasant surprise.

HISSING AND SPITTING
Cobras rear up off the ground and hiss to scare off an enemy. Most cobras inject deadly venom by biting, but spitting cobras squirt jets of venom into their attacker's eyes.

When they are alarmed, cobras spread the skin of their neck into a hood.

Monocled cobra (Naja naja kaouthia)

LOOKING FIERCE
When startled, the Australian frilled lizard (*Chlamydosaurus kingi*) erects a large, ruff-like flap of loose skin on its neck. This usually scares away the attacker.

NASTY SMELLS
The stinkpot turtle (*Sternotherus odoratus*) emits a foul-smelling yellow liquid to put off attackers.

SQUIRTING BLOOD
Some horned lizards (*Phrynosoma*) squirt drops of blood from their eyes at enemies. The blood may contain irritants.

REPTILE FACTS

• Some snakes push their windpipe out of their mouth to avoid being suffocated when swallowing a large animal.

• When a snake charmer's snake weaves to and fro, it is not dancing to the music, but following the snake charmer's movements.

• A chameleon's eyes can move independently. One eye can look up while the other looks down.

• Spitting cobras can squirt their venom up to 2.7m (9ft).

WALKING ON WATER
Basilisk lizards (*Basiliscus*) drop on to water and run across the surface on their back legs to escape from a predator.

"FLYING"
Some lizards, such as this flying dragon (*Draco volans*), escape attack by leaping and gliding from tree to tree.

DEADLIEST SNAKES

Some 50,000–100,000 people die each year from snake bites. These are some of the worse culprits.

Common name and distribution	Scientific name	No. of deaths per year (approx.)
Asian cobras (Asia)	*Naja*	15,000
Saw-scaled vipers (Asia and Africa)	*Echis*	10,000
Russell's viper (Asia)	*Daboia russelii*	5,000
Kraits (Asia)	*Bungarus*	3,000
Lance-headed vipers (Central and South America)	*Bothrops*	3,000

LOSING THE TAIL
Many lizards can shed their tail if an attacker grabs hold of it; this allows them to escape. A new tail eventually grows in its place.

This lizard has recently lost part of its tail while escaping from a predator.

Two months later the tail is growing back.

After eight months the tail has almost reached its original length.

The small vertebrae (back bones) along the lizard's tail have special weak points where the tail can break off.

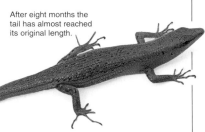

FISH

THERE IS NO SUCH thing as a typical fish: the three groups are as different from each other as a camel is from a crow. All fish live in water, although some species can spend time on land. Their habitats range from the cold, inky depths of the deepest oceans, to warm, sluggish, tropical rivers.

TYPES OF FISH
There are more than 20,000 species of fish, the vast majority of which are bony fish. Fish are divided into three classes (see p.72).

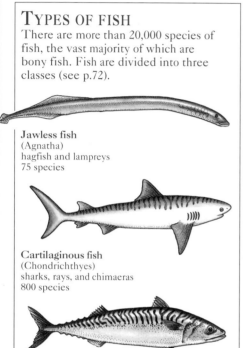

Jawless fish
(Agnatha)
hagfish and lampreys
75 species

Cartilaginous fish
(Chondrichthyes)
sharks, rays, and chimaeras
800 species

Bony fish
(Osteichthyes)
e.g. plaice, carp, cod
20,000–22,000 species

FISH RECORDS
LARGEST FISH
is the whale shark *(Rhincodon typus)*, which grows to more than 15m (50ft) long.

SMALLEST FISH
is the goby *(Pandaka pygmaea)*, which grows just 7.6mm (0.3in) long: smaller than a housefly.

FASTEST SWIMMER
is the tunny *(Thunnus)*, which has been recorded swimming at 71km/h (44mph).

SWIMMING
Fish swim by creating a series of S-shaped waves that travel along the body from head to tail.

PORTRAIT OF A FISH
Fish are vertebrates (see p.84). The most familiar and numerous are the bony fish, which have a skeleton made of bone, a swim bladder for buoyancy (floating), and a gill cover, called the operculum. Most fish are covered with scales.

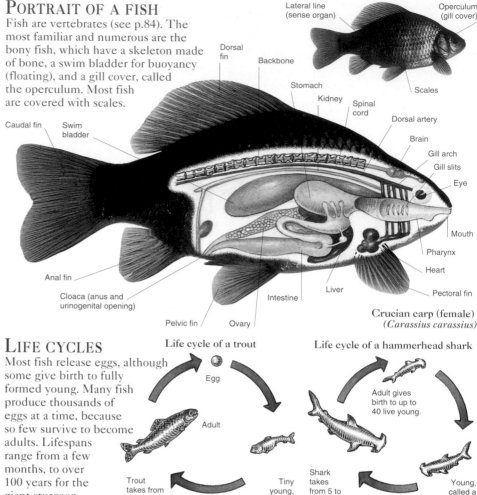

Lateral line (sense organ)
Operculum (gill cover)
Dorsal fin
Backbone
Stomach
Kidney
Spinal cord
Scales
Dorsal artery
Caudal fin
Swim bladder
Brain
Gill arch
Gill slits
Eye
Mouth
Pharynx
Heart
Anal fin
Pectoral fin
Cloaca (anus and urinogenital opening)
Intestine
Liver
Pelvic fin
Ovary

Crucian carp (female)
(Carassius carassius)

LIFE CYCLES
Most fish release eggs, although some give birth to fully formed young. Many fish produce thousands of eggs at a time, because so few survive to become adults. Lifespans range from a few months, to over 100 years for the giant sturgeon *(Huso huso)*.

Life cycle of a trout
Egg
Adult
Trout takes from 8 months to 3 years to mature, depending on species.
Tiny young, called a fry, resembles adult trout.

Life cycle of a hammerhead shark
Adult gives birth to up to 40 live young.
Young, called a pup, resembles adult, but its head projectiles are bent back.
Shark takes from 5 to 15 years to mature, depending on species.

HOW FISH BREATHE
Fish "breathe" using their gills. As water flows over the gills, oxygen passes through thin membranes (skins) into the blood.

Gill rakers sieve the water.
Pharynx (connects mouth with oesophagus).
The fish takes in water through its mouth.
Water flows out through the gill cover (operculum).
Water flows past the gills.

SMALL BEGINNINGS
An adult ocean sunfish *(Mola mola)* is about 60 million times bigger than its young: newly hatched sunfish are about 6mm (0.25in) long, while adults measure about 3m (10ft).

FISH MOVEMENT
Fish move in three dimensions: forwards and backwards; up and down; and left and right. They use different fins to control these movements.

ROLL
The fish uses its dorsal, pectoral, and pelvic fins to roll.

YAW
A combination of fin movements steers the fish to the left and right.

PITCH
The fish swivels its pectoral and pelvic fins to rise, stay level, and dive.

Dogfish
The S-shaped wave begins when the fish swings its head to the right.

First dorsal fin
Peak
Pelvic fin
The peak of the wave has travelled to the region of the pelvic and first dorsal fins.

Peak
The peak is now between the two dorsal fins, and the tail begins to thrust to the right.

Peak
The peak reaches the tail, and the head swings for the next wave.

CARING FOR YOUNG

Many fish do not look after their eggs and young, leaving them to fend for themselves. Others are caring parents, fiercely protecting their offspring from predators.

PROTECTIVE POUCH
The female seahorse lays her eggs into a special pouch on the male seahorse's body. The eggs develop inside the pouch, and are "born" when they are fully developed.

MOUTH BROODING
Many cichlids keep their eggs in their mouth while they develop. After hatching, the young usually stay in the mouth for safety, finally leaving it when they are mature enough.

PARENT NIBBLING
The common brown discus fish (*Symphysodon*) secretes a special nourishing substance from its skin for the young to nibble. They feed on their parents for about four weeks.

FISH SHAPES

Fish have evolved many different shapes to suit their particular way of life, from streamlined sharks shaped for fast swimming, to flatfish that lie motionless on the sea floor.

The John Dory (Zeus) approaches prey head-on. Its slim shape makes it difficult for the victim to spot.

FEEDING AND DIET

Fish feed in a variety of ways, depending on their diet. There are plant-eaters, meat-eaters, scavengers (feed on dead plants and animals), and parasites (see below).

FILTER FEEDING
Filter feeders, such as this paddlefish (*Polyodon spathula*), sift food from the water with their gill rakers.

Box-shaped body

Protective bony plates beneath the cowfish's skin give it a distinctive boxy shape.

TEARING TEETH
Many fish, such as this great white shark (*Carcharodan carcharias*), have razor-sharp teeth for biting chunks out of their prey.

SUCKING BLOOD
The lamprey is a parasitic fish (feeds on living things). It attaches itself to prey with a sucker, rasps at the flesh with its teeth, then sucks its blood.

Deep body

The freshwater hatchetfish "flies" for short distances above the water. Its deep body shape keeps it steady.

DEFENSIVE TACTICS

Many fish rely on camouflage to stay hidden from predators. Several species are poisonous, while the electric eel (*Electrophorus electricus*) can deliver a 500-volt shock.

The plaice's (Pleuronectes) flat shape allows it to remain almost invisible on the sea bed.

Plaice seen from above

FISH FACTS

• The basking shark (*Cetorhinus maximus*) filters about 1,500cu m (330,000 gallons) of water per hour: enough to fill 66,000 baths.

• Needlefish are the only fish that have green bones.

• It would take 2,000 gobies (smallest fish) to equal the length of a whale shark (largest fish).

• Some sharks give birth to just one live young: the first to develop inside the mother eats all the other eggs and embryos.

• In times of drought, the African lungfish (*Protopterus*) buries itself in mud. It can survive for at least three years by digesting its own muscles.

The long-nosed gar (Lepisosteus osseus) is a long, thin shape for quick dashes.

Poison is delivered through sharp spines.

PUFFING UP
When attacked, the porcupine fish inflates its body and erects its spines in the hope that it will be too large and prickly to be eaten.

POISON
More than 50 species of fish are poisonous. This lion fish (*Pterois volitans*) is one of the deadliest in the world.

CAMOUFLAGE
Some fish, such as these pipefish, look exactly like the vegetation where they make their homes.

The pipefish resembles a piece of seaweed.

FISH HABITATS

Mountain lakes and streams
Fish live at altitudes of up to 4,900m (16,000ft).

Loach: probably the highest living species

Lakes and rivers
Carp, characins, and catfish are some of the most common freshwater fish.

Upside-down catfish

Shoreline
Some species that live on the shoreline can survive for long periods out of the water.

Mudskipper

Coastal waters
In tropical coastal waters, coral reefs are home to many brightly coloured fish.

Mandarin fish

Open ocean
Many species of fish that live in the open ocean grow to a huge size.

Pacific manta ray

ON THE ATTACK

Most fish rely on speed and surprise to catch prey. Some species have developed other methods of attack.

SQUIRTING
The archer fish squirts water at its prey, knocking it into the water.

LURES
Some fish use lures to catch prey. Deep sea angler fish have a luminous organ on the end of a long, pole-like fin ray. Prey are attracted by the light, and are snapped up by the waiting fish.

Caves
Several species of cave fish have no eyes: they do not need them as they spend their lives in darkness.

Blind cave characin

Deep-ocean
Food is scarce here. Many fish have large jaws to make the most of feeding opportunities.

Gulper eel

Middle ocean depths
Light disappears and fish are fewer in deeper ocean waters.

Oarfish

BIRDS

THERE ARE MORE than 9,000 species of bird – about two for every species of mammal. All birds have feathers, and most can fly. They range in size from tiny hummingbirds, to the ostrich, which can grow one and a half times as tall as a human. Birds are found in almost all habitats.

PORTRAIT OF A BIRD

The body of a typical bird is superbly adapted for flight. The front limbs are modified to form wings, and the body is a streamlined shape. Birds have some hollow bones to keep them light.

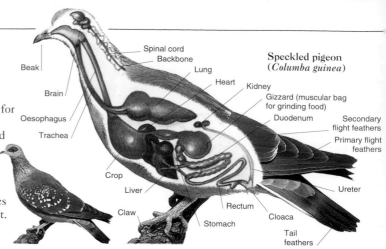

Beak
Brain
Oesophagus
Trachea
Spinal cord
Backbone
Lung
Heart
Kidney
Gizzard (muscular bag for grinding food)
Duodenum
Secondary flight feathers
Primary flight feathers
Ureter
Crop
Liver
Claw
Rectum
Stomach
Cloaca
Tail feathers

Speckled pigeon
(*Columba guinea*)

TYPES OF BIRD

The 9,000 or so known species of bird are divided into 28 orders (see p.72).

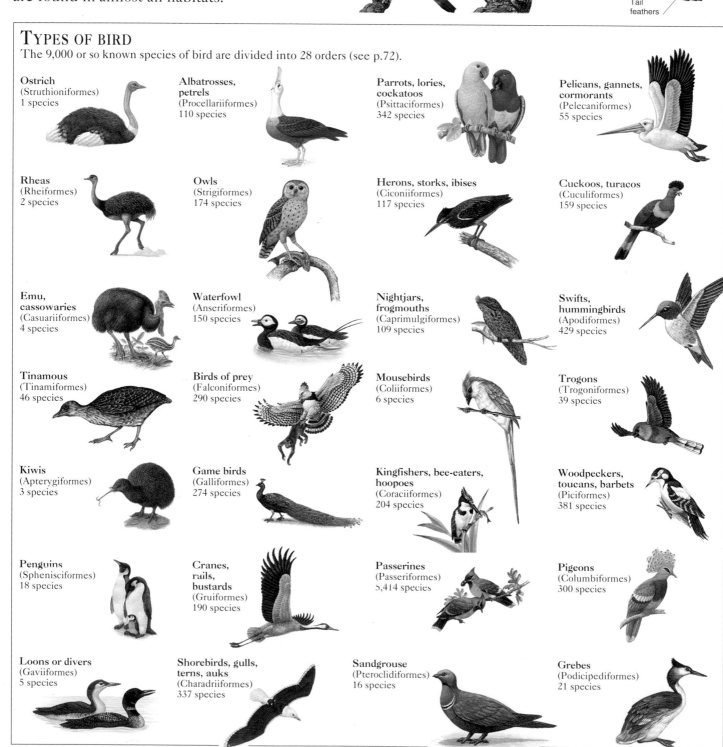

Ostrich
(Struthioniformes)
1 species

Rheas
(Rheiformes)
2 species

Emu, cassowaries
(Casuariiformes)
4 species

Tinamous
(Tinamiformes)
46 species

Kiwis
(Apterygiformes)
3 species

Penguins
(Sphenisciformes)
18 species

Loons or divers
(Gaviiformes)
5 species

Albatrosses, petrels
(Procellariiformes)
110 species

Owls
(Strigiformes)
174 species

Waterfowl
(Anseriformes)
150 species

Birds of prey
(Falconiformes)
290 species

Game birds
(Galliformes)
274 species

Cranes, rails, bustards
(Gruiformes)
190 species

Shorebirds, gulls, terns, auks
(Charadriiformes)
337 species

Parrots, lories, cockatoos
(Psittaciformes)
342 species

Herons, storks, ibises
(Ciconiiformes)
117 species

Nightjars, frogmouths
(Caprimulgiformes)
109 species

Mousebirds
(Coliiformes)
6 species

Kingfishers, bee-eaters, hoopoes
(Coraciiformes)
204 species

Passerines
(Passeriformes)
5,414 species

Sandgrouse
(Pteroclidiformes)
16 species

Pelicans, gannets, cormorants
(Pelecaniformes)
55 species

Cuckoos, turacos
(Cuculiformes)
159 species

Swifts, hummingbirds
(Apodiformes)
429 species

Trogons
(Trogoniformes)
39 species

Woodpeckers, toucans, barbets
(Piciformes)
381 species

Pigeons
(Columbiformes)
300 species

Grebes
(Podicipediformes)
21 species

LIFE CYCLE

Birds lay hard-shelled eggs which one or both parents usually incubate. The hatchlings of some species are blind and helpless, and have to be looked after for many weeks. Other species are able to leave the nest just one day after hatching. Lifespans range from 5 years for some species of hummingbird, to more than 72 years for the Andean condor (*Vultur gryphus*).

HATCHING OUT

Most types of chick are ready to hatch out of their egg a few weeks after it was laid. This sequence shows a duckling chipping its way out of its shell.

1 The duckling chips a hole in the blunt end of the shell with its special eggtooth. This tooth falls off after hatching.

2 The duckling turns as it chips, cutting a circle in its shell. It takes long rests between bursts of pecking.

3 When the circle is complete, the duckling straightens its neck to push the top of the egg away.

4 After a further push with its feet and shoulders, the duckling breaks off the end of the shell.

5 The duckling finally falls out of the egg. Its feathers are still wet.

6 Within two or three hours the duckling's soft, fluffy down feathers have dried. It will soon take to the water.

Life cycle of a moorhen (*Gallinula chloropus*)

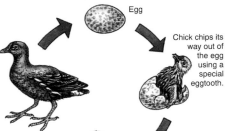

Egg

Chick chips its way out of the egg using a special eggtooth.

Young chick is covered in soft, fluffy down feathers.

After six to seven weeks the moorhen has its adult plumage and can fly.

CLOSE-UP OF A FEATHER

Feathers are strong and flexible. They are made from keratin: the same protein that hair, fingernails, and hooves contain.

Macaw feather

Shaft of feather is hollow.

Quill

Tip

Outer vane (windward edge)

Downcurved edge

Inner vane (leeward edge)

Upcurved edge

Barbs are locked tightly together to form a smooth surface.

TYPES OF FEATHER

There are four main types of feather, each with a different function.

Down feathers
These soft, fluffy feathers keep the bird warm.

Wing feathers
Strong wing feathers provide the surface the bird needs for flight.

Body feathers
Sleek body feathers emphasise the bird's streamlined shape.

Tail feathers
The bird uses its long tail feathers for steering, balance, and braking.

FEET SHAPES

Birds' feet come in many different shapes and sizes, to suit their various habitats and lifestyles.

The moorhen's long toes are widely spread, enabling the bird to walk across mud and floating vegetation.

*Water birds, such as Canada geese (*Branta canadensis*), have webbed feet to paddle through the water.*

Woodpeckers have two toes pointing forwards and two pointing backwards, to anchor them as they chip away at tree trunks.

Perching birds, such as crows, have a single hind toe that enables them to hold tightly on to branches.

Owls' legs and feet are covered in feathers to silence their approach as they swoop on prey.

The feet of birds of prey, such as hawks, are equipped with long, sharp talons for gripping prey.

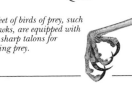

POISONOUS BIRD

The only known poisonous bird is the hooded pitohui (*Pitohui dichrous*) from New Guinea. Its skin, feathers, and internal organs contain a poison similar to that secreted by poison-dart frogs (see p.93).

WING SHAPES

Birds' wings are shaped to suit their lifestyles. They may be broad or slender; long or short.

Gulls have slender, pointed wings for gliding.

Woodpeckers have broad, rounded wings for manoeuvrability.

Geese have long, broad wings to lift their heavy body and keep it airborne.

Swifts have slender, curved wings for rapid and powerful flight.

The wings of flightless birds, such as rheas, are useless for flight.

Penguins have paddle shaped wings for swimming.

ATTRACTING A MATE

Birds go to great lengths to attract a mate. Usually, the males court the females: they may sing, dance, strut, or show off their colours to attract attention.

Display
Many birds display brightly coloured parts of the body to attract a female. The male raggiana bird of paradise (*Paradisaea raggiana*) may hang upside down as part of his display.

Presenting gifts
Some birds attract a female by presenting a gift. The male greater roadrunner (*Geococcyx californianus*) offers his mate a lizard, while the male sandwich tern (*Sterna sandvicensis*) (left) presents his with a fish.

Building a bower
Male bowerbirds build a bower to attract a mate. The male vogelkop gardener's (*Amblyornis inornatus*) bower is a complex shelter of twigs. The bower is only for attraction: after mating, the female builds her own nest in which to lay her eggs.

WIDEST WINGSPAN

The wandering albatross (*Diomedea exulans*) has the largest wingspan of any bird, measuring 3.6m (12ft) from wing tip to wing tip: greater than the length of a small car.

BIRDS' NESTS

Most birds build a nest in which to lay their eggs and rear their chicks. They range from simple scrapes, to intricately woven nests.

Simple nests
Some birds lay their eggs in a scrape in the ground. Others have no nest at all: guillemots (right) lay eggs on rocky ledges.

Burrows
Some birds, including puffins (*Fratercula arctica*) (right), nest inside a burrow.

Nests of mud
Flamingos build conical pots of sand and mud to lay their eggs in.

Woven nests
Many birds weave nests of grass, leaves, or twigs. Weaver birds build elaborate grass nests (right): the long entrance stops snakes from getting inside.

Nests of sticks
The hammerkop (*Scopus umbretta*) builds a huge, roofed nest of sticks, grass, and mud. The nest measures up to 1.5m (5ft) across.

Nests of saliva
Edible-nest swiftlets (*Collocalia fuciphaga*) build their nests from saliva. These nests are used to make birds nest soup: a food delicacy in China.

HIGH FLIER

Rüppell's griffons (*Gyps rueppelli*) are the highest flying birds. They can reach heights of 11,278m (37,000ft): as high as airliners fly.

BIRD RECORDS

LARGEST BIRD is the ostrich (*Struthio camelus*), which weighs up to 156kg (344lb), and grows up to 2.7m (8.9ft) tall.

SMALLEST BIRD is the bee hummingbird (*Mellisuga helenae*), which weighs about 1.6g (0.056oz) and grows just 5.7cm (2.24in) long.

FASTEST SWIMMER is the gentoo penguin (*Pygoscelis papua*), which can reach speeds of 27.4km/h (17mph).

MOST ABUNDANT BIRD is the red-billed quelea (*Quelea quelea*), with an adult population of about 1.5 billion. There may be up to 10 million birds in a single colony.

EGGS

The type and number of eggs a bird lays depends on its lifestyle and habitat. Some species lay just one egg; others lay several. Eggs vary widely in size and shape. Many are coloured and patterned for camouflage, making them difficult for predators, such as foxes, to spot.

The eggs of the bee hummingbird (Mellisuga helenae) are the smallest in the world, weighing only 0.25g (0.009oz).

Ostrich (Struthio camelus) eggs are the largest in the world, weighing up to 1.65kg (3.64lb), and measuring up to 20cm (8in) long.

DIETS AND BEAKS

Birds eat a huge variety of food, including meat, fish, seeds, insects, and fruit. Their beaks are adapted to suit their particular diets.

Serrated beaks
Birds do not have teeth, but some, such as mergansers (*Mergus*), have teeth-like structures on the sides of their beak. These serrations help them to catch fish.

Avocet beak
Avocets (*Recurvirostra*) have an upturned beak which they sweep from side to side to catch worms and other invertebrates in shallow estuary waters.

Fruit and nut eaters
Parrots' beaks are shaped for cracking nuts and eating fruit. The hook at the front of the beak is for tearing at fruit, and the strong base of the beak cracks open seeds.

Flamingo beak
Flamingos have a "bent" beak for sifting food from water. The tongue pumps water through fringes on either side of the bill, trapping small animals and plants.

Predators
Birds of prey, such as falcons (*Falco*), are carnivorous (meat-eating). They have a strong, hooked beak for tearing apart prey too large to be swallowed whole.

BIRD FACTS

- Hummingbirds need to eat half their body weight every day to stay alive.

- Pelican chicks can attract their parents' attention while still inside the egg: they call when they are too hot or too cold.

- Starlings are some of the best mimics in the bird world: they can mimic other birds, and even ringing telephones.

- Ostrich eggs are the largest single cells in the world.

- Once a young sooty tern (*Sterna fuscata*) takes to the wing, it may stay airborne for four years before returning to the ground to breed.

- Large birds, e.g. swans, may have more than 25,000 feathers.

- The peregrine falcon (*Falco peregrinus*) can reach speeds of 180km/h (112mph) during a stoop (dive).

FASTEST-FLYING BIRDS

Bird	Scientific name	Speed	
		km/h	mph
White-throated spine-tail swift	*Hirundapus caudacutus*	171	106
Alpine swift	*Apus melba*	160	99.4
Magnificent frigatebird	*Fregata magnificens*	159	99
Spurwing goose	*Plectropterus gambensis*	142	88
Red-breasted merganser	*Mergus serrator*	129	80

DOMESTIC BIRDS

DOMESTIC BIRDS ARE birds that are kept and bred by humans. They include chickens, ducks, and geese. Domestic birds are kept for various purposes: some are bred for their meat, eggs, or feathers; others for sports such as pigeon racing and falconry.

TURKEY FACTS
- Turkeys were first domesticated by the Aztec and Zuni Indians for food and sacrifice. They also used the feathers for decoration.
- Turkeys were first taken to Europe by the Spanish in about 1511.
- There are about 124 million domestic turkeys in the world.

CHICKEN FACTS
- Chickens were domesticated about 8,000 years ago.
- In the Middle Ages, chicken was only eaten by royalty and the aristocracy. The poor kept chickens for eggs and new chicks, and killed a hen only when it became too old to lay. Today, chicken is probably the most widely eaten meat in the world.
- Hens can lay about 250 eggs a year.

CHICKEN BREEDS
All chickens are descended from the red jungle fowl (*Gallus gallus*) of Southeast Asia, which is a member of the pheasant family. Chicken breeds are generally classified into American, Mediterranean, English, and Asian. Eight of the 150 breeds are illustrated here.

Salmon faverolle

Bantam Orpington Blue

Barred Plymouth Rock

White silky

Japanese yokohama

Silver braekel fowl

Red jungle fowl (Gallus gallus)

Turken

Mille fleur bantam

EGGSTRAORDINARY!

About 160 billion hens' eggs are laid every year in China: enough to make an omelette that would give every person in the world a piece measuring 1m (3.28ft) across.

DUCK FACT
- The Muscovy duck was first domesticated in South America by pre-Columbian Indians. The mallard (right) was domesticated in China at least 3,000 years ago.

DOMESTIC BIRD RECORDS
FASTEST EGG-LAYING CHICKEN was a white leghorn that laid 371 eggs in 364 days.

LARGEST CHICKEN'S EGG weighed 454g (16oz). It was laid by a white leghorn in Vineland, New Jersey, USA, in 1956.

MOST YOLKS in a chicken's egg was nine, laid by a hen in Mount Morris, New York, USA, in 1971.

LARGEST CHICKEN PRODUCER is the USA, which produces about 12 million tonnes of chicken meat a year.

LARGEST GOOSE EGG weighed 680g (24oz), laid by "Speckle" in Goshen, Ohio, USA.

GOOSE FACTS
- Geese were first domesticated more than 3,000 years ago.
- Goose was considered the finest poultry for festive occasions until the turkey became more popular in the 16th and 17th centuries.
- In the Middle Ages, gooseherds in Britain would drive flocks of up to 20,000 geese to be sold at goose fairs.

TYPES OF DOMESTIC BIRD

Domestic bird	Uses	Number of breeds (approx.)	Descended from
Chicken	Meat, eggs	150	Red jungle fowl (*Gallus gallus*)
Duck	Meat, eggs, down	97	Muscovy duck (*Cairina moschata*) and wild mallard (*Anas platyrhyncos*)
Goose	Meat, eggs, down	43	Most breeds from the greylag (*Anser anser*)
Turkey	Meat	33	Common turkey (*Meleagris gallopavo*)

OTHER DOMESTIC BIRDS

Racing pigeons (Columba livia) are kept for sport.

Racing pigeons are descended from the rock dove.

Guinea fowl (Numida), native to Africa and Madagascar, are now raised for their meat in many countries.

Long, tapering breast feathers

Swans are reared for their down, and as ornamental birds.

Hooked beak for tearing at prey.

Falcons are used in the sport of falconry.

Ostriches (Struthio camelus) are reared for their meat, and their decorative feathers.

Many types of bird are kept as pets. The budgerigar (Melopsittacus undulatus) is particularly popular.

The budgerigar is native to Australia.

Canaries (Serinus canaria) are kept as pets for their beautiful song.

Pheasants, native to Asia, are reared as game birds.

Pheasants have been introduced into Europe and North America.

Partridges are reared as game birds.

The partridge is native to Europe and Asia.

MAMMALS

MAMMALS RANGE IN size from tiny shrews to the blue whale – the largest animal that has ever lived on Earth. Mammals are found all over the world: on land, in oceans and rivers, and even, in the case of bats, in the air.

ARMADILLO SHELL-TER

Some ancient mammals grew to huge sizes. The ancestors of modern armadillos measured up to 3m (10ft) long. South American Indians used their shells as roofs.

PORTRAIT OF A MAMMAL

Mammals usually have fur or hair. Almost all species give birth to live young which they feed with milk produced in the female's body.

Male rabbit
(*Oryctolagus cuniculus*)

Eye

Furry skin

Tail

Pinna (ear flap) directs sounds towards inner ear.

Brain

Liver
Stomach
Kidney
Spinal cord

Gall bladder

Nasal cavity

Backbone

Colon

Ureter

Bladder

Reproductive organs

Mouth
Oesophagus
Trachea
Lung
Heart
Diaphragm

Anus

TYPES OF MAMMAL

There are more than 4,600 known species of mammal, divided into 21 orders (see p.72).

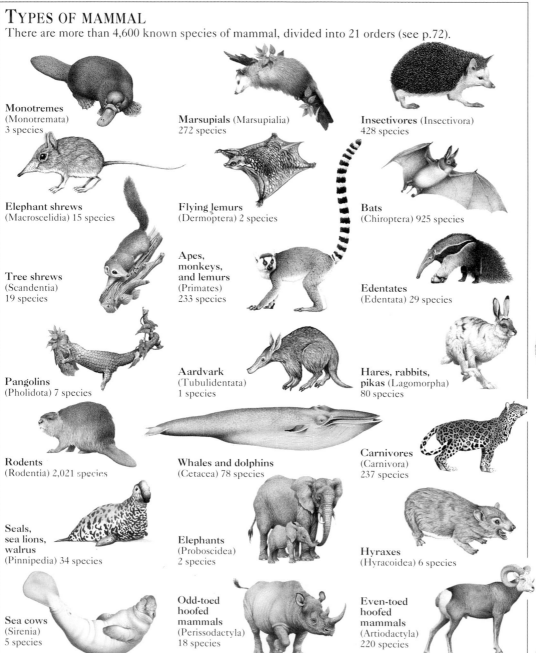

Monotremes (Monotremata) 3 species

Marsupials (Marsupialia) 272 species

Insectivores (Insectivora) 428 species

Elephant shrews (Macroscelidia) 15 species

Flying lemurs (Dermoptera) 2 species

Bats (Chiroptera) 925 species

Tree shrews (Scandentia) 19 species

Apes, monkeys, and lemurs (Primates) 233 species

Edentates (Edentata) 29 species

Pangolins (Pholidota) 7 species

Aardvark (Tubulidentata) 1 species

Hares, rabbits, pikas (Lagomorpha) 80 species

Rodents (Rodentia) 2,021 species

Whales and dolphins (Cetacea) 78 species

Carnivores (Carnivora) 237 species

Seals, sea lions, walrus (Pinnipedia) 34 species

Elephants (Proboscidea) 2 species

Hyraxes (Hyracoidea) 6 species

Sea cows (Sirenia) 5 species

Odd-toed hoofed mammals (Perissodactyla) 18 species

Even-toed hoofed mammals (Artiodactyla) 220 species

MAMMAL REPRODUCTION

EGG-LAYING MAMMALS

Monotremes are the only mammals that lay eggs. Female duck-billed platypuses (*Ornithorhynchus anatinus*) (right) incubate their eggs in a nest inside their burrow; female echidnas incubate their eggs in a pouch.

MARSUPIAL MAMMALS

Marsupials, such as kangaroos, give birth when the young are at a very early stage of development. The tiny baby crawls across its mother's belly to reach the pouch, where it latches on to a teat and feeds on milk. The baby remains in the pouch for many weeks, leaving it for longer periods as it grows older.

New-born joey (baby kangaroo) in the pouch.

PLACENTAL MAMMALS

Most mammals are placental: the young grow inside the female and receive nutrients via the placenta (a connection between the mother's and baby's blood systems). At birth, the young are physically well-developed

New-born kittens feeding on their mother's milk.

MAMMAL SKINS

FURRY SKIN
Fur and hair enable mammals to live in almost every climate. By trapping air, a furry coat, such as the Arctic fox's (*Alopex lagopus*), keeps out the cold, stops body heat from escaping, and protects the skin from wind, rain, and strong sunlight.

Arctic fox skin

CAMOUFLAGE PATTERNS
Many mammals have skins that are coloured and patterned for camouflage. This enables them to blend in with their background, hidden from enemies and prey. A jaguar's (*Panthera onca*) spots blend in with the dappled sunlight of the forest floor where it stalks its prey.

Jaguar skin

ARMOUR PLATING
Pangolins and armadillos are covered with bony plates and scales that provide a tough, armoured coat to protect them from predators. Some, such as the three-banded armadillo (*Tolypeutes*), can roll themselves up into a ball to defend their body completely.

Armadillo skin

CONFUSING PATTERNS
A zebra's (*Equus*) stripes break up its outline, making it more difficult for predators, such as lions (*Panthera leo*), to pick out one individual from the herd. This black and white pattern is particularly effective at night, protecting the herd from nocturnal hunters.

Zebra skin

NAKED SKIN
Hair or fur would slow down whales and dolphins in the water, so they have lost all but a few tufts. Naked mole rats (*Heterocephalus glaber*) have also lost their hair: it is easier for them to move forwards and backwards along a tunnel with a smooth, hairless skin.

Dolphin skin

SPINY SKIN
The hairs of hedgehogs and porcupines have developed into stiff, sharp spines that form an effective defence against predators. The European hedgehog (*Erinaceus europaeus*) has up to 5,000 spines. When it senses danger, it rolls itself up into a ball.

European hedgehog skin

LONGEST GESTATION PERIODS
The gestation period is the amount of time the young take to develop inside the mother. (Humans have a gestation period of nine months.)

Mammal	Scientific name	Gestation period
African elephant	*Loxodonta africana*	22 months
Asian elephant	*Elephas maximus*	22 months
Baird's beaked whale	*Berardius bairdii*	17 months
White rhinoceros	*Ceratotherium simum*	16 months

MAMMAL HANDS AND FEET
All early mammals probably had five fingers and toes on each hand and foot. Over time, these basic digits evolved to suit different lifestyles and habitats. Humans (*Homo sapiens*) have the five fingers and toes typical of many mammals. The colours of the various parts of a human hand (right) are repeated in the illustrations that follow, to show how those parts have developed to suit different animals' lifestyles.

Human hand
Finger bones (toe bones)
Wrist bones (ankle bones)
Palm bones (sole bones)
Lower arm bones (lower leg bones)

Cats walk on the tips of their toes. Each toe is armed with a sharp claw for catching prey.

Elephants have five toes on each foot, and a big fleshy pad to support their immense weight.

Tapirs' (Tapirus) front feet have four toes, while their back feet have three.

Gazelles have light, dainty, two-toed feet that enable them to run very fast.

Horses (Equus) have one long, strong toe on each foot, protected by a hoof.

Seals' hands and feet have evolved into large, paddle-shaped flippers for swimming.

Badgers' hands and feet are adapted for digging. They are broad and strong with wide claws.

MAMMAL RECORDS

LARGEST MAMMAL
is the blue whale (*Balaenoptera musculus*), which weighs up to 140 tonnes and grows up to 34m (111.5ft) long.

SMALLEST MAMMAL
is the Kitti's hog-nosed bat (*Craseonycteris thonglongyai*), which weighs only 1.5g (0.05oz) and is about the size of a large bumblebee.

Kitti's hog-nosed bat and bumblebee, shown actual size.

TALLEST MAMMAL
is the giraffe (*Giraffa camelopardalis*), which grows up to 5.9m (19.4ft) tall: more than three times the height of an adult human.

FASTEST SWIMMER
is the sei whale (*Balaenoptera borealis*), which can swim at speeds of up to 48km/h (29.8mph).

MAMMAL FACTS
• Some types of traditional Chinese warrior armour were based on the protective overlapping scales of the pangolin's skin.

• There are only two types of poisonous mammal: the duck-billed platypus, which injects poison through a sharp spur on its ankle; and some shrews, which paralyze the earthworms they feed on with poisonous saliva.

BIG HOUSE ON THE PRAIRIE
Black-tailed prairie dog (*Cynomys ludovicianus*) colonies can cover huge areas. A colony in Texas had an area of about 62,160sq km (24,000 sq miles): twice the size of Belgium.

TUSKS, HORNS, AND ANTLERS
Some mammals have antlers, horns, or tusks, that are used mainly for fighting and establishing dominance within their social group. Antlers are shed and regrown each year; horns grow steadily throughout an animal's life. Tusks are elongated, pointed teeth.

Black rhino (Diceros bicornis) horn

Elephant tusks grow about 17cm (7in) per year.

Red deer (Cervus elephus) antlers

Indian blackbuck (Antilope cervicapra) horn

MAMMAL TAILS

Most mammals have a tail. Tails have a variety of uses, including swatting flies, communication, and providing warmth.

The flying squirrel uses its flattened tail as a rudder for steering as it leaps from tree to tree. The tail also acts as an air brake.

A horse's (Equus) tail is made of many long, thick hairs. It is used mainly to keep flies and other pests away.

Some animals, for example spider monkeys (Ateles), have a prehensile tail that can grip branches like a fifth limb. This prehensile possum tail has scaly skin at the tip to give the animal a firm grip.

The fallow deer's (Dama dama) tail is dark on top and white underneath. If danger threatens, the deer holds up its tail to flash a warning to the other deer in the herd.

Elephants have wiry hair at the end of their tail. They sometimes hold each other's tails when walking along in single file.

Beavers use their flat, scaly tail as a rudder when swimming. They also slap it down on the water as a warning signal to other beavers when danger threatens.

Ring-tailed lemurs (Lemur catta) use their striped tail for signalling, and for spreading around their scent to establish dominance over other lemurs.

Foxes wrap their bushy tail around their body to keep warm. They also use their tail to signal to others in their family group.

Rats have a long, hairless, and scaly tail that they use for balance.

MAMMAL RECORDS

SHORTEST GESTATION PERIOD is that of the brindled bandicoot *(Isoodon macrourus)*. The young of this marsupial are born into the pouch after an average of just 12.5 days.

MOST TEATS are found on the common tenrec *(Tenrec ecaudatus)*, which has 29.

DEEPEST DIVER is the sperm whale *(Physeter macrocephalus)*, which can dive to depths of 1,200m (3,937ft) or more.

LONGEST LIFE-SPANS are those of the Asian elephant *(Elephas maximus)*, at up to 90 years, and humans *(Homo sapiens)*, at up to 120 years.

LARGEST ELEPHANT TUSK was 3.45m (11.3ft) long, and weighed 117kg (259lb).

LARGEST PRIMATE is the gorilla *(Gorilla gorilla)*, which weighs up to 220kg (485lb).

MAMMAL FACT

• The vampire bat *(Desmodus rotundus)* is the only mammal that lives on nothing but blood. In the 10 minutes or so it spends feeding on its victim, it can drink more than its own body weight in blood. The bat becomes so heavy that it is unable to fly for a while afterwards.

MAMMAL MOVEMENT

Most mammals walk and run on all fours. Some species have developed other ways of moving more suited to their habitat.

FLYING
Bats are the only mammals that can fly, although some, such as flying squirrels, can glide for long distances when leaping between trees.

SWIMMING
Many mammals can swim. Some, for example whales and dolphins, spend their entire life in the water.

BRACHIATION
Apes and monkeys swing through trees using their long arms. This method of movement is called brachiation. Gibbons *(Hylobytes)* can cover more than 3m (9.8ft) in a single swing.

BOUNDING
Kangaroos bound along when they need to move quickly. Their tails help them to balance. Some small rodents, for example jerboas, also move around by bounding.

BURROWING
Some mammals, such as moles, spend all their time under ground. Moles have broad front paws for burrowing, and strong hind legs for bracing themselves against tunnel walls.

FASTEST MAMMALS

Common name	Scientific name	Maximum speed km/h	mph
Cheetah	*Acinonyx jubatus*	105	65
Pronghorn antelope	*Antilocapra americana*	86	53
Mongolian gazelle	*Procapra gutturosa*	80	50
Springbok	*Antidorcas marsupialis*	80	50
Grant's gazelle	*Gazella granti*	76	47
Thomson's gazelle	*Gazella thomsoni*	76	47
European hare	*Lepus capensis*	72	45
Horse	*Equus*	70	43

FELINE PECKISH

A man-eating tiger *(Panthera tigris)* in Champawat district, India, was reputed to have killed 436 people. It was shot in 1907.

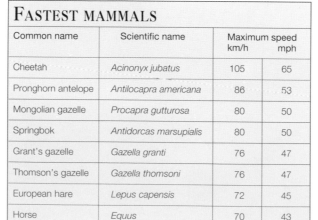

DOMESTIC MAMMALS

DOMESTIC MAMMALS are mammals that are kept and bred by humans. They include sheep, cattle, dogs, and cats. Many domestic mammals have been selectively bred over hundreds of years: today some breeds look and behave very differently from their wild counterparts.

TYPES OF DOMESTIC MAMMAL

Domestic mammal	Uses	Number of breeds (approx)
Sheep (Ovis aries)	Meat, wool	300
Llama (Llama glama)	Transport (pack animal), meat, wool, hides, dried dung for fuel, tallow for candles	2
Goat (Capra)	Milk, meat, cheese, hair, leather	300
Pig	Meat, leather	180
Cattle	Meat, milk and dairy products, leather, transport	280
Cat (Felis catus)	Pets, pest control	110
Dog (Canis familiaris)	Pets, working dogs, sports dogs	186
Buffalo	Milk, butter, transport	32
Bactrian camel (Camelus bactrianus)	Transport, wool, milk, hides, meat, dried dung for fuel (as for Bactrian camel)	3
Arabian camel (Camelus dromedarius)		4
Horse, donkey, mule (Equus)	Sport and leisure, transport, meat	100 (horse)

DOMESTIC MAMMAL RECORDS

LARGEST DOG BREED is the St. Bernard, which can weigh up to 77kg (170lb).

SMALLEST DOG BREED is the chihuahua, which weighs as little as 0.45kg (1lb).

COUNTRY WITH THE MOST SHEEP is Australia, which has about 167,781,000 individuals.

COUNTRY WITH THE MOST CATTLE is India, which has about 197,300,000.

COUNTRY WITH THE MOST CAMELS is Somalia, which has about 6,855,000 individuals.

SMALLEST CAT BREED is the Singapura, which weighs as little as 1.81kg (4lb).

LARGEST CAT BREEDS include the ragdoll : males can weigh up to 9.07kg (20lb).

Chihuahua   *St. Bernard*

Singapura

Ragdoll

EVOLUTION OF THE DOMESTIC DOG

Dogs were the first mammals to be domesticated. They were tamed by humans about 12,000 years ago. Every breed of dog is descended from the wolf (Canis lupus). This illustration shows the possible wolf ancestors of various dog breeds.

Gun dogs
Spaniels
Guard dogs
Hounds
Herding dogs
Greyhounds
Indian wolf
Feral dogs
Terriers
European wolf
Canis lupus
Chinese wolf
Oriental spaniels
European toy dogs
North American wolf
Oriental toy dogs
European spitz dogs
Oriental spitz dogs
Eskimo spitz dogs

CAT FACTS

• Cats were sacred to the ancient Egyptians. Many dead cats were mummified, and the Egyptians shaved off their eyebrows to mourn the loss of a cat.

• In 1951, a cat called Sugar travelled 2,414km (1,500 miles) to Oklahoma to rejoin the Woods family who had left him behind in California.

PIG FACTS

• Pigs are the most common provider of meat in China.

• In parts of Melanesia (see p.355), pigs are treated as members of the family.

• Pigs are often thought of as dirty animals, but in fact they keep themselves cleaner than most other domestic animals.

• Many Oceanic (see pp.352–53) peoples measure their wealth in terms of the number of pigs they own.

HORSES FOR COURSES

Every Thoroughbred racehorse is said to have descended from three desert stallions: the Darley Arabian, the Godolphin Barb, and the Byerly Turk. These stallions were taken to England between 1689 and 1724.

SHEEP FACTS

• The finest sheep's wool comes from the merino sheep.

• Astrakhan fur comes from the karakul sheep of central Asia.

• Parchment, an early type of writing paper, was made from untanned sheep hide.

MULE FACTS

• Mules are produced by crossing a donkey (Equus asinus) with a female horse. Mules are surer-footed and more intelligent than horses, but cannot reproduce.

• At one time there were many different types of mules, including draft mules, farm mules, sugar mules, cotton mules, and mining mules.

Mule: a cross between a donkey and a mare (female horse)

CATTLE FACTS

• There are about 1.21 billion cattle worldwide: more than the human population of China.

• Cattle are descended from the auroch, which once roamed across Asia and Europe. The last auroch died in 1627.

• Kenyan Masai warriors live almost entirely on blood and milk from their cattle.

ANIMAL SENSES AND BEHAVIOUR

ANIMALS HAVE EVOLVED senses and patterns of behaviour that ensure the survival of their species. Many animals have senses that are more highly developed than a human's.

COURTSHIP BEHAVIOUR

Female animals select the best available mate in order to produce strong and healthy offspring. To attract a female, male animals have evolved a fascinating range of courtship behaviour, including strutting, singing, and presenting gifts to the female.

To court a female, the peacock (Pavo cristatus) fans out and shakes his colourful tail.

ANIMAL SENSES

Many animals have excellent sight and hearing. Some have "sixth" senses that can detect magnetism, electricity, and even infra-red radiation.

An eagle's eyes see a magnified picture at the centre of its field of vision.

Many animals, e.g. foxes, can hear higher frequency sounds than humans.

Many mammals, e.g. dogs, have a highly developed sense of smell.

Sensitive whiskers help animals such as cats to find their way in the dark.

An invertebrate's antennae touch, taste, and smell its surroundings.

Spiders and scorpions have sensitive hairs that can detect the slightest air movements.

Fish have a lateral line: a row of sensitive pits that detect movements in the water.

Bats navigate by echolocation: they emit squeaks, and judge distances by how long the squeaks take to bounce back.

Sharks have sensors around their head that pick up electrical fields produced by prey.

Some migratory animals may navigate by sensing the Earth's magnetic field.

Pit vipers "see" an infra-red picture of their prey by detecting heat radiation given off by its body.

ATTACK AND DEFENCE BEHAVIOUR

Animals use a wide variety of attack and defence tactics. Attack strategies include stalking and pouncing; defensive tactics include stinging, and oozing poison.

The caracal (Lynx caracal) leaps into the air to catch birds.

Bombardier beetles (Brachinus) spray their attackers with hot, unpleasant chemicals.

SENSES AND BEHAVIOUR FACTS

• Net-casting spiders' eyes are 19 times more sensitive than a human's.

• The blue whale's (Balaenoptera musculus) call is the loudest noise made by any animal. It can travel up to 1,600km (1,000 miles).

FAKE SNAKE

Some animals mimic others to defend themselves. This Costa Rican moth caterpillar fools predators into thinking it is a poisonous snake.

TERRITORIAL BEHAVIOUR

Animals may fiercely defend their territory so that others cannot steal their food or harm their young. To let other animals know where their territorial boundaries lie, animals call, mark trees and bushes with scent, or leave piles of droppings.

A cheetah (Acinonyx jubatus) marking its territory.

• The mallee fowl's (Leipoa ocellata) beak acts as a thermometer. The bird incubates its eggs in a heap of rotting vegetation, checking the temperature with its beak.

• A hibernating mammal's body can be up to 32°C (90°F) below its normal temperature.

SOCIAL BEHAVIOUR

Animals that live in communities, such as chimpanzees *(Pan troglodytes)* and lions *(Panthera leo)*, have a social hierarchy ("pecking order"). This is reinforced in various ways.

Wolves use facial expressions to establish hierarchy, and cower in front of dominant members of the pack.

Herds of elephants are dominated by an elderly female: the matriarch. She keeps order and decides where the herd will go.

Matriarch

Herd is made up of adult females and young.

Young male

Six-year-old female

SURVIVING HEAT AND COLD

HIBERNATION

Many animals in cold climates hibernate to survive the harsh conditions and lack of food that winter brings. Their body temperature drops, their heartbeat slows down, and they go into a deep sleep, surviving on food reserves stored in the body.

AESTIVATION

Some animals aestivate to survive hot and dry periods, becoming sluggish or dormant until favourable conditions return. Many desert animals aestivate.

Dormice in cold countries hibernate for up to nine months of the year.

These snails are collecting together on grass stems ready to aestivate.

USING TOOLS

Some animals use tools to obtain food, e.g. chimpanzees poke twigs into termite mounds, and Egyptian vultures (Neophron percnopterus) throw stones at eggs to break them.

Sea otters (Enhydra lutris) smash sea urchins and shellfish on a stone which they place on their stomach.

MIGRATION AND HOMES

WHEN WINTER approaches, many animals migrate to warmer climates. Others rely on their homes to protect them from harsh conditions. Some animals live alone, while others live in pairs or in large, complex communities.

NAVIGATION

It is still a mystery how some migrating animals find their way. Most species probably use a combination of methods, including navigation by the Sun and stars, and using an inherited mental map.

Sight
Many birds can recognize physical features such as coastlines, mountain ranges, and deserts.

Using Earth's magnetic field
Some animals, e.g. monarch butterflies (*Danaus plexippus*) may navigate using a magnetic sense.

Smell
Atlantic salmon (*Salmo salar*) return to the river in which they hatched. They navigate by smell.

ANIMAL HOMES

Some animals do not build homes: they simply find a tree hole, perch on a branch, or hide under a stone for protection. Others construct intricate nests or burrows.

ANIMAL HOME NAMES

Animal	Description of home	Name of home
Squirrel	Nest of twigs	Drey
Badger	Underground chambers	Sett
Eagle	Nest of twigs	Eyrie
Rabbit	Burrow	Warren
River otter	Burrow in river bank	Holt

TYPES OF ANIMAL HOME

Nests
Many animals, including birds, mice, and ants, build nests. They use various materials such as twigs, mud, leaves, and hair.

Burrows
A burrow is a hole or tunnel dug by one or more animals. It may be a simple hole in the ground, or a complex network of tunnels and chambers, such as a rabbit warren.

Mounds
Termite colonies build complex mounds from mud. These structures have galleries, turrets, and towers, and even built-in air conditioning.

Termite mound

Pots
Potter wasps build tiny pots of mud to lay their eggs in. They build one pot for each egg.

Potter wasp's pot

Tree holes and caves
Many animals take advantage of ready-made homes, e.g. owls use tree holes, and bears often use caves.

Rabbit warren

KEY

← Blue whale 20,000km (12,500 miles)	← Monarch butterfly 5,600km (3,500 miles)
← Arctic tern 40,000km (24,855 miles)	← Green turtle over 2,000km (1,243 miles)
← Caribou 2,250 km (1,400 miles)	← Atlantic salmon over 2,000km (1,243 miles)

MIGRATION RECORDS

FURTHEST BIRD MIGRATION
and the longest migration of any animal, is that of the Arctic tern (*Sterna paradisaea*) (see map).

FURTHEST MAMMAL MIGRATION
is undertaken by the blue whale (*Balaenoptera musculus*) (see map).

LOADS OF LEMMINGS

Norway lemmings (*Lemmus lemmus*) migrate when population explosions occur. Their huge numbers stop traffic and trains. When they reach the coast, some swim out to sea and drown, hence the tales of lemming "mass suicides".

MIGRATION

Many animals migrate to avoid the cold weather and lack of food that winter brings. Some species migrate a few kilometres from high ground to low; others travel vast distances across continents and oceans.

FURTHEST INSECT MIGRATION
is undertaken by the painted lady butterfly (*Cynthia cardui*), which flies up to 8,500km (5,282 miles) a year. (This is not marked on the map, as it does not follow a set route).

ANIMAL RELATIONSHIPS

SOLITARY ANIMALS
The giant panda (*Ailuropoda melanoleuca*) spends most of its life alone, only meeting up for mating.

PAIRS AND FAMILIES
Golden eagles (*Aquila chrysaetos*) spend their life with the same mate, raising a family each year.

LARGE GROUPS
Meerkats (*Suricata suricatta*), a type of mongoose, live in large colonies with a complex social structure.

MUTUALISM
Some different species live together for mutual benefit: oxpeckers are picking ticks off this warthog.

COMMENSALISM
Two species may live together but only one benefits: this crab carries stinging anemones for protection.

PARASITISM
Parasites live in or on another species, causing it harm: this flea is sucking its host's blood.

ANIMAL COLONY FACT

• Australia's Great Barrier Reef is the largest structure in the world made by living things. It is more than 2,300km (1,429 miles) long, and has taken about 800 million years to build.

BEAVER DAM

Beavers dam a river, then construct their lodge on the shore, or on an island in the middle of the lake.

Upstream side of the dam is plastered with mud to make it watertight.

Winter food store

The only way into the lodge is through a tunnel that opens under water.

Lodge is a dome of branches, reeds and mud. The living chamber is inside.

Reed warbler's nest

FOOD CHAINS AND WEBS

A FOOD CHAIN shows how energy, in the form of food, passes from one living thing to another. At each chain's base is a primary producer – an organism that can make its own food. Most primary producers are plants.

FOOD CHAIN

Plant plankton is the primary producer at the bottom of this chain. When it is eaten, the plankton's energy is passed on to the next organism in the chain.

Plant plankton (microscopic water plants) use sunlight to produce energy.

Animal plankton eat plant plankton.

Insect larvae eat plankton.

Bears eat fish.

Fish eat insect larvae.

FOOD WEB

This illustration shows how the above food chain links with others to form the food web of a North American lake community. The arrows link each living thing to the organism that eats it, beginning with plankton at the bottom, and ending with carnivores (meat-eaters) at the top.

Bears

Otters

Beavers

Frogs

Beetles

Birds

Fish

Water plants

Freshwater molluscs

Freshwater shrimps

Insect larvae

Animal plankton

Plant plankton

ENERGY PYRAMID

About 90% of the energy a living thing takes in as food is used to make its body work. Only the remaining 10% is built into the body itself, and is therefore passed on to the next organism along the food chain. This means there is very little energy left towards the top of the food chain.

Trophic level 4

Energy loss

Trophic level 3

Energy loss

Trophic level 2

Trophic level 1

Only about 10% of energy is passed on to the next trophic level.

The amount of energy received by each successive link in the food chain decreases towards the top.

The various levels of an energy pyramid are called trophic levels.

Primary producers

POISONS IN THE FOOD CHAIN

Poisons, such as pesticides, are taken in by organisms at the lower end of a food chain. These poisons pass up the chain, and may eventually build into high concentrations in animals at the top of the chain. The process of poison building up in a food chain is called bioaccumulation.

Pesticides are sprayed on to crops to kill insect pests.

Small amounts of poison on each seed build up into larger amounts inside the bodies of seed-eating birds.

A bird of prey eats several seed-eating birds. Poison from all these birds collects in the bird of prey's body.

PRIMARY PRODUCTIVITY

The longest food chains occur where the amount of organic matter made by primary producers (primary productivity) is high. This table shows the primary productivity of various habitats.

Habitat	Primary productivity (grams of dry plant material per sq metre per year)
Coral reef	2,500
Tropical rainforest	2,200
Temperate forest	1,250
Savannah	900
Cultivated land	650
Open sea	125
Semi-desert	90

FOOD CHAIN FACTS

• The majority of food chains have three or four links.

• The only food chains that do not obtain energy from sunlight are those at deep sea vents, which derive energy from volcanic activity (see p.48).

TOXIC WHALES

Over the last 40 years, pollutants in Canada's St. Lawrence River have built up in the food chain, at the top of which is the beluga whale (*Delphinapterus leucas*). Chemicals are now so concentrated in these whales that, when they die, they are disposed of as toxic waste.

FOOD CHAIN RECORDS

SHORTEST FOOD CHAINS consist of only two organisms, for example the giant panda (*Ailuropoda melanoleuca*) and its major food source, bamboo.

Giant panda eating bamboo

LONGEST FOOD CHAINS often involve both land and water organisms, e.g. diatom (microscopic plant) to *Daphnia* (water flea), to newly hatched fish, to dragonfly larva, to adult fish, to heron.

ENDANGERED SPECIES

AN ENDANGERED SPECIES is a species that may become extinct in the near future. Throughout evolutionary history, millions of species have died out due to natural processes. Over the past 300 years, however, humans have speeded up the extinction rate more than 1,000 times: it is now estimated that one species dies out every 15 minutes.

THREATS TO WILDLIFE

Humans are responsible for almost all recent animal and plant extinctions. Threats to wildlife are caused by various human activities.

As the human population expands, more and more land is needed for planting crops, and for building settlements and roads. Natural vegetation and wildlife are destroyed.

Many animals are killed for their skins, bones, or horns. The jaguar (Panthera onca) and ocelot (Felis pardalis) are among the many species of cat that have become endangered through poaching for skins.

Pollution from industry and farming can poison wildlife. Chemical spills and acid rain (see p.65) can kill river life, and fertilizers and pesticides used in farming can upset natural systems and cycles.

When non-native animals are introduced to a country, they may have a disastrous impact on native wildlife, preying on animals and competing for food. The cane toad (Bufo marinus), introduced into Australia, has now overrun native species in some areas.

THREATENED ANIMALS

This table shows the number of threatened species in each animal group. Endangered species are monitored by the International Union for the Conservation of Nature, and recorded in their Red Data Book.

Animal group	Species at risk
Mammals	1,100
Birds	1,100
Reptiles	250
Amphibians	125
Fish	730
Insects	530
Other invertebrates	1,350

SAVING ENDANGERED SPECIES

Various measures are being used around the world in an effort to save endangered species from extinction.

Anti-poaching squads have been set up to protect animals such as rhinoceroses, elephants, and gorillas. Some countries, including Kenya, shoot poachers on sight.

The Arabian oryx (Oryx leucoryx) was hunted to extinction in the wild. After a captive-breeding programme in zoos, it was returned to its natural habitat.

DECLINING TIGER HABITAT

Tiger numbers have dropped dramatically in the last 100 years, because of the destruction of their habitat, and poaching. Tiger reserves have been established, but poaching is still a serious problem. This map shows the declining range of the tiger, and gives the estimated numbers of tigers left today.

KEY

Previous tiger range

Current, fragmented tiger range

RATES OF EXTINCTION

A species is considered to be extinct if it has not been found in the wild for 50 years. This graph illustrates the dramatic increase in the rate of extinction over the past 300 years.

The red line shows the number of species that became extinct in each year.

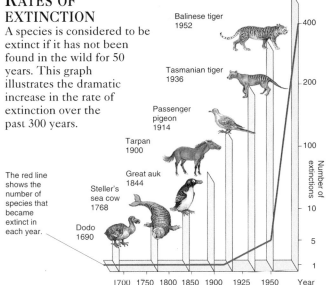

Balinese tiger 1952
Tasmanian tiger 1936
Passenger pigeon 1914
Tarpan 1900
Great auk 1844
Steller's sea cow 1768
Dodo 1690

Number of extinctions: 400, 200, 100, 10, 5, 1

1700 1750 1800 1850 1900 1925 1950 Year

MOST ENDANGERED ANIMALS

This table lists some of the rarest animal species in the world. Some endangered species are now extinct in the wild but are being bred in captivity. They will eventually be released into the wild if conditions are safe.

Common name	Scientific name	Distribution
Tiger	*Panthera tigris*	Asia
Black rhino	*Diceros bicornis*	Africa
Giant panda	*Ailuropoda melanoleuca*	China
Mountain gorilla	*Gorilla gorilla beringei*	Africa
Kakapo	*Strigops habroptilus*	New Zealand
Hawksbill sea turtle	*Fretmocholys imbricata*	Tropical seas
Spix's macaw	*Cyanopsitta spixii*	South America
California condor	*Gymnogyps californianus*	North America
Golden lancehead snake	*Bothrops insularis*	Brazil
Chinese alligator	*Alligator sinensis*	China
Yosemite toad	*Bufo canorus*	North America
Ganges shark	*Gylphis gangeticus*	Asia

Siberian tiger (250–400)
Caspian tiger (extinct)
South China tiger (30–80)
Indo-Chinese tiger (800–1,400)
Balinese tiger (extinct)
Bengal tiger (3,000–5,300)
Sumatran tiger (400–500)
Javan tiger (probably extinct)

ANIMAL RECORDS AND COMPARISONS

THERE IS A REMARKABLE DIVERSITY within the animal kingdom, from wasps no bigger than a full stop, to crabs that grow larger than people; from tiny, deadly cone shells, to the blue whale – the gentle giant of the oceans.

LARGEST WINGSPANS

BIRD
The wandering albatross *(Diomedea exulans)* has a wingspan measuring about 3.6m (12ft) across.
BAT
Flying foxes of the *Pteropus* genus are the largest bats in the world, with wingspans up to 2m (6.6ft) across.

Wandering albatross

Flying fox (Pteropus)

LARGEST ANIMALS

Largest mollusc
Giant Atlantic squid *(Archteuthis)*; 20m (66ft) long; North Atlantic Ocean

Largest insect
Goliath beetle *(Goliathus)* 110g (3.9oz) Equatorial Africa

Largest arachnid
Leblondis' goliath bird-eating spider *(Theraphosa leblondi)*; leg span 28cm (11in); Brazil, Venezuela, Guyana, French Guiana

Largest crustacean
Japanese spider crab *(Macrocheira kaempferi)* Leg span nearly 4m (13ft) Japan

Largest amphibian
Japanese giant salamander *(Andrias japonicus)* 1.5m (5ft) long Japan

Largest reptile
Saltwater crocodile *(Crocodylus porosus)*; 6m (20ft) long Southeast Asia, Indonesia, Philippines, New Guinea, Australia

Largest fish
Whale shark *(Rhincodon typus)* 15m (50ft) long; Atlantic, Pacific, and Indian Oceans

Largest bird
Ostrich *(Struthio camelus)* 2.7m (8.9ft) tall Mainly eastern and southern Africa

Largest mammal
Blue whale *(Balaenoptera musculus)* 34m (111.5ft) long; worldwide, particularly Southern Hemisphere

SMALLEST ANIMALS

Smallest insect
Fairyfly wasps 0.2mm long Worldwide

Smallest amphibian
Psyllophryne didactyla 10.4mm (0.41in) long Brazil

Smallest fish
Dwarf goby *(Pandaka pygmaea)* 7.6mm (0.3in) long Philippines

Smallest reptile
British Virgin Island gecko *(Sphaerodactylus parthenopion)* 18mm (0.7in) long Virgin Islands

Smallest bird
Bee hummingbird *(Mellisuga helenae)* 5.7cm (2.2in) long Cuba

Smallest mammal
Kitti's hog-nosed bat *(Craseonycteris thonglongyai)* 3.3cm (1.3in) long Thailand

LOUDEST ANIMALS

MARINE ANIMAL
The blue whale's *(Balaenoptera musculus)* call is the loudest noise made by any animal. It registers up to 188 decibels, and can be heard by other whales up to 1,600km (1,000 miles) away.

LAND ANIMAL
The howler monkey *(Alouatta)* can be heard up to 3km (2 miles) away.

Howler monkey

INSECT
Cicadas can be heard up to 400m (1,312ft) away.

Cicada

ANIMAL REPRODUCTION FACTS

• After spending a year or more as a larva, the adult mayfly *(Ephemera danica)* has only a day in which to mate and lay eggs before it dies.

• A tapeworm may release a million eggs a day for several years. Hardly any eggs survive.

• Many fish lay millions of eggs, because so few young survive. The ocean sunfish *(Mola mola)* lays about 30 million eggs.

ANIMAL LIFESPANS

Animals live from a few days to more than 200 years. The lifespans shown here are approximate maximum ages.

Housefly *(Musca domestica)* 3–12 weeks

Bedbug *(Cimex lectularius)* 6 months

Tooth carp 8 months

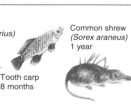
Common shrew *(Sorex araneus)* 1 year

Red fox *(Vulpes vulpes)* 8 years

Jewel beetle 30 years

Andean condor *(Vultur gryphus)* 72 years

Giant tortoise *(Megalochelys)* 150 years

Giant clam *(Tridacna)* 200 years

| 1 month | 3 months | 6 months | 9 months | 1 year | 5 years | 10 years | 50 years | 100 years | 150 years | 200 years |

POISONOUS ANIMALS

MOST POISONOUS MOLLUSCS

A sting from a blue-ringed octopus (*Hapalochlaena*) can kill a human. Three species of cone shell (*Conus*) (right) also have a deadly sting.

MOST POISONOUS FISH

When stepped on, the stonefish (*Synanceja*), which lurks in shallow waters in the Pacific and Indian Oceans, injects venom through spines in its dorsal fin, causing intense pain and sometimes death.

MOST POISONOUS FROG

The golden-yellow poison-dart frog (*Phyllobates terribilis*), which lives in Colombia, South America, oozes the strongest animal poison in the world from its skin. Toxin from a single frog could kill nearly 1,500 people.

MOST POISONOUS MAMMAL

The duck-billed platypus (*Ornithorhynchus anatinus*) injects venom through a spur on one of its hind legs. Its sting causes intense pain in humans. The platypus is one of only two species of poisonous mammal (see p.103).

MOST POISONOUS JELLYFISH

A human stung more than six times by a chironex (*Chironex fleckeri*) can die within two to three minutes. This jellyfish occurs in huge swarms off the northern coast of Australia.

MOST POISONOUS SPIDER

The Brazilian wandering spider (*Phoneutria*), which has a leg span of 10cm (4in), has the most poisonous of all spider bites. This spider has difficulty injecting venom into humans, so it causes few deaths.

MOST POISONOUS SNAKES

Sea snakes of the genus *Hydrophis* have extremely poisonous venom. The toxin of *Hydrophis belcheri*, which lives in the Timor Sea off northwestern Australia, is about 100 times as strong as that of the taipan (see below).

MOST POISONOUS BIRD

The only bird known to be poisonous is the hooded pitohui (*Pitohui dichrous*), from New Guinea. This brightly coloured bird secretes a poison similar to that produced by poison-dart frogs, although far less toxic.

TERRIBLE TAIPAN

The taipan (*Oxyuranus*) of northeastern Australia and New Guinea is one of the most poisonous snakes in the world. The venom from just one of these snakes could kill 125,000 mice.

LARGEST INSECT HOMES

Mounds built by termites can reach up to 12m (39ft) tall: more than six times the height of an adult human.

ANIMALS OF THE DEEP

The deepest-diving bird is the emperor penguin (*Aptenodytes forsteri*), which reaches depths of up to 265m (870ft).

The deepest-diving turtle is the leatherback turtle (*Dermochelys coriacea*), which dives down to 1,200m (3,937ft).

The deepest-diving mammal is the sperm whale (*Physeter macrocephalus*), which dives down to 1,200m (3,937ft).

Rat-tails are some of the deepest-living fish in the oceans.

TALLEST ANIMALS

MAMMAL

The giraffe (*Giraffa camelopardalis*) measures up to 5.9m (19.4ft) tall.

BIRDS

The tallest bird is the ostrich. The tallest flying birds are cranes: some species, e.g. the Japanese crane (*Grus japonensis*) (above), stand nearly 2m (6.6ft) high.

HEAVIEST ANIMALS

Animal	Scientific name	Weight kg	Weight lb
Blue whale	*Balaenoptera musculus*	190,000	418,878
African elephant	*Loxodonta africanus*	5,000	11,023
Asian elephant	*Elephas maximas*	4,000	8,818
White rhinoceros	*Ceratotherium simum*	2,200	4,850
Hippopotamus	*Hippopotamus amphibius*	2,000	4,409
Giraffe	*Giraffa camelopardalis*	1,200	2,646
Saltwater crocodile	*Crocodylus porosus*	1,100	2,425
Asian gaur	*Bos frontalis*	900	1,984
Bison	*Bison*	800	1,764
Kodiak bear	*Ursus arctos middendorffi*	800	1,764
Yak	*Bos grunniens*	800	1,764

ANIMAL SPEEDS

AIR

Dragonflies 50km/h (31mph) Fastest-flying insects

Racing pigeon (*Columba livia*) 85km/h (53mph)

White-throated spine-tail swift (*Hirundapus caudacutus*) 171km/h (106mph) Fastest-flying bird

Peregrine falcon (*Falco peregrinus*) 180km/h (112mph) Fastest bird in a dive

LAND

Brown hare (*Lepus capensis*) 25km/h (16mph)

Ostrich (*Struthio camelus*) 72km/h (45mph) Fastest-running bird

Pronghorn antelope (*Antilocapra americana*) 88km/h (55mph) Fastest mammal over long distances

Cheetah (*Acinonyx jubatus*) 105km/h (65mph) Fastest mammal over short distances

SEA

Gentoo penguin (*Pygoscelis papua*) 27km/h (17mph) Fastest-swimming bird

Sei whale (*Balaenoptera borealis*) 48km/h (29.8mph) Fastest-swimming mammal

Tunny (*Thunnus*) 71km/h (44mph) Fastest-swimming fish

| 0 | km/h | 10 | 20 | 30 | 40 | 50 | 60 | 70 | 80 | 90 | 100 | 150 | 200 |

LEAPS AND BOUNDS

The red kangaroo (*Macropus rufus*) can cover up to 12m (40ft) in a single bound.

The flying dragon (*Draco*) leaps up to 30m (100ft) from tree to tree.

The flying fish (*Cypselurus*) leaps out of the water for distances of up to 100m (328ft).

The sugar glider (*Petaurus breviceps*) can cover up to 90m (300ft) between trees.

The world long jump record for a human is 8.95m (29.4ft).

The African sharp-nosed frog (*Ptychadena oxyrhynchus*) can leap up to 5.35m (17.5ft).

| 0 | Distance (m) | 5 | | 10 | | 15 | | 20 | | 30 | 40 | 50 | 60 | 70 | 80 | 90 | 100 |

HIGHEST LEAPERS

Fleas are the highest leapers for their body size. The common flea (*Pulex irritans*) can leap up to 19cm (7.5in) high: about 130 times its own height.

LARGEST GROUPS

CRUSTACEANS

Swarms of krill (*Euphausia superba*) have been known to cover areas of ocean measuring up to 440sq km (170sq miles). These large swarms may contain up to 80 billion individuals: about 16 times the world's human population.

BIRDS

The red-billed quelea (*Quelea quelea*) gathers in roosts of up to 10 million birds.

Locust swarm

INSECTS

Locusts gather in enormous numbers. In 1873, a swarm of Rocky Mountain locusts estimated to contain 10,000 billion insects crossed the USA.

BEEFY BEETLE

One of the strongest insects is the Atlas beetle (*Chalcosoma atlas*). It can lift more than 800 times its own bodyweight – equivalent to a man lifting a *Leopard 2* tank.

ANIMAL ENERGY REQUIREMENTS

This table compares the kilojoules (kJ, see p.134) different animal species need per day for a moderate amount of activity.

Adult animal	Scientific name	kJ required
House mouse	*Mus musculus*	45.4
European robin	*Erithacus rubecula*	89.9
Peregrine falcon	*Falco peregrinus*	277
Grey squirrel	*Sciurus carolinensis*	386
Fennec fox	*Vulpes zerda*	1,067
Domestic cat	*Felis catus*	1,554
Baboon	*Papio hamadryas*	6,762
Giant anteater	*Myrmecophaga tridactyla*	7,392
Female human	*Homo sapiens*	10,080
Male human	*Homo sapiens*	13,713
Llama	*Llama glama*	16,128
Tiger	*Panthera tigris*	33,600
Gorilla	*Gorilla gorilla*	34,020
American black bear	*Ursus americanus*	38,556
Giraffe	*Giraffa camelopardalis*	152,754
Walrus	*Odobenus rosmarus*	159,852
Male Asian elephant	*Elephas maximus*	256,872

MOST DANGEROUS ANIMALS

50,000–100,000 people die every year from snake bites.

Mosquitoes transmit malaria, which kills between one and three million people every year.

Over a 217-year period in the USA, there were 1,291 recorded black widow spider (*Latrodectus mactans*) bites. Fifty-five of the victims died.

Sharks attack about 100 people per year: about 25 attacks result in death.

Saltwater crocodiles (*Crocodylus porosus*) (right) and Nile crocodiles (*C. niloticus*) kill hundreds of people every year.

About one person in 200 is allergic to bee and wasp venom. In the USA, between 50 and 100 people die every year from bee and wasp stings.

In the Sunderbans region of India, 521 people were killed by tigers between 1975 and mid-1989.

GESTATION PERIODS

The gestation period is the length of time an animal takes to develop inside its mother before it is born.

Virginia opossum (*Didelphis virginiana*) *12 days; 8–14 young*

Golden hamster (*Mesocricetus auratus*) *15 days; 6–8 young*

House mouse (*Mus musculus*) *20 days; 6–8 young*

Red kangaroo (*Macropus rufus*) *33 days; 1 young*

Lion (*Panthera leo*) *105–108 days; 3–4 young*

Goat (*Capra*) *150 days; 1–2 young*

Orang utan (*Pongo pygmaeus*) *250 days; 1 young*

Human (Homo sapiens) *267 days; 1 young*

Cow *278 days; 1 young*

Dolphin *360 days; 1 young*

Asian elephant (*Elephas maximus*) *660 days; 1 young*

HUMAN BODY

Stunning detailed illustrations, supported by a wealth of facts and figures, show the amazing workings of the human body. Other topics include evolution, reproduction and growth, the history of medicine, traditional medicine, nutrition, and first aid.

Humankind • Human Body • The Brain • Nervous System • Eyes • Ears
Skin, Hair, and Nails • Smell, Taste, and Throat • Skeleton and Teeth • Muscles
Heart • Circulation and Blood • Respiratory System • Digestion • Urinary System
Endocrine System • Reproduction and Growth • Medicine • Nutrition
Traditional Medicine • First Aid

HUMANKIND

SCIENTISTS BELIEVE the first living thing on Earth was a single-celled organism that developed almost four billion years ago. From that organism, plant and animal life evolved. Finally, just five million years ago, hominids appeared.

Aegyptopithecus
30 million years ago
Ancestor of monkeys, apes, and humans

BRAIN POWER

Homo habilis had a larger brain than the first ape people, but it was only half the size of a modern human brain. As the brain grew in size, people developed greater powers of reasoning and survival.

Australopithecus

Homo habilis

Homo sapiens

HUMAN FOSSILS

The structure of human remains and where they are found tell us a great deal about the growth and development of the human race.

 ● **Lucy**
A three million-year-old *Australopithecus* skeleton, found in Ethiopia.
 ● **Homo habilis skull**
Fossils and tools found in same area in East Africa.
 ● **Beijing man**
Homo erectus skull found. Evidence of fire in area.
 ● **Neanderthals**
Fossils found in Europe.

EVOLUTION FACTS

● Early humans used wisdom teeth to eat roots and berries. Today, some people do not even develop them.

● Neanderthals had a slightly bigger brain than humans today. It may have signified a stronger body, not high intelligence.

EVOLUTIONARY CLOCK

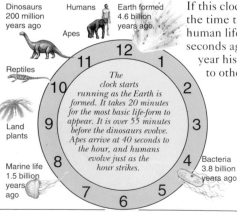

Dinosaurs 200 million years ago

Humans

Apes

Earth formed 4.6 billion years ago.

Reptiles

The clock starts running as the Earth is formed. It takes 20 minutes for the most basic life-form to appear. It is over 55 minutes before the dinosaurs evolve. Apes arrive at 40 seconds to the hour, and humans evolve just as the hour strikes.

Land plants

Marine life 1.5 billion years ago

Bacteria 3.8 billion years ago

If this clock face represents the time the Earth has existed, human life began only a few seconds ago. Our five-million-year history is short compared to other life-forms.

HUMAN FAMILY TREE

Sivapithecus
7–13 million years ago
Early ancestor of the orang utan

Orang utan
Differences in skull shape put them in a separate family from humans and gorillas.

Australopithecus
1.5–5 million years ago
Earliest ape people to walk upright

Chimpanzee/gorilla
Skull shape links them to human family, but they do not walk upright and brain is smaller.

Homo habilis
1.5–2 million years ago
Made tools to assist with hunter-scavenger lifestyle.

Homo sapiens sapiens
40,000 years ago
Modern humans were the first artists. Emerged in Africa and spread to all continents by 11,000 years ago.

Homo erectus
0.5–1.5 million years ago
Used fire and dwellings to survive in cooler climates.

Homo sapiens neanderthalensis
40,000–100,000 years ago
Sub-species of modern humans with overhanging brow. First burial ceremonies

SKELETON SHAPES

The human skeleton is designed for upright walking. Human toes point forwards, whereas a gorilla's big toe is at an angle for grasping. The *Homo sapiens* hip bone is shorter than a gorilla's for easy striding. The human head is more centrally balanced on the backbone than a gorilla's.

Gorilla foot

Human

Gorilla

Human foot

THE ICEMAN

In 1991 the oldest complete *Homo sapiens* corpse was found in a glacier in the European Alps. His internal organs, skin, and even his eyes were intact.

The Iceman had been frozen for 5,300 years.

HUMAN FAMILY

As humans spread across the world, they gradually evolved different features, such as dark and light hair, that were suited, for example, to a particular climate.

East Indian

Native American

Australian Aboriginal

Caucasoid

Black African

Mongoloid

PILTDOWN HOAX

Remains found in Piltdown, England, were first thought to show a missing link between apes and humans. But in 1953, tests showed them to be the skull of a 14th-century man and the jaw of a 15th-century orang utan.

HUMAN BODY

EACH BODY SYSTEM is composed of organs made from different types of tissue. Tissue is made from cells all performing a similar function. There are roughly 50 billion cells in the body.

CELL GROWTH

As cells divide and multiply, children and young people grow. In later life, some cells still multiply, but this is to replace the millions of cells that die every second.

Nucleus starts to grow.

Nucleus starts to divide.

First nucleus, then cell divides in two.

Each cell may grow to size of parent cell.

THE BODY AT WORK

Each body system combines cells, tissue, and organs.

There are many millions of nerve cells in the human body.

Individual cells combine to make cell tissue, such as major nerves.

Cells, tissue, and nerves make up the brain and spinal cord: the major organs of the human nervous system.

INSIDE A CELL

Nearly all human cells are too small to see without a microscope: the average diameter is 0.02mm. Inside each there are organelles that control and run the cell.

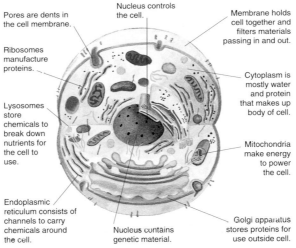

Pores are dents in the cell membrane.

Ribosomes manufacture proteins.

Lysosomes store chemicals to break down nutrients for the cell to use.

Endoplasmic reticulum consists of channels to carry chemicals around the cell.

Nucleus controls the cell.

Membrane holds cell together and filters materials passing in and out.

Cytoplasm is mostly water and protein that makes up body of cell.

Mitochondria make energy to power the cell.

Nucleus contains genetic material.

Golgi apparatus stores proteins for use outside cell.

CELL DISCOVERY

In 1838, German botanist Matthias Schleiden recognized that plants are made up of cells. In 1839, German physiologist Theodor Schwann extended this theory to animal life. Schwann cells are so-named because of his research on the nervous system.

Matthias Schleiden (1804–81)

Theodor Schwann (1810–82)

CELL FACTS

• Some gut cells have a life expectancy of only three days. A brain cell can last for life.

• An egg cell (ovum) is the largest human cell and can just be seen without a microscope.

• Red blood cells are the only cells without a nucleus.

• Cancer causes cells in many body systems to multiply uncontrollably, form tumours, and invade neighbouring tissue.

• All humans develop from just two cells: an ovum and a sperm.

• Neurons, the message carriers of the nervous system, are the longest cells in the human body. Some are up to 1.2m (4ft) long.

TYPES OF CELL

More than 200 cell types each perform specialized functions.

Duodenal cells use mucus to protect against stomach acid.

Secretory thyroid gland cells control the metabolism.

Sperm cells can live in the female tract for up to seven days.

Red blood cells carry oxygen and live for about 120 days.

Brain cell: after 18 years we lose more than 1,000 a day.

Bone-maintaining cells develop from bone-forming cells.

CELL, CELL, CELL!

If all the cells in a human body were put end to end, they would stretch for 1,000km (620 miles): from Paris to Rome.

BODY SYSTEMS

The major systems shown here work together to help the body function efficiently. Each system consists of organs that carry out a similar task.

Respiratory system draws oxygen into the body and expels carbon dioxide.

Excretory system filters waste from the blood.

Digestive system processes food, absorbs nutrients, and expels waste.

Skeletal system is usually made up of 206 individual bones.

Circulatory system consists of the heart, blood, and blood vessels.

Muscular system has 650 muscles that exert pulling power on bones.

Nervous system carries messages to and from the brain. Endocrine system carries hormones.

Skin system consists of the skin, nails, and hair covering the body.

THE BRAIN

THE BRAIN IS THE major organ of the nervous system. It is the control centre of the body, responsible for thought, memory, language, and emotion. The brain is protected by the skull, which encases it, and the cerebro-spinal fluid, which cushions it.

SENSORY AREAS

Different parts of the brain carry out specialized functions. For example, the occipital lobe deals with vision, an area in the frontal lobe controls speech, and the temporal lobe receives and interprets information from the ears.

Skilled movements
Sensation
Basic movements
Behaviour and emotion
Vision
Speech
Hearing
Balance and muscle co-ordination

BRAIN FUNCTIONS

The brain stem controls digestion, breathing, and heartbeat, and the cerebellum controls muscle co-ordination. These are all involuntary activities (see p.117). Conscious functions, such as memory, learning, speech, and the conscious control of movement, take place in the cerebrum. Thoughts also occur here.

BRAIN COMPARISONS

Animals have brains of varying shapes and sizes. Some have larger brains than humans, including dolphins, elephants, and whales. An elephant's brain is four times as heavy as a human's. However, human brains are much heavier in relation to body weight than the brains of any other animal.

MEGAMEMORY

In 1974, a man named Bhandanta Vicitsara recited 16,000 pages of Buddhist text from memory: enough to fill books equalling the height of a six-year-old.

Hemispheres have a cortex of nerve cells (grey matter), and inner areas of nerve fibres (white matter).
Right cerebral hemisphere
Corpus callosum
Periosteum (skull membrane)
Frontal lobe
Occipitofrontalis (muscle sheet)
Skull
Fat
Skin
Frontal sinus
Nasal cavity
Hypothalamus controls part of the nervous system.
Pituitary gland (see p.129)
Brain stem
Spinal cord
Optic nerves (see p.118)

Parietal lobe
Three layers, called meninges, cover the brain.
Dura mater: toughest layer
Arachnoid layer: contains blood vessels and fluid.
Pia mater: nourishes the brain.
Left cerebral hemisphere
Occipital lobe
Cerebellum
Temporal lobe

STRUCTURE OF THE BRAIN

The brain has three main regions: the brain stem, which merges with the spinal cord; the cerebellum; and the cerebrum, which contains the two cerebral hemispheres. The cerebrum makes up 90% of the brain.

BRAIN POWER

The brain sends and receives messages as impulses of electrical energy. The energy travels via nerve cells, called neurons, that run down the spinal cord to the rest of the body. Each neuron ends in a network of fine branches, called dendrites.

Information passes between nerve cells at the synapses: the points where the tips of dendrites from different cells meet.

Close-up of a synapse transferring information from one nerve cell to another.

CEREBRAL HEMISPHERES

The cerebrum is divided into two halves, called cerebral hemispheres. The left half is usually dominant and controls speech and thought; the right half manages artistic and imaginative activity. The corpus callosum joins the two hemispheres.

The left side of the brain is responsible for logical activities such as language and numeracy.

The right side mainly controls the imagination, and artistic activities such as music and painting.

Human brain: the size of a cauliflower

Dolphin brain

Ape brain

Bird brain

Snake brain

Fish brain

MEMORY

Memory works in three ways: iconic memory briefly remembers things seen for a split-second; short-term memory stores things for about five minutes; and long-term memory can store things for a lifetime.

BRAIN WAVES

An electroencephalogram (EEG) records tiny electrical impulses produced by brain activity.

Alpha waves
Awake and relaxed

Beta waves
Concentrating

Delta waves
Asleep

Theta waves
Meditation and creative thought

MEMORY FACTS

• Short-term memory can hold about seven unrelated facts at any one time.

• As a person gets older, it becomes easier for them to remember past events than to remember recent events.

• The brain has to forget certain things in order to make room for new memories.

BRAIN FACTS

• A typical adult brain weighs about 1.3kg (3lb).

• About 0.85 litres (1.8 pints) of blood travel through the brain every minute.

• A human brain contains about fifteen billion cells.

• The grey matter of a brain's cortex, laid out flat, would cover an office desk.

COMMON ILLNESSES

Name	Description
Encephalitis	Inflammation of the brain; usually caused by viral infection
Meningitis	Inflammation of the meninges; usually caused by bacterial or viral infection
Alzheimer's disease	Deterioration of memory and thought processes

NERVOUS SYSTEM

THE NERVOUS SYSTEM is a huge communications network of nerves. This network allows us to feel, see, and hear the world, and to detect and respond quickly to changes inside and outside the body.

NEURONS (NERVE CELLS)

Neurons are the building blocks of the nervous system. Each consists of a cell body containing the nucleus, and a long, thread-like nerve fibre called the axon.

The axon carries impulses away from the cell.

An insulating layer of myelin (a fatty material) protects the axon and speeds up the electrical impulses.

Nerve fibres consist of the axon and dendrites of a neuron.

The cell body contains the nucleus.

Synapses are gaps where the axon of one neuron meets the dendrites of the next.

Dendrites are nerve fibres that carry impulses towards a cell body.

INVOLUNTARY ACTIONS

Automatic actions that the brain does not consciously decide on, such as heartbeat, are called involuntary actions. They include the actions of internal organs (autonomic actions), and reflex actions. This sequence shows how the nervous system produces an involuntary reflex action in response to touching a flame.

1 When the hand touches a hot object, sensory neurons produce a signal.

2 The signal passes along the neuron's axon to an association neuron in the spinal cord.

5 Signals also travel up to the brain. When they reach the cerebral cortex, the person feels pain.

4 A motor neuron makes the muscles contract, pulling the hand away from the source of pain.

3 The signal passes across a synapse to a motor neuron.

SPINAL CORD

The spinal cord is a bundle of nerves that runs down from the brain inside the backbone (see p.122). Spinal nerves branch out from the spinal cord through the gaps between the vertebrae.

Spinal cord
Vertebra
Nerve roots
Spinal nerve
Disc
Vertebra
Vertebral canal

STRUCTURE OF THE NERVOUS SYSTEM

The nervous system is made up of the central nervous system (CNS), which consists of the brain and spinal cord, and the peripheral nervous system, which consists of the nerves extending from the CNS to the rest of the body.

NERVES

There are millions of nerves and billions of nerve cells in the body. This close-up shows nerve cells in the brain.

NEURON FUNCTIONS

There are three types of neuron: sensory neurons send signals triggered by sensations to the CNS; motor neurons carry signals from the CNS to muscles to make them contract; and association neurons transfer signals between other neurons.

NERVE ENDINGS

There are several types of nerve ending. Each detects a different type of feeling.

Pressure   Touch

Cold   Heat   Pain

ACUPUNCTURE

This is an ancient Chinese method of treating illness by inserting fine needles into energy points on the body. These points are found along a system of channels, called meridians, that runs the length of the body, rather like the nervous system.

19th-century woodcut showing acupuncture points on the face, neck, shoulder, and hand.

NERVE FACTS

• Electric signals travel through some nerve fibres at more than 400km/h (248mph). Small axons conduct impulses more slowly.

• All the nerves in the body laid end to end would stretch for about 75km (47 miles).

• The tip of the index finger is one of the most sensitive parts of the body, with many thousands of sense receptors.

• The longest nerve is the sciatic nerve, stretching from base of the spine to the knee.

PHANTOM PAIN

People sometimes feel sensations in a limb they have lost. British Admiral Lord Nelson (1758–1805) had his arm cut off after it was fractured by gunshot. He felt pain in the non-existent arm for the rest of his life.

Cerebrum
Cerebellum
Cervical nerves
Brachial plexus
Spinal cord
Thoracic nerves
Radial nerve
Median nerve
Ulnar nerve
Sacral plexus
Lumbar nerves
Sacral nerves
Pudendal nerve
Femoral nerve
Sciatic nerve
Common peroneal nerve
Posterior tibial nerve
Superficial peroneal nerve
Deep peroneal nerve

COMMON ILLNESSES

Name	Description
Neuritis	Inflammation of a nerve
Neuralgia	Pain caused by an irritated or damaged nerve
Neuroma	Benign (will not spread) tumour of nerve tissue
Multiple sclerosis	Progressive disease of the central nervous system

EYES

THE EYES ARE probably the most important of the sense organs, enabling us to see and react to the world around us. They are positioned in protective bony sockets in the skull. Eyes work in pairs to transmit images to the brain via the optic nerves.

EYE FUNCTION

Light rays enter the eye through the pupil, and are focused by the cornea and the lens to form an image on the retina. Light-sensitive cells in the retina convert the image into nerve impulses that travel along the optic nerve to the brain.

Light rays reflected off the image travel to the eye.

Cornea partly focuses the rays.

Lens fine-focuses the image.

Image is reflected onto the retina.

Close-up of rods and cones

STEREOSCOPIC VISION

Two eyes give a wide range of vision, and enable us to judge depth, distance, and speed effectively. Each eye receives a slightly different view of the same object. The brain combines the two images to give a three-dimensional interpretation of the object.

SIGHT PROBLEMS

COLOUR BLINDNESS

Colour-blind people are unable to tell the difference between certain colours: usually red and green. The problem is normally caused by a defect in some of the retina's cone cells. True colour blindness, where people can only see shades of black and white, is very rare.

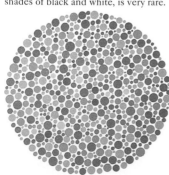

This is a test for colour blindness. If you have normal vision you can see the number 29. If you are colour blind you see the number 70.

EYE STRUCTURE

The eye is a round bag of clear, jelly-like fluid called vitreous humour, surrounded by a tough outer covering called the sclera. Each eyeball measures about 2.5cm (1in) across.

Area of optic disc (forms blind spot)

Optic nerve to brain

Retina: detects light

Retinal blood vessel

Choroid: contains nourishing blood vessels.

Medial rectus muscle

Image is upside-down, because light rays cross over behind the lens.

Image flashes along the optic nerve to the brain, where it is turned the right way up.

RODS AND CONES

Millions of light-sensitive cells, called rods and cones, pick up the image. Rods see black and white, and cones see colour.

Lateral rectus muscle

Vitreous humour allows light through to retina.

Conjunctiva: thin membrane of skin; keeps eye moist

Iris: muscular body; controls pupil size

Cornea bends light.

Pupil: hole through which light enters the eye. Dilates (widens) in dim light or shrinks in bright light.

Aqueous humour: watery fluid; fills chamber behind cornea

Pigments in iris give eye its colour.

Lens focuses light.

Sclera forms white of the eye.

Ciliary body: muscular ring; controls shape of lens

BLIND SPOT

This is a tiny, oval-shaped area on the retina where the optic nerve joins the eye. There are no rods or cones here, so this area of the retina cannot see.

Blind spot

Retina

Light rays

Optic nerve

EYE FACTS

• Most people blink about 15 times a minute.

• About one person in thirty is colour blind. More men are affected than women.

• The best photographic film is at least 1,000 times less sensitive than the human eye.

• Male eyes are about 0.5 mm bigger than female eyes.

• Carrots help you to see in the dark: they contain vitamin A, from which the light-sensitive chemical in the rods is made.

• The body produces excess tears in times of strong emotion. No-one knows why humans cry.

MUSCLES

Each eye has six muscles to move the eyeball around. Movements are co-ordinated, so it is impossible to look in two different directions at once.

Superior rectus: upwards, inwards, clockwise

Superior oblique: downwards, outwards, clockwise

Medial rectus: inwards

Lateral rectus: outwards

Inferior rectus: downwards, inwards, anticlockwise

Inferior oblique: upwards, outwards, anticlockwise

TEARS

Tears are necessary to keep the eyes moist and clean.

Eyelid washes tears across the eye.

Tear gland continually produces tears.

Surplus tear fluid drains down the tear ducts to the nose.

Visual region of the brain

Left eye receives this image.

Combined, three-dimensional image

Right eye receives this image.

SHARP EYES

The human eye is so sensitive that it can see a lighted candle positioned 1.6km (1 mile) away in the dark.

LONG- AND SHORT-SIGHTEDNESS

Short-sighted people cannot see distant objects clearly, and long-sighted people cannot see near objects clearly. These problems are caused by irregularly shaped eyeballs.

Long-sightedness: rays focused behind the retina. Convex lens corrects focus.

Short-sightedness: rays focused in front of the retina. Concave lens corrects focus.

COMMON PROBLEMS

Name	Description
Cataracts	Loss of transparency of the lens. Causes short-sightedness and distorted vision or blindness
Conjunctivitis	Inflammation of the conjunctiva. Causes redness, discomfort, and discharge
Glaucoma	Abnormally high pressure of fluid in the eye. Causes severe pain, and partial or complete loss of vision

EARS

EARS ARE THE organs of hearing and balance. Set on either side of the head, only part of each ear is visible; the rest is protected by the bones of the skull. Ears work in pairs to collect sound vibrations and turn them into signals, which are then passed to the brain, enabling us to hear.

EAR BONES

The three tiny ossicles in the middle ear are named the hammer, the anvil, and the stirrup, because of their shapes.

Stirrup
Anvil
Hammer
Eardrum

BALANCE

Every time the body moves, fluid, called perilymph, flows around the three semicircular canals. Tiny hair cells sense the movement and send signals to the brain to communicate the body's position. This helps the body to keep its balance.

HEARING RANGES

Animals hear different levels of sound frequency (see p.233). This diagram compares the hearing ranges of some animals.

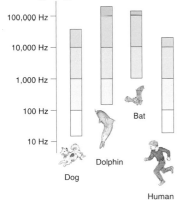

100,000 Hz
10,000 Hz
1,000 Hz
100 Hz
10 Hz

Bat
Dolphin
Dog
Human

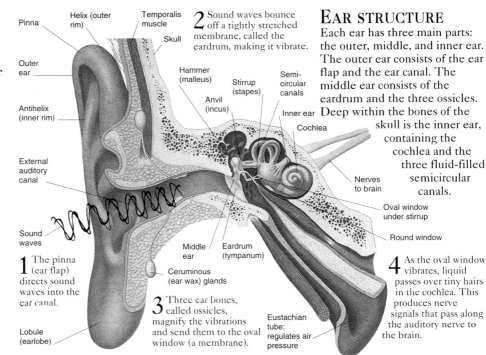

Pinna
Helix (outer rim)
Temporalis muscle
Skull
Outer ear
Antihelix (inner rim)
External auditory canal
Sound waves
Hammer (malleus)
Anvil (incus)
Stirrup (stapes)
Semicircular canals
Inner ear
Cochlea
Nerves to brain
Oval window under stirrup
Round window
Middle ear
Eardrum (tympanum)
Ceruminous (ear wax) glands
Eustachian tube: regulates air pressure
Lobule (earlobe)

2 Sound waves bounce off a tightly stretched membrane, called the eardrum, making it vibrate.

1 The pinna (ear flap) directs sound waves into the ear canal.

3 Three ear bones, called ossicles, magnify the vibrations and send them to the oval window (a membrane).

EAR STRUCTURE

Each ear has three main parts: the outer, middle, and inner ear. The outer ear consists of the ear flap and the ear canal. The middle ear consists of the eardrum and the three ossicles. Deep within the bones of the skull is the inner ear, containing the cochlea and the three fluid-filled semicircular canals.

4 As the oval window vibrates, liquid passes over tiny hairs in the cochlea. This produces nerve signals that pass along the auditory nerve to the brain.

Perilymph in bony labyrinth
Nerves
Semicircular canals
Cochlea

Fluid flows over more than 20,000 fine hairs inside the cochlea.

NOISE LEVELS

Loudness of sound is measured in decibels (dB). Sounds above 90dB cause pain to the human ear. Sounds above 130dB can damage the ear, and may cause deafness. This diagram compares some noise levels.

EAR FACTS

- Stirrup is the smallest bone in the human body, at only 3mm (0.12in) long.

- Sensation of ears "popping" is caused by the eustachian tube opening to equalize air pressure in the middle ear.

- Ear canal is about 2.5cm (1in) in length.

- Ears can detect the direction of a sound within three degrees.

- Children usually have more sensitive ears than adults.

- Ears can detect 1,500 different tones, and 350 degrees of loudness.

DIZZINESS

If you spin round and round and then stop, the fluid in the semicircular canals continues to move for a while. This confuses the brain, causing dizziness.

EAR WAX

Glands in the skin lining the ear canal produce ear wax. This wax protects the eardrum from dirt and dust, and its unpleasant smell discourages insects from entering the ear.

Aeroplane at 100m
Heavy traffic
Quiet street
Pneumatic drill
Office
Whispering

120
110
100
90
80
70
60
50
40
30
20
Decibels

PERFECT BALANCE

In 1973, Frenchman Henri Rochatain (b. 1926) spent 185 days on a tightrope 25m (82ft) above a supermarket in St. Etienne, France.

HEARING AIDS

In the past, people with hearing difficulties used large ear trumpets. Modern hearing aids are smaller and less noticeable.

Modern hearing aid consisting of a microphone, amplifier, and battery; worn behind the ear.

This tiny hearing aid fits inside the ear where it is almost completely hidden.

Ear trumpets were held against the ear to amplify (increase) sound.

This ear trumpet is 30cm (12in) long.

This hearing aid fits onto the frame of spectacles.

Volume control
Earphone (receiver)

COMMON PROBLEMS

Name	Description
Deafness	Inability to hear
Tinnitus	Noises, such as ringing or buzzing, heard inside the ear
Ménière's disease	Inner ear disorder. May cause tinnitus, deafness, and vertigo (illusion of spinning)
Earache	Pain often caused by infection of the middle ear

SKIN, HAIR, AND NAILS

THE SKIN IS THE largest organ of the body. It is waterproof, bacteria-proof, and repairs itself. Hair and nails are extensions of the skin and are mainly composed of keratin, a protein that also protects the skin. The skin has nerve cells that respond to touch, heat, and pain. Hair and nails, however, lack nerve cells.

HAIR STRUCTURE

A tube of the protein keratin is pushed up from the hair follicle to form the hair shaft. Each hair is attached to a tiny muscle that allows it to move independently.

- Medulla
- Cortex
- Melanin granule
- Cell nucleus residue
- Macrofibril
- Cuticle

HAIR TYPES

The shape of the hair follicle determines whether the hair grows straight, wavy, or curly.

Curly hair grows from an oval follicle.

Wavy hair grows from a flat follicle.

Straight hair grows from a round follicle.

HAIR FACTS

- There are about 100,000 hairs on the head; 80 fall out every day.
- Hair grows about 2–3mm (0.08–0.1in) in a week.

RARE HAIR

These two boys have a rare medical condition known as "werewolf syndrome". Their faces are covered in hair.

Movement of hairs creates the sensation of touch.

Outer layers consist of dead skin cells containing a hard protein called keratin.

Sebaceous glands coat hair and skin in waterproof oil.

Hair follicles are surrounded by touch sensitive nerve endings.

Hair erector muscle tightens in the cold, causing hairs to stand on end and trap warmth.

Sweat gland produces sweat to cool down body temperature.

SKIN STRUCTURE

The skin has two main layers: the outer epidermis and the inner dermis. The surface of the epidermis consists of dead skin cells. These are worn away and replaced by new skin cells from deep in the epidermis. The dermis is living and contains vital nerves, glands, hairs, and blood vessels.

Epidermis contains layers of new and dead skin cells.

Basal cell layer produces new cells which continually move towards the surface.

Blood vessels expand when body is hot. The skin flushes and heat is rapidly lost.

Beneath the skin is an insulating layer of fat.

The dermis is about four times thicker than the epidermis.

Sense receptor cells

SKIN FACTS

- Protects internal organs from injury and infection.
- Sweat glands control body temperature by pushing water and salt to the surface.
- Contains thousands of nerve cells that can detect pressure, temperature, and pain.
- Contains the pigment melanin that gives the skin its colour and protects against the Sun's rays. Dark skin contains more melanin than fair.
- In most places skin is about 2mm (0.08in) thick.
- Freckles are due to an uneven production of melanin.
- Household dust is mostly made up of dead skin cells.

NAIL STRUCTURE

Nails are made of a tough protein called keratin. The half-moon at the base of each nail – the lunula – is covered by a flap of skin called the cuticle.

Lunula

Nail

Dermis

Nail root: a flap of skin from which the nail grows.

Bone

Fatty pad cushions the sensitive skin of the fingertip.

NAIL FACTS

- Fingernails take six months to grow from the base to the tip.
- Nails grow at a rate of 0.5mm (0.02in) per week. They can grow up to 30cm (12in) long.

BLOOD CLOTTING

Red blood cells help cuts to heal quickly by binding together and forming a clot.

1 A cut in the skin triggers the release of substances to make blood cells, called platelets, sticky.

Red blood cells

2 White blood cells fight infection in the cut. Fibrin threads are made from blood-clotting factors.

White blood cell

3 Fibrin threads contract and bind red blood cells into a clot. This hardens to a scab which protects the cut as it heals.

Fibrin threads stop blood flow

FINGERPRINTS

The patterns made by the ridges on your fingertips are called fingerprints. The patterns are formed months before birth, and no two fingerprint patterns are the same.

SKIN LOSS

The body sheds about 18kg (40lb) of dead skin in a lifetime: about the weight of a six- to seven-year-old child.

SKIN'S SURFACE

These magnified images show details of the skin's surface.

Sweat pores allow fluid to escape. This cools the skin.

Hair grows out of pits called hair follicles.

COMMON PROBLEMS

Name	Description
Acne	Skin disorder: raised red spots that may scar
Eczema	Itchy skin inflammation: may cause blisters and scaling
Psoriasis	Skin disorder: patches of red skin often covered with silvery scales
Alopecia	Patchy loss of hair, usually on scalp

SMELL, TASTE, AND THROAT

SMELL AND TASTE are closely linked. The sensation of flavour combines messages from taste buds and smell receptors, as well as heat, texture, and sharpness. A 30 per cent change in the strength of a smell or taste is needed for the brain to register it. Humans can distinguish 2,000 to 4,000 different smells.

SENSE OF SMELL
There are specialized nerve endings at the back of the nose called smell receptors. These are sensitive to chemicals in the airstream deposited in mucus.

Air passes over smell receptors attached to the olfactory bulb. These are made up of thousands of cells bearing microscopic hairs that are sensitive to chemicals in the mucus.

Olfactory bulb

The smell receptors send a message to the brain through the olfactory nerve.

Olfactory nerve

Nasal cavity

Chemicals from the airstream are deposited in the mucus.

The nasal cavity is lined with a very thin skin called the mucus membrane, which secretes mucus.

Nasal hairs filter particles as they are breathed in.

Mucus moves back towards the throat. Harmful micro-organisms are swallowed and made safe by acids in the stomach.

TONGUE AND TASTE
The human tongue measures about 10cm (4in) in length, and is covered with taste buds. These microscopic nerve endings are the main organs of taste. Different areas detect different tastes. There are four basic tastes: sweet, sour, salt, and bitter.

Tongue surface magnified to show sensory nerve endings.

Bitter tastes such as coffee are tasted at the back of the tongue.

Sour tastes such as lemon along the edges at the back

Salt is tasted along the sides at the front.

Sweet tastes such as sugar at the tip

No taste buds in centre

THE VOICE
Sounds are made by forcing air from the lungs up the trachea and through the vocal cords, causing them to vibrate. The tongue, throat, mouth, and lips change the sounds into words.

Nasal cavity and mouth passage join at the throat (pharynx).

Epiglottis flap

Tongue

Larynx (voice box)

Vocal cords

Trachea (windpipe) expels air through vocal cords.

Oesophagus carries food down to the stomach.

Relaxed chords
Vocal chords are far apart for low-pitched noise and breathing.

Active chords
Muscles bring vocal chords close together for high-pitched sound.

VOICE RECORDS
LOUDEST RECORDED
shout measured 119 decibels – louder than a loud rock concert.

FASTEST SPEAKERS
can say more than 300 words per minute and still be understood.

SNEEZING RECORD
An Englishwoman sneezed about 2.7 million times over 2.5 years. With each sneeze she expelled about six litres of air. During her world-record sneezing fit, she blew out enough air to fill eight hot air balloons.

LOSS OF SMELL
Immediately after birth the efficiency of our smell receptors begins to decline. This graph shows how the sense of smell deteriorates as we age.

82% Age 20
38% Age 60
28% Age 80

SMELL FACTS
• You can smell better if you sniff hard because more chemicals reach the receptors in your nose.

• The brain can become used to smells, even the most horrible ones. It simply switches off and you stop detecting them.

VOICE BOX
The vocal cords are two rubbery ligaments in the larynx.

The harder air is forced through the vocal cords, the louder the sound they make.

Thyroid cartilage (Adam's apple)

Rings of cartilage hold trachea open to allow air through.

Epiglottis flap closes when we swallow to stop food from going wrong way.

Trachea (windpipe) shown sliced open and laid flat.

TASTE FACTS
• Taste buds only work when saliva dissolves chemicals in food and washes over the buds.

• Babies are born with taste buds all over their mouth. They gradually disappear, remaining only on the tongue. Adults have about 1,000 taste buds.

VOICE FACTS
• The larynx is larger in men, which is why they can produce deeper sounds.

• A boy's voice "breaks" when the larynx enlarges at puberty.

• If the larynx lining is tickled by a food particle, a reflex contraction causes coughing, which ejects the foreign body.

COMMON PROBLEMS

Name	Description
Allergic rhinitis (hay fever)	Inflammation of mucus membrane caused by allergy to pollen or dust
Common cold	Viral infection causing stuffed up, runny nose and sneezing
Laryngitis	Inflammation of the larynx caused by infection, resulting in loss of voice

SKELETON AND TEETH

THE FRAMEWORK OF bones in the human body, including the teeth, is called the skeleton, and it supports and protects delicate internal organs, such as the brain, lungs, and heart. The skeleton also provides strong, fixed points of attachment for muscles. Bones contain marrow, which generates red and white blood cells.

BONE STRUCTURE

Bones contain calcium and phosphorus, which make them hard. The strongest part of a bone is its compact outer layer. Inside longer bones, softer living tissue, called marrow, produces red and white blood cells, and stores fat.

Compact bone
Spongy bone
Fatty bone marrow
Micrograph of marrow

Cross-section of a humerus (upper arm bone)

JOINTS

Where bones meet, a joint forms. In a mobile joint, the bone surface is coated with slippery cartilage and lubricated with synovial fluid. Most joints are held together by cords or bands called ligaments. Below are several types of joints.

Ball-and-socket
Ball-and-socket joints (e.g. shoulder, hip) allow the most movement of any joint.

Hinge
Hinge joints (e.g. elbow, knee) allow movement in just one plane.

Fixed
Some bones lock together, allowing no movement at all (e.g. cranial joints).

Pivot
A pivot joint consists of a bony projection that pivots within a ring (e.g. skull on vertebra).

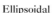

Ellipsoidal
An ellipsoidal joint (e.g. wrist) is one where an oval bone fits into an oval cavity.

A BONE TO PICK

A small piece of bone could support a nine-tonne weight. The same weight would crush a piece of cement of the same size.

BONE RECORDS

LARGEST BONE in the body is the thigh bone (femur): average male length 46cm (18.1in)

SMALLEST BONE is the stirrup (stapes) bone in the middle ear, 2.6–3.4mm (0.1–0.13in) long.

TEETH

Teeth are covered with enamel, the hardest substance made by animals. They are connected to the jaw by strong fibres that allow slight movement when chewing or biting. Humans have two sets of teeth: the first, of 20, called "milk" teeth, starts to fall out at about age 6; the second, of 32, replaces the first and is permanent.

Upper jaw
Canine
Premolars
Molars
Incisors

Lower jaw
Molars
Incisors
Premolars
Canine

TOOTH TYPES
Our front 12 teeth (incisors and canines) are sharp; they grip and tear off pieces of food. Our back 20 teeth (premolars and molars) grind and crush food for later digestion. The third molars, or wisdom teeth, sometimes remain embedded beneath gum in the jawbone.

TOOTH STRUCTURE
Enamel forms the hard, non-living, surface of the tooth. The pulp contains vessels that bring blood to the tooth, enabling it to live and grow.

Fissure
Cusp
Enamel
Dentine
Gum
Pulp
Jaw-bone
Nerve
Blood vessels
Root canal

Structure of a tooth

Mandible (jaw-bone)
Cranium (skull)
Clavicle
Ribs
Humerus (upper arm bone)
Vertebrae (spine)
Radius
Ulna
Carpals (wrist bones)
Sacrum
Pelvis (hip bone)
Metacarpals (finger bones)
Femur (thigh bone)
Patella
Tibia (shin-bone)
Fibula (calf-bone)
Foot-bones (tarsals and metatarsals)

Cervical
Thoracic
Vertebral disc
Lumbar
Sacrum
Coccyx

SKELETON

The average person has 206 bones. Some people have extra bones in their thumbs or big toes, called sesamoid bones. Women have shallower and wider pelvic bones than men, to help with childbirth.

BONE FACTS

• Some people have an extra (thirteenth) pair of ribs.

• A giraffe's neck contains the same number of bones as the human neck.

• The bones in a baby's head are not fused – they can overlap slightly to ease birth.

• Babies have more than 300 bones – they fuse together later.

SPINAL COLUMN

The spinal column has four curves: cervical, thoracic, lumbar, and sacral. Each bone in the spine is called a vertebra, and most are cushioned from their neighbours by a piece of cartilage called a vertebral disc. Vertebrae interlock with each other in sliding joints.

TOOTH FACTS

• Teeth decay more easily during the first 25 years of life; mature enamel is more resistant to attack.

• Some babies are born with a full set of teeth – King Louis XIV of France, for instance.

• Some adults' four back molars (wisdom teeth) never fully grow.

CARING FOR TEETH
Tooth decay can be reduced by cutting down on the sugar and starch we eat and by brushing (with a fluoride-based toothpaste) and flossing after meals.

Correct brushing

Correct flossing

COMMON PROBLEMS

Name	Description
Osteoarthritis	Degeneration of cartilage or bone ends in the joints
Osteoporosis	Thinning of bone, with ageing. Bone fractures easily
Caries	Patches of decay and erosion of tooth enamel and dentine by plaque (bacteria, saliva, and food remains)
Gingivitis	Inflammation of the gums, due to infection

MUSCLES

MUSCLES CARRY OUT all the body's movements. They number more than 600, accounting for about half the body's weight. Muscles are arranged in groups of fibres that contract when triggered by nerves. Regular, vigorous exercise increases a muscle's size and improves its circulation of blood.

TYPES OF MUSCLE
Voluntary muscles (e.g. biceps) can be consciously controlled; involuntary ones do internal jobs, such as the muscles of the intestine, which move food through the digestive system.

Voluntary muscle
Voluntary (skeletal) muscle cells appear striped close up. The muscle fibres are bundled together for quick contraction.

Involuntary muscle
Involuntary (smooth) muscle cells are tapered and loosely woven, and contract more slowly than other muscle types.

Cardiac muscle
Cardiac (heart) muscle has short, branching cells; these help spread the nerve signals that cause contraction.

CONTRACTION
Muscle fibre contains tiny strands called myofibrils. A myofibril contains overlapping layers of two proteins: actin and myosin. When triggered by an electrical nerve signal, the actin and myosin attract each other, and their layers slide closer together. The myofibril shortens; the muscle contracts.

Structure of a muscle

Myofibril
Muscle fibre
Actin
Myosin
Bundle of muscle fibres
Relaxed myofibril
Contracted myofibril
Overlapping and interlocking myosin and actin proteins
Tough membrane protects muscle.

MULTI-MUSCLE MOVER
Humans have more than 600 muscles, but an average-sized caterpillar has over 2,000.

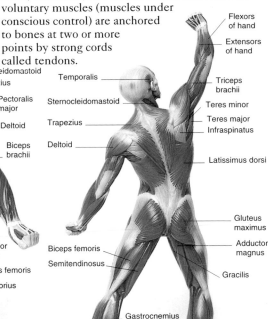

Flexors of forearm
Brachioradialis
Frontalis
Brachialis
Sternocleidomastoid
Trapezius
Pectoralis major
Deltoid
Biceps brachii
Rectus abdominis
Linea alba
External oblique
Tensor fasciae latae
Iliopsoas
Pectineus
Vastus lateralis
Serratus anterior
Adductor longus
Rectus femoris
Sartorius
Gracilis
Vastus medialis
Gastrocnemius
Tibialis anterior
Extensor muscles of foot
Flexor muscles of foot

Flexors of hand
Extensors of hand
Temporalis
Triceps brachii
Sternocleidomastoid
Teres minor
Trapezius
Teres major
Deltoid
Infraspinatus
Latissimus dorsi
Gluteus maximus
Biceps femoris
Adductor magnus
Semitendinosus
Gracilis
Gastrocnemius
Soleus
Peroneus brevis

MUSCLE SYSTEM
Muscles warm up when used, providing about four-fifths of the body's heat. Many organs, such as the heart, intestines, and bladder, have muscles. Most voluntary muscles (muscles under conscious control) are anchored to bones at two or more points by strong cords called tendons.

MUSCLE RECORDS
LONGEST MUSCLE is the sartorius, which runs from the pelvis to just below the knee.

BIGGEST MUSCLE is the gluteus maximus (buttock).

SMALLEST MUSCLE is the stapedius in the middle ear – less than 1.27mm (0.05in) long.

FASTEST MUSCLE blinks the eyelids up to five times every second.

MUSCLE ACTION
Muscles can only pull, not push. So, they often work in opposing pairs called antagonists; one muscle in the pair contracts while the other relaxes.

Biceps relaxes.
Triceps contracts.
Tendon attaches muscle to bone.
Muscles straighten the forearm.

Biceps contracts.
Triceps relaxes.
Muscles lift the forearm.

TYPES OF EXERCISE
Muscles normally use glucose and oxygen for day-to-day (aerobic) exercise. If glucose or oxygen are in short supply, muscles use their own energy stores. This anaerobic exercise generates lactic acid, which causes muscles to tire and ache, and makes us gasp for replacement oxygen.

Aerobic exercise
Anaerobic exercise

MUSCLE FUNCTIONS
• Move bones at joints.
• Force food through intestines.
• Blink the eyelids.
• Smile or make other facial expressions.
• Make breathing movements of chest and diaphragm.
• Contract walls of blood vessels.

MUSCLE FACTS
• Muscle cells can contract by up to one-third of their length.
• The muscles that work a gnat's wings can make them beat over 1,000 times a second.
• When we walk, we use more than 200 different muscles.

COMMON PROBLEMS

Name	Description
Cramp	Painful spasm from lactic acid build-up in muscles
Strain	Tear in muscle, causing bleeding and swelling
Tetanus	Toxin makes muscle contract continuously
Muscular dystrophy	Gradual wasting of muscle fibres, an inherited illness
Tendinitis	Inflammation of tendon, usually caused by injury

HEART

THE HEART IS a fist-sized muscular pump that carries blood around the body. It has two sides, and each side has two chambers. These chambers contract and relax about once every four-fifths of a second, ensuring that blood continually flows in the right direction.

Heart lies in middle of chest; it feels further left since left side beats stronger.

HEARTBEAT CYCLE

The heart is a special kind of muscle, a cardiac muscle, that works automatically. A heartbeat has four phases, or stages, and lasts for about four-fifths of a second.

Pulmonary valve shuts. Aortic valve shuts.

1 The left and right atria relax. Blood fills them through pulmonary veins and vena cava.

Tricuspid valve opens. Mitral valve opens.

2 Blood passes through tricuspid and mitral valves from atria into right and left ventricles.

Tricuspid valve shuts. Mitral valve shuts.

3 Ventricles contract and force blood through aortic and pulmonary valves into main arteries.

Pulmonary valve shuts. Aortic valve shuts.

4 Pulmonary and aortic valves close as ventricles relax. Cycle restarts at phase one.

HEART STRUCTURE

The septum divides the two sides of the heart. Each side has two chambers: an atrium and a ventricle, separated by valves. The stronger left side pumps oxygenated blood from the lungs to the rest of the body; the right brings deoxygenated (used) blood back to the lungs.

Right pulmonary artery

Location of sinoatrial node

Right pulmonary vein

Right pulmonary vein

Myocardium

Pericardium

Right ventricle

Superior vena cava

Aorta

Artery to head

Cardiac nerves

Right atrium

Pulmonary valve

Tricuspid valve

Cardiac nerves stimulate the heart muscle, passing electrical signals from the brain to tell the heart how fast it should beat.

Valves stop blood from going the wrong way when the heart muscle contracts.

Left pulmonary artery

Aortic valve

Left atrium

Left pulmonary vein

Mitral valve

Tendon supporting valve

Septum

Coronary vein

Coronary artery

Fat

Left ventricle

Muscular column supporting valve tendons

Aorta

Inferior vena cava

HEART FACTS

• Heart sounds are caused by the valves snapping shut, and the whoosh of blood leaving the heart.

• Bicuspid valves have two flaps; tricuspid have three.

• A heart beats more than 30 million times a year, and about 2 billion times in a lifetime.

• Our heart rate increases when we exercise, to supply our muscles with extra oxygen.

• The heart rests between beats. In an average lifetime of 70 years, the heart will be at rest for about 40 years.

HEART RECORDS

LONGEST CARDIAC ARREST lasted four hours – Norwegian fisherman Egil Refsdahl (b.1936), later revived.

FIRST HUMAN HEART TRANSPLANT was performed on 3 December 1967 by South African surgeon Christiaan Barnard, on grocer Louis Washkansky.

LONGEST-SURVIVING TRANSPLANTEE survived for 22 years, 10 months, 24 days.

HEARTBEAT PACEMAKER

The heart has a built-in pacemaker that keeps it beating rhythmically. It lies at the top of the heart, at the sinoatrial node, and sends an electrical signal around the heart just before every beat. An electrocardiograph machine can record these impulses painlessly.

Electrocardiogram of electrical impulse just before a heartbeat

ECG (electrocardiogram) of a normal heartbeat

ECG of complete heart block (chambers beat independently)

BLOOD WAGON

The heart ejects about 80ml (0.14 pints) of blood with every beat. If an adult heart were connected to an 8,000-litre (1,760-gallon) container lorry, it could fill it in a single day, with blood to spare.

HOLE IN THE HEART

Sometimes the right and left sides of the heart connect through a hole in the septum. Holes are closed by surgery; otherwise, fresh blood from the lungs returns there directly, without going around the body.

Septum

Surgical seal

Ventricular septal defect (hole in the septum)

ARTIFICIAL VALVES

Caged-ball valve

Closed   Open

Tilting disc valve

Closed   Open

Modified pig's valve

Sometimes valves do not work properly, and blood flows the wrong way. Surgeons replace them with real valves from pigs or artificial, mechanical ones.

COMMON PROBLEMS

Name	Description
Angina	Tight heart pain caused by lack of oxygen, often from narrowed arteries
Coronary heart disease	Reduced blood supply from narrowed arteries
Cardiac arrest	Part or all of heart muscle stops beating
Endo-carditis	Infection of the heart valves, usually after rheumatic fever
Arrhythmia	Disturbance in heartbeat

CIRCULATION AND BLOOD

THE CIRCULATORY SYSTEM supplies each body cell with life-giving blood. Blood flows around the body in a continuous circuit, through a network of vessels that is thousands of kilometres long. The heart acts as a pump, keeping the entire system moving.

THE CIRCULATORY SYSTEM

Veins bring deoxygenated blood from the body to the right-hand side of the heart. The right ventricle pumps it to the lungs, where it becomes saturated with oxygen. This blood returns to the left atrium of the heart and enters the left ventricle. The ventricle then pumps it into the network of arteries, keeping the body constantly supplied with oxygen.

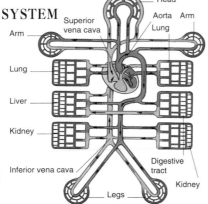

Head
Aorta
Arm
Superior vena cava
Arm
Lung
Lung
Liver
Kidney
Inferior vena cava
Digestive tract
Kidney
Legs

ARTERIES

Common carotid artery
Subclavian artery
Aortic arch
Pulmonary artery
Axillary artery
Coronary artery
Brachial artery
Gastric artery
Hepatic artery
Renal artery
Superior mesenteric artery
Inferior mesenteric artery
Ovarian artery
Palmar arch
Digital artery
Ulnar artery
Radial artery
Common iliac artery
External iliac artery
Femoral artery
Popliteal artery
Peroneal artery
Anterior tibial artery
Posterior tibial artery
Lateral plantar artery
Dorsal metatarsal artery

VEINS

Internal jugular vein
Brachiocephalic vein
Subclavian vein
Axillary vein
Superior vena cava
Pulmonary vein
Cephalic vein
Basilic vein
Hepatic portal vein
Gastroepiploic vein
Median cubital vein
Anterior median vein
Inferior vena cava
Inferior mesenteric vein
Ovarian vein
Palmar vein
Digital vein
Common iliac vein
External iliac vein
Femoral vein
Great saphenous vein
Short saphenous vein
Dorsal venous arch
Digital vein

BLOOD

White blood cell (lymphocyte)
Platelet
Red blood cell (erythrocyte)

Blood consists of red blood cells, white blood cells, and cell fragments called platelets, floating in a fluid called plasma. Proteins, hormones, and minerals are dissolved in the plasma. Red blood cells contain haemoglobin, which stores oxygen and releases it to the body. White blood cells fight infection. Platelets help blood to clot when we cut our skin.

VESSEL RECORDS

LARGEST ARTERY
is the aorta. It has an internal diameter of 2.5cm (1in).

LARGEST VEIN
is the vena cava. It has an internal diameter of 2.5cm (1in).

LEECH LUNCH

Leeches attach themselves with suckers to animals and feed off their blood. They can drink up to ten times their own bodyweight of blood – enough to last them for nine months.

BLOOD VESSELS

Muscular-walled arteries divide into smaller arterioles, then into capillaries, which have thin walls through which oxygen can pass. Deoxygenated blood returns via venules, which join up into wider, thin-walled veins.

Artery
Arteriole
Endothelium
Fatty deposits
Muscle fibres
Vein
Venule
Single cell layer
Capillary
Valve action in vein
Valve open
Valve shut

BLOOD FACTS

- There are four main types, or groups, of blood: A, B, AB, and O. Blood transfusions (transfers) must use compatible groups.

- Red blood cells last about four months and make about 172,000 circuits around the body.

BLOOD PRESSURE

Blood circulates under pressure. This is measured using two figures: the systole, or first figure, gives the pressure as the heart pumps blood into the system; the diastole, or second figure, gives the pressure when the heart rests between beats.

A nurse or doctor measures blood pressure.

HIV AND AIDS

The HIV virus that causes AIDS disables the immune system. One way it achieves this is by destroying the T4-lymphocytes (white blood cells) that help "killer" lymphocytes attack invaders.

Micrograph of an HIV virus bursting from a T4-lymphocyte

Pressure
180
140
100
60
Time 8 AM 9 10 11 12 1
Exercise raises pressure
Getting up raises pressure
Systolic
Diastolic

PRESSURE CHANGES

Blood pressure is low when we sleep, and rises during exercise. Also, it may rise as we grow older. A 20-year-old might have a pressure of 110/70mm mercury; a 60-year-old of 160/90mm.

COMMON PROBLEMS

Name	Description
Haemophilia	Deficiency of a blood-clotting factor
Anaemia	Haemoglobin deficiency causing lack of oxygen
Arterio-sclerosis	Thickening of artery wall due to deposits of fat
Varicose vein	Swelling, twisting, and distortion of a vein
Aneurysm	Thinning and dilation (widening) of artery wall

RESPIRATORY SYSTEM

WHEN WE BREATHE IN, we supply our bodies with oxygen from the air, and when we breathe out, we expel a waste gas, carbon dioxide. We breathe about six litres (10.56 pints) of air every minute, and adult lungs hold about three litres (5.28 pints) of air.

Location of respiratory system

RESPIRATORY SYSTEM

Air enters the body at the upper respiratory tract (nose, mouth, and trachea). The trachea splits into two bronchi (tubes), which divide into narrower bronchioles, leading to tiny, hollow, capsules called alveoli. Air is drawn in and out of this system by the action of the diaphragm muscle.

ALVEOLI

The lungs' 700 million microscopic alveoli are hollow and covered in a network of capillary arteries and veins. Their moist walls are so thin that blood passing by can release its waste carbon dioxide and take up oxygen. The capillaries then join up to form the pulmonary vein.

Epiglottis
Hyoid bone
Thyroid cartilage
Thyroid gland
Cricoid cartilage
Trachea
Apex of lung
Aorta
Superior vena cava
Left pulmonary artery
Upper lobe
Secondary bronchus

Mucous membrane
Smooth muscles
Cartilage
Capillary network
Elastic fibres
Alveolus

Lower lobe
Middle lobe of right lung
Oesophagus
Heart
Muscular wall of diaphragm
Tertiary bronchus

Alveoli

RESPIRATION FACTS

• The left lung has two lobes, or sections, and the right has three. Each lung is encased in a

lubricated skin called a pleural membrane. It allows the lungs to slide easily during breathing.

X-ray of lungs

• Rings of cartilage reinforce the trachea and bronchioles to prevent them from collapsing.

• Thousands of tiny hairs, called cilia, line the walls of the airways. They carry dust and bacteria away from the lungs. A mucous lining also catches dust.

• We can survive with just one fully working lung.

Oxygen: 21%
Nitrogen: 75%
Carbon dioxide: 4%
Composition of inhaled air

Oxygen: 16%
Nitrogen: 75%
Carbon dioxide: 9%
Composition of exhaled air

• Nitrogen dissolves in blood plasma, but is not used in any of the body's processes.

ACE AIRWAYS

If the inner surfaces of the lungs were laid out flat, their total area would be 180sq m (1,938sq ft). This would cover more than two-thirds of a tennis court.

BREATHING

BREATHING IN

Intercostal (rib) muscles contract.
Ribs lift upwards and outwards.
Lungs expand, drawing in air.
Diaphragm contracts and flattens.

BREATHING OUT

Intercostal (rib) muscles relax.
Ribs move downwards and in.
Lungs contract, forcing air out.
Diaphragm returns to natural arch shape.

The bases of our lungs rest on the diaphragm, a dome-shaped muscle. When we inhale, it pulls the bases down, and chest (intercostal) muscles expand the ribcage. Air rushes into the lungs through the trachea.

• Hiccups are caused by the rapid contraction of the diaphragm. Air is drawn in very rapidly and the vocal cords snap quickly shut, causing the noise we hear as a hiccup.

• Between the trachea and the alveoli the airways divide 23 times, making a total of 2,400km (1,491 miles) of airways.

HIC HICK

American farmer Charles Osborne (1894–1991) began hiccuping in 1922. He continued until 1990, after 68 years of constant hiccups.

Healthy lung   *Smoker's lung*

LUNGS AND SMOKING

More than 4,000 chemicals have been identified in cigarette smoke, and many of these irritate the lungs and cause cancer. Many people die each year from the effects of smoking.

COMMON PROBLEMS

Name	Description
Asthma	Causes wheezing and difficulty of breathing out
Bronchitis	Inflammation of the bronchi
Pneumonia	Inflammation of lungs caused by infection
Lung cancer	Malignant tumours of the lung
Emphysema	Damage to alveoli, causes breathlessness

SMOKING HEALTH RISK

Cigarettes per day	Lung cancer deaths per year per 100,000 males
0	10
1–14	78
15–24	127

DIGESTION

FOOD HAS TO BE broken down into small particles before the body can make use of its energy and nutrients. This process is called digestion and happens in the digestive tract, a tube 9m (29.5ft) long.

DIGESTIVE TRACT

The digestive tract runs from the mouth to the anus. Organs such as the liver, pancreas, and gall bladder connect with the tract and help it to break down and absorb food.

THE LIVER

Right lobe
Left lobe
Inferior vena cava
Gall bladder

The liver receives blood from the hepatic artery and the portal (gastrointestinal) vein, and has many functions, including:
- Makes bile for digesting fat.
- Helps maintain blood sugar levels.
- Makes blood proteins.
- Helps blood to clot.
- Controls blood cell formation and destruction.
- Stores vitamins.
- Removes poisons from body.
- Stores energy.
- Makes heat.
- Destroys micro-organisms.

ABSORBING FOOD

The lining of the small intestine has millions of microscopic, finger-like projections called villi. They are packed with blood and lymph vessels and have thin walls through which nutrients from the partly digested food can easily pass.

1 MOUTH AND THROAT

Digestion begins as soon as you take a bite of food: chewing breaks down food into smaller lumps; enzymes (proteins that speed up chemical reactions) in saliva begin to break down complex carbohydrates into simpler sugars. The tongue rolls food into a bolus (lump) and pushes it to the back of the throat, where a swallowing reflex is activated. The bolus passes down the oesophagus (food pipe) towards the stomach.

Oesophagus

2 STOMACH

The lining of the stomach gives out highly acidic juices and enzymes that break down food. Acid helps the enzymes work and kills bacteria. The resulting soupy liquid is called chyme.

Stomach

3 DUODENUM

The duodenum receives bile (green, watery fluid) from the liver and juices from the pancreas. Pancreatic juice continues to break down food, but also neutralizes stomach acids so that other enzymes can act. Bile emulsifies (splits up) fats for later digestion.

Duodenum

4 ILEUM (SMALL INTESTINE)

Food is absorbed in the ileum, and some substances, such as fats, lactose, and sucrose are finally digested here. Nutrients absorbed into the blood are sent to the liver for processing. *Colon*

Villus: 1mm (0.04in) long
Capillaries
Lacteal
Epithelium
Muscles contract and relax to squeeze food along.
Mucosa layer contains venules, arterioles, and thin muscle sheets.

5 COLON AND RECTUM (LARGE INTESTINE)

Water and fibre from food pass into the colon, where much of the water is aborbed into the body. The large intestine does not secrete enzymes, but contains bacteria which break down the fibrous, undigested leftovers. This semi-solid waste, called faeces, then passes into the rectum, and is later expelled through the anus.

Tongue
Trachea
Maxilla (upper jaw)
Mandible (lower jaw)
Epiglottis
Oesophagus
Fold of mucous membrane
Stomach
Liver
Pancreas | Spleen
Appendix
Colon
Small intestine
Rectum
Anal sphincter muscle
Ileum
Anus

IRON AND FIBRE

Since 1966, Frenchman Michel Lolito, "Monsieur Mangetout", has eaten and digested ten bicycles, seven TVs, six chandeliers, and a Cessna light aircraft.

DIGESTION FACTS

- Food spends 3 to 5 hours in the stomach, and 6 to 20 hours in the large intestine.
- The stomach wall is protected by a mucus lining; otherwise, it would start to digest itself.
- When we swallow, a lid called the epiglottis covers the trachea to stop food from entering.

PERISTALSIS

Circular muscle contracts.
Bolus
Circular muscle relaxes.
Muscular wall of tract
Bolus pushed downwards.

A muscular, wave-like movement called peristalsis pushes food through the digestive tract. The walls of the tract contain rings and lengths of muscle. These contract and relax alternately to propel food through the system.

X-ray of faeces passing through the colon

KEY ENZYMES

Region	Enzymes produced	Foods acted on by enzymes
Mouth	Salivary amylase	Starch (carbohydrate)
Stomach	Pepsin and rennin	Proteins and milk protein
Duodenum	Trypsin, amylase, lipase	Proteins, peptides, starch, and fats
Ileum	Trypsin, amylase, lipase	Peptides, fats, maltose, sucrose, lactose
Colon	Bacterial enzymes	Vegetable and undigested fibre

COMMON PROBLEMS

Name	Description
Indigestion	Stomach pain, when stomach stretches with gas or acid build-up
Diarrhoea	Liquid or semi-liquid faeces caused by poisoned food or infection
Constipation	Slow bowel actions, can be caused by lack of fibre in diet
Cirrhosis	Scarring and breakdown of liver commonly caused by alcohol abuse
Hepatitis	Inflammation of liver caused by viral infection, drugs, or poisons

URINARY SYSTEM

THE KIDNEYS CONTROL the amount of water and minerals in our blood by getting rid of unwanted substances in the form of urine. Urine is expelled from the body via a muscular reservoir called the bladder. This system is known as the urinary or excretory system. The kidneys filter all the blood in the body every five minutes.

Location of urinary system

THE KIDNEYS

The two kidneys contain about 1.3 million tiny tubes, called nephrons, that cleanse the blood. As blood passes through the tubes into a network of tiny blood vessels, called the glomerulus, wastes and water are filtered out into a cup-shaped organ called a Bowman's capsule. Some of this filtrate is reabsorbed into the blood. The rest, now concentrated, travels down the ureter towards the bladder.

Glomerulus and Bowman's capsule

Renal cortex

Medulla

U-shaped collecting tubule

Urine-collecting tubule

Section through kidney

URINARY FACTS

• Up to about two years of age, the bladder is emptied by a reflex action. After this age, a child learns to control the bladder.

• ADH (anti-diuretic hormone), made in the pituitary gland, controls the uptake of water in the kidneys.

• We can survive with only one kidney. If one stops working the other enlarges in order to do the work for both.

KIDNEY FILTRATES

This table shows percentages of major substances in the blood serum (plasma), and how much is then filtered out by the kidneys as urine.

Compounds	Blood %	Urine %
Proteins	7–9	0
Urea	0.03	2
Uric Acid	0.005	0.05
Ammonium	0.0001	0.04
Water	90–93	95

KIDNEY STONES

Sometimes, minerals from urine solidify and block the tubes inside the kidneys, forming kidney stones. Some are smooth, like pebbles, while others, called stag-horn stones, are spiked. Passing a small stone causes intense pain. Larger stones can be broken up by ultrasound waves, or removed by surgery.

Dissected kidney with stones

WASTE NOT

Our word "lotion" comes from the Latin word for urine, *lotium*. Romans used stale urine as a hair lotion because it prevented dandruff and killed lice. It was also used to help dye clothes.

1 KIDNEYS
Blood enters the kidneys and flows into the nephrons. Each nephron contains a filtering unit called a glomerulus. Water and salts pass from the blood into collecting tubules.

Suprarenal gland

Kidney

Renal artery

Renal vein

Pelvis

Testicular artery

Testicular vein

Fat

Medulla: light inner core

Cortex: dark outer region

2 URETER
The filtrate of water and salts, called urine, produced in the nephrons, leaves the kidney via a tube called the ureter.

Vas deferens: carries sperm from testes.

Ureter

3 BLADDER
Day and night urine trickles down the two ureters into a stretchable, muscular bag called the bladder. The adult bladder can store well over half a litre (19fl oz) of urine, until it can be released from the body at a suitable time. Urine leaves through the urethral opening in the base.

Inner bladder

Muscle layer

Pubic bone

Seminal vesicle

Prostate

Ampulla

Fatty pad

Ischium of pelvis

4 URETHRA
Urine leaves the body through a tube called the urethra. The male urethra is about 20cm (8in) long and stretches to the tip of the penis. The female urethra is much shorter: about 4cm (1.4in) long.

Bulb of penis

Vas deferens

Urethra

PROSTATE GLAND

This gland, found only in males, surrounds the part of the urethra nearest the bladder. It secretes a milky fluid into the urethra, which forms about 30% of the seminal fluid in which sperm are ejaculated. After the age of about 50, this gland naturally enlarges. However, sometimes it may squash the urethra and make urination difficult. Treatment usually involves removal of all or part of the gland.

X-ray showing enlarged prostate gland

KIDNEY DIALYSIS AND TRANSPLANT

If the kidneys fail completely, a dialysis machine can be used to filter blood. Blood passes through the machine 20 times before it is properly cleansed, and the patient must have two to three of these filtering sessions every week. More often, kidney failure is treated by transplanting a healthy organ. Drugs then prevent the body from rejecting the new kidney. Kidneys are the most commonly transplanted organ.

Patient connected to a kidney dialysis machine

COMMON PROBLEMS

Name	Description
Cystitis	Inflammation of inside of bladder caused by bacterial infection; more common in women than in men
Pyelonephritis	Infection of the kidney caused by bacteria
Kidney stones	Stones formed from salts in urine
Polycystic kidneys	Multiple fluid sacs that grow in kidneys
Bladder stones	Stones formed in bladder resulting from solidified salts in urine; can block urethral opening

ENDOCRINE SYSTEM

ENDOCRINE GLANDS produce chemicals that the body needs in order to grow properly and work smoothly. The chemicals that these glands (e.g. pituitary, thyroid gland) produce are called hormones and are released directly into the bloodstream. Tiny amounts can have great effects on the body's systems.

MAJOR ENDOCRINE GLANDS

Endocrine glands have no ducts or openings, but the hormones they produce enter the bloodstream as it passes through the gland. Hormones released by endocrine glands tend to have slow-acting, profound effects.

THE PITUITARY GLAND

The pituitary gland, situated in the brain, is often called the master gland; it secretes more than 10 hormones that act on other glands (e.g. thyroid, adrenals, ovaries, testes, mammary glands) to help them produce hormones of their own. Some of the functions of the pituitary gland are controlled by an area of the brain that lies just above it, called the hypothalamus. It also produces ADH (anti-diuretic hormone), which controls the level of water in the body.

Micrograph showing cross-section of pituitary gland

Pituitary gland

Thyroid gland

Parathyroid glands

Adrenal gland

Pancreas

Ovaries

In women, the ovaries produce oestrogen and progesterone, which control the development of sexual characteristics at puberty, such as breast growth and pubic hair, and aspects of menstruation.

The liver controls the duration of some hormones' action. When hormones pass through the liver, they are made inactive and pass, via the kidneys, into urine. (So, doctors test for pregnancy by analysing urine for hormone changes.)

Testis

In men, the testes produce testosterone, a hormone that controls the development of sexual characteristics at puberty, such as pubic and body hair, and voice pitch.

FIGHT AND FLIGHT

In situations of fear, anger, or shock, adrenal glands produce adrenalin, which mobilizes the body in preparation for strong physical exertion. Levels return to normal after exercise.

Heart rate (beats/min) — 180, 120, 60, 0
Time (mins) — 30, 60

HORMONE IMBALANCE

One of the hormones produced by the pituitary controls our rate of growth. Too much can cause gigantism (excessive growth). Too little causes short stature.

Tallest person: 2.7m (8ft 11in) tall

Smallest person: 61cm (24 in) tall

NERVOUS ENERGY

When Mrs. Maxwell Rogers of Florida, US, found her son pinned underneath their car, fear and adrenalin gave her the strength to lift the 1.6 tonne vehicle. She cracked several vertebrae.

ENDOCRINE GLANDS AND THEIR HORMONES

Gland	Hormones produced	Function	Effect of deficiency	Effect of excess
Thyroid	Thyroxine, triiodothyronine	Regulate chemical activity in cells. Essential for normal physical growth and mental development in children	In children, retards growth and mental development (cretinism)	Thyrotoxicosis: over-activity, anxiety, weight loss, diarrhoea, rapid pulse
Pituitary	Growth hormone TSH Prolactin ACTH LH and FSH MSH ADH Oxytocin	Stimulates cell growth in bone, cartilage, and soft tissue Stimulates thyroid gland to secrete hormones Stimulates breast growth and milk production Stimulates adrenal glands to secrete hormones Controls functioning of sexual organs Controls skin darkening Acts on kidneys to decrease water loss Stimulates uterus contraction during birth	Short stature Slow metabolism, bloating Reduced sex drive Can cause infertility Increases water loss Prolonged labour	Gigantism Overproduction of eggs Causes fluid retention, bloating
Parathyroid	Parathyroid hormone (PTH)	Regulates blood calcium levels; important for nerves and muscle functioning	Tetany: spasm and twitching of the muscles	May cause thinning of bones (osteoporosis), or kidney stones
Adrenal	Adrenalin Cortisone Aldosterone	Mobilizes body in response to fear, anger, shock Controls metabolism, body shape Controls level of salts in body	Addison's disease: salt imbalance, low blood pressure, weakness, weight loss, intestinal upsets	Cushing's disease: obesity, moon face, high blood pressure, high blood sugar levels, hairiness
Pancreas	Insulin Glucagon	Control level of sugar in blood	Diabetes: excess sugar in blood	Rare: Coma due to reduced sugar in blood
Kidneys	Erythropoietin 1,25 dihydroxychole-calciferol Renin	Acts on bone marrow to produce red blood cells Raises amount of calcium absorbed in gut, formed from Vitamin D Helps control blood pressure	Anaemia Rickets, osteomalacia	High blood pressure
Ovaries	Oestrogen Progesterone	Stimulates breast growth and egg production, pubic and body hair, changes distribution of body fat at puberty. Thickens uterus walls after ovulation	Infertility	Levels naturally high during pregnancy: at other times, can cause blood clots
Testes	Testosterone	Stimulates sperm production, muscle and bone enlargement, deepening of voice, pubic and body hair. Small amounts present in females	In males, low sperm count and sex drive. Hair thinning	Excessive muscular development and body hair. In males, can cause painful, persistent erection (priapism)

REPRODUCTION AND GROWTH

PLANTS AND ANIMALS produce young like themselves. This creation of life is called reproduction. Humans reproduce sexually: male and female mate to produce their young. A new human life begins when a sperm cell from the father joins an egg cell from the mother. This cell divides into many cells, until it begins to look like a baby.

REPRODUCTION SYSTEMS

FEMALE SEX ORGANS
Eggs are stored in both ovaries. Each month, during the menstrual cycle, one egg ripens, leaves the ovary, and enters the fallopian tube. If it is then fertilized by sperm, it becomes implanted in the uterus. If it is not fertilized, it breaks up and is shed from the body (menstruation).

The woman's main sex organs, the two ovaries, are inside the abdomen.

Fallopian tube
Eggs stored in the ovary
Ovary
Uterus (womb)
The neck of the womb (cervix) opens into the vagina.
Vagina

MALE SEX ORGANS
The two testes produce fresh sperm cells every day. The cells are stored in the testes and epididymides. If the sperm are not released, the cells break down and are reabsorbed into the bloodstream.

The man's main sex organs, the testes and penis, are outside the abdomen.

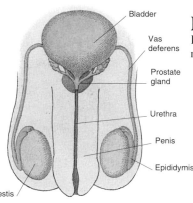

Bladder
Vas deferens
Prostate gland
Urethra
Penis
Epididymis
Testis

MENSTRUAL CYCLE

From puberty (10 to 16 years of age) a woman has monthly menstrual cycles (menstruation), during which she loses blood.

Egg ripening

Endometrium

Ripened egg leaving the ovary

1 An egg starts to ripen in one of the ovaries. The lining of the uterus, called the endometrium, swells with blood in preparation for the egg.

2 About two weeks later, the ripe egg enters the fallopian tube. It is now ready to be fertilized.

Fallopian tube

Lining of the uterus breaks down and passes out of the vagina.

Ripe egg

3 The egg reaches the uterus. If the egg is not fertilized, it begins to break up.

4 The lining of the uterus breaks down and passes, along with the unfertilized egg, out of the vagina as menstrual blood flow.

REPRODUCTION FACTS

• The sperm cell is about 0.05mm (0.002in) long and can be seen only with a microscope. It can swim at about 18cm (7in) per hour and takes on average two hours to reach the egg.

• The testes are kept outside the body in the scrotum, as they need to be 4°C (7°F) cooler than body temperature. If they heat up, sperm production slows down and infertility may result.

• The biggest human cell is the egg cell; it measures 0.1–0.2mm (0.004–0.008in) in diameter and is just visible to the naked eye.

Types of contraceptive

Oral contraceptive pills

The cap

Rubber condom

CONTRACEPTION

Contraceptives are used to prevent conception (pregnancy). A rubber sheath, or condom, fits over the penis to catch semen. Hormones in the oral contraceptive pill prevent eggs from being released. The cap is placed over the cervix to stop sperm from entering the uterus.

SEXUAL INTERCOURSE

For the egg to be fertilized by sperm, a man and woman must have sexual intercourse. The man's penis becomes erect and enters the woman's vagina. When the man climaxes, he ejaculates a fluid, semen, which contains sperm cells. The cells swim into the fallopian tube. One of these cells may reach the egg and fertilize it.

Vagina
Penis

SPERM RACE

More than 300 million sperm are ejaculated into the vagina; 50–150 sperm reach the egg in the fallopian tube, but only one may fertilize the egg.

FERTILIZATION

After sexual intercourse, sperm cells enter the uterus and travel along the fallopian tube. Only one sperm cell may break through the outer layer of the egg cell. Once the egg is fertilized, it divides into two cells, then into four, and so on.

Tadpole-shaped sperm cells are propelled by their tails.

Only one sperm cell can penetrate the outer layer of the egg.

Egg cell

IMPLANTATION

Once an egg has been fertilized, it divides into a ball of cells, called the morula, as it travels down the fallopian tube. After five days, the cells form a hollow ball, or blastocyst. About a week after fertilization, the blastocyst becomes implanted in the rich lining of the uterus.

Egg divides into two cells within 36 hours.

The cells form a ball of cells, or blastocyst.

The egg subdivides further to form a ball of cells, called the morula.

Uterus

STAGES OF GROWTH

FOUR-WEEK EMBRYO

The blastocyst quickly develops to form the placenta, umbilical cord, and the developing baby, or embryo. The embryo is protected by amniotic fluid. About now, its heart begins to beat.

Eye begins to form

Leg bud

Arm bud

Vertebra, or backbone

EIGHT-WEEK FOETUS

The embryo is 2.5cm (1in) long and is now called a foetus. All the internal organs have developed.

Wall of uterus

Fallopian tube

Placenta

TWELVE WEEKS

All the foetus' organs are fully formed. From this stage on, the foetus develops quickly.

Umbilical cord, made up of three intertwined blood vessels

BABY IN WOMB

The baby receives food and oxygen from the mother's bloodstream via the placenta, a disc-shaped organ that is attached to the baby by the umbilical cord. The baby's waste products pass back into the mother's bloodstream for excretion. The baby is surrounded by amniotic fluid, which cushions it from knocks and bumps.

Psoas muscle

Chorion membrane

Amnion membrane, containing amniotic fluid

TWENTY-WEEK FOETUS

During the last six months of growth the baby develops fine details like fingernails and hair. From 16 to 20 weeks, it starts to move and kick. This is called quickening. The baby can now hear, tell light from dark, and can swallow and suck its thumb.

During the last few weeks of pregnancy, the baby turns round so its head is facing downwards, ready to be born.

Vagina

Placenta

CHILD DEVELOPMENT

SIX-MONTH BABY

Most babies sit propped up and can support the weight of their head. They will start to make word sounds such as "Da-Da" or "Ma-Ma". The first teeth start to show.

NINE- TO TWELVE-MONTH BABY

Most babies learn to crawl, can pull themselves upright on furniture, and stand unsupported for a second or two. By 12 months, they may have up to eight teeth and weigh three times their birth weight.

EIGHTEEN-MONTH CHILD

Most children can walk unaided. They will know at least six words, usually many more, and can put words together to make simple phrases. They can climb stairs and make towers of bricks.

TWO- TO THREE-YEAR-OLD CHILD

Children can hold a pencil and draw. Aged three, they can talk in simple sentences and copy basic shapes.

NEW-BORN BABY

After about 40 weeks, or 9 months, of development, the baby is ready to be born. The muscles of the uterus contract and the cervix dilates, pushing the baby out, usually head first. The baby soon takes its first breath of fresh air. The new-born baby can hear well but cannot focus its eyes properly.

New-born baby

PUBERTY FACTS

- When children reach puberty, they undergo physical and psychological changes that prepare them for sexual maturity.

- A girl's ovaries produce the hormones progesterone and oestrogen. These cause breasts to develop, hips to broaden, and pubic hair to grow. At this time menstruation begins.

- A boy's testes produce the hormone testosterone. This causes muscles to develop, hair to grow on the face and body, the voice to deepen, and sperm to be produced.

GENETICS

Egg and sperm cells each contain 23 chromosomes. When an egg and a sperm cell join, the new cell has 46 chromosomes – the same as all other types of cell in the human body. A baby's sex is determined by one chromosome, X or Y. The egg carries only X, but the sperm can carry either X or Y. If the egg is fertilized by a sperm carrying an X, the sex will be female (XX), if the sperm carries a Y, the sex will be male (XY).

Father (XY) *Mother (XX)*

Girl (XX) *Boy (XY)* *Girl (XX)* *Boy (XY)*

GROWTH FACTS

- The proportions of our bodies change as we grow. A baby's head accounts for about one quarter of its body length. By adulthood, the proportion has reduced to one eighth.

- Girls grow faster than boys during the early stages of growth. A girl is about three-quarters of her adult height by the age of 7½; a boy reaches this height by the age of 9.

- A person is about 1cm (0.4in) taller in the morning than in the evening. This is because the pads of cartilage in the spine become more compressed during the day.

COMMON PROBLEMS

Ectopic pregnancy	Foetus implanted outside the womb.
Infertility	Inability to conceive a child.
Miscarriage	Premature ending of pregnancy on or before 24 weeks.
Pre-eclampsia	High blood pressure developed during pregnancy.

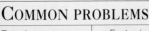

MEDICINE

THROUGHOUT THE AGES, people have tried to find ways to cure illness. In early times, people believed that disease was a punishment from the gods. Today, scientists are constantly searching for new ways of treating and preventing illness.

c.10,000 B.C. Trepanning is practised in Europe and America. Holes are drilled into a person's skull to cure illness. People believed that evil spirits left through these holes.

Trepanning

2700 B.C. First named doctor is Imhotep of Egypt. He acquired a great reputation for healing. He later became known as the Egyptian god of medicine.

Imhotep

| 10,000 B.C. | 10,000 B.C. | 3000 B.C. | 2700 B.C. |

c.A.D. 130 Galen, a Greek physician, introduces the idea that a person's mood depends on the balancing of four fluids, or humours, in the body: black bile (melancholy), yellow bile (choleric), blood (sanguine), and phlegm (phlegmatic).

The four humours: choleric (with lion), sanguine (with ape), phlegmatic (with sheep), and melancholic (with hog).

1300s Leeches are used to suck blood from the body, as it was believed that too much blood was the cause of some illnesses. Blood-letting is used to treat a variety of illnesses, such as tumours, fevers, and gout.

Leech

1543 First accurate anatomical drawings of the human body are drawn by Flemish doctor, Andreas Vesalius (1514–64). Stolen corpses are used for his studies.

First anatomical drawings

c.1590 Compound microscope invented. Dutchman, Zacharias Janssen (1580–c.1638) makes lenses held in two iron tubes, one inside the other.

Early microscope

| A.D. 100 | A.D. 130 | 1300 | 1300 | 1500 | 1543 | 1590 |

1683 Bacteria first seen under a microscope by Antonie van Leeuwenhoek (1632–1723), a Dutch scientist.

Antonie van Leeuwenhoek

1796 Vaccination against smallpox is discovered by English doctor, Edward Jenner (1749–1823). He innoculates an eight-year-old boy with cowpox taken from a sore on the hand of a dairymaid.

Medal issued c.1800 to celebrate Edward Jenner's discovery of vaccination.

1800 Effects of electricity on muscles described by Italian physicist, Volta (1745–1827).

1805 Morphine, a painkiller, is separated from opium.

1810 Homeopathy is introduced by German physician, Samuel Hahnemann (1755–1843). This new system is based on the principle of curing like with like.

Samuel Hahnemann

| 1680 | 1683 | 1796 | 1800 | 1800 | 1805 | 1810 |

1854 Florence Nightingale (1820–1910), born in Florence, Italy, nurses soldiers during the Crimean War (1854–56) in the hospital at Scutari, Turkey. She becomes known as "the lady with the lamp". Four years later, she opens the Nightingale Training School for nurses in London, which greatly improves nursing standards.

Florence Nightingale

1860 Antiseptic, in the form of weak carbolic acid, is used to prevent infections during operations by English surgeon, Joseph Lister (1827–1912).

Joseph Lister

1864 Red Cross Society founded in Geneva, Switzerland, by Swiss businessman, Henri Dunant (1829–1910), after helping casualties at the Battle of Solferino (1859).

Henri Dunant

| 1850 | 1854 | 1860 | 1860 | 1864 |

1895 X-rays discovered by German physicist, Wilhelm Roentgen (1845–1923). He uses his wife's hand for the first pictures.

One of the first X-rays

1895 Psychoanalysis founded by Austrian doctor, Sigmund Freud (1856–1939). He treats people with mental disorders by talking to them about their dreams and childhood experiences.

Sigmund Freud

1902 Radium and polonium discovered by Polish-born Marie Curie (1867–1934) and her husband, Pierre Curie (1859–1906), of France. These elements are now used in radiotherapy to treat cancer.

Marie and Pierre Curie

1910 Four blood groups, A, B, AB, O, discovered by Austrian pathologist, Dr. Karl Landsteiner (1868–1943).

1912 Vitamins discovered by British biochemist, Sir Frederick Gowland Hopkins (1861–1947).

1920 First EE machine is developed to re electrical brain waves.

1921 First birt control clinic founded by Mar Stopes (1880–19 in London.

| 1890 | 1895 | 1900 | 1902 | 1910 | 1912 | 1920 | 1921 |

1952 Vaccine against polio produced by American scientist, Jonas Salk (1914–1995).

Jonas Salk

1953 Structure of genetic material (DNA) discovered by American biologist, James Watson (born 1928) and English biochemist, Francis Crick (born 1916).

Watson and Crick

1954 Heart–lung machine developed for use during heart surgery.

1954 First internal heart pacemaker fitted in Stockholm, Sweden.

1958 Endoscope, a telescope that looks inside the body, developed.

1967 First heart transplant, performed by South African surgeon, Christiaan Barnard (born 1922). The patient survives 18 days.

1970 Heart pacemakers in general use.

Christiaan Barnard

| 1952 | 1952 | 1953 | 1954 | 1958 | 1967 | 1970 | 1970 |

B.C. *The Canons of ine* is written in China. ...udes an account of blood ...ation.

...B.C. Surgery practised ...a. Surgeons perform ...ations, skin grafts, and ...e cataracts from eyes.

400 B.C. Greek physician, Hippocrates (c.460–377 B.C.) teaches that the first duty of a doctor is to do what is best for his patients, and makes rules for his pupils to follow. They form the basis of the Hippocratic Oath, which doctors still follow today.

2 B.C. Acupuncture, puncturing the skin with needles to cure illness, is practised in China.

Hippocrates

Acupuncture chart

| ...B.C. | 1000 B.C. | 1000 B.C. | 400 B.C. | 400 B.C. | 2 B.C. |

...Quinine is used to ...nalaria in South ...ca.

First thermometer ...king human ...erature invented by ...n physician, Sanctorius ...–1636).

Sanctorius' thermometer

1628 First description of the circulation of the blood by Englishman William Harvey (1578–1657), physician to King James I and King Charles I of England.

William Harvey with Charles I

| 1600 | 1615 | 1628 |

First stethoscope ... from a roll of paper ...ench doctor, René ...nec (1781–1826).

Laughing gas ...us oxide) is first used ...eneral anaesthetic by ...e Wells (1815–48).

René Laënnec

1846 Ether used as an anaesthetic by William Morton (1819–68), an American dentist.

1847 Chloroform is used as an anaesthetic by Sir James Young Simpson (1811–70).

1849 First female medical graduate in the USA is Elizabeth Blackwell (1821–1910).

Elizabeth Blackwell

| 1844 | 1846 | 1847 | 1849 |

Elizabeth ...ett Anderson is ...oman to practise ...cine in Britain.

...urization invented ...enchman, Louis ...ur (1822–95) to ...reat food and kill ...ria.

Louis Pasteur

1883 Bacteria that cause tuberculosis and cholera discovered by German scientist, Robert Koch (1843–1910).

1883 Cocaine used as a local anaesthetic during an eye operation.

1886 Surgical instruments are sterilized by steam. Masks, gowns, and capes are used by surgeons in operations.

Operation, 1880s

| 1880 | 1883 | 1886 |

First injection of insulin given, ...-year-old boy.

...Penicillin ...ered by Scottish ...iologist, Sir ...der Fleming ...–1955), in a green ...growing on a plate.

Alexander Fleming

1928 The Iron Lung is developed in Boston, Massachusetts, USA. It saves the life of a paralysed boy in 1932.

1950 First kidney transplant performed in Chicago, USA.

1950s Birth control pill developed for women. By the early 1960s it is widely used.

Birth control pill

| 1928 | 1950 | 1950 |

...CT (computerized ...graphy) scan introduced. ...ces more detailed picture of ...al organs than an X-ray.

...(magnetic resonance ...ng) scan uses radio waves ...duce pictures of the ...of the body.

MRI scan

1976 Transistorized bionic, arm is fitted to the victim of a road accident in Australia.

1978 First test-tube baby, Louise Brown, is born in Britain.

1980s–1990s Laser surgery used in eye operations and to remove cancer cells.
Keyhole surgery is practised: operations are performed through small incisions in the body.
Gene transplants performed: defective or missing genes are replaced with artificial copies.

| 1976 | 1978 | 1980 | 1990 |

BRANCHES OF MEDICINE

Name	What it deals with
Cardiology	Heart and arteries
Chiropody	Feet
Dermatology	Skin
Endocrinology	Hormones
Gastroenterology	Stomach, intestines
Geriatrics	Elderly people
Gynaecology	Female reproductive organs
Haematology	Blood
Neurology	Brain and nerves
Obstetrics	Pregnancy
Oncology	Growths and tumours
Ophthalmology	Eyes
Orthopaedics	Bones, joints, muscles
Osteopathy	Manipulation of back and limbs to ease pain
Paediatrics	Children
Pathology	Body tissues and fluids
Pharmacology	Drugs
Physiotherapy	Exercise and massage of the body
Psychiatry	Mental illness
Radiology	X-rays for diagnosis
Radiotherapy	Use of X-rays to kill unwanted cells
Renal medicine	Kidneys

DRUG TYPES

Name	Use
Analgesic	Provides relief from pain, such as headache and stomach-ache.
Antacid	Counteracts acid in the stomach to relieve heartburn, indigestion, etc.
Antibiotic	Treats infections by killing bacteria in the body.
Antihistamine	Counteracts allergies such as hay fever.
Antipyretic	Reduces fevers, such as influenza.
Bronchodilator	Eases breathing in diseases such as asthma.
Decongestant	Common cold treatment; works by unblocking nasal passages.

RETURN OF THE LEECH

Leeches are being used again in modern medicine. After certain operations, they are used to restore blood circulation and to prevent the blood from clotting.

NUTRITION

A GOOD DIET is an essential part of a healthy lifestyle for children and adults. Rich in vitamins, minerals, and other nutrients, a balanced diet will assist growth and help fight against disease.

VITAL COMPONENTS OF FOOD

Nutrients are the essential elements for healthy eating and include:

Vitamins
These aid the release of energy from glucose, and assist the body's growth and repair.

Minerals
These help growth and repair processes, the release of energy from nutrients, and help form new tissues.

Fibre
The indigestible part of fruit, vegetables, bread, and cereals, fibre aids normal bowel function.

Carbohydrates
These are compounds of carbon, hydrogen, and oxygen, such as starch and sugar, that provide the body with energy.

Fats
These supply concentrated energy. They also help form chemical "messengers", such as hormones.

Protein
This is a substance the body needs for growth and repair. It is found in foods such as meat, fish, cheese, and beans.

A BALANCED DIET

The food pyramid was developed by American nutritionists at the beginning of the 1990s. It represents the proportions in which the five food groups should be eaten each day for a balanced diet.

Sugars, fats, and oils (use sparingly)

Dairy products (2–3 servings)

Meat,. seafood, eggs, pulses, nuts (2–3 servings)

Vegetables (3–5 servings)

Fruit (2–4 servings)

Carbohydrates (6-11 servings)

FOOD FACTS

• Surprisingly, frozen vegetables are just as good for you as fresh vegetables.
• In India, many people are vegetarian, following the Hindu belief that all life is sacred.
• All vegetables contain some protein, but dried peas and beans have large amounts.

FOOD WORDS

Acid A substance produced by the stomach that helps digest food.
Antibodies Proteins in the blood that protect the body by fighting bacteria and viruses.
Antioxidant A substance added to foods to prevent them from oxidizing and so going stale.
Carnivore Person who eats meat.
Cholesterol A chemical found in certain foods, such as eggs, and produced in the liver from saturated fats.
Digestion The breaking down of food in the stomach so that nutrients may be absorbed into the body.
Glucose A sugar, released from the digestion of starch and sucrose, that is the body's main energy source.
Hormone Chemical "messenger" that moves in the bloodstream and controls the functions of the body.
Kilocalorie A unit used to measure the energy content of foods.
Kilojoule A unit of measurement showing energy content in food. One kilojoule equals 1,000 joules.
Metabolism The chemical processes occurring in the body that result in growth, production of energy, and elimination of waste.
Nutrient The essential dietary factors – carbohydrates, fats, proteins, vitamins, and minerals.
Saturated fat Fat that tends to increase the amount of unwanted cholesterol in the blood. Mostly found in animal fats.
Starch A polymer found in plants that is an important part of the human diet.
Unsaturated fat Fat that helps decrease unwanted types of cholesterol in the blood. Most vegetable fats are unsaturated.
Vegan Person who does not eat or use any products or byproducts from animals.
Vegetarian Person who does not eat animal products, sometimes with the exception of fish and eggs.

MAIN VITAMIN SOURCES AND REQUIREMENTS

Type of vitamin	Where found	Required for
Vitamin A	Liver, fish-liver oils, egg yolk, and yellow-orange coloured fruit and vegetables	Growth, healthy eyes and skin. Fights infection.
Vitamin B$_1$ (Thiamine)	Whole grains (wholemeal bread and pasta), brown rice, liver, beans, peas, and eggs	Healthy functioning of nervous and digestive systems.
Vitamin B$_2$ (Riboflavin)	Milk, liver, cheese, eggs, green vegetables, brewer's yeast, whole grains, and wheatgerm	Metabolism of protein, fat, and carbohydrates. Keeps tissues healthy.
Vitamin B$_3$ (Niacin)	Liver, lean meats, poultry, fish, nuts, and dried beans	Production of energy and a healthy skin.
Vitamin B$_6$ (Pyridoxine)	Liver, poultry, pork, fish, bananas, potatoes, dried beans, and most fruit and vegetables	Metabolism of protein and production of red blood cells.
Vitamin C	Citrus fruit, strawberries, and potatoes	Healthy skin, teeth, bones, and tissues, and for fighting disease.
Vitamin D	Oily fish (such as salmon), liver, eggs, cod-liver oil, and some cereals	The absorption of calcium and phosphate.
Vitamin E	Margarine, whole grain cereals, and nuts	The formation of new red blood cells. Protection of cell linings in the lungs.

BURNING KILOJOULES

The energy from food is measured in kilojoules (kJ). One kilocalorie (kcal) is equivalent to 4.2 kilojoules, and if your kilojoule intake exceeds your energy and body maintenance requirements, you will put on weight. Various physical activities (see right) help you avoid putting on weight by burning off kilojoules.

Judo
Male: 3,420kJ per hour
Female: 2,950kJ per hour

Running
Male: 3,400kJ per hour
Female: 2,900 kJ per hour

Basketball
Male: 2,430kJ per hour
Female: 2,080kJ per hour

ALTERNATIVE MEDICINE

MORE AND MORE people are now turning to traditional, or alternative, forms of medicine to improve their health or simply to stay well. Many of these therapies treat the whole person, and aim to restore the body's natural state of balance, or harmony.

This detail from the 12th-century Persian Book of Antidotes shows the growing of plants for medicinal purposes.

EARLY HEALING

For thousands of years, people have used plants and minerals to ease pain, heal wounds, and relieve the symptoms of illness. In ancient Egypt, records from about 1600 B.C. list plant remedies, such as gentian, senna, and thyme, that are still used today. Archaeologists have also found in China lists of herbs carved on oracle bones dated about the same time.

ACUPUNCTURE

Acupuncturists treat illness by inserting needles into the skin at particular points. These points lie along invisible energy channels, known as meridians, that are linked to internal organs. The needles unblock, increase, or decrease the flow of energy (called Qi) to restore balance and health.

The acupuncture points on each meridian are numbered.

ALEXANDER TECHNIQUE

This therapy aims to treat and prevent a range of disorders by improving posture. Australian actor, F. Matthias Alexander (1869–1955) developed the technique when he found that bad posture had caused him to lose his voice.

A correct posture, far right, based on the Alexander technique.

AROMATHERAPY

This form of treatment uses highly concentrated oils extracted from plants. The oils can be used in massage, added to baths, or inhaled. French chemist, Réné Gattefossé (1881-1950), who treated soldiers in the First World War, was a pioneer of modern aromatherapy.

Rose oil has a soothing effect.

AYURVEDA

The oldest system of Indian medicine is Ayurveda, from the Sanskrit word meaning "the science of life". Remedies, mainly plants, are chosen for their ability to harmonize the balance between a patient and the basic influences of life, such as diet, work, or home life.

Om – the symbol for the life force in Ayurvedic medicine.

CHINESE HERBALISM

This natural method of treatment is based on restoring the balance of Yin (female) and Yang (male) in the body's energy channels. Combinations of herbs are selected and supplied in the form of tea, powder, pills, or pastes.

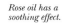

In Chinese medicine, the five elements of wood, fire, earth, metal, and water are used in diagnosis.

CHIROPRACTIC

Chiropractic relieves pain by manipulating the joints, especially those of the spine. It can be used to correct disorders of the joints, muscles, and spine. American David Daniel Palmer (1845–1913) is considered the founder of modern chiropractic.

A chiropractor checks the spine.

HOMEOPATHY

Homeopathy uses a minute dose of a substance that, in large amounts, produces the same symptoms from which the patient is suffering. The aim is to stimulate the body's defences so they fight the disease. Its founder was German physician Samuel Hahnemann (1755–1843).

Samuel Hahnemann

HYDROTHERAPY

Water, in the form of hot and cold baths or sprays, is used in hydrotherapy to stimulate the body's power to heal itself. The first hydrotherapy centre in Britain was founded by a Dominican monk, Sebastian Kneipp (1821–97).

Hot and cold water sprays stimulate circulation.

OSTEOPATHY

When the body's framework is out of alignment, osteopaths can diagnose and treat disorders. They use their hands to massage and manipulate the joints to restore normal movement. Osteopathy was founded by American doctor Andrew Taylor Still (1828–1917).

Shoulders and spine out of alignment

REFLEXOLOGY

In this form of therapy, areas on the feet, known as reflex areas, relate to certain parts of the body. By skillful massage of the relevant area, blockages in the energy channels are released allowing the affected part of the body to heal. The practice was developed in the United States by Eunice Ingham (1889–1974).

Reflex areas

SHIATSU

Shiatsu is a Japanese word meaning "finger pressure". The therapist uses pressure on hundreds of surface points along the body's meridians to rebalance the quality and quantity of energy. The system was popularized by Tokujiro Namikoshi (1905–94).

The yin-yang symbol represents harmony or balance in the body.

YOGA

This well-known Hindu system combines physical, mental, and spiritual health. The most common form is Hatha yoga, a course of exercises and postures designed to promote physical and mental well-being. Yoga has been practised in India for thousands of years.

The lotus position

Feverfew can help relieve migraines and arthritis.

Evening primrose is used for skin problems.

PLANTS IN MEDICINE

Wild flowers such as evening primrose (*Oenothera biennis*) and feverfew (*Tanacetum parthenium*) are among the most widely used medicinal herbs. Research has confirmed their power to heal.

MEDICINE FACTS

• Chinese medicine uses dried seahorse in preparations to treat kidney problems.

• In Ayurvedic medicine, the flesh from a pit viper is given to relieve muscular pain.

FIRST AID

FIRST AID IS the first assistance or treatment given to a person for any injury or sudden illness, before the arrival of an ambulance, doctor, or other qualified help. The main aim of first aid is to prevent the injury from becoming worse.

Keep the head tilted back.

Use two fingers to check pulse.

CHECK FOR A PULSE

If the heart is beating, there will be a pulse in the neck. Tilt the head back and feel for the Adam's apple with the pads of two fingers. Slide your fingers back into the gap between the windpipe and the muscle that runs beside it. Feel for ten seconds before deciding that the pulse is absent.

CALL AN AMBULANCE OR DOCTOR FOR:

• Unexplained drowsiness or loss of consciousness
• Severe bleeding
• Unexplained fits of any sort
• Difficulty in breathing
• Severe abdominal pain
• Sudden blurred vision or seeing coloured haloes around lights

FIRST-AID KIT

Every home and car should have a first-aid kit containing items needed for emergency treatment. Keep the box clean and clearly labelled, and out of reach of children. Replace items as soon as you use them.

Tweezers for removing splinters

Cotton wool is useful for cleaning wounds.

Adhesive dressings protect minor cuts and scrapes while they heal.

Elastic bandages stretch to provide support for sprained ankles.

Scissors for cutting bandages

Different injuries require a variety of dressings and bandages.

Safety pins to hold dressings in place.

Eye bath is useful for washing the eye clean of chemicals such as bleach.

Antiseptic cream protects minor cuts against infection.

LEARNING THE A, B, AND C

The A (Airway), B (Breathing), and C (Circulation) of any unconscious person must be established within three minutes in order to prevent permanent injury.

A IS FOR AIRWAY
Airway must be opened and kept open. Tilt the head of the injured person (casualty) back and lift the chin forward to open the airway.

B IS FOR BREATHING
Breathing must be established and maintained. If breathing has stopped, then start mouth-to-mouth ventilation by blowing your own expelled air into the casualty's lungs.

C IS FOR CIRCULATION
Circulation of blood must be maintained. Check the heart is beating by feeling for a pulse. If the heart has stopped "chest compressions" can be applied, together with artificial ventilation. In some countries the hand nearest the casualty's feet should be used for compressions.

RECOVERY POSITION

If an injured child is unconscious, but still breathing and has a pulse, place her or him in the recovery position.

Place foot flat on the ground.

Clasp under thigh and bend at knee.

Keep this leg straight.

First, lie the child on her back and straighten her legs. Bend the arm nearest to you and lay it on the ground with the palm up. Bring the other arm across her chest and hold the palm of your hand against her cheek. Use your free hand to pull her knee up.

Adjust child's hand under her cheek.

Bend top leg into a right angle to prevent her from rolling forward.

Gently pull on the thigh of the bent leg, and roll the patient towards you and on to her side. Bend this same leg into a right angle to prevent her from rolling forward. Tilt her head back to make sure the airway is still open. Call an ambulance.

ADVICE NOTE
This page supplies some basic information on first aid. It does not offer complete procedures, and readers are advised to refer to a first-aid manual for full guidance.

HOME SAFETY FACTS

Although most people think of home as the safest place, you are more likely to have an accident in the home than at work or school. To make the home a safer place:

• Do not use electrical equipment in the bathroom or near water.

• Keep saucepan handles turned inward so they do not hang over the work surface, and use the back rings of a hob first.

• Store dangerous items in a high cupboard, out of the reach of children.

• Do not put toxic substances in a familiar food or drink container.

• Run the cold water into the bath first, and keep testing the temperature as you add the hot water.

• Do not hold a hot drink when you have a baby on your lap.

• Do not put an iron on the floor to cool; put it out of reach.

BELIEFS, CUSTOMS, AND SOCIETY

Focusing on the way we live, this section provides detailed facts and figures on religion, politics, philosophy, and money around the world, as well as describing all kinds of strange customs and rituals.

Myths and Legends • Faith Systems • Other Faiths
Great Thinkers • Patterns of Family and Society • Customs and Rituals
Celebration and Decoration • Money • Politics • Law and Order

On pages 139 to 143, B.C.E. (Before the Common Era)
and C.E. (Common Era) stand for the same dates
as B.C. and A.D.

MYTHS AND LEGENDS

FROM ANCIENT TIMES people have invented stories to explain the world around them. Myths help explain events such as how the world was created and why people die, as well as natural phenomena such as the weather. Legends are closely related to myths but may be based on actual events.

AN AZTEC MYTH
Quetzalcoatl, the chief god of the Aztecs who lived in Central Mexico, took the form of a feathered serpent. He created humans and gave them knowledge, but then he sailed away on a raft of serpents. The Aztecs believed that, upon his return, their world would end.

This mask, representing the god Quetzalcoatl, is made of turquoise mosaic.

FIGURE OF VENUS
This clay figure from Austria shows the Venus of Willendorf, dated 25,000 B.C. Her full figure represents the fertility of the goddess.

EARTH GODDESS
For thousands of years, people in different parts of the world worshipped images of the Earth Goddess, or Great Mother. As the "mother of the world," she was believed to give life to plants, animals, and humans. Because the power of fertility ensures the future of humanity, earth goddesses have always played an important role in mythology.

KING ARTHUR
A famous Arthurian legend tells how the magic sword Excalibur was given to King Arthur by the Lady of the Lake. Another version tells how he proved himself king by pulling the sword from a stone. It is thought that Arthur may have been a real king or chieftain in 5th-century Britain.

Arthur watches the sword Excalibur rise from the lake.

CREATION MYTHS
Stories that try to answer the mystery of how the world began are called creation myths.

IZANAGI AND IZANAMI
The Japanese thought the Earth was once a shapeless mass. A god and goddess, Izanagi and Izanami, stirred the mass with a long spear. Gradually the mixture thickened and dropped off the spear to form an island. The god and goddess married and had children who became the eight islands of Japan.

THE RAVEN
A Native American myth tells how a raven, flying over water, could find nowhere to land. He dropped pebbles to make islands and then created trees. Beasts lived in the forests and fish in the sea. When the raven had made the first man and woman out of wood and clay, the world was complete.

SACRED SITES

Mount Shasta, California, is a Native American site where the power of the Earth Spirit is strong.

Glastonbury Tor, England, is one of the reputed resting places of the Holy Grail, the cup Christ drank from at the Last Supper.

Uluru, Australia, is a special place to the Aboriginals. Paintings in rock shelters show the journeys of the ancestral beings who formed its features.

Uluru (Ayers Rock)

Cape Reinga, New Zealand, is where spirits of the dead depart for Hawaiki, far away in the mystical beginnings of Polynesia.

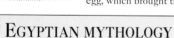

THE WORLD EGG
In Egyptian mythology, life began from water. The first dry land – a primeval mound – rose above the water. A large bird called the Great Cackler alighted on the land and laid the world egg, which brought the first life.

EGYPTIAN MYTHOLOGY
Gods in Egypt often had a human body and the head of an animal or bird to represent their power.

Name	Form
Ra (Amun-Ra)	Universal god, takes many forms
Anubis	Jackal or dog
Apis	Bull
Bastet	Cat
Hathor	Cow
Isis	Woman with a throne on her head
Khepri	Scarab
Mut	Vulture
Nut	Woman with long body, or cow
Osiris	Mummified man
Set, or Seth	Fantastic beast
Sobek	Crocodile
Tefnut	Lioness
Thoth	Ibis or baboon

MYTHICAL BEASTS
There are some frightening creatures in mythology that may have been created to represent evil. Some appear as half-human, half-animal; others take on shapes they can change at will.

DEMONS
Demons, or evil spirits, are often shown as grotesque beings who haunt cemeteries and force people to commit violent acts. They appear in various forms in the religions of the world, sometimes with cloven feet, horns, and a long tail.

MONSTERS
This figure shows a gorgon, a female monster from Greek mythology, who had snakes for hair. Medusa is the most famous of the three gorgons. After she was beheaded by the hero Perseus, her head had the power to turn anyone who looked at it into stone.

GREEK AND ROMAN MYTHOLOGY
The Greeks had 12 main gods and goddesses who cared for different aspects of their life. The Romans later adopted many Greek gods as their own, but with new names.

Greek	Roman	Role
Zeus	Jupiter	King of the gods, god of thunder
Hera	Juno	Queen of the gods, protector of women
Aphrodite	Venus	Goddess of beauty and love
Apollo	Apollo	Sun god, and god of prophecy
Ares	Mars	God of war
Artemis	Diana	Goddess of hunting, protector of animals and children
Athene	Minerva	Goddess of wisdom and war
Demeter	Ceres	Goddess of fertility, and of fruit and crops
Hephaestus	Vulcan	God of fire
Hermes	Mercury	Messenger god, god of travellers
Hestia	Vesta	Goddess of the hearth and home
Poseidon	Neptune	God of the sea

FAITH SYSTEMS

FAITH SYSTEMS ARE sets of beliefs that help to explain some of the mysteries of life and death. Most people who have a faith believe in either one god or several gods.

TOP SIX FAITHS

Faith	Number of followers
Christianity	1,833 million
Islam	971 million
Hinduism	733 million
Buddhism	315 million
Sikhism	13.5–16 million
Judaism	13–14.3 million

DIVISION OF MAJOR FAITHS BY GEOGRAPHIC AREA
Figures are given in percentages. (L.A. = Latin America. N.A. = North America)

Faith	Africa	Asia	Europe	L.A.	N.A.	Oceania	Eurasia	Total
Christianity	17.9	15.6	22.55	23.75	13.0	1.2	6.0	(100%)
Islam	28.66	65.56	1.3	0.14	0.29	0.01	4.04	(100%)
Hinduism	0.2	99.37	0.1	0.1	0.17	0.059	0.001	(100%)
Buddhism	0.01	99.42	0.08	0.17	0.18	0.01	0.13	(100%)
Sikhism	0.14	97.2	1.2	0.05	1.36	0.05	0.00	(100%)
Judaism	1.89	31.35	8.24	6.13	39.29	0.55	12.55	(100%)

WORLD PERCENTAGES

This bar chart shows the percentage distribution of the major world faiths. The figure for "Others" includes those who do not follow a faith system.

Judaism 0.3%
Sikhism 0.3%
Buddhism 5.7%
Hinduism 13.4%
Islam 17.7%
Others 29.2%
Christianity 33.4%

HISTORY OF RELIGIONS
B.C.E. (Before the Common Era) and C.E. (Common Era) stand for the same dates as B.C. and A.D.

JUDAISM
c.2000 B.C.E. | c.1200 B.C.E. | c.900 B.C.E. | 587 B.C.E. | C.E. 70

c.2000 B.C.E. Abraham, prophet of Judaism, Christianity, and Islam, is born in Ur, in present-day Iraq.

c.1200 B.C.E. Hebrews settle in Canaan, mainly present-day Israel, after the Exodus from Egypt.

931 B.C.E. Hebrew kingdom divides into Israel and Judah.
c.900 B.C.E. Torah, the first five books of the Bible, is written.

587 B.C.E. Jerusalem, in present-day Israel, is captured by the Babylonians and the Jews sent into exile.

Herod's Temple

C.E. 70 Herod's Temple, Jerusalem, is destroyed by the Romans. Today, only the Western Wall remains.

ISLAM
c.2000 B.C.E. | C.E. 570 | c.C.E. 622

c.2000 B.C.E. Abraham and his son, Ishmael, build Ka'ba, an Islamic shrine, in Mecca *(Makkah)*, in present-day Saudi Arabia.

c.C.E. 570–632 Muhammad, the last and most important Islamic prophet, is born in Mecca.

Mecca, Saudi Arabia

c.C.E. 610–632 Koran (*Qur'an*), the Islamic scriptures, is revealed to Muhammad by the angel Gabriel.

c.C.E. 622 Muhammad goes to Medina, in present-day Saudi Arabia. This marks the beginning of the Islamic calendar.

HINDUISM
c.1750 B.C.E. | c.1700 B.C.E. | c.1400 B.C.E. | c.800 B.C.E.

c.1750 B.C.E. Beginning of Hinduism in India is influenced by the Aryan people, who worship many gods.

c.1700 B.C.E. Hindu beliefs are revealed to the *rishis*, or holy men, and passed on by word of mouth. *The rishis*

c.1400 B.C.E. *Rig Veda*, the earliest and most important book of the *Vedas*, which contain Hindu beliefs, is written.

c.800 B.C.E. The *Upanishads*, the final books of the *Vedas*, are written. They develop the idea of Brahman, the soul of the Universe.

Brahma, the creator god, the masculine form of Brahman

BUDDHISM
c.563 B.C.E. | c.100 B.C.E. | c.C.E. 20

c.563–483 B.C.E. Siddharta Gautama, later known as Buddha, founder of Buddhism, is born in northeast India.

c.100 B.C.E. The *Pali Canon*, or *Tripitaka* (three baskets), the holy book of Theravada Buddhists, is written.
The Buddhist wheel of life

c.C.E. 20–200 The *Sutras* (collections of sayings), the earliest holy books of Mahayana Buddhists, is written.
Shwedagon Pagoda

c.1300 Shwedagon Pagoda, major Buddhist temple, is built in Rangoon in Burma. It is said to contain the hairs of Buddha.

CHRISTIANITY
c.4 B.C.E. | c.C.E. 40

c.4 B.C.E. Jesus Christ, founder of Christianity, is born in Bethlehem, in present-day Israel.

c.C.E. 30 Jesus is crucified on a cross. Three days later he is raised from the dead (the Resurrection).
The Crucifixion

c.C.E. 40–100 New Testament of the Christian Bible is written. Christianity spreads throughout the Roman empire.

c.1506 St. Peter's Basilica, a major Christian church, is built in Rome. (Original built in c.C.E. 330.)

St. Peter's, Rome

SIKHISM
c.1469 | c.1600

1469–1539 Guru Nanak, leader and founder of Sikhism, is born in the Punjab region of north India and Pakistan.

Guru Nanak and the other nine Gurus who developed Sikhism.

c.1600 Golden Temple of Amritsar, major Sikh temple, is built in the Punjab by Guru Arjan (1563–1606), the fifth Guru.

c.1604 *Adi Granth*, Sikh holy book, is compiled by Guru Arjan. This was later added to and called the *Guru Granth Sahib*.

A Sikh reading the Guru Granth.

CHRISTIANITY

CHRISTIANS BELIEVE THAT Jesus Christ is the Son of God. Their symbol is a cross, which stands for the cross on which Jesus was crucified.

ORIGIN
Christianity originated in about C.E. 30 in Jerusalem, in present-day Israel. Today, it is practised throughout the world.

JESUS CHRIST
Jesus was born in Bethlehem, Israel, in c.4 B.C.E. From the age of 30, he began to preach and heal the sick. A few years later he was tried and executed for having beliefs against Hebrew law.

TEN COMMANDMENTS
Christians obey these ten rules adapted from the Jewish scriptures (which Christians call the Old Testament).
1 Worship only one God.
2 Make no image of God.
3 Respect God's name.
4 Keep Sunday holy.
5 Honour your parents.
6 Do not kill.
7 Do not commit adultery.
8 Do not steal.
9 Do not tell lies.
10 Do not be envious.

KEY POINTS
• Jesus rose from the dead.

• The Holy Trinity is God as the Father, Son, and Holy Spirit.

• Jesus taught that people must love God, and love their neighbour as they love themselves.

BAPTISM
The ceremony of being dipped in water is called baptism. It is practised by Christians throughout the world, upon entering the faith. This practice dates from when Jesus was baptized by John the Baptist.

John the Baptist baptized Jesus in the River Jordan.

BIBLE
This holy book is made up of two parts, the Old and the New Testaments. The Old Testament contains the sacred writings of the Jews. The New Testament is about the life of Jesus and the growth of the early Church.

First printed Bible, 1455, by Johannes Gutenberg.

TYPES OF CHRISTIAN

Eastern Orthodox	Others	Protestants	Roman Catholics
9.3%	10.2%	24.5%	56%

CHRISTIAN HOLY DAYS

Name	Event
Christmas	The birthday of Jesus Christ
Good Friday	Jesus is crucified on a cross
Easter	Jesus is resurrected from the dead
Pentecost	Coming of the Holy Spirit

ST. PETER'S BASILICA
This Roman Catholic church in the Vatican City, Rome, Italy, took more than 100 years to build. Ten architects worked on it, including Michelangelo, who designed the dome.

CHRISTIAN WORDS
Advent Preparation for birth of Jesus.
Ascension Raising of Jesus to Heaven.
Eucharist Bread and wine taken in memory of Jesus.
Evangelist One of the four Gospel writers.
Gospel One of four accounts of Jesus' life in the New Testament.
Lent Forty days of preparation for Easter.

ISLAM

THE ISLAMIC FAITH is based on belief in one God, Allah. Followers of Islam are called Muslims. Their symbol is a star and a crescent moon.

ORIGIN
Islam originated in about C.E. 600 in Mecca (Makkah), in present-day Saudi Arabia. It is now practised throughout the world.

Shahadah

MUHAMMAD
The last and greatest of the 26 Islamic prophets was Muhammad, born in Mecca in c.C.E. 570. The *shahadah* states that Muhammad is Allah's messenger.

PILLARS OF ISLAM
Muslims must obey these five rules:
1 **Shahadah** Allah is the only god, and Muhammad is his messenger.
2 **Salah** Pray five times a day.
3 **Zakah** Give aid to charity.
4 **Sawm** Fast during month of Ramadan.
5 **Hajj** Make at least one pilgrimage to Mecca in a lifetime.

KEY POINTS
• Muslims promise to obey the will of Allah.

• Islam is Allah's chosen faith for the human race.

• Muhammad is Allah's main messenger.

• The Islamic calendar has no leap years.

MECCA (MAKKAH)
This city in Saudi Arabia is the most sacred place in the Muslim world. It contains a cube-shaped shrine, the Ka'ba, believed to have been built by Abraham and Ishmael nearly 4,000 years ago. Every year, especially during their month of pilgrimage, Muslims flock to Mecca and gather around the Ka'ba.

KORAN (QUR'AN)
In this sacred book of Islam, Allah revealed to Muhammad how humankind should live on Earth. Muslims treat the book with great respect. They keep it in a clean place and wash before touching it.

TYPES OF MUSLIM

Others	Shi'ites	Sunnis
1%	16%	83%

ISLAMIC FESTIVALS

Name	Event
Mawlid al-Nabi	Birthday of Muhammad
Layl'at al-Qadr	Koran revealed to Muhammad
Id al-Fitr	Celebration of end of Ramadan
Id al-Adha	End of pilgrimage to Mecca

AT PRAYER
Muslims often pray together in groups. They kneel, facing Mecca, on clean ground, or on fabric; this may be a woven carpet, straw mat, or even a handkerchief.

ISLAMIC WORDS
Ayatollah Shi'ite leader.
Hadith Stories about Muhammad.
Hafiz Muslim who has memorized the Koran.
Hajji One who has fulfilled the *Hajj*.
Jihad Striving to spread the Islamic way of life.
Shari'ah Islamic law.
Masjid Place of worship.
Mulla Scholar.

HINDUISM

MOST HINDUS BELIEVE in many gods, but in one underlying Reality, and that when a person dies the soul is reborn again in another body. Their symbol is a sacred sound, OM.

ORIGIN
Hinduism originated in India, in about 1750 B.C.E. Today it has spread throughout much of southeast Asia.

FOUNDERS
Hinduism has no single founder. Its early gods were brought by the Aryan people who invaded India. Shiva is one of the main Hindu gods.

Shiva

HINDU GODS
These are some of the most important gods:
Brahman Divine, absolute reality.
Vishnu Life-giver.
Shiva God of good and evil.
Sarasvati Goddess of truth.
Indra God of war.
Lakshmi Goddess of beauty.
Kali Goddess of death.
Krishna Hero and lover.

KEY POINTS
• People living good lives are born again in a higher life; bad lives lead to a lower life.

• Hindus aim to be free from the cycle of rebirth to become one with Brahman.

HOLY CITY
Varanasi, or Benares, in India, is one of the oldest cities in the world and the chief place of Hindu pilgrimage. Every year millions come to bathe in its sacred river, the Ganges. The waters are believed to wash away sin. People's ashes are often scattered on the river.

Rig Veda

VEDAS
The earliest Hindu beliefs were written down as the *Vedas* in c.1400 B.C.E., which consists of hymns and chants. The *Rig Veda* is the most important book of the *Vedas*.

TYPES OF HINDU
- Others 5%
- Vishnu 25%
- Vaishnavites 70%

HINDU HOLY DAYS

Name	Event
Diwali	New Year Festival of Lights
Holi	Spring Festival
Janmashtami	Birthday of Krishna
Shiva Ratri	Main festival of Shiva

SACRED COW
Hindus respect all animals, especially cows, as sacred beings. Most Hindus are vegetarians. The cow is a symbol of the Earth and feeding a cow is considered an act of worship.

HINDU WORDS
Atman Individual soul.
Avatar Appearance of Vishnu on Earth.
Guru Religious teacher.
Karma Moral law.
Mantra Sacred chant, hymn, or poem.
Moksha Release from the life cycle.
Nirvana Total peace.
Puja Worship.
Sanskrit Hindu language.
Yogi Holy man.

BUDDHISM

THE BUDDHIST FAITH is based on the teachings of the Buddha. Its symbol is an eight-spoked wheel.

ORIGIN
Buddhism originated in northern India in about 500 B.C.E. Today it has spread throughout most of southeast Asia.

BUDDHA
Siddharta Gautama was born in India c.563 B.C.E. Brought up as a prince, he left his home, aged 29, to lead a life of meditation and preaching. He was named Buddha, "the enlightened one".

FOUR TRUTHS
These holy principles are contained in the scripture, the *Dhammapada*.
1 Dukkha To live is to suffer.
2 Samudaya Desire or craving causes suffering.
3 Nirodha Freedom from desire leads to the end of suffering.
4 Magga Freedom can be found by following the Eightfold Path of Buddhism.

KEY POINTS
• Spiritual fulfilment comes from right actions and thoughts.

• Life is a sequence of birth, death, and rebirth.

GOLDEN PAGODA
The Shwedagon pagoda in Rangoon, Burma, is one of the earliest and most important Buddhist temples of worship. It is covered with gold and is topped by an "umbrella" of more than 4,000 diamonds.

Shwedagon pagoda

MONKS
Buddhist monks live a simple life, giving up most of their possessions. They pray, teach, meditate, and beg for their food.

Monks wear saffron-yellow robes.

Begging bowl

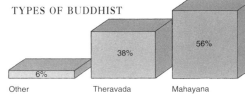

HOLY TEXT
Extracts from the Pali Canon
The *Dhammapada* is the best-known part of the *Pali Canon*, the collected teachings of Buddha. It contains the Four Truths, and the Eightfold Path: rightness of views, intention, speech, action, way of life, effort, awareness, and concentration.

TYPES OF BUDDHIST
- Other 6%
- Theravada 38%
- Mahayana 56%

BUDDHIST HOLY DAYS

Name	Event
Sakyamuni (or Wesak)	Birth of Siddharta Gautama
Bodhi Day	Buddha's enlightenment
Parinirvana	Buddha's ascent from Earth
Phagguna	Origin of life cycle

BUDDHIST WORDS
Anatta No such thing as self.
Anicca Self is impermanent.
Arahat Worthy, used to describe Buddha.
Bhikkhu Monk.
Jataka Accounts of Buddha's lives.
Nibbana State of peace.
Sangha Order of monks.
Vihaia Monastery.

SIKHISM

THE SIKH faith is based on the worship of one God and on the cycle of rebirth. God is the eternal Guru who inspires all religious teachers. The Sikh symbol is the Khanda, a design of weapons.

KEY POINTS
- God is found in all things.
- All humans will be reborn.
- All people are equal in the eyes of God.

FIVE K'S
The Khalsa (Pure Ones) are deeply committed to Sikhism. They must wear five items:
1 **Kesh** Uncut hair, worn in a turban if a man.
2 **Kara** Steel bracelet.
3 **Kangha** Hair comb.
4 **Kirpan** Sword.
5 **Kaccha** Short trousers often worn as an undergarment.

Turban
Sword
Steel bracelet

SIKH HOLY DAYS
Name	Event
Baisakhi	New Year and formation of Khalsa
Diwali	Release from prison of Guru Hargobind, the sixth Guru
Guru Nanak	Birthday of the Founder

ORIGIN
Sikhism began in the Punjab region of north India and Pakistan in about 1500 C.E. Today, it has spread to Britain and North America.

Punjab
Pakistan
India

AMRITSAR
This town in the Punjab is sacred to Sikhs. They make pilgrimages to its Golden Temple, which is situated in the middle of a lake.

MEDITATION
Sikhs believe that God is inside everybody. Guru Nanak taught the importance of meditation to strengthen a person's sense of God. Sikhs often use beads (*Mala*) during meditation.

A Sikh meditating

GURU NANAK

Guru Nanak was born in the Punjab region in 1469. At the age of 30, he underwent a religious experience and founded the Sikh religion. He was succeeded by nine other Gurus.

Guru Granth Sahib

GURU GRANTH
The *Guru Granth Sahib* contains hymns and poems written by the Gurus, especially Guru Arjan, the fifth Guru. The book is central to Sikh ritual and is treated with great respect. Sikhs bow down before the book, which is placed under a special canopy.

SIKH WORDS
Darbar Sahib Name for Golden Temple.
Diwan Group worship.
Gurdwara Place of worship.
Guru Name for leader, scripture, and God.
Japji Morning prayer.
Kaur Female surname.
Mool Mantra Statement of belief.
Mukti Freedom of the spirit from the cycle.
Singh Male surname.

JUDAISM

FOLLOWERS OF Judaism are called Jews. They believe in one God, who revealed the Law to his people. Their symbol is the Star of David.

RULES AND RITUALS
These are some of the traditions of Jewish life:
- Baby boys are circumcised eight days after birth.
- The Sabbath day (Saturday) is the holy day of rest.
- Pork and shellfish must not be eaten.
- A Jewish boy becomes *bar mitzvah*, an adult member of Jewish life, when he is 13.

KEY POINTS
- God created the world and all its history.
- The Jews are descendants of the Hebrew people.
- The Jews are God's chosen people, "a light to all nations".

ORIGIN
Judaism originated in about 2000 B.C.E. in Canaan, the Promised Land, mainly present-day Israel. Today, it has spread throughout the world.

Lebanon
Israel
Jordan
Egypt

WESTERN WALL
This wall in Jerusalem, also known as the Wailing Wall, is the only remaining part of Herod's Temple, which was destroyed in C.E. 70. Today, Jews come here to pray and to tuck written prayers and requests in between the huge blocks of stone.

ABRAHAM
Abraham, the first leader of the Hebrews, was born in Ur, in present-day Iraq, in about 2000 B.C.E. At God's command, he later settled in Canaan.

TENAKH
The Jewish Bible is called the *Tenakh*. It tells the history of the Jewish people. The most important part is the *Torah*, the first five books of the Bible. It contains the laws, including the Ten Commandments, that God revealed to Moses.

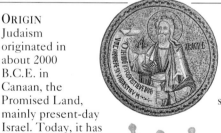

Tenakh scroll

TYPES OF JEW

5% Sephardis
10% Orientals
85% Ashkenazim

JEWISH HOLY DAYS
Name	Event
Hannukah	Festival of Lights
Pesach/Passover	Deliverance from slavery in Egypt
Yom Kippur	Day of Atonement

Taliith, or prayer shawl

Menorah, or branched candlestick

Yarmulke, or skull cap

The *Tenakh*

JEWISH WORDS
Diaspora Dispersion, or spread, of Jews.
Exodus Israelites' escape from Egypt.
Gentiles Non-Jewish people.
Kaddish Synagogue prayer.
Rabbi Teacher and leader.
Synagogue Place of worship.
Tephillin Prayer box containing words from the *Torah* worn strapped to forehead and arm.

OTHER FAITHS

THERE ARE thousands of faith systems, with millions of followers all around the world. Apart from the six major faiths already discussed, the faiths below are amongst the best-known. Each has an organized structure and established beliefs.

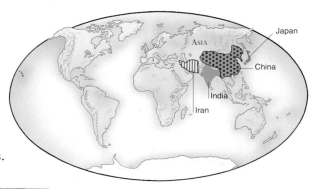

ORIGIN OF OTHER FAITHS

- Baha'ism (Iran)
- Confucianism (China)
- Jainism (India)
- Shintoism (Japan)
- Taoism (China)
- Zoroastrianism (Iran)

BAHA'I FAITH

The Baha'i faith is based on the worship of one God, who is at the root of all religions. The Baha'i symbol is a nine-pointed star that stands for this combination of faiths.

WORLD CENTRE
Baha'is worship in private homes and Houses of Worship. The most famous is the World Centre in Haifa, Israel, which is also the centre of administration.

FACTS
- Founded in Persia (present-day Iran) in the 19th century.
- The founder was Baha'u'llah (1817–1892).
- *Al-Kitab al-Aqdas* is the most important scripture.
- There are about 6 million followers; many of them are in India and South America.

CONFUCIANISM

Confucianism is not based on the worship of a god, but on following *The Tao* (The Way). It teaches the wisdom of living a balanced life that is in harmony with nature.

CONFUCIUS
Confucius, or K'ung Fu Tze, (551–479 B.C.E.) was the founder of Confucianism. Born in China, he worked as a government administrator, and became a respected teacher and moral philosopher. He was known for his wise sayings, such as, "A good man is never alone".

FACTS
- Confucianism originated in the Shantung province of China c.6th century B.C.E.
- The *Analects* are the major scriptures.
- Confucianism is practised throughout China.
- Its main teaching is, "Never do to others what you would not like them to do to you".

JAINISM

Jains do not believe in a god. Their faith is based on non-violence to all living things, or *ahimsa*. Jains believe in the cycle of rebirth. A good person is born again into a higher life.

JAIN NUN
Jain nuns and monks lead a life of poverty, obedience, and chastity. They must protect all forms of life. They use a brush to sweep the ground in front of them, for fear of treading on any insects, and wear masks to prevent insects from entering their mouths.

FACTS
- Founded in India, in the 6th century B.C.E.
- The founder was Mahavira (c.540–468 B.C.E.).
- Jains worship in temples, or in shrines in the home.
- There are approximately 4 million Jains; most of them live in India.

SHINTOISM

This faith is based on the worship of the gods of nature. Its symbol is the outline of a temple gateway.

MOUNT FUJI
Shintoists love nature. Many Shinto shrines are in parks, gardens, and on mountains. Mount Fuji, in Japan, is a Shinto god. People come to pray at a shrine on its summit.

FACTS
- Shintoism started in Japan in the 8th century B.C.E.
- The *Chronicles of Japan* and the *Record of Ancient Things* contain Shinto stories.
- Shintoists worship alone, not in groups.
- One of the chief Shinto deities is Amaterasu, the Sun Goddess.
- Most followers live in Japan.

TAOISM

Taoists believe in many gods. They aim to live in harmony with nature. Their symbol, *Yin Yang*, stands for balance and harmony.

LAO TZU
Lao Tzu, the founder of Taoism, was born in about the 4th century B.C.E. His name means "Old Master". According to legend, he was born with white hair.

FACTS
- Taoism originated in China in about the 4th century B.C.E.
- The *Tao Te Ching* is the most important scripture.
- Most Taoists live in China and the Far East.
- Taoists aim to balance the calm, feminine side of the body (*Yin*), with the active, male side (*Yang*).

ZOROASTRIANISM

This faith is based on two gods: Ahura Mazda, a good spirit; and Angra Mainyu, an evil spirit. Its symbol is a winged image of Ahura.

FIRE TEMPLE
Sacred fires, symbolizing Ahura Mazda, burn continually in Zoroastrian fire temples. Priests cover their mouths when tending the sacrificial fires.

FACTS
- Founded in Persia (present-day Iran), c.1000 B.C.E.
- Zoroaster, or Zarathustra, was the major prophet.
- The scripture is the *Avesta*, which explains the struggle between good and evil.
- There are about 140,000 followers; most of them are in India and Iran.

GREAT THINKERS

FROM EARLY TIMES, philosophers have used argument and reason to try to understand the world and our place in it. They question the meaning of ideas such as reality, right and wrong, and art.

624 B.C. Thales (624–550 B.C.) is born in Miletus, Greece. He is interested in astronomy and politics, as well as philosophy. He became known as the first Western philosopher.

Thales

Pythagoras (c.580–500 B.C.), Greek philosopher, explores the importance of numbers. He discovers the mathematical relationship between sound pitch and the length of a string or pipe.

Pythagoras

PYTACORA
PHYLOLAVS

650 B.C. | 624 B.C. | 600 B.C. | 580 B.C. | 500 B.C.

Aristotle (384–322 B.C.) is the last and most influential of the Greek philosophers. He stresses the importance of logic, or reasoning, in philosophy.

Aristotle tutoring Alexander the Great (356-323 B.C.).

St. Augustine (A.D. 354–430), North African philosopher, uses Plato's philosophy to express Christian ideas.

1225–74 St. Thomas Aquinas, Italian friar, aims to make Christian teaching consistent with Aristotle's philosophy.

St. Thomas Aquinas

Thomas Hobbes (1588–1679), English political philosopher, says that giving all power to the state is the only way to avoid chaos and endless war. He writes the *Leviath* in 1651.

400 B.C. | 384 B.C. | A.D 300 | A.D. 354 | 1200 | 1225 | 1500 | 1588

George Berkeley (1685–1753), Irish bishop and idealist philosopher, believes that objects, such as tables and chairs, are collections of ideas, and exist only if a person perceives (is aware of) them.

David Hume (1711–76), Scottish empiricist and sceptic, states that all knowledge is taken from ideas and experience, but denies that this knowledge can ever be proved.

David Hume

Jean-Jacques Rousseau (1712–78), French political philosopher, is against the limitations of civilized society and advises a return to nature.

Rousseau

Immanuel Kant (1724–1804), German thinker, says that we gain knowledge through both experience and understanding.

Immanuel Kant

1650 | 1685 | 1700 | 1711 | 1712 | 1724

John Stuart Mill (1806–73), English utilitarian, emphasizes that some pleasures are worthier than others. He writes *On Liberty* in 1859.

John Stuart Mill

Søren Kierkegaard (1813–55), Danish founder of existentialism and religious writer, claims that the only real thing is individual existence.

Karl Marx (1818–83), German revolutionary thinker, founds Communism, adapting ideas from Hegel's philosophy. He writes *Das Kapital* in 1867.

Karl Marx

William James (1842–1910), American psychologist and pragmatist, sees the truthfulness of any idea in terms of the usefulness of its results.

1800 | 1806 | 1810 | 1813 | 1818 | 1840 | 1842

Bertrand Russell (1872–1970), English thinker and political activist, tries to provide firm foundations in philosophy for mathematics.

Bertrand Russell

Martin Heidegger (1889–1976), German existentialist, writes *Being and Time* in 1927.

Ludwig Wittgenstein (1889–1951), Austrian analytic philosopher, explores the relationship between language and the world. He argues that everything that can be thought can also be said.

Ludwig Wittgenstein

Jean-Paul Sartre (1905–80), French existentialist, says there is no fixed human nature or destiny, and that people are free to choose their actions without following society's rules.

Sartre

1870 | 1872 | 1890 | 1889 | 1889 | 1900 | 1905

FAMOUS PHILOSOPHICAL SAYINGS

Philosopher	Dates	Nationality	Quotation
Protagoras	c.485-410 B.C.	Greek	*Man is the measure of all things.*
Socrates	470-399 B.C.	Greek	*The unexamined life is not worth living.*
Francis Bacon	1561-1626	English	*Knowledge is power.*
René Descartes	1596-1650	French	*I think, therefore I am.*
George Berkeley	1685-1753	Irish	*To be is to be perceived.*
David Hume	1711-76	Scottish	*Beauty in things exists in the mind which contemplates them.*
Jean-Jacques Rousseau	1712-78	French	*Man is born free, and everywhere he is in chains.*
G.W.F. Hegel	1770-1831	German	*History teaches us that people have never learnt anything from history.*
John Stuart Mill	1806-73	English	*Ask yourself whether you are happy, and you cease to be so.*
Karl Marx	1818-83	German	*Philosophers have only interpreted the world, the point is to change it.*
Friedrich Nietzsche	1844-1900	German	*God is dead.*
Ludwig Wittgenstein	1889-1951	Austrian	*The limits of my language are the limits of my world.*

WARM THOUGHTS

In 1620, René Descartes thought up his most famous statement, "I think, therefore I am", as he kept warm by a stove while on military service in Bavaria, Germany.

70–399 B.C. Socrates, Greek
...losopher, and Plato's teacher, uses
...uestion and answer method of
...quiry. His main concern is morality
...ght and wrong). He is accused of
... state of corrupting young people
...d is sentenced to death.

*Socrates is forced to
drink hemlock, a poison.*

Plato (c.428–347 B.C.),
of Athens, Greece,
founds the Academy (a
university) in Athens and
teaches Aristotle there.
He outlines his ideal city-
state in *The Republic*.

Plato's Academy

| 470 B.C. | | 470 B.C. | 428 B.C. |

...né Descartes (1596–1650),
...ench dualist, rationalist
...losopher, and mathematician,
...onsidered the first modern
...ilosopher. He bases all
...nowledge on one truth: that we
...nnot doubt the existence of
... own thoughts.

Descartes

John Locke (1632–1704), English
philosopher and political writer, founds
classical British empiricism. His
political writings form the foundations
of modern democracy. He wrote *Two
Treatises of Government* in 1690.

John Locke

| 1596 | | 1600 | 1632 |

Jeremy Bentham
(1748–1832), English
utilitarian, judges an
action to be right by the
extent to which it
promotes happiness or
minimizes pain.

G.W.F. Hegel
(1770–1831), German
idealist, says that the
history of events and
thoughts is a process of
conflict, which will lead to
an inevitable conclusion.

Hegel

Arthur Schopenhauer
(1788–1860),
German idealist, saw
art as the only
escape from a world
without reason.

Schopenhauer

| 1740 | 1748 | 1770 | | 1788 |

...riedrich Wilhelm Nietzsche
...844–1900), German
...ilosopher,
...gues that people are driven in life
... the "will to power", and that society
...ll evolve into a race of "supermen".
... rejects Christianity, and influences
... Nazi party.

Edmund Husserl (1859–1938),
German philosopher, develops
the basic ideas of phenomenology
(descriptions of human
experience).

Nietzsche's "Ubermenschen" ("supermen")

| ...44 | | 1850 | 1859 |

...imone de Beauvoir (1908–86),
...rench existentialist and founder
... modern feminist philosophy.

...illard van Orme Quine (born
...08), American pragmatist,
...ints out inconsistencies in early
...alytic philosophy.

Simone de Beauvoir

Michel Foucault
(1926–84), French
philosopher, looks
at ways in which
the individual is
controlled by
society's rules.

Jacques Derrida (born
1930), French founder of
deconstructionism, which
rejects the idea of any fixed
truths in language and
philosophy.

Michel Foucault

| 1906 | 1908 | 1920 | 1926 | 1930 | 1930 |

PHILOSOPHY FACTS

Pythagoras refused to eat beans,
...s he believed that they had souls.

English philosopher, Francis
...acon (1561–1626), died of
...neumonia, caught while stuffing a
...ead chicken with snow on
...ampstead Heath, London, in an
...arly attempt to preserve it by
...efrigeration.

The most influential philosopher
...f the 20th century, Ludwig
...Wittgenstein, published one work
...n his lifetime. Parts of his
...*Tractatus Logico-philosophicus* were
...ritten in the trenches during
...World War I (1914–18), while he
...as on sentry duty.

• In his will, Jeremy Bentham
left his body to University
College, London. His corpse
was preserved and dressed, and
crowned with a wax head. The
corpse was kept in a glass case,
along with his real head, which

Jeremy Bentham

was mummified. Bentham's
dressed corpse is still on display
at the university.

• René Descartes was tutor to
the Swedish monarch, Queen
Christina (1626–89). She made
him give her philosophy lessons
at dawn, even though she knew
his preference for lying in bed
and meditating until 11 o'clock
in the morning.

• Until the 18th and 19th
centuries, the term
"philosophy" included many
branches that have since
become areas of study in their
own right: physics, biology,
mathematics, and engineering.

PHILOSOPHY WORDS

Analytic Movement that considers
philosophy to be based essentially
on logic.
A priori Knowledge based on
reasoning rather than experience.
Determinism Idea that all
things, including "free
will", are already fixed, or
determined.
Dualism Belief that there
are two distinct types of
substance in the world: the physical
and the mental.
Empiricism Belief that all
knowledge is based on experience.
At birth, the mind is a blank sheet,
on which experience then makes
its mark.
Epistemology Study of the theory
of knowledge: what knowledge
is, how we come to know things,
how much we can hope to
know, etc.
Ethics Study of moral systems, or
ideas about how people ought to
live and behave.
Existentialism Belief that the
individual has free will, and must
take responsibility for his or her
actions in a world where there are
no definite rights or wrongs.
Idealism Belief that the world is in
some way created by the mind.
Idealists do not deny that the
world exists, but deny it can be
separated from the mind.
Logic Series of statements that
necessarily follow on from each
other. Also called a chain of
reasoning.
Materialism Belief that everything
that exists is either matter
(substance), or is dependent on
matter for its existence.
Metaphysics Study of principles of
nature, such as being, identity,
substance, time,
and space.
Objectivity
Existence outside a
person's mind; the
opposite of
subjectivity.
Pragmatism A practical view
of philosophy: the truthfulness of
an idea is seen in terms of the
usefulness of its results.
Rationalism Belief that reason
alone, without any reliance on
experience, can reveal the basic
truths of the Universe, and that
everything can be explained by a
single system.
Realism Belief, usually contrasted
with idealism, that physical objects
exist independently of the mind.
Relativism Belief that there are no
universal standards or truths;
usually a rejection of absolute
rights and wrongs.
Scepticism Belief that nothing
can be known for certain.
Subjectivity Existence inside a
person's mind; the opposite of
objectivity.
Solipsism Belief that the only
reality is inside your own mind.
Utilitarianism Belief that
actions are right if they
result in happiness,
wrong if they
result in
unhappiness.

PATTERNS OF FAMILY AND SOCIETY

EVERY HUMAN SOCIETY (community of people) in the world is based on the family. Types of family and marriage arrangements, however, vary from one society to the next. Organization and living habits can also be very different, according to how and where people live and work.

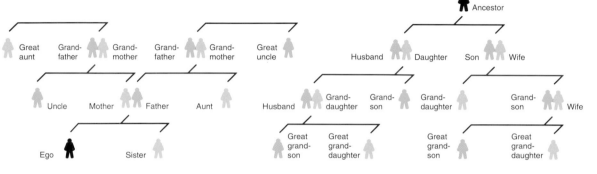

Aboriginal Rainbow Snake Dreaming

DREAMING
Aboriginal Australians believe the land and all living creatures were formed by spirit ancestors in the dawn of time called the Dreaming.

KINSHIP
Kinship is a way of describing bonds between people of the same family. A family may be defined as just parents and children, or it may include other types of relatives.

KEY

= Male   = Female

EGO-FOCUSED KINSHIP
People can use themselves as the starting point from which to construct a family tree. They trace their roots back as far as they can through both their fathers' and mothers' families. This is called ego-focused kinship.

ANCESTOR-FOCUSED KINSHIP
People can trace their roots to a known ancestor who starts off the family tree. This is called ancestor-focused kinship and is found, for example, in Scottish clans where everyone shares the same surname.

FAMILY WORDS

Ancestor An earlier member of the family.

Clan A family group descended from a common ancestor.

Dowry A wedding payment from the bride to the groom.

Lineage A line of family relations.

Marriage A legal bond between two people.

Tribe A group of people linked to an ancestor.

Western society People living in industrialized areas.

DESCENT
The system linking families to their ancestors is called descent. Inheritance of family property and titles is based on rules of descent.

Duke of Westminster, a British aristocrat

Green line shows patrilineal line of descent

Trobriand Island mother and child

Orange line shows matrilineal line of descent

PATRILINEAL DESCENT
Descent traced through the male line is called patrilineal descent. The Duke of Westminster inherited his title as the first-born son – a feature of a type of European patrilineal descent.

MATRILINEAL DESCENT
Matrilineal families trace their descent through female relatives. Many tribal societies, such as that of the Trobriand Islanders of the southwestern Pacific, are matrilineal.

HOUSEHOLDS
A household is a group of people who live together as a family. The number of people in a family household can vary widely around the world; so can the way in which members of a household organize family life and bring up their children.

Kibbutzim
In communities in Israel called kibbutzim families live and work together, helping to bring up each others' children.

Extended family
In many tribal societies several generations of the same family live together and share the responsibility for domestic duties.

Nuclear family
Anthropologists use the term nuclear family to mean a household consisting of two parents who bring up their own children.

MARRIAGE TYPES

Endogamy Marriage between members of the same family or clan.

Exogamy Marriage between members of a different family or clan.

Monogamy Marriage of one man to one wife.

Bigamy Marriage of one man to two wives or one woman to two husbands.

Polygamy Marriage of one man or one woman to several wives or several husbands at the same time.

Polyandry Marriage of one woman to several husbands at the same time.

Polygyny Marriage of one man to several wives at the same time.

Levirate Remarriage of a woman to her dead husband's brother.

Sororate Remarriage of a man to his dead wife's sister.

TAKING THE PLUNGE

On 13 September 1991, Dustin and Becca Webster of California, USA, completed their wedding by diving 21.30m (70 ft) into a swimming pool.

MARRIAGE RECORDS

LARGEST GROUP WEDDING was between 60,000 members of the Unificationist Church on 25 August 1992, in the Seoul Olympic Stadium, Korea.

MOST EXPENSIVE WEDDING was 20 million US dollars for Mohammed, son of Sheik Rashid Bin Saeed Al Maktoum, and Princess Salama, in Dubai, in May 1981.

MOST MARRIED MAN was Giovanni Vigliotto from New York, USA, who married 104 times in 15 different countries, from 1949 to 1981.

TRADITIONAL BRIDES

Brides who want a traditional wedding can choose from many different styles of outfit.

Chinese brides may wear a traditional head-dress of pierced metal strips, often silver, with a veil made from feathers and pearls.

Western brides wear a long dress and veil in white, symbolizing purity and innocence. This custom dates from the 19th century.

Japanese brides may dress in a brightly coloured traditional kimono. This contrasts with the black costumes of the brides' attendants.

Hindu brides wear a red dress and both bride and groom wear colourful garlands of flowers around their necks.

MARRIAGE AND DIVORCE STATISTICS

Country	Marriages per year 1981	Marriages per year 1994	Divorces per year 1981	Divorces per year 1994
USA	10.6	9.1	5.3	4.6
South Africa	8.2	10.7	2.0	2.5
UK	7.1	5.9	2.8	3.1
Japan	6.6	6.4	1.3	1.5
Belgium	6.5	5.1	1.6	2.2
Finland	6.3	4.9	2.0	2.7
Germany	6.2	5.4	2.0	2.0
France	5.8	4.4	1.6	1.9
Italy	5.6	5.0	0.2	0.5
Denmark	5.0	6.8	2.8	2.6

(figures given per thousand people)

WEDDING CUSTOMS

- Ancient Romans first gave pieces of wedding cake to guests.

- Greek Orthodox couples wear wedding crowns linked by a red ribbon.

- Indian couples tie their clothes together and walk seven times around a fire.

- In Egypt the bride's father signs her wedding contract while she sits alone in a separate room.

- Japanese couples take three sips of sake (rice wine) to complete their wedding ceremony.

- Jewish couples do not eat or drink on their wedding day until the ceremony is over.

SYMBOLS

A symbol is something, such as an object, a sign, or a mark, that stands for something else. All the symbols shown below have a clear meaning.

Wedding ring A wedding ring is worn by both the bride and the groom to show their bond to each other.

The Scout Association The symbol of the Scout Association stands for this worldwide movement for boys and girls, which started in 1908.

US Navy Commander Three equal lace stripes on the sleeve are worn by US Navy commanders.

Olympic rings Five coloured rings are the symbol that stands for the International Olympic Committee.

SOCIETY TYPES

Work and home life influence how people live.

City dwellers Many city dwellers live on housing estates or in blocks of flats.

Hunter-gatherers Hunters and gatherers live in small groups of several families. They move home from one place to another in search of wild animals and plants to eat.

Nomads Nomads are groups of people who have no fixed home, but who move with their animals from one grazing ground to another.

SOCIETY WORDS

Rural People who live and work in the countryside.

Urban People who live and work in towns or cities.

Suburban People who live on the edges of a large city.

Migrant People who have moved from one region to another, or one country to another.

ONE WORLD

Different societies' customs can travel all over the world via film and television. A Campa Indian boy from Peru now enjoys a game with a frisbee.

CUSTOMS AND RITUALS

THROUGHOUT THE WORLD, different societies have their own traditions for marking important events such as the birth of a child, or the harvesting of crops. These traditions are called customs and rituals, and many are based around the cycles of nature, and the mystery of life and death.

THE JAPANESE TEA CEREMONY
In Japan, drinking tea is a long-established ritual that is based on the teachings of Zen Buddhism. Tea is prepared and served in a special tea room or tea house.

BIRTH RITES
The Azande people of the Sudan gently wave newborn babies through smoke to protect them against witchcraft and to help them grow up strong and healthy.

Azande birth rites

DEATH RITES
Traditional Taoist (see p.143) funerals involve the burning of imitation money. The smoke will carry it to the dead to spend in a future life.

Taoist funeral

BIRTH AND DEATH FACTS
- Many Christian babies are baptised in holy water in a church font.
- Jewish baby boys are circumcised eight days after birth.
- Romany gypsies press a gold ring against their baby's hand to bring it wealth.
- Pregnant women in New Guinea live alone until their baby is born.
- Death rites in Melanesia last for several years, until the deceased becomes an ancestor.
- Chinese coffins are painted white to give the dead a happy future life.

GREETINGS
A greeting is a means of friendly communication. between two or more people.

Hand-shake
The gripping and shaking of hands is a formal greeting around the world.

Bow
Bowing is a greeting in the Far East, showing politeness by lowering the head.

Nose rub
This Maori greeting is called a hongi. It is usually made on ceremonial occasions.

Wave
A friendly waving of the hand and arm means hello or goodbye, all around the world.

GESTURES
A gesture is an action that sends a visual signal to an onlooker.

Thumbs up
Raising the thumb is a friendly gesture. It is a sign of approval.or that all is going well.

V for victory
This victory gesture was made famous by Sir Winston Churchill during World War II.

Ssshh!
A finger pressed to the lips is a worldwide sign meaning "keep quiet" or "keep this a secret".

Beautiful!
This Native American gesture means beauty. It combines the signs for "good" and "looking".

INITIATION RITES
Initiation is a rite to welcome adolescents into adulthood in many traditional societies. The White Mountain Apache from North America perform a ritual for teenage girls, called the Sunrise Dance.

1 Ground-up plants and coloured rocks are daubed over the girl's head with a brush made from plant stalks.

2 The girl kneels facing the sun, and acts out the legend of the creation of the First Woman. Finally, as a woman, she is given the powers of a goddess for four days.

CHARMS
People keep or carry certain objects to bring them good luck or to ward off evil.

Pocket-sized Buddhas are popular good-luck charms worldwide.

Horseshoe
Hanging a horseshoe over the doorway brings good luck to the household.

Cork & coin
A coin wedged into a champagne cork acts as a lucky charm.

4-leaved clover
Finding a rare four-leaved clover is said to bring good luck.

Charm bracelet
This chain holds a variety of tiny lucky charms.

Garlic
A clove of garlic has many powers: it cures warts and keeps vampires away!

Sugar skull
This lucky sweet is eaten during the Mexican Day of the Dead Festival.

CELEBRATION AND DECORATION

CELEBRATIONS that involve the whole community mark events such as the passing of the seasons, and holy days. These events contain a mixture of customs, using music, dance, and costume.

Mexican Day of the Dead Festival

CELEBRATION FACTS

- Dragon Boat Festival of China is held to give thanks for food and water in the dry season, with races of decorated boats.

- On Thanksgiving Day in the USA and Canada, families sit down to a special meal in celebration of the harvest.

- Diwali Festival in India celebrates the harvest with decorative lights, and offerings to Lakshmi, Hindu goddess of prosperity.

- Inti Raymi is the Peruvian Festival of the Sun god, Inti, held in an Inca fortress.

- Rio de Janeiro Carnival is a mass parade of costume and dance, based on the Christian celebration of the end of Lent.

Rio de Janeiro Carnival

DRESS CODES

Wearing certain items of clothing helps to identify what a person is or does.

Mortar-board

Graduate's gown
University students wear a black gown and a hat called a mortar-board at their graduation ceremony.

Wimple

Nun's habit
Nuns wear a plain robe called a habit. Their head is covered by a hood called a wimple.

Eye-slits

Arab burka
The burka is a single length of cloth worn by Arab women. It covers the body, except for the eyes.

Devil mask

Bolivian dancer's mask
This Devil mask is worn as part of the colourful costume at the annual Diablada Festival in Bolivia.

Bearskin

Welsh Guard
Various army regiments, such as the Welsh Guards, wear ceremonial uniforms topped by hats made of bear fur.

Toque

Chef's whites
Chefs wear starched white clothing they call their whites, and a tall white cloth hat called a toque.

DANCING FOR JOY

Dancing is one of the earliest known activities of humankind. Some dances are purely for fun; others are important rituals.

A ritual tribal dance from Kenya.

The jitterbug, popular in the USA in the 1940's.

BODY DECORATION

Decorative jewellery and body scars are part of a person's appearance. Each society, however, has different ideas about what makes the body beautiful.

Forehead spot
Hindu women paint a red spot on their forehead called a *Tilak*, as a symbol of wisdom.

Earring
A ring through the ear draws attention to the eyes and adds to the beauty of the face.

Lip plug
Kaiapo men from the Brazilian Amazon wear a wooden lip plug to decorate their mouths.

MOST TATTOOS

Tom Leppard, a Scotsman, has leopard skin tattoos covering 99.2% of his body.

Scarification
Many African tribal people decorate their face and body with scars to add to their beauty.

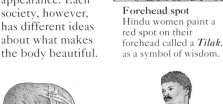

Samoan tattoo
Men from the Pacific islands of Samoa are tattooed all over the body as a sign of manliness.

Punk jewellery
Safety pins and other unusual objects are worn as jewellery for their startling effect.

Sikh hand-painting
Sikh brides paint decorative patterns on their hands with dye from the henna plant.

COSMETIC SURGERY

The three most popular cosmetic surgery operations in the USA in 1994 were:

Women (88% of all operations)	Men (12% of all operations)
Liposuction	Nose reshaping
Eyelid surgery	Eyelid surgery
Breast augmentation	Liposuction

MONEY

MONEY COMES IN the form of cash, which consists of coins and banknotes. Anything that represents cash, such as the computer records of a bank account, a cheque, or a credit card, is also money. Today, many people prefer to pay for things with cards rather than carry around cash.

EARLY MONEY
The oldest recorded use of money was in ancient Mesopotamia (Iraq), about 4,500 years ago. Inscribed tablets describe payments made with weighed amounts of silver. Other earlier forms of money include cowrie shells, used in ancient Egypt, and feather money on Santa Cruz Island, Pacific Ocean.

THE FIRST COINS
The first known coins were made 2,700 years ago in Lydia, Turkey, from a mixture of gold and silver called electrum. They were stamped at mints to confirm their weight and value. Today, most coins are made out of cheaper metals.

BANKNOTES
Banknotes have extremely complicated designs with special security features, to make it as difficult as possible for forgers to copy them. The four main stages of making a banknote are design, papermaking, ink-mixing, and printing. When the notes are printed, three separate processes are used.

SKETCHES
An artist makes two preliminary sketches for the note: the first one shows the main features; the second shows the background details.

Position of main features

Coloured background

PAPER MONEY
Paper money – banknotes – was invented by the Chinese in the 10th century. People tired of carrying coins around and left them with merchants instead. Merchants provided vouchers (receipts) for the money and people exchanged the vouchers among themselves, rather than turn them back into cash.

BACKGROUND DESIGN
This design uses eight different coloured inks. First, these are printed on three sheets in groups of colours: blues, yellows, and reds.

Inks for each colour group are combined on a single sheet.

FINISHED NOTE
This type of specimen banknote is produced by the company, Thomas de La Rue, to show to its customers all over the world.

Sharp burins

Burnisher for smoothing

INTAGLIO ENGRAVING
The features of the note are engraved on to a steel plate by hand, using special sharp tools, called burins. The engraved area is then inked.

SECURITY THREAD
Banknote paper is made with a plastic thread sealed inside it. This feature is extremely difficult for forgers to copy.

NUMBERING
Numbering barrels print a different serial number on each banknote.

MONEY RECORDS
BIGGEST MINT in the world is in Philadelphia, USA, where 15 billion coins are made each year.

FIRST CREDIT CARD was the Diners Club card, issued in the USA in 1950. The card enabled the first 200 members to eat on credit at 27 New York restaurants.

GREATEST GOLD RESERVES are held by the United States at Fort Knox, Kentucky. The gold bars are stored in bomb-proof vaults, surrounded by armed guards.

AMAZING MONEY
The people of Yap, a Pacific island, used large stone discs for money. The largest was about 4m (12ft) across – as big as two adults standing on each other's shoulders.

WORLD'S RICHEST PEOPLE
(excluding heads of state)

Name	Country	Business
Bill Gates	USA	Computer software
Warren Buffett	USA	Textiles
Hans Rausing	Sweden	Packaging
Yoshiaki Tsutsumi	Japan	Land, railways, leisure
Paul Sacher	Switzerland	Drug company
Tsai Wan-lin	Taiwan	Insurance

MONEY FACTS
• The ancient Greeks put a silver coin into the mouths of corpses. The purpose was to pay the ferryman, Charon, to carry their souls across the River Styx.

• Numismatists are people who collect coins. Gold coins are the oldest and most precious.

• Forgers try to make copies of notes and pass them off as genuine. Forgers are highly skilled professionals.

• "Piggy banks" have been used for saving money since the 14th century. The first pigs were of pottery and had to be smashed to extract the money.

Fort Knox

BANKS

Most people find it convenient to keep their money in a bank. The bank keeps a record of how much each person takes out or puts into their account. This information is printed out in the form of a bank statement.

Automatic telling machine

STOCKS AND SHARES

People can invest in a company by buying shares (stocks) in it. If the company makes a profit, the shareholders are entitled to some of it. Share prices can rise or fall according to the company's performance. Share prices are displayed in the financial sections of newspapers.

THE STOCK MARKET

The stock market is a place where shares are bought and sold. People who want to invest in a company employ a stockbroker who buys and sells the shares for them. The activity of a stock market reflects the economic performance and prospects of a country.

Tokyo Stock Exchange

Company	Price	Weekly change + / -
Birch Interiors	69	-1
Gunzi Properties	44	-2
Kennedy Holdings PLC	46	+2
Kruger Corporation	162	+7
Shaw Associates	121	+5

Shares listing (imaginary) as shown in many newspapers

KEY STOCK EXCHANGES

Country	City	Index
Japan	Tokyo	Nikkei Average
United States	New York	Dow-Jones
United Kingdom	London	FTSE-100*
Germany	Frankfurt	DAX**

* Financial Times Stock Exchange 100

** Deutsche Aktien Index

BANKING FACTS

• Cash-dispensing machines allow people to withdraw money from their bank account 24 hours a day.

• Banks today arrange insurance, pensions, and mortgages (loans to buy houses), as well as keeping money safe.

• Cheques, written instructions to make payments, can be written on anything, even a cow.

• Banking began in the 14th century, in Lombardy, northern Italy.

FINANCIAL WORDS

Accountant A person who keeps and checks financial records for a person or business.

Credit An amount of money made available to make purchases on the basis that they will be paid for later.

Crash A very quick and very large drop in the price of shares, causing people to lose a great deal of money.

Dividend Share of a company's profits that is paid out to shareholders.

Exchange rate The amount of one country's currency needed to buy a fixed amount of another country's currency.

Merchant bank A bank that deals in finance and loans for businesses.

Share index Shows the price of selected shares being traded.

Stockbroker/Broker A member of a stock exchange who buys and sells shares.

Take-over When one company buys another.

FOREIGN CURRENCY

Every country has its own money, or currency. Some currencies hold their value longer than others because they reflect the economic strength of the country. Stable, widely traded currencies are hard currencies. Dealers buy and sell them on foreign currency markets.

THE EURO

In 1999, eleven of the countries of the European Union (EU) started to use a new, common currency – the Euro. After some years the Euro will replace the currencies of all members of the EU except those of Britain, Denmark, Sweden, and Greece.

GALLOPING INFLATION

Inflation results when prices increase and the purchasing power of money decreases. Very rapid price rises, called "hyper-inflation", took place in Germany between 1921 and 1923. At this time, money was worth so little that children used banknotes for building bricks.

German inflation, 1923

CURRENCY VALUES (1997)

Nearly every country has its own money, or currency. Usually each currency can be broken down into 100 smaller units. Currencies are worth different amounts, as you can see from the cost of an ounce (28.35g) of gold in each currency in this table.

Country	Currency	Value	Cost for an ounce of gold
Chile	Peso	100 centavos	150,916
China	Yuan	100 fen, 10 jiao	2,938
Ethiopia	Birr	100 cents	2,215
Germany	Deutschmark	100 pfennigs	570.72
India	Rupee	100 paise	12,697
Japan	Yen	100 sen	41,487
Poland	Zloty	100 groszy	1,030
South Africa	Rand	100 cents	1,646
United Kingdom	Pound	100 pence	212.34
USA	Dollar	100 cents	354.20

TODAY'S MONEY

Increasingly, plastic cards are taking the place of cash and cheques as a form of payment. Banks, credit companies, and stores issue credit, or charge, cards. These allow people to buy things and pay for them later. The latest cards, smart cards, use microchips to store information.

SMART CARDS

Money from a bank account can be transferred on to a smart card. This card can then be used to pay for many things, from goods in shops to electricity bills,

CHARGE CARDS

You can pay for something with a charge card at a store, or pay for goods over the phone. The credit company records all transactions and sends a bill each month.

Charge cards

Smart card

POLITICS

POLITICS IS CONCERNED with the organization of society. Political parties are groups of people who agree about the way in which a country should be run and who seek to gain power in government.

POLITICAL SYSTEMS

Every political system has a central authority called a government that is responsible for organizing the duties of the state. The most common form of government in the world today is the presidential system. This system has three branches.

Pericles, leader of Athens at the height of its power

THE BIRTH OF DEMOCRACY

Democracy means "rule by the people". Democratic traditions of debate and voting first appeared 2,500 years ago in the ancient Greek city-state of Athens. A regular general assembly was held where every male citizen was free to speak and vote. Daily running of the city was in the hands of an elected "Council of Five Hundred". Women and slaves, however, were not allowed to vote.

Bill Clinton is sworn in as US President.

PRESIDENT

In a presidential system, an elected president is the head of state and chief executive. He or she proposes new laws and passes them to the legislature, which may or may not pass them and can also refuse to pass laws proposed by the legislature. The president is Commander-in-Chief of the army and controls foreign policy.

US Congress, Washington D.C.

LEGISLATURE

The legislature is an assembly of elected representatives. Every new law must be passed by this assembly. It may propose laws itself and votes on those proposed by the president. In most presidential systems, the legislature is composed of two assemblies, or houses. In the US, the legislature is called Congress.

US Supreme Court, Washington D.C.

JUDICIARY

The judiciary is a legal body that reviews the laws passed by the legislature and ensures that they are in line with the country's written Constitution. In the US, the highest legal body is the Supreme Court. It can judge the activities of the executive and legislative branches, and reverse judicial decisions made by lower courts.

EXECUTIVE

US State Department

The president, as chief executive, is responsible for the administration of the state and for putting into practice new acts of law. He or she appoints the heads of the many administrative departments such as Defence, Trade, Education, Agriculture, and State.

PARLIAMENTARY SYSTEM

In a parliamentary system, political activity focuses on an assembly where matters are debated and laws are passed. Citizens elect members to act as their representatives. In Britain, the political party with the largest number of members elected to the House of Commons forms the government. The leader of that party becomes the Prime Minister, or chief executive. All executive power is held by the Prime Minister and his or her cabinet.

House of Commons – the political focus of Parliament and of British democracy

PEACEFUL PARLIAMENT

During debates in the British House of Commons, the leaders of the government and opposition stand at two swords' lengths from each other. This is a symbol of the parliamentary rule that members should never use violence to solve political problems.

POLITICAL FACTS

• The word "government" comes from the latin word *gubernare*, meaning "to steer".

• In Switzerland, voting in elections is compulsory – it is regarded as every citizen's duty.

• Until the 1980s, Soviet leaders were able to rule Communist USSR as virtual dictators – with more power than US presidents.

• The terms right and left wing come from France's Assembly of the 1790s: conservatives sat on the right of the speaker's chair, and reformers sat on its left.

French Assembly, c.1865

POLITICAL RECORDS

OLDEST RECORDED LAW-MAKING BODY is the Althing in Iceland. It was formed in about A.D. 930 and consisted of 40 local priest-chieftains. It was abolished in 1800 but then restored in 1843.

OLDEST CONSTITUTION still in use is that of the US, which was written in 1787.

LARGEST LAW-MAKING BODY is the National People's Congress of the People's Republic of China.

COMMUNISM

German thinker Karl Marx (1818–83) devised a new political and economic system, which he called Communism, in which all property is owned by the community and everyone shares in the country's wealth. In 1917, the USSR became the first communist state. Wealth was shared out more or less equally but, unlike Marx's ideal communist state, a single party, the Soviet Communist party, wielded total power and was able to use it unfairly.

Communist magazine, showing a worker smashing the chains of capitalism.

COMMUNISM

Under Communism, workers own the factories and share their profits equally.

CAPITALISM

Under capitalism, a few people own all the factories, but do not share profits with the workers.

POLITICAL ORGANIZATIONS AND PRESSURE GROUPS

Throughout the world, people and countries with shared interests form organizations to promote and defend their interests. Some, such as the United Nations, the Arab League, and the European Community, are concerned with the common interests of member states. Others, such as the environmental group Greenpeace and the human rights group Amnesty International, devote themselves to a particular cause.

Members of Greenpeace protest against plans for a nuclear power station.

VOTING

People hold elections to choose people to represent them. Each person usually casts one vote, and the candidate who receives the most votes is elected to office. This system is used in electing one representative for each constituency. An alternative system, proportional representation, allocates the seats in numbers proportional to the total number of votes given for each party.

South African citizen casts her vote in 1994 elections for president and parliament.

WOMEN'S VOTES

Women have not always shared in decisions about the way they were governed.

Country	First vote
New Zealand	1893
Australia	1902
Finland	1906
Norway	1913
Denmark	1915
Former USSR	1917
Britain	1918
USA	1920
South Africa (whites)	1930
Japan	1945

Emmeline Pankhurst, a British supporter of women's voting rights, arrested during a protest.

GOVERNMENT EXAMPLES AROUND THE WORLD

Power may be held by groups or individuals. Democracies may differ in structure.

 Monarchies
Saudi Arabia is an absolute monarchy with no political parties.

 Totalitarian regimes
China is ruled by one party, the Communist Party, and other parties are forbidden.

 Facade democracies
Iran holds elections for its presidency, but candidates are chosen by those in power.

 Military dictatorships
Myanmar (Burma) is ruled by a 19-member military council.

 Presidential republics
France's democracy has both a president and prime minister.

KEY POLITICAL THINKERS

Thinker	Dates	Biographical details
Plato	429–347 B.C.	Greek philosopher, rejected democracy in *The Republic* and insisted that government was a science, requiring experts.
Niccolo Machiavelli	1469–1527	Italian political thinker and diplomat, wrote a book, *The Prince*, that described methods of achieving political unity.
Thomas Hobbes	1588–1679	English philosopher, argued in *Leviathan* that human nature made absolute monarchy desirable and inevitable.
Jean-Jacques Rousseau	1712–78	French philosopher. His *Social Contract* argued that people sacrifice their rights in return for protection by a head of state.
Comte de Saint-Simon	1760–1825	French social scientist, believed that society should be organized along industrial lines.
John Stuart Mill	1806–73	English philosopher and political activist, argued for truly representative democracy.
Karl Marx	1818–83	German philosopher and economist, founder of Communism. Wrote *Das Kapital*.
Emile Durkheim	1858–1917	French founder of sociology.
Max Weber	1864–1920	German economist. Described the relationship between economy and society.

FALSE STARTER

Bolivia's political system has experienced great turmoil. In the 156 years from its independence from Spain (1825) to 1981, Bolivia has had 192 changes of government. This is an average of a new government every ten months.

POLITICAL WORDS

Anarchism Movement in favour of the abolition of the state.

Cabinet Group of ministers responsible for government in a parliamentary system.

Capitalism Economic system where invested capital (accumulated wealth) and profit-making drives industry.

Coalition Temporary alliance between different parties for combined action.

Communism Political and economic system in which all property is commonly owned and each person is paid according to their needs and abilities.

Congress US legislature composed of two houses – the Senate and the House of Representatives.

Constituency Geographical area representing a body of voters.

Constitution Basic set of laws that set out the institutions through which political power is exercised.

Constitutional monarchy System of government authorized by a constitution with a monarch as the head of state.

Coup d'Etat Violent or illegal seizure of power.

Democracy System of government by whole population or its representatives.

Dictatorship Government by a ruler with unrestricted authority.

Electorate Body of people entitled to vote in an election.

Executive Branch of government that carries out laws and performs general administration.

Fascism Extreme right-wing nationalist movement.

House of Commons In Britain, the elected chamber of Parliament.

Judiciary All the nation's judges.

Legislature Assembly or group that passes laws.

Lobby Group of people seeking to influence law-makers.

Prime minister Chief executive of government in countries with a parliamentary system.

Republic State in which power is held by the people or their elected representatives.

Revolution Forcible overthrow of a government or social order.

Socialism System in which the means of production (factories, etc.) and distribution are owned by the community as a whole.

Suffrage Right to vote in a political election.

Suffragette A woman who protests for her right to vote.

Trade union Group of workers or professionals united to protect and promote their rights and interests.

Totalitarianism Dictatorial system of government that extends its control to all social institutions.

LAW AND ORDER

EVERY COUNTRY HAS a set of rules or laws to protect the rights of its citizens. Laws are usually enforced by government through the police and the courts. In most countries, legal systems are the result of years of development, change, and reform.

EARLY LAW

About 4,000 years ago, King Hammurabi of Babylon set out some of the first recorded codes of behaviour. He devised laws, as well as penalties, covering family, property, slaves, and wages. These laws were engraved on a stone pillar.

Hammurabi meets the god of justice.

SCALES OF JUSTICE

The Statue of Justice at the Old Bailey, London (above), holds scales to show that justice weighs opposing evidence the way a balance weighs goods. The sword represents punishment. Some countries abuse their legal powers and remove freedoms instead of upholding them.

THE FIRST COURTS

In about 450 B.C., the Romans formed a system of courts where trials were held, and judges decided if a person had broken the law. In serious cases the accused paid a lawyer, called an *advocatus*, to speak for him. Most European law is based on Roman law.

TRIAL BY JURY

Anyone accused of a serious crime has the right to a trial by a jury, usually 12 men and women, chosen at random. South Africa does not have the jury system.

The judge helps the jury on points of the law, listens to the evidence, and passes sentence if there is a guilty verdict.

Prisoner on trial (the accused)

Prosecuting lawyer

COURT PROCEDURE

A prosecuting lawyer tries to convince the jury that the accused is guilty, while a defence lawyer sets out to prove the person's innocence. After listening to evidence from various witnesses, the jury has to decide whether the prosecution has proved guilt.

Prosecution tries to prove guilt.

Defence tries to convince the jury that the prisoner is not guilty.

TYPES OF LAW

There are several branches of the law, each devised to meet the different problems of society.

CRIMINAL LAW

This branch of the law covers acts such as murder, arson, rape, and robbery. In the USA, these are broken down into first, second, third, and fourth degrees, depending on the state of mind of the accused.

CIVIL LAW

This law deals with cases in which no crime has taken place, but someone's rights have been infringed. It covers day-to-day events such as buying a house or making a will, as well as resolving disputes between companies.

RELIGIOUS LAW

This law deals with cases in which religious code determines the law. For example, Islamic Law is based on the Koran and the teachings of Muhammad and is the basis for the law in North Africa and the Middle East.

Jury of 12 men and women chosen from members of the public aged over 18

PRISON POPULATION WESTERN EUROPE (1994)

Country	Prisoners per 100,000 population
UK	92.1
Spain	91.8
Austria	87.5
Switzerland	84.9
France	83.9
Portugal	82.0
Germany	78.8
Denmark	63.0
Finland	62.6
Belgium	60.5

PRISON FACTS

- Early prisons were filthy, and people often died of a kind of typhus known as "jail fever".

- The longest prison sentence was 141,078 years, passed on a woman in Thailand, for fraud.

- The world's most secure prison was Alcatraz, on an island off the California coast. Although 24 convicts tried to break free, no one ever managed to escape.

THE DEATH PENALTY

The death penalty is still legal in 105 countries, although many of them never carry out the sentence. Offences range from murder to drug trafficking. The first country to abolish the death penalty was Austria, in 1787. From 1995 the death penalty is unconstitutional in South Africa.

LEGAL WORDS

Accused Person charged with committing a crime.
Arson Criminal damage caused by fire.

Arson

Assault Threat or attempt to physically harm a person.
Bail Money given to gain temporary release of a prisoner facing trial.
Bankruptcy Situation in which a person is unable to pay their debts.
Barrister Lawyer who practises in the higher courts.
Damages Money claimed or awarded as compensation for loss or injury.
Defence Defendant's case in a law suit.
Defendant Person prosecuted in a criminal action.
Evidence The means used for proving a disputed fact in a legal action.
Felony A crime regarded by the law as serious, usually involving violence.

English judge

Fraud Deliberate trickery to gain an advantage, often financial.
Insolvent Situation in which a company is unable to pay its debts.
Judge Official who hears and tries cases in a court of law.
Jury Group of people who give a verdict in criminal cases on the basis of evidence given in court.
Kidnap Carry off a person against their will.
Libel Words published about a person that may harm their good character.
Murder To kill a person.
Oath Formal declaration as to the truth of something.
Perjury Wilfully tell an untruth when under oath.
Probation An alternative to a prison sentence whereby an offender must report regularly to a probation officer.
Prosecution The carrying on of legal proceedings.
Rape Force a person to have sexual intercourse against their will.
Slander Words spoken about a person that may harm their good character.
Solicitor Lawyer who advises clients and instructs barristers.
Subpoena A written demand that a person appear in court.
Sue To begin legal proceedings.
Summons Call to appear before a judge or magistrate.

Subpoena

Theft Take another's property without their consent.
Trial Legal proceedings to determine issues between parties.
Verdict Decision made in a criminal case.
Warrant Written authorization allowing police to search property and make arrests.

ARTS AND THE MEDIA

All the major art forms, from architecture to music, are given detailed treatment in this section. Timelines present key developments in the arts, and tables list famous painters, composers, architects, and writers. The media pages feature the latest in modern technology, including virtual reality.

Architecture • Fine Arts • Artists and Materials • Photography
Theatre • Dance • Ballet and Modern Dance • Traditional World Dance
Music • Classical Music • Popular Music • Musical Instruments
Writing • Printing • Radio • Television • Cinema • Animation
Video • Newspapers

ARCHITECTURE

ARCHITECTURE IS THE art and science of designing and constructing buildings. Modern steel-and-glass structures are now a feature of cities worldwide.

Step Pyramid

c.6500 B.C. Çatal Hüyük in Turkey, one of the first known towns, has rectangular houses built from mud bricks.

c.2650–2150 B.C. Pyramids are constructed in the lower Nile Valley, Egypt. The famous Step Pyramid at Saqqara is designed by Imhotep, a high priest and the first recorded architect.

c.2200 B.C. Stonehenge, a massive stone circle that is one of prehistoric Europe's most comple stone monuments, is erected for religious purposes.

6500 B.C. • *2600 B.C.* • *2200 B.C.*

700–400 B.C. Classical Greece. Architects of Greek temples develop three architectural "orders": Doric, Ionic, and Corinthian. Each order has its own style and proportions, based on mathematics and geometry, that are thought to be pleasing to the Greek gods.

Parthenon, Athens

Indian stupa

c.300 B.C. Buddhist stupas appear in India and Southeast Asia. These solid mounds symbolize the dome of heaven and contain sacred Buddhist relics.

c.200 B.C.–A.D. 500 Roman architect takes over the Greek orders and Etruscan arch. The Roman develop concrete and us construct huge vaults domes. Their public buildings include bath houses, templ amphitheatres.

Colosseum, Rome

700 B.C. • *300 B.C.* • *200 B.C.*

607–670 Japan's temple of the Horyuji Buddhist monastery, Nara, is the world's oldest surviving wooden building.

618–782 China. Nanchan Buddhist temple, Shaanxi province, built on a holy mountain, is the earliest surviving traditional Chinese timber-framed building.

Horyuji Temple

690–850 Early Islamic mosques, palaces, and houses are designed around courtyards. Mosques have minarets (prayer towers), arcades, and vaulted porches. Surface decoration is often mosaic – patterns of glass, stone, or marble pieces.

778–850 Borobudur Buddhist temple, Indonesia, has 8 stone terraces and 72 bell-shaped stupas.

Great Mosque, Samarra

c.900–1150 Roman style of architecture develops in western Europe. Romanesque churches have massive rubble-filled walls wi small windows. Arche semi-circular in shape stand on top of huge cylindrical columns.

Pisa Cathedral, Italy

600 • *607* • *618* • *700* • *778* • *900*

c.1420 Renaissance begins in Florence, Italy. Key figures are Brunelleschi (1377–1446) and Alberti (1404–72). This study of and adaptation of classical Roman styles and building techniques soon spreads through western Europe.

The Duomo, Florence, Italy

c.1650 Baroque style in Europe re-interprets Roman and Renaissance styles. Architects are commissioned by the Catholic Church and royalty to build large-scale, grand, and very ornate churches and palaces.

Church of St. Nicholas, Prague

1750–1840 Neo-Classicism Architects rediscover the proportions and details of Roman and then Greek classical architecture. A fine example is the church of Sainte Geneviève, Paris, later renamed the "Panthéon".

Pan

1400 • *c.1420* • *1600* • *c.1650* • *1700* • *1750*

1900–40s American architect Frank Lloyd Wright (1867–1959) promotes "organic" architecture – buildings that blend in with nature, such as Falling Water, Pennsylvania, USA.

Falling Water

1919–33 Bauhaus, Germany, an influential design school led by Walter Gropius (1883–1969), teaches design based on modern industrial technologies.

Bauhaus, Dessau

1920s International Modernism. Leading Swiss-born architect, Le Corbusier (1887–1965) defines a house as "a machine for living in".

Le Corbusier

1970s High-Tech sty In the steel-and-glass buildings of Richard Rogers (born 1933) an Norman Foster (born 1935), parts of the structure and services (pipes) are left expose A typical example is th Lloyds Building, Lond

1900 • *1919* • *1920* • *1970*

ORDERS

In classical Greek architecture, an order consists of an upright column supporting a horizontal entablature. A cornice, a frieze, and an architrave make up the entablature itself. The three Greek orders are Doric, Ionic, and Corinthian.

cornice
frieze
architrave
entablature
column

Doric
The Greeks used this order from about 700 B.C.

Ionic
From 600 B.C., this order appeared in western Asia.

Corinthian
This decorative order originated in Athens in 500 B.C.

Caryatids
These female statues are used as supporting columns.

Atlas (male caryatid)

Pedestal

Ziggurat, Ur

2095 B.C.
...ans build ziggurats, ...stepped temples of ...cks, in Mesopotamia.

c.1700–1200 B.C. Beehive tomb *(tholos)* is constructed by the Mycenean civilization on the Greek mainland.

c.1500 B.C. Minoan Palace of Knossos is rebuilt on the island of Crete, Greece. Paintings decorate the walls.

800–200 B.C. Etruscans, in modern-day Tuscany, Italy, use the arch in the construction of their buildings.

Palace of Knossos, Crete

1700 B.C. / 1500 B.C. / 800 B.C.

DOMES
These curved roofs are convex (arched) in shape, and are often a feature of religious buildings worldwide.

Hemispherical dome

Onion dome   *Polyhedral dome*   *Saucer dome*

...00–1540 Pre-Columbian
...ions build stepped pyramids ..., crowned with temples. ...he finest to survive is the ...pyramid, known as the ...guar, built before ...0 in the ceremonial ...x at Tikal, ...ala.

Giant Jaguar

A.D. 330–1453 Byzantine architecture develops when the new Roman Imperial capital moves to Byzantium (now Istanbul). It reflects Roman and Middle Eastern styles. The largest domed church of its day, Hagia Sophia, Istanbul, is completed in 537.

Hagia Sophia

A.D. 300 / 330

ROOFS
Roofs are defined by the shape and structure of their supporting frames. Coverings range from tiles to reeds.

Hipped roof

c.1100–1500 Gothic style is first used for Christian churches in northern Europe. New construction methods – the pointed arch and the flying buttress – result in much taller, lighter structures.

Amiens Cathedral, France

Angkor Wat

1113–c.1150 Angkor Wat, a vast stone temple city, is built by the Khmers at their capital in Cambodia. It is crowned with lotus-bud spires and covers almost 200 hectares (495 acres).

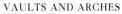

1100 / 1113

Pavilion roof   *Turret roof*   *Gable-and-valley roof*

VAULTS AND ARCHES
Vaults are arched roofs or ceilings, and there are four main types. Arches span openings and carry weight.

Barrel vault

...–1930s Gothic ...l. Architects attempt ...ture the style of ...al buildings. They also ...reate a new style ...odern building ...ds and materials as in ...nsylvania Academy of ...rts, Philadelphia, USA.

Home Insurance Building, Chicago

19th-century Industrial Revolution results in mass-produced materials that transform construction. Plate glass is used from the 1840s, steel from 1856, and reinforced concrete from the 1860s. Following the invention of the lift, steel-framed skyscrapers are first erected in Chicago, USA.

Casa Batlló, Barcelona

1890– early 1900s Art Nouveau – "new art" – is inspired by plant forms. Buildings are very ornate.

1890

Groin vault   *Rib vault*   *Fan vault*

Mid-1970s Postmodernism develops, a style that refers to past styles, sometimes in a humorous way. Buildings often feature strong, bright colours, such as the Neue Staatsgalerie, Stuttgart, Germany.

Neue Staatsgalerie

1990s Sustainable architecture provides a means of maintaining an ecological balance between human needs and preservation of the environment. Architects employ technology that manages nature in their designs.

Lloyds Building

1990

Pointed arch   *Horseshoe arch*   *Lobed arch*

WINDOWS
A window is an opening to let in light and air. Its materials, shape, and design reflect a building's architectural style.

Casement window

...APITALS
...he top section, or head, of a ...lumn is called a capital.

...gyptian capital   *Romanesque capital*   *Korean capital*

BUTTRESSES
Made of stone or brickwork, buttresses are built against walls to strengthen them. Flying buttresses transfer the weight of the upper part of a wall to an exterior support.

Flying buttress

Oeil-de-Boeuf (Ox-eye) window

Fanlight

SEVEN WONDERS OF THE WORLD

Temple of Artemis
Originally erected in about 550 B.C., this marble temple was burned down and later rebuilt. The gold statue of Artemis was destroyed, and only one of the original 127 Ionic columns remains.

Mausoleum at Halicarnassus
This vast marble tomb of Turkish ruler Mausolos was built in about 350 B.C. On site, only the foundations remain, but some statues are in London's British Museum.

Pharos of Alexandria
Built in about 297 B.C., this lighthouse stood on the island of Pharos, Alexandria, Egypt. At night a fire burned, reflected by bronze mirrors. Three earthquakes reduced the building to rubble.

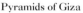

Pyramids of Giza
These pyramids were built at Giza, Egypt, between about 2575 and 2465 B.C. The Great Pyramid of Cheops is said to have taken 100,000 men 20 years to build.

Statue of Zeus, Olympia
This huge statue of the king of the gods was made from ivory and gold. The head alone measured 13m (43ft) in height.

Colossus of Rhodes
This bronze statue of the Sun god, Helios, stood more than 35m (110ft) high at the entrance to Rhodes harbour, Greece. An earthquake toppled it.

Hanging Gardens of Babylon
Nebuchadnezzar II (c.605–562 B.C.), King of Babylon, built these magnificent terraced gardens for one of his wives. Although descriptions exist, archaeologists are still looking for the site.

ARCHITECTURE FACTS

- Ancient Greeks painted the inside and outside of their temples in brilliant colours. The present whitened marble is due to weathering and bleaching by the hot sun.

- There is about 100 times more stone and brick in the Great Pyramid of Cheops than there is in the Empire State Building.

- Our ancestors' homes were dark caves. Today, in the mining community of Coober Pedy, Australia, people live in well-equipped dugouts with TVs and showers.

RECORDS

BIGGEST CASTLE
in the world is Prague Castle in the Czech Republic. Founded in about 850, the castle now covers about 8 hectares (20 acres).

TALLEST RESIDENTIAL BLOCK OF FLATS
is Lake Point Tower, Chicago, Illinois. It has 70 storeys and is 195m (639ft) high.

BIGGEST SHOPPING CENTRE
in the world is West Edmonton Mall, Alberta, Canada, which is as big as 90 American football fields.

TRADITIONAL HOMES AROUND THE WORLD

AFRICA

Zulu kraal, South Africa
Kraals are traditional dome-shaped, grass-covered houses with low openings at the front.

Masai house, Kenya
The Masai people build their rounded houses from bent branches covered with cow dung.

Algerian desert village
Houses are packed tightly together, so that as little of the house as possible is exposed to the blistering heat of the sun.

Dogon village, Mali
In these West African villages, houses are built of mud-brick, and storehouse roofs are thatched.

OCEANIA
Longhouse
These communal houses are raised on wooden stilts to keep animals out.

EUROPE

Swiss chalet
Traditional wooden chalets have sloping roofs to stop too much snow from collecting on them.

Scandinavian house
Roofs of traditionally built houses in such cold climates are turf covered to keep in the heat.

Mediterranean village house
The whitewashed stone houses of this region reflect the sun's heat, keeping the interior cool.

ASIA

Yurt
Nomads from Iran to Mongolia live in these willow-framed tents covered in felt and canvas.

Japanese house
Traditional timber-framed houses have sliding walls and doors that can be opened to the outside.

Chinese house
In China, traditional houses are arranged around a courtyard. The main part is on the north side.

AMERICAS

Amyara Indian house
On Lake Titicaca, Bolivia, Amyara Indians live in houses constructed from woven reeds.

Adobe houses
In New Mexico, traditional houses are built with adobe – bricks of sun-baked mud.

New England house
The walls of these North American houses have overlapping wooden boards (clapboards).

CROSS-SECTION OF A SKYSCRAPER, HONG KONG AND SHANGHAI BANK, HONG KONG

Mast
Illuminated display
External maintenance crane
Curved glass
Circular access platform
Face panel
Mullion
Steel column
Hanger
Escalator
Handrail
Fire escape staircase
Top beam
Outer diagonal beam
External staircase
Inner diagonal beam
Hanger
Terrace
Full-height glazing
Hanger
Glazed curtain wall
Lightweight steel and concrete floor
Entrance lobby
South face
Plaza

KEY ARCHITECTS

Name	Dates	Nationality	Building
Filippo Brunelleschi	1377–1446	Italian	Santa Maria del Fiore, Florence, Italy
Michelangelo Buonarroti	1475–1564	Italian	Dome of St. Peter's, Vatican City
Andrea Palladio	1508–80	Italian	Villa Rotonda, Vicenza, Italy
Inigo Jones	1573–1652	British	Banqueting House, London, England
François Mansart	1598–1666	French	Chateau de Maisons, Paris, France
Christopher Wren	1632–1723	British	St. Paul's, London, England
Jacques-Germain Soufflot	1713–80	French	The Panthéon, Paris, France
Andreyan Zakharov	1761–1811	Russian	The Admiralty, St. Petersburg, Russia
Karl Friedrich Schinkel	1781–1841	German	Altes Museum, Berlin, Germany
Antonio Gaudi	1852–1926	Spanish	La Sagrada Familia, Barcelona, Spain
Frank Lloyd Wright	1867–1959	American	Falling Water, Pennsylvania, USA
Edwin Lutyens	1869–1944	British	Viceroy's House, New Delhi, India
Adolf Loos	1870–1933	Czech	Scheu House, Vienna, Austria
Walter Gropius	1883–1969	German	Bauhaus, Dessau, Germany
Mies van der Rohe	1886–1969	German	Seagram Building, New York, USA
Erich Mendelsohn	1887–1953	German	Einstein Tower, Potsdam, Germany
Le Corbusier	1887–1965	Swiss	Notre Dame du Haut, Ronchamp, France
R. Buckminster Fuller	1895–1983	American	USA Pavilion, Expo 67, Montreal, Canada
Philip Johnson	b.1906	American	The Glass House, Connecticut, USA
Oscar Niemeyer	b.1907	Brazilian	Government Buildings, Brasilia, Brazil
Ieoh Ming Pei	b.1917	American	Louvre Pyramid, Paris, France
Richard Rogers	b.1933	British	Lloyds Building, London, England
Michael Graves	b.1934	American	Public Service Building, Oregon, USA
Norman Foster	b.1935	British	Hong Kong and Shanghai Bank, Hong Kong

ON A HIGH

When the Manhattan skyscrapers were erected, red-hot rivets were driven into holes in narrow steel beams hundreds of metres up in the air with nothing beneath. Iroquois and Mohawk Indians show no fear of heights and have put up many of these skyscrapers.

TALLEST BUILDINGS

Towers	Height	
	m	ft
KTHI-TV Mast, North Dakota, USA	629	2,064
KSFX-TV Mast, Texas, USA	615	2,018
TV Tower, Devers, Texas, USA	607	1,991
Building and location		
1 Petronas Towers, K L, Malaysia	452	1,483
2 Sears Tower, Chicago, USA	443	1,453
3 Jin Mao Building, Shanghai, China	420	1,378
4 World Trade Center, New York, USA	417	1,368
5 Empire State Building, New York, USA	381	1,250
6 Central Plaza, Hong Kong, China	374	1,227
7 Bank of China, Hong Kong, China	368	1,207
8 T and C-T Tower, Kaoshiung, Taiwan	348	1,142
9 Amoco Building, Chicago, USA	346	1,135
10 John Hancock Center, Chicago, USA	344	1,129

Petronas Towers, Malaysia

FINE ARTS

EVERY CULTURE HAS its own works of art. In some cultures, artistic styles have changed significantly; others have remained more or less the same over thousands of years. Movements in Western art have been given names and dates by specialists called art historians.

c.27,000 B.C. "Venus" figurines, small clay statues of pregnant women, appear across Europe.

Figurine, Lespugue, France

Horse, Lascaux

27,000 B.C.

c.500–323 B.C. Greek Classical sculptors study the form of the human body and explore its movement, making perfect figures of gods and athletes in marble, bronze, and clay. Phidias, a famous sculptor, makes a huge statue of Athena for the Parthenon, Athens, between 445 and 432 B.C.

Bronze charioteer, Greece

323–31 B.C. Greek Hellenistic sculptors make statues that emphasize the body's gracefulness. The portrait is developed and profiles of Greek rulers appear on coins.

Detail, Trajan's column

c.100 B.C.–A.D. 400 Roman decorative art flourishes. Relief carvings (standing out from the surface), often depicting Roman military victories, adorn arches and columns.

A.D. 100–400 Gandharan sculpture, influenced by Greek art, develops in the Indus Valley region (Pakistan). Sculptures show scenes from the Buddha's life.

Gandhara Buddha teaching

300 B.C. | 100 B.C. | A.D. 100

1000–1200 Romanesque style in Europe is displayed in church sculpture and mural painting, and in embroideries such as the Bayeux Tapestry, showing the Norman conquest of England.

Detail, Bayeux Tapestry, 1066

1000–1600 Easter Island (Polynesia). Gigantic, half-length figures up to 10m (33ft) in height are carved from volcanic rock and erected facing the sea.

Statue, Easter Island

1368–1644 Ming Dynasty in China is famous for its glazed blue-painted porcelain bowls and vases.

1450s Printing process develops in Germany. Illustrations are first printed using carved woodblocks; images are then engraved on to copper for greater detail.

1000 | 1200 | 1368 | 1400

1600s Dutch Golden Age painters represent scenes from everyday life, portraits and still-life subjects (such as fruit and flowers), and landscapes. Key artists are Rembrandt van Rijn (1606–69) and Jan Vermeer (1632–75).

Saskia as Flora, Rembrandt, c.1635

1600s Baroque style develops in Europe. Paintings feature energetic movement and strong contrasts of light and shadow to create dramatic effects. Michelangelo da Caravaggio (1573–1610) is one of the most influential artists.

Late 1700s to mid-1800s Romantic school of painting reflects the power of human emotions and nature. Key painters include J.M.W. Turner (1775–1851) and Caspar David Friedrich (1774–1840).

Norham Castle, Turner, 1824

1600 | 1700

1880–1905 Post-Impressionist artists Paul Cézanne (1839–1906), Vincent Van Gogh (1853–90), and Paul Gauguin (1848–1903), develop in their own different directions.

White Horse, Gauguin, 1898

1880s–90s Expressionism develops in Europe. Intense colour and free brushstrokes communicate artists' feelings. Ernst Ludwig Kirchner (1880–1938) is a key figure in Germany.

Drawing, Kirchner

1880s–90s Symbolist artists create images that portray inner feelings and suggest what may lie beneath the surface of things. Key painters include Gustave Moreau (1826–98).

1905–7 Fauves, a group of French painters that includes Henri Matisse (1869–1954), represent the world in brilliant colour harmonies.

1880 | 1900

1920s Surrealism develops from Dada and Freud's theories of psychoanalysis (see p.132). Artists such as Salvador Dali (1904–89) and Max Ernst (1891–1976) use dreams to explore their hidden feelings.

Salvador Dali, 1971

1940s Abstract Expressionism appears in New York, USA. Artists create abstract images, while experimenting with the physical properties of paint and different ways of applying it to the canvas. Jackson Pollock (1912–56) develops his paint-dripping technique as a way of expressing his feelings more directly.

Mid-1950s Pop Art develops in the USA and Britain. Artists use consumer goods and images from the media in their work. A key figure is Andy Warhol (1928–87).

Andy Warhol, 1971

Late 1950s Performance artists combine different art forms – painting, music, theatre, film, video – in their work. Key figures are Gilbert (born 1943) and George (born 1942), and Joseph Beuys (1921–86).

Planted, Gilbert and George, 1

1920 | 1940 | 1950 | 1960

,000 B.C. Lascaux ...es, France, are ...rated with images ...nimals. Artists use ...ral mineral colours, ...ying them with ...ers, brushes, and by ...ving through hollow ...ls.

c.4000–1000 B.C. Egyptian art includes painted statues sculpted from limestone, wall and scroll paintings, and fine gold jewellery, set with precious stones.

Nefertiti, Queen of Egypt

Bull-leaping, Crete

2000–1100 B.C. Minoans on Crete, an island near Greece, decorate the walls of their huge palaces with coloured murals.

1600–1027 Shang Dynasty craftsmen, China, discover how to cast in bronze and make beautiful decorated vessels for food and wine.

c.500 B.C. Nok culture, Nigeria, West Africa, produces lifelike terracotta figurines of humans with individual features emphasized.

Nok terracotta head

.000 B.C. | **5,000 B.C.** | **1,500 B.C.** | **500 B.C.**

D. 100–1000 ...yan carvings ...abine ornate ...man figures with ...roglyphs ...cture-writing). ...ving is done ...hout metal tools.

Mayan incense burner

400–1100 Medieval European monks produce illuminated manuscripts, such as the Book of Kells – the four gospels copied out and illustrated by a 9th-century Irish friar.

600–1185 Icons (religious portraits) are developed. Painters in the Eastern Christian Church follow strict rules that govern how religious figures must be shown.

Icon, Madonna and Child

618–907 T'ang Dynasty, a golden age in Chinese art. In this period, the great tradition of Chinese landscape painting develops, and figure (people) painting continues.

T'ang "blue and green" landscape

A.D. 500 | **600**

1400–1500 Early Renaissance starts in Florence, Italy, with a revival of interest in Classical sculpture and architecture. Masaccio (1401–28) is the first painter to use perspective (see p.162).

The Flood, Paolo Uccello, c.1445

Late 1400s Islamic miniature painting flourishes in Persia (Iran). Paintings are brightly coloured and highly detailed.

15th-century miniature

The Annunciation, Leonardo da Vinci

1500s–1600s High Renaissance period in Italy, particularly Rome and Venice. Major artists are Leonardo da Vinci (1452-1519), Raphael (1483–1520), and Michelangelo (1475–1564).

1500

40s Realism develops in ...ance with painters such as ...ustave Courbet (1819–77) ...o show ordinary people and ...eir surroundings in a direct, ...tural, and lifelike way.

The Winnowers, Courbet, 1855

1848 Pre-Raphaelites in England are inspired by painters before Raphael but develop their own style and symbols. The group includes Dante Gabriel Rossetti (1828–82) and J.E. Millais (1829–96).

1860s–90s Impressionism originates in France. Painters, notably Claude Monet (1840–1926) and Edouard Manet (1832–83), try to capture their impressions, in particular the light, of a fleeting moment in time. **Neo-Impressionism** develops, led by Georges Seurat (1859–91), whose work is based on dots of pure colour.

Waterlilies, Monet, 1916–19

1800 | **1848** | **1850**

907–1920s Cubism ...evelops in Paris, ...ance, with Pablo ...icasso (1881–1973) ...d Georges Braque ...882–1963), who use ...eometric shapes to ...ortray what they see.

...icasso, 1955

1910–50 Abstract movement, in which artists' paintings and sculptures do not directly resemble people or things in everyday life. The first abstract painting may be a work (c.1910) by Wassily Kandinsky (1866–1944).

Hornform, Kandinsky, 1924

1916 Dada movement, originally a protest against World War I, rejects traditional forms of art. Marcel Duchamp (1887–1968), selects and displays everyday objects, which he calls "ready-mades".

MOST EXPENSIVE PAINTINGS SOLD AT AUCTION

Title, artist, date sold	Price in US$
Portrait of Dr. Gachet, Van Gogh, 1990	82,500,000
Au Moulin de la Galette, Renoir, 1990	78,100,000
Self Portrait, Van Gogh, 1998	71,500,000
Still Life with Curtain, Pitcher, and Bowl of Fruit, Cezanne, 1999	60,500,000
Irises, Van Gogh, 1987	53,900,000
Les Noces de Pierrette, Picasso, 1989	51,895,000
Self Portrait: Yo Picasso, Picasso, 1989	47,850,000
Au Lapin Agile, Picasso, 1989	40,700,000

Source: Sotheby's, London

1910 | **1915** | **1916**

From 1970s Video Artists use video and computer technology. Their installations (exhibitions) feature video projection. A key figure is Korean-born Nam Jun Paik (born 1932).

1980s Art in Nature. Artists such as Richard Long (born 1945) and Andy Goldsworthy (born 1956) create outdoor works of art that are in harmony with the landscape. Materials – stones, leaves, etc. – are found on-site.

Flower, Andy Goldsworthy, 1992

1970 | **1990**

ARTISTS AND MATERIALS

ARTISTS USE PAINT to create images of the world as they see it. Originally they painted on cave walls using the most basic materials. Today, an artist can choose different materials and techniques to express his or her ideas and feelings.

MATERIALS

Artists paint on many surfaces using a range of materials. One person may spread thick blobs of oil paint on a canvas with a knife, while another will apply delicate brushstrokes of watercolour on to a sheet of paper. Some artists paint with their fingers, or employ traditional methods such as egg tempera.

Varnish
Paint layers
Drawing layer
Imprimatura
Priming
Size
Ground

LAYERS OF A PAINTING

There are several layers to an oil painting. These can help modern historians to date a picture accurately, and also to spot whether it is a fake. This artwork, showing a section of Caravaggio's *Youth with a Ram*, reveals the layers through a typical 17th-century oil painting.

ARTIST FACTS

• Architect and artist Leon Battista Alberti (1404–72) wrote a key book about perspective in 1436. His methods enabled artists to create a geometrically controlled space on a two-dimensional surface.

• Making copies of paintings by Old Masters was considered an essential part of a young painter's training. Edouard Manet made copies of both Delacroix and Titian while working as a student.

• Pablo Picasso's famous work *Guernica* (1937) depicts scenes from the Spanish Civil War. Picasso refused to let the painting hang in Spain until the country was free. It remained in New York until 1981, when democracy was restored.

• Katsushika Hokusai (1760–1849) was a master of the Japanese ukiyo-e (pictures of the floating world) school. He made beautiful wood-block colour prints showing views of Mt. Fuji.

PIGMENTS

Paint is made from pigments (powdered colours). Pigments were first found in natural substances such as carbon (black), chalk (white), and red and yellow earths. The ancient Egyptians added mineral colours such as malachite (green) from copper, and ultramarine (blue) from lapis lazuli.

Malachite

Lapis lazuli

DRAWING TOOLS

Artists often make sketches (quick drawings) to record what they see, or to prepare for a finished work. Many drawings are sold as finished works of art. A variety of tools is available.

Conté crayon
Charcoal
Pencil
Graphite stick
Reed pen and ink

BRUSHES

Paintbrushes fall into two main groups, soft-hair brushes, mostly used for watercolours, and bristle brushes, used in oil painting and acrylics. Within these groups there are three main types (round, flat, and filbert) identified by the length and shape of the hairs.

Round
Flat
Filbert

MATERIAL FACTS

• The pigment Indian yellow used to be made by boiling the urine of cows fed only on mango leaves. The urine was mixed with earth, heated, and dried.

• Brushes were once made by tying white hog bristles to a stick. The brush was then used to whitewash a wall until the bristles became supple.

• Thousands of years ago, artists in Australia mixed paint, such as red ochre or charcoal, in their mouths and spat the colour into paintings on the cave walls.

PAINTS

Oil paints
These are a mixture of dry pigment and an oil – usually linseed oil. They were first used by 15th-century painters, such as Jan van Eyck.

Watercolour paints
These are pigments bound with gum arabic and diluted with water. They became popular with 18th-century landscape artists, such as J.M.W. Turner.

Acrylic paints
These were developed in the USA during the 1920s. Acrylic is applied with a knife, or diluted and used with a brush. Acrylic was used by Andy Warhol.

Oil paint
Watercolour paint
Acrylic paint

FAKE FACTS

• Paint can be dated by analysing its content. Cobalt blue, for example, was not produced before 1802, but is used by forgers when they need a cheap substitute for ultramarine.

• Many signed drawings and paintings, supposedly by Rembrandt, were actually done by artists of his school.

• Leonardo da Vinci's *Mona Lisa* was stolen from the Louvre in 1912. It took three years to find, during which time six forgeries turned up in the USA, each selling for a very high price.

POPULAR EUROPEAN GALLERIES (1996)

Art Gallery	Visitors
National Gallery, London	5,000,000
Louvre, Paris	4,700,000
Prado, Madrid	1,814,892
Uffizi Gallery, Florence	1,106,173
Van Gogh Museum, Amsterdam	971,479
Alte Pinakothek, Munich	335,000

SCULPTOR FACTS

• When Rodin exhibited his first major work, *The Age of Bronze* (1878), it caused a sensation. The figure was so lifelike he was accused of casting it from a living model.

• Henry Moore's work was influenced by the carvings of the Aztecs. A sculpture of their ancient rain god, Tlaloc, gave him the idea for his statues of *Reclining Women*.

LABOUR OF LOVE

Michelangelo painted the ceiling of the Sistine Chapel in Rome. The fresco covers more than 900sq m (9,688sq ft), and took four and a half years to complete.

ARTISTS' WORDS

Airbrushing Spraying on colour under pressure with an airbrush.

Alla prima A direct form of painting made in one session. Used by artists when they want to paint spontaneously.

Casting To make an object, often a sculpture, by pouring metal into a mould and letting it harden.

Chiaroscuro The treatment of light and shade in drawing and painting.

Chroma The intensity or saturation of a colour.

Collage A pictorial technique in which various materials are arranged and fixed to a backing.

Craquelure The network of small cracks that appears on a painting when, in the course of time, the pigment's varnish has become brittle.

Craquelure

Engraving The various processes of cutting a design into a plate or block of metal or wood, and the prints taken from these plates or blocks.

Etching A method of engraving in which a corrosive acid "eats" a design into a metal plate.

Ferrule The metal part of a brush which surrounds and retains the hairs.

Fresco Powdered pigments mixed in water and applied to wet lime plaster. Fresco means "fresh" in Italian.

Gesso A traditional surface for tempera and oil painting on a panel made of glue and plaster of paris.

Glaze Film of transparent colour laid over a painting once it has dried.

Gouache Similar technique to watercolour but glue is used to bind the colour together. Used since the 18th century.

Ground The surface on which colour is applied.

Gum arabic Gum from the acacia tree, which is used as a binding material in the manufacture of watercolour paints.

S'graffito

Impasto Paint put on so thickly that it stands up from the surface.

Imprimatura A thin overall film or stain of translucent colour over a white priming.

Pigment The colouring matter, usually powder, which forms the basis of all paint.

Priming The preliminary coating that is put on to the support before painting.

S'graffito A technique using a scalpel or sharp knife in which dried paint is scraped off the painted surface. Used to create texture.

Size Material such as glue or gelatine used to prepare canvas prior to priming or to reduce the absorbency of paper.

Support The material on which a painting is made, such as paper, canvas, or a wooden panel.

Tempera Usually refers to egg tempera, a pigment bound with egg white instead of glue. Most important technique for panel painting (wood) in Europe from 13th to 15th centuries before oil. Layers of paint are built up slowly.

Tone The degree of darkness or lightness of a colour.

Trompe-l'oeil A still-life painting designed to give an illusion of reality.

Varnish Protective surface over a finished painting that gives a glossy or matt appearance.

Wash A thin, transparent layer of paint.

Wash

KEY ARTISTS

Name	Dates	Nationality	Key work
Donatello	c.1386–1466	Italian	*David*
Jan van Eyck	c.1390–1441	Flemish	*Arnolfini and his Wife*
Piero della Francesca	c.1420–92	Italian	*Dream of Constantine*
Sandro Botticelli	c.1445–1510	Italian	*Birth of Venus*
Albrecht Dürer	1471–1528	German	*Melancholia*
Michelangelo Buonarroti	1475–1564	Italian	*David, The Creation of Adam*
Raphael	1483–1520	Italian	*The Sistine Madonna*
Titian	c.1487–1576	Italian	*Assumption of the Madonna*
Leonardo da Vinci	1452–1519	Italian	*Mona Lisa*
Pieter Bruegel the Elder	c.1525–69	Flemish	*A Country Wedding*
Michelangelo da Caravaggio	1573–1610	Italian	*The Supper at Emmaus*
Peter Paul Rubens	1577–1640	Flemish	*Peace and War*
Frans Hals	1580–1666	Flemish	*Laughing Cavalier*
Artemisia Gentileschi	1593–1651	Italian	*Judith and Holofernes*
Nicholas Poussin	1594–1665	French	*Et in Arcadia Ego*
Diego do Velázquez	1599–1660	Spanish	*Las Meninas*
Claude Lorrain	1600–82	French	*Landscape with Sacrifice to Apollo*
Rembrandt van Rijn	1606–69	Dutch	*The Night Watch*
Jan Vermeer	1632–75	Dutch	*Young Woman with a Water Jug*
Antoine Watteau	1684–1721	French	*Embarcation for the Isle of Cythera*
Antonio Canaletto	1697–1768	Italian	*The Stonemason's Yard*
Thomas Gainsborough	1727–88	English	*The Blue Boy*
Francisco de Goya y Lucientes	1746–1828	Spanish	*The Second of May*
Jacques-Louis David	1748–1825	French	*The Death of Marat*
Caspar David Friedrich	1774–1840	German	*Solitary Tree*
Joseph Mallord William Turner	1775–1851	English	*The Fighting Temeraire*
John Constable	1776–1837	English	*The Hay Wain*
Eugène Delacroix	1798–1863	French	*The Massacre at Chios*
Gustave Courbet	1819–77	French	*The Peasants of Flagey*
Edouard Manet	1832–83	French	*Dejeuner sur l'herbe*
Paul Cézanne	1839–1906	French	*Mont Ste. Victoire*
Auguste Rodin	1840–1917	French	*The Kiss*
Claude Monet	1840–1926	French	*The Water Lilies*
Auguste Renoir	1841–1919	French	*Le Moulin de la Galette*
Mary Cassatt	1844–1926	American	*La Loge*
Paul Gauguin	1848–1903	French	*Te Rereioa (Rest)*
Vincent van Gogh	1853–90	Dutch	*Sunflowers*
Georges Seurat	1859–91	French	*A Summer Sunday at La Grande Jatte*
Gustave Klimt	1862–1918	Austrian	*The Kiss*
Edvard Munch	1863–1944	Norwegian	*The Scream*
Henri de Toulouse-Lautrec	1864–1901	French	*Le Moulin Rouge*
Wassily Kandinsky	1866–1944	Russian	*Shrill-Peaceful Pink*
Käthe Kollwitz	1867–1945	German	*Bread*
Pierre Bonnard	1867–1947	French	*At the Table*
Henri Matisse	1869–1954	French	*La Danse*
Piet Mondrian	1872–1944	Dutch	*New York City I*
Constantin Brancusi	1876–1957	Romanian	*Endless Column*
Paul Klee	1879–1940	Swiss	*Ambassador of Autumn*
Fernand Léger	1881–1955	French	*The Outing*
Pablo Picasso	1881–1973	Spanish	*Les Demoiselles d'Avignon*
Georges Braque	1882–1963	French	*Man with a Pipe*
Marcel Duchamp	1887–1968	French	*The Large Glass*
Georgia O'Keeffe	1887–1986	American	*Lilies*
Egon Schiele	1890–1918	Austrian	*Death and the Maiden*
Max Ernst	1891–1976	German	*On the Threshold of Liberty*
Joan Miró	1893–1983	Spanish	*The Birth of the World*
René Magritte	1898–1967	Belgian	*The Use of Words*
Henry Moore	1898–1986	English	*Reclining Figure*
Alberto Giacometti	1901–66	Swiss	*The Forest*
Mark Rothko	1903–70	American	*Blue, Orange, and Red*
Barbara Hepworth	1903–75	English	*Wave*
Salvador Dali	1904–89	Spanish	*Premonition of a Civil War*
Francis Bacon	1909–92	English	*The Screaming Pope*
Jackson Pollock	1912–56	American	*Lavender Mist*
Joseph Beuys	1921–86	German	*The Pack*
Jean Tinguely	1925–91	Swiss	*Homage to New York*
Robert Rauschenberg	1925–	American	*Bed*
Andy Warhol	1928–87	American	*Marilyn Monroe*
Jasper Johns	b.1930–	American	*Three Flags*
Bridget Riley	b.1931–	English	*Late Morning*
David Hockney	b.1937–	English	*A Bigger Splash*
Gilbert and George	b.1943–, 1942–	English	*Underneath the Arches*
Anselm Kiefer	b.1945–	German	*Scorched Earth*

PHOTOGRAPHY

PHOTOGRAPHY IS a way of recording images using a lens and some light-sensitive material. Taking a good photograph depends more on the photographer's visual skills than on the equipment used.

11th century Camera obscura ("dark room") is invented in Arabia for observing solar eclipses. It later forms the basis of photography.

18th-century camera obscura includes a mirror.

1727 Johann Schulze (1687–1744), a German doctor, discovers that silver nitrate darkens when exposed to light.

1827 First photographic image is produced by Joseph Nicéphore Niepce (1765–1833). It takes eight hours of exposure time.

First photographic image

1100 | 1700 | 1727 | 1800 | 1827

1839 Daguerreotype process is developed by Frenchman Louis Daguerre (1757–1851).

Daguerreotype camera

1839 Calotype process is invented by Englishman William Fox Talbot (1800–77). This negative-positive process allows photographs to be copied.

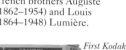
William Fox Talbot

1851 Collodion process is developed by English sculptor Frederick Archer (1813–57). His glass-plate negatives allow paper prints to be made.

Frederick Archer

1907 First practical colour photographic process is introduced by French brothers Auguste (1862–1954) and Louis (1864–1948) Lumière.

First Kodak colour film

1913 35mm film is used for the first time.

Auguste and Louis Lumière

1800 | 1839 | 1851 | 1900 | 1913

1924 The Leica I, the first 35mm camera, is launched commercially. Its frame counter runs to 36 exposures, setting the standard for later cameras.

Leica I

1935 Kodachrome film is invented, allowing colour transparencies to be both projected and reproduced.

1939 First important negative colour film is produced by Agfa.

Edwin Land

1947 First instant picture camera, invented by American Edwin Land (1909–90), is marketed by Polaroid Corporation.

1975 Using special cameras and lights, an American scientist photographs a bullet passing through an apple at one three-millionth of a second exposure.

1976 First compact camera with automatic focusing is produced in Japan by Konica. It is called the Konica C35AF.

1990 First "Eye-Start" system is introduced. The camera lens automatically zooms in on the subject when you look through the viewfinder.

1990s Digital cameras are introduced. Images are stored on disks.

1900 | 1924 | 1935 | 1939 | 1947 | 1975 | 1976 | 1990 | 1999

TYPES OF CAMERA

Automatic SLR camera

Manual SLR camera

Basic compact camera

Advanced compact camera

6cm x 4.5cm roll-film camera

6cm x 6cm roll-film camera

Direct vision camera

6cm x 7cm roll-film camera

6cm x 9cm roll-film camera

Instant camera

Waterproof camera

Wide-view camera

Panoramic camera

Large-format camera

Single-use camera

PHOTOGRAPHY FACTS

• The first successful camera weighed 23kg (51lb), which is the same weight as a red-necked wallaby.

• Every day, more than two million photographs are taken around the world.

• Until about 1930, photographers made flash lights by creating small explosions with magnesium powder.

• One 35mm transparency (slide) can hold as much information as a single high-density floppy disk for a personal computer.

STIFF SHOT

The first cameras required long exposure times, so people had to stand still for long periods in order to avoid a blurred image. The photographer also attached a clamp to the subject's head and body.

PHOTOGRAPHY WORDS

Aperture The opening in the camera lens that controls the amount of light passing on to the film.

Auto-focus A system in the camera which adjusts the focus automatically.

Darkroom A lightproof room used for developing photographic film.

Electronic flash The light source on a camera that is needed for taking pictures after dark, indoors, or in dim light.

Enlargement A photographic print that is larger than the negative from which it was developed.

Motor-drive The device on a camera that enables you to take a rapid sequence of photographs.

SLR (single-lens reflex) A type of camera where the view through the viewfinder is what will actually be recorded on the film.

Transparency A positive image, in black and white or colour, that is produced on a transparent film.

Tripod A stand that supports a camera to keep it steady and avoid blurred images.

Viewfinder The device on a camera that shows what will be in the photograph.

INSIDE A CAMERA

A camera is basically a lightproof box that has a hole, or lens, at one end. An open lens allows light to enter and shine on a piece of film (light-sensitive paper) inside the camera, forming an image. The most important parts of a camera are the lens, shutter, and diaphragm.

Rear viewfinder camera

Flash hot shoe

Frame counter

Shutter speed dial

Shutter release button

Strap attachment

Film

Film take-up spool

Internal lens elements

Lens housing

Aperture control ring

Light path through the camera

Front lens element

THE LIGHT PATH INSIDE THE CAMERA

This diagram shows how light is adjusted when it travels through the camera to form an image on the light-sensitive film.

Light source The light illuminating the subject is reflected through the camera lens.

Lens A piece of curved glass that reflects the light rays.

Diaphragm A device for controlling the amount of light entering the camera, made of metal plates. It forms an adjustable aperture (hole).

Shutter The shutter can be set to open and close at different speeds, which determines for how long the film is exposed to the light.

Focal plane and film The focal plane is where the light from the lens is brought into focus, coinciding with the position of the film.

TYPES OF LENSES

Lenses can be fitted on to the basic camera lens of certain types of cameras to create different effects in a photograph or to help take a better picture of difficult subjects.

Wide-angle lens allows 50% more of the subject to appear on the film than a standard lens.

Wide-angle lens

Telephoto lens is used to take close-ups of subjects from a distance and to make them appear bigger.

Telephoto lens

Fisheye lens is a wide-angle lens which covers up to 210° of vision.

Fisheye lens

Standard lens shows the scene almost as it appears to the naked eye.

Standard lens

Super telephoto lens is a specialist lens that needs a tripod to support its weight.

Super telephoto lens

Filters are flat coloured discs that are attached to the front of a camera lens to alter or distort the subject.

Green

Purple

Orange

Red

Yellow

FILM SPEED

Film comes in various speeds, which are shown on the package as ISO (International Standards Organization) numbers. This table shows their uses for different situations and subjects.

ISO	Speed	Situations and subjects
32	Slow	Well lit, still life
200	Medium	General subjects and lighting levels
400	Moderate-fast	Dimly lit, moving subjects

FAMOUS PHOTOGRAPHERS

Julia Margaret Cameron (1815–79) British-born portrait photographer.

Robert Capa (1913–54) Hungarian-born war photographer. In 1947 Capa and Cartier-Bresson founded Magnum Studios.

Henri Cartier-Bresson (born 1908) French photographer who did much to establish photo-journalism as an art form.

Richard Avedon (born 1923) American photographer famous for portraits and fashion pictures.

DEVELOPING

A photograph is developed by fixing the image on to special photographic paper using chemicals. This process is done in the dark.

1 Each grain of silver on the film changes when it is exposed to light. The film must be processed before the image can be seen.

2 Developing and fixing chemicals imprint the image on to the film.

Equipment

3 The pictures on the film are called negatives because the light and dark areas are reversed.

Negatives

4 The negative is printed onto white paper using an enlarger.

5 The exposed white paper is developed and set with chemicals.

Enlarger

6 After the print has been developed, it is washed and dried.

Finished print

Colour film has three layers of light-sensitive emulsion. Each reacts to a colour – either blue, green, or red. The emulsion layers record how much of each colour there is in the image.

Developing tray

THEATRE

MODERN WESTERN THEATRE has its origins in Ancient Greece. The word itself comes from the Ancient Greek word *theatron*, meaning "place for viewing".

c. 3000 B.C. Religious ceremonies all over the world include music, dance, and elements of drama.

Egyptian hunters

c. 1000 B.C. Chinese and Indian dance-dramas develop and become more formalized in style.

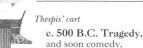
Thespis' cart

534 B.C. Thespis, the first actor to step outside the chorus of singers and dancers, arrives in Athens.

c. 500 B.C. Tragedy, and soon comedy, develops in Greece.

384–322 B.C. Aristotle Greek philosopher, explains his theories of tragedy in *The Poetics*.

3000 B.C. | 1000 B.C. | 534 B.C. | 500 B.C. | 320 B.C.

c. 200 B.C. Romans adapt Greek comedies. Plautus (c.254–184) and Terence (c.190–159) are among the most popular playwrights.

c. A.D. 1 Sanskrit theatre quickly flourishes in India.

Pantomimus

c. A.D. 1–100 Pantomimus, a form of theatre in which actors used gesture and movement to act out tragic stories, was popular in Rome throughout the first century.

c. 1200 Travelling story-tellers in Middle Eastern countries use mime to break through language barriers.

c. 1300 Indian folk theatre develops, following the decline of Sanskrit theatre. Noh theatre becomes the dominant form in Japan.

1453 The Renaissance begins in Italy, and soon spreads to the rest of Europe. Roman plays are revived, and buildings reflect the style of classical architecture.

c. 1500 Commedia dell'Arte companies from Italy travel widely in Europe, greatly influencing theatrical styles.

Harlequin

200 B.C. | A.D. 1 | A.D. 1–100 | 1200 | 1300 | 1453 | 1500

1564 William Shakespeare, an English dramatist, is born.

c. 1600 Kathakali (meaning story-play) is created in India. Actors use body language and mime to tell popular Hindu epic stories.

Kathakali

1603 Okuni, a young Japanese woman, creates a new dance called **Kabuki**.

1653 Japanese authorities allow only adult males to perform Kabuki, and it begins to develop a more theatrical style.

1678 Aphra Behn (1640–1689), an English dramatist, stages *The Rover*, a Restoration comedy. Behn is the first British woman to write plays for a living. She is also a spy.

Aphra Behn

1782 Friedrich von Schiller (1759–1805), a German dramatist, stages *The Robbers*. This play is among those that inspire the German Romantic movement of the late 18th and early 19th centuries (see p.161).

Friedrich von Schiller

1564 | 1600 | 1603 | 1653 | 1678 | 1782

c. 1800 Peking Opera begins in China. The performances are a mixture of mime, song, dance, dialogue, and acrobatics. In Vietnam, **Hat Boi** uses a similar theatrical style to dramatize tales of war and suffering.

Peking Opera

1877 Henrik Ibsen (1828–1906), a Norwegian dramatist, stages *The Pillars of Society*.

c. 1890 Symbolism (see p.160) begins in the German theatre.

1894 George Bernard Shaw (1856–1950), an Irish dramatist, stages *Arms and the Man*.

1894 The Olympia Theater is the first to open on Broadway, New York, USA.

1896 Alfred Jarry (1873–1907), a French dramatist, stages *Ubu Roi* in Paris. The play later influences the movement called *Theatre of the Absurd*.

Poster for Ubu Roi

c. 1910 Expressionism (see p.161) emerges in Germany. Georg Kaiser (1878–1945) and Ernst Toller (1893–1939) are popular playwrights.

1800 | 1877 | 1890 | 1894 | 1896 | 1910

1905 The Russian Revolution creates a need for *Agit-prop* (agitational propaganda) theatre. Actors act out political events, replacing newspapers for the many people who cannot read.

Agit-prop

1935 Antonin Artaud (1896–1948), a French dramatist, stages *Les Cenci*, the first play to represent *Theatre of Cruelty*. This style of theatre is intended to horrify the audience.

Bertolt Brecht

1949 Bertolt Brecht (1898–1956), a German dramatist, founds the Berliner Ensemble. The company stages plays in Brecht's "epic" style, always reminding the audience that it is watching a play, and not real events.

1950 Eugène Ionesco (1912–1994), a French dramatist, stages *The Bald Primadonna*, the first example of his *Theatre of the Absurd*.

1955 Tennessee Williams (1911–1983), an American dramatist, stages *Cat on a Hot Tin Roof*.

1905 | 1935 | 1949 | 1950 | 1955

Look Back in Anger

1956 John Osborne (1929-1994), an English dramatist, stages *Look Back in Anger*. The term "kitchen sink drama" is used to describe its realistic coverage of everyday life.

1986 Wole Soyinka (born 1934), a Nigerian dramatist, is the first black African to win the Nobel Prize for literature. He was imprisoned from 1967 to 1969 for criticizing the Nigerian government.

Wole Soyinka

1990s Musicals, especially revivals such as *Crazy for You*, are the most popular form in most commercial western theatres.

1996 Globe Theatre opens in London. It is a reconstruction of the venue in which Shakespeare's plays were originally performed.

Crazy for You

1956 | 1959 | 1986

A MODERN THEATRE

Many modern theatres are designed like this one, with a proscenium arch separating the real world of the audience from the pretend world of the actors. The word "proscenium" comes from the Ancient Greek *pro skene*, meaning "in front of the stage".

Upstage (furthest from the audience) actors are well lit, and draw the audience's attention. Actors are sometimes accused of "upstaging" each other.

Props (properties) are objects that the actors carry on stage. They are kept on a table in the wings.

Wings at each side of the stage provide space for scenery and costumes that will be used later.

Scenery is suspended by ropes from a grid above the stage. This area is called the "flies".

Curtain is usually lowered while stagehands change the set (scenery).

Iron, or safety curtain, separates stage and auditorium so that a fire cannot spread too quickly.

Proscenium arch frames the acting area.

FOLLOW-SPOT OPERATOR

The follow-spot operator controls a heavy spotlight, directing the beam of light so that a moving actor is always lit. The follow-spot is usually either in the lighting box, or high up at one side of the auditorium.

Dressing rooms are usually shared by members of the company.

Green room is where actors rest between scenes.

Dressing room for an actor who is taking a leading role.

Wardrobe department makes and looks after costumes.

Scenery is made and stored in the workshop.

Downstage (towards the pit) the audience's attention can easily be distracted. Actors use this area when another actor has more important lines.

Lifts like this one can make actors or scenery appear and disappear to surprise the audience. Some theatres have two or more lifts.

Orchestra pit is in front of the stage. In many theatres the pit can be covered, and the stage can be extended, or extra seating added.

Lighting operators control lighting using a board, or console. Computerized boards control every light in the theatre.

Stage manager gives "calls" to make sure that scenery moves and actors make their entrances on time.

WILLIAM SHAKESPEARE (1564–1616)

William Shakespeare was born in Stratford-upon-Avon, England, but moved to London in about 1590. There he became an actor and playwright, and a shareholder in the Globe Theatre. Today Shakespeare is the most often performed playwright in the world. He is thought to have written 37 plays, with more than 100,000 lines. The longest Shakespearean role is Hamlet, which has a total of 1,530 lines.

MOST POPULAR PLAYS 1996 (BY SCRIPT SALES)

Title	First staged	Playwright
Top Girls	1982	Caryl Churchill (born 1938)
Streetcar Named Desire	1948	Tennessee Williams (1911–83)
Our Country's Good	1988	Timberlake Wertenbaker (1951–)
The Doll's House	1879	Henrik Ibsen (1828–1906)
Educating Rita	1980	Willy Russell (born 1947)

THEATRE RECORDS

SMALLEST PROFESSIONAL THEATRE is the Piccolo in Hamburg, Germany. It can seat no more than 30 people.

LONGEST RUNNING PLAY is *The Mousetrap*, which has been running in London since 1952.

EARLIEST KNOWN STONE AMPHITHEATRE was built in Rome in about 55 B.C. It held roughly 40,000 people.

SHORTEST RECORDED PLAY, *Breath*, by Samuel Beckett, consists of 35 seconds of human cries and breaths.

THE IMAGINARY INVALID

Molière (1622–1673), France's most famous dramatist, acted and managed a theatrical company as well as writing plays. He died within hours of collapsing on stage in a production of his own play, *Le Malade Imaginaire (The Imaginary Invalid)*.

THEATRE FACTS

• Until the invention of greasepaint in the 1860s, stage make-up contained lead. Many actors died from lead poisoning.

• The title of *Macbeth* is considered unlucky in the theatre. Instead, the play is called "the Scottish play".

BUILDING THEATRES

Since the Ancient Greeks built the first theatres in the 5th century B.C. the style of theatrical buildings has altered constantly to suit the demands of the plays performed in them. In many modern theatres, the shape and size of the stage can be changed for each production.

Ancient Greek theatres had seats built into the sides of a natural bowl. The centre was used for singing and dancing, and the small stage for acting.

Roman theatres were built of wood or stone in a semi-circular shape. A permanent roof sheltered the actors on stage.

Renaissance theatres were loosely based on those of Ancient Rome, with the audience on one side only.

Elizabethan English theatres had several entrances and exits, used for acting out complex plots.

Modern stages take many forms. One is theatre-in-the-round, where the audience surrounds the stage.

JAPANESE THEATRE

The two traditional forms of Japanese theatre are *Noh* and *Kabuki*. The actors are male, and usually trained by their fathers to act a particular role. *Noh* actors wear masks, and *Kabuki* actors use make-up.

KABUKI CHARACTERS

Noble male   *Crab*   *Wicked male*

A Noh actor

CABARET

Cabaret may be pure entertainment, or it can contain political statements. Writers and performers often use cabaret to comment on society or challenge fixed ideas.

Au und aus, performed at the Admirals Palast, Berlin, 1926

PUPPETS AND PUPPETRY

There have been puppet shows in Europe since at least 500 B.C., and probably even earlier than this in other parts of the world.

ANIMATRONICS
The term *animatronics* is used to describe a puppet that is partly controlled by electronics. Operators control the facial movements from a distance by sending electronic signals through a cable.

SHADOW PUPPETS
Shadow puppets are one of the most versatile kinds of puppet. They are controlled by sticks joined to their arms and legs. In Indonesia shadow puppetry is called *Wayang Kulit*.

STRING PUPPETS
In some parts of the world string puppets perform complete operas or tragedies. The puppeteers move the puppets' limbs from above using strings.

FINGER PUPPETS
Finger puppets are easy to make and operate, but limited in movement. Glove puppets fit over the whole hand, and each finger moves a different part of the puppet.

The operator inside moves the puppet's body and limbs.

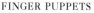

MIME

Mime, or the art of gesture and movement, has always been part of acting. But modern mime, which developed mainly in France, does not use the spoken word at all. One of the most famous mime artists is the Frenchman, Marcel Marceau (born 1923).

Tying a love knot means marriage.

COSTUMES

Costumes play an important part in any production. They can change an actor's appearance by altering shape or height, indicate the period and country in which a play is set, or completely transform an actor into an animal, an object, or a fantasy figure.

Ancient Greek actors wore masks, and often platform shoes, to make them appear god-like.

Animal costumes are usually padded and heavy, and can be difficult to move in.

Modern costumes tell us about the period as well as the character.

PUPPET FACTS
- *Wayang Kulit* plays may last a whole week, and some use as many as 200 puppets.
- Punch and Judy (British) and Petrushka (Russian) grew out of characters in *Commedia dell'Arte* (see p.166).
- It takes three puppeteers to control each of the *Bunraku* doll puppets of Japan.

LONGEST RUNNING PLAYS, UK (1999)

Play	Years
The Mousetrap	46
Cats	18
Starlight Express	15
Les Miserables	13
The Phantom of the Opera	12
Blood Brothers	11
Reduced Shakespeare	11
The Woman in Black	10
Miss Saigon	9
Buddy	9

THEATRE WORDS

Angel Someone who provides the financial backing for a production.

Apron The part of the stage in front of the proscenium arch (see p.167).

Arena A stage that is surrounded by seating for the audience.

Block To set the actors' movements around the stage.

Chorus Actors in Ancient Greek drama who sang and commented on the action.

Corpse To burst into laughter on stage.

Deus ex machina (God from the machine) a god brought in to resolve the plot in Ancient Greek drama.

Deus ex machina

Director The person who has artistic control of a production, interpreting the script and rehearsing the actors.

Dress rehearsal The last rehearsal before the opening night, with costumes, lights, and scenery.

Dry To forget one's lines.

Flats Screens painted with scenery, often on both sides, which can be moved around the stage for different effects.

Footlights Lights at the front of the stage, near the auditorium.

Fringe theatre Alternative theatre, including unconventional plays, venues, or theatrical styles.

Gallery Seats at the top rear of the auditorium. Also called "the gods".

Ham A bad actor, usually one who overacts.

House The audience.

Limelight Powerful light, like that once produced by burning lime.

Open stage A stage without a proscenium arch, with the audience seated on three sides.

Ham

Producer The person responsible for financial and practical aspects of a production. A theatrical producer is not usually involved in artistic direction.

Prompt To whisper lines to an actor who has forgotten them. A "prompt" is someone employed for this purpose.

Rake The angle of the stage. In modern theatres the rake can be altered for different productions.

Rake

Trap A trapdoor that opens into the area below the stage. Often used together with a "lift" for surprise entrances (see p.167).

Walk-on A non-speaking part.

DANCE

PEOPLE HAVE been dancing since prehistoric times. Over thousands of years, many different styles of dance have developed all over the world.

c.15,000 B.C. Stone Age rock paintings in Europe and Africa show people in dance-like ritual formation.

Tanzanian Stone Age rock painting

3000–1000 B.C. Ancient Egyptians use ritual and ceremonial dance in the worship of gods and goddesses such as Isis.

Fresco (wall painting) from Thebes, showing dancers at a banquet, 1425 B.C.

15,000 B.C.		3000 B.C.

c.1400 B.C. Bull dancing is a popular entertainment in Crete. People dance around a bull, springing on and off its back or leaping between its horns.

Bronze sculpture of boy leaping over a bull

c.1000 B.C. Chinese shamans (healers and spirit guides) use dance to bring spirits down to Earth.

c.500–400 B.C. Spartan warriors in Greece use dance as part of their training. Socrates (470–399 B.C.), Greek philosopher, states "The best dancer is also the best warrior".

Spartan warriors

c.150 B.C. Romans close all dance schools. Cicero (106–43 B.C.), Roman consul, states that no man dances unless he is insane.

c.A.D. 400 Kagura dances performed to religious chants at Shinto shrines in Japan. Dancers accompanied by drums, brass, gongs, and flutes.

Kagura dancer

c.800 Early Christians include traditional pagan dances in Christian ceremonies. Charlemagne (742–814), the Holy Roman Emperor, bans dancing, but the ban is ignored.

1000 B.C.	500–400 B.C.	A.D. 400	400	800

1300s Ballroom dancing emerges in the royal palaces of Europe.

1300–1500 Mass dances in Europe cause frenzy and often trances. In Italy the *tarantella* is devised to sweat the poison from a spider's bite out of the victim's body.

Medieval German peasants

1416 First European dancing manual, *On the Art of Dancing and Directing Choruses*, is published.

Late 1400s Ballo, Italian dance performance with a storyline, is the earliest form of ballet.

c.1600 Kathakali (see p.171) emerges in India.

Louis XIV in Le Ballet de la Nuit

1653 Louis XIV (1638–1715), 14-year-old French king, appears in *Le Ballet de la Nuit* (Ballet of the Night).

1681 Women are now allowed to dance in ballets, although long, bulky skirts get in the way.

1700s The waltz develops from German folk dances, and will become popular in European courts.

Waltzers in The Court Ball

1300	1400	1416	1600	1653	1681	1700

Late 1700s French ballet masters, frustrated by lack of opportunity, travel to Russia and develop the full-length story-ballet.

1830–1840s Romantic ballet develops and flourishes. The ballerina is the most important dancer in the performance.

Cancan dancer

1832 Marie Taglioni (1804–84), Italian, is the first ballerina to go *en pointe* (on points).

1870s The cancan, a high-kicking dance, becomes very fashionable in France.

Marie Taglioni

1880s–1890s Classical ballet (see p.170) reaches its peak in Russia.

1892 Loie Fuller (1862–1928), American dancer, uses fabric and lighting in her *Serpentine Dance* to create a dreamlike effect.

Loie Fuller, 1897

c.1900 American Isadora Duncan (1877–1927), the first modern dancer, develops freer forms of dance.

1909 Serge Diaghilev (1872–1929), Russian arts promoter, presents his Ballets Russes company in Paris. Dancers include Vaslav Nijinsky (1889–1950) and Anna Pavlova (1881–1931).

1700	1830	1832	1880	1892	1900	1909

1913 Nijinsky uses turned-in feet in his ballet, *The Rite of Spring*.

1920s Tap, charleston, jazz, and many other dance forms influenced by African-American dancing, are increasingly popular.

Nijinsky in Giselle

1927 Rudolf von Laban (1879–1958), Hungarian dancer and choreographer, invents a method of recording ballet movements using geometric sketches, called Labanotation.

1927 Martha Graham, (1894–1991), American modern dancer and choreographer, founds her own company.

Martha Graham

1930s Jitterbug and jive are two lively, popular jazz dances.

1933 Ted Shawn (1891–1972), American dancer, forms an all-male company to show men as dancers in their own right, not just as supports for women.

1933 Fred Astaire (1899–1987) and Ginger Rogers (1911–1995), American dancers, appear in the film *Flying Down to Rio*. More films follow including *The Gay Divorcée* and *Top Hat*.

Fred Astaire

1910	1913	1920	1927	1930	1933

1945 Latin American rumba, samba, calypso, and cha-cha-cha are added to the established ballroom dances.

1950s Rock and roll develops as a social dance, mainly for teenagers.

1952 Merce Cunningham (born 1919), American dancer and choreographer, forms his own company. He uses natural movement to create a free-flowing effect.

Rock and roll dancers, 1956

1960s Post-modern dance develops in New York. It is experimental, and often improvised.

1970s Disco dancing is popular in Europe and the USA.

1976 Twyla Tharp (born 1942), American dancer, choreographs *Push Comes to Shove*. Tharp uses elements of many other styles in her dances.

Break dancing

1980s Break dancing and body-popping are born. Dancers spin around on their backs and heads, and imitate robotic movements. These styles appear in other media, such as film.

1990s DV8 and other companies design dances for television as well as stage.

DV8 Physical Theatre

1940	1945	1950	1952	1960	1970	1976	1980	1990

BALLET AND MODERN DANCE

BALLET IS A combination of music, dance, and mime, with set steps and techniques. Modern dance developed from it as a freer, more natural form.

BALLET STYLES

The three main styles of ballet are Romantic, Classical, and modern. The style of ballet is usually reflected in the type of costume that the dancers wear.

Most Romantic ballets feature spirits and magic. Dancers often wear white, calf-length dresses.

In Classical ballets, dancers wear short dresses, called tutus, to show off their footwork.

In modern ballets, dancers usually wear simple costumes.

THE FIVE POSITIONS

In ballet there are five basic positions for the arms, and five for the feet.

Positions of the arms
Second, fourth, and fifth positions have variations, e.g. in *demi-seconde*, the arms are raised half-way between first and second positions.

First position

Second position

Third position

Fourth position

Fifth position

Positions of the feet
Almost every movement danced in a ballet begins and ends with one of the five positions of the feet.

First position

Second position

Third position

Fourth position

Fifth position

MODERN DANCE

In the late 1800s, Isadora Duncan and Loie Fuller (see p.169) felt ballet movements were unnatural, and developed a new, freer style. Martha Graham and Merce Cunningham (see p.169) are the two most famous dancer-choreographers of the modern dance movement.

Isadora Duncan pioneered modern dance.

Twyla Tharp (see p.169) was a later modern dance innovator.

Today, new modern dance techniques are still being developed.

FAMOUS 20TH CENTURY DANCERS

Many dancers have become choreographers and teachers, passing their style and skills on to others.

Marie Rambert (1888–1982) Polish teacher and dancer, founded the Ballet Rambert (now the Rambert Dance Company).

Vaslav Nijinsky (1890–1950) Russian Classical dancer, was famous for his athletic style and innovative choreography. He was the star of the Ballets Russes.

Margot Fonteyn (1919–91) British, and **Rudolf Nureyev** (1938–93), Russian, formed the world's most famous and most popular partnership.

Arthur Mitchell (born 1934) American dancer. In 1969 he founded the Dance Theater of Harlem, the first dance company with only black dancers.

DANCE NOTATION

Like music, dance is written down using a system of symbols. There are two forms of dance notation: Benesh and Laban. The Benesh method, which is usually used for ballet, was devised by Rudolf (1916–75) and Joan Benesh (born 1920). Labanotation, named after Rudolf von Laban (see p.169), is mainly used to record modern dance.

| | Top of head |
| Top of shoulder |
| Waist |
| Knee |
| Floor |

Grand plié in Benesh notation

This grand plié (a deep knee bend) is recorded (right) in two forms of dance notation.

Grand plié in Labanotation

BALLET RECORDS

MOST CURTAIN CALLS was 89, taken by Margot Fonteyn and Rudolf Nureyev after a performance of *Swan Lake* in Austria in 1964.

MOST EXPENSIVE COSTUME was made for the part of the Chinese conjurer in *Parade*, premièred in Paris in 1917. Designed by Pablo Picasso (see p.161), the costume fetched £28,000 at auction in 1984.

FAMOUS BALLETS

Title	Choreographer	First danced
La Sylphide	Filippo Taglioni (1777–1871), Italian	1832
Nutcracker	Lev Ivanov (1834–1901), Russian	1892
Swan Lake	Lev Ivanov and Marius Petipa (1818–1910), French	1895
Manon	Kenneth MacMillan (1929–93), British	1974

BALLET FACTS

• A ballerina who dances regularly wears out about ten pairs of *pointe* shoes each month.

• During the average length career, dancers practise for eight hours a day, six days a week: in total, about five-and-a-half years.

CHOREOGRAPHY

Choreography is the art of designing and devising the steps of a ballet or dance routine. The term comes from the ancient Greek words *khoreia* (dancing) and *graphos* (writing). Choreographers – the people who devise dance routines – work with dancers to compose a dance sequence, then record it using notation.

BALLET TERMS

Barre The bar that dancers use to help them balance during exercises

Battement A beating movement of the leg (many forms)

Corps de ballet The chorus of dancers (those not dancing solo roles)

Jeté A jump from one leg to the other

Pas de chat A jumping step

Pas de deux A dance for two people (male and female), usually the principals

Pirouette A complete 360° turn on one leg

Pas de deux

Plié A knee-bending movement

Pointe On the points or the tips of the toes (female dancers)

FEET FEAT

British dancer Wayne Sleep (born 1948) achieved six *entrechats* in 1973, crossing and uncrossing his legs six times while still in the air.

TRADITIONAL WORLD DANCE

MOST COUNTRIES OF the world have a traditional form of dance that has evolved over many years. These dances have often developed from simple religious or tribal rituals into complex dance forms with set movements.

SOUTHEAST ASIA
Classical dance is performed by highly trained artists. Dancing is slow, with complex hand movements.

POLYNESIAN DANCE
Dance plays an important role in traditional Polynesian culture. Women often swing and rotate their hips rapidly, e.g. in the Hawaiian hula.

AMERICAN DANCE
Native Americans dance at special ceremonies to win the goodwill of spirits, ancestors, and gods.

Thai classical dancer

Polynesian dancer

Native American dancer

European folk dancers

Japanese gagaku *dancer*

African tribal dancer

Indian temple dancer

EUROPEAN DANCE
Many traditional European folk dances have their roots in religious rituals. For example, dancing in a circle probably originated from circling around an object of worship.

EAST ASIA
Most East Asian dance forms part of theatrical dance drama, e.g. Chinese opera. Japanese *gagaku* and *bugaka* are the world's oldest forms of traditional court dance.

AFRICAN DANCE
Most African dance has its roots in tribal rituals. It includes Sun- and Moon-worshipping dances, weapon, fertility, and hunting dances.

INDIA
Indian classical dance developed from religious rituals in which dancers told stories about the lives of the gods. There are six styles of dance, including *kathakali* and *bharata natyam*.

TRANCE DANCES
In many cultures, people dance themselves into a trance as a way of communicating with spirits and gods. They may perform acts that would normally be dangerous, but which leave them unharmed.

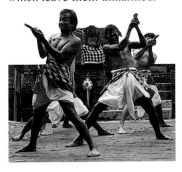

Barong dancers in Bali strike themselves with daggers while in a trance.

DANCE PROPS
Props (items in addition to costume that a dancer may use) are important in many traditional dances.

Prop	Country	Significance
Maypole	England	The maypole is a fertility object symbolizing a tree. People dance around it, holding ribbons that represent branches.
Weapons	Worldwide	The use of weapons, e.g. swords, clubs, and shields, dates back to religious ceremonies in which the gods were asked for help in battle.
Snakes	N. America	The Hopi people use snakes in their rain dances. Snakes are believed to be brothers of the spirits that control clouds and rain.
Instruments	Worldwide	Dancers often wear or use instruments to accentuate (bring out) the rhythm of a dance, e.g. castanets in Spanish flamenco; bells worn by classical Indian dancers.

LOW-DOWN LIMBO
Caribbean limbo dancers can pass underneath bars as low as 15.25cm (6in) off the ground.

DANCE FACTS
• In North Africa, belly dancers are judged by how well they move their shoulders.

• Judges at Irish jigging contests sit under the stage to assess the speed and precision of the dancers' steps.

• The cakewalk was the first African-American dance to be taken up by white Americans. It developed from dance competitions where the prize was usually a cake.

• Between 1910 and 1920, animal dances such as the chicken scratch and the grizzly bear were popular in the USA. Not everyone approved: a woman was jailed for 50 days for doing the turkey trot, a dance that was officially denounced by the Vatican.

• Flamenco dancers can tap their heels at a rate of up to 16 taps per second.

FACE FACTS

Kathakali dancers take up to four hours to apply their make-up. They have such control over their facial muscles that they can laugh with one side of their face and cry with the other.

DANCE RECORDS
FASTEST TAP DANCE was 32 taps per second by Englishman Stephen Gare (born 1967), in 1990.

LONGEST CONGA was the Miami Super Conga in 1988, which consisted of 119,986 people.

MUSIC

FROM A PRIMITIVE war cry to the complex sound of a symphony orchestra, music has been created by every known society. Vibrations are the source of all musical sound.

MUSICAL TONE AND NOTATION

Most Western music is based on major and minor scales – traditional patterns of pitches that sound pleasing to the ear. Composers write down these pitches using notation – a code of signs and symbols that enables a musician to interpret and play a musical composition.

A key is a set of related notes. The key signature shows which key the music is in.

The tempo marking tells the musician how fast the music should go. *Allegro* means fast.

When more than two notes are played together, the tones produced are called a chord.

Sharps and flats are signs before a note that indicate a note should be raised by half a tone (sharp) or lowered by half a tone (flat).

A natural sign cancels the preceding sharp or flat on that particular note.

A piece of music is divided into measures called bars, each with the same number of beats. The bar line shows where the measure ends.

The five horizontal lines are called the stave, or staff.

Rests show the musician where, and for how long, to be silent.

The clef, here a treble clef, shows which pitches are represented by the lines and spaces of the stave.

Dynamic markings tell the player how loud or soft to play the music. *mf* stands for *mezzo-forte*, or moderately loud.

The stem and colouring of a note indicates its length. These are quavers.

The time signature shows the number of beats in a measure and which type of note gets one beat.

This sign, meaning *crescendo*, indicates that the music becomes gradually louder.

Sforzando means that the note should be played loudly with special emphasis.

SCALE

Pitches are named from low to high using seven letters: A, B, C, D, E, F, and G. This series of letters is repeated as the notes continue to ascend in pitch.

Pitches lying in between stave's lines and spaces are shown using sharp (#) and flat (♭) signs.

One octave (eight notes) of the scale of C major

C D E F G A B C

C major notes on stave correspond to white keys on keyboard.

Black keys represent the notes that lie between some of the notes of the C major scale.

C D E F G A B C D E

White key on keyboard

MUSICAL WORDS

Pianissimo (pp) Very softly

Piano (p) Softly

Mezzo-piano (mp) Quite softly

Mezzo-forte (mf) Quite loudly

Forte (f) Loudly

Fortissimo (ff) Very loudly

Forte-piano (fp) Loud then suddenly soft

Crescendo (cresc.) Getting louder

Diminuendo (dim.) Getting softer

Dolce Sweetly

Legato Smoothly

Leggiero Lightly

Pizzicato (pizz.) Marking for stringed instruments meaning that the player should pluck the string

Accelerando (accel.) Accelerate or speed up

Ritardando (rit.) or rallentando Slow down

Sforzando (sf) Note or chord to be played loudly with special emphasis

Staccato Short, separated notes

Con brio With fire

TIME SIGNATURES

Time signature	Meaning	Examples
2/4	2 beats per measure; crotchet = 1 beat	*Twinkle, twinkle little star;* Beethoven's *Fifth Symphony*
3/4	3 beats per measure; crotchet = 1 beat	*Happy Birthday;* *God Save the Queen*
4/4	4 beats per measure; crotchet = 1 beat	*Auld Lang Syne;* *Yesterday*
6/8	2 beats per measure; 3 quavers = 1 beat	*For He's a Jolly Good Fellow* *Pop Goes the Weasel*

WORLD MUSIC FACTS

• Indian music uses patterns of notes called ragas. There are about 130 commonly used ragas, and each one has a special association. It can be an emotion, a time of day, or a season of the year.

• Strings on one African drum can vary the tension in the drum-head to produce different notes. Players can use it to recreate the changing tones of their language.

Nigerian "talking" drum

TEMPO MARKINGS

Largo Very slow and broad

Grave Very slow and solemn

Adagio Slow and leisurely

Andante Moderately slow

Allegretto Moderately fast

Allegro Fast and brisk

Vivace Lively and quick

Presto Very fast

Prestissimo Extremely fast

NOTE VALUES

Name	Sign	Rest
Semibreve (whole-note)	o	—
Minim (half-note)	♩	—
Crotchet (quarter-note)	♩	𝄽
Quaver (eighth-note)	♪	𝄾
Semiquaver (16th-note)	♫	𝄿
Demisemiquaver (32nd-note)	♬	𝅀

DATES IN MUSIC HISTORY

c.4000 B.C. Flutes and harps played in Egypt.

Egyptian tomb painting showing court musicians

A.D. 600 Schola Cantorum founded in Rome. This was an early music school, founded on the order of Pope Gregory the Great (c.540–604).

725 Orchestra developed in China. These orchestras included flutes, guitars, gongs, and drums.

Traditional Chinese orchestra

1480 First printed music in Europe.

Early music printed from carved woodblocks.

1553 Violin design developed into its early form in Europe.

1600s Opera begins to be developed by the *Camerata* – a group of poets and musicians – in Florence, Italy.

1709 Early pianoforte built by Italian Bartolomeo Cristofori (1655–1731).

1727 German J.S. Bach (1685–1750) composes choral work *St. Matthew Passion.*

J.S.Bach

| 4000 B.C. | A.D.600 | 725 | 1480 | 1553 | 1600 | 1709 | 1727 |

MUSICAL GROUPS

Groups range from duos, which have two performers, to symphony orchestras, which contain up to 120 (see p.174). Most classical music groups play written music. Jazz groups take a theme and invent variations on it as they play.

Duo

In a duo, one player usually plays a brass, string, or wind instrument and the other a piano. Pieces for two players are called duets.

Cello and piano duo

Trio

Trios have three players. A string trio uses a violin, viola, and cello. Piano trios are written for violin, cello, and piano.

String trio

Quartet

Jazz groups often use quartets (groups of four players). String quartets consist of two violins, a viola, and a cello.

Jazz quartet

Quintet

Quintets use five players and usually contain wind or brass instruments or instruments from different families.

Mixed quintet

Choir

A choir is a group of singers. A mixed voice choir contains men and women, who sing four parts. Most choirs sing religious music.

Small church choir

LARGER GROUPS

• Large groups of brass instrument players, called brass bands, are used in many military and civic ceremonies.

• A larger string group, often including a few wind instruments, is called a chamber orchestra. It may accompany a soloist in a piece called a concerto.

MAJOR COMPOSERS IN WESTERN MUSIC

Composer	Nationality, dates	Major work(s), date(s) composed
Renaissance (1450–1600) Guillaume Dufay	Flemish, c.1400–74	Church music and secular pieces
Josquin des Prés	Flemish, c.1445–1521	Choral church and secular music
Giovanni Palestrina	Italian, c.1525–94	Choral church and secular music
William Byrd	English, 1543–1623	Church music, string music, keyboard music, and madrigals
Baroque (1600–1750) Claudio Monteverdi	Italian, 1567–1643	*Orfeo* (1607), *Vespers* (1610)
Heinrich Schütz	German, 1585–1672	*Symphoniae Sacrae* (1650)
Jean Baptiste Lully	French, 1632–87	Operas, church compositions
Henry Purcell	English, 1659–95	*Dido and Aeneas* (1689)
Antonio Vivaldi	Italian, 1678–1741	*Four Seasons* (1725)
Jean Phillippe Rameau	French, 1683–1764	*Castor and Pollux* (1737)
Johann Sebastian Bach	German, 1685–1750	*Brandenburg Concertos* (1721), *St. Matthew Passion* (1727)
George Frederic Handel	German, 1685–1759	*The Messiah* (1741), *Music for the Royal Fireworks* (1749)
Classical (1750–1820) Joseph Haydn	Austrian, 1732–1809	*London Symphonies*: 1st set (1791–92) *London Symphonies*: 2nd set (1793–95),
Wolfgang Amadeus Mozart	Austrian, 1756–91	*Piano Concertos in C major and D minor* (1785), *The Marriage of Figaro* (1786), *Don Giovanni* (1787)
Ludwig van Beethoven	German, 1770–1827	*Symphonies No. 3* (1802), *No. 5* (1809), and *No. 9* (1823)
Romantic (1820–1900) Franz Schubert	Austrian, 1797–1828	*Piano Quintet in A* (1819), *"Unfinished" Symphony No. 8* (1822)
Hector Berlioz	French, 1803–69	*Symphonie Fantastique* (1830), *The Trojans* (1859)
Frederic Chopin	Polish, 1810–49	Piano compositions, *Preludes* (1839)
Franz Liszt	Hungarian, 1811–86	*Piano Sonata in B min* (1853), *Hungarian Rhapsodies* (1839–85)
Richard Wagner	German, 1813–83	*The Flying Dutchman* (1841), *The Ring of the Nibelung* (1848–74)
Giuseppe Verdi	Italian, 1813–1901	*Aida* (1871), *Requiem Mass* (1873), *Otello* (1887)
Johannes Brahms	German, 1833–97	*Violin Concerto in D major* (1878), *Symphony No. 4* (1884)
Peter Ilyich Tchaikovsky	Russian, 1840–93	*Piano Concerto No 1* (1874–5), *Swan Lake* (1876)
Edvard Grieg	Norwegian, 1843–1907	*Piano Concerto in A minor* (1869), *Peer Gynt* (1876)
Edward Elgar	English, 1857–1934	*Enigma Variations* (1899), *Violin Concerto* (1910)
Modern (1900 to present) Claude Debussy	French, 1862–1918	*Pelléas and Mélisande* (1892–1902), *Images* (1905-07)
Arnold Schoenberg	Austrian, 1874–1951	*First String Quartet* (1897), *Pierrot Lunaire* (1912)
Béla Bartók	Hungarian, 1881–1945	*Six String Quartets* (1939), *Concerto for Orchestra* (1944)
Igor Stravinsky	Russian, 1882–1971	*The Firebird* (1910), *The Rite of Spring* (1913)
Sergei Prokofiev	Russian, 1891–1953	*Romeo and Juliet* (1935), *Peter and the Wolf* (1936)
Lili Boulanger	French, 1893–1918	*Faust and Helène* (1913)
George Gershwin	American, 1898–1937	*Rhapsody in Blue* (1924), *Porgy and Bess* (1935)
Dmitry Shostakovich	Russian, 1906–75	*Symphonies No.5* (1937) and *No.10* (1953)
John Cage	American, 1912–92	*Music of Changes* (1951), *4' 33"* (1954)
Pierre Boulez	French, born 1925	*Le Marteau sans Maître* (1954), *Memoriales* (1975)
Karlheinz Stockhausen	German, born 1928	*Groups* (1955–57)
Philip Glass	American, born 1937	*Einstein on the Beach* (1976)

Austrian composer
(W)ang A. Mozart (1756–91)
(compo)ses opera, *Don Giovanni.*

(Youn)g Mozart (at) the piano

1808 German composer Ludwig van Beethoven (1770–1827) composes Symphonies No.5 and No.6.

Ludwig van Beethoven

1874 German composer Richard Wagner (1813–83) finishes *The Ring of the Nibelung.*

c.1900 Jazz music appears in New Orleans, USA. It combines African rhythms with Western harmony.

Early jazz music

1940 Synthesizers appear, giving composer complete control over sound.

1950 Rock music appears in US.

Rock singer Chuck Berry

1787   1808   1874   1900   1950

OFF BEAT

Jean Baptiste Lully (1632–87), court musician to Louis XIV of France, stabbed his foot with the long staff that he banged on the floor in order to keep his orchestra in time. He later died from an abscess caused by this injury.

CLASSICAL MUSIC

WHEN PEOPLE think of classical music, most think of orchestras and symphonies, and opera.

PERCUSSION

WOODWIND

BRASS

BRASS

Symphony
Symphonies are pieces of music written for a full range of orchestral instruments. There is no dominant soloist.

Concerto
In a concerto, a soloist is accompanied by an orchestra. A concerto orchestra usually has fewer brass and percussion instruments, which allows the soloist to be heard more clearly.

STRINGS

ORCHESTRA
The orchestra is the largest grouping of instruments in classical music.

STRINGS

Conductor

An orchestra usually contains about 90 people.

CONDUCTOR
A conductor directs the performance, indicating the pace of the music. He or she traces patterns through the air with a baton, according to the time signature of the piece.

Two beats in a bar

Three beats in a bar

Four beats in a bar

Five beats in a bar

Diagrams show traditional baton movements.

BOUNCING BACK
In *Tosca*, the heroine jumps to her death from castle battlements. In 1960, angry stagehands backstage substituted a trampoline for the usual mattress. Tosca reappeared 15 times before the curtain fell.

OPERA
Operas are musical dramas in which singers, accompanied by an orchestra, act out a story. They can be sung throughout, or sung and spoken.

Royal Opera House production, London

Madam Butterfly sings soprano part.

Madam Butterfly, a moving love story, was created by Puccini in 1904. It centres on a Japanese heroine, Madam Butterfly, whose betrayal by an American sailor ends in her suicide.

US Navy Lieutenant F.B. Pinkerton sings tenor part.

Solos by major characters are called arias.

KEY OPERA SINGERS

Tito Gobbi (1915–84), Italian operatic baritone, made his debut in Rome in 1938.

Kathleen Ferrier (1912–53), English contralto singer, made her debut as Lucretia in Benjamin Britten's *The Rape of Lucretia* in 1946.

Luciano Pavarotti (born 1935), Italian operatic tenor, made his international debut as Rudolfo in Puccini's *La Bohème* in 1961.

Kiri Te Kanawa (born 1944), New Zealand operatic soprano, made her international debut in 1971, as the Countess in Mozart's *The Marriage of Figaro*.

OPERA FACTS
• There are six commonly accepted ranges of voice. From lowest to highest these are: bass, baritone, tenor, contralto, mezzo-soprano, and soprano.

• Many people believe that the quality of an opera singer's voice improves with extra body-weight. In fact, a person's weight is irrelevant: thin people may possess the finest voices.

• Many people can identify the pitch of any note that they hear, without needing to refer to an instrument. This ability is called "perfect pitch".

KEY OPERAS

Title	Composer	First performed
The Marriage of Figaro	Wolfgang Amadeus Mozart (1756–91), Austrian	1786 Vienna
The Barber of Seville	Gioacchino Rossini (1792–1868), Italian	1816 Rome
Otello	Giuseppe Verdi (1813–1901), Italian	1887 Milan, Italy
The Ring of the Nibelung	Richard Wagner (1813–83), German	1876 Bayreuth, Germany
Carmen	Georges Bizet (1838–75), French	1875 Paris
La Bohème	Giacomo Puccini (1858–1924), Italian	1896 Turin, Italy
Peter Grimes	Benjamin Britten (1913–76), British	1945 London

POPULAR MUSIC

MANY DIFFERENT styles of music have evolved in the twentieth century. Here the most popular Western styles are described.

FOLK MUSIC

In the 19th century, America's southern black population, including transport workers on the railways and riverboats, as well as cotton workers, sang and listened to folk songs at work, or at the end of the day. They created a new kind of folk song in which they mixed the complex, overlapping rhythms and free melodies of West African music with the harmonies of Western music. This combination formed the foundation for music that would dominate popular tastes during the 20th century.

Album cover from a collection of early Afro-American songs

BLUES

The blues express the troubles and emotions of the performer in a simple but strict form. The performer sets three lines of poetry to 12 bars of music. The blues use a basic, set pattern of harmonies (chords), over which the performer invents variations.

Leadbelly
Leadbelly's Last Sessions

JAZZ

Jazz emerged in the early 1900s in New Orleans, USA, as a mixture of blues, religious gospel singing, and European influences. Driven by the urgent rhythms of West African music and using the melodic style of the Blues, jazz musicians improvise – they recreate the melody of a piece each time it is performed. This allows each player to express their emotions through their special version of the music. Major artists of the "jazz age" of the 1920s included American trumpeters Louis "Satchmo" Armstrong (c.1898–1971), Bix Beiderbecke (1903–31), and the orchestral composer George Gershwin (1898–1937).

Louis Armstrong
Laughing Louis

BIG BANDS AND BE-BOP

In the 1930s and early 1940s, swing, a form of jazz, was played by "big bands," under great bandleaders such as Duke Ellington (1899–1974). Later, a new style emerged, called be-bop. It was pioneered by trumpeter Dizzy Gillespie (1917–1993) and saxophonist Charlie Parker (1920–55). Be-bop led to more complex schemes of harmony. Major artists included trumpeter Miles Davis (1926–91) and saxophonist John Coltrane (1926–67).

Charlie Parker Bird Lives

COUNTRY AND WESTERN

Country and Western music takes its inspiration from the country life of the American West. Its performers, often dressed as cowboys of the old West, sing with the accent of the southern USA and are accompanied by instruments such as the banjo, fiddle, and guitar. Performers include Hank Williams (1923–1952), Johnny Cash (born 1932), and Tammy Wynette (born 1942).

Johnny Cash
The Johnny Cash Collection

ROCK AND ROLL

Rock and roll began in the 1950s as a mix of rhythm-and-blues and country music and was played loudly on newly invented electric guitars. Although this style arose in black communities, white singer and guitarist Elvis Presley (1935–77) greatly increased its popularity.

Elvis Presley Elvis Presley

ROCK

In the 1960s, rock and roll was abbreviated to "rock" music. Rock music has a heavy, driving rhythm, with eight quavers on the bar and accents on the second and fourth beats. Early rock bands included The Beatles, The Rolling Stones, Pink Floyd, The Who, and The Jimi Hendrix Experience.

The Rolling Stones
Their Satanic Majesties
Request

REGGAE

West Indian reggae music was spread abroad by West Indian communities overseas. It is closely associated with the Rastafarian religion. Its most famous artist was Bob Marley (1945–81), whose music calls for an end to racism and political repression.

Bob Marley & The Wailers

DISCO

In the 1970s, new music centred around the disco movement. It was promoted by films such as *Saturday Night Fever* and by a revival of interest in 1950s music by black artists such as James Brown (born 1933). Disco artists include The Bee Gees and Donna Summer.

The Bee Gees
Saturday Night Fever

PUNK

Punk music exploded on to the scene at the close of the 1970s, led by the British groups The Sex Pistols and The Clash. It had a savage character, and appealed to young people whose dress, language, and behaviour were designed to outrage traditional tastes.

The Damned

1980S POP MUSIC

Pop music in the 1980s became lighter and more concerned with dance rhythms. Major pop artists and groups included Michael Jackson, The Pet Shop Boys, Madonna, and Duran Duran. Pop videos, in which the music was set to a piece of film, made it possible for a performer to be seen on television by millions at the same time as the release of their record.

Michael Jackson Thriller

1990S POPULAR MUSIC

A specialized form of dance music, called house music, emerged in the 1980s, based on very rapid rhythms and electronic sounds. The technology for making and mixing these new sounds is now widely available to musicians and their music has since branched into the related styles of acid house, techno, trance, ambient, and jungle music.

The Orb Blue Room

BEST-SELLING SINGLES WORLDWIDE

Single	Performer/group	Copies sold (approx.)
Candle In The Wind	Elton John	35,000,000
White Christmas	Bing Crosby	30,000,000
Rock Around the Clock	Bill Haley and His Comets	17,000,000
I Want to Hold Your Hand	The Beatles	12,000,000
It's Now or Never	Elvis Presley	10,000,000
I Will Always Love You	Whitney Houston	10,000,000
Hound Dog/Don't Be Cruel	Elvis Presley	9,000,000
Diana	Paul Anka	9,000,000
Hey Jude	The Beatles	8,000,000
I'm a Believer	The Monkees	8,000,000

POP MUSIC RECORDS

MOST EXPENSIVE GUITAR was a Fender Stratocaster belonging to Jimi Hendrix (1942–70). It was sold for £180,000 (US $275,940) at Sotheby's, London, in 1990.

MOST SUCCESSFUL SONGWRITERS are Paul McCartney (born 1942), who has had 32 number one singles in the USA and 28 in the UK, and John Lennon (1940–80), with 26 number one singles in the USA and 29 in the UK.

MUSICAL INSTRUMENTS

MUSICAL INSTRUMENTS are designed to make vibrations that our ears and brain recognize as musical sounds. They are usually classified into percussion, stringed, woodwind, brass, and keyboard. Archaeologists excavating the sites of ancient Mesopotamian cities (see p.375) have found evidence for every basic instrument type.

VIOLIN
The violin is the smallest stringed instrument. It also produces the highest sound. The player holds the violin between the chin and the shoulder, drawing the bow across the strings to produce a clear tone.

Violin bow

F-shaped sound hole typical of violin family

Tuning peg connected to each string

Thinnest string produces highest notes.

Chin-rest

Bridge supports strings.

Frog provides grip for bow.

Screw

STRINGED INSTRUMENTS
A stringed instrument consists of a series of stretched strings connected to a hollow box that amplifies the string's vibrations. The string is set in motion by being plucked, as with a harp; by the friction of a bow, as with a violin; or by being struck, as with a piano.

Horse-hair strings

Ivory tuning peg

Carved pegbox

Heart-shaped sound hole

Triangular-shaped body

Fish-shaped body

Spike to keep instrument steady

Iranian spike fiddle, Middle-Eastern ancestor of the violin, typically has a long neck.

Russian balalaika uses two to four strings and may sit on the ground.

Portuguese rajao is a folk music instrument originating in Madeira, an island off North Africa.

WOODWIND INSTRUMENTS
A woodwind instrument is either a tube that the player blows across or into, or a tube that amplifies the vibrations of a thin reed at one end. Most woodwind instruments have holes running down the tube. The player covers and uncovers them to produce different notes.

Mouthpiece with reed

Neck

Upper octave key

Pads lined with cork and felt cover toneholes.

Key to operate pad.

Bell projects sound.

Holder allows thumb to support instrument body.

SAXOPHONE
The saxophone, like the flute, is a woodwind instrument made of metal. It can produce a harsh, raw tone, but it also carries a smooth, lilting melody with great sensitivity. Clarinettists may easily play the saxophone since they share a common type of reed.

Ornate lacquer decoration

Ring for neck sling

Curved tube for deep sound

Double reed

Flute blown through hole cut in side.

Thumb knuckle operates these keys.

Opening adjusted by hand to change note.

Carved wooden dragon's head

Alto clarinet produces a deeper sound than a standard clarinet.

Dragon flute or lung-ti flute, is used in Chinese ceremonies.

Oboe, an orchestral instrument, is used to tune the orchestra.

Guyanese flute with pitch controlled by hand.

DOUBLE REED
A double reed is made by binding the ends of a bent strip of cane and fitting them into a staple (cork tube). The bend is then sliced off.

PIED PIPERS
In 1454, French knights from the Order of the Golden Fleece held a banquet in which more than 20 musicians emerged from a giant pie to entertain the guests.

BRASS INSTRUMENTS
Brass instruments have a mouthpiece shaped like a funnel. Vibrations are produced not by the instrument itself, but by the player's lips pressed against this mouthpiece. The player alters the pitch by changing the tension in the lips, and by changing the length of tubing through which the vibrating air passes.

Moroccan nfīr is a trumpet used in Islamic religious festivals. It is 1.5m (5ft) long and is made from brass sections that are fixed together and taken apart after use.

THE TRUMPET
This trumpet is a modern version of the oldest brass instrument. It has changed very little since its invention, and is the dominant instrument in many bands and orchestras.

Cup-shaped mouthpiece allows variety of notes to be made with lips.

Pistons enable the pitch of the note to be changed.

Water key drains trumpet of condensed water.

Mouthpiece

Detachable brass section

Decorative carrying cord

Slim brass bell

Tenor horn is a descendant of the bugle.

1780s horn is coiled for ease of playing.

French horn has a wide flared bell.

Serpent horn has two sets of fingerholes.

PERCUSSION INSTRUMENTS

Percussion instruments are played by being struck, rubbed, or shaken; they usually provide the rhythmic beat in an instrumental group. They include snare drums, bass drums, tambourines, cymbals, gongs, castanets, maracas, tom-toms, timpani, bells, the xylophone, celesta, marimba, vibraphone, and chimes.

DRUM KIT
A drum kit consists of different types of drums and cymbals. The player uses both hands and feet to operate it.

Crash cymbal loosely fitted to allow vibrations

High-hat uses two cymbals.

Tom-tom drums

Ride cymbal

Snare drum

Key to adjust height

Floor tom-tom

Bass drum pedal

Felt-covered beater

Bass drum gives deep thud.

Egyptian darabuka
is an example of the goblet drum popular in many Arab countries.

Oriental gong
is struck in the centre to cause the greatest vibrations.

Nigerian gourd rattle

Chinese rattle drum

Gourd

Brazilian berimbau
with resonating gourd.

Tambourine
has cymbals set into frame, which sound when shaken.

KEYBOARD INSTRUMENTS

Keyboard instruments have an arrangement of levers or keys that activate the source of sound. Their popularity arose from a capacity to play melody and accompaniment at the same time. The three major keyboard instruments are the pianoforte or piano, the harpsichord, and the organ.

PIANOFORTE

The keys of a pianoforte manipulate felt-covered hammers. These strike wire strings, causing them to resonate. The player can sound many notes at once and can vary the loudness of individual notes.

Strings

Heavy iron frame

Hammers

88-note keyboard

Tuning pins

Raised lid gives fuller sound.

Left or soft pedal moves hammer nearer to strings, allowing softer tone.

Right or sustaining pedal controls duration of sound.

Square pianoforte
made in England in 1773.

Italian spinet
of 1550s used a four-octave keyboard.

Strings plucked by wooden jacks.

Wooden soundboard

ELECTRONIC INSTRUMENTS

The electronic synthesizer creates sound by artificial means. It changes electric impulses into sound, and every aspect of the sound can be controlled. The synthesizer player can generate virtually any sound imaginable, from those of the natural world or of traditional instruments, to new, unique, "space-age" sounds.

Electronic keyboard
can change a sound wave to produce a great variety of sounds.

Drum pad
emits electric signal when struck, to produce electronic drum sound.

1950s electric guitar
pioneered rock as musical form. Most bands have three guitars, a lead, rhythm, and bass.

Output socket

Futuristic V-shaped wooden body

Pick-ups that convert string vibrations into electrical impulses.

MOST EXPENSIVE INSTRUMENTS

Instrument	Date made	Value $
"Mendelssohn" violin by Stradivari	1720	1,382,766
"Cholmondeley" cello by Stradivari	1698	950,460
"Bonjour" cello by Stradivari	1690	927,465
Violin by Joseph del Gesu	1743	797,160
"Marie Hall" violin by Stradivari	1709	659,190
"Schreiber" violin by Stradivari	1712	539,616
Violin by Pietro Guarneri	1715	339,560
"Ex-Kosman" violin by G. Guadagnini	c.1750	339,560
"Montagnana" violin by D. Montagnana	1741	314,265
Jimi Hendrix's *Stratocaster* guitar	1968	275,940

MUSIC FACTS

• Italian violinist Niccolò Paganini (1782–1840) was the most skilled violin virtuoso of the 19th century. He was the fastest violinist in the world, playing his own *Mouvement Perpetuel* in three minutes, three seconds. This translates as 12 notes per second.

• In 1846, Belgian instrument maker Adolphe Sax invented the saxophone.

• The harmonica is the world's most popular instrument. In 1965, more than 28 million were sold in the USA.

• The drum used on British explorer Sir Francis Drake's ship hangs in Buckland Abbey, England. It is believed to roll by itself when England faces danger. It was last heard in World War I (1914–18).

• In 1709, the first piano was built by Italian Bartolomeo Cristofori (1655-1731). The first iron-framed piano appeared in 1859.

WRITING

THE FIRST WRITING began as a way to keep accounts and to record details of history. Today people read books for pleasure and to learn about the world.

3000 B.C. The Egyptians invent a form of writing using picture signs called hieroglyphs. They write on scrolls made from papyrus reed.

Egyptian hieroglyphs

2000 B.C. Sumerian epic poem *Gilgamesh* is recorded on 12 clay tablets using cuneiform, a script named after the wedge-shaped pen used for writing.

600 B.C. Greek writer Aesop composes his fables, including the story of *The Boy Who Cried Wolf*, and *The Crow and Pitcher*.

| 3000 B.C. | 3000–2000 B.C. | 2000 B.C. | 2000 B.C. | 1000 B.C. | 600 B.C. |

610–580 B.C. Female poet Sappho, from the Greek island of Lesbos, composes lyrical poetry on themes of love and jealousy.

Greek poet Sappho

500 B.C. The most famous Hindu text, the *Bhagavadgita*, is written in form of a conversation between Arjuna and Krishna.

200 B.C. Parchment (the skin of sheep or goats treated to make a smooth surface) is invented in the Greek city of Pergamum. Parchment is used in the West for 1,000 years.

A.D. 100 Plutarch writes first biography, *Parallel Lives*, which details the lives of Greek soldiers.

Plutarch (A.D.46–119)

A.D. 105 Chinese invent paper which they make from the pulp of fibres from mulberry trees. They keep invention a secret for 600 years.

Making paper

868 A.D. The earliest known wood-block printed book, with wood-cut illustrations, is the *Diamond Sutra*, printed in China.

| 610 B.C. | 500–200 B.C. | A.D.100 | A.D.105 | A.D. 868 |

1007 Murasaki Shikibu (973–1014) writes *The Tale of Genji*, based on life in the Heian court of Japan. It is the world's first novel.

1048–1123 Persian poet Omar Khayyam writes the *The Rubáiyát*.

1190-1320 Writers in Iceland begin to record the oral part of their history as a story. This is known as a *saga*.

c.1450 Johann Gutenberg (c.1398–1468) invents printing by movable type. First printing is 170 bibles.

1593 William Shakespeare writes one of his first plays, *The Taming of the Shrew*.

Gutenberg bible

1605 Miguel de Cervantes (1547–1616) writes *Don Quixote*, a comic satire about the travels of an elderly Spanish knight.

1697 French author Charles Perrault writes *Tales of Mother Goose*, a collection of oral folk tales that includes *Cinderella* and *Beauty and the Beast*.

1719 Englishman Daniel Defoe (1660–1731) writes *Robinson Crusoe*. Defoe is one of the first people to write major works of literature in an "ordinary" or natural style.

Early copy of Robinson Crusoe

| 1000 | 1007-1320 | 1400 | 1450 | 1593 | 1600 | 1605 | 1697 | 1700 | 1719 |

1800s Charles Dickens' novel, *The Old Curiosity Shop*, is published a chapter a month. Crowds at New York docks shout "is Little Nell Dead?" as ship arrives with the next instalment.

Scene with Little Nell

1837 First book for the blind, *A Summary of French History, Century by Century*, is printed using braille, a system of raised dots invented by Louis Braille (1809–52).

1841 American author, Edgar Allan Poe (1809–49), creates *The Murders in the Rue Morgue*, which is the first true detective story.

1847 Charlotte Brontë writes *Jane Eyre*, a love story that breaks the rules of Victorian society. She uses the false name of Currer Bell, as it is still unacceptable for women to write fiction.

Charlotte Brontë (1816–55)

1852 Harriet Beecher Stowe book, *Uncle Tom's Cabin*, draws attention to the injustice of slavery in the United States.

Scene from Uncle Tom's Cabin

| 1800 | 1800 | 1830 | 1837 | 1841 | 1847 | 1850 |

1864 Jules Verne (1828–1905) writes *Journey to the Centre of the Earth*, which is the first science fiction story.

An illustration from Journey to the Centre of the Earth

1873 First typewriter in the world is produced and sold by the American Remington Company.

Early typewriter

1901 French poet Sully Prudhomme (1839–1907) becomes first person to win Nobel Prize for literature. His work includes *The Broken Vase* and *Solitude*.

1910 First children's encyclopedia is compiled and published by Arthur Mee (1875–1943). It is called *The Children's Encyclopedia* in Great Britain.

World War I soldiers shown in action

1914–18 World War I. A group of English poets that includes Rupert Brooke, Wilfred Owen, and Siegfried Sassoon, record with great emotions the horror of life for soldiers in the war.

| 1860 | 1864 | 1873 | 1890 | 1901 | 1910 | 1914-18 |

1935 Penguin paperback books appear in English-speaking countries. The first title is *Ariel* by André Maurois (1885–1967) with a printing of 25,000 copies.

Penguin paperbacks

Anne Frank (1929–45)

1943 Anne Frank, a young Jewish girl hiding from the Nazis in occupied Holland, writes a diary that is published after her capture and death in a concentration camp.

1944 English author George Orwell writes *Animal Farm*, a satire about a group of animals who overthrow their master.

1970s Desktop publishing arrives. Word processors and computers revolutionize book printing. *Word processor*

1986 The first book on CD-ROM, called *Electronic Encyclopedia*, is published in the USA by Grolier Electronic Publishing, Inc. It contains the full-text version of 20 volumes of the *Academic American Encyclopedia*.

| 1930 | 1935 | 1940 | 1943 | 1944 | 1970s | 1986 | 1990 |

1995 Production and marketing of CD-ROM titles increases significantly.

LITERARY WORDS

Allegory A story with a second meaning hidden beneath its obvious meaning.

Alliteration The repetition of the same sounds (usually consonants of words or stressed syllables) e.g. "landscape-lover, lord of language" (Alfred Lord Tennyson).

Allusion An indirect reference to some event, person, place, or work of art; its nature or relevance is not explained by the writer but relies on the reader's familiarity with what is mentioned.

Autobiography An account of a person's life that is written or recorded by that person.

Biography An account of a person's life written by another.

Character A person in a story or drama, or a sketch describing some recognizable type of person.

The character Huckleberry Finn

Cliché A phrase or saying made commonplace by overuse.

Couplet A pair of rhyming verse lines.

Criticism The reasoned discussion of literary works.

Drama A story written in dialogue, or conversational, form so that it can be spoken and acted.

Elegy A poem lamenting the death of a friend or public figure, or reflecting seriously on a solemn subject.

Epic A long narrative poem celebrating, in a grand style, the great deeds of one or more legendary heroes.

Fable A short story, often about animals who behave and talk as humans, which teaches about right and wrong.

Fiction Something that is not true. A category used to describe a novel.

Genre French term for a type, species, or class of composition.

Gothic novel A story of terror and suspense, usually set in a gloomy castle or monastery.

A Gothic castle

Lyric Expressing the writer's personal feelings and thoughts. Used to describe poetry.

Metaphor A word or phrase used about a thing or an action that is not literally true, but describes it imaginatively.

Non-fiction A written work that is based on fact.

Novel An invented, or fictitious, story that usually deals with human relationships, often in a specified setting.

Onomatopoeia The use of words that seem to imitate the sounds they refer to (e.g. buzz, crackle, hiss, snap, splash).

Oral Anything that is spoken or verbal.

Plot The pattern of events in a story or a play.

Rhetoric Eloquence in public speaking or writing for the most persuasive effect.

Satire A kind of writing that makes fun of the failings of individuals, or societies, such as William Golding's *Lord of the Flies*.

Sonnet A lyric poem of 14 rhyming lines of equal length.

Tragedy A serious work representing the unhappy downfall of a central character, such as William Shakespeare's *Hamlet*.

KEY WRITERS

Name	Dates	Nationality	Key work
Homer	c.800 B.C.	Greek	*The Iliad*
Virgil	70–1 B.C.	Roman	*The Aeneid*
Dante Alighieri	1265–1321	Italian	*The Divine Comedy*
Giovanni Boccaccio	1313–75	Italian	*The Decameron*
Geoffrey Chaucer	1343–1400	English	*The Canterbury Tales*
Miguel de Cervantes	1547–1616	Spanish	*Don Quixote*
Edmund Spenser	1552–99	English	*The Faerie Queene*
John Milton	1608–74	English	*Paradise Lost*
John Bunyan	1628–88	English	*The Pilgrim's Progress*
Henry Fielding	1707–54	English	*Tom Jones*
Laurence Sterne	1713–68	Irish	*Tristram Shandy*
J. W. Von Goethe	1748–1832	German	*Faust*
William Wordsworth	1770–1850	English	*Lyrical Ballads*
Jane Austen	1775–1817	English	*Pride and Prejudice*
Mary Shelley	1797–1851	English	*Frankenstein*
Honoré de Balzac	1799–1850	French	*Old Goriot*
Victor Hugo	1802–85	French	*Les Misérables*
Charles Dickens	1812–70	English	*Oliver Twist*
Charlotte Brontë	1816–55	English	*Jane Eyre*
Emily Brontë	1818–48	English	*Wuthering Heights*
George Eliot	1819–80	English	*Middlemarch*
Herman Melville	1819–91	American	*Moby Dick*
Walt Whitman	1819–92	American	*Leaves of Grass*
Gustave Flaubert	1821–80	French	*Madame Bovary*
Feyodor Dostoyevsky	1821–81	Russian	*Crime and Punishment*
Leo Tolstoy	1828–1910	Russian	*War and Peace*
Émile Zola	1840–1902	French	*Germinal*
Thomas Hardy	1840–1928	English	*Tess of the d'Urbervilles*
Henry James	1843–1916	American	*Portrait of a Lady*
Joseph Conrad	1857–1924	British	*Heart of Darkness*
Rabindranath Tagore	1861–1941	Indian	*Gitanjali*
W. B. Yeats	1865–1939	Irish	*The Tower*
Marcel Proust	1871–1922	French	*Remembrance of Things Past*
Thomas Mann	1875–1955	German	*The Magic Mountain*
E. M. Forster	1879–1970	English	*Passage to India*
James Joyce	1882–1941	Irish	*Ulysses*
Virginia Woolf	1882–1941	English	*To the Lighthouse*
Franz Kafka	1883–1924	Czechoslovakian	*The Trial*
D. H. Lawrence	1885–1930	English	*Sons and Lovers*
Ezra Pound	1885–1972	American	*The Cantos*
T. S. Eliot	1888–1965	American	*The Waste Land*
Boris Pasternak	1890–1960	Russian	*Dr. Zhivago*
Aldous Huxley	1894–1963	English	*Brave New World*
F. Scott Fitzgerald	1896–1940	American	*The Great Gatsby*
Ernest Hemingway	1899–1961	American	*A Farewell to Arms*
Vladimir Nabokov	1899–1977	Russian	*Lolita*
Jorge Luis Borges	1899–1986	Argentinian	*Labyrinths*
John Steinbeck	1902–68	American	*The Grapes of Wrath*
George Orwell	1903–50	English	*Animal Farm*
Evelyn Waugh	1903–66	English	*Brideshead Revisited*
Pablo Neruda	1904–73	Chilean	*Great Song*
Graham Greene	1904–91	English	*The Power and the Glory*
William Golding	1911–93	English	*Lord of the Flies*
Patrick White	1912–90	Australian	*Voss*
Albert Camus	1913–60	French	*The Outsider*
Dylan Thomas	1914–53	Welsh	*Under Milk Wood*
Anthony Burgess	1917–93	English	*A Clockwork Orange*
Doris Lessing	b.1919–	English	*The Golden Notebook*
Iris Murdoch	b.1919–	English	*Bruno's Dream*
Italo Calvino	1923–85	Italian	*The Path to the Nest of Spiders*
Yukio Mishima	1925–1970	Japanese	*The Sound of Waves*
Günter Grass	b.1927–	German	*The Tin Drum*
Gabriel García Márquez	b.1928–	Colombian	*One Hundred Years of Solitude*
Toni Morrison	b.1931–	American	*Beloved*

PRINTING

BEFORE PRINTING WAS invented, information was written by hand. The introduction of printing with movable type (one block for each character or letter) meant that many copies of an original work could be made quickly and cheaply. Today, many stages of print production are done by computer.

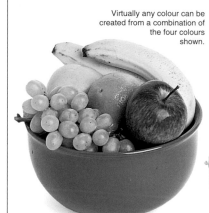

Virtually any colour can be created from a combination of the four colours shown.

Yellow

Magenta

Cyan

Black

PRINTING PRESS

After colour separation, the details on each of the coloured films is transferred on to a plate. Each plate is treated with chemicals, then fitted to rollers on a press. The paper feeds through, and as it comes into contact with each plate, the four colours are added one by one.

TYPOGRAPHY

Typography is the design of letters and words printed on a page. Typographers create a page of print using different type styles, which when put together, make the page look appealing and easy to read. Typefaces can be divided into two main groups:

SERIF
Serif faces have little strokes (serifs) at the end of many letters. The serifs form a link between the letters, which helps bind them together as words.

TYPEFACES
There are thousands of different typefaces. Some of the most common are shown on the right. A typeface comes in a range of styles (such as italics) and sizes, which are measured in points. This book is set in the Caslon typeface.

Typeface
Caslon Roman, 30 point

Typeface
Caslon italic, 30 point

Typeface
Caslon bold, 30 point

SANS SERIF
Sans serif typefaces do not have serifs. They are harder to read than serif faces.

COLOUR SEPARATION

Colour illustrations are separated into four colours (magenta, cyan, yellow, and black) by an electronic scanner before printing. A laser scans the pictures four times, once for each separation. This process results in four pieces of film, one for each colour.

The illustration is placed on a revolving drum and is scanned by a laser.

Paper is fed through the press, and comes into contact with each of the colour plates in turn.

The final full-colour printed sheets appear at the far end of the press.

TYPESETTING
Today, this is mainly done by computer. The typeface and text width is set, and any corrections can be made on screen. A laser printer, which is connected to the computer, prints the words on to a sheet of light-sensitive film, or type film.

Helvetica ABCDEFGHIJKLMNOPQR STUVWXYZ

Times ABCDEFGHIJKLMNOPQ RSTUVWXYZ

Futura ABCDEFGHIJKLMNOPQRST UVWXYZ

Baskerville ABCDEFGHIJKLMNOPQRSTUVWXYZ

PRINTING WORDS

Ascender Part of a lower-case letter that is above the x-height.
Bromide Photosensitive paper on which an image is created. *ascender*
Cold type Modern method of printing that produces a photographic image.
Colour correction Changing the strength of colours in an illustration before going to print.
Cropping Trimming and shaping illustrations. *flat colour*
Descender Part of a lower-case letter that is below the x-height.
Em Unit of measurement.
Flat colour Area of printed colour without variations in tone.
Flop Reversal of an illustration.
Font Set of typed characters of the same style.
Format Size of a book or a page.
Gutter Margin that runs down the centre of a spread.
Hot metal Traditional method of printing in which type is cast from molten lead.
Kerning Adjusting the space between letters.
Leading Space between lines of type.
Lower case Letters that are not capitals.
Measure Length of a line of type.
Mechanical Illustrations and text drawn up for reproduction.
Orphan The start of a paragraph at the foot of the page.
Ozalid Reproduction of *x-height* printed material on to chemically treated, usually blue, paper.
Phototypesetting Setting of type on film or photographic paper.
Pica Unit of type measurement equal to 12 points.
Point A measurement type equal to 0.351457mm (0.013837in).
Proof A reproduction of illustrations or text before the printing stage.
Range Lining up of type either vertically or horizontally. *descender*
Reproduction Process by which artwork is reproduced, through colour separation, before printing.
Upper case Letters that are capitals.
Widow A short line.
X-height The height of a letter that does not include its ascender or descender.

PRINTING FACTS
● First printers were the Chinese, who printed scrolls and books using wooden blocks in about A.D. 770.

Chinese wooden block

● Today, there are more than 11,000 Western typefaces.

RADIO

RADIO WAVES WERE first used for communication some 30 years before television appeared. The invention of radio also made television broadcasting possible.

1888 Heinrich Hertz (1857–1894), German physicist, discovers radio waves.

Heinrich Hertz

1894 Guglielmo Marconi (1874–1937), Italian-born physicist, sends radio waves across a room, making a bell ring.

1901 Morse code (see p.269) is transmitted across the Atlantic by Marconi.

Guglielmo Marconi

| 1800 | 1888 | 1890 | 1894 | 1900 | 1901 |

RMS Titanic

1912 Titanic sends an emergency signal by radio after hitting an iceberg.

1920 First commercial radio station, KDKA of Pittsburgh, USA, starts broadcasting with a transmission of the presidential election results.

BBC Radio microphone

1927 BBC (British Broadcasting Corporation) is granted its first charter (licence).

1932 Frequency Modulation, which reduces interference, is invented by American inventor Edwin Armstrong (1890–1954).

1954 First transistor radio appears in the USA. Transistors replace valves.

Early transistor radio

1960 First VHF-FM stereo broadcasts, from KDKA-FM (see 1920).

1988 Radio Data System (automatic station identification and traffic news for car radios) is introduced in the UK and Sweden.

| 1910 | 1912 | 1920 | 1920 | 1927 | 1930 | 1932 | 1950 | 1954 | 1960 | 1960 | 1980 | 1988 |

RADIO FACTS

- Australian RPH radio stations broadcast only programmes for the vision impaired.

- During the five days in 1991 that Cyclone Val pounded Samoa, the island's only link with the outside world was amateur radio.

- Digital Audio Broadcasting (DAB) is a new radio system that produces CD-quality digital sound.

- The distance radio waves travel around the Earth depends partly on the number of sunspots at the time.

TOP RADIO OWNERS

Country	Radios per person
USA	2.1
Bermuda	1.4
Australia	1.3
Gibraltar	1.2
United Kingdom	1.1

RADIO FREQUENCIES

Radio waves are waves of electromagnetic energy that have varying lengths and that vibrate at varying speeds. The rate of vibration is called frequency. Radio stations use long, medium or short waves. TV satellite link-ups and microwave ovens also use radio waves.

Frequency bands are divided between radio stations so each station can broadcast on its own frequency and no clashes with other stations occur.

Radio receivers select a single radio channel and convert the waves back into sound.

Satellites provide communication between very distant locations with microwaves.

Long waves (LW) can travel almost 2,000km (1,240m). They are used for some national broadcasts.

Medium waves (MW) travel for a few hundred kms. National and local radio stations often transmit in MW.

Very high frequency waves (VHF) travel short distances.

Short waves (SW) travel thousands of kilometres. International radio stations use SW.

RADIOS OLD AND NEW

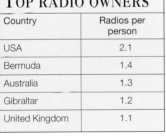

1930s
This 1936 set was 41cm (16in) tall, 33cm (13in) wide, and used valves.

TODAY
Radios can now be fitted inside wrist-watches.

RADIO RECORDS

LARGEST AUDIENCE is for the BBC's World Service, with at least 140 million regular listeners around the world.

LONGEST-RUNNING SHOW is *Rambling with Gambling* on WOR-NY (New York, USA), first broadcast in 1925.

LONGEST-RUNNING SOAP is *The Archers*, first broadcast by the BBC in 1950.

ALIEN ATTACK!

In 1938 American actor and director Orson Welles (1915-85) dramatised H.G. Wells' *War of the Worlds*, in which Earth is invaded by aliens. Thousands of people panicked, believing the programme to be a news bulletin.

TELEVISION

TELEVISION SETS convert radio waves into pictures and sound. A single event can be watched live by billions of people all over the world.

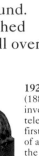

Paul Nipkow

1884 Nipkow disc is invented by Paul Nipkow (1860–1940), a German inventor. The spinning disc is an early alternative to the cathode ray tube.

1897 Cathode-ray tube is invented by German physicist Karl Ferdinand Braun (1850–1918). It is the forerunner of the modern TV receiver tube.

Cathode ray tube

1880   1884   1897

1926 John Logie Baird (1888–1946), a Scottish inventor, demonstrates television by showing the first recognizable pictures of a human face. He uses the Nipkow disc.

1929 Late-night transmissions of Baird's 30-line pictures are broadcast by the British Broadcasting Corporation (BBC).

1930 Sound is added to Baird's 30-line television pictures and transmitted by the BBC.

1932 First practical television camera is demonstrated by Russian-born American Vladimir Kosma Zworykin (1889–1982). It is fully electronic, unlike Baird's mechanical camera.

Baird's system

Vladimir Zworykin

1920   1926   1929   1930   1930   1931

1950 Colour television system is developed by the American company CBS.

1954 Eurovision formed to share transmission of programmes across Europe.

1960–61 All-transistor televisions appear for the first time in the United States.

1962 First transatlantic pictures are broadcast live from the communications satellite Telstar, launched by NASA.

Telstar satellite

1969 First Moon landing is seen by millions all over the world, filmed in colour by the Apollo XI crew.

First man on the moon

1970 Transmission direct from satellite to high-definition television (HDTV) is developed by Japan Broadcasting System (NHK).

1973 Ceefax, an information system using the spare lines on a 625-line television system, is developed in Britain.

1950   1954   1960   1961   1962   1969   1970   1973

1979 First regular direct broadcasting system (DBS) by satellite is launched in Canada. A dish is needed to receive broadcasts.

Satellite receiver dish

1979 Pocket television set is invented by Japanese firm Matsushita. It is no bigger than a video cassette.

Pocket TV set

1980 Cable News Network (CNN) officially begins in June. This American 24-hour television channel relies on satellites for news reporting and gives up-to-the minute news coverage in times of crisis.

1981 Camcorder revolutionises TV news gathering (see p.187).

1991 Hi-Vision, a high definition TV service, is broadcast for eight hours daily by NHK of Japan.

1999 Digital TV promises a huge increase in the number of channels.

1979   1980   1981   1986   1991   1999

TV SETS OLD AND NEW

TV technology has advanced rapidly over its brief history.

1930s
Early sets had small black- and- white screens but contained so much electronic equipment that they were housed in large boxes.

1960s
In the 1960s smaller, colour TVs became common. Transistors replaced valves.

TODAY
Pocket-sized TVs are now widely available. Very small sets often use liquid crystal screens.

TELEVISION RECORDS

WORLD'S LONGEST-RUNNING TV SHOW
is NBC's *Meet the Press*, first shown in the USA in 1947.

WORLD'S SMALLEST TV SET
is Seiko's TV-Wrist Watch, launched in 1982. It has a 1.2inch (30.5mm) screen.

LONGEST CONTINUOUS BROADCAST
was by GTV 9, Australia, lasting 163 hrs 18 mins, of Apollo XI's Moon mission (19-26 July 1969).

FIRST DAILY BROADCASTS
were made by the BBC, broadcasting from London, starting 10 November 1936.

TV GENERATION
Americans watch more television than any other nationality. In an average household the TV set is turned on for seven hours a day. By the time they are 65 years old, most Americans have watched more than nine years' worth of television.

POPULAR TELEVISION

SOAP OPERAS ("SOAPS")
Soaps are dramas with continuous storylines screened in regular episodes. The world's longest-running soap is *Coronation Street*, first shown on British TV in 1960. The earliest American soaps of the 1950s were sponsored by soap-powder companies.

SPORTS PROGRAMMES
One of the biggest TV audiences was about 26.5 billion for the 1990 World Cup finals.

World Cup finals, 1990

CHAT SHOWS
Chat shows are programmes where a host asks members of the audience to talk about their lives. The popularity of American chat show, *Oprah*, has made its host, Oprah Winfrey, the highest paid entertainer in the world. In 1994–5 she allegedly earned $146 million.

CHILDREN'S PROGRAMMES
Children's programmes show a wide range of material suitable for a younger audience. *Sesame Street*, first shown in the USA in 1969, is seen in 80 countries.

MAKING A DOCUMENTARY
This diagram shows one way of making a documentary. The two main players are the production company, which makes the film, and the TV station, which broadcasts it. The three main stages of the process are pre-production (organization of the shoot), production (filming) and post-production (editing).

Idea is taken to the production company that will make the programme and arrange for it to be shown on TV.

Go ahead
Preliminary research into subject and possible locations (recce) is undertaken.

Finance committee
Committee, which includes accountants, commissioning editor, and controller, approves project and budget.

Treatment
This written outline is taken to a TV station.

Commissioning editor
Commissioning editor, a TV executive, receives and approves treatment.

Rushes
If shot on videotape, material can be checked instantly on playback. If film has been used, previous day's work, developed overnight, is viewed daily.

Production
Shooting begins. Crew go on location.

Pre-production
Equipment and crew hired, interviews set up, locations found, filming permissions obtained.

Contract
After signing, preparation and shooting of documentary can begin.

Post-production
Editor and director put the programme together in its finished version, adding sound and titles.

Delivery
Completed film is delivered to TV station.

Transmission
Programme is broadcast by TV station.

Viewing
Documentary is seen on television.

INSIDE A TELEVISION SET
The TV set's aerial picks up radio waves and converts them into electronic signals. These signals in turn are converted into pictures by the picture tube.

Electron guns fire streams of electrons (see p.226) that sweep across the inside of the screen, building up the image.

Picture tube is the most important single component of a TV set. All the air has been pumped out of the tube to allow free flow of electrons.

Coils produce magnetic fields that deflect the electron beams, creating a new picture 25 times a second.

Phosphor strips coat the inside of the screen. Three different types of phosphor are used: one which glows red when struck by electrons; one green; and one blue.

Shadow mask has slots which ensure that the electrons light phosphor of the correct colour.

WORLD TV VIEWING

Country	Hours per week
United States	49.35
Italy	28.93
Hong Kong	28.70
Colombia	23.80
United Kingdom	23.80
Australia	21.98
Chile	17.50
China	10.59
Malaysia	10.50
World average	19.67

TELEVISION FACTS
• By 1993 there were 746,829,000 homes with a TV set world-wide. By 2005 there will be an estimated billion.

• In 1977 hundreds of bald men invaded an English farm after a BBC April fool joke suggested that water there had hair-restoring properties.

• High-definition TV, which uses twice as many lines to build up each frame as ordinary TV, gives a much sharper picture.

• Virtual Vision Sport is a TV system in which the viewer wears a pair of special glasses. They create a colour picture that appears to be 1.5m (5ft) wide floating in space about 3m (10ft) away.

Virtual vision glasses

CINEMA

CINEMA IS A MILLION-dollar industry that makes, sells, and shows movies worldwide. Film stars attract publicity and often become household names.

1879 Zoogyroscope (later renamed Zoopraxiscope) is developed by English photographer Eadweard Muybridge (1830-1904). It projects images of a series of photographs on to a screen, in quick succession, creating the illusion of movement.

Zoogyroscope

1881 Etienne Marey (1830-1904), French photographic pioneer, invents a camera, shaped like a gun, which takes pictures on a revolving plate.

Etienne Marey

| 1870 | 1879 | 1880 | 1881 |

1885 Paper roll film is invented by American George Eastman (1854-1932).

1894 Kinetograph (film camera) and Kinetoscope (film viewer) are marketed by Americans Thomas Edison (1847-1931) and W.K.L. Dickson (1860-1933), using celluloid roll film.

1895 Projection system is invented by French brothers August (1862-1954) and Louis (1864-1948) Lumière, and publicly demonstrated for the first time in Paris.

Lumière projector

1908 Kinemacolour is invented by Englishman George Albert Smith (1864-1959) and demonstrated in London. It uses two colour filters and two reels of film.

1913 Hollywood's first feature film, *Squaw Man*, is made by American directors Jesse Lasky (1880-1958), Cecil B. de Mille (1881-1959), and Samuel Goldwyn (1879-1974).

1920s First studios in India appear, including Bombay Talkies, Ranjit Film Company, and Prabhat Film Company.

Indian film posters

| 1880 | 1885 | 1894 | 1890 | 1895 | 1900 | 1908 | 1913 |

1920s-30s Picture palaces are at the peak of their popularity, offering movie-goers magic and luxury.

1927 The first "talkie" is *The Jazz Singer*. The soundtrack to the film is recorded on a disc.

Jazz singer poster

1928 Sound is recorded on to the film itself. The first all-talking picture is *The Lights of New York*.

1929 First Oscars (Academy Awards) include Emil Jannings (best actor) and Janet Gaynor (best actress).

Oscar

1932 Technicolor process is perfected and three-colour Technicolor cameras are developed.

1937 *Becky Sharp* is the first film to be made entirely in three-strip colour.

1920s picture palace

| 1920 | 1920 | 1927 | 1928 | 1929 | 1930 | 1932 | 1937 |

1952 Eastman color takes over from Technicolor. A negative three-colour movie is made from which Technicolor or Eastman color prints can be taken.

Scene from Eastman color movie, Doctor at Large

1952 *Bwana Devil* is the first 3-D film in Natural Vision (a large screen process using natural colour).

1953 CinemaScope is developed by Fox studios. This wide-screen process forces Hollywood to film on location as sets are harder to hide. *The Robe* is the first CinemaScope film.

3-D glasses

1970 Steadycam is invented. It is a camera that remains completely steady while strapped to a freely moving cameraman.

1976 OMNIMAX projection is first demonstrated. OMNIMAX films are shown on a huge dome-like screen that towers above and around the audience.

| 1950 | 1952 | 1953 | 1970 | 1970 | 1976 |

POPULAR FILMS

Three of the most popular types of film at the cinema are science fiction (sci-fi), action, and horror.

SCIENCE FICTION
The most expensive film ever made was the sci-fi adventure *Waterworld*. The film cost 160 million US dollars. The second most expensive film was *Terminator 2*.

ACTION
The three *Indiana Jones* films were all in the top ten most successful films of the 1980s. Each film earned at least 100 million US dollars.

HORROR
Count Dracula, the vampire, is the most frequently filmed horror character. Since his screen debut in 1931, he has appeared on film more than 160 times.

Arnold Schwarzenegger in Terminator 2

FILM FORMATS

One minute of a movie uses over 27m (90ft) of film, and a full-length feature about 2.5km (1.5 miles). The standard size used now is 35mm (standard gauge).

This 9.5mm film was introduced by the French Pathé company in 1922 for amateur films.

The standard 35mm film

Sound is recorded on this squiggly line.

Scene from an IMAX film

IMAX

The IMAX projection system was first demonstrated in Japan in 1970. The films are shown on giant screens with a full range of digital sound. 70mm film is used with special cameras and projectors to create very clear, vivid pictures on screen.

MOVIE MAKERS

This diagram shows many of the most important people involved in making a movie. The producer has overall financial responsibility and the director has overall creative control.

PRE-PRODUCTION
All the necessary arrangements are made to ensure that filming runs smoothly.

Producer
The producer raises money for the film and puts together the creative package: director, script, and actors. Once finance has been raised, filming begins.

Scriptwriter
Works on story to make it attractive to stars as well as to financial backers.

Production manager
Controls the budget and expenditure; oversees practicalities of the shoot such as scheduling, travel, and accommodation.

Director
Liaises with producer over script, hiring of stars, and key crew.

Finance
Once enough money has been raised, filming can begin.

Stars
Popular actors are important for the success of the film.

Casting director
Works with the director, selecting actors.

Location manager
Finds suitable locations and arranges for their use.

Production co-ordinator
Runs production office and makes sure information is circulated to crew and cast.

Production assistant
Performs a variety of tasks including liaising between office and set, and administration.

Cast
Actors for each speaking part in the script.

PRODUCTION
Filming begins. The director is helped by experts in the various departments. Each take (uninterrupted sequence of filming) begins with the filming of a clapperboard, which is then slammed shut, making a noise on the soundtrack. This way, sound and image can be synchronized when the film is edited.

Director
The director is the creative force behind the film, controlling the action and bringing the script to life.

Director of photography
Responsible for lighting, composition, and choice of camera, lens, and film.

Production designer
Responsible for the overall design of the film, including sets and costumes.

First assitant director
Controls day-to-day filming on the set. Ensures schedule of film is on target.

Sound engineer
In charge of the sound quality of the film. Also supervises placing of microphones.

Camera operator works camera during shooting.

Focus puller adjusts focus on lens.

Clapper loader checks, cleans and loads the camera, operates the clapperboard, and sends film to the laboratory.

Grip lays tracks for dolly (support for camera that moves in any direction); moves dolly, as well as camera and camera equipment.

Gaffer is in charge of rigging and setting the lights.

Best boy assists the gaffer.

Art director draws up the designs for the sets on the film, supervises their construction, and orders the dressing of the set.

Construction manager is in charge of carpenters, painters, stagehands.

Set dresser places the many objects around the set that give it the appearance of reality.

Second assistant director helps First assistant director and co-ordinates cast, crew, and background action.

OTHER SERVICES
Costume design and costume department (buys and maintains costumes); make-up department (applies general and special effect make-up); transport; catering; stills photography (for publicity shots).

Boom operator positions and operates the microphone known as the boom.

POST-PRODUCTION
After all the film has been shot, the editor cuts up the individual film sequences and links them together. Working closely with the director, the editor then adds the sound. The finished version is sold for distribution to cinemas.

FAMOUS DIRECTORS
Fritz Lang (1890-1976), Austrian director of *Metropolis* (1926) and *Fury* (1936).

Sergei Eisenstein (1898-1948), Russian, directed *Battleship Potemkin* (1925) and *October/Ten Days That Shook the World* (1928).

Alfred Hitchcock (1899-1980), British director of *The Lady Vanishes* (1938), *Dial M for Murder* (1954), and *Psycho* (1960).

Contemporary poster advertising the film Metropolis

Akira Kurosawa (born 1910), Japanese director of *Rashomon* (1950) and *Hakuchi* (*The Idiot*)1951.

Ingmar Bergman (born 1918), Swedish director of *Smultronstallet* (*Wild Strawberries*) 1957.

Frederico Fellini (1920-1993), Italian, directed *Il Bidone* (*The Swindle*) 1955.

Satyajit Ray (1921–1992), Indian director of *The Apu Trilogy* (1955-1959).

Orson Welles (1915-1985), American who directed *Citizen Kane* (1940).

CINEMA FACTS
• Cinema screens are coated with minute plastic prisms which make the screen as bright as possible. Before their introduction, large screens were sprayed with water to improve reflection.

• First feature film was *The Story of the Kelly Gang*, made in Australia in 1906.

• Longest film ever made is *The Cure for Insomnia* (1987), directed by American J.H. Timmis. Lasts 85 hours.

MOST OSCARS WON

Name of film	Oscars
Ben Hur (1959)	11
Titanic (1998)	11
Gone with the Wind (1939)	10
West Side Story (1961)	10
Gandhi (1982)	9
The Last Emperor (1987)	9
The English Patient (1997)	9
Gigi (1958)	8
Cabaret (1972)	8
Amadeus (1984)	8

ANIMATION

ANIMATORS BRING drawings, models, or objects to life by filming them in detailed sequences. Computers are also used to create new techniques.

1832 Phenakistoscope is invented by Belgian Joseph Plateau (1801–83). Images painted in sequence on the disc seem to move when it is spun.

Phenakistoscope

1908 Emile Cohl (1857–1938), French animator, draws cartoons. His technique requires 16 pictures to make one second of screen time.

1914 Earl Hurd (1880–1950) and **J.R. Bray** (1879–1978), American animators, draw cartoons on clear celluloid sheets. The background does not have to be re-drawn for every frame (shot) of an animated sequence, only the moving parts.

1830 | 1832 | 1900 | 1908 | 1914

1919 Walt Disney (1901–66) meets Ub Iwerks (1901–71). These American animators refine and develop the celluloid-sheet technique. Disney Studios' Multiplane technique adds realism and depth to their cartoons.

1928 Mickey Mouse stars in Disney's *Steamboat Willie*, the first animated cartoon with synchronized sound. Disney himself provides Mickey's voice. The cartoon causes a sensation.

Mickey Mouse

1930s Len Lye (1901–80), New Zealand animator, makes short films by drawing abstract images directly on to the film itself, thus skipping the photographic process.

Len Lye

1939 Tom and Jerry, created by Americans Bill Hanna (born 1910) and Joe Barbera (born 1911), appear in their first cartoon, *Puss Gets the Boot*. They receive the first of their seven Oscars in 1943 for *Yankee Doodle Mouse*.

1915 | 1919 | 1920 | 1928 | 1930 | 1939 | 1940

1952 Norman McLaren (1914–87), Canadian animator, photographs real people frame by frame in his short film *Neighbours*, to make them look like animated robots.

Norman McLaren

1991 *Creature Comforts*, created by Aardman Animation (UK) and featuring clay zoo animals, wins an Oscar.

A gorilla from Creature Comforts

1990s Computer graphics may be used to enhance or manipulate hand-drawn images, as in *Aladdin* (1992). Some animators save time by using them to draw the intermediate images between the key, hand-drawn positions.

Aladdin

1950 | 1952 | 1990 | 1991

ANIMATION TYPES

ANIMATION
The twin Brothers Quay, born in Philadelphia in 1947, bring strange, dead objects to life in their animated films. *Street of Crocodiles*, made in 1986, features eyeless dolls. The brothers were influenced by Czech animator, Jan Svankmajer (born 1934).

CARTOONS
Walt Disney achieved huge popularity and won a special Oscar for the first feature-length cartoon, *Snow White and the Seven Dwarfs* (1937).

ANIMATION FACTS
• First ever motion-picture cartoon film was *Humorous Phases of Funny Faces* (1906), made by American J. Stuart Blackton (1875–1941) for Vitagraph. The cartoon required 3,000 drawings.

• First animated film nominated for an Oscar for best picture was the Disney production of *Beauty and the Beast* (1991).

• Since the 1930s cartoon characters have been drawn with only three fingers instead of four. This looks just as realistic and is much quicker for the animators.

TOP BOX OFFICE HITS

Film	Production company and date
The Lion King	Disney, 1994
Aladdin	Disney, 1992
Who Framed Roger Rabbit?	Disney, 1988
Snow White and the Seven Dwarfs	Disney, 1937
Toy Story	Disney, 1995
The Santa Clause	Disney, 1994
Pocahontas	Disney, 1995
The Jungle Book	Disney, 1967

MORPHING
This computer technique is used either to transform a person or object into something different, or to create animation in a live-action film. The illustration shows part of a morphing sequence.

The points of both objects, hand and spider, are plotted on the computer. When the two sets of points coincide the transformation is complete.

The outline of the spider is just visible.

The mid-point of the morphing process.

The spider is almost complete.

VIRTUAL REALITY
Virtual reality is a three-dimensional computer-generated world. The special headset contains miniature TV screens that provide stereo vision. If you wear the headset and move around, the virtual-reality world moves with you. The data glove allows you to operate tools in the virtual world.

VIDEO

THE TERM VIDEO refers to video cassettes, video recorders, and video cameras. Many TV programmes, advertisements, and pop promos are shot on video.

1929 Phonovision is introduced by John Logie Baird (1888–1946), Scottish inventor. This video system uses 12-inch discs with pictures recorded on to them.

Phonovision disc

1956 First working video recorder, the VR1000, is introduced by Ampex corporation of California, USA.

1965 First portable video camera introduced by Japanese Company Sony. It has a bulky separate unit containing the recording equipment, and records in black and white.

| 1920 | 1929 | | 1950 | 1956 | 1960 | 1965 |

1970 First video cassette is part of the U-Matic system, made by Sony.

Sony 1970 U-Matic video cassette

1972 First domestic video recorder is the N1500, brought out by Philips of Holland. It is the first video recorder to have its own tuner and timer.

1975 Laser Video Disc introduced by Sony/Philips.

1976 VHS system, launched by Japanese company JVC, proves more commercially successful than its rival Betamax.

An early camcorder

1981 Camcorder is invented. It is a camera with a built-in recorder, which records on to videotape instead of film.

1990s CDTV uses pre-recorded video discs similar to music CDs, instead of video tapes.

CDTV disc

| 1970 | 1972 | 1975 | 1976 | | 1980 | 1981 | 1990 |

VIDEO FACTS

• Approximately 25% of all video sales in the world are of animated films.

• Japanese companies account for over 80% of worldwide video recorder (VCR) production.

TOP VIDEO SPENDERS

Country	US $ Billions
USA	11.0
Japan	2.6
UK	1.4
Canada	1.2
France	0.7
Germany	0.7
Australia	0.7

• A basic VCR contains over 2,500 components, compared to about 360 in a colour TV set.

• Laser video discs spin approximately fifty times faster than a long-playing record. European models revolve 1,500 times a minute, and American and Japanese discs 1,800 times a minute.

• USA has the most video rental outlets in the world (55,000 in 1992). Japan is second with 11,500 stores.

• There are 230 million homes around the world with at least one VCR. The USA has the most video homes, with 65 million.

ELECTRONIC NEWS GATHERING

Electronic news gathering (ENG) teams use professional video cameras to record on to video cassettes. Unlike film, videos do not need to be processed before broadcasting.

On location abroad
ENG crew films news story.

Customized van
Cassette taken to van containing microwave transmitter. Pictures beamed home via nearby transmitting station.

Transmitting station
Signals received from van sent on to satellite.

Satellite
Signals beamed down to studio receiver dish.

Studio
TV station can broadcast immediately or tape pictures for later use.

At home
Viewer watches the news footage taken by the ENG team.

VIDEO CAMERAS

Early video cameras were carried on the shoulder and were connected by cables to separate recording equipment (called a portapak).

Portable video camera

Tripod

Video recorder

This camcorder films and records in one unit. It is small enough to be held in the palm of the hand.

The 1956 Ampex VR1000 video recorder weighed 665kg (1,465lb), the same as a small car, and used tape which was 4 times wider than that of today's VCRs.

VIDEO RECORDERS

The VR 1000 was 1.1m (3.7ft) high

Modern recorders like this one are only slightly larger than the cassette inside.

VIDEO RECORDS

FASTEST VIDEOTAPE ON SALE was the wedding of HRH Prince Andrew to Sarah Ferguson on 23 July 1986. The fully edited and packaged tapes were available in Virgin Megastore, London, UK, 5 hours 41 minutes after the event.

THE FIRST POP PROMO was for *Bohemian Rhapsody* by Queen, in 1975.

BEST-SELLING VIDEO is Disney's animated feature film *The Lion King* (1994), with the voices of Whoopi Goldberg and Jeremy Irons. By July 1996 it had sold 54 million copies.

NEWSPAPERS

NEWSPAPERS KEEP everyone in touch with local, national, and world events for a small price. They give more information on a wider range of topics and more detail than TV news.

59 B.C. Romans produce the *Acta diurna* (daily acts). They report on the social and political events of the day.

Roman reading a scroll.

A.D. 618 Newsletter reporting on court affairs is circulated by civil servants in Peking, China.

1440–50 Printing by movable type is invented by Johannes Gutenberg (c.1398–1468) of Germany. This leads to more printed material being produced and a growth in readership.

Johannes Gutenberg

60 B.C.	59 B.C.	A.D. 600	618	1440

1513 Newsbooks, forerunners of newspapers, produced. One surviving copy from England, *The Trew Encountre*, dated September 1513, gives a four-page eyewitness account of the Battle of Flodden Field.

1620 One of the first papers to be printed from movable type is a Dutch newspaper, called *Corantos* (currents of news). It contains extracts from foreign journals.

Corantos

1600s–1800s In Japan, people pay a small fee for the news to be read aloud to them. It is known as *yomiuri* (sell and read). *Kawara-ban* (tile-block printing) broadsheets are also produced.

In Japan, the news is read out loud for a fee.

1645 Oldest continuously published weekly newspaper, the *Post-och inrikes tidningar*, is published in Sweden.

1500	1513	1600	1620		1645

1703 Oldest surviving daily newspaper in the world is the *Wiener Zeitung* (Viennese newspaper), Austria.

Wiener Zeitung

1704 *The Boston Newsletter*, first official newspaper in the USA, appears. It replaces newsletters that had previously been sent from London.

The Boston Newsletter

1766 Sweden becomes the first country to guarantee freedom of the press.

1833 First successful penny paper, the *Sun*, appears in New York.

1842 *The Illustrated London News*, containing sketches by artists from all over the world, is established.

The Illustrated London News

1858 P. J. Reuter (1816–99), of Germany, starts a foreign news agency. It is now one of the biggest in the world.

P.J. Reuter

1700	1703	1704	1760	1766	1800	1833	1842	1858

1878 *The Hindu* is one of the first Indian newspapers to be established.

THE HINDU.

The Hindu

1903 First tabloid, the *Mirror*, is launched in Britain. The paper was half the size of other newspapers, had shortened articles, and was reasonably priced. Later, it became the *Daily Mirror*.

The Mirror

1910–20s American publisher, Edward Scripps (1854–1926), pioneers the collection and ownership of popular working-class newspapers. By the 1920s, there are about 6,000 newspapers in the USA.

Edward Scripps

1955 *The Village Voice* is published in New York. This paper brings a new, radical approach to news-reporting.

1970s Computers and new technology replace typesetters and printers.

1990s Many newspapers introduce web sites on the Internet.

1870	1878	1900	1903	1910	1920	1955	1970	1990

NEWSPAPER FACTS

• Sweden sells 574 newspapers for every 1,000 people: the highest sales in the world.

• First newspaper to achieve a circulation of one million was the French paper *Le Petit Journal*, in 1886.

COUNTRIES WITH THE MOST DAILY NEWSPAPERS

Country	Number
India	2,300
USA	1,586
Turkey	399
Brazil	373
Germany	355
Russia	339
Mexico	292
Pakistan	272
Argentina	190
Spain	148
Japan	124
UK	101

BEST-SELLING NEWSPAPERS IN THE WORLD

Newspaper	Country	Average daily circulation
Yomiuri Shimbun	Japan	8,700,000
Asahi Shimbun	Japan	7,400,000
People's Daily	China	6,000,000
Bild Zeitung	Germany	5,900,000
Sun	UK	4,006,979
Daily Mirror	UK	2,463,943
Daily Mail	UK	2,122,166
Wall Street Journal	USA	1,862,207
USA Today	USA	1,570,624
Daily Express	UK	1,215,509

NEWSPAPER WORDS

Broadsheet Newspaper with a large format, usually 61cm x 38cm (24in x 15in).
Circulation Number of newspapers sold each issue.
Editor Person with complete control over the contents of a newspaper.
Feature A non-news article.
Hard news Up-to-the-minute news.
Leader Article giving newspaper's own opinion.
Popular press, or tabloids. Newspapers aiming to provide lively news and entertainment for a mass readership. Also called tabloids, as they usually have a smaller format than broadsheets.
Quality press Newspapers aiming to provide serious news, information, and analysis. Also called broadsheets, as they usually have a large format.
Soft news Background news or news that is not up-to-the-minute.
Syndication Group of publishers who sell the reprint rights to articles all around the world.
Tabloid Newspaper with a smaller format, about half the size of broadsheets.

SPORTS

This factual survey covers every major sport from baseball to weightlifting, identifying Olympic sports and giving tables of Olympic events. For each sport, special clothing, and equipment are clearly illustrated, and all dimensions, weights, and distances are included. The section features rules and record breakers, glossaries to explain specialist terms, and amazing facts and comparisons.

Sports • Olympic Games • Track Events • Field Events • Weightlifting
Gymnastics • Combat Sports • Court Games • Basketball • Rugby • Football
Cricket • Baseball • Stick Games • Golf • Water Sports • Swimming
Equestrian • Winter Sports • Wheeled Sports • Target Sports

In this section the official measurements, whether
in metric or imperial, are given for each sport.

SPORTS

THE FIRST SPORTS, such as hunting and running, grew out of a need for survival. Today, people take part in sports for fitness and enjoyment.

c.3000–1500 B.C.
Wrestling and boxing are practised by the early Mediterranean civilizations.
Bull sports feature in Minoan festivals in Crete. Acrobats leap over the backs of running bulls.

Bull-leaping is practised in Crete.

c.1500 B.C.
Hunting, archery, wrestling, fighting, and organized running are practised in ancient Egypt.

An Egyptian nobleman hunts for birds with a curved stick.

| 3000 B.C. | 3000–1500 B.C. | 1500 B.C. | 1500 B.C. |

c.776 B.C. First Olympic Games held at Olympia, Greece. They last one day, with sacrifices to the gods followed by a single race, a sprint of 192m (630ft), the length of the stadium. Coroebus, a cook, wins the race.

c.200 B.C. Chariot racing is popular in Rome, where the Circus Maximus arena holds 200,000 people. Gladiators fight to the death in amphitheatres such as the Colosseum, Rome.

Chariot racing, Rome

c.20 B.C. Sumo wrestling develops in Japan from Chiao-Li, a form of wrestling used by the Chinese army in training.

Sumo wrestler, Japan

c.A.D. 400 Religious ball game, *tlachtli,* is played by the Aztec Indians of Central America. Players use their elbows, knees, and hips to hit a rubber ball.

Aztec ball court

| 800 B.C. | 776 B.C. | 200 B.C. | 200 B.C. | 20 B.C. | 20 B.C. | A.D. 400 | A.D. 400 |

c.1100 Knights take part in jousting tournaments in England and France to practise for warfare.

Knights jousting

1200s Real tennis played by the clergy and royalty in France.
Skating on frozen canals popular in Holland.
Bowls played in English gardens.

Skating, Holland

1400s Calcio (kick), a form of football, is played in Florence, Italy. Each side has 27 players.

1636 Lacrosse develops from baggataway, played by the American Indian Huron tribe in present-day Ontario, Canada. The word *Crosse* describes the stick used.

Early lacrosse

1777 People surfing off the islands of Tahiti and Oahu are seen by Captain James Cook (1728–79), British explorer. Surfing was later banned by missionaries who thought it immoral.

1811 First outdoor gymnasium is opened by German teacher Friedrich Jahn (1778–1852), inventor of rings and parallel bars.

Friedrich Jahn

| 1200 | 1200 | 1400 | 1630 | 1636 | 1770 | 1777 | 1810 | 1811 |

1823 Rugby is born when William Webb Ellis, a pupil at Rugby School, England, picks up the ball and runs with it during a game of soccer.
William Webb Ellis

c.1829 Baseball, derived from the English game of rounders, is first played in the USA.

Early baseball

1839 First Grand National steeplechase is held at Aintree, England.
Jumping the Brook at the Grand National, 1839

1843 First cross-country ski race held in Tromso, Norway.

1846 Soccer rules drawn up at Cambridge University, England.

1847 Tenpin bowling is born in Connecticut, USA. Ninepins had been banned, so a pin is added.

1860 First British Open Golf Championship held at Prestwick, Scotland.

1861 First hockey club formed in London.

1865 Gloved boxing develops from bare-knuckle fighting using the Marquess of Queensberry's rules.

Bare-knuckle fighter

| 1820 | 1823 | 1829 | 1830 | 1840 | 1843 | 1846 | 1847 | 1860 | 1860 | 1861 | 1865 |

1866 First show jumping event is held in Paris.

1874 American football is born when teams from McGill University, Canada, and Harvard, USA, play a game that is half soccer, half rugby.

1876 Modern badminton rules are drawn up in Poona, India.

1877 First cricket Test Match held between England and Australia in Melbourne.

England cricket team, 1886

1877 First Wimbledon lawn tennis championships held in England.

Wimbledon

1882 Judo developed by Jigoro Kano (1860–1938) in Japan.

1891 Basketball invented in Massachusetts, USA, by sports instructor Dr. James Naismith, who hangs two peach baskets on a verandah for goals.

Dr. James Naismith (1861-1939)

| 1866 | 1870 | 1874 | 1876 | 1877 | 1880 | 1882 | 1890 | 1891 |

1895 Volleyball devised by William G. Morgan in Massachusetts, USA.
First motor race held, Paris–Bordeaux–Paris.

1896 First modern Olympic Games held in Athens, inspired by Baron Pierre de Coubertin (1863-1937) of France.

1903 First Tour de France multi-stage cycle race.
1924 First Winter Olympics staged at Chamonix, France.

1930 Soccer's first World Cup is held in Uruguay.

1960 First Paralympics is held for handicapped people in Rome, Italy.

Canadian ice-hockey team, winners at the first Winter Olympics, 1924.

1972 At the Munich Olympics, Germany, Palestinian terrorists kill 11 members of the Israeli team.

1980–1990s Commercial sponsorship becomes more important in sport.

Satellites bring live international sport to worldwide TV audiences.
Regular mass marathons, with more than 15,000 entrants, are staged. Some marathons include wheelchair events.
Drugs testing becomes a feature of major competitions.

The London marathon

| 1895 | 1896 | 1900 | 1903 | 1924 | 1930 | 1960 | 1970 | 1970 | 1972 | 1980 | 1980 | 1990 | 1999 |

OLYMPIC GAMES

EVERY FOUR YEARS, athletes from all over the world meet to compete in the Summer Olympic Games. About 7,000 competitors take part in more than 20 different sports.

OLYMPIC SYMBOL
The Olympic symbol is made up of five interlocking rings, standing for Europe, Asia, Africa, Australia, and America.

OLYMPIC FLAME
This flame symbolizes the athlete's strive for perfection. A torch is carried by a series of runners from the site of the ancient Olympics in Greece to the stadium where the current Games are to be held.

CROWNING GLORY
In the ancient Olympic Games, winners were crowned with a sacred olive wreath.

MEDALS
Individuals and teams compete for gold (first), silver (second), and bronze (third) medals in the modern Games.

Gold medal from the 1984 Games

SUMMER OLYMPIC VENUES

Date	Place	Country
1896	Athens	Greece
1900	Paris	France
1904	St. Louis, Missouri	USA
1908	London	Britain
1912	Stockholm	Sweden
1920	Antwerp	Belgium
1924	Paris	France
1928	Amsterdam	Netherlands
1932	Los Angeles, California	USA
1936	Berlin	Germany
1948	London	Britain
1952	Helsinki	Finland
1956	Melbourne	Australia
1960	Rome	Italy
1964	Tokyo	Japan
1968	Mexico City	Mexico
1972	Munich	Germany
1976	Montreal	Canada
1980	Moscow	USSR
1984	Los Angeles, California	USA
1988	Seoul	South Korea
1992	Barcelona	Spain
1996	Atlanta, Georgia	USA
2000	Sydney	Australia

PARALYMPIC VENUES

Date	Place	Country
1960	Rome	Italy
1964	Tokyo	Japan
1968	Tel Aviv	Israel
1972	Heidelberg	Germany
1976	Toronto	Canada
1980	Arnhem	Netherlands
1984	New York	USA
1988	Seoul	South Korea
1992	Barcelona	Spain
1996	Atlanta, Georgia	USA
2000	Sydney	Australia

PARALYMPICS
Disabled people compete in the Paralympic Games, which are held every four years. Events include cycling and judo. The Winter Paralympics have been held since 1976.

WINTER OLYMPIC VENUES

Date	Place	Country
1924	Chamonix	France
1928	St. Moritz	Switzerland
1932	Lake Placid, New York	USA
1936	Garmisch-Partenkirchen	Germany
1948	St. Moritz	Switzerland
1952	Oslo	Norway
1956	Cortina d'Ampezzo	Italy
1960	Squaw Valley, California	USA
1964	Innsbruck	Austria
1968	Grenoble	France
1972	Sapporo	Japan
1976	Innsbruck	Austria
1980	Lake Placid, New York	USA
1984	Sarajevo	Yugoslavia
1988	Calgary, Alberta	Canada
1992	Albertville	France
1994	Lillehammer	Norway
1998	Nagano	Japan

WINTER OLYMPICS
Until 1992, the Winter Games were held in the same year as the Summer Olympics. Events include skiing, figure and speed skating, and ice-hockey.

CLASSIFICATION OF SPORTS
One way of classifying the many different types of sport is to put them into three basic groups, which can then be subdivided further.

This symbol is shown next to all Olympic sports featured on the pages following.

CLASSIFICATION

RACING			OPPONENT			ACHIEVEMENT		

| Body power | Extension of body power | Outside power source | Team | Court | Combat | Power | Display | Target |

Examples
Running
Hurdles
Swimming

Cycling
Skiing
Rowing

Motor racing
Motorcycle racing
Yacht racing

Baseball
Football
Ice-hockey

Tennis
Badminton
Squash

Boxing
Judo
Fencing

Long jump
Javelin
Weightlifting

Gymnastics
Show jumping
Figure skating

Golf
Archery
Darts

TRACK EVENTS

TRACK FACTS

- The standard track circuit, or lap, measures 400m and has 8 lanes.

- Races up to one lap in length are run in lanes.

- Races over 110m run anti-clockwise.

SHOES

Track-racing shoes are tight-fitting, lightweight, and have a maximum of 11 spikes. Road-racing shoes do not have spikes.

Sprinting shoe

Competitors wear a singlet, or vest, and shorts.

Spikes help the shoes grip the track.

PISTOL

A starting pistol is fired into the air to signal the beginning of a race. It automatically triggers an electronic timer.

STARTING BLOCKS

Starting blocks provide the runner with a firm base from which to push off. The blocks are fixed to the track just behind the starting, or scratch, line. Starting blocks are used in races up to 400m.

Adjustable foot plates

A built-in mechanism detects false starts.

STARTING POSITIONS

The 100m and 110m hurdles have a straight start. The 200m, 400m, and 800m races are staggered. Longer races start from curved lines.

Straight start

8 7 6 5 4 3 2 1

Staggered start

OLYMPIC AND WORLD CHAMPIONSHIP TRACK EVENTS

Event		Current Olympic record	
		Male (M)	Female (F)
Sprints	100m	9.84 secs	10.49 secs
	200m	19.32 secs	21.34 secs
	400m	43.49 secs	47.6 secs
Middle distance	800m	1 min 41.11 secs	1 min 53.28 secs
	1500m	3 mins 26 secs	3 mins 50.46 secs
Long distance	3,000m	–	8 mins 6.11 secs
	5,000m	12 mins 39.36 secs	14 mins 28.09 secs
	10,000m	26 mins 22.75 secs	29 mins 31.78 secs
Relays	4x100m	37.4 secs	41.37 secs
	4x400m	2 mins 54.2 secs	3 mins 15.17 secs
Hurdles	100m	–	12.21 secs
	110m	12.91 secs	–
	400m	46.78 secs	52.61 secs
Steeplechase	3,000m	7 mins 55.72 secs	–
Marathon	42.195km	2 hrs 6 mins 5 secs	2 hrs 20 mins 47 secs
Walks	10km	–	41 mins 56.23 secs
	20km	1 hr 17 mins 25.6 secs	–
	50km	3 hrs 40 mins 57.9 secs	–

TRACK

The starting lines for the track events are shown below.

International-level tracks have a synthetic surface, usually made of plastic or rubber.

1500m

3,000m and 5,000m Back straight 3,000m steeplechase

200m

Relays, 400m, 400m hurdles

10,000m

Home straight

100m
100m hurdles

110m hurdles

Finish line: the same for all events.

800m

SPRINT

On your marks The athlete moves to the starting blocks. He presses against them with the balls of his feet. He places his hands behind the starting line.

Set The athlete raises his body forwards. He waits in this position until the starting pistol is fired.

Fire The athlete lifts his hands up. He brings his rear leg forwards while pushing his other leg against the block.

The finish
The athletes push themselves forwards at the finish. The winner is the person whose torso, or trunk, crosses the finish line first.

Chest pushed forwards

He must not move before the gun is fired, or a false start is called.

RELAY

- Each of the four team members runs one stage, or leg, of a relay.

- A baton is carried by the first runner and passed on to the next team member in a take-over zone.

- A dropped baton must be picked up by the runner who dropped it.

4 x 100M
In this relay race, an athlete stretches back his hand to take the baton from his team mate, without looking behind him.

The take-over zone measures 20m (22yd)

BATON

The baton is a smooth, hollow tube made of wood, metal, or plastic.

Baton length: 28–30cm

4 x 400M
In this relay race, an athlete will look back to receive the baton from her team mate.

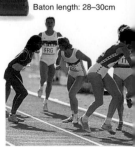

HURDLES

All races have ten hurdles in each lane.

An athlete is not disqualified for knocking down hurdles.

An athlete's rear leg must not trail around the outside of the hurdle.

TECHNIQUE
The athlete should clear each hurdle quickly and smoothly. In the 100m and 110m hurdles the athlete takes three strides between each hurdle.

Knee of lead leg is bent on approach.

Trail leg

The athlete stays in mid-flight for as short a time as possible, to minimize loss of speed.

He brings his trail leg forwards for the next stride.

Adjustable metal stand

Wooden bar is 1.2m wide.

Weights in the base of the stand keep the hurdle upright.

HURDLE HEIGHTS

Event	Height
100m (F)	0.838m
110m (M)	1.067m
400m (M)	0.914m
400m (F)	0.762m

MARATHON

• Marathons are run mainly on roads, but often start and finish in the stadium.

• Distances, in kilometres and miles, are shown to the runners during the race.

• Refreshments may be taken every 5km (3 miles).

Marathon race, 1988 Olympics

MARATHON ORIGIN

The marathon originated in 490 B.C. when a Greek messenger called Pheidippides ran 39km (24 miles) to report the Athenian victory over the Persians at the Battle of Marathon.

STEEPLECHASE

• At present, only men compete in the steeplechase.

• Athletes must make 28 jumps over hurdles and 7 over the water jump.

• Athletes can place their feet and hands on the hurdles when jumping over them.

WATER JUMP
The water jump is the fourth jump in each lap. The hurdle is the same height as the other hurdles, but sinks down into the ground on the far side.

Athletes clearing the water jump.

RACE WALKING

• A race walker must maintain unbroken contact with the ground, so his rear foot must not leave the ground until the front one has made contact.

• The leg must straighten for a moment, while the foot is on the ground.

Leg kept straight

By rotating his hips, the walker can increase the length of his stride.

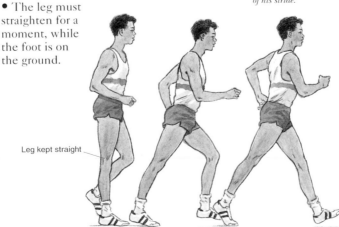

STEEPLECHASE HURDLE
These hurdles are placed on the three inside lanes of the track. They are much heavier than standard hurdles and will stand firm when struck by the athletes' feet.

Hurdle height: 91.4cm

Wooden bar is 3.96m wide

On the first lap, athletes run past the water jump.

Water jump

STEEPLECHASE TRACK
One water jump and four hurdles are placed on the three inside lanes of the track.

Roger Bannister

RECORD BREAKERS

FOUR-MINUTE MILE
was first broken in 1954 by Roger Bannister (born 1929), of Britain.

TEN-SECOND 100M
was first broken in 1968 by Jim Hines (born 1946), of the USA.

YOUNGEST INDIVIDUAL
world record breaker in athletics is Wang Yan (born 1971), of China. The 14-year-old girl set a women's 5,000m walk record at Jian, China, in 1986.

FIELD EVENTS

FIELD FACTS

• Field events include all the major athletic jumping and throwing sports.

• The Sydney games in 2000 will see women taking part in Olympic hammer and pole vault for the first time.

THROWING EVENTS

• Athletes must not touch any point outside the throwing area until their throw has landed.

• A white flag is shown for a correct attempt, a red flag signals a foul.

INFIELD
The positioning of the field areas varies from stadium to stadium, but, generally, events are held inside the track (the infield).

Shot put

Hammer and discus

Pole vault

Javelin

29° arc

40° arc

40° arc

High jump

Long jump

Triple jump

OLYMPIC THROWING EVENTS

Event	Weight	Current Olympic record
Javelin (F)	0.6kg	74.68m
Javelin (M)	0.8kg	89.66m
Discus (F)	1kg	72.30m
Discus (M)	2kg	69.40m
Shot put (F)	4kg	22.41m
Shot put (M)	7.26kg	22.47m
Hammer (M)	7.26kg	84.80m

JAVELIN

• The javelin is thrown from behind a curved line at the end of a run-up track, and must land within a 29° arc.

JAVELIN
The javelin looks like a spear. It has a long shaft, a cord grip, and a metal tip.

The length of the men's javelin is 260–270cm; the women's javelin measures 220–230cm.

THROWING THE JAVELIN
The athlete stretches his throwing arm behind him, to give him extra power. The javelin must land tip first, but it does not need to dig into the ground.

Sharply-pointed metal tip

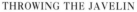

Cord grip

DISCUS

• The discus is thrown from a circle and must land within a 40° arc.

• Though any holding and throwing techniques are allowed, the discus is usually held and thrown with one hand.

DISCUS
The discus has a metal rim, with a metal weight at the

The width of the men's discus is 219–221mm; the width of the women's discus is 180–182mm.

THROWING THE DISCUS
The athlete stands with her back to the throwing area and turns one and a half times before releasing the discus.

The athlete usually takes one or two swings before starting to turn.

Her throwing arm is fully extended.

She turns one and a half times before release.

SHOT PUT

• The shot is thrown, or put, from a circle and must land within a 40° arc.

• Only one hand is used, and the put must not start from behind the line of the shoulders.

SHOT
The shot is a smooth metal ball. The men's shot is slightly larger than the women's.

PUTTING THE SHOT
The athlete puts the shot with a single pushing action. She must not let the hand holding the shot fall below its starting position.

She raises one leg and hops backwards.

Her body straightens on facing the throwing area.

She pushes the shot up and away from her.

The athlete nestles the shot under her chin.

Jesse Owens

RECORD BREAKERS

SIX WORLD RECORDS, including a long jump record of 8.13m that lasted 25 years, were set in 45 minutes by Jesse Owens (1913–80) of the USA in 1935 in Michigan, USA.

OLDEST FEMALE ATHLETE ever to win an Olympic title is Lia Manoliu (born 1932) of Romania, who was 36 years old when she won the discus at the 1968 Olympics in Mexico City.

HAMMER
The hammer is a metal ball that is attached to a handle by a length of steel wire. Although the hammer weighs the same as the men's shot, the different throwing technique means that it can travel much further.

HAMMER

• The hammer is thrown from a circle surrounded by a safety cage and must land within a 40° arc.

The hammer weighs the same as the men's shot.

THROWING THE HAMMER
The athlete throws the hammer using both hands. The head of the hammer may touch the ground during the first few swings.

The athlete turns two or three times before releasing the hammer.

OLYMPIC JUMPING EVENTS

Event	Current Olympic record
High jump (M)	2.39m
High jump (F)	2.05m
Pole vault (M)	5.92m
Long jump (M)	8.90m
Long jump (F)	7.40m
Triple jump (M)	18.09m
Triple jump (F)	15.33m

The athlete jumps backwards over the bar.

He lifts his legs clear of the bar.

COMBINED EVENTS

DECATHLON
● Men compete in the Decathlon, which covers ten events.

EVENTS

First day	Second day
100m race	110m hurdles
Long jump	Discus
Shot put	Pole vault
High jump	Javelin
400m race	1500m race

HEPTATHLON
● Women compete in the Heptathlon; it covers seven events.

EVENTS

First day	Second day
100m hurdles	Long jump
High jump	Javelin
Shot put	800m race
200m race	

MODERN PENTATHLON
● Men and women compete in the Modern Pentathlon, though only men in the Olympics; it covers five events.

EVENTS

Events
Fencing (Épée)
Freestyle swimming – 300m (M) and 200m (F)
Pistol shooting
Cross-country running – 4,000m (M) and 2,000m (F)
Riding

TRIATHLON
● Men and women compete in the Triathlon; it covers three events.

EVENTS

Course	Events		
	Swimming	Cycling	Running
Short Course	1.5km	40km	10km
Long Course	3.8km	180km	42.2km

FOSBURY FLOP
Most high-jumpers use a technique called the "Fosbury flop", in which the athlete jumps backwards over the bar.

HIGH JUMP
● The crossbar is raised for each round by a minimum of 2cm.

● The high jump has a fan-shaped run-up area.

POLE VAULT
● The crossbar is raised for each round by a minimum of 5cm.

● The pole vault has a straight run-up with a sunken box at the end.

● Poles may be of any size or material, but are usually made of fibreglass.

VAULTING OVER
The athlete must make an accurate run-up, to ensure that the pole is placed in the correct position for take-off. As he pushes off from the ground, the pole bends with the weight of his body. He levers himself over the bar, feet first.

JUMPING EVENTS
● In all jumping events, athletes may take any length of run and may place markers to help judge their approach.

The pole vaulter tucks himself under the pole until it straightens, and then rotates to come down facing the bar.

On leaving the ground, athletes may not climb the pole (by moving the lower hand above the upper hand).

LONG JUMP
● The athlete makes a straight run-up to a wooden take-off board which is sunk into the runway.

● Just beyond the take-off line is a soft substance that records foot faults.

● Jumps are measured to the nearest mark in the sand made by any part of the body.

TECHNIQUE
The athlete leaves the take-off board in an upright position. She increases the distance she travels by leaning back in mid-air before landing.

The athlete throws her legs forwards as she lands.

TRIPLE JUMP
● This event uses the same run-up and landing area as the long jump.

● The athlete must use a hop, step, and jump action.

THREE STAGES
Hop The athlete must land on the same foot that was used for take-off.

Step The athlete must land on the other foot.

Jump The athlete throws his arms and legs forwards, ready for landing.

Hop   *Step*   *Jump*

WEIGHTLIFTING

- Weightlifters compete in different classes according to their body-weight.

- There are two types of lifts: the snatch, and the clean and jerk.

- Men and women compete in weightlifting, but only men take part in Olympic events.

BAR
The weightlifting bar is made progressively heavier during each round of a competition. Discs of varying weights are loaded on to the bar, with the heaviest on the inside.

Length of bar: 2m

KIT
The weightlifter must wear a one-piece costume. He may wear a T-shirt underneath if he wishes. A wide belt may be worn to support the back.

Red (25kg)   Green (10kg)

The rubber- or plastic-covered discs are colour-coded according to weight.

Boots must give firm support and have a maximum height above the sole of 130mm.

DISC WEIGHTS
The cast-iron disc weights range from 0.25kg to 25kg. By adding a combination of discs, any weight can be added to the bar.

10kg

7.5kg (Not a current official weight)

5kg

2.5kg

1.5kg (Not a current official weight)

CLASSES OF WEIGHTLIFTING

Category	Weight (in kg)	
	Male	Female
1	54	46
2	59	50
3	64	54
4	70	59
5	76	64
6	83	70
7	91	76
8	99	83
9	108	Over 83
10	Over108	–

POWERLIFTING
Powerlifters can lift much heavier weights than weightlifters because they do not have to raise the bar above their heads.

TYPES OF POWERLIFTING
Squat The bar rests on a stand and the lifter squats below it. He must stand up and lift the bar across the shoulders.

Bench press The lifter lies on a bench with the bar resting on a stand above his chest. On the instruction "press", the lifter must push the bar up until both arms are straight.

Deadlift The competitor lifts the bar from the floor and rises to a standing position with the bar resting across the front of his thighs.

In the bench press, the athlete lifts the bar out of a stand.

The height of the bench is adjustable.

SNATCH

- The weightlifter must lift the bar in a single movement until the bar is above the head and the arms are fully extended.

- Once the bar is above his head, the weightlifter can take as much time as he needs to straighten his position (the recovery).

- On completing a lift, the weightlifter must hold the position until the referee signals to replace the bar.

The weightlifter uses chalk to help him grip the bar.

He may bend or split his legs during the lift.

He must not turn his wrists over until the bar is past head height.

He can take unlimited time over the recovery.

He must be completely still, and his arms and legs fully stretched, for the lift to be counted.

CLEAN AND JERK

- In the clean and jerk, the bar is lifted to the shoulders (the clean) and then to full arm's length overhead (the jerk).

- At the end of the clean, the lifter may rest the bar on the collarbones, chest, or fully bent arms, and may change his grip.

During the clean the lifter must not let his elbows or upper arms touch his knees or thighs.

The lifter must not let the bar touch his body until it has reached his shoulders.

Knees may be split or bent.

As in the snatch, the lifter can take any length of time over the recovery position.

RECORD BREAKERS
FIRST MAN TO CLEAN AND JERK more than three times his own body-weight was Stefan Topurov (born 1964), of Bulgaria, who lifted 180kg in Moscow, USSR, in 1983.

WEIGHTY MATTERS
Weightlifters can lift more than 2.5 times their own body-weight in the snatch, and more than 3 times their own body-weight in the clean and jerk. Powerlifters can lift more than 5 times their own body-weight.

Snatch

Clean and jerk

Powerlifting

GYMNASTICS

- The gymnast must combine acrobatic agility and muscle power with grace of movement.
- There are two Olympic events: artistic gymnastics, and rhythmic gymnastics, which is for women only.

ARTISTIC GYMNASTICS

- Gymnasts are awarded marks out of ten for their performances on various pieces of equipment.
- Women perform four types of exercise, men perform six.

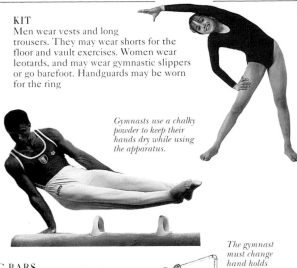

KIT
Men wear vests and long trousers. They may wear shorts for the floor and vault exercises. Women wear leotards, and may wear gymnastic slippers or go barefoot. Handguards may be worn for the ring

Gymnasts use a chalky powder to keep their hands dry while using the apparatus.

BEAM
This event is for women only. The whole routine should flow smoothly, and take between 70 and 90 seconds to complete.

Length: 5m   Height: 120cm (maximum)   Width: 10cm

The beam is made of wood and is covered with suede, which helps give the gymnast a good grip.

The gymnast walks, runs, leaps, and rolls along the beam, while keeping her balance throughout.

She will perform movements such as forward and backward somersaults, the splits, and handstands.

VAULT
Both men and women perform exercises on the vault. Women jump over the width of the vaulting horse, men jump over the length.

The horse is covered in smooth leather; it is set at different heights for male and female events.

Men's horse height: 135cm length: 160cm

Women's horse height: 120cm length: 160cm

The gymnast pushes off from the horse and performs twists or somersaults.

ASYMMETRIC BARS
This event is for women only. The gymnast must move from bar to bar using swinging and circular movements.

The whole routine should be rhythmic and continuous.

Height of higher bar: 235–240cm

Width between bars: 43cm

Height of lower bar: 140–160cm

Bars are made of wood or fibreglass.

The gymnast must change hand holds and direction constantly.

FLOOR
This event is for men and women. The women's routine is set to music and must last between 110 and 130 seconds. The men's exercise takes from 50 to 70 seconds to complete.

The gymnast performs a series of tumbling, leaping, and balancing movements, using the whole of the floor area.

RINGS
The rings are for men only. The gymnast demonstrates swinging movements, and holds positions for at least two seconds. He should not allow the rings to swing during the routine.

Steel wires   Canvas straps

Wooden rings

Height of frame: 575cm

The gymnast displays great strength in his arms and shoulders as he swings through his routine.

He holds positions such as the crucifix, or cross position.

POMMEL HORSE
This event is for men only. The gymnast supports himself above the pommel horse with his hands. He must make sure he does not touch the horse with any other part of his body.

The pommel horse is the same as the vaulting horse, but has wooden handles, or pommels, attached.

The gymnast makes continuous swinging movements with his legs.

HORIZONTAL BAR
This event is for men only. The gymnast performs continuous swings and circular movements on a steel bar which is 240cm wide and 275cm high. At least one release from the bar must be made.

PARALLEL BARS
This event is for men only. The gymnast performs swinging and balancing movements on the parallel bars. He will sometimes let go of the bars with both hands.

Adjustable wooden bars provide plenty of spring.

Length of bars: 350cm

Height: 195cm

Width between bars: 42cm

Weighted metal frame

RHYTHMIC GYMNASTICS

- Gymnasts perform routines set to music, using small, hand-held pieces of equipment, which must be kept moving at all times.
- Balletic, rather than acrobatic, movements are performed.

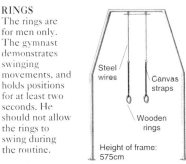

Ribbon The gymnast makes the ribbon form moving patterns in the air and on the floor.

Hoop The gymnast rotates the hoop around her, and throws and catches it.

Ball The gymnast bounces, throws, and catches the ball.

Clubs The gymnast throws, rolls, and juggles with two clubs.

Rope The gymnast jumps and skips while throwing and catching the rope.

COMBAT SPORTS

- In combat sports, competitors use either striking (e.g. boxing) or holding (e.g. judo) techniques against their opponents.

- Some combat sports, such as fencing and kendo, are armed.

GRADING SYSTEM

Contestants wear different coloured belts to show their grade. Black belt is usually the highest level reached, but there are even higher grades, awarded for length of service. A red-and-white striped belt is worn by the sixth, seventh, and eighth Dan. Very few people have ever reached ninth and tenth Dan.

Belt	Grade
	9–10th Dan
	1st–5th Dan
	1st Kyu
	2nd Kyu
	3rd Kyu
	4th Kyu
	5th Kyu

KIT
Contestants wear loose-fitting trousers, with a jacket which is held in at the waist with a cotton belt.

JUDO

- In judo ("the soft way"), competitors are judged on their throwing and holding techniques.

- A bout can last for up to 20 minutes.

White or off-white jacket and trousers are worn.

AREA
Contestants must fight within the contest area, and not step outside the danger zone.

The contest area is 9–10m x 9–10m.

Danger zone

Contest area

START
Competitors face each other at a distance of 4m and take a bow.

WEIGHT TABLE

Category	Male	Female
Bantam	under 60kg	under 48kg
Feather	under 65kg	under 52kg
Light	under 71kg	under 56kg
Light-middle	under 78kg	under 61kg
Middle	under 86kg	under 66kg
Light-heavy	under 95kg	under 72kg
Heavy	over 95kg	over 72kg

BOUT
The competitors are judged on their techniques. An outright winning technique scores an ippon (one point).

An ippon is awarded for:

Lifting the opponent above shoulder height.

A forceful throw

An effective stranglehold or arm-lock.

JUDO WORDS

Dan Leader or teacher.
Dojo Training hall.
Gake Hook or block.
Hajime Referee's call to begin.
Judo-gi Judo jacket and trousers.

Kyu Student grade.
Senshu Champion competitor.
Tsuri Lift up.
Waza-ari Half a point, awarded for a less than clean technique.

OTHER MARTIAL ARTS

Karate
Contestants aim punches and kicks at their opponents.

Aikido
Flowing movements are used to throw the opponent off balance.

Ju Jitsu
As in judo, throws and holds are used in this self-defence sport.

Kendo
Contestants in armour fight with bamboo swords.

FENCING

- In fencing, two opponents compete in a bout using one of three weapons: foil, épée, or sabre.

- A bout lasts until the agreed number of hits have been made, or until the time limit has been reached, e.g. five hits within a time limit of six minutes.

PISTE
The fencing area (piste) measures 14m x 2m.

Centre line

On-guard line

The foil

KIT
Competitors must wear white clothes that give freedom of movement and maximum protection.

A mask made of steel or plastic mesh is worn to protect the head.

In events using electronic equipment, a metallic overjacket is worn, to show when a hit has been scored.

A padded glove is worn on the sword-holding hand.

FENCING BOUT
At the start, the opponents face each other, 4m apart, at the centre of the piste. The president orders *en garde*, asks the players if they are ready, then calls *allez* to start a bout.

In the attack, the fencer threatens the target with his arm outstretched.

In the parry, the attacker's sword is deflected by the defender's sword.

WEAPONS AND TARGET AREAS

SABRE
The target area is the upper body and arms. The area must be struck with the point or with the blade edges.

Max weight: 500g
Blade length: 88cm

FOIL
The target area is the trunk only. The area must be struck with the point of the sword.

Max weight: 500g
Blade length: 90cm

EPEE
The target area is the whole body. The area must be struck with the point of the sword.

Max weight: 770g.
Blade length: 90cm

In the riposte, the defender makes a quick return thrust after the parry.

BOXING

In boxing, competitors use their gloved hands to punch each other in specific areas of the body.

Fights can be won on points, or because the opponent is counted out, retires, or is judged unfit to continue.

RING

Contests are held in a square "ring" surrounded by ropes.

Neutral corner

Red corner

Blue corner

Maximum size: 20ft square.

BOUT

The boxer must aim for the front or sides of his opponent's trunk, and the front or sides of the head. Points are given for good hits, and, in professional boxing, for defensive moves and style.

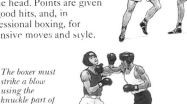

The boxer must strike a blow using the knuckle part of the glove.

KIT

Boxers wear padded, laced-up leather gloves. Professional boxers wear shorts only, amateurs wear shorts and a vest. The shorts are loose-fitting and traditionally made of satin. The "belt" of the shorts must be clearly shown by a contrasting colour, as hitting below the belt is against the rules.

Boxing boots are tall and lightweight; they provide support for the boxer's ankles and allow him to move quickly around the ring.

Amateur boxers wear headshields

Thin sole with no heel

A gumshield is worn to protect the mouth.

Hands are bandaged underneath the gloves for extra protection.

He may aim for the side of the head.

He must not hit below the waist.

Knock-down

In a knock-down, a count of ten begins. If the fallen boxer cannot rise before the count ends, he loses the fight. If he rises, and is judged by the referee to be fit to continue, the fight goes on.

BOXING WEIGHTS

Categories	Professional		Amateur
	lb	kg	kg
Mini flyweight/ straw weight	105	47.6	–
Light flyweight	108	49	48
Flyweight	112	50.8	51
Super flyweight	115	52.2	–
Bantamweight	118	53.5	54
Super bantamweight	122	55.3	–
Featherweight	126	57.2	57
Super featherweight	130	59	–
Lightweight	135	61.2	60
Light welterweight/ super lightweight	140	63.5	63.5
Welterweight	147	66.7	67
Super welterweight/ Light middleweight	154	70	71
Middleweight	160	72.6	75
Super middleweight	168	70.2	–
Light heavyweight	175	79.4	81
Cruiserweight	190	86.2	–
Heavyweight	over 190	over 86	91
Super heavyweight	–	–	over 91

FIGHTING FIT

The longest boxing fight on record lasted 7 hours, 19 minutes and was held in New Orleans, USA, in 1893. Andy Bowen fought Jack Burke over 110 rounds, and the match was finally declared a draw.

WRESTLING

• There are two Olympic wrestling events: freestyle and Greco-Roman.

• Points are awarded for successful moves and holds.

KIT

Wrestlers wear one-piece leotards that leave upper chest and shoulders bare. One competitor wears red, and the other blue. Wrestlers must not oil or grease their bodies.

Wrestling boots are tall and lightweight, have no heels, rings, or buckles.

FALL

The main aim in wrestling is to achieve a "fall", by forcing the opponent's shoulder blades onto the mat for one second, or for as long as it takes the referee to say to himself *tomber* (French for fall).

• In Greco-Roman contests, wrestlers must not use their legs or grip an opponent below the hips.

MAT

The contest circle, which includes the red band, is 9m in diameter.

Red corner

Wrestling surface

Blue corner

WRESTLING WEIGHTS

Category	Weight limits in kg
1	48
2	52
3	57
4	62
5	68
6	74
7	82
8	90
9	100
10	130

SUMO WRESTLING

• Ritual and tradition play an important part in Sumo wrestling.

• Bouts are won by pushing an opponent out of the ring, or by making him touch the ground with any part of his body other than the soles of his feet.

• Pushes, slaps, and holds are the main techniques.

Rice is thrown up at the beginning of the bout.

A loincloth is worn wrapped around the waist and between the legs.

SUMO GRADINGS

Sumo wrestlers are graded according to skill, not weight. There are ten grades:

Jonokuchi Novice
Jonidan Qualified
Sandanme Lower junior
Makushita Leading junior
Juryo Contender
Maegashira Senior

Komusubi Second grade junior champion
Sekiwake Junior champion
Ozeki Champion
Yokozuna Grand champion

HEAVY WEIGHTS

The heaviest Sumo wrestler weighs 250kg (551lb): equal to the total average weight of four teenage boys. This is about twice the weight of the heaviest world champion boxer, and almost twice the maximum weight permitted for an Olympic wrestler.

Boxer

Wrestler

Sumo wrestler

COURT GAMES

TENNIS

• The aim is to hit a ball over the net with a racket so that it lands inside the court, and cannot be returned.

• A match is divided into sets and ends when one player has won three sets (for men) or two sets (for women).

• Each set is divided into games, and a player must win at least six games, and have a two-game lead, to win a set.

• A tie-break is used if the set reaches six-all: the first player to score seven or more points, with a two-point lead, wins.

• A match lasts for a maximum of five sets for men and three sets for women.

SCORING A GAME

After scoring 4 points a player wins a game. But, if the players level at 3 points each (that is, 40-all, or *deuce*), play continues until one player has a 2-point lead.

SCORING A GAME

Points	Score
0	love
1	15
2	30
3	40

Martina Navratilova

RECORD BREAKERS

RECORD NUMBER OF WIMBLEDON SINGLES TITLES held is nine, by Martina Navratilova, USA (born in the former Czechoslovakia in 1956).
MOST SINGLES CHAMPIONSHIPS won in grand slam tournaments is 24, by Margaret Court, Australia (born 1942).
YOUNGEST MALE CHAMPION at Wimbledon is Boris Becker, Germany (born 1967), who won the singles title in 1985, aged 17.

KIT

Traditionally, clothing is white, though today the only professional tournament that insists on mostly white is Wimbledon, England. The kit, which is similar in all court sports, is a shirt and shorts for men, and a shirt and skirt, or a dress, for women.

Wristbands are worn for wiping the forehead and keeping palms dry.

Rubber-soled shoes

Socks are cushioned to protect soles and heels.

SERVING

The player serves behind the baseline. He throws the ball in the air and hits it before it touches the ground. The ball must pass over the net without bouncing and touch ground in the opposing service court.

PLAYING

The player receiving the serve must let the ball bounce once before returning it. A return is still good if the ball touches the net or passes outside the net post, so long as it lands in the opposing player's half of the court.

The shoulders turn as the racket swings back.

Knees are bent.

COURT

Tennis can be played indoors and outdoors. The court surface may be grass, wood, clay, or artificial.

Baseline

Height of net: 3ft 6in

Doubles sideline

Left service court

Right service court

Centre line

Length of court: 78ft

Singles sideline

The maximum length and width of the strung surface is 15.5in x 11.5in.

RACKET

Tennis racket frames are made from wood, metal, or a combination of materials.

Maximum length and width of the whole racket is 32in x 12.5in.

BALL

Tennis balls are yellow or white. They weigh about 2oz.

The ball is thrown up and to the right of the leading shoulder.

The racket arm is bent back behind the neck.

The racket arm is fully outstretched when hitting the ball.

The weight is thrown forwards.

In the follow through, the racket arm comes across the body.

Forehand drive

This is the most natural basic groundstroke in the game. A right-handed player plays it on his right side.

The racket is swung forwards to meet the ball.

Backhand drive

This basic stroke is less instinctive than the forehand drive. A right-handed player plays it on his left side.

The leading shoulder is turned away from the ball.

The ball is hit once it is to the front of the right foot.

In the follow through, the racket arm is fully extended.

The weight is put on to the front foot.

GRAND SLAM

Players who achieve the "grand slam" hold, all at the same time, the singles titles at these four major tournaments.

Tournament	Place	Surface
Wimbledon	London, England	Grass
United States Open	Flushing Meadow, New York, USA	Artificial material
Australian Open	Flinders Park, Melbourne, Australia	Synthetic grass
French Open	Roland Garros stadium, Paris, France	Clay

TENNIS WORDS

Ace A service beyond the reach of the receiver.
Advantage The first point scored after deuce.
Let A point that is played again.
Not up The ball has bounced twice before being hit.

Rally A long series of hits.
Seedings List showing where a player is expected to finish in a tournament.
Straight-sets Winning the match without losing a set.

BADMINTON

- In badminton, players hit a shuttlecock over a high net.

- In doubles and men's singles, the first side to score 15 points is the winner; in women's singles, it is the first player to score 11 points.

- Usually, a match is decided by the best of three games.

COURT

Short service line
Left service court
Right service court
Length of court: 44ft
Height of net: 5ft
Width of court: 20ft
Long service line for singles
Long service line for doubles

SHUTTLECOCK
At top-class level, the shuttlecock is made of a "skirt" of 14–16 goose feathers fixed in a cork base.

RACKET
These are usually made of metal or carbon fibre, and strung with gut.

SERVING
The player serves underarm and must hit the shuttlecock below waist level. If it is not returned, it must land within the service court diagonally opposite. Only the server can score points.

Arm is bent, and the racket held behind the shoulder.

Racket is angled downwards.

PLAYING
The receiver must return the shuttle over the net before it touches ground in the serving court. Most badminton shots are played overhead.

Racket is raised directly upwards.

The arm straightens on making contact with the shuttlecock.

Grip should be relaxed, not too tight, but not too loose.

TABLE TENNIS

- In this indoor game, the players use rackets, or bats, to hit a hollow ball across a table over a low net.

- The first side to score 21 points wins the game, but if the score reaches 20-all, the game continues until one side has a 2-point lead.

- A match is decided by the best of five games (for men), or three games (for women).

BAT
Originally, bats were made of wood only. The pimpled rubber face was added in the 1920s to allow players to give the ball spin.

Pimpled rubber

TABLE
The chipboard top is usually dark green.

Width: 1.52m
Height of net: 15.25cm
Length: 2.74m
Height: 76cm

BALL
The lightweight plastic ball is either white or yellow.

SERVING
The ball must be thrown vertically at least 16cm from the flat palm of the hand, and the ball must not spin. At the moment of striking, the racket must be behind the end of the table. The ball must bounce on the server's side first.

The ball is hit as it begins to fall.

GRIPS
There are two main grips used in table tennis.

Handshake grip
The bat is held as though the player is shaking hands.

Penholder grip
The bat is held as though the player is holding a pen.

SQUASH

- Squash is played using all four walls of an enclosed court.

- The ball is hit against the front wall first and must be returned before it has bounced twice on the floor.

- A match consists of the best of five games; the winner of a game is the first to nine points.

RACKET
The head of a squash racket is smaller and rounder than that of a badminton or tennis racket.

BALL
There are four varieties of squash ball: the slower balls are used in hot conditions, and the faster balls are used in cold conditions.

Yellow dot: very slow
White dot: slow
Red dot: fast
Blue dot: very fast

Out-of-court line
Cut line
Length: 32ft
Service box
Width: 21ft

COURT
The white, concrete walls of a squash court must be completely smooth. In tournaments, courts are often made of glass and Perspex, so that spectators can watch the match from all sides of the court. In the USA, squash is played on a narrower court with a harder ball.

SERVING
The player must stand with at least one foot in the service box, throw the ball into the air, and hit it at the first attempt. The ball must hit the front wall above the cut line, but below the out-of-court line, without bouncing elsewhere first.

The server can use any kind of stroke.

JAI ALAI

- In the fast court game of Jai alai, or Pelota, players use wicker baskets, called *cestas*, in place of rackets. The court is long and narrow and has three playing walls.

The player wears a rubber glove which is sewn on to the cesta.

RACQUETBALL

In racquetball, players use a short-handled racquet and a hollow rubber ball. The ball can be hit against the ceiling, as well as all four walls of the court.

The fast game of racquetball is similar in many ways to squash.

TOP BALL SPEEDS

Jai alai	302km/h (188mph)
Squash	232km/h (144mph)
Tennis	222km/h (138mph)
Badminton	200km/h (124mph)
Table tennis	170km/h (106mph)

BASKETBALL

FACTS

- The aim of basketball is to throw the ball into a basket at the opponent's end of the court.

- There are ten players in each team; only five are on the court at any one time.

- Players may throw and bounce the ball, but must not carry or kick it.

- A game consists of two halves of 20 minutes each.

KIT
Players wear brightly coloured singlets and shorts. Singlets have large numbers on the front and back.

Backboard

The rim of the net is 3.05m off the ground.

COURT
The dimensions given for this court are based on international rules. In the USA, the courts are slightly bigger.

Free-throw line.

Length: 28m

Three points are awarded for goals scored outside the semicircle.

Two points are awarded for goals scored inside the semicircle.

End line

Width: 15m

TIME RULES

Time limit	Action
3 seconds	A player may remain in the restricted area between his opponent's end line and the free-throw line.
5 seconds	A player may hold on to the ball.
10 seconds	The team with the ball must move from the back court to the front court.
30 seconds	The team with the ball must try for a goal.

BALL
The ball is made of rubber encased in leather, rubber, or synthetic material.

The high, padded sides of basketball boots give firm support.

BASKETBALL WORLD CHAMPIONS

Year	Men	Year	Women
1954	USA	1957	USA
1959	Brazil	1959	USSR
1963	Brazil	1964	USSR
1967	USSR	1967	USSR
1970	Yugoslavia	1971	USSR
1974	USSR	1975	USSR
1978	Yugoslavia	1979	USA
1982	USSR	1983	USSR
1986	USA	1986	USA
1990	Yugoslavia	1990	USA
1994	USA	1994	Brazil
1998	Yugoslavia	1998	USA

STARTING JUMP
At the beginning of a match, the referee throws the ball up and two opponents jump to hit it. A player may tap the ball twice after it has reached its highest point.

The player stands near the centre line, in his own half of the court.

SHOOTING
When attempting to score a goal, a player holds the ball high above his head and throws it towards the net.

MOVING WITH THE BALL
A player who has stopped while holding the ball may pivot on one foot, at the same time stepping in any direction with the other foot. A moving player may take one stride with the ball.

DRIBBLING
A player can progress with the ball by dribbling. He can take as many steps as he wishes while bouncing the ball.

VOLLEYBALL

- Volleyball is a ball game played between two teams of six players each.

- The aim of volleyball is to use any part of the body above the waist to send a ball over a net, so that the opposing team are unable to return it.

- A team may touch the ball up to three times before returning it over the net.

Length of court: 18m

Height of net: 1m

Width of court: 9m

UP AND OVER
Because of the height of the net, players have to jump up high in the air to hit the ball. Players must not touch or reach over the net. The ball is smaller than a basketball or netball.

NETBALL

- The aim in netball is to throw the ball into the opponent's net.

- The game is played between two teams of seven players each.

- Each player must keep to a particular area of the court.

NETBALL POSITIONS
Players wear letters to indicate their positions, and to show which zone they should stay in.

WA Wing attack

GS Goal shooter

GA Goal attack

WD Wing defence

C Centre

GD Goal defence

GK Goalkeeper

HANDBALL

- The aim is to pass or dribble the ball with the hands until a goal is scored.

- It is played between two teams of seven players each.

- Players may take three steps when holding the ball.

The player must not hold on to the ball for longer than three seconds.

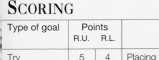

RUGBY

FACTS

- The aim of rugby is to score points by placing an oval-shaped ball on or over the opponent's goal line (a try), or by kicking it over the opponent's crossbar.

- Players may carry, pass, or kick the ball, but they cannot throw the ball in front of them.

- A game consists of two halves of 40 minutes each.

- There are two types of rugby: Rugby Union (R.U.), and Rugby League (R.L.).

SCORING

Type of goal	Points R.U.	R.L.	Action
Try	5	4	Placing the ball by hand on or over the goal line.
Dropped goal	3	1	Ball is dropped and kicked over the crossbar.
Penalty goal	3	2	A penalty kick awarded for a foul.
Conversion	2	2	A goal kick awarded after a try.

PASSING THE BALL

A player can run while holding the ball, but must not pass forwards. He should, however, pass to the front of the receiving player, to enable the player to run on to the ball.

Correct throw

Foul throw

LINE-OUT

A line-out is used to restart play after a ball crosses the touchline, or is "in-touch". At least two players from each team form separate lines at right angles to the touchline. The ball must be thrown straight between the two lines of players.

RUGBY LEAGUE

- This game developed from Rugby Union, and is played by professionals and amateurs.

- It is played by two teams of 13 players each.

- Rugby League, although very similar, follows slightly different rules to Rugby Union.

- One difference is that in Rugby League, players can restart the game after a tackle with the "play the ball" rule.

RUGBY UNION

- Rugby Union is the earliest and most widely played form of rugby.

- The game is traditionally played by amateurs (15 per team), but players can now also receive payment.

BALL

The oval-shaped ball is usually made of leather.

Length: 28cm

KIT

Although rugby is a tough game, players are not allowed to wear protective clothing, apart from a scrum cap made of soft leather, shin guards, and a gum shield. Sweat bands are also often worn.

BOOTS

Players may wear shoes similar to those worn by soccer players, or high-sided boots to support the ankles.

PITCH

The pitch usually has a grass surface, but may be made of clay or sand.

22m line

Length of pitch between the goal lines: 100m

Goal line

Dead ball line

Width of pitch: 69m

5m line

10m line

Halfway line

The goal is 5.6m wide; the height of the crossbar is 3m.

SCRUM

Players from both teams close up around the ball and link arms. The front row must be made up of three players: a "hooker" and two "props" who stand on each side of him. The ball is thrown into the scrum and the hooker will try to hook the ball to his team mates behind him.

A scrum is used to restart play, usually after a foul.

The scrum must not break up until the ball is cleared.

OLYMPIC RUGBY

Rugby was last staged at the Olympics in 1924, in Paris. There were three entrants: Romania, USA, and France. USA won the gold medal.

PLAY THE BALL RULE

A tackled player is allowed to drop the ball before kicking it in any direction, usually to a team mate behind him. This may be done for five consecutive tackles. After the sixth tackle, the team must give up possession.

Two members of the opposing team may stand directly in front of the player with the ball.

INTERNATIONAL RUGBY TEAMS

Each major international rugby team has its own symbol.

Australia

England

France

Ireland

New Zealand

Scotland

South Africa

Wales

RUGBY WORDS

Backs Players who position themselves behind a scrum.

Dummy Pretending to pass the ball to another player, while keeping possession.

Dropped goal Dropping the ball and kicking it over the cross bar after it touches the ground.

Goal Combination of a try and conversion.

Knock-on The ball bouncing forward off the hand or arm of a player.

Mark Place at which a free-kick or penalty kick is given.

Maul A scrum around a player carrying the ball.

Punt Dropping the ball and kicking it before it touches the ground.

Ruck A scrum around a player who has dropped the ball.

Touch-down A player grounding the ball in his own in-goal area.

Up-and-under A ball kicked high in the air, while players run upfield to catch it.

FOOTBALL

SOCCER

- Soccer, or Association football, is a ball game played by two teams of 11 players each.

- The aim is to hit the ball into the opponent's goal, and the team that scores the most goals wins.

- Players use their feet, head, thighs, and chest to hit or control the ball; only the goalkeeper may touch the ball with his hands or arms.

- A game consists of two periods, or halves, of 45 minutes each.

FORMATIONS
Soccer is a flexible game, but most teams start with players in a particular formation. The one shown below is 4–3–3. It uses four defenders, three midfielders, and three in attack.

The 4–3–3 formation

KIT
Players wear jerseys with numbers on the back. The soles of the boots may be fitted with studs or bars.

Soccer boot

Fat rubber studs for hard ground.

Aluminium for wet, slippery ground.

Nylon for soft ground.

Shin pads must be worn under socks.

Footballs used in top-class play are made of rubber encased in leather.

DRIBBLING
When dribbling, the player keeps the ball close to his feet, to prevent an opposing player taking the ball from him.

The player keeps close control of the ball while approaching his opponent.

In order to get round him, the player may pretend to go one way.

He then confuses his opponent by turning to go in the opposite direction.

PITCH

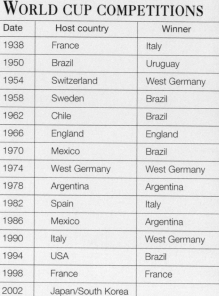

Width: 50-100yd

Centre circle

Length: 100–130yd

Penalty mark

Penalty area

Goal area

Goal line

Goalpost length: 8yd; height: 8ft

WORLD CUP COMPETITIONS

Date	Host country	Winner
1938	France	Italy
1950	Brazil	Uruguay
1954	Switzerland	West Germany
1958	Sweden	Brazil
1962	Chile	Brazil
1966	England	England
1970	Mexico	Brazil
1974	West Germany	West Germany
1978	Argentina	Argentina
1982	Spain	Italy
1986	Mexico	Argentina
1990	Italy	West Germany
1994	USA	Brazil
1998	France	France
2002	Japan/South Korea	

DEFENDING
A defender will often mark, or follow, one opponent throughout the game. Defenders must make strong tackles in order to take possession of the ball from their opponents.

Good timing is essential for a clean sliding tackle.

The defender must be careful not to foul his opponent.

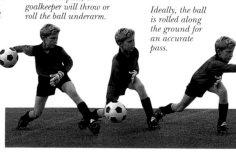

GOALKEEPING
The goalkeeper can touch the ball with his hands, but only within his own penalty area. He is not allowed to pick up a back pass from a team mate.

He slides down in front of his opponent and wins the ball.

For a short pass, a goalkeeper will throw or roll the ball underarm.

Ideally, the ball is rolled along the ground for an accurate pass.

GOAL SCORING
Any player in a team may score a goal, but the main goal-scorers are called strikers, who must be able to shoot and head the ball accurately.

Opportunist sliding shot into goal.

MAJOR TEAMS
These are the basic colours worn by some of the top international teams. The flags are not part of the kits.

Argentina Belgium Brazil Bulgaria Cameroon Colombia Denmark England France Germany Republic of Ireland

Italy Mexico Netherlands Nigeria Norway Poland Spain Sweden Switzerland Romania Uruguay USA

AMERICAN FOOTBALL

- American football is played by two teams of 11 players each, though frequent substitution is allowed, and up to 40 people can play for each team.

- A team earns points by making a touchdown (putting the ball behind the opposing team's goal line), or by kicking the ball between the goal posts.

- A game consists of four quarters, of 15 minutes each.

GRIDIRON
The field is commonly called the gridiron, because the lines make it look like a cooking grill. The field is marked out in yards to show how far a team has advanced.

End line
End zone
Yardline every 5 yds
Goal line
Length: 360ft
Height of crossbar: 10ft
Width of goal: 18ft 6in
Width: 160ft

KIT
There is a lot of physical contact in American football, and players wear several layers of protective clothing.

Chest protector
Groin protector
Shoulder pads
Leg pads
Helmets are made of tough plastic.
Face mask
Tight, knee-length trousers lace up at the front.

BALL

The oval-shaped ball is made of leather, and has laces and a pebbled finish to provide a good grip.

FOOTBALL LEAGUE
American football is the USA's major national sport. There are 28 teams in the National Football League (NFL), each with its own distinctive helmet design.

Atlanta Falcons

Buffalo Bills	*Chicago Bears*	*Cincinnati Bengals*
Cleveland Browns	*Dallas Cowboys*	*Denver Broncos*
Detroit Lions	*Green Bay Packers*	*Houston Oilers*
Indianapolis Colts	*Kansas City Chiefs*	*Oakland Raiders*
The Rams	*Miami Dolphins*	*Minnesota Vikings*
New England Patriots	*New Orleans Saints*	*New York Giants*
New York Jets	*Pittsburgh Steelers*	*Philadelphia Eagles*
Arizona Cardinals	*San Diego Chargers*	*San Francisco Forty-niners*
Seattle Seahawks	*Tampa Bay Buccaneers*	*Washington Redskins*

SHIRT NUMBERS
NFL players are numbered according to their positions.

Number	Position
1-19	Quarterbacks, punters, kickers
20-49	Running and defensive backs
50-59	Centres and linebackers
60-79	Defensive linemen, offensive guards, and tackles
80-89	Wide receivers and tight ends
90-99	Defensive linemen

OFFENCE
The team that is in possession of the ball is the offence, or attacking team. They are allowed four attempts, or downs, at advancing with the ball by at least 10yd. If they fail to do this, their opponents gain possession of the ball.

The snap is the start of the down.

BLOCKING
A blocker may use the upper part of his body to obstruct an opponent who does not have the ball. He may use his arms to push, but not grab hold of, him. Blocking is used by offensive and defensive players.

DEFENCE
The team that does not have the ball uses its defence players, usually the biggest men, to try to prevent the offence from advancing and scoring. A defender needs to be a good tackler. He is allowed to push, pull, or grab the person in possession of the ball, who is called the runner. If the defence manages to get hold of the ball, it is called a turnover, and possession changes to the other team.

SCORING

Score	Points	Action
Touchdown	6	Taking the ball across the opponent's goal line, or gaining possession within the opponents' end zone.
Field goal	3	Place-kicking the ball through the goal posts.
Safety	2	Tackling an opponent who is carrying the ball behind his own goal line.
Extra point (conversion)	1 or 2	A goal kick (1) or a pass into the end zone (2), after scoring a touchdown.

AUSTRALIAN FOOTBALL

- The game is played by two teams of 18 players. The aim is to score goals by kicking an oval-shaped ball between two tall posts.

- A player can kick, punch, and run with the ball, but he must not throw it.

- A game consists of 4 quarters, lasting 20 minutes each.

PLAYING FIELD
The game is played on an oval-shaped playing field. Six points are scored for kicking the ball between the two central "goal" posts.

One point is given for scoring between the outer, or "behind" posts.

CRICKET

FACTS

- Cricket is a ball game played by two teams of 11 players each.

- The teams take it in turns to bat and field.

- During each "innings", the batting side aims to score runs between two wickets; the fielding side aims to get the batting side out.

- A match consists of one or two innings per side.

KIT
Traditionally, cricketers wear white or cream shirts, trousers, and a sweater. Coloured clothing is worn during some one-day matches.

FIELD
The playing field surrounding the pitch can be any length. Below are the major fielding positions for a right-handed batsman.

The onside, or legside, is the side of the field behind the batsman as he stands waiting to receive a delivery; the offside is the area to the front of the batsman.

Batsmen and close fielders wear protective helmets made of metal or fibreglass.

Batting gloves give good protection, while allowing the batsman to grip and wield the bat.

Protective box

Shoes have spiked or rubber soles.

Leg pads are worn by batsmen and wicketkeepers.

WICKET
This has three stumps along which two bails are placed.

Bails

Width of wicket: 9in

BAT
The bat is made of willow, and has a cane handle covered with rubber.

Maximum length of bat: 3ft 2in

BALL
A cricket ball is made of layers of cork and wool, covered in red leather.

Wicketkeeper's gloves are heavily padded and are larger than batsmen's gloves.

Fielding positions:
Sightscreen, Long leg, Deep fine leg, Fine leg, Backward short leg, Third man, Leg slip, Short square leg, Deep square leg, Wicketkeeper, Square leg, Backward point, Gully, Slips, Batsman, Boundary line, Point, Silly point, Forward short leg, Mid wicket, Deep mid wicket, Silly mid off, Silly mid on, Short extra cover, Mid wicket, Cover, Extra cover, Bowler, Mid on, Deep extra cover, Mid off, Long on, Long off, Offside, Onside

PITCH
The pitch is the area between the two wickets, which are placed 66ft apart.

Popping crease
Bowling crease
Return crease

SCORING

Runs	Action
1 each	One run: every time the two batsmen pass other and reach the opposite wicket.
1	No ball: bowler steps outside the batting creases or throws, rather than bowls, the ball.
1	Wide: a delivery is too high or wide of the stumps for the batsman to play the ball.
4	The ball reaches the boundary after touching the ground.
6	The ball reaches the boundary without touching the ground.

DISMISSING THE BATSMAN
Bowled The ball breaks the striker's wicket.
Caught A fielder catches the ball after it has hit the batsman's bat or gloves.
Run out The wicket is broken by the fielding team before the batsman reaches the popping crease.
Leg Before Wicket (lbw) The batsman obstructs a delivery that would otherwise have touched the wicket, without previously playing the ball with his bat.
Stumped The wicketkeeper breaks the batsman's wicket while the batsman is outside his ground when receiving a ball.
Hit wicket The batsman breaks his wicket while playing a shot.

RECORD BREAKERS
MOST WICKETS
taken is 19 for 90 runs by Jim Laker (1922–86) for England against Australia in 1956.

FIRST BATSMAN TO SCORE SIX SIXES
in one over was Sir Garfield Sobers, West Indies (born 1936), for Nottinghamshire against Glamorgan, at Swansea, Wales, in 1968.

BOWLING

- Bowlers take it in turns to bowl "overs" of six (or eight) balls at alternate wickets.

- They must have part of the front foot behind the popping crease while making a delivery.

BOWLED OVER
Bowlers often rub the ball on their trousers to make the ball shiny on one side. This gives the ball extra swing, or movement, in mid-air. Bowlers use various techniques to achieve results. While a fast bowler uses speed and swing, a spin bowler will depend on spin to confuse the batsman.

The ball must be bowled with a straight arm, not thrown.

BATTING

- The aim of the batsman is to guard his wicket and to make runs.

BATTING STEADY
The batsman holds the bat with both hands. He must be able to read a delivery well, keep his eye firmly on the ball, and decide in an instant how to play the stroke.

In this forward defensive stroke, the batsman brings his left leg forwards.

The stroke is controlled with his left arm.

CRICKET WORDS
Bouncer A fast delivery, pitched short, that reaches the batsman at shoulder height or above.
Bye Run made when the ball passes the wicket untouched by the bat.
Close field Fielders close to the batsman.
Deep Part of the field near the boundary.
Delivery A bowled ball.
Duck A zero score.
Extras Runs made without the bat.
Follow-on The team batting second may be asked to bat again if their total falls short of their opponent's.
Leg-bye Run made when the ball is unintentionally deflected off the batsman's body in the process of playing a stroke.
Maiden over An over in which no runs are scored.

BASEBALL

FACTS

- Ball game played by two teams of nine players each.

- The game is similar to cricket in that teams take it in turns to bat and field.

- The aim of the batting side is to score runs around the four bases.

- A match consists of nine innings.

Catcher

Hard plastic helmet

Face mask

Padded chest-protector

Knee and shin guards

Batter

KIT

Players must not wear any emblems that may be mistaken for a baseball. The numbers on each shirt must be at least 6in high. The catcher wears more protective clothing than any other player.

Maximum length: 42in

BAT

Bats are made of wood, for top-class play, or aluminium. The barrel must be smooth and well rounded.

BALL

The ball is made of cork or rubber and is covered in cowhide or horsehide.

Each fielder wears a large leather glove.

The catcher's face mask is made of thick wire and foam padding.

Outfield

Second base

Third base

Infield

Pitcher's mound

First base

Home base, or home plate

FIELD

The playing field is made up of an infield and outfield, known as fair territory; any other area is foul territory.

MAJOR LEAGUES

There are two major baseball leagues in the USA. Each team has its own symbol.

AMERICAN LEAGUE

 Baltimore Orioles

 Boston Red Sox

California Angels

Chicago White Sox

Cleveland Indians

Detroit Tigers

Kansas City Royals

Milwaukee Brewers

Minnesota Twins

New York Yankees

Oakland Athletics

Seattle Mariners

Texas Rangers

Toronto Blue Jays

NATIONAL LEAGUE

 Atlanta Braves

Chicago Cubs

Cincinnati Reds

Colorado Rockies

Florida Marlins

 Houston Astros

Los Angeles Dodgers

Montreal Expos

New York Mets

Philadelphia Phillies

Pittsburgh Pirates

 St. Louis Cardinals

San Diego Padres

San Francisco Giants

PITCHING

- The pitcher tries to throw the ball through the strike zone; he must not pitch the ball directly at the batter.

- He may rub the ball with his hands, but must not shine it on his clothes, or rub it on the ground.

- He may throw the ball to a base before he pitches.

Pitchers can throw the ball at speeds of more than 145km/h (90mph).

BATTING

- The batter must stay within the batter's box on receiving the ball.

- Each ball, or pitch, delivered to the batter is either a strike or a ball.

STRIKE ZONE

This is the area over home plate and between the batter's armpits and knees. If the ball falls inside this zone and the batter fails to hit it, it is a strike. A ball is called when a pitch, thrown outside the strike zone, is not struck at by the batter. After four balls, the batter may walk to first base.

The blue balls indicate a strike.

The red balls indicate a ball.

RUNNING

- If a runner is approaching a base that already has a runner on it, then that runner must go on to the next base (force play).

- A runner must touch base before the fielder touches him or the base with the ball.

- A runner may run to a base while the ball is being pitched to a batter (a steal).

PUTTING OUT THE BATTER

Batted ball is caught before it bounces by a fielder.

Catcher catches the third strike and tags the batter or he throws the ball to first base.

Batter taps, or bunts, the ball down in front of him into foul territory; only the first two fouls count as strikes.

Batter strikes the ball three times, and is tagged before reaching first base.

RECORD BREAKERS

A PERFECT NINE INNINGS GAME (which means the pitcher allows the opposition no hits, no runs, and does not allow a player to reach first base) was first achieved by Lee Richmond (1857–1929) of the USA for Worcester against Cleveland in 1880.

MOST HOME RUNS

in a season is 61 by Roger Maris (1934–85) of the USA, for the New York Yankees in 1961. This beat the record of 60 that Babe Ruth (1895–1945) of the USA set in 1927.

STICK GAMES

HOCKEY

- Hockey is an 11-a-side game; the aim is to shoot a ball with hooked sticks into the opposing team's goal.

- Goals may be scored only from within the striking, or shooting, circle.

- A game consists of two 35-minute halves.

STICK
Hockey sticks are steam bent, so that the grain of the wood follows the bend. This helps to strengthen the stick. The ball may be struck with the flat face of the stick only.

The stick weighs between 12oz and 28oz for men, and up to 23oz for women.

BALL
The ball is traditionally white and is made of cork and twine, with a leather casing.

BULLY
The bully is a distinctive feature of hockey. It is used to restart the game after certain stoppages. A player from each side stands over the ball. They tap the ground and each other's sticks alternately three times before attempting to play the ball.

KIT
Players wear a shirt or shorts, or skirt (women) and guards on their shins and ankles. The goalkeeper wears extra protective clothing.

Helmet with face mask

Shoulder and elbow pads

Padded gauntlets

Light-weight leg guards

"Kickers" are worn over boots to protect the feet when kicking the hard ball.

Goalkeeper's kit

PITCH
Hockey is usually played outdoors, on grass or on artificial surfaces.

Width: 60yd

Length: 100yd

Goal height: 7ft
Goal width: 12ft

Shooting circle; goals can only be scored from inside here.

ICE-HOCKEY

- Ice-hockey is played six-a-side, with up to 14 substitutes.

- There are three periods, of 20 minutes each.

- Women's ice-hockey became an Olympic sport in 1998, at Nagano.

Puck is traditionally black and made from toughened rubber.

Width: 29–30m

Length: 60–61m

Goalkeeper's stick

Out-fielder's stick

ICE-HOCKEY STICKS
The out-fielder's stick has a shaft with an angled blade. The goalkeeper's stick is heavier and has a wider blade.

There are four face-off circles.

Goal width: 2.53m
Goal height: 1.22m

RINK
The rink is an iced surface surrounded by wooden boards.

LACROSSE

- Players use a net on the end of their stick (crosse) to carry and pass a ball and try to send it into the opposing team's goal.

- The men's and women's games are played under different rules. One of the main differences is that physical contact is allowed in the men's game, but not in the women's.

Women's lacrosse

LACROSSE RULES

Men's lacrosse	Women's lacrosse
10 players a-side; nine substitutes allowed.	12 players a-side; one substitute allowed.
Shoulder-to-shoulder contact and body-checking allowed.	No physical contact allowed.
Time: four 15-min periods.	Time: two 25-min periods.
Playing field usually measures 100m x 55m.	No measured boundaries.
Crosse measures: 1–1.8m.	Crosse measures: 0.9–1.1m.

OLYMPIC HOCKEY CHAMPIONS (MEN)

Year	Country
1920	Britain
1928	India
1932	India
1936	India
1948	India
1952	India
1956	India
1960	Pakistan
1964	India
1968	Pakistan
1972	West Germany
1976	New Zealand
1980	India
1984	Pakistan
1988	Britain
1992	Germany
1996	Netherlands

OLYMPIC HOCKEY CHAMPIONS (WOMEN)

Year	Country
1984	Netherlands
1988	Australia
1992	Spain
1996	Australia

ICE-HOCKEY PENALTIES

Type	Minutes in "Sin Bin"
Minor	2
Major	5
Misconduct	10*
Match	Rest of game**

*Substitute may replace immediately.
**Substitute may replace after 5 minutes.

OLYMPIC ICE-HOCKEY CHAMPIONS

Year	Country
1924	Canada
1928	Canada
1932	Canada
1936	Britain
1948	Canada
1952	Canada
1956	USSR
1960	USA
1964	USSR
1968	USSR
1972	USSR
1976	USSR
1980	USA
1984	USSR
1988	USSR
1992	CIS
1994	Sweden
1998	Czech Republic

HOCKEY SPEEDS
Ice-hockey is the fastest team game in the world. The puck is hit at speeds of up to 190km (118 miles) per hour. A hockey ball is hit at speeds of up to 160km (100 miles) per hour.

GOLF

FACTS

- A standard golf course has 18 holes of various lengths.

- There are two main types of competition: stroke play and match play.

- In stroke play, the player who completes a round in the fewest strokes wins the match; in match play the winner is the one who wins the most holes in a round.

Club-head cover

Score card

KIT
Comfortable clothes that allow the golfer to stretch and swing with ease are ideal.

Spike-studded shoes give a secure footing.

SWING TECHNIQUE
The swing is one continuous, smooth action.

The upper body turns as the arms swing up and back (the backswing).

As the club is brought down, the weight is moved from the back foot to the front foot.

Weight is fully on the left foot as the swing is followed through.

Wood
Woods are used for long shots. They are numbered 1–9. Their large heads may be made from wood, plastic, or light metal.

CLUBS
Players may not start or play a round of golf with more than 14 clubs. Most players use three or four woods, nine or ten irons, and one putter.

BAG
Beginners use a lightweight bag to carry a half set (seven clubs). Players with a full set of clubs use a trolley or have a caddy to assist them.

Bag stand   **Umbrella**

Iron
Irons are used for a variety of shots. The steel heads are numbered 1–10. The lower numbers hit the ball furthest and lowest.

Putter
Putters are used mainly on the putting green. Unlike the other clubs, they have two striking faces. They are the lightest of the clubs.

BALL
Golf balls are covered in more than 400 dimples. They help the ball travel further and straighter through the air.

TEES
Tees are small, usually plastic, pegs on which the ball is placed for the first shot to a hole.

COURSE
A standard course consists of 18 holes, varying in length from 90–550m (100–600yd). The length determines the "par" of each hole: the average number of strokes needed to get the ball into the hole.

STRIKING DISTANCES

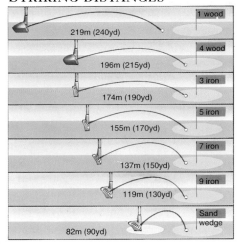

219m (240yd)   1 wood
196m (215yd)   4 wood
174m (190yd)   3 iron
155m (170yd)   5 iron
137m (150yd)   7 iron
119m (130yd)   9 iron
82m (90yd)   Sand wedge

The apron is the short grass surrounding the green.

The putting green is the smooth, grassy area that surrounds the hole.

Flagstick

Diameter of hole: 10.8cm (4.25in)

Sand bunker

Hazards may include ponds, streams, and sand bunkers.

The rough is uneven land surrounding the fairway.

The teeing ground, from which the first stroke is made, is a smooth, level area.

The head is kept down as the club makes contact with the ball.

The fairway is a closely mown strip of ground which stretches from tee to green, along which the players attempt to play the ball.

The body faces the target as the club is brought past the left shoulder.

MAJOR GOLF TOURNAMENTS

Tournament	First held
British Open	1860
US Open	1895
US PGA	1916
US Masters	1934
Ryder Cup (male team event)	1927
Curtis Cup (female team event)	1932

LONG SHOT
In a qualifying match in Pennsylvania, USA, in the early 1900s, one entrant drove her ball into a river at the 16th hole. She set out in a boat to reach it, and finally completed the hole in 166 shots.

GOLF WORDS

Approach Shot played to the green from the fairway or rough.

Birdie A score of one stroke under par for a hole.

Bogey A score of one stroke over par for a hole.

Eagle A score of two strokes under par for a hole.

Fourball Two play against two, each player having one ball, the lower score of each pair being their score at a hole.

Foursome Two play against two, each side having one ball and taking alternate strokes at each hole.

Handicap Number of strokes a player may subtract from his or her score for a round; enables players of different abilities to compete on equal terms.

Hole A complete section, from tee to putting green; the round hole into which the ball is played.

Par The standard score for a hole or round (18 holes) on a course, based on what a top player would be expected to shoot, and allowing for two putts.

Tee The ground that marks the start of a hole; a peg on which the ball is put for the first stroke of a hole.

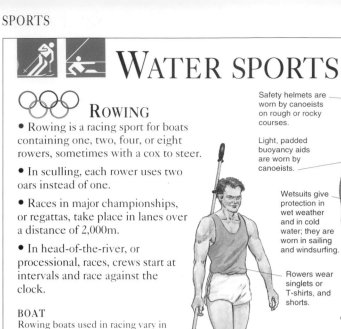

WATER SPORTS

ROWING

- Rowing is a racing sport for boats containing one, two, four, or eight rowers, sometimes with a cox to steer.

- In sculling, each rower uses two oars instead of one.

- Races in major championships, or regattas, take place in lanes over a distance of 2,000m.

- In head-of-the-river, or processional, races, crews start at intervals and race against the clock.

BOAT
Rowing boats used in racing vary in length depending on the event, but the basic design remains the same.

Safety helmets are worn by canoeists on rough or rocky courses.

Light, padded buoyancy aids are worn by canoeists.

Wetsuits give protection in wet weather and in cold water; they are worn in sailing and windsurfing.

Rowers wear singlets or T-shirts, and shorts.

WATER-SPORT KITS
Competitors must wear safety equipment for most water sports. Lifejackets are worn for yachting, water skiing, and motorboat racing. Buoyancy aids are less bulky than lifejackets and are worn in canoeing.

OLYMPIC ROWING EVENTS

Event	Approximate length of boat	
Sculls		8m (26ft)
Double sculls		10m (33ft)
Quadruple sculls		13m (43ft)
Coxless pairs		10m (33ft)
Coxed pairs (men only)		11m (36ft)
Coxless fours		13m (43ft)
Coxed fours (men only)		14m (46ft)
Eights		17m (56ft)

Boats are made from wood or reinforced plastic.

ROWING TECHNIQUE
The rowers lean forwards, legs are bent and arms are straight.

SCULLING TECHNIQUE
The rower holds the blades just above the water.

He leans forwards and bends his knees as he pulls the oars through the water.

He straightens his legs, and then his back when the oars are at right angles to the boat.

He leans back, arms bent, and pulls the oars up out of the water.

Their backs straighten as they pull the blades through the water.

They lean back, arms bent, as they pull the oars out of the water.

CANOEING

- There are two main types of competition canoes: the kayak and the Canadian canoe.

- The kayak has a closed deck. The canoeist sits inside, with legs outstretched underneath the deck. The paddle has a blade at each end.

- Most Canadian canoes have an open deck. The canoeist sits or kneels, and uses a single-bladed paddle.

Kayak

Stern

Cockpit

Bow

Double-bladed paddle

Canadian canoe

Bow

Stern

Thwart

Single-bladed paddle

OLYMPIC CANOEING EVENTS

Type of boat	Length (max.)	Event	
		Male	Female
K1	5.20m	500m, 1,000m, slalom	500m, slalom
K2	6.50m	500m, 1,000m	500m
K4	11m	1,000m	500m
C1	5.20m	500m, 1,000m, slalom	—
C2	6.50m	500m, 1,000m, slalom	—

K=Kayak, C=Canadian, 1=singles, 2=twos, 4=fours

SPRINT RACING
Sprint races take place on water that is as still as possible. Kayaks race in lanes, usually over distances of 500m or 1,000m. Some courses have windbreaks to limit the effect of crosswinds.

Men's K2 race

LONG-DISTANCE RACING
In 5,000m and 10,000m races, canoeists paddle round buoys at each end of the course. Canoe marathons range from 5km to 200km in length. Competitors avoid obstacles, such as locks or waterfalls, by carrying their canoes along the bank (portage).

Canoe marathon

WHITE-WATER RACING
There are two types of white-water racing. In wildwater racing, canoeists are timed over a course that includes obstacles such as rocks and rapids. In slalom, canoeists negotiate several "gates".

Slalom

SAILING

YACHT TYPES

- There are two types of yacht racing: inshore and offshore.
- Inshore racing takes place off the coast on courses marked by buoys. Offshore racing takes place across the sea or ocean.
- One-design events are for boats of the same class. Handicap events are for boats of different designs.

One-person dinghy
e.g. Optimist class.
National origin: USA.

Two-person boat with trapeze e.g. 470 class.
National origin: France.

Catamaran
e.g. Tornado class.
National origin: UK.

Two-person dinghy
e.g. Flying Dutchman.
National origin: Netherlands.

Ocean-going yacht
e.g. 12m class.
National origin: Europe.

WINDSURFING

- Windsurfing, or boardsailing, is a comparatively new sport that has developed in the last 20 years.
- The sailboard is a simple craft steered by means of the sail.
- There are three main types of competition: course racing, slalom, and wave performance.

SAILBOARD
The sailboard is made up of the rig (consisting of the sail, mast, and boom) connected to the board by a universal joint. The sailor supports the rig by holding the boom.

Mast

Sail

Window

Boom

Board

Universal joint

WINDSURFING WORDS

Boom Double, or wishbone, boom used for steering, changing speed, and maintaining balance.

Daggerboard Removable fin used to stop board from slipping sideways through the water.

Freestyle Competition or exhibition in which tricks are performed.

Funboard Board designed for sailing in strong winds and performing spectacular flying jumps.

Skeg Fin that helps to keep board on course.

Uphaul Rope used to pull rig out of the water.

Boom

Daggerboard

Skeg

Funboard

Uphaul

POWERBOAT RACING

- Motorboats range from big powerboats with cabins to small inflatable dinghies fitted with outboard motors.
- The two main types of powerboat racing are inshore and offshore. There are several classes, depending on size and type of engine.

Twin-hulled powerboat

SURFING

- Surfers paddle out to sea on lightweight boards, and "ride" the waves back to shore.
- Any type of board may be used, but most competition boards have three fins on the tail (tri-fins).

KIT

Boards are usually made of fibreglass.

Wetsuits are worn in cold conditions.

"Tube" rides are performed by riding in the hollow of the wave.

SURFING MOVES
Surfers perform a variety of moves. Judges assess surfers for style, grace, and timing, and award points, depending on the difficulty of the wave, for various aspects of the ride.

In a "turn", the surfer turns and cuts back through the wave.

WATER SPORT COMPARISONS

Water sport	First Olympics	Top speed	
		km/h	mph
Sailing	1900	69	43
Rowing	1900	21[1]	13
Powerboat racing	1908[2]	166[3]	103
Canoeing	1936	20[4]	12
Whitewater canoeing	1972	–	–
Windsurfing	1984	82	51
Water-skiing	–	230	143

(1) Average Olympic record speed for an eight over 2km. (2) Only inclusion. (3) Much higher speeds have been reached by boats specially designed for record breaking. (4) Average Olympic record speed for a K4 over 1km.

WATER-SKIING

- The water-skier is towed behind a motorboat, which needs a speed of at least 30km/h (19mph) to keep the skier upright. Competitions are divided into three sections.

Lifejacket

Ramp

SLALOM
Skiers negotiate a series of buoys while crossing the boat's wake. There are six buoys on each run, or pass, with a "gate" at each end. Each successive pass is made with a faster boat speed to a maximum of 58km/h (36mph) for men or 55km/h (34mph) for women.

JUMPING
This is performed from a ramp and is judged on distance.

TRICKS
Points are awarded for a variety of moves, such as a backward turn, performed while being towed.

SPEEDY SKIS
The world water-skiing speed record is more than 200km/h (124mph), which is more than three times the speed of the boat. A skier will cross from side to side behind the towing motorboat, and so can travel much faster.

SWIMMING AND DIVING

SWIMMING

• There are four strokes in competitive swimming: freestyle (swimmers always use the front crawl), backstroke, breaststroke, and butterfly.

• Competitors dive from starting blocks in all events (except for backstroke), and race in lanes.

• They are timed to one-thousandth of a second by touching sensitive pads at the end of the race.

RACING FACTS

• Swimmers must not leave their starting blocks until the starter fires the gun or, as in relay races, until the previous swimmer in their team has touched the electronic pad.

• Rules govern the style of each stroke (except for freestyle); including the turns made at the ends of the pool.

• In the individual medley race, competitors swim each quarter with a different stroke in the following order: butterfly, backstroke, breaststroke, and freestyle.

DIVING

• Competitive diving is a sport in which contestants are awarded points by judges.

• There are two divisions of diving: springboard and highboard, or platform, diving.

Forward dive

Forward dives may be performed from a run-up or standing position.

In the layout position, the body should not be bent at the hips or knees.

The diver must keep his feet together and his toes pointed.

He must keep his body as straight as possible when entering the water.

KIT

Bathing cap

Goggles are worn to protect the eyes from chemicals in the water.

Women wear light, tight-fitting nylon bathing suits; men wear trunks.

POOL

Length: 50m

Starting block

Width of each lane: 2.5m

STROKES

Front crawl
This is the fastest stroke and is used in freestyle races.

The swimmer moves his legs up and down from the hips.

His arms and legs move alternately.

He keeps his body as straight and flat as possible.

Breaststroke
This is the slowest stroke. Arms and legs stay underwater.

Her arms move together, circling from an outstretched position around and under the chin.

Her legs move together with a frog-like kick.

Backstroke
This is the only racing stroke in which the swimmers start in the water.

Her arms pull alternately in a "windmill" motion.

Her body is kept as straight as possible.

Butterfly
Like the breaststroke, this is a symmetrical stroke.

The swimmer uses a strong, double-arm pull to propel himself through the water.

He uses an up-and-down "dolphin kick" of the legs.

TYPES OF DIVE

The six types of dive are: forward, backward, twist, inward, reverse, and armstand. Within these six groups, there are many different starting positions and varieties of moves in the air, making a total of more than 100 recognized dives.

Backward dive

In the starting position, the diver must keep his body straight and his head up; his arms swing upwards just before leaving the platform or springboard.

Armstand dive

Armstand dives are made from the platform only.

Inward dive

An inward dive (body facing towards board or platform) in the pike position

Twist dive

The diver performs a twist in mid-air.

A forward somersault in the tuck position

OLYMPIC EVENTS

Event		Men	Women
Swimming			
Freestyle	50m	√	√
	100m	√	√
	200m	√	√
	400m	√	√
	800m		√
	1500m	√	
Backstroke	100m	√	√
	200m	√	√
Breaststroke	100m	√	√
	200m	√	√
Butterfly	100m	√	√
	200m	√	√
Individual	200m	√	√
medley	400m	√	√
Freestyle relays	4x100m	√	√
	4x200m	√	
Medley relay	4x100m	√	√
Diving			
Springboard		√	√
Highboard		√	√
Synchronized swimming			
Solo			√
Duet			√
Water Polo		√	

SYNCHRONIZED SWIMMING

• This sport is a kind of "water ballet", in which swimmers perform artistic movements under or on the water to music.

• There are solo, pair (duet), and team (four to eight swimmers) events.

Synchronized duet

WATER POLO

• This is played 7-a-side in water. Only the goalkeeper is allowed to stand to play the ball, touch it with both hands or punch it.

EQUESTRIAN

Gate

Triple bars

Start

Wall

Finish

SHOW JUMPING

• Riders take their mounts around a course of obstacles such as gates, walls, fences, and a water jump.

• Penalty faults are given for errors such as a refusal, knocking off a pole, or taking longer than the specified time.

SHOW-JUMPING FAULTS

Error	Faults
Fence (or part of fence) down	4
Foot in water	4
Refusal	3
2nd refusal	6
3rd refusal	Elimination
Fall (horse or rider)	8
Exceeding time allowance	1/4 per second
Taking jumps out of sequence	Elimination

KIT
Riders must wear a hard hat or crash helmet, and formal dress for show jumping and dressage competitions.

Riding hat

Jacket

Whip

Jodhpurs

Boots

Bridle, made of adjustable lengths of leather

Gloves

Saddle

JUMPING TECHNIQUE
When jumping, the rider should bend forwards from the hips and look up. On landing, the body must straighten up to take weight off the horse's front legs.

Take-off

Flight

Landing

DRESSAGE

• Riders take their mounts through an official test made up of a variety of paces, movements, and figures.

• Marks are awarded for the quality of the test performance.

Walk

Canter

Trot

THREE-DAY EVENTING

• Riders take their mounts through three disciplines over three days: day one, dressage; day two, speed and endurance; day three, show jumping.

• Speed and endurance is made up of four phases (see table).

Clearing a water jump in the three-day event.

SPEED AND ENDURANCE

Phase	Distance	Details
A Roads and tracks	16-20km	Trot or slow canter
B Steeplechase	approx. 3.5-4km	9 or 10 fences
C Roads and tracks	16-20km	Trot or slow canter
D Cross-country	up to 8km	28-32 obstacles

POLO

• Polo is a game played by two teams of four players. The aim is to hit a ball between the opposition's goalposts with a long stick called a mallet.

Polo

HARNESS RACING

• The horses pull their drivers round an oval track on light, two-wheeled "sulkies". Most races are 1 mile long.

HORSE RACING

• Flat races are for horses of 2 years old and over; most are from 5 furlongs to 1.5 miles long, with no jumps.

• Hurdle races are for 3-year-olds and over; they are from 2 to 3.25 miles long.

• Steeplechases have fences instead of hurdles. They are for 4-year-olds and over, and are from 2 to about 4.5 miles long.

MAJOR HORSE RACES

Race	Course	Distance	Type
2,000 Guineas	Newmarket, England	1 mile	Flat
1,000 Guineas (fillies)	Newmarket, England	1 mile	Flat
Derby	Epsom, England	1 mile, 4f*	Flat
Oaks (fillies)	Epsom, England	1 mile, 4f	Flat
St. Leger	Doncaster, England	1 mile, 6f, 132yd	Flat
Irish Derby	The Curragh, Ireland	1 mile, 4f	Flat
Arc de Triomphe	Longchamp, France	2,400m	Flat
Kentucky Derby	Churchill Downs, USA	1 mile, 2f	Flat
Melbourne Cup	Melbourne, Australia	3,200m	Flat
Grand National	Aintree, England	4 mile, 4f	Steeplechase
Cheltenham Gold Cup	Cheltenham, England	3 miles, 2f	Steeplechase
Champion Hurdle	Cheltenham, England	2 miles	Hurdle

*f = furlong (220yd); 8 furlongs = one miile

Harness racing

RECORD BREAKERS
ONLY THREE-TIME WINNER of the Grand National horse race in England is Red Rum, who won it in 1973, 1974, and 1977. MOST WINS IN HORSE RACING is 8,833 in 40,350 races by US jockey Bill Shoemaker (born 1931) who rode his first winner in March 1949 and retired in 1990.

WINTER SPORTS

SKIING

- There are two basic groups: alpine, which includes downhill and slalom racing, and nordic, which includes cross-country and ski jumping.

- Alpine skiing comes from the Alps; nordic skiing comes from northern Europe.

KIT
Skiers wear warm, wind- and waterproof clothing often in bright colours, so they can be seen clearly.

SKIS
Alpine skis vary in length depending on the event and the skier's own preference. Nordic skis are narrower and lighter than alpine skis.

Gloves

ALPINE SKIING
RACING
There are four main types:
Downhill This is the fastest race, in which skiers follow a set route down the mountain.
Slalom A short race downhill with quick turns through a series of "gates" – 55–75 for men, 40–60 for women.
Giant slalom This has fewer, wider gates than a slalom and takes place over a longer course.
Super giant slalom This is like a downhill race with gates; it contains up to two jumps.

FREESTYLE
There are three main types:
Aerials Acrobatics performed in mid-air after taking off from a ramp, judged on style and technique.
Mogul racing Skiing down a course of large round bumps, judged on skill as well as time.
Ballet Performed to music on smooth slopes, judged on grace and skill.

Aerials

SKI POLES
Poles should be made of a strong, light material such as aluminium. The basket stops the pole from sinking too deep into the snow. Nordic ski poles are longer than alpine poles.

Ski pole

Goggles

BOOTS
Alpine boots are attached to the ski, but have a mechanism that allows them to come off in a fall. Nordic boots are like trainers. The heel lifts free with each stride.

Basket

Alpine boot

Giant-slalom course
The gates are wider on a giant-slalom course. Each flag is set on a pair of poles.

Open gate

Blind gate

Slalom course
A slalom gate is represented by a pair of flags that are alternately blue and red.

NORDIC SKIING

CROSS-COUNTRY RACING
The cross-country course has no steep slopes or sharp turns, but is a test of stamina, with races ranging from 5 to 50km. Competitors start at 30-second intervals and time decides the placings.

Cross-country skier

Ski jumping
Two different ski towers, or ramps, are used from which skiers are expected to jump 70m and 90m respectively. Points are awarded for style as well as distance.

Take-off

Flight

Ski tower

The "norm point" is at the beginning of the expected landing area.

The "table point" is at the end of the expected landing area.

Inrun

Landing

Outrun area

OLYMPIC SKI AND SLED COMPETITIONS

Competition	Men	Women
Alpine ski racing		
Slalom	√	√
Giant slalom	√	√
Super giant slalom	√	√
Alpine combined (downhill and slalom)	√	√
Downhill	√	√
Freestyle		
Ballet	√	√
Moguls	√	√
Aerials	√	√
Nordic		
5km		√
10km	√	√
15km	√	√
30km	√	√
50km	√	
4 x 5km relay		√
4 x 10km relay	√	
Nordic combined		
Individual	√	
Team	√	
Ski jumping		
70m hill	√	
90m hill	√	
90m hill team	√	
Biathlon		
10km (M) / 7.5km (W)	√	√
20km (M) / 15km (W)	√	√
Relay 4 x 7.5km	√	
3 x 7.5km		√
Sled		
2-man bob	√	
4-man bob	√	
Single luge	√	√
Double luge	√	
Toboggan*	√	

*Held only on Cresta Run at St. Moritz, Switzerland (1928 and 1948).

OTHER NORDIC COMPETITIONS
Ski marathons Long-distance (40–150km) cross-country events with mass starts, also called "citizen racing".
Nordic combined Two-day event with ski jumping (70m hill) on the first day and cross-country (15km) on the second.
Relays Races between teams of four.
Biathlon Combination of cross-country skiing and rifle shooting. The skier carries his weapon on his back and stops regularly to shoot at targets, incurring time penalties for missing.

Rifle shooting at a biathlon

CAR SKIING
To find the best position for skiing in special high speed events on smooth slopes, a skier practises on top of a fast-moving car.

SLED RACING

LUGE TOBOGGANING
A luge is a one- or two-person toboggan with no steering or brakes. It is ridden face-up in a sitting or lying position.

BOBSLEIGH RACING
Bobsleighs, for two or four men, have metal runners, steering, and brakes.

SKELETON TOBOGGANING
Competitors ride face-down on an open toboggan. There is only one major competition, the Cresta Run at St. Moritz, Switzerland.

FIGURE SKATING

- Competitors perform routines to music containing compulsory movements and moves they choose themselves.

- A maximum of nine judges give marks for technical merit and artistic impression; 6.0 is the perfect score.

Top female skaters wear short fitted skirts or dresses.

SINGLES
Solo competitions, for men and women, have two parts: a short programme with compulsory moves and a long programme (freestyle).

Lutz jump

The skater increases her speed before attempting the jump.

She makes one turn, or two for a double lutz, in the air before landing.

The skater lifts one leg behind him, and holds it parallel to the ice.

Camel spin

ICE DANCE
Ice-dance competitions have three parts: compulsory dances, original set pattern dance, and free dance. Couples choose their own music and movements in the free dance. During their routine, they must not separate more than five times, or for longer than five seconds. Lifts must not be made above shoulder-height.

Expressiveness is important in ice dancing.

SPEED SKATING

- Competitors race in pairs against the clock around an oval two-lane track, 400m in length.

- Competitors switch lanes each lap in a change-over zone.

- In short-track speed skating, a maximum of six competitors race around a 110-metre oval track. The first to finish is the winner.

Competitors wear body-hugging suits to cut down air resistance.

Speed skates have a thin aluminium blade attached to a lightweight boot.

KIT
Top male skaters often wear all-in-one bodysuits made of stretch material.

Figure skating usually takes place on adapted ice-hockey rinks.

RINK
Maximum length: 60m
Maximum width: 30m

FIGURE SKATE
A figure skate has a steel blade about 3mm wide. The bottom of the blade is concave to make two edges. Figures are skated on one or other of these edges.

Toe-rake helps in spinning and in certain jumps.

PAIRS
Pair competitions are made up of two parts: a short programme and a free-skating programme.

A skating pair perform a high lift.

TRACK

Length of track: 400m

Width of lane: 4–5m

CURLING

- In curling, two four-a-side teams slide curling stones across the ice, aiming to get them as close as possible to the centre (tee) of a target area (house).

- Team-mates with brooms sweep the ice in front of the stones to change their speed and direction.

Curling

RECORD BREAKER
THREE CONSECUTIVE OLYMPIC GOLD MEDALS (1928–36) and ten consecutive world championships (1927–36) were won by Sonja Henie, a Norwegian figure skater. She then turned professional and made several Hollywood films featuring her grace and skills on ice.

OLYMPIC SKATING EVENTS

	Men	Women
Figure skating	√	√
Pairs	Together	
Ice dancing	Together	
Speed skating		
500m	√	√
1,000m	√	√
1500m	√	√
3,000m		√
5,000m	√	√
10,000m	√	
Short-track		
500m	√	√
1,000m	√	√
3,000m		√
5,000m	√	

WHEELED SPORTS

MOTOR RACING
• Competitions are held for different types of car on a variety of tracks. Races are held around circuits, on roads, and on grass and dirt tracks.

FORMULA 1
• Grand Prix races take place on circuits.

• Drivers and car-makers aim to win points for the world championships.

Straight

Spoon curve

S-curve

Start/Finish

RACE CIRCUIT
A Grand Prix circuit has corners and straights to test the drivers' car-handling skills. Above is a plan of the Suzuka circuit in Japan.

FLAG SIGNALS
Flags are held out during the race. Each colour has its own meaning.

Chequered: end of race

Yellow: danger

Red and yellow stripes: oil on course

White: service car on track

Black: car must stop in pits

Red: all cars must stop

INDYCAR RACING
• Most races take place in the USA, mainly on oval circuits.

• The annual championships are decided on points. The cars are similar to Formula One cars.

Turns bank at 9°

INDY 500
The most famous Indycar circuit is the Indianapolis, which is 4km long. The Indy 500 race is held over 200 laps of the circuit.

Pits area

Start/Finish

KARTING
• The simplest karts have a 100cc engine and no gearbox. The most powerful karts are like small racing cars and can reach speeds of 240 km/h (150 mph).

KIT
Motor-racing drivers wear a crash helmet and a thick, fire-resistant suit for protection in case of an accident.

Crash helmet

Face shield

Driving gloves

Aerofoil pushes the car down on the track.

Heavy-duty racing suit

Driving shoes

GRAND PRIX CIRCUITS

Grand Prix	Circuit	Length (km)	Laps
Argentina	Buenos Aires	4.26	72
Austria	A1-Ring	4.32	71
Australia	Adelaide	3.78	81
Belgium	Spa-Francorchamps	6.94	44
Brazil	Interlagos	4.32	71
Canada	Gilles Villeneuve	4.43	69
France	Magny-Cours	4.25	72
Germany	Hockenheim	6.81	45
Great Britain	Silverstone	5.23	59
Hungary	Hungaroring	3.97	77
Italy	Monza	5.80	53
Japan	Suzuka	5.86	53
Luxembourg	Nürburgring	4.57	67
Monaco	Monte Carlo	3.33	78
San Marino	Imola (Italy)	5.04	61
Spain	Catalunya	4.75	65

Smooth tyres called slicks for use in dry weather.

Body shell

Detachable steering wheel

Roll-over bar

FORMULA 1 RACING CAR
These streamlined cars are made of lightweight materials to make them go as fast as possible.

RALLY DRIVING
• In rally driving, strengthened saloon cars race against the clock, rather than each other. The route is divided into sections called "stages", with time-control points between them. Points are lost for exceeding time.

Rally cars are faster and stronger than ordinary cars.

RECENT FORMULA 1 WORLD CHAMPION DRIVERS

Year	Driver	Country of origin
1988	Ayrton Senna	Brazil
1989	Alain Prost	France
1990	Ayrton Senna	Brazil
1991	Ayrton Senna	Brazil
1992	Nigel Mansell	UK
1993	Alain Prost	France
1994	Michael Schumacher	Germany
1995	Michael Schumacher	Germany
1996	Damon Hill	UK
1997	Jacques Villeneuve	Canada
1998	Mika Hakkinen	Finland

DRAG RACING
• Races are held along straight 400m ($\frac{1}{4}$ mile) tracks called drag strips.

• Cars race in pairs. They reach speeds of 485km/h (300mph), and need parachutes to slow down.

DRAGSTER
A dragster has a lightweight body, with big wheels that give good grip at the back, and smaller, lighter front wheels. The fastest dragsters are called top-fuellers.

Aerofoil

Powerful, supercharged engine

Rear slicks

Lightweight front wheels

RECORD BREAKERS

MOST FORMULA 1 WORLD DRIVERS' CHAMPIONSHIP WINS is five by Juan Manuel Fangio (1911–1995) of Argentina.

CLOSEST FINISH TO A WORLD CHAMPIONSHIP GRAND PRIX RACE is 0.014 seconds, when Ayrton Senna (1960-94) of Brazil, beat Nigel Mansell (born 1953) of UK.

LONGEST ANNUALLY HELD RALLY RACE is the Safari Rally, Kenya. The race has covered up to 6234km (3874 miles).

MOTORCYCLE SPORT

There are a variety of competitions for different types of bike. They take place on circuits or cross-country tracks.

MOTORCYCLE RACING

• Grand Prix races take place on circuits.

• There are different classes for bikes of different engine sizes, and a class for sidecars.

RACING MOTORBIKE

The bikes are powerful machines designed for speed.

Streamlined plastic body

Light aluminium frame

WORLD CHAMPIONSHIP MOTORCYCLE CLASSES

Motorcycle	Racing	Motocross
500cc	√	√
250cc	√	√
125cc	√	√
80cc	√	
Sidecar	√	√

RACING SIDECAR

A racing sidecar is a bike and sidecar moulded together to make one piece. The driver and passenger work together as a team. The passenger leans over behind the driver to help with cornering. The passenger platform may be attached to either side of the bike.

Racing sidecar

MOTOCROSS

• Motocross, also known as scrambling, is the "cross-country" branch of motorcycle racing.

• Races take place on tracks that include muddy slopes, grass, and bumps.

MOTOCROSS BIKE

These bikes are adapted to cope with rough ground.

Swinging arm allows vertical movement of wheel.

Mudguard

Chunky-tread tyres for gripping loose surfaces

OTHER MOTORCYCLE SPORT

Speedway Riders race over four laps of a dirt track. The bikes have no brakes or gearbox so riders slow down by sliding their machines through turns.

Trials Riders negotiate a natural course with obstacles such as boulders, fast-flowing water, loose rocks, and deep mud, and lose points for putting a foot down or stopping.

CYCLE SPORTS

• Races range from track sprints held over 1,000m (1,094yd) to multi-stage road races lasting several weeks.

• The bicycles differ according to the type of race.

OLYMPIC CYCLING EVENTS

	Men	Women
Track:		
Sprint	√	√
Time trial	√	
Pursuit	√	√
Team pursuit	√	
Points race	√	
Road:		
Individual	√	√

ROAD RACING

• Races are run on courses set along ordinary roads.

• In stage races, such as the Tour de France, each stage is a race in itself, and the overall winner is the one with the lowest aggregate time.

KIT

Bicycle riders wear long close-fitting shorts to prevent thighs chafing against the saddle, and a top that allows the body to breathe and soaks up sweat.

A helmet is compulsory.

ROAD-RACING BICYCLE

The best bicycles are made of carbon tubing to save weight and are designed to be as streamlined as possible yet reliable and stable.

TOUR DE FRANCE

This famous race covers 3,400km in 24 one-day stages. Each year the route changes. The tour can even leave France and stretch over the border into neighbouring countries.

TRACK RACING

• Races take place on hard tracks including tightly banked wooden indoor tracks and almost flat asphalt outdoor tracks. Some are held on closed circuits (roads that have been closed to the public).

TYPES OF TRACK RACING

Points race Points are scored on each lap for crossing the line first, with double points on the last lap.

Sprint Riders spend most of the race jockeying for position before making a final dash for the line.

Individual pursuit Two riders start on opposite sides of the track, and the race is decided on time, or if one rider catches the other.

Team pursuit Similar to individual pursuit, but there are two teams of four riders. Only the times of the first three riders in each team are counted.

Italian pursuit For teams of up to five riders. The leading cyclist in each team drops out after each lap. The finishing time of the last rider of each team decides the race.

Devil-take-the-hindmost Last rider over the line at the end of each lap is eliminated.

Time trial Competitors ride on their own over a set distance from a standing start, and the rider with the fastest time wins.

OFF-ROAD RACING

• Cyclocross takes place on cross-country courses, and competitors may carry their bikes across obstacles.

• Mountain-bike racing includes several different styles, including trials and cross-country racing.

Tour de France route (1990)

Colour codes
Colour-coded jerseys help spectators identify leading riders in the Tour de France.

Yellow top is worn by the rider with the lowest overall time after each stage and by the ultimate winner of the Tour.

Polka-dot top is worn by the rider with most points from the climbing stages.

Green top worn by the rider with most points from sprints.

A cyclist carrying his bike across a river during a cyclocross race.

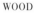

TARGET SPORTS

BOWLS

- Individuals or teams roll bowls, called woods, along a flat, smooth green, aiming at a target ball, or jack.

- A point is scored for each bowl that is nearer to the jack than any opponent's wood.

WOOD

Woods can be made of wood, rubber, or a composition material.

They are weighted, or biased, on one side so they curve when rolled.

Jack

BOULES

- In boules, which is similar to bowls, metal balls are thrown at a small wooden target ball.

- The game can be played on any bare stretch of land, but is usually played on sandy ground.

Boule

TENPIN BOWLING

- This is an indoor sport in which players roll a ball down an alley, aiming to knock down the pins.

- Points are scored for each pin knocked down. Bonuses are given for knocking down all ten pins in one go (a strike) or two goes (a spare).

BOWLING TECHNIQUES

In boules, the boule is lobbed.

In bowls, the wood must be rolled along the ground.

PINS
The pins are made from maple wood covered with plastic.

LANE
The pins are arranged in a triangular pattern at one end of the lane, which is made of plastic or wood.

TENPIN BALL
The bowling ball has three holes for the thumb and two middle fingers.

Ball made of hard rubber or plastic

ARCHERY

- Competitors use a bow to fire a certain number of arrows at targets set at different distances.

- The closer to the centre of the target an arrow lands, the higher the score.

BOW AND ARROWS
The bow is usually made of fibreglass. The arrow shafts are made of aluminium or carbon.

Plastic fletches

Aluminium or carbon shaft

Stabilizers keep the bow steady while shooting.

Quiver for carrying arrows

TARGET
There are five coloured rings, each with an inner and an outer part. Scores range from one point for the outer white, to ten points for the inner gold.

Straw butt

Bull's-eye

Paper target face

OLYMPIC ARCHERY QUALIFYING DISTANCES

	Men	Women
30m	√	√
50m	√	
60m		√
70m	√	√
90m	√	

DARTS

- Opponents take it in turns to throw three darts at a board from a distance of 2.4m.

- Each player usually starts with a score of 501 and must reduce it to the exact score of zero by finishing with a double or an inner bull.

DARTBOARD
The board is divided into different scoring sections, indicated by the numbers on the outer ring. Certain areas count double or treble.

Bull

Dart

Treble ring

Double ring

SHOOTING

- Rifles, pistols, and shotguns are used in shooting sports. The size of the target varies with the weapon and distance.

- Pistol shooting includes rapid-fire pistol shooting, in which 5 targets are exposed for only 4–8 seconds, and free pistol shooting in which competitors fire at a fixed target.

- Shotgun is firing with a double-barrelled gun at saucer-shaped targets released randomly from a spring-catapult.

RIFLE SHOOTING POSITIONS

Standing

Kneeling

Prone

OLYMPIC SHOOTING EVENTS

	Men	Women
Free pistol	√	
Rapid-fire pistol	√	
Air pistol	√	√
Sport pistol		√
Free rifle – prone – 3 positions	√ √	
Air rifle	√	√
Running target	√	
Standard rifle		√
Shotgun – Skeet – Trap – Double trap	√ √ √	√

SNOOKER

- Players score points by "potting" balls. A cue is used to hit a cue ball against a red or coloured ball, causing it to fall into a pocket.

TABLE

Pocket

Cushion

Black ball (7 points)

Fifteen red balls (1 point each)

Pink ball (6 points)

Blue ball (5 points)

Green ball (3 points)

Cue ball

Brown ball (4 points)

Yellow ball (2 points)

POOL

- One player tries to pot balls 1–7 (or colours) and then the black 8-ball to win, while the other player pots balls 9–15 (or stripes) and then black.

Chalk is rubbed on the tip of the cue to improve contact with the cue ball.

Seven colours

One black

Seven stripes

One white cue ball

A pool table is smaller than a snooker table.

CUE
The cue, used in both snooker and pool, is a tapered stick with a leather tip.

Two-piece cue

SCIENCE AND TECHNOLOGY

From the atom to the latest in information technology, this section offers a wealth of scientific facts and figures.

Matter • Atoms • Periodic Table • Energy
Forces and Machines • Electricity and Magnetism • Light and Colour
Sound • Electronics • Computers • Mathematics • Weights and Measures
Time • Engines • Space and Time • Natural Science
Physical Science • Weapons

MATTER

EVERYTHING IS MADE up of matter. It can be a solid, such as wood or iron, a liquid, such as water or oil, or a gas, such as air. Heat or pressure can change matter from one state into another.

Lead: solid

Glass: transparent solid

Terrarium, containing many types of matter

Droplets of water condensed from vapour

STATES OF MATTER

Matter exists in three basic forms, called states, depending on how their atoms and molecules (see p.222) are arranged.

GAS

A gas is a substance that does not have a fixed volume but fills all the space it occupies. Gas particles are not bound together and move fast and freely in all directions.

Gas particles, free to move around

LIQUID

A liquid has a fixed volume but can change shape to fit the space it occupies. Its particles are in contact with each other but can move around with some freedom.

Liquid particles, able to move short distances

SOLID

A solid is a substance with a definite size and shape. A solid's particles are tightly linked by strong bonds, making a firm structure.

Solid particles, held in a rigid pattern

THREE IN ONE

Water is one substance we often find in its different states.

ICE
Water is solid when its temperature is below 0°C (32°F) – what we know as ice.

Ice forms solid blocks with definite shapes.

WATER
Water is liquid when it has a temperature of between 0°C (32°F) and 100°C (212°F).

Liquid fills up its container to a horizontal surface.

STEAM
Water turns to steam, a gas, when it has a temperature of more than 100°C (212°F).

Liquid turns to gas.

TYPES OF MIXTURE

There are two main types of mixture: colloids and solutions. In a solution, two or more substances are broken down into individual atoms or molecules. A colloid is a mixture of larger particles of one substance, distributed in another.

Emulsion
Paint is an emulsion of oil particles dispersed in another liquid, water.

Gel
Hair gel is composed of particles of oil suspended in a solid.

Foam
Shaving foam is composed of bubbles of gas suspended in liquid.

Mist
Steam from a kettle is a mist of liquid particles suspended in a gas.

Smoke
A bonfire gives off a cloud of smoke composed of solid matter suspended in air.

Solution
A solvent, such as water, makes a solution by dissolving another substance, the solute.

CHANGING STATES

Evaporation and condensation
Particles can free themselves from the body of a liquid (evaporation). Above the boiling point, all of the liquid becomes gas. When the gas cools, it becomes a liquid (condenses) again.

Freezing and melting
A liquid becomes a solid (freezes) below a temperature called its freezing point. It becomes a liquid again (melts) if the temperature rises above the freezing point.

Sublimation
Some substances, such as carbon dioxide, will change from a solid to a gas when heated, without becoming liquid in between. This is sublimation. The reverse process, from a gas to a solid, is also called sublimation.

Changes of state

evaporating
subliming
condensing
subliming
freezing
melting

WEB FEAT

Some of the threads in a spider's web are stronger than a steel wire of the same width.

LIQUID GLASS

Over long periods of time, glass behaves like a liquid. Ancient Roman glassware has been found slightly flattened.

AIR SPEED

Each of the billions of air molecules that fill a balloon travels at the average speed of a jet plane.

COMPOUNDS

Elements that exist on their own are rare in the natural world. Most substances are made up of two or more elements bonded together by chemical reaction to form a compound. When iron and sulphur are heated together, a chemical reaction bonds their atoms into a solid structure.

MIXTURE

Iron filings and sulphur

Iron filings and sulphur can be mixed up together, but their atoms will not be chemically bound unless a chemical reaction takes place.

COMPOUND

A new substance, iron sulphide

When iron and sulphur are heated together, their atoms bind to form a new compound of iron sulphide. It is a completely new substance.

PHYSICAL PROPERTIES

There is a wide variety of matter, with a range of different properties. These properties help to identify the substance, and also determine to what use it can be put.

Viscosity
Viscous matter is liquid that does not flow easily. Friction between molecules makes a liquid viscous. Honey is highly viscous, whereas water is not.

Ductility and malleability
Ductile matter can be drawn out into a wire. Malleable matter can be moulded or beaten into other shapes.

Elasticity
Elastic matter can be stretched or squeezed and returns to its original size and shape.

Density
Two objects of the same size may not have the same mass, so they will not weigh the same. The denser of the two will weigh more, because it has more matter packed into the same space.

Dense tip

Conductivity
Matter that transfers heat and electricity is conductive. Many solids have a close-knit molecular structure that causes them to be cold to the touch, because it conducts heat away quickly.

Warm stone retains heat.

ANTIMATTER

For every type of particle that exists, such as the electron (see p.222) there is a corresponding antiparticle. Just as matter consists of particles, antimatter consists of antiparticles. If matter and antimatter are brought together, they will violently destroy each other, to become energy.

False-colour image of subatomic particles

COMBUSTION (BURNING)

A substance burns when it reacts with oxygen, releasing heat. A candle is made from carbon and hydrogen. These elements burn to form carbon dioxide and water.

Candle flame
A candle flame contains tiny particles of carbon. As they burn, they become so hot that they glow bright yellow.

Burning food
Food dissolved in your blood "burns" as it reacts with oxygen. The heat released provides you with the energy you need to live.

PLASTIC

Most synthetic plastics are made from chemicals in oil in a chemical process called polymerization. To make PVC, small molecules of chloroethene polymerize to form a long chain, or polymer.

Inflatable snake made of PVC (polyvinyl chloride).

Molecule of chloroethene (vinyl chloride)

Long chain molecule of PVC (polyvinyl chloride)

Polyvinyl chloride has a chain of molecules, from 70 to a million long.

KEY PLASTICS

Name	Uses
Polystyrene	Packaging, cups, bowls, ceiling tiles
Polyester	Artificial fibres, fibreglass
Polythene	Carrier bags, bottles, food wrapping
Nylon	Artificial fibres, carpets, fishing nets
PVC (Polyvinyl chloride)	Raincoats, garden hoses, guttering
Polyurethane	Plastic packaging foam, adhesives
Polymethyl methacrylate (perspex)	Substitute for glass

DEGRADABILITY

In time, most matter will degrade naturally, breaking down into simpler substances. Non-degradable pollution will remain in rivers, seas, and the atmosphere.

An apple core takes 20 days to decompose

Plastic can take more than 100 years to decompose.

Glass takes more than 4,000 years to decompose.

SAVOURY SEA

1cu metre (220 gallons) of typical sea water contains 23cu cm (1.4cu inches) of salt (sodium chloride). Sea water also contains other dissolved salts.

ACIDS AND ALKALIS

Acids are substances that dissolve in water to form sharp-tasting solutions. Alkalis dissolve in water to form soapy solutions. Both acids and alkalis can be corrosive. The strength of an acid or alkali is measured by its pH.

Caustic soda pH 14

Household cleaners pH 10

Liquid soaps pH 8

Pure water pH 7 (neutral)

Tap water pH 6

Vinegar (acetic acid) pH 4

The worst acid rain pH 1.5

Stomach acid pH 1

Alkaline
14
13
12
11
10
9
8
7
6
5
4
3
2
1
0
Acidic

ATOMS

EVERYTHING AROUND YOU is made up of tiny particles called atoms. Different atoms make up different kinds of matter.

ELEMENTS
Elements are substances made up of one kind of atom only. One element is fluorine.

INSIDE THE FLUORINE ATOM
If a fluorine atom could be cut open, it might look like this.

Nucleus
The central core of the atom is called the nucleus. It consists of protons and neutrons. The nucleus makes up 99.9% of an atom's mass, but only a tiny part of its volume.

Electrons
Electrons are negatively charged particles. They surround the nucleus in regions called orbitals.

Ions
When an atom loses or gains an electron, it becomes an ion. If it loses an electron, it becomes positively charged and is called a cation. If it gains an electron, it becomes negatively charged and is called an anion.

The illustration below distorts the real sizes of the atomic components – the nucleus is very large compared to electrons, and electrons orbit at a great distance from the nucleus.

Inner electron orbital

Neutrons
Neutrons are particles in a nucleus. They have no electric charge. They cling to the protons and to each other, keeping the nucleus together.

Protons
Protons are particles in a nucleus that carry a positive electric charge. The number of protons in an atom is called its atomic number. Fluorine has nine.

Quarks
Protons and neutrons are made up of even smaller particles, called quarks. There are two main types of quark. Up quarks have a positive charge. Down quarks have a negative one. Neutrons have one Up and two Down quarks. Protons have two Up and one Down.

Proton, with two Up quarks and one Down

ATOM FACTS
• Quarks are named after a word that appears in the novel *Finnegan's Wake* by Irish writer James Joyce (1882–1941).

• Some atomic isotopes are highly dangerous – if stored in large enough quantities, a nuclear reaction can occur.

• In 1995 physicists cooled several hundred atoms to a few billionths of a degree above absolute zero (-273°C), the lowest possible temperature. The atoms all became one super atom, known as a Bose-Einstein condensate.

ISOTOPES
Some atoms of the same element may have different numbers of neutrons. These different kinds of atoms are called isotopes. These two nuclei are from isotopes of fluorine. Fluorine–19 has 10 neutrons, while fluorine–18 has 9 neutrons.

Fluorine–19 nucleus

Extra neutron

Fluorine–18 nucleus

INTO THE ATOM
What would happen if you could tear this book in half, and then in half again and again – until you broke it down into the tiniest particles possible?

The book becomes…

scraps of paper, which become…

wood pulp fibres, which become…

molecules of cellulose, which become…

atoms of the different substances that made up the molecules, which can be divided into…

protons, neutrons and electrons. Protons and neutrons are each made up of…

quarks.

MOLECULES
There are only about 100 kinds of atom, but there are millions of different compounds. Most compounds are made of particular combinations of atoms joined together, called molecules.

Double bond

Carbon nucleus

Hydrogen atom

Molecule of ethene (C₂H₄)

ATOMIC BONDING
Atoms join to form molecules. They do this by bonding (sticking together). There are two main types of bonding: ionic and covalent. In each case, the electrons form the bond.

IONIC BOND
In an ionic bond, atoms lose or gain electrons to form ions of opposite charge. These opposite charges attract each other, and bond the two ions together.

Electron

Molecule of lithium fluoride

Fluorine atom

Lithium atom loses electron to become a positive ion, or cation.

Fluorine atom gains electron to become a negative ion, or anion.

Ions attract each other to form a molecule of lithium fluoride.

COVALENT BOND
A covalent bond occurs where electrons are shared between atoms. This sharing keeps the atoms together. One or two, or occasionally three, nuclei are attracted to the same electrons at once. Water and nitrogen gas are substances with covalent bonds.

Shared electron

Hydrogen atom

Fluorine atom

Both fluorine and hydrogen atoms need one electron to become stable.

Atoms form a covalent bond, becoming stable as they do so.

FORCES OF ATTRACTION
If an atom's nucleus were the size of a sports stadium, some of its electrons would revolve at the distance of a low-orbiting satellite.

RADIOACTIVITY

Large nuclei can be unstable, and they can decay. When they do, charged particles are lost from them. This process is called radioactivity. Most elements have unstable forms, called radioisotopes. Some occur naturally, others are made in nuclear reactors. The most radioactive substances have the highest number of particles in their nuclei. Uranium has 238.

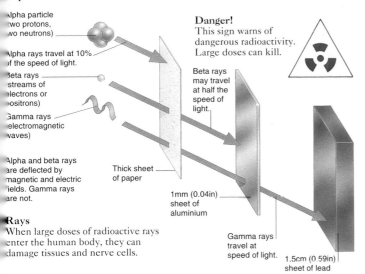

Alpha particle (two protons, two neutrons)

Alpha rays travel at 10% of the speed of light.

Beta rays (streams of electrons or positrons)

Gamma rays (electromagnetic waves)

Alpha and beta rays are deflected by magnetic and electric fields. Gamma rays are not.

Danger!
This sign warns of dangerous radioactivity. Large doses can kill.

Beta rays may travel at half the speed of light.

Thick sheet of paper

1mm (0.04in) sheet of aluminium

Gamma rays travel at speed of light.

1.5cm (0.59in) sheet of lead

Rays
When large doses of radioactive rays enter the human body, they can damage tissues and nerve cells.

RADIATION FACTS

- Levels of radiation can be measured with a device called a Geiger counter. A probe filled with gas at low pressure triggers an electric pulse, heard as a click, when radiation is near.

- About 200 million gamma rays pass through the body every hour from soil and buildings.

- All-out nuclear war would force people to live underground for months, and possibly years.

- Exposure to gamma rays can kill bacteria in food. This process, called irradiation, keeps the food fresh for longer, but many people are afraid of its possible long-term health risks.

NUCLEAR REACTIONS

There are two kinds of nuclear reaction – fission and fusion. Both are a release of the "binding energy" that keeps the nucleus of an atom together. Atoms are called "stable" if they have a lot of binding energy, "unstable" if they have little.

NUCLEAR FISSION

If a neutron hits the nucleus of the unstable element uranium–235, the nucleus splits into two lighter nuclei. More neutrons shoot off to bombard other nuclei in a chain reaction. Energy is released. In nuclear power stations, this energy is used to generate electricity.

Neutron

Uranium–235 nucleus

Nuclear fission reaction

Krypton atom

Neutron

Neutron

Energy released

SUBATOMIC PARTICLES

Many types of particle other than electrons, protons, and neutrons are known to exist, and are generally referred to as subatomic particles. More and more particles are being discovered, through the use of particle accelerators, and physicists face the task of making sense of them all. One of the greatest puzzles concerns neutrinos – particles produced during nuclear reactions in the Sun. Neutrinos are elusive particles, and strange experiments are performed to detect them and measure their mass.

USES OF RADIATION

ALPHA RADIATION
Alpha rays are charged particles of two protons and two neutrons. Nuclear batteries, which give off harmless alpha rays, power heart pacemakers, because they last much longer than normal ones.

Alpha rays from the radio-isotope plutonium power heart pacemakers.

Heart pacemaker

BETA RADIATION
During radioactive decay, a neutron can change into a proton, and vice versa. Streams of electrons or positrons are given off in this process – these are beta rays. The isotope carbon–14, found in all living things, produces beta radiation as it decays. Scientists can date once-living things by seeing how much carbon–14 has decayed. This is called carbon dating.

Once thought to be the 2,000-year-old death shroud of Jesus Christ, the cloth was carbon dated and found to be only 600 years old.

The Turin shroud

GAMMA RADIATION
Gamma radiation, an electromagnetic wave, travels at the speed of light, but with much more energy. These waves, like light or radio waves, are given off when a nucleus has too much energy. Not often found on their own, they are given off with alpha and beta particles.

Person undergoes radiotherapy (cancer treatment)

Cobalt–60 produces gamma radiation. Here, it is being used to kill cancerous body cells. It can also be used to sterilize medical instruments.

KEY HALF-LIVES
The half-life of an element is the time it takes for half its atoms to decay into other materials. A strongly radioactive substance has a short half-life – it decays quickly.

Isotope	Half-life	Type of decay	Use
Radium–221	30 sec	Alpha and gamma	Cancer therapy
Iron (Fe–59)	45 days	Beta and gamma	Testing car parts
Carbon–14	5570 yrs	Beta and gamma	Carbon dating
Uranium–238	500 million yrs	Alpha and gamma	Nuclear energy

Helium nucleus

Barium atom

Energy released

Hydrogen isotope deuterium

Nuclear fusion reaction

Hydrogen nuclei fuse

Hydrogen isotope tritium

Neutron released

NUCLEAR FUSION
When the nuclei of lighter elements are forced together they combine and form a new, heavier nucleus, releasing energy. In the Sun, hydrogen atoms fuse together to make helium, and produce the Sun's heat. Scientists hope to find a safe way of creating fusion on Earth.

MARIE CURIE
French scientist Marie Curie (1867–1934) pioneered the study of radiation. A flask that she used in her experiments turned blue after constant exposure to radioactive ores.

COLD ENERGY
In 1989, Stanley Pons and Martin Fleischmann claimed to have succeeded in making fusion reactions at room temperature. This claim has since been shown to be false.

PERIODIC TABLE

THE ELEMENTS THAT MAKE UP all of the matter around us can be arranged into a table. The table is arranged in vertical columns, called groups, and in horizontal rows, called periods. The complete table includes elements that do not occur naturally, but have been made artificially.

6   **12**

C

Carbon

Atomic number
The number of protons in the nucleus defines what element a particular atom is. This is the atomic number.

Atomic mass
Carbon occurs with 6, 7, 8, and 9 neutrons in its nucleus, in addition to its 6 protons, giving it a mass of between 12 and 15.

Chemical symbol
Each element has a symbol; it is used for identification in chemical equations.

Carbon–12 nucleus

Proton – total number is atomic number

Neutron – with protons, makes atomic mass

TABLE PATTERNS

We can tell a lot about an element from its position on the periodic table. Elements situated in the same area behave in the same way.

☐ **Metals**
Metals are mostly solids, and are all good conductors of heat and electricity.

▨ **Non-metals**
Non-metals are not good conductors of heat or electricity, and can be solid, liquid, or gas.

▨ **Metalloids**
Metalloids, also called semi-metals, are non-metals that behave like metals in some ways, or in some conditions.

■ **Noble gases**
Noble gases are also called inert gases because they are not reactive. They are all gas at room temperature.

▨ **Lanthanides and actinides**
These elements are separated out from the table to give it a regular shape.

PERIODIC PIONEER

The first person to arrange the elements into the shape of a table was Russian chemist, Dmitri Mendeleyev (1834–1907). In 1869, he made cards for each element, and laid them out according to the property of each element. The cards formed the periodic table.

1   **1**

H

Hydrogen

Elements on handwritten cards were known in Mendeleyev's time.

3   **7**   **4**   **9**

Li   *Be*

Lithium   *Beryllium*

11   **23**   **12**   **24**

Na   *Mg*

Sodium   *Magnesium*

SODIUM
There are about 18,000,000,000,000 tonnes of this element in the world's oceans; most of it is in a solution of sodium chloride.

RUBIDIUM
Rubidium is typical of elements in its group. It reacts violently with water or even air, catching fire immediately. Its salts give a red flame when heated.

19 39	20 40	21 45	22 48	23 51	24 52	25 55	26 56	27 5
K	*Ca*	**Sc**	*Ti*	*V*	*Cr*	*Mn*	*Fe*	*Co*
Potassium	*Calcium*	*Scandium*	*Titanium*	*Vanadium*	*Chromium*	*Manganese*	*Iron*	*Cobalt*
37 85	38 88	39 89	40 91	41 93	42 96	43 97	44 101	45 10
Rb	*Sr*	*Y*	*Zr*	*Nb*	*Mo*	**Tc**	*Ru*	*Rh*
Rubidium	*Strontium*	*Yttrium*	*Zirconium*	*Niobium*	*Molybdenum*	*Technetium*	*Ruthenium*	*Rhodium*
55 133	56 137	57 139	72 180	73 181	74 184	75 187	76 190	77 19
Cs	*Ba*	*La*	**Hf**	*Ta*	**W**	**Re**	*Os*	*Ir*
Caesium	*Barium*	*Lanthanum*	*Hafnium*	*Tantalum*	*Tungsten*	*Rhenium*	*Osmium*	*Iridium*
87 223	88 226	89 227	104 260	105 262	106 263	107 262	108 265	109 266
Fr	**Ra**	**Ac**	**Db**	**Jl**	**Rf**	**Bh**	**Hn**	**Mt**
Francium	*Radium*	*Actinium*	*Dubnium*	*Joliotium*	*Rutherfordium*	*Bohrium*	*Hahnium*	*Meitnerium*

GROUPS AND PERIODS

☐ **Groups**
Each element is similar to a handful of others. The periodic table is arranged so that similar elements are put together in vertical columns, or groups.

☐ **Periods**
Elements are arranged into horizontal rows, or periods. The electron arrangement around the nucleus (see p.222) determines the period's length.

CAESIUM
The nucleus of this element can be made to vibrate at an extremely reliable rate – 9,192,631,770 times every second. Caesium is used in atomic clocks, which are accurate to one second in thousands of years.

Lanthanides

58 140	59 141	60 142	61 145	62 152	63 153	64 158
Ce	**Pr**	**Nd**	**Pm**	**Sm**	**Eu**	**Gd**
Cerium	*Praseodymium*	*Neodymium*	*Promethium*	*Samarium*	*Europium*	*Gadolinium*

Actinides

90 232	91 231	92 238	93 237	94 244	95 243	96 247
Th	**Pa**	*U*	**Np**	**Pu**	**Am**	**Cm**
Thorium	*Protactinium*	*Uranium*	*Neptunium*	*Plutonium*	*Americium*	*Curium*

URANIUM
There are two main types, or isotopes, of uranium. Uranium–238 (with 92 protons and 146 neutrons) accounts for 99% of all uranium. The isotope that is useful in nuclear reactors, uranium–235 (with 92 protons and 143 neutrons), accounts for only about 1%.

TUNGSTEN
Tungsten has the highest boiling point of all the elements. It boils at a temperature of 6,200°C (11,190°F), which makes it useful for filaments in electric light bulbs. Their temperatures would melt most of the other elements.

ABUNDANT ELEMENTS

The most abundant elements in the Earth's crust (by mass), in elemental or compound form

Element	Abundance (%)
Oxygen	49
Silicon	26
Aluminium	7
Iron	4
Calcium	3

FLUORINE
Fluorine is very reactive – a typical property of the elements in its group. It is often added to water supplies and to toothpaste in the form of fluoride ions (fluorine atoms with an extra electron).

MERCURY
Used in thermometers, mercury is the only metal that is liquid at room temperature. It is very poisonous, and affects mental health. The phrase "mad as a hatter" arose because hatters, who used mercury, often went mad.

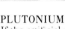

ELEMENT RECORDS

RAREST METAL
is Rhodium. Just 3 tonnes are produced each year, compared with 1,500 tonnes of gold.

MOST COMMON ELEMENT
in the Universe is hydrogen; the next is helium.

NITROGEN
Nitrogen accounts for over 75% of the Earth's atmosphere and is essential to plants and animals. It is an ingredient in fertilizers, and plants need it to help them grow.

ELEMENT FACTS

• In 1994, elements 104–109 were renamed by an international commission. Disputes over who had discovered them first had led to a temporary system of naming by their atomic number.

HELIUM
The lowest possible temperature is 0K (-273.16°C/-459.69°F). Helium has the lowest boiling point of any element: 4.23K (-268.93°C/-453.07°F).

• The element dysprosium is named after the Greek word *dysprositos*, which means "difficult to obtain".

• Helium was discovered by analyzing light from the Sun. Its name comes from *helios*, the Greek word for Sun.

HEAVY METAL
The densest element is osmium; a cube 33x33x33cm (13x13x13in) weighs as much as a small car.

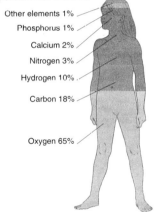

BODY ELEMENTS
Many elements are essential to the human body. Minute amounts of certain elements, called trace elements, are important for health.

Other elements 1%
Phosphorus 1%
Calcium 2%
Nitrogen 3%
Hydrogen 10%
Carbon 18%
Oxygen 65%

2	4
He	
Helium	

5	11	6	12	7	14	8	16	9	19
B		*C*		*N*		*O*		*F*	
Boron		*Carbon*		*Nitrogen*		*Oxygen*		*Fluorine*	

10	20
Ne	
Neon	

13	27	14	28	15	31	16	32	17	35·5
Al		*Si*		*P*		*S*		*Cl*	
Aluminium		*Silicon*		*Phosphorus*		*Sulphur*		*Chlorine*	

18	40
Ar	
Argon	

28	59	29	63·5	30	65	31	69	32	74	33	75	34	79	35	80
Ni		*Cu*		*Zn*		Ga		Ge		*As*		*Se*		*Br*	
Nickel		*Copper*		*Zinc*		*Gallium*		*Germanium*		*Arsenic*		*Selenium*		*Bromine*	

36	84
Kr	
Krypton	

46	106	47	108	48	112	49	115	50	119	51	122	52	128	53	127
Pd		*Ag*		*Cd*		*In*		*Sn*		*Sb*		*Te*		*I*	
Palladium		*Silver*		*Cadmium*		*Indium*		*Tin*		*Antimony*		*Tellurium*		*Iodine*	

54	132
Xe	
Xenon	

78	195	79	197	80	201	81	204	82	207	83	209	84	209
Pt		*Au*		*Hg*		*Tl*		*Pb*		*Bi*		**Po**	
Platinum		*Gold*		*Mercury*		*Thallium*		*Lead*		*Bismuth*		*Polonium*	

85	210
At	
Astatine	

86	222
Rn	
Radon	

PLUTONIUM
If the artificial element plutonium–239 is not produced and stored in quantities of less than 300g (0.66lb), a spontaneous nuclear reaction begins, and dangerous amounts of energy are released.

SILICON
Pure silicon, a semiconductor, is used in electronic devices to provide a base for minute integrated circuits.

65	159	66	164	67	165	68	167	69	169	70	174	71	175
Tb		Dy		Ho		*Er*		Tm		Yb		Lu	
Terbium		*Dysprosium*		*Holmium*		*Erbium*		*Thulium*		*Ytterbium*		*Lutetium*	

97	247	98	251	99	254	100	257	101	258	102	255	103	256
Bk		Cf		Es		Fm		Md		No		Lr	
Berkelium		*Californium*		*Einsteinium*		*Fermium*		*Mendelevium*		*Nobelium*		*Lawrencium*	

TECHNETIUM
This element does not occur naturally, and was the first of many elements to be made artificially, in nuclear reactions. It is used to some extent in medical diagnosis.

IODINE
Once prepared from seaweed, iodine is essential to the human diet. It turns into a violet vapour when heated.

HEAVY ELEMENTS
Uranium (atomic number 92) is the element with the heaviest atoms that exist naturally on Earth. Since 1940 several heavier – transuranium – elements have been produced in laboratories.

Element	Atomic number	Year produced
Neptunium	93	1940
Curium	96	1944
Californium	98	1950
Fermium	100	1952
Nobelium	102	1958
Lawrencium	103	1961
Element 107	107	1976
Element 108	108	1984
Element 109	109	1985
Element 110	110	1994
Element 111	111	1994
Element 112	112	1996

ENERGY

ENERGY AND FORCES constantly change the world. Energy takes many forms – the only visible one is light energy – and people have built many types of machine to convert and control all its forms.

The car has a certain mass, which gives it a certain weight.

The tension in the rope is a force, which pulls the car up the slope.

The total energy expended is the same as if the car were lifted vertically.

The person is using energy to produce a force on the handle of the winch.

Friction is a force that acts in the opposite direction to the movement of the car.

Gears magnify the force produced by the person, but the rope moves much more slowly than the winch handle.

Weight is a force.

The ramp is a machine.

ENERGY AND FORCE

How can one person lift a heavy car? He or she can use a force, applied through a machine such as a winch, but must still provide the total amount of energy required to lift the car. Twice as much energy is needed to lift the car twice as high, or if the car is twice as heavy.

ENERGY CONVERSION

Energy can be neither destroyed, nor can it be created from nothing. Whenever anything happens, one form of energy is simply changed into another.

TEMPERATURE SCALE

Temperature is measured in degrees of Fahrenheit or Celsius, but also in kelvins (K).

Burning point of wood: 523K; 250°C; 482°F

Explosion point of nitro-glycerine: 491K; 218°C; 424°F

Sauna bath: 413K; 140°C; 284°F

Boiling point of water: 373K; 100°C; 212°F

Midday heat in Death Valley, California: 329.7K; 56.7°C; 134°F

Human body temperature: 310K; 37°C; 98.6°F

Body temperature of spiny anteater: 295K; 22°C; 71.6°F

Freezing point of pure water: 273K; 0°C; 32°F

Freezing point of mercury: 234K; -39°C; -38°F

Absolute zero: 0K; -273°C; -459°F

ENERGY CONVERSION IN A CAR JOURNEY

Chemical energy
Petrol releases lots of energy when ignited under pressure.

Sound energy
Radio and loudspeakers convert electrical energy into sound.

Kinetic energy
Any moving object possesses kinetic energy. The faster it moves and the greater its mass, the greater its kinetic energy.

Electrical energy
Movement of car's wheels recharges battery.

Light energy
Car headlights are powered by battery.

Potential energy
Energy that is "stored" is potential energy. When released, it is converted into other forms.

Heat energy
Movement of engine parts generates heat.

Heat energy (brakes)
When brakes are applied, friction between car tyres and ground generates heat.

ENERGY MEASURE

All forms of energy – potential, kinetic, sound, chemical, light, heat, etc. – can be measured in units called joules.

Energy of a thunderstorm
About 1,000 million million joules of heat and potential (stored) energy.

Energy released by a lightning strike
100 million joules of electrical energy becoming 100 million joules of heat energy.

An apple lifted 1m (3.28ft)
1 joule of muscle energy becoming 1 joule of potential (stored) energy.

1 second of a 100-watt light bulb
100 joules of electrical energy becoming 15 joules of light energy and 85 joules of heat energy.

1 second of Itaipu Dam, Brazil
Potential energy becoming 12.6 million joules of electrical energy.

EVER READY

The amount of atomic energy in a kilogram of radioactive uranium–235 would keep a 100-watt light bulb alight for 27,400 years.

TEMPERATURE

The particles that make up all matter, such as atoms, are constantly in motion, vibrating to and fro or speeding through space. The temperature of matter is the average energy of its particles. Matter with more energy can raise the temperature of other matter around it.

Hot water molecules transfer kinetic energy to ice molecules – ice melts.

Ice molecules have low energy.

Hot water molecules have more energy.

Hot water

ENERGY UNITS

Other energy units can be converted into joules

Unit	Joule equivalent
Joule (J)	
Watts (W)	1J per second
Horsepower (Hp)	2,600,000 J
Calories (Cal)	4,184 J
Kilowatt hour (kWh)	3,600,000 J

FORCES

A FORCE IS a push or a pull. A force can start an object moving, slow it down, or change its direction. Forces can also change the shape of an object.

GRAVITY

One of the most familiar forces is a force of attraction between objects, called gravity. Gravity keeps us on the Earth and gives us weight. Anything with mass exerts gravity, and the size of this force depends on the masses of the objects and the distance between them. It becomes weaker as bodies move further apart or lose mass.

Moon gravity
The Moon exerts less gravitational force than Earth because it has less mass.

Earth gravity
Earth's large mass makes things on its surface weigh six times more than on the Moon.

ADDING FORCES TOGETHER

If more than one force acts on an object, the overall effect will be the same as one force acting in one direction. This force is called the resultant.

BOW AND ARROW
The force of an arrow fired from a bow is the resultant of the two forces that act along the upper and lower halves of the bowstring.

TUG OF WAR
In a tug of war, the resultant force is almost zero, because the two forces on the rope act in exactly opposite directions.

Opposing forces

TURNING FORCES

Forces can turn objects. The greater the force, and the greater its distance from the turning point, the greater the turning force.

TURNING NUTS
The spanner is useful for turning a nut because its long handle means that you can apply a force far away from the nut. This produces a stronger turning force (moment).

NEWTON'S LAWS OF MOTION

In 1687, English mathematician Isaac Newton (1642–1725) identified three laws that describe the motion of objects under the influence of forces.

NEWTON'S FIRST LAW

An object will not change its motion unless a force acts upon it.

A frog will stay still unless a force makes it move. If the frog was drifting along at a constant speed, it would continue to do so until a force stopped it, slowed it down, or made it speed up.

NEWTON'S SECOND LAW

A change in an object's motion depends upon the force acting on it, and on the mass of the object.

The frog needs twice as much force to change its motion twice as much.

MACHINES

A machine is a device that can change the size and direction of a force. With a block and tackle, for example, a person can lift a very heavy load. This is because the arrangement of ropes in the block and tackle means that the person needs to pull a long length of rope to lift the load a small distance.

PULLEY
Effort is magnified by the rope and the wheels in order to lift the load.

WEDGE
The slope allows less effort to lift the load than by picking it up vertically.

SCREW
Effort is magnified by the thread, acting as a long slope wrapped around the screw.

WHEEL AND AXLE
Effort applied to the wheel is magnified by the axle, turning it with greater force.

LEVER
Effort applied at one end of a bar is magnified by the fulcrum to lift the load at the other end.

CIRCULAR MOTION

A moving object will travel in a straight line, unless a force changes its direction.

Hammer thrower
To make a hammer go in a circle, an athlete must supply a force, called centripetal force, that constantly pulls it around in a circle. As soon as the athlete lets go, the hammer flies off in a straight line.

Athlete uses centripetal force to throw hammer.

PRESSURE

Pressure is a measure of how "concentrated" a force is. A force applied over a small area exerts more pressure than the same force applied over a large area.

PRESSURE AND AREA
If a watering can and trowel are pushed into sand with about the same force, the trowel sinks further into the sand. This is because the force is exerted over a smaller area – the trowel's thin blade.

Larger handle produces greater turning force.

NEWTON'S THIRD LAW

For every force there is an equal force acting in the other direction.

Forces come in pairs. The frog and the lilypad push against each other.

FORCES WORDS

Acceleration Rate of change of velocity.

Centre of gravity The point on an object at which it balances.

Equilibrium State produced when forces acting on an object balance, so that there is no resultant.

Momentum Mass of an object multiplied by its velocity.

Newton Unit of force. One newton (1N) causes a mass of one kilogram to move with an acceleration of one metre (3.28ft) per second per second.

Resultant Force produced by combining two or more forces.

Velocity Speed and direction of an object.

BRAIN POWER

The ancient Greek scientist Archimedes was said to have constructed a pulley mechanism that enabled a ship that had run aground to be dragged into open water by just one man.

ELECTRICITY AND MAGNETISM

PUT A PIN CLOSE to a magnet, and it will cling to the magnet. Rub a balloon on a sweater and the balloon will cling to a wall. These things happen because invisible forces are at work – electricity and magnetism. These forces are important, as they hold almost everything together.

Electron — An electron carries negative electric charge. When millions of electrons flow in a conductor, an electric current is produced.

Proton — A proton carries a positive charge. Protons lie in the nucleus of the atom.

Atom — Nucleus

Normally, atoms have no electrical charge – the charges from the protons in the nucleus and electrons orbiting around the nucleus cancel each other out.

Location of one of atom's electrons

CURRENT ELECTRICITY

The unit of charge is the coulomb. One coulomb is equal to the charge of 6 million million million electrons. An electric current is a flow of electrons. A current of one ampere (see below) means that a charge of one coulomb is flowing per second.

Electron — Direction of electron flow
Plastic insulator

STATIC ELECTRICITY

When you rub a balloon on a jumper, some electrons get separated from their atoms. This creates an electrical charge. Charges of the same type repel (push each other away). Opposite charges attract. The balloon gains a negative charge. This gives the wall a positive charge, and the balloon clings to it.

Positive charge
Negative charge

Comb negatively charged by being run through hair.

Negatively charged leaves repel each other.

ELECTROSCOPE

An electroscope is an instrument for detecting electric charge. It has two pieces of gold leaf fixed to a brass rod. The leaves separate when an electric charge is brought near to the rod.

ELECTRICITY WORDS

Ampere The unit of current. If a wire carries one ampere (1A), one coulomb (1C) of charge is flowing along the wire each second.

Volt The unit of voltage or electromotive force. This is a measure of how much energy charges have. One volt (1V) means that each coulomb (1C) has one joule (1J) of energy.

Ohm The unit of resistance. If a wire has a one ohm (1Ω) resistance, a voltage of one volt will produce a current of one ampere.

Watt The unit used to measure power. An electric current of one ampere (1A) at one volt (1V) will have a power of one watt (1W).

SHOCKING CURE

The bite of the South American Bushmaster snake can be treated by a series of short electric shocks at around 20,000–25,000V. In remote areas, car or outboard motors are sometimes used to deliver the voltage.

ELECTRIC FACTS

• The word "electricity" comes from the Greek word for amber, *elektron*. The ancient Greeks noticed that when amber was rubbed with a cloth, small objects would cling to it.

• A television on "standby" uses one-third as much electrical power as a television that is switched on.

• The body's nerves carry electric currents to and from the brain at speeds of up to 400km/h (249mph).

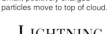

Small, positively charged particles move to top of cloud.

Large, negatively charged particles move to bottom of cloud.

Negative cloud charge induces positive ground charge.

Lightning conductor

LIGHTNING

Lightning is a tremendous spark of electricity, caused by a build-up of electric charge in clouds. The spark passes between clouds, or from the cloud to the ground. Many buildings are fitted with lightning conductors, which reduce the risk of lightning striking by draining electric charge away from clouds.

BATTERY

Inside a battery, chemical reactions separate electrons from atoms of the chemicals present. These electrons move around a circuit from the negative to the positive terminal.

Positive terminal
Carbon rod
Ammonium chloride paste
Negative terminal
Electron flow

SERIES AND PARALLEL CIRCUITS

Two bulbs one after the other in a circuit are said to be "in series". Each bulb only gets half the energy (voltage), so they shine dimly. In parallel, the bulbs would shine more brightly, since each bulb gets the full voltage – but the current will be doubled.

Bulbs in series – only receive half the voltage.

Batteries

Wire insulated by plastic coating

Bulbs in parallel – receive the batteries' full voltage.

Current flows round the circuit unless a break occurs.

Switch

RESISTANCE

The resistance of a material is a measure of how easily electric current will flow through it. Resistance depends upon the material, its width and its length.

Bright bulb
Battery
Low resistance from short length of lead
Dim bulb
High resistance from longer length of lead

MAGNETISM

Certain materials exert invisible forces, similar to electric forces. A magnet will attract objects made of iron, and a few other metals. Also magnets will attract or repel other magnets. Every magnet has two ends, called poles, where the forces it exerts are strongest. One is called the north pole and the other is called the south pole.

Magnet exerts force around it in an area called a magnetic field.

Iron filings and compasses show magnetic lines of force.

North pole

South pole

Lines of force loop around magnet and splay out from poles.

Unlike poles attract
If unlike poles – one north and one south – are placed together, they attract each other.

Fields of attracting magnets

Like poles repel
If like poles – both north or both south – are put together they repel each other.

Fields of repelling magnets

Iron filings show distortion of normal lines of force when two magnets meet.

Magnet
When a magnet attracts objects, the objects become magnetized and can attract other objects.

Each steel ball acts as a magnet.

LODESTONE

Metal objects, such as pins, are attracted to the lodestone.

Lodestone is a magnetic rock of iron oxide that occurs naturally. In ancient times people used lodestones as compasses and later to make magnetic compass needles.

EARTH MAGNET

The Earth's metallic core is a giant magnet, which lines up near to the true North Pole and South Pole, moving slightly every year. A compass contains a magnetized needle, which always points towards the magnetic north and south poles, enabling navigators to find their way.

Magnetic north

True North

Lines of magnetic force

Earth's magnetic field

DOMAINS

Magnetic objects contain small regions, between 0.1 and 1mm across, called domains. Each domain has two poles, and most of a magnet's domains lie in the same direction. If the domains are made to point in different directions the magnet will lose its magnetism.

Domain poles not in line

Poles line up.

Domains are jumbled up in unmagnetized iron or steel.

Domains may be aligned by stroking with another magnet.

Magnets also demagnetized by heating

Striking with a hammer jumbles up domains, demagnetizing the bar.

ELECTROMAGNETISM

Magnetic forces are not only produced by magnets. Magnetism is also produced by an electric current flowing through a wire. This magnetism can be made stronger by wrapping the wire around an iron core, such as a nail.

Insulated copper wire wrapped around iron nail

Wire connected to a battery

Metal objects are attracted to electromagnet.

ELECTRIC MAGNET

The magnetism produced by an electric current is exactly the same as magnetism produced by a magnet – it has a magnetic field, and a north and south pole. It can be switched on and off, however, with the electric current.

Magnetic field

North pole

South pole

Flow of current

BARKING MAD

Scottish physicist James Clerk Maxwell, who first explained the relationship between electricity and magnetism, used to talk through his theories with his dog, often at noisy parties.

MAGNETISM FACTS

• A wire carrying an electric current straight into this page would have a magnetic field going clockwise around it.

• Keepers are pieces of iron that help a magnet keep its power.

• Near the North and South Poles, the Earth's magnetic field traps charged particles emitted by the Sun. These particles react with the Earth's field to produce layers of coloured lights in the night sky, called Northern Lights or aurora borealis in the North, and Southern Lights or aurora australis in the south.

MAGNETIC FIELDS

Field	Strength in tesla (unit of field measurement)
Weakest measured field	0.000000000008T
Earth's field	0.00003T
Powerful magnet	1T
Highest field on record	30.1T

ELECTRIC MOTOR

An electric motor contains magnets and coils of wire. When current passes through the coil, it produces magnetism, which makes the coil turn in the magnetic field of the magnets.

Magnetic field

Direction of rotation

Permanent magnet

Direction of current

Coil

Brush

In an electric motor, the magnetic fields of the coil and magnet interact and force the coil to rotate. This rotational motion can be harnessed to provide power for machines.

Commutator – reverses flow of current at each half-turn, reversing the coil's magnetic field and keeping coil moving.

Battery

Simple direct current motor

GENERATOR

A generator is like a motor in reverse. Turning the coil inside the magnet's field produces an electric current. Power stations use huge generators to produce electricity for homes, schools, and factories.

Handle turns coil inside magnet and commutator.

Commutator

Direction of current flow

Coil

Permanent magnet

Magnetic field of magnet

Bulb lights up when handle is turned.

Current is generated in coil when it cuts through lines of force of magnet.

Simple direct current generator

Direction of current reverses at every half-turn of the handle – one brush is always negative, the other positive, producing direct current in the circuit.

LIGHT AND COLOUR

WITHOUT LIGHT, WE would not be able to see. Nature provides our most important light source – the Sun – and its light, either directly, or by bouncing off our surroundings, enters our eyes and enables us to recognize our world.

LIGHT LAWS

Law of reflection
The angle at which light hits a mirror is equal to the angle that light leaves the mirror.

Incident light ray (ray approaching mirror)   Reflected light ray

Law of refraction
Light changes speed when it passes from one material to another. The more it slows down, the more it bends.

Angle of incidence   Normal   Transparent solid   Angle of refraction

Ray of light passes from less dense medium (air) a more dense one (glass)

LIGHT ACTION
Light travels in straight lines at 300 million m/sec (980 million ft/sec). It creates shadows, bounces or reflects off smooth surfaces, and bends when it passes through different transparent materials.

LIGHT SPEED
Knowing the speed of light, astronomers have measured the distance to the Moon very accurately, by bouncing a laser beam off a mirror left there by astronauts, and timing its return journey.

REFLECTION
When light bounces off a surface, we say it is reflected. Few things we see give off their own light – we see them only because of reflection. Flat and shiny surfaces, such as mirrors, reflect light evenly to form an image, or picture.

Surface reflection
Most surfaces are not flat, even if they seem to be. When light reflects from an irregular surface, the reflected rays return at many different angles.

Shadow   Opaque object

SHADOW
Light travels through transparent substances, such as water or glass, in straight lines. Non-transparent (opaque) materials, such as wood or metal, do not allow light to pass through them. They cause a shadow to be cast on the opposite side from the light source.

Mirror – flat and shiny surface

Image appears "behind" mirror.

REFRACTION
Light changes direction when it passes from one transparent material to another. This happens because light travels at different speeds through different materials. The change in direction is called refraction.

Glass – denser substance than air

Angle of light ray changes.

Emerging light ray is parallel to original ray but shifted to left.

BRIGHTNESS
Light is given off by many different light sources, such as candles and light bulbs. Some light sources are brighter than others, and will provide better illumination.

Brightness in candela
The luminous intensity (brightness) of a light source is measured in candela (cd). One candela is approximately equal to the brightness of a candle.

Surface: 1lux

Candle: 1cd

Illumination in lux
Light from a source illuminates a surface placed in its path. This illumination is measured in lux (lx). From a distance of 1m (3.28ft) away, a source of light intensity one candela (1cd) will illuminate a 1sq m (10.8sq ft) surface with an illumination of 1lux.

EYE SEE
When comparing areas of different colour, in good light and using both eyes, the human eye can distinguish surfaces of 10 million different colours. No machine yet invented can distinguish as many colours.

LENSES
Lenses are specially shaped pieces of glass, or other transparent substances, that focus or disperse light evenly.

Convex lens
A block of glass that curves outwards is called a convex lens. Its shape focuses light on a point. It is used in cameras, magnifying glasses, and microscopes.

Lens   Focus

Focal length

Parallel light

Concave lens
A block of glass that curves inwards is called a concave lens. Its shape causes light to diverge (spread out). It is used in wide-angle and telephoto lenses.

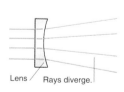

Lens   Rays diverge.

MIRROR
If the light falls on a completely smooth surface, all the rays are reflected regularly, at the same angle. An image forms, and the object looks as if it is behind the mirror.

Eye of observer   Mirror   Image of cup and saucer forms behind mirror.

HOW LIGHT IS MADE
There are two ways of making light – incandescence and luminescence. Incandescence happens when something gets very hot. Luminescence happens in four major ways.

Incandescence
In a light bulb, the fine filament heats up and gives out incandescent light. Other forms of incandescent light are candle flames, or the red glow from an electric element.

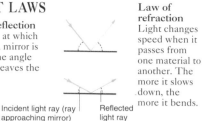

Phosphorescence
Phophorescent paint makes the numbers on clock faces glow in the dark. The paint stores energy when light falls on it. The energy is slowly released, as light, so the paint can be seen at night.

Fluorescence
Fluorescent chemicals in some washing powders make clothes look brighter in sunlight. Ultraviolet light energy is briefly stored, then released as visible light.

Bioluminescence
Some animals, such as the firefly, produce chemicals that release light energy when combined in their bodies.

Triboluminescence
Some substances, such as sugar, give out light when suddenly broken apart or crushed.

ELECTROMAGNETIC SPECTRUM

Light is part of a range of radiation called the electromagnetic spectrum. Different parts of the spectrum have different energy – from low-energy radio waves to high-energy gamma rays. Wavelengths can be as short as one nanometre (nm – one thousand millionth of a metre).

Television waves – about 1m (3.28ft)

Infrared – about 1mm

Ultraviolet – 100nm

X-rays – 1nm

Radio waves – up to 1km (0.62 miles)

Microwaves – about 1cm (0.37in)

Visible light – 400–700nm

Wavelength of electromagnetic wave (number given after type of light)

SKY COLOUR

Tiny particles in the sky scatter sunlight in all directions as it penetrates the Earth's atmosphere. They scatter blue light better than red, yellow, and green.

Daytime

Light of longer wavelength passes through atmosphere.

Sun appears yellow to observer.

Blue light scattered in atmosphere.

BLUE SKIES

During the day, the blue parts of sunlight are scattered in all directions, making the sky look blue. The rest of the light gets through, to give the Sun a yellow appearance.

Dusk or dawn

Sun appears red-orange to observer.

Some green and yellow light scattered.

SUNSET RED

In the evening, sunlight passes through a longer distance in the atmosphere. This means that some green and yellow light also gets scattered. Only orange and red light gets through, so the Sun looks orange-red.

MIRAGES

Light is refracted as it passes through layers of air at different temperatures. This can make objects seem nearer than they are and can make hot air layers look like water. When hot air lies above cool air, objects far away, such as ships, can seem to loom upside down. This occurs because light rays travelling from cool to hot air bend down and form an inverted image.

Observer

Warm air

Cool air

Inverted image of ship seen by observer.

VISIBLE SPECTRUM

Ordinary white light is made up of a range of colours. When white light passes through a prism, a triangular transparent block, the prism splits up its various wavelengths and all the colours can be seen separately. This range of colours is called the spectrum.

White light

Glass prism

Prism bends different wavelengths of light by different amounts.

Different colours that make up white light emerge from prism at different angles.

Violet light has shortest wavelength.

Red light has longest wavelength.

RAINBOW

When white sunlight falls on rain, the colours are split up and reflected inside the droplets, just as they are in a prism. The colours form a rainbow.

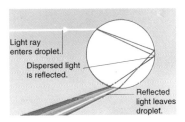

Light ray enters droplet.

Dispersed light is reflected.

Reflected light leaves droplet.

Rainbow

Red seen at 42° to the horizontal.

Observer

Violet seen at 40° to the horizontal.

MIXING COLOURS

Magenta

Blue

Black

Red

Yellow

Cyan

Green

PIGMENTS

Any colour of paint, ink, or dye can be formed from the three "secondary" colours of magenta, cyan, and yellow. Together they produce black.

INTERFERENCE

When light strikes a bubble, it is reflected off both the inside and outside surfaces. The two rays combine in a process called interference and create beautiful colours on the thin surface.

Colours vary with thickness of bubble.

Colours on bubble surface

Red light

Blue light

Red and blue give magenta.

Green light

Red and green give yellow.

White light

Blue and green give cyan.

LIGHT

Beams of light of the "primary" colours of red, green, and blue, can be mixed to form any other colour. When all the primaries are mixed, we get white light.

LIGHT AND ATMOSPHERE

Not every wavelength of light from space reaches the ground. Some infrared waves (1,100–2,300nm) are absorbed by carbon dioxide, water vapour, and ozone. "Hard" ultraviolet waves (about 220nm) are filtered out by ozone.

Effects of atmosphere on wavelengths of light

COLOUR WAVELENGTHS

Colour	Wavelength (Nanometres)
Violet	370–440
Blue	440–500
Green	500–575
Yellow	575–580
Orange	580–610
Red	610–720

LASERS

When certain materials are given enough energy, their atoms begin to give off light. Inside a laser, mirrors reflect this light back and forth until it is intense enough to escape at one end. Laser light is special because it is light of just one wavelength, and its waves are all aligned with each other. This means it can be very powerful and precise.

Mirror reflects light.

Material produces laser light.

Power supply excites light-producing material.

Laser light emerges from hole in mirror.

LIGHT FACTS

• Electromagnetic radiation can be thought of as waves. The higher the energy, the shorter the wavelength.

• Bees' eyes can detect ultraviolet light. A flower looks bright to a bee because the petals reflect a lot of ultraviolet.

• The word laser stands for Light Amplification by Stimulated Emission of Radiation.

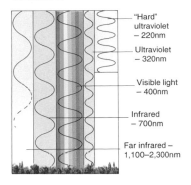

"Hard" ultraviolet – 220nm

Ultraviolet – 320nm

Visible light – 400nm

Infrared – 700nm

Far infrared – 1,100–2,300nm

SOUND

SOUND IS PRODUCED by objects vibrating. This vibration first pushes the air forwards, compressing (squashing) it, then pulls it back, causing it to expand. These contractions and expansions travel through the air as vibrations, called sound waves.

Tough, elastic strips covered with membrane

SOUND WAVE

When people shout, they use the vocal cords in their throat to make a sound. Vocal cords vibrate as air passes through them.

Vocal cords
Larynx muscles stretch vocal cords loosely for low sounds, tightly for high sounds.

Rarefaction
When air expands, the molecules are spread out. This is called rarefaction. The air exerts less pressure than normal.

Compression
When air is compressed, all its molecules are pushed together. The air exerts more pressure than normal.

THE DECIBEL SCALE

The loudness of sound is measured in decibels (db). A 10-db sound increase corresponds to a ten*fold* increase in loudness.

Decibel scale

130db Noise this loud is dangerous!

120db Jet aircraft taking off 100m (330ft) away

100db Loud rock concert

80db Pneumatic drill, 20m (66ft) away

10db Someone whispering 5m (16ft) away

0db A sound you can only just hear.

SOUND FACTS

• Sometimes, a sound and its echo are so close together they seem to be one long sound. This is called reverberation.

• You can hear the sound of a horse's hooves a long time before it arrives, by putting your ear to the ground. Sound waves travel much faster through the ground than through air.

• Sound travels quickly, but light travels much more quickly. You can work out how far away a storm is from the time between the lightning flash and the thunder. Sound travels at about 334m/s (1,096ft/sec). So a storm is about 1km (0.62 miles) away for every three seconds.

SOUND SPEEDS

Sound travels at different speeds through different materials.

Material	Speed	
	m/sec	ft/sec
Rubber	54	177
Air at 0°C	334	1,096
Air at 100°C	366	1,201
Water	1,284	4,213
Mercury	1,452	4,764
Wood (Oak)	3,850	12,631
Iron	5,000	16,404
Glass	5,000	16,404

ECHOES

An echo is heard when a sound wave bounces off a hard surface. The length of time between the original sound and the echo depends on how far the sound travels before it bounces back. The further it travels, the longer it is before the echo is heard. Most sounds we hear arrive at our ears as a mixture of direct waves and echoes bouncing off surrounding surfaces.

ULTRASOUND

Ultrasound is sound at a frequency too high for humans to hear. Some animals can hear ultrasounds by echolocation and some make ultrasounds. Bats use ultrasound to catch their food. Depending on their frequency, the sounds they make bounce off flying insects, which the bat can locate and catch.

Echo

Listener hears one sound only, because sound wave travels quickly from hands to wall and back.

Handclap compresses air, creating sound wave.

Outgoing wave

Wall acts as barrier to sound wave. Distant barriers, such as cliffs or hills, will create separate echo, heard slightly later.

Echo from insect

Ultrasound waves

SOUND MAN

One of the most important contributors to our understanding of how we hear sounds was Georg von Békésy. In his research into hearing, he examined the ears of a dead zoo elephant that he had rescued from a glue factory.

SONIC BOOM

A sonic boom happens when the source of a sound, such as a jet aircraft, travels faster than the sound it produces (at about 1,200km/h, or 745mph). At such times, many wave fronts reach the ears of people standing directly below at the same time, making a very loud noise like a huge clap of thunder.

Subsonic flight

When flying below speed of sound, jet aircraft compresses air in front of it. Near to speed of sound, a wall or barrier of compressed air forms.

Supersonic flight

When aircraft reaches speed of sound, air pressure wave at nose produces massive shock wave. This causes sonic boom.

FREQUENCY

Frequency is the number of sound waves per second. The higher the number, the higher the pitch of the sound. Frequency is measured in hertz (Hz).

Peak
Trough
Amplitude
Wavelength

Sound wave The loudness of a sound depends on its amplitude. This is the difference between the point in a sound wave where the air is exerting the least pressure, and the point where it exerts the most.

Soft sound
There is not much difference between the low-pressure area of the sound wave and the high-pressure area.

Loud sound
As a sound gets louder, there is a greater difference between areas of high and low pressure.

Low sound
Low-pitched sounds have low frequency – fewer waves per second.

High sound
The sound waves are closer together – there are more of them per second.

SHATTERED

If a sound makes an object vibrate at its natural frequency, the vibrations will build to a greater and greater amplitude. This effect is called resonance, and it can even make an object break.

DOPPLER EFFECT

A police car's siren becomes more high-pitched as it approaches, and less high-pitched as it moves away. This is called the Doppler effect, and is caused by sound waves being pushed together in front of a moving source of sound, and spaced out behind it.

Waves compressed as car moves

Waves spread out behind car as it moves forwards.

Pitch of note lowers for listener when car passes.

1 As the sound gets nearer, the waves are pushed closer together and are heard at a higher frequency.

2 As the sound moves away, the waves are further apart and the sound is heard at a lower frequency.

KEY FREQUENCY RANGES
Various animals and machines make or detect sounds over different ranges of frequency. The human voice creates sound over a relatively narrow range of frequencies.

Human
Hears: 20–20,000Hz
Makes: 85–1,100Hz

Bat
Hears: 1,000–120,000Hz
Makes: 10,000–120,000Hz

Ultrasound scanner
Makes and receives:
3,500,000–
7,500,000Hz

SONAR ECHO
SONAR (Sound Navigation and Ranging) is a way of using echoes from ultrasound to detect the presence of objects. The echoes are used to form a picture on a screen.

Pictures from sound
Waves of ultrasound can be directed into the human body – to an unborn child, for example. The ultrasound echoes off the unborn child, then the ultrasound equipment picks up the echo and turns it into electrical impulses. These form a picture of the baby on a screen.

Frequency scale
Infrasound
Audible sounds
Ultrasounds

Elephant
Hears: 1–20,000Hz
Makes: 12Hz–unknown

Nuclear explosion:
as low as 0.01Hz

Dog
Hears: 15–50,000Hz
Makes: 450–1,080Hz

Porpoise
Hears: 150–150,000Hz
Makes: 7,000–120,000Hz

Ultrasound scan of foetus in womb

MUSIC
Musical instruments may make the same notes (sounds of different pitch) but they sound different because each one has its own quality. Although the main frequency is the same for each, they also produce overtones of other frequencies. These vary for each instrument.

Ranges
Some instruments produce a greater range of frequency than others.

Pipe organ
10–8,000Hz

Violin
200–2,650Hz

Trumpet
190–990Hz

Clarinet 75–1,800Hz

Comparison of instrument ranges

Piano
30–4,100Hz

RECORDING SOUND
There are several different ways of recording sound. All recorders work by turning the sound into some sort of electrical signal, which can be turned back into a sound later.

Vinyl records
These record signals appear as a wavy groove. They make the stylus vibrate, which in turn creates electrical signals that can be turned into sound.

Cassette tapes
Sounds are recorded as signals on a magnetic tape. A pattern of strong or weak magnetic signals forms on the tape. This can be played back, making electrical signals later used to make a sound.

Compact discs
Sounds are recorded in the CD's surface as tiny pits, which pass under a laser beam. Reflections from the beam are turned into electrical signals and used to make sound.

Vinyl record

Cassette tape

Compact disc

Record player's stylus fits into spiral groove.

Contours in groove wall record loudness and frequency of sound.

Magnetic alignment of particles on tape records sound.

Track is thinner than a hair and several kilometres long.

Sequence of microscopic pits records sound.

ELECTRONICS

ELECTRONICS, WHICH IS concerned with the movement and control of electrons, plays a crucial role in the efficient operation of modern technology.

1879 Cathode rays observed by English physicist William Crookes (1832–1919), using a specially designed vacuum tube. He finds that the rays, which he calls cathode rays, are deflected by magnetic fields.

Crookes tube

1880 American inventor Thomas Edison (1847–1931) observes tiny currents flowing from a lamp filament. This becomes known as the Edison effect.

1882 Edison effect investigated by Englishman John Ambrose Fleming (1849–1945).

Thomas Edison

| 1850 | 1879 | 1880 | 1882 |

1906 Use of crystals as radio wave detectors discovered independently by Americans H.H.C. Dunwoody and G.W. Pickard.

Early crystal radio set (c.1920)

1917 First crystal grown by artificial means by German J. Czochralski (1885–1953).

1918/19 Switching circuits devised by British scientists W.H. Eccles and F.W. Jordan.

1931 Electron microscope invented by German scientists Ernst Ruska (1906–88) and Max Knoll (1897–1969).

Image from modern electron microscope

1940 Electronic computers (using valv developed. These first computers are as l as buildings.

1943 Printed circuit boards perfected Austrian-born Paul Eisler (1907–92).

1947 Transistor invented by Americans William Shockley (1910–89), John Barde (1908–91), and Walter Brattain (1902–87)

| 1917 | 1918 | 1931 | 1940 | 1943 | 1947 |

TRANSISTOR

The transistor, the most important component in electronics, replaced the valve (below). It can turn a current on and off, and it can alter its strength. If enough transistors are connected together, their particular state at any time (on or off) can be used by computers to store and manipulate numbers, words, and pictures.

Audion valve of 1907, invented by Lee de Forest

Plate (anode)

Grid gives off weak signal.

Filament (cathode) gives off electrons.

VALVE

Valves control the strength and direction of a current. A red-hot filament (cathode) in a vacuum tube gives off streams of electrons. These are attracted towards a positively charged plate (anode), but a grid placed in the flow's path and given its own current will copy any variations in its current on to the larger current.

MINIATURIZED TRANSISTOR

A transistor can permit or prevent a current from flowing using a small charge.

1. A small, positive electric charge is given to a layer of conductive polysilicon that is embedded in non-conductive silicon dioxide.

2. The positive charge in the polysilicon attracts electrons from the base layer of P-type silicon (see below).

3. The flow of electrons towards the polysilicon makes current flow from the N-type silicon point, called the source, to another, the drain.

4. When current flows between source and drain in this way, the transistor is switched on. If the polysilicon is negatively charged, current stops, and the transistor switches off.

Semiconductors

Silicon is used for microchips because it is a semiconductor – it varies in conductivity. Different types of silicon – N-type and P-type – placed side-by-side, allow current flow to be directed. This property directs current in miniature transistors.

Aluminium lead

Polysilicon

Non-conductive silicon dioxide

Aluminium lead

Polysilicon

Aluminium lead

Source   **Drain**

N-type silicon

N-type silicon

P-type silicon

+

–

Electron-poor P-type silicon

Electron-rich N-type silicon

Current only flows from N- to P-type

CIRCUIT SYMBOLS

Diode

Light-emitting diode

Photodiode

N-P-N transistor

P-N-P transistor

Resistor

Speaker

Bulb

Transformer

Battery

CHIP RESULT

A single microchip produced in 1994 contained 9 million transistors. A similar number of transistors in 1950 would cover an area larger than eight football fields.

MAKING A MICROCHIP

Thousands of tiny transistors (above) and other components can be put on one tiny slice of silicon to make a complete electronic circuit – an integrated circuit, or microchip. Most electronic devices contain one or more of these silicon chips.

Design

The first stage in making a microchip is to plan and map the thousands of transistors and other components that the chip needs to perform its tasks. Modern chips are so complicated that most of this work is done by computers, not people.

Photography and checking

Once the circuit has been planned, computers check the proposed chip for possible design weaknesses. Microchips contain layers of different materials, and transparent, enlarged plans are used to check that each layer fits precisely with all the others.

7 **Electron discovered** by English sicist J.J.Thomson (1856–1940)

Vacuum tube

Anodes

Cathode

Thomson's tube

Fleming's diode

1904 Diode valve produced by John Ambrose Fleming. It is the first practical electronic device and conducts current in one direction only.

1906 Triode invented by American inventor Lee de Forest (1873–1961). His valve can amplify (make stronger) weak electric signals and becomes crucial to the development of electronics.

Lee de Forest

1907 Electric charge of electron measured by American physicist Robert Millikan (1868–1953).

1912 Electronic circuits using valves devised. This leads to broadcasting and radio communication.

| 1897 | 1900 | 1904 | 1906 | 1907 | 1912 |

8 **First integrated** uit, made from single ce of semiconductor erial, produced by erican Jack Kilby n 1923).

59–60 egrated circuit duction begins.

Modern circuit board with components

1971 First microprocessor developed by the Intel Corporation.

1973 Home video recorders (VCR) produced.

1983 First mobile telephone network introduced in Chicago, USA.

1987 Transatlantic optical fibre telephone cable laid, enlarging capacity of communications network.

1997 MMX processor chip introduced for multimedia computers.

1998 Iridium telephone network begins operation, using satellites in low orbits to offer global coverage for mobile telephones.

| 1958 | 1959 | | 1971 | 1973 | 1983 | 1987 | 1997 | 1998 |

Shockley, Bardeen, and Brattain, at Bell Laboratories, US

Fibre-optic installation

EVERYDAY ELECTRONICS

Modern car control systems

Automatic camera

Washing machine

Medical scanner

Mobile telephone

Radar system

Factory robot

Electronic shaver

LIQUID CRYSTAL DISPLAYS
Liquid crystals have a regular structure. Controlled currents force their molecules to allow or prevent the passage of light. Liquid crystal displays can display colour images as well as black and white. They are used mainly for portable electronic items, such as computers and hand-held games.

ELECTRONICS WORDS

Analogue signal Electrical copy of sound, vision, or other form of information.

Cathode Negative electrode in a valve or tube.

Digital signal Electrical stream of information in the form of on or off pulses.

Diode Permits electric current in circuit to travel in one direction only.

LED Light-emitting diode.

Microprocessor Integrated circuit that can decode instructions and manipulate information.

Resistor Controls amount of current flowing in a circuit.

Semiconductor Substance that conducts slightly; it can be combined with other substances to control conductivity.

Solid-state Using the electronic properties of solids, especially semiconductors, to act as valves.

Transistor Miniature electronic device that can amplify electric current and turn it on or off.

ELECTRONICS RECORDS
DENSEST MICROCHIP (1996) is a thumbnail-sized microprocessor which contains 125 million transistors.

LARGEST VALVES are about 2m (6.6ft) long and handle about 10 million watts. They are used in military radars and particle accelerators.

ELECTRONICS FACTS
• Microchips are the size of a fingernail, and yet a drawing showing all their workings in detail would be bigger than a detailed map of a major city.

• Fibre-optic cables, made of hair-fine glass, transmit information in the form of pulses of light. They are able to carry much more data than traditional copper cables.

• Filmmakers use electronics to generate astonishing special effects in their films. Animation, once produced by hand, can now be done by computers.

Electronics in special effects – scene from Disney film Tron

Pocket calculators – covered and uncovered

Liquid crystal display

Microchip

Uncovered keyboard

Silicon slice
Silicon metal, which is cheap and strong, needs to be highly refined before it can be used in chips. A pure enough piece, sliced and polished into thin wafers, is treated in a chemical process that etches the grid of components and tracks onto its surface,

Chemical and heat treatment
The potential microchip is now heated to a high temperature at which the chemicals that will form its several layers can fix on to the etched silicon surface. The delicacy of this process requires extreme cleanliness. All workers wear gowns and gloves.

Integrated circuit (chip)

Protective plastic casing

Chip with connections
When the silicon slice has been fully treated, it is placed on a plastic base and connected to metal leads that expand and connect to other parts of a circuit. These conductive leads send out the chip's signals and receive signals from other components.

Product
The pocket calculator (above) uses just one integrated circuit, but most modern appliances contain several. Other types of electronic items, such as liquid crystal displays, may be included in a final product.

COMPUTERS

COMPUTERS ARE AUTOMATIC electronic devices that can perform complex tasks by breaking them down into many simple calculations and doing them extremely quickly. Their ability to store, manipulate, and communicate information has had a massive impact on our lives.

1945 First electronic general-purpose calculator, ENIAC (Electronic Numerical Integrator and Calculator), built in US. Using valves, it weighs 30 tonnes, consumes 150kW, and averages 5,000 operations per second. The US Army uses it to calculate artillery aiming tables.

ENIAC

1964 BASIC (Beginners All-Purpose Symbolic Instruction Code) programming language is created by professors at Dartmouth College, USA. BASIC later becomes popular among users of personal computers.

1965 First commercially successful minicomputer, DEC PDP–8, is produced in USA. It sits on a desk-top.

1971 First microprocessor chip, the Intel 4004, produced in USA. It performs 60,000 operations per second.

1975 Microsoft founded by American businessmen Bill Gates (born 1955) and Paul Allen (born 1953). They develop DOS, which later becomes the dominant operating system for computers.

1976 Cray–1 supercomputer built. Word processor for personal computers, *Electric Pencil,* developed. **Apple** computer company formed.

1977 Mass-produced personal computer, Commodore PET (Personal Electronic Transactor), appears.

Early Commodore personal computer

1979 Applicati **software** for personal computers, Visicalc, appear A spreadsheet program, it sells 100,000 copies i its first year.

Timeline: 1940 ... 1945 ... 1960 1964 1965 1971 1975 1976 1977 1979

ANATOMY OF A COMPUTER

Every computer has four basic parts, or units: an input unit, such as a keyboard, that feeds information into the computer; a central processing unit (CPU) that performs the computer's tasks; an output unit, such as a monitor, that displays the results; a memory unit for storing information and instructions.

Input and output devices
These allow the computer to communicate with people and other computers. The keyboard and mouse are input devices. The monitor and printer are output devices.

Microprocessor
The microprocessor is the central control unit. It carries out a program's instructions and controls the information flowing around the computer on the Bus and the input and output devices.

Bus
The Bus links the microprocessor, memory, and input and output devices.

RAM (Random-Access Memory)
RAM is used to store programs that are being run. When a computer is switched off the information in the RAM is lost.

ROM (Read-Only Memory)
When you switch on a computer, a program that is permanently stored in the ROM checks the computer and makes it ready for use. The ROM's program cannot be changed.

Monitor

Cards for different systems can be added, e.g. modem, sound card, video card.

Power supply

CD–ROM drive

Floppy disk drive

Compact disc

Hard disk

Floppy disk

Mouse pad

Mouse

Keyboard

COMPUTER WORDS

Applications software Software used for specific tasks, e.g. word processors, databases.

Bit Binary digit (a 1 or a 0).

Bug Error in a program.

Byte Piece of information. One byte contains eight bits.

Database Set of data on computer accessible in various ways.

Hardware Machinery and components of the computer.

Internet Worldwide network of computer networks.

Megabyte One million bytes.

Modem Device that allows computers to exchange information using the telephone network.

Operating system The program that enables the computer to perform general operations.

Software The variety of programs used by a computer.

CD–ROM drive
Compact discs, read using lasers, store more data than floppy disks.

Hard disk
The hard disk stores data when the computer is switched off. It is usually used to store larger amounts of data than the RAM.

Floppy disks
These can be used to transfer data between computers.

GENERATIONS OF COMPUTER

Generation	Dates	Characteristic
1st	1944–59	Use valves (vacuum tubes)
2nd	1959–64	Use transistors
3rd	1964–75	Large Scale Integrated Circuits (LSI)
4th	1975–	Very Large Scale Integrated Circuits (VLSI)
5th	Under development	"Artificial Intelligence"-based computers

MODERN COMPUTERS

• In 1996 the first ever computer that can carry out one trillion calculations per second was unveiled.

• Digital versatile disc, or digital video disc, (DVD) was released in 1996. It began to replace CD-ROMs and may soon become standard on personal computers.

• In 1997 a computer called Deep Blue 2 beat the reigning world chess champion, Garry Kasparov.

7 Transistor, ...ntial storage device ...omputers, invented ...merican engineers ...am Shockley ...0–89), John Bardeen ...8–91), and Walter ...tain (1902–87).

1948 First stored-program computer, Manchester Mark 1, built in UK. Using valves, it can perform about 500 operations per second and has the first RAM (see opposite). It fills a room the size of a small office.

Visible portion of Manchester Mark 1 computer

1951 Early computer game, *Nim,* played by Ferranti Nimrod Computer at the Festival of Britain.

1957 FORTRAN (Formula Translator) programming language invented at IBM.

1958 Integrated circuit (microchip) produced by American engineer Jack Kilby (born 1923). His circuit is made on a single piece of semiconductor.

Jack Kilby

| 1947 | 1948 | 1950 | 1951 | 1957 | 1958 |

1 First portable computer, ...orne 1, produced. At the size and ...ght of a sewing machine, however, it is ...h less convenient than current ...able computers.

Osborne 1 portable computer

1981 IBM launches IBM PC on the personal computer market. IBM makes the first massive sales in the personal computer market.

1984 Apple Macintosh computer (or Apple Mac) becomes first successful personal computer with a mouse (see opposite) and easy-to-use Graphical User Interface (GUI).

1985 Microsoft launches Windows for the PC. Windows is a Graphical User Interface similar to the Apple Mac's, making personal computers much easier to use.

Microsoft Windows title screen

1990 IBM Pentium PC produced. It holds up to 4,000 megabytes of RAM and can perform up to 112 million instructions per second. The microprocessor chip at the heart of the computer measures 16mm by 17mm and contains 3.1 million transistors. It is designed using a system called VLSI (Very Large Scale Integration).

| 80 | 1981 | 1984 | 1985 | 1990 |

OMPUTER FACTS

...ll the data that computers use is ...inary code: a signal of electrical ...ses that is either on (1) or off ... Words, numbers, and pictures ...n he expressed as sequences of ...ary code.

CD-ROM is useful for reference books and can use sound and moving images.

...CD–ROM is a form of compact ...sc player modified for computers. ...Ds for CD–ROM can store 450 ...nes as much data as can be held ...a floppy disk.

Computer viruses may multiply in a computer's memory like bacteria.

- Computer viruses are programs that destroy stored information. A virus may enter the computer's memory and copy itself so many times that it uses up all the memory, or it may make the computer destroy all the data in its memory.
- Computers can communicate with each other over a telephone line, using a machine called a modem.
- Computer performance increased by a factor of about a million between 1950 and 1990.

PROGRAMS

A program is the set of instructions that a computer needs to carry out a particular task, such as word processing. Instructions may be written in "machine code", or other computer languages, such as BASIC or FORTRAN.

A computer's program may be printed out.

SUPERCOMPUTERS

Computers designed to operate at the highest possible speeds are called supercomputers. By performing several processes at once and by being cooled – which causes their components to conduct electricity more efficiently – they can calculate at a very fast rate.

Cray X–MP/48 supercomputer, used in study of particle physics at CERN, Switzerland.

OW A FLOPPY DISK WORKS

...mputer users can store data on floppy disks ...d transfer it to other computers.

1 The surface of a floppy disk is coated with iron particles. Small bands of these particles can be made to line up in one direction or another by an electromagnet inside the computer.

2 Current is passed down a coil, magnetizing an iron core and forcing the iron particles to line up. If current is reversed, the particles line up in the other direction.

3 One pair of particle bands makes up a bit of data. If the bands in the pair lie in the same direction, they represent the binary number 0. If not, the pair represents 1.

IMAGES ON SCREEN

A computer screen consists of a grid of small picture cells called pixels. Each pixel has a horizontal and vertical position code and a colour code. The computer's microprocessor generates the picture as a series of these codes, lighting up each pixel in a certain colour.

Example of screen image, showing enlarged area with individual pixels.

Horizontal position code

Vertical position code

Colour codes:
0 White
1 Black
2 Red
3 Green
4 Blue
5 Cyan
6 Yellow
7 Magenta

	58	59	60	61	62
73	0	0	0	0	0
74	0	0	2	2	0
75	0	0	0	2	0
76	0	0	2	0	0
77	0	2	0	0	0
78	0	0	0	0	0

COMPUTER-AIDED DESIGN

Computers allow engineers to test new designs without having to build prototype models. They can also be used to help model complex systems, such as weather systems.

Computer model of airflow over aeroplane

BRAIN DRAIN

The first all-purpose computer, ENIAC, required so much electricity to process information that the lights in a nearby town dimmed each time it was used.

MATHEMATICS

MATHEMATICS IS THE study of numbers and shapes. It is a vital tool, not only for scientists and engineers, but for everyone. Algebra is the branch of mathematics that uses abstract symbols in place of numbers, while geometry deals with shapes and lines.

MATHS TOOLS

Set squares and compasses enable us to draw shapes precisely, such as circles and squares. Electronic tools, such as the calculator, save time.

Compasses

Protractor for measuring angles

Set square

Calculator

ONE TO TEN: SYMBOL SYSTEMS

Different civilizations have used different symbols for numbers, and some do not include a zero symbol.

Number	Babylonian	Roman	Mayan	Arabic
Zero				0
One		I	•	1
Two		II	••	2
Three		III	•••	3
Four		IV	••••	4
Five		V	—	5
Six		VI		6
Seven		VII		7
Eight		VIII		8
Nine		IX		9
Ten		X		10

NEGATIVE NUMBERS

Sometimes it is useful to use numbers less than zero – negative numbers. For example, if the temperature on a winter's day falls below zero, it is referred to as a negative number, such as -3.

-5 -4 -3 -2 -1 0 1 2 3 4 5

Number line

9-dot matrix, 3-by-3 square

SQUARE NUMBERS

When a number is multiplied by itself, it is said to be squared. This is usually written as the number, with a small 2 next to and above it. So, three squared is $3^2 = 3 \times 3 = 9$.

BINARY SYSTEM

We use a number system based on the number ten, but a number system can be based on any number. Computers use binary numbers, based on the number two. Binary uses only two digits: 0 and 1.

Base 10 number	Binary number
1	1
2	10
3	11
4	100
5	101
6	110
7	111

PRIME NUMBERS

Prime numbers are those that can be divided only by themselves and 1, e.g., 17. 12 is not a prime, since it can be divided by 2, 3, 4, and 6, as well as by itself and 1.

2	3	5	7
11	13	17	19
23	29	31	37
41	43	47	53
59	61	67	71
73	79	83	89
97	101	103	107
109	113	127	131

FRACTIONS

When a cake is halved, each piece is equivalent to the whole divided by two. This is written $1/2$, the line meaning "divided by". So, $3/4$ (three-quarters) means three divided by four.

PERCENTAGES

It is sometimes useful to write fractions as percentages. Per cent means "for each hundred". Written as a percentage, $1/2$ becomes 50%, since half of 100 is 50.

DECIMALS

Numbers less than one can be written as decimals. A decimal point is used. The number after the decimal point represents a number of tenths. So, one-half is written as 0.5 ($5/10$).

STYLE TABLE

Fractions	Decimals	Percentages
$1/2$	0.5	50%
$1/4$	0.25	25%
$1/10$	0.1	10%
$1/100$	0.01	1%

MATHEMATICAL SYMBOLS

Symbol	Meaning	Symbol	Meaning	Symbol	Meaning
+	Add (plus)	=	Equal to	√	Square root of
−	Subtract (minus)	≠	Not equal to	%	Per cent
×	Multiply (times)	<	Less than	≤	Less than or equal to
÷	Divided by	>	Greater than	≥	Greater than or equal to

CHAOS THEORY

The intricate pattern (below) was created using a simple mathematical equation. These equations are a product of a recent field of mathematics called chaos theory.

Fractal (computer-generated image)

SCIENTIFIC NOTATION

Very large or small numbers are often written using a system called scientific notation.

Number	Number between 1 and 10	Power of ten	Scientific notation
10	1	10	1×10
150	1.5	$10^2 (= 100)$	1.5×10^2
274,000,000	2.74	$10^8 (= 100,000,000)$	2.74×10^8
0.0023	2.3	$10^{-3} (= 0.001)$	2.3×10^{-3}

DEAD RIGHT

At 20 years of age, Pierre Galois wrote his most important mathematical ideas in a letter to a friend, the night before he was killed in a duel. His results are still used today.

GEOMETRY

Geometry is the study of lines, angles, solid shapes, and surfaces.

PLANE FIGURES

Any two-dimensional (flat) shape, such as a circle, is a plane figure. A polygon is a plane figure with three or more straight sides.

Area

The area of a shape or surface is a measure of the size of the surface. For example, the area of a football pitch is greater than the area of a tennis court.

SOLIDS

Solids are not flat, but three-dimensional (they take up space). A polyhedron is a solid that has plane (flat) faces.

Volume

The volume of a solid is the amount of space it takes up. For example, a football has a greater volume than that of a golf ball.

Square *Polygon with four equal sides, all meeting at right angles*
Area = length²

Circle *Curve on which all points are equidistant from the centre*
Area = π x radius²

Equilateral triangle *Has three equal sides*
Area (of any triangle) = ¹/₂ x base x height

Isosceles triangle *Triangle with two equal sides*
Area = ¹/₂ x base x height

Quadrilateral *Polygon with four sides*

Rhombus *Quadrilateral with sides of equal length*
Area = 2x (a x b)

Rectangle *Quadrilateral with opposite sides of equal length that meet at right angles*
Area = base x height

Parallelogram *Quadrilateral with opposite sides that are parallel and of equal length*
Area = a x b

Trapezium *Quadrilateral with only two sides parallel*
Area = ¹/₂ x sum of parallel sides x distance between them

Pentagon *Polygon with five sides*

Hexagon *Polygon with six sides*

Octagon *Polygon with eight sides*

Tetrahedron *Polyhedron with four triangles as faces*

Cube *Six squares of equal sides as faces*
Volume = length³

Octahedron *Polyhedron with eight faces*

Square pyramid *Pentahedron with one square face and four triangular faces*

Triangular prism *Solid figure with two triangular ends*
Volume = area of triangular ends x distance between them

Rectangular block
Volume = length x breadth x height

Sphere *Globe-shaped figure with every point on its surface equidistant from its centre*
Volume = ⁴/₃ x π x radius³
Surface area = 4 x π x radius²

Hemisphere *Half-sphere*

Spheroid *Egg shaped figure*

Apex

Cone *Circular base, narrowing to a point, or apex*
Volume = ¹/₃ x π x radius² x height

Cylinder *Two circular faces, connected by a tube*
Surface area = π x diameter x length
Volume = π x radius² x length

CIRCLE TERMS

Arc Part of curve.

Circumference Distance around edge of circle.

Chord Straight line joining any two points on circumference.

Diameter Line from one side of circle to other, passing through centre.

Pi (π) Ratio of circumference to diameter (approx. 3.14159, same for all circles).

Radius Distance from centre of circle to edge.

Sector Slice of circle between two radii.

Segment Part of circle between chord and edge.

PYTHAGORAS' THEOREM

For any right-angled triangle, the squares of the two sides adjacent to the right angle (B and C, below) add up to the square of the longest side, or hypotenuse (A).

$$A^2 = B^2 + C^2$$

Right angle

ANGLE

An angle is a measure of the space between two lines, formed when one line is rotated (turned). The hands of a clock form an angle between each other as they turn. Angles are measured in degrees (°), or radians.

Obtuse angle
90°
130°
45°
0°
360°
Reflex angle
Right angle
Acute angle
Round angle
240°

TRIGONOMETRY

Trigonometry is the study of the relationships between the sides and angles of triangles.

TRIGONOMETRIC RATIOS

Three simple relationships, or ratios, are commonly used in trigonometry: sine (sin), cosine (cos), and tangent (tan). The sine of an angle in a right-angled triangle is given by dividing the length of the side opposite the angle by the length of the hypotenuse.

Right-angled triangle
Hypotenuse
Opposite
Adjacent

$$\sin = \frac{\text{length of opposite}}{\text{length of hypotenuse}}$$

$$\cos = \frac{\text{length of adjacent}}{\text{length of hypotenuse}}$$

$$\tan = \frac{\text{length of opposite}}{\text{length of adjacent}}$$

Trigonometry calculation
To find the height of the tower, multiply the tangent (tan) of the angle from the ground to the top of the tower by the distance from the building – 659m (2,162ft). This gives a height of 553m (1,814ft).

659m (2,162ft)
40°
Position of observer

KEY MATHEMATICIANS

Euclid (c.300 B.C.), Greek mathematician, whose geometric proofs in *The Elements* were taught in schools for 2,000 years. He studied irrational numbers (numbers, such as √2, that cannot be written as fractions or decimals).

Gottfried Wilhelm Leibniz (1646–1716), German mathematician and philosopher, independently invented the theory of calculus, at the same time as Isaac Newton. He built a mechanical multiplying machine.

Karl Friedrich Gauss (1777–1855), German mathematician and astronomer. He wrote first major book on number theory, which included a theory of complex numbers. He contributed to many areas.

Baron Augustin-Louis Cauchy (1789–1857), French mathematician, modernized the calculus, contributed to an area of mathematics called group theory. He is said to have more theorems named after him than any other mathematician.

MATHS FACTS

• Perfect numbers are those that are equal to the sum of their factors (a number that divides equally into another number). The first perfect number is six, since 1 + 2 + 3 = 6.

• The theorem that Greek mathematician Pythagoras discovered and that bears his name was known by Babylonian and Egyptian mathematicians hundreds of years earlier.

• The Maya in South America were the first people to invent a symbol for the number zero.

• There is an infinite number of prime numbers.

• The mathematical term "algorithm" is derived from the name of the 9th-century Arabic mathematician al-Khwarizmi. The term "algebra" comes from the title of his book.

WEIGHTS AND MEASURES

THERE ARE TWO MAJOR systems of measurement. The metric system, based on the number ten, is the most common and is used by scientists worldwide. Certain countries, such as the USA, use the older imperial system. You can convert between systems using conversion tables (right).

5 kite

4 deben

2 kite

1 kite

ANCIENT MEASURES

MAYAN NUMBER KNOTS
The ancient Maya of Central America used an arrangement of knotted strings, called a quipu, to record numerical information. The type and position of knot and the length and colour of string were all significant.

Mayan quipu

ASSYRIAN WEIGHTS
The first standard system of weights arose when traders needed to measure quantities of goods. Assyrian weights (right) were made for King Shalmaneser III.

Assyrian ingot weights

EGYPTIAN WEIGHTS
Ancient Egyptians used a weight called a deben, made of copper. The value of the standard deben was later increased, and divided into ten "kite".

INDUS VALLEY WEIGHTS
The people of Mohenjo-Daro, a city of the Indus valley civilization (c. 2500 B.C.) used cubic weights made of a stone called chert. The largest of these weights could not be lifted by one person alone.

Indus valley chert weights

THE SEVEN BASE SI UNITS

SI (Système Internationale d'Unités) is the standard system of units for scientists throughout the world. There are seven base units, from which the other units are derived (shown below).

Quantity	Unit	Symbol
Mass	Kilogram	kg
Length	Metre	m
Time	Second	s
Electric current	Ampere	A
Temperature	Kelvin	K
Luminous intensity	Candela	cd
Amount of substance	Mole	mole

MEASUREMENT FACTS

• The metric system was first adopted in France in 1791. King Louis XVI approved it the day before he attempted to flee the revolution that was unfolding.

• China was the first country to use a decimal system. Wooden rulers divided into units of ten that date back to the 6th century B.C. have been found.

• Units used today in the imperial system have evolved over centuries, mainly by custom. The origins of some of these units can be found in the earliest civilizations of the Near and Middle East. The metric system commonly used today – the SI system – was devised by scientists and adopted in a single period by many nations.

STANDARDS
To ensure that everyone means the same thing when stating measurements, several units have very precisely defined standards. A few are defined below.

THE STANDARD SECOND
One second is defined as "the duration of 9,192,631,770 periods of the radiation corresponding to the transition between the two hyperfine levels of the ground state of the caesium–133 atom."

Caesium clock

THE STANDARD KILOGRAM
A kilogram of the metal platinum was made as a worldwide standard for the kilogram. It is kept under carefully controlled conditions at the International Bureau of Weights and Measures at Sèvres, France.

Standard kilogram

THE STANDARD METRE
One metre is defined as "the length equal to 1,650,763.73 wavelengths, in a vacuum, of the radiation corresponding to the transition between the levels 2p10 and 5d5 of the krypton–86 atom."

Krypton gas

DERIVED UNITS
This table shows a selection of the derived units in the SI (Système Internationale d'Unités).

Quantity	Unit	Symbol
Frequency	Hertz	Hz
Energy	Joule	J
Force	Newton	N
Power	Watt	W
Pressure	Pascal	Pa
Electric charge	Coulomb	C
Electrical resistance	Ohm	Ω
Electric potential difference	Volt	V
Radiation activity	Becquerel	Bq

MUSICAL MEASURE
In ancient China, a vessel that was used to measure out grain or wine was known to contain the correct volume of goods if it made the right sound when struck.

NUMBER TERMS: GREAT AND SMALL
Prefixes inserted before a unit signify multiples or fractions of that unit.

Prefix	Symbol	Meaning	Prefix	Symbol	Meaning
tera	T	One million million	deci	d	One-tenth
giga	G	One thousand million	centi	c	One-hundredth
mega	M	One million	milli	m	One-thousandth
kilo	k	One thousand	micro	μ	One-millionth
hecto	h	One hundred	nano	n	One-thousand millionth

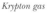

LENGTH

1 inch (in)	
1 foot (ft)	12 in
1 yard (yd)	3 ft
1 mile	1,760 yd
1 millimetre (mm)	
1 centimetre (cm)	10 mm
1 metre (m)	100 cm
1 kilometre (km)	1,000 m

AREA

1 square inch (in²)	
1 sq foot (ft²)	144 in²
1 sq yard (yd²)	9 ft²
1 acre	4,840 yd²
1 sq mile	640 acres
1 sq millimetre (mm²)	
1 sq centimetre (cm²)	100 mm²
1 sq metre (m²)	10,000 cm²
1 hectare (ha)	10,000 m²
1 sq kilometre (km²)	1,000,000 m²

VOLUME

1 cubic inch (in³)	
1 cubic foot (ft³)	1,728 in³
1 cubic yard (yd³)	27 ft³
1 fluid ounce (fl oz)	
1 pint (pt)	20 fl oz
1 gallon (gal)	8 pt
1 cubic mm (mm³)	
1 cubic cm (cm³)	1,000 mm³
1 cubic metre (m³)	1,000,000 cm³
1 litre (l)	1,000 cm³

MASS AND WEIGHT

1 ounce (oz)	
1 pound (lb)	16 oz
1 stone	14 lb
1 hundredweight (cwt)	8 stones
1 ton	20 cwt
1 gram (g)	
1 kilogram (kg)	1,000 g
1 tonne (t)	1,000 kg

BODY MEASURE

Ancient civilizations used proportions of the body as units of measurement because of their convenience. Since the unit varied slightly according to the size of the person making the measurement, a master unit, or standard was often made.

In ancient Egypt, the cubit was from the tip of the forefinger to the elbow.

A royal master of black granite cubit was made as a standard.

A hand was divided into four fingers.

The foot was used as a unit of measurement in ancient Greece and Rome.

Two steps = one pace

The mile originated in Rome – it consisted of 1,000 paces, each of which was two steps.

LENGTH CONVERSION

To convert:	Into:	Multiply by:
Inches	Centimetres	2.54
Feet	Metres	0.3048
Yards	Metres	0.9144
Miles	Kilometres	1.6093
Centimetres	Inches	0.3937
Metres	Feet	3.2808
Metres	Yards	1.0936
Kilometres	Miles	0.6214

VOLUME CONVERSION

To convert:	Into:	Multiply by:
Cubic inches	Cubic centimetres (millilitres)	16.3871
Cubic feet	Litres	28.3169
Cubic yards	Cubic metres	0.7646
Fluid ounces	Cubic centimetres (millilitres)	28.4131
Pints	Litres	0.5683
Gallons	Litres	4.5461
Cubic centimetres (millilitres)	Cubic inches	0.0610
	Fluid ounces	0.0352
Litres	Cubic feet	0.0353
Cubic metres	Cubic yards	1.3080
Cubic centimetres (millilitres)	Fluid ounces	0.0352
Litres	Pints	1.7598
	Gallons	0.2200

AREA CONVERSION

To convert:	Into:	Multiply by:
Sq inches	Sq centimetres	6.4516
Sq feet	Sq metres	0.0929
Sq yards	Sq metres	0.8361
Acres	Hectares	0.4047
Sq miles	Sq kilometres	2.5900
Sq centimetres	Sq inches	0.155
Sq metres	Sq feet	10.7639
Sq metres	Sq yards	1.1960
Hectares	Acres	2.4711
Sq kilometres	Sq miles	0.3861

MASS AND WEIGHT CONVERSIONS

To convert:	Into:	Multiply by:
Ounces	Grams	28.3495
Pounds	Kilograms	0.4536
Stones	Kilograms	6.3503
Hundredweights	Kilograms	50.802
Tons	Tonnes	1.0161
Grams	Ounces	0.0352
Kilograms	Pounds	2.2046
	Stones	0.1575
	Hundredweights	0.0197
Tonnes	Tons	0.9842

TEMPERATURE CONVERSION

To convert Fahrenheit (°F) into centigrade (°C), use the following formula:
$$°C = (°F - 32) \div 1.8$$

To convert centigrade (°C) into Fahrenheit (°F), use the following formula:
$$°F = (°C \times 1.8) + 32$$

SPEED CONVERSION

To convert:	Into:	Multiply by:
Miles per hour	Kilometres per hour Metres per second	1.6093 0.4470
Kilometres per hour	Miles per hour	0.6214
Metres per second	Miles per hour	2.2370
Feet per second	Miles per hour	0.6818

MEASURING MARATHON

An acre was originally defined as the area of land that a pair of oxen could plough in one day.

TIME

TIME IS THE INTERVAL between one instant and another. People measure time by recording the movements of the Earth travelling in space: one Earth spin is a day and one orbit of the Earth around the Sun is a year. People keep time with mechanical timekeepers such as clocks and watches.

NATURAL TIME

DAYS AND YEARS

The Earth orbits the Sun in one year. At the same time, the Earth spins on its own axis. It completes one spin in a single day and 365 1/4 spins in a year. The quarter day is impractical, so after four years they are added together, and every fourth year has 366 days, a leap year.

Day

The Earth completes one spin on its axis in one day.

Year

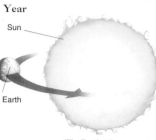

Sun

Earth

The Earth takes a year to travel round the Sun.

MONTH

While the Earth orbits the Sun, the Moon orbits the Earth. The phases of the moon add up to 29.5 days. This cycle is the lunar month and is the basis of our present-day months.

Earth

Moon

STANDARD TIME

The time measured at Greenwich, London, is the standard time for the whole world. For every 15 degrees of longitude east or west of Greenwich, the time is one hour ahead of or behind Greenwich time.

Moscow, Russia: 3.00 p.m.

London, England: 12.00 noon

New York, USA: 7.00 a.m.

Tokyo, Japan: 9.00 p.m.

Rio de Janeiro, Brazil: 9.00 a.m.

There are 24 time zones around the globe.

TIME FACTS

• The Earth is slowing down: a few million years from now leap years will not be needed.

• The Sumerians of Mesopotamia (present-day Iraq) first divided hours into 60 minutes, and minutes into 60 seconds in about 3000 B.C. They used 60, because it was easily divisible by 2, 3, and 4.

TIME WORDS

a.m. Before noon (ante meridiem)

Equinox The two times in a year when the Sun crosses the Equator and day and night are of equal length.

Local time The time at points that are on the same meridian.

Meridian Line of longitude

p.m. After noon (post meridiem)

Solstice The two times in the year when the Sun is farthest from the Equator. These are the shortest and the longest days.

HISTORY OF TIMEKEEPING

People originally measured time by the position of the Sun in the sky. Later, they began to rely on machines for timekeeping, with mechanical motions that were repeated over and over again. Today, people use clocks and watches that can measure time in fractions of a second.

c.2200 B.C. Stonehenge stone circles, England, may have been used by Neolithic people to tell the time. The position of the circles allows the Sun to shine through or rise above certain stones.

Stonehenge

c.1500 B.C. Sundials are used by the Egyptians. A shadow cast by the Sun's rays indicates the time on a marked surface.

Position of the stars is used by the peoples of Babylon, Egypt, and China to tell the time.

Sun

2200 B.C.   1500 B.C.   1500 B.C.

1335 First mechanical clock is erected in Milan, Italy. The turret, or tower, clock has no face, but simply strikes the hours. Turret clocks are later built throughout Europe.

1364 First known domestic clocks made by Giovanni Dondi (1318–89) of Italy. These early clocks are small versions of turret clocks, with the addition of an hour hand.

1386 Oldest mechanical clock still working is built at Salisbury Cathedral, England.

The clock in Salisbury Cathedral is driven by a revolving drum.

1510 First portable clocks made by Peter Henlein (1479–1542), a German locksmith. These small clocks are driven by a spring. The open face has an hour hand only.

Early portable clock

1330   1335   1360   1364   1380   1386   1500   1510

c.1730 Cuckoo clocks first introduced in the Black Forest, Germany.

1754 Lever escapement combined with the balance spring, gives an accuracy to within ten seconds a day.

Cuckoo clock

1759 An accurate marine timekeeper, Harrison 4, is introduced by Englishman John Harrison (1693-1776). It can withstand the changing movement and temperatures on board ship and has less than one minute of error after five months at sea.

1880 Greenwich time, time measured at the Royal Observatory, Greenwich, becomes standard time in Britain. Four years later it becomes standard time for the whole world.

c.1900 First wrist-watches introduced. At first only women wear them, until World War I (1914–18), when they become popular with men in the trenches.

Early electric clock

1730   1730   1754   1759   1800   1880   1900   1900

GREGORIAN CALENDAR

Most Western countries use the Gregorian calendar, which is based on the time it takes for the Earth to circle the Sun. At first, the Romans began their year in March, which is why September to December are named after the Latin numbers seven to ten. Later, in about 150 B.C., January became the first month of the year.

NAMES OF THE MONTHS

January Janus, god of gateways

February Februa, festival of purification

March Mars, god of war

April Aperire, to open

May Maia, goddess of fertility

June Juno, goddess of the Moon

July Julius Caesar

August Augustus, the first Roman emperor

September Septem, seven
October Octo, eight
November Novem, nine
December Decem, ten

LONGEST YEAR

The longest year ever was 46 B.C., which lasted for 455 days. Lengthened by 90 days to bring it in line with the solar year, it became known as the Year of Confusion.

HEBREW AND MUSLIM CALENDARS

These are based on the Moon's cycle.

Hebrew months	Muslim months	Gregorian date
Tishri	Muharram	Sept. to Oct.
Heshvan	Safar	Oct. to Nov.
Kislev	Rabi I	Nov. to Dec.
Tevet	Rabi II	Dec. to Jan.
Shevat	Jumada I	Jan. to Feb.
Adar	Jumada II	Feb. to Mar.
Nisan	Rajab	Mar. to Apr.
Iyar	Sha'ban	Apr. to May
Sivan	Ramadan	May to June
Tammuz	Shawwal	June to July
Av	Dhu al-Qa'dah	July to Aug.
Elul	Dhu al-Hijjah	Aug. to Sept.

ANCIENT CHINESE CALENDAR

This calendar, based on the Sun and the Moon, is no longer used in China, but is still in use in some Asian countries. It is divided into 24 seasons.

Season	Meaning	Gregorian date
Li Chun	Spring begins	5 Feb. to 19 Feb.
Yu Shui	Rain water	19 Feb. to 5 Mar.
Jing Zhe	Excited insects	5 Mar. to 20 Mar.
Chun Fen	Vernal equinox	20 Mar. to 5 Apr.
Qing Ming	Clear and bright	5 Apr. to 20 Apr.
Gu Yu	Grain rains	20 Apr. to 5 May
Li Xia	Summer begins	5 May to 21 May
Xiao Man	Grain fills	21 May to 5 June
Mang Zhong	Grain in ear	5 June to 21 June
Xia Zhi	Summer solstice	21 June to 7 July
Xiao Shu	Slight heat	7 July to 23 July
Da Shu	Great heat	23 July to 7 Aug.
Li Qiu	Autumn begins	7 Aug. to 23 Aug.
Chu Shu	Limit of heat	23 Aug. to 7 Sept.
Bai Lu	White dew	7 Sept. to 23 Sept.
Qui Fen	Autumn equinox	23 Sept. to 8 Oct.
Han Lu	Cold dew	8 Oct. to 23 Oct.
Shuang Jiang	Frost descends	23 Oct. to 7 Nov.
Li Dong	Winter begins	7 Nov. to 22 Nov.
Xiao Xue	Little snow	22 Nov. to 7 Dec.
Da Xue	Heavy snow	7 Dec. to 22 Dec.
Dong Zhi	Winter solstice	22 Dec. to 6 Jan.
Xiao Han	Little cold	6 Jan. to 21 Jan.
Da Han	Severe cold	21 Jan. to 5 Feb.

1400 B.C. Water clocks [ar]e used by the Egyptians. [A] bowl with a hole in the [bo]ttom is filled with water. [T]he passing of time is [sh]own by a drop in the level [of] water, which lines up [wi]th one of the marks [ca]rved into the bowl.

Water clock

c.A.D. 890 Clock candles are used by the English king, Alfred the Great (849–899). When a candle, which has hours marked down its length, has burnt down to a mark, it indicates that an hour has passed by.

1100s Hourglasses used in navigation, by physicians to time a pulse, and by teachers and preachers to time lessons and sermons. Sand drains from the top glass bulb to the bottom. Some glasses measure 15 or 30 minutes as well as up to one or two hours.

1300s Monasteries use simple machinery that sounds bells at regular intervals to call worshippers to prayer. A person called a clock jack rings the bells.

Hourglass

0 B.C.	1400 B.C.	A.D. 500	A.D. 890	1100 / 1100	1300 / 1300

1582 Regularity of [a] pendulum's swing [is] shown by Italian [sc]ientist, Galileo (1564–1642).

Galileo's design for a pendulum

1657 First pendulum clock is made by Dutch astronomer, Christiaan Huygens (1629–95). The pendulum controls the rotation of the wheels of the clock.

1670 Long, or seconds, pendulum is introduced by William Clement (c.1638–1704), an English clockmaker.

1675 Spiral balance spring, giving clocks an accuracy to within two minutes a day, is invented by Huygens.

Huygens' balance spring

c.1690s Astronomers at the Royal Observatory, Greenwich, London, measure the stars to determine time.

Royal Observatory

1582	1650 / 1657 / 1670 / 1670	1675	1690 / 1690		

1939 First quartz [c]rystal clock is [in]stalled at Greenwich. [T]he crystals' vibrations [ar]e controlled, counted, [re]corded, and used to [e]stablish precise time.

Early wrist-watch

1948 First atomic clock developed in the USA. It works by counting the natural vibrations of caesium atoms, which vibrate 9,192,631,770 times per second. Time for the whole world is now established by using 80 atomic clocks from 24 countries.

1970 Atomic clock is accurate to one second in 30,000 years.

1970s–1990s Digital watches are popular. A microchip changes the numbers every second, so that the time kept is very precise.

Early atomic clock

1990s Global positioning system (GPS) employs geostationary satellites, each with three atomic clocks.

1997 Caesium fountain atomic clock tells time to an accuracy of one second in 3 million years.

1930	1939	1940 / 1948	1970 / 1970	1990 / 1997	2000

ENGINES

AN ENGINE TURNS different forms of energy into motion, or kinetic energy. In the last two centuries, engine efficiency has substantially improved.

50 B.C. Chinese engineers build water wheels that use the energy of moving water.

A.D. c.600 Early windmills appear, converting wind energy into mechanical motion.

1712 Practical steam engine using piston and cylinder built by English inventor Thomas Newcomen (1663–1729).

1769 Steam carriage built by French military engineer Nicolas-Joseph Cugnot (1725–1804).

Watt's rotative engine

1783 Steam-powered paddleboat, *Pyroscaphe,* sailed up Saône River, France, by French engineer Jouffroy d'Abbans (1751–1832).

1782 Rotative steam engine built by Scottish engineer James Watt (1736–1819). Watt's engine is much more efficient and practical than Newcomen's engine.

| 50 B.C. | A.D. 1 | 600 | 1700 | 1712 | 1769 | 1782 | 1783 |

1892 German Rudolf Diesel (1858–1913) invents engine (later named diesel engine) with fuel that ignites on compression. When later built, the engine is more efficient than existing internal combustion engines.

1897 Ship powered by new steam turbine launched by British engineer Charles Parsons (1854–1931), revolutionizing marine engineering. His ship, *Turbinia,* unexpectedly appears at a British naval review and, at 34.5 knots, easily outruns the launch sent to stop it.
Queen (1904), fitted with marine turbine

1903 Powered flight by American brothers, Orville (1871–1948) and Wilbur (1867–1912) Wright, using internal combustion engine.

First sustained powered flight of Kitty Hawk

1907 Supercharger used on a car by American engineer Lee S. Chadwick.

1926 Liquid-fuel rocket launched by American Robert Goddard (1882–1945).

Robert Goddard

| 1892 | 1897 | 1900 | 1903 | 1907 | 1926 |

INTERNAL COMBUSTION ENGINE

The internal combustion engine, developed in the 19th century, has several advantages over earlier types of engine: it does not require stoking, like a steam engine; it is portable, unlike windmills or water wheels; and its fuel is highly efficient.

FOUR-STROKE ENGINE CYCLE

1 Inlet valve opens. Piston slides down cylinder, sucking in a mixture of fuel and air, called the charge.
Induction stroke

3 Spark ignites compressed charge. Expanding gases force piston down cylinder. Piston spins crankshaft.
Power stroke

2 Inlet valve snaps shut and piston rises, squeezing charge into small space, under pressure.
Compression stroke

4 Exhaust valve opens. Hot gases escape, pushed out by rising piston. Cycle restarts.
Exhaust stroke

Spring snaps valve shut.
Distributor
Camshaft controls opening and closing of valves.
Rocker arm pushes valve open.
Channels for cooling water
Valve
Cylinder
Piston
Flywheel
Clutch disconnects engine while driver changes gear.
Crankshaft drives wheels via gearbox and clutch.
Oilpan contains reservoir of oil for lubricating engine parts.
Crankshaft bearing where crankshaft runs through engine block
Dipstick for checking level of lubricating oil
Fanbelt drives a cooling fan.

ENGINE WORDS

Carburettor Device that mixes fuel and air before its combustion in the cylinder.

Catalytic converter Device fitted to exhaust that converts pollutant gases into harmless products.

Crankshaft Shaft that turns the up and down movement of the pistons into rotary (spinning) movement.

Distributor Device that sends a spark to each cylinder at the right moment to ignite fuel.

Flywheel Heavy wheel attached to the crankshaft to smooth out the power from individual cylinders.

Horsepower Measure of the power of an engine; one horsepower is equal to 746 watts.

Internal combustion engine Engine in which fuel is burned (combusted) inside the cylinder of the engine, e.g., petrol engine.

Throttle Flap controlling flow of air and fuel through carburettor.

r.p.m. Revolutions (of the crankshaft) per minute.

TYPES OF ENGINE

The first engines harnessed natural forces to produce motive force. In the 20th century, several new types appeared.

WINDMILL
The force of the wind across the sails produces a stronger driving force at the central shaft.

STEAM ENGINE
Water, heated by a furnace, produces steam. Expanding steam drives a piston back and forth.

PETROL ENGINE
Hot gases from an ignited petrol and air mixture push a piston down a cylinder, moving a crankshaft.

TURBO JET
Jet engines, used mainly in planes, draw in, compress, and throw out air at high speeds.

LINEAR ENGINE
Magnetic fields lift the train from the track, and shifting fields then propel it along the track.

ROCKET
Rocket fuel burns in a combustion chamber and the resultant hot gases drive the rocket forwards.

ION MOTOR
Ionized molecules (see p.222) are made to rush out by an electrical process in the motor.

STEAM ENGINE

Water in a boiler is heated by a coal fire and turns to steam. The expanding steam, fed into a cylinder, moves a piston back and forth, and the piston turns the train's wheels via a connecting rod and crank. Ships were also powered by steam engines.

Steam engines are external combustion engines, since their fuel is burned outside the cylinder.

Furnace
Steam is fed into the cylinder under high pressure.
Cylinder
Water turns to steam in the boiler.
Piston

800 First engine to use high pressure steam built by English engineer Richard Trevithick (1771–1833).

852 Steam-powered ship built by French engineer Henri Giffard (825–82).

1859 Internal combustion engine built by Belgian-French inventor Etienne Lenoir (1822–1900).

1877 Four-stroke internal combustion engine built by German Nikolaus Otto (1832–91).

Etienne Lenoir's internal combustion engine

1883 High-speed internal combustion engine built by German Gottlieb W. Daimler (1834–1900).

1884 Steam turbine generator for electricity is built by English engineer Charles Parsons (1854–1931).

1885 Motorbike engine built by Daimler. **Three-wheeled automobile,** built by German Karl Benz (1844–1929), is the first petrol driven motor vehicle.

| 1800 | 1852 | 1859 | 1877 | 1883 | 1884 | 1885 |

937 First working jet engine built by British engineer Frank Whittle (907–1996).

1939 First plane with a jet engine, Heinkel *He178,* built and flown by German engineer Hans von Ohain.

Frank Whittle (right) with early jet engine

1962 First nuclear-powered ship, *USS Savannah,* begins sea trials.

1970 Bypass ("turbofan") jet engine used, now the most common type of jet engine; *Boeing 747 "Jumbo Jet"* goes into service.

1979 Catalytic converter developed by British firm, Ricardo Consulting Engineers, to remove harmful gases from exhaust fumes.

USS Savannah

1990s Alternative fuel research begins. Possibilities include hydrogen fuel cells and liquid nitrogen.

1999 Aerospike rocket engine successfully tested.

| 1937 | 1939 | 1960 | 1962 | 1970 | 1979 | 1990 | 1999 |

JET ENGINE

A jet engine sucks in and compresses air using fan blades. When this air is ignited with kerosene, the hot gases produced thrust the engine forwards. Before leaving the exhaust nozzle, these gases pass over and drive turbines that are connected to the initial compressor blades. In a turbofan jet engine, air flows around the engine, cooling and quietening it.

Fan blade

Blades rotate and compress incoming air.

Bypass air duct

Inner drive shaft

Fuel inlet

Fuel and air ignited.

Bypass air provides main thrust.

Outer drive shaft

Turbine spins outer shaft, driving compressor.

HOW A TURBOFAN WORKS

ROCKET ENGINE

Rockets, the simplest and most powerful type of engine, are powered by solid or liquid fuel. The fuel burns in a combustion chamber with one open end, and the escaping hot gases thrust the rocket upwards.

Saturn V rocket at take-off

Most liquid-fuel rockets use liquid hydrogen and liquid oxygen.

Casing of rocket

Combustion chamber

Escaping gases provide thrust for rocket.

ENGINE EFFICIENCY

An engine with 100% efficiency converts all its fuel's energy into useful work.

Engine Type		Efficiency
Steam		7%
Internal combustion	Petrol	25–35%
	Diesel	30–40%
Power station (oil or coal-burning)		35%
Hydro-electric plant		80%

Inlet cone (rotates)

Low-pressure fan

Oil tank

High-pressure compressor

Fuel nozzle

Combustion chamber

High-pressure turbine

Exhaust cone

Fan duct

Fuel shut-off valve cable

Low-pressure turbine

Electronic engine control unit

MODERN TURBOFAN JET ENGINE – CANADA PW 305
Most jet aircraft, including passenger airliners, use turbofan engines. Their main thrust comes from the air that bypasses the engine itself. Fuel and fan adjustments are controlled electronically.

HOT ROD

The temperature inside the cylinders of an internal combustion engine can reach 1,700°C (3,100°F) – as hot as molten lava.

EXTRA POWER

There are several ways of getting more power from an engine.

SUPERCHARGERS AND TURBOCHARGERS
Petrol and diesel engines can be fitted with pumps that force the fuel and air mixture into the cylinders. This increases the strength of the explosion on the power stroke. Two types of pump are used – supercharger and turbocharger.

Supercharged 1935 Auburn Speedster

Supercharger
A supercharger is driven by a belt or gears from the engine itself.

AFTERBURNERS
Afterburners inject extra fuel into the hot jet exhaust, giving the engine extra thrust, almost like a rocket. Jet aircraft such as Concorde use afterburners for take-off, or for sudden, fast manoeuvres. They use much more fuel and are extremely loud.

Afterburners on a jet-fighter aircraft

LINEAR ENGINE

A linear engine uses powerful magnetism to lift a train off its track and propel it forwards. These trains are called maglev (magnetic levitation) trains, because they glide along just above their tracks.

Maglev train, Birmingham airport, UK

ENGINE RECORDS

SMALLEST INTERNAL COMBUSTION ENGINE is the 0.1cc model aircraft.

LARGEST INTERNAL COMBUSTION ENGINES are Sulzer ship engines, providing up to 60,000 horsepower, at 100 r.p.m.

Turbocharger

Inlet duct

Inlet rotor squeezes extra fuel and air into cylinder.

Turbocharger
Turbochargers are more common today; they are driven directly by the engine's exhaust gases.

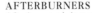

SPACE AND TIME

THE UNIVERSE IN WHICH we live is vast, and it has existed for a very long time. Everything we see or do takes place in space and time. Objects in space have physical dimensions and mass. Time runs from the past into the future, never the other way around.

TIME SLOWED DOWN

The Theory of Relativity (below) describes how space and time are related. It shows that, since the speed of light is always the same, time may speed up or slow down, and space may stretch or shrink.

Two rockets fly past Earth at a speed close to that of light. To the astronauts aboard, a flash of light sent from one to the other seems to travel in a straight line between them. To an observer on Earth, the flash follows a diagonal line. Since light travels at a constant speed, its crossing time for those on Earth must be longer than for those on board. Time passes at different rates for different observers.

JET SET

Relativity states that clocks run faster in weaker gravity. In 1975, this was proved using two atomic clocks. One, carried in a plane at high altitude, ran faster.

To observers on Earth, a light flash between rockets appears to follow a long path, and take a longer time to cross space.

To astronauts on rocket, same light flash follows shorter route straight between rockets, taking a short time to cross.

Rockets travel at speed close to speed of light.

Time, like length, can be divided only a finite number of times.

TIME PERIODS

Time is usually measured in seconds, or hours and minutes.

Time period		Example
0.000 000 000 001	second	A gas molecule to spin around once
0.000 000 001	second	The time it takes light to travel 30cm in air
0.000 001	second	The duration of a flash of lightning
0.001	second	The time it takes sound to travel 30cm in air
0.1	second	Olympic sprinter to run 1m
1	second	Quartz in a watch to vibrate 32,768 times
1 000	seconds	Time for a snail to move 10m
1 000 000	seconds	11.5 days
1 000 000 000	seconds	Time for Saturn to orbit the Sun once
1 000 000 000 000	seconds	Age of the earliest cave paintings

TIME AND SPACE FACTS

• The smallest unit of time that scientists believe we can measure is called the "Planck time". One second contains 600,000,000,000, 000,000,000,000,000,000,000, 000,000,000 Planck times.

• Gravity has an effect on the passage of time. Time runs more quickly at the top of a mountain, where gravity is weaker, than at sea level.

• In a famous experiment during a solar eclipse in 1919, it was shown that light from a distant star was "bent". The strong gravity of the Sun has a tiny effect on time and space nearby, not normally visible.

Solar eclipse of 1919 showed bending of light – the first evidence in support of Einstein's Theory of Relativity.

DISTANCES: SMALL AND GREAT

The range of distances in the Universe is vast. The table below gives a scale of distances in metres.

Distance		Example
0.000 000 000 000 001	m	The diameter of an atomic nucleus
0.000 000 000 001	m	The wavelength of high energy X-rays
0.000 000 001	m	The diameter of an oil molecule
0.000 001	m	The diameter of a single-celled organism
0.001	m	The wavelength of microwave radiation
0.1	m	The diameter of a croquet ball
1	m	Height of a child
1 000	m	One kilometre
1 000 000	m	The width of Egypt
1 000 000 000	m	The diameter of the Sun
1 000 000 000 000	m	The distance from Saturn to the Sun
1 000 000 000 000 000	m	1/40 the distance to the nearest star

RELATIVITY

In 1905, German scientist Albert Einstein (1879–1955) published the *Special Theory of Relativity*. It shocked the scientific world because it showed that time and space are not fixed things. His *General Theory of Relativity* (1915) later suggested that space is distorted by matter. In this theory, space and time co-exist as spacetime. Spacetime can be visualized as a rubber sheet, which stretches as objects are placed upon it. Objects with mass deform real spacetime in a similar way. The larger the mass, the more spacetime deforms.

Albert Einstein

NATURAL SCIENCE

THE STUDY OF the origins and processes of life is called natural science. Scientific discoveries have helped us to understand and influence these processes.

Aristotle

c.350–340 B.C. Greek thinker Aristotle (384–322B.C.) attempts **system of animal classification,** distinguishing between animals with blood and animals without.

1543 Science of anatomy developed by Flemish doctor Andreas Vesalius (1514–64). His accurate illustrations of dissected bodies appear in *The Fabric of the Human Body* (1543).

Andreas Vesalius

400 B.C.	350	A.D. 1	1500	1543

1665 English scientist Robert Hooke (1635–1703) publishes *Micrographia,* showing detailed microscopic drawings. He introduced the term "cell" to biology and helped improve the design of the compound microscope.

Drawing of magnified slice of cork

1677 Protozoa discovered by Dutch scientist Antonie van Leeuwenhoek (1632–1723), using a simple microscope. He later becomes first person to observe bacteria.

1701 Asexual reproduction first observed by Antonie van Leeuwenhoek, while watching hydra under a microscope (see p.83).

Hydra

1735 System of classification of living organisms invented by Swedish botanist Carolus Linnaeus (1707–78). His binomial (two-part) system identifies each species and shows its relation to others.

Carolus Linnaeus

1600	1665	1677	1700	1701	1735

1749 French naturalist Georges-Louis Buffon (1707–88) suggests that some species of plants or animals give rise to others.

1771 Connection between muscle movements and electrical impulses discovered by Italian anatomist Luigi Galvani (1737–98), while experimenting on the leg muscles of a dissected frog.

Galvani demonstrates nerve impulses.

1779 Process of photosynthesis discovered by Dutch-born scientist Jan Ingenhousz (1730–99).

1805 Term "biology" coined by Jean-Baptiste Lamarck (1744–1829) and Gottfried Treviranus (1776–1837). Science of anthropology founded by German Johann Blumenbach (1750–1840).

1812 Science of palaeontology (fossil studies) developed by pioneer French zoologist Georges Cuvier (1769–1832). He showed the connection between patterns of rock layers and patterns of fossil remains.

Fossil jawbone of a palaeotherium

Diagram of typical cell

1749	1771	1779	1800	1805	1812

1839 Cell theory founded by German scientists Theodor Schwann (1810–82) and Matthias Schleiden (1804–81), which holds that all living things are made from cells. Also observed that single egg cells grow into organisms.

1855 Theory of homeostasis proposed by French physiologist Claude Bernard (1813–78), describing how organs interact to maintain steady internal conditions.

1856 French chemist Louis Pasteur (1822–95) disproves long-held idea that living organisms could grow from non-living matter (spontaneous generation).

Louis Pasteur

1859 Charles Darwin (1809–82) publishes *Origin of Species,* which explains his principle of natural selection and theory of evolution (see p.68).

Cartoon of Charles Darwin, mocking idea that humans are descended from apes

1839	1855	1856	1859

1860s Science of heredity (how characteristics are inherited) pioneered by Austrian monk and botanist Gregor Mendel (1822–84), after long experimentation on pea plants.

Gregor Mendel

1889 Important role of acids in food digestion discovered by German researchers. **Russian scientist Ivan Pavlov** (1849–1936) shows that reflex actions can be conditioned (learned), and are not just inbuilt. His proof involves teaching dogs to salivate at the ring of a bell.

1937 Chemistry of respiration, the way that food is converted into energy in cells, discovered by German-born biochemist Hans Krebs (1900–81). The series of chemical reactions that he identifies is central to nearly all metabolic reactions (reactions in living organisms).

Spiral of DNA

1953 Double-helix structure of DNA, the substance responsible for heredity, discovered by American and British biologists James Watson (born 1928) and Francis Crick (born 1916).

1860	1889	1900	1937	1953

1963 Mechanism by which nerves convey messages explained by Australian John Eccles (born 1903) and British doctors Andrew Huxley (born 1917) and Alan Hodgkin (born 1914).

Eccles receives Nobel prize

1974 Oldest and most complete skeleton of early upright-walking hominid discovered by American anthropologists in Ethiopia. This hominid, *Lucy,* is estimated to be 3–3.5 million years old.

Bone fragments from Lucy

1979 "Gaia" theory proposed by British scientist James Lovelock (born 1919). He suggests that the Earth is a living, self-regulating organism.

1984 Genetic fingerprinting developed by British scientist Alec Jeffreys.

James Lovelock

1990 Human genome project begins in several countries. It aims to map the position of all the genetic material in human chromosomes. This will enable scientists to eradicate inherited diseases.

1996 Dolly the sheep is born, a clone of a single cell from an adult sheep – the first time this is achieved in a mammal.

1963	1974	1979	1984	1000	1996

PHYSICAL SCIENCE

EVEN BEFORE THE TERM science was coined, people devised experiments to test their ideas about the physical universe.

Democritus

c.400 B.C. Greek thinker Democritus (c.460–361 B.C.) teaches that matter consists of small, hard, indivisible particles, called atoms.

c.260 B.C. Flotation principle discovered by Greek scientist Archimedes (c.287–212 B.C.). He also studied principles of levers and invented many machines.

Archimedes realizes that the volume of his body is equal to the volume of water spilled from full bath.

400 B.C.   260   *200 B.C.*

1643 Air pressure discovered and measured by Italian scientist and pupil of Galileo, Evangelista Torricelli (1608–47). He measures it using mercury barometer, his invention.

Mercury barometer

1687 Laws of motion and law of gravitation formulated by English mathematician Isaac Newton (1642–1727) in *Principia Mathematica*. Also discovers that white light is made up of a spectrum of colours.

Isaac Newton

1701 French scientist Joseph Sauveur (1653–1716) studies relationship between sound waves and vibrations and suggests term "acoustics" for the science of sound.

1706 Friction machine to generate electrical sparks made by English scientist Francis Hauksbee (1666–1713).

1712 Successful steam engine, with piston and cylinder, built by English engineer Thomas Newcomen (1663–1729).

Newcomen's engine, used for draining mines.

1643   1687   *1700*   1701   1706   1712

1800 Infrared waves discovered by Anglo-German astronomer William Herschel (1738–1822). Infrared is an invisible form of electromagnetic wave (see p.231). Herschel discovered Uranus and hundreds of stars and nebulae.

William Herschel

1803 Atomic theory of matter proposed by Englishman John Dalton (1766–1844), introducing modern ideas about elements and compounds made of atoms and molecules.

Dalton's atomic models

1807–8 Potassium, sodium, magnesium, barium, calcium, and strontium discovered by British chemist Humphry Davy (1778–1829).

Davy performs a public experiment.

1811 Avogadr[o's] Law formulat[ed] by Italian phys[icist] Amedeo Avoga[dro] (1776–1856). T[he] law states that [the] same volume of any gas contain[s] the same numb[er] of molecules.

1800   1803   1807   1811

1843 Relationship between heat, power, and work investigated and formulated by English scientist James Joule (1818–89).

Joule's machine for measuring energy conversion

1846 Laws of thermodynamics developed by British physicist William Thomson (1824–1907), later Lord Kelvin. In 1862 he uses them to estimate Earth's age.

1865 Relationship between electricity and magnetism formulated by Scottish physicist James Clerk Maxwell (1831–79).

1869 Periodic Table devised by Russian schoolteacher Dmitri Mendeleyev (1834–1907). It classifies elements into family groups by atomic weight.

James Clerk Maxwell

1876 Telephone invented by Scottish-b[orn] speech therapist and inventor Alexander Graham Bell (1847–1922). His device use[s] thin diaphragm to convert the vibrations [of] the human voice into electrical signals, th[en] reconverts them into sound waves.

Alexan[der] Graham [Bell's] telephon[e]

1840   1843   1846   1865   18[76]

1900 Quantum theory proposed by German physicist Max Planck (1858–1947), stating that energy consists of small units, called "quanta". This leads to theory that light acts as both a wave and particles.

Albert Einstein

1905 *Special Theory of Relativity* published by German physicist Albert Einstein (1879–1955). Together with *General Theory* (1915), it revolutionizes the foundations of physics.

Albert Einstein

1909 First stable plastic, "Bakelite", developed by American chemist Leo Henrick Baekeland (1863–1944). This helped to found plastics industry.

Telephone receiver made of early plastic

1911 Atomic nucleus discovered by New Zeala[nd] born physicist Ernest Rutherford (1871–1937).

1913 Electron shells around nuclei discovered by Danish physicist Niels Bohr (1885–1962).

Electron shells

1900   1905   1909   1911   1913

1938 Nuclear fission, splitting of nuclei to release energy, discovered by German physicists Otto Hahn (1879–1968) and Fritz Strassmann (1902–80).

Uranium fission reaction

1939 Nature of the chemical bond between atoms and molecules explained by American chemist Linus Pauling (1901–94).

1942 First nuclear reactor built by Italian physicist Enrico Fermi (1901–54).

Fermi's reactor, built in a squash court at Chicago University

1945 Heating effect of microwaves discovered by American engineer Percy Le Baron Spencer (1894–1970), when a sweet melts in his pocket during experiments with microwaves.

1946 Carbon dating invented by American scientist Willard Frank Libby (1908–80).

1960 First laser built by American physicist Theodore Maiman (born 1927), based on work of American physicist Gordon Gould in 1957.

Replica of early transistor

1938   1939   1942   1945   1946   1947   1960

A.D. 1100s Compass used by Italian and Chinese navigators. They independently discover that a free or floating magnetic needle always indicates north.

1600 English doctor William Gilbert (1544–1603), in his book *De Magnete*, claims that the core of the Earth is a great magnet with poles at its north and south points.

Diagram showing dip of compass at different latitudes.

1620s Modern scientific method developed by English philosopher Francis Bacon (1561–1626). He advocates experiment as the best basis for knowledge.

1638 Science of mechanics founded by Italian scientist Galileo Galilei (1564–1642) in *Dialogue Concerning Two New Sciences*. He investigated how force causes acceleration and discovered the properties of the pendulum.

Apparatus to demonstrate Galileo's work on the paths of projectiles (objects thrown up and along)

1000 — 1100 — 1600 — 1620 — 1638

1755 Carbon dioxide discovered by Scottish chemist Joseph Black (1728–99), who calls it "fixed air".

1765 First efficient steam engine built by Scottish engineer James Watt (1736–1819).

1766 Hydrogen discovered by English chemist Henry Cavendish (1731–1810), who calls the gas "inflammable air".

Henry Cavendish

1779 Oxygen named by French chemist Antoine Lavoisier (1743–94), who demonstrates its role in combustion. Also shows air to be a mixture of gases, and that water is a compound of oxygen and hydrogen.

Antoine Lavoisier with wife and co-worker Marie-Anne

1799 Battery invented by Italian chemist Alessandro Volta (1745–1827), using different metals separated by salt solutions.

— Cell

Voltaic pile or battery (collection of cells)

1755 — 1765 — 1766 — 1779 — 1799

1830s German chemists focus on carbon as the basis of the organic chemistry of living things. Carbon takes many forms, from coal to diamonds.

1831 English scientist Michael Faraday (1791–1867) uses magnetism to make electricity, a process called electromagnetic induction. American Joseph Henry (1797–1878) makes same discovery independently.

Faraday's induction ring

1836 Catalysts discovered by Swedish scientist Jöns Berzelius (1779–1848). Catalysts speed up certain chemical reactions without themselves being used in the reactions.

1839 Practical photographic processes invented independently by Englishman William Fox Talbot (1800–77) and Frenchman Louis Daguerre (1789–1851).

Daguerreotype image on copper plate

1831 — 1836 — 1839

1888 Existence of radio waves demonstrated by German physicist Heinrich Hertz (1857–94). **Induction motor** invented by Croatian-born physicist Nikolai Tesla (1856–1943).

Heinrich Hertz

Marconi

1894 Radio communication invented by 20-year-old Italian Guglielmo Marconi (1874–1937).

1895 X-rays discovered by German physicist Wilhelm Roentgen (1845–1925).

1896 Effects of radioactivity discovered by French physicist Antoine-Henri Becquerel (1852–1908).

1897 Electron discovered by British physicist Joseph John Thompson (1856–1940).

1898 Elements radium and polonium isolated by Polish-born chemist Marie Curie (1867–1934) and Pierre Curie (1859–1906). She calls the powerful emissions of radiation "radioactivity".

Marie and Pierre Curie

1876 — 1888 — 1894 — 1895 — 1896 — 1897 — 1898

1915 X-ray crystallography, a way of finding out the structure of crystals, invented by British father and son physicists, William H. Bragg (1862–1942) and Lawrence Bragg (1890–1971).

Mineral with crystalline atomic structure

1919 New Zealand-born physicist Ernest Rutherford (1871–1937) changes one element into another. He converts nitrogen nuclei into oxygen nuclei.

Ernest Rutherford

1931 Neutron (particle in nucleus) discovered by British physicist James Chadwick (1891–1974).

1932 First subatomic particle accelerator built by British physicists J. Cockcroft (1897–1967) and Ernest Walton (1903–1995). **Positron**, a particle of antimatter, discovered by American physicist Carl David Anderson (1905–1991).

1935 Nylon developed by American chemist Wallace H. Carothers (1896–1937).

First particle accelerator, built at Manchester University, UK

1915 — 1919 — 1920 — 1931 — 1932 — 1935

1964 Existence of quarks, the constituent parts of neutrons and protons, proposed by Murray Gell-Mann, American physicist (born 1929).

1980s Chaos theory developed by American mathematicians, based on the unpredictability of nature. Chaos theory is used to try to predict complex systems.

Atomic nucleus, showing quarks

1986 Superconductors, substances with extremely low resistance to electricity, are developed.

Fractal: computer-generated pattern derived from chaos theory

1990s "Theory of everything" is worked on by physicists as a means of explaining the origin of matter, energy, and forces.

1990s Scanning probe microscopes, first invented in the 1980s, give chemists their first glimpses of actual atoms, linked together to form surfaces of materials.

1997 "Atom laser", giving a beam of individual atoms, is built by American scientists. It may be used to build tiny structures.

1964 — 1980 — 1986 — 1990 — 1997

WEAPONS

WEAPONS ARE TOOLS for attacking people and animals. Technology has made weapons increasingly efficient in their ability to wound and kill.

Flint handaxe

c.100,000 B.C. Neanderthal people use sharpened wooden spear point and simple stone axe.

c.2800–2000 B.C. Composite bow, first effective military bow, developed in Middle East. Made of strips of wood, animal horn, and sinew, glued together.

Egyptian battle chariot

c.2000–1500 B.C. Two-wheeled fighting chariot introduced. Provides fast and stable platform for archers and spearmen.

c.1000 B.C. Iron sword developed in southern and central Europe. Far superior to weapons made from bronze, iron is hard and sharp.

100,000 B.C.	2800	2000 B.C.	1000	

Viking sword, c.1000

200 B.C.–A.D. 400 Siege weapons used by Roman soldiers to batter down walls of enemies.

Ballista (giant crossbow)

Bolt

1100 Mace becomes a common weapon of war. It can smash human bones protected by plate armour or chain mail.
Crossbow developed and used for 400 years, a powerful weapon that can be used with little training.

Bronze mace on modern haft

1340–1400 Cannons introduced into warfare. Powered by gunpowder, they fire small stone balls or large crossbow-type arrows. Large cannon, called bombards, lay open castles to attack.

Replica of small early cannon   Muzzle

1500 Arquebus developed, a hand-held firearm capable of being operated by a single infantryman.

1550 Naval warfare revolutionized as ships are fitted with cannons.

1680 Flintlock musket is dominant weapon for infantry soldiers for next 140 years. A piece of flint ignites gunpowder in musket's barrel.

A.D. 1	1000	1100	1340	1500	1550	1680

1836 First effective revolver developed by American gunsmith Samuel Colt (1814–62). Revolvers can fire several shots in a row before they need reloading.

Five-shot Colt police revolver from 1862

1837 Bolt-action, breech-loading rifle developed by Prussian gunsmith J. N. Dreyse (1787–1867), with increased accuracy and firing rate. Soon all armies are armed with this type of rifle. It remains in use today.

1890s Belt-fed machine guns introduced. Allows two people to fire at great speed. Fires 600 bullets per minute, over 1km (0.62 miles).

RAF No.1 Squadron of 1918

1915 Aircraft first used as weapons when armed with machine guns.

1916 First tank used in war during Battle of the Somme. Although slow and unreliable, the lumbering British tanks cause panic among German troops.

Early British tank

1800	1836	1837	1890	1900	1915	1916

1940s Submarines, with torpedoes, become a decisive weapon of war. German U-boats almost defeat Allies in Battle of the Atlantic (1939–44).

German U-boat submarine

1945 Dropping of atomic bomb on Japan changes nature of warfare. Now a single bomb can destroy a whole city.

1950s Missiles become effective weapons delivery system. Inter-Continental Ballistic Missiles (ICBMs) carry nuclear warheads thousands of kilometres; smaller missiles are used to knock out fighter aircraft and tanks.

1960s Assault rifle introduced in large numbers. It provides infantrymen with a light weapon capable of full automatic fire.

US M16A1 assault rifle fitted with 40mm grenade launcher

1980s Attack helicopter, armed with laser-guided missiles and machine guns, proves highly effective in battle. It becomes a key element in rapid reaction forces.

Tiger anti-tank attack helicopter

1940	1945	1950	1960	1980

AUTOMATIC PISTOL

A pistol is loaded with cartridges, each containing a lead bullet and a casing packed with explosive. When the trigger is pulled, the hammer forces the firing pin into the back of the cartridge, igniting the explosive. The force of this explosion drives the bullet down the barrel and it leaves the pistol at high speed.

Rear sight   Firing pin   Front sight

Hammer

Trigger

Cartridge   Slide

Pulling trigger makes firing pin strike cartridge and ignite explosive.

Slide ejects used cartridge case and lets new cartridge spring into the barrel.

Slide pushes cartridge into place and returns to rest.

Automatic weapons
In automatic weapons, the force of the departing bullet (the recoil) ejects the spent cartridge casing from the gun, allowing a new cartridge into the barrel.

WEAPONS FACTS

• Powered by their own nuclear reactors, nuclear submarines can remain underwater for months on end, and can fire nuclear missiles over thousands of kilometres without being detected. They are the deadliest of modern weapons systems.

• "Smart" weapons allow a warhead to be guided directly on to its target. Some "smart" missiles have television cameras in their nose, while others use radar or infrared homing to reach their targets.

Tomahawk Cruise missile, with 454kg (1,000lb) warhead, locates and destroys target below in pre-programmed attack.

READY... AIM...

In 1830, a musket could fire a maximum of four bullets every minute. A modern M61 cannon will fire up to 100 bullets every second.

• In the 19th century, the development of rifled barrels (with spiral grooves running inside the barrel) made guns much more accurate. They made the bullet spin in flight, allowing it to travel further and straighter.

TRANSPORT, COMMUNICATIONS, AND INDUSTRY

Factual coverage of every major transport group and major world industries, plus global communications, including alphabets and major languages.

Cars • Bicycles • Motorcyles • Trains • Boats • Warships and Submarines
Aircraft • Airline Insignia • Communications • Language • Alphabets and Scripts
Energy • Major Industries • Roads • Construction

CARS

THE FIRST mass-produced car, the Oldsmobile, appeared less than a hundred years ago. Since then, car ownership around the world has grown dramatically: there will probably be a billion cars on the road by the year 2025.

Gear lever changes the gears. These enable the engine to run at efficient speeds while the car slows down or speeds up.

Silencer reduces noise made by the exhaust.

Sun roof

Rear-view mirror

Windscreen

The steering wheel is connected to two rods that swivel the front wheels.

Rear light

Shock absorber

Rear bumper

Fuel tank

Half-shafts link the driving wheels to the differential.

The differential contains a set of interlocking gears. It allows the rear wheels to turn at different speeds when the car turns a corner.

Drive shaft transmits the movements of the engine to the wheels.

Handbrake and ratchet

The distributor ensures that the spark plugs fire in a particular sequence.

PARTS OF A CAR

Most cars have four wheels, an engine in the front, and room for at least two passengers. This illustration shows the parts of a rear-wheel drive hatchback.

Windscreen wipers

Air filter cleans the air before it is mixed with the petrol.

Battery

Headlight

Front bumper

The fan helps to cool water in the radiator.

The radiator cools the water that flows around the engine.

The generator produces electricity when the engine is running. This electricity is stored in the battery.

TYPES OF CAR

Veteran car
Veteran cars are the oldest surviving cars. They were built between 1896 and 1903.

Vintage car
Vintage cars are those that were built between 1904 and 1930.

Classic car
Classic cars are outstanding examples of design and engineering.

Saloon (sedan)
Saloon cars can usually carry four passengers, and have a boot for luggage.

Estate (station wagon)
Estate cars are similar to saloons, with a large loading space at the rear.

Hatchback
Hatchbacks have a rear door that lifts upwards for easy access to the loading space.

Convertible
These are open-topped cars. The roof folds back, or can be lifted off.

Coupé
Coupés have a sloping roof. They are usually two-seater cars.

Limousine
These extended cars are designed for comfort and luxury. Some have a television and cocktail cabinet.

Sports car
Sports cars display a high performance and good road handling. Most have two seats.

Racing car
Racing cars are purpose-built for racing on a track. There are several types (see p.255).

Tourer
Tourers were designed for touring, with room for several passengers and plenty of luggage.

Custom car
Custom cars are adapted by their owners to their personal preferences.

Off-road car
Off-road cars are designed for driving on rough terrain. They have four-wheel drive.

Gull-wing car
These cars have upswinging doors that, when open, resemble the wings of a seagull.

CAR FACTS

• After WWII, British motor manufacturers turned down the chance to make the German Beetle on the grounds that it was too ugly and would not sell. It has since become the best-selling car of all time, with more than 20 million produced.

Volkswagen Beetle

• This "motorized orange" was manufactured during the 1970s by a firm that sold fruit. It had a Mini engine with a specially built chassis and fibreglass skin.

• The most widely travelled car is the Moon Buggy, which the US astronauts drove on the Moon in 1971/72. It also has one of the lowest recorded mileages, at only 29km (18 miles).

HISTORY OF CARS

1886 Gottlieb Daimler (1834–1900, German) fixes an engine to a horse-drawn carriage.

1891 Frenchmen René Panhard (1841–1908) **and Emile Levassor** (1844–97) produce a car that establishes the classic layout.

1901 First mass-produced car, the Oldsmobile, is produced by Ransom Eli Olds (1864–1950, American).

Oldsmobile

1906 Charles Rolls (1877–1910, British) **and Henry Royce** (see opposite page) introduce their 40/50 horsepower Rolls-Royce car series, which includes the *Silver Ghost*.

1910 First car to be assembled on a moving production line was the Model T, created by Henry Ford (see opposite page).

Model T

1913 Mass-production begins in Britain with William Morris's (see opposite page) Morris Oxford.

Morris Oxford

| 1880 | 1886 | 1890 | 1891 | 1900 | 1901 | 1906 | 1910 | 1910 | 1913 |

FASTEST LUXURY SALOON CARS

Car	Top speed km/h	mph
Lotus Carlton	282	175
Maserati Quattroporte	264	164
Mercedes S600	256	159
BMW M5	254	158
Audi A8 4.2 Quattro	249	155
BMW 7501	249	155
BMW 540i	249	155
Jaguar XJ12	249	155
Lexus LS400	249	155
Mercedes S500	249	155

TOP CAR-OWNING COUNTRIES

Country	Total cars registered
USA	141,251,695
Japan	30,776,243
Germany	29,190,322
Italy	23,500,000
France	22,370,000
UK	20,923,423
CIS	15,874,700
Canada	11,900,000
Brazil	11,760,459
Spain	10,787,424

CAR FACTS

• The luxurious interior of a 1927 Rolls-Royce Phantom 1 was upholstered in Aubusson silk tapestry.

• William Morris hated the popular Morris Minor, which was built for 31 years. He called it the "poached egg".

WORLD'S TOP CAR MANUFACTURERS

Company	Total annual car production
General Motors	5,662,843
Ford Motor Company	4,234,583
Toyota	3,093,692
Volkswagen	2,748,152
Peugeot-Citroën	2,227,528
Nissan	2,016,626
Fiat	1,790,631
Renault	1,767,516

FAMOUS MOTOR MEN

Henry Royce (1863–1933, British) was the engineering partner of Rolls-Royce. He once said: "There is no such thing as good enough".

Henry Ford (1863–1947) a talented American mechanic, revolutionized the motor industry by introducing assembly-line production.

Herbert Austin (1866–1941) set up his own company in Britain after working for the car builders Wolseley.

Frederick Lanchester (1868–1946) designed cars in Britain from 1896. His key inventions included a semi-automatic gearbox.

William Morris (1877–1963) produced the "Bullnose" Morris, and played an important role in the British motor industry.

Ettore Bugatti (1882–1947) was an Italian engineer who built the Classic type 35 racing car, as well as beautiful touring models.

Kiichiro Toyoda (1895–1952) founded Toyota cars in Japan. His dream was to see as many cars on the streets of Japan as on those of America.

Alexander Issigonis (1904–88) was a Turkish car designer who went to the UK in 1922. He designed the Morris Minor and the Mini.

HELPING HAND

Before indicators were invented, drivers used hand signals. This false hand clipped on to the car door. It mimicked each signal.

TOP CAR-PRODUCING COUNTRIES

Country	Total annual production
Japan	9,052,406
USA	6,823,097
Germany	4,563,673
France	3,409,017
Italy	1,971,969

CAR RECORDS

WORLD LAND SPEED RECORD is 1,227km/h (763mph), achieved in October 1997 by Briton Andy Green driving the jet car *Thrust SSC*. The record is 208km/h (130mph) faster than the previous record set in *Thrust II*.

Thrust II

LONGEST PRODUCTION CAR was the Bugatti Royale (below) with a length of more than 6.7m (22ft). The first was produced in 1927, but only six were made.

MOST ECONOMICAL PRODUCTION CAR is the Daihatsu Charade Diesel Turbo (below), which can achieve 28km/l (79.1mpg) at a steady 90km/h (56mph).

HIGHEST PRICE PAID FOR A CAR THROUGH PRIVATE SALE was over $15 million for a 1962 Ferrari 250 GTO (below) in 1989. The vendor had bought the car for $7,665 in 1971.

Frenchman André ën (1878–1935) uces front-wheel (*traction avant*). This opment bankrupts ën, who dies a year

1935 World's first parking meter is installed, in Oklahoma, USA.
1936 Austrian Dr. Ferdinand Porsche (1875–1951) is instructed by Hitler (see p.404) to make a "people's car", and develops the Beetle.

1949 The Citroën 2CV, the people's car of France, is launched.

1958 The Austin Mini is launched. It can seat four people despite its small size.

1979 The catalytic converter is introduced. It reduces pollution from car exhausts.
1988 Fastest speed by a solar-powered vehicle is achieved by the General Motors *Sunraycer* (see p.254), which reaches 78.4km/h (48.71mph).

1990s New safety features, such as air bags, are developed. Other safety options are researched; the experimental *Venus* has two cameras to help the driver see the road in bad conditions.

1930s Citroën

Beetle

Citroën 2CV

Austin Mini

Venus

| 1934 | 1935 | 1936 | 1940 | 1949 | 1950 | 1958 | 1270 | 1979 | 1960 | 1000 | 1990 |

MARQUES AND MAKES

Motor manufacturers each have a badge, called a marque, to identify their vehicles. Some well-known marques are shown below.

MOTORING WORDS

Air bag A safety device that fills with air on impact to protect the driver in a collision.

Anti-lock braking system (ABS) A system that prevents skidding by detecting if a wheel is about to lock during braking.

Brake horsepower (BHP) The power of an engine calculated in terms of the force needed to stop it.

Catalytic converter A filter that absorbs many exhaust pollutants.

Fuel-injection (FI) The direct introduction of fuel under pressure into the engine.

Ignition The mechanism that starts a car's engine.

Power steering A steering system that reduces the effort needed to park and manoeuvre at low speeds.

Roll-bar An overhead bar that strengthens the car, protecting passengers if the vehicle overturns.

Spoiler An extension that improves a car's road-holding at high speeds.

Supercharger A mechanism that supplies air or fuel to the engine at above-normal pressure to increase efficiency.

Turbocharger A supercharger driven by a turbine powered by the engine's exhaust gases.

CAR FACTS

• André Citroën (see p.253) used many attention-grabbing forms of publicity. He once hired the Eiffel Tower in Paris, and had his name picked out in lights down the side. More than 250,000 light bulbs were used.

• The car that reached a production of one million in the shortest time was the Volkswagen Golf. Introduced in 1974, it passed the million mark in 31 months.

MANY IN A MINI

Since the Austin Mini was first produced (see p.253), records have been set and broken for how many people can squeeze inside one. The record currently stands at 24.

• A Lincoln Continental presidential limousine built in the USA in 1968 weighed 5.35 tonnes (5.9 tons), more than half of which was protective armour plating.

• In the early days of motoring, Italians drove on the right-hand side of the road in the country, and on the left in towns. One of the last towns to end this practice was Milan, in 1926.

• From 1865 to 1896, British law stated that every car on the road had to have a person running along in front of it waving a red flag.

AMAZING CARS

Car designers have produced some unusual models over the years. Some have been built purely to break records, others as experiments in car design.

Honda's *Genius E* holds the record for lowest petrol consumption. It achieved 2,279km/l (6,409mpg).

The *Peel* is one of the smallest cars ever built, at only 1.34m (4.4ft) long. It has no reverse gear.

The *Sunraycer* runs on solar energy. It has special panels that convert sunlight into electrical energy.

A limousine built in the USA had 26 wheels and was more than 30m (98ft) long. It had a swimming pool and a helicopter landing pad.

MOST EXPENSIVE CARS SOLD AT AUCTION

Make	Car	Price US$
Any car	1962 Ferrari 250 Gran Turismo Berlinetta Competition GTO	8,853,690
Bugatti	1931 Bugatti Type 41 Royale Sports Coupé	7,665,000
Rolls Royce	1907 Rolls-Royce Silver Ghost 40/50hp tourer	2,386,706
Mercedes-Benz	1936 Mercedes-Benz 500 K Special Roadster	2,222,850

DASHBOARD AND CONTROLS

Pedals to control the car's acceleration, clutch, and brakes are situated on the car floor. Instruments to indicate speed, fuel levels, temperature, and so on are usually found on the dashboard.

Indicator lights are flicked on and off with this lever.

The driver slows down and stops the car with the brake pedal.

The driver pushes down the clutch pedal when changing gear.

Accelerator controls the car's speed.

Speedometer indicates the car's speed.

Steering wheel

Small items are stored in the glove box.

Gear lever

Handbrake stops the car from moving when it is parked.

RACING CARS

RACING CARS ARE designed to compete on a race track. They range from simple stock cars to high-technology Formula 1 racing cars, which can achieve speeds of more than 300km/h (190mph).

MOTOR RACING FACTS

• Ferrari are the only motor racing team to have competed in the Formula 1 world championship every year since it started in 1950.

• The youngest world champion racing driver was Brazilian Emerson Fittipaldi (born 1946), who won his first world championship in 1972, at the age of 25 years and 9 months.

Emerson Fittipaldi

• The oldest world champion racing driver was Argentinian Juan Manuel Fangio (1911–1995). When Fangio won his last world championship race in 1957, he was 46 years and 41 days old.

TYPES OF RACING CAR

Formula 1
These are the fastest racing cars. They compete in races called Grand Prix.

Formula 2
These are the second most powerful class of racing car after Formula 1.

Formula 3
These racing cars have engines of up to 2,000cc.

Rally cars
Rally cars are usually ordinary cars with specially strengthened bodies.

Indycars
Indycars are similar to Formula 1 cars, but are larger. They are named after the Indianapolis 500, the most famous race in which they compete.

Le Mans
These racing cars are specially adapted sports cars that race at the 24-hour Le Mans circuit in France.

US stock cars
These are simple cars that are raced around oval dirt tracks.

Dragsters
Dragsters race a short distance along a straight track, at speeds of more than 485km/h (300mph).

WINNING FORMULA

It takes 150 Renault-Sport staff to produce one of their Formula 1 engines, including 35 mechanics and 25 engineers.

RACING RECORDS

FASTEST PIT STOP
(break in a race for refuelling or servicing) was four seconds, made by American Robert William "Bobby" Unser (born 1934) in the 1976 Indianapolis 500.

COUNTRY WITH MOST FORMULA 1 DRIVERS
from 1950 to 1993 was Great Britain, which had 131 drivers (21% of total drivers).

WORST CRASH
in a motor race occurred at Le Mans in 1955: 83 spectators were killed and more than 100 were injured when a car somersaulted over the safety barrier, burst into flames, and disintegrated. The driver also died.

LONGEST RALLY
was from Covent Garden, London, UK, to the Sydney Opera House, Australia: a distance of 31,107km (19,329 miles).

HISTORY OF MOTOR RACING

1895 First motor race to include petrol-engine vehicles takes place, from Paris, France, to Bordeaux and back. The first car past the finishing line averages 24km/h (15mph) for the race.

1906 First Grand Prix in Le Mans, France, is won by Austro-Hungarian Ferencz Szisz (1873–1970).

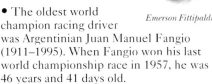
Ferencz Szisz

1907 First track constructed for motor car racing opens: the Brooklands Motor Course, UK.

1911 First Indianapolis 500 race takes place in Indianapolis, USA.

1929 Bentley cars take first, second, third, and fourth places at Le Mans.

| 1895 | 1900 | 1906 | 1907 | 1910 | 1911 | 1920 | 1929 |

1950 First international Formula 1 race, the Pau Grand Prix, is held in France. It is won by Juan Manuel Fangio (see above). Formula 1 cars are cigar-shaped with front-mounted engines. The driver sits in an upright position.

1951 Fangio wins the first of five World Drivers' Championships.
1958 First rear-mounted engines appear in Formula 1 cars.

Cooper 45, 1958

1960s Formula 1 drivers wear helmets and fireproof overalls, and sit in a more reclined position.

1968 Aerofoil wings are introduced by Ferrari and Brabham to produce downforce (holds the car flat on the track).

1988 Raised noses are introduced on Formula 1 cars. They improve air flow past the chassis.
1993 Use of electronic aids is outlawed.

| 1950 | 1950 | 1951 | 1958 | 1960 | 1968 | 1970 | 1980 | 1990 | 1993 |

BICYCLES

BICYCLES ARE RIDDEN by millions of people around the world. They range from simple models with no gears, to sophisticated, multi-geared mountain bicycles and racers. Bicycles are the most energy-efficient of all forms of transport.

PARTS OF A BICYCLE

The basic design of all bicycles (bikes) is the same. They are made up of a frame, wheels, transmission (cogs, chains, and gears), brakes, stem, handlebars, and saddle. This photograph shows the parts of a racing bike.

Handlebar · Brake lever · Stem · Saddle · Brake cable · Gear lever · Tyre · Spoke · Rim · Brake block · Front derailleur · Sprockets or cogs · Rear derailleur · Fork blade · Hub axle or spindle · Toe clip · Pedal · Chainrings · Valve · Chain · Sidewall

TYPES OF BICYCLE

Racing bicycle
Racing bicycles are fast, lightweight, and multi-geared, with drop handlebars.

Mountain bicycle
These bicycles are built for off-road cycling. They have thick tyres, a lightweight frame, and a wide range of gears.

BMX (Bicycle Motocross)
The BMX bike is designed for rough-terrain cycling, and is often used for acrobatics and tricks.

Tandem
Tandems are bicycles for two riders, with two saddles, two handlebars, and two wheels.

Bicycle rickshaw
Rickshaws are bicycles adapted to carry two passengers behind or in front, in a wheeled chair.

BICYCLE OWNERSHIP AROUND THE WORLD

This table shows the number of bicycles owned in various different countries.

Country	Bicycles (millions)
China	300
USA	103
Japan	60
India	45
Mexico	12
Netherlands	11
Australia	6.8
South Korea	6
Argentina	4.5
Egypt	1.5
Tanzania	0.5

GEAR SYSTEMS

Many bicycles have gear systems that enable the cyclist to travel quickly or slowly while pedalling at a comfortable rate. By moving the gear lever, the cyclist lifts the chain from one cog to another.

A small cog turns the wheel quickly, producing extra force for climbing uphill.

A large cog turns the wheel slowly, allowing the bicycle to travel fast downhill or on flat ground.

BICYCLE RECORDS

LONGEST BICYCLE is 22.24m (72.96ft) long. Built in 1988, it was ridden by four riders for a distance of 246m (807ft).

LARGEST BICYCLE (front-wheel diameter) is the *Frankencycle*, with a diameter of 3.05m (10ft).

BICYCLE FACTS

• There are 800 million bicycles in the world: they outnumber cars two to one.
• The Belgian army added elbow rests to the bicycles ridden by their regimental bands, so that they could play their instruments whilst cycling.

HISTORY OF BICYCLES

1790 The *célérifère*, a wooden, hobby horse-like machine, is built by a Frenchman, the Compte de Sivrac.

1813 The *Draisienne* is built by Carl Von Drais (1785–1851, German). It has a steerable front wheel and a saddle.

1839 First bicycle with pedals to turn the rear wheel is built. It is nicknamed the "Boneshaker".

1790 | 1790 | 1800 | 1813 | 1830 | 1839

PEDAL POWER

The fastest speed on a bicycle was 245.08km/h (152.3mph), achieved by American John Howard in 1985. He was helped by the slipstreaming effect of the leading vehicle.

1861 First bicycle with pedals on the front wheel is built. The saddle is mounted on a spring for comfort, and there is a braking system for the front wheel.

c.1870 The Penny Farthing, named after two British coins, is developed. It proves unsafe.

1879 First commercial bicycle, the Bicyclette, is patented.

1959 First new bicycle design for 50 years – the Moulton – is produced.

1970s BMX bikes are launched. They appeal particularly to children.

1990s Human-powered vehicles (HPVs), such as this *Windcheetah SL*, are developed. They can reach greater speeds than ordinary bicycles.

1990s Lightweight composite materials, such as carbon fibre, and new aerodynamic shapes revolutionize bicycle design.

1860 | 1861 | 1870 | 1879 | 1950 | 1959 | 1990

MOTORCYCLES

THE BASIC DESIGN of a motorcycle consists of a bicycle powered by an engine. Motorcycles range from small-engined mopeds, to racing motorcycles that can reach speeds of more than 500km/h (311mph).

PARTS OF A MOTORCYCLE

The largest to the smallest machines are all built in a similar way, with a piston engine and telescopic forks. Motorcycle engine sizes range from 50cc (cubic centimetres) to more than 1,000cc. This Yamaha motorcycle has a 1,002cc engine.

Windscreen

Mirror

The throttle is on the handlebars.

Air scoops feed the air box to supply the carburettors.

Twin spar chassis

This motorcycle can reach a speed of 269km/h (167mph).

Saddle

Four-cylinder engine

Indicator light

Exhaust

Three-spoke wheels

Chain

This motorcycle has upside-down telescopic forks; the lower section of the fork slides into the upper.

Radiator

The fairing (front enclosure) has been removed to show the engine.

1992 Yamaha FZR 1000 Exup

TYPES OF MOTORCYCLE

Motorcycle rickshaw
These three-wheeled taxis are adapted motorcycles.

Trail bike
Lightweight trail motorcycles are designed for rough terrain.

Custom motorcycle
These motorcycles are adapted by their owners to individual specifications.

Moped
Mopeds are 50cc motorcycles restricted by law to 48km/h (30mph).

Scooter
Scooters are small-wheeled motorcycles.

Combination
Combination or outfit motorcycles are those with a sidecar attached.

MOTORCYCLE RECORDS

LONGEST JUMP FROM A RAMP
was 76.5m (251ft), by American Doug Danger on a 991 Honda CR 500.

LONGEST WHEELIE
(travelling non-stop on the rear wheel) was 331km (205.7 miles), by Yasuyuki Kudoh of Japan.

LARGEST MOTORCYCLE PYRAMID
consisted of 45 riders of the Indian Army motorcycle display team. They rode eight motorcycles a distance of 800m (2,625ft).

LONGEST STREET-LEGAL MOTORCYCLE
was 4.57m (15ft) long, built by American Gregg Reid.

SMALLEST MOTORCYCLE
had a wheelbase of 10.79cm (4.25in), a seat height of 9.5cm (3.75in), a front wheel diameter of 1.9cm (0.75in), and a back wheel diameter of 2.41cm (0.95in). It was ridden over a distance of 1m (3.3ft).

Smallest motorcycle

FASTEST PRODUCTION MOTORCYCLES
(Motorcycles built for general sale)

Motorcycle	Speed	
	km/h	mph
Bimota YB11	289.6	180
Honda Blackbird	281.6	175
Kawasaki ZZR1100	273.6	170
Yamaha Thunder Ace	268.7	167

MOST EXPENSIVE PRODUCTION MOTORCYCLES

Motorcycle	Price US$
Bimota Tesi 1D ES	35,259
Bimota Tesi 1D SR	33,343
Bimota YB10 Furano	32,193

HISTORY OF MOTORCYCLES

1818 First idea for a motorcycle, a steam-driven *Velocipedraisiavaporianna,* appears in a cartoon in Paris, France.

1884 Britain's first motorcycle, the *Petrolcycle,* is patented. It is not built until 1888.

1885 Germans Wilhelm Maybach (1846–1929) and Gottlieb Daimler (1834–1900) build a motorcycle with a wooden frame and wheels, powered by Daimler's four-stroke internal combustion engine. Daimler's son rides 10km (6 miles) before the saddle catches fire.

1818 | 1818 | 1884 | 1885

MOTORCYCLE MADNESS

The most people to ride one motorcycle was 47, in 1995. The riders were members of the Army Corps of Brasília, Brazil, on a 1200cc Harley Davidson.

1892 First commercially produced motorcycle is launched.

1901 One of the first practical motorcycles, the new Werner, is produced.

1904 Harley Davidson begin motorcycle production with their *Silent Grey Fellow.*

1907 First TT (Tourist Trophy) race is held in the Isle of Man, UK.

1910 Sidecars become popular.

1959 Triumph introduce their most famous motorcycle, the high performance Bonneville.

1972 First superbike produced by Honda.

1978 New motorcycle speed record set by Donald Vesco (born 1939), who reaches 512km/h (318mph) (below).

1990s The R1100, with computerized engine management, is launched by German company BMW.

1890 | 1892 | 1900 | 1901 | 1904 | 1907 | 1910 | 1950 | 1959 | 1970 | 1972 | 1978 | 1990

TRAINS

A TRAIN IS A SERIES of vehicles pushed or pulled along a track (a railway) by a locomotive. Trains are an efficient method of transport: they use less fuel than cars and lorries.

TYPES OF TRAIN

Electric locomotive

Diesel locomotive

Steam locomotive

Underground train

Funicular train

Monorail

Tilting train

PARTS OF A TRAIN

This illustration shows the *Train à Grande Vitesse* (TGV) – the French high-speed train. It runs on specially built tracks with gentle grades and curves. The TGV was introduced in 1983.

The pantograph picks up an electric current from overhead cables.

Air-conditioned carriages

An air-powered suspension system and large shock absorbers enable the train to run smoothly.

Trains run on "trucks", which have four or more wheels. The trucks swivel to enable the train to go around curves.

The wheels under the power cars and the leading carriage are driven by electric motors.

The power cars pull and push the train.

The driver's cab has a computer that checks for faults on the train, and a radio that keeps the driver in touch with the signalling centre and other trains.

The TGV's streamlined shape reduces air resistance, enabling it to travel at high speeds.

TRAIN FACTS

• Steam trains are still used in several countries, including Zimbabwe, India, and China.

• The first toilets on trains appeared in the 1850s, in the USA and Europe.

RAILS AND SWITCHES

Rails are usually welded into one continuous track as they are laid, allowing trains to run smoothly. Switches, or points, are intersections in the rails that move trains on to a new section of track.

When a switch takes place, one rail of the track on to which the train will pass slides up against the far rail of the track on which it has been travelling.

A small gap opens in the near rail of the old track, and the train moves on to the new track.

The track rests on beams of wood or concrete called ties or sleepers.

BRING YOUR OWN CARRIAGE

On some of the earliest trains, passengers' own carriages were attached to wagons pulled behind the locomotive. Passengers sat in them during the journey.

RAILWAY GAUGES

The gauge of a railway is the distance between the two running rails. Railways are laid to different gauges in different parts of the world. This table shows some of the countries that have the various gauges.

Gauge		Countries
metric	imperial	
1,676mm	5ft 6in	Argentina, Chile, India, Pakistan, Portugal, Spain
1,600mm	5ft 3in	Brazil, Ireland, South Australia, Victoria (Australia)
1,520mm	5ft	Finland, former USSR
1,435mm	4ft 8.5in	Canada, China, France, Germany, Great Britain, Italy, New South Wales (Australia), Scandinavia (except Finland), USA
1,067mm	3ft 6in	Japan, Queensland, Tasmania, Western Australia (Australia), South Africa, Zimbabwe
1m	3ft 3in	Argentina, Brazil, Burma, Chile, East Africa, Thailand

HISTORY OF TRAINS

Pre-19th century
Wagons are pulled along tracks by horses and humans.

Stones being hauled along a track

1804 First successful steam railway locomotive built by Richard Trevithick (1771–1833, English) for the Pen-y-darren ironworks in South Wales, UK.

1829 *Rocket* **built by Robert Stephenson** (see opposite page). It is the first locomotive to incorporate modern features.

1830 First public steam railway for goods and passengers, the Liverpool and Manchester railway, UK, opens.

1881 World's first public electric railway opens, in Germany.

1890 World's first electric underground railway, the City and South London Line, UK opens (below).

| B.C. | 1800 | 1804 | 1829 | 1830 | 1881 | 1890 |

TRAIN RECORDS

MOST POWERFUL SINGLE-UNIT DIESEL-ELECTRIC LOCOMOTIVES
are 6,600 horsepower, owned by the US Union Pacific Railroad.

LONGEST AND HEAVIEST FREIGHT TRAIN
was a 660-car iron ore train that stretched for 7.3km (4.5 miles) and weighed 69,393 tonnes. It ran on the Sishen and Saldanha railroad, South Africa.

Grand Central Terminal, New York

LARGEST STATION
is the Grand Central Terminal in New York, USA, which has 44 platforms.

HIGHEST STATION
is at Condor, Bolivia. It is situated at an altitude of 4,787m (15,705ft).

OLDEST SURVIVING STATION
is Liverpool Road, Manchester, UK, which opened in 1830. It is now part of the Museum of Science and Industry.

MAJOR PASSENGER RAILWAY USERS

This table shows the countries with the highest passenger railway usage.

Country	Distance travelled (in billions)	
	km	miles
Russia	410.7	255.2
Japan	390	242
Germany	65.9	40.9
France	64.3	40.0
Italy	44.4	27.6
UK	33.2	20.6

FAMOUS TRAINS

ROCKET
This early steam engine was designed by English engineers Robert Stephenson (1803–59) and Henry Booth in 1829. It reached 47km/h (29mph), and heralded the age of the passenger train.

THE GENERAL
This train was built for the Western and Atlantic Railroad in 1855. It was typical of the steam engines that opened up the American West, with a cowcatcher on the front, and a large funnel for catching sparks.

ORIENT EXPRESS
The luxurious *Orient Express* was introduced in 1883. It ran between London, Paris, Vienna, Budapest, and Constantinople (Istanbul). So many secret agents used this train that it became known as the "Spies Express".

TWENTIETH CENTURY LTD
This luxury train was run by the New York Central and Hudson River Railroad. It ran between New York and Chicago from 1902 to 1967, and had a rear observation car and on-board barber shop.

TRAIN FACTS
- A high-speed diesel railcar introduced in Germany in 1933 ran at speeds of 161km/h (100mph) between Berlin and Hamburg. It was widely known as the *Flying Hamburger*.

TRANS-SIBERIAN EXPRESS
This service runs from Moscow to Vladivostock, taking almost eight days to cover 9,297km (5,777 miles) – the longest regular train journey in the world. The first through Trans-Siberian train ran in 1914.

FLYING SCOTSMAN
Flying Scotsman – London and North Eastern Railway locomotive No. 4472 – was built in 1923. It hauled express passenger trains between London, England, and Edinburgh, Scotland, until 1963.

HIAWATHA
Hiawatha was a steam-powered train built to provide a high-speed passenger service in the USA. It began in 1935, and travelled between Chicago and Minneapolis-St. Paul, taking just five hours and five minutes.

MALLARD
This steam locomotive – London and North Eastern Railway locomotive No. 4468 – holds the world speed record for steam traction. In 1938 it reached a speed of 203km/h (126mph), pulling a seven-coach train.

Steam locomotive works, Newcastle, UK, 1864

BLUE TRAIN
The *Blue Train* is probably the most luxurious train in the world: it has been described as "a five-star hotel on wheels". Introduced in 1939, it runs between the South African cities of Pretoria and Cape Town.

"BIG BOYS"
These locomotives were built from 1941 to 1944 by the American Locomotive Company, for the Union Pacific Railroad. They were among the largest conventional steam locomotives ever built.

ETR450 TILTING TRAIN
This Italian train was introduced in 1988. It runs fast passenger services on routes between Rome and other cities in Italy. It can tilt at an angle of up to 10°, and has a maximum speed of 250km/h (155mph).

BULLET TRAIN
This is the nickname of Japan's high-speed train, which began running between Tokyo and Osaka in 1965. The Bullet Train's aerodynamic shape enables it to travel at speeds of up to 210km/h (130mph).

- Between 1804 and 1968, more than 130,000 steam locomotives were built in Britain.

- The first railway to serve meals on a train was the US Baltimore and Ohio Railroad, in 1853.

1895 Electric traction is introduced in the USA, on a 6km (3.7 mile) stretch of track in Baltimore.

1913 First diesel-powered railcar, built in Sweden, enters service.

1923 Flying Scotsman (see above) enters service.

1934 Pioneer Zephyr, a streamlined diesel-electric train, is introduced in the USA. It sets the long-distance non-stop speed record.

1968 Last scheduled passenger steam train runs on British Railways: the 21.15 Preston to Liverpool.

1987 World speed record for diesel traction is set by British Railways' High-Speed Train, which achieves 283.9km/h (176.4mph).

1990 World speed record for an electric locomotive is set by the French TGV. It achieves a speed of 515km/h (320mph).

Flying Scotsman

Pioneer Zephyr

British Rail High-Speed Train

5 | 1900 | 1913 | 1920 | 1923 | 1930 | 1934 | 1960 | 1968 | 1980 | 1987 | 1990

BOATS

FROM HUGE OIL tankers to simple dugout canoes, boats play a vital role in the transport of people and goods. For many centuries, much of the world's trade has depended on shipping.

SAILS

Sails catch the wind to provide power for boats.

Mainmast

Foremast (front mast)

Main sail

Fore sail (front sail)

Chesapeake Bay bateau

PARTS OF A BOAT

Sailing has its own language, with special terms to describe many of the features found on boats. This racing yacht shows most of the parts of a modern boat.

Mast

Shrouds support the mast.

Forestay

Pulpit

Halyards hoist (raise) or lower the sails.

Stay supports the mast.

Mainhatch is watertight when closed.

Handholds (grabrails)

Vang (kicking strap) holds the boom down.

Boom

Sheet controls the position of the sail relative to the wind.

Steering compass

Bow (front)

Port (left-hand side)

Winch

Guardrails stop crew from falling over the side.

Navigation system antenna

Lifesaving gear

Deck

Backstay

Starboard (right-hand side)

Tiller controls the rudder.

Toerail stops feet sliding over the side.

Gunwales: the tops of the boat's sides

Navigation instruments

Spinnaker sheet

Genoa sheet

Hull (main body of the boat)

Cockpit

Blocks enclose rotating pulleys.

Cleat

Pushpit

Transom

Stern (rear)

Navigation light

Offshore racing yacht

TYPES OF SHIP AND BOAT

Boats can be divided into various categories according to their function: passenger, cargo, sport, service, fishing, or military (see p.262).

PASSENGER/CARGO

Liner

Ferry

Hovercraft

Hydrofoil

Paddle steamer (sternwheeler)

Pacific Island canoe

MAINLY CARGO

Oil tanker

Container ship

Barge

Dhow

Clipper

Junk

Sampan

Tramp steamer

Heavy lift

SERVICE

Police patrol boat

Dredger

Lifeboat

Weather ship

Lightship

Tug

Icebreaker

Submersible

SPORT AND LEISURE

Powerboat

Motor cruiser

Steam river launch

Jet ski

Racing four

Rowing boat

Kayak

Punt

FISHING

Stern trawler

Seiner netter

Factory ship

Titicaca reed boat

Grand Banks dory

Coracle

HISTORY OF BOATS

c.3500 B.C. Early Egyptian boats are made from bundles of reeds.

Egyptian reed sailing boat

c.2450 B.C. Egyptians develop ocean-going planked boats, powered by about 30 rowers.

c.500–c.323 B.C. The age of the trireme: ancient Greek warships powered by oars, with a bronze ram at the bow for piercing enemy ships.

Greek trireme

489 B.C. Battle of Salamis: Greeks defeat the much larger Persian forces in a major sea battle.

A.D. 400–1200 Viking longships dominate north European waters.

Viking longship

1000 Vikings land in North America.

c.1240 Centreline rudder introduced in Europe.

Centreline rudder

1492 Italian explor Christopher Colum (1451–1506) lands the Caribbean.

Santa Maria

| 3500 B.C. | 2500 B.C. | 500 B.C. | 489 | A.D. | 400 | 1000 | 1200 | 1240 | 1400 | 1492 |

SAILING WORDS

Aft At or near the stern.

Beating Sailing into the wind; wind coming from the bow.

Forward At or towards the bow.

Gangplank Portable bridge for boarding or leaving the boat.

Gybing Turning the stern of a boat through the wind.

Heave-to To slow or stop a boat using the sails and rudder.

Knot Unit of speed used by ships and aircraft: one knot = one nautical mph.

Log The record of a ship's voyage.

Nautical mile Unit of length used in sailing: one nautical mile = 1,852m (6,076ft). (One land mile = 1,609m/5,279ft.)

Reaching Sailing across the wind; wind coming from the beam (side).

Running Sailing with the wind coming from astern.

Tacking Turning the bow of a boat through the wind.

SHIP RECORDS

LARGEST SAILING SHIP was the *France*, which measured 127.7m (418.8ft) long.

LARGEST CONTAINER SHIPS are owned by American President Lines. Five of their ships are 275m (902ft) long. These ships are too large for the Panama Canal, and are known as *Post-Panamax* ships.

Queen Elizabeth

LARGEST PASSENGER LINER is the *France/Norway*, which is 1,035ft (315.5m) long. The *Queen Elizabeth*, launched in 1938, was 314m (1,031ft) long.

FAMOUS SHIPS

SANTA MARIA
This was the flagship of Italian explorer Christopher Columbus (1451–1506) on his voyage of discovery to the West Indies in 1492. *Santa Maria* was wrecked, and Columbus continued on the *Nina*.

BOUNTY
In 1788, a famous mutiny took place on the *Bounty*. Lieutenant Fletcher Christian (1764–c.1790) led a revolt against commanding officer William Bligh (1754–1817) after the ship had collected breadfruit from Tahiti.

MAYFLOWER
This square-rigged sailing ship took 100 Puritans from Southampton, England, in 1620, to form the first permanent European colony in New England, USA. Plymouth, Massachussets now stands on the site.

CUTTY SARK
This was the most famous of the clippers. By the time the *Cutty Sark* was launched in 1869, the Suez Canal was open and steamships could travel east economically. The era of the sailing ship was drawing to an end.

ENDEAVOUR
Captain James Cook (1728–79) undertook his first scientific and exploratory voyage in this ship, in 1768. During this three-year voyage, Cook mapped 8,000km (5,000 miles) of coastline.

KON TIKI
Norwegian Thor Heyerdahl (born 1914) built the raft *Kon Tiki* in 1947 to prove that the Polynesian islands could have been populated from South America. He sailed 6,115km (3,800 miles) from Peru to Raroia.

VIKING VERY LONG SHIP
The world's largest ship is the Norwegian oil tanker *Jahre Viking*, which is 458m (1,503ft) long. It takes five minutes to walk from one end to the other.

SHIPWRECKS AND DISASTERS

Ship	Date	Shipwreck/disaster
Armada	1588	Spanish fleet of 130 ships sent to invade England. After losing the battle, the surviving ships fled north around Scotland and Ireland where many were wrecked by storms. Only 60 ships returned to Spain; about 15,000 sailors died.
Marie Celeste	1872	Found abandoned and empty, with no trace of the ten people originally on board.
Titanic	1912	Struck an iceberg and sank, with the loss of about 1,500 lives.
Lusitania	1915	Torpedoed with the loss of 1,198 lives.
Wilhelm Gustloff	1945	Torpedoed with the loss of more than 7,000 lives.
Dona Paz	1963	Collided with motor tanker *Vector*: 4,386 people died.
Queen Elizabeth	1972	Burned and sank in Hong Kong harbour whilst being refitted.
Amoco Cadiz	1978	Spilled 223,000 tonnes of oil, with drastic environmental consequences.

SHIP FACTS

• Japanese companies own 3,041 large- and medium-sized ships (those with more than 1,000 gross tonnes); Greek companies own 2,773, and US companies own 1,654.

• A large oil tanker carries about 132,925,040 litres (29,240,000 gallons) of petrol: this is enough to enable a car to drive around the Earth nearly 47,000 times.

• About 92% of the world's trading goods are carried by ships.

SUPERSTORER
Large container ships can carry about 2,700 containers. Stacked, they would stand almost twice as high as Mt. Everest.

–22 First –mnavigation –e world by –guese –rer –nand –llan –1521).

c.1700 Introduction of the steering wheel.

Ship's steering wheel

1838 First crossing of the Atlantic entirely under steam, by *Sirius*.

Sirius

1850–59 Heyday of the clipper: fast sailing ship that transports tea from China to Europe and North America.

Clipper

1968–69 First non-stop solo circumnavigation of the world from west to east, by English yachtsman Robin Knox-Johnston (born 1939), in *Suhaili*.

Suhaili

1994 Englishman Mike Golding (born 1960) breaks east-west, single-handed, non-stop round-the-world record, in *Group 4* (sloop). Voyage takes 161 days, 16 hours, 32 minutes.

| 1519 | 1700 | 1800 | 1838 | 1850 | 1900 | 1968 | 1994 |

WARSHIPS AND SUBMARINES

THERE ARE MANY types of fighting vessel, from light, speedy frigates, to massive aircraft carriers and nuclear-powered submarines. A country or state's fighting force of ships and submarines is called its navy.

TYPES OF WARSHIP

The main function of a warship is to defend its country, sea-lanes, and shipping from enemy attack.

Aircraft carrier
The aircraft carrier is the largest of all warships. It acts as a floating airfield for up to 100 aircraft, and may have a crew of more than 2,000, plus a flying crew of more than 1,000.

Cruiser
The cruiser's speed and endurance are considered more important than its protection (self-defence) and weapons. Cruiser functions vary from navy to navy.

Battleship
Before aircraft carriers were built, the battleship was the most heavily armed and armoured ship. There are now very few battleships remaining in service.

Destroyer
The destroyer was originally intended to defend fleets against attack from torpedo boats. Today's destroyers are armed with guided missiles.

Frigate
The frigate was developed during World War II to escort convoys and protect them from submarines. Today's frigates perform a variety of functions.

Minesweeper
Minesweepers have special equipment for locating and destroying mines. They are usually small craft of 400–800 tonnes (440–880 tons).

PARTS OF A WARSHIP

Modern warships are armed with guns and guided missiles for attack and defence. Most are also equipped with advanced electronic equipment for detecting targets.

Frigate

Surveillance radar · Navigation/helicopter control radar antenna · Mast · Radar for gunnery and missile control · Signalling lamp · Exocet missile launcher · Gun turret · 11cm (4.4in) gun · Funnel · Seacat missile launcher · Ensign staff · Lynx helicopter · Sonar torpedo decoy · Variable pitch propeller · Rudder · Anti-submarine torpedo tube · Liferaft cylinder · Rocket launcher · Pennant number · Porthole · Sonar bulge · Anchor · F174

SUBMARINES

There are two main types of military submarine: patrol submarines, which seek and destroy ships, and missile-carrying submarines. Today's nuclear missile-carrying submarines are the most powerful weapons carriers of all time.

Stabilized fin · Aft hydroplane · Main turbine · Snort mast · Conning tower · Control room · Periscope · Senior ratings' mess · Galley · Officers' mess · Propeller · Lower rudder · Diesel motor compartment · Reactor space · Junior rating's mess · Torpedo compartment · Torpedo tube

Nuclear-powered submarine

WARSHIP AND SUBMARINE RECORDS

Russian Typhoon class submarine

LARGEST SUBMARINE is the Russian Typhoon class, which measures about 170m (558ft) long.

FASTEST SUBMARINE is the Russian *Alpha*, which can probably exceed 42 knots (see p.261) when submerged.

WARSHIP WITH THE LARGEST NUMBER OF HEAVY GUNS was the battleship *Agincourt*, built in 1914, which had fourteen 30.5cm (12in) guns.

WARSHIP HARDSHIP

During the late 18th century, only about 9% of deaths on British Royal Navy warships were due to enemy action. About 50% were caused by disease, 31% by accidents, and about 10% by fires and wrecks.

FAMOUS FIGHTING SHIPS

VICTORY
The *Victory*, built in 1765, was British Admiral Lord Nelson's (1758–1805) flagship. It had 100 guns and a crew of 850.

BISMARCK
This German WWII battleship, launched in 1939 and sunk in May 1941, had eight 38cm (15in) guns.

WARRIOR
The *Warrior*, built in 1860, was the first iron battleship. This British ship was protected by a 114mm (4.5in) iron belt.

YAMATO
This Japanese battleship, launched in 1940, was the largest battleship of all time. It was sunk in 1945.

MONITOR
In 1862, during the American Civil War, the US *Monitor* took part in the first battle between ironclad warships.

ESSEX
The US aircraft carrier *Essex*, launched in 1942, could carry 91 aircraft and achieve a speed of 32 knots.

DREADNOUGHT
This British ship, built in 1906, was the first modern battleship. It was armed with heavy guns and protected by thick steel.

NIMITZ
The US nuclear-powered aircraft carrier *Nimitz* was completed in 1975. It carries 90 aircraft.

AIRCRAFT

THE TERM AIRCRAFT refers to all flying machines, including aeroplanes, helicopters, and hot-air balloons. Aircraft range from simple hang-gliders to the enormous Boeing 747, which can carry more than 550 people.

Piper Cherokee

The fin stops the back of the plane swinging from side to side.

The elevators control the plane's ascent and descent.

Fuselage

Pilot's seat

Wings are covered with thin aluminium sheeting.

Fuel tanks in the wings and wing tips hold up to 320 litres (70 gallons) of fuel.

Engine

The rudder steers the plane.

Strong metal cables run from the pilot's control stick and rudder pedals to the control surfaces.

Spinner

Ailerons control the plane's balance and, together with the rudder, steer the plane.

Flap

Propeller

Nose landing gear

Wings are made from spars. These are long, strong rods that stretch from the fuselage to the wing tip.

Undercarriage (main landing gear)

PARTS OF AN AIRCRAFT
This small, propelled light aircraft shows the features of a typical aeroplane. Its main structures are the fuselage, wings, tailplane, and fin, which together are called the airframe.

TYPES OF AEROPLANE
Aeroplanes (planes) are powered, heavier-than-air aircraft with fixed wings. There are many different types of aeroplane; their uses include transport, warfare, and sport.

Jet aircraft
Jet aircraft are powered by jet engines (see p.247). Most civil airliners (large passenger aircraft) and military planes have jet engines.

Propellered plane
Propellered planes are cheaper to run than jet aircraft, and can take off easily from short runways. Many airlines use turboprop aircraft for regional air services. The propellers of these planes are driven by gas turbines.

Biplane
Biplanes have two sets of wings, one above the other, braced with wires. Early planes were built in this style because two wings were stronger than one long, single wing. Today's biplanes are strong enough to withstand aerobatic displays.

Light aircraft
Light aircraft are powered by piston engines similar to those found in cars. These small aeroplanes are used mainly for leisure and short business trips.

Observation plane
Observation planes are used by police, rescue services, and armies. They are used mainly as standard light aircraft, although the *Edgeley Optica* (above) is a purpose-built model.

Supersonic plane
Supersonic planes are jet aircraft that can fly faster than the speed of sound (see p.236). Their shape is different from that of conventional aeroplanes, because air flows in a different way at such high speeds.

Seaplane
Seaplanes can take off from and land on water. They are used mainly in remote areas with few airfields, such as northern Canada and Alaska, where the country is undeveloped and there are many lakes.

FLIGHT DECK
The flight deck contains the controls and data-display instruments. Today's flight decks, such as this 1980s airliner cockpit, have CRTs (cathode-ray tubes). These display computerized information on screens that can be changed at the touch of a button.

Primary flight display CRT: includes artificial horizon, altimeter, and airspeed indicator.

Landing and taxi light switches

Warning lights

Second CRT displays navigational information, and functions as a simple compass, radar screen, or map display.

Engine throttles

Navigation computer equipment

Independent weather radar

Wing flap control

FLYING A PLANE
Aeroplanes have three main controls: the throttle, which controls the speed; the rudder pedals, and the control column.

Rolling
To roll, the pilot moves the control column to the left or right, raising the ailerons on one wing and lowering them on the other.

The plane rolls when the ailerons are raised and lowered.

Control column

Aileron

Elevator

Pitching
To pitch the plane up or down, the pilot pushes or pulls the control column, raising or lowering the elevator flaps on the tail wing.

Yawing
To make the plane yaw (swerve) to the left or right, the pilot swivels the rudder bar with the feet. This turns the upright rudder on the tail.

Rudder pedals steer the plane to the left and right.

Rudder

The control column tilts the aircraft to either side (rolling), and up and down (pitching).

Plane banks in order to turn.

Banking
Aeroplanes have to bank in order to turn. The pilot uses the control column and the rudder pedals together, so that the aircraft rolls and yaws at the same time.

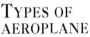

HISTORY OF FLIGHT

For centuries, people tried to fly. They made elaborate wings, launching themselves from high places, often with fatal results. Only in the last 100 years have humans learned to fly, advancing from simple machines to jet aeroplanes.

Daedalus

c.2000 B.C. According to legend, Daedalus, a craftsman working on the labyrinth for King Minos of Crete, makes wings for himself and his son to escape the island.

1010 Oliver of Malmesbury (c.980–1066), a Benedictine monk, attaches wings to his arms and jumps from a tower. He travels for a short distance, but breaks his legs.

1486–1500 Italian artist Leonardo da Vinci (1452–1519) sketches designs for flapping wing craft (ornithopters), as well as parachutes and helicopters.

2000 B.C.	A.D.	1000	1010	1400	1486

1853 Sir George Cayley builds a full-size glider which, it is claimed, carries his coachman across a small valley.

1891–96 The world's first aviator, German Otto Lilienthal (1848–96), invents a practical hang-glider and becomes the first person to make repeated controlled flights.

Otto Lilienthal, 1896

1896 American scientist Samuel Langley (1834–1906) builds a tandem-winged, steam-powered model, the *Aerodrome*.

Samuel Langley flew 1km (0.6 miles) in the Aerodrome.

1903 The world's first powered aeroplane flight is made by the Wright brothers, Orville (1871–1948) and Wilbur (1867–1912), who fly 26 (853ft) at Kitty Hawk, eastern U

1853	1891	1896	1900	1903

1919 First non-stop flight across the Atlantic is made by British aviators John Alcock (1892–1919) and Arthur Whitten-Brown (1886–1948), in a Vickers Vimy with Rolls-Royce engines. It takes 16 hours.

Alcock and Brown

1920s Vast airships fly people across the Atlantic in ocean-liner style.

1924 Hugo Junkers (1859–1935, German) produces a pioneering all-metal three-engined monoplane airliner.

All-metal Junkers airliner

1927 First solo flight across the Atlantic is made by American Charles Lindbergh (1902–74) in a Ryan monoplane, *Spirit of St. Louis.*

Spirit of St. Louis

1928 First flight the mid-Pacific is by Australian Char Kingsford Smith (1897–1935).

1928 World's first modern airport at Croydon, near London, UK.

1919	1920	1924	1927	1928

1937 First experimental jet engine is designed by British engineer Frank Whittle (born 1907) (above right).

1939 First jet-propelled flight is made by a Heinkel He178, powered by an engine designed by German Hans von Ohain (born 1911).

Heinkel He178

1940 Battle of Britain: the victory of the British Royal Air Force over the German Luftwaffe ensures Britain is not invaded.

Gloster E28/39

1941 Frank Whittle's jet engine is used in the Gloster E28/39.

1947 The Bell X-1 experimental rocket plane, piloted by American Chuck Yeager (born 1923), breaks the sound barrier.

Bell X-1

1952 The world's first jetlin the De Havilland Comet, com into service, halving internatio flight times. Two years later it withdrawn following crashes to metal fatigue.

1939	1940	1940	1941	1947	1950	1952

OTHER AIRCRAFT TYPES

HOT-AIR BALLOON

Hot-air balloons are used mainly for recreation. Modern hot-air balloons use propane burners carried above the balloon's basket to heat up the air.

AIRSHIP

Modern airships are filled with helium or hot air. Their long, thin shape keeps them stable. Airships can be steered, and many have swivelling propellers to assist with take-off and landing. Airships are sometimes used for advertising, with messages displayed on their sides.

GLIDER

Gliders are unpowered planes with a wide wingspan measuring up to 25m (82ft). They use currents of hot, rising air (thermals) to stay aloft, and are controlled with a rudder, elevators, and ailerons (see p.263).

HANG-GLIDER

Hang-gliders are made of material stretched across a simple frame, forming wings. The pilot hangs beneath the wings in a harness or body-bag, and steers by shifting his or her weight from side to side. Hang-gliders are not powered: the pilot relies on thermals for lift.

MICROLIGHT

A microlight is basically a powered hang-glider. It has a small engine and an open fibreglass car, called a trike, that can hold a crew of two. The trike is suspended on a strong frame, and the pilot steers by shifting his or her weight against the frame. Microlights can reach speeds of up to 160km/h (100mph).

HELICOPTER

Helicopters are powered, lifted, and steered by rotating blades. They take off vertically, fly slowly and hover, and move in any direction. This manoeuvrability makes them ideal for functions such as crop-spraying, traffic surveillance, and rescue.

French brothers
h and Etienne
golfier (1740–1810;
99) launch a balloon
ersailles, France,
cockerel, a sheep,
duck on board. A few
later they fly a new
n carrying two men.

*Montgolfier brothers'
balloon*

1804 British baronet
Sir George Cayley
(1773–1857) invents the
practical aeroplane: he
builds a model glider
that provides the basis
for later aircraft design.

*Aerial Steam
Carriage
design*

**1844 First design for
a complete
mechanically powered
aeroplane:** William
Henson (1812–88,
British) designs the
Aerial Steam Carriage
and makes a 6m (20ft)
model version.

**1852 First
airship** is built
and flown by
Henri Giffard
(1825–82, French).
It is a cigar-shaped
balloon powered
by a steam engine.

*Henri Giffard's
airship*

| 1783 | 1800 | 1804 | 1844 | 1850 | 1852 |

**1907 First helicopter flight is
made** by French mechanic Paul
Cornu (1881–1944). He lifts off
the ground for 20 seconds.

*Paul Cornu's
helicopter*

**1909 First flight across the
English Channel** is made by
Louis Blériot (1872–1936,
French), who flies from
France to England in a
monoplane.

*Blériot's monoplane,
the Blériot Type XI*

**1909 Baroness
de Laroche**
(?–1919) is the
first woman to
make a solo flight.

*Baroness de
Laroche*

**1914–18 WWI: first use of aircraft
in war.** The aeroplane becomes a
weapon; there is a huge increase in
speed, range, and strength.

*WWI German
biplanes*

| 1907 | 1909 | 1909 |

British aviator Amy Mollison
Johnson) (1903–41) flies solo
England to Australia in *Gypsy Moth*.

1932 American aviator
Amelia Earhart (1898–1937)
is the first woman to fly solo
across the Atlantic.

*Macchi
M72*

**1933 World's first modern
airliner, the Boeing 247,** is
launched.

Boeing 247

1934 Italian Macchi M72
floatplane sets the world
speed record
at 708km/h
(440mph).

**1936 First practical
helicopter, the Focke
Achgelis FW-61,** flies.

Foche Achgelis FW-61

1937 The airship *Hindenburg*
is destroyed in an accident,
killing 35 people.

| 1932 | 1933 | 1934 | 1936 | 1937 |

The Hawker P1127
es the first hovering trials
jet thrust. It is the
ecessor of the Harrier, the
VTOL (vertical take-off
and landing) aircraft to
enter service.

Hawker P1127

1965 The Lockheed
SR71 Blackbird spy
plane sets a new world
speed record of 3,331km/h
(2,070mph).

Blackbird

**1970 The first wide-
bodied jet, the Boeing 747
"Jumbo Jet",** comes into
service. It carries up to 550
passengers, and makes
international jet travel
commonplace.

*Boeing
747*

Concorde

**1976
The Anglo-
French supersonic**
airliner Concorde goes into
service, reaching speeds
of 2,494km/h (1,550mph).

*Right: Gossamer Albatross,
designed by American Paul
Macready (born 1925)*

**1979 First
human-powered
aircraft,** the
Gossamer Albatross,
crosses the
English Channel.

**1986 First non-stop
round-the-world flight,** by
Americans J. Yeager (born
1936) and D. Rutan (born
1952), in *Rutan Voyager.*

| 1960 | 1965 | 1970 | 1970 | 1976 |

AIRCRAFT FACTS

• One of first airline services was
provided by German Zeppelin
airships. They carried a total of
35,000 passengers between Lake
Constance, Berlin, and other cities.

• The world's first electrically
powered aircraft, the MB–E1, flew in
1973, in Germany.

WINGED THING
In the 1890s, Horatio
Phillips (1845–1926,
British) built a
plane with 20
sets of wings.
It looked like
a venetian
blind.

AIRCRAFT RECORDS
LARGEST AIRCRAFT WINGSPAN
is that of the Hughes H4 Hercules
flying boat *Spruce Goose*, which
measures 97.51m (319.9ft) across.

Hughes H4 Hercules flying boat Spruce Goose

SMALLEST BIPLANE
is *Bumble Bee Two*, which is just
2.64m (8.7ft) long, and weighs
179.6kg (396lb).

HEAVIEST AIRCRAFT
is the Antonov An-225 Mriya
(*Dream*), which weighs 600 tonnes.

WORST AIR DISASTERS

Year	Incident	Number of people killed
1977	Two Boeing 747s (KLM and Pan Am) collided on the runway at Tenerife, Canary Islands.	583
1985	A Japan Airlines Boeing 747 crashed en route from Tokyo to Osaka.	520
1996	A Saudi Arabian Boeing 747 collided above India with a Kazakh Airways Ilyushin 76.	350
1974	A Turkish Airlines DC-10 crashed at Ermenonville, France, immediately after take-off from Paris.	346
1985	An Air India Boeing 747 exploded in mid-air off the Irish coast, en route from Vancouver to Delhi.	329

LARGEST AIRLINER
is the Boeing 747-400,
which has a wingspan of
64.4m (211fr). It can carry
up to 567 passengers.

TYPES OF WARPLANE

Fighter
Fighter planes are designed to win air superiority so that other, slower aircraft, such as bombers and observers, can operate over battle zones. Fighters also attack enemy bombers.

Bomber
Bombers can carry a wide range of weapons and bombs, including nuclear weapons, and special bombs for destroying runways.

Transport aircraft
Modern armies rely on transport planes and helicopters to move troops and equipment rapidly into battle zones.

Helicopter gunship
Helicopter gunships are heavily armed helicopters, with rapid-fire machine guns that fire from the turret. They were widely used by US forces in Vietnam (see p.409).

Aerial reconnaissance plane
Army commanders rely on airborne observers to report on the movements of enemy forces. Observation planes are a prime target for enemy fighters, so pilotless, remote-controlled aircraft (RPVs) are often used.

VTOL aircraft
VTOL (vertical take-off and landing) aircraft use the immense power of the jet engine to rise vertically, or after a short run. VTOL craft do not need a long runway, and can therefore be hidden near the battlefront.

PARTS OF A FIGHTER
Modern fighter planes are equipped with sophisticated electronic instruments for detecting and attacking enemy aircraft and ground targets. This fighter can fly at more than 2,980km/h (1,852mph), at a height of 18,288m (60,000ft).

Two turbofan (jet) engines

F-15E Eagle

This fighter carries a crew of two: the pilot, and the weapon systems operator.

The crew can escape from ejector seats if the aircraft is in danger of crashing.

The large, transparent canopy gives the crew a good range of vision.

An infrared heat-sensitive camera enables the crew to fly in the dark.

Radar antennae detect other aircraft.

The rotary cannon can fire more than 6,000 rounds of ammunition per minute.

Four air-to-air missiles for shooting down enemy aircraft.

The plane's fuselage is made of composite plastic materials and light metal alloys.

Terrain-following radar enables the plane to fly at high speeds close to the ground.

AIRCREW
Aircrew consists of flying crew, who fly in the planes, and ground crew. Armourers ensure that the planes are adequately equipped with ammunition and bombs.

The pilot flies the aircraft. He or she carries flight plans in knee pads.

Women flying crew do not usually fly aircraft in battles.

Aircraft engineers check the planes after every flight.

The ground crew carry out maintenance and repair of the aircraft.

FAMOUS WAR PLANES

FOKKER TRIPLANE
German WWI flying ace Manfred von Richthofen (1892–1918), the "Red Baron", flew many aircraft. The best-known was the Fokker Triplane.

SPITFIRE
The Spitfire was the fastest and most effective British fighter plane of WWII. It had a Rolls-Royce Merlin engine, and could reach a speed of 684km/h (425mph).

FOCKE-WULF FW 190A
Brought into operation in 1941, the powerful FW 190A became one of the German Luftwaffe's principal fighter aircraft during World War II.

FLYING FORTRESS
These heavily armed US WWII bombers were designed for daylight raids. Fortresses were meant to fly in formation and protect each other, but this strategy failed. They were only safe when escorted by fighters.

AVRO LANCASTER
This was the main British bomber used by the RAF during WWII. It flew mainly at night to avoid detection by enemy fighters.

TORNADO
The Tornado is NATO's (see p.406) most powerful fighting plane. It is built in two forms: one carries bombs and guided weapons for ground attack; the other attacks enemy fighters.

VULCAN
The Vulcan was the main British nuclear attack aircraft in the 1950s and 1960s. Although it was not supersonic, its large delta wing allowed it to fly higher than Soviet fighters.

MIG 25
The Russian MIG 25 is one of the fastest aircraft in service, reaching speeds of Mach 2.8 (see p.236). It was developed to counter the threat of American supersonic nuclear bombers.

NORTHROP B-2 "STEALTH" BOMBER
This US bomber is designed to absorb or deflect enemy radar, so that it can remain undetected when approaching its targets. It is made of composite plastics.

MIRAGE
This plane is used by air forces around the world. Different models are used as fighters, fighter-bombers, and for reconnaissance.

KING OF THE ACES
During WWII, German Major Erich Hartmann (1922–93) shot down 352 planes, making him the war's top air ace.

AIR FORCE RECORDS
LARGEST AIR FORCE ever was the US Army Air Corps (now the US Air Force), which in 1944 numbered 79,908 aircraft and 2,411,294 personnel.

HEAVIEST BOMBER is the Boeing B-52H Stratofortress (below). It has a max. take-off weight of 221,353kg (488,000lb), and can carry 12 SRAM thermo-nuclear short-range missiles or 24 340kg (750lb) bombs under its wings, and 8 SRAMS or 84 227kg (500lb) bombs in the fuselage.

TOP WOMAN ACE was Junior Lieutenant Lydia Litvak (1921–43) of the USSR, who shot down 12 planes between 1941 and 1943.

TOP JET ACE was Captain Joseph McConnell Jr. (1922–54), of the US Air Force, who shot down 16 planes in the Korean War.

AIRLINE INSIGNIA

MOST COUNTRIES OF the world have a national airline. Each airline has its own distinctive insignia (emblem) and colours, which make its aircraft easy to identify. A selection of airline insignia is shown here.

 Aer Lingus
Irish airlines

 AEROLINEAS ARGENTINAS

 AIR ALGERIE

 AIR FRANCE

 Air Namibia

 air new zealand

 AIRLANKA

 AUSTRIAN AIRLINES

 Avianca
The Airline of Colombia

 Bahamasair

 BALKAN
BULGARIAN AIRLINES

 BRITISH AIRWAYS

 BWIA
WE ARE THE CARIBBEAN

 CAMEROON AIRLINES

 Canadian
Canadian Airlines International

 CROATIA AIRLINES

 CYPRUS AIRWAYS

 EGYPTAIR

 EL AL
Israel airlines

 ETHIOPIAN AIRLINES

 FINNAIR

 Garuda Indonesia

 GHANA AIRWAYS

 GULF AIR

 IBERIA
Spanish airline

 ICELANDAIR

 İstanbul Airlines
Ihre türkischen Ferienflieger

 JAL
Japan Airlines

 JERSEY EUROPEAN

 Kenya Airways
The Pride of Africa

 KLM
KLM Royal Dutch Airlines

 KOREAN AIR

 Lauda-air
Independent airline

 POLISH AIRLINES LOT

 Lufthansa
German airlines

 LUXAIR
Luxembourg airlines

 malaysia

 MEA
Middle East Airlines

 NIGERIA AIRWAYS LIMITED

 NORTHWEST AIRLINES
American airline

 OLYMPIC AIRWAYS
Greek airlines

 Philippine Airlines

 PIA
Pakistan International Airlines

 QANTAS
Australian airlines

 sabena
Belgian airlines

 SAS
Scandinavian Airlines System

 saudia
SAUDI ARABIAN AIRLINES

 SINGAPORE AIRLINES

 SAA
SOUTH AFRICAN AIRWAYS

 swissair

 Thai
Thai Airways International Limited

 TURKISH AIRLINES

 UZBEKISTAN
airways

 VARIG
Brazilian Airlines

 virgin atlantic

COMMUNICATIONS

DEVELOPMENTS IN COMMUNICATION systems have changed people's lives. Today, a person can make instant contact, whether by phone or fax, with someone on the other side of the world. People can travel to distant countries in a matter of hours. Advances in computer technology have transformed many workplaces.

TELECOMMUNICATIONS

Telecommunications covers communication by telephone, fax, television, and radio. All these forms of communication need a transmitter to send out the information, something to carry the signal, and a receiver to convert the signal back into an understandable message.

FIBRE OPTICS

Today, most international calls are routed through fibre optic cables, which lie on the sea bed. A telephone call is carried as a pulse of light along a cable that is made up of a few fine strands of pure glass, called optical fibres.

Fibre optic cable

POSTAL COMMUNICATIONS

One of the earliest, cheapest, and most reliable forms of communication is the postal service. Letters and parcels can be sent by air from one part of the world to another in a matter of days.

FIBRE OPTIC SUBMARINE SYSTEMS

This map shows the fibre optic routes existing today; many more are in the process of being built.

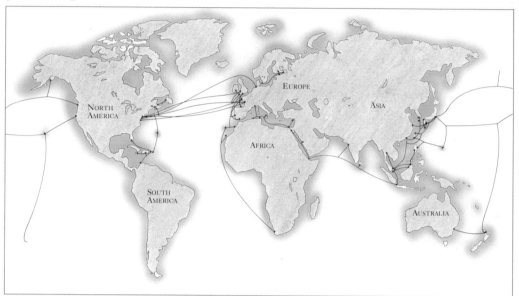

POSTAL STAGES

1 Letters and small packages are dropped in a letter box.

2 They are collected by postal workers and taken to the local sorting office.

3 Letters and packages are sorted and put in a sack with others going to the same area.

4 They are transported by road, rail, or air to their destination.

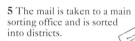

5 The mail is taken to a main sorting office and is sorted into districts.

6 It is taken to a local sorting office.

7 The letters are sorted by street.

8 They are then delivered by foot, bicycle, or van.

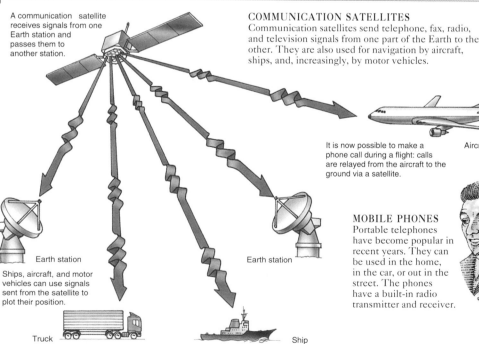

A communication satellite receives signals from one Earth station and passes them to another station.

COMMUNICATION SATELLITES

Communication satellites send telephone, fax, radio, and television signals from one part of the Earth to the other. They are also used for navigation by aircraft, ships, and, increasingly, by motor vehicles.

It is now possible to make a phone call during a flight: calls are relayed from the aircraft to the ground via a satellite.

Aircraft

Earth station

Earth station

Ships, aircraft, and motor vehicles can use signals sent from the satellite to plot their position.

Truck

Ship

MOBILE PHONES

Portable telephones have become popular in recent years. They can be used in the home, in the car, or out in the street. The phones have a built-in radio transmitter and receiver.

POSTAL SORTING

Most letter sorting in post offices is done by machine. An operator reads the address on a letter and punches a keyboard that prints a code of dots or bars. Other sorting machines "read" the codes and sort the letters further.

Letter sorting

MORSE CODE

The earliest form of telecommunication was the electric telegraph. An electric current was sent along a wire in long and short bursts, known as Morse code.

AIR TRAVEL

There are hundreds of airline companies operating throughout the world, offering safe, affordable travel to billions of people.

AIR TRAVEL FACTS

• Chicago International Airport in the USA is the busiest airport in the world. Aircraft take off or land about every 40 seconds.
• London's Heathrow Airport handles the most international flights in the world.

A MAJOR AIRLINE'S WORLD ROUTES

NORTH AMERICA
EUROPE
ASIA
AFRICA
AUSTRALIA
SOUTH AMERICA

AIR TRAFFIC CONTROL

Aeroplanes carry a device, called a transponder, which sends out a signal when it receives a pulse of radio energy from the secondary scanner. This signal tells air traffic control the aircraft's identity, height, and speed.

The aircraft reflects the pulses back to the scanner.

The aircraft replies with a signal only when it receives a pulse from the secondary scanner.

The radar sends out pulses to the aircraft.

Secondary radar system sends out pulses to the aircraft, and receives signals from the aircraft's transponder.

Radar antenna spins slowly, scanning for aircraft coming in different directions.

BUSINESS COMMUNICATIONS

The development of communications technology in the workplace has changed the way many people do their work. Because of the speed of communication possible with the use of fax machines, electronic mail, and telephone systems, it is likely that in the future more people will be able to work from home.

VIDEO CONFERENCE

Instead of spending time and money travelling to meetings, people can now communicate with each other by going to video conference centres. People speak through microphones and are able to see each other on screens. Although not yet widespread, video conferences are expected to become more common in the future.

At video conference centres, people can see each other on screen.

Computer screen

Keyboard

FAX MACHINE

Text and illustrations can be sent through a facsimile (fax) machine. Whatever is written or drawn on the page is transmitted in the same way as a telephone message.

Fax machine

COMMUNICATION WORDS

Cable television Television programmes delivered by a metal or fibre optic cable.
CD-ROM Compact Disc Read-Only Memory: a laser disc used to store computer data. The data cannot be removed, and new data cannot be recorded.
Database Information stored on a computer.
Navigation Finding a route between two places.
Network A system of interconnected pieces of equipment that communicate with each other.
Satellite An object held in orbit around a planet.

COMPUTERS

Information can be collected, stored, processed, and transmitted very quickly on computer.

INTERNET

The world's largest computer network is called the Internet. It enables all types of computer to share services and communicate directly.

INTERNET SERVICES

Some of the services available on Internet include:
Electronic mail (E-mail) This allows messages to be sent from one computer to another.
CU SeeMe This enables up to eight people to see and hear each other on their computer screens.
Usernet A collection of electronic bulletin boards (called Newsgroups) set up by subject matter. It is used for news and information.

COMMUNICATION FACTS

• A post office sorting machine can sort about 36,000 letters an hour.

• A pair of optical fibres can hold up to 61,440 telephone conversations at any one time.

• First country to introduce car navigation systems was Japan, in 1990.

• More than 4,000,000,000 messages are sent by E-mail in North America each year.

SEMAPHORE

Semaphore flag signals were used for signalling between ships until the early 1900s and by the army. It remains a quick method of visual signalling, and is still used for passing messages between ships sailing close to each other.

A B C D E F G H I J K L M N
O P Q R S T U V W X Y Z

LANGUAGE

LANGUAGE is a system of sounds and signs that people use to express their thoughts and communicate with others. There are thousands of languages throughout the world.

There are 845 languages in India, more than any other country in the world.

COMMON WORLD LANGUAGES
This map shows the distribution of the major world languages. It shows how European nations, when they explored the world, brought their languages to other countries; for example, English settlers brought their language to North America and Australia.

Mandarin Chinese		French
English		Portuguese
Russian		Arabic
Spanish		Other

MOST COMMON LANGUAGES

Language	Number of speakers
Chinese (Mandarin)	1,093 million
English	450 million
Hindi	367 million
Spanish	352 million
Russian	204 million
Arabic	202 million
Bengali	187 million
Portuguese	175 million
Malay-Indonesian	145 million
Japanese	126 million

HOW TO SAY "YES" AND "NO" IN DIFFERENT LANGUAGES AROUND THE WORLD
Words in brackets are a guide to pronunciation.

Language	Yes	No	Language	Yes	No	Language	Yes	No
Arabic	نَعَم (Na'am)	لا (La'a)	German	Ja	Nein	Polish	Tak	Nie
Bengali	হ্যাঁ (Haa)	না (Naa)	Greek	Ne	Óhee	Portuguese	Sim	Não
Bulgarian	Da	He	Hebrew	כֵּן (Ken)	לא (Lo)	Punjabi	ਹਾਂ (Haan)	ਨਹੀਂ (Nahi)
Chinese (Cantonese)	係 (Hai)	唔係 (M hai)	Hindi	हां (Haan)	नहीं (Nahi)	Romanian	Da	Nu
Chinese (Mandarin)	是 (Shi)	不是 (Bu shi)	Hungarian	Igen	Nem	Russian	Да (Dah)	Нет (Nyet)
Czech	Ano	Ne	Icelandic	Já	Nei	Serbo-Croat	Da	Ne
Danish	Ja	Nej	Indonesian	Ja	Tidak	Slovak	Áno	Nie
Dutch	Ja	Nee	Italian	Sì	No	Spanish	Si	No
English	Yes	No	Japanese	はい (Hai)	いいえ (Lie)	Swedish	Ja	Nej
Finnish	Kyllä	Ei	Korean	네 (Ne)	아니오 (A-ni-yo)	Thai	ค่ะ (Kha [female])	ไม่ค่ะ (Mai kha [female])
Flemish	Ja	Nee	Malay	Ya	Tidak	Thai	ครับ (Khrap [male])	ไม่ครับ (Mai khrap [male])
French	Oui	Non	Norwegian	Ja	Nei	Turkish	Evet	Hayir

SIGN LANGUAGE
People who cannot hear or speak can communicate through sign language. Signs may stand for whole words as well as individual letters. There are many different sign language systems. The example shown is used in Britain.

A B C D E F G H I J K L M
N O P Q R S T U V W X Y Z

SCRIPTS

SCRIPTS ARE SETS of symbols that we use to write things down. One script can be used to form different languages, for example, the Roman alphabet is used in many European languages, such as English and French.

PICTOGRAMS

The first scripts were pictograms. Pictures were drawn of an object or idea. These pictures were gradually simplified, to make them quicker and easier to write.

CUNEIFORM

The first successful pictogram script was cuneiform, which means "wedge-shaped". It was invented by the Sumerians of Mesopotamia (present-day Iraq) in about 3000 B.C. The script was written on damp clay with a wedge shaped stylus. After a while, the pictograms were written sideways and developed into simple, stylized symbols.

Bird

Ox

PRESENT-DAY SCRIPTS

CYRILLIC (RUSSIAN)

The Cyrillic alphabet is named after St. Cyril, who spread the Christian faith to the Slavonic peoples in A.D. 800.

А Б В Г Д Е Ж З И І Й К Л М Н О П Р С
Т У Ф Х Ц Ч Ш Щ Ъ Ы Ь Ѣ Э Ю Я Ѳ Ѵ

DEVANAGARI (HINDI)

There are about 200 Indian scripts in use today. The most widely known is Devanagari.

अ आ इ ई उ ऊ
ऋ ए ऐ ओ औ क ख ग घ ङ च छ ज
झ ञ ट ठ ड ढ ण त थ द ध न प फ ब
भ म य र ल व श ष स ह

BRAILLE

People who are blind or have poor eyesight can read by using Braille, invented by Frenchman Louis Braille (1809–1852). People read texts by touching a raised pattern of dots with their fingertips.

Braille

CHINESE

The Chinese use more than 50,000 signs, but only a few thousand are commonly used. A character is made up of a combination of up to 26 different strokes, which must be made in a particular order.

This character, "Yong", is made up of the five basic strokes.

First stroke

Second stroke

Third stroke

Fourth stroke

Fifth stroke

HIEROGLYPHS

The ancient Egyptians had a system of picture writing called hieroglyphs, meaning "sacred carvings". They were carved and painted on temple walls and tombs.

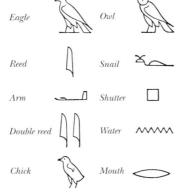

Eagle

Reed

Arm

Double reed

Chick

Leg

Owl

Snail

Shutter

Water

Mouth

Lion

JAPANESE

The Japanese adapted Chinese characters so that they could write down their spoken language, which in fact belongs to a different family from Chinese. Japanese, like Chinese, is written and read in vertical columns from right to left.

Japanese book

ALPHABETS

The letters of an alphabet are signs that represent sounds. This way of writing was quicker and easier to remember than pictogram writing.

DEVELOPMENT OF ALPHABETS

The Phoenicians developed the first alphabet around 1600 B.C. The Greek alphabet was adapted by the Etruscans in about 700 B.C. The Romans based their alphabet on the Etruscans'. The modern Hebrew alphabet has changed little from the original biblical Hebrew, and has similarities to the Phoenician alphabet.

GREEK WORDS

The ancient Greeks based their own alphabet on the Phoenician one. To begin with, they wrote in almost any direction, even in a spiral.

Greek inscription

Phoenician	Modern Hebrew	Early Greek	Classical Greek	Etruscan	Classical Roman	Modern Roman
∢	א	A	A	A	A	A
٩	ב	B	B	B	B	B
٦	ג	٦	Γ	⊃	C	C
◁	ד	Δ	Δ	⋂	D	D
⅄	ה	∃	E	∃	E	E
�	ו	⅂		⅄	F	F
						G
I	ז	I	Z	I		
⊟	ח	⊟	H	⊟	H	H
⊗	ט	⊗	θ	⊗		
Z	י	⟨	I	I	I	I
						J
Y	כ	⅄	K	⅄	K	K
レ	ל	⅂	Λ	⅃	L	L
⋎	מ	⋔	M	⋎	M	M
⅄	נ	⅄	N	⅄	N	N
‡	ס	☰	Ξ	⊞		
O	ע	O	O	O	O	O
⌐	פ	⌐	Π	⌐	P	P
⋔	צ	M		M		
φ	ק	φ		φ	Q	Q
٩	ר	٩	P	٩	R	R
W	ש	₤	Σ	₤	S	S
✝	ת	X	T	T	T	T
						U
		Y		V	V	V
						W
		Φ				
		X			X	X
		Ψ				
		Ω				
					Y	Y
					Z	Z

SCRIPT FACTS

• The oldest letter still in use is "O", which has not changed its shape since it was part of the Phoenician alphabet in about 1600 B.C.

• Children in Japan are taught 881 characters in their first six years at school.

• The longest alphabet is Cambodian (Khmer), with 74 letters.

ENERGY RESOURCES

INDUSTRY, TRANSPORT, and homes require energy to power everything from furnaces to televisions. Much of this energy is produced by burning fossil fuels, such as oil. Renewable energy sources, such as wind and solar power, are also playing an increasing role in energy generation.

FOSSIL FUELS

Oil, coal, and natural gas are called fossil fuels because they are made of the remains of long-dead plants and animals. When burned they release energy, which is used to generate power. Fossil fuels are non-renewable energy sources, because they will eventually run out.

COAL
About 20% of the world's energy is generated from coal, and its use is increasing.

OIL AND NATURAL GAS
About 60% of the world's energy comes from oil and natural gas. Oil is the main fuel used in transportation, and both oil and gas are burned to produce heat.

Some heat escapes through the chimney.

Cooling tower

Coal is crushed in a mill, and the powder is blown to the furnace.

Water from the condenser flows to cooling towers. Here it is sprayed into the air for cooling.

Furnace

Condenser

Steam turns the turbines.

Electricity generator

Transformer changes the voltage before it is supplied to homes and factories.

GENERATING ELECTRICITY
This illustration shows a coal-fired power station. Coal is burned in a furnace to heat water and produce steam. The steam drives a turbine attached to an electricity generator, which sends electricity down a network of cables called a grid.

MAJOR OIL PRODUCERS

Country	Million tonnes per year
CIS	570
USA	417.6
Saudi Arabia	327.1
Iran	155.3
Mexico	145.3
China	139
Venezuela	119.4

FOSSIL FUELS IN RESERVE
In 1960, it was estimated that existing underground fossil fuels would last for about 40 years. By 1990, more reserves had been found, but the rate at which they were being used had increased. In 1990, the reserves were still estimated to last about 40 years.

41 billion tonnes of known reserves

1.1 billion tonnes used in 1960

142 billion tonnes of known reserves

3 billion tonnes used in 1990

1960 fossil fuel consumption

1990 fossil fuel consumption

RENEWABLE ENERGY SOURCES
Renewable energy sources are those that will not run out in the foreseeable future. Most "renewables" are cleaner and less harmful to the environment than fossil fuels.

WIND POWER
Wind turbines generate electricity at "wind farms", such as the one at Altmont Pass, California, USA (right). During the 1980s more than 20,000 wind turbines were erected worldwide. Scientists estimate that by 2030, wind power could provide more than 10% of the world's electricity.

SOLAR POWER
The Sun is a non-polluting source of renewable energy. Solar energy is converted into electricity in photovoltaic (solar) cells, which are used to power various devices, including calculators, space satellites, and telephone links in remote areas. The Sun's heat is also used to heat water in many hot countries.

TIDAL POWER
Tidal power is generated at barrages (barriers) built across estuaries. As the tide rises or falls, water is kept at high or low tide level inside the barrage. When the water level differs by about 3m (10ft) water flows through huge turbines.

HYDROELECTRIC POWER
Hydroelectric power is generated at dams and waterfalls. Falling water drives turbines, which in turn drive electricity generators. About 7% of the world's energy is provided by hydroelectricity.

GEOTHERMAL ENERGY
Geothermal energy is generated by heat energy in the Earth's crust. At present, most geothermal energy is generated in volcanically active regions, such as Iceland and New Zealand. Approximately 20 countries use geothermal energy for heating, or for generating electricity.

WAVE POWER
Wave power is still being researched and developed. Several experimental generators have been built. Some are sited on the seashore. Others are designed for the deep sea, where the energy content per metre of wave can be equivalent to the power source for 50 single-bar electric fires.

BIOMASS ENERGY
Biomass energy is derived from organic matter, such as wood and agricultural waste. Biomass power plants are being built in many countries. They produce little air pollution and do not usually contribute to global warming.

ENERGY FACTS
• Watching colour television accounts for 20% of the average British person's energy consumption.

• Worldwide, lighting accounts for about 17% of electricity use.

• The average person in the UK uses 10 times more energy each year than the average person in India.

MAJOR WOOD USERS
Many developing countries depend on wood for fuel and energy production.

Country	Wood as % of total energy consumption
Mali	97
Rwanda	96
Tanzania	94
Burkina	94
Ethiopia	93
Central African Republic	91
Somalia	90

NUCLEAR ENERGY

Nuclear energy is generated by the breakdown of uranium and plutonium atoms. There are about 350 nuclear power stations around the world, and they supply more than 5% of the world's electricity. Nuclear power stations do not emit polluting gases or contribute to global warming, but accidents and the disposal of fuel rods pose serious risks.

The core is surrounded by a thick concrete shield that absorbs radiation.

Cooling tower

Heated fluid is used to produce steam.

The steam is piped to turbines linked to electricity generators.

Pellet of uranium or uranium dioxide

Fuel rods are made of several pellets.

The fuel rods are embedded in a material that slows down the neutrons (see pp.226–227), called a moderator.

There are about 90,000 fuel rods in the nuclear reactor core.

Fluid circulates through the core to carry away heat produced by nuclear fission.

NUCLEAR ENERGY RISKS

Nuclear waste remains dangerously radioactive for thousands of years, and has to be buried deep underground or at sea. Accidents at nuclear power plants, such as the Chernobyl disaster in Ukraine in 1986, can expose hundreds of thousands of people to radiation and contaminate millions of square kilometres of land.

MAJOR NUCLEAR POWER USERS

Country	% of total electricity generated by nuclear power
Lithuania	85.59
France	76.14
Belgium	55.52
Sweden	46.61
Bulgaria	46.43
Slovakia	44.14
Hungary	42.30
Switzerland	39.92
Slovenia	39.46
Ukraine	37.83

MAJOR ENERGY CONSUMERS

This table includes commercially traded fuels (oil, coal, gas, etc.) only. Fuels such as wood and animal waste are excluded, as figures are unreliable.

Country	Consumption as % of world total
USA	24.6
CIS	16.8
China	8.4
Japan	5.4
Germany	4.3
Central Europe	4.2
Canada	3
France	2.6

ENERGY CONSUMPTION OF VARIOUS HOUSEHOLD PRODUCTS IN THE USA

Household product	% of homes with product	Typical energy consumption (kilowatts per year)
Freezer (frost-free)	34.5	1,820
Refrigerator	84.6	1,591
Aquarium/terrarium	15	200–1,000
Colour television	98	75–1,000
Electric stove or oven	61.5	650
Personal computer	23.3	25–400
Dishwasher	45.2	165
Iron	40	20–150
Clock	100	17–50
Video recorder	98	10–70

RENEWABLE ENERGY FACTS

• The amount of sunshine that falls on roads in the USA in one year contains twice as much energy as all the coal and oil used worldwide in a year.

• Owing to better energy efficiency standards, new houses in Sweden use at least three times less energy to keep their houses warm in winter than the average British home.

Energy-efficient Swedish village

• Tokyo, Japan, has more than 1.5 million solar collectors for domestic water heating.

• About 90% of Israel's domestic hot water is supplied by solar heating.

GREAT LENGTHS

The world's largest wind turbines have blades up to 50m (164ft) long. One hundred people could stand side by side on a single blade.

ALTERNATIVE VEHICLE ENERGY

Oil will eventually run out, and in the meantime vehicle exhaust fumes are polluting the atmosphere. It is therefore important that clean, renewable energy sources are developed. Those being researched include compressed natural gas, electricity, hydrogen, ethanol (grain alcohol), and methanol (wood alcohol).

Hydrogen-powered car

OIL FACTS

• About 500,000 different materials can be made from crude oil. The products on the right are all made from materials derived from crude oil. They include wax, plastics, fertilizers, and detergents.

• One day's world oil supply took 110,000 years to fossilize.

• More than 500 oil wells are drilled every week in the USA.

• If all the barrels of oil produced worldwide in one day were laid end to end, they would stretch twice around the Equator.

HOW THE WORLD OBTAINS ITS ENERGY

This diagram shows the percentage of each energy source currently used worldwide.

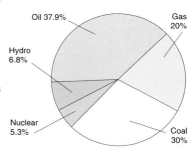

Oil 37.9%
Gas 20%
Hydro 6.8%
Nuclear 5.3%
Coal 30%

INDUSTRY

INDUSTRY IS AN organized economic activity. It deals with the extraction and use of raw materials, with manufacturing and construction, and with putting the products of these activities to profitable use.

CLASSIFICATION OF INDUSTRIES

There are three basic types of industry.

PRIMARY
These industries are concerned with the extraction of basic raw materials. Examples include agriculture, forestry, fishing, and mining.

Forestry industry

SECONDARY
These industries convert raw materials into other products. They can be further divided into heavy industry, e.g. shipbuilding, and light industry, e.g. textiles and clothing.

Clothing industry

TERTIARY
Tertiary (third order) industries offer a service rather than a product, e.g. banking and tourism. Today, this type of industry is expanding.

Cashier at work in a building society.

MAJOR INDUSTRIAL PRODUCERS

All total figures given are in millions, except where indicated. Where a country has a large share of the market, producer and figure are given in parentheses.

Industry	Top producers	Total (in millions)	World total (in millions)
Transport Cars, buses, and trucks	Europe	15 (Germany: 4.5)	45
	Asia	14 (Japan: 9.7)	
	North America	12	
Commercial aircraft	North America	2203*	3,207*
	Europe	814*	
Ships	Asia	814 (Japan: 535)*	1,452*
	Europe	546*	
Bicycles	Asia	59 (China: 36)	84
	Europe	10	
Communications TV and radio	Asia	172 (China: 42)	253
	Europe	32	
Telephones	Asia	66	107
	North America	18.7	
Electronic components	Japan	78,000	81,000
	North America	480	
Fuel Coal	Asia	1,421 tonnes (China:1,100)	3,453 tonnes
	North America	873 tonnes	
	Europe	525 tonnes	
Crude oil	Asia	1,094 tonnes (Saudi Arabia: 404)	2,971 tonnes
	North America	597 tonnes	
Construction and engineering Cement	Asia	588 tonnes (China: 244)	1,148 tonnes
	Europe	232 tonnes	
Pig-iron for steel-making	Asia	216 tonnes	526 tonnes
	Europe	123 tonnes	
Timber	Asia	1,074 cubic metres	3,450 cubic metres
	North America	717 cubic metres	

* Figures for commercial aircraft and ships are not in millions.

DISTRIBUTION OF MAJOR INDUSTRIES

Cars, buses, and trucks

Commercial aircraft

Ships

Bicycles

TV and radio sets

Telephones

Transistors and semiconductors

Coal

Crude oil

Cement

Pig-iron for steel-making

Timber

INDUSTRY FACTS

• Japan, which lacks most of the important industrial minerals, depends heavily on imports, importing about 95% of its iron ore, tin, copper, zinc, and lead. It is the world's largest importer of coal, natural gas, and oil.

• Mexico produces one-fifth of the world's silver.

• British Columbia produces about one-quarter of the marketable timber in North America. It also supplies the world with chopsticks.

• Wind power from approximately 1,100 windmills in Denmark supplies 3% of its energy needs.

• Gold provides between 20% and 30% of South Africa's export earnings.

274

OIL INDUSTRY

Oil is found under the sea bed or in places that were once covered by sea. Complex technology is used to drill deep wells and extract oil from the sea bed. Despite concerns about pollution and oil wells running dry, there is no sign of any fall in the demand for oil for fuel and for making chemicals.

TYPES OF OIL RIG

Shallow water
A jack-up rig is used. Its legs extend to the sea bed.

Deep water
A tension-leg rig is used. It floats, but is chained to the sea bed.

Very deep water
Ships are used. The oil drill comes out through a hole in the hull.

COAL INDUSTRY

Coal is valuable as an industrial fuel and for making chemicals. It is formed from the remains of decaying plant life, which solidified into coal over millions of years.

TYPES OF COAL MINE

Shaft mine

Drift mine

Open-cast mine

Shaft mine
Miners tunnel vertically when coal is deep under the ground.

Drift mine
Miners tunnel horizontally if a coal seam emerges near the surface of the ground.

Open-cast mine
If the coal is near the surface, the covering layers of ground are stripped away to reveal the coal.

FOOD INDUSTRY

The food industry processes much of our food so that it is safe to eat, looks appealing, and will remain fresh for a longer period of time. Food can be processed in many different ways.

MILK INTO CHEESE

There are many types of cheese, but most of them share the same basic stages of production.

A tanker will transport milk to the dairy.

The milk is pasteurized to destroy bacteria.

Another type of bacteria is added to the milk to produce lactic acid. The acid thickens the milk and turns it sour.

The milk is warmed, and rennet, which comes from a calf's stomach, is added. This makes the milk lumpy.

The watery part of the milk (the whey) is drained away and made into food for farm animals, leaving solid lumps, called curds.

Salt is added to the curds, which are pressed to get rid of any remaining whey. The curds are shaped into moulds. They are left in a cool place to ripen into cheese.

WAYS OF PROCESSING FOOD

Canning
Foods are boiled, put in cans, then heated to kill any remaining bacteria. The cans are then sealed to prevent air from bringing oxygen and bacteria to the food.

Cans on an assembly line

Freeze-drying
Food is frozen, and the water is removed. This kills all the bacteria, which cannot live without water.

Astronauts in space use freeze-dried food.

Pasteurizing
Liquids such as milk are heated to 70°C (160°F) for 15 seconds and then cooled quickly. This preserves the flavour while killing the bacteria.

Freezing
In fluidized freezing, small food items, such as peas, pass over very cold air (-34°C/-29°F) on a conveyer belt. The food freezes in minutes.

The cold air makes the peas rise.

ADDITIVES
Additives are natural or synthetic chemicals that are added to food to prevent it from going bad too quickly, and to make food look appetizing.

Beta carotene, a natural colouring from carrots, may be added to orange juice to strengthen colour.

Synthetic chemicals are added to cola to improve flavour.

Emulsifiers ensure fat and water remain combined. They are used in such foods as yoghurt.

The synthetic chemical – butylated hydroxytoluene (BHT) – stops the fat in corn chips from decaying.

Colourings and flavourings
Natural colour pigments may break up, so artificial or natural colourings are used as a replacement. Synthetic flavourings, which copy natural flavourings, may also be used.

In biscuits, bases such as sodium and ammonium hydrogen carbonate improve flavour and prevent changes in acidity and colour.

The preservative sodium nitrite is added to salami and hot dogs.

In bread rolls, a natural chemical such as vitamin C stops oxygen reacting with the fat in bread.

PAPER INDUSTRY

Paper is made in large factories called paper mills. Wood is ground down, mixed with water, and turned into wood pulp. The pulp is then pressed and rolled by machine into a layer of paper.

Most paper comes from softwood trees, such as spruce and pine.

Wood chips are heated to a pulp to release fibres.

Trees are cut into logs and transported to a paper mill.

The logs are broken down into chips.

Wastepaper is added and the fibres are reused to make recycled paper.

Fibres are mixed with fillers and dyes.

Wastepaper is taken back for recycling.

Water is removed from the pulp by suction.

Rollers remove any remaining water, and compress the paper.

Tissue is made from fibres that are lifted from the paper as it rolls off the machine.

A large roll of paper is finally produced.

PAPER PRODUCTS

Other paper products, such as tissue and cardboard, are made in a similar way to paper. The colour, strength, and texture of paper can be changed by dyeing, printing, and by mixing it with other materials, such as wax or plastic.

MOTOR INDUSTRY

In the motor industry, computer-controlled robots are programmed to carry out repetitive jobs previously performed by people. Robots are used to weld, paint, or drill engine parts. This has helped to improve efficiency in car factories.

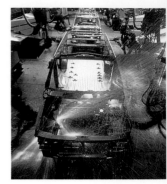

Motor cars being spray-painted by robots.

CERAMIC INDUSTRY

Ceramics may be divided into two groups: materials that are moulded into shape before being heated, such as pottery and bricks, and materials that are shaped after being treated by heat, such as cement.

Building bricks

Ceramic head made from cement mixture.

POTTERY INDUSTRY

Pottery clay is a mixture of two clays: kaolin (china clay), which gives clay its smooth texture, and ball clay, which adds strength. The moist clay is moulded, then placed in a kiln and heated until it hardens.

Detailed decorative work is still done by hand.

ELECTRICITY FACTS

- The amount of electricity a country produces is closely related to its industrial activity.
- Electricity production is measured in units, or kilowatt-hours. One unit is equivalent to leaving a hundred-watt light bulb on for ten hours.
- A typical household uses 6,000 units in a year.
- The world production of electricity is more than 12 trillion units.
- About 60% of production is used in industry, commerce, transport, and for public lighting.

MAJOR ELECTRICITY PRODUCERS

Producer	Units produced
North America	3.774 trillion
Asia (mostly Japan and the Pacific Coast)	2.7 trillion
Europe	2.0 trillion

GLASS INDUSTRY

Glass has many advantages. It is easily shaped, it is rust-proof, it is cheap to make, and it can be recycled.

Sodium carbonate

Limestone (calcium carbonate)

Glass

Sand

Limestone, waste glass (for recycling), sand, and sodium carbonate are put into a furnace.

Moulds are used to make glass bottles: a lump of hot, molten glass (a gob) is placed in a bottle-shaped mould.

Air is blown into the mould to make the glass inflate into a bubble, which expands to fit the shape of the mould.

Once hardened, the glass bottle is removed from the mould.

To make sheets of glass for windows, the molten glass is poured on to a pool of molten tin: this makes the glass spread out, until it is as smooth as the molten tin.

The glass is cooled slowly on rollers.

When the glass has cooled and hardened, it is cut with a diamond-tipped cutter.

INDUSTRIAL WORDS

Automation Repetitive work carried out by machines that need little human control.

Component One part of a finished product.

Consumerism Economic system based on the continued increase of goods produced to satisfy increased human need.

Depression A period of low output in trade and industry.

Economy The administration of a country's trade, industry, and money supply.

GNP Gross National Product. The total value of a country's industrial production.

Mass production Manufacture of goods repeating the same processes on a large scale.

Nationalize To make an industry operate under state control.

Production line The assembling, in several stages, of a product by the workforce.

Robotics Use of computer-controlled machines that carry out jobs previously done by humans.

Staple industry A country's most important industry.

ROADS

THE FIRST MAJOR road builders were the Romans, who built roads for their armies and messengers. Today, networks of roads and motorways cover most countries, linking cities, towns, and country areas. Increasing numbers of cars, buses, coaches, and trucks use the roads to transport people and goods.

ANCIENT ROADS
The Romans created a system of roads to serve their empire in Europe from about 400 B.C. to A.D. 400. The straight, wide roads were made up of several layers. Many of these roads are still in use today.

Large paving stones

Ditch for drainage of water

Crushed stone

Slabs of stone in cement

Sand

COUNTRIES WITH THE BUSIEST ROADS

Country	Distance travelled by a vehicle per km of road	
	x 1,000km	x 1,000 miles
Portugal	1,716	1,066
UK	1,140	708
Italy	1,138	707
Netherlands	896	557
Germany	866	538
Spain	687	427
Switzerland	628	390
Finland	513	319
USA	510	317
Sweden	435	270

COUNTRIES WITH DENSEST ROAD NETWORK

Country	km (per 1,000 sq km of land)	miles
Belgium	4,205	2,613
Japan	3,002	1,865
Netherlands	2,478	1,540
Luxembourg	1,970	1,224
Germany	1,900	1,181
Switzerland	1,722	1,070
Denmark	1,643	1,021
UK	1,553	965

COUNTRIES WITH MOST ROADS

Country	x 1,000km of road	x 1,000 miles of road
USA	6,328	3,932
Russia	1,588	987
Japan	1,120	696
France	811	504
Germany	549	341
UK	380	236

MODERN ROADS
Today's roads are built to withstand heavy traffic. First, the ground is levelled and trenches are dug. Drains are laid to carry water away. The road is composed of several layers of crushed stone and soil, with a top layer of concrete or asphalt and stone chips.

Tarmac, cement, or concrete

Sand, gravel, or stone

COUNTRIES WITH MOST MOTORWAYS

Country	x 1,000km of motorway	x 1,000 miles of motorway
USA	84.9	52.8
Germany	10.8	6.7
France	7.6	4.7
Italy	6.8	4.2
Japan	4.9	3.0
UK	3.2	2.0

ROAD NETWORK
Different types of road have different functions. Motorways and dual carriageways link towns and cities. Smaller roads intersect towns and cities to connect neighbourhoods and homes. In most countries people drive on the right-hand side of the road. In some countries, such as Australia, Britain, and Japan, people drive on the left-hand side.

MOTORWAY
A wide road, usually consisting of three lanes in each direction, a motorway is specially designed for fast-moving traffic travelling long distances.

BYPASS
This type of road carries traffic around the edges of cities, avoiding city centres.

Bypass

Crossroads

Roundabout

ROUNDABOUT
A roundabout allows traffic to change direction without crossing other lines of traffic.

CROSSROADS
When roads meet at a crossroads, traffic on one road is stopped by traffic lights to give way to traffic on the other road.

ROAD RECORDS

EARLIEST LONG DISTANCE road was the Persian Royal Road, which was 2,857km (1,775 miles) long. It ran from Susa in the Middle East to Smyrna, present-day Izmir in Turkey.

LONGEST ROAD is the Pan-American Highway. It runs from Alaska, USA, to Brasilia, Brazil, and is more than 24,140km (15,000 miles) in length.

HIGHEST ROAD lies between Tibet and Xinjiang, China. In places it is 5,633m (18,480ft) above sea level.

LOWEST ROAD is by the Dead Sea in Israel. It lies 393m (1,290ft) below sea level.

CONSTRUCTION

FROM EARLY TIMES, people have built all kinds of structures: tunnels and bridges to cross natural barriers; canals for transporting goods and for irrigation. Today, engineers are constantly improving construction methods and materials to produce canals that link oceans, and skyscrapers that are more than a hundred storeys high.

BRIDGES

The first bridges were made by placing tree trunks across rivers, and laying flat stones on rocks in the middle of streams. Today, bridges made of concrete and steel span lakes, rivers, deep valleys, roads, and railway lines.

Early clapper bridge, England

TYPES OF BRIDGE

Suspension
The deck, or roadway, is suspended from long steel cables attached to tall towers standing near each end of the bridge. The cables are made of thousands of steel wires bound tightly together.

Arch
This type of bridge is supported by an arch, propped up by abutments. The deck is usually straight, and does not follow the curve of the arch. It is sometimes built below, as well as above, the arch.

Bascule
This is a type of drawbridge. Its two sections can be raised at an angle to allow ships to pass through.

Beam
Most bridges with a short span are beam bridges. Each end of the bridge rests on the ground or on piers.

Swing
This type of bridge can be swung to one side to allow ships to pass through.

This swing bridge, in the foreground of the picture, is in Newcastle-upon-Tyne, England.

Suspension bridge

Arch bridge

Cantilever bridge

Cable-stayed bridge

Bascule bridge

Beam bridge

Cantilever
This is a type of beam bridge. Each half of the bridge balances on a supporting pier that is embedded in the river.

Cable-stayed
The deck is supported by steel cables connected to towers. Early cable-stayed bridges had pairs of towers, but today, single towers are also built in the centre of the deck. Its style is midway between a beam bridge and a suspension bridge. It requires fewer piers than a beam bridge, and does not need the heavy anchorages of a suspension bridge.

Pontoon
This type of bridge floats on the water. The deck rests on hollow concrete blocks, called pontoons, which lie on the water. Each pontoon is anchored to concrete blocks which are buried in the bed of the lake.

Pontoon bridge, Istanbul, Turkey

BRIDGES HOLDING WORLD RECORD FOR LONGEST MAIN SPAN

Bridge	Country	Date built	Type	Length m	ft
Ponte D'Augusto	Italy	220 B.C.	stone arch	30	98
Martorell	Spain	218 B.C.	stone arch	37	121
Chaochow	China	A.D. 617	stone arch	37	121
Bern	Switzerland	1204	stone arch	46	151
Scaligero	Italy	1356	stone arch	49	161
Trezzo over R. Adda (destroyed in 1416)	Italy	1377	stone arch	72	236
Schaffhausen	Switzerland	1755	wooden arch	59	193
Reichenau	Switzerland	1758	wooden arch	73	239
Union Bridge	Scotland	1820	suspension	137	449
Menai Straits	Wales	1826	suspension	177	581
Fribourg	Switzerland	1834	suspension	265	869
Cincinnati	USA	1867	suspension	323	1,060
Brooklyn	USA	1883	suspension	487	1,598
Forth Rail	Scotland	1889	cantilever	521	1,709
Quebec	Canada	1917	cantilever	549	1,801
Ambassador	Canada/USA	1929	suspension	565	1,854
George Washington	USA	1931	suspension	1,067	3,501
Golden Gate	USA	1937	suspension	1,280	4,199
Verrazano Narrows	USA	1964	suspension	1,298	4,258
Humber	England	1981	suspension	1,410	4,626
Great Belt East	Denmark	1997	suspension	1,624	5,328
Akashi Kaikyo	Japan	1998	suspension	1,990	6,529

SUSPENSION BRIDGES WITH LONGEST MAIN SPAN

Bridge	Country	Date built	Length m	ft
Akashi Kaikyo, Hyogo	Japan	1998	1,990	6,529
Great Belt East	Denmark	1997	1,624	5,328
Humber	England	1981	1,410	4,626
Tsing Ma	Hong Kong	1997	1,377	4,518
Verrazano Narrows	USA	1964	1,298	4,258
Golden Gate	USA	1937	1,280	4,199
Höga Kusten	Sweden	2000*	1,210	3,970
Mackinac Straits	USA	1957	1,158	3,799
Minami Bisan Seto	Japan	1988	1,100	3,609
Bosphorus 2	Turkey	1988	1,090	3,576
Bosphorus 1	Turkey	1973	1,074	3,524
George Washington	USA	1931	1,067	3,501
Kurushima 3, Ehime	Japan	1999	1,030	3,379
Kurushima 2, Ehime	Japan	1999	1,020	3,346
April 25	Portugal	1966	1,013	3,323
Forth Road	Scotland	1964	1,006	3,300
Kita Bisan Seto, Kagawa	Japan	1988	990	3,248
Severn	England	1966	988	3,241
Shimotsui	Japan	1988	940	3,084
Ohnaruto	Japan	1985	876	2,874

* Planned completion date

BRIDGE FACTS

• The first bridge made of iron was built in 1779 in Shropshire, England.

Ironbridge, England

• The longest bridge in the world is the Second Lake Pontchartrain Causeway, in Louisiana, USA. Each of its concrete spans measures 17m (56ft). The total length of the bridge is nearly 38km (24 miles). Land cannot be seen from its centre.

• The Tay Bridge in Scotland had been standing for just over two years when it collapsed during a stormy night in 1879. A train was crossing the wrought-iron bridge at the time, and 75 people were killed.

BRIDGE WORDS

Pier

Abutment End support for an arch.
Aqueduct Water-carrying bridge.
Box girder Hollow girder, or beam, built in the shape of a box for strength.
Caisson Water-tight structure used for preventing water and mud from flowing into foundation excavations.

Box girder

Clapper A type of bridge made of large slabs of stone placed over boulders.

Clapper bridge

Cofferdam Temporary dam used to keep out water while people work on a riverbed.
Creep Gradual change in shape of certain materials when under pressure.
Formwork Structure built to form, or shape, concrete on a bridge and to hold it while it hardens.
Hangers The wires or bars that connect the cables to the deck in a suspension bridge.
Lift bridge A bridge with a deck that rises in the air, like a lift.
Pier A support for the middle spans of a beam or arch bridge. The foundation of the tower on a suspension or cantilever bridge.
Reinforced concrete Concrete that contains steel rods, bars, wires, or mesh.
Viaduct A bridge carrying a road or railway.
Wrought iron Iron that is hammered into shape.

Lift bridge

CANALS

Canals are man-made waterways. Most canals are used by boats to transport cargo and people, others are used to take water to dry land, or drain water from marshy ground. Some canals, such as the Suez Canal in the Middle East and the Panama Canal in Central America, link seas and oceans.

HOW A LOCK WORKS

A canal lock is used to change the water level. A lock is a section of canal, large enough to take one or more boats, that has large, water-tight gates at each end. By opening and closing paddles, or valves, in one pair of gates, water is allowed to run into or out of the lock, and so raise or lower the water level to the same height as that in the next section of canal.

The narrowboat passes through the open gate into the lock.

Open gates

Upper water level

Closed gates

Lower water level

The paddles, or valves, in the lower gates are opened to let water out and the narrowboat is carried down with the dropping water level.

Gates are now closed.

The narrowboat is fully inside the lock.

Paddles are opened, and water rushes out.

The lower gates can now be opened for the boat to pass through.

Lower water level

Gates are opened.

Upper water level

DAMS

People need a constant supply of water to live. Efficient collection and storage of water is essential, especially in countries where there is little rainfall. Dams are built either to divert or store water.

DAM RECORDS

OLDEST KNOWN DAM in the world is the Sadd el-Kafara in Egypt. It was built out of earth and rock in about 3000 B.C.

LARGEST DAM in the world is the Syncrude Tailings dam in Canada, at 540,000,000 cu m (706,000,000cu ft).

LONGEST SEA DAM in the world is the Afsluitdijk in the Netherlands. Built in two sections, its total length is 62.5km (38.8 miles).

LONGEST SHIP CANALS

Canal	Location	Date built	Length km	Length miles
Suez	Links the Red Sea with the Mediterranean Sea	1869	174	108
Kiel	Links the North Sea with the Baltic Sea, Germany	1895	99	61
Panama	Links the Atlantic Ocean and the Caribbean Sea with the Pacific Ocean	1914	81	50
Manchester	England	1894	57	35

CANAL FACTS

• The Chinese were the first people to build canal locks along the Great Canal of China, which ran from Peking to Hangzhou. The canal was built during the 1200s and is still used today.

• Leonardo da Vinci (1452–1519), Italian artist and engineer, designed locks for the Languedoc Canal, France, which was completed in 1681. It linked the Mediterranean Sea with the Atlantic Ocean.

• The largest lock in the world is the Berendrecht lock in Antwerp, Belgium. It is 500m (1,640ft) long and 68m (223ft) wide. It has four sliding lock gates.

• The Netherlands has more than 8,000km (4,971 miles) of canals.

TYPES OF DAM

Arch dam
This has a curved shape, with the inside of the curve facing downstream.

Arch dam

Buttress dam
This has a series of props, or buttresses, which are on the side of the dam facing downstream.

Buttress dam

Embankment dam
This is made of a huge pile of soil or rocks. Like the massive dam, the embankment dam relies on its sheer bulk to hold back water.

Embankment dam

Massive dam
This is built of concrete and relies on its size and weight to withstand the pressure of a huge amount of stored water.

Massive dam

TALLEST DAMS

Dam	Location	Date built	Height m	Height ft
Rogun	Tajikistan	1989	325	1066
Nourek	Tajikistan	1979	317	1040
Grande Dixence	Switzerland	1962	285	935
Inguri	Georgia, USA	1979	271	889
Vaiont	Italy	1961	265	869
Mica	British Columbia, Canada	1973	244	800

TUNNELS

Tunnels have a variety of uses. Many are built for transport purposes: to pass through or under obstacles such as mountains, rivers, and busy roads. They are also used to carry sewage, water from reservoirs, power and communication cables, and in mining.

TYPES OF TUNNEL
Road tunnels
These are built to allow traffic to pass through mountains, under rivers and busy crossroads.

Pedestrian tunnels
These allow people to cross busy streets safely.

Train tunnels
There are underground train systems in many of the major cities of the world. They offer a fast form of transport, and save valuable space above ground.

Pedestrian tunnel

Train tunnel

Road tunnel

Water tunnel

Water tunnels
These are built just underneath the surface. Some carry fresh water, others carry sewage.

HOW A TUNNEL IS BUILT
Tunnelling shields are used to drive a tunnel through soft ground. As the shield moves forwards, the front cutting edge bores through rock and earth. Tunnel lining, fitted behind the shield, prevents the walls and roof of the tunnel from collapsing. In hard ground, huge drilling machines, called moles, are often used.

SKYSCRAPERS

From early times, people have built tall buildings. The Romans built blocks of flats 15 storeys high. Today, advances in construction methods have resulted in many high-rise buildings, such as the Sears Tower, USA, which is 110 storeys high.

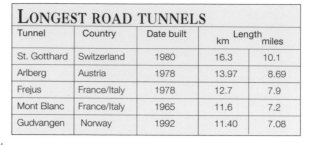

LONGEST ROAD TUNNELS

Tunnel	Country	Date built	Length	
			km	miles
St. Gotthard	Switzerland	1980	16.3	10.1
Arlberg	Austria	1978	13.97	8.69
Frejus	France/Italy	1978	12.7	7.9
Mont Blanc	France/Italy	1965	11.6	7.2
Gudvangen	Norway	1992	11.40	7.08

A tunnelling shield breaking through earth

BUILDING A SKYSCRAPER
A skyscraper has an inner frame made of steel or concrete. The frame holds the floors and walls (often made of glass) together. The building is supported by a foundation – usually a pit containing reinforced concrete.

TUNNEL FACTS

• The Channel Tunnel, which links England and France, was completed in 1994. Trains carry people, cars, and goods through the tunnel. It is 51.8km (32.2 miles) long.

• The longest water tunnel in the world is the Delaware Aqueduct, built in 1944. It is 168.9km (104.9 miles) long, more than twice the length of the second longest, the Orange-Fish in South Africa.

• The fastest rate of tunnel-driving in soft ground, using a tunnelling shield, is 501m (1,644ft) in five days, on the London Ring Main Tunnel in 1992.

LONGEST RAILWAY TUNNELS

Tunnel	Country	Date built	Length	
			km	miles
AlpTransit Link	Switzerland	2007*	57	35.4
Seikan	Japan	1985	53.9	33.5
Channel	France/England	1994	51.8	32.2
Northern line	England	1939	27.8	17.3
Daishimizu	Japan	1982	22.2	13.8
Simplon 2	Switzerland/Italy	1922	19.8	12.3
Simplon 1	Switzerland/Italy	1906	19.8	12.3
Shin Kanmon	Japan	1973	18.7	11.6
Apennines	Italy	1931	18.6	11.5
Rokko	Japan	1971	16.2	10
Henderson	USA	1975	15.8	9.8
Haruna	Japan	1982	15.4	9.6
St. Gotthard	Switzerland	1882	15	9.3
Nakayama	Japan	1982	14.8	9.2
Lötschberg	Switzerland	1913	14.5	9

* Planned completion date

TALLEST TOWERS

Tower	Location	Date built	Height	
			m	ft
KTHI-TV Mast	North Dakota, USA	1963	629	2,064
KSLA-TV Mast	Louisiana, USA	1982	579	1,900
CN Tower	Toronto, Canada	1975	555	1,821
Ostankino TV Tower	Moscow, Russia	1967	537	1,762
WTVM & WRBL TV Mast	Georgia, USA	1962	533	1,749
WBIR TV Mast	Tennessee, USA	1963	533	1,749
KFVS TV Mast	Cape Girardeau, USA	1960	511	1,676

Liquid concrete is pumped to the upper levels of the skyscraper.

Concrete is mixed in a revolving drum to stop it from setting.

TALLEST OFFICE BLOCKS

Office block	Location	Date built	Height	
			m	ft
Shanghai World Finance Centre	Shanghai, China	2001*	460	1,509
Chongqing Tower	Chongqing, China	2000*	457	1,499
Petronas Tower	Kuala Lumpur, Malaysia	1996	452	1,483
Sears Tower	Chicago, USA	1974	443	1,453
Jin Mao Building	Shanghai, China	1997	420	1,378
Tour Sans Fin	Paris, France	2000*	419	1,375
World Trade Center	New York, USA	1973	417	1,368
Empire State Building	New York, USA	1931	381	1,250
T & C Tower	Kao-hsiung, Taiwan	1997	348	1,142

INTERNATIONAL WORLD

In this section, the latest computer-generated maps show all the countries of the world in amazing detail. Data boxes provide up-to-date statistics, and lifestyle facts, prepared in association with embassies worldwide, give authoritative information about how people live today.

The Physical World • The Political World • How To Use The Map Pages
All the Countries and Continents of the World • Flags • Mapping
Raw Materials • Farming and Fisheries • Population
Living Standards • Debt and Wealth

THE PHYSICAL WORLD

Severnaya Zemlya

Svalbard

Franz Josef Land

Laptev Sea

New Siberian Islands

E.a.

Novaya Zemlya

Kara Sea

Barents Sea

Central Siberian Plateau

Denmark Strait

Iceland

Norwegian

Faeroe Islands

Lake Saimaa

Lake Onega

Lake Ladoga

Ural Mts.

Ob'

Yenisey

S i b e r i a

Lena

Sea Okho

Kam

British Isles

North Sea

Baltic Sea

Volga

Lake Baikal

A S I A

E U R O P E

Dnieper

Do

Kirghiz Steppe

Lake Balkhash

Amur

Kuril

Alps

Carpathians

Danube

Aral Sea

Altai Mts.

Manchurian Plain

Sea of Japan

Bay of Biscay

Black Sea

Caucasus Mts.

Caspian Sea

Kara Kum

Tien Shan

Gobi Desert

Yellow River

Great Plain of China

Yellow Sea

Japan

Mediterranean Sea

Taurus Mts.

Taklamakan Desert

Kunlun

Madeira Islands

Syrian Desert

Zagros Mts.

Hindu Kush

Plateau of Tibet

Yangtze

East China Sea

Bonin Islands

Canary Islands

Atlas Mts.

Dead Sea

Iranian Plateau

H i m a l a y a s

Thar Desert

Ganges

Mekong

Libyan Desert

The Gulf

Gulf of Oman

Deccan

S a h a r a

Nile

Red Sea

Rub al Khali

Arabian Sea

Bay of Bengal

Philippine Sea

Mariana Islands

Niger

A F R I C A

Gulf of Aden

Lakshadweep

Andaman Islands

South China Sea

Gulf of Thailand

Caroline

Cape Verde Islands

Ethiopian Highlands

Laccadive Sea

Sri Lanka

Nicobar Islands

Borneo

Bismarck Archipelago

Gulf of Guinea

Congo (Zaire)

Lake Victoria

Maldive Islands

Java Sea

New Guinea

Ascension Island

Lake Tanganyika

Seychelles

Chagos Archipelago

Sumatra

Arafura Sea

A T L A N T I C

Lake Nyasa (Lake Malawi)

Comoros

Agalega Islands

I N D I A N

Cocos Islands

Timor Sea

St. Helena

Zambezi

Mozambique Channel

Agalega Islands

AUSTRALIA

O C E A N

Madagascar

Mascarene Islands

O C E A N

Great Sandy Desert

Kalahari Desert

Gibson Desert

Lake Eyre

Orange River

Great Victoria Desert

Darling

Tristan da Cunha

Cape of Good Hope

Great Australian Bight

Murray

Tas

Se

Gough Island

South East Cape

Crozet Islands

Prince Edward Islands

Kerguélen Islands

Heard & McDonald Islands

Bouvet Island

S O U T H E R N   O C E A N

Davis Sea

Dumont D'Urville Sea

Fimbul Ice Shelf

Amery Ice Shelf

A N T A R C T I C A

0°

30°E

60°E

90°E

120°E

150°E

ARCTIC OCEAN

Chukchi
Sea

Queen Elizabeth Islands

Baffin
Bay

Greenland

Greenland Sea

Beaufort
Sea

Davis Strait

Arctic Circle

Bering
Sea

Yukon

Mackenzie

Great Bear
Lake

Great Slave
Lake

Hudson
Bay

Labrador
Sea

60°N

Aleutian Islands

Gulf of
Alaska

Coast Ranges

Rocky Mountains

Missouri

NORTH
AMERICA

Great Lakes

Appalachian

Newfoundland

ATLANTIC
OCEAN

Azores

Midway Islands

Hawaiian Islands

Sonoran
Desert

Rio Grande

Sierra Madre

Mississippi

Gulf of
Mexico

Bahamas

Bermuda
Islands

30°N

Tropic of Cancer

PACIFIC

OCEAN

Islands

Line Islands

Phoenix Islands

CENTRAL
AMERICA

Galápagos
Islands

Greater Antilles

Caribbean Sea

Leeward
Islands

Windward
Islands

Tuvalu

Samoa

Marquesas Islands

Amazon

Amazonia

SOUTH
AMERICA

São Francisco

Andes

Llanos

Equator 0°

Fiji

Society Islands

Tahiti

Tuamotu

Tubuai
Islands

Cook Islands

Lake Titicaca

Plateau of
Mato Grosso

Tropic of Capricorn

Pitcairn Islands

Sala y Gómez

Easter Island

Juan Fernández
Islands

Atacama Desert

Pampas

Paraná

30°S

New
Zealand

Chatham Islands

Patagonia

Falkland
Islands

ATLANTIC

OCEAN

Bounty Islands

Antipodes
Islands

Cape Horn

Drake Passage

Scotia Sea

South Orkney
Islands

South
Sandwich
Islands

60°S

South Shetland
Islands

Antarctic Circle

Ross Sea

Amundsen Sea

Bellingshausen
Sea

ANTARCTICA

Weddell Sea

180°   150°W   120°W   90°W   60°W   30°W

283

THE POLITICAL WORLD

THE COUNTRIES OF the world, which number 192, are
spread over seven continents and vary greatly in size. The
Russian Federation, for example, is almost 39 million times
bigger than the Vatican City.

INTERNATIONAL TIME ZONES

The world is made up of 24 different time zones, as
shown on the map below. In each zone, the clocks a
set to a different time of day. Time zones ensure th
noon in each country is fixed at about midday, and
that midnight falls in the middle of the night.

TIME ZONES	23hours	24h	1h	2h	3h	4h	5h	6h	7h	8h	9h

KEY
1 NETHERLANDS
2 BELGIUM
3 LUXEMBOURG
4 SWITZERLAND
5 LIECHTENSTEIN
6 MOLDAVIA
7 ANDORRA
8 MONACO
9 SAN MARINO
10 VATICAN CITY
11 SLOVENIA
12 CROATIA
13 BOSNIA & HERZEGOVINA
14 YUGOSLAVIA
15 ALBANIA
16 MACEDONIA
17 *Ceuta* (Spain)
18 *Melilla* (Spain)

ANTARCTICA
Many countries claim
territories in Antarctica.

Chile &
UK

Argentina,
Chile, &
UK

Argentina
& UK

Chile

UK

Unclaimed

Norway

New
Zealand

Australia

Australia

France

RECORDS

CONTINENT WITH MOST COUNTRIES
is Africa with 54 countries.

**ONLY CONTINENT THAT IS ALSO
A COUNTRY** is Australia.

LARGEST ISLAND
is Greenland, at 2,175,219sq km (839,852sq miles).

LARGEST COUNTRY
is the Russian Federation, with an area of
17,075,400sq km (6,592,846sq miles).

SMALLEST COUNTRY
is the Vatican City with an area of just
0.44sq km (0.17sq miles).

**INTERNATIONAL
DATE LINE**
When you cross this imaginary
line from east to west, the date
changes. The western side is a day
ahead of the eastern side.

KEY
20 *Cayman Is.* (UK)
21 *Navassa Island* (USA)
22 *Virgin Is.* (USA)
23 ST. KITTS & NEVIS
24 *Montserrat* (UK)
25 *Martinique* (France)
26 ST. VINCENT & THE GRENADINES
27 *Netherlands Antilles* (Netherlands)
28 *Aruba* (Netherlands)

285

HOW TO USE THE MAP PAGES

THE MAPS IN International World are organized into sections, based on continents. There is a section for North America, South America, Europe, Africa, Asia, and Australasia. At the start of each section there is a map showing the whole continent, followed by maps of the countries in that continent. This page explains the information and symbols that appear on and around these country maps.

DATA BOXES

Every country in this section has a box with important statistics about that country. Some of the main countries contain more detailed information than others.

Flag
The national flag for each country or territory is shown at the top of the data box.

Area
The figure shown is the total area of the country, and includes all inland water (e.g. lakes, reservoirs, and rivers).

Government
The type of government ruling the country at time of going to press is described. Some governments, however, are fairly unstable and may change at short notice.

Independence
This is the date when a country broke free from the control of another power and became independent. The date when a republic was formed, or a state was declared, may also be given.

Currency
The paper or metal money used as the system of exchange, and in current use in that country, is named.

Population
This figure is the number of people registered in the most recent census as living in the country. Most countries round up their estimated population to the nearest thousand. Migration and famine will affect these figures.

Density
The average number of people occupying each square kilometre or square mile of the country is given. The figure is based on land area only and not on the total area.

Official Language
This language, or languages, is used by the government, and is not necessarily the most widely spoken language.

✝ Major Religions
The percentage breakdown of religions currently practised by the population is shown. A religious symbol, such as this cross for Christianity, appears when a religion is followed by 75% or more of the population.

LOCATOR MAPS
The red area on the globe shows the location of the countries on the page, or spre[ad] in relation to the continent.

LANGUAGE
This spells out a traditional greeting in the main language of the country.

INTERNATIONAL WORLD

ICELAND

ICELAND, EUROPE'S second largest island, has the lowest population density in Europe. The remote interior can be reached only by special vehicle, pony, or small plane.

LAND PROFILE

Area 103,000sq km (39,769sq miles)
Government Presidential republic
Independence 1944, from British and US control during World War II
Currency Icelandic króna
Population 300,000
Density 3 sq km (8 per sq mile)
Official Language Icelandic
✝ **Major Religions** Evangelical Lutheran Church of Iceland 96%, other Protestant and Roman Catholic 3%, non-religious 1%

LIFESTYLE FACTS
• The Althing, the Icelandic parliament, has been in existence since the 13th century and is one of the oldest surviving assemblies in the world.

• Iceland has the most solfataras (volcanic vents) and hot springs in the world. Many of its towns are heated by underground hot water.

• Iceland produces more than a third of the world's cod-liver oil, and is the biggest consumer of it.

LANGUAGE
A traditional greeting in Icelandic is *góðan daginn.*

ICELAND

HOT SPRINGS
Deildartunguhver hot springs blow out 250 litres (55 gallons) of hot water every second. Over a 24-hour period, they produce enough water to fill 105,600 baths.

WEATHER FACTS
30°C (86°F) — 860mm (33.9in) — -36°C (-32.8°F)
10.6°C (51.8°F) — 0.2°C (32.4°F)

DENMARK

DENMARK, WHICH IS divided into numerous islands, has a 4,500-mile (7,300km) coastline. It was the first Scandinavian country to belong to the European Community (EC).

100 kroner

Area 43,070sq km (16,629sq miles)
Government Constitutional monarchy
State founded c. 950
Territories Faeroe Islands, Greenland
Currency Danish krone
Population 5,200,000
Density 123 per sq km (319 per sq mile)
Official Language Danish
✝ **Major Religions** Evangelical Lutheran Church 91%, Roman Catholic 2%, other and non-religious 7%

LANGUAGE
A traditional greeting in Danish is *goddag.*

LIFESTYLE FACTS
• Lego was created by a Danish carpenter in the 1930s. Legoland Park is a miniature, working village created from 35 million plastic bricks.

• Denmark has one of the lowest private ownerships of cars in Europe. Cyclists are encouraged with special lanes, and Copenhagen was the first city to create a pedestrian street.

• Denmark has over twice as many pigs as humans, and Danish bacon is a successful export product. Danish farmers produce three times more food than is needed to feed the population.

WEATHER FACTS
35°C (95°F) — 704mm (27.7in) — -24°C (-11.2°F)
16.3°C (61.3°F) — 1.3°C (34.3°F)

LAND PROFILE
Almost two-thirds of the land is farmed.

LITTLE MERMAID
Situated by Copenhagen harbour, this statue of the mermaid from Hans C. Andersen's fairy tale was sculpted in 1913 by Edvard Eriksen (1876–1959). In 1964, her head was sawn off, but was soon replaced.

NORWAY

NORWAY MEANS "the way to the north". It is a land of beautiful fjords (valleys flooded by risin[g] levels); the longest is Sogne Fj[ord] at 203 kilometres (126 miles).

Area 323,900sq km (125,058sq miles)
Government Constitutional monarc[hy]
Independence from Sweden, 1[905]
Territories Svalbard archipelago, Ja[n] Mayen Island
Currency Norwegian krone
Population 4,233,116
Density 14 per sq km (36 per sq mile)
Official Language Nynorsk (new Norwegian) and Bokmaal (older)
✝ **Major Religions** Evangelical Lutheran and other Protestant 87.9%, Roman Catholic 0.8%, other 11.3%

WEATHER FACTS
34°C (93°F) — 730mm (28.7in) — -26°C
16.3°C (61.3°F) — -3.5°C (25.7[°F])

LAND PROFILE

WEATHER FACTS

Country's hottest recorded temperature

Country's coldest recorded temperature

Average annual rainfall in capital city

35°C (95°F) — 704mm (27.7in) — -24°C (-11.2°F)

16.3°C (61.3°F) — 1.3°C (34.3°F)

Average summer temperature in capital city

Average winter temperature in capital city

LANDMARK
This is the country's most recognizable building or statue, and has been chosen by the embassy or consulate of the featured country. The map shows the location of the landmark, with an illustration similar to the photograph.

LAND PROFILE
This artwork shows how the land in a country divides into areas such as forest or desert, how much is built on (urban), and how much is available for farming (agriculture). Barren land indicates areas such as the bare rocks of mountain tops, or salt flats.

KEY

- Urban
- Agriculture
- Forest
- Wetland
- Grassland
- Desert
- Tundra
- Barren

KEY TO MAPS
The maps in this section have been created to give an accurate representation of the landscape.

COLOURS
The different physical features and climate zones are listed below.

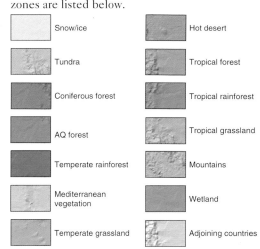

- Snow/ice
- Hot desert
- Tundra
- Tropical forest
- Coniferous forest
- Tropical rainforest
- AQ forest
- Tropical rainforest
- Temperate rainforest
- Mountains
- Mediterranean vegetation
- Wetland
- Temperate grassland
- Adjoining countries
- Cold desert

SYMBOLS
The symbols below appear on the map to represent places and physical features.

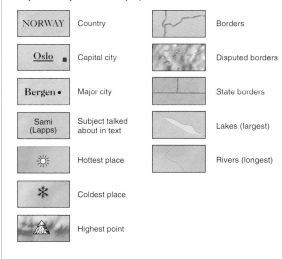

- NORWAY — Country
- Borders
- Oslo — Capital city
- Disputed borders
- Bergen — Major city
- State borders
- Sami (Lapps) — Subject talked about in text
- Lakes (largest)
- Hottest place
- Rivers (longest)
- Coldest place
- Highest point

SWEDEN
THIRDS OF the land in Sweden covered by forests, and there are 0 lakes. Timber products, including paper, account for nearly fth of all Swedish exports.

Area 449,960sq km (173,730sq miles)
Government Constitutional monarchy established 1523
Currency Swedish krona
Population 8,585,907
Density 21 per sq km (54 per sq mile)
Official Language Swedish
Major Religions Evangelical Lutheran Church of Sweden 89%, other Protestant 8%, Roman Catholic 1.7%, other 1.3%

PRIZES
B. Nobel (1833–96) was a Swedish chemist and inventor of dynamite. He set up a fund for the Nobel prizes, awarded each year for sciences, literature, peace, to those who have given the greatest benefit to humankind.

LANGUAGE
A traditional greeting in Swedish is *god dag*.

LANGUAGE
A traditional greeting in Norwegian is *go dag*.

LAND PROFILE
The land is mainly forested or used for farming.

LIFESTYLE FACTS
- Each year 12,000 cross-country skiers take part in a race from Salen to Mora in central Sweden. The course is 90km (56 miles) long.
- In 1910, Sweden was the first European country to establish national parks. Animals that can be found in the parks include lynx, bear, and moose.
- Stockholm's waterways are so pure that people can safely swim and fish in them.

WEATHER FACTS
35°C (95°F) 622mm (24.5in) -38°C (-36.4°F)
16.5°C (61.7°F) -2°C (28.4°F)

CITY HALL
Stockholm's fine City Hall, called the Stadshus, was built between 1911 and 1923. Its Golden Hall has 19 million gilded tiles.

HOLMENKOLLEN
The ski-jump at Holmenkollen, outside Oslo, is the oldest in existence. The first ski-jump competition was held in 1892, and the event continues to be held every March.

LIFESTYLE FACTS
At Hammerfest, the world's most northerly town, the sun shines at midnight for just over two months in the summer.

Norway's annual contribution of its national income (1.17%) towards foreign aid is the highest proportion in the world.

Norwegians read more newspapers than anyone else in the world, and buy more English books than any other non-English-speaking country.

THE SAMI
The Sami (Lapps) have inhabited the arctic regions of Norway and Sweden since ancient times. Today, there are about 60,000 and 70% speak the Sami language. About 70,000 reindeer live in Sami territories, and the main occupation of the people is reindeer breeding. The woven clothes worn by the Sami are practical and beautiful.

More than 50% of Norwegian families have a weekend home in the mountains or by the sea. These second homes are made of wood, and some have turf-covered roofs.

Name	m	Height ft
Utigord	800	2,625
Mongefossen	774	2,540
Ostre Mardola Foss	657	2,154
Tyssetrengane	646	2,120
Kjelfossen	561	1,841

HIGHEST WATERFALLS

TABLES
These provide easy-to-follow information about the top features of a country. They may list the highest waterfalls, as shown here, or the most cars manufactured, or chief exports.

LIFESTYLE FACTS
These facts give details about food, sports, industry, events that are unique to that country. They have been chosen from information supplied by the country itself and realistically reflect life in that country.

SCALE
This shows how distance on the map relates to kilometres and miles, and can be used to see how big a country is. Not all maps are drawn to the same scale.

COMPASS POINT
This fixes the direction of North (N), and gives the position of the country in relation to North.

NORTH AND CENTRAL AMERICA

CANADA AND THE United States of America cover most of the continent of North America. To the south lie Mexico and the seven small countries of Central America. The western side of the continent is dominated by the Rocky Mountains, which run from Canada to Mexico.

Area 24,238,000sq km (9,358,340sq miles)
Countries 24
Largest Canada
Smallest Grenada
Population 431,352,677
Density 20 per sq km (52 per sq mile)
Major Languages English, Spanish, French, Amerindian and Inuit languages, Nahuatl (Aztec)

▲ **Highest point** Mount McKinley, Alaska, 6,194m (20,320ft)
▼ **Lowest point** Death Valley, California 86m (282ft) below sea level
☼ **Highest temperature** 57°C (135°F) Death Valley, California
❆ **Lowest temperature** -66°C (-87°F) Northice, Greenland

COUNTRIES, TERRITORIES, AND CAPITALS

Name	Capital	Name	Capital
Antigua and Barbuda	St. John's	Guatemala	Guatemala City
Bahamas	Nassau	Haiti	Port-au-Prince
Barbados	Bridgetown	Honduras	Tegucigalpa
Belize	Belmopan	Jamaica	Kingston
Canada	Ottawa	Mexico	Mexico City
Costa Rica	San José	Nicaragua	Managua
Cuba	Havana	Panama	Panama City
Dominica	Roseau	St. Kitts and Nevis	Basseterre
Dominican Republic	Santo Domingo	St. Lucia	Castries
El Salvador	San Salvador	St. Vincent and the Grenadines	Kingstown
Greenland	Godthåb	Trinidad and Tobago	Port of Spain
Grenada	St. George's	USA	Washington, D.C.

GRAND CANYON
The Grand Canyon was gouged out of rock by the Colorado River. The canyon is 349km (217 miles) long, up to 30km (19 miles) wide, and 1.6km (1 mile) deep. At its deepest point it cuts through rock 2,000 million years old.

LONGEST ROADS (see map on pages 292-3)

Trans-Canada Highway: St. John's, Newfoundland to Victoria, B.C. 7,821km (4,860 miles)

US 20: Boston, Massachusetts to Newport, Oregon 5,415km (3,365 miles)

US 6: Provincetown, Massachusetts to Bishop, California 5,229km (3,249 miles)

US 30: Atlantic City, N.J. to Astoria, Oregon 5,019km (3,119 miles)

TIME ZONES

4:00 Vancouver | 6:00 Mexico City | 9:00 Godthåb | 12:00 Greenwich

TOP CITY POPULATIONS

Mexico City, Mexico 15,047,685
Los Angeles, USA 11,400,000
New York, USA 8,546,846
Chicago, USA 8,000,000
Toronto, Canada 3,893,000

CLIMATE ZONES

KEY
- Polar and tundra
- Mountain regions
- Taiga
- Temperate forest
- Dry grassland
- Hot desert
- Tropical grassland
- Rainforest

RUSSIAN FEDERATION — Bering Strait — ALA (US
Mount McKin 6,19 (20,32
Bering Sea
Aleutian Islands

CONTINENT FACTS
- British Columbia produces 25% of the timber sold in North America. It also supplies the world with chopsticks.
- Grenada is the only country in the Western world where spices such as nutmeg, cinnamon, and cloves grow in abundance.

- Surfing as a competitive sport began on the island of Oahu in Hawaii. Surfing waves can reach about 8m (26ft) high.

Midway Islands (USA)
Hawaiian Islands
PACIFIC OCEAN

AGE BREAKDOWN

Under 15 years	15 to 65 years	Over 65 years

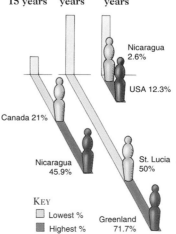

Nicaragua 2.6%
USA 12.3%
Canada 21%
Nicaragua 45.9%
St. Lucia 50%
Greenland 71.7%

KEY
- Lowest %
- Highest %

FEWEST DOCTORS

Haiti	1 to 7,040 people
St. Vincent	1 to 3,760 people
Honduras	1 to 2,330 people
El Salvador	1 to 2,312 people
St. Kitts and Nevis	1 to 2,180 people

LONGEST LIFESPAN

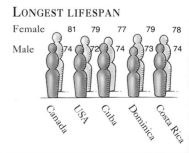

	Canada	USA	Cuba	Dominica	Costa Rica
Female	81	79	77	79	78
Male	74	72	74	73	74

CROSS-SECTION ACROSS CONTINENT

Coast Range
Pacific Ocean
Great Basin
Rocky Mts.
Mississippi
Lake Michigan
Lake Erie
Appalachian Mts.
Atlantic Ocean

3,000m (9,84 ft)
0 Sea level
-4,500m (-14,764ft)

Length: 5,800km (3,600 miles)

LARGEST LAKES
The largest lakes, except for Lake Michigan (USA), lie partly or completely in Canada.

Lake Superior 83,270sq km (32,140sq miles)
Lake Huron 60,700sq km (23,430sq miles)
Lake Michigan 58,020sq km (22,395sq miles)
Great Bear Lake 31,790sq km (12,270sq miles)
Great Slave Lake 28,440sq km (10,980sq miles)

WILDLIFE
North America has an amazing variety of animals and plants.

FAUNA
Moose (*Alces alces*) is the largest deer in the world. A male can weigh up to 450kg (992lb) Broad hooves help the moose walk in deep snow.

Solenodon (*Solenodon cubanus*) is found only on the island of Cuba.

Fer-de-lance (*Bothrops atrox*) of Central America is one of the world's most aggressive snakes.

FLORA
Frangipani (*Plumeria rubra*) is a large shrub with fragrant flowers. It is also known as West Indian jasmine.

Cotton (*Gossypium hirsutum*) is grown in the United States and Mexico. Fibre from the plant is harvested and used to make cloth.

Coast redwoods (*Sequoia sempervirens*) are the tallest living trees. They can grow to 90m (300ft) tall.

LAND PROFILE
Almost one-third of the continent is agricultural land.

- 0.5% Urban
- 2.5% Wetlands
- 4.5% Barren lands
- 9% Desert
- 11% Grasslands
- 17% Tundra
- 23% Agriculture
- 32.5% Forest

SUGAR CANE
One of the major crops in Central America is sugar cane. Sugar is extracted from the cane, which grows rapidly in the hot, humid climate.

Country	Production (1998)
Guatemala	18,189,380 tonnes
El Salvador	4,500,000 tonnes
Nicaragua	3,842,540 tonnes
Honduras	3,580,045 tonnes
Costa Rica	3,550,000 tonnes
Panama	2,032,668 tonnes
Belize	1,208,830 tonnes

CANADA

CANADA IS THE second largest country in the world. Across the centre of the country lie the Prairies, a flat plain used for growing wheat and grazing cattle. Most Canadians live around the Great Lakes and the St. Lawrence River.

Area 9,976,140sq km (3,851,788sq miles)
Government Federal democracy, with British sovereign as constitutional monarch
Independence 1931, from Britain
Currency Canadian dollar
Population 29,500,000
Density 3 per sq km (8 per sq mile)
Official Languages English, French
Major Religions Roman Catholic 46%, Protestant 30%, other 24%

LIFESTYLE FACTS

• Canada is such a vast country that it takes 3 days and 3 nights to travel by train from Toronto to Vancouver – a distance of 4,467 km (2,776 miles).

• Dinosaur Provincial Park, on the banks of the Red Deer River in Alberta, is one of the greatest sites for dinosaur remains in the world. The *Albertosaurus* is one of the large dinosaurs that once roamed around this area.

• Canada produces 75% of the world's maple syrup. Each March, sap is collected from sugar maple trees and boiled down into syrup. A maple leaf is the symbol of Canada.

• Some places in Canada are freezing cold for months on end. A family can flood their garden and use it as an ice-hockey rink.

CANADIAN PEOPLE
Many people have settled in Canada. The largest ethnic groups, after the British and French, are Italian and German.

Languages spoken	% of population
English	66.3
French	23.2
Italian	5.9
German	1.1
Chinese	0.4
Other	3.1

WEATHER FACTS

45°C (113°F)   87.2mm (34in)   -63°C (-81.4°F)
19.2°C (66.6°F)   -11°C (12°F)

LAND PROFILE
More than half the land in Canada is covered by forest.

%
0.5
1
2
5
5.5
27
59

WOOD AND PAPER EXPORTS (1992)
Canada is the world's largest exporter of forest products. These include timber for building as well as wood pulp for paper.

Destination	Amount (in tonnes)
United States	9,508,754
Europe	4,877,883
Asia	1,728,895
South America	657,159
Central America	211,608

10 Canadian dollars

THE CN TOWER
The Canadian National (CN) Tower in Toronto is the tallest free-standing structure in Canada at 555m (1,821ft) high. It was built as a TV transmitter and was completed in 1975.

TORONTO SKYDOME
• SkyDome is the world's first stadium with a moving roof. Seating is on four levels and can hold 50,000 people.

• The field is covered with 106 rolls of Astroturf, joined together with 12.8km (8 miles) of zip fasteners.

CITY OF MONTREAL
This square in Montreal was named after Jacques Cartier (1491–1557), the explorer who claimed Canada for the French in 1535. Today, Canada is a bilingual country and two-thirds of the people in Montreal still speak French.

GREENLAND

THE WORLD'S LARGEST island, Greenland is part of Denmark. Almost all of Greenland lies within the Arctic Circle. Most of the island is permanently covered with ice and is uninhabited.

Area 2,175,600sq km (840,004sq miles)
Government Constitutional monarchy, as part of kingdom of Denmark
Currency Danish krone
Population 55,732
Density 0.16 per sq km (0.4 per sq mile)
Official Language Greenlandic, Danish
✝ **Major Religions** Evangelical Lutheran 99%, Roman Catholic 1%

LIFESTYLE FACTS

• Greenland's 55,000-plus inhabitants live in the capital, Godthåb, 16 small towns, and 66 other settlements. There are no roads or rail links between areas so travel is by air or sea.

• In winter the skidoo, a kind of motorcycle on skis, is used to move across the snow.

• More than 85% of Greenland is a massive ice sheet with an average thickness of 1,524m (5,000ft). Icebreaker ships are used to keep the sea channels open.

• Only low-growing plants with shallow roots, such as the Arctic rhododendron, Arctic poppy, saxifrage, and bilberry, can survive the harsh climate.

Arctic rhododendron (Rhododendron lapponicum)   *Arctic poppy (Papaver lapponicum)*   *Saxifrage (Saxifraga sp.)*

This fishing community lies near Cape Farvel on the southernmost tip of Greenland.

ALONG THE COAST

Greenland has more than 39,315km (24,430 miles) of jagged coastline. Most people live along the coast and work in the fishing industry. In the south, the Gulf Stream current helps keep the sea free of ice.

FISH EXPORTS

Greenland's fishing rights cover more than 2,000,000sq km (772,204,000sq miles) of sea. Shrimp accounts for 80% of the country's exports. Cod, salmon, haddock, and other fish make up the remaining 20%.

WILDLIFE

Conditions within the Arctic Circle are harsh, but the animals that live there are well adapted to the ice and snow.

Caribou *(Rangifer tarandus)* has broad hooves to walk in snow.

Hooded seal *(Cystophora cristata)* lives in the seas around the polar ice cap.

Walrus *(Odobenus rosmarus)* has long tusks which it uses to haul itself up on to the ice.

Polar bear *(Thalarctos maritimus)* feeds on seals which it catches through holes in the ice.

Arctic fox *(Alopex lagopus)* has fur that changes from brown to pure white in winter.

INUIT ART

Kenojuak, a famous Inuit painter, is shown with her work. Inuit art also includes fine carvings in ivory and bone.

Lincoln Sea
Wandel Sea
Greenland Sea
GREENLAND (Denmark)
Davis Strait
Disko I.
• Ilulissat
Gunnbjørn Fjeld 3,702m (12,146ft)
• Sisimrut
Denmark Strait
Arctic Circle
• Godthåb (Nuuk)
N
ATLANTIC OCEAN
0 — 700 km
0 — 400 miles
Cape Farvel
Labrador Sea
Newfoundland
swick • St. John's
e Edward
d St. Pierre & Miquelon (France)
rlottetown
cton
lifax
otia
ble

INUIT FACTS

• Large areas of Canada and Greenland are still inhabited by the original settlers of these lands. They are called the Inuit, which means "people."

• Inuit build temporary snowhouses (correctly called *illuviga*) when they go hunting. Igloo is their word for any other kind of house.

• The main food source for the Inuit is the animals they hunt. Hunting is vital to their survival and provides food and clothing. Inuit hunt caribou, seal, walrus, and fish.

• Some words we use, such as kayak and anorak, are taken from the Inuit language.

Inuit child from Hudson Bay, Canada

THE NUNAVUT AGREEMENT

This agreement took effect in 1999. It is the largest land claim in Canadian history. Its terms include:

• The Inuit receive title to 350,000sq km (135,136sq miles) of land in 1999.

• They also have 36,257sq km (13,999sq miles) of underground mineral rights.

• The Inuit are granted $1.15 billion by Canada in compensation to be paid over 14 years (this sum based on value with interest by end of 14-year period).

UNITED STATES OF AMERICA

THE UNITED STATES of America (USA) is made up of 50 states plus the District of Columbia. Two of the states, Alaska and Hawaii, are separate from the others. The USA is the world's wealthiest country with vast areas of rich farmland and supplies of coal, oil, and minerals.

Area 9,372,610sq km (3,618,783sq miles)
Government Federal democracy
Independence 1776, from Britain
Territories Northern Mariana Islands, Puerto Rico, American Samoa, Guam, United States Virgin Islands, Johnston Atoll, Line Islands, Midway Islands, Wake Island, Baker and Howland Islands, Jarvis Island, Kingman Reef, Navassa Island, Palmyra Atoll
Currency United States dollar
Population 263,300,000
Density 29 per sq km (75 per sq mile)
Official Language English
Major Religions Protestant 56%, Roman Catholic 28%, Jewish 2%, other 14%

WEATHER FACTS

57°C (135°F)   976mm (38.4in)   -62°C (-79.6°F)

24°C (75.2°F)   2.2°C (36°F)

LAND PROFILE
More than one-third of the country is covered in forest.

%
0.5
2.5
3.5
5
9.5
12
29.5
37.5

MAJOR AREAS OF WILD LANDS (1994)
Large areas of wild land have been set aside as parks and nature reserves.

State	% of state	Key animal
Alaska	15.03	Moose
Idaho	6.98	Cougar
Washington	5.91	Grizzly bear
California	5.81	Mountain lion
Wyoming	4.91	American buffalo
Florida	3.78	Manatee

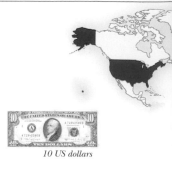

10 US dollars

LIFESTYLE FACTS
• Alaska was bought from Russia in 1867 for 2 cents an acre. Today the state is rich in oil and other natural resources.

• Inland storms called tornadoes, or twisters, suck up dust as they swirl across the landscape.

• The average American eats 50kg (110lb) of meat each year; more than twice as much as the average European.

• The USA is the major producer of household waste. Every day, the average person produces about 1.8kg (4lb) of rubbish.

• There is one television for every 1.2 people living in the United States.

HOLLYWOOD
Hollywood is the film capital of America. The fine weather and varied landscape attracted film directors from the East Coast to a small town called Hollywood in about 1910.

THE FIRST AMERICANS
The first people to live in North America arrived from Asia more than 20,000 years ago. This Native American, Chief Looking Horse (above), is a member of the Sioux from a reservation at Wounded Knee in South Dakota.

NATIVE AMERICAN FACTS
• Today 544 tribes of about 1.5 million Native Americans live on reservations which they govern themselves.

• The Navajo of Arizona, New Mexico, and Utah is the biggest tribe. People still practise traditional pottery and weaving: Navajo rugs are woven into geometric patterns, and are coloured with natural dyes.

HAWAIIAN ISLANDS
Hawaii is a group of 20 volcanic islands in the Pacific Ocean. One of the largest active volcanoes in the world, Mauna Loa, is located on the main island of Hawaii. It last erupted in 1984. Two types of lava, *aa* and *pahoehoe*, get their names from Hawaiian words.

WHEATFIELDS OF NEBRASKA

The United States is the largest exporter of wheat and produces more than half the world's maize. This supply of food is grown on the open plains, or prairies, which stretch across the Midwest.

WASHINGTON, DISTRICT OF COLUMBIA

Washington is the capital city of the USA. It is home to the Capitol Building, which is the centre of government and houses the Senate and the House of Representatives.

BASEBALL

Baseball is America's national sport. The first game between two organized teams was played in New Jersey in 1846.

THE CAR INDUSTRY

The USA has more cars on the road than any other country (see page 277 for longest roads). It also has the highest ratio of cars, with 570 for every 1,000 persons.

BEST-SELLING CARS (1998)

Model	Number sold
Toyota Camry	429,575
Honda Accord	401,071
Ford Taurus	371,074
Honda Civic	334,562
Ford Escort	291,936
Chevrolet Cavalier	256,099
Toyota Corolla	250,501
Saturn	231,703
Chevrolet Malibu	223,703
Pontiac Grand Am	180,428

AMISH

The Amish are a Protestant group who came to America from Switzerland in the 18th century. Members do not conform to modern ways of life: they reject the use of electric lights and telephones, and drive horses and carriages rather than cars.

STATUE OF LIBERTY, NEW YORK

• The statue was given to the USA by France in 1884. It was designed by Auguste Bartholdi (1834–1904) and shipped across the Atlantic, packed in 210 crates.

• 300 sheets of copper were beaten into a thin sheet to act as the lady's "skin".

• Visitors can climb 171 steps up to the viewing gallery in the head of the statue for a spectacular view of the New York skyline.

MISSISSIPPI RIVER

The Mississippi is one of the world's busiest waterways. Ships can travel for nearly 2,900km (1,802 miles) from Minneapolis to New Orleans. The first steamboat appeared on the Mississippi in 1811.

EVERGLADES FACTS

• Southern Florida has a vast area of cypress swamp called the Everglades. It is home to many rare animals and plants.

• The green tree frog has sticky suction pads on its toes that help it to grip the slippery branches.

Tree frog

• The American alligator grows up to 3.6m (12ft) long and may live for 50 years. It propels itself through the water with its tail.

ARCHITECTURE

The many different styles of American architecture reflect the diverse climate and conditions of the USA.

Plantation homes
People who grew rich on the profits of the plantations in the 19th century built grand mansions in European styles.

Art deco style
William van Alen (1882–1954) designed the Chrysler building in the 1920s.

Clapboard
Houses in the eastern states are often built of overlapping wooden boards, known as clapboard, to keep out rain.

Major American architect
Frank Lloyd Wright (1867–1959) designed houses that blend with the landscape.

UNITED STATES OF AMERICA: STATES OF THE UNION

THE UNITED STATES of America originally consisted of 13 colonies on the East Coast, all of them ruled by Britain until independence in 1776. Today there are 50 states, ruled by the federal government in Washington, D.C., each with its own set of laws. For example, the age for holding a driving licence varies, as does the number of states that uphold the death sentence for murder.

The bald eagle is the national symbol of the USA.

ALABAMA

Area 133,916sq km (51,705sq miles)
Capital Montgomery
Population 4,252,938
Entry into Union 14 December, 1819
✿ **State flower** Camellia

ALASKA

Area 1,530,690sq km (591,000sq miles)
Capital Juneau
Population 603,617
Entry into Union 3 January, 1959
✿ **State flower** Forget-me-not

ARIZONA

Area 295,260sq km (114,000sq miles)
Capital Phoenix
Population 4,217,940
Entry into Union 14 February, 1912
✿ **State flower** Saguaro blossom

ARKANSAS

Area 137,754sq km (53,187sq miles)
Capital Little Rock
Population 2,483,769
Entry into Union 15 June, 1836
✿ **State flower** Apple blossom

Stretch limo

CALIFORNIA

Area 411,049sq km (158,707sq miles)
Capital Sacramento
Population 31,589,153
Entry into Union 9 September, 1850
✿ **State flower** California poppy

COLORADO

Area 269,596sq km (104,091sq miles)
Capital Denver
Population 3,746,585
Entry into Union 1 August, 1876
✿ **State flower** Columbine

CONNECTICUT

Area 12,997sq km (5,018sq miles)
Capital Hartford
Population 3,274,662
Entry into Union 9 January, 1788
✿ **State flower** Mountain laurel

DELAWARE

Area 5,297sq km (2,045sq miles)
Capital Dover
Population 717,917
Entry into Union 7 December, 1787
✿ **State flower** Peach blossom

FLORIDA

Area 151,940sq km (58,664sq miles)
Capital Tallahassee
Population 14,165,570
Entry into Union 3 March, 1845
✿ **State flower** Orange blossom

Baseball game

GEORGIA

Area 152,577sq km (58,910sq miles)
Capital Atlanta
Population 7,200,882
Entry into Union 2 January, 1788
✿ **State flower** Cherokee rose

Surfer

HAWAII

Area 16,760sq km (6,471sq miles)
Capital Honolulu
Population 1,186,815
Entry into Union 21 August, 1959
✿ **State flower** Yellow hibiscus

IDAHO

Area 231,971sq km (89,564sq miles)
Capital Boise
Population 1,163,261
Entry into Union 3 July, 1890
✿ **State flower** Mock orange

ILLINOIS

Area 145,933sq km (56,345sq miles)
Capital Springfield
Population 11,829,940
Entry into Union 3 December, 1818
✿ **State flower** Native violet

Appaloosa horse

INDIANA

Area 93,719sq km (36,185sq miles)
Capital Indianapolis
Population 5,803,471
Entry into Union 11 December, 1816
✿ **State flower** Peony

IOWA

Area 145,752sq km (56,275sq miles)
Capital Des Moines
Population 2,841,764
Entry into Union 28 December, 1846
✿ **State flower** Wild rose

KANSAS
Area 213,097sq km (82,277sq miles)
Capital Topeka
Population 2,565,328
Entry into Union 29 January, 1861
✿ **State flower** Native sunflower

Cowboy hat

KENTUCKY
Area 104,662sq km (40,410sq miles)
Capital Frankfort
Population 3,860,219
Entry into Union 1 June, 1792
✿ **State flower** Golden rod

LOUISIANA

Area 123,678sq km (47,752sq miles)
Capital Baton Rouge
Population 4,342,334
Entry into Union 30 April, 1812
✿ **State flower** Southern magnolia

MAINE
 Blueberries

Area 86,156sq km (33,265sq miles)
Capital Augusta
Population 1,241,382
Entry into Union 15 March, 1820
✿ **State flower** White pine cone

MARYLAND

Area 27,091sq km (10,460sq miles)
Capital Annapolis
Population 5,042,438
Entry into Union 28 April, 1788
✿ **State flower** Black-eyed susan

MASSACHUSETTS

Area 21,456sq km (8,284sq miles)
Capital Boston
Population 6,073,550
Entry into Union 6 February, 1788
✿ **State flower** Mayflower

MICHIGAN

Area 151,585sq km (56,527sq miles)
Capital Lansing
Population 9,549,353
Entry into Union 26 January, 1837
✿ **State flower** Apple blossom

THE WHITE HOUSE
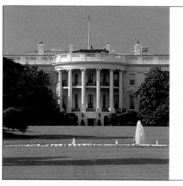
The White House in Washington, D.C., is the official residence of the president and his family. The 3-storey, 100-room mansion was designed by Irish-born architect James Hoban (1762–1831) and completed in 1800. The building is made of grey sandstone painted white, which is how it got its name.

American beaver

MINNESOTA

Area 218,601sq km (84,402sq miles)
Capital St. Paul
Population 4,609,548
Entry into Union 11 May, 1858
✿ **State flower** Showy lady's slipper

Dixieland jazz band

MISSISSIPPI
Area 123,515sq km (47,689sq miles)
Capital Jackson
Population 2,697,243
Entry into Union 10 December, 1817
✿ **State flower** Magnolia

MISSOURI

Area 180,515sq km
(69,697sq km)
Capital Jefferson City
Population 5,323,523
Entry into Union 10 August, 1821
❋ **State flower** Hawthorn

MONTANA

Area 380,849sq km
(147,046sq miles)
Capital Helena
Population 870,281
Entry into Union 8 November, 1889
❋ **State flower** Bitterroot

American football

NEBRASKA

Area 200,349sq km
(77,355sq miles)
Capital Lincoln
Population 1,637,112
Entry into Union 1 March, 1867
❋ **State flower** Golden rod

NEVADA

Area 286,353sq km
(110,561sq miles)
Capital Carson City
Population 1,530,108
Entry into Union 31 October, 1864
❋ **State flower** Sagebrush

NEW HAMPSHIRE

Area 24,033sq km
(9,279sq miles)
Capital Concord
Population 1,148,253
Entry into Union 21 June, 1788
❋ **State flower** Lilac

Yellow taxicab

NEW JERSEY
Area 20,168sq km
(7,787sq miles)
Capital Trenton
Population 7,945,298
Entry into Union 18 December, 1787
❋ **State flower** Purple violet

Roadrunner

NEW MEXICO
Area 314,926sq km
(121,593sq miles)
Capital Sante Fe
Population 1,685,401
Entry into Union 6 January, 1912
❋ **State flower** Yucca

New York skyline

NEW YORK

Area 127,190sq km
(49,108sq miles)
Capital Albany
Population 18,136,081
Entry into Union 26 July, 1788
❋ **State flower** Rose

NORTH CAROLINA

Area 136,490sq km
(52,699sq miles)
Capital Raleigh
Population 7,195,138
Entry into Union 21 November, 1789
❋ **State flower** Flowering dogwood

NORTH DAKOTA
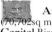
Area 183,118sq km
(70,702sq miles)
Capital Bismarck
Population 641,367
Entry into Union 2 November, 1889
❋ **State flower** Wild prairie rose

OHIO

Area 107,045sq km
(41,330sq miles)
Capital Columbus
Population 11,150,506
Entry into Union 1 March, 1803
❋ **State flower** Scarlet carnation

OKLAHOMA

Area 181,090sq km
(69,919sq miles)
Capital Oklahoma City
Population 3,277,687
Entry into Union 16 November, 1907
❋ **State flower** Mistletoe

OREGON

Area 251,419sq km
(97,073sq miles)
Capital Salem
Population 3,140,585
Entry into Union 14 February, 1859
❋ **State flower** Oregon grape

PENNSYLVANIA

Area 117,348sq km
(45,308sq miles)
Capital Harrisburg
Population 12,071,842
Entry into Union 12 December, 1787
❋ **State flower** Mountain laurel

RHODE ISLAND

Area 3,139sq km
(1,212sq miles)
Capital Providence
Population 989,794
Entry into Union 29 May, 1790
❋ **State flower** Violet

Chopper bike

SOUTH CAROLINA

Area 199,730sq km
(77,116sq miles)
Capital Columbia
Population 3,673,287
Entry into Union 23 May, 1788
❋ **State flower** Yellow jessamine

*Mount Rushmore
National Monument*

SOUTH DAKOTA

Area 199,730sq km
(77,116sq miles)
Capital Pierre
Population 729,034
Entry into Union 2 November, 1889
❋ **State flower** Pasqueflower

TENNESSEE

Area 109,152sq km
(42,144sq miles)
Capital Nashville
Population 5,256,051
Entry into Union 1 June, 1796
❋ **State flower** Iris

Cowboys roping cattle

TEXAS

Area 691,030sq km
(266,807sq miles)
Capital Austin
Population 18,723,991
Entry into Union 29 December, 1845
❋ **State flower** Bluebonnet

UTAH

Area 219,888sq km
(84,899sq miles)
Capital Salt Lake City
Population 1,951,408
Entry into Union 4 January, 1896
❋ **State flower** Sego lily

STATE FACTS

• Only about 800 grizzly bears are left in the USA; many of them roam wild in the mountain forests of Idaho and Wyoming.

• Georgia grows nearly half the USA's total crop of peanuts. Half the crop is used for making peanut butter, the rest for edible oil and animal feed.

• Rhode Island is the smallest state. It gave its name to a chicken, the Rhode Island Red, first bred in 1857.

Halloween lantern

VERMONT

Area 24,900sq km
(9,614sq miles)
Capital Montpelier
Population 584,771
Entry into Union 4 March, 1791
❋ **State flower** Red clover

VIRGINIA

Area 105,586sq km
(40,767sq miles)
Capital Richmond
Population 6,618,358
Entry into Union 25 June, 1788
❋ **State flower** Flowering dogwood

WASHINGTON

Area 176,480sq km
(68,139sq miles)
Capital Olympia
Population 5,430,940
Entry into Union 11 November, 1889
❋ **State flower** Coast rhododendron

WEST VIRGINIA

Area 62,761sq km
(24,232sq miles)
Capital Charleston
Population 1,828,140
Entry into Union 20 June, 1863
❋ **State flower** Rhododendron

WISCONSIN

Area 145,436sq km
(56,153sq miles)
Capital Madison
Population 5,122,871
Entry into Union 29 May, 1848
❋ **State flower** Wood violet

WYOMING
Area 253,325sq km
(97,809sq miles)
Capital Cheyenne
Population 480,184
Entry into Union 10 July, 1890
❋ **State flower** Indian paintbrush

• There are more engineers and scientists in New Jersey than in any other state.

• The Stock Exchange on Wall Street, New York, is the largest in the world, handling more than 100 million shares a day.

• Silicon Valley, south of San Francisco, has one of the world's largest concentrations of high-technology industry.

• One-third of the world's cherry crop is grown along the shores of Lake Michigan.

• The USA's top tourist destinations include Disney World in Florida, with more than 20 million visitors a year.

MEXICO

THIS IS A land of contrasts with snow-capped mountains, a high central plateau, and tropical rainforests. It is the world's leading producer of silver. The capital, Mexico City, is the largest city in the world. Southern Mexico is often affected by earthquakes.

 Area 1,958,200sq km (756,061sq miles)
Government Multiparty republic
Independence 1821, from Spain
Currency Mexican new peso
Population 93,700,000
Density 49 per sq km (127 per sq mile)
Official Language Spanish
Major Religions Roman Catholic 89%, Protestant 6%, other 5%

WEATHER FACTS

47°C (117°F)   929mm (36in)   -4°C (25°F)

22.8°C (73°F)   17.8°C (64°F)

LAND PROFILE

More than one-third of Mexico is desert.

%
0.5
0.5
15.5
20.5
26
37

LIFESTYLE FACTS

• There are more Spanish speakers in Mexico than in any other country.

• Bee-keeping is an important activity, especially in the south. Mexico is one of the world's main exporters of natural honey.

• Mexicans eat a variety of spicy foods using chillies. Pancakes, called *tortillas*, are made from maize flour and filled with meat, vegetables, and cheese.

• Many familiar garden plants, such as poinsettias, marigolds, and dahlias, originated in Mexico.

• Mexico has more than 9,650km (6,000 miles) of coastline, and fishing for shrimp is an important industry. Natural bath sponges are harvested in the Gulf of Mexico.

FEAST DAY

Day of the Dead (November 1) is a feast day when food and drink are offered to dead relatives. Bakers sell sweets in the shapes of skulls and coffins.

DESERT FACTS

• The largest of all cacti is the giant saguaro from the Sonoran Desert. It can grow to 18m (60ft) high.

• The tiny elf owl hides from the heat of the day in the cool branches of the saguaro.

Elf owl

10 Mexican pesos

LANGUAGE

A traditional greeting in Spanish is *buenos días*.

JAGUAR

The jaguar *(Panthera onca)* lives in the jungles of Central America. Its spotted coat acts as a camouflage.

SILVER

Mexico is rich in minerals and supplies one-fifth of the world's silver. Some of the silver is made into jewellery; it is also used as a coating for photographic film.

Silver jewellery

ACAPULCO BEACH

Tourism is a vital part of Mexico's economy. The busy resort of Acapulco, on the Pacific Coast, has more than 1,900,000 visitors every year.

GUATEMALA

HIGH MOUNTAINS AND volcanoes, tropical forests, and lakes cover Guatemala. More than half the population are Maya Indians.

 Area 108,890sq km (42,043sq miles)
Government Multiparty republic
Independence 1821, from Spain
Currency Quetzal
Population 10,600,000
Density 98 per sq km (255 per sq mile)
Official Language Spanish
Major Religions Roman Catholic 65%, Protestant 33%, other 2%

NATIONAL BIRD

The quetzal bird *(Pharomachrus mocinno)* is found in Guatemala. The male has long tail feathers to help him attract a mate.

WEAVING

Traditional textiles from Guatemala are made in more than 325 variations of style and colour. Every Maya village has its unique style of dress made from handwoven textiles.

EL SALVADOR

A LINE OF volcanoes dominates El Salvador. The layers of volcanic ash and lava make fertile soil for growing coffee.

Area 21,040sq km (8,124sq miles)
Government Multiparty republic
Independence 1821, from Spain
Currency Salvadorean colon
Population 5,800,000
Density 280 per sq km (726 per sq mile)
Official Language Spanish
Major Religions Roman Catholic 75%, other 25%

HONDURAS

MOST PEOPLE WORK on small farms growing rice, beans, and maize for themselves. Cattle are raised for beef exports.

Area 112,090sq km (43,278sq miles)
Government Multiparty republic
Independence 1821, from Spain
Currency Lempira
Population 5,700,000
Density 51 per sq km (133 per sq mile)
Official Language Spanish
Major Religions Roman Catholic 97%, other 3%

BELIZE

BELIZE IS A land of tropical jungles, mountains, and swamps. The climate is ideal for growing citrus fruits, as well as sugar cane.

PEOPLE OF BELIZE
More than half the population of Belize are Creole. All Creoles are of African descent and speak the English-Creole dialect.

 Area 22,960sq km (8,865sq miles)
Government Parliamentary democracy
Independence 1981, from Britain
Currency Belizean dollar
Population 200,000
Density 9 per sq km (23 per sq mile)
Official Language English
Major Religions Christian 87%, other 13%

PALENQUE, CITY OF THE MAYA
For many years, Mexico was home to a series of native American peoples. One of the most important groups, the Maya, built the city of Palenque in about 500 A.D.

ANCIENT SITES IN CENTRAL AMERICA		
Site	Culture	Country
Tula	Toltec	Mexico
Tenochtitlán	Aztec	Mexico
Copán	Maya	Honduras
Tikal	Maya	Guatemala
Cerros	Maya	Belize

LAKE NICARAGUA
Lake Nicaragua is the only freshwater lake to contain ocean animals such as the bullshark. The lake was once part of an ocean bay which was cut off by volcanic activity.

CACAO PLANT FACTS
• Central America is a major exporter of cacao, from which cocoa and chocolate are made.
• The cacao tree is a tropical plant. It sprouts long, thin pods, called cherelles, which grow to about 25cm (10in) long.
• Each pod contains 30 to 40 beans. In the 16th century, cacao beans were considered so valuable the Aztecs used them as money.

PANAMA

PANAMA FORMS A land link between the North and South American continents. The country is cut through by the Panama Canal, which links the Caribbean Sea with the Pacific Ocean.

NICARAGUA

THE LARGEST COUNTRY in Central America after Mexico, Nicaragua has large forests and a swampy Caribbean shore, called the Mosquito Coast.

 Area 130,000sq km (50,193sq miles)
Government Multiparty republic
Independence 1821, from Spain
Currency Cordoba
Population 4,400,000
Density 37 per sq km (96 per sq mile)
Official Language Spanish
Major Religions Roman Catholic 95%, other 5%

COSTA RICA

ONE-THIRD OF Costa Rica, which means "rich coast", is covered with forests that include mahogany and tropical cedar trees.

Area 51,100sq km (19,730sq miles)
Government Multiparty republic
Independence 1821, from Spain
Currency Costa Rican colon
Population 3,400,000
Density 67 per sq km (174 per sq mile)
Official Language Spanish
Major Religions Roman Catholic 95%, other 5%

Area 77,080sq km (29,761sq miles)
Government Multiparty republic
Independence 1903, from Colombia
Currency Balboa
Population 2,600,000
Density 34 per sq km (88 per sq mile)
Official Language Spanish
Major Religions Roman Catholic 93%, other 7%

PANAMA CANAL FACTS
• The canal opened in 1914 and cut the sailing distance from New York to San Francisco by 13,000km (8,000 miles).
• More than 153 million cubic metres (200 million cubic yards) of rubble were removed to make room for the 80-km (50-mile) canal.

297

THE CARIBBEAN

THESE ISLANDS, ALSO known as the West Indies, form a 3,200-km (2,000-mile) chain stretching from the coast of Florida almost to Venezuela. Tourists flock to the beautiful beaches: 1.5 million people each year to the Bahamas alone.

CUBA

CUBA IS THE only communist state in the Western Hemisphere, and Fidel Castro has been its leader since January 1959. World-famous Cuban cigars are a major export.

Area 110,860sq km (42,803sq miles)
Government Socialist republic
Independence 1898, from Spain. US troops withdrew in 1902
Currency Cuban peso
Population 10,800,000
Density 97 per sq km (251 per sq mile)
Official Language Spanish
Major Religions Roman Catholic 85%, other 15%

THE SMALLEST BIRD
Cuba is the home of the world's smallest bird. The Bee Hummingbird, known in Cuba as the *zunzuncito*, is just 6cm (2.4in) long: roughly the same size as a Red Admiral butterfly.

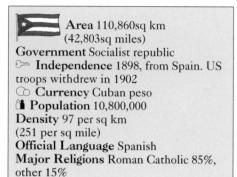

Bee Hummingbird

Red Admiral

JAMAICA

JAMAICA, THE HOME of reggae music, is the third largest of the Caribbean islands. Most of its income is derived from mining bauxite, the chief source of aluminium, and the tourist industry.

Area 10,990sq km (4,243sq miles)
Government Parliamentary democracy, member of the British Commonwealth
Independence 1962, from Britain
Currency Jamaican dollar
Population 2,400,000
Density 222 per sq km (577 per sq mile)
Official Language English
Major Religions Christian 60%, other 40%

NATIONAL HERO Marcus Garvey (1887-1940) is one of Jamaica's national heroes. He founded the Universal Negro Improvement Association in 1914.

MAJOR TOURIST DESTINATIONS (Figures show visitors per year)

Cayman Islands 381,188
Barbados 447,083
US Virgin Islands 562,062
Jamaica 1,056,000
Bahamas 1,368,038

BAHAMAS

THE BAHAMAS are made up of more than 700 islands and cays (small islands). Only about 30 of these are inhabited.

Area 13,880sq km (5,359sq miles)
Independence 1973, from Britain
Currency Bahamian dollar
Population 300,000
Official Language English

HAITI

THE PEOPLE of this mountainous country are French-speaking, and many practise the folk religion called voodoo.

Area 27,750sq km (10,714sq miles)
Independence 1804, from France
Currency Gourde
Population 7,200,000
Official Languages French, French Creole

DOMINICA

THE IMPERIAL parrot, shown on the Dominican flag, is found only in the dense tropical forests of the northern mountains.

Area 750sq km (290sq miles)
Independence 1978, from Britain
Currency East Caribbean dollar
Population 71,000
Official Language English

ST. LUCIA

THE PITONS, twin volcanic peaks that rise about 800m (2,600ft) above the lush forests, are St. Lucia's best-known landmarks.

Area 620sq km (239sq miles)
Independence 1979, from Britain
Currency East Caribbean dollar
Population 145,000
Official Language English

BEST-KNOWN
CARIBBEAN FRUIT

Guava
The guava is a pear-shaped fruit with cream or pink flesh.

Pawpaw
The flesh of the pawpaw is orange, like an apricot's.

Mango
The juicy mango is green, red, or orange-pink in colour.

DOMINICAN REPUBLIC

THE DOMINICAN REPUBLIC is called *Quisqueya* in native Arawak Indian. It is the second largest country in the Caribbean.

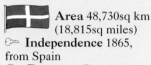
Area 48,730sq km (18,815sq miles)
Independence 1865, from Spain
Currency Dominican Republic peso
Population 7,800,000
Official Language Spanish

ANTIGUA AND BARBUDA

SUGAR WAS once the main export from these islands. Today tourism is more important and Barbuda is also an animal reserve.

Area 440sq km (170sq miles)
Independence 1981, from Britain
Currency East Caribbean dollar
Population 65,000
Official Language English

BARBADOS

TOURISM IS the leading industry in Barbados, employing almost 40% of the workforce. Sugar is an important export, and a traditional local dish is the famous flying fish.

Area 430sq km (166sq miles)
Independence 1966, from Britain
Currency Barbados dollar
Population 300,000
Official Language English

CARIBBEAN MUSIC AND DANCE FACTS
• The biggest and most famous carnival in the Caribbean takes place in Trinidad and Tobago every year. People spend months creating the costumes.

• Calypso music originated in Trinidad, although it is popular throughout the Caribbean. Steel bands are musicians who play calypso and their drums, called pans, are made out of oil drums. The rhythms of calypso music show a strong African influence.

• Reggae music emerged in Jamaica in the 1970s and developed from earlier Jamaican musical styles. Reggae has achieved worldwide popularity through the songs of musicians such as Bob Marley.

• Bob Marley (1945–81) was the most famous Jamaican reggae singer, who had hit records around the world in the 1970s. He believed in world peace and equality among people, and his songs were a powerful means of spreading this message.

GRENADA

ON GRENADA, the "spice island", nutmeg, cloves, cinnamon, and saffron grow abundantly. Cacao is also an important export.

Area 340sq km (131sq miles)
Independence 1974, from Britain
Currency East Caribbean dollar
Population 92,000
Official Language English

GREATEST WEST INDIES BATSMEN (1994)

Cricketer	Tests	Runs
I.V.A. Richards	121	8,540
G.S. Sobers	93	8,032
C.G. Greenidge	108	7,558
C.H. Lloyd	110	7,515
D.L. Haynes	103	7,487

REGIONAL WEATHER
Records
5°C (41°F)
38°C (100.4°F)
Averages
27°C (80.6°F) 1,529mm (60in) 24.5°C (76°F)

ST. KITTS AND NEVIS

ST. CHRISTOPHER is commonly known as St. Kitts. It is separated from its sister island, Nevis, by a 3-km-wide (2 mile) sea channel.

Area 360sq km (140sq miles)
Independence 1983, from Britain
Currency East Caribbean dollar
Population 44,000
Official Language English

ST. VINCENT AND THE GRENADINES

ST. VINCENT, the largest of the islands of this nation, has black volcanic beaches. The Grenadines group consists of 32 smaller islands.

Area 340sq km (131sq miles)
Independence 1979, from Britain
Currency East Caribbean dollar
Population 111,000
Official Language English

TRINIDAD AND TOBAGO

TRINIDAD, the larger of these two islands, is rich in oil and natural gas. Tobago has fine beaches and an 18-hole championship golf course.

Area 5,130sq km (1,980sq miles)
Independence 1962, from Britain
Currency Trinidad & Tobago dollar
Population 1,300,000
Official Language English

SOUTH AMERICA

THE CONTINENT OF South America is dominated by the Andes, the world's longest mountain chain, passing through seven countries. Brazil is the largest country, occupying almost half of the continent.

Area 17,716,530sq km (6,840,388sq miles)
Countries 12
Largest Brazil 8,511,970sq km (3,286,489sq miles)
Smallest Surinam 163,270sq km (63,039sq miles)
Population 305,074,803
Density 17 per sq km (44 per sq mile)
Major Languages Spanish, Portuguese, Quechua, Guarani, Aymara
▲ **Highest point** Mount Aconcagua 6,959m (22,831ft)
▼ **Lowest point** Valdés Peninsula 40m (131ft) below sea level
☼ **Highest temperature** 49°C (120°F) Rivadavia, Argentina
❄ **Lowest temperature** -33°C (-27°F) Sarmiento, Argentina

CLIMATE ZONES

KEY

⬜	Polar and tundra
⬜	Mountain region
⬛	Mediterranean
⬜	Dry grassland
⬜	Hot desert
⬜	Rainforest
⬜	Tropical grassland

TIME ZONES

7:00 Lima	8:00 Caracas	9:00 Buenos Aires	12:00 Greenwich

FEWEST DOCTORS

Guyana	1 to 6,200 people
Chile	1 to 2,150 people
Surinam	1 to 1,800 people
Uruguay	1 to 1,500 people

CONTINENT FACTS

● At 4,000m (13,000ft) above sea level, Lake Titicaca is the world's highest lake. It lies across the borders of Peru and Bolivia.

● The continent of South America experiences extremes of weather. In parts of Colombia, more than 11,700mm (460in) of rain falls per year, while the Atacama Desert, Chile, is the world's driest place.

● Both the tomato and the potato originated in South America. Andean farmers grow potatoes at altitudes of more than 2,000m (6,550ft).

COUNTRIES AND CAPITALS

Name	Capital
Argentina	Buenos Aires
Bolivia	La Paz
Brazil	Brasilia
Chile	Santiago
Colombia	Santa Fe de Bogotá
Ecuador	Quito
Guyana	Georgetown
Paraguay	Asunción
Peru	Lima
Surinam	Paramaribo
Uruguay	Montevideo
Venezuela	Caracas

AGE BREAKDOWN

Under 15 years
15 to 65 years
Over 65 years

3.4% Paraguay
11.4% Uruguay
25.8% Uruguay
42.5% Bolivia
54.1% Bolivia
63.6% Chile

KEY
⬜ Lowest %
⬛ Highest %

LONGEST LIFESPAN

Female 77 76 75 73 72
Male 70 68 68 67 66

Uruguay Chile Argentina Venezuela Colombia

NATIVE PEOPLE

The homes of the Quechua Indians of Ecuador and Peru are some of the highest settlements in the world. These Andean peoples have adapted physically to the low-oxygen atmosphere.

Quechua children outside their school

TOP CITY POPULATIONS
(Metropolitan Area)

Santiago Chile 5,170,293
Lima Peru 5,706,127
Rio de Janeiro Brazil 10,192,097
Buenos Aires Argentina 11,255,618
São Paulo Brazil 16,583,234

RAINFOREST AREA

The Amazonian rainforest is 12.8 times bigger than France.

Amazon area 7 million sq km (2.7 million sq miles)

France area 545,630sq km (210,669sq miles)

HIGHEST WATERFALLS

Angel Falls 979m (3,212ft)
Cuquenan 610m (2,000ft)

WORLD'S LONGEST MOUNTAIN RANGES

Mt. Aconcagua
Andes 7,200km (4,500 miles)

Mt. McKinley
Rocky Mountains, USA 4,800km (3,600 miles)

COFFEE TREE

Coffee is the fruit of the coffee tree, an evergreen that reaches a height of 2–3m (6.6–9.9ft). After or at the same time as flowering, the branches bear green "cherries" that ripen to red. The cherries split open to reveal two seeds – the coffee beans – which are then washed, dried, and roasted.

TOP COFFEE EXPORTERS (1997)

Country	Bags	Tonnes
Brazil	14,484,300	869,058
Colombia	10,294,116	617,647
Peru	1,468,217	88,093
Ecuador	658,450	39,507

WILDLIFE

Rainforests and mountains are home to a huge variety of animals and plants.

FAUNA

Giant armadillo
(*Priodontes giganteus*) has the biggest claws of any living animal.

Toco toucan
(*Ramphastos toco*) has the largest bill of all the toucans.

Llama
(*Llama glama*) is most important for transport in the Andes.

FLORA

Opuntia
(*Cactaceae*) bear pear-shaped fruits known as prickly pears.

Puya
(*Puya raimondii*) is the world's tallest herb and has 8,000 flowers.

Monkey puzzle
(*Araucaria araucana*), the Chile Pine, is native to the Andes.

CROSS-SECTION

4,500m
(14,764ft)
0 Sea level
-6,000m
(-19,686ft)
Peru-Chile
trench

Pacific
Ocean
Andes
Amazon
Basin
Guiana
Highlands
Atlantic
Ocean

Length: 4,400km (2,700 miles)

LAND PROFILE

Urban 0.5%
Wetlands 1%
Barren land 4%
Desert 4%
Agriculture 5%
Grassland 19%
Forest 66.5%

Map labels

Caribbean Sea
Margarita I.
Caracas
VENEZUELA
Lake Maracaibo
ANAMA
Georgetown
Paramaribo
GUYANA
SURINAM
FRENCH GUIANA
(France)
Cayenne
Angel Falls
Orinoco
Llanos
Cordillera Oriental
Bogotá
COLOMBIA
Guiana Highlands
pelo I.
ombia)
Caquetá
Cordillera
Quito
EQUATOR
UADOR
Marañón
Río Negro
Amazon
Amazonia
Tocantins
Rocas I.
(Brazil)
Fernando de
Noronha I.
(Brazil)
PERU
Selvas
Madeira
BRAZIL
São Francisco
Lima
Brazilian Highlands
BOLIVIA
Plateau of
Mato Grosso
Brasília
Lake Titicaca
La Paz
Altiplano
L. Poopó
Salar de
Uyuni
Paraguay
Paraná
Paranaíba
Rio de Janeiro
PARAGUAY
Atacama Desert
Rivadavia
São Paulo
Tropic of Capricorn
Gran Chaco
Asunción
San Ambrosio I.
(Chile)
Pampas
Paraná
Aconcagua 6,960m
(22,836ft)
URUGUAY
nández
(Chile)
Santiago
Buenos Aires
Montevideo
Plate
ARGENTINA
Valdés Peninsula
-40m (-131ft)
CHILE
ANDES
Patagonia
Los Chonos
Archipelago
Sarmiento
Gulf of San
Jorge
Lake
Buenos
Aires
Falkland
Islands
(UK)
Lake
Argentino
Bahía
Grande
Strait of Magellan
Tierra del Fuego
Cape Horn

N

0   500km
0   300 miles

301

COLOMBIA

COLOMBIA IS FAMOUS for producing high-quality coffee – its major cash crop. Some of the finest emeralds are mined here and account for 90 per cent of world output.

Area 1,038,910sq km (439,733sq miles)
Government Multiparty republic
Independence 1819, from Spain
Territories San Andres, Providencia, San Bernardo, Islas del Rosario, Isla Fuerte and Gorgona, Gorgonilla, and Malpelo
Currency Colombian peso
Population 35,100,000
Density 34 per sq km (88 per sq mile)
Official Language Spanish
Major Religions Roman Catholic 95%, other 5%

ECUADOR

ECUADOR'S NAME COMES from its position on the Equator. It is a country of very varied landscape, from low coastal regions to high Andean peaks and dense jungle.

Area 283,560sq km (109,480sq miles)
Government Multiparty republic
Independence 1830, from Spain
Currency Sucre
Population 11,500,000
Density 42 per sq km (109 per sq mile)
Official Language Spanish
Major Religions Roman Catholic 95%, other 5%

LAND PROFILE

More than 90% of Ecuador is forested or used for farming.

%
.5
5
41.5
53

GALAPAGOS ISLANDS

The Galapagos islands lie 970km (603 miles) off the coast of Ecuador. Many of the animals there are not found anywhere else. British scientist Charles Darwin (1809–82) made important discoveries there concerning his theory of natural selection (see p.68).

Galapagos tortoise

WEATHER FACTS

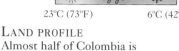

49°C (120°F)   444mm (17.4in)   -10°C (14°F)

23°C (73°F)   6°C (42°F)

LAND PROFILE

Almost half of Colombia is covered with dense forest.

%
0.5
1
1
16
33
48.5

LIFESTYLE FACTS

• Many great writers have come from Colombia, including world-famous novelist Gabriel García Márquez (born 1928), who won the Nobel Prize for literature in 1982.

• Colombia is one of the world's biggest exporters of quality coffee.

• Colombians are great music lovers. The *tiple*, a small guitar, is the national instrument.

• Ninety-six per cent of Colombians live on less than half the land area. Almost all live in the west of the country.

10,000 pesos

ORCHID

Colombia's national symbol is the orchid.

THE WALLED CITY

Cartagena, in northern Colombia, became famous in the 16th century. Spanish ships stopped off there to collect South American gold.

THE ANDES

The Andes mountain range stretches from the top to the bottom of South America. It runs through seven countries.

VENEZUELA

VENEZUELA IS THE world's third greatest oil producer. Oil provides 80 per cent of export earnings and has made Venezuela one of the richest countries in South America.

Area 912,050sq km (352,143sq miles)
Government Presidential republic
Independence 1821, from Spain
Currency Bolivar
Population 21,800,000
Density 25 per sq km (65 per sq mile)
Official Language Spanish
Major Religions Roman Catholic 96%, Protestant 2%, other 2%

WEATHER FACTS

49°C (120°F)   444mm (17.4in)   -10°C (14°F)
23°C (73°F)   6°C (42°F)

LAND PROFILE
More than half of Venezuela is densely forested.

%
1
2
5
34
58

ANGEL FALLS
The Angel Falls, in southeastern Venezuela, is the highest waterfall in the world, with a drop of 979m (3,212ft) The falls are named after American pilot Jimmy Angel (died 1956), who found them in 1935.

BOLIVIA

BOLIVIA IS A mountainous country with no coastline. Farmers make up half of its population; many of them are very poor, and grow just enough food for their families to live on.

Area 1,098,580sq km (424,160sq miles)
Government Multiparty republic
Independence 1825, from Spain
Currency Boliviano
Population 7,400,000
Density 7 per sq km (18 per sq mile)
Official Languages Spanish, Quechua, and Aymara
Major Religions Roman Catholic 95%, other 5%

LAND PROFILE
Two-thirds of Peru is jungle.

%
0.5
7
13
13
66.5

PERU

PERU CONTAINS many spectacular ruins. They were built during the time of the Inca empire (see p.389), which was destroyed by Spanish invaders in the 16th century.

Area 1,285,220sq km (496,223sq miles)
Government Multiparty republic
Independence 1824, from Spain
Currency Nuevo sol
Population 23,800,000
Density 19 per sq km (49 per sq mile)
Official Languages Spanish and Quechua
Major Religions Roman Catholic 95%, other 5%

WEATHER FACTS

49°C (120°F)   444mm (17.4in)   -10°C (14°F)
23°C (73°F)   6°C (42°F)

NAZCA LINES
Huge animal figures and strange shapes were cut into the ground in southern Peru thousands of years ago. The whole design can be seen only from the air.

Nazca hummingbird figure

HIGHEST TRACK
The highest section of railway track in the world, in Peru, lies at an altitude of 4,782m (15,688ft). The track passes through a tunnel on the Morochocha branch of Peruvian State Railways.

Andean condor

ANDEAN CONDOR
The Andean condor is the heaviest bird of prey in the world, with a wingspan of more than 3m (10ft). It lives in the highest parts of the Andes mountains and feeds on dead animals.

Highest railway in the world

GUYANA

A FERTILE COASTAL strip of land just 16km (10 miles) wide is where 90 per cent of the population lives. Much of the rest of Guyana is covered with dense rainforest.

Area 214,970sq km (83,000sq miles)
Independence 1966, from Britian
Currency Guyana dollar
Population 800,000
Official Language English

SURINAM

SURINAM'S CLIMATE is humid and tropical. Its rich wildlife includes jaguars, pumas, and ocelots, plus a variety of reptiles such as iguanas, rattlesnakes and boa constrictors.

Area 163,270sq km (63,039sq miles)
Independence 1975, from Netherlands
Currency Surinam guilder
Population 400,000
Official Language Dutch

FRENCH GUIANA

FRENCH GUIANA IS the only European colony in South America. It is a part of France, and sends two members to the French National Assembly (parliament).

Area 90,000sq km (34,750sq miles)
Currency French franc
Population 118,000
Official Language French

ARGENTINA

CENTRAL ARGENTINA is covered with lush grasslands called the *pampas*, where crops are grown and cattle and sheep are reared. This area produces three-quarters of Argentina's income.

Area 2,766,890sq km (1,068,296sq miles)
Government Multiparty republic
Independence 1816, from Spain
Currency Argentinian peso
Population 34,600,000
Density 13 per sq km (34 per sq mile)
Official Language Spanish
Major Religions Roman Catholic 90%, Jewish 2%, others 8%

WEATHER FACTS

47°C (117°F)   950mm (37.4in)   -8.8°C (16°F)
22.5°C (72.5°F)   10.2°C (50.4°F)

LIFESTYLE FACTS

• Soccer is the national sport. Argentina hosted and won the World Cup in 1978, then won again in Mexico City in 1986.

• The Argentinian daily drink is a tea called *maté*. It is made from a tree used since ancient times by native South Americans.

• *Gauchos*, cowboys who work on the huge Argentinian cattle ranches, are folklore heroes. They also created dances which feature fast, complex footwork.

PATAGONIA

The region of Patagonia in southern Argentina is home to unique wildlife such as the pudu, the smallest known deer.

Pudu

THE CEIBO FLOWER

The ceibo is Argentina's national flower.

PALACIO DEL CONGRESO

The Argentinian government meets in the magnificent *Palacio del Congreso* (Congress building) in the *centro* (city centre) area of the capital, Buenos Aires.

WELSH TEAS

Welsh immigrants settled in Patagonia more than 100 years ago. Their descendants still follow Welsh traditions, such as eating porridge for breakfast, drinking tea, and singing Welsh songs.

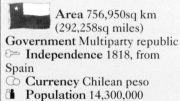

CHILE

CHILE RETURNED to being a democracy in 1989: elections were held for the first time in nearly 20 years.

Area 756,950sq km (292,258sq miles)
Government Multiparty republic
Independence 1818, from Spain
Currency Chilean peso
Population 14,300,000
Density 19 per sq km (49 per sq mile)
Official Language Spanish
Major Religions Roman Catholic 89%, Protestant 11%

WEATHER FACTS

37°C (98.6°F°)   361mm (14.2in)   -12°C (11°F)
20°C (68°F)   9.3°C (48.7°F)

LIFESTYLE FACTS

• Soccer is the sport with the largest following in Chile. Skiing is popular in winter; the world speed ski record of 171km/h (106mph) was set there.

• More copper is produced in Chile than any other country in the world.

• Chileans are very well educated: 94% of the population can read and write.

• Chile is famous for its fine wines. Chilean grapes are also used to make *pisco*, a spirit.

PARAGUAY

NINETY PER CENT of Paraguayans are *Mestizo* – a mixture of native Guarani Indian and Spanish blood. Half of the working population is employed in agriculture.

Area 406,750sq km (157,046sq miles)
Independence 1811, from Spain
Currency Guarani
Population 5,000,000
Official Language Spanish

URUGUAY

ALMOST HALF of Uruguay's population lives in the capital city, Montevideo. Much of the city's electricity is provided by hydroelectric dams.

Area 174,810sq km (67,494sq miles)
Independence 1825, from Spain
Currency Uruguayan peso
Population 3,200,000
Official Language Spanish

BRAZIL

BRAZIL OCCUPIES NEARLY half the continent of South America and is the fifth largest country in the world. The country supplies 85 per cent of the world's orange juice and is the largest producer of coffee. Around 70 per cent of the population is aged under 30.

Area 8,511,970sq km (3,286,472sq miles)
Government Multiparty republic
Independence 1822, from Portugal
Currency Real, formerly cruzeiro
Population 161,800,000
Density 19 per sq km (49 per sq mile)
Official Language Portuguese
Major Religions Roman Catholic 90%, others 10%

WEATHER FACTS

41°C (105.8°F)   1603mm (63.1 in)   -4°C (24.8°F)
22.3°C (72°F)   19.8°C (68°F)

LAND PROFILE

Tropical rainforests cover almost 60% of Brazil.

%
0.3
0.5
10
29.7
59.5

LIFESTYLE FACTS

● More than 1.5 million of Rio de Janeiro's 5 million plus population live in shanty towns known as *favelas*.

● Football is Brazil's favourite sport, and the country has more than 20,000 soccer teams. The brilliant Brazilian player, Pélé, is known throughout the world.

● Brasilia, the capital city since 1960, was built on the Central Plains to help develop inland areas of Brazil. The modern cathedral is the city's main landmark.

1,000 cruzeiros

LANGUAGE

A traditional greeting in Portuguese is *bom dia*.

BRAZILIAN INSTANT COFFEE EXPORTS (1997)

Destination	Tonnes
Eastern Europe	29,240
North America	8,771
Far East	7,196
South America	1,372

AMAZON RAINFOREST FACTS

● The Amazon Basin lies across the Equator. This hot, wet, region contains the world's largest tropical rainforest, which is 12 times the size of France.

● The Amazon River and its tributaries make up 20% of the world's supply of fresh water. This powerful river delivers an average of 773 billion litres (170 billion gallons) of water per hour into the Atlantic Ocean.

MAJOR RAINFOREST PEOPLES

Name of tribe and territory	Estimated population
Tikuna	25,000
Yanomami	7,500
Guajajara	7,000
Xavante	5,000
Sateré Maué	4,700

The Yanomami live in vine and leaf-thatched homes in the forests of northern Brazil and southern Venezuela.

RAINFOREST WILDLIFE FACTS

● The rainforest is home to 250 varieties of mammals, 1,800 species of birds, and more than 10,000 species of trees.

● The humming-bird beats its wings 55 times per second – 200 times per second during courtship flights. It can also hover in one place, or even fly backwards.

● The two-toed sloth is the world's slowest animal. It takes 6.5 hours to cover just 1.6km (1 mile). The sloth also spends 21.5 hours asleep each day.

● The anaconda is the world's heaviest snake, and can weigh up to 230kg (507lb).

CHRIST THE REDEEMER

The statue of Christ the Redeemer overlooks Rio de Janeiro from Mount Corcovado. It was designed by French sculptor Paul Landowsky, and was completed in 1931.

RIO CARNIVAL

The carnival in Rio de Janeiro is the biggest in the world and takes place every year before Lent. The highlight of the carnival is the parade of the Samba schools.

EUROPE

EUROPE IS THE second smallest continent and has a varied landscape and climate. Southern Europe is mostly hilly or mountainous and generally warm and dry. The north is wetter and cooler with flat plains and thick forests. Europe includes the western third of the Russian Federation.

Area 23,947,919sq km (9,246,339sq miles)
Countries 48
Largest Russian Federation 17,075,400sq km (6,592,846sq miles): European Russia 3,955,818sq km (1,527,349sq miles)
Smallest Vatican City 0.44sq km (0.17sq miles)
Population 750,582,660
Density 31 per sq km (80 per sq mile)

Major Languages Russian, German, Turkish, Italian, English
▲ **Highest point** Mount El'brus, Russian Federation 5,642m (18,510 ft)
▼ **Lowest point** Caspian Sea 28m (92ft) below sea level
☀ **Highest temperature** 50°C (122°F), Seville, Spain
❄ **Lowest temperature** -55°C (-67°F), Ust 'Shchugor, Russian Federation

TIME ZONES

| 12.00 Greenwich | 13.00 Berlin | 14.00 Athens | 15.00 Moscow |

LONGEST RIVERS

Volga 3,530km (2,194 miles)
Danube 2,858km (1,776 miles)
Ural 2,534km (1,575 miles)
Dnieper 2,285km (1,420 miles)
Don 1,969km (1,224 miles)

CLIMATE ZONES
KEY
- Temperate forest
- Mediterranean
- Dry grassland
- Polar and tundra
- Taiga
- Mountain regions

MOST POPULAR CITIES
The cities of Europe are popular with tourists from all over the world. The most visited cities in 1993 were, in order, London, Paris, Rome, Vienna, and Madrid

TOP CITY POPULATIONS

St. Petersburg, Russian Federation 4,446,000
Istanbul, Turkey 6,748,000
London, UK 6,803,100
Paris, France 9,318,000
Moscow, Russian Federation 8,717,000

COUNTRIES, TERRITORIES, AND CAPITALS

Name	Capital	Name	Capital
Albania	Tirana	Liechtenstein	Vaduz
Andorra	Andorra la Vella	Lithuania	Vilnius
Armenia	Yerevan	Luxembourg	Luxembourg
Austria	Vienna	Macedonia	Skopje
Azerbaijan	Baku	Malta	Valetta
Belgium	Brussels	Moldavia	Kishinev or Chisinau
Belorussia	Minsk	Monaco	Monaco
Bosnia & Herzegovina	Sarajevo	Netherlands	Amsterdam
Bulgaria	Sofia	Norway	Oslo
Croatia	Zagreb	Poland	Warsaw
Cyprus	Nicosia	Portugal	Lisbon
Czech Republic	Prague	Romania	Bucharest
Denmark	Copenhagen	Russian Federation	Moscow
Estonia	Tallinn	San Marino	San Marino
Finland	Helsinki	Slovakia	Bratislava
France	Paris	Slovenia	Ljubljana
Georgia	Tbilisi	Spain	Madrid
Germany	Berlin	Sweden	Stockholm
Greece	Athens	Switzerland	Berne
Hungary	Budapest	Turkey	Ankara
Iceland	Reykjavik	Ukraine	Kiev
Ireland, Republic of	Dublin	United Kingdom	London
Italy	Rome	Vatican City	Vatican City
Latvia	Riga	Yugoslavia	Belgrade

AGE BREAKDOWN

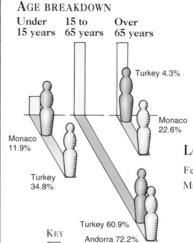

| Under 15 years | 15 to 65 years | Over 65 years |

Monaco 11.9%
Turkey 34.8%
Turkey 60.9%
Turkey 4.3%
Monaco 22.6%
Andorra 72.2%

KEY
- Lowest %
- Highest %

FEWEST DOCTORS

Ukraine	1 to 1,260 people
Cyprus	1 to 1,100 people
Ireland	1 to 630 people
Switzerland	1 to 630 people
Bosnia/Herz.	1 to 600 people

LONGEST LIFESPAN

	Switzerland	Sweden	Italy	Iceland	Norway
Female	81	81	81	80	80
Male	74	75	74	75	74

CONTINENT FACTS
• Most of the world's amber is found along the Baltic coast of Lithuania. Amber, the fossilized sap of ancient trees, is a precious stone. It is used in the treatment of arthritis.

• The French are the world's greatest snail eaters. They eat about 25,000 tonnes each year. Snails, *Helix pomatia* and *Helix aspersa*, are gathered from the wild.

• Germany is Europe's leading producer of chemicals; they are used in industry to make paint, cosmetics, and medicines.

• The Vatican City is the only place in the world where Latin is the official language.

• The St. Gotthard tunnel in Switzerland is the world's longest road tunnel. It is 16.3 km (10.1 miles) long.

• The largest cotton mill in Europe is in Estonia. Cotton is grown in the Baltic States.

WILDLIFE
The woodlands of Europe provide food and shelter for a variety of animals.

European badger
(Meles meles) has strong front legs and long claws to dig underground burrows up to 20m (66ft) long.

European hedgehog
(Erinaceus europaeus) has up to 5,000 spines on its back. Hedgehogs hibernate in the cold months of winter.

ARCTIC OCEAN

Franz Josef Land
(Russian Federation)

Svalbard
(Norway)

Bear I.
(Norway)

Novaya Zemlya

Kara Sea

Barents Sea

Jan Mayen
(Norway)

Arctic Circle   Arctic Circle

ICELAND

Ust 'Shchugor

Faeroe Islands

Norwegian Sea

NORWAY   SWEDEN   FINLAND

Gulf of Bothnia

L. Saimaa   *L. Onega*

L. Ladoga

St. Petersburg

RUSSIAN FEDERATION

Ural Mountains

Volga

North Sea

DENMARK

ESTONIA

LATVIA

LITHUANIA

RUSS. FED.

Baltic Sea

Gulf of Finland

Moscow

UNITED KINGDOM

NETHERLANDS

Berlin

GERMANY

POLAND

BELORUSSIA

Dnieper

Ural

REPUBLIC OF IRELAND

London

English Channel

Channel Islands
(UK)

BELGIUM

LUXEMBOURG

CZECH REPUBLIC

SLOVAKIA

UKRAINE

Don

KAZAKHSTAN

Paris

FRANCE

SWITZERLAND

LIECHTENSTEIN

AUSTRIA

SLOVENIA

HUNGARY

MOLDAVIA

Bay of Biscay

ALPS

CROATIA

ROMANIA

Danube

Carpathians

ANDORRA

Pyrenees

Corsica
(France)

BOSNIA AND HERZEGOVINA

YUGOSLAVIA

Sea of Azov

▲ **Mt. El'brus**
5,462m
(18,510ft)

▽ **Caspian Sea**
-28m (-92ft)

Adriatic Sea

BULGARIA

MACEDONIA

Black Sea

GEORGIA

Caucasus Mountains

N

SPAIN

PORTUGAL

Balearic Islands

Sardinia
(Italy)

ITALY

ALBANIA

GREECE

Aegean Sea

Istanbul

TURKEY

ARMENIA   AZERBAIJAN

Lake Van

Taurus Mts.

IRAN

Seville ☀

Strait of Gibraltar

Gibraltar
(UK)

Mediterranean Sea

Sicily

Athens

Crete

CYPRUS

SYRIA   IRAQ

ALGERIA

TUNISIA

MALTA

MOROCCO

Madeira
(Portugal)

0		500km
0		300 miles

CROSS-SECTION

3,000m
(9,843ft)

0 Sea level

Atlantic Ocean

Bay of Biscay

Alps

Adriatic Sea

Dinaric Alps

Transylvanian Alps

Black Sea

Crimea

Kerch Strait

-4,500m
(14,764ft)

Length:4,500km (2,800 miles)

LAND PROFILE
Most of Europe is covered with forest and agricultural land.

Wetlands 0.5%

Barren land 3%

Urban 4%

Grassland 6%

Agriculture 37.5%

Tundra 5.5%

Forest 43.5%

ICELAND

ICELAND, EUROPE'S second largest island, has the lowest population density in Europe. The remote interior can be reached only by special vehicle, pony, or small plane.

Area 103,000sq km (39,770sq miles)
Government Constitutional republic
Independence 1944, from British and US control during World War II
Currency Icelandic króna
Population 300,000
Density 3 per sq km (8 per sq mile)
Official Language Icelandic
✝ **Major Religions** Evangelical Lutheran Church of Iceland 96%, other Protestant and Roman Catholic 3%, non-religious 1%

WEATHER FACTS

30°C (86°F)   860mm (33.9in)   -36°C (-32.8°F)
10.6°C (51.8°F)   0.2°C (32.4°F)

LAND PROFILE

%
0.5
24
75.5

LIFESTYLE FACTS

• The Althing, the Icelandic parliament, has been in existence since the 13th century and is one of the oldest surviving assemblies in the world.

• Iceland has the most solfataras (volcanic vents) and hot springs in the world. Many of its towns are heated by underground hot water.

• Iceland produces more than a third of the world's cod-liver oil, and is the biggest consumer of it.

HOT SPRINGS

Deildartunguhver hot springs blow out 250 litres (55 gallons) of hot water every second. Over a 24-hour period, they produce enough water to fill 105,600 baths.

100 krónur

LANGUAGE

A traditional greeting in Icelandic is *gódan daginn*.

Arctic Circle
Siglufjördur
Akureyri
Herdubreid
ICELAND
Thjorsa   Vatnajökunll
Deildartunguhver
Thingvallavatn   Teiga
Reykjavik
Hafnarfjördhur   Kópavogur   Hvannadalshnúkur 2,119m (6,954ft)

N

0   500km
0   300 miles

DENMARK

DENMARK, WHICH IS divided into numerous islands, has a 4,500-mile (7,300km) coastline. It was the first Scandinavian country to belong to the European Community (EC).

Area 43,069sq km (16,629sq miles)
Government Constitutional monarchy
State founded c. 950
Territories Faeroe Islands, Greenland
Currency Danish krone
Population 5,200,000
Density 123 per sq km (319 per sq mile)
Official Language Danish
✝ **Major Religions** Evangelical Lutheran Church 91%, Roman Catholic 2%, other and non-religious 7%

WEATHER FACTS

35°C (95°F)   704mm (27.7in)   -24°C (-11.2°F)
16.3°C (61.3°F)   1.3°C (34.3°F)

LAND PROFILE

Almost two-thirds of the land is farmed.

%
2
11
87

100 kroner

LANGUAGE

A traditional greeting in Danish is *goddag*.

LIFESTYLE FACTS

• Lego was created by a Danish carpenter in the 1930s. Legoland Park is a miniature, working village created from 35 million plastic bricks.

• Denmark has one of the lowest private ownerships of cars in Europe. Cyclists are encouraged with special lanes, and Copenhagen was the first city to create a pedestrian street.

• Denmark has over twice as many pigs as humans, and Danish bacon is a successful export product. Danish farmers produce three times more food than is needed to feed the population.

LITTLE MERMAID

Situated by Copenhagen harbour, this statue of the mermaid from Hans C. Andersen's fairy tale was sculpted in 1913 by Edvard Eriksen (1876–1959). Her head has had to be replaced several times.

NORWAY

NORWAY IS A LAND of beautiful fjords (valleys flooded by rising sea levels after the last ice age): the longest is Sogne Fjord, at 203 kilometres (126 miles).

Area 323,900sq km (125,060sq miles)
Government Constitutional monarchy
Independence from Sweden, 1905
Territories Svalbard archipelago, Jan Mayen Island
Currency Norwegian krone
Population 4,300,000
Density 14 per sq km (36 per sq mile)
Official Language Nynorsk (new Norwegian) and Bokmaal (older)
✝ **Major Religions** Evangelical Lutheran and other Protestant 88%, other Christian 12%

WEATHER FACTS

34°C (93°F)   730mm (28.7in)   -26°C (-15°F)
16.3°C (61.3°F)   -3.5°C (25.7°F)

LAND PROFILE

%
1
9
18
24.5
47.5

SWEDEN

TWO-THIRDS OF the land in Sweden is covered by forests, and there are 100,000 lakes. Timber products, including paper, account for nearly one-fifth of all Swedish exports.

Area 449,960sq km (173,730sq miles)
Government Constitutional monarchy
State established 1523
Currency Swedish krona
Population 8,800,000
Density 20 per sq km (50 per sq mile)
Official Language Swedish
✝ Major Religions Evangelical Lutheran Church of Sweden 94%, Roman Catholic 2%, other 4%

NOBEL PRIZES
Alfred B. Nobel (1833–96) was a Swedish scientist and inventor of dynamite. He created a fund for the Nobel prizes, awarded each year for sciences, literature, and peace, to those who have given the greatest benefit to humankind.

100 kroner

LANGUAGE
A traditional greeting in Norwegian is *go dag.*

HOLMENKOLLEN
The ski jump at Holmenkollen, outside Oslo, is the oldest in existence. The first ski-jump competition was held in 1892, and the event continues to be held every March.

LIFESTYLE FACTS
• In Hammerfest, the world's most northerly town, the sun shines at midnight for just over two months in the summer.

• Norway's annual contribution of its national income (1.17%) towards foreign aid is the highest proportion in the world.

• Norwegians read more newspapers than anyone else in the world, and buy more English books than any other non-English-speaking country.

100 kronor

LANGUAGE
A traditional greeting in Swedish is *god dag.*

LAND PROFILE
The land is mainly forested or used for farming.

%
2.5
4.5
5.5
12.5
75

LIFESTYLE FACTS
• Each year 12,000 cross-country skiers take part in a race from Salen to Mora in central Sweden. The course is 90km (56 miles) long.

• In 1910, Sweden was the first European country to establish national parks. Animals that can be found in the parks include lynx, bear, and moose.

• Stockholm's waterways are so pure that people can safely swim and fish in them.

WEATHER FACTS

35°C (95°F) 622mm (24.5in) -38°C (-36.4°F)
16.5°C (61.7°F) -2°C (28.4°F)

CITY HALL
Stockholm's fine City Hall, called the Stadshus, was built between 1911 and 1923. Its Golden Hall has 19 million gilded tiles.

BARENTS SEA
• Hammerfest
Sami (Lapps)
Lofoten Islands
Kebnekaise 2,111m (6,928ft)
Padjelanta National Park
Arctic Circle
• Piteå
Trondheim
Galdhøpiggen 2,469m (8,103ft)
Femund
Sogne Fjord
Lillehammer
Bergen
Mjøsa
Holmenkollen
Mora
Salen
Oslo
Drammen
Uppsala
Stavanger
Stockholm
Örebro
Vänern
Norrköping
Stadshus
Linköping
Gotland
Gothenburg
Öland
Skagerrak
NORTH SEA
Ålborg
DENMARK
Yding Skovhøj 179m (587ft)
Legoland
L. Arre
Fanø
Copenhagen • Malmö
Odense
Little Mermaid
GERMANY
Baltic Sea
Kattegat
NORWAY
SWEDEN
FINLAND
Gulf of Bothnia

N

0   500km
0   300 miles

THE SAMI
The Sami (Lapps) have inhabited the arctic regions of Norway and Sweden since ancient times. Today, there are about 60,000 and 70% speak the Sami language. About 70,000 reindeer live in Sami territories, and the main occupation of the people is reindeer breeding. The woven clothes worn by the Sami are practical and beautiful.

• More than 50% of Norwegian families have a weekend home in the mountains or by the sea. These second homes are made of wood, and some have turf-covered roofs.

HIGHEST WATERFALLS

Name	Height	
	m	ft
Utigord	800	2,625
Mongefossen	774	2,540
Ostre Mardola Foss	657	2,154
Tyssetrengane	646	2,120
Kjellfossen	561	1,841

UNITED KINGDOM

THE UNITED KINGDOM, also known as Britain, is made up of England, Wales, Scotland, and Northern Ireland. London, the capital, has a population of almost 7 million, and is the political and financial centre.

Area 244,880sq km (94,550sq miles)
Government Constitutional monarchy
Unification 1707, between England/Wales and Scotland; 1801, between Britain and Ireland
Territories Anguilla, Bermuda, British Antarctic Territory, British India Ocean Territory, British Virgin Islands, Cayman Islands, Falkland Islands, Gibraltar, Montserrat, Pitcairn Islands, St. Helena and dependencies, South Georgia and the South Sandwich Islands, Turks and Caicos Islands
Currency Pound sterling
Population 58,300,000
Density 241 per sq km (625 per sq mile)
Official Language English
Major Religions Protestant 52%, Roman Catholic 9%, Muslim 3%, other 36%

WEATHER FACTS

34°C (93°F)   593mm (23in)   -17°C (2°F)
14.6°C (58.3°F)   6.5°C (43.7°F)

LAND PROFILE

Almost three-quarters of the land is farmed.

%
4
11
14
71

LIFESTYLE FACTS

• There are more than 25,000 different names for the public houses (pubs) where people in Britain meet to talk and drink. The most popular name is *The Red Lion*.

• The Eistedfodd is a Welsh arts festival held every August. The festival dates back to 1176 when competitions were held for poet-musicians. The winner was awarded a "chair", or position, in the royal court.

HOUSES OF PARLIAMENT
This palace is the headquarters of the British Government. Its famous clock tower has a great bell called Big Ben.

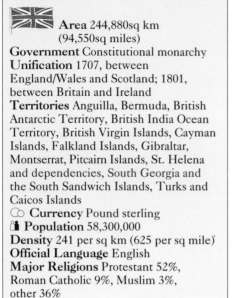

SCOTTISH TARTAN
Members of a Scottish clan have their own tartan. This cloth, often worn as a kilt, is woven with a criss-cross pattern. There are more than 2,000 varieties of tartan.

LANGUAGE
A traditional greeting in English is hello.

0   150km
0   100 miles

Shetland Is.
Orkney Is.
Outer Hebrides
Lewis
North Uist
Skye
South Uist
North West Highlands
Moray Firth
Ben Nevis 1,343m (4,406ft)
SCOTLAND
Islay
Glasgow   Edinburgh
Southern Uplands
Newcastle upon Tyne
UNITED KINGDOM
North Sea
ATLANTIC OCEAN
NORTHERN IRELAND
Donegal Bay
Belfast
Lough Neagh
Isle of Man
Irish Sea
REPUBLIC OF IRELAND
Mullingar
Dublin
Trinity College
Dun Laoghaire
Galway
Shannon
Liverpool   Manchester
Anglesey
Limerick
Wicklow Mts.
Cardigan Bay
Cambrian Mts.
Severn
Birmingham
Carantuohill 1,041m (3,416ft)
Waterford
WALES
ENGLAND
Cork
St. George's Channel
Brecon Beacons
The Wash
Cardiff
Thames
London
Houses of Parliament
Bristol Channel
Stonehenge
Strait of
Plymouth
Isle of Wight
N
Isles of Scilly
English Channel
Guernsey
Channel Islands Jersey (U.K.)

10 pounds sterling

SYMBOLS
England, rose; Wales, daffodil; Scotland, thistle; and Ireland, shamrock.

STONEHENGE
This prehistoric stone circle in southern England was completed in about 1600 B.C.

REPUBLIC OF IRELAND

IRELAND IS A mainly rural country. It has a wet and mild climate with rich grass for dairy farming. Tourists come to fish in the rivers and lakes.

Area 70,280sq km (27,135sq miles)
Government Multiparty republic
Independence 1921, Irish Free State granted 26 counties
Currency Punt
Population 3,600,000
Density 52 per sq km (135 per sq mile)
Official Language Irish
Major Religions Roman Catholic 93%, Anglican 5%, other 2%

1 Irish punt

WEATHER FACTS

30°C (86°F)   762mm (30in)   -12°C (10°F)
12.6°C (54.6°F)   6.4°C (43.5°F)

LAND PROFILE

Almost all of Ireland is farmland.

%
0.5
1
3.5
14.5
80.5

BOOK OF KELLS
This page is from the *Book of Kells*, the four gospels set down by a 8th-century Irish monk. It is displayed in the Trinity College Library, Dublin, where a page is turned each day.

SPAIN

SPAIN IS THE SECOND largest country in Europe, and one of the most mountainous. Madrid, the capital, is Europe's highest city. Spain's warm climate and fine beaches attract 50 million visitors a year.

Area 504,780sq km (194,900sq miles)
Government Constitutional monarchy
Independence 1469, reunification of Spain against Moorish invaders
Territories Canary Islands, Balearic Islands, Ceuta, Melilla, Islas Chafarinas; Peñón de Vélez de la Gomera; Peñón de Alhucemas
Currency Peseta
Population 39,600,000
Density 79 per sq km (205 per sq mile)
Official Language Castilian Spanish
Major Religions Roman Catholic 99%, other 1%

ALHAMBRA PALACE

This beautiful palace of the Moorish (Muslim) rulers of 14th-century Spain sits high above the city of Granada. Also a fortress with huge towers, Alhambra means "red castle".

WEATHER FACTS

49°C (120°F) 444mm (17.4in) -20°C (-6°F)
19.3°C (66.7°F) 8.5°C (47.3°F)

LAND PROFILE

Almost half of Spain's land is farmed.

%
0.5
0.5
1
20
28.5
49.5

LIFESTYLE FACTS

• Spain is the world's third largest wine producer. Famous Spanish wines include sherry, first produced in the town of Jerez.

• During the "running of the bulls" in Pamplona, men test their courage by running in front of a herd of bulls.

LANGUAGE

A traditional greeting in Castilian Spanish is *buenos días*.

FLOWER

The red carnation is the Spanish national flower.

AMAZING OLIVES

Spain is the world's top producer of olives and olive products. In one year, enough olives are grown to supply every person in the world with 70 each.

Map of the Iberian Peninsula

Bay of Biscay
La Coruña • Gijón •
• Bilbao
Cantabrian Mountains Pamplona •
FRANCE
Pyrenees
ANDORRA
Andorra-La Vella
• Vigo
Bragança • Valladolid Duero Zaragoza
Oporto • Douro Barcelona •
SPAIN Hospitalet
Coimbra Estrela 1993m (6500 ft) Madrid Serrania de Cuenca
PORTUGAL Sierra de Gredos Cuenca
Tagus Alcántara Reservoir Tagus Valencia
Lisbon Guadiana
Sierra Morena Alicante
Guadalquivir Murcia •
Córdoba • Alhambra Palace
Seville • Granada Mulhacén 3478 m (11,411 ft)
• Jérez Málaga •
GIBRALTAR (UK)

ATLANTIC OCEAN
Balearic Islands Minorca
Majorca
• Palma
Ibiza
MEDITERRANEAN SEA

N

0   100   200 km
0   125 miles

The cockerel is Portugal's national symbol.

PORTUGAL

IN THE 15TH CENTURY Portugal was a great seafaring nation with many famous explorers. Today, Portuguese is the seventh most spoken language in the world.

LANGUAGE

A traditional greeting in Portuguese is *bom dia*.

Area 92,390sq km (35,670sq miles)
Government Multiparty republic
Independence 1910, Republic declared
Territories Azores, Madeiras, Macao
Currency Escudo
Population 9,800,000
Density 107 per sq km (277 per sq mile)
Official Languages Portuguese
Major Religions Roman Catholic 97%, Protestant 1%, other 2%

WEATHER FACTS

49°C (120°F) 708mm (27.8in) -12°C (10°F)
21.5°C (70.7°F) 11.5°C (52.7°F)

LAND PROFILE

Two-thirds of Portugal is farmland and forest.

%
1
15
39
45

CORK FACTS

• Cork is made from the bark of the cork oak tree.

• Portugal supplies more than half the world's cork.

• The main product made from cork is the bottle stopper.

ANDORRA

ANDORRA IS TUCKED away in the high valleys of the Pyrenees and its perpetual snow attracts many skiers. It is the fourth smallest independent state in Europe.

Area 468sq km (181sq miles)
Government Co-principality (France and Spain)
Independence 1278, established as a state
Currencies French franc and Spanish peseta
Population 64,000
Density 138 per sq km (357 per sq mile)
Official language Catalan

NETHERLANDS

THE DUTCH PEOPLE made their fortunes from the sea in the 17th century with a worldwide trading network. Today, Rotterdam is the world's largest and busiest port.

 Area 37,330sq km (14,410sq miles)
Government Constitutional monarchy
Kingdom established 1830
Territories Aruba, Netherlands Antilles
Currency Guilder
Population 15,500,000
Density 457 per sq km (1,188 per sq mile)
Official Language Dutch
Major Religions Roman Catholic 36%, Protestant 27%, other 37%

DUTCH WATER FACTS

• Without protective dunes and dykes, half the land area of the Netherlands would be flooded by the sea twice a day.

• Almost 20% of the Netherlands is made up of inland water. Windmills once pumped out water; now, the pumps are electric.

BELGIUM

BELGIUM COMBINES two cultures: the French-speaking Walloons and the Dutch-speaking Flemings. Brussels, the capital, is host to the Commission of the European Union (EU).

Area 33,100sq km (12,780sq miles)
Currency Belgian franc
Government Constitutional monarchy
Independence 1830, from the Netherlands
Population 10,100,000
Density 308 per sq km (798 per sq mile)
Official Languages French, Dutch, and German
✝ **Major Religions** Roman Catholic 75%, other 25%

ATOMIUM

Erected in 1958 in Brussels, this space-age structure, called the Atomium, represents an iron crystal. It houses a permanent scientific exhibition on the history of medicine.

LAND PROFILE

The Netherlands is intensively farmed.

%
3.5
12
84.5

LIFESTYLE FACTS

• There are 14 million bicycles between 15 million people in the Netherlands. This is the highest proportion in the world.

 • If the canals freeze over, the Dutch take part in a *tocht*, a long skating tour. Official tour routes between villages are announced on TV and radio.

• More Dutch cheese is exported than any other cheese in the world. Half of all milk produced is made into cheese.

FLOWER POWER

The Netherlands is the world's largest exporter of flowers and bulbs. In spring, fields packed with brightly coloured tulips attract thousands of visitors.

0   75km
0   40 miles

100 Belgium francs

WEATHER FACTS

37°C (98.6°F)   825mm (32in)   -18°C (0°F)
17°C (62.6°F)   2.6°C (36.7°F)

LAND PROFILE

%
7
35
58

LIFESTYLE FACTS

 • Belgium is the third biggest producer of chocolates in the world.

• Belgians spend more on food and drink than their European neighbours. Brussels has 25 restaurants holding a prized Michelin rosette – more than twice as many as London, which is eight times bigger.

• Bruges is the centre of European lacemaking; women have made exquisite lace here for centuries.

• Belgium has the world's densest railway system: there are 8,408km (5,224 miles) of tracks.

25 guilders

WEATHER FACTS

37°C (98.6°F)   580mm (23in)   -25°C (-13°F)
16.5°C (61.7°F)   2.3°C (36.1°F)

LUXEMBOURG

LUXEMBOURG IS A Grand Duchy, with a Grand Duke as Head of State. Luxembourg City is a major international banking centre.

Area 2,586sq km (998sq miles)
Currency Luxembourg franc, Belgian franc
Government Constitutional monarchy
Independence 1839, from the Netherlands
Population 400,000
Density 155 per sq km (403 per sq mile)
Official Language Luxembourgish
✝ **Major Religions** Roman Catholic 97%, other 3%

*Map labels:*
Frisian Islands
Waddenzee
NORTH SEA
Groningen
Bulbfields
IJsselmeer
Bulbfields
Amsterdam
De Bilt
NETHERLANDS
The Hague   Utrecht   Arnhem
Rotterdam   Rhine
Zeeland   Meuse
Eindhoven
Bruges   Antwerp
Ghent   Scheldt   Atomium
Brussels   Vaalserberg 321m (1,054ft)
BELGIUM   Liège
Charleroi   Meuse
Botrange 692m (2,271ft)
GERMANY
Buurgplaatz 560m (1,838ft)
Sûre
FRANCE   LUXEMBOURG
Luxembourg
Virton   Moselle
N

FRANCE

FRANCE IS THE LARGEST of the fifteen countries in the European Union (EU), and its leading agricultural power. Ninety per cent of the land is farmed, and one in five French people lives and works in the countryside.

Area 551,500sq km (219,930sq miles)
Government Multiparty republic
Independence 1789
Territories Corsica, French Guiana, Guadeloupe, Martinique, Reunion, Mayotte, St. Pierre & Miquelon, Bassas da India, Clipperton Island, Europa Island, French Polynesia, French Southern and Antarctic Lands, Juan de Nova Island, New Caledonia, Glorioso Islands, Tromelin Island, Wallis, Futuna
Currency Franc
Population 58,000,000
Density 105 per sq km (272 per sq mile)
Official Language French
Major Religions Roman Catholic 90%, other 10%

EIFFEL TOWER
A.G. Eiffel (1832–1923) designed this famous tower. It is 300m (984ft) high and was built for the Paris World Exposition of 1889.

WEATHER FACTS

39°C (102°F) 444mm (17.4in) -17°C (1°F)
23°C (73°F) 6°C (42°F)

LAND PROFILE
The majority of land is farmed and there are extensive forests.

%
1
3
36
60

LIFESTYLE FACTS
• France is the world's second biggest producer of cheese and curd. There is a different cheese for every single day of the year.

• Cycle races are a top spectator sport in France. The Tour de France is the world's longest cycle race. It covers 3,720km (2,312 miles) and takes three weeks. The first race was held in 1913.

FASTEST TRAIN
France holds the record for the fastest train, the TGV. It reached 515.3km/h (320.1mph) in 1990. The fastest recorded journey is between Paris and Mâcon, covered at an average speed of 217km/h (135mph).

100 French francs

LANGUAGE
A traditional greeting in French is *bonjour*.

PARIS, CITY OF CULTURE
Paris is a very successful mix of different architectural styles, from world-famous historic monuments to ultra-modern glass-and-steel structures.

The *Grand Louvre* museum, France's second most visited monument, houses the world-famous *Mona Lisa*. The glass pyramid over the entrance was built in 1989.

The *Centre Georges Pompidou*, which contains France's National Museum of Modern Art, is the most visited public building in the country. The centre was opened in 1977.

BEST CELLAR
France, along with Italy, is the world's leading wine producer. In 1997, wine production totalled 7,400,000,000 bottles: enough for a bottle taller than the Statue of Liberty.

MONACO

THE TINY COUNTRY of Monaco, which has an orchestra larger than its army, is the most densely populated country in Europe.

Area 1.95sq km (0.75sq mile)
Government Constitutional monarchy
Independence 1861, state established
Currency French franc
Population 31,000
Density 15,897 per sq km (41,332 per sq mile)
Official Language French
Major Religions Roman Catholic 95%, other 5%

Lille
Lens
Valenciennes
BELGIUM
LUXEMBOURG
GERMANY
English
Channel Islands (UK)
Le Havre
Rouen
Reims
Brest
Paris
Eiffel Tower
Seine
Nancy
Strasbourg
Rennes
Le Mans
Orléans
Loire
Mulhouse
Nantes
Tours
Dijon
Vosges
Jura
SWITZERLAND
FRANCE
Poitiers
Lake Geneva
Mâcon
Mont Blanc 4810m (15,782ft)
Clermont-Ferrand
Lyon
Angoulême
St. Étienne
Massif Central
Grenoble
ITALY
Bordeaux
Rhône
Garonne
Toulouse
Montpellier
MONACO
Nice
Marseille
Toulon
Pyrenees
MEDITERRANEAN SEA
SPAIN
ANDORRA
ATLANTIC OCEAN
Les Landes

0   100km
0   100 miles

N

Ligurian Sea
Corsica
Ajaccio
Mediterranean Sea

GERMANY

THE FEDERAL REPUBLIC of Germany holds a key position in Central Europe. A divided country for 41 years, reunification with the German Democratic Republic took place on 3 October 1990.

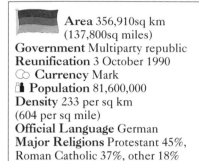

Area 356,910sq km (137,800sq miles)
Government Multiparty republic
Reunification 3 October 1990
Currency Mark
Population 81,600,000
Density 233 per sq km (604 per sq mile)
Official Language German
Major Religions Protestant 45%, Roman Catholic 37%, other 18%

WEATHER FACTS

39°C (101°F)   619mm (24.4in)   -30°C (-21°F)
14.3°C (57.7°F)   3°C (37.4°F)

LAND PROFILE

	%
	0.5
	5.5
	45.5
	48.5

BRANDENBURG GATE

From 1961, this last town gateway was blocked, separating East Berlin from West Berlin. On 22 December 1989, the gate was re-opened.

10 Deutschmark

LANGUAGE

A traditional greeting in German is *Guten Tag*.

LIFESTYLE FACTS

• West Germany's football team won the World Cup championship three times: Berne in 1954, Munich in 1974, and Rome in 1990.

• 40 million Germans travel abroad for their holidays every year: this represents 51% of the population.

• The Federal Republic is the third largest producer of cars in the world, after Japan and the United States. In 1991, 4.6 million cars were produced, and 2.2 million of these were exported.

• Wurst (sausage) is a traditional and popular German food. There are about 1,500 varieties.

FAIRS AND FESTIVALS

• Frankfurt Book Fair, held every October, attracts publishers and booksellers from all over the world. In 1996, there were 274,000 visitors and 6,819 exhibitors.

FAIRYTALE CASTLE

Neuschwanstein Castle, one of the most fantastic, fairytale castles in the world, was dreamed up by King Ludwig II of Bavaria (1845–86). Sadly, Ludwig, who had a two-storey room built for his gold and ivory throne, died before the castle was completed.

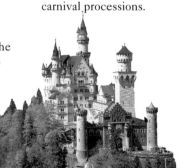

• Since 1810, Europe's best-known beer festival has been held at Munich. In 1993, visitors drank 4.8 million litres of beer.

• Each spring, the world's biggest trade fair is held in Hanover. Exhibitors from 50 countries display the latest industrial technology.

• Cologne carnival is a five-day festival held seven weeks before Easter. The most important day is Rose Monday, when chocolates and gifts are thrown to the crowd from carnival processions.

BAYREUTH

Each year, the Bavarian city of Bayreuth hosts a festival in honour of the famous composer Richard Wagner (1813–83). His operas are staged in the purpose-built *Festspielhaus* (Festival Theatre).

Wagner's Opera Lohengrin

TOP GERMAN CAR MANUFACTURERS (1997)	
Manufacturer	Number of cars produced
Volkswagen	1,188,601
Opel	1,040,298
Ford	754,140
Mercedes-Benz	696,445
BMW	599,493
Audi	557,777

NORTH SEA
North Frisian Is.
DENMARK
BALTIC SEA
East Frisian Is.
NETHERLANDS
Hamburg
Oderhaff
Bremen
Elbe
Oder
POLAND
Berlin
Hanover
Brandenburg Gate
GERMANY
Harz Mts.
Brocken 1,142m (3,747ft)
Essen Dortmund
Leipzig
Duisburg
Düsseldorf
Thuringian Forest
Cologne
Grosser Beerberg 982m (3,222ft)
Ore Mts.
BELGIUM
Bonn
Wasser Kuppe 950m (3,117ft)
Neisse
CZECH. REP.
LUX.
Frankfurt
Bayreuth
Main
Franconian Jura
Bohemian Forest
Nuremberg
Rhine
Stuttgart
Danube
Black Forest
Swabian Jura
Munich
FRANCE
Freiburg im Breisgau
Lake Constance
Rhine
Neuschwanstein
Bavarian Alps
AUSTRIA
SWITZERLAND
Zugspitze 2,963m (9,271ft)
N

0   150km
0   100 miles

SWITZERLAND

JUST ONE-QUARTER of Switzerland is habitable: the remaining land consists of mountains, forests, and ice. Every minute, 20 to 30 square metres of Swiss land are built on.

 Area 41,290sq km (15,940sq miles)
Government Federal republic
Independence 1648, from the Holy Roman Empire
Currency Swiss franc
Population 7,200,000
Density 181 per sq km (469 per sq mile)
Official Languages German, French, Italian
† **Major Religions** Roman Catholic 48%, Protestant 44%, other 8%

JET D'EAU
The water from the jet d'eau, the famous fountain situated in the centre of Geneva's harbour, gushes 140 metres (460ft) in the air.

WEATHER FACTS
38°C (100°F)   444mm (17.5in)   -30°C (-23°F)
23°C (73.4°F)   6°C (42.8°F)

LAND PROFILE
%
2
21
34.5
42.5

LIFESTYLE FACTS
• The Swiss are famous bankers, and their banks attract money from investors all over the world. There is a bank for every 1,600 Swiss people.

• Watches are Switzerland's best-known export. The watchmaking centre in Neuchâtel developed both the quartz watch and the atomic clock.

• The surplus of home-produced milk led to two important Swiss inventions, baby food and condensed milk. Other Swiss milk products are cheese and fine chocolate.

50 Swiss francs

LANGUAGE
A traditional greeting in French is *Bonjour*; in German *Guten Tag*; in Italian *Buongiorno*.

TOP CHOCOLATE EATERS		
Country	Amount per person kg	lb
Switzerland	10.18	22.45
Norway	10.12	22.31
Belgium	10.06	22.18

N

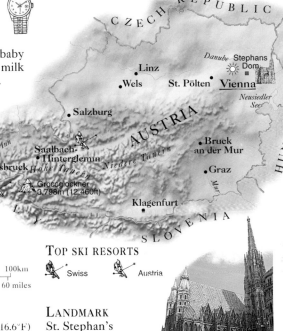

AUSTRIA

AUSTRIA'S FINE CITIES and beautiful, mountainous landscape – 40 per cent of the land lies at an altitude of more than 1,000 metres – attract about 18 million visitors a year.

 Area 83,850sq km (32,375sq miles)
Government Multiparty republic
Independence 1918, Republic declared
Currency Schilling
Population 8,000,000
Density 97 per sq km (251 per sq mile)
Official Language German
† **Major Religions** Roman Catholic 85%, Evangelical 6%, other 9%

LANGUAGE
A traditional greeting in German is *Guten Tag*.

100 Austrian schillings

WEATHER FACTS
38°C (100.4°F)   640mm (25.2in)   -27°C (-16.6°F)
19.3°C (66.7°F)   0°C (32°F)

LAND PROFILE
Almost two-thirds of the land is farmed.
%
1
4
30
65

LIFESTYLE FACTS
• Many great composers were Austrian; they include Mozart (1756–91), Haydn (1732–1809), Schubert (1797–1828), and Johann Strauss (1825–99), who composed the famous Viennese waltz, *The Blue Danube*.

• Skiing is Austria's national sport. The first ski school was set up at St. Anton am Arlberg, and Austrian Annemarie Moser-Proll (b. 1953) is a celebrated woman skier.

TOP SKI RESORTS
Swiss   Austria

LANDMARK
St. Stephan's Cathedral, more than 600 years old, is one of Vienna's most famous buildings.

LIECHTENSTEIN

THIS TINY COUNTRY is ruled by a prince. Liechtenstein is famous for its royal art collection and its postage stamps. One of the principal exports is false teeth.

Area 160sq km (62sq miles)
Government Constitutional monarchy
Independence 1866, from the German Confederation
Currency Swiss franc
Population 30,630
Density 191 per sq km (495 per sq mile)
Official Language German

ITALY

THIS IMPORTANT INDUSTRIAL nation has most of its factories as well as rich farmland concentrated in the north. The south is mountainous and farmers grow olives, and grapes for making wine. Italy includes the large islands of Sicily and Sardinia.

Area 301,270sq km (116,320sq miles)
Government Multiparty republic
Republic Declared in 1948
Currency Lira
Population 57,200,000
Density 195 per sq km (505 per sq mile)
Official Language Italian
✝ **Major Religions** Roman Catholic 99%, other 1%

WEATHER FACTS

42°C (107.6°F) 744mm (29in) -11°C (13°F)
19°C (66.2°F) 12.3°C (54.1°F)

LAND PROFILE

More than 68% of Italy is agricultural land.

%
1.5
2.5
27.5
68.5

LIFESTYLE FACTS

- The Palio of Siena is a twice yearly bareback horse race round the city's main square. The palio is the silk banner awarded to the winner.

- The most popular resort is Venice, with more than 7.5 million tourists a year. The city has 118 islands, 177

VATICAN CITY

- The Vatican City in Rome is the world's smallest independent state. It is the world centre for the Roman Catholic religion and its ruler is the pope.

- There has been a pope for more than 1,900 years – since the time of St. Peter, who was the first pope.

- St. Peter's is the largest and most important cathedral in the Christian world, first built by the Roman Emperor Constantine in about A.D.330.

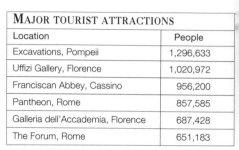

1,000 lira

LANGUAGE

A traditional greeting in Italian is *buongiorno*.

MAJOR TOURIST ATTRACTIONS

Location	People
Excavations, Pompeii	1,296,633
Uffizi Gallery, Florence	1,020,972
Franciscan Abbey, Cassino	956,200
Pantheon, Rome	857,585
Galleria dell'Accademia, Florence	687,428
The Forum, Rome	651,183

FOOD FACTS

- There are more than 600 different types of pasta.

- More than 4 million tonnes of tomatoes are grown in Italy every year. Many are used to make sauces for pasta dishes.

- Genuine mozzarella cheese is made from the milk of the water buffalo. It is made fresh daily in many parts of Italy.

TOWER OF PISA

The leaning tower of Pisa is made of white marble and was built between 1174 and 1350. It is 54m (177ft) tall and leans at an angle of 11.3 degrees from the vertical.

SAN MARINO

THE TINY REPUBLIC of San Marino is located in the mountains of central Italy. Tourism accounts for 60 per cent of the country's income.

Area 61sq km (24sq miles)
Independence 1631, recognition as a city state
Currency Italian lira
Population 24,000
Official Language Italian

MALTA

MALTA IS AN island country in the Mediterranean. The climate is warm but there are no rivers and little rain to provide water for crops.

Area 320sq km (124sq miles)
Independence 1964, from Britain
Currency Maltese lira
Population 400,000
Official Languages English, Maltese

MEDITERRANEAN SEA

Pollution is a problem in the Mediterranean because no strong currents wash away waste. The waters are completely changed with those of the Atlantic only once every 100 years.

FINLAND

A COUNTRY WITH 187,888 lakes, Finland also has vast forests of pine and spruce. Timber, used to make paper and furniture, provides most of the wealth of the country. Finland also includes part of Lapland.

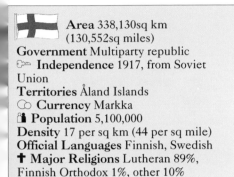

Area 338,130sq km (130,552sq miles)
Government Multiparty republic
Independence 1917, from Soviet Union
Territories Åland Islands
Currency Markka
Population 5,100,000
Density 17 per sq km (44 per sq mile)
Official Languages Finnish, Swedish
✝ **Major Religions** Lutheran 89%, Finnish Orthodox 1%, other 10%

LIFESTYLE FACTS

• Finnish women were the first in Europe to get the vote, in 1906.

• The world's longest cross-country ski race is held in March each year. Skiers race from Kuusamo on the Russian border to Tornio on the Swedish border, across southern Lapland.

• Savonlinna Opera Festival is the most successful cultural event in Finland. It was founded in 1912 by opera singer Aino Ackte and is held in the courtyard of the medieval Olavinlinna Castle.

ESTONIA

MUCH OF ESTONIA is flat countryside with fields and forests, marshes and lakes. The main industries include engineering and textiles.

Area 45,125sq km (17,423sq miles)
Government Multiparty republic
Independence 1991, from Soviet Union
Currency Kroon
Population 1,600,000
Density 37 per sq km (86 per sq mile)
Official Language Estonian
Major Religions No figures available. Most people Evangelical Lutheran, also Russian Orthodox

HELPING HANDS

In 1989, the Estonians formed a chain across their land, and into Latvia and Lithuania. The 644-km (400-mile) link symbolized their bid for freedom from the Soviet Union.

33°C (91.4°F)   688mm (27in)   -41°C (-43°F)
20.3°C (68.5°F)   -2.6°C (27.3°F)

LATVIA

A MIXTURE OF forested hills and plains, Latvia is often called Amberland because so much amber can be found on its Baltic shore.

Area 64,589sq km (24,938sq miles)
Government Multiparty republic
Independence 1991, from Soviet Union
Currency Lats
Population 2,600,000
Density 40 per sq km (104 per sq mile)
Official Language Latvian
Major Religions No figures available. Predominantly Lutheran, also Roman Catholic and Russian Orthodox

100 markka

LANGUAGE

A traditional greeting in Finnish is *hyvää päivää*.

LAND PROFILE

Forests cover 80% of the total area of Finland.

FINNISH TIMBER EXPORTS (1997)	
Europe	78%
Asia	10%
North America	5%
Africa	3%
South America	2%
Oceania	2%

HELSINKI CATHEDRAL

This fine cathedral was designed in the 19th century by architect Carl Engel. It was laid out in its present form of a Greek cross with a central tower.

SAUNA BOX

The sauna is a national tradition and Finns have at least one a week. There are about 1.4 million saunas in Finland: one for every 3.5 people.

LITHUANIA

MOST OF LITHUANIA is a low-lying plain with many small lakes formed by glaciers. Winter temperatures can fall below freezing for four months.

Area 65,200sq km (25,174sq miles)
Government Multiparty republic
Independence 1991, from Soviet Union
Currency Litas
Population 3,700,000
Density 57 per sq km (148 per sq mile)
Official Language Lithuanian
Major Religions No figures available. Predominantly Roman Catholic, also Evangelical Lutheran and Reformist

POLAND

POLAND IS AN industrial country rich in coal and copper. It has large textile, iron, steel, and shipbuilding industries. Much of the landscape is flat and about one third of the people work on the land.

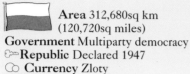

Area 312,680sq km (120,720sq miles)
Government Multiparty democracy
Republic Declared 1947
Currency Zloty
Population 38,400,000
Density 126 per sq km (326 per sq mile)
Official Language Polish
✝ **Major Religions** Roman Catholic 95%, other 5%

CZECH REPUBLIC

THE HOMELAND OF the Czechs was originally called Bohemia. Much of the country is flat farmland. Prague, the capital, has many churches with gilded roofs which gave the city the name *zlata Praha*, or golden Prague.

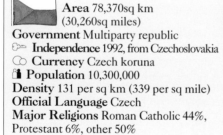

Area 78,370sq km (30,260sq miles)
Government Multiparty republic
Independence 1992, from Czechoslovakia
Currency Czech koruna
Population 10,300,000
Density 131 per sq km (339 per sq mile)
Official Language Czech
Major Religions Roman Catholic 44%, Protestant 6%, other 50%

SLOVAKIA

FORMERLY PART OF the kingdom of Hungary, Slovakia is a hilly country of thick forests dominated by the Carpathian Mountains. Bratislava, on the Danube, is the capital city and main export point.

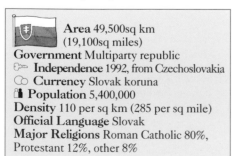

Area 49,500sq km (19,100sq miles)
Government Multiparty republic
Independence 1992, from Czechoslovakia
Currency Slovak koruna
Population 5,400,000
Density 110 per sq km (285 per sq mile)
Official Language Slovak
Major Religions Roman Catholic 80%, Protestant 12%, other 8%

WEATHER FACTS

39°C (102.2°F) 550mm (22in) -28°C (-18°F)
18.9°C (66°F) -3.9°C (25°F)

LAND PROFILE

%
1.5
47
51.5

LIFESTYLE FACTS

• Poland has Europe's oldest operating salt mine at Wieliczka, near Kraków. The layers of salt go down to 327m (1,073ft).

• Education is compulsory between the ages of 7 and 18, and 98 per cent of Poles can read and write.

• Open-air museums, known as *skansens*, exhibit a selection of typical, old wooden buildings such as barns, churches, and windmills.

PRAGUE'S CLOCK
The astronomical clock in the Old Town Hall, Prague, was installed in 1410. The clock's interlocking circles show phases of the Sun and Moon. It has run non-stop since 1572.

100,000 zloty

LANGUAGE
A traditional greeting in Polish is *dzien dóbry*.

WAWEL CASTLE
Wawel Castle is built on a rocky embankment of the Vistula River in the old capital of Kraków. Many Polish kings are buried in the castle's underground crypts.

TRADITIONAL POLISH FOOD
Poland can be extremely cold, so many dishes are planned to be warm and filling.
Krupnik A thick soup made with barley or buckwheat. Also the name of a strong drink.
Pierozki Dumplings filled with meat, mushrooms, cooked cabbage or cheese.
Bigos A meat stew using wild boar, hare, or venison and *wiejska*, a Polish sausage.

Polish dumplings

UKRAINE

MUCH OF THE Ukraine consists of vast flat plains called steppes. Chief crops include winter wheat, maize, barley, sugar beet, and potatoes.

Area 603,700sq km (233,090sq miles)
Government Multiparty republic
Independence 1991, from USSR
Currency Karbovanets (temporary)
Population 51,400,000
Density 85 per sq km (220 per sq mile)
Official Language Ukrainian
Major Religions No figures available

UKRAINE CROPS (1998)
(in thousand tonnes)

17,500 — Potatoes
16,000 — Sugar beet
14,900 — Wheat
6,215 — Vegetables

BISON
The Bialowieza Forest is the largest ancient forest in Europe. It is home to the last 500 or so remaining European bison. The bison is the biggest European mammal and can measure 2m (6.6ft).

BELORUSSIA

AGRICULTURE IS THE main occupation in Belorussia, despite poor soil. The capital city, Minsk, produces agricultural machinery.

Area 207,600sq km (80,154sq miles)
Government Multiparty republic
Independence 1991, from USSR
Currency Belorussian rouble
Population 10,199,709
Density 50 per sq km (129 per sq mile)
Official Language Belorussian
Major Religions Russian Orthodox 60%, Roman Catholic 8%, other 32%

ROMANIA

FORESTS COVER ABOUT a quarter of Romania and timber is an important product. The River Danube is used for transport and as a source of hydroelectric power.

Area 237,500sq km (91,700sq miles)
Government Multiparty republic
Independence 1881, from Ottoman Empire
Currency Leu
Population 22,800,000
Density 99 per sq km (257 per sq mile)
Official Language Romanian
Major Religions Romanian Orthodox 70%, Roman Catholic 6%, Catholic Eastern Rite 3%, Protestant 6%, other 15%

MOLDAVIA

WARM SUMMERS AND mild winters make Moldavia ideal for growing fruit, especially grapes. Moldavian people are Romanian in origin.

Area 33,700sq km (13,000sq miles)
Government Multiparty republic
Independence 1991, from USSR
Currency Moldavian leu
Population 4,400,000
Density 131 per sq km (339 per sq mile)
Official Language Romanian
Major Religions Romanian Orthodox 98%, other 2%

HUNGARY

HUNGARY HAS FERTILE soil and farmers grow wheat, sugar beet, and tobacco. The capital, Budapest, was originally Buda and Pest, two towns on either side of the River Danube.

Area 93,030sq km (35,919sq miles)
Government Multiparty republic
Independence 1918, after collapse of Austro-Hungarian monarchy
Currency Forint
Population 10,100,000
Density 109 per sq km (282 per sq mile)
Official Language Hungarian
Major Religions Roman Catholic 68%, Protestant 25%, other 7%

FACTS ABOUT ROMANIA AND HUNGARY
- There are about 410,000 gypsies (or Romanies) in Romania. The gypsies are thought to have arrived from India (via the Middle East) in about the 5th century A.D.

- Transylvania, which means "beyond the forest", is an area of Romania where music and folk art remain untouched. This wayside cross shows the skill of the woodcarver.

- Sunflowers are grown in Hungary for the oil which is extracted from their seeds. The stems of sunflowers turn so that the flowers can always face towards the sun.

- Peppers are cultivated in Hungary and ground into the spice, paprika. The rose paprika of Hungary has a special sweet flavour and is used in stews such as *gulyas*, or goulash. Paprika is made from the pods of the pepper *Capsicum annuum*.

Hand-carved wooden cross from Romania

The Gellert Baths in Budapest

- Hungary is famous for its medicinal waters, and Budapest has at least 120 hot springs. Every day, about 70 million litres (15.4 million gallons) of water well up to the surface, allowing thousands of people to enjoy the healing baths.

- The River Danube rises in the Alps of Germany and flows through eight countries on its journey to the Black Sea. The Danube is also called the Donau, Danuj, Duna, Dunav, Dunarea, and Dunay.

FEDERATION
Kharkiv
N E
Dnipropetrovs'k
Donets'k
Zaporizhzhya
...ovka Reservoir
Sea of Azov
...a
S E A

BULGARIA

BULGARIA HAS HIGH mountains and more than 600 natural springs. Grapes grow abundantly on the fertile plains, making Bulgaria the world's fourth largest wine exporter.

Area 110,910sq km (42,822sq miles)
Government Multiparty republic
Republic declared 1946
⚭ **Currency** Lev
👤 **Population** 8,800,000
Density 80 per sq km (207 per sq mile)
Official Language Bulgarian
✝ **Major Religions** Bulgarian Orthodox (Christian) 85%, Muslim 13%, Jewish 1%, other 1%

LANDMARK
St. Alexander Nevsky Cathedral, Sofia, completed in 1912, was built in honour of the Russian soldiers who died in the 1877–78 Russo–Turkish War.

GREECE

MORE THAN 1,400 islands surround Greece's heavily indented coastline; only 154 are inhabited. Greece has the second largest fleet of merchant ships in the world.

Area 131,990sq km (50,961sq miles)
Government Multiparty republic
⚭ **Independence** 1829, from Ottoman Empire
⚭ **Currency** Drachma
👤 **Population** 10,500,000
Density 80 per sq km (207 per sq mile)
Official Language Greek
✝ **Major Religions** Greek Orthodox (Christian) 98%, Muslim 1%, other 1%

LAND PROFILE
Even though 80% of Greece is mountainous, almost two-thirds of the land is used for farming and grazing.

5,000 drachmas

% 1 26 73

WEATHER FACTS

40.6°C (104°F)   635mm (25in)   -25°C (-13°F)

20°C (69°F)   -2.2°C (28°F)

LIFESTYLE FACTS

● Rose oil is one of the most precious ingredients of perfume. Bulgaria is the major supplier of rose oil and has the world's largest rose gardens at Kazanluk.

● Bulgarians nod their heads when they mean "no" and shake them when they mean "yes".

● In Gabrovo, Bulgaria, there is a national museum devoted entirely to humour called The House of Humour and Satire.

OLIVE
The national symbol of Greece is the olive branch.

LANGUAGE
A traditional greeting in Greek is *kalimera.* καλημερα

WEATHER FACTS

44°C (111°F)   414mm (16.3in)   -12°C (10°F)

28.2°C (82.8°F)   8.6°C (47°F)

GREEK MUSIC
One of the most important instruments in traditional Greek music is the bouzouki, which has metal strings. Traditional music is played at religious festivals and special occasions such as weddings.

LANGUAGE
A traditional greeting in Bulgarian is *dobró útro.*

LAND PROFILE
Bulgaria has extensive forests, and the land is mainly used for farming.

% 2 39 59

LION
The lion is the national symbol of Bulgaria and is depicted on its coat of arms.

PARTHENON
The Parthenon is a world-famous classical Greek temple dedicated to the goddess of Athens, Athena. It sits on a hill in Athens called the Acropolis, and was constructed between 447 and 432 B.C.

TURKEY

TURKEY LIES IN both Europe and Asia. The two continents are separated by the Bosphorus, site of the beautiful city of Istanbul, and one of the world's busiest waterways.

 Area 779,450sq km (300,950sq miles)
Government Multiparty republic
Republic declared 1923
Currency Turkish lira
Population 61,000,000
Density 80 per sq km (207 per sq mile)
Official Language Turkish
Major Religions Muslim 99%, Orthodox Christian, Roman Catholic, Protestant, Jewish 1%

WEATHER FACTS

43°C (109°F)   367mm (14.4in)   -36°C (-33°F)
23°C (73°F)   0.3°C (32.5°F)

LAND PROFILE

Land use in Turkey is predominantly agricultural.

%
0.75
4.25
23.5
28.0
43.5

LIFESTYLE FACTS

• Grapes, one of the world's oldest crops, were first grown in Anatolia. From here they spread to other parts of the world.

• Turkey's national sport is wrestling. *Kirkpinar*, the feast of wrestling, has been held each spring for 626 years.

PAMUKKALE

Pamukkale, meaning "cotton castle", is a brilliant-white hillside of cascading thermal pools fringed with stalactites. People have bathed in the warm, healing waters since Roman times.

LANGUAGE

A traditional greeting in Turkish is *iyi günler*.

TURKISH CARPETS

Turkey produces about 44 million sq m (474 million sq ft) of carpets each year. There are about 400 types of carpet, produced in centres such as Hereke, Malatya, Konya, and Kayseri.

• Turkey is the world's leading grower and exporter of figs, producing between 51,000 and 61,000 tonnes every year. Fresh, ripe figs are picked for eating from mid-July, or left to dry first on the tree branches, and then for a further two to four days in the hot sun.

TULIP

Turkey's national symbol is the tulip.

LIFESTYLE FACTS

• Greece, with its many mountains, has the greatest number of hill-farms in Europe. Goats are ideally suited to the terrain.

• In summer the flat roofs of houses on Greek islands are used for drying fruit and, in winter, for collecting rainwater.

• 8.2 million tourists visit Greece every year, drawn there by its ancient sites and sunny beaches.

TOP GREEK TOURIST RESORTS (1997)

Resort	Visitor-nights
Crete	10,619,000
Rhodes	8,238,000
Athens	3,438,000
Corfu	2,819,000

Source: Greek National Tourism Office

ALBANIA

MOST ALBANIANS live in remote mountain villages in this tiny, mountainous country. Albania's main crops are wheat, barley, tobacco, potatoes, and fruit.

 Area 28,750sq km (11,100sq miles)
Government Multiparty republic
Independence 1912, from Turkey
Currency Lek
Population 3,400,000
Density 124 per sq km (321 per sq mile)
Official Language Albanian
Major Religions Muslim 70%, Greek Orthodox 20%, Roman Catholic 10%

LIFESTYLE FACTS

• Since World War II, Albania has had the fastest-growing population in Europe. Good health care services for mother and child receive the highest priority from the government.

• More than half of the Albanian people earn their living from farming.

• In 1992, there were only about 6,000 telephones in the whole of Albania – one for every 550 people.

CYPRUS

CYPRUS IS THE LARGEST island in the eastern Mediterranean. It has both Greek and Turkish communities and, since 1974, the island has been split into two parts.

Area 9,251sq km (3,572sq miles)
Government Multiparty republic
Independence 1960, from Britain
Currency Cyprus pound/Turkish lira
Population 700,000
Density 77 per sq km (197 per sq mile)
Official Languages Greek and Turkish
Major Religions Greek Orthodox (Christian) 77%, Muslim 18%, other 5%

LIFESTYLE FACTS

• The ancient monuments of Cyprus are so important that some have been added to the UNESCO World Cultural Heritage list.

• Clothing, footwear, potatoes, grapes, and citrus fruit are Cyprus' main exports.

• The moufflon (*Ovis musimon*), a reddish-brown wild sheep, is native to Cyprus. It is the smallest wild sheep, reaching a height of just 74cm (29in).

SLOVENIA

SLOVENIA IS AN industrialized country with supplies of iron and steel. It is also a major producer of mercury, which is used in thermometers.

Area 20,250sq km (7,820sq miles)
Government Multiparty democracy
Currency Tolar
Population 1,900,000
Density 94 per sq km (244 per sq mile)
Official Language Slovene
Major Religions Roman Catholic 96%, other 4%

CROATIA

PART OF CROATIA runs along the coast of the Adriatic Sea, and was once a popular tourist destination. Supplies of limestone around Split help support the concrete industry.

Area 56,540sq km (21,830sq miles)
Government Multiparty democracy
Currency Kuna
Population 4,500,000
Density 80 per sq km (207 per sq mile)
Official Language Croatian
✝ **Major Religions** Roman Catholic 77%, Orthodox 11%, Muslim 1%, other 11%

LANGUAGE
A traditional greeting in Serbo-Croat is *dobró utro*.

REGIONAL LIFESTYLE FACTS

- The Dalmatian dog is named after the coastal region of Dalmatia in Croatia, which was its first known home.
- Walnuts grow well in the warm summers and well-drained soils of Yugoslavia.
- Dubrovnik, a city on Croatia's Adriatic coast, is famous for its traditional costumes of white dresses, embroidered blouses, and waistcoats.
- The picturesque city of Ljubljana is surrounded by mountains. Dominated by a medieval fortress, the city has an opera house, an art gallery, and a museum.

Traditional costume from Dubrovnik

YUGOSLAVIA

MADE UP OF the republics of Serbia and Montenegro, Yugoslavia is mountainous in the south, while the north is flat farmland. The capital, Belgrade, lies on the River Danube.

Area 102,173sq km (39,449sq miles)
Government Presidential republic
Currency Dinar
Population 10,580,892
Density 104 per sq km (269 per sq mile)
Official Language Serbian
Major Religions Christian 65%, Muslim 19%, other 16%

BOSNIA AND HERZEGOVINA

MINING FOR MINERALS, such as iron, copper, and silver, is an important part of the country's economy. Farmers grow olives, pomegranates, figs, rice, and tobacco.

Area 51,130sq km (19,741sq miles)
Government Parliamentary republic
Currency Bosnian dinar
Population 3,500,000
Density 68 per sq km (176 per sq mile)
Official Language Serbo-Croat
Major Religions Muslim 40%, Orthodox Catholic 31%, other 29%

CIVIL WAR
In 1990, Yugoslavia began to break up into independent countries. Serbia resisted this process, and in 1991 fighting broke out in Slovenia, Croatia, and Bosnia and Herzegovina. In 1995 the Dayton agreement separated the country into a Serb republic and a federation of Muslims and Croats.

The war-torn city of Sarajevo

MACEDONIA

ONCE PART OF YUGOSLAVIA, Macedonia is a mountainous region. Farmers grow wheat, millet, and barley in the upland valleys. Tobacco is the main crop grown for export.

Area 25,715sq km (9,929sq miles)
Government Parliamentary republic
Currency Denar
Population 1,900,000
Density 74 per sq km (192 per sq mile)
Official Language Macedonian
Major Religions Christian 64.5%, Muslim 21%, other 14.5%

GEORGIA

MOST OF GEORGIA is mountainous. The Black Sea coast is popular with tourists. The country has a humid climate that is ideal for growing tea and citrus fruits.

 Area 69,700sq km (26,911sq miles)
Government Republic
Independence 1991, from Soviet Union
Currency Coupons
Population 5,500,000
Official Language Georgian
† Major Religions Georgian Orthodox 70%, Russian Orthodox 10%, other 20%

LIFESTYLE FACTS
• Vines thrive on the warm, sunny hills of eastern Georgia, where wine and brandy are produced.
• Visitors are attracted to Georgia's health spas, waterfalls, and natural caves.

• Sweet tea, served black and strong, is a popular drink throughout the countries that lie around the Caucasus Mountains. Crops for both green and black teas are grown on large plantations in Georgia.

THE BLACK SEA
Tourism is a major part of the Georgian economy. Many resorts and spas, with beaches and forests, attract tourists to the coast of the Black Sea.

The Black Sea resort of Bat'umi

LANGUAGE
A traditional greeting in Georgian is *garmardzobat*.

TEXTILES
Georgia is famous for its silk and textiles. Brightly patterned cloth is woven with gold and silver thread. The cloth is often worn as a headscarf.

N

0 —— 150km
0 —— 80 miles

ARMENIA

ARMENIA IS A mainly mountainous country, and most people live in the foothills or around the Ararat Plain. Crops include orchard fruits such as peaches, apricots, and cherries.

 Area 29,000sq km (11,505sq miles)
Government Multiparty republic
Independence 1991, from Soviet Union
Currency Dram
Population 3,600,000
Official Language Armenian
† Major Religions Armenian Apostolic 90%, other 10%

LIFESTYLE FACTS

• Armenia grows rare plants used in perfumery and medicine, including geranium, rose, peppermint, cinchona bark, and basma.
• Lake Sevan is a major recreation area and offers windsurfing, sailing, swimming, and water skiing.

MAIN AGRICULTURAL PRODUCTS (1998)	
Product	Amount (thousand tonnes)
Vegetables	452
Potatoes	425
Fruit	295
Wheat	165
Grapes	150
Meat	42

AZERBAIJAN

OIL AND NATURAL gas are the most important products in Azerbaijan and Baku, the capital, is the major industrial centre. Fruit, walnuts, and hazelnuts are valuable export crops.

 Area 86,600sq km (33,436sq miles)
Government Multiparty republic
Independence 1991, from Soviet Union
Currency Manat
Population 7,600,000
Official Language Azerbaijani
♪ Major Religions Muslim 83%, Armenian Apostolic and Russian Orthodox 17%

LIFESTYLE FACTS
• In the warm climate around Länkäran, farmers grow oranges, lemons, and figs.
• Light industry in Azerbaijan includes cotton and woollen goods, footwear, traditional household items, and souvenirs.

WILDLIFE FACTS
• The mountains and forests of Azerbaijan are home to a variety of wildlife, including wild boar, brown bears, European bison, chamois, and leopards, although the leopard is now very rare.

Chamois

• The mild winters attract many birds to the coast of the Caspian Sea. A reservation provides a seasonal resting place for flamingoes, swans, pelicans, herons, and buzzards.

Pelican

• Musical tradition is strong in Azerbaijan. The music of the *ashugs*, who improvise songs to their own accompaniment on a stringed instrument called a *kobuz*, is extremely popular.

• Almost 90% of Azerbaijan's electricity is produced at hydroelectric power stations throughout the country.

RUSSIAN FEDERATION

THE LARGEST COUNTRY in the world, the Russian Federation stretches across two continents – Europe and Asia – that are separated by the Ural Mountains. Most people live in the western third of the country.

Area 17,075,400sq km (6,592,800sq miles)
Government Presidential republic
Independence 1991, from the former Soviet Union
Currency Rouble
Population 147,021,869
Density 9 per sq km (23 per sq mile)
Official Language Russian
Major Religions Russian Orthodox 80%, others (including Jewish and Muslim) 20%

WEATHER FACTS

39°C (102°F)   575mm (22.6in)   -68°C (-90°F)
18.9°C (66°F)   -9°C (16°F)

LAND PROFILE
Half the land in the Russian Federation is covered in forest.

%
0.5
2
6
10
13
18.5
50

ST. BASIL'S CATHEDRAL
The 16th-century St. Basil's Cathedral in Moscow is a magnificent example of old Russian architecture. It is situated within the Kremlin, the original fortress at the historic heart of the city. The cathedral was completed in 1560 and has nine great domes. It is now open as a museum.

St. Basil's was built on the orders of Tsar Ivan IV the Terrible in gratitude for his military victories.

LANGUAGE
A traditional greeting in Russian is *zdravstvuyitye*.
Здравствуйте

NATIONAL ANIMAL
The brown bear *(Ursus arctos)* is the national symbol of Russia. In folklore it is linked with kindness and wisdom. Bears eat fruits, berries, and bulbs that they dig up with their claws.

0   600km
0   300 miles

Barents Sea
Arctic Circle
NORWAY
FINLAND
Novaya Ze
R U S S
St. Petersburg
ESTONIA
LATVIA
LITHUANIA
BELORUSSIA
RUSSIAN FED.
Moscow
Nizhniy Novgorod
Chelyabinsk
Ural Mountai
UKRAINE
KAZAKH
Astrakhan
Black Sea
Caucasus Mountains
Caspian Sea

LIFESTYLE FACTS
• Ballet is a popular form of entertainment in Russia. The dance company that became the Bolshoi Ballet was founded in 1773. It is famous for classical ballets such as *Swan Lake*.

• From October to March, Moscow receives an average of 15 minutes sunshine a day. Snow can lie on the ground for up to five months every year.

• Russians love to eat ice-cream, which can be bought from places marked *morozhenoe*.

ST. PETERSBURG
St. Petersburg, formerly called Leningrad, is a major industrial centre. The centre of the city is the Nevsky Prospekt, a street lined with shops, cafés, and theatres.

PASTIMES
• One of the most famous circuses in the world is in Russia. The acrobats of the New Moscow Circus are highly skilled.

• Chess is a popular game, and many people practise in Gorky Park, Moscow.

TOLSTOY
Leo Tolstoy (1828–1910) is one of the world's greatest novelists. His most famous book, *War and Peace*, is set in Russia during the Napoleonic Wars. It examines the feelings of the Russians as the French invade their country in 1812.

FAMOUS RUSSIAN WRITERS

Name	Date	Key work
Alexander Pushkin	1799–1837	*Eugene Onegin*
Fyodor Dostoyevsky	1821–81	*Crime and Punishment*
Boris Pasternak	1890–1960	*Dr. Zhivago*
Vladimir Nabokov	1899–1977	*Lolita*
Alexander Solzhenitsyn	b.1918–	*The Gulag Archipelago*

• The former Soviet Union had more than half of all cinemas in the world, selling an average of 80 million tickets a week. Sergei Eisenstein, a famous Russian film maker from the 1920s, made *Battleship Potemkin*.

• Reading is popular in Russia. Men spend one-eighth of their free time reading a book or newspaper. Women spend one-sixth of their free time reading.

POPULAR RUSSIAN FOOD
Russians have a fattening diet that includes potatoes, fats, and sugar. Their food energy intake is 70% higher than the USA's.
Borscht This pinkish-red soup is made from beetroot, and can be eaten hot or cold. It is often served with sour cream.
Blinis These pancakes are made using buckwheat, filled with meat or cheese, and then browned.
Charlotte Russe This special pudding was created for Russian royalty. It is made in a mould lined with sponge, and filled with both ice-cream and whipped cream.

A plate of blinis served with red caviar.

SIBERIAN WEALTH
Beneath its icy surface, western Siberia has vast reserves of coal, gas, and oil. The area provides fuel for the industries of western Russia, and gas is piped to western Europe.

SIBERIA FACTS
• The region of Siberia covers 12.5 million sq km (4.8 million sq miles) of the eastern, or Asiatic, part of Russia. Its name comes from the word "sibi" which means "sleeping land".
• In the north lies the tundra, where the ground is frozen for much of the year. This is known as permafrost.
• The snowy owl (*Nyctea scandiaca*) glides over the tundra hunting for small mammals.

• South of the tundra, vast expanses of conifer trees make up the largest forest in the world. The cones of the larch, fir, and spruce trees provide food for animals during the long winter.

• The Chukchi people live on the Kamchatka peninsula and survive by hunting, herding reindeer, and fishing. The Siberian husky dog was first raised by the Chukchi, who used the dogs as companions and to pull their sleds.

GOLD AND DIAMONDS
During the 1840s, prospectors found gold in the area around the River Lena, in northern Siberia. Today the area has four major gold fields as well as 800 diamond mines.

Heavy-duty machinery digs for minerals in northern Siberia.

URAL MOUNTAIN FACTS
• The Ural Mountains stretch for 2,100km (1,300 miles) from the Kara Sea in the north to Kazakhstan in the south.
• Only 40–200km (25–125 miles) wide, the mountains left Russia open to attack in its early history.

RUSSIAN ICONS
Beautiful icons, religious images painted on wood, adorn Russian churches and homes. For many years Christians were persecuted in the old Soviet Union.

This icon shows the Madonna and Child.

TIME DIFFERENCE
The Russian Federation covers 10 time zones. This means that when it is morning in the west, it is already early evening in the east.

Time to get up in St. Petersburg

At school in Irkutsk

Getting ready for bed in Anadyr'

TRANS-SIBERIAN EXPRESS
The longest railway line in the world crosses the Russian Federation. Started in 1881, the railway was vital for the mining and transport of Siberia's minerals. The journey from Moscow to Vladivostock takes about 165 hours.

Moscow	3,219km (2,000 miles)	Novosibirsk	1,609km (1,000 miles)	Irkutsk	1,448km (900 miles)	Chita	3,621km (2,250 miles)	Vladivostok

AFRICA

AFRICA IS THE second largest and warmest of the continents. It is also the only continent through which the Equator and both Tropics pass. Landscape and vegetation include rainforest, grassy savannah, and hot desert.

CLIMATE ZONES

KEY

▨	Mediterranean
▨	Dry grassland
▨	Hot desert
▨	Rainforest
▨	Tropical grassland

Area 30,131,536sq km (11,633,846sq miles)
Countries 54
Largest Sudan 2,505,810sq km (967,498sq miles)
Smallest Seychelles 280sq km (108sq miles)
🏠 **Population** 678,428,967
Density 21 per sq km (54 per sq mile)
Major Languages Arabic, Swahili, Hausa, Somali, Amharic

▲ **Highest point** Kilimanjaro, Tanzania 5,895m (19,341ft)
◪ **Lowest point** Lake Assal, Djibouti 156m (512ft) below sea level
☀ **Highest temperature** 58°C (136°F) Al' Aziziyah, Libya
✳ **Lowest temperature** -24°C (-11°F) Ilfrane, Morocco

TIME ZONES

| 12:00 Greenwich | 13:00 Libreville | 14:00 Cairo | 15:00 Addis Ababa |

CONTINENT FACTS

• The world's largest desert is the African Sahara, with an area of 8,600,000sq km (3,320,000sq miles). It is bigger than all of Australia.

• Half of all Africans are under 15, making Africa the continent with the world's highest percentage of young people. Only 3 out of 100 can expect to live to be 65 years of age.

• Western Sahara, with just one person per sq km (2.6 per sq mile), is the world's least densely populated country.

• The earliest evidence of humans – the oldest known human footprints – were found in the Olduvai Gorge, Tanzania.

• Africa has more countries than any other continent: 54 in total.

COUNTRIES, TERRITORIES, AND CAPITALS

Name	Capital
Algeria	Algiers
Angola	Luanda
Benin	Porto-Novo
Botswana	Gaborone
Burkina	Ouagadougou
Burundi	Bujumbura
Cameroon	Yaoundé
Cape Verde	Praia
Central African Republic	Bangui
Chad	N'Djamena
Comoros	Moroni
Congo	Brazzaville
Djibouti	Djibouti
Egypt	Cairo
Equatorial Guinea	Malabo
Eritrea	Asmara
Ethiopia	Addis Ababa
Gabon	Libreville
Gambia	Banjul
Ghana	Accra
Guinea	Conakry
Guinea-Bissau	Bissau
Ivory Coast	Yamoussoukro
Kenya	Nairobi
Lesotho	Maseru
Liberia	Monrovia
Libya	Tripoli

Name	Capital
Madagascar	Antananarivo
Malawi	Lilongwe
Mali	Bamako
Mauritania	Nouakchott
Mauritius	Port Louis
Morocco	Rabat
Mozambique	Maputo
Namibia	Windhoek
Niger	Niamey
Nigeria	Abuja
Rwanda	Kigali
Sao Tome and Principe	São Tomé
Senegal	Dakar
Seychelles	Victoria
Sierra Leone	Freetown
Somalia	Mogadishu
South Africa	Pretoria
Sudan	Khartoum
Swaziland	Mbabane
Tanzania	Dodoma
Togo	Lomé
Tunisia	Tunis
Uganda	Kampala
Western Sahara	Laâyoune
Zaire	Kinshasa
Zambia	Lusaka
Zimbabwe	Harare

AGE BREAKDOWN

| Under 15 years | 15 to 65 years | Over 65 years |

Zambia 2.2%
Seychelles 6%
Mauritius 29.4%
Kenya 49.9%
Kenya 47.3%
Mauritius 65.2%

KEY
▨ Lowest %
▨ Highest %

FEWEST DOCTORS

Rwanda	1 to 72,990 people
Burkina	1 to 57,320 people
Botswana	1 to 51,590 people
Guinea	1 to 46,000 people
Malawi	1 to 45,740 people

LONGEST LIFESPAN

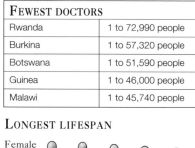

Female
Male

74 73 69 68 67
65 67 65 66 64

Seychelles Mauritius Botswana Tunisia Sao Tome and Principe

GREAT RIFT VALLEY

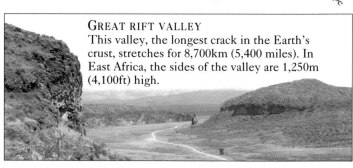

This valley, the longest crack in the Earth's crust, stretches for 8,700km (5,400 miles). In East Africa, the sides of the valley are 1,250m (4,100ft) high.

TOP CITY POPULATIONS

Abidjan, Ivory Coast 1,929,079
Casablanca, Morocco 3,200,000
Alexandria, Egypt 3,328,000
Kinshasa, Zaire 3,741,000
Cairo, Egypt 6,452,000

LONGEST RIVERS

Zambesi 2,735km (1,700 miles)
Niger 4,167km (2,589 miles)
Congo (Zaire) 4,373km (2,717 miles)
Nile 6,695km (4,160 miles)
Cairo
Lake Victoria

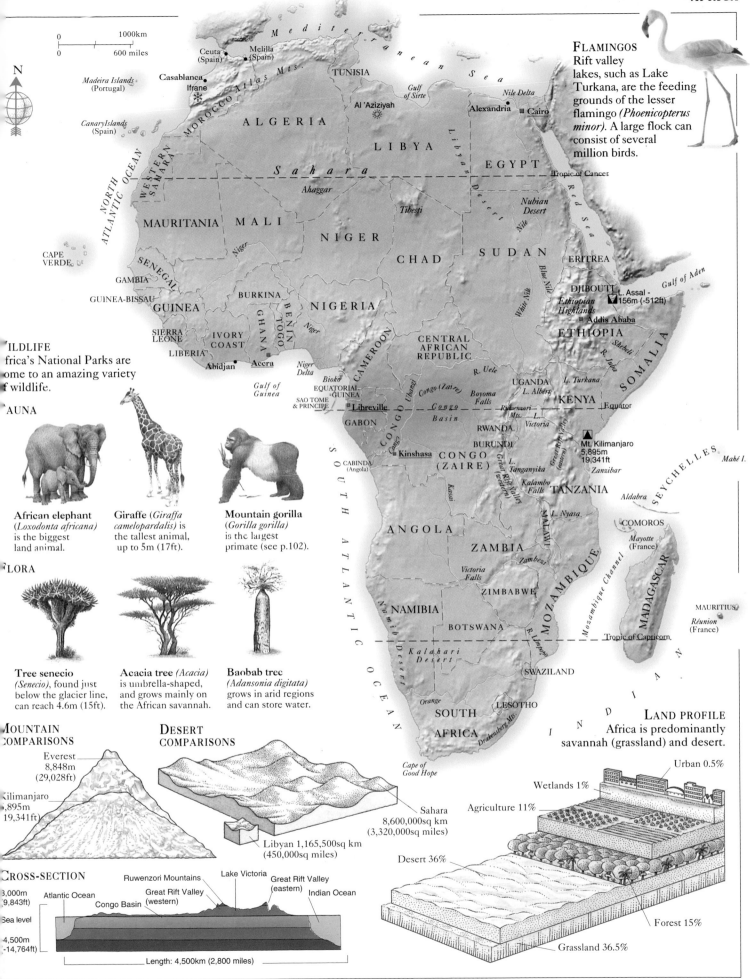

FLAMINGOS
Rift valley lakes, such as Lake Turkana, are the feeding grounds of the lesser flamingo (*Phoenicopterus minor*). A large flock can consist of several million birds.

WILDLIFE
Africa's National Parks are home to an amazing variety of wildlife.

FAUNA

African elephant (*Loxodonta africana*) is the biggest land animal.

Giraffe (*Giraffa camelopardalis*) is the tallest animal, up to 5m (17ft).

Mountain gorilla (*Gorilla gorilla*) is the largest primate (see p.102).

FLORA

Tree senecio (*Senecio*), found just below the glacier line, can reach 4.6m (15ft).

Acacia tree (*Acacia*) is umbrella-shaped, and grows mainly on the African savannah.

Baobab tree (*Adansonia digitata*) grows in arid regions and can store water.

MOUNTAIN COMPARISONS

Everest 8,848m (29,028ft)

Kilimanjaro 5,895m 19,341ft

DESERT COMPARISONS

Sahara 8,600,000sq km (3,320,000sq miles)

Libyan 1,165,500sq km (450,000sq miles)

CROSS-SECTION

3,000m (9,843ft)
Sea level
4,500m (14,764ft)

Atlantic Ocean
Congo Basin
Great Rift Valley (western)
Ruwenzori Mountains
Lake Victoria
Great Rift Valley (eastern)
Indian Ocean

Length: 4,500km (2,800 miles)

LAND PROFILE
Africa is predominantly savannah (grassland) and desert.

Urban 0.5%
Wetlands 1%
Agriculture 11%
Desert 36%
Forest 15%
Grassland 36.5%

327

EGYPT

MOST OF EGYPT is barren desert, with 99 per cent of the population living by the River Nile. Farmers, called *fellahin*, grow cotton, wheat, rice, and vegetables. The Great Pyramid at Giza is one of the seven wonders of the ancient world.

Area 1,001,450sq km (386,662sq miles)
Government Presidential republic
Independence 1936, from Britain
Currency Egyptian pound
Population 62,900,000
Density 63 per sq km (163 per sq mile)
Official Language Arabic
Major Religions Muslim 94%, other 6%

WEATHER FACTS

51°C (124°F) 29mm (1.1in) 1°C (34°F)
28.2°C (82.8°F) 14.3°C (57.8°F)

LAND PROFILE
Only 4.5 per cent of the land in Egypt can be cultivated.

%
0.5
0.5
4.5
6.5
88.0

LIFESTYLE FACTS
• Overpopulation is a problem in Egypt. The estimated birth rate is one baby born every 24 seconds.

• Egypt is the world's top producer of dates, and the fourth largest producer of water-melons.

• Tolls from the Suez Canal, completed in 1869, now bring the Egyptian government more than US $500 million each year.

One Egyptian pound

LANGUAGE
A traditional greeting in Arabic is *ahlan wasahlan.* اَهلاً وَسَهلاً

GREAT PYRAMIDS
The pyramids at Giza were built in about 2600 B.C. to house the mummified bodies of Egyptian kings, or pharaohs. The largest pyramid contains more than 2 million stone blocks and took 100,000 men more than 20 years to build.

MAJOR COTTON IMPORTERS FROM ALL SOURCES (1996)

Destination	Amount in thousand US$
China	1,276,438
Italy	786,089
South Korea	717,276
Thailand	693,224
Indonesia	680,256

SUDAN

SUDAN IS THE largest country in Africa and includes the swampy Sudd region. Sudan exports gum arabic, used in watercolour painting.

Area 2,505,815sq km (967,493sq miles)
Independence 1956, from Anglo-Egyptian agreement
Currency Sudanese dinar
Population 28,100,000
Official Language Arabic
Major Religions Muslim 70%, Christian 5%, traditional beliefs 20%, other 5%

ETHIOPIA

FOUR OUT OF five Ethiopians work on the land, with coffee as the main cash crop. The Blue Nile flows from Lake Tana in the north.

Area 1,221,900sq km (471,778sq miles)
Foundation More than 2,000 years; never colonized
Currency Birr
Population 51,300,000
Official Language Amharic
Major Religions Muslim 40%, Ethiopian Orthodox 40%, traditional beliefs 15%, other 5%

LOCUST ATTACK
Massive swarms of locusts sometimes sweep across the African continent, destroying huge areas of crops in just minutes. Large swarms can weigh up to 50,000 tonnes.

SOMALIA

SOMALIA'S ECONOMY is based on rearing animals for use or profit. Bananas, a major export, are grown on riverside plantations.

Area 637,660sq km (246,200sq miles)
Independence 1960, formation of Somali Republic
Currency Somali shilling
Population 9,300,000
Official Languages Arabic, Somali
Major Religions Muslim 99%, other 1%

WATER FACTS
• Two billion people in the world lack access to safe water.

• A family of six needs about 91 litres (20 gallons) of water a day for basic needs, such as drinking and keeping clean.

• In Ethiopia 39.5 million people have no access to a safe supply of water. In Sudan the figure is 14.7 million, in Somalia, 4.8 million.

• In the Sudan it takes at least 2 hours, or a journey of 8km (5 miles), every day to fetch water. The work is usually done by women and children.

DJIBOUTI

DJIBOUTI IS AN important trading port for Ethiopia and occupies a prime site between the Indian Ocean and the Red Sea.

Area 23,200sq km (8,958sq miles)
Independence 1977, from France
Currency Djibouti franc
Population 500,000
Official Language Arabic, French
Major Religions Muslim 94%, other 6%

ERITREA

ERITREA IS A hot country with very little rainfall and locust plagues that make farming difficult. Many people live as nomads.

Area 93,679sq km (36,170sq miles)
Independence 1993, from Ethiopia
Currency Birr
Population 3,500,000
Official Language Amharic
Major Religions No figures available. People of the mountains are Christians; lowland Eritreans are Muslim

TANZANIA

THE MAIN EXPORT crops of Tanzania include sisal, which is used to make rope. Most of the world's cloves grow on the islands of Zanzibar.

Area 945,090sq km (364,900sq miles)
Independence 1961, from Britain
Currency Tanzanian shilling
Population 29,700,000
Official Language English, Swahili
Major Religions Traditional beliefs 42%, Christian 27%, Muslim 31%

N

KENYA

KENYA LIES ON the Equator. It consists of dry grasslands, which are home to wildlife such as elephants, lions, and zebras. Most people live in the highlands of the southwest, where there is enough rain to grow crops and graze cattle and sheep.

Area 580,370sq km (224,081sq miles)
Government Presidential republic
Independence 1963, from Britain
Currency Kenya shilling
Population 28,300,000
Density 50 per sq km (130 per sq mile)
Official Language Swahili
Major Religions Christian 66%, Traditional beliefs 26%, other 8%

WEATHER FACTS

37°C (98°F)   959mm (37.7in)   5°C (41°F)

18.6°C (65.6°F)   16.5°C (61.7°F)

LIFESTYLE FACTS

• Kenya has the world's youngest population with about 50% of the people under 15 years of age.

• There are two rainy seasons in Kenya. The "long" rains are between March and May and "short" rains between October and November.

• Kenya produces 80% of the world's pyrethrum. The flowers of this type of chrysanthemum are dried and used for making insecticide.

LAND PROFILE

Almost two-thirds of Kenya is covered in grassland.

%
0.5
2.6
8.6
10.7
14.9
62.7

Masai warriors

MASAI FACTS

• The Masai are a tribe of nomadic herders who live on the borders of Kenya and Tanzania.

• They survive on the meat, blood, and milk of their herds.

• Between the ages of 14 and 30, the young men live in the bush learning the skills that will make them great warriors.

UGANDA

ONE-FIFTH OF Uganda consists of large lakes and swamps. Most farmers grow their own food, such as sweet potatoes, maize, and beans, although coffee is grown for export.

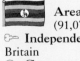

Area 235,880sq km (91,073sq miles)
Independence 1962, from Britain
Currency New Uganda shilling
Population 21,300,000
Official Languages English, Swahili
Major Religions Christian 66%, Traditional beliefs 18%, Muslim 16%

MAJOR NATIONAL PARKS AND GAME RESERVES

Name	Size	Key animal
Selous Tanzania, Tanzania	45,000sq km (17,375sq miles)	
Tsavo National Park, Kenya	20,812sq km (8,035sq miles)	
Serengeti National Park, Tanzania	14,76 sq km (5,700sq miles)	
Ruaha National Park, Tanzania	12,950sq km (5,000sq miles)	
Ngorongoro Conservation Area, Tanzania	8,292sq km (3,201sq miles)	

MOROCCO

MOROCCO HAS MILD winters and hot, dry summers. On the fertile coastal plains farmers grow fruits and vegetables that are canned for export. Most people are Berbers, the name given to them by their Arab conquerors in the 7th century.

Area 698,670sq km (269,757sq miles)
Government Constitutional monarchy
Independence 1956, from France
Currency Moroccan dirham
Population 27,000,000
Density 60 per sq km (155 per sq mile)
Official Language Arabic
♪ **Major Religions** Sunni Muslim 99%, Christian, Jewish and other 1%

WEATHER FACTS

49°C (120°F)   -3°C (27°F)
503mm (20in)
22.2°C (72°F)   13°C (55.4°F)

LAND PROFILE

Almost 40% of Morocco is grassland.

%
0.2
2.3
11.1
23.0
24.5
38.9

FLOWER FACTS

• In Morocco, roses, gladioli, carnations, irises, and marigolds are grown for export. In 1991, production reached 2,500 tonnes.

• Saffron, used to flavour rice, is produced in the eastern region of Morocco. Saffron comes from the crocus flower, and it takes about 400,000 stamens to make 1kg (2.2lb).

LIFESTYLE FACTS

• A covered market, called a souk, is where Moroccan traders sell spices, fruits, and textiles.

• Skilled craftworkers make beautiful pictures using wood from lemon, cedar, and sandalwood trees.

• The Moroccan leather industry produces shoes, bags, and clothes. Tanning, the process of turning animal skins into leather, is also an important industry.

FANTASIA

Every year in Morocco there is an event called the Fantasia. Two groups of horsemen in traditional dress charge the length of the arena, firing rifles. The spectacle dates back to the ancient warfare tactics of Berber horsemen.

LANGUAGE

A traditional greeting in Arabic is *ahlan wasahlan*.

أَهْلاً وَسَهْلاً

MARRAKESH MOSQUE

The Koutoubia Mosque, Marrakesh, was built during the 11th century on the orders of Yacoub El Mansour. Its minaret stands 70m (230ft) tall. It is known as the booksellers' mosque because traders used to gather outside to sell their books.

MAJOR EXPORTS (1996–97)	
Product	Value in US$
Canned fish	180,624,000
Tomatoes	90,894,000
Green beans	893,000
Apricots	59,000
Olives	58,000

WESTERN SAHARA

WESTERN SAHARA IS the emptiest country in the world with just one person per sq km (2.6 per sq mile). Few crops are grown, but farmers raise goats and sheep.

Area 252,120sq km (97,344sq miles)
Independence 1976, from Spain; currently occupied by Morocco
Currency Moroccan dirham
Population 200,000
Official Language None; most people speak different Arabic dialects
♪ **Major Religion** Muslim 100%

MALI

ONLY ABOUT 2 per cent of Mali is arable land. Cotton and groundnuts are the main crops. The Malinke and Songhai tribes have a reputation for fine music and dancing.

Area 1,240,190sq km (478,837sq miles)
Independence 1960, from France
Currency CFA franc
Population 10,800,000
Official Language French
♪ **Major Religions** Muslim 80%, Christian and other 2%, traditional beliefs 18%

MAURITANIA

MAURITANIA IS HOT and dry, and sand dunes cover half the country. Antelopes, lions, and elephants live in the southern grasslands. Fish from the Atlantic are exported.

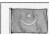

Area 1,025,520sq km (395,955sq miles)
Independence 1960, from France
Currency Ouguiya
Population 2,200,000
Official Language Arabic
♪ **Major Religions** Sunni Muslim 99%, other 1%

NIGER

NORTHERN NIGER IS almost empty and most people live in the south. One-sixth of the population still lives as nomads. Niger is one of the world's top producers of uranium.

Area 1,267,000 sq km (489,188sq miles)
Independence 1960, from France
Currency CFA franc
Population 9,200,000
Official Language French
♪ **Major Religions** Muslim 85%, traditional beliefs 14%, Christian 1%

CAPE VERDE

THE VOLCANIC Cape Verde islands are divided into the Windward and Leeward groups. Most of the people are Creole, and the main crops include bananas and sugar-cane.

Area 4,030sq km (1,556sq miles)
Independence 1975, from Portugal
Currency Cape Verde escudo
Population 400,000
Official Language Portuguese
✝ **Major Religions** Roman Catholic 98%, Protestant and other 2%

ALGERIA

MORE THAN 80 per cent of Algeria lies within the Sahara desert. The discovery of oil and natural gas in the desert has made these the country's main exports.

Area 2,381,740sq km (919,590sq miles)
Independence 1962, from France
Currency Algerian dinar
Population 27,900,000
Official Language Arabic
Major Religions Sunni Muslim 99%, Christian, Jewish and other 1%

ROCK ART
This rock painting from Tassili N'Ajjer, dated about 6000 B.C., shows nomadic herders. Until about 4500 B.C., the Sahara was not a desert. There was enough rain to support animals, such as gazelles and buffaloes.

SAHARA FACTS
• The Sahara (the word means desert) is the world's largest desert and covers 8,600,000 sq km (3,320,000sq miles): almost as large as the United States of America.

• The dromedary camel is adapted to life in the desert. It can travel 160km (100 miles) a day for eight days without drinking any water.

• Despite its popular image, only about 20% of the Sahara is continuous sand. The sand often forms into pyramid-shaped dunes which can be up to 230m (750ft) tall.

PIPED WATER
Beneath the Sahara there are vast underground supplies of water. The Libyans have built a series of pipelines to carry water to the coastal areas for increased crop production.

DESERT TRIBES
The Tuareg, who are of Berber origin, are nomadic tribes who live on the edge of the Sahara. Long scarves protect them from the heat and dust.

TUNISIA

GENERALLY TUNISIA HAS poor soil and relies on tourism for most of its income. Esparto grass, which grows on the plains, is used to make quality paper.

Area 163,610sq km (63,170sq miles)
Independence 1956, from France
Currency Tunisian dinar
Population 8,900,000
Official Language Arabic
Major Religions Muslim 99%, Christian, Jewish, and other 1%

FALCONRY
In Tunisia, falcons are used to hunt quail, hare, and partridge during the summer.

LIBYA

LIBYA IS ONE of the world's leading producers of oil. Although the country is mainly desert, citrus fruits, figs, and dates are grown in the southern oases.

Area 1,759,540sq km (679,358sq miles)
Independence 1951, from Italy
Currency Libyan dinar
Population 5,400,000
Official Language Arabic
Major Religions Sunni Muslim 97%, other 3%

CHAD

CHAD HAS A landscape of desert, grassland, and tropical forests. Most crops, including cotton, are grown in the south. Sodium bicarbonate (natron) is mined near Lake Chad.

Area 1,284,000sq km (495,752sq miles)
Independence 1960, from France
Currency CFA franc
Population 6,400,000
Official Languages Arabic, French
Major Religions Muslim 44%, Christian 33%, traditional beliefs 23%

Map labels

MEDITERRANEAN SEA
Strait of Gibraltar
Ceuta (Spain)
Melilla (Spain)
Rabat
Koutoubia Mosque (Marrakesh)
Algiers
Tunis
Chambi 1,544m (5,066ft)
Chott Melrhir
Chott El Jerid
TUNISIA
Tripoli
Gulf of Sirte
Libyan Desert
EGYPT
ATLANTIC OCEAN
MOROCCO
ATLAS MOUNTAINS
Oued er Rbia
Chelif
Medjerda
Laâyoune
WESTERN SAHARA
ALGERIA
LIBYA
SAHARA
Tassili N'Ajjer
Kediet Ijill 915m (3,002ft)
Tahat 2,918m (9,574ft)
Ahaggar
Plateau du Manguéni
Rette 2,286m (7,500ft)
Tibesti
Emi Koussi 3,415m (11,205ft)
MAURITANIA
Nouakchott
L. Rkiz
MALI
L.Faguibine
Ténéré du Tafassasset
Talak Air
Bagzane 2,022m (6,634ft)
NIGER
CHAD
Senegal
SENEGAL
Niger
Niger
Niamey
L.Chad
N'Djamena
Bamako
765m (2,510ft)
BURKINA
GUINEA
IVORY COAST
NIGERIA
CAMEROON
SUDAN
Chari
CENTRAL AFRICAN REPUBLIC

CAPE VERDE
São Tiago
Praia

N

0   75km
0   40 miles

NIGERIA

NIGERIA IS AFRICA'S most heavily populated country, and two-thirds of the people live in farming villages. The most valuable crops are cacao, palm products, and rubber, with oil as the main export.

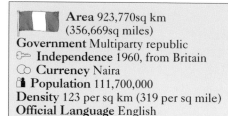
Area 923,770sq km (356,669sq miles)
Government Multiparty republic
⚷ **Independence** 1960, from Britain
◯ **Currency** Naira
🛄 **Population** 111,700,000
Density 123 per sq km (319 per sq mile)
Official Language English

LAND PROFILE
More than half of Nigeria is grassland.

%
0.2
3.5
4.5
25.5
66.3

LIFESTYLE FACTS
• Nigeria spends a lot of money on education. The country has 33 universities with more than 243,000 students.

• All twins in Nigeria, boys and girls, are given the same names. The firstborn is called Taiwo, the second is Kehinde.

• The main ethnic groups in Nigeria are the Hausa (north), the Ibo (east), and the Yoruba (south and west).

10 naira

A traditional greeting in the Hausa language is *ina-kwna.*

MARKETS
This scene in Benin City shows a woman buying chillis for the hot sauce used in cooking. She wears a length of patterned cloth, called a *pagne*, around her waist.

SENEGAL

IN THIS FLAT country, peanuts (groundnuts) are grown to make oil for export. The capital, Dakar, is West Africa's most important port.

Area 196,720sq km (75,950sq miles)
⚷ **Independence** 1960, from France; republic declared
◯ **Currency** CFA franc
🛄 **Population** 8,300,000
Official Language French

THE GAMBIA

GAMBIA IS AFRICA'S smallest country, and stretches for 320km (200 miles) on either side of the River Gambia. The main cash crop is peanuts.

Area 11,300sq km (4,363sq miles)
⚷ **Independence** 1965, from Britain; 1970, republic declared.
◯ **Currency** Dalasi
🛄 **Population** 1,100,000
Official Language English

PEANUT FACTS
• Peanuts (or groundnuts) are a major crop in West Africa. Despite the name, it is not a true nut.

• The pod, or peanut, has the unusual habit of ripening underground.

• There are about 300 by-products of peanuts, including flour, soap, and plastics.

GUINEA-BISSAU

THE COAST HAS a monsoon climate with heavy rainfall between May and October. Water birds include pelicans and flamingos.

Area 36,120sq km (13,940sq miles)
⚷ **Independence** 1974, from Portugal
◯ **Currency** Guinea peso
🛄 **Population** 1,100,000
Official Language Portuguese

GUINEA

GUINEA IS THE world's second biggest producer of the mineral bauxite. Iron ore, gold, and diamonds are also mined here.

Area 245,860sq km (94,926sq miles)
⚷ **Independence** 1958, from France
◯ **Currency** Guinean franc
🛄 **Population** 6,700,000
Official Language French

SIERRA LEONE

PORTUGUESE EXPLORERS in the 15th century named this country, which means "lion mountain". Diamonds and bauxite are the main exports.

Area 71,740sq km (27,699sq miles)
⚷ **Independence** 1961, from Britain
◯ **Currency** Leone
🛄 **Population** 4,500,000
Official Language English

LANGUAGE RHYTHMS

The Ashanti language of West Africa is a tonal language, and a special drum can be played to reproduce the tonal pattern of a word. Drum language, which has its own vocabulary, can be used to send messages from one village to another.

TALKING DRUMS

The *kalungu*, or talking drum, is held together with thongs that link the two skins. When the "waist" is squeezed, the sound can be changed.

animal skin

"waist"

leather thongs

LIBERIA

LIBERIA WAS FOUNDED as a home for freed slaves from the USA. High-quality iron ore has replaced rubber as the country's most valuable product.

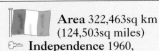

Area 111,370sq km (43,000sq miles)
Independence 1847, independent state founded
Currency Liberian dollar
Population 3,000,000
Official Language English

IVORY COAST

THERE ARE 66 different tribes living in the Ivory Coast. One tribe, the Dan, carve beautiful masks for use in their traditional ceremonies.

Area 322,463sq km (124,503sq miles)
Independence 1960, from France
Currency CFA franc
Population 14,500,000
Official Language French

BURKINA

BURKINA IS AN inland country on the southern edge of the Sahara Desert. Infertile soils mean that less than 10 per cent of the land can be farmed.

Area 274,200sq km (105,850sq miles)
Independence 1960, from France
Currency CFA franc
Population 10,300,000
Official Language French

NIGERIA WEATHER FACTS

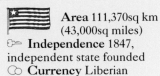

46°C (114°F) 1838mm (72in) 6°C (43°F)

27.6°C (81.7°F) 26°C (78.8°F)

ANCIENT KINGDOM OF BENIN

The kingdom of Benin, founded in the forests of what is now Nigeria, rose to power during the 14th century. Its skilled craftworkers made spectacular bronze heads and figures.

(map)

N I G E R

C H A D

L. Chad

Komadugu Yobe

Kano

agadougou

INA

B E N I N

641m (2,103ft)

Atako Mts.

Oueme

N I G E R I A

Niger

Abuja

Dimlang 2,042m (6,700ft)

C A M E R O O N

Togo

Mono

Agou 986m (3,235ft)

Lagos

Porto-Novo

Lomé

Benin City

Bight of Benin

Niger Delta

WEST AFRICAN RELIGIONS
Percentages of population

	Muslim	Christian	Traditional
Benin	15	18	67
Burkina	35	10	55
Gambia	90	9	1
Ghana	12	43	45
Guinea	95	1.5	3.5
Guinea-Bissau	38	8	54
Ivory Coast	23	12	65
Liberia	14	68	18
Nigeria	50	40	10
Senegal	90	5	5
Sierra Leone	30	10	60
Togo	15	35	50

GHANA

GHANA WAS THE first African country to win its independence. Ghana exports more cacao than any other country in the world.

Area 238,540sq km (92,100sq miles)
Independence 1957, from Britain
Currency Cedi
Population 17,500,000
Official Language English

TOGO

THE POPULATION OF Togo has about 30 ethnic groups, many from other parts of West Africa. Nearly half the people are under 15 years of age.

Area 56,790sq km (21,927sq miles)
Independence 1960, from France
Currency CFA franc
Population 4,100,000
Official Language French

BENIN

BENIN HAS A coastline fringed with saltwater lakes. Lake villages and old palaces make Benin popular with tourists.

Area 112,620sq km (43,480sq miles)
Independence 1960, from France
Currency CFA franc
Population 5,400,000
Official Language French

GABON

GABON LIES ACROSS the Equator and is hot and rainy. About 75 per cent of the country is rainforest. Gabon is the world's fourth largest producer of manganese.

 Area 267,670sq km (103,347sq miles)
Independence 1960, from France
Currency CFA franc
Population 1,300,000
Official Language French
Major Religions Roman Catholic and other Christians 96%, Muslim 2%, other 2%

TRADITIONAL BELIEFS

• Many Africans follow religious systems that existed before the introduction of the major faiths, such as Islam and Christianity.

• Many of these traditions suggest that natural objects, such as mountains and rivers, have a spirit. Spirits can be good or evil.

• Fetishes are figures that are thought to be inhabited by a spirit. A good spirit can be activated by rubbing the figure's nose or forehead and offering a prayer.

EQUATORIAL GUINEA

THIS COUNTRY IS made up of Rio Muni, on the mainland, and the island of Bioko. Most people belong to the Fang, a group who are known for their storytelling and music.

Area 28,050sq km (108,30sq miles)
Independence 1968, from Spain
Currency CFA franc
Population 400,000
Official Language Spanish
✝ **Major Religions** Roman Catholic 89%, other 11%

TURTLE BEACH
In January and February each year, thousands of turtles come to the south shore of the island of Bioko, to lay their eggs. Only one in every 100 will survive.

Green turtle

CAMEROON

TROPICAL RAINFORESTS COVER much of the Republic of Cameroon. The country's main export is cacao, which is used to make cocoa and chocolate.

 Area 475,440sq km (183,570sq miles)
Independence 1960, from France
Currency CFA franc
Population 12,500,000
Official Languages English, French
Major Religions Traditional beliefs 51%, Christian 33%, Muslim 16%

LIVING IN THE RAINFOREST

• Large areas of Central Africa are covered in rainforest. The forest is warm and damp and home to wildlife such as chimpanzees, leopards, and a wealth of birdlife.

• In the rainforests, there are groups of people commonly known as pygmies (a name they dislike). They survive by hunting animals and gathering wild plants, nuts, and honey.

• Forest homes are made from a framework of poles tied together and thatched with large leaves. The people do not plant crops so have no need to cut down their forest retreat.

• The main forest people are the Twa, the BaKa, and the Mbuti, who live in an area that covers parts of Gabon, Congo, Central African Republic, Cameroon, and Zaire.

SAO TOME AND PRINCIPE

THESE VOLCANIC ISLANDS lie in the Gulf of Guinea. About 40 per cent of the land is planted with cacao trees. Most people live in São Tomé.

 Area 964sq km (372sq miles)
Independence 1975, from Portugal
Currency Dobra
Population 125,000
Official Language Portuguese
✝ **Major Religions** Roman Catholic 90%, other Christian 10%

YAOUNDÉ
Yaoundé is the capital city and business centre of Cameroon. It also has many schools and research institutes.

CENTRAL AFRICAN REPUBLIC

TIMBER, COFFEE, and cotton are the main exports here. Along the rivers, used for access to the sea, there are hippopotamuses and crocodiles.

 Area 622,980sq km (240,530sq miles)
Independence 1960, from France
Currency CFA franc
Population 3,300,000
Official Languages French, Sango
Major Religions Christian 50%, traditional beliefs 27%, Muslim 15%, other 8%

CONGO

ALMOST TWO-THIRDS of the Congo is covered with tropical rainforests. The coast and swamps contain coconut palms and mangrove forests.

 Area 342,000sq km (132,040sq miles)
Independence 1960, from France
Currency CFA franc
Population 2,600,000
Official Language French
Major Religions Roman Catholic 50%, traditional beliefs 48%, other 2%

ANGOLA

THE MAIN PRODUCTS of Angola are oil and diamonds. The long coastline also provides good fishing for sardines and mackerel.

 Area 1,246,700sq km (481,551sq miles)
Independence 1975, from Portugal
Currency New kwanza
Population 11,100,000
Official Language Portuguese
✝ **Major Religions** Christian 64%, traditional beliefs 34%, other 2%

Mt.Toussoro
1,330m (4,364ft)

Cameroon Mountain
4,095m (13,436ft)

Margherita Peak
5,110m (16,766ft)

Mont Tembo
1,200m (3,937ft)

Monts de la Lékéti
1,040m (3,412ft)

Karisimbi
4,507m (14,787ft)

2,067m
(6,782ft)

Serra do Môco
2,620m (8,596ft)

Equator

RWANDA

RWANDA IS ONE of Africa's most densely populated countries. Main exports include coffee, tungsten, tea, and pyrethrum.

Area 26,340sq km (10,170sq miles)
Independence 1962, from Belgium
Currency Rwanda franc
Population 8,000,000
Official Languages Kinyarwanda, French
Major Religions Christian 74%, traditional beliefs 25%, other 1%

GORILLAS OF RWANDA
One of the last remaining sanctuaries of the mountain gorilla is in Rwanda. The largest of all primates, gorillas live in female groups with one male.

BURUNDI

A TINY, DENSELY populated country, Burundi is only 265 km (165 miles) wide. Nickel, copper, and cobalt are mined in the southeast.

Area 27,830sq km (10,745sq miles)
Independence 1962, from Belgium
Currency Burundi franc
Population 6,400,000
Official Languages French, Kirundi
Major Religions Christian 68%, traditional beliefs 32%

ZAMBIA

ZAMBIA IS A large, land-locked country. The economy relies on road and rail transport through the port of Dar-es-Salaam in Tanzania.

Area 740,720sq km (285,992sq miles)
Independence 1964, from Britain
Currency Zambian kwacha
Population 9,500,000
Official Language English
Major Religions Christian 63%, traditional beliefs 35%, other 2%

FISHING METHODS
The coasts of Angola are dotted with fishing villages. Some fish are caught by using conical traps that hang from specially built scaffolding.

REGIONAL LIFESTYLE FACTS
• Sao Tome has the highest literacy rate in Central Africa (63%) and the third highest life expectancy in all of Africa.
• The wooden masks of Central Africa inspired the Spanish painter Picasso (see p.163).

Mask from Congo (Zaire)

CONGO (ZAIRE)

THIS COUNTRY IS the world's largest producer of industrial diamonds. Minerals, mainly copper, make up 80 per cent of total exports.

Area 2,345,410sq km (905,563sq miles)
Independence 1960, from Belgium
Currency Zaire
Population 43,900,000
Official Language French
Major Religions Christian 70%, Traditional beliefs 20%, Muslim 10%

• A vegetarian dish from the Central African Republic is made with spinach or greens mixed with peanut butter to make a thick stew. It is served with rice or cornmeal.
• Makossa, the music of Cameroon, is popular all over Africa. Musicians use a thumb piano (sanza), flute, and percussion.

Thumb piano

• In parts of Zambia, areas of dense forest are burned to clear the land for farming. The ash acts as a fertilizer.

VICTORIA FALLS
Victoria Falls lies on the border of Zambia and Zimbabwe. Water falls 108m (354ft), and has twice the drop of Niagara Falls. The spray can be seen from 65km (40 miles) away.

SOUTH AFRICA

MOST OF South Africa lies on a plateau, or tableland, about 900 metres (2,953 feet) above sea level. Land is used for grazing and wool is an important export. Minerals, such as gold, platinum, diamonds, and coal, provide most of the wealth.

Area 1,221,040sq km (471,443sq miles)
Government Multiparty democracy
Foundation 1910, declaration of Union of South Africa
Territories Transkei, Bophuthatswana, Ciskei, and Venda
Currency Rand
Population 41,500,000
Density 34 per sq km (88 per sq mile)
Official Languages Afrikaans, English
Major Religions Christian 64%, Hindu and Muslim 2%, other 34%

CENTRE OF GOVERNMENT
The Parliament Building in Cape Town was used for the first time in 1885. The building provided chambers for the two Houses of the Cape Parliament, as well as a large library. Nelson Mandela took up his post here as the first black president of South Africa in May 1994.

MAJOR SOUTH AFRICAN LANGUAGES

Language	Number of speakers
Zulu	8,343,590
Xhosa	6,646,568
Afrikaans	5,702,535
Tswana	3,482,657
North Sotho	3,530,616
English	3,414,900

NAMIBIA

THIS HOT DRY country includes the barren Namib Desert and part of the Kalahari. Namibia's main exports are diamonds and minerals.

Area 824,290sq km (318,260sq miles)
Independence 1990, from South Africa
Currency Namibian dollar
Population 1,500,000
Official Language English
✝ **Major Religions** Christian 90%, traditional beliefs 10%

WEATHER FACTS
42°C (107°F)   784mm (31in)   -9°C (16°F)

21.5°C (70.7°F)   13.9°C (57°F)

LAND PROFILE
In South Africa 27% of the land is used for agriculture.

%
0.5
10
12.5
27
50

LIFESTYLE FACTS

• In April 1994, the first-ever free elections were held. These followed years of apartheid, which denied black South Africans any voting power.
• Every year Zulus celebrate Shaka Day. Between 1818 and 1828, a great warrior called Shaka created the Zulu nation from many black clans in South Africa.
• South Africa has the fourth largest Indian community in the world.
• South Africa has the world's deepest gold mine. It is 4,200m (13,780 ft) deep.

SWAZILAND

THIS SMALL COUNTRY lies within South Africa. It is well-watered from four rivers which provide irrigation for citrus fruits and sugar-cane.

Area 17,360sq km (6,703sq miles)
Independence 1968, from Britain
Currency Lilangeni
Population 900,000
Official Languages English, Swazi
Major Religions Christian 60%, traditional beliefs 40%

SAVANNAH FACTS

• The springbok, a small antelope, lives on the grasslands. If alarmed, it can leap 3.5m (11.5ft) in the air with its back arched. This is called "pronking".
• The trees in the African savannah include several species of acacia. The sweet-thorn acacia sends tap roots down 65m (213ft) to seek out water.

• The oldest surviving inhabitants of southern Africa are the San (Bushmen). These people now live in the semi-desert regions of Botswana and Namibia.

10 rand

LANGUAGE
A traditional greeting in Zulu is *kunjani.*

NATIONAL BIRD
The blue crane is the national bird, and lives in protected areas throughout South Africa.

PRECIOUS MINERALS
South Africa is the world's leading supplier of gold and platinum. The country produces 40% of the world's gold, and 72% of its platinum.

MAJOR PLATINUM MARKETS (1992)

Destination	Amount in grams/ounces
Japan	52,731,000g (1,860,000oz)
Western Europe	23,814,000g (840,000oz)
North America	20,270,250g (715,000oz)
Other	10,914,750g (385,000oz)

LESOTHO

LESOTHO IS AN independent kingdom within South Africa. The mountain slopes provide good pasture for cattle and sheep.

Area 30,350sq km (11,718sq miles)
Independence 1966, from Britain
Currency Loti
Population 2,100,000
Official Languages English, Sotho
✝ **Major Religions** Christian 93%, traditional beliefs 7%

BOTSWANA

THE KALAHARI, A semi-desert with grass and thorn bushes, covers much of Botswana. Most of its income comes from mining diamonds.

Area 581,730sq km (224,600sq miles)
Independence 1966, from Britain
Currency Pula
Population 1,500,000
Official Language English
Major Religions Traditional beliefs 50%, Christian 50%

ZIMBABWE

MOST PEOPLE IN the land-locked country of Zimbabwe belong to the Shona or Ndebele tribes. Main cash crops are tobacco, cotton, and sugar.

 Area 390,580sq km (150,800sq miles)

Independence 1980, from Britain

Currency Zimbabwe dollar

Population 11,300,000

Official Language English

Major Religions Syncretic (part Christian, part traditional beliefs) 50%, Christian 26%, traditional beliefs 24%

CAPITAL OF ZIMBABWE
Harare, named after the African chief Neharawe, is the capital of Zimbabwe. It is a modern city with wide, tree-lined streets.

NDEBELE HOMES
Ndebele women decorate their homes with bright geometric patterns.

COMOROS

THE THREE MAIN islands of Comoros lie between mainland Africa and Madagascar. More than half of its food has to be imported.

 Area 2,230sq km (861sq miles)

Independence 1975, from France

Currency CFA franc

Population 600,000

Official Languages Arabic, French

Major Religions Muslim 86%, Roman Catholic 14%

MADAGASCAR

THE MAIN EXPORTS of Madagascar are coffee, cloves, and vanilla. The fourth largest island in the world, Madagascar has a varied climate and a wide range of wildlife.

 Area 587,040sq km (226,600sq miles)

Independence 1960, from France

Currency Malagasy franc

Population 14,800,000

Official Languages French, Malagasy

Major Religions Traditional beliefs 52%, Christian 41%, Muslim 7%

MADAGASCAR WILDLIFE FACTS
- Many unique animals evolved on Madagascar, which is isolated from mainland Africa.
- Two-thirds of the world's chameleons live on the island. These animals can change colour when threatened.
- Madagascar is also home to the Indri, the largest of the world's lemurs.

PEOPLE OF MADAGASCAR
The fertility rate of women here is one of the highest in the world. More than two-fifths of the population is under 15 years of age.

MALAWI

THIS NARROW COUNTRY is only 160km (100 miles) wide. Tobacco has recently overtaken tea as Malawi's major cash crop.

 Area 118,840sq km (45,745sq miles)

Independence 1964, from Britain

Currency Malawi kwacha

Population 11,100,000

Official Language English

Major Religions Christian 66%, traditional beliefs 18%, other 16%

MOZAMBIQUE

MOZAMBIQUE IS ONE of the poorest countries in the world. Most farms are state owned and exports include coconuts, cotton, tea, and sugar.

 Area 801,590sq km (309,493sq miles)

Independence 1975, from Portugal

Currency Metical

Population 16,000,000

Official Language Portuguese

Major Religions Traditional beliefs 60%, Christian 30%, Muslim 10%

COCONUT
Copra, the dried flesh of the coconut, is used to make soap, shampoo, and margarine.

ASIA

ASIA IS THE world's largest continent and includes hot, dry deserts, icy tundra, and tropical rainforests. Asia also has the largest population of any continent with sixty per cent of the world's people.

Area 44,680,718sq km (17,251,315sq miles)
Countries 44
Largest Russian Federation 17,075,400sq km (6,592,846sq miles)
Smallest Maldives 300sq km (116 sq miles)
Population 3,184,078,671
Density 73per sq km (189per sq mile)
Major Languages Chinese, Hindi, Japanese, Bengali, Punjabi

▲ **Highest point** Mount Everest, Nepal/China 8,848m (29,029ft)
▼ **Lowest point** Dead Sea, Israel/Jordan 400m (1,312ft) below sea level
☀ **Highest temperature** 54°C (129°F), Tirat Tsvi, Israel
❄ **Lowest temperature** -68°C (-90°F) Verkhoyansk and Oimekon, Russian Federation

CLIMATE ZONES

KEY

- Mountain regions
- Polar and tundra
- Taiga
- Dry grassland

- Mediterranean
- Temperate forest
- Rainforest
- Tropical grassland
- Hot desert

TIME ZONES

12:00 Greenwich | 15:30 Tehran | 17:30 New Delhi | 21:00 Tokyo

TOP CITY POPULATIONS

Tokyo, Japan 7,968,000
Delhi, India 8,419,084
Shanghai, China 8,760,000
Calcutta, India 11,021,000
Bombay, India 12,596,000

COUNTRIES, TERRITORIES AND CAPITALS

Name	Capital
Afghanistan	Kabul
Bahrain	Al Manama
Bangladesh	Dhaka
Bhutan	Thimphu
Brunei	Bandar Seri Begawan
Burma	Rangoon
Cambodia	Phnom Penh
China	Beijing
India	New Delhi
Indonesia	Jakarta
Iran	Tehran
Iraq	Baghdad
Israel	Jerusalem
Japan	Tokyo
Jordan	Amman
Kazakhstan	Astana (Akmola)
Kuwait	Kuwait
Kyrgyzstan	Bishkek
Laos	Vientiane
Lebanon	Beirut
Malaysia	Kuala Lumpur
Maldives	Male

Name	Capital
Mongolia	Ulan Bator
Nepal	Kathmandu
North Korea	Pyongyang
Oman	Muscat
Pakistan	Islamabad
Philippines	Manila
Qatar	Doha
Russian Federation	Moscow
Saudi Arabia	Riyadh
Singapore	Singapore
South Korea	Seoul
Sri Lanka	Colombo
Syria	Damascus
Taiwan	Taipei
Tajikistan	Dushanbe
Thailand	Bangkok
Turkmenistan	Ashkhabad
United Arab Emirates	Abu Dhabi
Uzbekistan	Tashkent
Vietnam	Hanoi
Yemen	Sana

AGE BREAKDOWN

Under 15 years | 15 to 65 years | Over 65 years

Qatar 1%
Israel 8.9%
Hong Kong 21%
Yemen 49%
Yemen 48%
Qatar 71%

KEY
- Lowest %
- Highest %

FEWEST DOCTORS

Cambodia	1 to 25,000 people
Maldives	1 to 20,300 people
Nepal	1 to 16,830 people
Bhutan	1 to 13,110 people
Indonesia	1 to 7,050 people

LONGEST LIFESPAN

Female 82 78 77 77 76
Male 76 74 74 71 72

Japan | Israel | Brunei | Singapore | Kuwait

GROWING RICE

Ninety per cent of the world's rice is grown in Asia. Rice, along with wheat and maize, supplies the basic food needs for more than half the population of the world.

ASIA FACTS

- Lake Baikal in the Russian Federation is the world's deepest lake at 1,620m (5,315ft). It is home to the world's only freshwater seal.

Baikal seal

- The world's top five tea growers are all in Asia – India, China, Sri Lanka, Japan, and the Russian Federation.

- All the world's major religions originated in Asia. They include Christianity, Islam, Judaism, Hinduism, Buddhism, and Sikhism.

- The highest city in the world is Lhasa, in Tibet, which lies at 3,650m (11,975ft) above sea level.

TALLEST MOUNTAINS

K2 (Mount Godwin Austen), Kashmir/China, 8,611m (28,251ft)

Mount Everest, Nepal/China, 8,848m (29,030ft)

Lhotse, Tibet/Nepal 8,516m (27,940ft)

Kangchenjunga, India/Nepal, 8,586m (28,169ft)

Makalu, Tibet/Nepal, 8,463m (27,766ft)

CROSS-SECTION (NORTH AND SOUTH)

Arctic Ocean
Kara Sea
Ural Mountains
Kirghiz Steppe
Kara Kum
Aral Sea
Iranian Plateau
Arabian Sea

1,500m (4,921ft)
0 Sea level
-3,000m (-9,843ft)

Length: 8,000km (5,000 miles)

CROSS-SECTION (WEST AND EAST)

8,848m (29,029ft)
Himalayas
Thar Desert
Plateau of Tibet
Daxue Shan
Great Plain of China
Red Basin
Yellow Sea
Korea
Sea of Japan
Honshu

Sea level 0
-4,500m (-14,76ft)

Length: 8,000km (5,000 miles)

0 —— 1500km
0 —— 750 miles

KEY
1. Mount Everest
2. K2
3. Kangchenjunga
4. Lhotse
5. Makalu

ARCTIC OCEAN
Kara Sea
Taymyr Peninsula
Laptev Sea
East Siberian Sea
Verkhoyansk ✳
Arctic Circle
Siberia
RUSSIAN FEDERATION
Ural Mountains
Ob'
L. Baikal
Lena
Bering Sea
Kamchatka
Sea of Okhotsk
Amur

Kirghiz Steppe
KAZAKHSTAN
Altai Mountains
MONGOLIA
Aral Sea
L. Balkhash
Tien Shan
Gobi Desert
Manchurian Plain
Sea of Japan
Honshu

ARMENIA AZERBAIJAN
UZBEKISTAN
Issyk-Kul
KYRGYZSTAN
Yellow River
NORTH KOREA
SOUTH KOREA
JAPAN
Tokyo

URKEY
Caspian Sea
Kara Kum
TURKMENISTAN
TAJIKISTAN
Taklamakan Desert
Kunlun Shan
CHINA
Yellow Sea
East China Sea

SYRIA
Tehran
Hindu Kush
Plateau of Tibet
ON
Dead Sea
IRAQ
Iranian Plateau
AFGHANISTAN
Mt. Everest
8,848m (29,030ft)
Red Basin
Yangtze
Shanghai
JORDAN
KUWAIT
PAKISTAN
NEPAL
BHUTAN
Great Plain of China

BAHRAIN
QATAR
U.A.E.
Thar Desert
New Delhi
BANGLADESH
TAIWAN

c of Cancer
SAUDI ARABIA
Rub 'al Khali
Arabian Sea
Calcutta
BURMA
LAOS

Red Sea
YEMEN OMAN
Bombay
INDIA
Bay of Bengal
THAILAND
CAMBODIA
VIETNAM
South China Sea
Luzon
PHILIPPINES
Mindanao

Socotra
Lakshadweep (India)
Andaman Is.
Nicobar Is.
MALAYSIA
BRUNEI

SRI LANKA
Sumatra
SINGAPORE
Equator
INDONESIA
Java
New Guinea
INDIAN OCEAN
Arafura Sea

PACIFIC OCEAN

N

LAND PROFILE
Almost one-third of Asia is forested land.

Urban 0.5%
Wetlands 3.5%
Desert 4%
Tundra 5%
Barren land 9.5%
Agriculture 20%
Grassland 25%
Forest 32.5%

WILDLIFE
Asia has an amazing variety of wildlife that represents the wide range of habitats.

FAUNA

Siberian tiger (*Pantherus tigris altaica*) is the largest cat in the world. The heaviest specimen weighed 384kg (847lb).

Orang-utan (*Pongo pygmaeus*) is found only in the jungles of Borneo and Sumatra.

Bactrian camel (*Camelus bactrianus*) has two humps. It lives wild in the Gobi Desert.

FLORA

Rhododendron (*Rhododendron arboreum*), from India and Sri Lanka, can reach 12m (40ft) in height.

Bamboo (*Bambusa multiplex*) is classified as a grass. It can grow at the rate of 40cm (16in) a day.

ISRAEL

ABOUT FOUR-FIFTHS of Israelis are Jewish, and many Jews all over the world consider the State of Israel their homeland. The average age in Israel is very young: 25.6 years.

Area 20,700sq km (7,992sq miles)
Government Multiparty republic
Independence 1948, from Britain
Territories Disputes over land with Jordan and Syria
Currency New shekel
Population 5,600,000
Density 251 per sq km (650 per sq mile)
Official Languages Hebrew and Arabic
Major Religions Jewish 83%, Muslim 13%, Christian 2%

LAND PROFILE
Almost half of Israel is desert.

%
1.5
5.0
20.5
29.5
43.5

50 New shekels

LIFESTYLE FACTS
● Israel produces 95% of its own food, including delicious oranges, bananas, and avocados.

WESTERN WALL
Also called the Wailing Wall, this is a most sacred Jewish place of prayer and pilgrimage. It is all that remains of the Second Temple of Solomon, built about 200 B.C.

● 3% of Israelis live on 270 *kibbutzim*. These are communities, often farms, where families live together and share decision-making, work, and property.

DEAD SEA
This inland sea lies 400m (1,300ft) below sea level, and is the lowest point on Earth. Its water is the saltiest known, and this allows people to float easily.

LEBANON

UNTIL THE outbreak of civil war in 1975, Lebanon was the trading and financial centre of the Middle East. Its fertile inland plain yields fruits, vegetables, grains, and tobacco.

Area 10,400sq km (4,015sq miles)
Government Multiparty republic
Independence 1941, from France
Currency Lebanese pound
Population 3,000,000
Official Language Arabic
Major Religions Muslim 57%, Christian 43%

SYRIA

THIS LAND OF rocky deserts and ancient cities has been called the cradle of civilization: the world's first alphabet was found in Ugarit.

Area 185,180sq km (71,500sq miles)
Government Single party republic
Independence 1946, from France
Currency Syrian pound
Population 14,700,000
Official Language Arabic
Major Religions Sunni Muslim 74%, Alawite, Druze, and other Muslim sects 16%, Christian 10%

DAMASCUS
The capital of Syria, Damascus is the world's most ancient inhabited city. It is famous for its souqs (markets).

PALMYRA
Palmyra (city of palms) now lies in ruins. It was once a major stopping place for travelling merchants taking the shortest route to the Mediterranean.

JORDAN

THE ARABIAN desert covers almost two-thirds of Jordan. Nomadic bedouin herders were the first desert-dwellers; now their numbers are dwindling.

Area 89,210sq km (34,440sq miles)
Government Constitutional monarchy
Independence 1946, from Britain
Currency Jordanian dinar
Population 5,400,000
Official Language Arabic
Major Religions Muslim 95%, Christian 5%

PETRA
This beautiful, rose-red city was carved from solid rock more than 2,000 years ago.

REGIONAL WEATHER FACTS
Records

-13°C (8.6°F)

54°C (129.2°F)

Averages

484mm (19.1in)

24.3°C (75.7°F)   -10°C (14°F)

IRAQ

IRAQ'S STATE religion is Islam, and its followers are called Muslims. From 1980 to 1988, Iraq was at war with Iran.

 Area 438,320sq km (169,235sq miles)
☞ **Independence** 1932, from Britain
♻ **Currency** Iraqi dinar
🛉 **Population** 20,400,000

ARABIC
Arabic is the religious language of Muslims all over the world, whether they are Arabs or not.

LANGUAGE
A traditional greeting in Arabic is *ahlan wasahlan*.

SAUDI ARABIA

THIS KINGDOM is the world's leading producer and exporter of oil, and holds 25 per cent of world oil reserves.

Area 2,149,690sq km (829,995sq miles)
☞ **Independence and Unification** 1932
♻ **Currency** Saudi riyal
🛉 **Population** 17,900,000

ARAB HOUSES
Most Arabs are of the Muslim faith, which says that women must cover themselves from everyone except their families. Muslim houses have a screened balcony that shields women from the outside, and also keeps the house cool.

KUWAIT

IRAQ INVADED oil-rich Kuwait in 1990. The Iraqis were driven out seven months later during the Gulf War.

 Area 17,820sq km (6,880sq miles)
🛉 **Independence** 1961, from Britain
♻ **Currency** Kuwaiti dinar
🛉 **Population** 1,500,000

BAHRAIN

BAHRAIN IS MADE up of 33 islands in the west of the Arabian Gulf. It was the first Arab nation to strike oil, in 1932.

 Area 680sq km (263sq miles)
☞ **Independence** 1971, from Britain
♻ **Currency** Bahrain dinar
🛉 **Population** 600,000

ARAB HEADDRESS
Headcloths are worn by both men and women to protect them from the sun. Arab women often wear a veil or mask.

Chequered headcloth, or smagh *White headcloth, or ghoutra* *Headcloth, or misfa, worn with a veil* *Misfa worn with a mask*

MAJOR OIL PRODUCERS
The countries in the table are members of OPEC (Organization of Petroleum Exporting Countries), which was formed in 1960.

Country	Barrels per day (1998)
Saudi Arabia	8,248,000
Iran	3,586,000
United Arab Emirates	2,261,000
Kuwait	2,074,000
Data supplied by OPEC bulletin	

YEMEN

NORTH AND South Yemen were united in 1990 to form the Republic of Yemen. Oil finds are small compared to wealthy neighbouring countries.

 Area 527,970sq km (203,849sq miles)
Unification 1990
♻ **Currency** Northern riyal and southern dinar
🛉 **Population** 14,500,000

OMAN

SINCE 1970, when Sultan Qaboos took power, Oman's oil wealth has been used to develop industry, education, and health care.

 Area 212,460sq km (82,030sq miles)
☞ **Independence** 1951, from Britain
♻ **Currency** Omani rial
🛉 **Population** 2,200,000

QATAR

UP TO 70 per cent of Qatar's people were attracted there by jobs in the oil industry. Qatar has one of the lowest death rates in the world.

Area 11,000sq km (4,247sq miles)
☞ **Independence** 1971, from Britain
♻ **Currency** Qatar riyal
🛉 **Population** 600,000

UNITED ARAB EMIRATES

THE UAE HAS some of the richest oil deposits in the world. Money from oil is used to turn the desert into farmland.

 Area 83,600sq km (32,278sq miles)
☞ **Independence** 1971, from Britain
♻ **Currency** UAE dirham
🛉 **Population** 1,900,000

IRAN

IRAN, ORIGINALLY CALLED Persia, is a flat, mainly barren land surrounded by mountains. The only fertile areas are near the Caspian Sea and the mountain foothills. The country has large reserves of oil, natural gas, and minerals.

 Area 1,648,000sq km (636,293sq miles)
Government Islamic republic
Independence 1925, from Britain
Currency Iranian rial
Population 67,300,000
Density 41 per sq km (106 per sq mile)
Official Language Farsi (Persian)
Major Religions Shi'ite Muslim 95%, Sunni Muslim 4%, Baha'i, Christian, Jewish, Zoroastrian 1%

ARCHITECTURE
The Imam Mosque is in the traditional Islamic architectural style. The mosque, built in 1020, is decorated with fine tile work.

Imam Mosque, Isfahan

The modern Shayad Monument was built to commemorate King Cyrus' birth, 2,500 years ago. He united the Persian Empire.

Shayad Monument, Tehran

WEATHER FACTS

51°C (123.8°F)   246mm (9.7in)   -21°C (-5°F)
29.4°C (85°F)   2.2°C (36°F)

LAND PROFILE
Only 6.5% of Iran is agricultural land.

%
0.5
0.5
6.5
11.5
22
59

LIFESTYLE FACTS

• All Iranian men have to join the armed forces at the age of 16. The only reasons for exemption are poor health or the death of a brother in military service since 1979.

• Wrestling and horse-racing are traditional sports, although rugby and volleyball are the most popular modern games.

• Iran is the world's second largest oil producer. Oil accounts for 80% of revenue and 95% of foreign exchange earnings.

• Most towns get their water supply from a series of long irrigation tunnels, called *qanat*, which bring water from the mountains.

MUSLIM FACTS

• Muslims believe that the greatest and last of the prophets was Muhammad, who was born in Arabia in A.D. 570. Islam is the name that the prophet Muhammad gave to the religion of the Muslims.

• All women in Iran, even tourists, must cover their bodies. Only hands, feet, and face may show. Records are kept of anyone breaking this law.

Iranian woman in traditional headcloth

LANGUAGE
A traditional greeting in Farsi is *salam*.

سلام

MAJOR OIL MARKETS	
Importer	Thousand barrels per day
Western Europe	1,195
Asia and Far East	938
Eastern Europe	185
Latin America	125
Africa	45
Middle East	30

PERSIAN CARPETS
Hand-woven carpets are Iran's second largest export. Persian carpets have different patterns according to their region of origin. These include Isfahan, Kashan, Kerman, Qom, Shiraz, and Tabriz.

• After Muhammad's death, there was a dispute among his followers about who should lead the Muslims. The Sunnis followed the Caliphs while the Shi'ites decided to follow Muhammad's cousin, Ali.

• Under Islam it is possible for a man to have four wives, but he must treat them all equally.

• The Koran is the Holy Book of the Muslims. It is the basis for Muslim law on all important aspects of life, and is treated with great respect.

TURKMENISTAN

TURKMENISTAN IS AN extremely dry land, with large supplies of natural gas beneath the Kara Kum desert. In irrigated areas, farmers grow cotton, wheat, grapes, and melons.

 Area 488,100sq km (188,455sq miles)
Government Single party republic
Independence 1991, from Soviet Union
Currency Manat
Population 4,100,000
Density 8 per sq km (21 per sq mile)
Official Language Turkmen
Major Religions Muslim 85%, Eastern Orthodox 10%, other 5%

AFGHANISTAN

THIS AGRICULTURAL COUNTRY is divided by the Hindu Kush Mountains, where many people still live as nomads. In villages, farmers raise sheep to export the lambskins.

 Area 652,090sq km (251,770sq miles)
Government Mujahideen coalition
Independence 1919, from Britain
Currency Afghani
Population 20,100,000
Density 31 per sq km (80 per sq mile)
Official Languages Dari (Persian) and Pashtu
Major Religions Sunni Muslim 84%, Shi'ite Muslim 15%, Hindu, Jewish, Sikh 1%

TAJIKISTAN

THE PAMIR MOUNTAINS of Tajikistan have one of the world's longest mountain glaciers – 72 km (45 miles) long. In the valleys, farmers grow fruit, rice, and cotton.

 Area 143,100sq km (55,251sq miles)
Government Single party republic
Independence 1991, from Soviet Union
Currency Rouble
Population 6,100,000
Density 43 per sq km (111 per sq mile)
Official Language Tajik
Major Religions Sunni Muslim 85%, Shi'ite Muslim 5%, other 10%

KAZAKHSTAN

MOST OF KAZAKHSTAN is a dry plain, with mountains to the southeast. The main crop is wheat which is grown in the north. Industries include mining for copper, lead, gold, and silver.

Area 2,717,300sq km (1,049,150sq miles)
Government Multiparty republic
Independence 1991, from Soviet Union
Currency Tenge
Population 17,100,000
Density 6 per sq km (16 per sq mile)
Official Language Kazakh
Major Religions Muslim 47%, other (mostly Russian Orthodox and Lutheran) 53%

YURTS
Yurts, traditional homes of the Kazakhs, can be 1.5m (5ft) high and 6m (20ft) across. Their collapsible frameworks of wood are held tight by leather thongs. Felt is then stretched over the frame and lashed into position.

leather thong

felt covering

UZBEKISTAN

MUCH OF UZBEKISTAN is desert. In the east, mountain streams irrigate the land, and farmers can grow cotton, rice, and mulberry trees for feeding silkworms.

Area 439,733sq km (172,742sq miles)
Government Single party republic
Independence 1991, from Soviet Union
Currency Sum
Population 22,800,000
Density 51 per sq km (132 per sq mile)
Official Language Uzbek
Major Religions Muslim 88%, Orthodox Christian 12%

KYRGYZSTAN

MANY OF THE Kyrgyz people are nomads who tend their flocks on the slopes of the Tien Shan Mountains. In Bishkek, there are factories for processing leather and soap.

Area 198,500sq km (76,640sq miles)
Government Multiparty republic
Independence 1991, from Soviet Union.
Currency Som
Population 4,700,000
Density 24 per sq km (62 per sq mile)
Official Language Kyrgyz
Major Religion Muslim 65%, other 35%

CASPIAN SEA
- The Caspian Sea is the largest inland lake in the world and covers an area of 371,000 sq km (143,205 sq miles).

- Sturgeon, a kind of fish, are found in the Caspian Sea. They can grow up to 7m (23ft) long, and their eggs, called caviar, are an expensive delicacy. Caviar is a major export from Iran.

- Salmon, bream, mullet, carp, catfish, and perch are also caught for export.

MAKING SILK
Silk is produced by the white moth caterpillar, or silkworm. After caterpillars have spun a silken cocoon, they are put into boiling water. The silk is removed and spun into threads.

mulberry leaves

silkworm

INDIA

INDIA HAS THE world's second largest population, and a wide variety of peoples, religions, and languages. The mountainous north contrasts with the low-lying south.

Area 3,287,590sq km (1,269,338sq miles)
Government Multiparty republic
Independence 1947, from Britain
Currency Indian rupee
Population 935,700,000
Density 315 per sq km (816 per sq mile)
Official Languages Hindi, English, Bengali, Punjabi, Gujarati; 19 languages recognized constitutionally
ॐ **Major Religions** Hindu 83%, Muslim 11%, Christian 2%, Sikh 2%, Buddhist 1%, Jain 0.5%, Parsee and Jewish 0.43%, other 0.07%

WEATHER FACTS

46°C (114.8°F)   -14°C (6.8°F)
642mm (25.3in)
31.6°C (88.9°F)   14°C (57.2°F)

100 Indian rupees

LAND PROFILE
Forest, rainforest, and crops, such as rice, flourish in India.

%
1
1.5
4
11.5
40
42

LANGUAGE
A traditional greeting in Hindi is *namaskar*. नमस्कार

Traditional seven-stringed sitar

LIFESTYLE FACTS
• Each Indian region has its own unique range of dishes. There are at least a hundred different ways of preparing curry sauces, and up to 30 spices to choose from.

• Kabaddi is an ancient sport, popular all over India. Two teams (women or men) play on a pitch, raiding each other's territory, while chanting.

• In classical Indian music, rhythms are very complicated, and the ability to sing is very highly regarded. The tabla (twin drums) and stringed instruments, such as the tambura and sitar, accompany the voice.

• India produces more films than any other country in the world: more than 800 every year. Bombay is the centre of the Indian film industry.

NATIONAL SYMBOL
India's national symbol is the Royal Bengal tiger, which is a protected species.

TAJ MAHAL
The Taj Mahal, situated just outside Agra, was built by Mughal emperor Shah Jahan (1592–1666) as a tomb and monument to his favourite wife, Mumtaz Mahal. Her body lies beneath it. The Taj Mahal took 22 years to build and is one of the most visited buildings in the world.

INDIAN TEA PRODUCTION, (1996)

Area	Tonnes
Assam, Bengal, Bihar, and Tripura	565,422
Punjab, Uttar Pradesh, and Himachal Pradesh	2,551
South India	185,949
Total	753,922
Source: International Tea Committee	

TEXTILES
Textiles and clothing together make up India's second biggest export sector, after gems and jewellery. Textiles and clothes are produced in factories, but many people still work at home to produce beautiful, and often ancient, designs.

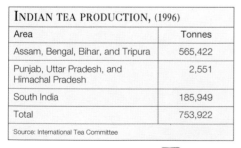

RAINFALL
The rainiest town in the world is Cherrapunji, northeastern India, with an average 11,437mm (450in) of rainfall per year. This amount of rain would almost cover six adults standing on each other's shoulders.

344

PAKISTAN

IN 1988, BENAZIR BHUTTO became the only woman to lead a Muslim country when she was first elected prime minister of Pakistan.

 Area 796,100sq km (307,374sq miles)
Government Federal parliamentary democracy
Independence 1947, from Britain
Currency Pakistani rupee
Population 140,500,000
Density 182 per sq km (472 per sq mile)
Official Language Urdu
Major Religions Muslim 97%, Hindu 2%, Christian 1%

WEATHER FACTS

53°C (127.4°F)   900mm (35.4in)   -4°C (24.8°F)

30.6°C (87.1°F)   11.3°C (52.3°F)

LAND PROFILE

Pakistan is mostly covered in grassland and desert.

%
1
1.5
4
11.5
40
42

LIFESTYLE FACTS

• Pakistan's population, with one of the world's highest growth rates, is set to reach 150 million by the 21st century. Half the population is less than 15 years old.

• Pakistan has one of the world's best cricket teams. They won the cricket world cup in 1992 under captain Imran Khan.

LANGUAGE

A traditional greeting in Nepali is *namaste*.

100 Pakistani rupees

MINAR-E

The Minar-e-Pakistan is a fine tower in Lahore. It was built on a historic spot in 1940 to commemorate Pakistan Day.

• Pakistan's male squash players are the best in the world. Jahangir Khan (b.1963) remained unbeaten for 5 years, 7 months, and one day: an all-time world record.

LANGUAGE

A traditional greeting in Urdu is *assalm-u-alaikum*. السلام عليكم

NEPAL

NEPAL IS A mountainous country, lying mostly in the Himalayas. About 250,000 people visit each year, mainly for mountain trekking.

LIFESTYLE FACTS

• In Nepal the traditional greeting is to press the palms together in a prayer-like gesture.

• The Nepalese celebrate 50 religious festivals each year, involving 120 days of celebrations. They are so frequent that they often overlap.

LANGUAGE

A traditional greeting in Nepali is *namaste*.

HINDU STATE

Nepal is the world's only Hindu state. Its many superb temples include gold-roofed Pashupatinath, the holiest of all the Nepalese temples dedicated to the god Shiva. Non-Hindus are not allowed to enter the temple.

 Area 140,800sq km (54,363sq miles)
Government Constitutional monarchy
State established 1869
Currency Nepalese rupee
Population 21,100,000
Density 151 per sq km (391 per sq miles)
Official Language Nepali
Major Religions Hindu 90%, Buddhist 5.3%, Muslim 2.7%, Christian 0.21%, other 1.79%

BHUTAN

BHUTAN IS A Buddhist state, ruled by a king who allows only 2,250 tourists per year. Nine out of ten Bhutanese are farmers and herders.

 Area 47,000sq km (18,147sq miles)
Government Constitutional monarchy
Independence 1949, from Britain
Currency Ngultrum
Population 1,600,000
Density 34 per sq km (88 per sq miles)
Official Language Dzongkha
Major Religions Mahayana Buddhist 70%, Hindu 24%, other 6%

VEGETATION

m
7,500

Bare rock; nothing can survive

Shrubs and dry alpine scrub

4,600

Coniferous forest

4,000

Evergreen and broadleaf forest

3,000

2,000

Tropical forest

1,000

0

LIFESTYLE FACTS

• Bhutanese food is hot and spicy. The national dish is *emadatsi*, made of chilli peppers in cheese sauce.

• Rare blue sheep and snow leopards live on high ground.

• Archery is the Bhutanese national sport. Competitors may distract each other by jumping in front of the targets.

BANGLADESH

BANGLADESH IS A low, flat land, and hundreds of square kilometres are flooded every year. It is the world's most densely populated country.

 Area 143,998sq km (55,598sq miles)
Government Multiparty republic
Independence 1971, from Pakistan
Currency Taka
Population 120,400,000
Density 899 per sq km (2,330 per sq miles)
Official Language Bengali
Major Religions Muslim 83%, Hindu 16%, Buddhist and Christian 1%

FLOOD PLAIN

Bangladesh, located on a low-lying delta, is flooded by monsoon rainfall from June to the end of September.

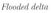

Normal delta

Flooded delta

LIFESTYLE FACTS

• Bangladesh's economy is based mainly on agriculture; the main export is jute, a plant used like cotton.

• Rivers form a huge transport network: there are about 8,370 kilometres of waterways in Bangladesh.

SRI LANKA

FORMERLY CALLED CEYLON, Sri Lanka is an island country off the southeast coast of India. It has a warm, tropical climate with two monsoon seasons each year. Tea and rubber plantations cover much of the land. Gemstones and spices are important exports.

Area 65,610sq km (25,332sq miles)
Government Multiparty republic
Currency Sri Lanka rupee
Population 18,400,000
Density 284 per sq km (736 per sq mile)
Official Languages Sinhala, Tamil
Major Religions Buddhist 70%, Hindu 15%, Christian 8%, Muslim 7%

WEATHER FACTS

40°C (104°F)   2,527mm (99.5in)   -3°C (27°F)
27.2°C (81°F)   26.7°C (80°F)

LANGUAGE

A traditional greeting in Sinhalese is *aubowan.*

NATIONAL LANDMARK

The city of Kandy is home to the 16th-century Buddhist Temple of the Tooth *(Dalada Maligawa).* This is where a sacred tooth, said to be one of Buddha's, is kept in a special casket.

INDIAN ELEPHANT

The Indian elephant *(Elephas maximus)* is similar to its African relative, but it has smaller ears and four nails on each back foot instead of three.

LIFESTYLE FACTS

• Most Sri Lankans make their own curry powder by grinding a mixture of local spices and herbs with a mortar and pestle.

• Every summer there is a festival when elephants in beautiful embroidered cloth parade through the city of Kandy.

• Sri Lanka has 242 species of butterfly. During March and April, the seasonal migration is a spectacular sight.

TEA GROWING

Sri Lanka is one of the world's top tea growers. Each year, more than 182 million kg (400 million lb) of tea are exported worldwide. Expert tasters will check the quality and value before making a purchase.

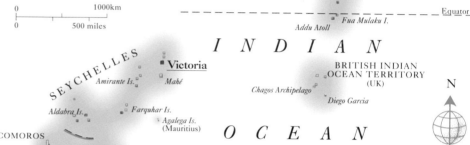

ISLAND PARADISE

The island of Mauritius is a popular tourist destination. Almost 50% of the visitors are European, most of them from France.

MALDIVES

THE HOT, TROPICAL climate of the Maldives means that most islands are covered with lush vegetation. Tourist resorts on the island of Male help to boost the economy.

Area 300sq km (116sq miles)
Government Republic
Currency Rufiyaa
Population 300,000
Official Language Dhivehi (Maldivian)
Major Religions Sunni Muslim 100%

SEYCHELLES

MAHÉ IS THE largest of the 115 islands that form the Seychelles. Tourism is the most important industry, along with exports of fish, copra, and cinnamon.

Area 280sq km (108sq miles)
Government Multiparty republic
Currency Seychelles rupee
Population 73,000
Official Language Seselwa (French Creole)
Major Religions Roman Catholic 90%, other 10%

MAURITIUS

MAURITIUS LIES ABOUT 2,000 km (1,200 miles) off the coast of Africa. The most important crops are sugar cane, tea, and aloe – a medicinal and cosmetic plant.

Area 1,860sq km (718sq miles)
Government Multiparty republic
Currency Mauritian rupee
Population 1,100,000
Official Language English
Major Religions Hindu 52%, Roman Catholic 26%, Muslim 17%, other 5%

THAILAND

THAILAND IS THE world's leading exporter of rice, and paddy fields cover much of the land. Most Thais are Buddhists and the country has more than 30,000 Buddhist temples.

Area 513,120sq km (198,116sq miles)
Government Constitutional monarchy
Unification 1782, Thailand never colonized
Currency Baht
Population 58,800,000
Density 115 per sq km (298 per sq mile)
Official Language Thai
Major Religions Buddhist 95%, Muslim 3.8%, Christian 0.5%, Hindu 0.1%, other 0.6%

BURMA

THE NORTH OF Burma is flat and farmers grow peanuts, millet, and cotton. Teak forests cover the south. The timber is hauled to rivers by elephants, and floated to sawmills.

Area 676,550sq km (261,200sq miles)
Government Military regime
Independence 1948, from Britain
Currency Kyat
Population 46,500,000
Density 71 per sq km (184 per sq mile)
Official Language Burmese
Major Religions Buddhist 89%, Muslim 4%, other 7%

REGIONAL WEATHER FACTS

1744mm (68.7in)

27°C (80.6°F)   25.4°C (77.7°F)

MONSOON
Most of Southeast Asia is affected by the monsoon winds, which bring heavy rainfall every year from May to October. Monsoon comes from the Arabic word meaning "season". Although the rains are vital for crops, such as rice, they can also cause disastrous floods.

LIFESTYLE FACTS
• Burma's rubies are considered the finest in the world. In the East, a ruby is thought to protect the wearer from harm.

• All young men in Thailand are expected to become monks for at least three months of their lives and reject all material wealth.

LANGUAGE
A traditional greeting in Thai is *sawatdee.* สวัสดี

THAI BOXING
Thai boxers use their feet, knees, elbows and fists to fight.

ANGKOR WAT
The magnificent temple city of Angkor Wat in Cambodia was built by the Khmers in the 12th century A.D.

CAMBODIA

MOST PEOPLE IN Cambodia are descendants of the Khmers who arrived in Southeast Asia in about 2000 B.C. Today, farmers grow rice, bananas, coconuts, and cotton.

Area 181,040sq km (69,000sq miles)
Government Parliamentary democracy
Independence 1953, from France
Currency Riel
Population 10,300,000
Density 58 per sq km (150 per sq mile)
Official Language Khmer
Major Religions Buddhist 88%, Muslim 20%, other 10%

LAOS

LAOS HAS MANY mountains and forests, and most people live in the Mekong River valley. Only about 4 per cent of the land is suitable for agriculture. Tin is mined for export.

Area 236,800sq km (91,429sq miles)
Government Single party republic
Independence 1949, from France. 1954 independent state established
Currency Kip
Population 4,900,000
Density 21 per sq km (54 per sq mile)
Official Language Laotian
Major Religions Buddhist 85%, Christian 2%, other 13%

VIETNAM

VIETNAM IS A WARM, monsoon land with heavy rainfall and thick forests. Many forests were destroyed during the Vietnam War. Rice, maize, and sweet potatoes are the main crops.

Area 329,560sq km (127,243sq miles)
Government Communist state
Unification 1976, proclamation of Socialist Republic of Vietnam
Currency New dong
Population 74,500,000
Density 229 per sq km (593 per sq mile)
Official Language Vietnamese
Major Religions Buddhist 55%, Christian 7%, other 38%

347

CHINA

THE THIRD LARGEST country in the world, China contains almost a quarter of the world's people. The landscape varies enormously. In the north there are dry deserts, while the south is warm and humid. Rice grows well in the warm, moist soil.

 Area 9,396,960sq km (3,628,166sq miles)
Government Single party republic
Unification 221 B.C., separate states united under First Emperor
Currency Yuan
Population 1.2 billion
Density 131 per sq km (340 per sq mile)
Official Language Mandarin Chinese
Major Religions Confucianist 20%, Buddhist 6%, Taoist 2%, other 72%

WEATHER FACTS

44°C (111°F)   623mm (24in)   -34°C (-30°F)
26°C (79°F)   -4.4°C (24°F)

GREAT WALL OF CHINA
The Great Wall of China is the longest man-made structure in the world. In 214 B.C. the First Emperor ordered one huge wall over 2,350km (1,460 miles) long to guard the northern frontier.

MONGOLIA

THE CLIMATE IN Mongolia is severe and it is one of the least populated countries in the world. Most people were nomadic herders but land is now organized into state farms.

 Area 1,565,000sq km (604,247sq miles)
Government Constitutional monarchy
Republic Mongolian People's Republic declared, 1924
Currency Tughrik
Population 2,400,000
Density 2 per sq km (5 per sq mile)
Official Language Khalka Mongol
Major Religions Limited religious practice due to former communist regime. Principal religion is Tibetan Buddhist, with 4% Muslim

LAND PROFILE

Most Chinese live in just 15% of the total land area.

%
1.5
2
6.5
9
21
24
36

LIFESTYLE FACTS

• The population in China increases by about 17 million people a year. To try to limit the expansion, one-child families are given priority for housing and medical care.

• One in five Chinese live in large cities, the rest live in the countryside. Most people travel by bicycle and there are 17,500,000 made in China every year.

REGIONAL CHINESE FOOD

• Peking (now Beijing) dishes often include duck and sweet and sour sauces.

• Food from the region of Sichuan is usually spicy, with garlic, chillies, and ginger.

• Cantonese cooking often features shellfish and other seafoods.

 • Shanghainese dishes can include steamed dumplings, as well as bird's nest soup made from the nests of cave swiftlets in southeast China.

TIBET FACTS

• Tibet lies in the highlands of southwest China at an average height of 4,500m (14,800ft). This is higher than most European mountains.

• Prayer flags are a Tibetan tradition symbolizing the Buddhist faith. Before the Chinese occupation, they flew from every home as a symbol of good luck.

Tibetan prayer flags

MONGOLIAN LIFESTYLE FACTS

• One third of Mongolia is covered by the vast Gobi Desert. Gobi is the Mongolian word for "waterless place".

• Mongols are expert horsemen. The Three Games of Men festival takes place every July and includes a 32-km (20-mile) horse race for children aged seven to twelve, wrestling, and archery.

• Mongolia has resources of coal, oil, and gold. The main coal mines are found near the capital city of Ulan Bator.

10 yuan

LANGUAGE

A traditional greeting in Mandarin is *nin hao*. 你好

IMPERIAL PALACE, BEIJING

The Imperial Palace in Beijing was built for the Emperor Zhu Di during the Ming Dynasty (1368–1644). The palace complex contains nearly 1,000 buildings. Only the emperor's family and people doing business were allowed into the central palace, which became known as the Forbidden City.

MAIN CHINESE OCCUPATIONS (1992)

Agriculture and fishing   Manufacturing   Services

350,170,000 people   99,490,000 people   40,180,000 people

• The Dalai Lama is the head of the Tibetan Buddhists. He went into exile in India after Tibet was invaded by China in 1950. Dalai Lama is a Mongolian word meaning "great ocean".

• Tibetans consider it bad luck if it snows during a marriage procession. But it is good luck to meet a funeral procession or a passer-by carrying a pitcher of water.

• Because of the cool, dry air of Tibet, grain can be stored for up to 60 years.

MACAO

THIS SMALL TERRITORY lies on the south coast of China. Textiles, incense, and fireworks are Macao's major exports.

 Area 20sq km (8sq miles)
Government Under Chinese administration
Currency Pataca
Population 355,693
Official Languages Cantonese, Portuguese

SOUTH KOREA

FORESTS COVER 70 per cent of the land in South Korea. The country's chief crops are rice and tobacco, and fishing is an important industry.

Area 99,020sq km (38,232sq miles)
Government Multiparty republice
Republic Republic of Korea declared, 1948
Currency South Korean won
Population 45,000,000
Density 456 per sq km (1,182 per sq mile)
Official Language Korean
Major Religions Mahayana Buddhist 47%, Protestant 38%, Roman Catholic 11%, Confucian 3%, other 1%

NORTH KOREA

NORTH KOREA IS a mountainous country and most people live on coastal plains in the east. Minerals such as copper and zinc are mined.

Area 120,540sq km (46,540sq miles)
Government Single party republic
Republic Democratic People's Republic of Korea founded in 1948
Currency North Korean won
Population 23,900,000
Density 198 per sq km (515 per sq mile)
Official Language Korean
Major Religions Organized religion not encouraged by the state

NORTH AND SOUTH KOREA FACTS

- Korean ginseng is a plant that is highly valued for its ability to improve memory and restore energy. The plant takes about seven years to mature.

- For centuries women divers, called *haenyo*, have collected seaweed and sea cucumbers from the coast off Cheju Island. A *haenyo* can dive to 18m (60ft) and hold her breath for four minutes.

- The remains of the oldest observatory in the world are in eastern South Korea. It was built in about A.D. 643.

TAIWAN

THE MOUNTAINOUS ISLAND of Taiwan lies on the Tropic of Cancer and has a warm, humid climate. Taiwan has modern factories and exports its goods all over the world.

Area 36,179sq km (13,969sq miles)
Government Multiparty republic
State founded In 1949
Currency New Taiwan dollar
Population 20,900,000
Density 645 per sq km (1,670 per sq mile)
Official Language Mandarin Chinese
Major Religions Buddhist-Confucian-Taoist 93%, Christian, Muslim, other 7%

PANDAS

Pandas feed on the bamboo shoots which grow in the forests of the Sichuan Mountains.

TAIWAN'S TOP EXPORTS (1996)

Product	US$ m
Data-processing machines	16,253
Electronic components	8,146
Textiles	4,823
Plastics	4,780
Transmission apparatus	2,772
Electric motors & generators	1,852
Sports equipment	1,516

HONG KONG

- Hong Kong is a small, densely populated area with 5,859 people per sq km (15,175 per sq mile).

- Hong Kong is a major financial centre and attracts investors from around the world.

- In 1842, Britain took control of Hong Kong under the Treaty of Nanjing. In 1898, Britain agreed to rent the island and part of the mainland for 99 years. On 1 July 1997, it was handed back to China.

JAPAN

JAPAN IS MADE up of a chain of about 3,900 volcanic islands. The four main islands are Hokkaido, Honshu, Shikoku, and Kyushu. Tokyo, the capital, is one of the most densely populated cities in the world.

Area 377,800sq km (145,869sq miles)
Government Constitutional monarchy
🗝 **Independence** Restored, 1952, after World War II occupation
Territories Ogasawara Islands
◎ **Currency** Yen
👤 **Population** 125,100,000
Density 322 per sq km (834 per sq mile)
Official Language Japanese
❋ **Major Religions** Shinto and Buddhist 76%, Buddhist 16%, other 8%

WEATHER FACTS

38°C (100.4°F)   1460mm (57.5in)   -24°C (-11.2°F)
23.8°C (74.8°F)   4.3°C (39.7°F)

1,000 Japanese yen

LANGUAGE

A traditional greeting in Japanese is *konnichiwa*. こんにちは

BLOSSOM

Cherry blossom is the national flower of Japan and is celebrated with festivals in spring.

LIFESTYLE FACTS

• A Japanese employee works longer hours (2,100 hours per year) than a worker in the United States (1,900 hours), or in Germany or France (1,600 hours).

• Japan has more golf courses per sq km than any other country. Due to lack of suitable space, there are multi-storey driving ranges.

• The Ainu, the aboriginal people of Japan, have their own culture, language, and religion. They live on Hokkaido island.

• In Japan, traditional flower arranging is called *ikebana*. The display is based on three main lines that symbolize heaven, earth, and humankind.

HORIYUJI TEMPLE

Buddhism was introduced into Japan in A.D. 538. The Horyuji Temple in Nara, first built in 607, is the world's oldest wooden building.

Map labels: Sea of Okhotsk, Kurile Islands, Iturup, Kunashir, Shikotan, Hokkaido, Ishikari Mts., Sapporo, Tsugaru Strait, Ou Mountains, Akita, Sado, Shinano, Honshu, Sea of Japan, Oki Is., Mt. Fuji 3,776m (12,385ft), L. Biwa, Nagoya, JAPAN, Kobe, Osaka, Nara, Chugoku Mts., Tsushima, Shikoku, Kyushu, PACIFIC OCEAN, Imperial Palace, Tokyo, Yokohama, N, East China Sea, Osumi Is., Amami Is., Ryukyu Islands, Okinawa

PHEASANT

The pheasant often appears in Japanese folklore and is the national bird.

IMPERIAL PALACE

The Imperial Palace was built on the grounds of Tokyo Castle. It is the official residence of the Japanese royal family. The present emperor, Akihito, is a direct descendant of the legendary first emperor Jimmu (660-585 B.C.).

FOOD FROM THE SEA

• Japan is the world's greatest fishing nation in terms of volume of catch. Almost 10 million tonnes of fish are caught each year.

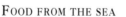

• Fish is the major source of protein and each person in Japan eats an average of 30kg (66lb) of fish a year.

• Life expectancy in Japan is the highest in the world: 81.8 years for women and 75.9 years for men.

SUMO WRESTLERS

Sumo wrestlers may weigh up to 280kg (617lb). To maintain this colossal weight, a wrestler eats a daily stew of seafood, meat, vegetables, and tofu, called *chanko-nabe*.

MOUNT FUJI FACTS

• Mount Fuji is one of Japan's 60 active volcanoes. It has not erupted since 1707.

• Mount Fuji is sacred to the Japanese, and in summer people climb to the shrine on the summit.

LAND PROFILE

Most of Japan is mountainous. Only 15% is suitable for farming.

%
4
5.5
90.5

TOP ELECTRONIC EXPORTS (1996)
(Value in US $1,000's)

Export	Value
TV cameras	4,078,154
Video recorders	2,826,193
Televisions	2,031,576
Tape recorders	1,904,653
Radios	1,518,825

Scale: 0 — 250km, 0 — 150 miles

INDONESIA

INDONESIA IS THE world's biggest island chain. It has more than 17,000 islands and covers three time zones. The weather is hot, wet, and humid. Rice is the most important food crop.

Area 1,904,570sq km (735,555sq miles)
Government Multiparty republic
⚷ **Independence** 1949, declared Republic of the United States of Indonesia
♾ **Currency** Rupiah
❖ **Population** 197,600,000
Density 109 per sq km (282 per sq mile)
Official Language Bahasa Indonesia
☽ **Major Religions** Muslim 87%, Christian 10%, Hindu 2%, Buddhist 1%

REGIONAL WEATHER FACTS

2403mm (94.6in)

26.8°C (80.2°F)   26.7°C (80.1°F)

REGIONAL FACTS

• In Malaysia, workers collect latex from rubber trees. They make a diagonal cut in the tree and then collect the white latex, or rubber, that oozes from the cut.

• Java produces the world's finest batik: traditional cloth decorated using wax and dyes.

• Indonesia is the largest Islamic country in the world.

LANGUAGE
A traditional greeting in Bahasa is *selamat pagi*.

PHILIPPINES

THE PHILIPPINES IS a collection of more than 7,000 islands. Rainfall can be heavy, and typhoons sweep through the northern islands.

Area 300,000sq km (115,830sq miles)
Government Multiparty republic
⚷ **Independence** 1946, from United States
♾ **Currency** Philippine peso
❖ **Population** 67,600,000
Density 227 per sq km (588 per sq mile)
Official Languages Filipino, English
✝ **Major Religions** Roman Catholic 83%, Protestant 9%, Muslim 5%, Buddhist and other 3%

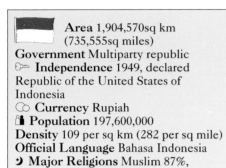

KOMODO DRAGON
The world's largest lizard is found on the island of Komodo. It eats anything it can catch, even people.

MALAYSIA

THE COUNTRY OF Malaysia covers the Malay Peninsula and northern Borneo. Malaysia is the world's leading producer of natural rubber.

Area 329,750sq km (127,317sq miles)
Government Federal constitutional monarchy
⚷ **Independence** 1957, from Britain
♾ **Currency** Ringgit
❖ **Population** 20,100,000
Density 61 per sq km (158 per sq mile)
Official Languages Bahasa Malaysia, English
Major Religions Muslim 53%, Buddhist 19%, Chinese faiths 11.6%, Christian 7%, Hindu 6.9%, traditional beliefs 2%, Sikh and other 0.5%

SINGAPORE

SINGAPORE IS A small and successful country. Most people work in industries making electrical goods, clothes, and transport items.

Area 620.5sq km (239sq miles)
Government Multiparty democracy
⚷ **Independence** 1965, breaks away from Malaysia
♾ **Currency** Singapore dollar
❖ **Population** 2,800,000
Density 4,590 per sq km (11,894 per sq mile)
Official Languages Bahasa Malaysia, English, Mandarin, Tamil
Major Religions Buddhist 30%, Christian 20%, Muslim 17%, other 33%

BRUNEI

BRUNEI IS A tiny, but extremely rich, country on the island of Borneo. The wealth comes from local oil, and the people of Brunei pay no taxes.

Area 5,770sq km (2,228sq miles)
Government Absolute monarchy
⚷ **Independence** 1984, from British control
♾ **Currency** Brunei dollar
❖ **Population** 300,000
Density 57 per sq km (148 per sq mile)
Official Languages Malay, English
Major Religions Muslim 63% (mainly Sunni), Buddhist 14%, Christian 10%, other 13%

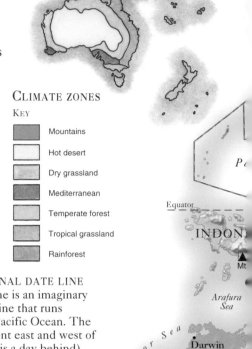

AUSTRALASIA AND OCEANIA

THIS AREA COVERS the continent of Australia, as well as New Zealand and numerous island groups in the Pacific Ocean. Climate zones vary greatly across the region, and include the wet, tropical conditions of the Pacific Islands as well as the hot, dry deserts of central Australia.

Area 8,508,238sq km (3,285,048sq miles)
Countries 13
Largest Australia 7,686,850sq km (2,967,908sq miles)
Smallest Nauru 21sq km (8sq miles)
Population 26,370,088
Density 3 per sq km (8 per sq mile)
Major Languages English, Italian (Australia), Fijian (Fiji), Hindi (Fiji), Greek (Australia)

▲ **Highest point** Mt. Wilhelm, Papua New Guinea 4,509 m (14,794 ft)
▼ **Lowest point** Lake Eyre, Australia -16m (-52ft)
☼ **Highest temperature** 53°C (128°F), Bourke, Australia
❄ **Lowest temperature** -22°C (-8°F), Canberra, Australia

CLIMATE ZONES

KEY

	Mountains
	Hot desert
	Dry grassland
	Mediterranean
	Temperate forest
	Tropical grassland
	Rainforest

COUNTRIES, TERRITORIES, AND CAPITALS

Name	Capital
Australia	Canberra
Fiji	Suva
Kiribati	Bairiki
Marshall Islands	Majuro
Micronesia (Federated States of)	Palikir
Nauru	No capital
New Zealand	Wellington
Palau	Oreor
Papua New Guinea	Port Moresby
Samoa	Apia
Solomon Islands	Honiara
Tonga	Nuku'alofa
Tuvalu	Fongafale
Vanuatu	Vila

TIME ZONES

Greenwich 12:00 | Perth 20:00 | Sydney 22:00 | Majuro 24:00 (midnight)

INTERNATIONAL DATE LINE
The Date Line is an imaginary north–south line that runs through the Pacific Ocean. The date is different east and west of the line (east is a day behind).

TOP CITY POPULATIONS

Adelaide, Australia 1,080,000 | Perth, Australia 1,262,000 | Brisbane, Australia 1,488,000 | Melbourne, Australia 3,217,000 | Sydney, Australia 3,770,000

MILFORD SOUND
Milford Sound in New Zealand is a spectacular fjord that was created when the sea flooded a glaciated valley.

CONTINENT FACTS
• In Australia, the Royal Flying Doctor Service provides emergency medical treatment for people who live vast distances from the nearest source of medical help.

• New Zealand's North Island is a volcanic region, with three active volcanoes, hot springs, geysers, and boiling mud pools.

• There are about 25,000 islands in the Pacific Ocean, but only a few thousand are inhabited. The islands stretch across an area that is larger than the entire continent of Asia.

LARGEST DESERTS

Great Victoria 647,000sq km (260,000sq miles)

Great Sandy 407,000sq km (157,000sq miles)

Gibson 310,800sq km (120,000sq miles)

Simpson 103,600sq km (40,000sq miles)

AGE BREAKDOWN

Under 15 years | 15 to 65 years | Over 65 years

Papua New Guinea 2.7%
Australia 11.2%
Tuvalu 31.8%
Marshall Islands 48.8%
Marshall Islands 48%
Australia 66.9%

KEY
☐ Lowest %
☐ Highest %

FEWEST DOCTORS

Papua New Guinea	1 to 12,870 people
Solomon Islands	1 to 10,000 people
Vanuatu	1 to 5,500 people
Marshall Islands	1 to 4,000 people
Tuvalu	1 to 2,500 people

LONGEST LIFESPAN

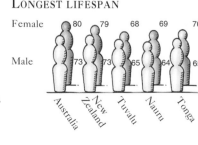

Female | 80 | 79 | 68 | 69 | 70
Male | 73 | 73 | 65 | 64 | 65
Australia | New Zealand | Tuvalu | Nauru | Tonga

Map labels

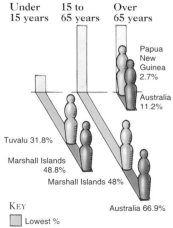

Equator
INDON
Mt
Arafura Sea
Timor Sea
Darwin
Kimberley Plateau
INDIAN OCEAN
Hamersley Range
Great Sandy Desert
Macdonell Range
AUSTRAL
Gibson Desert
Simpson Desert
Coon
Great Victoria Desert
Lake Ey -15m (-49
Perth
Great Australian Bight
Ad
Pe

CROSS-SECTION

3,000m
(9,843ft)
0 Sea level

-4,500m
(-14,764ft)

Indian Ocean · Mt. Bruce · Great Victoria Desert · Great Dividing Range · Tasman Sea · New Zealand · Pacific Ocean

Length: 7,250km (4,500 miles)

P A C I F I C   O C E A N

Wake I. (USA)

MARSHALL ISLANDS

Majuro

Caroline Islands

MICRONESIA

Palmyra I. (USA)

Line Islands

N

thern ariana lands

marck Sea

NAURU

APUA NEW INEA

SOLOMON ISLANDS

Gilbert Islands

K I R I B A T I

Phoenix Islands

TUVALU

Tokelau (New Zealand)

Marquesas Islands

Wallis & Futuna (France)

WESTERN SAMOA

American Samoa (USA)

Coral Sea Islands (Australia)

VANUATU

FIJI

TONGA

Niue (NZ)

Cook Islands (New Zealand)

French Polynesia (France)

New Caledonia (France)

Tropic of Capricorn

Pitcairn Islands (UK)

● Brisbane

Norfolk I. (Australia)

Kermadec Islands (New Zealand)

0   1000km
0   600 miles

Great Barrier Reef

Great Dividing Range

● Sydney

■ Canberra

lbourne

Tasman Sea

NEW ZEALAND

North Island

■ Wellington

International Date Line

Tasmania

● Hobart

South Island

Milford Sound

Southern Alps

Stewart I.

Chatham Islands

Bounty Islands

Antipodes Islands

Auckland Islands

Campbell I.

LAND PROFILE
Almost half the continent is covered in desert.

Barren land 0.25%   Urban 0.25%

Wetlands 3%

Agriculture 10.5%

Grassland 36%

Forest 5%

Desert 45%

WILDLIFE
Many of these animals and plants are unique to Australasia and Oceania.

FAUNA

Tasmanian devil (*Sarcophilus harrisi*) is found only in Tasmania. It eats all of its prey – bones, fur, and feathers – until nothing is left.

Queen Alexandra's butterfly (*Ornithoptera alexandrae*) is the world's largest butterfly with a wingspan that can measure up to 28cm (11in) across.

Red kangaroo (*Macropus rufus*) is the biggest marsupial in the world. A large male kangaroo can clear more than 8m (26ft) in one leap.

FLORA

Spinning gum (*Eucalyptus perriniana*), from Australia, is so-called because some leaves form spinning discs.

353

NEW ZEALAND

TWO MAIN ISLANDS and a number of smaller islands make up New Zealand. Its rich pastureland makes it one of the world's main producers of meat, dairy products, and wool. New Zealand is in an earthquake zone, and tremors are felt every year.

 Area 268,860sq km (103,730sq miles)
Government Unitarian parliamentary democracy, with British sovereign as constitutional monarch
Independence 1947, from Britain
Territories Cook Islands, Niue, Tokelau
Currency New Zealand dollar
Population 3,600,000
Density 13 per sq km (34 per sq mile)
Official Languages English, Maori
✝ **Major Religions** Protestant 62%, Roman Catholic 18%, other 20%

BEEHIVE BUILDING

This circular building, in the capital city of Wellington, is one of three parliament buildings. It was designed by British architect Sir Basil Spence (1907–76) and was opened in 1977.

SHEEP FARMING

The mild climate of New Zealand provides permanent pasture for the country's 52.6 million sheep. About 340,000 tonnes of wool are shorn a year, most of it used to supply high-class knitting yarns for export.

MAORI FACTS

• New Zealand's first settlers were the Maori – Polynesians who arrived in about A.D. 950. They called the country Aotearoa, which means "the land of the long white cloud."

• At the time of the 1991 census, the Maori population of New Zealand stood at 434,847, with 89% living on North Island. Almost one-third of Maoris are under 10 years of age.

• *Maoritanga* is the word for Maori culture, and traditional Maori art is preserved through woodcarving and stone sculpture.

WEATHER FACTS

35°C (95°F)   1,205mm (47.4in)   -6°C (21.2°F)
16.3°C (61.3°F)   9.5°C (49.1°F)

LIFESTYLE FACTS

• Sport is important to the people of New Zealand. The most popular sports for people over 15 years of age are swimming, diving, waterpolo, cycling, snooker and pool, tennis, and aerobics.

• In 1893, New Zealand became the first country where women could vote in national elections.

• Orchards produce a wide range of fruits ranging from apples to tamarillos, avocadoes, and kiwi fruit.

kiwi fruit

• Hiking is a popular pastime in New Zealand, where 13% of the land is turned over to National Parks.

NEW ZEALAND

Auckland
Hamilton   Bay of Plenty
NORTH ISLAND   L. Taupo
Hastings
Tasman Sea
Cook Strait
Wellington
Mt. Cook 3,754m (12,317ft)   Christchurch
Chatham Islands
Southern Alps
SOUTH ISLAND
Dunedin
Stewart I.
Snares Islands   Bounty Islands
Antipodes Islands
Auckland Islands
Campbell I.
0   1750km
0   1000 miles
PACIFIC OCEAN

PAPUA NEW GUINEA

PAPUA NEW GUINEA occupies the eastern half of a large island. The land is mountainous, and there are deposits of gold, oil, and copper.

 Area 462,840sq km (178,700sq miles)
Government Parliamentary democracy
Independence 1975, from Australian administration
Currency Kina
Population 5,000,000
Density 13 per sq km (34 per sq mile)
Official Language English

10 New Zealand dollars

LAND PROFILE

More than two-thirds of the land is used for grazing.

%
1.5
5
20
32
41.4

MICRONESIA

MORE THAN 600 islands and islets make up the Federated States of Micronesia. Plants include black pepper, which is grown for export.

Area 2,900sq km (1,120sq miles)
Independence 1986, from United States administration
Currency United States dollar
Population 107,000
Density 152 per sq km (394 per sq mile)
Official Language English

NAURU

THE SMALL ISLAND of Nauru is surrounded by a coral reef. The country has very little agriculture because of the infertile soil.

Area 21sq km (8sq miles)
Independence 1968, from UN supervision
Currency Australian dollar
Population 10,000
Density 476 per sq km (1,233 per sq mile)
Official Language Nauruan

SOLOMON ISLANDS

MOST OF THE eight main islands in this group are thickly forested and have a hot, wet climate. Islanders catch tuna for export.

 Area 28,900sq km (11,158sq miles)
Independence 1978, from Britain
Currency Solomon Islands dollar
Population 400,000
Density 11 per sq km (28 per sq mile)
Official Language English

MARSHALL ISLANDS

THE MARSHALL ISLANDS consist of two parallel chains of coral atolls. Farming and fishing, as well as raising pigs are the main activities.

Area 181sq km (70sq miles)

Independence 1986, from UN supervision

Currency United States dollar

Population 48,000

Density 265 per sq km (686 per sq mile)

Official Language English

SAMOA

THE PEOPLE OF Samoa are mainly Polynesians, descendants of the Maori. Frequent typhoons cause widespread damage to the islands.

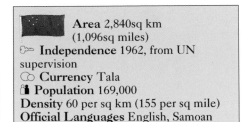

Area 2,840sq km (1,096sq miles)

Independence 1962, from UN supervision

Currency Tala

Population 169,000

Density 60 per sq km (155 per sq mile)

Official Languages English, Samoan

KIRIBATI

THE ISLANDS OF Kiribati have poor soil, so people rely on fishing. They use leaves from the pandanus tree to thatch their traditional homes.

Area 710sq km (274sq miles)

Republic Declared 1979

Currency Australian dollar

Population 66,000

Density 93 per sq km (241 per sq mile)

Official Language English

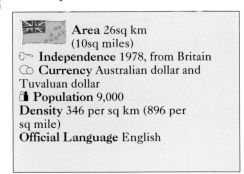

KIRIBATI CANOE
Fishing from canoes is traditional for the Pacific Ocean islanders. This fisherman from Kiribati has an outrigger, or float, on his canoe to help balance in rough seas.

TUVALU

TUVALU, FORMERLY the Ellice Islands, is made up of nine small coral atolls. Sales of postage stamps is an important source of income.

Area 26sq km (10sq miles)

Independence 1978, from Britain

Currency Australian dollar and Tuvaluan dollar

Population 9,000

Density 346 per sq km (896 per sq mile)

Official Language English

FIJI

MADE UP OF 322 islands, more than half of Fiji's land area is covered with forests. Coconuts are grown on plantations around the coasts.

Area 18,270sq km (7,054sq miles)

Independence 1970, from Britain

Currency Fiji dollar

Population 800,000

Density 44 per sq km (114 per sq mile)

Official Language English

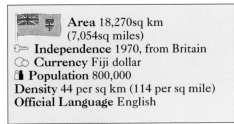

SUGAR CANE
Sugar is the main cash crop in Fiji. Women cut the cane using machetes.

VANUATU

THE VANUATU ISLANDS form a chain about 800km (497 miles) long. Bananas, oranges, and pineapples are grown in the fertile volcanic soil.

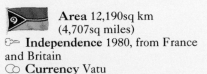

Area 12,190sq km (4,707sq miles)

Independence 1980, from France and Britain

Currency Vatu

Population 163,000

Density 13 per sq km (34 per sq mile)

Official Languages Bislama, English, French

TONGA

THERE ARE 169 islands in Tonga, some made of coral and some that are volcanic. Tonga is the last remaining Polynesian kingdom.

Area 750sq km (290sq miles)

Independence 1970, from Britain

Currency Pa'anga

Population 94,000

Density 131 per sq km (339 per sq mile)

Official Languages English, Tongan

AUSTRALIA

AUSTRALIA IS ONE of the oldest landmasses and is the flattest of the continents. Much of the country is hot and dry and farmers graze sheep and cattle, growing crops in places where irrigation is possible. Most people live in cooler coastal cities.

Area 7,686,850sq km (2,967,908sq miles)
Government Parliamentary democracy with British monarch as head of state
Independence 1901, Commonwealth of Australia created
Territories Australian Antarctic Territory, Christmas Island, Cocos (Keeling) Islands, Norfolk Island, Heard and McDonald Islands, Ashmore and Cartier Islands, Coral Sea Islands.
Currency Australian dollar
Population 18,758,000
Density 2 per sq km (5 per sq mile)
Official Language English
Major Religions Protestant 60%, Roman Catholic 26%, other 14%

An Aboriginal rock painting that shows a Dreamtime ancestor.

THE FIRST AUSTRALIANS
The Aboriginals were the first people to live in Australia about 50,000 years ago. They hold deep spiritual links with the land, believing it and all living things were created by their ancestor beings at the beginning of time.

MINING AND MINERALS
Australia is a major source of minerals. It is the world's largest exporter of coal, and has the world's most productive diamond mine near Lake Argyle in Western Australia.

MAJOR MINERAL EXPORTS (1996)

Mineral	Value in thousand US$
Coal	6,123,550
Gold	4,101,202
Iron ore	2,278,644
Aluminium ores	1,994,489
Zinc ores	348,540

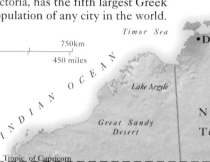

AUSTRALIAN MARSUPIAL FACTS
• Marsupials are animals that carry and suckle their young in a pouch in front of their body.

• The koala feeds on the leaves of eucalyptus trees found in Eastern Australia.

• The grey kangaroo has powerful hind legs and can jump at least 8m (26ft).

• The striped possum eats ants, bees, and termites in the rainforests of Queensland.

Koala

WEATHER FACTS

52°C (126°F)   629mm (24.8in)   -22°C (-7.6°F)
20.2°C (68.4°F)   6.7°C (44.1°F)

LAND PROFILE
Forests cover 5.5% of the land in Australia.

%
0.5
1
5.5
7.5
38.5
47

LIFESTYLE FACTS
• Voting is compulsory in Australia. Failure to vote is punishable by a fine.

• Australia is the world's leading producer of wool (30%). There are about 7 sheep for every person in Australia.

• Melbourne, the state capital of Victoria, has the fifth largest Greek population of any city in the world.

ISLAND STATE
Tasmania is the smallest of the Australian states. The south-west of the island is a natural wilderness and has been made a World Heritage Site.

MOST POPULAR SPORTS (1998)
Australians are keen on sport and will host the Olympic Games in the year 2000.

Sport	Club members
Swimming	1,628,800
Fitness	1,379,200
Golf	1,116,200
Tennis	937,800
Fishing	641,500
Cycling	626,000
Tenpin bowling	438,000

20 Australian dollars

GREAT BARRIER REEF
This reef, the largest structure built by living creatures, stretches for 2,000km (1,243 miles) off the Queensland coast. There are more than 400 types of coral and 1,500 species of fish.

AUSTRALIAN FLOWER
The national flower is the golden wattle.

Arafura Sea   *Torres Strait*
Timor Sea
• Darwin   *Gulf of Carpentaria*   *Coral Sea*
0   750km
0   450 miles
Lake Argyle
Great Sandy Desert   **Northern Territory**   **Queensland**
Tropic of Capricorn
Gibson Desert   Uluru (Ayers Rock)   A U S T R A L I A   *Great Dividing Range*
Western Australia   *Simpson Desert*   Brisbane •
Great Victoria Desert   L. Eyre
South Australia   Bourke •   *Great Range*   Sydney Opera House
• Perth   **New South Wales**
Great Australian Bight   Australian Capital Territory   **Sydney**
Adelaide •   *Murray*   **Canberra**
N   **Victoria**   Kosciuszko 2,228m (7,310ft)
Melbourne •   *Bass Strait*   *Tasman Sea*
Tasmania
• Hobart

INDIAN OCEAN   *PACIFIC OCEAN*

SYDNEY OPERA HOUSE
Sydney Opera House, designed by Danish architect Jörn Utzon (born 1918), was completed in 1973. The shell-shaped roofs are covered with more than one million Swedish ceramic tiles.

ANTARCTICA

ANTARCTICA IS THE coldest, windiest place on Earth. The harsh conditions mean there are no permanent inhabitants, only visiting scientists working in research stations. The land is rich in oil and minerals, but mining is prohibited under the laws of the Antarctic Treaty.

WEATHER FACTS

15°C (59°F)   303mm (12in)   -89°C (-128.2°F)

N

Area 14,200,000sq km (5,500,000sq miles)
Government None
Currency Not applicable
Population Staff of scientific stations – in winter about 1,000 people, in summer about 4,000
Density Not applicable
Official Language Not applicable
Major Religions Not applicable

THE ANTARCTIC TREATY
Antarctica is owned by no-one. In 1959, a group of nations agreed to set the land aside for peaceful uses only, and suspended the issue of territorial rights. The Antarctic Treaty was originally signed by Argentina, Australia, Belgium, Chile, France, Japan, New Zealand, Norway, South Africa, Russia, the UK, and USA. Since 1959, a further 28 countries have joined the Treaty.

LIFESTYLE FACTS
• Between 2,000 and 3,000 tourists a year admire the dramatic beauty of the landscape from the comfort of their cruise ships.

• Scientists in Antarctica carry out many experiments, such as studying the effect of the Antarctic ice sheet on the world's weather patterns, or observing the behaviour of marine life.

• Polar clothing is designed to keep the body warm, especially fingers and toes. Goggles help to protect eyes from the glare of the ice.

PROTECTING THE LAND
In 1987, British scientists discovered a hole in the ozone layer above Antarctica. The Greenpeace environmental organization would like Antarctica to be a World Park to protect the land for the future.

A Greenpeace boat patrols the icy seas.

South Orkney Islands (UK)
Scotia Sea
South Shetland Islands (UK)
Palmer Archipelago
Drake Passage
Antarctic Circle
Antarctic Peninsula
Alexander I.
Bellingshausen Sea
Peter I st I. (Norway)
Thurston I.
Amundsen Sea
Carney I.
Siple I.
PACIFIC OCEAN
Siple
Vinson Massif 5,140m (16,864ft)
Ellsworth Mts.
West Antarctica
Ross Ice Shelf
Roosevelt I.
Scott I.
Balleny Islands
Ross Sea
Vanda
Weddell Sea
Berkner Island
Ronne Ice Shelf
ATLANTIC OCEAN
Fimbul Ice Shelf
Riiser-Larsen Ice Shelf
Lyddan I.
ANTARCTICA
East Antarctica
South Pole
Vostok
Transantarctic Mountains
Amery Ice Shelf
West Ice Shelf
Davis Sea
Shackleton Ice Shelf
Mill I.
Casey
Dumont d'Urville Sea
INDIAN OCEAN
Antarctic Circle

0 — 750km
0 — 400 miles

CROSS-SECTION OF ANTARCTICA
Most of Antarctica is covered by a huge sheet of ice up to 2km (1.2 miles) thick.

West Antarctic Ice Sheet | Transantarctic Mountains | East Antarctic Ice Sheet
Siple | Casey
3,000m (9,843ft)
0 Sea level
-2,000m (-6,562ft)

0 km/miles | 2,000 km (1,243 miles) | 4,000 km (2,486 miles) | 6,000 km (3,729 miles)

ROSS ICE SHELF
Antarctica has the world's largest floating body of ice, the Ross Ice Shelf (shown left), which is as large as France. At some points the ice reaches 60m (197ft) high. Its flat surface provides the best approach to the interior.

SOUTH POLE
At the beginning of this century, many nations tried to reach the South Pole. On 14 December, 1911, Norwegian Roald Amundsen became the first person to reach the South Pole.

WILDLIFE
Antarctica is too cold for any land animals except the smallest insects. But the sea is rich in food, and many sea birds and sea mammals live on and around the nearby islands.

Blue whale (*Balaenoptera musculus*) is the largest animal ever to have lived, and can be up to 30m (98ft) long. It spends summers in Antarctic waters.

Emperor penguin (*Aptenodytes forsteri*) is the world's largest penguin, and can grow up to 1.2m (4ft) tall. The female lays one egg, which the male carries on his feet until the egg hatches.

FLAGS

THESE NATIONAL FLAGS represent the 198 main countries and territories of the world. The designs usually reflect the country's culture or religion.

Guatemala

Honduras

Belize

Barbados

Bahamas

Antigua & Barbuda

SOUTH AMERICA
The three-striped flag, or tricolour, is often used here.

Surinam

Brazil

Argentina

Chile

Uruguay

Paraguay

EUROPE
Many of the European flags use a variation of the cross.

England

Wales

Northern Ireland

Republic of Ireland

Spain

Portugal

Andorra

Netherlands

Belgium

Luxembourg

France

Monaco

Germany

Austria

Switzerland

Liechtenstein

Italy

Vatican City

Malta

San Marino

Finland

Lithuania

Latvia

Estonia

Ukraine

Poland

Czech Republic

Hungary

Romania

Moldavia

Belorussia

Slovakia

Turkey

Greece

Bulgaria

Albania

Cyprus

Yugoslavia

Croatia

Bosnia and Herzegovina

Slovenia

Macedonia

Armenia

Azerbaijan

Georgia

Russian Federation

AFRICA
Many African flags include the colours green, yellow, and red.

Uganda

Somalia

Sudan

Eritrea

Djibouti

Algeria

Egypt

Ethiopia

Kenya

Tanzania

NORTH AND CENTRAL AMERICA
Blue appears in many flags here.

Canada

Greenland

USA

Mexico

Nicaragua

Panama

El Salvador

Costa Rica

Cuba

Haiti

Jamaica

Trinidad & Tobago

Dominican Republic

Barbados

Antigua & Barbuda

Dominica

Grenada

St. Christopher & Nevis

St. Lucia

St. Vincent & The Grenadines

Colombia

Peru

Venezuela

Bolivia

Ecuador

Guyana

Sweden

Denmark

Norway

Iceland

United Kingdom

Scotland

FLAG FACTS
• Vexillology is the word for the study of flags. The name comes from the Latin *vexillum*, a banner carried by Roman soldiers.
• Throughout the world, a white flag is flown to indicate a truce.
• At sea, lowering the ship's flag, or ensign, is a sign of surrender.
• The continent of Antarctica has no flags. The land belongs to no-one and can be used only for peaceful research.

AFRICA
(Flags of Africa continued)

Mali

Mauritania

Morocco

Libya

Tunisia

Western Sahara

Nigeria

Niger

Chad

Cape Verde

Guinea

Liberia

Burkina

Benin

Sierra Leone

Togo

Gambia

Guinea-Bissau

Congo (Zaire)

Zambia

Angola

Cameroon

Central African Republic

Congo

Gabon

Burundi

Rwanda

Equatorial Guinea

Sao Tome & Principe

South Africa

Zimbabwe

Mozambique

Madagascar

Namibia

Malawi

Botswana

Lesotho

Swaziland

Comoros

INTERPRETING THE FLAG

Cap · 50 stars · 13 horizontal stripes · Flagstaff · Halyard

THE STARS AND STRIPES
The American flag has 50 stars – one for each of today's states. The horizontal stripes represent the country's original 13 states.

ASIA
Symbols of the Sun and the crescent of Islam can be seen.

Israel

Syria

Lebanon

Jordan

Iraq

Saudi Arabia

Kuwait

Yemen

United Arab Emirates

Oman

Qatar

Bahrain

Iran

Afghanistan

Kazakhstan

Uzbekistan

Kyrgyzstan

Tajikistan

Turkmenistan

India

Pakistan

Bangladesh

Nepal

Bhutan

Sri Lanka

Seychelles

Maldives

Mauritius

Vietnam

Thailand

Burma

Cambodia

Laos

China

South Korea

Taiwan

North Korea

Mongolia

Hong Kong

Japan

Indonesia

Malaysia

Philippines

Singapore

Brunei

AUSTRALASIA AND OCEANIA
Navigational stars are often used.

Australia

Papua New Guinea

Fiji

Solomon Islands

Vanuatu

New Zealand

Samoa

Marshall Islands

Tonga

Kiribati

Micronesia

Tuvalu

Nauru

Palau

MAPPING

TODAY, MOST PLACES in the world have been visited and mapped; and photographs taken from space have given us an accurate picture of the Earth's surface. Over the years, mapmakers, known as cartographers, have created maps for different purposes. People can use an atlas to find a particular place, or a smaller-scale map to drive or walk from one place to another.

EARLY MAPPING

Before the world was mapped out as it is today, people understood only the world that they knew. This clay tablet shows the earliest map of the world, which was made in Babylon (now Iraq) in about 1000 B.C. The outer circle is marked as the ocean with the known world depicted in the centre.

READING A MAP

A map is like an aerial photograph of the landscape and is designed to show a detailed part of the Earth's surface. To make good use of a map you must know how to "read" it.

The map (right) shows the landscape that appears in the photograph below.

Tree symbols show that an area is wooded.

Contour lines are imaginary lines joining places of the same height above sea level.

The church on the map is shown by a circle and a cross.

Legend

Dotted green lines on the map show the route of footpaths between fields.

The bigger a place is, the bigger its name appears on the map.

The steeper the hill, the closer together the contour lines.

LEGEND
Modern maps have a panel called a legend, or key, explaining what the symbols mean. These symbols are designed to save space, so that the mapmakers can include more information and place names on the map.

SCALE
A graduated line shows the real distance that 1 inch or 1 centimetre represents on the map.

1,000m   Metres   Kilometres   1km

1,000 yd   Yards   0   Miles

USING A COMPASS

A compass is an instrument used to find directions. The Earth's magnetism pulls the magnetised compass needle so that it points north. However, it points to magnetic north, which is not true north. Markers within the compass also show south, west, east, and the angles in between.

North
Northwest   Northeast
West   East
Southwest   Southeast
South

LONGITUDE AND LATITUDE

Lines of longitude are vertical lines that run through the Poles, while lines of latitude are horizontal lines that run parallel to the Equator. These imaginary lines on the Earth's surface help map readers to locate places on a map.

North Pole 90°   Greenwich meridian
60°   60°   Tropic of Cancer
30°   30°
0°   0°
Equator
30°
Tropic of Capricorn   60°   60°   30°
90° South Pole

Lines of latitude run parallel to the Equator.

Lines of longitude run north to south between the Poles.

PROJECTIONS

To show the Earth on a flat sheet of paper, mapmakers use a projection. Imagine a glass globe with a light at its centre. This light projects shadows on to a sheet of paper, which forms the basis of the map.

CONICAL
In this projection, the imaginary sheet of paper forms a cone, touching the Earth along a particular line of latitude. This system shows the least distortion to areas.

Conical projection

CYLINDRICAL
The paper is rolled around the Earth, touching it at the Equator. This shows north at the top, but the areas are distorted.

Cylindrical projection

ZENITHAL
The paper touches the globe at one point. If this point is the Pole, then the lines of longitude show their correct angles.

Zenithal projection

MERCATOR

Gerard Kremer (1512–94) was a Flemish geographer who found a way to show the globe on a flat map. He was called Mercator, or merchant, because he made maps for ocean-going traders.

WORLD MAPS

Mercator's world map was made in 1569. His projection shows the correct shapes of the continents but distorts their areas. Arno Peters' projection, made in 1977, distorts the shapes of countries but shows their true size.

Mercator's projection

Peters' projection

MAP FACTS

• Amerigo Vespucci (1454–1512) made maps of the New World based on the reports of his sea captains. His maps were referred to as Amerigo's land, or America.

• In 1884, when Britain was a great sea power, Greenwich was chosen as the place from which all measurements of longitude were to be made.

SATELLITE MAPS

With space technology, we can now compile maps from satellite photographs. This view of the Earth from space was made using thousands of separate images.

RAW MATERIALS

NATURAL SUBSTANCES THAT are extracted from the ground, from water, or from the air are called raw materials. These substances can be changed by chemical processes into many different types of material that can be put to everyday use.

DISTRIBUTION OF RAW MATERIALS

- Bauxite (aluminium oxide)
- Copper
- Kaolin (clay)
- Oil
- Sulphur
- Coal
- Iron ore
- Natural gas
- Cement
- Wood

RAW MATERIAL FACTS

- Copper is a good conductor of heat and electricity. It lasts a long time because it does not rust easily and is ideal for making wires and hot-water pipes.

- Aluminium, extracted from bauxite ore, is lightweight, easy to work and shape, yet durable. It is ideal for making bicycle frames, aircraft, and motor-vehicle parts.

OIL

Crude oil, from which thousands of products are made, is found under the ground or sea. The oil is separated into various parts by a process called fractional distillation: it is heated to form different gases, then each gas condenses back into a liquid at a different temperature.

LEADING PRODUCERS OF RAW MATERIALS

Material	Top producers	Total* (in millions)	World total* (in millions)
Bauxite (aluminium oxide)	Australia	37.4	
	Guinea	16.5	1,064
Coal	China	1,054	
	USA	889	5,882
Copper	Chile	1.6	
	USA	1.5	9.2
Natural Gas	CIS	796,000m³	
	USA	488,749m³	2,100,000 m³
Iron ore	CIS	241	
	China	165	984
Kaolin (clay)	CIS	2.0	
	Republic of Korea	1.3	23.1
Oil	CIS	607	
	USA	373	
	Saudi Arabia	257	2,987
Salt	USA	35.5	
	China	28.3	189
Sulphur	USA	11.6	
	China	7.4	60.3
Wood	USA	1,109m³	
	CIS	862m³	7,147m³

*All figures in tonnes apart from m³ = cubic metres.

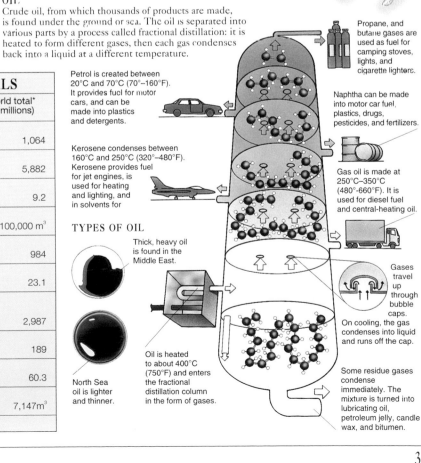

Propane, and butane gases are used as fuel for camping stoves, lights, and cigarette lighters.

Petrol is created between 20°C and 70°C (70°–160°F). It provides fuel for motor cars, and can be made into plastics and detergents.

Naphtha can be made into motor car fuel, plastics, drugs, pesticides, and fertilizers.

Kerosene condenses between 160°C and 250°C (320°–480°F). Kerosene provides fuel for jet engines, is used for heating and lighting, and in solvents for

Gas oil is made at 250°C–350°C (480°–660°F). It is used for diesel fuel and central-heating oil.

TYPES OF OIL

Thick, heavy oil is found in the Middle East.

Gases travel up through bubble caps. On cooling, the gas condenses into liquid and runs off the cap.

North Sea oil is lighter and thinner.

Oil is heated to about 400°C (750°F) and enters the fractional distillation column in the form of gases.

Some residue gases condense immediately. The mixture is turned into lubricating oil, petroleum jelly, candle wax, and bitumen.

FARMING AND FISHERIES

IN 9000 B.C., people in the Middle East began to grow crops. They were the first farmers. Since then, people have tried many different ways of producing crops, rearing animals, and catching fish. Today, farming and fishing are major international industries.

MAJOR WORLD CROPS AND LIVESTOCK

This map shows the top producer of each crop or livestock.

Cattle — Maize — Soy beans
Coffee — Oats — Tea
Cotton — Potatoes — Tobacco
Cow's milk — Rice — Wheat
Hen's eggs — Rubber — Wood
Hogs — Sheep — Wool

TOP AGRICULTURAL PRODUCERS

Product	Top Producer	Second	Third
Cattle	Australia	Brazil	USA
Coffee	Brazil	Colombia	Indonesia
Cotton	China	USA	Former USSR
Cow's milk	USA	Germany	Russia
Hen's eggs	China	USA	Russia
Hogs	China	USA	Russia
Maize	USA	China	Brazil
Oats	Former USSR	USA	Canada
Potatoes	Russia	Poland	China
Rice	China	India	Indonesia
Rubber	Malaysia	Indonesia	Thailand
Sheep	Australia	China	New Zealand
Soy beans	USA	Brazil	China
Tea	India	China	Sri Lanka
Tobacco	China	USA	India
Wheat	China	Former USSR	USA
Wood	USA	Russia	China
Wool	Australia	Former USSR	New Zealand

CROP FACTS

• More than half the world's population relies on three grains – wheat, maize, and rice – for their basic food needs.

• Asia produces more than nine-tenths of the world's rice, and could not feed itself on any other crop.

• More than 500 varieties of grape are grown along the Black Sea coast in Georgia.

• Eighty-five per cent of the world's orange juice is supplied by Brazil.

• Malaysia's rubber trees are descended from about 11 seedlings, sent to Malaysia from Kew Gardens, England, in 1877.

SHEEP JAM

In New Zealand, sheep outnumber people by 20 to 1, and have right of way on the roads.

SELECTING AND CULTIVATING CROPS

Only the strongest plants are selected and cultivated. This has caused the size, shape, and flavour of many crops to change over the years.

Wild tomatoes

Though smaller, wild tomatoes are sweeter and more strongly flavoured than cultivated tomatoes.

Cultivated tomato

Cultivated corn cob

Wild carrot

Cultivated carrot

Early corn cob

A wild cabbage has bitter-tasting, leathery leaves.

A cultivated cabbage has tightly packed leaves.

FROM GRAIN TO FOOD

The wide variety of grain grown can be made into many different types of food.

Bread wheat

Bread wheat's large grains have a high gluten content – this makes bread dough elastic.

Whole-wheat flour

White bread, from bleached flour

Brown bread, from unbleached flour

Long grain rice

Rice plant

Durum wheat has a low gluten content, and is used to make pasta and biscuits.

Types of pasta

Pasta comes in a variety of shapes and sizes.

Ruotedi carro, or "cartwheels"

Spaghetti

FARMING PROCESSES

SUBSISTENCE FARMING

When farmers grow enough food to support themselves and their families, but leave little or nothing to be sold, this is known as subsistence farming. Subsistence farming is more common in developing countries, such as Kenya, Africa.

Subsistence farming in Sudan

INTENSIVE FARMING

In this type of farming, production of crops and livestock is maximized by the use of machinery and chemicals. Up to ten people can be fed from land that once fed one person.

In spring the soil is ploughed into furrows ready for planting.

A seed drill plants the seeds in the prepared soil and covers them again with soil.

Once the grain is ripe, it is cut by a combine harvester and taken away for storage.

A sprayer is used to spray crops with pesticides to kill any insects that may harm the young plants.

Battery hens

One disadvantage of intensive farming is that it can lead to animals being treated in an unnatural way. Egg-laying hens are often kept in cages in buildings called batteries where they do not have enough space to flap their wings or turn around. Because of concern for animal welfare and a preference for naturally grown food, more people are returning to natural, or organic, farming methods.

Battery hens, Texas, USA

FISHING INDUSTRY

Most fish are caught in the seas near the coast, above the continental shelf. Different fishing methods are used, largely depending on whether the fish swim near the surface of the sea (pelagic fish) or on or near the sea bed (demersal fish).

WAYS OF CATCHING FISH

Deep-water trawling

Cone-shaped nets, about 30m (100ft) wide, are pulled along the sea bed by a trawler. Used to catch demersal fish, such as cod.

Mid-water trawling

Trawling nets are towed by either one or two trawlers. Used to catch pelagic fish, such as herring.

Trawler

Drift nets

Long nets, up to 95km (60 miles) in length, are left to drift in the water and used to catch pelagic fish.

Drift nets are attached to a boat.

Purse-seining

Pelagic fish are surrounded by a huge net and the net lines are drawn together, like purse strings, until the fish are completely enclosed in the net.

Lining

Long lines with baited hooks are laid, either on the sea bed, to catch demersal fish, or near the surface, to catch tuna and mackerel.

Baskets or netting pots

These are used to catch shellfish, such as crabs and lobsters. The openings are designed so the fish can easily swim inside but find it difficult to get out.

FISHING GROUNDS

The continental shelf (shown in blue on the map) is the land surrounding each continent, covered by shallow sea water. It is rich in nutrients, and is an excellent feeding ground for fish.

FISHING FACTS

• At least 25% of the world's diet of animal protein is derived from fish and other seafood.

• Japan catches about 10 million tonnes of fish each year, more than any other country in the world.

• Fish and fish products account for about 70% of Iceland's export earnings. They consume more cod-liver oil than any other nation, and produce more than one third of the world's supply.

• In Vietnam, bomb craters remaining after the Indochinese conflicts (1946–75) have since been turned into pools for farming fish.

WORLD DISTRIBUTION OF FISH CATCHES

Area	Catch in million metric tonnes (1989–91)
Pacific Ocean	48.32
Atlantic Ocean	20.17
Indian Ocean	5.93
Mediterranean and Black Sea	1.29
Antarctic	0.40
World total	76.11

FISH PRODUCTS

Meal and oil 29.7%
Fresh 23.8%
Frozen 21.1%
Cured 13.4%
Canned 12%

FISH FARMING

Some types of fish, such as trout and carp, are kept on fish farms. Enclosures are built on lakes, ponds, or estuaries. Most fish farming occurs in fresh water, but in some countries, such as Japan, fish farms have been built along sheltered coastal waters.

Salmon farm, Norway

AGRICULTURAL WORDS

Agroforestry System of growing trees and crops together.
Biotechnology To scientifically change plants and animals for the benefit of humans.
Cash crops Crops grown for trade.
Hydroponics Growing plants without soil using water and nutrients.

Irrigation To water dried-up land by using water channels, pipes, or sprinklers.
Nomadic Moving from place to place to find new grazing land, food, and water.
Rainforest A forest that grows in hot, tropical areas that have high rainfall.
Subsoil Layer of soil underneath topsoil.
Topsoil The uppermost, fertile layer of soil.

POPULATION

THE TOTAL POPULATION of the world now stands at 5.6 billion. Some continents are experiencing a population explosion, others are beginning to stabilize their growth. Many people think that an increasing population is the greatest problem facing the world.

WORLD POPULATION

Europe: 750,582,660 13.9% of world population

North/Central America: 431,352,677. 8% of world population

South America: 305,074,803 5.6% of world population

Oceania: 26,370,088 0.5% of world population

Asia: 3,184,078,671 59.3% of world population

Africa: 678,428,967 12.7% of world population

MOST POPULATED COUNTRIES

Country	Total population (in millions)
China	1,200.0
India	935.7
United States	263.3
Indonesia	197.6
Brazil	161.8
Russia	149.9
Pakistan	140.5
Japan	125.1
Bangladesh	120.4
Nigeria	111.7
Mexico	93.7
Germany	81.6
Vietnam	74.5
Philippines	67.6

Source: Population Concern

FERTILITY RATES

The fertility rate corresponds to the average number of children born to a woman in her lifetime. Even if every couple had only two children starting tomorrow, the world's population would still grow to at least 8 billion.

8.5   7.6   6.4   5.1   4.5   3.9   2.2   1.5

Rwanda   Malawi   Saudi Arabia   Nicaragua   Cambodia   India   China   Germany

POPULATION GROWTH RATES

This table shows the current rate of population increase and the time it will take each region to double in size.

Region	Increase (annual %)	Doubling Time (years)
Africa	2.9	24
Latin America	2.0	35
Asia	1.7	41
Oceania	1.2	57
North America	0.7	98
Europe	0.1	1,025

Source: Population Concern

GROWTH FACT
● About 97% of global population growth between now and 2050 is projected to occur in Africa, Asia, and Latin America – the countries least able to absorb such increases.

POPULATION MOMENTUM
Three people are born every second, nearly 11,000 every hour, and more than 255,000 every day.

POPULATION FACTS
● One-third of the world's people are under the age of 15.

● By 2025, the total number of people aged 60 and over will be about 1.2 billion (14% of the world's population). The majority of them, almost 71%, will be living in the developed countries.

● 75% of the world's population cannot be expected to reach their sixtieth birthday.

LEAST DENSELY POPULATED COUNTRIES

Country	Population per sq km	per sq mile
Western Sahara	1	2.6
Mongolia	1	2.6
Namibia	2	5.2
Australia	2	5.2

AGEING POPULATION
Ageing populations occur in more developed countries. Here, people choose not to have many children because infant mortality is low and the cost of living high. Advanced medicines help to increase life expectancy and enable the existing population to live longer.

YOUNG POPULATION
People in developing countries have more children. Health care is poor, many babies die at birth, and people do not have long lives. In such countries, numbers of young people have increased dramatically: in Africa almost half the population is under the age of 15.

URBANIZATION

Modern technology has enabled more people to live in a smaller space. Today, nearly 50% of the world's population, about 2.6 billion people, live in cities. Of these urban dwellers, half live in cities of more than 500,000 people.

Sprawling suburbs of Mexico City

WORLD URBAN GROWTH

KEY
2000
1990
1970
1950

London
New York
Mexico City
Tokyo
Shanghai
Cairo
Tehran
Bangkok
Bombay
São Paulo

This map shows major world city populations in millions from 1950 projected to 2000.

POPULATION MANAGEMENT

The education of women is now recognized as the most important factor in population control. Programmes that give women choice in matters of family planning and contraception (see p.130) are becoming more widespread.

Urban and rural population predictions

These diagrams show the proportion of the world's population living in urban and rural areas. The chart for 2025 forecasts the majority of the developing world living in urban areas.

Urban (developing world): 25%
Urban (developed world): 17%
Rural (developed world): 6%
Rural (developing world): 52%
1990 World population

Urban (developing world): 46%
Urban (developed world): 13%
Rural (developed world): 4%
Rural (developing world): 37%
2025 World population

THE CAIRO CONFERENCE

In 1994, the Cairo Conference on world population agreed on a twenty-year programme that laid emphasis on giving women greater power in matters of family planning. The UN claims that if this programme succeeds, world population will rise to 7.27 billion by 2015. If it fails, the population will reach 7.92 billion people by 2015, and 12.5 billion by 2050.

Delegates at the Cairo Conference

WORLD'S LARGEST CITIES

City (metropolitan area)	Total Population (millions)
Tokyo, Japan	27.242
Mexico City, Mexico	16.908
São Paulo, Brazil	16.792
New York, USA	16.390
Bombay, India	15.725
Shanghai, China	13.659
Los Angeles, USA	12.576
Calcutta, India	12.118
Buenos Aires, Argentina	11.931
Seoul, South Korea	11.768

Source: UN "Urban Agglomerations"

YEAR ZERO

When the Khmer Rouge took power in Cambodia in 1976, they said that cities were corrupt places. They hoped to begin a new era by forcing people to abandon them.

FAMILY PLANNING FACTS

- Less than 2% of government spending in the developing world, and less than 2% of all international aid, is currently devoted to family planning programmes.

- Financial incentives are used in China to promote a policy of one child per family.

SHIFTING POPULATIONS

Refugees are people who have fled their country in fear; today they number 20 million. People become refugees for many reasons such as war, politics, and religious and racial discrimination. Some refugees, like the Vietnamese boat people, have undertaken difficult and dangerous journeys to safety.

THE REFUGEE POPULATION

Country of origin	Number of refugees (millions)
Afghanistan	4.0
Rwanda	3.0
Palestine	2.8
Former Yugoslavia	1.3
Burundi	0.8
Mozambique	0.7
Liberia	0.7
Angola	0.5
Sri Lanka	0.5
Sudan	0.4
Azerbaijan	0.3

Source: The Refugee Council

MASS MIGRATIONS

Throughout history, people have chosen to leave their homelands or have abandoned them against their will.

- From 1600 to 1810, ten million Africans were taken as slaves to the Americas to work on plantations.

- Expansion in North America came via mass immigration: from 1860 to 1910, the population rose from 31 to 92 million.

SPACE POPULATIONS

Scientists explore ways to enable people to live on other planets. An experiment in Texas to create an artificial atmosphere was called Biosphere II. Although it failed, there is still hope that one day people may live in artificial atmospheres on the Moon.

LIVING STANDARDS

HIGH STANDARDS IN health, nutrition, and education are considered fundamental to the well-being of a nation. Generally, if a country is wealthy, its population will enjoy a high standard of living. If it is poor, people may not get enough to eat and may also lack social services such as hospitals and schools. Poverty also exists in developed countries, where a high standard of living for a few people can mean that others struggle to afford necessities.

World Health Organization

CHILD MORTALITY RATES

This table shows how many children under 5 die each year per 1,000 children.

Country	Infant deaths
Niger	320
Angola	292
Mozambique	287
Afghanistan	257
Sierra Leone	249
Finland	7
Singapore	7
Sweden	7
Japan	6

Source: UNICEF (1992)

BIRTH AND DEATH RATES

Region	Births (millions per year)	Deaths (millions per year)
Asia	84.8	27.1
Africa	29.4	9.1
South America	12.7	3.3
Europe	8.7	8.0
North America	4.6	2.6
Oceania	0.6	0.2

LIFE EXPECTANCY

The graph below shows the average age to which men and women are expected to live.

Afghanistan 41 42
Burkina 45 49
China 68 71
India 55 56
Australia 74 80
USA 72 79

Women
Men

DISEASE

In tropical countries, infections are spread by organisms that carry disease from person to person. Developing countries also tend to suffer from diseases carried by contaminated food and water. In these countries, children are most at risk: life expectancy is low and disease cripples many. Diseases linked with industrialization and wealth, such as cancer and heart disease, have brought new health problems to developed countries.

DISEASE FACTS

• Measles, diarrhoea, and pneumonia kill an estimated 7 million children a year.

• Tetanus kills 600,000 babies each year even though immunization exists.

• Every year polio cripples 140,000 children.

• Following WWI, a global influenza epidemic killed nearly 22 million people between 1918 and 1920.

• Infectious diseases account for 25% of all deaths in the developing world, compared with just 1.4% of total deaths in the developed world.

SAFE WATER

UNICEF (United Nations Children's Fund) defines safe water as "20 litres per person per day, at a source within one kilometre from the user's dwelling". Most diseases are spread through water contaminated by waste. Dehydration also causes many deaths. WHO aims to provide as many people as possible with clean water and proper sanitation.

Children collecting water in Africa.

WATER FACTS

• 22% of Mozambique's population has safe water.

• Two-thirds of the world's families do not have running water in their homes.

• If clean, safe water was made available for the world's population, 80% of sickness and disease would be prevented.

• Almost 2 billion people, most of them in the developing world, do not have access to the minimum level of safe drinking water.

SALAAM BOMBAY

Every year, an estimated 13 million children die, the equivalent of the entire population of Bombay, India.

HEALTH AND SICKNESS

The World Health Organization (WHO) defines "health" as a state of physical, mental, and social well-being. The absence of adequate food and sanitation causes much sickness around the world. The availability of doctors and hospitals also contributes to maintaining a nation's health.

Malaria has killed more than any other disease in recorded history. It kills at least 2 million people every year, most of them children in Africa, and infects 10 million with the disease. Mosquitoes carry the malarial protozoa, which is becoming increasingly resistant to western medicines.

AIDS stands for Acquired Immune Deficiency Syndrome. In 1990, it was believed that more than 80% of the estimated 8.8 million people infected with HIV (see p.125) live in developing countries. More than 1.8 million people will have died as a result of AIDS by the year 2000.

DOCTORS PER POPULATION

The graph below shows how many people there are per doctor in each country.

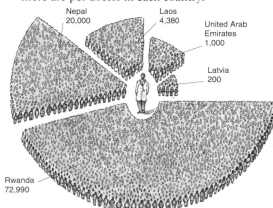

Nepal 20,000
Laos 4,380
United Arab Emirates 1,000
Latvia 200
Rwanda 72,990

FOOD AND NUTRITION

Food production has been increased to deal with the growing world population. Nutrition is not just a matter of good food; immunization, safe water supply, and a basic education would all reduce child malnutrition. Millions of people, most of them in the developing world, still suffer from malnutrition.

Undernourished child

FOOD PRODUCTION

The Food and Agriculture Organization (FAO) was set up in 1945, as part of the United Nations. It aims to reduce malnutrition, to improve efficiency in food production and distribution, and to improve life in rural areas.

Food and Agriculture Organization

EDUCATION

Education remains the single most important factor in creating a better world. Educating women has been shown to improve health care, reduce infant mortality, and lead to greater control over population growth.

Family planning in Africa

EDUCATION FACTS

• In 1993, almost 130 million children, two-thirds of them girls, were denied primary education.

• About one billion adults cannot read or write.

FOOD SUPPLY

The "Dietary energy supply" (DES) is the amount of food available per person per day, and is measured in calories. The table below compares the DES in some developed and developing countries.

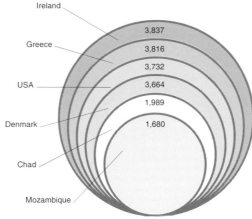

Ireland	3,837
Greece	3,816
USA	3,732
Denmark	3,664
Chad	1,989
Mozambique	1,680

ADULT LITERACY RATES

This table shows the percentage of each region's male and female population aged over 15 years who can read and write.

	F	M
Africa	38.5	61.7
America	89.2	90.8
Asia	66	76.6
Europe	96.2	97.7
Oceania	91.1	92.5

HIGHEST SPENDERS ON EDUCATION

This table shows % of income (GNP) spent on education.

Country	% of GNP
Liechtenstein	11.8
Surinam	9.7
Libya	9.6
Algeria	9.1
Seychelles	9.1

LOWEST SPENDERS ON EDUCATION

This table shows % of income (GNP) spent on education.

Country	% of GNP
Somalia	0.4
Indonesia	0.9
Congo (Zaire)	0.9
Paraguay	1.0
Laos	1.2

NUTRITION FACTS

• About one-third of the developing world's children are underweight.

• 80% of the food for home consumption in Africa is grown by women.

SCHOOL'S OUT

Almost 80 million children in developing countries do not attend primary school.

BEST PUPIL/ TEACHER RATIO

Country	Pupils per teacher
San Marino	6
Sweden	6
Austria	11
Qatar	11

WORST PUPIL/ TEACHER RATIO

Country	Pupils per teacher
Central African Republic	90
Equatorial Guinea	68
Chad	67
Burundi	67

NORTH–SOUTH DIVIDE

Economic differences between developed and developing countries are also seen as a physical divide. The developed countries mainly occupy the northern part of the planet and the developing countries the south. This is known as the "North–South divide".

ECONOMIC FACTS

• A person from a developed nation consumes 20 to 30 times more of the world's resources than a person from the developing world.

• The average Ghanaian spends $5 a year in the shops compared to $9,000 for the average Japanese.

THE HUMAN INDEX

Many people now consider GNP (see p.368) to be an unreliable reflection of a nation's development. The United Nations publishes "The Human Development Index", which is an alternative way of measuring the well-being and economic progress of a nation. Different indicators of living standards are recorded (e.g. education, life expectancy, nutrition, access to water), to help to establish an accurate world ranking for development. This index also recognizes poor living standards in the developed world.

HIGHEST LIVING STANDARDS

Country	Rank	Assessment
Japan	1	High income and savings by individuals
Canada	2	Among the highest figures of GNP per person
Norway	3	High standards of health and social services
Switzerland	4	High income per person

Source: United Nations (1993)

LOWEST LIVING STANDARDS

Country	Rank	Assessment
Guinea	173	Just 32% of population has access to safe water
Sierra Leone	172	Daily calorie supply is only 79% of requirements
Afghanistan	171	Average life expectancy is about 40 years
Burkina	170	69% of population have access to safe water

Source: United Nations (1993)

DEBT AND WEALTH

LEVELS OF PROSPERITY around the world differ from country to country. Although the wealth of a nation is not simply a matter of money, what a country has or owes can indicate its prosperity.

Out of sight, out of mind: a South American shanty town situated on the fringe of the city.

WEALTH AND TRADE

A country's wealth depends on factors of production such as natural resources, capital, and labour. Some countries are rich in large amounts of mineral deposits like coal, oil, gold, and copper. Others may have a large amount of capital in the form of money from business, or a highly skilled workforce. These resources are traded within a country, as well as on the world market.

IMPORTS AND EXPORTS

Imports are what one country buys from another; exports are what it sells to another. By trading internationally, a country can sell what it produces to pay for things it is unable to produce itself. When a country does not produce enough wealth, it must borrow money from another country to pay for its imports.

Imports

India imports cars from Japan and oil from the Arabian peninsula. It exports tea and textiles to Europe, and rice to Australia.

Exports

THE UNEQUAL WORLD

The world has experienced an exceptional growth in wealth since the 1950s with technology making the means of production more efficient. Many countries, particularly those situated in the southern hemisphere of the planet, have not benefited from this growth and are known as "developing" countries. The resulting inequality is known as the "North–South" divide.

THE DEBT CRISIS

Some developing countries borrow money for development from banking organizations like the World Bank. These institutions charge interest on the money borrowed. The longer a country takes to pay back the loan, the more interest they are charged. Some countries have to use much of the money they earn from trade to repay this interest, instead of using it for development. Developed countries have been criticized for controlling developing countries through debt.

IMF AND WORLD BANK

The International Monetary Fund (IMF) and World Bank were set up after World War II to help Europe redevelop. When developing countries became independent they also turned to these banks for aid.

International Monetary Fund

The World Bank

Economic inequalities

Economic alliances between developed countries have widened the gap between rich and poor nations.

Production *Trade* *Aid*

| ▨ | Rest of the world | ☐ | 24 richest countries |

Chart of debt in comparison with GNP

Brazil   Mexico   Indonesia   India

| ▨ Total GNP | ☐ Total debt |

NOT-SO-GOLDEN HANDSHAKE

Ten countries are home to three-quarters of the world's poor, and yet they receive only 26% of total global aid.

RICHEST AND POOREST

Economists judge a nation's wealth by looking at its Gross National Product, or GNP (the income generated per year). GNP per capita shows the average income of each person. Although useful, many believe that this does not reflect the true prosperity of a country.

Country	GNP per capita (US$)	Country	GNP per capita (US$)
Switzerland	37,930	Rwanda	80
Japan	34,630	Mozambique	90
Denmark	27,970	Ethiopia	100
Norway	26,390	Eritrea	100
USA	25,880	Somalia	120
Germany	25,580	Tanzania	140
Austria	24,630	Burundi	160
Sweden	23,530	Sierra Leone	160
France	23,420	Malawi	170

OIL WEALTH

Producers of particular goods have formed alliances to protect their mutual economic interests. OPEC, the Organization of Petroleum Exporting Countries, was set up to represent the interests of petroleum-exporting, developing countries. The price of oil has a greater effect on the international economy than any other product.

Representatives at an OPEC conference

OIL CRISIS

In 1973, OPEC restricted the amount of oil it was exporting, which in turn increased the price of oil around the world. This affected the wealth of many countries, especially the USA with its high consumption of oil by industry. To save petrol, the American authorities had to introduce a 50km/h (30mph) speed limit.

Cars queuing for petrol during the oil crisis.

TOP AID DONORS

Aid supplier	Aid as % of GNP (1994)
Norway	1.05
Denmark	1.03
Sweden	0.96
Netherlands	0.76
France	0.64
Canada	0.43

Source: UNICEF "The Progress of Nations"

HISTORY

Spanning the period from 40,000 B.C. to the present day, this extensive and absorbing section includes all the key dates and events in world history. Comparative timelines provide a global overview of events in each continent at any given time, and detailed tables list key personalities for every historical era.

Early Toolmakers and Artists • Early Farmers and Towns • Egypt and Mesopotamia
Expanding Empires and Mediterranean Trade • Ancient Greece and the Rise of Rome
Imperial Rome and Christianity • Islam and the Vikings • Mongols and Crusaders
Marco Polo and the Black Death • Renaissance and the Americas
Religious Conflict and Akbar • Manchu China, Supreme Rulers, and Slavery
Enlightenment, Revolution, and Napoleon • Europe in Turmoil and the British Empire
American Civil War and the Scramble for Africa • World War I and the Russian Revolution
Interwar Years and Communists in China • World War II • Cold War and the Middle East
African Independence • Middle East and the End of the Cold War • Great Civilizations
Rulers and Leaders • Presidents and Prime Ministers • Explorers • Battles and Wars
Revolutions and Rights • Archaeology and History

40,000 B.C.

AFRICA			**30,000** Disappearance of the Neanderthals
ASIA **40,000** Cro-Magnon humans living at Skhül and Kafzel (Israel)			**27,000–19,000** Female statuettes made at various sites, including locations in Russia
EUROPE **40,000** Neanderthals active in France at La Chapelle-Aux-Saints, La Ferassie, and La Quina. Cro-Magnons start to spread to Europe	**35,000** Start of Upper Paleolithic Period (flaked stone tools, bone and horn implements)		**30,000** Probable date of earliest figurative art in Fra (Dordogne). Disappearance of Neanderthals **27,000–19,000** Female statuettes at various sites in France and Italy
AMERICAS	**35,000** First humans arrive in North America from Asia		
OCEANIA **40,000** Probable arrival of Aboriginals in Australia			

THE FIRST TOOLMAKERS

In this period our human ancestors *(Homo sapiens sapiens)* became the dominant species on Earth. These early humans made great advances in toolmaking, and examples of their tools survive today. With great skill, they shaped stone and other materials, such as bone and wood, to produce a useful toolkit.

Area of skilfully flaked flint points. Use of nets and snares

Advanced flintwork, spear throwers, lamps and palettes for cave painting

Advanced bone carving, grain mills, bowls

Basic stone and flint tools

Widespread flint- and bone work

● Toolmaking region

REGIONS OF TOOLMAKING INDUSTRIES

Where early humans found such raw materials as stone, flint, bone, antler, shell, wood, and ivory, they started up toolmaking industries. Examples of tools have been found in continental and southern Europe, in southern Africa, Mesopotamia, and the Americas.

Felled trees allow greater use of timber for homes and tools.

Binding a wooden haft to a stone axehead allowed user to swing it with great force.

The sickle's long edge could be used to reap corn.

Toolmaker fits flints into shaft.

When a flint piece became blunt it could be replaced easily.

Handaxe used to skin animal.

Flint flakes from handaxe kept to make other tools.

Point and double edge allow many uses.

Toolmaker uses burin to carve antler.

Antler

Axe-head

Split shaft

Pin

Flint axe-head fitted on to haft

1 FLINT HANDAXE

The most commonly found tool of early humans is the flint handaxe. Toolmakers used such techniques as pressure flaking, which controls the size of the chip, to give the stone a fine point and a sharp, straight, double edge.

Flint handaxe

2 STONE BURIN

After the handaxe, toolmakers developed the burin. This smaller, thinner stone tool was used to carve materials other than stone, such as antler and bone. Toolmakers made fine items including needles, fish hooks, and spear throwers.

Burin

Hafted axe

3 COMBINING MATERIALS

The next advances came when toolmakers found they could combine different materials.

Small, sharp pieces of flint

Split bone shaft

KEY INNOVATIONS

Spear rests on end of thrower.

Thrower acts as extension of arm.

Carved stone arrowhead

SPEAR THROWER

The spear thrower acted as an extension of the arm, enabling early hunters to throw their weapons with extra force.

Early human hunter

Modern Aboriginal using spear thrower

Bow and arrow

BOW AND ARROW

Between 30,000 B.C. and 15,000 B.C. toolmakers in northern Africa made the first bows. They carved fine stone arrowheads.

ANCIENT TECHNOLOGY

Item	Function	Location of find
	Comb	Mesopotamia
	Needle	Eastern Mediterranean
	Harpoon	Continental Europe
	Fish hook	Continental Europe
	Beads	Eastern Mediterranean

B.C.   **10,000 B.C.**

15,000 Last rainy period in northern Africa

16,000 Coldest point in glaciation

12,500 Rise of Magdalenian toolmakers (bone and antler harpoons, fishing spears)

14,000–11,000 El-Kebareh culture (Israel), with free-standing round huts

11,000 Rise of Natufian culture.

10,500 Earliest pottery: Fukui cave, Japan

15,000 Cave paintings, Lascaux, France

12,500 Rise of Magdalenian toolmakers (bone and antler harpoons, fishing spears)

15,000–10,000 Magdalenian culture, high point of mural and portable art

11,000 Cave paintings, Altimira, Spain

) Cave dwellers present in Brazil

15,000 Cave art begins in Brazil (shelter of Toca do Boqueirao de Pedra Furada)

24,000 Earliest known cremation, Lake Mungo, New South Wales, Australia

16,000 Cave art, north coast of Australia

THE FIRST ARTISTS

Creating art is an activity that marks out humans from other animals. Early artists used the walls of caves to paint animals and images, but they rarely painted people, and never landscapes. They did, though, carve small statues of people.

Brown powder sprayed on

LASCAUX ART
This painted horse of about 15,000 B.C. was found in the Lascaux caves, France. The feathered dots may have been magical hunting symbols.

ARTISTS' METHODS
Early artists used natural materials for different coloured paints. They painted with brushes of hair or sticks, or pads made from moss or animal skin. They drew lines with sharp stones.

Charcoal, for black

Clay, for brown

Green clay, for green

LOCATIONS OF ANCIENT ART
The best-preserved paintings are on the walls of caves in France and Spain that remained undiscovered until this century. Objects carved in wood, stone, or bone are known as portable art objects.

Altimira   EUROPE

Lascaux   *Günnersdorf*

Poch Merle   *Petersfels*

Mas d'Azil   *Dolni Vestonice*

Willendorf

Cave and portable art site   • Portable art site

CAVE ART FACTS
● In cave art, pictures of rarer animals (bears, big cats, rhinoceroses) often appear in more remote parts of the cave; common ones (aurochs, deer, mammoths) often appear at the entrance.

● The Lascaux paintings have suffered more in the last 50 years from human perspiration, body heat, and micro-organisms than in the 15,000-year period during which they lay undisturbed.

● Artists may have applied some colours by blowing paint through hollow reeds on to the cave wall.

"VENUS" FIGURINES
Several small female statues, called "Venus" figurines, have been found across Europe, and may represent goddesses; their large size may symbolize pregnancy (for fertility worship) or obesity (for abundant food).

A CAVE DISCOVERED
In 1940 Marcel Ravidat led three friends to a hole he had spied while walking his dog at Lascaux, France. He dropped down through the hole into a cave. By matchlight he saw beautiful paintings, made thousands of years earlier.

ICE-AGE LIFE

For at least the last two million years the world's climate has regularly swung between cold and warm periods. When cold struck, landscapes, rivers, lakes, and vegetation changed greatly. Humans had to adapt to the new environment to survive.

Ice-Age hunters trap a mammoth

ICE-AGE HUNTERS
Ice-Age people used many parts of the animals that they hunted: they made warm clothes from their fur and skin, and some used mammoth bones to support the animal-skin walls of their huts.

Mammoth bone hut

Harpoon

ICE-AGE SPREAD
At the peak of the last Ice Age, ice sheets covered huge areas of the world, and sea levels dropped. Emerging land formed bridges between continents separated today.

   Ice-Age coast

- - - Present-day coast

   Ice sheet c.18,000 B.C.

TROPICAL THAMES
The world experienced warm periods as well as ice ages. Bones found underneath Trafalgar Square, London, prove that hippopotamuses swam in the River Thames during one of these warmer spells.

NATUFIAN CULTURE
In 11,000 B.C. the Natufians of Palestine became probably the first people to abandon a hunter-based, nomadic lifestyle and settle down. They began to live permanently in caves, or in circular huts.

Grain store   Huts of mud, reed, and timber

Natufians gathered wild grain and stored it in huts.   House

Wild grain made coarse bread that wore down Natufians' teeth.

Headdress of shell beads

Burial customs
Natufians often buried their dead with personal items: necklaces and bracelets of bone or beads.

Natufian woman

10,000 B.C.

AFRICA 10,000 Hunting camps established in Sahara region after Ice Age ends	8500 First rock paintings, Sahara region	8000 Pottery made in Sahara region

ASIA 10,000 Ice cap retreats	9000–8000 Cereals (wheat and barley) grown in Jordan and Syria. Pottery made at Mureybet, Syria. Domestication of goats and sheep in Iran and Jordan	8000 Jericho, the first town, appears. Ice Age ends in Far East	7500 Domestication of pigs, Crimea

EUROPE 10,000 Ice cap retreats	8300 Retreat of glaciers

AMERICAS	9000 First people reach southern tip of South America	8500 Cultivation of wild grasses and beans, Peru	8000 Semi-permanent settlements, North America 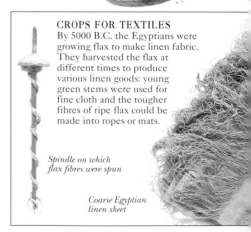

OCEANIA

THE FIRST FARMERS

In 8000 B.C., people in the Middle East cultivated crops for the first time. They grew mainly varieties of wheat and barley. The new strains of wheat they developed slowly spread around the Mediterranean, then further afield.

EARLY CROPS
Wild species of wheat were not ideal as food crops because their seed heads would shatter when ripe. Farmers solved this by hybridization (combining different wheat strains) to create new types of wheat.

Wild and hybridized species of grain

Wild einkorn   Einkorn   Wild emmer   Emmer

Wheat
Early cereal grain used for bread

Barley
Milled for bread, also used for beer

Lentil
Pulse, dried or eaten fresh

Yam
Large tuber, high in starch

Millet
Asian cereal high in protein

Rice
High-protein cereal

Maize
Grows in cobs (heads)

Tapioca
From root of manioc plant

THE SPREAD OF AGRICULTURE
In western Asia and Europe knowledge of farming spread from the central area of Syria, Palestine, Iran, Iraq, and Turkey. Farmers in Southeast Asia developed their crops independently, while in the Americas farmers appeared later, in about 7000 B.C.

DOMESTICATED ANIMALS
When they began to grow crops, farmers also domesticated wild animals. Domestication often changed a species' appearance.

Wild Animal   Domesticated Animal

Asiatic moufflon   *Sheep*
Near East 8000 B.C.

Wild Animal   Domesticated Animal

Wolf   *Dog*
Near East 11,000 B.C.

Wild boar   *Pig*
Near East 7500 B.C.

Bezoar goat   *Goat*
Near East 8900 B.C.

Aurochs   *Cow*
Near East 7000 B.C.

GREEN SAHARA
The Sahara Desert was once a fertile region with organized communities. 8,000-year-old paintings on cliff walls at Tassili-n-Ajjer, Libya, show many species of animal, hunters, a woman pounding flour, wedding ceremonies, and a family with a pet dog.

DOLMENS
Chûn Quoit, Cornwall, U.K.
Dolmens are the first great stone monuments of Europe and date from about 4500 B.C. They are the remains of ancient chamber tombs, and consist of a large, flat, stone, supported by upright stones. Their existence shows a great knowledge of engineering.

EARLY BREADMAKING
Early humans collected the seed heads of wild wheats and ground them using a stone quern (hand-mill). After separating the husks from the coarse flour, they mixed the flour with water and baked unleavened (unrisen) bread.

Clay oven
Baked bread
Sealed opening
Smooth pestle
Wheat seed-heads
Stone quern

CROPS FOR TEXTILES
By 5000 B.C. the Egyptians were growing flax to make linen fabric. They harvested the flax at different times to produce various linen goods: young green stems were used for fine cloth and the tougher fibres of ripe flax could be made into ropes or mats.

Spindle on which flax fibres were spun

Coarse Egyptian linen sheet

6500 Cattle domesticated

6500–5700 Çatal Hüyük, Turkey, important early town

0–6500 Domestication of n, eastern Mediterranean

6500 Date of earliest surviving textile, Çatal Hüyük

6200 Copper smelted, central Turkey

5000 Irrigation in Mesopotamia. Rice farming in China. Ubaid culture in Mesopotamia

4500 Farming around River Ganges, India

4400 Horses domesticated in Russia

6500 Britain separated from mainland as ice melts

6500 First farming communities, south-east Europe

5000 Farming begins, western Europe. Gold and copper used in Balkans

4500 First megalithic tombs, Brittany and Portugal

6500 Cultivation of potato, Peru

5000 First settlements in Anáhuac, Mexico. Maize grown, Mexico. Beginnings of domestication of llama and alpaca in Andes

5000 New Guinea and Tasmania separated from Australia as sea level rises

THE FIRST TOWNS

Towns and trade began to develop at the same time as agriculture and in the same parts of the world. The first townspeople were craft workers, priests, and traders. They depended on nearby farmers for food and on areas further afield for trade.

Reconstruction of Çatal Hüyük

Sometimes a courtyard was used as a rubbish dump by surrounding houses.

Mud-brick walls

Ladder

Entrance through rooftop

Timber and reed support roofs

Lack of streets made town easy to defend.

JERICHO
Jericho in the Near East was probably the first town, built in about 8000 B.C. It had a strong stone wall, a tower and defensive ditch, and a large and well-organized population.

Stone tower at Jericho

Staircase

Doorway

Cross-section of Jericho Tower, 10m (32ft) wide

Ditch

ÇATAL HÜYÜK
Çatal Hüyük is the site of a well-preserved town in Turkey from 6500 B.C. Its mud-brick houses had shared walls; there were no streets. Its people went about by climbing over the rooftops.

TRADERS
Goods from distant lands were found in the ruins of Çatal Hüyük: obsidian (volcanic glass), cowrie shells from the Mediterranean, and turquoise from Sinai.

Turkish obsidian   *Turquoise*   *Cowrie shells*

SMALL WORLD
In 10,000 B.C. the entire population of the world was about 12 million. This is two-thirds of the current population of New York State.

EVIDENCE OF RELIGION

Human skulls
Jericho's dead were sometimes buried beneath the floors of the houses with their skulls (though not the jaw) removed and decorated.

Cowrie shells   Plaster

Shrine paintings
Some rooms in Çatal Hüyük were decorated with religious images. Here vultures with human legs (perhaps priests in costume) attack a headless figure.

Early clay stamps

• From about 6000 B.C. town dwellers in the Middle East began using clay stamps to mark their personal property. Traders may also have used them to mark their goods.

KEY EARLY TOWNS

Town	Area	Date	Industry/Craft
Jericho	Eastern Mediterranean	8000 B.C.	Pottery
Çatal Hüyük	Turkey	7000 B.C.	Obsidian toolmaking
Jarmo	Iraq	c.7000 B.C.	Textile weaving
Khirokitia	Cyprus	c.6000 B.C.	Stone and wood articles

TOWN FACTS
• Early towns were sited in places with reliable springs; with mountains nearby where wild crops could grow; and with enough rainfall for the crops.

• In Çatal Hüyük, the average man lived to the age of 34, the average woman to the age of 30.

• Excavations at Jarmo revealed eleven towns, each one built on top of the other at different times.

FIRST POTTERY
The earliest pottery is more than 12,000 years old and comes from Japan. People from Africa and the Near East discovered it about 3,000 years later.

Pinching method

Potter hollows out solid lump of clay.

Potter coils single stretched piece of clay.

Coiling method

Decorated pot from Nasunahara, Japan: one of the earliest-known pottery vessels

FIRST METALWORKERS
In 7000–6000 B.C. people discovered that certain rocks, called ores, would release pure metal when heated. The metal could then be beaten into shape to make useful objects, or be melted and poured directly into moulds.

Copper spearhead

Furnace at c.1200°C (c.2200°F)

Molten metal is poured into mould.

Bag bellows   Clay nozzle

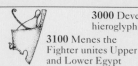

	4000 B.C.				
AFRICA		3750 First bronze alloy (also used by Sumerians)	3500 First sailing vessels, Egypt	3000 Development of hieroglyphic writing	2590 Building of G Pyramid of Khufu a
				3100 Menes the Fighter unites Upper and Lower Egypt	2686 Beginning of Egyptian Old Kingdom
					2646 Pyramid of Zoser at Sa
ASIA	4000 Beginning of bronze casting, Middle East		3500 Earliest Chinese city, Liang-ch'eng chen. Mesopotamians invent wheel and plough	3000 Development of Sumerian cities	
			3250 Earliest pictographic writing, Mesopotamia	2850 Legendary Golden Age in China	
				2750 Gilgamesh, legendary king of Ur	
EUROPE			3200 Beginnings of early Cycladic civilization in Aegean islands	3000 Spread of copper use	
				2900 Danubian culture, central Europe	
AMERICAS			3200 Maize farmed in South America	3000 First pottery in Americas	
OCEANIA				3000 Probable introduction of dogs in Australia	

ANCIENT EGYPT

In about 3500 B.C. Egyptians established one of the world's longest-lasting civilizations along the fertile banks of the Nile. Ruled by pharaohs (kings) and serviced by a large priesthood, Egyptians were famous for their stone building skills, their hieroglyphic writing, and their elaborate cult of the dead.

PYRAMID BUILDERS

Egyptians had a ready supply of stone, a good transport system on the Nile, and a large labour force. This enabled them to become the first people to build in stone on a large scale. The details of their building methods, however, have been lost.

Saqqara Earliest pyramid (stepped) and first known stone building

Dahshur Bent pyramid of King Snefru, about 100m (330ft) high

Giza Khufu's tomb and world's largest stone structure

• City
Ancient coastline

• Heliopolis
• Memphis

• Thebes

LANDMARKS IN STONE

From the Nile delta as far south as modern-day Sudan, Egyptians built pyramid tombs in various styles, and temples to their gods. Many of these monuments are still standing.

Abu Simbel Temple of Rameses II, cut into solid rock face

Sphinx Khafre's guard, 73m (240ft) long

KEY INNOVATIONS

SAIL

Egyptians constructed sailing ships from about 3500 B.C. Ships were first built from the Nile's reeds, and later from foreign timber.

POTTERY KILN

Kilns, invented in both Egypt and Mesopotamia, produced better-quality pots.

BURIAL FACTS

• Any important Egyptian was carefully mummified after death. Internal organs were placed in jars, and the body preserved with natron (salts) and wrapped in linen bandages.

• Egyptians placed mummies in a series of decorated cases, often painted with a portrait of the dead person. The nest of cases was then placed in a stone coffin, called a sarcophagus.

Mummy
Cartonnage (papier-mâché) mummy-case
Canopic jar for internal organs

Probable method of pyramid construction

Slave team
Temporary ramp
Stones dragged up on rollers

HIEROGLYPHIC WRITING

Egyptians used hieroglyphs for temple inscriptions and religious texts. A hieroglyph can stand for an object, an idea, or a sound. Scribes and priests, who alone understood hieroglyphs, grew more powerful when their writing skills were needed for administration.

Tutan-khamun's cartouche (name inscription)

KEY PHARAOHS

Zoser (c.2700 B.C.) – first pyramid builder.

Hatshepsut (c.1473–58 B.C.) – first female ruler in history.

Thutmose III (1479–25 B.C.) expanded empire's territories.

Akhenaton (1370–52 B.C.) started a new religion.

Tutankhamun (1353–35 B.C.), a boy-king, revived old gods.

Rameses II (1290–24 B.C.) – last great military pharaoh.

STONEHENGE

Stonehenge is a circle of stones on Salisbury Plain, England. Construction began in about 2200 B.C. Some of the huge stones had to be transported more than 216km (134 miles), from Wales. On the summer solstice, the sun rises directly over the axis of the monument.

Lintel stone
Sarsen stone
Timber platform used to raise lintel
Foundation pit

Builders drag stones into place using rollers.

Probable method of construction of Stonehenge

INDUS VALLEY CIVILIZATION

In 1921 archaeologists discovered remains of a unknown civilization from about 2500 B.C. Based in the Indian cities of Harappa and Mohenjo-Daro, its people lived in mud-brick houses and had baths, vast granaries, and drainage systems. Their writing appears on seals, but it has never been deciphered.

Mohenjo-Daro sculpture (c.2100 B.C.), probably of a priest or divine king

Great Bath, Mohenjo-Daro

Ritual baths
The size of the Great Bath at Mohenjo-Daro and the footbath at its entrance suggest that it was used for purifying rituals, perhaps by priests.

Beginnings of desiccation
(drying out) of Sahara region

2133 Beginning of
Egyptian Middle Kingdom

1786 End of Egyptian
Middle Kingdom

1652 War between Egypt
and Hyksos people from Asia

2150 End of Egyptian
Old Kingdom

1550 Beginning of
Egyptian New Kingdom

Beginnings of Indus civilization.
domesticated, Central Asia

2000 Hittites begin
invasions of Anatolia

1800 Beginnings of
Assyrian empire

1500 Chinese
ideographic
script in use

2371 Semites under Sargon of Akkad
begin to occupy entire plain of Shinar –
greatest Mesopotamian empire established

1900 Decline of Indus civilization

1792 Birth of Hammurabi,
founder of Babylonian empire

Earliest barrow burials in Britain.
nings of Dolmen period of
navian Neolithic age

2200 Building of Stonehenge starts.
End of Scandinavian Dolmen period

1600 Beginnings of
Mycenean civilization, Greece

1500 Linear B
script in use
on Crete

2000 Beginnings of
Minoan civilization, Crete

Earliest large settlements in
area, with temple mounds

2000 First metalworking, Peru.
Inuits reach northern Greenland

2000 Beginnings of settlement
of Melanesia, South Pacific

MESOPOTAMIA

The fertile region of Mesopotamia, between
the rivers Tigris and Euphrates, nurtured
some of the world's most influential
civilizations. This area saw the invention of
writing, the birth of mathematics, and great
experiments in irrigation.

Irrigation for
farming often
caused the
Tigris and
Euphrates
rivers to
change
course.

Centuries of
silt extended
the coastline

- - - Ancient
river
Ancient
coastline

MESOPOTAMIAN CITY-STATES

Mesopotamia lies in modern-day Iraq. Different
cities dominated the region at different times: Agade
in about 2300 B.C.; Ur from 2112 B.C. to 2095 B.C.;
Babylon after 1750 B.C. At other times the cities
shared power over the region.

ONE FOR THE ROAD

Kings and their servants
were often found in the
same grave. In the Royal
Graves at Ur small cups lay
near the skeletons of the
king's servants, which may
have contained poison.

MESOPOTAMIAN INNOVATIONS

WHEEL
Mesopotamians invented
the wheel between 3500
and 3250 B.C. Their
wheels were strong and
solid, but heavy.

PLOUGH
The plough appeared
c.3500 B.C. Pulled by
oxen, it made the job
of sowing seeds much
quicker and easier.

WRITING
Picture-writing
appeared c.3000 B.C.
The pictures grew more
abstract, becoming
cuneiform script.

EPIC
The Epic of Gilgamesh, the
first epic story to be
written down (c.2000
B.C.), tells of godlike
Gilgamesh of Uruk.

THE STANDARD OF UR
A famous inlaid box (c.2600 B.C.), called the
Standard of Ur, was found in the grave pits at Ur. It
shows kings, priests, musicians, soldiers, wheeled
chariots, farmers, fishermen, and many animals.
No-one knows what it was used for.

BABYLON'S HEYDAY
Under King Hammurabi
(c.1792–50 B.C.) the city of
Babylon became a centre of law,
mathematics, medicine, and
literature. The king had his legal
code, the first known, carved on
a famous granite stela (pillar).

ZIGGURAT
Mesopotamians built great mud-brick temples,
called ziggurats, to their sun and moon gods. The
huge size of many of these ziggurats
suggests that religion was very
important in Mesopotamian
society.

*Ziggurat at Ur –
about 45m*

*Arc de
Triomphe,
Paris – 50m
(164ft) high*

MINOAN CULTURE

Minoans were Mediterranean
traders. Their civilization
lasted from 2000 B.C. to
1400 B.C. and was centred
around huge palaces, the
largest of which was the
palace of Minos (after the
legendary King Minos) in
Knossos, Crete. Sea trade
made Minoans very wealthy.

MINOAN WALL-PAINTINGS
The walls of Minoan palaces were
decorated with colourful murals. One
famous painting shows a religious
ceremony in which young athletes
somersault over the horns of a bull.

MINOAN FACTS
- Minoan women wore colourful,
topless dresses, sometimes with
layered skirts.

- Minoans developed a script, later
named Linear B. British architect
Michael Ventris deciphered it in 1952.
An earlier Minoan script, Linear A,
remains undeciphered.

- Palaces not only served as royal
residences, but also as stores for farm
produce, as craft workshops, and as
depots for sea trade.

BIG URNERS
Archaeologists found
enormous clay jars
called *pithoi* at
Knossos, some over
5ft (1.5m) tall.
Minoans used the
jars to store their
trade goods: grain,
wine, and olive oil.

1500 B.C.

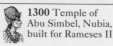

AFRICA

1300 Temple of Abu Simbel, Nubia, built for Rameses II

1218 First invasion of Egypt by Sea Peoples

1182 Second invasion of Egypt by Sea Peoples

ASIA **1500** People from Thrace, Balkans, move to Asia Minor, leading to establishment of Phrygia. Composition of hymns of Rig Veda

1400 Chinese capital moved to Anyang, present-day S. Korea. Extensive use of iron in Asia Minor and India

1200 Hittite Empire collapses. Jews settle in Palestine

1100 Phoenicians begin to spread out from eastern Mediterranean

1027 Chou overthrow Sh dynasty in C

EUROPE **1500** Beginning of Bronze Age in Scandinavia

1450 End of Minoan civilization, Crete

1200 Decline of Mycenaean culture, Greece

AMERICAS

1300 Beginning of Olmec civilization in Mexico

OCEANIA

1200 First settlers from Indonesia and Philippines arrive in Fiji and spread throughout Polynesia

---

EXPANDING EMPIRES

After the first civilizations were established in the Middle East, their peoples began to expand their territories and build large empires. These warlike peoples used their military might to conquer weaker groups and extracted tax, tribute, or trading advantages from their victims.

ASSYRIAN EMPIRE

Nineveh • Dur-Sharrukin
• Nimrud
MESOPOTAMIA
Babylon •

NEW KINGDOM EGYPT

Ancient coastline
Qadesh •
Beth-shan •
Memphis •
• Jerusalem
• Thebes
NUBIA
• Temple of Abu Simbel

EMPIRE TIMESCALE

Empire	Dates
Hittite	c.1400–1200 B.C.
Assyrian	1500–612 B.C.
New Kingdom Egypt	1550–1050 B.C.
Neo-Babylonian (Chaldean)	626–539 B.C.

HITTITE EMPIRE

• Hattusas
ASIA MINOR
• Qadesh

Hittite fortress

Hittite soldier

HITTITES

The Hittites settled in Asia Minor in about 2000 B.C. and built an empire under King Suppiluliuma (c.1386–48 B.C.) In 1294 B.C. Hittites fought Egyptians at Qadesh in a great battle for control of Palestine. Egypt claimed victory, but withdrew.

Hittite culture

10,000 cuneiform tablets, found at the Hittite capital of Hattusas, tell us most of what we know of their later history. Few Hittite artefacts survive.

ASSYRIANS

Tiglath-Pileser I (1114–1076 B.C.) ruled the Assyrian empire at its height. Assyrians were known for their cruelty, and used fear and threats to plunder their neighbours.

Royal hunter

Beautiful reliefs decorated Assyrian palace walls. King Ashurbanipal I kills a lion (right).

Ivory decorations

Assyrians demanded payment from their defeated enemies. The Phoenician ivory carving (left) is from Nimrud.

Assyrian soldier

EGYPTIANS

The New Kingdom, established in Egypt in 1550 B.C., covered Palestine (including Canaan), Syria, and the southern Nile (Nubia). It was the greatest Egyptian empire of all time.

Egyptian soldier

Buhen fortress, Egypt

Hebrews

When Egypt invaded Canaan, many inhabitants (Hebrews) hid in the hills of Judea.

Amarna letters

The Amarna letters record some of Egypt's diplomatic dealings. A rival king wrote to ask Pharaoh Amenophis IV for his continued friendship (right).

NEO-BABYLONIAN EMPIRE

Nineveh •
MESOPOTAMIA
• Jerusalem
Babylon •

Babylon's Ishtar Gate

CHALDEANS

Nebuchadnezzar II rebuilt the city of Babylon in 605 B.C. He created its famous Hanging Gardens for his homesick Persian wife.

Chaldean soldier

Cylinder seals

Chaldeans marked their property using inscribed cylinders. They rolled them over wet clay or soft wax.

KEY INNOVATIONS

HITTITE CHARIOTS

Hittites were the first systematic users of chariots to break through enemy infantry.

ASSYRIAN FLOAT

Assyrian soldiers used inflatable animal skins to help them swim across fast rivers.

EGYPTIAN MATHS

The Rhind Papyrus, from about 1600 B.C., shows that Egyptians were advanced mathematicians, skilled in geometry and arithmetic.

STARGAZERS

Chaldeans were the first people to make long-term astronomical records, which they wrote on wax-covered boards.

.C.

900 Foundation of kingdom of Kush in Nubia

814 Phoenicians found their colony at Carthage

600 Phoenicians sail around Africa

kingdom of Israel
King David

800 Aryans from present-day Iran expand into southern India

771 Chou state collapses in China

721–05 Assyrian Empire at its greatest extent

660 Jimmu, legendary first Japanese emperor

650 Chinese begin to use iron

612 Decline of Assyrian power after Medes and Scythians destroy Nineveh

604 Nebuchadnezzar II is ruler of Babylonian Empire

Etruscans
n Italy

776 First recorded Olympic Games, Greece

753 Traditional date of foundation of Rome

750 Greek city-states establish settlements around Mediterranean

700 Beginning of Halstatt culture (Iron Age) in central and western Europe

650 Earliest surviving Latin inscriptions

621 First written laws of Athens (Laws of Dracon)

900 Height of Chavin civilization in Andes

800 Zapotec civilization of Central America produces first writing in Americas

Most of Polynesian Islands settled

OLMECS
The Olmecs were one of the earliest civilizations of Central America (1300–400 B.C.). They lived between the Gulf of Mexico and the Pacific Ocean, and traded with present-day Mexico and Costa Rica. Some of their colossal carved stone heads are still standing.

Basalt head of an Olmec king

CHAVIN
Chavin was one of the earliest civilizations of South America (c.900 B.C.). Based in the Andes (Peru), its people were farmers, and built a canal that ran for 9km (5.6 miles), partly underground.

Chavin carving of warrior with severed enemy head

ETRUSCANS
Etruscans lived in northern Italy from about 1000 B.C. in loosely connected city-states. Etruscan farmers supplied the Greek markets, and their craftsmen produced high-quality bronzes, pottery, and wall paintings. The Romans later destroyed their race and language.

Etruscan tomb fresco (wall painting) showing musician and dancer.

SHANG CHINA
Kings of the Shang dynasty ruled China from about 1600 B.C. until 1027 B.C. Shang people produced: amazing bronzework, carts with harnesses, writing, and had a highly developed urban culture. They used cowrie shells for money, and traded far and wide in beautiful jade carvings.

Fang Ding (four-legged food vessel)

Wine vessel

WHAT'S COOKING?
Shang people made predictions by engraving questions about the future on cattle bones, then interpreting the cracks that appeared after they had heated up the bones.

TRAVELLERS AND TRADERS
The Mycenaeans were sea-going Greeks who built a Mediterranean empire based on a mixture of war and trade. They were followed by the more peaceful Phoenicians from northern Palestine, who set up trading bases along the Mediterranean coast.

MYCENAEAN RICHES
Amazing gold items have been found at Mycenaean sites, such as the death mask of a Mycenaean king (left).

Gold Mycenaean death mask

Ashlar stone blocks

Vault – 13.1m (43ft) high

Doorway – 5.8m (19ft) high

Mycenaean tomb

MYCENAEAN MONUMENTS
Mycenaeans built great stone tombs for their kings. The Treasury of Atreus (above) was built in about 1250 B.C. of ashlar stone, and was covered by an artificial mound of earth.

PHOENICIAN TRADERS
Phoenician sailors built colonies throughout the Mediterranean, trading in glassware and their famous purple cloth dyed with an extract from the murex shell. Their ships' timber came from the forests of the Phoenician homeland in northern Palestine.

Mycenae

Panormus

Byblos
Sidon
Tyre

Gades

Leptis Minor

Carthage

Knossos

Hippo Regius

Leptis Magna

MYCENAEANS AND PHOENICIANS
Mycenaeans dominated southern Greece from about 1600 B.C. to 1200 B.C. In about 1000 B.C. the Phoenicians began colonizing the coast from their homeland cities of Tyre, Sidon, and Byblos in present-day Lebanon.

Mycenaean empire

• Mycenaean city

• Phoenician city

Phoenician sailors trade cloth and glass for ivory at an Egyptian port.

Coloured glass jars

Egyptian ivory

Phoenician merchant

Egyptian merchant

KEY PEOPLE

Name	Dates	Biographical details
Rameses II	r.1279–13 B.C.	Great military pharaoh, fought Hittites at Qadesh
David	d.962 B.C.	Israelite king, unified Israel with Jerusalem as capital
Homer	c.800 B.C.	Blind Greek epic poet, author of *Iliad* and *Odyssey*
Romulus	c.700 B.C.	Legendary founder of Rome (with brother Remus)
Nebuchadnezzar	630–562 B.C.	Chaldean king, captured Jerusalem, rebuilt Babylon
Ashurbanipal	d.627 B.C.	Last great Assyrian king, founded first catalogued library of ancient Middle East at Nineveh
Sappho	c.600 B.C.	Greek lyric poetess from island of Lesbos

600 B.C.

AFRICA   **600** Building of temple of the Sun at Meroë, Sudan   **500** Iron Age in sub-Saharan Africa. Beginning of Nok culture in northern Nigeria   **304** Egyp[t] independ[ent] under Pto[lemy]

ASIA   **560** *Tao Te Ching* appears, Taoist philosophical work by Lao-Tze   **539** Persians conquer Neo-Babylonian Empire   **500** Caste system established in India   **479** Death of Confucius (b.551)   **334–26** Alexander the Great (b.356) co[nquers] Asia Minor, Persia, and parts of India

550 Cyrus II of Persia defeats Medes and founds Persian Empire   **521** Height of the Persian Empire under Darius I   **486** Death of Buddha   **403** Start of "Warring States" period in China   **323** Death of Alexander the Great and division of his empi[re]   **322** Chandragupta founds Mauryan Empire in India

EUROPE   **510** Foundation of Roman Republic   **478** Confederacy of Delos (Athenian League) founded   **338** Macedonians gain control of Greece at Battle of Chaeronea

505 Establishment of democracy in Athens   **480** Greeks defeat Persians at Battle of Salamis

490 Greeks defeat Persians at Battle of Marathon   **450** La Tène (Iron Age) culture in central and western Europe

431–04 Peloponnesian Wars: Sparta defeats Athens

AMERICAS   **400** Decline of Olmec civilization

OCEANIA   **500** Trading contacts established in South Pacific islands

---

ANCIENT GREECE

In the fifth century B.C., Greek civilization produced arts, philosophy, and political ideas that have had a deep and lasting effect on later societies, especially in the West. Early in the century, Greece united to defeat Persia; later rivalries led to a long internal war that weakened and finally destroyed Greek dominance in the Mediterranean.

ATHENS

Athens was the most important city of ancient Greece. With a long coastline for shipping trade, and with rich silver mines, the city-state of Athens grew wealthy. Its leaders, notably Pericles, built great temples and state buildings on the Acropolis, the city's old fortress. The Parthenon was the largest of all.

The Propylaea: grand entrance to the Acropolis

Temple of Athena Nike

Voting disc (guilty)   *Voting disc (not guilty)*

BIRTH OF DEMOCRACY

Athenians were the first people to have the chance to vote on how their city or state was run. Male citizens met in the agora (market-place) to discuss politics as well as to do business, but women and slaves were not allowed to vote.

The Parthenon: the marble temple of goddess Athena, built by Pericles in 447–432 B.C. It contained a 12m (40ft) gold and ivory statue of Athena.

Sanctuary of Asclepius: medical and religious centre dedicated to the god of healing

Theatre of Dionysus: festival performances twice a year with prizes for best writer, play, producer, and actor

Delphi ·   · Athens   Corinth ·   · Sparta

ANCIENT GREECE

The Greek world consisted of many city-states (independent cities with surrounding territory). In the later fifth century B.C., two city-states, Athens and Sparta, grew more powerful, and began to compete for dominance of the Mediterranean.

ANCIENT GREECE FACTS

• Greek artists were the first to use an understanding of human anatomy to make their art more realistic. They sculpted in marble, bronze, and clay, and painted beautiful scenes on their pottery and walls.

• Sparta was ruled by a small military aristocracy (the Spartiates). Spartan men began military training at the age of seven, but weaker boys were abandoned at birth.

Spartan runner

• A united Greek force defeated invading Persians on the plains at Marathon in 490 B.C., and at the sea battle of Salamis in 480 B.C. This later victory led to Athenian dominance.

• Sparta defeated Athens in the Peloponnesian Wars (431–404 B.C.), and ruled Greece until 371 B.C.

KEY PEOPLE OF ANCIENT GREECE

Name	Dates	Biographical details
Peisistratus	c.580–527	Tyrant of ancient Athens, encouraged trade and arts
Themistocles	c.524–460	Athenian politician and soldier, defeated Xerxes at Salamis, saving Greece from Persian domination
Pericles	c.495–429	Athenian leader, empire builder; developed democracy; made Athens cultural focus of Greece
Thucydides	c.465–403	Athenian historian, recorded Peloponnesian Wars

---

ALEXANDER

In just eight years Alexander the Great (356–323 B.C.) built the largest empire the world had ever seen. He helped spread Greek, or Hellenistic, culture all over Asia, but his early death, at the age of 33, left his empire leaderless and divided.

Pella   Gaugamela   Issus   Kabul   Alexandria   Babylon   Persepolis

Alexander at Issus

→ Alexander's route

■ Alexander's empire

BATTLE OF ISSUS

Outnumbered six to one, Alexander defeated the Persian Emperor, Darius, at Issus in 333 B.C.

ALEXANDER'S CONQUESTS

Alexander led his forces to victory from Greece as far as the Indus valley. He took with him not only soldiers, but engineers, artists, and philosophers. He founded some 70 cities, notably Alexandria in Egypt.

BRIDE BRIBE

After conquering Darius, Alexander encouraged the Hellenistic and Persian cultures to mix. He offered money to the first 10,000 Macedonian soldiers who wished to marry Persian women.

C.   **1 B.C.**

90 Foundation of library at Alexandria, Egypt

149–6 Rome destroys Carthage in Third Punic War, founding province of Africa

100 Camel introduced into Sahara region

30 Egypt becomes Roman province on death of Mark Antony (b.82) and Cleopatra (b.69)

---

262 Mauryan Emperor Asoka converts to Buddhism

221 Ch'in Shih huang-ti (c.259–210), the first emperor, unites China

185 Bactrians from present-day Afghanistan conquer northwest India

112 "Silk Road" opens up, giving West some access to China

240 Beginning of Parthian dynasty in northern Persia

207 Chinese unity disintegrates

64 Roman general Pompey (106–28) conquers Syria

202 China reunited under Han dynasty

53 Parthia halts Roman eastward expansion

---

90 Rome gains control of central Italy

264–41 First Punic War (Rome versus Carthage): Rome wins control of Sicily

218–01 Second Punic War: Roman general Scipio defeats Hannibal

49 Julius Caesar invades Gaul

31 Battle of Actium gives Octavian (later Emperor Augustus) power over Rome

46 Julius Caesar reforms calendar

45 Julius Caesar becomes sole ruler of Rome after civil war

27 Roman Empire replaces Republic

44 Julius Caesar murdered

...eight of North American mound-building cultures. ...ning of Early Maya Period, Central America

200 Height of Nazca civilization, Peru, South America

100 Anasazi, Hohokam, and Mogollon peoples begin farming in southwestern North America. Okvik hunters settle in northern Alaska

---

THE RISE OF ROME

From a shepherds' village in central Italy, Rome grew to be the focus of an empire that controlled most of western Europe. Its rise to power was based on discipline, virtue, and military prowess, but it took centuries of warfare for Romans to secure their empire. They exported Rome's lifestyle and technology to all their provinces.

Patricians *Soldier and slave* *Plebeians*

201 B.C.
44 B.C.
A.D.14
A.D.117

ROME'S EXPANSION AND EMPIRE

Rome secured the Mediterranean only after three long wars, the Punic Wars, in which it defeated the sea-based empire of Carthage. Julius Caesar later conquered Gaul.

Londinium
Trier
GAUL
Byzantium
Rome
Antioch
Carthage
Alexandria

ROMAN SOCIETY

Roman society was divided into several levels: patricians (aristocrats), plebeians (citizens), subjects (in the provinces), and slaves. Women were expected to be mothers, but rich females had some freedom.

KEY INNOVATIONS

HEATED BATHS

Roman baths were heated by external fires, stoked by slaves. The fire's hot air circulated underneath a raised floor and heated the water above.

AQUEDUCTS

Roman engineers built great aqueducts. Water in this one at Nîmes dropped only 17m (56ft) over 50km (31 miles).

Nîmes aqueduct

THE ROMAN ARMY

Legate (general)

Centurion *Aquilifer (standard bearer)*

Trumpeter *Auxiliary*

Foreign legions

When their empire began to expand, Romans had to recruit soldiers, called auxiliaries, from the countries they had conquered. After 25 years auxiliaries could become Roman citizens.

Boulders placed here.

Protected battering ram

Frame built to withstand high tension.

Twisted cord

Soldiers collect ammunition.

Siege tower

Testudo

Army structure and command

The Roman army was divided into about 28 legions of about 5,000 infantry soldiers each; a legion contained 10 cohorts; a cohort contained 6 centuries of 80 men each. Officers called centurions commanded each century, and wore crests on their helmets so that they could easily be seen in battle.

Military technology

The Roman catapult, or *ballista*, could launch boulders or arrows over an enemy's defences. Covered siege towers and battering rams protected soldiers inside.

Roman tactics

Soldiers advancing under attack would form a *testudo* (tortoise), a formation of upheld shields that protected them from arrows, missiles, or burning oil.

MAURYAN EMPIRE

Mauryan emperor Asoka conquered and unified India. In 262 B.C. he became a Buddhist and set up thousands of stupas (monuments) to Buddha around the empire. Each is said to contain a part of Buddha's body.

Buddhist stupa at Sanchi, India, c.150 B.C.

CH'IN DYNASTY OF CHINA

In 221 B.C. China was unified under its first emperor, Ch'in Shih huang-ti (c.259–210 B.C.). He centralized the government, standardized money, weights and measures, and built grand monuments in his own honour.

The Great Wall: a 3,000km- (1,900mile-) long defence against northern Huns

Terracotta army

Ch'in Shih huang-ti built himself a great underground tomb.

Tomb had 7,000 statues of fully armed warriors, some with horses.

ADENA AND HOPEWELL

From 700 B.C. to A.D. 400 the Adena, and later the Hopewell, farming societies flourished in North America. They built huge, mysterious, earth mounds, and filled their graves with beautifully carved objects.

Serpent mound, Ohio: 1,310ft (400m) uncoiled

A.D. 1

AFRICA

50 Kingdom of Axum (Ethiopia) begins to expand

150 Berbers and Mandingos start to dominate Sudan area

250 Axum controls trade in Red Sea

ASIA

9 Han dynasty overthrown in China
25 Han dynasty restored
30 Jesus Christ crucified in Jerusalem
46–57 St. Paul's missionary journeys
60 Beginning of Kushan Empire in India

70 Romans seize Jerusalem and destroy Jewish temple
105 Paper first used in China
132 Jewish revolt against Rome, leading to dispersal of Jews

200 Completion of Mishnah (Jewish law). Composition of Ramayana, Mahabharata (Indian epics), and Bhagavad Gita (Hindu scripture)
220 Han dynasty ends; China divided into three state
224 Sassanian dynasty founded in Persia
245 China and Funan (first Southeast Asian state) in co

EUROPE

43 Romans invade Great Britain

79 Eruption of Vesuvius, southern Italy

117 Roman Empire reaches its maximum extent

238 Goths begin to encroach on Roman Empire

293 Empe Diocletia reorganiz Roman E

AMERICAS

1 Beginning of Moche civilization in northern Peru

OCEANIA

1–100 Hindu-Buddhists from Southeast Asia colonize Sumatra and Java

---

IMPERIAL ROME

The Roman Republic was shaken by a series of civil wars that began in 49 B.C. In 27 B.C., the general and adopted son of Julius Caesar, Octavian, defeated his rival Mark Antony and, as Augustus, became the first emperor. His reforms brought peace and prosperity to the Empire and created a power structure that lasted until the last emperor, Romulus Augustulus, was deposed in A.D. 476.

AUGUSTUS

Though he preserved many of the Republic's old institutions, Augustus (previously Octavian) had overall power; he even encouraged a cult of Augustus, in which he was worshipped as a god. He passed his title and powers on to his son Tiberius in A.D. 14.

Emperor Augustus

ROMAN CHARIOT RACES

Rome's *Circus Maximus* was a great stadium in which chariot races were held. Races were often dangerous and the teams (reds, blues, greens, whites) inspired fans throughout the empire.

IMPERIAL TRIUMPH

Emperors used military triumphs to reinforce their power. They paraded defeated enemies through Rome to the cheers of onlookers.

KEY PEOPLE OF ANCIENT ROME

Name	Dates	Biographical details
Julius Caesar	100–44 B.C.	Conquered Gaul, won civil war, dictator of Rome (46–44), murdered 44 B.C.
Augustus	63 B.C.–A.D.19	Julius Caesar's adopted son, defeated Mark Antony to become first emperor
Trajan	A.D. 53–117	Popular emperor, extended Empire eastward, began vast building programme
Hadrian	A.D. 76–138	Emperor, secured boundaries of Empire, built Hadrian's Wall as defence
Diocletian	A.D. 245–316	Emperor, restored order after near anarchy. Last persecutor of Christians

DECLINE OF THE ROMAN EMPIRE

Reliance on army

The emperor Septimius Severus ended a civil war in A.D. 193, but his reliance on the army to restore order showed that no future emperor could enjoy total power: he would need the support of the army.

Collaboration with barbarians

In the third century A.D., hostile barbarians from northern Europe stepped up pressure on the Empire's borders. Rome increasingly relied on local forces in their provinces and many locals rose to important government positions. Later, these leaders took more power into their own hands.

Shifting centre

In the fourth and fifth centuries A.D., the Empire gradually fragmented; there were capitals at different times at Ravenna, Milan, Trier, Sirmium, and Constantinople.

Visigoth

DIVISION OF EMPIRE

In A.D. 293, Emperor Diocletian changed the structure of the empire. He divided it into two parts (east and west), each with an emperor and a deputy. He ruled the east, and gave the west to Maximian. He called the new system a tetrarchy, and it helped him deal with the growing problem of civil unrest.

The four tetrarchs

PAVING THE WAY

By the early 4th century A.D., Romans had built a road network of 85,000km (52,800 miles). It took six days to go from Londinium (London) to Rome. In the 1800s the journey took just as long.

Imperial border — Division of the Empire

Londinium, Trier, Byzantium, Rome, Carthage

→ Visigoths → Vandals → Burgundians
→ Ostrogoths → Franks → Angles

ROME UNDER SIEGE

Rome devoted much of its resources to defending its long borders. From the 4th century A.D., economic problems forced a weakening in defence. Visigoths under Alaric captured and sacked Rome in A.D. 410, and Attila the Hun invaded Gaul in A.D. 451.

325 Axum destroys kingdom of Meroë

400 Christianity adopted in Axum
439 Vandals establish kingdom in northern Africa

533 Emperor Justinian wins back northern Africa for Rome

4 Invasion of Huns ...her splits up China

320 Chandragupta I founds Gupta Empire in northern India

480 End of Gupta Empire

520 Rise of mathematics in India; decimal number system invented
531 Height of Sassanian Empire
550 Buddhism introduced into Japan
589 China reunified under Sui dynasty

313 Toleration of Christians in Roman Empire as result of Edict of Milan
330 Emperor Constantine moves capital of Roman Empire to Constantinople
370 Huns appear in Europe

410 Visigoths invade Italy and Spain, sack Rome
450 Angles, Jutes, and Saxons settle in Great Britain
476 Last western Roman emperor, Romulus Augustulus, overthrown
486 Clovis establishes Frankish kingdom in present-day northern France, Belgium, and parts of western Germany
493 Ostrogoths take over in Italy

552 Emperor Justinian restores Italy to Roman control
568 Lombards take over northern Italy
590 Pope Gregory the Great (c.540–604) expands papal power

...reat civilized states in Mexico ...e Alban, Teotihuacán)

600 Height of Mayan civilization, central America

...astern Polynesia settled

THE COMING OF CHRISTIANITY

Christianity began as a minor sect in a remote corner of the Roman Empire. A series of events brought it wider fame, until Emperor Constantine was himself converted. In A.D. 391, Emperor Theodosius I made it Rome's official religion and banned all other religions.

Mainly Christian by A.D. 600
· Christian centre

Cantauri
Augusta Treverorum
Turones
Arelate
Toletum
Roma
Byzantium
Ephesus
Carthage
Edessa
Antioch
Damascus
Jerusalem
Alexandria
Artashat

JESUS OF NAZARETH
In about A.D. 30, the Jewish teacher Jesus of Nazareth, who was seen by the Roman and Jewish authorities as a revolutionary, was crucified. His apostles, or followers, spread his message.

SPREAD OF CHRISTIANITY
After Jesus' death, his apostles took his message abroad. Christianity spread rapidly within the Roman Empire. The centres of Antioch and Edessa carried it eastward into Persia. Later it reached China and India.

ST. PAUL'S JOURNEYS
Paul of Tarsus, one of Jesus' apostles, made four journeys around the Mediterranean coast, preaching Christianity. This new faith excluded no-one, offering salvation to rich and poor alike, and Christian martyrs inspired many people to convert.

St. Paul, in a mosaic from St. Peter's, Rome

EARLY CHRISTIANITY FACTS

Christian fish symbol

• The fish was an early Christian symbol. In Greek, the letters of the word for fish stand for, "Jesus Christ, God's Son, Saviour."

Captive lion

• Christians were persecuted in the Roman Empire. Emperor Nero had Christians thrown to the lions, and Diocletian had priests tortured.

Fragment of Gospel text

• Key books of the New Testament – the gospels of disciples Matthew, Mark, and Luke – were written in A.D. 65–70.

CONSTANTINE
In A.D. 313 Emperor Constantine became a Christian and gave Christians freedom to worship with the Edict of Milan. The Church could then flourish.

SASSANIAN EMPIRE
The Sassanian Empire lasted from A.D. 224 to 641 and was centred around the city of Ctesiphon (Baghdad). At its height under King Khosrow (A.D. 531- 79), it stretched from the River Indus to the Euphrates. Sassanians were great architects and followed the Zoroastrian religion (see p.143).

Ramparts form perfect circle 2km (1.2 miles) in diameter
Circular city at Firuzabad

MAYAN CIVILIZATION
The Mayan civilization of Central America flourished between A.D. 300 and 900. Mayans built great pyramidal temples; they also developed writing and advanced mathematics. Mayan astronomers had calculated the exact length of the solar year and lunar month and could predict eclipses. They played a form of basketball that was half religious ceremony, half sport. Anyone who scored had the right to demand the property of any spectator they managed to catch.

Players could only use hips, elbows, and ankles to control the ball.

ROME AND JUDAISM
From A.D. 66 to 70, Jews in Palestine, led by important priests and Pharisees, revolted against Roman rule. Emperor Vespasian, with his son Titus, brutally suppressed the revolt. A second Jewish rebellion of A.D. 132 to 135 was put down by Emperor Hadrian.

Capture of Jerusalem
In A.D. 70, Titus captured Jerusalem, plundering and destroying its great Jewish temple. The resulting diaspora (dispersal) of Jews carried Judaism as far as Spain and Africa.

Sacking of the temple of Jerusalem

Masada
In A.D. 73 the last Jewish stronghold, at Masada on the shores of the Dead Sea, fell to the Romans. When the Romans broke into the fortress, they found that all 960 Jews inside had killed themselves rather than be captured.

Remains of siege ramp
Fortress at Masada

AXUM
In the 4th century A.D., Axum in northeastern Africa overthrew the rule of the city of Meroë and became an important power. Its exports of African ivory and sea trade brought great wealth. Axumites built great granite towers, or stelas, as monuments to their civilization. The tallest surviving stela stands at 23m (75.5ft) high – as high as 16 people standing on each other's shoulders.

Great Stela at Axum

600

AFRICA

c.700 Kingdom of Ghana prospers on trans-Saharan trade. Bantu Africans cross the River Limpopo, taking iron-working technology to the south

ASIA

618 China reunified by T'ang dynasty

637 Muslims conquer Jerusalem

647 Central Asian Hun tribes invade India, causing decline of Gupta Empire

786 Harun-al-Rashid becomes caliph of Baghdad

802 Khmers found c in Cambodia and La

622 Year One of Islamic calendar, the year of Muhammad's flight from Mecca to Medina

642 Islam replaces Zoroastrianism as major religion in Persia

674 Islam reaches modern Pakistan

751 Muslims defeat Mongols at Samarkand

794 Kyoto, ancient capital of Japan, is established

814 Arabs adop Indian numeral

EUROPE

711 Moors invade Spain

732 Muslims defeated at Tours by Frankish leader Charles Martel (c.688–741), halting Islam's advance in Europe

800 Charlemagne, Kir the Franks, is crowned first Holy Roman Emp

AMERICAS

OCEANIA

RISE AND SPREAD OF ISLAM

In 610, an Arab merchant called Muhammad (c.570–632) founded a new religion: Islam. His teachings were an inspiration to the Arab peoples, and by 750, Muslims (the followers of Islam) had gained control of a massive area stretching from Spain to Afghanistan. The Muslim advance spread trade, culture, and science, as well as Islam.

	622–32
	632–44
	644–750
	750–850

Córdoba · Samarkand · Antioch · Damascus · Jerusalem · Alexandria · Medina · Mecca

EXPANSION OF ISLAM

Muhammad died in 632, but his teachings spread rapidly after his death. By 850, Muslims had made Islam the most important civilization after China.

Great Mosque at Córdoba

CÓRDOBA'S GREAT MOSQUE

Arab colonists built the Great Mosque at Córdoba, southern Spain, between 784 and 990. One of the largest and most complex Islamic mosques, it has 850 marble columns supporting arches on two levels.

El Cid

EL CID

Rodrigo Diaz de Vivar (c.1043–99) was the real name of "El Cid", a Spanish knight and outlaw who fought against Muslim colonists. His greatest achievement was the capture of the Spanish city of Valencia in 1094, which made him a national hero.

Muslim at prayer

Prayer rug

MUHAMMAD'S JOURNEY

Muhammad's religious ideas were initially unpopular. In 622, established merchants forced him to flee Mecca for Medina, but in 630, Muhammad returned to the city in triumph. Since then, Muslims at prayer have always faced Mecca.

HARUN-AL-RASHID

Harun-al-Rashid (766–809) ruled the Islamic world at its height. The wealth and culture of his court at Baghdad inspired the tales of *The Thousand and One Nights*. His wife would drink only from gold and silver gem-studded vessels.

Harun-al-Rashid

ARAB TECHNOLOGY

PAPER
Following the capture of Chinese papermakers in 751, Arabs spread their craft throughout the Islamic world.

WINDMILL
Arab colonists brought windmill technology to Spain from Persia in the 10th century.

OPTICS
Arabic scholar Alhazen (c.965–1039) wrote the first accurate account of vision. He gave us the term "lens".

CHARLEMAGNE

King Charlemagne of the Franks (742–814) conquered most of the Christian lands of western Europe and founded the Holy Roman Empire in 800. He encouraged learning with a new, clear, script called Carolingian miniscule.

KEY PEOPLE

Name	Dates	Biographical details
Muhammad	c.570–632	Arab merchant and religious teacher, founder of Islam
Rabiah-al-Adawiyah	712–801	Female Arab mystic and religious teacher
Charlemagne	742–814	King of the Franks (people of northwestern Europe), conquered Western Europe, spread Christianity
Harun-al-Rashid	766–809	Caliph of Baghdad, ruled Islamic world at its height
Leif Eriksson	c.1000	Viking explorer, reached North American coast in 1000
William of Normandy	c.1028–87	Duke of Normandy, conquered England in 1066
El Cid	c.1043–99	Spanish knight and outlaw, fought Muslims in Spain

POPE SYLVESTER

Pope Sylvester II (940–1003) introduced Arabic numerals (0-9) and the astrolabe (an aid to navigation) to Europe from Muslim Spain.

Astrolabe

900 Hausa kingdom of Daura founded in northern Nigeria

920 Ghana's Golden Age begins

980 Arab traders settle on East African coast

1054 Ghana conquered by Muslim Almoravid dynasty

888 Chola dynasty of Tamil kings replaces the Pallavas in southern India and Sri Lanka

935–41 Civil war in Japan

960 Sung Dynasty takes over China

861 The Vikings discover Iceland

Kenneth MacAlpine (d. 858) eats the Picts and unites Scotland

911 The Viking Rollo is granted Normandy

930 Cordoba becomes seat of Arab learning in Spain

966 Poles converted to Christianity

982 Erik the Red settles in Greenland

997 Stephen I (977–1038) becomes first King of Hungary

1000 Leif Eriksson, son of Erik the Red, sails down North American coast. He names it "Vinland"

1066 William of Normandy invades England

1096 First Crusade begins

900 Mixtec civilization begins in Mexico

980 Toltecs set up capital at Tula (Mexico)

1000 Chimu civilization of Peru founded

950 Polynesian navigator Kupe discovers New Zealand, and first Maori settlers arrive

TRADERS AND RAIDERS

Late in the eighth century people from present-day Denmark, Norway, and Sweden, called Vikings, began to leave their overcrowded homelands in search of treasure to plunder or new land to settle. Their golden age of trade, exploration, and colonization lasted until 1100.

Viking homeland
Settlement
Sea route
River route

York
Dublin
Novgorod
Dilka
Byzantium (Istanbul)
Baghdad
L'Anse aux Meadows

ROUTES OF VIKING TRAVEL
Vikings were great traders. They dealt in many goods, exchanging slaves, fur, wood, honey, walrus tusks, whale oil, feathers, and down for silver, silk, spices, and wine.

Viking trading post

Viking traders carried their goods in knorrs – small, stable ships.

Carved figurehead

VIKING LONGSHIPS
The key to Viking success was their skill in building and sailing ships. Their longships were the fastest ships of the time; they had both sail and oar, and their flat bottoms enabled them to navigate both seas and inland rivers.

Battle helmet
Handaxe

BERSERKERS
Some warriors were called "berserkers" – from *bare sark*, meaning shirtless. A berserker with battle-fever was said to have the strength of a bull and would fight without shirt or armour. Our word "berserk" comes from the name for these Viking madmen.

VIKING TRADING POSTS
Many great cities such as York, England, and Dublin, Ireland, started as places where Vikings met with locals to exchange goods.

Novgorod

VIKING FACTS
• Viking graffiti can still be seen in a gallery of Istanbul's great mosque, Hagia Sophia.

• Vikings reached the Americas in 1000, 500 years before Christopher Columbus.

• After a battle, Viking women would feed those with belly wounds a strong-smelling soup of onions and herbs. If, later, they smelled this mix at the wound, they knew that the intestine had been pierced and that the victim would soon die.

VIKING SUPERMEN
The Emperor of Byzantium was so impressed by the courage, strength, and size of the Viking warriors he had seen that he recruited them for his personal bodyguard. It was called the Varangian guard.

Broadsword

Varangian guard

ROLLO OF NORMANDY
In 911, Rollo, a Norseman chief, was granted land in northern France by the King of France, in return for his promise to defend it. William the Conqueror was Rollo's descendant.

Rollo of Normandy

NORMANDY

BIRTH OF RUSSIA
According to the 12th-century Russian Chronicle, Novgorod Slavs invited Vikings to rule over them. Vikings were also called "Rus", so when they took over the area it was called the Land of Rus, and later, Russia.

KING WENCESLAS
Wenceslas (907–29) was the first ruler of Bohemia, central Europe. He became a Christian and helped spread Christianity in Bohemia. Murdered outside his church by his own brother, Wenceslas was later made the patron saint of Hungary, Poland, and Bohemia.

KEY INVENTIONS

GUNPOWDER
In 1044, Chinese chemist Wu Ching Tsao Yao published the first known recipe for gunpowder. The explosive mix was first used for fireworks.

FIRST PRINTED BOOKS
The Diamond Sutra, dated 868, is the world's oldest printed book. It is a Buddhist scripture printed from blocks of wood on to sheets of paper and joined into a scroll.

FIRST NOVEL
In 1007, a Japanese noblewoman called Murasaki Shikibu wrote the first novel. Over 600,000 words long, *The Tale of Genji* tells of a prince's quest for true love and wisdom.

1100

AFRICA **c.1100** First Iron Age
settlement in Zimbabwe

1169 Saladin (1137–9
becomes ruler of Egy

ASIA **1104** Crusaders capture Acre

1156 Civil war between rival
clans in Japan leads to
domination by samurai warlords

EUROPE **1115** French philosopher Peter Abelard (1079–1142)
begins teaching in Paris. St. Bernard (1090–1153)
founds important monastery at Clairvaux
1119 Bologna University, one of Europe's oldest, founded in Italy

1143 Alfonso Henriques (c.1109–85)
becomes first King of Portugal

1170 Murder of
Thomas Becket
(1118–70), Archbi
of Canterbury, E

AMERICAS **1151** Fall of the Toltec
Empire in Mexico

OCEANIA **1100s** Giant statues first erected
on Easter Island, South Pacific

MONGOL EXPANSION

In the late 1100s, Temujin, a young chieftain of central Asia, united a group of tribes to form a powerful Mongol army. In 1211, the Mongols invaded China, then swept through Asia. Temujin was later proclaimed as Genghis Khan, which means "Universal Ruler".

Genghis Khan

--- Genghis' campaigns
→ Successors' campaigns

Area under direct Mongol control
Area under loose Mongol control

Karakorum · Peking
Novgorod
Bolgar
Legnica
New Sarai · Kashgar · Canton
Gran
Tiflis
Jerusalem · Baghdad

GENGHIS KHAN
Genghis Khan was born just as his father had killed a rival chief named Temujin. As a baby he was given the name Temujin because it was believed that the courage of a defeated enemy magically entered the newborn.

POWDERED MILK
Mongols would mix sun-dried mare's milk with water in the morning, and place it in their saddlebags. By the evening the shaken mix had formed an edible porridge.

ROUTES OF MONGOL CONQUEST
At its height, the greatest land empire in the history of the world spanned almost all of Asia, from Korea in the east to Poland in the west, and from the Arctic south to Persia.

Strengthened leather armour

Mongol cavalrymen

MONGOL CAVALRY
Mongol cavalrymen had immense advantages over their enemies. They could ride up to 120km (75 miles) a day with just one stop for food and water, and hit targets at full gallop.

SORROW AND SLAUGHTER
In 1227, Genghis Khan grew ill and died while on campaign in China. When his men brought his body back to Mongolia for burial, they killed every living creature that crossed the path of the homebound procession. At his funeral forty jewelled slave girls and forty horses were slaughtered in his honour.

MONGOL FACTS
• Mongol archers had whistling arrows for signalling, armour-piercing arrows, and even arrows tipped with grenades.

• From the age of three, Mongol children were regularly strapped onto their ponies to help them learn to ride.

Whistling arrowheads

• One of Genghis Khan's tactics was to set fire to live animals, such as elephants and horses, and send them rushing at the enemy's battle lines.

• Genghis lived in simple Mongol style even at the height of his power.

• Mongols were the first to use gunpowder as a military weapon.

MONGOL HOME LIFE
Mongols were nomads and lived in moveable tents, or yurts, made of animal skins or textiles stretched over a wooden frame. The women kept herds of livestock and tribes competed with each other for the best grazing lands.

A SPORTING CONTEST TO THE DEATH

In 1180, one of the greatest medieval tournaments was staged at Lagny-sur-Marne, France. More than 3,000 armed and mounted knights jousted for sport and honour, "with no holds barred".

KEY PEOPLE

Name	Dates	Biographical details
Genghis Khan	1162–1227	Mongolian warrior, conqueror, and Emperor of China, Iran, Iraq, and Central Asia
Saladin	1137–93	Sultan of Egypt and Muslim hero of Third Crusade famed for his chivalry and courage
Richard I	1157–99	Popular English king and English hero of Third Crusade, also called "Richard The Lionheart"
St. Francis of Assisi	1181–1226	Founder of Franciscan order and leader of Church reform
Sun Diata	d.1255	Founder of Mali Empire, West Africa, established unity and brought prosperity to empire

1244 Egyptians retake Jerusalem

1190 Lalibela becomes Emperor of Ethiopia

1235 Sun Diata (d.1255) founds empire of Mali, West Africa

187 Saladin captures ~~rusalem from Crusaders~~

1191 Zen Buddhism first introduced to Japan

1206 Genghis Khan (1162–1227) founds Mongol Empire. Islam takes root in new Kingdom of Delhi, India, founded by Aibak, a former slave

1229 Sixth Crusaders recapture Jerusalem

1237 Mongol army begins to conquer Russia

1232 Explosive rockets used in war between Chinese and conquering Mongols

~~Work begins on~~ ~~ndon Bridge,~~ ~~n Bridge, and~~ "Leaning Tower"

1204 Fourth Crusaders sack and loot Constantinople. King John of England (1167–1216) loses French lands

1209 St. Francis (1181–1226) founds Franciscan order

1215 St. Dominic (1170–1221) founds Dominican Order. King John of England seals Magna Carta

1240s German towns begin regional trades, later forming powerful and protective trading alliance, the Hanseatic League

c.1200 Cuzco, Peru, becomes an Inca centre. First maize farmers settle along banks of Mississippi

ZEN BUDDHISM
In 1191, Zen Buddhism was introduced to Japan by a monk named Eisai (1141–1215). Zen Buddhism stressed personal instruction by a master (rather than the study of scriptures) as the path to self-knowledge.

MAGNA CARTA
In 1215, King John of England was forced to seal the Magna Carta, or Great Charter. It gave political rights to his most powerful subjects and made the king subject to law.

Royal seal

THIRTEENTH-CENTURY BUILDINGS
Chartres Cathedral, the finest example of French Gothic architecture, took 31 years to build in the mid-13th century. At the same time, the Mayans of Central America began building the massive temples of their new capital at Mayapan, in modern-day Mexico.

North spire (burned down 1194, rebuilt by 1513)

South spire (1160)

Mayan Temple

Only priests were allowed to go to the top of the steps

Chartres Cathedral

THE CRUSADES
By 1095 the Saracens (Muslims) had gained control of the holy lands in the Middle East. European Christians, urged on by Pope Urban II, organized armed expeditions, or crusades, to recapture the lands. The First Crusade was a triumph. Others were less successful, and the last ended in 1291.

— 1st Crusade
---- 2nd Crusade
— 3rd Crusade

Paris · Bruges · Vienna · Genoa · Toulouse · Marseilles · Rome · Constantinople · Damascus · Acre · Jerusalem

CRUSADE ROUTES
The first two crusader armies assembled at meeting points in Europe, and fought their way overland across Asia Minor. Later, European control of the Mediterranean allowed crusaders to take a sea route to the Holy Land.

Conical helmet
Nasal (nose-guard)
Shield

CHILDREN'S CRUSADE
In 1212, thousands of unarmed children believing in the power of innocence set off from Europe for the Holy Land. Most died on the way, or were sold as slaves in Africa.

Helmet
Surcoat
Hauberk (chain mail shirt)

CRUSADER
Crusaders took their name from the cross (Latin *crux*) that was sewn on to their clothing. Crusader knights wore suits of armour and vowed to follow strict codes of chivalry.

Chausses (chain-mail leggings)

Typical Crusader of the order of Knights Templar

Scimitar

SARACEN WARRIOR
The term Saracen was used to describe any Arab, Turk, or other follower of Islam. They used a shield of Persian design and a long, curved sword called a scimitar.

Saracen warrior

DOME OF THE ROCK
The magnificent Dome of the Rock mosque in Jerusalem was built by an Arab caliph between 685 and 691 on a Jewish temple site. When the crusaders controlled Jerusalem, however, they turned it into a Christian church.

 Shield of the order of Knights Hospitaller

 Shield of the order of Teutonic Knights

KRAK DES CHEVALIERS
Begun in 1142, and now in modern-day Syria, this is the most impressive crusader fortress. Its storerooms could provide hundreds of people with food for five years.

MAJOR CRUSADES

Crusade	Dates	Result
First Crusade	1096–99	Crusaders take Antioch, then Jerusalem in July 1099
Second Crusade	1147–49	Incompetence leads to Crusader defeat in Anatolia
Third Crusade	1189–92	Crusaders win coast from Tyre to Jaffa but Jerusalem remains uncaptured
Fourth Crusade	1202–04	Crusaders loot Constantinople
Children's Crusade	1212	Thousands of innocent children march to death and slavery in North Africa
5th–8th	1218–91	Partial and short-lived Crusader victories

1250

AFRICA	**1250** Mamelukes, rebel slave-soldiers, become rulers of Egypt		**1300** Foundation of Benin kingdom in Nigeria	**1324** Mansa Musa (d.1332), emperor of Mali, makes pilgrimage to Mecca	**1348** Plague devastates E...
ASIA	**1250** A Japanese monk, Nicherin (1222–82), proclaims *Lotus Sutra* the supreme Buddhist scripture	**1260** Mamelukes halt Mongol advance at Battle of Ain Jalut in Palestine	**1281** The *Kamikaze* (Divine Wind) drives Mongol invaders from Japan	**1291** Saracens capture Acre, ending the Crusades **c.1294** Persians convert to Islam	**1340** Hindu empire of Vijayanagar in India becomes centre of resistance to Islam
EUROPE		**1273** Rudolf Habsburg (1218–91) becomes ruler of Germany, founding the powerful Habsburg dynasty		**1309** Pope moves to Avignon, leading to great rift in Western Church (1378)	**1346** Battle of Crécy Hundred Years War b... England and France **1347** Plague (Blac... Death) reaches E...
AMERICAS	**c.1250** Mayans restore empire and build new capital at Mayapan. Incas expand their capital at Chan-chan in northern Peru			**c.1300** Incas begin major expansion through Andes	**1325** Aztecs found their capital at Tenochtitlán (now Mexico City)
OCEANIA	**c.1250** Religious assembly platforms built throughout Polynesian Islands				

MARCO POLO'S EPIC JOURNEY

In 1271, brothers Niccolo and Maffeo Polo, merchants of Venice, Italy, took Niccolo's 16-year-old son Marco on their second trading journey to the East. Marco had many amazing experiences in the depths of China, and when he returned to Europe 24 years later, he was able to give the first detailed account of daily life in the East.

POLO'S FOOTSTEPS

On their second journey the Polos travelled the ancient Silk Route of central Asia, which, before the Mongol Empire, could only be used by Arab traders. They took three-and-a-half years to reach the palace of the Mongol emperor, including a year's rest for Marco to recover from illness.

Venice, Constantinople, Shangtu, Peking, Kashgar, Nanking, Cheng-tu, Foochow, HIMALAYAS, Yunnan, Acre, Pagan, Jerusalem

Polo's journey (1271–95)

VENICE

In the 13th century, Venice was the busiest port in the world. Venetian traders supplied Europe's markets with the precious products of the East: silk, spices, and porcelain.

Polos leave Venice

PASTA AND ICE-CREAM

The Chinese invented two of modern Italy's most famous dishes: pasta and ice-cream. Italian merchants returning from the East brought back the recipes.

The court of Kublai Khan

KUBLAI KHAN

Mongol Emperor Kublai Khan, was eager to learn about European society and he welcomed the Polos at his palace in Shangtu, China.

HUMAN KITE-RIDERS

Marco Polo told terrifying tales of wickerwork kites. These hoisted live prisoners into the sky, both to test the wind and to bring good luck before ships sailed. Few of the prisoners survived.

POLO TELLS HIS STORY

In 1298, Marco Polo was locked up in Genoa, Italy. There he dictated the story of his journey to a fellow prisoner called Rustichello. The tale amazed Europeans and was translated into several languages.

POLO'S TRUE STORIES

- Polo described Eastern springs that gushed oil. Europeans had doubts, but Polo had not lied: he had seen the Baku oilfields in modern-day Azerbaijan.

- Polo spoke of rocks that could be ground up and spun into a fireproof cloth: they were asbestos rocks, well known in China, but unheard-of in 13th-century Europe.

- The Chinese were the first people to use paper money as currency. Venetian merchants, who still used gold and silver coins as currency, could not believe this.

Early Chinese paper money

KAMIKAZE – DIVINE WIND OF JAPAN

In 1281, the Mongols attacked Japan by sea, hoping to enlarge their vast empire. A timely typhoon destroyed their fleet and put to flight those Mongols already on land. The Japanese named this typhoon the "Divine Wind" or *Kamikaze*.

The Mongol fleet breaks up on Japan's coast

KEY INNOVATIONS

SPECTACLES

By the early 14th century, reading glasses with curved lenses were being made in a Venice factory.

ACCOUNTANCY

From the 1340s, European merchants began using double-entry book-keeping to record their business.

JOAN OF ARC

In 1431, Joan of Arc (1412–31) was tried by her English enemies and burned as a witch. Inspired by divine visions, the young French shepherdess had led the armies of King Charles VII to a great victory that proved to be the turning point of the Hundred Years War. Since that time she has been honoured as a saint.

52 Moroccan scholar
Battuta (1304–68)
kes his great journey
oss Sahara to Mali

c.1400 Kingdom of Zimbabwe
thrives on gold trade

1432 Portuguese explorers
reach the Azores

Majapahit Empire
ed in Java

1368 Tai Tsu (1328–98),
founder of Ming dynasty,
drives Mongols from China

1398 Mongol leader Tamerlane
(1336–1405) sacks Delhi

1405 Death of Tamerlane
and fall of Mongol Empire

1404–33 Chinese navigator
Cheng Ho (1371–1435)
explores India and East Africa

1411 Ahmad Shah founds
Ahmadabad, important
commercial city in India

1448 Major reforms
in Thailand under
King Traillok
(1431–88)

1358 The *Jacquerie*:
French peasants
revolt against raised
taxes. Rebel peasants
defeated and killed

1380 Russians halt Tatar
Mongols at Battle of Kulikovo

1381 Peasants' Revolt in England
led by Wat Tyler and John Ball

1389 Ottoman Turks crush Serbs
and neighbours at Battle of Kosovo

1429 Siege of Orléans
lifted by French soldier-
saint Joan of Arc's forces

Acamapitzin becomes Aztec ruler,
sing Aztec power

1400 Viracocha (d.1438): first Inca overlord to
establish permanent rule over conquered tribes

1438 Inca overlord Pachacuti (d.1471)
greatly enlarges Inca Empire

Maoris create rock
New Zealand

MANSA MUSA
The African empire of Mansa Musa (d.1332)
was famed for its size and wealth. Stopping in
Egypt during a pilgrimage to Mecca, Mansa Musa,
his 80 camels laden with gold, spent so much that
prices rose dramatically all over Egypt. On his return
he had a great mosque
built at
Timbuktu.

Mansa Musa
Gold nugget

Great Mosque at Timbuktu

KEY PEOPLE

Name	Date	Biographical details
Kublai Khan	1215–94	Mongol Emperor of China, patronized the arts
Marco Polo	c.1254–1324	Venetian merchant-explorer, reached court of Kublai Khan and served as his envoy
Ibn Battuta	1304–68	Moroccan explorer of Africa, India, Russia, China
Mansa Musa	d.1332	Wealthy Emperor of Mali, conquered Songhai empire
Tamerlane	1336–1405	Mongol conqueror of modern-day Iraq and Iran
Joan of Arc	1412–31	French soldier-saint, heroine of Hundred Years War
Pachacuti	d.1471	Inca overlord, started great expansion of Empire

THE BLACK DEATH
In 1347, a horrific disease hit Europe: the
Black Death. A combination of bubonic
and pneumonic plague, it caused one of the
worst disasters in human
history, wiping out a quarter
of the European population
in just four
years.

Warsaw
c.1353
FLANDERS
London
c.1351
1350
1349
POLAND
Black Death Timetable
Autumn 1348
Paris
Summer 1348
Extent by 1347
Prague
Milan
Genoa
Marseilles

THE JOURNEY OF DEATH
Genoese traders brought the Black Death to Sicily in
1347. It took hold of the ports of Pisa, Genoa, and
Marseilles, then swept into France and Spain. A few
areas escaped: Milan, Flanders, and parts of Poland.

SCALE OF DEATH
The Black Death
claimed an enormous
25 million lives in
Europe alone: at least a
quarter of its population.
This is more than three
times the number of
soldiers killed in
World War I.

25m

8m

Black
Death

World
War I

= 2 million
dead

HOW THE PLAGUE SPREAD
Fleas on animals, such as rats, carried and transmitted
the Black Death. Humans caught the disease either
from fleabites or from other infected people. Even
when all ships were quarantined for 40 days, rats
living on board could simply swim ashore.

BLACK DEATH FACTS
• The term "bubonic plague" comes from the
buboes, or dark swellings, that appear in the
armpits and groin of an infected person.

• At the height of the Black Death, the Rhône
river in France was consecrated
as a graveyard; many
hundreds of victims
were thrown into it.

• Milan, Italy,
survived the first
plague because the
Bishop ordered the
first three houses that it
struck to be walled up. The
dead, sick, and healthy were all trapped inside.

Condemned homes

• In 1348 the Black Death killed the great
Italian historian Giovanni Villani (b.1275). His
writings end in mid-sentence, with, "And this
plague lasted until....."

FLAGELLANTS
Many believed that the
plague was God's
punishment for their
sins. Some, called
Flagellants, would whip
themselves until they
bled, hoping for salvation.

PEASANTS' REVOLTS
Survivors of the plague,
which had greatly
reduced Europe's
workforce, demanded
higher pay and better
conditions. French
peasants revolted in 1358;
English peasants in 1381.
Both revolts were crushed
and their leaders killed.

Rebel leader Wat Tyler is murdered.

HOT UNDER THE COLLAR
On doctors' orders, Pope
Clement VI spent the hot
summer of 1348
sitting between two
fires that were
kept permanently
stoked. Although
he didn't know
it, the heat
probably kept
the fleas at bay,
and he survived.

1450

1464 Sonni Ali (d.1492) becomes ruler of Songhai in West Africa

1482 Portuguese begin settling on Gold Coast, West Africa

1488 Portuguese navigator Bartolomeu Diaz (1450–1500) rounds Cape of Good Hope, South Africa, opening the sea route from Europe to Asia

1467 Onin War, lasting over 100 years, begins in Japan. Leads to end of feudal system and rise of large territories

1497–98 Portuguese navigator Vasco Gama (1460–1524) reaches India via

1450 Florence, Milan, and Naples form alliance

1450s German craftsman Johannes Gutenberg (c.1398–1468) produces first printed books in Europe

1453 Constantinople falls, ending Byzantine empire

1463 Turkey and Venice fight for control of Mediterranean until 1479

1478 Ivan III (1440–1505) begins to unify Russia

1479 Marriage of Ferdinand of Aragon and Isabella of Castille unites Spain. Lorenzo de Medici (1449–92) becomes unofficial ruler of Florence

1492 Conquest of Granada ends Moorish Spain and results in expulsion of Jews

1494 Under Treaty of Tordesillas, Spain Portugal agree to divide unexplored worl

1492 Italian explorer Christopher Columbus (1451–1506) discovers the Caribbean

1497 Italian explorer John Cabot (c.1450–c.1498) discovers Newfoundl

FALL OF BYZANTIUM

In 1453, Constantinople, capital of the centuries-old Byzantine Empire, fell to the Ottoman sultan Muhammad II. He had dragged 70 ships overland to avoid a huge iron chain protecting the waterway into the city.

PRINCE DRACULA (THE IMPALER)

The cruelties of the sadistic Romanian prince Vlad Dracul or "Vlad the Impaler" inspired the Dracula legend. He reigned for less than ten years, yet caused at least 50,000 deaths. After his own violent death in 1476, his severed head was impaled on a stake for public display.

FERDINAND AND ISABELLA

In 1479, Ferdinand of Aragon and Isabella of Castille married and formed a larger, Christian Spanish kingdom. In 1492, their forces captured Granada, the last Muslim outpost in Spain. The new rulers were intolerant of other religions: 165,000 Jews were told to convert to Christianity or leave Spain.

THE RENAISSANCE

15th-century Europe experienced a great cultural movement called the Renaissance (meaning "rebirth"). It began in the prosperous cities of Italy and was inspired by the rediscovery of ancient Greek and Roman ideas on art, literature, and science.

RENAISSANCE FLORENCE

At the height of its power, Florence was run by the Medici family, the greatest financiers in Europe. They were educated in the classics and supported new artists and their ideas. Michelangelo's first commissions came from Lorenzo de Medici, and it was Medici money that attracted Leonardo da Vinci to the city.

RENAISSANCE INNOVATIONS

COAL MINING
In the 1520s, the first coal mines were opened in Newcastle, England, and Liège, Belgium.

FLIGHT DESIGNS
Leonardo da Vinci made detailed designs for a flying machine, a parachute, and a helicopter.

PRINTING PRESS
German printer Johannes Gutenberg (d.1468) made the first European moveable-type printing press in Mainz, Germany.

LUCREZIA BORGIA

Lucrezia Borgia (1480–1519) was the daughter of Rodrigo Borgia (Pope Alexander VI). She was famed for her charity and great learning – she wrote poetry in three languages. Exhausted by eleven pregnancies, she died in childbirth.

ENIGMATIC SMILE

Leonardo da Vinci's greatest painting, the *Mona Lisa*, was sold to Francis I of France. He kept it in his bathroom.

MICHELANGELO

By studying Greek and Roman art, Renaissance artists learned how to draw "in perspective" – to show depth on a flat canvas – and how to depict the proportions of the body. Michelangelo's huge statue of the biblical hero David, completed in Florence in 1504, is the most famous example of classical Renaissance sculpture.

David – height 5.49m (18ft)

RENAISSANCE FIGURES

Name	Dates	Biographical details
Lorenzo de Medici	1449–92	Florentine patron of the arts, poet, classical scholar, banker, ruler of Florence
Leonardo da Vinci	1452–1519	Italian artist, sculptor, architect, engineer, inventor, anatomist
Desiderius Erasmus	1466–1536	Influential Dutch Renaissance thinker and priest, critical of the church
Niccolo Machiavelli	1469–1527	Florentine statesman, author of political masterpiece *The Prince*
Albrecht Dürer	1471–1528	German artist of the Northern Renaissance; painter and printmaker
Michelangelo	1475–1564	Italian painter, sculptor, and architect; painted ceiling of Sistine Chapel, Vatican
Andreas Vesalius	1514–64	Anatomist and physician; wrote first complete description of the human body

Bantus in southern
trade with Europeans.
states develop in
Africa

1517 Egypt conquered
by Ottomans

Safavid dynasty
ns in Persia

1517 Syria conquered
by Ottomans

1520–21 Portuguese traders reach China
1526 Babur becomes first Mogul Emperor of India

1542 Portuguese traders reach Japan

1546 Burma united
under King Tabin Shweti

503 Leonardo da
nci (1452–1519)
nts *Mona Lisa*

1512 Italian artist Michelangelo (1475–1564)
completes ceiling of Sistine Chapel

1517 German monk Martin
Luther (1483–1546) sets off
the Reformation

1529 Ottoman Turks
besiege Vienna

1520 Suleiman I (1494–1566) begins
greatest reign of Ottoman empire

1533 Ivan the Terrible
comes to the throne in Russia

1541 French Protestant
reformer Jean Calvin (1509–64)
sets up Puritan state in Geneva

1545 Council of Trent starts
Catholic Counter-Reformation

02 Italian Amerigo Vespucci
–1512) explores coast of
. African slaves
to the
Indies

1519 Portuguese explorer Ferdinand
Magellan (1480–1521) sails across
Pacific Ocean. Spaniard Hernán Cortés
(1485–1547) overthrows Aztec empire

1532 Spaniard Francisco Pizarro (1475–1541)
brings down Inca empire, South America

1534 French explorer Jacques
Cartier (1491–1557) sails St. Lawrence River, Canada

1526 Portuguese landings in Polynesia

1550 Maoris settle on
South Island, New Zealand

Battle of Mohács

SULEIMAN THE MAGNIFICENT
Suleiman I, "The Magnificent" (1494–1566), was the
greatest of the Ottoman (Turkish) sultans. He
reformed the educational and legal systems, and built
great mosques, bridges, fortresses, and aqueducts. At
the Battle of Mohács in 1526, his huge victory over
Hungary marked the height of the Ottoman empire.

MAORI MIGRATION
Around 1550, Maoris sailed from
North Island, New Zealand, in
large double canoes to settle
South Island. Overcrowding on
North Island had led to violent
competition for new lands.

BABUR I OF INDIA
Babur (1483–1530), a
descendant of Genghis
Khan, was the first Mogul
Emperor of India and made
Delhi his capital in 1526. He
was a brilliant military leader,
but was also fascinated by
art and poetry.

LUTHER'S THESES
In 1517 a German monk
called Martin Luther
(1483–1546) nailed a list of
complaints, his "95 Theses",
to the door of his church at
Wittenberg. He criticized
the Catholic Church for its
increasing corruption and
called for reform. This
sparked off a movement
called the Reformation, and
led to the formation of the
Protestant churches
(churches of protest).

AZTECS AND INCAS
Advanced civilizations were
established in the Americas long before
the Europeans arrived: the Aztec capital
was bigger than any city in Europe.
Astronomy, mathematics, and the arts
flourished, and great temples were raised in
honour of their gods.

Favoured
subjects
Montezuma
Nobles
Steps
War Council
Wise men

*Montezuma's court
and ceremonial
chamber*

TWO GREAT EMPIRES
The Aztecs controlled an empire of
500 towns and 15 million people in
modern-day Mexico. The Inca
Empire stretched hundreds of
miles down the Pacific coast.

Aztec
empire

Inca
empire

CALENDAR SYSTEM
Aztecs had a sophisticated
calendar system that enabled
them to date events centuries-
apart with great accuracy.

Sacrificial ceremony

MONTEZUMA, AZTEC KING
Montezuma II (1466–1520) was
elected king in 1503. In 1520 he was
murdered by the Spanish conqueror
Hernan Cortés (1485–1547).

AZTEC AND INCA FACTS
• Before Europeans arrived,
neither Aztecs nor Incas had
seen horses. Incas used runners,
trained from birth, to deliver
official messages.

• The Aztec punishment for
thieves was for them to repay
twice what they had stolen.

• The Aztecs' lucky number
was 13.

• Aztecs feared that the world
might end every 52 years, and
threw away all their possessions
in preparation.

HUMAN SACRIFICE
Both Aztecs and Incas believed
their angry gods were only
soothed by blood sacrifice.
In the early 1500s, Aztec
priests were tearing the
hearts from an estimated
20,000 people every year.

FALL OF THE INCAS
In 1532, the Spaniard Francisco
Pizarro (1475–1541) marched into
Peru with just 200 soldiers and
kidnapped the Inca Emperor
Atahualpa (1502–33). Pizarro
asked for a ransom of a room full
of gold, then murdered
Atahualpa. The leaderless
empire crumbled.

COUNTER-REFORMATION
In 1545 Catholic leaders met at the Council of Trent
in northern Italy to settle the main principles of
Catholicism and
to organize a
campaign against
the spread of the
Reformation.
This movement
was called the
Counter-
Reformation.

Council of Trent

FIELD OF THE CLOTH OF GOLD
In 1520 the French King Francis I, met the English
King Henry VIII, at a lavish ceremony in France to
sign a peace treaty. The field was named after the
fabulous cloth of their royal tents.

Timeline 1550

AFRICA					**1591** Moroccans and Europea[n] mercenaries destroy Songhai e[mpire]
ASIA		**1566** Death of Suleiman I: Ottoman empire at greatest extent	**1577** Akbar the Great (1542–1605) completes unification of northern India	**1590** Shah Abbas of Persia (1557– makes peace with Ottoman Turke[y] **1592** Japan invades Korea commander Hideyoshi
EUROPE	**1555** Peace of Augsburg permits each German ruler to decide religion of subjects	**1564** Death of Michelangelo. Shakespeare born	**1571** Battle of Lepanto: Christian European alliance defeats Ottoman Turkish fleet **1572** St. Bartholomew's Day Massacre of Protestants in France	**1588** England defeats Spanish Armada **1582** Gregorian calendar reform introduced in Catholic countries	**1598** Edict of Na[ntes] ends civil war in F[rance] giving Catholics a[nd] Huguenots equal [rights]
AMERICAS		**1567** Portuguese establish Rio de Janeiro, Brazil	**1579** Francis Drake (c.1540-96) establishes British claim to west coast of North America		
OCEANIA		**1567** Spanish explorer Mendaña (1541–95) becomes first European to reach Solomon Islands		**1595** Mendaña lands on Mar[quesas] Islands, central South Pacific

RELIGION DIVIDES EUROPE

Luther's protests led to the formation of Protestant churches and split Christians in Europe into violent rival groups. War often broke out as each country struggled with the new religious alliances.

Battle of Lepanto

BATTLE OF LEPANTO
In 1571 an alliance of European sea powers led by the Pope defeated the Ottoman fleet at the Battle of Lepanto, Greece. The battle ended Turkish threats to Europe by sea, and allowed Catholics to turn to their struggles with European Protestants.

DIVINE DICTATION
St. Mary-Magdalen dei Pazzi (1566–1607) was famed for the length of her religious trances, during which she was thought to speak sacred truths. Six secretaries would record her words for hours, and sometimes days, at a time.

ELIZABETH I OF ENGLAND
The Protestant Elizabeth I ruled England from 1558 to 1603 and showed tolerance towards other religions. She never married and so avoided sharing her power with a foreign king.

PHILIP OF SPAIN
Philip II of Spain was the most powerful Catholic monarch in Europe. When Queen Elizabeth I executed the Catholic Mary Queen of Scots, he organized a fleet (the Spanish Armada) to invade England and restore Catholic rule. It set sail in July 1588.

The Spanish had 130 ships. The English had less than 100.

Battle of the Spanish Armada

SPANISH ARMADA
In August 1588 the English fleet defeated Philip's massive invasion fleet, the Spanish Armada. The victory was a triumph for Protestantism.

RETRACTABLE BLADE
Witch-hunters claimed that witches felt no pain when stabbed. When the witch-hunters wanted to condemn a person of a different religion from their own, they used a retractable blade.

Spring

Blade does not pierce skin

LANDMARKS OF A RELIGIOUS AGE

St. Bartholomew's Day Massacre

Catherine de Medici with Huguenots

St. Bartholomew's Day Massacre
On 24 August 1572, the Catholic queen regent of France, Catherine de Medici, secretly ordered the massacre of thousands of French Protestants (Huguenots). This St. Bartholomew's Day Massacre was meant to destroy the Huguenots; instead it re-opened hostilities between Huguenots and Catholics.

Edict of Nantes (1598)
In 1593, the Protestant Henry of Navarre became a Catholic in order to be confirmed as Henry IV of France. His law, the Edict of Nantes, ended France's religious wars by allowing Protestants to worship.

Gunpowder Plot
In 1605, a Catholic plot to murder James I of England was discovered. Guy Fawkes was planning to light gunpowder in the cellars of Parliament while James was giving an address; he was caught and executed after torture. The discovery of the Gunpowder Plot led to greater persecution of English Catholics.

Guy Fawkes' signature before his torture

Guy Fawkes' signature after his torture

Jesuit missionaries
Spanish nobleman Ignatius de Loyola founded the Society of Jesus, or the Jesuits, as the missionaries of the Catholic Counter-Reformation. From 1550, Jesuits were in action all over Europe, and soon they began converting the peoples of the Americas to Christianity. Wherever traders went, Jesuits followed.

Persecuted Puritans
Rival groups of Protestants sometimes persecuted each other. In 1620, a group of Puritans called the Pilgrim Fathers set sail from Plymouth, England, to North America in search of religious freedom.

The Mayflower

All major European powers
...ish trading posts on African coast

1620s Queen Nzinga of Mbundu
defeats the Portuguese

...Beginning of Tokugawa period in Japan.
...h East India Company founded
...602 Dutch East India Company founded

1604 Russians settle in Siberia

1610 Assassination of French
King Henry IV (b.1553)

1618 Beginning of
Thirty Years War

1631 Sacking of
Magdeburg, Germany:
worst atrocity of
Thirty Years War

1605 Failure of Gunpowder Plot
and arrest of Guy Fawkes

1613 Michael Romanov (r.1613–45)
becomes first Russian Romanov tsar

1607 John Smith (1580–1631) founds
colony of Virginia at Jamestown

1608 Quebec founded

1609 Henry Hudson (c.1565–1611)
sails up Hudson river

1620 Mayflower
sets sail for
North America

1625 French begin
to settle West Indies

1626 Dutch found New
Amsterdam (now New York)

1630 Dutch East India
Company seizes part of
Brazil for its sugar and silver

1629 Massachusetts colony founded

 1606 Portuguese navigator De Quiros arrives at Tahiti, and Spanish
navigator Luis Vaez de Torres sails between Australia and New Guinea

AKBAR THE GREAT

The Mogul Emperor Akbar (1542–1605) gave
his expanding empire a superb structure of
government. Although he was a Muslim, he
also won the support of non-Muslims by
his tolerance of other religions. He even
tried to start a new religion – Din Illahl –
and supported many Hindu practices.

HINDU MARRIAGES

In 1562 and 1570, Akbar married
Hindu Rajput princesses, despite
his Islamic beliefs. The marriages
demonstrated his respect for his
Hindu subjects.

*Muslim Emperor Akbar
with his Hindu bride*

*Extent of
Mogul Empire*

AKBAR'S MOGUL EMPIRE
At his death Akbar's empire stretched from
Afghanistan in the north, to Bengal in the east,
and Gujarat in the west.

AKBAR'S FAVOURITE
Akbar, a keen hunter, trained
cheetahs to catch and kill his prey.
His favourite once jumped a
ravine to kill a blackbuck deer.
From then it was carried into the
hunt on a cushioned litter.

*Festivities at
the birth of
Akbar's son*

AKBAR'S ART
The arts blossomed
under Akbar. A
series of beautiful
paintings, called *The
Annals of Akbar*, were
prepared in the late
1590s and show
scenes from his life.

INABAT-KHANA
In 1575, Akbar built
the Inabat-Khana
(house of worship) in
which Muslims of
many traditions,
Zoroastrians, Hindu
pandits, and yogis
came to discuss their
religious beliefs.

*Akbar in religious
discussion*

TOKUGAWA JAPAN

In 1603 Ieyasu (1543–1616) of the
Tokugawa clan became *shogun* (ruler) of
Japan after defeating his rivals at the Battle
of Sekigahara (1600). He placed the
government in Edo (now Tokyo) and
forced his remaining rivals to move there.

Sloping roof gives
view of enemy.

Decorative
gable

Fireproof and
bulletproof plaster

Windows
could be
used as
gunports.

*Gatehouse of
Edo Castle,
Tokyo,
Japan*

Stone
rampart

DISTRACTING HIS RIVALS
From 1604 to 1614, Ieyasu forced his rival *daimyo*
(samurai warlords) to build and enlarge a castle at
Edo. By the time he died he had built
the world's biggest castle.

Dutch trading post

JAPAN IN ISOLATION
In 1636, the Tokugawa regime prevented all Japanese
from travelling abroad, and in 1641 expelled all
foreigners. A Dutch trading post in Nagasaki Bay was
the only contact with the outside world until 1854.

KEY PEOPLE

Name	Dates	Biographical details
Ignatius de Loyola	1491–1556	Spanish ex-soldier and priest, founded Society of Jesus (Jesuits) in 1534
Philip II	1527–98	King of Spain and Portugal, champion of the Catholic Counter-Reformation
Elizabeth I	1533–1603	Queen of England during period of naval supremacy, artistic excellence, and international trade
Akbar	1542–1605	Mogul emperor, famous for religious tolerance and support of the arts
Tokugawa Ieyasu	1543–1616	Shogun (ruler) of Japan, ended wars, unified country, banned Christianity
Henry IV	1553–1610	King of France, converted to Catholicism from Protestantism to re-unify France
William Shakespeare	1564–1616	English dramatist and poet; plays include Hamlet and King Lear

KEY INNOVATIONS

PENCILS
Pencils were first produced
in England in 1565.

MERCATOR'S MAP
In 1569, Flemish
geographer Gerhard
Mercator (1512–94)
published a map on his
new projection, which
is still in use today.

1640

| AFRICA | **1652** Dutch found Cape colony in southern Africa | **1663** Death of Queen Nzinga of Mbundu | **1670s** French settle in Senegal | **1690s** Ashanti kingdom established on Gold Coast |

| ASIA | **1644** Manchu dynasty replaces Ming dynasty in China | **1657** Edo (Tokyo) is destroyed by a great fire | **1661** English East India Company acquires Bombay | **1662** K'ang Hsi begins reign in China | **1669** Mogul Emperor Aurangzeb prohibits Hinduism | **1683** K'ang Hsi conquers Formosa (Taiwan) | **1688** Genroku Period, rise of merchant class in Japan (until |

| EUROPE | **1642** Civil War in England | **1643** Louis XIV begins reign | **1649** Charles I of England executed. Commonwealth set up under Oliver Cromwell | **1648** End of the Thirty Years War | **1660** English monarchy restored | **1661** Bank of Sweden issues first European bank notes | **1672** Third Anglo-Dutch trade war begins | **1677** Ottomans at war with Russia | **1682** Peter the Great begins reign | **1683** Siege of Vienna by Ottoman forces fails | **1688** England's "Glorious Revolution" | **1690** Battle of the Boyne. Protestant William of Orange defeats Catholic James |

| AMERICAS | **1642** French explorer De Maisonneuve founds Ville-Marie (now Montreal) | **1664** England seizes New Amsterdam (now New York) from Dutch | **1670** Colony of South Carolina founded. English Hudson's Bay Company founded | **1675** War between colonists and Native Americans devastates New England | **1680** French explorer Robert Cavalier de la Salle claims Mississippi valley for France | **1683** William Penn signs treaty with Native Americans | **1692** Salem witch trials, New England |

| OCEANIA | **1642** Dutch explorer Abel Tasman becomes first European to reach Van Diemen's Land (Tasmania) | | **1680** The dodo becomes extinct |

MANCHU CHINA

In 1644, the Manchus invaded China at the request of an unhappy Ming (Chinese) general. After the conquest, however, the Manchu leader Fu-lin (r.1638–61) made himself emperor. The *Ch'ing*, or Pure, dynasty that he founded ruled China for more than 250 years.

Under Manchu control by:
- 1644
- 1660
- 1760

MANCHURIAN EMPIRE
Manchuria lies in the northeastern region of modern-day China.

MING MANDARINS
Mandarins were the top officials of Ming China and were famed for their organizing skills. When the Manchus conquered China the mandarins were left to carry on with their work.

Manchus forced the Chinese to braid their hair, as they did, into a queue, or pigtail, as a sign of inferiority.

Manchu lord with Ming Chinese

Art of Manchu period

ART AND LEARNING
The second Emperor K'ang Hsi (1654–1722), like Fu-lin, saw the value of Ming culture. He requested scholars to write a Ming history, as well as dictionaries, encyclopedias, and technical works.

SUPREME RULERS

Kings and queens held massive political power in seventeenth-century Europe. Louis XIV of France (1638–1715), the most powerful of all, made decisions without regard to parliament or leading aristocrats.

THE AGE OF LOUIS XIV
- Louis ruled France for 62 years – during this time it became the most powerful country in Europe.
- Louis forced the nobles to live at his Versailles palace so that he could watch them closely.
- Louis' keen support of the arts earned him the nickname "The Sun King", after Apollo, Greek god of the arts.
- In 1685, Louis abolished a law called the Edict of Nantes, which had protected the rights of French Protestants (Huguenots). Many went to England, where their businesses and crafts were successful.

Hall of Mirrors at Versailles

CHARLES I
In 1649, the unpopular Charles I (1600–49) was beheaded by his English subjects, an event that shocked Europe. Parliament limited his successors' powers.

Execution of Charles I

A boyar (Russian noble)

Peter the Great forces the old-fashioned boyars, or nobles, to shave their beards in modern European style.

King Louis XIV of France in classical costume

SUICIDAL CHEF
In 1676, Le Grand Vatel, the famous chef to the Prince de Condé, committed suicide because a meal he had prepared for Louis XIV did not meet with the king's full approval.

PETER THE GREAT
In 1682, Peter the Great (1672–1725) became Tsar of Russia. He was a leader of great energy and re-organized the army, founded the navy, and built a new capital at St. Petersburg.

KEY PEOPLE

Name	Dates	Biographical details
Nzinga of Mbundu	1582–1663	Queen of Mbundu, West Africa, fought Portuguese slave traders, offered shelter to runaway slaves from neighbouring states
Oliver Cromwell	1599–1658	Victorious commander of English Parliamentary forces in civil war of 1642–48, Lord Protector (ruler) of England, 1653–58
Charles I	1600–49	British king executed after losing civil war against Parliamentary armies
Louis XIV	1638–1715	Absolute ruler during period when France led in politics, arts, and culture
Fu-lin	r.1638–61	First Manchu Emperor of China, increased number of Chinese in government
Peter the Great	1672–1725	Tsar of Russia, imported Western Europe's ideas and technology

02 French win Asiento (monopoly on ipping of Africans to Spanish colonies)

1712 Rise of Futa Jalon kingdom in West Africa

1713 King Philip V of Spain grants Asiento to England

1707 Death of Aurangzeb leads to fall of Mogul Empire and opportunities for European traders

1708 Jesuit map-makers plot accurate maps of China

1727 Border fixed between China and Russia

1739 Nadir Shah captures Delhi with a Persian army, defeating the Moguls

1740s Anglo-French rivalry in India until 1760s

Charles II of Spain dies g French heir: starts War of h Succession (1701–13)

1703 Hungary revolts against Austria. Peter the Great founds St. Petersburg

1707 England and Scotland united

1709 English ironmaster Abraham Darby produces coke, and uses it to smelt (extract metal from) iron ore, starting Industrial Revolution

1709 Russia conquers Swedish Baltic provinces

1748 Marie Theresa becomes Empress of Austria

1746 Culloden: last infantry battle in Britain ends Scottish revolt

1709 Mass emigration of Germans to America begins

1710 South Sea Company increases British trade with South America

1720–22 Spain occupies Texas. English South Sea and French Mississippi Companies collapse

1733 Molasses Act: England forbids trade between American and West Indian colonies. Colony of Georgia founded

1739 Slave uprising in South Carolina

1722 Dutch navigator Roggeveen reaches Samoa and Easter Island

---

THE SLAVE TRADE

When Europeans settled in the Americas, they transported Africans to work as slaves on the cotton, sugar, and tobacco plantations and in the silver mines. Slaves were forced to travel in horrific conditions, and were often worked to death once they had arrived.

Sugar, cotton, and rum

Arab-owned slaves

English-owned and French-owned slaves

Portuguese-owned slaves

Slaves packed in as tightly as possible.

Plan of slave ship owned by Brookes of Liverpool, England

THE MIDDLE PASSAGE

The slave ship shown was designed to carry more than 400 people on the journey from Africa to America, called the Middle Passage. The supersonic jet *Concorde* would require three trips to transport 400 people over the Atlantic, yet *Concorde* is three times this ship's length.

Size comparison of slave ship and Concorde

Queen Nzinga seated on her attendant's back meets with the Portuguese at Luanda.

QUEEN NZINGA

Queen Nzinga of Mbundu, West Africa, opposed European slave traders. Her army was swelled by runaway slaves who had fled to her lands.

THE TRIANGULAR SLAVE ROUTE

Slave ships took a triangular route. They sailed from Europe to Africa to get slaves, over to the Americas to exchange slaves for sugar, cotton, and rum, then returned to Europe to sell those goods.

TRADER PORTS PROSPER

Atlantic ports such as Bristol, England, and Bordeaux, France, grew rich due to their strategic position between Europe, Africa, and the West Indies.

Branding mark burned into skin.

Bristol docks

MARKETS FOR PEOPLE

Once slaves reached the Caribbean, South America, or the colonies of North America, they were sold to the highest bidder. If different traders had used the same ship they had their own slaves branded with hot irons to identify them after the journey.

European slave traders assemble their captured slaves for sale.

SLAVE TRADE FACTS

• Between 1500 and 1800, European ships transported about 12 million people from their homes in Africa to the colonies of the Americas – two million more than the entire population of 15th-century North America.

• By 1800, the total African slave population of South America was just 1.2 million; most slaves died of overwork within a few years of arriving.

• The slave trade was more profitable than the trade in ebony, ivory, or gold.

• The Portuguese called their slave ships *tumbeiros*, meaning coffins, because they lost more than 30% of their human cargo during the voyage.

• In 1781, the captain of the *Zong* threw 132 slaves overboard to collect the insurance.

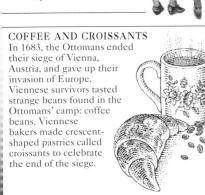

KING AGAJA

King Agaja (1673–1740) of Dahomey raided and enslaved his weaker neighbours. European and Arab traders bought his captives as slaves.

COFFEE AND CROISSANTS

In 1683, the Ottomans ended their siege of Vienna, Austria, and gave up their invasion of Europe. Viennese survivors tasted strange beans found in the Ottomans' camp: coffee beans. Viennese bakers made crescent-shaped pastries called croissants to celebrate the end of the siege.

KEY INNOVATIONS

18th-century orrery shows planetary motion

STRADIVARIUS' VIOLIN

Italian craftsman Antonio Stradivarius (c.1644–1737) perfected the art of violin-making. The secret of his varnish has never been discovered.

NEWTON'S LAWS

English scientist Isaac Newton (1642–1727) first formulated the laws of gravity in his book *Principia* (1687).

IRON SMELTING

In 1709, Englishman Abraham Darby (c.1678–1717) made the first industrial iron by smelting pig iron with coke, not charcoal.

1750

AFRICA
1768 Ali Bey becomes ruler of independent Egypt

ASIA 1750 China conquers Tibet   1757 Battle of Plassey: British conquer Bengal   1761 Battle of Panipat: Marathas defeated by Afghans

EUROPE
1755 Earthquake at Lisbon, Portugal
1756–63 Seven Years War between Britain and France
1757 First English canal built
1762 Catherine the Great begins reign over Russia
1769 Richard Arkwright builds first cotton factory
1772 First Partition of Poland between Prussia, Russia, and Austria
1771 Russia conquers Crimea
1789 Storming of the Ba French Revolution begi
1781 Joseph II abolishes serfdom (a form of peasant slavery) in Austrian Empire

AMERICAS
1759 English forces defeat French on Plains of Abraham, Quebec
1763 Pontiac (1720–69) leads Native American uprising against British in North America
1773 Boston Tea Party: protest against British tea tax
1775–83 American War of Independence
1776 US Declaration of Independence signed
1780 Tupac Amara leads Incas of Peru in revolt against Spain
1787–9 US Constitution an Bill of Rights written and ra

OCEANIA
1768–71 Captain Cook's first voyage on *Endeavour*
1788 British colony of Ne South Wales, Australia, fo

THE ENLIGHTENMENT
Followers of the 18th-century movement called the Enlightenment believed that reason and science could help to free people from rigid governments and religious intolerance. Enlightenment ideas about justice, equality, and freedom for all inspired the American and French revolutions.

THE ENCYCLOPEDIA
French philosophers Denis Diderot and Jean Le Rond d'Alembert collected and published the ideas of the Enlightenment in the multi-volume *L'Encyclopédie* between 1751 and 1786. It included contributions by thinkers such as Voltaire and Rousseau.

L'Encyclopédie

VOLTAIRE
The French thinker Voltaire (1694–1778) was a key figure in the Enlightenment. His witty writings criticized religious intolerance and backward governments and rulers.

Marble sculpture of Voltaire

BENJAMIN FRANKLIN
American Benjamin Franklin (1706–90) was a typical Enlightenment figure – scientist, philosopher, and statesman. In 1776, he went to France to raise support for the American struggle against British rule.

Benjamin Franklin

CAPTAIN COOK
English navigator James Cook (1728–79) explored the South Pacific. He sensibly kept his ships clean and well ventilated; he gave his crews fresh vegetables and lime juice which saved them from scurvy.

Ship's cloth   Lobster

Cook trades with Islanders

COWPOX FOR SMALLPOX
Catherine the Great of Russia, who used to write to Voltaire, set an example to her fearful subjects when she had herself and her heir vaccinated by cowpox against smallpox.

REVOLUTION AND UNREST

Washington crosses the Delaware River before battle.

American War of Independence 1775–83
Americans disliked paying taxes to a government in which they had no representation. Led by George Washington, they had won independence by 1783.

French Revolution, 1789
In return for funding the bankrupt Louis XVI, the French lords, clergy, and commons demanded more power. On 14 July 1789, their supporters in Paris stormed the Bastille prison, an ancient symbol of royal authority, and launched the French Revolution.

Reign of Terror
In 1792, France chose a new form of government: a republic. Louis XVI was executed in January 1793, and from mid-1793 to July 1794 anti-republicans were executed, often without trial. The period was called "The Terror".

Guillotine

Execution of Louis XVI

Toussaint L'Ouverture
In 1791, slaves in the French colony of Sainte Domingue (Haiti) rose up to fight for their freedom. Their leader Toussaint L'Ouverture (1743–1803) was himself a former slave. In spite of his successes he was captured by Napoleon and died a prisoner in France.

KEY PEOPLE

Name	Dates	Biographical details
Voltaire	1694–1778	Key French intellectual of the Enlightenment, wrote novel, *Candide* (1759)
Benjamin Franklin	1706–90	American author, publisher, inventor, scientist, and diplomat, helped frame the US Declaration of Independence, inspired French revolutionaries
Jean–Jacques Rousseau	1712–78	French philosopher and political writer, inspired leaders of revolution
Catherine the Great	1729–96	Empress of Russia, brought Russia fully into Western European cultural life
George Washington	1732–99	American commander-in-chief (1775–83) and first US President (1789–97)
Napoleon Bonaparte	1769–1821	French general, later emperor, established the principles of the French Revolution in law and government and spread them by military conquest

EUROPE COLONIZES OCEANIA
In 1788, the first 750 European settlers in Australia set up camp on the shores of Sydney Harbour. They were convicts who had been shipped from the overcrowded prisons of repressive, 18th-century Britain.

Convicts disembark at Sydney Cove.

1804 British win control
of Cape of Good Hope

1822 Liberia founded for freed slaves

1824–7 First Ashanti War
between Britain and the Ashanti
of the Gold Coast (Ghana)

1794 Qaja Dynasty of Persia
begins; rules until 1925

1819 Singapore founded by
Stamford Raffles (1721–1826)

1824 Britain and
Burma at war

93 Louis XVI executed.
cond Partition of Poland

1796 Napoleon's Italian campaigns.
Jenner introduces smallpox vaccine

1804 Napoleon becomes Emperor of the French
1805 Battle of Trafalgar   1815 Battle of Waterloo

1821–9 Greek War of Independence
from Ottoman Turkey

95 New French government,
Directory, set up

1801 Union of Great
Britain and Ireland

1814 Congress of Vienna
restores European monarchies

1825 First passenger
railway opened
in England

91 Constitutional Act creates Upper Canada (Ontario)
d Lower Canada (Quebec). Revolution in Haiti
by former slave Toussaint L'Ouverture (1743–1803)

93 York (now Toronto) founded

1810 Buenos Aires gains independence

1811 Paraguay and Venezuela gain independence

1812–14 US and
Britain at war:
Washington DC burned

1818 Chile gains independence

1819 US purchases
Florida from Spain

1821 Mexico gains independence

1822 Brazil gains independence

1823 Monroe Doctrine:
US declares Americas free
from European intervention

1806 First white women
arrive in New Zealand

1817 First European emigrants
settle Australian grasslands

1825 Van Diemen's Land
becomes separate colony

KEY INNOVATIONS

SPINNING JENNY
In 1764, English weaver
James Hargreaves invented
his "Spinning Jenny". It
enabled one worker to spin
several threads at once.

Spinning Jenny

COTTON MILLS
In 1769, English businessman Richard Arkwright
(1732–92) set up the first cotton "mill" or factory.

FIRST TRAINS
In 1829, English engineer
George Stephenson built
one of the first steam
locomotives, *The Rocket*.

HOT AIR BALLOON
The first manned flight took place in
1783 in a hot air balloon made and flown
by the French Montgolfier brothers.
They sailed over Paris for 25 minutes.

BLACK HOLE OF CALCUTTA
The Black Hole of Calcutta was a
suffocatingly small cell in
which a local Indian official
held 64 British prisoners in
1756. The British publicized
the resulting deaths of 43 of
the prisoners in its campaign
for total control of India.

Cell measured 5.5m (18ft)
by 4.5m (14ft 10in)

British prisoners in Calcutta

CHAKA: ZULU WARLORD
The great Zulu warlord Chaka (d.1828) owed
his success to a brilliantly organized and
highly trained army. For greater speed,
his warriors went
into battle
barefoot. They
were not allowed
to marry until the
age of 40, when
they could leave
the army.

— Chaka replaced javelins
with short assegais

— Reinforced shield
of strong leather

Chaka in battle dress

NAPOLEON'S IMPACT

By 1812, the brilliant French general
Napoleon Bonaparte (1769–1821) had
conquered almost all of Europe. He gave
himself great power, but also made the
French government and army more
efficient and open.

*Napoleon
crowned himself
Emperor of
the French
in 1804.*

× Major battle
------- French border
→ Campaign route
French empire

NAPOLEON'S CAMPAIGNS
Napoleon's greatest campaigns were
fought in Italy in 1796 and in Austria,
Prussia, and the Rhine in 1806–7. His
Russian campaign of 1812 was a
disaster and he was defeated for good
at Waterloo, Belgium, in 1815.

JOSEPHINE
Josephine de Beauharnais (1763–1814),
Napoleon's first wife, had political
connections that were very useful to
him in his early career.

NAPOLEON FACTS
• On 5 October 1795, Napoleon saved
the post-revolutionary government
when he ordered his artillery to shoot
down royalist rebels in Paris.

• Many ancient monuments, including
the Sphinx, were excavated on
Napoleon's Egyptian campaigns.

• Napoleon owed the success of his
own career to talent. So, he made
promotion in his army depend on
ability, rather than on birth and money.

• In 1812, Napoleon fought his way to
Moscow with 450,000 men. Russians
burned the city and he was forced to
return to France. 440,000 of his men
died of cold and hunger.

SIMON BOLIVAR
While Napoleon was conquering
Spain, the Spanish colonies of South
America, led by Simon Bolivar and
José de San Martin, rose up in
rebellion. By 1825, they had all
gained full independence.

EROICA SYMPHONY
German composer Ludwig van
Beethoven (1770–1827) dedicated
his Third Symphony to Napoleon,
whom he saw as a champion of
democracy. After Napoleon made
himself Emperor of the French,
Beethoven crossed out the
dedication on his manuscript copy.

Ludwig van Beethoven

*Simon
Bolivar*

DEADLY DECOR
Napoleon was finally
exiled to the Atlantic
island of St. Helena.
Mould in the green dye
(arsenic oxide) of his
bedroom wallpaper is
now thought to have
contributed to his
slow death.

1830

AFRICA	**1830** French invade Algeria. British and Boers (Dutch South Africans) clash in South Africa	**1836** Start of Great Trek of the Boer farmers to establish independent Transvaal	**1839** British capture Aden **1838** Boers defeat Zulus at the Battle of Blood River	**1843** Natal be British colony
ASIA			**1839–42** China seizes opium imports from India, starting First Opium War	**1842** Treaty of Na opens Chinese por British trade and gi Hong Kong to Brita
EUROPE	**1830** July Revolution overthrows King Charles X of France. Belgium declares independence from Netherlands	**1832** First Reform Act extends voting rights in Britain	**1837** Queen Victoria begins reign	**1840** Penny postage introduced in Britain
AMERICAS		**1832** Samuel Morse (1791–1872) invents electric telegraph	**1836** Texas wins independence from Mexico and becomes a republic	**1839** American Charles Goodyear (1800–60) vulcanizes rubber, making it stable at both high and low temperatures	**1842** First use general anaesth by American C. W. Long (18
OCEANIA				**1840** New Zealand: Treaty of Waitangi. Last convict-settlers arrive in Australia

EUROPE IN TURMOIL

In 1848, demands for democracy and national independence shook Europe's towns and cities. Industrial growth had made many people rich; now they wanted their fair share of political power. They rose up with students and workers and called for equality and democracy.

Karl Marx

FLASHPOINTS OF REVOLUTION
In the first four months of 1848, Europe was rocked by almost 50 separate revolutions in France, Prussia, Austria, and almost all the minor German and Italian states.

▼ Centre of revolution

KARL MARX
In 1848 German thinkers Karl Marx (1818–83) and Friedrich Engels (1820–95) published the *Communist Manifesto*. It described a just society, without classes of people or private property: a communist society.

GARIBALDI AND RISORGIMENTO
The Italian revolts of 1848–9 failed, but the 1860 *Risorgimento* (Reawakening) was a triumph. Patriot and leader of the "Redshirts", Giuseppe Garibaldi used guerilla war tactics in the struggle for Italian unification. He captured Sicily and southern Italy to form a new Italian state.

Garibaldi

CONCENTRATION OF POWER
In no European nation of 1830 did voters exceed more than 5% of the population. This meant only one in twenty had a say in their government.

CHOLERA
Cholera, caused by drinking contaminated water, spread easily in the overcrowded cities of industrial Europe. Public panic about the disease encouraged revolution.

MONARCHIES IN CRISIS
The last king of France
In 1848, the unpopular King Louis Philippe of France abdicated. Louis Napoleon became president of the new republic; monarchy was over in France.

Frankfurt parliament
In 1848, Germans in Frankfurt set up their first national parliament. Though it soon failed, this parliament fuelled hopes of a unified German nation.

Boy emperor
In 1848, 18-year-old Franz Joseph became emperor of the troubled Habsburg realms of central Europe. His uncle, Ferdinand I, had abdicated in the Vienna revolution.

Emperor Franz Joseph

FAMINE AND EMIGRATION
In the 1840s, sometimes called "The Hungry Forties", famine struck much of Europe – it killed more than one million people in Ireland alone. As a result many Europeans emigrated, chiefly to the Americas.

KEY INNOVATIONS

FARADAY'S COIL
English scientist Michael Faraday's copper coil (see p.229) demonstrated the connection between electricity and magnetism.

PHOTOGRAPHY
In 1839, French artist and physicist Louis Jacques Daguerre developed his superior photographic process, the Daguerreotype.

POSTAGE STAMPS
Postage stamps were first issued in Britain in 1840, and in the US in 1847. The first stamp was the "penny black"

RAIL NETWORK
By 1847, steam-powered trains served all parts of Britain. The rest of the world soon built rail networks.

THE LURE OF GOLD
American carpenter John Marshall discovered flakes of gold on land in California in 1848. Despite his efforts to keep the discovery secret, the news soon broke out and people rushed from Europe and from the eastern US in the hope of finding their fortunes. A similar gold rush occurred in New South Wales, Australia, in 1851.

Gold nugget

1847 Bantus defeated by British in southern Africa

1854 Independent Orange Free State and Transvaal set up, South Africa

1855 Livingstone discovers Victoria Falls, sparking off European exploration of the African interior

...49 British and Sikhs : Sikh defeat leads ...ish rule over their ...and, the Punjab

1848 Nasir ad-Din begins reign as Shah (ruler) of Persia

1850–64 Taiping revolt in China

1852–53 Second war between England and Burma

1853–54 US forces Japan to open up to Western trade

1856 Persia's seizure of Herat, Afghanistan, leads to war with Britain, until 1857

1857 Britain governs India directly after "Indian Mutiny"

1858 Treaty of Tientsin forces China to trade with West

...46 Failure of ...r crop in Ireland ...to severe famine

1848 Year of Revolution in Europe

1849 Collapse of revolutionary movements

1851 Great Exhibition held in London

1852 Louis Napoleon Bonaparte becomes Napoleon III

1853–56 Crimean War between Russia, Britain and France

1856 Bessemer invents industrial steel-making process

1858 *S.S. Great Eastern*, largest ship of its time, launched

1859–61 War of Italian unification

...Texas and Florida ...e US states

1846 US and Mexico ...at war over Texas

1848 California Gold Rush helps open up west US. First US women's rights convention in New York State

1851 I. S. Singer makes first pedal-powered sewing machine

1850 California becomes a US state

1853 Completion of railroad from New York to Chicago

1850 Australian Colonies Act enables New South Wales, Tasmania, and South Australia to have virtual self-government

1851 Australian Gold Rush begins

THE BRITISH EMPIRE

Between 1830 and 1860, Western powers forced isolated countries to open their ports to Western goods: Turkey, Egypt, Persia, China, then Japan. The British, with the strongest navy and the most advanced industries in the world, took control of these rich eastern markets by diplomacy or force, and built a vast trading empire.

QUEEN VICTORIA
Queen Victoria (r.1837–1901) had the longest reign of any British monarch. She presided over the peak of the British Industrial Revolution and over the development of an enormous colonial empire.

British empire | Under British influence

THE BRITISH EMPIRE
In 1860, the British had either direct control or great influence over territories throughout the world. Important groups of islands gave them control of the major sea routes and trading advantages.

Chinese opium smokers

THE FIRST OPIUM WAR
Opium grown in India was bought by the British and sold in China for silks, spices, and tea. In 1839 Britain crushed a Manchu attempt to stop the drug trade at Canton. They forced the Chinese to grant trade and land rights to Western powers.

TREATY OF WAITANGI
In 1840 Britain and the Maori leaders of North Island, New Zealand, made an agreement which gave Britain formal possession in return for recognizing ancient Maori land rights.

Ceremonial dress of Maori leader

British and Maoris at Waitangi

LADY WITH THE LAMP
In 1854, Florence Nightingale (1820–1910) pioneered modern nursing by organizing the care of British soldiers during the Crimean War. Every night she walked 6km (4 miles) on her ward rounds.

GREAT EXHIBITION FACTS

Visitors at the Great Exhibition

• In 1851, London hosted the first international exhibition. The Great Exhibition showed 14,000 objects in celebration of the industrial age.

• Victoria's adored husband Prince Albert (1819–61) made the exhibition his pet project and much of its success was due to him. He died of typhoid, caused, ironically, by inferior, old-fashioned sanitation.

• The exhibition was housed in a glass and cast iron building called the Crystal Palace. It was built in five months in Hyde Park and covered 7.7 hectares.

INDIAN UPRISING
The "Indian Mutiny" of 1857 began when Indian soldiers refused to bite open cartridges greased with animal fats, forbidden to Hindus and Muslims. The rebellion became a massive protest against British rule.

US OPENS JAPAN TO TRADE
In 1853, Commodore Perry of the US Navy steamed into Tokyo Bay to demand that Japan open its ports to trade. His "black ships" forced the Japanese to give in.

KEY PEOPLE

Name	Dates	Biographical details
Michael Faraday	1791–1867	English scientist, discovered relationship between electricity and magnetism
Samuel Morse	1791–1872	American inventor of electric telegraph and developer of Morse code (1838)
Giuseppe Garibaldi	1807–82	Italian leader of Risorgimento "Redshirts", refused honours for service
David Livingstone	1813–73	Scottish missionary and explorer, influenced Western attitudes towards Africa
Karl Marx	1818–83	Philosopher and economist, wrote The Communist Manifesto and Das Kapital
Victoria	1819–1901	Queen of Great Britain and Ireland, Empress of India from 1876, revived popularity of monarchy in Britain over her long and stable reign
Florence Nightingale	1820–1910	English nurse, pioneered nursing as a profession during Crimean War (1853–6)

1860

| AFRICA | **1860s** Britain, France, Belgium, Germany, and Portugal begin to explore and colonize inner Africa | **1869** Suez Canal opens | **1879** Zulu War: British defeat Zulu Cetewayo at Ulundi in South Africa |

| ASIA | **1861** Empress Tze Hsi begins 47-year rule of China | **1870s** Japan industrializes | **1872** Samurai's feudal control of Japan ends. Compulsory education introduced |

| EUROPE | **1864** International Red Cross founded by Swiss Henri Dunant. Otto von Bismarck leads Prussia to victory against Denmark | **1866** Dynamite invented by Swedish chemist Alfred Nobel. Prussia, led by Bismarck, defeats Austria | **1870s** Most Western European countries industrialize **1871** Bismarck invades and defeats France. Britain legalizes trade unions | **1876** French build refrigerated cargo ships |

| AMERICAS | **1861** US Civil War begins **1862** Billy Barker strikes gold in Williams Creek, British Columbia | **1865** Union wins Civil War. Lincoln assassinated **1867** Mexicans force French withdrawal from Mexico. British North America Act brings Dominion of Canada into being, with Sir John A. Macdonald as first prime minister. US buys Alaska from Russia **1869** First transcontinental railroad completed across US | **1876** Sioux and Cheyenne tribes defeat Custer at the Battle of Little Bighorn **1877–1911** Rule of Porfirio Diaz in Mexico **1879** Chile defeats Peru and Bolivia in war over nitrates (ends 1883). Electric light bulb invented |

| OCEANIA | **1860–70** Maori Wars in New Zealand: Maoris fight white settlers | | **1876** New Zealand–Australia telegraph cable laid |

AMERICAN CIVIL WAR

In 1861, deep divisions between northern and southern American states plunged the country into open warfare. The agricultural South, with its workforce of black slaves, feared the industrial North's economic power and resented its efforts to ban the spread of slavery. In 1865, the North won, but more than 600,000 had died in the fight.

NORTH AGAINST SOUTH

The 11 southern states of the Confederacy made Richmond, Virginia, their capital, while the 23 Union states were based at Washington. In 1861, the Confederates won the first major battle of the war at Bull Run, Virginia, and almost overran Washington. But the great Union victory at Gettysburg (1863) foreshadowed the end of Confederate resistance.

Union states

Slave states remaining in the Union

Confederate states

Washington
Richmond

CIVIL WAR FACTS

• More than 200,000 black soldiers fought for the Union.

• Twice as many men died of disease as died in battle.

• The 1860 election of anti-slavery president Abraham Lincoln was the immediate cause of war. His leadership brought victory to the Union and an end to slavery, but he was shot dead at a theatre by a Confederate just five days after their surrender.

Union general   *Confederate general*

FORCES OF WAR

The northern, or Union, states had more soldiers, industry, and money than the southern, or Confederate, states. The Union also held the navy, and used it to block supplies reaching the South, but the Confederacy had excellent generals.

WHITE ELEPHANTS

The King of Siam, Southeast Asia, offered Abraham Lincoln the use of a troop of his war elephants in the fight to preserve the Union. The President declined the offer.

KEY BATTLES

Battle	Date	Victor	Details
Bull Run	July 1861	Confederacy	5,000 dead
Antietam	Sep 1862	Union	21,000 dead in one day
Gettysburg	July 1863	Union	40,000 dead

LEVI'S JEANS

In the 1860s, American tailor Levi Strauss made the first pair of denim jeans. The tough cotton fabric, woven only in Nîmes, France, was ideal for miners of the Gold Rush. Later, workers, railwaymen, farmers, and cowboys began wearing jeans.

WOMEN VOTERS

In 1893, New Zealand became the first country to give women the right to vote in national elections. Almost a quarter of the female population had signed petitions demanding votes.

BOXER REBELS

In the late 19th century, economic and natural disasters weakened China's government. Western powers there grew stronger until, in 1899, an officially supported peasant rebellion, the Boxer Rebellion, tried to rid China of all foreigners. It was soon crushed by Western forces.

BISMARCK

Otto von Bismarck

Otto von Bismarck (1815–98) was the chief minister of Prussia, Germany. He led Prussia to victory against Denmark (1864), Austria (1866), and France (1871). He then founded a German Empire with Prussian King William I (1797–1888) as emperor.

GERMANY FACTS

• Before 1867, Germany consisted of more than 38 states. After 1871, Bismarck proclaimed all Germany an empire.

• After political unification, Germany rapidly built up its industries and armies. By 1914, the German army was twice the size of France's, and 12 times the size of Britain's.

• Bismarck was known as the "Iron Chancellor". In reality, he was prone to nervous attacks.

KEY PEOPLE

Name	Dates	Biographical details
Abraham Lincoln	1809–65	US President, preserved Union in US Civil War, emancipated slaves. Shot dead while at theatre
Otto von Bismarck	1815–98	Founder and first Chancellor of German Empire
Susan B. Anthony	1820–1906	Crusader for US women's right to vote
Harriet Tubman	1821–1913	Escaped US slave, helped 300 slaves flee to North
Alfred Nobel	1833–96	Swedish chemist, invented dynamite in 1866
Karl Benz	1844–1929	German engineer, built first practical car
Sigmund Freud	1856–1939	Austrian doctor, founder of psychoanalysis

1881 First Anglo-Boer War

1882 British begin rule in Egypt

1886 Gold discovered in South Africa

1895–96 Italy and Ethiopia at war: Ethiopia wins

1899 Second Boer War

Britain and France into Burma and Vietnam

1885 Indian National Congress Party formed

1899 Boxer Rebellion of Chinese peasants

1884 Berlin conference decides colonial divisions in Africa. First deep underground railway built in London

1885 Karl Benz builds first car driven by internal combustion engine

1888 Scottish surgeon John Dunlop (1840–1921) patents pneumatic (air-filled) tyre

1889 English chemist Frederick Abel invents cordite (explosive)

1896 Modern Olympic Games introduced in Greece

1897 Greece and Turkey at war

1882 Thomas Edison designs first hydroelectric power station

1884 First skyscraper built in Chicago

1889 Pedro II abdicates and Brazil declared a republic

1890 Battle of Wounded Knee: last massacre of Native Americans in US. First moving picture (film) shows appear in New York

1895 Cuban revolt against Spanish rule

1896 Gold struck in Klondike, Canada

1898 US wins Spanish-American War and takes over the Philippines. Cuba obtains independence from Spain

1884 Volcano erupts on island of Krakatau

1885 Britain and Germany divide up New Guinea

1893 Women granted the vote in New Zealand. New Zealand Prime Minister Richard Seddon introduces advanced social reforms

---

INDUSTRY AND INNOVATION

The later 19th century saw a dramatic growth in technology and industry. Factories multiplied and cities expanded, aided by improved transport, such as railways, and new inventions.

SOCIALISM
Many people who worked in the new factories lived in bad conditions. They began to demand rights through trade unions and socialist organizations.

INDUSTRY FACTS
• With industrial growth came an explosion in the size and population of cities. Germany in 1871 consisted mainly of small towns. By 1914 it had 30 cities of more than 100,000 people.

• After 1870, new industries – the chemical and electrical industries – joined the older coal, iron, and textile industries as a result of scientific discoveries.

KEY INNOVATIONS

SKYSCRAPERS
The large-scale production of steel made it possible for architects to construct buildings around steel "skeletons". The first skyscraper, the Chicago Home Insurance Building, was built in 1884.

LIGHT BULB
Englishman Joseph Swan and American Thomas Edison invented light bulbs in the late 1870s.

CAR
In 1885, German engineer Karl Benz built the first car driven by an internal combustion engine. He fitted the engine on to a two-seat tricycle and patented the invention in 1886.

TELEPHONE
Scottish-born speech therapist Alexander Graham Bell invented the telephone in 1876.

SCRAMBLE FOR AFRICA

Before 1870, European interest in Africa was confined to coastal towns that were important for sea trade. In the 1870s European armies followed missionaries and explorers into the interior, and by 1914 nearly all Africa had been colonized.

CARVING UP AFRICA
France and Britain held the greatest proportion of African territories. Germany, Italy, Portugal, and Belgium also held territories. Most of today's borders come from the lines drawn by Europeans at an 1884 conference in Berlin. No native Africans were invited to attend.

ICE TO DIAMONDS
Cecil Rhodes, the empire-builder of British South Africa, began his career selling ice to diamond-mine workers. He later gained control of 90% of the world's production of diamonds.

The British wanted to unite their southern and northern territories in Africa; the French, their western and eastern lands.

Emperor Menelik of Ethiopia

Map labels: Spanish Morocco, Tunisia, Morocco, Ifni, Algeria, Libya, Egypt, Rio de Oro, Portuguese Guinea, French West Africa, Sudan (governed jointly by Britain and Egypt), Eritrea, Gambia, Sierra Leone, Nigeria, British Somaliland, Liberia, Togo, Gold Coast, Cameroon, Rio Muni, Ethiopia, Italian Somaliland, Uganda, Kenya, Belgian Congo, German East Africa, Cabinda, Angola, Northern Rhodesia, Mozambique, Southern Rhodesia, Madagascar, German South West Africa, Bechuanaland, Swaziland, Basutoland, Union of South Africa

- French
- British
- Portuguese
- German
- Belgian
- Spanish
- Italian
- Independent

No African group accepted colonization without resistance.

1. Independent Liberia
Liberia was the first African country to become independent, in 1847. It was founded by freed American slaves.

2. Menelik's victory
Though Europeans had guns, African resistance to the European advance was often fierce. In 1896, Emperor Menelik of Ethiopia defeated the Italians at a famous battle at Adowa and secured Ethiopia's independence.

Stanley's hat

Livingstone's hat

3. Intrepid explorers
From 1850, several Europeans, including Richard Burton, Henry Speke, Mary Kingsley, David Livingstone, and Henry Stanley, explored Central Africa.

4. Fight for South Africa
In South Africa, Africans had to fight both British and Boers (white Dutch settlers). Zulus, led by King Cetewayo, held out, but were finally defeated by Britain in 1879.

Zulu shield

5. The Boers
In 1899, a major war broke out between the British and the Boers. By 1902, Britain had defeated the Boers, who were mostly farmers. Within ten years, though, Britain gave Boers the power to rule South Africa.

1900

AFRICA			

1902 Ovimbundu people of Angola revolt against Portuguese rule

1905 Maji Maji rebellion in Tanzania against German rule leaves 75,000 dead.

ASIA

1901 Peace of Peking ends Boxer Rebellion in China

1905 Japan wins Russo-Japanese War

1907 British company discovers oil in Persia

1909 China atta Tibet

EUROPE

1900 German navy law calls for increases in sea power. Britain responds with similar increases; arms race begins

1903 Women's Union formed in Britain by suffragette Emmeline Pankhurst. First Tour de France cycle race

1905 October Manifesto: Tsar of Russia forced to grant democratic rights. Einstein formulates his Special Theory of Relativity

1908 First steel and glass bui AEG turbine factory, Berlin

1904 Entente Cordiale (friendly understanding) between Britain and France

AMERICAS

1900 Coca Cola first produced

1902 British and German fleets seize Venezuelan navy. Plastic invented in USA

1906 US forces occupy Cuba. Earthquake in San Francisco, USA

1909 US explor Robert Peary (1856–1920) cla to have reached North Pole

1901 Theodore Roosevelt becomes youngest-ever US president after assassination of President McKinley

1903 US bicyclemakers Orville and Wilbur Wright build first aeroplane and make first successful powered flight

1907 First comic strips appear in USA

OCEANIA

1901 Commonwealth of Australia proclaimed. New Zealand takes over Cook Islands

1907 New Zealand becomes a dominion. Federal basic wage set in Australia

WORLD WAR I

In the early 1900s, Europe was kept at peace by a complex system of alliances. When the heir to the Austro-Hungarian Empire, Archduke Ferdinand, was shot dead in 1914, the system collapsed, and war broke out. A combination of new weapons with old tactics resulted in war on a huge scale and a vast death toll: more than 20 million dead.

KEY BATTLES

Battle	Date	Outcome
Tannenberg	Aug 1914	Germans halt Russian advance
The Marne	Sep 1914	Last mobile action of western war; Germans pushed back to trench front
Passchendaele	July 1917	British defeated in sea of mud
Cambrai	Nov 1917	First successes with British tanks

BATTLE OF THE SOMME

More people – 1,265,000 – died in the Battle of the Somme in 1916 than in any other World War I battle. Artillery gunfire from the battle could be heard in England.

Somme death toll

650,000 German

420,000 British

195,000 French

WAR ON TWO FRONTS

World War I involved so many countries that it became known as the Great War. Although it was fought mainly in Europe, other nations, notably Japan and the USA, were also involved. In western Europe, French and Commonwealth forces fought Germans around Belgium and France.

Soldiers lived, slept, ate, fought, and often died in trenches. Heavy guns would pound an enemy's trenches before an attack.

British trench

Allied powers		Front lines
Central powers		——— 1914
Neutral states		- - - - 1915
		—— 1918

TRENCH WARFARE

Much fighting took place between lines of trenches dug by soldiers. When one army charged at another, many died, since both sides had machine guns. The area between trenches, called No Man's Land, was often a muddy wasteland covered in dead bodies and craters. Conditions were terrible and disease was rife.

German trench

FIRST WARPLANES

Aircraft were first used to spy on enemy trenches, but later were fitted with bombs and machine guns. The most successful fighter pilots, such as the German Baron von Richthofen who was credited with shooting down 80 enemy planes, were called aces.

WORLD WAR I FACTS

- World War I was the first to make use of entire adult populations. Men were conscripted (called up) into the armed forces, and women worked in armaments factories and on farms. It changed the way wars were fought forever.

- Poison gas, in this case chlorine, was first used in war by Germans at the Battle of Ypres (1915).

- Governments concealed the extent of the slaughter from the public by publishing false statistics.

- The Germans surrendered at 11.00 a.m. on the 11th of November 1918. On every anniversary of this day the war dead are remembered in religious services around the world.

SINKING OF THE LUSITANIA

On 7 May 1915, the British passenger liner *Lusitania* was sunk by a German submarine. It went down with 1,198 civilians, including 198 Americans. The attack hastened US entry into the war.

Victims from the Lusitania

KEY INNOVATIONS

MACHINE GUN
Machine guns turned the western front from a mobile war into a static, trench war. A few could kill thousands.

TANKS
The first practical tank, *Big Willie*, was built by the British in 1916. Tanks proved slow but effective.

Union of Africa formed	**1911** Lamogi people of Uganda rebel against British rule **1912** African National Congress formed in South Africa to fight for black people's rights		**1917** Rebellion against French rule in Chad forces 3-year French withdrawal
Japan takes Korea	**1911** Chinese revolution overthrows Manchu dynasty **1912** British arrest Mohandas Gandhi (1869–1948)	**1915** Mohandas Gandhi becomes leader of Indian National Congress Party	**1917** China joins Allies
Halley's appears	**1911** Norwegian explorer Roald Amundsen (1872–1928) reaches South Pole **1912** Sinking of *Titanic* **1912–13** Balkan Wars: Greece, Serbia, Bulgaria, Montenegro against Turkey	**1914** World War I begins **1915** British liner *Lusitania* sunk by German torpedo. Bulgaria joins Central Powers (Germany, Austro-Hungary). Italy joins Allies (Britain, France, Russia, Serbia)	**1916** Irish revolt against British rule **1917** Russian Revolution: Communists take over from Tsar. Russia leaves World War I and civil war breaks out. Greece joins Allies **1918** World War I ends
	1911 Mexican dictator Diaz overthrown in revolution **1912–33** US troops occupy Nicaragua	**1914** Panama Canal opens **1915–16** US troops put down disorders in Haiti and Dominican Republic	**1917** US enters World War I

1914 Australia and New Zealand join Allies in World War I

RUSSIAN REVOLUTION

In the early 20th century, rapid industrialization threatened the rule of the tyrannical Tsar Nicholas II, when workers began to demand their rights. In 1917, Vladimir Lenin, leader of the Bolshevik Party, led a revolution that overthrew tzarist rule. In its place he set up the world's first Communist regime and pulled Russia out of World War I.

RUSSIAN REVOLUTION FACTS

• In March 1917, food and fuel were in short supply in the cities. Angry citizens in St. Petersburg began strikes and riots. Troops ordered to break up the riots joined the rioters instead. The Tsar abdicated, and a temporary government was set up.

• In November 1917, the war was going badly for Russia and the temporary government had failed to ease the food and fuel shortages. The Bolsheviks were able to seize power after besieging the government in the Winter Palace in St. Petersburg.

• In July 1918, Tsar Nicholas II and his family were shot by the Bolsheviks.

• The "October Revolution" actually happened in November, because at that time Russians used a different calendar from the rest of the world. Lenin brought it into line in 1918.

• Lenin's Communists were called the Red Army, and were led by Trotsky.

Aurora

Winter Palace, St. Petersburg

The Bolsheviks had supporters in the Navy. During the October Revolution, the cruiser *Aurora* steamed upriver towards St. Petersburg. It fired blanks over the roof of the Winter Palace during the siege of the temporary government.

• Lenin gave land from old estates to the peasants, gave workers the power to run their factories, and confiscated the property of the Church. He faced armed opposition from "White" Russians, who wanted the Tsar restored. A civil war began, ending in 1921 with the Red Army triumphant.

REVOLUTION EXPRESS

Until April 1917, Lenin had been in exile in Switzerland. When Russian communists gained permission for him to return, the German government agreed, on condition that he remain on a sealed train until his destination.

KEY PEOPLE OF THE REVOLUTION

Tsar Nicholas II (1868–1918) became unpopular after his 1905 promises of democracy proved empty. When he became personally involved in the war, he also took the blame for the army's successive defeats.

Vladimir Lenin (1870–1924) formed the Social Democratic Party in 1898, which had to meet in secret, as the tsarist government immediately banned it. When the time came, Lenin's followers, the Bolsheviks, were ready.

Leon Trotsky (1879–1940) was a brilliant writer and speaker, and the most popular leader after Lenin. He created the Red Army, led it to victory in the Civil War, and defeated a Polish invasion.

Josef Stalin (1879–1953) was a key administrator in the Bolshevik party. When Lenin died in 1924, Stalin struggled with Trotsky for power. Stalin succeeded and ruled the country until 1953.

RUSSO–JAPANESE WAR 1904–05

In 1904, Japan, hoping to capture Manchuria, launched a surprise attack on Russian forces there. Japan won a series of victories ending in 1905 with the total destruction of the Russian fleet. It was the first time in modern history that an Asian power had defeated a European power.

Battle of Liao-Yang, 1904

SINKING OF THE TITANIC

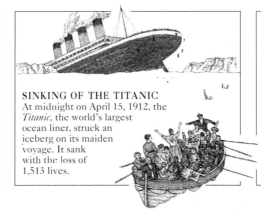

At midnight on April 15, 1912, the *Titanic*, the world's largest ocean liner, struck an iceberg on its maiden voyage. It sank with the loss of 1,513 lives.

IRELAND AND THE EASTER RISING

In 1912, Britain agreed to give Ireland home rule, but when World War I began, the plan was postponed. In 1916, those Irish who wanted independence organized armies, took control of Dublin, and declared a republic. Britain put down this "Easter Rising", but it led to greater support for a republic.

Dublin barricades

AFRICA
1922 Egypt wins conditional independence from Britain
1923 Ethiopia joins League of Nations

ASIA
1919 Amritsar Massacre: 379 people die when British fire on peaceful Indian protest

1923 Earthquake in Tokyo. Ottoman Empire ends

EUROPE
1919 Paris Peace Conference. First international daily air service between London and Paris
1921 Heavy German reparations announced
1922 Mussolini (1883–1945) forms Italian government
1924 Lenin (born 1870) dies. Stalin (1879–1953) succeeds as leader of Russia
1926 General strike in Britain

1920 Red Army wins Russian Civil War. Poland takes advantage of Russian turmoil and attacks Russia, claiming much new territory
1923 Ireland wins partial independence from Britain

AMERICAS
1920 Manufacture and sale of alcohol banned in USA. Women granted vote in USA
1924 US military planes make first airborne trip around the world
1927 *The Jazz Singer*, the first film with speaking and singing, is released

OCEANIA
1919 Australia acquires former German colonies in the Pacific
1923 Ross area of Antarctica becomes New Zealand dependency
1927 Canberra becomes capital of Australia

AFTERMATH OF WAR

After World War I, various plans were laid to make sure such a war could never happen again. Germany was blamed and severely punished, while the Allies drew together and formed a pact to protect themselves from further attacks. The victors thought they had secured lasting peace.

PARIS PEACE CONFERENCE

In 1919, the victors organized a conference at which Germany lost much of its territory, including its African colonies. It was forced to disarm and make huge reparations (compensation). Many felt that the Allies had treated Germany harshly and unfairly.

The signing of the peace treaty between the Allies and Germany in the Hall of Mirrors at Versailles in 1919

THE WORLD BETWEEN THE WARS

• The victors joined together to form the League of Nations and promised to seek peaceful solutions to problems. Defeated countries were not allowed to join and the USA preferred to stay out of world affairs.

• Hitler's economic policies eased Germany's crisis, and few stood against his 1934 seizure of power.

• In the late 1920s Stalin forced Russia to industrialize very quickly; millions died of starvation. Later he enforced his rule by intimidating and murdering millions of Soviet citizens.

Soviet (Russian) worker

THE POST-WAR SETTLEMENT

The defeat of Germany, the destruction of the Austro-Hungarian Empire, and the Bolshevik Revolution, completely changed the map of Europe. Several states, such as Poland, and the Baltic and Yugoslavian states, gained independence.

REPARATIONS

The reparations the Allies forced on the Germans gave their economy no chance to recover, and they had to borrow again to keep paying. In 1923, it took a whole wheelbarrow of German marks to buy a loaf of bread.

Amount borrowed: 33 million marks

Reparation payments: 36.1 million marks

1918–1931

Map legend:
- German Empire 1914
- Russian Empire 1914
- Austro-Hungarian Empire 1914
- Post-war borders

THE GREAT DEPRESSION

In October 1929, share dealers in New York, having pushed share prices above their real value, panicked, and sold 13 million shares in one day. This event, called the Wall Street Crash, was a major cause of the worldwide economic crisis that followed. Millions of people lost jobs, businesses, savings, and homes.

THE DUST BOWL

Drought struck the midwestern and western USA at the time of the Crash, and the soil of the farmlands was blown away in strong winds. Their land now a desert, many farmers lost everything and went west. The region was called the Dust Bowl.

Homeless victims of the Great Depression

GREAT DEPRESSION FACTS

• By 1933 the USA had 14 million unemployed. Franklin D. Roosevelt, elected president in 1932, devised his "New Deal" policy to create jobs and ease the depression.

• German factory production levels halved between 1929 and 1932. Germans blamed their system of government, a view that the Nazis later used to take absolute power.

• Britain's Labour government failed to deal with the depression. In 1931, the National government, made up from every party, took over, but it was largely conservative.

• Japan's rice and textile markets suffered greatly and the military used widespread economic misery to seize power from the elected rulers.

A FISTFUL OF WOOD

In 1932, a shortage of ready cash led the authorities of Tenino, Washington, USA, to issue "notes" made of wood. There were notes worth $10, $5, $1, 50¢, and 25¢.

KEY PEOPLE

Name	Dates	Biographical details
Mohandas Gandhi	1869–1948	Crusader for Indian independence, founder of modern Indian state
Adolf Hitler	1889–1945	*Führer* (leader) of the German Nazi Party, dictator from August 1934
Francisco Franco	1892–1975	Spanish general and dictator 1939–75
Haile Selassie	1892–1975	Progressive Emperor of Ethiopia
Al Capone	1899–1947	Notorious gangster in Chicago, USA
Jesse Owens	1913–80	Black US Olympic athlete, challenged Hitler's belief in white superiority

GANGSTERS

The sale of alcohol was banned in the USA in 1920. An illegal trade in alcohol immediately sprang up in major cities, backed by gangs of criminals. Gang leaders, such as Al "Scarface" Capone, grew very powerful. Capone was eventually jailed in 1930, for tax evasion.

Al Capone (centre)

1930 Ras (Prince) Tafari crowned as Haile Selassie I in Ethiopia

1931 South Africa gains independence from Britain

1934 Lagos Youth Movement formed, demanding self-government for Nigeria
1935 Italy invades Ethiopia

1930s Gandhi leads non-violent opposition to British rule in India

1934–35 Long March in China

1936 Japan signs alliance with Germany

1937 Japan and China at war. Japan occupies much of Chinese coast

Penicillin discovered

1931 Spain becomes a republic. "National" Government formed in Britain

1933 Adolf Hitler, (1889–1945), *führer* (leader) of Nazi Party, becomes German Chancellor

1936 Germany hosts Olympic Games in Berlin

1936–39 Spanish Civil War between Republicans and Nationalists: Nationalist victory

1937 Jet engine invented in Britain

1938 Hitler takes over Czechoslovakia

1929 Wall Street Crash: prices of shares on American stock exchange fall rapidly

1931 British Parliament gives Canada independence

1933 Franklin D. Roosevelt becomes US President. Ban on sale and manufacture of alcohol lifted

1931 First solo flight between Australia and New Zealand. Airmail service from Australia to Britain introduced

1937 Royal New Zealand Air Force formed

REVOLUTION IN CHINA

Between the wars, Communism rose to be the major force in China. From 1927, Communists led by Mao Tse-tung tried to overthrow Chiang Kai-shek's corrupt Nationalist government in a bloody civil war. In 1937, Japan took advantage of China's domestic turmoil by invading the north, further damaging Chiang's power. Mao and Communism triumphed in 1949.

TURMOIL IN THE EAST

Chiang Kai-shek's forces, called the Kuomintang (Nationalists), drove the Communists into the southern hills of Jiangxi. Although the Kuomintang ruled most of China, Communists held many remote, agricultural areas.

- Area of early Communist rule
- Route of the Long March
- Under Japanese rule by 1938
- Under Communist rule by 1945
- Communist base

During the 10,000-km Long March, more than three-quarters of the original 100,000 died of cold, hunger, or from attacks by Chiang's forces or local warlords.

KEY LEADERS

Chiang Kai-shek (1887–1975), although at first allied with the Communists who helped him take power in 1925, broke with them soon after. His rule was harsh and corrupt, and the fortunes he amassed while his people starved made him unpopular.

Mao Tse-tung (1893–1976) drew support from peasants, but early in the Civil War was outfought by Chiang's armies. On the Long March, he became leader of the party and wrote the *Red Book*, which described life under Communism.

CHINA FACTS

- Mao Tse-tung was born a peasant and educated himself. He became involved in peasant affairs in 1921.

- In April 1927, Chiang Kai-shek had several hundred Communists and union organizers shot in Shanghai. The ensuing chaos in the Communist Party enabled him to seize power.

- In 1929, Mao established a strong Communist base in Kiangsi. Communist troops from all over China fled there after Chiang Kai-shek broke his alliance with the Communists.

- Mao was forced to leave behind his two children on the Long March. He never located them after the war.

THE LONG MARCH

In October 1934, 100,000 Communists, mainly peasants, marched for a year across swamps, mountains, and large rivers, to escape Chiang Kai-shek's armies. Survivors set up a base at Yenan, in a deep gorge where they lived in cliff caves.

HEN HORNS
Hens in crates on boats on the crowded Shanghai River acted as horns, warning other craft at night.

THE RISE OF JAPAN

- In the late 1930s, Japan's military seized power and were keen to show Japan's strength in war and empire-building. They invaded China in 1937 and occupied much territory.

- Japan withdrew after defeat in World War II, but its occupation had weakened Chiang's armies and helped bring Mao to power.

JAPANESE MILITARY BUILD-UP	1919	1932
Battleships, cruisers	41	45
Destroyers	73	101
Submarines	20	61
Aircraft	630	1,025

1939

| AFRICA | | **1940** British Navy sinks French fleet at Oran to prevent its capture by Germany | **1941** Allied troops overrun Italy's African colonies. German forces, led by Erwin Rommel, arrive in Libya to help Italy |

| ASIA | | | **1941** Japan takes over French colonies in Southeast Asia and attacks US Navy at Pearl Harbor |
| | | | **1941–42** Japan captures Hong Kong, Philippines, Malaya, Singapore, Burma, and Indonesia |

| EUROPE | **1939** Germany invades Poland; Britain and France declare war on Germany | **1940** Germany occupies Denmark, Norway, France, Belgium, and the Netherlands. Italy joins war to help Germany. Winston Churchill becomes Prime Minister of Britain. Battle of Britain: British air force fights off German air attack, preventing German invasion of Britain | **1941** Germans in eastern Europe take over Hungary, Bulgaria, Greece, and parts of Yugoslavia and Russia |

| AMERICAS | | **1940** Xerox copying machine invented. Antibiotics (e.g. penicillin) developed | **1941** US Navy attacked by Japanese planes at Pearl Harbor in Hawaii. USA joins Allies in war against Germany and Japa |

| OCEANIA | **1939** Australia and New Zealand join Allied forces | **1940s** Australia prepares for Japanese invasion, which never comes |

WORLD WAR II

Militaristic and nationalistic governments rose to power in Germany, Italy, and Japan, as a result of the Great Depression of the 1930s and the Versailles Treaty of World War I. All were intent on expanding their power and territory. Global war broke out with Germany's invasion of Poland in 1939, eventually costing over 50 million lives.

LEADERS OF THE AXIS POWERS

Adolf Hitler
(1889–1945)
founded the Nazi Party in the 1920s. He seized power in 1933, and quickly destroyed all opposition. His dreams of empire ended with the failure of his Russian invasion. At the war's end he shot himself.

Benito Mussolini
(1883–1945) founded the Fascist movement in Italy in 1919. In 1922, he gained power, and ruled as a dictator. He took Italy into the war in 1940 on the Axis side and, after their defeat, was captured and executed by Italian rebels in April 1945.

Emperor Hirohito
(1901–89), though seen as a god in Japan, had little power. Japanese pilots thought it an honour to die for the Emperor. They went on *kamikaze* missions in which they flew into Allied ships in planes packed with explosives.

WORLD WAR II FACTS

• Germany brutally put down any resistance to its rule. Those suspected of opposing German occupation were often tortured or killed by the feared Nazi police, the Gestapo. In occupied countries many joined secret resistance groups.

• In August 1939, the USSR signed a pact with Germany, called the Nazi–Soviet pact, which carved up Poland and the Baltic states between the two. In June 1941, Germany's invasion of Russia, called "Operation Barbarossa", broke the pact.

• The Nazis passed laws to discriminate against Jews. During the war they built camps around Europe, called concentration camps, where they killed six million Jews, along with Slavs, Gypsies, homosexuals, and political prisoners.

Belsen concentration camp

German soldier   *Italian soldier*   *Japanese soldier*

The 1940 "Blitz" of London was the first long, large-scale bombing campaign from the air.

Leningrad
·Moscow
London·
·Berlin
Paris·
·Stalingrad
Rome·

■ Maximum extent of Axis empire (1942)
□ Allied states
□ Neutral states
→ British and US advances (1943–5)
→ Russian advances (1943–5)

THE OCCUPATION OF EUROPE

By 1942, Germany had conquered most of Europe and a great area of Russia. Its *blitzkrieg* (lightning campaign) tactics devastated the Allies and it was not until 1943, with US entry into the war and the Allies' huge rearmament programmes, that the tide turned against Germany. In June 1944, the Allies landed in Normandy, France. Russia matched their successes, and by May 1945 the war in Europe was over.

BOMBING AND THE BLITZ

World War II marked the first use of large-scale bombing raids, or blitzes, to try to destroy civilian morale and industrial efficiency. In 1945, a single British raid on the German city of Dresden killed more people than either of the atomic bombs dropped on Japan.

KEY GENERALS

Name	Dates	Biographical details
D. MacArthur	1880–1964	US general, recaptured much of South Pacific from Japanese, received Japanese surrender aboard USS *Missouri*
B. L. Montgomery	1887–1976	British general, defeated Rommel, led Allied invasion of France
Erwin Rommel	1891–1944	German tank commander, won huge victories in North Africa
G. K. Zhukov	1896–1974	Red Army (Russian) commander, recaptured Russian lands; his troops were first to enter Berlin at end of war

llied troops land in Morocco and force
el's troops to retreat from El Alamein

'S Navy defeats Japan in Coral Sea
v Guinea and at Midway Island

1943–44 Series of island-hopping
victories by USA pushes Japanese back

1944 Japan attacks India
but is defeated at Kohima

1945 USA drops first atomic bombs on Japanese
cities of Hiroshima and Nagasaki. Emperor
Hirohito authorizes Japanese surrender

1943 Allies invade Italy
1943–44 Germans driven out of Russia

1944 Allies invade France
and drive back Germans

1945 German forces surrender

Enrico Fermi builds first nuclear
, USA. Mexico and Brazil join Allies

1943 Argentine Revolution brings
Juan Perón to power as virtual dictator

1945 US tests first atomic
bomb in New Mexico

apanese bomb Darwin, Australia,
ade New Guinea and part of Papua

1944 Japanese prisoners of war
in Australia stage mass breakout

1945 Australia recovers New Guinea
and Papua territory from Japan

LEADERS OF THE ALLIED POWERS

Josef Stalin
(1879–1953) was taken
by surprise when
Germany invaded.
Hitler's troops
came very close to
Moscow, but were
pushed back by
cold, hunger, and
the bravery of Soviet
troops: millions of them
died on the eastern front.

Winston Churchill
(1874–1965), a veteran
of World War I, had
warned against the
rise of Hitler and
Nazism during the
1930s. Britain
turned to him for
leadership in the war,
and his many rousing
speeches on the radio
inspired the Allies to victory.

**Franklin D.
Roosevelt**
(1882–1945), US
President, urged
America into the
war despite its
initial reluctance.
He supported the
Allies with large
amounts of arms and
food. He died just
before the Allied victory.

KEY INNOVATIONS

RADAR
Britain developed the first
radar powerful enough to
detect approaching enemy
aircraft. It gave Britain a
huge advantage in the air.

NYLON
In 1942, nylon was first
produced in the USA. It
was first used for hosiery
and parachutes.

Russian soldier   *British soldier*   *American soldier*

WORLD WAR II IN ASIA AND THE PACIFIC
In December 1941, Japan made a surprise attack on the USA Navy
at Pearl Harbor, Hawaii, sinking or damaging 18 ships, and
destroying 200 aircraft. The USA immediately declared
war, but within six months Japan had conquered the
USA, British, and Dutch colonies in the Indian and
Pacific Oceans. Japan could not, however, defend
such a vast empire and by 1943 the USA had begun
a series of bitterly fought, island-hopping, victories.

Maximum extent of
Japanese occupation,
August 1942

US, British, Common-
wealth advances (1943–5)

Soviet advances (1943–5)

Nagasaki · Tokyo
Hiroshima

· Hong Kong

· Singapore

WORLD WAR II LIFESTYLE FACTS
• In cities throughout Europe,
children were evacuated to safer
homes in the countryside. Those
left often slept in underground
train stations, or air-raid shelters.

• At night, the smallest amount of light was
visible from the air, so cities introduced
blackouts to make it hard for enemy pilots
to find targets. Curtains had to be closed
and the use of car headlights minimized.

• Some foods, such as
meat, eggs, and
sweets, were scarce
during the war, so
families had "ration
books" showing their
weekly allowance.

• The army floated huge balloons over
London. Enemy planes had to avoid the
steel cables that tied them to the ground,
and so could not get close to their targets.

THE ATOMIC BOMB
On 6 August 1945, US President Harry
Truman ordered an atomic bomb to be
dropped on Hiroshima, Japan. It
instantly killed about 80,000 people. A second was
dropped on Nagasaki three days later and
led to Japan's surrender. The war was
over, but people were still dying from
radiation sickness decades later.

Mushroom cloud following bombing of Nagasaki

KEY BATTLES

Battle	Date	Victor
Crossing of the Meuse	1940	Germany pierces French "Maginot Line" defences
Battle of Britain	1941	Britain's air defence prevents German seaborne invasion
Midway	1942	US cripples Japanese Navy
El Alamein	1942	British push back Rommel
Normandy (D-Day)	1944	Largest seaborne attack ever: Allies force German retreat

THE HUMAN COST OF WORLD WAR II
Estimates of total deaths in World War II vary
between 40 and 60 million, because the mass
dispersal of armies and huge migrations at the
war's end made it impossible to compile
statistics. More civilians died than soldiers,
largely from famine, disease, air raids, and
executions by occupying forces. Poland lost
20% of its pre-war population.

Italy: 395,000

Britain: 357,000

USA: 298,000

Japan: 1,972,000   Germany: 4,200,000   USSR: 18,000,000

1946

AFRICA		**1948** National Party under leadership of D.F. Malan came into power in South Africa	**1950** Group Areas Act, South Africa orders segregation of races (apartheid) **1951** Libyan independence from Italy sanctioned by UN	

ASIA **1947** India wins independence from Great Britain amid riots that kill half a million **1948** Gandhi assassinated in India; Nehru takes over. State of Israel created **1950** China occupies Tibet. Korean War begins between North Korea (supported by China) and South Korea (supported by UN); ends 1953 **1949** Mao Tse-tung proclaims new Communist Republic of China. Vietnam, with aid from China, fights French rule

EUROPE $ **1947** Marshall Plan offers US aid to European countries to help rebuild their economies after World War II **1949** Germany split into East and West. NATO formed **1952** Greece and Turkey join NATO
1948 Berlin Airlift overcomes USSR's blockade of West Berlin. Communist coup in Czechoslovakia

AMERICAS **1948** Harry Truman (1884–1972) wins US Presidential election **1950** US Senator Joseph McCarthy begins anti-Communist "witch-hunts"

OCEANIA **1947** South Pacific Commission formed to discuss economic and health issues of South Pacific islands **1951** Australia, New Zealand, and USA sign ANZUS Pact defence alliance

THE COLD WAR

After World War II, Europe was split by an "iron curtain" dividing USSR-backed East from US-backed West. This rivalry was known as the Cold War, with each side distrusting the other and expecting an attack at any time. The USA and the USSR began stockpiling nuclear weapons, and the arms race was born. In 1945, there were only three nuclear weapons in the world; in 1962, there were 2,000. Later, each side had enough to destroy the world many times over.

THE TWO GERMANIES

Germany was carved up by its conquerors at the end of World War II. The USA, France, and Great Britain controlled the West and the USSR controlled the East. The old capital, Berlin, was in East Germany, but was also divided between the two sides, by a wall erected in August 1961.

The Berlin Wall

NATO FACTS

• The North Atlantic Treaty Organization, NATO, was founded in 1949 by the Western countries to protect themselves against attack from the USSR and its allies.

• The USA provided over $25 billion of military aid in NATO's first 20 years, a third of its total funds.

• By 1959, the USA had more than 1,400 military bases, including 275 bases for nuclear bombers, in 31 countries around the world.

• The first hydrogen bomb, tested in 1952, was as powerful as the total of all bombs dropped on Germany and Japan during World War II, including the atomic bombs dropped on Hiroshima and Nagasaki.

• Between 1950 and 1954, Senator Joe McCarthy led a "witch-hunt" to identify Communist sympathizers in the USA. In some areas of society people were encouraged to betray friends and colleagues. Many were wrongly accused and lost their jobs; some were imprisoned.

■ USSR and aligned Communist countries

■ NATO countries and allies

THE WEST

In response to the growing threat of Communism in the East, the countries of Western Europe formed a military alliance with North America. The USA, via the Marshall Plan, funded these countries to help them rebuild their economies after World War II.

THE EAST

Immediately after World War II, Stalin closed the borders of Eastern Europe and placed the countries bordering Russia under the control of the USSR. Opponents of Communism were imprisoned and more than a million were killed.

WARSAW PACT FACTS

• The Warsaw Pact was founded in 1955. It allowed Soviet troops to be stationed in any Communist Eastern European country.

• Between 1949 and 1958, three million people escaped from East to West Berlin. In 1961, East Germany erected the Berlin Wall to close off access between the two sectors.

• The USSR's inter-continental ballistic missiles (ICBMs), first developed in 1957, had a range of 11,300km (7,000 miles).

HUNGARIAN UPRISING

In 1956, many Hungarians rebelled against Soviet domination and communist rule of their country, and Hungary tried to leave the Warsaw Pact. However, tanks and troops from the USSR quickly ended their revolt and killed the leaders.

Hungarian rebel

THE THIRD WAY

The USA and the USSR encouraged many countries to take sides in the Cold War. Some, like India, Egypt, and Yugoslavia chose the "Third Way" and stayed out of the conflict.

Nasser (Egypt), Nehru (India), and Tito (Yugoslavia)

AERIAL ASSISTANCE

In 1948, the USSR blockaded Berlin, forcing the West to deliver supplies by air. For five months, planes landed at Tempelhof airport, Berlin, every four minutes. There was only one accident.

ARMS COMPARISON, 1960

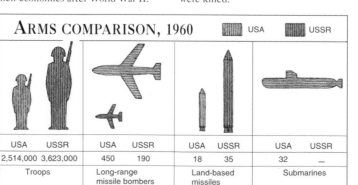

▨ USA ▨ USSR

USA	USSR	USA	USSR	USA	USSR	USA	USSR
2,514,000	3,623,000	450	190	18	35	32	—
Troops		Long-range missile bombers		Land-based missiles		Submarines	

Military coup in Egypt ends
chy and establishes a republic

1954 Algerian National Liberation
Front formed to fight French rule

1955 ANC pressure group in South
Africa adopts anti-racist Freedom Charter

1956 Suez Crisis: French and
British troops forced to withdraw

Edmund Hillary and Sherpa Tenzing Norgay climb Everest

1954 French defeated at Dien Bien Phu,
north Vietnam. Vietnam divided into
communist North and US-backed South

1956 Sinai Campaign: Israel
captures Sinai peninsula from
Arab forces in eight days

1958 Military revolt in Iraq removes King Faisal II; republic formed

1959 Tibetan uprising crushed
by Chinese; Dalai Lama flees

1955 Warsaw Pact defence treaty signed by
Communist nations. West Germany joins
NATO; East Germany joins Warsaw Pact

1957 European Common Market formed.
USSR launches Sputnik I, the world's first satellite

1956 Soviet troops put down anti-Communist uprising in Hungary

Link between smoking and
cancer first established in USA

1955 Military coup in Argentina overthrows
President Juan Perón (1895–1974)

1958 First atomic-powered submarine, USS *Nautilus*,
makes first undersea crossing of North Pole

1954 US Supreme Court prohibits
racial separation in schools

1959 Revolution in Cuba; Communist guerrilla
Fidel Castro overthrows dictator Batista

1956 Olympics held in Melbourne, Australia.
British nuclear testing in Maralinga, Australia

1959 Antarctic Treaty
preserves area for research

THE MIDDLE EAST

During the 1930s and 1940s, many Jews fled from Hitler's persecution to their ancient homeland in British-controlled Palestine. They claimed the territory as their own and set up the state of Israel. In 1948, Britain gave control of the area to the United Nations, and decades of conflict between Arabs and Israelis began.

NASSER
Egyptian leader Gamal A. Nasser (1918–70) planned to unite the Arab countries against Israel. In 1956, he took over the important Suez Canal Company, owned by Britain and France, and became even more popular.

Arab woman during failed Anglo-French attempt to recapture Suez Canal

ALGERIAN WAR
Civil war broke out in Algeria in 1954, with Ahmed Ben Bella's National Liberation Front (FLN) seeking Algerian independence from France. A guerrilla war between the FLN and colonists ended in a French withdrawal in 1962.

MIDDLE EAST MAP
The Middle East was governed by Great Britain and France between the two World Wars. In 1917, Britain had promised to create a Jewish homeland, and in 1948, Palestine was divided between Jordan and the new Jewish settlers. Israel was created in place of Palestine.

French soldiers check Algerian identity papers

THE UNITED NATIONS
The United Nations (UN) was established in 1945, in the hope that international disputes could be solved without war and to foster friendly relations between nations. Its offices opened in New York.

UN peacekeeper

WELL OILED
Oil was first discovered in the Middle East in 1908, but major production did not begin until the 1940s. In 1945, 101,156 barrels of oil were produced. By 1959, the figure had risen to 1,055,986 barrels.

1945   1959

ARAB-ISRAELI CONFLICT

War of Independence, 1948
When Israel became independent in 1948, the surrounding Arab countries immediately invaded. After 15 months' fighting, Jordan controlled much of the West Bank of the River Jordan.

- Under Jordanian rule
- Under Egyptian rule

Sinai Campaign, 1956
Owing to increased Arab trade blockades, Israel invaded the Sinai peninsula in October 1956 and captured the entire area in eight days. Following a UN peace-keeping mission, Israel withdrew.

- Area captured (1956) and returned (1957) by Israel
- Under Jordanian rule

THE DALAI LAMA
Tibet's spiritual leader, the Dalai Lama, was forced to flee the country with 100,000 followers in 1959 after an unsuccessful Tibetan revolt against Chinese occupation. He has lived in exile ever since, travelling the world and gaining support for the Tibetan cause. He won the Nobel Peace Prize in 1989 for this work.

KEY PEOPLE

Name	Dates	Biographical details
Ho Chi Minh	1890–1969	Leader of North Vietnam, 1945–69. Led fight against French colonial rule
Charles de Gaulle	1890–1970	President of French Fifth Republic 1958–69. Offered independence to African colonies
Nikita Khrushchev	1894–1971	Soviet leader during Cold War years 1953–64
Edmund Hillary	born 1919	New Zealand explorer and first, with Nepalese Sherpa Tenzing Norgay, to climb Everest (1953)
Dalai Lama	born 1935	Spiritual ruler of Tibet, fled to India after failed 1959 revolt against Chinese occupation. Lives in exile

KEY INNOVATIONS

HEART PACEMAKER
In 1951, the first heart pacemaker was invented. It used electric shocks to stabilize the heartbeat.

Heart pacemaker

NON-STICK FRYING PAN
The first non-stick frying pan, lined with a low-friction plastic, appeared in 1956.

SATELLITE
In 1957, the USSR launched Sputnik 1, the world's first space satellite. It stayed in orbit until early 1958, when it burned up in Earth's atmosphere.

Sputnik 1

1960

1960 17 African colonies gain independence. Peaceful demonstration at Sharpeville against white rule in South Africa; 69 protestors killed and ANC banned
1961 Patrice Lumumba, first Prime Minister of Congo, assassinated
1962 UN imposes sanctions on South Africa in protest at apartheid

1964 ANC leader Nelson Mandela jailed in South Africa
1965 White-ruled Rhodesia declares independence from Britain

1963 Diem, leader of South Vietnam, assassinated in military coup
1964–65 War between Indonesia and Malaysia

1965 USA starts bombing North Vietnam
1966 Cultural Revolution begins in China; Red Guard formed

1961 Berlin Wall built. Russian cosmonaut Yuri Gagarin is first man in space
1963 Russian Valentina Tereshkova is first woman in space
1964 Fighting between Greeks and Turks in Cyprus

1961 John F. Kennedy (1917–63) becomes youngest elected US President
1962 Cuban Missile Crisis
1963 President Kennedy assassinated
1965 Civil rights leader Malcolm X assassinated. Riots in Chicago and Los Angeles

1965 Ferdinand E. Marcos (1917–89) elected President of the Philippines

AFRICAN INDEPENDENCE

Weakened by World War II, France and Britain found it hard to maintain their overseas colonies. During the 1950s and 1960s, many African countries gained independence. These new states faced great financial problems and were dependent on aid donated by richer countries. Many also suffered civil wars as military leaders seized control.

NELSON MANDELA
The African National Congress (ANC), a black political party, was banned in South Africa in 1960. In 1964, its leader, Nelson Mandela, was imprisoned for life. In 1990 he was released and in 1994 he became president of South Africa.

Ian Smith

RHODESIA
In 1965, the white government of Rhodesia, led by Ian Smith, declared independence from Britain. After a long guerrilla war, the black majority finally won power in 1980, and Rhodesia was renamed Zimbabwe.

TRUNK ROAD
In 1971, an East German woman was smuggled from East to West by her French fiancé. She spent a 70-minute train journey hidden inside two adjacent suitcases. Her fiancé had removed two of the side panels before the train's inspectors arrived.

KEY INNOVATIONS

LASER
In 1960, American physicist T.H. Maiman made the first laser, using a synthetic ruby crystal. Lasers are used in industry and medicine.

CONCORDE
In 1969, the first supersonic airliner, *Concorde*, crossed the Atlantic in three hours, flying at 1,600km/h (1,000mph).

POCKET CALCULATOR
From 1972, many companies made pocket calculators. These small computers were made possible by the production of tiny electronic circuits, called silicon chips.

AFRICAN INDEPENDENCE TABLE

	Country	Independence	Details
	Ghana	1957, from Great Britain	First leader, Kwame Nkrumah (1909–72), became one of Africa's most powerful politicians, but corruption led to his defeat in 1966
	Congo	1960, from France	First president Fulbert Youlou was forced to resign in 1963. Congo then had a Marxist government until elections were held in 1992.
	Senegal	1960, from France	Able leader and distinguished poet, Léopold Senghor (b.1906), ruled for two decades following independence
	Nigeria	1960, from Great Britain	Military coups have left the army in control of the country for 25 of the 34 years since independence
	Mauritania	1960, from France	Mokhtar Ould Daddah (b.1924), first Mauritanian lawyer, led the country from independence until the military overthrew him in 1978
	Uganda	1962, from Great Britain	Following independence, the government changed seven times, four of them resulting in violence, and there were two civil wars
	Kenya	1963, from Great Britain	Jomo Kenyatta (c.1894–1978), who had fought against British rule in the 1950s, became the country's first leader
	Mozambique	1975, from Portugal	Independence leader, Samora Machel (1933–86), set out to provide education and health care for all, despite his country's debts
	Angola	1975, from Portugal	Independence led to a civil war that has continued for more than 20 years

KEY PEOPLE

Name	Dates	Biographical details
Antonio Salazar	1889–1970	Dictator of Portugal, 1932–68. Kept Portugal's African colonies while other countries decolonized
Kwame Nkrumah	1909–72	Independence leader and first President of Ghana
Richard Nixon	1913–94	US President 1969–74. Began bombing of Cambodia. Resigned over Watergate scandal
Yuri Gagarin	1934–68	Russian cosmonaut. First man in space, aboard spacecraft Vostok 1. Orbited Earth in 89 minutes
The Beatles	1960s	British pop group; most influential of the period. Hits include *She Loves You* and *Let It Be*

CASTRO AND CUBA
In 1962, the Cuban dictator Fidel Castro (born 1926) allowed the USSR to build missile bases in Cuba, which threatened the USA. President Kennedy ordered the USA Navy to blockade Cuba and the Russians agreed to withdraw.

Fidel Castro

MOON LANDING
In July 1969, 600 million television viewers saw US astronaut Neil Armstrong become the first person to set foot on the moon. He and two other astronauts arrived there after a four-day journey aboard the spacecraft Apollo 11.

Neil Armstrong

Civil War in Nigeria. Biafra region
...s away from Nigerian Federation.
...hristian Barnard completes first
...t transplant in South Africa

1970 Biafra defeated by Federal
Nigerian Government in a civil war

1975 Portugal grants
independence to its
African colonies

Six-Day War between Israelis and Arabs

1968 US troops kill hundreds of
unarmed civilians in Vietnamese
village of My Lai

1971 Indian troops defeat West Pakistan
in Kashmir. Newly independent East
Pakistan becomes Bangladesh

1970 USA bombs Cambodia

1972 Ceylon becomes republic, as Sri Lanka

1973 October War: Arab states attack Israel.
Arab states restrict oil supplies and start
world economic crisis

Military coup in Greece

1969 Britain sends troops to Northern Ireland

1968 Riots in Paris by students and workers.
Anti-communist uprising in Prague

1971 Women granted the
right to vote in Switzerland

1973 Britain, Ireland
and Denmark join the
Common Market

1975 Spanish dictator
Franco dies; Juan
Carlos becomes king

1968 Civil rights leader Martin Luther
King, Jr. assassinated in Memphis

1969 American Neil Armstrong
the first person on the moon

1973 Military coup in Chile removes
Marxist President Salvador Allende

1974 US President Richard
Nixon resigns over Watergate scandal

New Zealand vote extended to 20-
...olds. Aboriginals become Australian
...ns and gain full voting rights

1973 Sydney Opera
House opens

1975 Papua New Guinea
becomes independent

SOCIAL REVOLUTION

During the 1960s and 1970s, people all over
the world began to demand greater rights.
Some protested against sexual and racial
discrimination, and against war. Others used
the new freedom to express themselves
through music, cinema, and literature.
During this period people questioned many
old traditions and chose different lifestyles.

CIVIL RIGHTS

Following independence
movements in Africa, many
black Americans sought
more rights. Leaders, such as
Martin Luther King, Jr. and
Malcolm X, staged protests
demanding equality.

WOMEN'S MOVEMENT

Women all over the
world began to demand
equality with men and
more recognition. The
contraceptive pill and
legalized abortion gave
many women much
greater freedom.

ANTI-GOVERNMENT PROTESTS

Protests against governments broke out in countries
on both sides in the Cold War. In 1968, students
rioted in Paris and took over the universities. In the
same year, Soviet troops invaded Prague to crush the
reforms of Czech leader Alexander Dubcek, which
they feared would weaken the Warsaw Pact. In the
USA, huge demonstrations against involvement in
the Vietnam War took place across the country.

MUSIC

Popular music became a way of
criticizing war. In 1969, 400,000
people attended a concert near
Woodstock, New York, to hear
singers such as Joan Baez and Jimi
Hendrix. Meanwhile, the Beatles
and the Rolling Stones (left) were
selling millions of records a year.

CIVIL RIGHTS FACTS

• Until the Civil Rights Act (1964),
shops, cinemas, and libraries could be
divided into separate areas for blacks
and whites.

• In August 1965, civil unrest led to
five days of rioting on the streets of
Los Angeles. 35 people were killed,
$175 million of damage was caused,
and 14,000 National Guardsmen were
called in to control rioters and looters.

HIPPIES

Hippies felt that the
West was dominated
by big business, so
they "dropped out" of
society. Some lived in
communes and grew
their own food. They
were also associated
with the use of
narcotics (drugs).

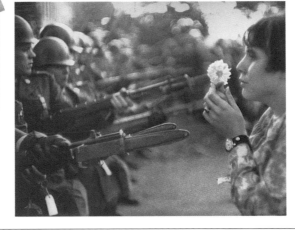

VIETNAM WAR

In 1965, the USA, with Australia
and New Zealand, sent troops to
help South Vietnam fight the
communist North. By 1973,
terrible casualties led all allied
troops to withdraw and Vietnam
became a communist country.

CIVILIAN SUFFERING

Intensive bombing
left hundreds of
thousands of
civilians dead or
injured and
countless others as
homeless refugees.

VIETNAM WAR FACTS

 • Money: the USA spent
$150 billion on the war.

 • Deaths: two million
Vietnamese and 58,000 allied
soldiers and nurses died in
Vietnam.

 • Trees: chemicals such as
Agent Orange destroyed large
parts of Vietnam's jungle;
much is still deforested today.

KEY ASSASSINATIONS

John F. Kennedy
(1917–63) became the
youngest elected US
President in
1961. He was
shot in
a motorcade
in Dallas,
Texas.
Controversy
surrounds
his death.

Malcolm X (1925–65)
was a militant Muslim
black rights leader. After
hostility with a
rival Muslim
group, he
was shot at
a rally in
Harlem,
New York.

Martin Luther King, Jr.
(1929–68), a black
Baptist minister, was a
brilliant speaker for the
Civil Rights
Movement.
He was shot
in Memphis,
Tennessee.

Robert Kennedy
(1925–68), US Attorney
General, Senator, and
John Kennedy's
brother, was
shot while
campaigning
for the US
Presidential
nomination.

THE CULTURAL REVOLUTION IN CHINA

In China, Mao Tse-tung began his own social
revolution. From 1966 to 1977, he brought industry
and agriculture under state control. He closed schools
and colleges and forced teachers and students to work
on the land. Any opposition was brutally put down by
the Red Guards, or Communist Party police.

*Children recite
phrases from the
Red Book during
the Cultural
Revolution.*

1976

| AFRICA | **1976** Riots in black townships across South Africa | **1979** Ugandan leader Idi Amin (born 1925) ousted by Tanzanian-backed rebels | **1980** Robert Mugabe (born 1924) becomes first leader of an independent Zimbabwe | **1983** Famine in Ethiopia |

| ASIA | **1976** North and South Vietnam reunited after 22 years of separation | **1978** UN intervenes in Lebanon. Vietnam invades Cambodia | **1979** Russian intervention in Afghanistan (until 1988). Camp David peace treaty between Egypt and Israel. Iranian Revolution. US hostage crisis (until 1981) **1980–88** Iran-Iraq War | **1984** Sikh extremists forced from Golden Temple at Amritsar, Ind in bloody siege. Prime Minister Indira Gandhi (born 1917) later assassinated by her Sikh bodygu |

| EUROPE | **1979** Margaret Thatcher (born 1925) becomes Britain's first woman prime minister *SOLIDARNOŚĆ* | **1980** President Tito (born 1892) of Yugoslavia dies. Lech Walesa leads Solidarity trade union **1981** 11 Irish republicans die on hunger strike | **1984** French and US scientists independently identify AIDS vi |

| AMERICAS | **1977** Jimmy Carter (born 1924) becomes US President | **1979** Marxist (Communist) Sandinistas take power in Nicaragua | **1981** Ronald Reagan (born 1911) becomes US President **1982** Falklands War: Argentine forces driven from British-held islands after brief occupation. Canada creates constitution independent of UK and passes Canada Act with Charter of Rights and Freed |

| OCEANIA | **1978** Solomon Islands, Tuvalu, and Dominica become independent nations | **1984** New Zealand declares itself a nuclear-free zone |

THE MIDDLE EAST

During the 1970s and 1980s, violent conflict continued to break out in the Middle East. The main causes of war and unrest were religious differences and territorial disputes. Oil brought great wealth to the region.

Iranian supporters of the Ayatollah Khomeini

IRANIAN REVOLUTION
In 1979, a revolution overthrew the Shah (King) of Iran and brought the Ayatollah Khomeini to power. The Ayatollah, a fundamentalist (strict) Muslim, was hostile to the West. When the Shah entered the USA, Iranian students stormed the US embassy in Tehran and held 53 Americans hostage for more than a year.

Oil fields in Libya

PLO members

OIL
In 1973, Arab states raised their oil prices, causing economic disaster in many countries that depended on their oil. In 1990, Saddam Hussein, the Iraqi leader, invaded oil-rich Kuwait. He was expelled by a United Nations coalition force.

PLO AND ISRAEL
The Palestine Liberation Organization (PLO) represents Palestinians living in exile or under Israeli rule. It was responsible for bombings, hijackings, and attacks on Israelis. In 1993, the PLO and Israel agreed to make peace. A year later, PLO leader Yasir Arafat returned from exile in Tunis and Palestinians in the Gaza Strip became self-governing.

KEY MIDDLE-EAST LEADERS

Anwar Sadat (1918–81), president of Egypt from 1970, unsuccessfully invaded Israeli-held territory in 1973. He signed first major Arab peace treaty with Israel and was assassinated by Muslim fundamentalists.

Saddam Hussein (born 1937), president of Iraq since coup in 1968, put down opposition using secret police, warred with Iran (1980–88), and unsuccessfully invaded Kuwait in 1990.

Muammar Gaddafi (born 1942), leader of Libya since coup in 1969, made Libya strictly Muslim, nationalized the oil industry, promoted Arab unity, and funded terrorist groups worldwide.

Ayatollah Khomeini (1900–89), political and religious leader of Iran after revolution of 1979, declared Iran a strictly Islamic republic.

Yasir Arafat (born 1929), leader of Palestinians-in-exile and chairman of PLO from 1968, eventually secured Palestinian independence from Israel in the Gaza Strip in 1993.

KEY CONFLICTS OF THE MIDDLE EAST

Region/conflict	Year	Details
Mecca, Saudi Arabia	1979	Muslim extremists seize Grand Mosque. Saudis recapture it after bloody battle
Iran–Iraq War	1980–88	War begins when Iraqi forces attack the world's largest oil refinery at Abadan, Iran. Iraq gains minimal territory. More than a million lives are lost
Lebanon	1982	Israel invades Lebanon, destroys PLO power base, and forces PLO to evacuate
West Bank, Gaza Strip (see p.340)	1987–8	Intifada (Palestinian uprising) leads to rioting and unrest in Israeli-held territories. Severely suppressed by Israeli military: 300 killed, thousands wounded
Gulf War	1990–91	Iraq invades oil-rich Kuwait. US-led UN forces expel Sadam Hussein's troops

KEY INNOVATIONS

TEST-TUBE BABY
In 1978, the first human conceived outside the mother's body – an English girl called Louise Brown – was born.

VIDEO RECORDER
In 1975, the first home videotape system – the *Betamax* system – was launched by the Japanese company, Sony.

PERSONAL COMPUTER
In 1981, the American company IBM produced the first desktop computer, the IBM-PC.

GENOME PROJECT
Since 1991, scientists have been trying to map all the genetic material in human chromosomes – the human genome.

RISE OF ASIAN ECONOMIES
Since the 1960s, the economies of many East Asian countries have expanded and prospered. With stable governments, advanced factories, and plentiful, cheap labour, living standards have risen dramatically in Japan, Hong Kong, Singapore, South Korea, and Taiwan. From 1997, economic turmoil has made this process falter.

Japanese executives at a business training camp

1990 Namibia gains independence. Three-year civil war begins in Liberia

1991 Government rule in Somalia collapses

1993 Eritrea gains independence from Ethiopia

1992 UN troops led by USA enter Somalia

1994 ANC wins South Africa's first free elections. Civil war in Rwanda

...6 President Marcos (1917–89) ...s the Philippines. Corazon Aquino ...n 1933) becomes president

1987 Palestinian *Intifada* (uprising) erupts

1989 Chinese security forces kill pro-democracy protestors in Beijing's Tiananmen Square. Martial law imposed in Lhasa, Tibet, after anti-Chinese protests

1990 Iraq invades Kuwait

1991 Gulf War. Iraq driven from Kuwait. Indonesian forces kill pro-independence protestors in Dili, East Timor

1992 Muslim-Hindu riots spread across India

1994 PLO gains autonomy in Gaza Strip

1995 Israel's Prime Minister, Yitzhak Rabin, is assassinated

1989 Communist governments overthrown in Romania, Hungary, East Germany, and Czechoslovakia

1991 Break-up of Soviet Union

1992 Civil war begins in former Yugoslavia

1996 A peace agreement is signed in Northern Ireland

...6 "Irangate" scandal: US ...sident Reagan admits to ...et arms deals with Iran

1989 USA invades Panama. George Bush (born 1924) becomes US President

1993 Bill Clinton (born 1946) becomes US President

1997 Bill Clinton starts second term of office

1999 Inuit people are given control of Nunavut, a huge territory in Northern Canada

1991 Paul Keating (born 1944) becomes Prime Minister of Australia

1996 John Howard becomes Prime Minister of Australia

THE COLD WAR ENDS

Communist leader Mikhail Gorbachev launched a new era of freedom in the USSR. The failure of his economic plans made him and his party unpopular, and in 1991 democrat Boris Yeltsin gained power in the country's first free elections.

GLASNOST AND PERESTROIKA

When Mikhail Gorbachev came to power he pressed for economic reforms. His policy of *glasnost* (openness) revealed how weak the Soviet Union had become, but his *perestroika* (remodelling) policy failed to solve his country's problems.

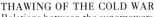

Queues for food in Soviet Russia

THAWING OF THE COLD WAR

Relations between the superpowers – the USA and USSR – improved greatly after Gorbachev came to power. In 1987, Gorbachev and US President Ronald Reagan agreed to reduce the number of nuclear weapons in their countries.

Gorbachev and Reagan meet.

Anti-communists remove statue of Felix Dzerzhinsky, founder of USSR's secret service.

AUGUST COUP

In August 1991, a powerful group of Communists who wished to halt the progress of reform took Gorbachev prisoner and, with the support of the army, seized power. The radical reformer Boris Yeltsin and the people of Moscow gathered in defiance around the Russian Parliament building, and the coup soon failed. A few days later, Yeltsin and Gorbachev banned the Communist party. Communist rule in the Soviet Union was over.

SOVIET SPLIT

The USSR was home to more than 140 different national groups. When Communism weakened, many of these called for, and were given, self-rule. On 21 December 1991, the Soviet Union ceased to exist.

THE FALL OF COMMUNISM

Glasnost encouraged open demands for independence from republics and allies of the USSR. When economic hardship caused unrest in some of these states, Gorbachev was unwilling to intervene using force. In December 1989, the Berlin Wall came down. Within two years, people in the USSR's allied states had toppled their Communist leaders.

Yeltsin outside Russian Parliament during 1991 coup.

GLOBAL AWARENESS

Today, aided by campaigning environmental groups, people have become more aware of the terrible damage inflicted on the Earth by industrial pollution, overuse of natural resources, overpopulation, and widespread deforestation.

Hole in ozone layer

False-colour satellite image of Earth's atmosphere above South Pole

ENVIRONMENTAL FACTS

● In 1987, 33 countries agreed to phase out the use of CFCs, the industrial gases responsible for damage to the ozone layer.

● In 1984, the leakage of poisonous gas from an American-owned pesticide company caused the death of more than 2,500 people in Bhopal, India.

● In 1986, the world's worst nuclear accident occurred at Chernobyl, Ukraine. Clouds of radiation spread over Europe and beyond.

● In 1992, the Earth Summit in Rio de Janeiro, Brazil, brought together representatives from more than 170 countries to discuss global environmental issues.

AFRICAN FAMINE

In the 1970s and 1980s, famine and war hit Africa. Ethiopia, the Sudan, Angola, and people living along the southern Sahara suffered most, and millions died. Western aid has helped, but has not cured, these countries' problems.

Live Aid benefit concert for African famine

KEY PEOPLE

Name	Dates	Biographical details
Nelson Mandela	born 1918	Leader of ANC, jailed for 26 years, elected president in South Africa's first free elections (1994)
Margaret Thatcher	born 1925	Britain's first woman prime minister, developed a rigid (strict) style of politics called Thatcherism
Mikhail Gorbachev	born 1931	Reformist Soviet leader, initiated nuclear disarmament and presided over end of Cold War
Boris Yeltsin	born 1931	First elected president of Russian Federation
Lech Walesa	born 1943	Polish trade union leader, led anti-communist Solidarity movement. President 1990–1995

WAR IN FORMER YUGOSLAVIA

From 1991 Yugoslavia started disintegrating: national and religious divisions led to bloody fighting. In 1995 Bosnia settled down to an uneasy peace, but in 1999 war broke out between NATO countries and Serbia.

Woman in Sarajevo mourns child, shot by sniper.

GREAT CIVILIZATIONS

7000–1580 B.C.
Jericho
Region Jordan
Major cities Jericho
Features of civilization First true urban settlement; fortifications (including ramps); plastered skulls

1600–1027 B.C.
Shang China
Region China
Major cities Zhengzhou, Anyang
Features of civilization Ideographic script; development of bronze casting; bone oracles

c.3400 B.C.
Sumerian
Region Lower Mesopotamia
Major cities Ur, Eridu, Lagash, Uruk
Features of civilization Early cities; advances in architecture (ziggurats), and sculpture; invention of writing (cuneiform); legal codes; money economy; division of labour

c.1500–1300 B.C.
Mycenean
Region Mainland southern Greece, Crete
Major cities Mycenae, Tiryns, Pylos
Features of civilization Architecture (fortified cities, megaron houses, and tholos tombs); ivory-, gold-, and bronzework; linear B script

3050–322 B.C.
Egyptian
Region Nile Valley
Major cities Saqqara, Giza, Luxor, Thebes
Features of civilization Stone building; hieroglyphic writing (also demotic and hieratic writing); funerary art; sailing boats; agriculture

1027–256 B.C.
Chou China
Region China (for some time divided into eastern and western sections)
Major cities Loyang
Features of civilization Jadework and cast ironworking; composite bow; Confucianism, Taoism

c.2500–1400 B.C.
Minoan
Region Crete
Major cities Knossos, Mallia, Phaistos
Features of civilization Palace architecture and interior decoration; linear scripts; decorated pottery; bronze- and goldwork

c.1000–574 B.C.
Phoenician
Region Coastal plane of Lebanon and Syria; then trading posts or colonies around Mediterranean
Major cities Tyre, Sidon, Byblos, Carthage
Features of civilization Ships and trading; purple dye from murex shells; alphabet

c.2600–2000 B.C.
Indus
Region Indus Valley, Pakistan
Major cities Mohenjo-Daro, Harappa
Features of civilization Town planning (grid plans and drains, granaries); seal stones with indecipherable script; copper-bronze technology; standardized weights and measures

1000–600 B.C.
Olmec
Region Mexico
Major cities San Lorenzo, Tenochtitlán
Features of civilization Stone carvings (masks); jade carvings

c.1750–1200 B.C.
Hittite
Region Anatolia (Turkey), and outposts in northern Syria
Major cities Boghazköy
Features of civilization Fortifications; iron smelting; use of chariot in warfare

c.1000–200 B.C.
Chavin
Region Peru, Andes
Major cities Chavin de Huantár
Features of civilization Pottery; metalwork; sculpture (human and jaguar heads)

c.1792–c.1595 B.C.
Babylonian
Later Neo-Babylonian, 626–539 B.C.
Region Mesopotamia
Major cities Babylon
Features of civilization Fortifications (Ishtar Gate and great fortified city walls); astronomy and mathematics; law-making; famous for "Hanging Gardens"

c.900–100 B.C.
Etruscan
Region Northern Italy
Major cities Populonia, Tarquinia, Caere (modern Tuscany)
Features of civilization Bronzeworking; sculpture

883–612 B.C. (at height)
Assyrian
Region Mesopotamia, Iran, Turkey, Syria
Major cities Assur, Nineveh, Nimrud, Khorsabad
Features of civilization Palace and temple complexes; sculpture, especially carved reliefs; military conquests

A.D. 330–1453
Byzantine
Region Eastern Roman Empire
Major cities Constantinople
Features of civilization Mosaic art and wall paintings; jewellery and metalwork; fortifications; legal codes; philosophy; history; literature

750 B.C.–A.D. 350
Meroë
Region Sudan (Nubia)
Major cities Meroë
Features of civilization Ironworking; trade in gold, ivory, and raw materials; temple architecture

A.D. 600–794
Nara
Region Japan
Major cities Nara
Features of civilization Buddhist culture including pagoda-type temples

c.800–300 B.C.
Classical Greek
Region Greece, Aegean Sea
Major cities Athens, Sparta, Delphi
Features of civilization Classical architecture; flourishing of literature (drama, poetry, philosophy, history); pottery (vase painting), and sculpture; politics (democracy)

A.D. 900–1168
Toltec
Region Central Mexico
Major cities Tula, Chichen Itza
Features of civilization Continuation of Maya culture; use of metals

509 B.C.–A.D. 410
Roman
Region Mediterranean, Middle East, Italy, Spain, France, Britain
Major cities Rome
Features of civilization Building and civil engineering using vaults, arches, concrete (temples, walls, roads, aqueducts, amphitheatres); military organization and technology

A.D. c. 900–1400
Khmer
Region Cambodia
Major cities Angkor
Features of civilization Temple architecture; relief sculpture; agricultural irrigation programme

221–206 B.C.
Ch'in China
Region China
Major cities Hsienyang, Loyang, Chinyuan, Lingling
Features of civilization Great Wall; imperial tombs; standardization of script, weights and measures, and currency; unification of China

A.D. 1100–1350
Ife
Region Southwest Nigeria
Major cities Ife
Features of civilization Sculpture (human heads) in terracotta, or cast in copper or brass

321–187 B.C.
Mauryan
Region India
Major cities Pataliputra (Patoa), Sanchi
Features of civilization Adoption of Buddhism, stupas; road network; unification of India

A.D. 1200–1572
Inca
Region Peru
Major cities Cuzco, Machu Picchu
Features of civilization Stone building: roads, palaces, fortifications, and temples; quipus (form of writing using knots); textiles

A.D. 300–900
Maya (Classic)
Region Mexico, Guatemala
Major cities Tikal, Copan, Chichen Itza
Features of civilization Pictorial writing; astronomy, mathematics, and calendar system; stone temples on stepped pyramids; decorative art

A.D. 1345–1521
Aztec
Region Mexico
Major cities Tenochtitlán
Features of civilization Jewellery and featherwork; codex-form books; military organization; religious architecture

RULERS AND LEADERS

EGYPTIAN PERIODS AND DYNASTIES

Period	Dynasty	Dates	Main pharaohs
Early dynastic	1-2	c.3100–c.2686 B.C.	Narmer (Menes)
Old Kingdom	3-6	c.2686–c.2160 B.C.	Zoser
			Khufu
First Intermediate Period	7-10	c.2160–c.2130 B.C.	
Middle Kingdom	11-12	c.2130–c.1786 B.C.	Mentuhotep II
Second Intermediate Period	13-17	c.1786–c.1550 B.C.	Hyksos rule
New Kingdom	18-20	c.1550–c.1050 B.C.	Amenhotep I
			Queen Hatshepsut
			Thutmose III
			Akhenaton
			Tutankhamun
			Rameses II
Third Intermediate Period	21-25	c.1085–667 B.C.	Nubian rule
Late Period	26-31	c.664–333 B.C.	Darius III
Foreign rulers		333–30 B.C.	Alexander the Great
			Ptolemy I Soter
			Queen Cleopatra VII

(Note: Hatshepsut and Cleopatra strictly queen regents)

ANCIENT EMPIRES FACTS

• Under the Roman Emperor Augustus, the Empire, arts, and literature flourished, and the era was called the Golden Age. Augustus came to be regarded as a god, and from then on all successful emperors were worshipped as gods after their deaths.

• The Roman Emperor Caligula was thought to have had his father, mother, and two elder brothers murdered in order to become emperor. Nero had his mother and his first wife murdered. Both Emperors were so hated that their reigns were erased from the official Roman records.

• China got its name in the 3rd century B.C. It comes from the ruling name of the first emperor, Ch'in Shih huang-ti (221–202 B.C.).

• When the daughter of the T'ang dynasty Emperor Yizong fell ill, twenty leading doctors were called to the capital to cure her. All failed, and all were beheaded.

• Egyptian Emperor Rameses II (c.1250–1213 B.C.) was a captain in the army and had his own harem by the time he was ten years old. By the end of his reign, at the age of 90, he had fathered 111 sons and 67 daughters.

CHINESE DYNASTIES AND REPUBLICS

Dynasty	Dates	Main rulers
Hsia	c.2200–c.1600 B.C.	
Shang	c.1600–c.1027 B.C.	Wu-ting
Chou	c.1027–c.256 B.C.	Wen-wang
Qin (Ch'in)	221–206 B.C.	Ch'in Shih huang-ti
Early Han	206 B.C.–A.D. 9	Wu-ti
Hsin	A.D. 9–25	Wang Mang
Later Han	25–220	Kuang-wuti
Three Kingdoms	220–265	
Western Chin	265–317	Liu Yüan
Eastern Chin	317–420	
Southern	420–589	Wu-ti
Sui	581–618	Wen-ti
T'ang	618–690	T'ai-tsung
Chou	690–705	Wu-hou
T'ang	705–907	Hsüan-tsung
Northern Five, Southern Ten	907–960	
Song (Sung)	960–1279	T'ai-tsu
Yuan (Mongol)	1279–1368	Kublai Khan
Ming	1368–1644	Ch'eng Tsu
Qing (Manchu)	1644–1911	Ch'ien-lung
Republic (Nationalist)	1911–1949	Sun Yat-sen, Chiang Kai-shek
People's Republic (Communist)	1949–	Mao Tse-tung, Deng Xiaoping

Emperor Wu-ti

KEY ROMAN RULERS

ROMAN REPUBLIC

Ruler	Reign
Lucius Cornelius Sulla	82–78 B.C.
Pompey, Crassus, Caesar	
(First Triumvirate)	60–53 B.C.
Pompey	52–47 B.C.
Julius Caesar	46–44 B.C.
Mark Antony, Octavian, Lepidus	
(Second Triumvirate)	43–31 B.C.

ROMAN EMPIRE

Emperor	Reign
Augustus (Octavian)	27 B.C.–A.D. 14
Tiberius	14–37
Caligula	37–41
Claudius	41–54
Nero	54–68
Vespasian	69–79
Titus	79–81
Domitian	81–96
Trajan	98–117
Hadrian	117–138
Antoninus Pius	138–161
Marcus Aurelius	161–180
Commodus	180–192
Septimius Severus	193–211
Alexander Severus	222–235
Valerian	253–259
Diocletian (in the east)	284–305
Maximian (in the west)	286–305
Constantine the Great	311–337
Valentinian I (west)	364–375
Valens (east)	364–378
Theodosius the Great (east; and, after 394, west)	379–395
Honorius (west)	395–423
Theodosius II (east)	408–450
Valentinian III (west)	425–455
Zeno (east)	474–491
Romulus Augustulus (west)	475–476

JAPANESE PERIODS

Periods	Dates
Yamato	250–710
Nara	710–794
Heian	794–1192
Kamakura	1192–1333
Muromachi	1333–1573
Momoyama	1573–1603
Edo	1603–1867
Meiji	1867–1912
Taisho	1912–1926
Showa	1926–1989
Heisei	1989–

• Few Japanese emperors have wielded true power. Aristocrats and, later, military dictatorship, or shogunates, ruled in the emperor's name. The last shoguns were the Tokugawa clan, a clan that held power throughout the Edo Period.

• The Japanese people saw their emperors as gods. After Japan's defeat in World War II, Emperor Hirohito (Showa) renounced his divinity.

KEY HOLY ROMAN EMPERORS

Emperor	Reign
Charlemagne	800–814
Otto I, the Great	936–973
Henry IV	1056–1106
Frederick I, Barbarossa	1152–90
Frederick II	1212–50
Rudolf I	1273–92
Adolf of Nassau	1292–98
Albrecht I, King of Germany	1298–1308
Albrecht II	1437–39
Frederick III	1440–93
Maximilian I	1493–1519
Charles V (Charles I of Spain)	1519–56
Ferdinand I	1556–64
Maximilian II	1564–76
Rudolf II	1576–1612
Matthias	1612–19
Ferdinand II	1619–37
Ferdinand III	1637–57
Leopold I	1658–1705
Joseph I	1705–11
Charles VI	1711–40
(War of Austrian Succession	1740–48)
Charles VII of Bavaria	1742–45
Francis I of Lorraine	1745–65
Joseph II	1765–90
Leopold II	1790–92
Francis II	1792–1806
(Last Holy Roman Emperor)	

• From 1437 to 1806, all the Holy Roman Emperors came from the Habsburg dynasty.

RUSSIAN RULERS

Tsars and Tsarinas	Reign
Ivan III, the Great	1462–1505
Basil III	1505–33
Ivan IV, the Terrible	1533–84
Fyodor I	1584–98
Boris Godunov	1598–1605
Fyodor II	1605
Demetrius	1605–06
Basil (IV) Shuiski	1606–10
Interregnum	1610–13
Michael Romanov	1613–45
Alexis	1645–76
Fyodor III	1676–82
Ivan V and	
Peter the Great	1682–89
Peter I	1689–1725
Catherine I	1725–27
Peter II	1727–30
Anna	1730–40
Ivan VI	1740–41
Elizabeth	1741–1762
Peter III	1762
Catherine II, the Great	1762–96
Paul I	1796–1801
Alexander I	1801–25
Nicholas I	1825–55
Alexander II	1855–81
Alexander III	1881–94
Nicholas II	1894–1917

KEY POPES

Pope	Reign
St. Peter	c.42–67
St. Clement I	c.88–97
St. Stephen I	254–257
St. Leo I, the Great	440–461
St. Gregory I, the Great	590–604
St. Leo IX	1049–54
St. Gregory VII	1073–85
Urban II	1088–99
Innocent III	1198–1216
Alexander VI	1492–1503
Paul III	1534–49
Gregory XIII	1572–85
Pius IX	1846–78
John XXIII	1958–63
John Paul II	1978–

POPE FACTS

• The pope is the chief bishop of the Roman Catholic Church. He is considered the successor to St. Peter, the first pope.

• New popes are elected by the College of Cardinals in the Vatican, Rome, at a secret meeting. The Cardinals may not leave the Vatican until a new pope has been chosen.

• There have been more than 30 antipopes, rivals to the officially elected popes.

• Pope John XXI served for 9 months, but was killed in 1277 when a ceiling collapsed on him.

• The shortest-serving pope was Urban VII, who reigned for just 12 days in 1590.

• The longest-serving pope, Pius IX, had 31 years in office and died at the age of 85.

FRENCH RULERS

Name	Reign	Name	Reign
Carolingians		Charles VII	1422–61
Louis IV	936–954	Louis XI	1461–83
Lothair	954–986	Charles VIII	1483–98
Louis V	986–987	Louis XII	1498–1515
Capets		Francis I	1515–47
Hugh Capet	987–996	Henry II	1547–59
Robert II, the Pious	996–1031	Francis II	1559–60
Henry I	1031–60	Charles IX	1560–74
Philip I	1060–1108	Henry III	1574–89
Louis VI	1108–37	**Bourbon**	
Louis VII	1137–80	Henry IV, of Navarre	1589–1610
Philip II	1180–1223	Louis XIII	1610–43
Louis VIII	1223–26	Louis XIV	1643–1715
Louis IX	1226–70	Louis XV	1715–74
Philip III	1270–85	Louis XVI	1774–93
Philip IV	1285–1314		
Louis X	1314–16	**First Republic and Empire**	
Philip V	1316–22	Napoleon Bonaparte	1799–1814
Charles IV	1322–28	(After 1804, as Emperor Napoleon I)	
Valois		**Restoration of monarchy**	
Philip VI	1328–50	Louis XVIII	1814–24
John II	1350–64	Charles X	1824–30
Charles V	1364–80	Louis Philippe	1830–48
Charles VI	1380–1422	**Second to Fifth Republics**	1848–

Francis I

SPANISH RULERS

Name	Reign	Name	Reign
Ferdinand II of Aragon	1479–1516	Ferdinand VII	1808
and Isabella I of Castille	1474–1504	(Joseph Bonaparte	1808–13)
Habsburgs		Ferdinand VII (2nd time)	1814–33
Charles I	1516–56	Isabella II	1833–68
Philip II	1556–98	Amadeus of Savoy	1870–73
Philip III	1598–1621	**First Republic**	1873–74
Philip IV	1621–65	**Bourbons (restored)**	
Charles II	1665–1700	Alfonso XII	1874–85
Bourbons		Maria Cristina (Regent)	1885–86
Philip V (abdicated)	1700–24	Alfonso XIII	1886–1931
Louis I	1724	**Second Republic**	1931–39
Philip V (restored)	1724–46	Francisco Franco (Dictator)	1939–75
Ferdinand VI	1746–59	**Bourbons (restored)**	
Charles III	1759–88	Juan Carlos I	1975–
Charles IV	1788–1808		

KINGS AND QUEENS OF GREAT BRITAIN

ENGLAND

Monarch	Reign
Saxons	
Egbert	827–839
Ethelwulf	839–858
Ethelbald	858–860
Ethelbert	860–865
Ethelred I	865–871
Alfred the Great	871–899
Edward the Elder	899–924
Athelstan	924–939
Edmund	939–946
Edred	946–955
Edwy	955–959
Edgar	959–975
Edward the Martyr	975–978
Ethelred II, the Unready	978–1016
Edmund Ironside	1016
Danes	
Canute	1016–35
Harold I Harefoot	1035–40
Hardicanute	1040–42
Saxons	
Edward the Confessor	1042–66
Harold II	1066
Normans	
William I, the Conqueror	1066–87
William II	1087–1100
Henry I	1100–35
Stephen	1135–54
Plantagenets	
Henry II	1154–89
Richard I	1189–99
John	1199–1216
Henry III	1216–72
Edward I	1272–1307
Edward II	1307–27
Edward III	1327–77
Richard II	1377–99
Lancaster	
Henry IV	1399–1413
Henry V	1413–22
Henry VI	1422–61

Alfred the Great

Monarch	Reign
York	
Edward IV	1461–83
Edward V	1483
Richard III	1483–85
Tudors	
Henry VII	1485–1509
Henry VIII	1509–47
Edward VI	1547–53
Mary I	1553–58
Elizabeth I	1558–1603

Henry VIII

BRITAIN

Monarch	Reign
Stuarts	
James I, VI of Scotland	1603–25
Charles I	1625–49
Commonwealth	1649–60
Stuarts (restoration)	
Charles II	1660–85
James II	1685–88
William III, jointly with	1689–1702
Mary II	1689–94
Anne	1702–14
House of Hanover	
George I	1714–27
George II	1727–60
George III	1760–1820
George IV	1820–30
William IV	1830–37
Victoria	1837–1901
House of Saxe-Coburg	
Edward VII	1901–10
House of Windsor	
George V	1910–36
Edward VIII	1936
George VI	1936–52
Elizabeth II	1952–

Elizabeth II

SCOTLAND

Monarch	Reign
Malcolm II	1005–34
Duncan I	1034–40
Macbeth	1040–57
Malcolm III Canmore	1058–93
Donald Bane	1093–94
Duncan II	1094
Donald Bane (restored)	1094–97
Edgar	1097–1107
Alexander I	1107–24
David I	1124–53
Malcolm IV	1153–65
William the Lion	1165–1214
Alexander II	1214–49
Alexander III	1249–86
Margaret of Norway	1286–90
Interregnum	1290–92
John Balliol	1292–96
Interregnum	1296–1306
Robert I, the Bruce	1306–29
David II	1329–71
Stuarts	
Robert II	1371–90
Robert III	1390–1406
James I	1406–37
James II	1437–60
James III	1460–88
James IV	1488–1513
James V	1513–42
Mary, Queen of Scots	1542–67
James VI, I of England	1567–1625

Mary, Queen of Scots

SAFE RAVEN

Legend has it that when ravens leave the Tower of London, the throne of England will fall. So, a family of ravens is kept at the tower with their wings clipped.

PRESIDENTS OF THE UNITED STATES

President	Term of office	President	Term of office	President	Term of office
George Washington	1789–97	Abraham Lincoln	1861–65	Herbert C. Hoover	1929–33
John Adams	1797–1801	Andrew Johnson	1865–69	Franklin D.	
Thomas Jefferson	1801–09	Ulysses S. Grant	1869–77	Roosevelt	1933–45
James Madison	1809–17	Rutherford B. Hayes	1877–81	Harry S. Truman	1945–53
James Monroe	1817–25	James A. Garfield	Mar–Sept 1881	Dwight D.	
John Quincy Adams	1825–29	Chester A. Arthur	1881–85	Eisenhower	1953–61
Andrew Jackson	1829–37	Grover S. Cleveland	1885–89	John F. Kennedy	1961–63
Martin van Buren	1837–41	Benjamin Harrison	1889–93	Lyndon B. Johnson	1963–69
William H. Harrison	Mar–April 1841	Grover S. Cleveland	1893–97	Richard M. Nixon	1969–74
John Tyler	1841–45	William McKinley	1897–1901	Gerald R. Ford	1974–77
James K. Polk	1845–49	Theodore Roosevelt	1901–09	James E. Carter	1977–81
Zachary Taylor	1849–50	William H. Taft	1909–13	Ronald W. Reagan	1981–89
Millard Fillmore	1850–53	Woodrow Wilson	1913–21	George Bush	1989–93
Franklin Pierce	1853–57	Warren G. Harding	1921–23	William J. Clinton	1993–
James Buchanan	1857–61	Calvin Coolidge	1923–29		

F. D. Roosevelt

BRITISH PRIME MINISTERS

Prime Minister	Term of office
Sir Robert Walpole	1721–42
Earl of Wilmington	1742–43
Henry Pelham	1743–54
Duke of Newcastle	1754–56
Duke of Devonshire	1756–57
Duke of Newcastle	1757–62
Earl of Bute	1762–63
George Grenville	1763–65
Marquess of Rockingham	1765–66
Earl of Chatham (Pitt the Elder)	1766–67
Duke of Grafton	1767–70
Lord North	1770–82
Marquess of Rockingham	1782
Earl of Shelburne	1782–1783
Duke of Portland	1783
William Pitt, the Younger	1783–1801
Henry Addington	1801–04
William Pitt	1804–06
Lord Grenville	1806–07
Duke of Portland	1807–09
Spencer Perceval	1809–12
Earl of Liverpool	1812–27
George Canning	1827
Viscount Goderich	1827–28
Duke of Wellington	1828–30
Earl Grey	1830–34
Viscount Melbourne	1834
Sir Robert Peel	1834–35
Viscount Melbourne	1835–41
Sir Robert Peel	1841–46
Lord John Russell	1846–52
Earl of Derby	1852
Earl of Aberdeen	1852–55
Viscount Palmerston	1855–58
Earl of Derby	1858–59
Viscount Palmerston	1859–65

Robert Walpole

Pitt the Younger

Prime Minister	Term of office
Earl Russell	1865–66
Earl of Derby	1866–68
Benjamin Disraeli	1868
William Gladstone	1868–74
Benjamin Disraeli	1874–80
William Gladstone	1880–85
Marquess of Salisbury	1885–86
William Gladstone	1886
Marquess of Salisbury	1886–92
William Gladstone	1892–94
Earl of Rosebery	1894–95
Marquess of Salisbury	1895–1902
Arthur Balfour	1902–05
Sir Henry Campbell-Bannerman	1905–08
Herbert Asquith	1908–16
David Lloyd-George	1916–22
Andrew Bonar Law	1922–23
Stanley Baldwin	1923–24
James Ramsay-MacDonald	1924
Stanley Baldwin	1924–29
James Ramsay-MacDonald	1929–35
Stanley Baldwin	1935–37
Neville Chamberlain	1937–40
Winston Churchill	1940–45
Clement Attlee	1945–51
Sir Winston Churchill	1951–55
Sir Anthony Eden	1955–57
Harold Macmillan	1957–63
Sir Alec Douglas-Home	1963–64
Harold Wilson	1964–70
Edward Heath	1970–74
Harold Wilson	1974–76
James Callaghan	1976–79
Margaret Thatcher	1979–90
John Major	1990–97
Tony Blair	1997–

Winston Churchill

AUSTRALIAN PRIME MINISTERS

Prime Minister	Term of office
Edmund Barton	1901–03
Alfred Deakin	1903–04
John C. Watson	1904
George Houston Reid	1904–05
Alfred Deakin	1905–08
Andrew Fisher	1908–09
Alfred Deakin	1909–10
Andrew Fisher	1910–13
Joseph Cook	1913–14
Andrew Fisher	1914–15
William M. Hughes	1915–23
Stanley M. Bruce	1923–29
James H. Scullin	1929–32
Joseph A. Lyons	1932–39
Robert Gordon Menzies	1939–41
Arthur William Fadden	1941
John Curtin	1941–45
Joseph Benedict Chifley	1945–49
Robert Gordon Menzies	1949–66
Harold Edward Holt	1966–67
John Grey Gorton	1968–71
William McMahon	1971–72
Edward Gough Whitlam	1972–75
John Malcolm Fraser	1975–83
Robert James Hawke	1983–91
Paul Keating	1991–96
John Howard	1996–

Stanley M. Bruce

BRITISH GOVERNORS AT THE CAPE, 1806-1910

Prime Minister	Term of office
Sir David Baird (acting)	1806–07
Count Caledon	1807–11
Sir John Francis Cradock	1811–14
Lord Charles H. Somerset	1814–26
Sir Rufane S. Donkin (acting)	1820–21
Sir Richard Bourke (acting)	1826–28
Sir Galbraith L. Cole	1828–33
Sir Benjamin D'Urban	1834–38
Sir George T. Napier	1838–44
Sir Peregrine Maitland	1844–47
Sir Harry Smith	1847–52
Sir George Cathcart	1852–54
Sir George Grey	1854–61
Sir Philip Wodehouse	1862–70
Sir Henry Barkly	1870–77
Sir Henry B. E. Frere	1877–80
Sir Hercules G. Robinson	1881–89
Lord Henry B. Loch	1889–95
Sir Hercules G. Robinson	1895–97
Lord Alfred Milner	1897–01
Sir W. F. Hely-Hutchinson	1901–10

RUSSIAN LEADERS

General secretaries	Term of office
Vladimir Illich Lenin	1917–22
Josef Stalin	1922–53
Nikita Khrushchev	1953–64
Leonid Brezhnev	1964–82
Yuri Andropov	1982–84
Konstantin Chernenko	1984–85
Mikhail Gorbachev	1985–92
Russian presidents	
Boris Yeltsin	1992–

INDIAN PRIME MINISTERS

Prime Minister	Term of office
Jawaharlal Nehru	1947–64
Lal Bahadur Shastri	1964–66
Indira Gandhi	1966–77
Morarji Desai	1977–79
Indira Gandhi	1980–84
Rajiv Gandhi	1984–89
V.P. Singh	1989–90
Chandra Shekhar	1990–91
P.V. Narasima Rao	1991–96
H.D. Deve Gowda	1996-

Indira Gandhi

WORLD LEADER FACTS

• In 1803, Thomas Jefferson wanted to buy part of the French colony of Louisiana for the US and was prepared to pay up to $10 million. France, however, threatened by war in Europe, agreed to sell much more land. Jefferson was able to double the size of the US for just $15 million.

• William Pitt the Younger, prime minister of Britain at the end of the 18th century, took office at the very young age of 24.

• In 1809, George Canning, Britain's foreign minister, who later became prime minister, fought a duel with Lord Castlereagh, the war minister. Canning was wounded in the leg, and both Ministers resigned afterwards.

• The White House, the US president's official home, is built from sandstone that is naturally grey. Only after it was burned in a major fire in 1814 was it painted white to hide the smoke stains.

READY TEDDY GO

Teddy bears get their name from US President Theodore "Teddy" Roosevelt, who, when on a hunting trip in Mississippi, refused to shoot a bear cub.

EXPLORERS

PEOPLE HAVE ALWAYS WANTED to travel to distant regions that are unknown to them, for various reasons. Trade, conquest, and settlement were common motives in the past; scientific research or sheer adventure often inspire today's explorers. Some explorers, such as the Polynesians who sailed across the Pacific Ocean, are little known to us, as they left no written records of their journeys.

NORTH ATLANTIC OCEAN AND NORTH AMERICA

c.330 B.C. Pytheas, Greek, sails into North Atlantic, around Britain and "Thule" (Iceland or Norway).

800–1100 Viking travellers (Leif Eriksson, Erik the Red) cross North Atlantic, starting settlements in Newfoundland and Greenland; they discover "Vinland" (modern USA).

1527–28 Pánfilo de Narváez, Spanish, reached Florida, USA.

1534–42 Jacques Cartier, French, sailed through the Gulf of St. Lawrence into the St. Lawrence River, in Canada. Huron Indian villages that he found became Quebec and Montreal.

1615–16 Samuel de Champlain, French, founder of French Canada, helped establish the fur trade.

NORTH AND CENTRAL AMERICA

1492–93 Christopher Columbus, Italian, backed by the Spanish, sailed the Atlantic to the West Indies and, on later voyages, the coasts of Central and South America. Columbus died believing that he had been the first European to find a westerly route to Asia, not the first European in Central America.

1519–21 Hernán Cortés, Spanish, captured Mexico for Spain. He conquered the massive Aztec empire of Mexico with the help of thousands of local rebels.

1528–36 Álvar Núñez Cabeza de Vaca, Spanish, travelled to Florida with Spanish *conquistador* (conqueror) Pánfilo de Narváez. Starvation, disease, and hostility killed most of the company. De Vaca was saved by Yaqui tribesmen and journeyed into Mexico.

1678–80 Robert Cavelier de la Salle, French, explored the Great Lakes and sailed down the Mississippi River to the Gulf of Mexico. In 1687, his expedition to find the Mississippi delta from the sea ended in failure and his death.

BURNING BOATS
When Cortés decided to invade the Aztec empire with a force of just 508 soldiers and 100 sailors, he burned his ships, so that his men would see victory or death.

1804–06 Meriwether Lewis and William Clark, Americans, were sent by US President Thomas Jefferson to search for a route to the Pacific Ocean from St. Louis. Their journeys took them along the Missouri, Yellowstone, and Columbia rivers by canoe, meeting with local peoples on the way.

NORTHERN PASSAGES
NORTH-WEST PASSAGE (NWP)

1497 John Cabot, Italian, backed by British merchants, reached Newfoundland in Canada in search of NWP. He believed he had found Asia. A second voyage in 1498 ended in mystery, as Cabot was never seen again.

Cabot's men could scoop up cod from the Grand Banks.

1576 Martin Frobisher, British, reached Baffin Island in search of NWP. Found Frobisher Bay.

1610–11 Henry Hudson, British, backed by Dutch, reached Hudson Bay in search of NWP. Abandoned to die after his crew mutinied.

1845–47 John Franklin, British, died west of King William Island in search of NWP. Ship stuck in ice.

NORTH-EAST PASSAGE (NEP)

1596–98 Willem Barents, Dutch, reached Kara Sea in search of NEP.

1878–79 Nils Nordenskjold, Norwegian, first explorer to complete the NEP. Also a scientific expedition.

Greenland

Baffin Island

Frobisher Bay

Hudson Bay

NORTH AMERICA

Great Lakes

ATLANTIC OCEAN

Newfoundland

St. Lawrence River

Mississippi River

West Indies

CENTRAL AMERICA

River Niger

River Amazon

SOUTH AMERICA

SOUTH AMERICA
1531–33 Francisco Pizarro, Spanish, conquered Inca empire.

1735–44 Charles de la Condamine, French, explored River Amazon and northwest coast of South America.

1799–1804 Alexander von Humboldt, German naturalist, explored northwest South America.

1831–35 Charles Darwin, British, explored South America and Galapagos Islands.

CIRCUMNAVIGATIONS
1519–22 Ferdinand Magellan, Portuguese, set off to circumnavigate the globe. Just one of his 5 ships and 18 of his 260-man crew survived. In 1521, Magellan himself was killed by locals in the Philippines. Sebastián de Elcano took command.

1577–80 Francis Drake, English, circumnavigated the globe in the *Golden Hind*, plundering Spanish ships and lands on the way.

Ferdinand Magellan

Antarctic region

SOUTH POLE
1839 James Clark Ross, British, explored Antarctic coast and ice sheet in his ships *Erebus* and *Terror*.

1910–12 Roald Amundsen, Norwegian, was first to reach South Pole. He used sleds pulled by dogs.

1910–13 Robert Falcon Scott, British, was just beaten to Pole by Amundsen. He used both ponies and dogs, but difficult conditions killed all the animals. The four-man team died on the return journey.

Amundsen's team

NORTH POLE

1871 Charles Hall, American, made three expeditions, came close to North Pole. Died three weeks after third and last expedition.

1893–96 Fridtjof Nansen, Norwegian, attempted and failed to reach North Pole by ship and sled. Nansen was picked up by a British ship on Franz Joseph Land.

1908–09 Robert Peary, American, after last of eight expeditions, claimed to have reached Pole; there is still doubt about his claim.

Nansen's ship Fram *was designed to move with ice floes, without being crushed*

EURASIA

138–116 B.C. Chang Ch'ien, Chinese, travelled westwards across Asia to Samarkand and beyond, to find allies for emperor Wu-Ti.

Chang Ch'ien at the court of Wu-Ti

A.D. 399–414 Fa Hsien, Chinese, travelled across Asia on the Silk Road to Khotan, then down into India, before crossing the sea to Sri Lanka. He was a Buddhist monk, and wanted to learn more about the origins and texts of Buddhism.

629–649 Hsüan Tsang, Chinese, followed Fa Hsien's route to India, and travelled extensively there.

800–1100 Viking travellers and traders sailed along Dnieper and Volga Rivers, and reached Constantinople and Baghdad.

1260–71 Polo brothers Niccolo and Maffeo, and Niccolo's son Marco, from Venice, travelled across Asia to China. Marco stayed for 20 years, working for Kublai Khan.

1541–52 Francis Xavier, Spanish Jesuit, sailed to Japan. First European to visit Japan.

1602–07 Bento de Goes, Portuguese, joined Jesuits in India and went from Agra across Asia as far as Suchow.

1661–64 John Grueber and Albert d'Orville, German and Belgian, were the first Europeans to reach Lhasa, Tibet, from China.

1725–29 and 1734–41 Vitus Bering, Danish, appointed by Tzar of Russia, crossed Asia by land before going out to find out whether Russia and America were joined.

Map labels

KARA SEA

EURASIA

River Volga

CHINA

INDIA

PACIFIC OCEAN

INDIAN OCEAN

River Congo

Zambezi River

Cape Cross

Cape of Good Hope

AUSTRALIA

Darling River

AUSTRALIA

1828–30 and 1844–45 Charles Sturt, British, mapped Murray and Darling Rivers, then explored central Australia.

1840–41 Edward Eyre, British, found land route along south coast from Adelaide to Albany.

1860–61 Robert Burke, William Wills, Irish and English, make south–north journey across Australia from Melbourne.

1861–62 John Stuart, Scottish, crossed Australia from Adelaide to Darwin (south to north).

Burke and Wills, who died on their return journey to Melbourne

PACIFIC

1567–1607 Mendaña, Quirós, Torres, Spanish, made various voyages across Pacific from South America past Pacific islands and, on one journey, as far as Manila.

1642–43 Abel Janszoon Tasman, Dutch, sailed from Mauritius to Tasmania, New Zealand, Fiji, New Guinea, Java.

1766–69 Louis Bougainville, French, sailed from Falklands, across Pacific to Great Barrier Reef, then to New Guinea and Java.

1768–79 James Cook, British, made three voyages around Pacific, visiting New Zealand and Australia. Extensive mapping of southern Pacific and its islands.

Cook's ship Endeavour

AFRICA

c.1500 B.C. Queen Hatshepsut, Egyptian, sent explorers to the land of Punt (possibly East Africa).

c.500 B.C. Hanno, Phoenician, sailed from Carthage, down the West African coast, and up the River Senegal, looking for sites for Phoenician colonies.

1324–53 Ibn Battuta, from Tangier, North Africa, travelled through Sahara to Mali and Timbuktu, also travelled extensively in Middle East and Arabia.

1795–97, 1805–06 Mungo Park, Scottish, reached River Niger in West Africa, later followed it upstream.

1827–28 René Caillié, French, travelled from West Africa across Sahara to Tangier. First European in Timbuktu.

Livingstone on the Zambezi River, Africa

1841–73 David Livingstone, Scottish, four expeditions, crossed southern Africa and travelled south to Cape Town and Port Elizabeth.

1844–45, 1850–55 Heinrich Barth, German, travelled across Sahara and in West Africa.

1857–63 Richard Burton and John Hanning Speke, British, made three expeditions to Africa.

1871–89 Henry Morton Stanley, American, made three expeditions, across Africa and up River Congo.

SOUTH ATLANTIC OCEAN AND AFRICA

1485–86 Diogo Cão, Portuguese, first of the professional explorers, sailed down the West African coast as far as Cape Cross.

1487–88 Bartolemeu Días, Portuguese, sailed down the West African coast, past the southernmost point, the Cape of Good Hope. He then entered the Indian Ocean, before turning back.

1497–98 Vasco da Gama, Portuguese, sailed down the West African coast, around the Cape of Good Hope, up the East African coast and across the Indian Ocean to Calicut, India. He was the first European to reach India by sea.

BATTLES AND WARS

MAJOR WARS

B.C. c.3100	First recorded war in history, between Upper and Lower Egypt. Pharaoh Narmer (Menes) unified Egypt.
c.1600–600	Continual warring between the three great powers of the Middle East: Egypt, Babylon, and Assyria.
c.1200 **Trojan War**	Legendary war between Greeks and Trojans, described in Homer's *Iliad*. However, legend was probably based on a real war between Greeks and people of Troy.
490–479 **Persian Wars**	Fought between Persia and anti-Persian alliance of Sparta and Athens. Persia ultimately defeated.
431–404 **Peloponnesian War**	Fought between Athens and Sparta, two long-standing rivals. Sparta was the land power, Athens the sea power. Sparta was victorious.
264–146 **Punic Wars**	Prolonged struggle between Rome and Carthage. Ended in Rome's victory and total destruction of Carthage.
A.D. c.1096–1291 **Crusades**	Series of warring pilgrimages undertaken by European Christians to recapture Jerusalem from Turkish Muslims. In 1099, Crusaders captured Jerusalem but in 1187 Saladin recaptured the city. In 1291, the Crusaders were finally thrown out.
c.1337–1453 **Hundred Years War**	Irregular succession of wars between France and England. Ended in victory for France.
1455–85 **Wars of the Roses**	English war between Houses of Lancaster and York. House of Lancaster was victorious.
1618–48 **Thirty Years War**	Complex European war fought mainly on German soil. Began as a struggle of German Protestants against Habsburgs, Catholics, and the Holy Roman Empire. War gradually involved most European powers, and ended with Protestant victory.
1642–49 **English Civil War**	Fought between Parliament (Roundheads) and Royalists (Cavaliers). Parliament victorious. War ended with execution of King Charles I. Monarchy later restored.
1700–21 **Great Northern War**	Fought between Russia and Sweden. Sweden defeated.
1701–13 **War of the Spanish Succession**	Struggle between France and Austria over who was to rule Spain. France defeated.
1756–63 **Seven Years War**	Fought between Austria, France, Russia, and Sweden on one side; Britain, Hanover, and Prussia on the other. Britain and the German states victorious.
1775–83 **American Revolution**	Fought between British-ruled American colonies and Britain. Colonies gained independence and formed United States of America.
1792–1815 **Napoleonic Wars**	Fought between France and an alliance between Austria, Britain, Russia, Prussia, and Sweden. France defeated.
1812–14 **War of 1812**	Fought between United States and Britain. USA victorious.
1821–29 **Greek War of Independence**	Greece fought for and gained independence from Turkey.
1839–42 **First Opium War**	Trade war between Britain and China. China forced to open trade ports to Western countries.
1846–48 **Mexican-American War**	Fought between USA and Mexico. Mexico was defeated.
1853–56 **Crimean War**	Britain, France, Sardinia, and Turkey fought against Russia, and won.
1861–65 **American Civil War**	Fought between Union (northern states) and Confederacy (southern states). Union victorious. First war to be photographed extensively.
1866 **Austro-Prussian War**	Fought between Austria and Prussia. Austria defeated.
1870–71 **Franco-Prussian War**	Prussia and other German states fought France, and won.
1894–95 **Chinese-Japanese War**	Fought between China and Japan. Japan victorious.
1898–99 **Spanish-American War**	Fought between USA and Spain. USA victorious.
1899–1902 **Second Boer War**	Britain and Commonwealth countries fought Boers and won control of South Africa.
1904–05 **Russo-Japanese War**	Fought between Russia and Japan. Japan victorious.
1914–18 **World War I (The Great War)**	Fought between Germany, Austria-Hungary, and Turkey on one side; British Commonwealth, Belgium, France, Italy, Russia, and USA on the other. Germany defeated.
1918–21 **Russian Civil War**	Fought between Reds (Bolsheviks) and anti-Communists, known as Whites. Bolsheviks victorious.
1931–1933 **Chinese-Japanese War**	Fought between Japan and China. Japan victorious.
1936–39 **Spanish Civil War**	Anarchist uprising that became a struggle between Nationalists (Fascists) and Republicans. Nationalists won.
1937–45 **Chinese-Japanese War**	Fought between China and Japan. China victorious.
1939–45 **World War II**	Global conflict involving every major world power. Fought between Axis powers of Nazi Germany, Italy, and Japan on one side; Allied powers of British Commonwealth, USSR, and USA, on the other. Germany and the Axis powers defeated. USA and USSR become global "superpowers".

1950–53 **Korean War**	Fought between North Korea (aided by China) and South Korea (aided by USA and allies). Ceasefire negotiated.	**1971** **Pakistan Civil War**	Fought between Bangladesh (east Pakistan) and west Pakistan. Bangladesh victorious.
1965–75 **Vietnam War**	Fought between North (Communist) Vietnam and South Vietnam (aided by USA and allies). USA withdrew in 1973. In 1975, North Vietnam won the war.	**1973** **October War**	Arabs and Israelis fought. United Nations (UN) called a ceasefire.
1967 **Six-Day War**	Fought between Israel and Arab forces led by Egypt. Israel won.	**1980–88** **Iran-Iraq War**	Iran and Iraq fought. Ceasefire was negotiated.
1967–70 **Nigerian Civil War**	Fought between Biafra and Federal Government. Biafra was defeated.	**1991** **Gulf War**	Iraq fought UN forces, headed by USA. Iraq defeated and Kuwait liberated.
1968– **Northern Ireland**	Prolonged conflict between Protestants and Catholics. Peace agreement was signed on Good Friday 1998.	**1991–** **Civil War, former Yugoslavia**	Prolonged ethnic, territorial, and religious conflict involving Serbs, Croats, Bosnians, and Albanians. In 1999 NATO intervened against the Serbs.

MAJOR BATTLES

B.C. **490** **Marathon (Greece)**	10,000 Athenians and allies defeated 50,000 Persian troops. After battle, Pheidippides, a runner, ran to Athens to report victory. Exhausted, he delivered message and died. The modern marathon is named after his achievement.	**732** **Tours (France)**	The Franks, led by Charles Martel, defeated Muslim invaders from Spain, securing Western European independence.
480 **Salamis (Greece)**	Combined Greek fleet, led by Athenian Themistocles and Spartan Eurybiades, defeated larger invading Persian fleet under King Xerxes. Secured Greek independence in the Mediterranean.	**1260** **Ain Jalut (Palestine)**	Muslim general Kutuz defeated combined Mongol and Christian mounted forces. First major victory against massive Mongol empire, also ended Crusaders' hopes of recovering Holy Land.
415–413 **Siege of Syracuse (Sicily)**	40,000-strong Athenian force massacred in failed invasion of Syracuse. Ended Athenian military supremacy over Greek world.	**1066** **Hastings (Britain)**	Norman (French) soldiers, led by William the Conqueror, crossed English Channel and defeated Saxon forces, led by Harold II. Norman conquest brought England into realm of Western Europe and created a unified, centralized state.
405 **Aegispotamoi (Turkey)**	Spartan fleet under Lysander defeated last Athenian fleet, ending Peloponnesian War.	**1415** **Agincourt (France)**	10,000 English under Henry V defeated 30,000 French, and recaptured Normandy. Demonstrated superiority of English longbowmen over French knights.
331 **Gaugamela (Persia)**	Alexander the Great's supreme victory. He defeated Persian King Darius and opened up the East to Greek ideas and culture.	**1429** **Siege of Orléans (France)**	English siege of Orléans lifted by French forces. England's hopes of total conquest of France destroyed by Joan of Arc, who revived French unity and courage. Decisive moment of Hundred Years War.
202 **Zama (Tunisia)**	Roman force under Scipio ended Punic Wars against Carthage with a massive victory over Hannibal. End of 400-year-old Carthaginian empire.	**1453** **Siege of Constantinople (Turkey)**	Ottoman Turks, led by Sultan Mehmed II, besieged and captured Constantinople (Istanbul). Marked end of the Byzantine Empire.
31 **Actium (Greece)**	Octavian (later Augustus) defeated Mark Antony and Cleopatra at sea, ending decades of civil war. Marked end of Roman Republic and beginning of Imperial Rome.	**1521** **Siege of Tenochtitlán (Mexico)**	Landing with a small force, Spanish explorer Hernán Cortés won allies from enemies of Aztecs, and attacked Aztec capital, Tenochtitlán. Siege ended in total defeat of Aztecs, who had the greatest empire in Americas. Started European colonization.
A.D. **378** **Adrianople (Turkey)**	Goths (Germanic tribes) inflicted a crippling defeat on Roman army, sending panic throughout Roman Empire. Emperor Valens was killed in the battle, and Roman tactics shown to be outdated.	**1571** **Lepanto (Greece)**	Christian fleet of more than 200 galleys, led by Don John of Austria, defeated Turkish fleet of more than 200 galleys, led by Ali Pasha. More than 30,000 men drowned in one afternoon. Last major naval battle to use oar-powered galleys.
636 **Yarmuk (Israel)**	Arab leader Khalid ibn-al Walid, with 25,000 men, defeated and killed 50,000-strong Byzantine force in a desert sandstorm. Brought Jerusalem under Arab control, and opened the way to Arab expansion in Egypt, North Africa, and Spain.	**1588** **Spanish Armada (Britain)**	Spanish fleet of 130 ships, led by Duke of Medina Sidonia, defeated by 97 English ships and by heavy storms. 86 Spanish ships survived. Major blow to Counter-Reformation.
718 **Siege of Constantinople (Turkey)**	Leo the Isaurian, Emperor of Byzantium, defeated Saracen Arabs using "greek fire", an inflammable substance that ignited on contact with water. Halted Arab advance into Western Europe.		

1645 **Naseby (Britain)**	14,000 British Parliamentary troops, under Fairfax, defeated 10,000 Royalist troops under Prince Rupert. Spelled the end of Charles I's power and beginning of Republican rule.	**1876** **Little Bighorn (United States)**	About 3,000 Sioux and Cheyenne warriors, led by Sitting Bull and Crazy Horse, destroyed part of the 7th US Cavalry, led by Colonel George Custer. The only survivor from Custer's force was a horse.
1704 **Blenheim (Germany)**	British-Austrian army, under Duke of Marlborough, defeated a French-Bavarian force, under Marshal Tallard. Ended Stuart claims to throne of England, and prevented French domination in Europe.	**1905** **Tsushima (West of Japan)**	Japanese fleet under Admiral Togo destroyed Russian fleet, under Rozhdestvenski. Decisive battle of Russo-Japanese War.
1709 **Poltava (Ukraine)**	Russian Tsar, Peter the Great, defeated Sweden for control of Baltic Sea. Ended 80 years of Swedish military domination and began Russian empire's expansion.	**1914** **The Marne (France)**	Strategic victory for French and British Commonwealth forces that halted the German advance. Last mobile battle in the west in World War I. Long trench battles followed.
1757 **Plassey (India)**	Robert Clive's 3,200-strong British force defeated 50,000-strong Bengali army to install a puppet nawab (king) and to seize power for British East India Company. First step on road to British domination of India.	**1916** **The Somme (France)**	The Somme was the bloodiest battle of World War I, taking 1,265,000 lives. British Commonwealth and French forces captured just 320sq km (125sq miles) of ground.
1759 **Quebec (Canada)**	British general James Wolfe defeated French forces under the Marquis de Montcalm in a night attack on the Plains of Abraham outside Quebec. Gave Britain control of Canada. Both generals died in battle.	**1917** **Passchendaele (Belgium)**	5-month battle of trench warfare. British Commonwealth gained 8km (5 miles) and lost more than 400,000 men. 57,000 were killed in just a few hours on 1 July 1917.
1777 **Saratoga (United States)**	Decisive American victory in American Revolution. British troops, led by Burgoyne, surrendered to Americans.	**1940** **Britain**	German air force of 2,500 planes launched attack on Britain. Smaller Royal Air Force defeated them and prevented planned seaborne invasion.
1781 **Yorktown (United States)**	General Cornwallis, with 8,000 British troops, was hemmed in, and surrendered to a larger American force under George Washington. End of American Revolution.	**1942** **Midway (Pacific)**	Japanese attempt to capture Midway Island defeated by US Navy. First naval battle in which opposing ships never saw each other. Marked the new dominance of the aircraft carrier.
1805 **Trafalgar (South of Spain)**	Nelson destroyed French-Spanish fleet south of Cadiz, Spain, and with it Napoleon's plans to invade England.	**1942** **El Alamein (Egypt)**	Allied forces, led by General Montgomery (British), drove German Afrika Korps, under Erwin Rommel, out of Egypt, deep into Libya. Britain's greatest victory of WWII.
1805 **Austerlitz (Czech Republic)**	65,000 French troops, led by Napoleon Bonaparte, defeated 83,000 Austrian and Russian forces. Napoleon's greatest victory.	**1942–43** **Stalingrad (Russia)**	German forces surrendered to Soviet Russians after long siege of Stalingrad (Volgograd). One of the bloodiest battles in history: more than 600,000 Soviet soldiers killed and more than 1 million dead in total.
1815 **Waterloo (Belgium)**	Napoleon was defeated by combined British, Dutch, Belgian, and Prussian forces. This finally ended Napoleonic Wars.	**1944** **Normandy (France) D-Day**	Allied forces, led by General Eisenhower (American), invaded German-occupied northern France. Largest-ever seaborne attack: 38 convoys of 745 ships, with more than 4,000 landing craft, 156,000 men, and 300 minesweepers.
1854 **Balaclava (Crimea)**	British defeat of a Russian attack in the Crimean War. Famous for charge of Lord Cardigan's Light Brigade, which only one-third of his men survived.		
1863 **Gettysburg (United States)**	Decisive battle of American Civil War. Federal forces under George Meade defeated Confederates under Robert E. Lee. Heavy losses on both sides: approximately 40,000 Union and Confederate troops killed.	**1954** **Dien Bien Phu (Vietnam)**	Vietnamese defeated French forces, ending French control of Vietnam. Led to establishment of North and South Vietnam: one Communist, the other US-aided.
1870 **Sedan (France)**	Prussia, led by Moltke, inflicted crushing defeat on France. This ended Second Empire and forced abdication of Emperor Napoleon III.	**1991** **Operation Desert Storm (Iraq)**	Airborne attack on Iraq by United Nations Coalition forces. Broke Iraqi resistance and led to swift end of Gulf War.

WAR FACTS

- The Geneva Convention of 1949 separates civilians from the military in four major ways: the military wear clothes that show they are soldiers, openly carry weapons, are under the control of a commander, and obey the laws and customs of war.

- Germ warfare's use was first recorded in the 14th century. Tartars, besieging a Crimean city, catapulted plague-infected corpses over the walls, spreading disease among the inhabitants.

- War in this century has killed more than 100 million people; 20 million since 1945.

- In 1905, Russia's Baltic fleet took seven months to reach its enemy, Japan. Japanese Navy destroyed it in 36 hours.

- In World War I, about 19 million died: 95% soldiers, 5% civilians. In World War II, more than 50 million died: 50% soldiers, 50% civilians.

WAR RECORDS

MOST WARLIKE LEADER was Sargon of Akkad (c.2370 B.C.), who waged 34 wars in 55 years.

SHORTEST WAR lasted just 38 minutes, between Britain and Zanzibar (East Africa) in 1896.

REVOLUTIONS AND RIGHTS

FRENCH REVOLUTION

1788 France bankrupt
King Louis XVI, nobles, and Church hold power. Louis summons Estates-General (ancient parliament) to raise extra taxes.

1789 Meeting of Estates-General at Versailles, 5 May. Third Estate (middle-class representatives) demands democratic reforms.

National Assembly set up by Third Estate rebels to rule France, 10 June. Louis sends troops to Versailles.

Storming of the Bastille (royal fortress and hated symbol of tyranny) by people of Paris, 14 July. Revolution spreads around France. Peasants burn chateaux and manors.

Declaration of the Rights of Man adopted by Assembly, 27 August.

1790 Nobility abolished.

1791 Royal family flee Paris, but are captured, June.

1792 Revolutionary War begins, as Austria and Prussia attack France. Monarchy abolished; France declared a republic.

1793 Louis XVI executed (Jan. 21).

Jacobins (extreme revolutionary group) take power in July.

Reign of Terror, from September 1793 to July 1794. 300,000 people arrested and about 17,000 guillotined.

1795 The Directory (a five-man executive body) takes power.

1799 Napoleon Bonaparte overthrows Directory and takes power.

Guillotine of the French Revolution, invented as a humane method of execution.

KEY PEOPLE

Name	Dates	Biographical details
Louis XVI	1754–93	King of France, opposed to reform. Tried for treason and guillotined
Georges Danton	1759–94	Jacobin leader and Minister of Justice. Voted for execution of King but opposed Reign of Terror. Arrested and guillotined
Maximilien Robespierre	1758–94	Lawyer and Jacobin revolutionary. Head of Committee of Public Safety. Key figure in Reign of Terror. Arrested and guillotined
Olympes de Gouges	1748–94	Revolutionary. Wrote *Declaration of the Rights of Women and Citizens*. Arrested and guillotined

RUSSIAN REVOLUTION

1917 Petrograd bread riots (8 March). Army joins with workers. Soviets (councils) of soldiers, peasants, and workers set up all over Russia.

Tsar abdicates (15 March). Moderate provisional (temporary) government set up. Power struggles begin between government and soviets, and between Mensheviks (moderates) and Bolsheviks (Communists).

Lenin returns to Russia (April). His "April Theses" declare independence of Bolsheviks, and call for revolution.

Bolsheviks take over Petrograd, led by Trotsky (7–8 November).

Bolsheviks seize control of Moscow and European Russia. Lenin passes law giving land to peasants. Creates Cheka (secret police force) to enforce party's decisions. Abolishes ranks in society and army. Nationalizes all factories and banks. Takes schools from Church and gives to state (November–December).

1918 Russia leaves World War I after Treaty of Brest-Litovsk between Russia and Germany, 3 March.

Tsar and royal family executed, in Yekaterinburg (now Sverdlovsk), July.

KEY PEOPLE

Name	Dates	Biographical details
Nicholas II	1868–1918	Last Tsar of Russia, overthrown in revolution
Vladimir Illich Lenin	1870–1924	Founder of Bolshevik Party and leader of revolution. Ruled Soviet Union 1917–24
Leon Trotsky	1879–1940	Bolshevik and head of Red Army. Organized revolution with Lenin; murdered by Stalin
Josef Stalin	1879–1953	Succeeded Lenin. Forced intense industrialization and collectivization of land

1918–21 Civil War between Reds (Bolsheviks) and Whites (anti-Bolsheviks) results in Red victory. More than 20 million die.

1918–22 Socialist reforms

1922 Soviet Union established, the world's first Communist state.

CHINESE REVOLUTION

1921 Chinese Communist Party holds first meeting in Shanghai.

1926 Northern Expedition Communists and Nationalists unite against tyrannical warlords.

1927 Nationalist leader Chiang Kai-shek executes hundreds of Communists in lightning coup, April.

Chinese Communist Party cap

1934–35 Long March. Communists retreat 8,000km (5,000 miles) to escape Nationalist forces. Mao Tse-tung emerges as Communist Party leader.

1945 Civil war erupts between Communists and Nationalists after Japanese surrender in World War II.

1946 Communists wage successful guerilla war against Nationalists.

1947 People's Liberation Army organized by Communist leader and military genius, Lin Bao. Mao Tse-tung establishes Communist capital at Shih-chia-chuang (November). Peasant uprisings throughout China.

KEY PEOPLE

Name	Dates	Biographical details
Chiang Kai-shek	1887–1975	Chinese general. President of Chinese Republic and head of Kuomintang (Nationalist party). Fled to Taiwan following Communist victory
Mao Tse-tung	1893–1976	Chinese Communist leader and first chairman of the People's Republic
Lin Bao	1907–71	Founder and leader of People's Liberation Army

1949 Communists capture Peking (Beijing). Nationalist resistance collapses. Chiang Kai-shek flees to Taiwan and sets up Nationalist Government.

Mao Tse-tung proclaims People's Republic of China, (1 October), in Peking (Beijing), with himself as leader. People's Liberation Army control entire Chinese mainland.

BLACK RIGHTS

1600–1810 Ten million Africans are taken to the Americas as slaves.

1823–33 Anti-slavery society set up in Britain to end slavery in colonies.

1909 W.E.B. Du Bois (1889–1963) helps found National Association for the Advancement of Coloured People to end racial inequality in the USA.

1912 African National Congress (ANC) founded in South Africa to secure racial equality and black representation in parliament.

1914 Marcus Garvey (1887–1940) founds Universal Negro Improvement Association in Harlem, New York.

1925 A. Philip Randolph (1889–1979) organizes and leads the first successful black trade union.

1950–59 Apartheid laws set up in South Africa. These discriminate against blacks, "coloureds" and Asians.

1954 US Supreme Court rules that segregated education (by colour) is "inherently unequal".

1955 Martin Luther King, Jr. (1929–68) organizes campaign to desegregate bus service in Montgomery, Alabama. This becomes a mass protest across southern USA.

1960 Sharpeville Massacre. 69 die and 200 injured in protest against South Africa's racist "Pass Laws".

1964 Nelson Mandela (born 1918), leader of military wing of ANC, jailed for life in South Africa.

1965–68 US Congress outlaws discrimination. Martin Luther King assassinated.

1990 F.W. De Klerk, president of South Africa, lifts ban on ANC and releases Nelson Mandela.

1994 First all-party elections in South Africa. ANC wins 62% of vote; Nelson Mandela becomes president.

ARCHAEOLOGY AND HISTORY

ARCHAEOLOGISTS HELP US to understand the past by digging up ancient sites and studying what they find there. In the past, they often looked only for treasure. Today, archaeologists use science to piece together a full picture of an ancient society.

At every stage of an excavation, archaeologists take photographs, make drawings, and write detailed notes on everything they find, and where they find it.

EXCAVATION

When archaeologists discover a site that they wish to investigate, they organize an excavation, or "dig". They work in teams, and each person has a different skill, such as surveying, excavation, drawing, or photography. Most archaeologists today work on "rescue" digs, where construction work, such as city centre redevelopment, threatens to disturb or destroy ancient remains.

The site's finds are later processed. This includes recording, labelling, bagging, examining, drawing, conserving, and documenting.

ANALYSIS METHODS

Human skull

Comparisons of skulls can also show where they fit into an evolutionary pattern.

• Looking at bone finds can tell scientists about the diet and health of ancient peoples, as well as their burial customs.

• Analysis of materials such as seeds, pollen, and animal remains builds up a picture of the ancient environment. It can show which crops were grown for food, and how people lived.

• Dendrochronology is the study of tree rings to date wooden objects. In a good year, trees grow more and have larger rings than in a bad year. Rings on the object can be identified with those of other timbers that have already been dated.

Tree sections show ring matches.

• Many sites have had different inhabitants at different times. Archaeologists dig a vertical cross-section through the earth of a site. This reveals the "layers" of time, the most recent occurring at the top.

• Radio-carbon dating is a very accurate scientific method of dating. All living things contain some radioactive carbon (C-14). After a living thing dies, this C-14 decays (its atoms break down) at a known rate. If the amount of C-14 in an organic find (wood, antler, etc.) is known, its age can be estimated.

DETECTION METHODS

• Using geophysics, we can show what lies underground without excavating. One technique, called resistivity, uses two electrical probes driven into the ground at different places. The resistance of the ground to the current can indicate underground remains.

• X-rays can reveal details of objects that are too brittle to be handled, or encrusted with rock.

AERIAL PHOTOGRAPHY

Sun at noon

During the daytime, the slight bumps made by buried remains cannot be seen clearly.

Sun at dawn or dusk
Shadows form.

At sunset or dawn, bumps cast shadows easily seen from the air.

Crop growth can be affected by old earthworks or stoneworks, and this can be seen easily from the air.

PHASES OF HISTORY

Phase		Historian	Characteristics
Ancient Near Eastern:		Egyptian/Mesopotamian chroniclers	Recorded and praised the deeds of kings and emperors with little concern for accuracy
Classical:	Greece	Herodotus (c.484–c.425 B.C.)	His histories tell of famous military and political activities
		Thucydides (455–400 B.C.)	Closely examined military events of his time and their political consequences
	Rome	Livy (c.60 B.C.–A.D. 17)	Interested in historical figures and morality. He tried to be unbiased
		Tacitus (c.A.D. 56–120)	Wrote vivid, detailed accounts with some accuracy
Medieval:	Europe	Orosius (c.417)	First Christian historian. Promoted Christian world view over Paganism
		Bede (c.672–735)	"The Father of English History", who carefully researched the reliability of his sources
		Villehardouin (c.1150–c.1213)	His histories included eyewitness accounts of military activity
		Froissart (c.1333–1401)	His closely researched accounts emphasized the lives and battles of knights
	Muslim World	Al-Tabari (c.923)	Produced a religious history of the conflicts and customs of Muslims
		Ibn Khaldun (1332–1406)	Wrote political, economic, and social history
Renaissance:		Biondo (1392–1463)	Used many accurate sources in his chronological history of Italy
		Guicciardini (1483–1540)	Described historical events in a clear and methodical manner
Enlightenment:	18th Century	Gibbon (1737–94)	His writings examined the movement and patterns of historical events
	19th Century	Ranke (1795–1886)	Attempted to understand the past through scientific research methods
	20th Century	Febvre (1878–1956) Braudel (1902–85)	They broadened the subject matter by emphasizing social and economic matters, as well as describing military, political, and geographical affairs

INDEX AND CREDITS

INDEX

Page numbers in **bold** type refer to main entries

Q

PICTURE SOURCES

The publisher would like to thank the following for their kind permission to reproduce the photographs:

ABBREVIATIONS
t-top
b-bottom
l-left
r-right
tl-top left
tr-top right
cla-centre left above
cra-centre right above
cl-centre left
cr-centre right
clb-centre left below
crb-centre right below
bl-bottom left
br-bottom right
c-centre
ca-centre above
cb-centre below
bc-bottom centre
tc-top centre

A

©**Aardman Animations** 186c.
Action Plus 199clb/Chris Barry 213c;
R.Francis 197cb, 199bl; Tony Henshaw
193c, 199c, 215cr; Mike Hewitt 212br;
Glyn Kirk 212crb, 215tc; Robert Lewis
190br. **Lorna Ainger** 162b, 178tc.
AKG, London 132cb, 133crb, 144cb,
145c, 172bl, 188tr, l, 242crb.
Allsport/David Klutho 201bc.
Alton Telegraph Photo/Robert Graul
129car. **Ampex** 187bl. **Ancient Art
and Architecture Collection** 32cl,
135bc, 142cr, 166tl, cal, 382cl, 384tl,
385cl/Ronald Sheridan 373br.
Animals Unlimited 105cl. **Directed
and Produced by Animation City/
AC Live** 184bc. **Archiv fur Kunst
und Geschicte, Berlin** 182tc, 184tr,
380c, 381cl, bl, 390bl. **Ardea**/
Liz Bomford 97tc. **Art Directors**/
Carl Young 152c. **Aviation
Photographers International** 265cb.

B

B&U International Picture Service
279c. **BFI Stills, Posters & Designs**
164cra, 186tr. **Barnaby's Picture
Library**/Georg Sturm 142c. **Michael
Barrett Levy** 182bl, 187cr. **Norman
Barratt** 190. **Basketball Hall of Fame,
Springfield, Massachusetts** 190crb.
©**Bayreuther Festspiele GmbH**/
Wilhelm Rauh 314bc. **Bibliotheque
de L'Assemblée Nationale,Paris**
190cra. **Biofotos**/Heather Angel 92crb.
©**1993 Boeing Commercial Airplane
Group** 265br. **Bridgeman Art Library**/
Bodleian Library, Oxford 386tl; British
Museum, London 160cr; Christie's,
London 162cr; City of Bristol
Museum & Art Gallery 393cr;
British Library, London 350ca, 392bl;
Department of the Environment,
London 385tc; Egyptian National
Museum, Cairo 374ca; Fervers Gallery,
London 169cr; Giraudon 69cr, 161cl;
Greater London Council 132cl;
Hermitage, St.Petersburg 160cl;
Historiches Museum Der Stadt,Vienna
169cr; Institute of Directors, London
397cra; Sir Godfrey Kneller 145cra;
Louvre, Paris 374bc; Musée de
L'Armée, Paris/Giraudon 395c;
Museum of Mankind 138tc;
Nationalgalerie, Berlin, *Hornform*,
1924, Wassily Kandinsky © ADAGP,
Paris & DACS, London, 1995 161cb;
Prado, Madrid 390cl;
Private Collection 133clb, 190ca, 390tl,
397tl; Salvator Rosa 145tl; Royal College
of Physicians, London 133cra;
Tretyakov Gallery, Moscow 324c;
Trinity College, Dublin 310br;
by courtesy of the Board of Trustees of
the V&A, London 391cl, 169c. **British
Library** 141cra. **British Red Cross**
132crb. **Brothers Quay** 186cl.
**Bureau International des Poids et
Mesure Sevres** 240clb.

C

Camera Press/Curtis/RBO 409bcl;
Karsh of Ottawa 409bl; Herbie Knott
410c; Ian Stone 409br; Eli Weinberg
408tl. **California Institute of
Technology** 44bl. **J.Allan Cash Ltd.**
140bc, 340br, 342cl, 348cb, 379bl, 390br.
Casio Electronics Co.Ltd. 182cb, bc.
Jean-Loup Charmet 166cbr, 173br,
239br. **Lester Cheeseman** 143cl.
Chicago Historical Institute 157cl.
Christies Colour Library 47br.
Bruce Coleman Ltd./Fred Bruemmer
291cr; Jane Burton 86cr, 93cbr;
Alain Compost 95cb; Gerald Cubitt
336cl, 354bl; Peter Davey 101cb;
Andrew Davies 272bl; Jack Dermid 93crb;
Keith Gunnar 43ct; David C.Houston
288clb; Stephen J.Krasemann 63crb,
106bl; S.Nielsen 23cr; Dieter & Mary
Plage 335cr; Dr.Eckart Pott 108bc,
101bc, 291tr; Andy Price 354br;
Mr.Jens Rydell 235c; John Shaw 50clb;
Austin James Steven 93tr, 95tl;
Kim Taylor 95tr, 236crb; Barrie
Wilkins 106c; Gunter Ziesler 112cl;
Christian Zuber 329c. **Colorsport**
194bc, 196cr, 197c, cr, 199bc, 200cl,
210bl, bc, 213cr, 214c, cr, 215bl/ ©
duomo-David Madison 191cra,
William R.Sallaz 214cl/Olympia,
Roberto Bettini 217cb/Sipa Sport,
Pascal Huit 216cb, Lacombe 217c,
R.Martin 215bc. **Comstock** 379br,
381tr.**Michael Copsey** 46cb, 53tr &
cra, 56cla, cl, 75tl, 138cl, 141tl, 242c,
326br, 344cl, 352c.

D

Daihatsu 253cr. **James Davis Travel
Photography** 142bl, 143cr, 171bl, 303ca,
350bc. **Dessau**/Peter Kuhn 156cb.
©**The Walt Disney Company** 186tl,
cl, cb. **C.M. Dixon** 161tc, tr, 373cra,
377tc, 378bc. Courtesy **Anthony
d'Offay Gallery, London** 161bl.
Dominic Photography/Catherine
Ashmore 174c. **Dr. Peter Dorrell**
373tl. **Dulceana**/J.D. Sharp 184cl.

E

E.T.Archive 139cb, 169tr, 374br,
377cl, 395bc, 398br, 401bl, 402tl/
Biblioteca Marciana, Venice 190cla;
Metropolitan Museum of Art 176br;
Plymouth City Art Gallery 176bc.
Mary Evans Picture Library 18cla,
18cra, 32tr, tl, cla, c, cra & clb, 68cr,
69cl, 71tr, cla, 132cra, 133tr, 140cra,
143cr, bl, 144cr, cra, crb, 145ca, cra,
152tc, cr, 167cl, cr, 169cla, 176cb,
178ca, cl, clb, 190c, cr, 239cr, cb, 247tr,
cra, cl, clb, 248tc, 249tl, cr, cb, 264ca,
265cra, cl, cr, 357crb, 380cl, 386c,
388tc, 389br, 393cl, 394cra, 396clb, c,
397ca, 398bl, 399tr, cr, 402tr, 415cr, 416,
417tl, cl, c, Elenore Plaisted Abbott
178cr; Carrey, Le Petit Parisien 264cra;
A.W. Diggelmann in La Conquete du
Ciel 264cr; Explorer 133cla, 169ca;
G.W. Lambert 419c; Alexander
Meledin Collection 402bl, 420br; J.K.
Stieler 395crb; Steve Rumney 169cl;
N.C. Wyeth 138tr.

F

Werner Forman Archive/
Anthropology Museum, Veracruz
University, Jalapa 377tl;
British Museum, London 190tr;
J. Paul Getty Museum, Malibu, USA
190cal; Private Collection, Prague 354cl;
Tanzania National Museum, Dar es
Salaam 169tc. **Fotomas Index** 395bl.
**John Frost Historical Newspaper
Service** 188cla, cl, c, cb. **Fuji** 164bc.

G

Genesis 34bl. **Geoscience Features**
51clb. courtesy of Andy Goldsworthy
161bc. **Ronald Grant Archive** 169crb,
184ca, clb, 185bl. **Greenpeace**/Gleizes
153tc; Morgan 357bl.

H

Sonia Halliday Photographs 135tc,
157ca, 160tc, 188tc, 381tl, l,
Laura Lushington 381bc;
James Wellard 331tr. **Robert Harding
Picture Library** 42cl, 71tl, 171tr, 290bl,
309br, 330tr, 331bl, 340c, crb, 345tr,
366bc, 371tl, 374c, cra, cb, crb, 377clb,
385bl, 392tr, Mohamed Amin 31bc;
Bildagentur Schuster/Kim Hart

309bl/Layda 348cra; C.Bowman 293bl;
Cordier/Explorer 336bc; K.Gillham
317cr; Ian Griffiths 334c; Kosel 51cl;
J.Desmarteau 394tc;
FPG International 398clb, 400bl;
Robert Francis 46c; Robert Frerck/
Odyssey/Chicago 278bc;
David Hughes 157cla; F.Jackson 342cr,
343bl; Krafft 43tc; Robert McLeod 62bl,
410br; Geoff Renner 55bl; Christopher
Rennie 383bl; Rolf Richardson 320cl,
379bc; Paul van Riel 411cl;
Sackim 315cr; Andy Williams 279tl;
JHC Wilson 184cra; Adam Woolfitt
319br, 342cla; Earl Young 152tr, 293tc;
John Hedgecoe 165cl, c.
The Hindu Newspaper 188clb.
Michael Holford 89clb, 154tl, 160tl,
374cr, 375c, cra, 376clb, cb, cl, cbr, crb,
377bl, 380cb, 394cl, 378cr.
Rebecca Hossack Gallery 146tr.
Hulton-Deutsch Collection 18ca,
34tl, 45c, 132br, 144clb, 145clb, 151cr,
153c, 156crb, 160crb, bl, 165c, 166bar,
169bl, 170clb, crb, 174cra, cr, 176bl,
178br, bc, 181tc, tr, tl, ca, 182tl, 188cr,
190c, bl, 193crb, 194crb, 245cla, 261bl,
264cl, c, clb, crb, 396tl, 398cra, 400crb,
401br, 406tc, cl, br, 407tr, 408tc, 417tr,
bc, 422crb/ Bettmann Archive 182cra;
Terry Fincher 407tl.
Robert Hunt Library 404tc.
**Henry E. Huntington Library &
Art Gallery** 18clb.
Hutchison Library 171c, 337br/
H.R.Dorig 377cla; Sarah Errington
148ca, 363tl; Melanie Friend 141bl;
Julia Highet 171cra; Michael McIntyre
139cr, 146cb, 171lc, 347c;
Christine Pemberton 141tr;
Pern 146bc; Bernard Regent 143tl;
John Ryle 148tl; Liba Taylor 142cra;
Anna Tully 171tl.

I

The Image Bank/Charles S.Allen
272cl; Alan Becker 314c; A.Boccaccio
274tl; Lionel F.Brown 236cr;
Gary Cralle 53crb; Fotoworld 308bc;
Chris Hackett 294cr; G.Heisler 276tr;
Lionel Isy-Schwart 171t, 354cra;
Ronald Johnson 272clb; Tadao Kimura
379cra; Kim Keitt/Stockphotos,Inc.
169bc; Romilly Lockyer 310bl;
Michael Melford 109clb;
Arthur Meyerson 363tr; Alfred Pasieka
268tr; Co.Rentmeester 274cla; Guido
Alberto Rossi 53br, 320br, 346cr,
363crb; Steve Satushek 321c; Michael
Skott 367bl; Harold Sund 293tl, 324ca;
A.T.Willett 245br; Trevor Wood 43cl.
Image Select 129tr, 132clb, 172bc, br,
bl, 178cb, crb, 392cl.
©**Imax Corporation** 184br.
Impact Photos/Steve Benbow 297tc;
John Cole 293cr. A.J.Deane 319clb;
Paul Forster 354cl; Alan Keohane

147bc; Peter Menzel 149tc; Tony Page 156cra.
Institut Pasteur 133cl. **International Coffee Organization** 301tr. **By courtesy of the Israel Antiquities Authority** 371br.

JKL
Japan Archive 169cra. **Robert Jones** 355bl. **A.F.Kersting** 378cra. **Keymed Ltd.**127tc, clb. **David King Collection** 144crb, 152bc, 166bal. **Kobal Collection** 31cr, 184cla, bl, 236c. **Konica** 164c. **Frank Lane Picture Agency** 79cl/ Silvestris 62clb, 63br, 87tc; T&P Gardner 109bl; R.Wilmshurst 106cr. **Leica** 164cl. **Eleni Leoussi** 169br. **Mike Linley** 93clb.

M
Magnum Photos Ltd. 165cb, 334tr/ Abbas 342c, 365tl; Collection Astier 401crb; Bruno Barbey 143br; Ian Berry 18crb; Cagnoni 408bc; Bruce Davidson 409tl; Stuart Franklin 365clb; Ernst Haas 364bl; Philippe Halsman 169cb; David Hurn 148cr, 365br; S. Meiselas 152tl; Wayne Miller 403tl; Michael K.Nichols 364bc; Pinkhassov 411tc; Raghu Rai 365cl; Marc Riboud 409c; David Scherman 165cr; Nicolas Tikhomiroff 407c. **Mander & Mitcheson** 166c, cr, bl, 168cl, 169clb, 170cla, c. ©**Moroccan Embassy**/Philippe Ploquin 330ca.

N
NASA 21tr, 27bl, 29cr, 34cra, c, cr, cb, 35c, cr, br, 36cb, br, 45br, 60br, 182c, cr, 245bl, 275c, 408br, 411cr/ JPL 35ca, cra. **NHPA**/Stephen Dalton 95clb; Manfred Danegger 101br; Douglas Dickens 109 c, cb; George Gainsburgh 75cla; Peter Parks 87tl; John Shaw 79tr; Martin Wendler 95tc, 109tl, cl. **Edmund Nagele, FRPS** 296cra. **National Film Board of Canada** 186cla. **National Maritime Museum** 390tc. **National Motor Museum, Beaulieu** 253tl, cla, cl.ca, c, cr, br, 255. **Nationwide Building Society** 274cl. **Natural History Museum Publications** 105clb. **Nature Photographers Ltd.**/ J.F.Reynolds 101crb. **Network Photographers**/Roger Hutchings 322bc. ©**Nobel Foundation**/Svensk Reportaget Janst 309c. **Northern Ireland Tourist Board** 46cla. **Novosti** 34tl, 35tl, 323ca, 383cr.

OP
The Open University 32bc. **Oxford Scientific Films**/Animals,Animals/ Raymond A.Mendex 95ca/ Breck P.Kent 85c; Fred Bavendam 87tr & cra; G.I. Bernard 91cl;

Fredrik Ehrenstrom 85br; Michael Fogden 92ca, cra; Rudie Kuiter 97tl; London Scientific Films 85cla; Root Okapia 102crb; Kjell Sandved 86cra. **Panos Pictures**/Rob Cousins 367cl; Jean-Leo Dugast 346cl; Ron Giling 367tr; Trevor Page 367tl; Nick Robinson 366cr; Liba Taylor 337tc; Penny Tweedie 146bl. **Ann & Bury Peerless** 139cl, bl, br, 140tr, 141cr, 142tr, tc. **Chris Pellant** 46bc. **Planet Earth Pictures**/Peter David 97bl; Robert Hessler 43tl; A.Kerstitch 87cla; Ken Lucas 97ca, cal; Paulo de Oliveira 97tcr. **Philips** 187ca. **Photostage**/Donald Cooper 166cbl, br, 174crb, br. **Pictor International** 340cra, 345c, 346tc/Leo Aarons 376cr. **Pictorial Press Ltd.** 409tc. **Richard Platt** 368tc. **Polish Cultural Institute** 318cra. **Popperfoto** 190cl, 247bl, 298cr, 401ca, cb, cra, 402bc, 404e, 405tl, tc, tr, crb, 407crb, 409cl, bc, bcr, 411cb, br. The Post Office 268bl, **Press Association** 152cb. **Q&A Pictures** 280c.

R
Range 145crb, 160br/Bettmann 132bc, 133cr, 159bl, 244ca, tr, 248clb, 253tc, 255crb, 265bc/Bettmann; UPI 165crb, 188crb, 245cra, 246bc. **Redferns**/David Redfern 173bc. **Retna Pictures Ltd.**/Adrian Boot 299ca. **Reuters**/Visnews Library 365cr. **Rex Features Ltd.** 152ca, 265cb, crb, 273cb, 409tr, 411bl/Collection Privee/Sipa 292c, 404tr; D.Turner Givens 350cr; Dave Hogan 305bl; Peter Lomas 120bl; Mark Sherman 368bc; Sipa Press 292c, 403bl, 409cr, 410tl, tctr, cr/Cheryl Hatch 410cb/F.Mitri 410cl/Robert 411clb/ Setboun 410crb; Ian Waldie 149br; Markus Zeffler 153cl. **Michael Roaf** 156ca. **Roger-Viollet** 245tc. **Ann Ronan at Image Select** 32tc, 115cl, cr, 132tl, cla, ca, cr, c, 133tc, 135clb, 144c, cla, cl, 145cla, tr, 164bc, 172bcl, 173bcl, 224cra, 242br, 243clb, 244tc, cla, 248tr, c, 249tc, 259crb, 396cr, 418bl/ WHO Jean Mohr 132bl **Royal Britannic Gardens, Kew** 77br.

S
©**Fotograf H.J.Schuffenhauer** 314cl. **The Science Museum/Science and Society Picture Library** 239bc. **Science Photo Library** 123cla, 128crb, 249c/Bill van Aken/CSIRO 65cr; Argonne National Laboratory 248bc; Alex Bartel 245cr; Biofoto Associates 117tc; Martin Bond 65bc, 272crb, 273cl; Dr. Goran Bredberg 119c; Dr. Jeremy Burgess 120crb, 248ca; CNRI 83crb, 115ca, cra,cb,120br,127cb, br, 237cr/ Prof. C.Ferlaud 121 / Secchi, Lecaque, Roussel, Uclaf 115cr; Jean-Loup Charmet 32ca; Martin Dohrn 366tr; Ralph Eagle 118cl; Prof. Harold Edgerton 164cr;

Fred Espenak 24tr; Simon Fraser 272c; Stevie Grand 227cra; Hale Observatories 24crb; Adam Hart-Davis 118bl; Anthony Howarth 247br, 64br; Dr. William Hsin-Min Ku 19cb; Manfred Kage 123tl; John Mead 272ca; Astrid & Hans-Frieder Michler 115tr, 129cl; Laurence Migdale 366cra; Hank Morgan 128bc; Prof. P. Motta, Dept. of Anatomy,University "La Sapienza", Rome 122tc; NASA 34crb, 35cla, cl, crb, 36cr, 51cr; NIBSC 125cl; National Library of Medicine 117bc; Novosti Press Agency 31crb, 34cl, 35tc, tr; Omikron 121 ; David Parker 45bl; Pekka Parviainen 30br; Alfred Pasieka 126clb; Petit Format/CSI 84crb; Petit Format, Institut Pasteur, Charles Dauguet 125br; Phillipe Plailly 225bl; Chris Priest & Mark Clarke 125cb; J. C. Revy 133bl; Royal Observatory, Edinburgh 30ca; Gregory Sams 238br, 249br; John Sanford 31cl; Tom van Sant/ Geosphere Project, Santa Monica 368br; Francoise Sauze 135cr; Dr. Klaus Schiller 121, 127cl; Science Source 123cl; Sinclair Stammers 85cl, crb; James Stevenson 126cb, 131cr; Prof. Yoshiaki Sofoe 19clb; Andrew Syred 85bc; Gianni Tortoli 227tr; Alexander Tsiaras 240cl; U. S. Dept. of Energy 272br; Dr. E.Walker 128cb; M.I.Walker 247ca; John Walsh 84cb, 115c SPL/ 186br/ **Scala**/Biblioteca Nazionale, Firenze 389bl. **Mark Shearman** 195cr. **Harry Smith**/PoluninCollection 75c. **Sony UK Ltd.** 187tl, c, bc. **Sotheby's** 242bl. **South American Pictures**/Marion Morrison 302br; Tony Morrison 303cb, crb **Frank SpoonerPictures**/Gamma/ Novosti 324tr/Daniel Simon 368bl. **Sporting Pictures(UK)Ltd.**183tl, 191c, 192br, 193cl, 195crb, 201bl, 208cl, bl, 211cr, 213br, bl, 217br. **Stadelsches Kunstinstitut, Frankfurt a.m.**/Ursula Edelmann, Frankfurt a.m. 160cb. **Starland Picture Library**/AT&T Bell Laboratories 32bl. **Dr. F.Richard Stephenson** 22bl. **Still Pictures** 332tr/ Andy Crump 355tr; Mark Edwards 147cb, 305cr; Julio Etchart/ Reportage 300cr; John Maier 368tr. **Tony Stone Images** 296bl, 296c, 297cl/Doug Armand 299cb; Oliver Benn 315cl; 382cla; Jon Bradley 157c; Julian Calder 312c; John Callahan 349br; Tony Craddock 51cr, 312bl; John Edwards 290tr; David H.Endersbee 278bl; Robert Everts 309tr; Robert Frerck 311cl; Jon Gray 56tl; Michael Harris 141c; David Hiser 291bl; John Lamb 315cra; Ian Murphy171tc; Hugh Sitton 338cb; Nabeel Turner 139tl, 140bl, 341c. **Sygma** 114cb/David Gomle 146clb; Bill Nation 147tc.

Syndication International/Macdonald, Aldus Archive 182clb,390bc.

T
Telegraph Colour Library 365bl/ Colorific!/JaakkoAvikainen 324bl; John de Visser/Black Star 324tl. **Telesat, Canada** 182cl. **Time UK** 243bl. **Toyota** 253clb. **TRH Pictures**/ DOD 262c; U.S.A.F. 266br.

UWZ
UPI, Bettmann 18cb, 32cb & crb. **Vireo**/Academy of Natural Sciences, Philadelphia 99tr. **Wedgwood** 276cr. **Straker Welds** 181bl. **Wellcome Institute Library, London** 133cra. **West Africa** 166bc. **Wiedenfeld & Nicolson Archives**/British Museum 393tl. **Rodney Wilson** 156c, clb, 318c, 372c. ©**The Wimbledon Lawn Tennis Museum** 190cb. **ZEFA** 135cb, 147br, 148tr, 151tl, cl, 271cb, 275cra, 357cb/ Damm 171cl; W.F.Davidson 278tc; J.Distler 302cra; A.Edgeworth 146br; Goebel 305cra; Hackenberg 157cb; Harlicek 331cl; K.Lehnartz 147c; G.Mebbs 243crb; Resea 150br; S.Velberg 149tr. **ZEON** 181bc. **Zoological Society of London** 95c. **Sam Zwemmer** 340bc.

Other photography by Max Alexander; Sue Barnes; Geoff Brightling; Peter Chadwick; Andy Crawford; Geoff Dann; Richard Davies (Oxford Scientific Film); Philip Dowell©pp 80, 81, 83, 96, 321, 372; Mike Dunning; Neil Fletcher; Jo Foord; Philip Gatward; Frank Greenaway; Steve Gorton; Peter Hayman; Stephen Hayward; John Heseltine; Chas Howson; Colin Keates; Dave King; Bob Langrish; C. Laubscher; Mike Linley; Andrew McRobb; E.Meacher; Stephen Oliver; Roger Phillips; Martin Phomer; Steve Ridley; Tim Ridley; Kim Sayer; Karl Shone; James Stephenson; Harry Taylor; Kim Taylor; Andreas Von Einsiedel; Matthew Ward; Jerry Young© pp84, 89, 91, 93, 94, 95, 104, 106

With thanks to: British Museum, British Library, Museum of London, Natural History Museum, Naturmuseum, Senkenberg Frankfurt, Beaulieu National Motor Museum, National Maritime Museum, National Gallery, Science Museum,

Every effort has been made to trace the copyright holders and we apologize for any unintentional omissions. We would be pleased to insert the appropriate acknowledgement in any subsequent edition of this publication.

ILLUSTRATORS

ACKNOWLEDGEMENTS

Additional editorial and research assistance
Céline Carez, Christiane Gunzi, Robin Griffiths, Kitty Hauser,
Francesca Stich

Additional design assistance
Chetan Joshi, Duncan Brown, Diane Clouting, Sharon Grant, Jill Planck

Indexer Hilary Bird

Proofreader Jill Somerscales

In addition, Dorling Kindersley would like to thank the following people and organizations for their assistance in the production of this book:

All embassies, consulates, and high commissions for supplying information; Alpine Club Library; American Society of Plastic and Reconstructive Surgeons; Amstrad; ; Anglo-American Corporation; Dr. Louis Arrington, University of Wisconsin; *Automotive News*; Baha'i Faith National Centre; BBC Engineering Department; BBC Radio; BBC TV; Bernafron UK Ltd; Ian Blatchford; Blockbuster Entertainment; British Film Institute; British Geological Survey; British Humanities Library; British Library Environmental Information Service; British Meteorological Office; British Olympic Association; British Olympic Federation; British Paralympic Association; British Science Library; British Telecom; British Trust for Ornithology; Broadcasters' Audience Research Board Ltd; Buddhist Society; Carluccio's; Centre for Global Energy Studies; Dr. Gerry Cherry, University of Georgia; Christie's International Fine Art Auctioneers; Church of Scientology; Confederation of European Paper Industries; Cousins' Properties; Mick Czaky, Antelope Films; Far East Trading Service Inc; First Interstate World Center; Food and Agriculture Organization; Stephanie Giordano; Great British China Centre; Greenpeace; Linda Hoyt, Maguire Thomas Partners; Independent Television Library; Institute for African Alternatives; International Coffee Organisation; International Olympic Committee; John Oliver Jones; Kenya Wildlife Service; Julie Kusminska, London Video Access; Language of Dance Centre; Bernard Lavery; London Contemporary Dance Theatre; Mac Warehouse; Magnetic Trading Company; Margarita Publications Ltd; Sir Robert Menzies Centre for Australian Studies; Ministry of Agriculture, Fisheries and Food; *Motor Trend* Magazine; MTV International; Museum of Mankind; National Agricultural Centre; National Earthquake Information Center, US Geological Survey; National Motor Museum, Beaulieu; National Society's Religious Education Centre; Natural History Museum; OPEC; Overseas Development Administration; OXFAM; Oxford Museum of the History of Science; Philips Corporation; Pilkington Research Laboratories; Population Concern, Fiona Barr; Refugee Council, Jill Rutter; Andy Roor, US Department of Agriculture; Royal Air Force Museum; Royal Botanic Gardens, Kew; Royal Institute of the Blind; Royal National Institute for the Deaf; Scout Association; *Screen Digest*; Dr Kanwaljit Singh; Smithsonian Institution; Sony; STC Submarine Systems Ltd; Survival International, London; Swiss Bank Corporation, Leslie Prescott; Tea Board of India; Theatre Museum; UNESCO; UNICEF, Anne Luzeekyi; United Airlines; United Nations; Virtual Vision; Voluntary Services Overseas, Tom Crick; Wales Green Party; Professor David A. Warrell, John Radcliffe Hospital, Oxford University; Water Aid; Wellcome Foundation Ltd; Dr. Andrew Wilkins, MRC, The Gambia; Andrew Wilson, Department of Anthropology Oxford University; Woodlands Heritage Museum; World Bank; World Conservation Monitoring Centre; World Health Organization

Logos and Insignias
The Major League Baseball Club insignias depicted in this book are reproduced with the permission of Major League Baseball Properties and are the exclusive property of the respective Major League Clubs and may not be reproduced without their written consent.

The helmet logos on page 205 are registered trademarks of the Teams indicated.

The Silver Fern Device and the New Zealand Rugby Union logo on page 203 are trademarked and owned by the New Zealand Rugby Football Union and used with their permission.

Model of dinosaur page 70, Roby Braun